BIRMINGHAM CITY
A COMPLETE RECORD

BIRMINGHAM CITY
A COMPLETE RECORD

TONY MATTHEWS

Breedon Books
Publishing Company
Derby

First published in Great Britain by
The Breedon Books Publishing Company Limited
44 Friar Gate, Derby, DE1 1DA.
1995

ISBN 1 85983 010 2

Printed and bound by Butler & Tanner, Frome, Somerset.

Contents

Acknowledgements

THE author wishes to thank the following: Roger Baker, for his dedicated enthusiasm with regard to the players' biographies; Dave Page and Dafydd Williams for their contributions to the original edition of this book; former Blues players George Edwards and Ambrose Mulraney; statisticians Jim Creasey and Mike Davage; Ivan Barnsley from Four Oaks; the Birmingham Mail Picture Library; and my wife, Margaret, who has once again shown great patience and offered encouragement whilst this work was in preparation. The author also acknowledges the use of material from Simon Inglis's *The Football Grounds of England and Wales*.

Introduction

THE West Midlands, one of the cradles of professional football, has always been rich in soccer folklore, with the names of Aston Villa, West Bromwich Albion and Wolverhampton Wanderers dominating the game there. At their sides, Birmingham City have not always found it easy to exist in what has often been a rarefied atmosphere of success. Yet the Blues of St Andrew's have their own special place in soccer.

Although, they have never won the championship of the top division and still await that glorious moment when a Blues skipper lifts the FA Cup at Wembley, Birmingham City are a much-loved club and Blues have made their mark on the history of football.

In 1888 they were the first club to be formed into a limited company. In 1960 they were the first British club to reach a European Final, when they met Barcelona in the Inter Cities Fairs Cup. They lifted the Football League Cup in 1963 and were victorious in the Leyland Daf Cup and Auto Windscreens Shield Finals of 1991 and 1993 respectively. There has been a host of great names, from Joe Bradford to Trevor Francis, Harry Hibbs to Gil Merrick.

There have been the good times, when Birmingham City fans have had special reasons to hold their heads high, and then that great battle hymn *Keep Right on to the End of the Road* has reverberated around St Andrew's and elsewhere.

There is much tradition to suggest that this famous old club will once more rub shoulders with the game's élite, especially after their Second Division championship success in 1995. In the meantime, we hope that this book will rekindle some golden memories, answer some questions and, most important, give pleasure to the supporters of one of the warmest, friendliest clubs in football.

The Birmingham City Story

LIKE so many football clubs which began life in the last quarter of the 19th century, the origins of Birmingham City FC lie in the church. Indeed, the Birmingham club is one of soccer's oldest institutions, being founded in September 1875 under the name of Small Heath Alliance by a number of young cricketers from the Holy Trinity CC, based in Bordesley Green. Here again, the birth of Birmingham City was typical. The cricketers wanted something to keep them together in the winter months and conceived the idea that the new pastime of association football would be an ideal vehicle.

Interest was high from the very beginning and soon there were 12 members of the new club, eager to play against neighbouring opposition which arrived in the form of Holte Wanderers from Aston. The match took place on a bitterly cold November afternoon, the result was a 1-1 draw and Small Heath Alliance fielded these players: W.Edden; A.Wright, F.James; T.James, G.Edden, W.Edmunds (captain), T.Edden, D.Keys, C.Barmore, C.Barr, J.Sparrow and R.Morris. The latter was a late introduction when it was learnt that the Wanderers had 12 players on the field. David Keys was credited with the first-ever Blues' goal.

The Alliance played only a handful of games in their first season, but interest was such that the playing strength doubled and the annual subscription was raised from three halfpence per man, to twopence after the first year and then, in 1877, it was increased to threepence after the club had moved to their first enclosed ground, which had a capacity of 3,000, in Ladybrook Road, Sparkbrook.

On 11 September 1877, Small Heath moved headquarters again, paying a yearly rent of £5 for the privilege of playing at the Muntz Street ground. This was to be home for the Heathens, as they were called at this time, for 29 years. When they vacated that ground in December 1906, it was costing them £375 a year.

Small Heath impressed in their first season at Muntz Street, going through their 22-match programme undefeated, with Bill Edmunds and Arthur James sharing the captaincy and Charlie Barr, Tom Edden and Jack Sparrow scoring most of the goals. James was club skipper from 1878 to 1885 and, so great was his popularity, that he was affectionately known as 'The People's Pet'. He represented the Birmingham Association many times in challenge matches against Sheffield, Glasgow, London and other leading associations in contests which assumed considerable importance.

W.H.'Bill' Edwards was the club's first honorary secretary and he was followed into office by various city 'gents' including Walter W.Hart, Alfred 'Inky' Jones (1885-86) – a manufacturer of scales who was asked to balance the club's accounts – and Will Edden, who was the first in a long line of fine goalkeepers to have served the club down the years. Known as 'Pouncer', Edden won representative honours.

On 27 September 1879, the Heathens had an engagement at Muntz Street which was to form the beginnings of that great Midlands rivalry with Aston Villa. It was Small Heath who scored a victory which was recorded as 'one goal, and a disputed goal, to nil'. This historic occasion failed to get a mention in the local Press, the Birchfield Harriers Sports meeting taking priority.

Muntz Street was not the greatest of grounds, its playing surface being rather bumpy, which annoyed a lot of visiting teams. Small Heath, however, loved the place and suffered relatively few upsets during a five-year spell from 1878 to 1883. Opposing teams, though, were keen to avoid playing there and in 1882-83, a Walsall Cup-tie against Wednesbury Old Athletic was switched from Muntz Street to the Wednesbury club's ground after Athletic had offered £5 to give up home advantage. The Heathens duly obliged, collected their fiver and won 4-1. They went on to win the Walsall Cup – their first trophy.

The Birmingham club can claim precious few 'firsts' in football, yet one of their boasts is that they were one of the pioneers of professional soccer. They joined the paid ranks in August 1885, simply because their players could not afford to lose money by taking time off work to train for and play football.

The previous season, an 18-year-old called Harry Morris gained his place in the first team and few men did more sterling work on behalf of the Blues than this fellow. He went on to captain the side and was later a powerful figure in the boardroom. Morris was no business tycoon when he first joined the club. He was an apprentice plumber, earning half a crown (13p) a week. But he also pocketed cash from his soccer career and carefully saved this until he had amassed the princely sum of £85. When his playing days were over, he was in the position to rent a shop near to the club's former ground in Arthur Street. He bought a handcart, a few tools and set up a business on his own as a master-plumber. It was this same man – Harry Morris – who was to show great foresight again, when he saw 'a wilderness of stagnant water and muddy slopes' off Garrison Lane, Bordesley Green, and visualised a soccer arena arising out of that wilderness. It was this man who 'found' St Andrew's in 1906, when he was then a director of the club.

Another man whose name is linked with the club's early days is Alfred Jones – known universally as 'Inky' – who was appointed secretary in 1885-86. He succeeded Walter Hart, who was later to become chairman of the club. In 1892, 'Inky' Jones became the first paid secretary of Blues and he was widely regarded as one of the most capable executives in football.

In his first season as secretary, Jones saw the Heathens reach the semi-finals of the FA Cup (known then as the English Cup). On their way to the last four, they accounted for Burton Wanderers (9-2), Darwen (3-1), Derby County (4-2), Davenham (2-1) and Redcar (2-0), all at home. At the Aston Lower Grounds, however, against West Bromwich Albion, they crashed 4-0. Albion were a powerful side in those days and were too strong for Small Heath, who fielded Hedges (later to become an Albion director); Hare, Events, F.James, Felton, Simms, Davenport, Morris, Stanley, Figures and Hill. Their share of the gate receipts from this semi-final amounted to a mere £4 5s 0d. Some years later, defender Charlie 'Bowie' Simms revealed that each player was given half a crown for playing in that semi-final plus 1s 6d for a meal and 1s 0d for cab fare.

In 1886, the Heathens signed amateur goalkeeper Chris Charsley, who went on to become the only member of the club, when it was known as Small Heath Alliance, to represent England, being capped against Ireland in 1893. Charsley later joined the police force and became Chief Constable of Coventry.

Two years later another fine player, Billy Walton, was signed and went on to serve the club until 1902. Walton had been a supporter of the Small Heath club and was present at their semi-final against West Brom in 1886. In 1906, he attended the first game ever to be played at St Andrew's and helped clear snow off the pitch before the kick-off against Middlesbrough. In 1956, at the age of 84, he watched Blues play Manchester City in the FA Cup Final at Wembley. As a player, Walton gave Blues tremendous service at inside-forward and is a major personality in the club's history.

The 1886 semi-final against the Baggies was a significant stepping-stone for Small Heath, even though the players did not make a fortune from that fine Cup run. The kudos of reaching the semi-final stage, though, perhaps meant more than cash and certainly at this juncture the club could boast of some wonderfully loyal and dedicated servants. Charlie Simms proved a fitting example of a loyal club man. He served blues as a player from 1884 until 1892, then as a trainer and finally as groundsman before leaving the club in 1914, after 30 years' service.

The Heathens continued to operate as Small Heath Alliance until 24 July 1888, when the decision was taken to drop the word 'Alliance' and they became known as Small Heath Football Club Limited. That brought them another claim to fame, for they became the first club to introduce football directors. The first chairman of their board was Walter W.Hart. In the first year the club was 'in business' he was able to reveal glowing reports to his fellow directors, stating that in 1888-89, Small Heath had made a considerable profit which enabled the club to pay a five per cent dividend.

It was not all plain sailing, however, during these early years. Small Heath were elected to the Football Alliance in 1889, an organisation which included the likes of The Wednesday club (later Sheffield Wednesday), Stoke, Nottingham Forest, Sunderland Albion and St George's, a powerful Birmingham side. For three seasons, Small Heath remained members of the Alliance but achieved little.

In their initial season of 1889-90 – the Football League had been formed a season earlier – they managed only 17 points out of a possible 44 and finished third from bottom. The following season, after starting off with an emphatic 4-0 win over Aston Villa in a friendly at Perry Barr, their league form again left a lot to be desired and Small Heath once more finished third from bottom, with one point less.

There seemed a general lack of interest in the affairs of the club and this led to a public meeting being arranged at the Jenkins Street Board School, at which several of the 'football magnates' sought to whip up enthusiasm. They were successful to the extent that an extra 207 shares were put on the market.

Matters improved and in 1891-92, Small Heath took third place in the table, behind the champions, Nottingham Forest, and Newton Heath (now Manchester United). They also did well in the FA Cup, knocking out Leicester Fosse, Burton Wanderers, Brierley Hill and Woolwich Arsenal before succumbing to The Wednesday in the second round proper. This tie was scheduled to take place at Muntz Street, but the Sheffield club offered Small Heath £200 to play the match at Owlerton. The Birmingham side collected the fee and were duly dumped out of the competition, much to the annoyance of their supporters. Soon after the kick-off there were crowd disturbances and the FA later closed Wednesday's ground for 14 days.

The previous season (1890-91) Small Heath had been disqualified from the Cup when a man called Charlie Short, a former Unity Gas FC player, had not been properly registered. This came to light after the Heathens had eliminated Hednesford Town and Wednesbury Old Athletic.

The Devey family was a force to be reckoned with around this era and there were five brothers of some standing who were all useful footballers. Aston Villa claimed three of the brothers, while Small Heath took the other two, Will and Ted, both of whom were to render yeoman service to the club in the years ahead. Will Devey skippered the side from 1888 to 1891 and he was paid 12s 6d per week – good wages in those days.

Billy Walton was now showing off his scintillating skills at inside-forward and among the other stars of that period were goalkeeper Charsley, Tommy Hands, Frank Mobley, Billy Ollis, Freddie Wheldon – who later became an England international – and Caesar Augustus Llewellyn Jenkyns, a burly centre-half with a fearsome shoulder-charge.

Jenkyns had a magnificent physique and plenty of skill. He took over the club captaincy from Will Devey and won the first four of his eight Welsh caps with Small Heath. Solid, pale of complexion, moustachio'd and a player of immense power, he was a sight to inspire his own teammates and to strike fear into the hearts of the opposition. He could head a ball half the length of the field and once, it is alleged, kicked a dead-ball from one goal-line to the other. He was often in trouble with referees and was sent off at least four times during his career. Legends abounded and in one game he directed a shoulder-charge at an opponent in the centre of the field and onlookers swore that the poor fellow went flying for a distance of 30 yards before coming to rest in a heap against the wire ropes which surrounded the pitch.

In 1892, the Second Division of the Football League was formed and Small Heath, along with other members of the Football Alliance, were elected members. With Jenkins at the helm, the Heathens gave their opponents short shrift indeed. They scored 90 goals in only 22 matches and carried off the Second Division championship in style. Yet they were unable to claim a First Division place, losing in the Test Matches – forerunners of today's Play-offs. They were paired with Newton Heath and, after drawing at neutral Stoke, they lost the replay 5-2 at Sheffield and with it their hopes of gaining a place with the footballing élite.

Thus, Small Heath's achievement of winning the first-ever Second Division championship was not sufficient to see them promoted. In 1893-94, they finished runners-up in the Second Division and again had to take part in the Test Matches to see whether First Division football would be staged at Muntz Street – the ground was now known now as the 'celery trenches' – the following season. This time they came through with flying colours, beating Darwen 3-1 at Stoke. This was the team that won that game on 28 April 1894: Charsley; Short, Purves, Ollis, Jenkyns, E.Devey, Hallam, Walton, Mobley, Wheldon and Hands.

A train, with the club colours of royal blue and white draped around the funnel of the engine, was greeted by some 1,000 fans as it pulled into New Street Station from Stoke. They were already relishing the prospect of First Division football, especially the matches against arch rivals and neighbours, Aston Villa.

Small Heath's stay in Division One was destined to be short-lived, however, and after only two seasons they were relegated. Indeed, Blues might well have returned to the Second Division after only a season. They survived by the narrowest of margins after winning their final game of the 1894-95 campaign at Sheffield United 2-0, thus avoiding

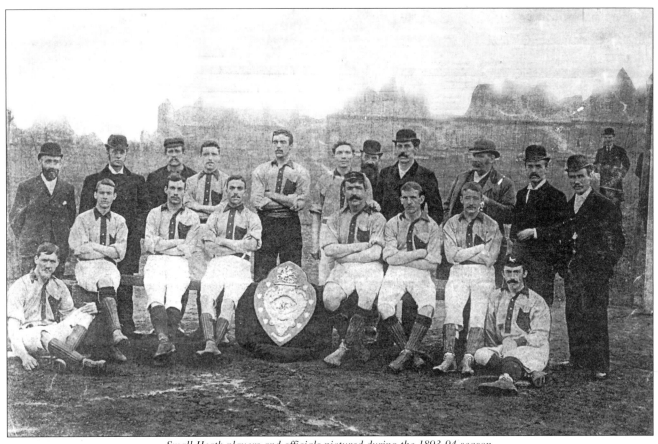

Small Heath players and officials pictured during the 1893-94 season.

another Test Match showdown.

These were hard times for Small Heath. Lack of cash hampered their recruitment of new players and the club's directors seemed to be waging a perpetual war against the spectre of debt. Even so, they kept battling and somehow managed to get together a brand-new side, although it is recorded that wages and other expenses were reduced. Among the new faces to arrive at the club was that of the

First League Match
Small Heath 5 Burslem Port Vale 1

NOTWITHSTANDING the wet and windy weather, which was 'rather uninviting' according to the *Birmingham Daily Gazette* reporter, a crowd of 2,500 saw the Blues' first-ever Football League game on 3 September 1893. But they had to wait quite some time before the Second Division match kicked-off. The visitors did not arrive at the Coventry Road ground until 4pm – half an hour after the scheduled kick-off time – and then they had a player missing, centre-forward Beats having missed his train.

That handicap of playing with ten men proved too much for Vale. Small Heath, backed by a gale-force wind, took the initiative from the start, peppering the Vale goal from all angles. Freddie Wheldon and Tommy Hands both went close with well-struck shots and George Short hit the woodwork.

The first goal came after five minutes. A 'rush' by Wheldon, Short and Harry Edwards resulted in Wheldon registering the Blues' opening goal. Vale responded with a shot from Scarratt, held comfortably by Chris Charsley, but the Blues always had the edge, playing a 'scientific' game, despite the gusty conditions.

Frail, the Vale goalkeeper, was warned by the referee for a bad foul on Wheldon but it was the 'keeper's mistake which led to the Blues' second goal, scored in splendid style by Short in the 37th minute. Six minutes later, following a 'scrimmage', Wheldon bundled the ball over the line to give the Blues a 3-0 advantage.

Vale bravely went forward in search of a consolation goal but the Blues were in complete control. Five minutes after the interval, Jack Hallam let fly with a right-foot 'rocket' from fully 20 yards to make it 4-0. All credit to Vale, though. They never gave in and, following a neat movement involving Walker and Bliss, the latter scored with a 'swift shot'.

Immediately afterwards Edwards skimmed a post for the Blues, Hallam fired over and Wheldon missed a 'sitter' from six yards. Scarratt had a fierce shot well-saved by Charsley, but in the dying seconds, a breakaway goal from Edwards made the final score 5-1 in the Blues' favour – a fine start to their League career.

Small Heath: Charsley; Bailey, Speller, Ollis, Jenkyns, E.Devey, Hallam, Edwards, Short, Wheldon, Hands.

Burslem Port Vale: Frail; Clutton, Elson, Farrington, McCrindle, Delves, Walker, Scarratt, Bliss, Jones (ten men only).

Attendance: 2,500

Referee: E.Aitchison (Long Eaton)

former Aston Villa and England forward, Dennis Hodgetts. He was well past his best but still gave Small Heath grand service as captain. At the end of the 1896-97 season they finished in fourth place in Division Two, then slipped down two places the following season, overall things were not looking too bright. Their support was waning and to reap some ready cash, the club staged a summer sports meeting which realised over £211 to boost the funds.

In the summer of 1898, Small Heath signed Bob McRoberts from Gainsborough Trinity and this great-hearted forward went on to give his all for the Birmingham club, who duly presented him with an illuminated address in April 1903, in recognition of five years' magnificent service.

By this time Caesar Jenkyns had moved on – to Woolwich Arsenal where he became skipper – and his place at centre-half was filled by Alex Leake. Birmingham-born and bred, Leake was a jovial fellow and soon became a great favourite at Small Heath. He eventually left them, following in the footsteps of Freddie Wheldon who had been transferred across the city to Aston Villa, and it was with Villa that he became an England international.

Another player of the same era was a left winger by the name of Sid Wharton. A 'Brummie', he served the club from 1897 until 1903, and he too graduated to international football with England. Later, he became a successful bookmaker and was also an excellent after-dinner speaker and an MC at boxing tournaments.

If Aston Villa could be thankful to Small Heath for the transfer of Messrs Wheldon and Leake, Blues could be grateful to their neighbours and keenest rivals for the transfer, not of a player, but of a valuable piece of property – Villa's old stand from Perry Barr which the Blues bought and erected behind the goal at the Muntz Street end of their ground in 1897.

The following year, in four consecutive games played at Muntz Street with that newly-erected stand full of cheering supporters, Blues rattled in no fewer than 35 goals. Their goalkeeper, Clutterbuck, was more or less a spectator as Chirk (8-0), Luton Town (9-0), Druids (10-0) and Darwen (8-0) succumbed to the power of the Blues forwards.

The wins over Chirk and Druids came in the FA Cup and soon after Burslem were hammered 7-0 and Manchester City 3-2 in the same competition, before Stoke finally ended Small Heath's impressive run in the second round proper.

It was around this period that support for Blues began to increase and on one occasion the club announced a profit of £755 18s 1d. But First Division football was still a distant vision and more money was still needed to boost the playing side. A little cash was gained from a bazaar and with it Blues went into the transfer market once more, this time securing the services of another Gainsborough star, Walter Wigmore. Bought initially to replace the injured McRoberts, he later switched into defence where he became a brilliant centre-half, the strongest man in the side.

In 1899-1900, Blues suffered what was described as a 'heavy loss' – more than £800 – and they took third place in Division Two. The club's directors courageously faced the deficit and firmly declined a tempting bait from Aston Villa to part with McRoberts.

At the turn of the century, Blues' exploits in the FA Cup were mediocre to say the least, after hammering luckless Oswestry 10-2 and Wrexham 6-1, they went out to Walsall in a replay, losing 2-0, with former Small Heath player Caesar Jenkyns performing splendidly for the Saddlers. The following year they lost in another replay, this time to Aston Villa; in 1901-02, Portsmouth dealt the knock-out blow in the first round; and 12 months later, Blues fell at the first hurdle, beaten by Derby County.

In the League, however, things looked brighter, especially in 1900-01 when Blues again won promotion from the Second Division, finishing runners-up to Grimsby Town. They lost only five out of 34 games during the course of the season and not one visiting team scored more than one goal against Blues at Muntz Street. A total of 48 points were gained and the defence gave away only 24 goals.

That 'cast-iron' rearguard in 1900-01 included goalkeeper 'Nat' Robinson and half-backs Walter Wigmore and Alex Leake, all three players having a terrific season.

Blues Hit a Dozen
Small Heath 12 Doncaster Rovers 0

THE *Birmingham Daily Gazette* correspondent described this victory on 11 April 1903 as 'emphatic, characterised by expressiveness, forceful finishing and unselfishness'. Rovers were completely 'overwhelmed, outplayed in every department and their defenders were powerless against constant Blues' attacking'.

The Blues scored three times in the first 45 minutes, through Arthur Leonard (18 minutes) and Freddie Wilcox (29 and 40 minutes). Wilcox's second followed a magnificent run by Charlie Field, who went past four defenders in a 40-yard dribble before setting up Wilcox ten yards from goal.

Eggett, in the visitors' goal, performed miracles during the first period. He saved twice from Wilcox, once each from Field, Leonard, Charlie Athersmith and Bob McRoberts, and then deflected a stunning 30-yard drive from Billy Beer on to the crossbar with his outstretched leg.

McRoberts, who insisted on playing despite suffering from a heavy cold, had a hand in eight of the nine goals the Blues ran in during a one-sided second half. He and Leonard were in brilliant form. Rovers were torn to shreds as the rampaging Small Heath pressed home their advantage. The Blues, in fact, seemed to have far too much time and both McRoberts and Field fluffed easy chances. then the floodgates reopened and the hapless Eggett in the visitors' goal could do nothing as the goals rained in.

Leonard and Wilcox each took their tallies to four goals apiece, Leonard's third coming from 40 yards, after a brave run by full-back Archie Goldie. Wilcox's fourth was a superb right-foot volley after a devastating run and dribble by McRoberts. Athersmith, Field, McRoberts and Jack Dougherty rounded off the massacre with Field's goal the 'pick of the bunch'.

Small Heath: Dorrington; Goldie, Wassell, Beer, Dougherty, Howard, Athersmith, Leonard, McRoberts, Wilcox, Field.

Doncaster Rovers: Eggett; Simpson, Layton, Murphy, Aston, Wright, Langham, Richards, Price, Ratcliffe, Robinson.

Attendance: 8,000

Referee: D.Hammond (Heywood, Lancashire)

Birmingham in 1905-06. Back row (left to right): Simms (assistant trainer), Norman (trainer), Glover, Robinson, W.Adams, Stokes, Howard, Dougherty, Dr Stanley, Alf Jones (secretary). Front row: Beer, Green, Mounteney, Wigmore, W.H.Jones, Wilcox, Field.

But that glory soon faded as Blues, under considerable pressure from the start of their first season back in the top-flight since 1895-96, slumped alarmingly and were immediately relegated. They struggled from start to finish and at once earned the reputation as the Midlands 'Yo-Yo' team. So far as the Blues' supporters were concerned, the only thing worth cheering in 1902 was the fact that the Boer War had been brought to a conclusion. Yet Small Heath could have saved themselves at the death. They had to win their last game, against Notts County, to avoid the drop. They managed only a goalless draw and went down with Manchester City.

Remarkably, Blues returned to Division One in 1903, along with Manchester City. Promotion, though, was not forthcoming without a bout of end-of-season nerves and anxieties as Blues stuttered over the last couple of weeks, with Woolwich Arsenal hot on their heels.

Harry Morris, who had played for the club for some 11 years, was invited to join the board of directors in 1903 and, with William Adams as president, things began to take a turn for the better as new players were enlisted, among them Jack Glover (from Liverpool), Ben Green (from Barnsley) and Frank Stokes (from Reading). Already well established in the side were goalkeeper Robinson; Billy Beer, a wonderful half-back bought from Sheffield United; former Aston Villa and England winger Charlie Athersmith; and of course, Wigmore and McRoberts, while in the forward-line W.H.'Bullet' Jones was also making a name for himself. Beer, incidentally, later became manager of the club.

Blues perhaps had their best season to date in 1904-05. Indeed, many old-time supporters reckoned that this was the best side that played under the title of Small Heath. The team had a reasonable League campaign (finishing seventh) and, despite going out of the FA Cup to Portsmouth in the opening round, they went on to win three important local trophies: The Lord Mayor of Birmingham's Charity Cup, the Birmingham Senior Cup and the Staffordshire Senior Cup. The season also

signalled the end of an era, for it was the last under the name of Small Heath.

In March 1905, Birmingham Football Club came into being. At a dinner for the players at the Swan Hotel, Yardley, director Mr T.D.Todd proposed an important change – that as the Blues were the only Football League club within the city of Birmingham, the time was ripe to call them Birmingham City.

Mr Todd, as it turned out, was some way before his time, because the club's shareholders refused to back him 100 per cent and the word 'City' was deleted from the original proposal. Thus Small Heath became Birmingham. Even then, some people did not take wholeheartedly to the change and one reporter referred to 'the Small Heath club now masquerading as Birmingham'.

In season 1905-06, Blues got the better of Aston Villa for the first time in a League fixture, defeating them 2-0 at Muntz Street on 16 September 1905 in front of a crowd estimated at 32,000. Blues again took seventh place in the final table and did very well in the FA Cup, dismissing Preston, Stoke and Tottenham Hotspur before losing in a fourth-round replay to Newcastle United.

So Birmingham were going places and with their fans ever-increasing in numbers, it was decided that Muntz Street could no longer cope with large attendances. A new ground was required and it was now that Harry Morris again stepped forward to convince his fellow directors that a desolate piece of wasteland – a wilderness of stagnant water and muddy slopes – off Garrison Lane, Bordesley Green – could be successfully converted into a soccer ground good enough to stage major competitive matches.

Chairman Walter Hart backed Harry Morris to the hilt and a debenture scheme was launched. Money was duly raised and in February 1906, the land was acquired on a 21-year lease at what was then described as 'advantageous terms'. A new ground committee was immediately appointed and everyone got down to the task of ensuring that everything ran smoothly. It was hard work, requiring an enormous amount

Birmingham in 1908-09. Back row (left to right): Beer, W.S.Corbett, Wigmore, Dorrington, Fairman, Kearns. Front row: Green, Williams, Jones, Smith, Eyre.

of effort with the clerk of the works, T.W.Turley and his committee, comprising Walter Hart, Harry Morris, Richard Todd, Thomas Wittell and Walter H.Bull, encouraging their assistants at every opportunity.

Plans were drawn up but, surprisingly, Blues did not appoint a professional architect for the task and were quite happy to rely upon a carpenter, Harry Pumfrey, who had been a fanatical supporter of the club for many years. The committee's faith was well founded, for Pumfrey had studied at the Birmingham School of Art and he forwarded a set of plans and drawings which, according to a spokesman, 'would have done credit to the most expensive professional architect'. Two vast pools had to be drained; tons of rubble had to be shifted and rolled down; and 10,000 square yards of turf had to be laid – all by the end of June, 1906. The second stage of the ground operation was to 'build' the Spion Kop and the original site was offered as a tip. That meant the dumping of thousands of tons of refuse on the site by the general public. This realised around £800 and the 'Kop' was there.

A grandstand on the Garrison side of the ground was erected, 123 yards long with close on half-a-million bricks holding up the roof. From that vast wasteland, the new and splendid ground, known as St Andrew's, was established with a capacity of 75,000. It had taken almost ten months of ceaseless toil to build but it was all worthwhile and Harry Morris's lifelong ambition had been fulfilled. St Andrew's was officially opened on Boxing Day 1906, for the First Division match between Birmingham and Middlesbrough.

For a time it was doubtful whether the game would be

staged because heavy snow covered the ground on Christmas Day night. But scores of volunteers battled away to clear the pitch and the match went ahead, ending in a goalless draw after 90 minutes of fierce endeavour. Ben Green had the pleasure of scoring the first goal at St Andrew's, for Blues against Preston three days later – and for his efforts he won a piano.

Season 1906-07 saw Blues take ninth place in the League and suffer an early Cup defeat (against Liverpool). But there was one consolation, in as much that St Andrew's was chosen as the venue for the FA Cup semi-final that season between Arsenal and Sheffield Wednesday.

After christening St Andrew's to good effect, Blues crashed alarmingly in 1907-08 and were relegated to the Second Division, finishing at the foot of the table. And worse was to follow. Two years later they finished last in Division Two but, fortunately for Blues, there was no automatic relegation and they topped the re-election poll on the first occasion they had sunk so low in the Football League.

There were the odd moments to enjoy during those disastrous campaigns, including away wins over Liverpool (4-3) and Sheffield Wednesday (4-1) in 1907-08; and a 5-0 home triumph over Gainsborough Trinity in 1909-10. Also in 1907-08, Blues' goalkeeper Jack Dorrington saved two penalties from that great marksman Harry Hampton in a Lord Mayor's Charity Cup-tie against Aston Villa.

Players inevitably left the club and new faces arrived. McRoberts departed in 1905, being the first player signed by Chelsea when they joined the Football League. He later returned as manager of Blues, when his trainer was the

Burnley's Hopes Dashed
Birmingham 4 Burnley 0

WHEN Burnley arrived at St Andrew's for this Second Division match on 6 April 1912, they were sitting proudly on top of the League table, their thoughts firmly set on winning promotion. But what a shock they had in store.

The Blues were in the middle of the pack and playing out the season, yet they completely outplayed Burnley, denting their promotion ambitions enormously. Indeed, the visitors failed to win First Division status at the end of the season.

A crowd of 35,000 – the biggest of the season at St Andrew's – saw a young amateur from Doncaster, Arthur Reed, make his debut for the Blues at centre-forward. He had a marvellous baptism, scoring twice, and gave the Burnley defence a 'right royal roasting.'

The Blues had the advantage of a strong wind behind them in the first half and Burnley had to face an exceptionally bright sun. It was the home side who dominated the early play with a series of attacks down the left wing.

After Dawson, in the Burnley goal, had saved three good efforts from Jack Hall, George Robertson and Dickie Gibson, debut-boy Reed was denied a goal through offside.

The Blues went ahead after 20 minutes. Some excellent work by Robertson and Albert Gardner set up Hall, whose powerful right-foot shot left Dawson stranded. Six minutes later, Reed celebrated his first senior outing for the Blues by making it 2-0 with a sweetly-struck shot from the edge of the area, after Hall and Walter Hastings had created the opening.

Dawson continued to perform heroics in the Burnley goal, stopping three efforts in four minutes as the Blues piled on the pressure. Birmingham were enjoying themselves immensely and in the 61st minute, Gibson broke away down the right and from his pin-point cross, Hastings cut in from the opposite flank and blasted in goal number-three. With 15 minutes remaining and Burnley looking rather despondent, Reed grabbed a fourth to give the Blues an inspired victory.

Birmingham: Bailey; Ball, Womack, Gardner, Tinkler, Bumphrey, Gibson, Hall, Reed, Robertson, Hastings.
Burnley: Dawson; Reid, Taylor, McLaren, Boyle, Watson, Nesbitt, Hodgson, Freeman, Weightman, Harris.
Attendance: 35,000
Referee: T.Kirkham (Burslem)

---

former Aston Villa goalkeeper, Billy George. Walter Wigmore's career was slowly drawing to a close and Billy Beer left, along with Messrs Green, Glover and Stokes.

Players recruited included Frank Womack, destined to become one of the club's greatest defenders, Jimmy Bumphrey and Charlie Millington. From 1910 to 1915, Blues had an undistinguished record, although they narrowly missed out on gaining promotion once more in 1912-13, failing by four points to overhaul runners-up Burnley. They never ventured beyond the first round of the FA Cup in four successive season up to 1912-13 and were knocked out in the third round in each of the next two campaigns, by Queen's Park Rangers and Oldham Athletic respectively.

In 1913 there were two major bribery scandals in Midlands football. One surrounded Jesse Pennington, the West Bromwich Albion and England footballer; the other was linked with Frank Womack of Blues. Womack, then Birmingham's captain, was approached in November 1913 by a fellow who offered him 55 guineas (£57.75) to help fix the game against Grimsby Town at St Andrew's so that it would end in a draw. Womack reported the matter to the police via club officials and the culprit was eventually dealt with in the Assize Court. For the record, the game ended in a 2-1 win for Grimsby.

Birmingham went reasonably close to regaining their First Division status in the first post-war season of 1919-20. In their side they had the former Villa star, Harry Hampton, Jack Jones from Sunderland, goalkeeper Dan Tremelling, formerly with Lincoln City, Joe Lane, Charlie Whitehouse and Alex McClure, who had progressed through the ranks after first signing for Birmingham in 1911-12. He later went to Aston Villa.

Blues took third spot in the table that season, beaten comfortably by the two promoted teams, Spurs and Huddersfield. The battling Brummies were exceptionally well served by Tremelling in goal. He played for 13 years with Blues, before handing over to another great goalkeeper,

Harry Hibbs. A tremendous favourite with the fans, Tremelling made almost 400 senior appearances (1919-31) before moving to Bury. It was his selection for England in an international match against Wales in 1928 which let in Hibbs and so well did Hibbs perform that when Tremelling returned, he found himself playing second fiddle to the man who was to become a household name with Blues.

It was Tremelling, though, who prevented Cardiff City from winning the Football League Championship in 1924. The Welsh club needed to beat Blues on the last day of the season to pip Huddersfield for the title and with the scores level they were awarded a penalty. Len Davies took the kick, Tremelling saved it and Cardiff missed out by a single point.

One lapse of memory meant that Blues did not enter the FA Cup competition in 1920-21. Secretary Frank Richards simply forgot to send in the club's application form and consequently they were not put in the hat for the first round draw. Richards admitted: "It was just one of those things – it could have happened even in the best regulated families."

Birmingham made up for that embarrassing Cup lapse by winning promotion that season. In 1920, Blues made a bargain signing when they lured Scot Johnny Crosbie, from Ayr United, down to St Andrew's for £3,000. Crosbie was rated one of the finest investments the club ever made. He was a dazzling ball-player who provided the ammunition for that great centre-forward, Joe Bradford, to score many of the 249 goals he amassed for Blues from 1921 to 1935.

It was Crosbie who guided Blues to the Second Division championship, appearing in all 42 matches. He and skipper Womack were in superb form throughout the campaign which saw Blues win 24 of their 42 matches, losing only eight. They scored 79 goals, conceded 38 and totalled 58 points.

This was the second time Blues had won the Division Two title. On the previous occasion, of course, they failed to win promotion after losing a Test Match against Newton Heath. Now promotion was automatic and Birmingham

Blistering Blues Fell Forest
Birmingham 8 Nottingham Forest 0

THE newspaper headlines which greeted this emphatic victory on 10 March 1920 contained those of 'Blistering Birmingham', 'Forest felled by Birmingham's new blood' and 'Scoring was like clockwork'.

Some of the Blues' best performances during this first post-war season had been given on away grounds, notably at Barnsley and Stoke, and it was gratifying when, in this rearranged home League match, the team chose to display their skills in front of their own supporters in such fine style.

The Blues introduced two new forwards to their line-up, Harry Hampton, (ex-Aston Villa and England) and Joe Lane (formerly of Blackpool, who cost a record £6,500). They linked up splendidly as the Blues registered their brightest victory of the season.

The work of Hampton was a revelation, while Lane, all muscle and aggression, also put in a sterling performance against a tough-tackling defence. 'This new strike-force was unstoppable going down the centre of the pitch,' reported the *Birmingham Gazette*. The Blues were in with a great chance of promotion to the First Division – they were lying second in the table, behind Tottenham Hotspur, with Huddersfield a close third – and

they controlled the play for long periods, more so after Forest had lost their centre-forward Hart with a fractured leg four minutes before the interval.

Early on, Forest went close on a couple of occasions through Shearman and Lithgoe, but gradually the Blues took charge and although their two first-half goals, both scored by Hampton, were somewhat fortunate, they went in at half-time in complete control.

Hampton's initial strike was a header in the 20th minute, after George Davis'; centre had eluded two Forest defenders. The ball dropped over the line off the far upright with 'keeper Johnson scrambling after it. Hampton's second, six minutes later, was a tap-in from six yards after Lane's shot had rebounded straight to him off the 'keeper's body and an upright.

In the second period, the Blues simply overwhelmed their visitors and the goals came with regularity. On 48 minutes Davies' cross was hammered, right-footed, into the net by Lane for a wonderful goal.

Fifteen minutes later Lane thundered in a shot which almost cracked the crossbar and Hampton was on hand to head in the rebound. It was 5-0 in the 68th minute, after

Lawrie Burkinshaw had slammed in a spectacular 30-yarder.

Five minutes later, the dazzling wing play of Davies caused havoc in the Forest defence and Burkinshaw was well-placed to turn in his pin-point centre. Fifteen minutes from time, Jack Whitehouse's blockbusting effort was superbly saved by the diving Johnson but the ball bounced perfectly for Hampton, who completed his afternoon with his fourth and Blues' seventh goal.

Lane rounded things off with number eight in the 89th minute, tucking away Davies' cunning centre after Barrett and Lowe had got themselves in a 'right old tizzy'.

The Blues missed promotion, finishing third behind Spurs and Huddersfield. But they did regain their First Division status the following season, going up as champions.

Birmingham: Tremelling; White, Womack, Evans, Millard, Roulson, Burkinshaw, Hampton, Lane, Whitehouse, Davies.
Nottingham Forest: Johnson; Barrett, Jones, Belton, Lowe, Armstrong, Davis, Spaven, Hart, Lithgoe, Shearman.

Attendance: 15,000
Referee: E.Pullan (Leeds)

---

made absolutely certain with some brilliant performances, including five-goal home wins over Hull, Leicester and Stockport, a 4-0 win at Coventry and a 3-0 triumph at Wolves. Yet the title was only achieved on goal-average from Cardiff.

In the early 1920s, some of the finest players ever to pull on the famous blue jersey of Birmingham joined the club. George Liddell, Dickie Dale, George Briggs, Jimmy Cringan, Ernie Islip and, of course, Harry Hibbs and Joe Bradford formed the backbone of the team which established the Blues as a First Division club for 18 seasons from 1921-22 to 1938-39 inclusive.

They did not exactly set the football world alight in the top flight, however, finishing in 18th position in 1921-22, 17th the following season and 14th the season after that. In 1924-25 Blues took eighth place, but then came a string of disappointing campaigns (1925-26 to 1930-31) when they never rose above halfway.

In 1927-28 Birmingham were desperately short of goals as they drew more matches (15) than they won (13) or lost (14). Indeed it took Blues nine seasons before they could boast a better 'goals for' column than 'goals against', this being in 1929-30.

Eight times they finished in the bottom six of the First Division between the wars, narrowly avoiding relegation in

1933-34 (20th) and 1930-31 (19th). They were always flirting with danger, continually struggling below the halfway mark in the table. Their form left a lot to be desired, yet the crowds were always willing to turn out at St Andrew's to cheer Blues. Average home attendances during the 1920s and 1930s were exceptionally good.

It must be said that the St Andrew's loyalists never got value for money. Time and again it was the presence of just three or four players that helped keep Blues in with a chance of taking something from the match in question. Goalkeeper Harry Hibbs was one of these star performers, following in the footsteps of great 'keepers like Charsley, Robinson, Hauser and Tremelling. Hibbs played for Blues from 1924 to 1940, making his debut at Aston Villa and his farewell appearance in a wartime testimonial against Villa at St Andrew's 16 years later.

During those seasons of First Division struggle, many fans claimed – and with some justification – that it was Hibbs, more than anyone else, who kept Birmingham going week after week, season after season. He stood between Blues and potential disaster as they struggled to keep their opponents at bay and were unable to hit the net at the other end.

A glance through the First Division tables of the inter-war period shows quite plainly that Blues just could not score the

Birmingham goalkeeper Dan Tremelling fails to clear the ball at White Hart Lane in December 1925 and Spurs' Jimmy Seed gets in a header.

A Tough Cup Battle
Birmingham 4 Peterborough & Fletton United 3

ON paper there seemed only one possible result – a home win – when the Blues took on non-Leaguers Peterborough & Fletton United in a third round FA Cup-tie at St Andrew's on 14 January 1928. It was the first time that Peterborough had reached this stage in the competition and they brought over 4,000 supporters with them.

The Blues were hot favourites and when Welsh international Stan Davies put them in front after seven minutes, running on to a centre from Benny Bond to crack the ball right-footed past Whitehead from 15 yards, the home crowd sat back in anticipation of seeing an onslaught. Indeed it was all Blues in the opening quarter of an hour, Davies and Joe Bradford having shots saved by the alert Whitehead.

But after 19 minutes, a breakaway saw Peterborough scramble an equaliser through Bruton, after Dan Tremelling in the Blues' goal had failed to hold a shot from Willis. Birmingham were now under heavy pressure and five minutes later, Peterborough went ahead in a simple and surprising way.

A free-kick conceded by Jimmy Cringan after a foul on MacNaughton resulted in Forrester firing the ball straight at Tremelling, who again fumbled it, allowing Bruton to easily slip it into the unguarded net.

Davies had a great chance of equalising as the Blues counter-attacked, but he shot over the bar from point-blank range after being set up by Bradford. It was a crucial miss, because two minutes from half-time, Peterborough went 3-1 up when McGuigan shot home following a wonderful run and cross from left winger Willis.

After half-time the Blues attacked straight from the whistle, Whitehead saving twice from Ellis and Davies. On the hour, Johnny Crosbie laid on a pin-point pass for Bradford to hammer home the Blues' second goal. Fifteen minutes later it was Crosbie, again, who carved out another opening for Bradford to coolly slot in the equaliser. Peterborough began to lose their momentum but as the Blues powered forward, so Whitehead and his co-defenders held firm and a replay looked on the cards. Then, with barely four minutes remaining, Crosbie sliced open the opponents' rearguard with a marvellous 30-yard pass which let in Bradford for his hat-trick.

It was tough on Peterborough, who had battled throughout. The Blues accounted for Wrexham in the next round before being knocked out by Manchester United, one step from the quarter-final.

Birmingham: Tremelling; Womack, Randle, Morrall, Cringan, Leslie, Bond, Crosbie, Bradford, Davies, Ellis.
Peterborough & Fletton United: Whitehead; Hutchinson, Betteridge, Dickinson, Forrester, Irving, McGuigan, MacNaughton, Bruton, Lowson, Willis.
Attendance: 38,128
Referee: I.Stouther (Nottingham)

It's all stripes. Blues goalkeeper Harry Hibbs fists at the ball against Chelsea in the 1931 FA Cup quarter-final at St Andrew's.

goals which would have brought them infinitely many more points and a greater assurance of First Division safety. Only five times did they finish above halfway and only twice in 18 seasons did they score more goals than they conceded. These statistics emphasise what an enormous burden the Blues defence had to carry, with Hibbs the kingpin in that overworked rearguard.

Yet, by a strange paradox, Blues had the players who, individually, were fine footballers, players who could match the best in the country. Billy Harvey was a grand winger and also a cricketer of some note; Joe Barrett and Aubrey Scriven were class performers, as were Welshman Ernie Curtis, George Morrall, Ned Barkas, who became club captain, the lanky Tom Fillingham, Bob Gregg, who came from Sheffield Wednesday, and Tom Grosvenor, later to move to Hillsborough.

Bradford was a magnificent goalscorer whose club record

of 32 goals in a season still stands. He set the record in 1927-28, including all four in a match against Blackburn Rovers and a terrific second-half hat-trick against Peterborough & Fletton United in the FA Cup, this after the non-League club had led 3-1 at half-time.

If Blues' League form was not up to scratch, they certainly made amends in the FA Cup, having good runs in 1924-25, 1927-28, 1930-31, 1932-33, 1933-34, 1934-35 and 1938-39. In 1930-31 the club reached its first-ever FA Cup Final, shortly after the appointment of Leslie Knighton as team manager. He arrived from Third Division Bournemouth in 1928-29, when Blues were really struggling, and set about a difficult task so well that his 'rescue act' culminated in Blues' appearance in the 1931 FA Cup Final against neighbours West Bromwich Albion at Wembley.

Knighton became known as 'football's lifeboatman' and he discovered Tom Grosvenor, a rock-like defender who

Blues Scale New Heights
Birmingham 2 Sunderland 0

ON their way to their first-ever FA Cup Final appearance, Birmingham knocked out some useful sides including Liverpool and Chelsea. Their semi-final game against Sunderland at Elland Road on 14 March 1931 saw the Blues scale new heights as they strode through to Wembley.

The Wearsiders were favourites to go on to their second Cup Final (they were beaten by Villa in the 1913 game) but on an afternoon when nervousness was commonplace and mistakes plentiful, it was the Blues, backed by 15,000 supporters, who maintained their discipline and withstood intense late pressure to record a grand victory.

A near full-house of around 43,500 saw this action-packed semi-final in which both goalkeepers were kept on their toes throughout the entire 90 minutes. Harry Hibbs was perhaps busiest and, according to Bobby Gurney, the Sunderland centre-forward, played 'an absolute blinder'.

But as far as the Sunderland fans were concerned, they blamed their inside-right 'Hookey' Leonard for the defeat, claiming that he missed four clear-cut chances with only Hibbs to beat. On the other hand, Hibbs possessed the extraordinary gift of anticipation which enabled him to get his body behind the ball when saving the hardest shot. And he was so quick off his line, cutting down the angle in a split second. Blues fans argued that their goalkeeper saved those shots, rather than Leonard missing the chances.

Ernie Curtis was the other Blues hero. A modest little Welshman, who four years earlier had played a prominent part in Cardiff City's sensational FA Cup Final victory over Arsenal, he scored both goals to ensure the Blues a place at Wembley.

After an even opening half-hour when Joe Bradford (twice) and Jack Firth had gone close for Birmingham and Gurney, Leonard and Eden had tested Hibbs, the dynamic Curtis struck his first blow.

The move was started by Jimmy Cringan in centre-field and George Briggs carried it on, skipping past full-back Murray before setting up Curtis. Although challenged strongly by Hastings and Andrews, he got in a powerful left-foot shot which flew past Middleton and into the far corner of the net via an upright. Sunderland hit back immediately. Gurney grazing the crossbar with a 20-yarder and O'Connor heading inches wide after Ned Barkas had slipped in trying to cut out a centre from the right.

The Blues held on until half-time but they lived dangerously early in the second period when Leonard, in the space of five minutes, missed two chances, Hibbs smothering the ball on each occasion. Bradford went close, as did Johnny Crosbie, and then Leonard (twice), Gurney and the industrious Eden tested Hibbs with crisp ground-shots.

With only three minutes left and the Blues under pressure, Curtis made certain of victory. Bradford, hovering on the right wing, picked out Curtis, who had moved into the centre-forward position. The Welshman's first shot was saved by the diving Middleton but he was on the rebound in a flash and thumped the ball into the net.

Birmingham: Hibbs; Liddell, Barkas, Cringan, Morrall, Leslie, Briggs, Crosbie, Bradford, Firth, Curtis.
Sunderland: Middleton; Murray, Shaw, Hastings, McDougall, Andrews, Eden, Devine, Gurney, Leonard, O'Connor.
Attendance: 43,570
Referee: A.E.Fogg (Bolton)

came into the Birmingham side after the 1930-31 season. He also signed Barkas and Fillingham, as well as Gregg and Stoker, and had a bid for the great Alex James turned down. At one time he had four international goalkeepers to choose from – Tremelling and Hibbs both full England caps, Ken Tewkesbury, an England amateur player, and Arthur Slater, a junior international.

With Knighton in charge and Ned Barkas driving the team from the back, Crosbie oiling the midfield and Joe Bradford scoring goals., Blues began their march on Wembley with a 2-0 third-round win at Liverpool and repeated the scoreline in round four, at home to Port Vale. Unlike Blues' League fortunes, in the Cup every shot seemed to go in. Even a few injury problems did not deter Blues, who stormed on with a fifth-round 3-0 victory over Watford.

In the quarter-finals they met Chelsea at St Andrew's and drew 2-2 after a tense struggle. The midweek replay at Stamford Bridge drew a crowd of 74,365, with a further 6,000 locked outside. Those present witnessed a cracking contest, won in style by Blues, 3-0. Briggs made all the goals, for Jack Firth and Joe Bradford (2). In the semi-final for the first time since 1886, Blues met Sunderland at Elland Road, Leeds, and this time they achieved their ambition, winning 2-0 to earn a Wembley place against West Brom.

At this juncture in the season Blues were still striving to avoid relegation. Prior to the third round, they had gone through a terrible period, losing 9-1 at Hillsborough – it would have been ten had not Hibbs saved a penalty – and going down at home to Leeds United and Derby County.

Injury problems plagued the Blues right up to the eve of the 1931 FA Cup Final. Briggs and Cringan both suffered knocks and there was a serious doubt over Joe Bradford, whose damaged knee was not responding to treatment. In their League programme, Birmingham lost match after match and their confidence dwindled. 'Gentleman' Joe Bradford pronounced himself fit on the morning of the Final but still had to turn out with one leg heavily bandaged.

Albion, then in Division Two had beaten the favourites, Everton, in the semi-final and were quietly confident of causing another upset. Blues were able to field their strongest side which was: Hibbs; Liddell, Barkas, Cringan, Morrall, Leslie, Briggs, Crosbie, Bradford, Gregg, Curtis. Albion lined up: Pearson; Shaw, Trentham, Magee, W.Richardson, Edwards, Glidden, Carter, W.G.Richardson, Sandford, Wood. The referee was A.H.Kingscott from Derby. The outcome was a 2-1 win for Albion. W.G.Richardson scored both their goals, the winner only seconds after Joe Bradford had equalised for Blues.

It was a hard-fought Final, not a classic by any means. Albion just about deserved their success but the whole context or the match could well have been different had Bob Gregg's early 'goal' for Blues been allowed to stand. Instead it was ruled out for offside and Albion took full advantage of this let-off. 'WG' scored first after 25 minutes, Bradford

Birmingham's Gregg gets the ball into the West Brom net early in the 1931 FA Cup Final at Wembley but the goal was disallowed.

First Wembley Appearance
Birmingham 1 West Bromwich Albion 2

AFTER 50 years of trying, Birmingham at last reached their first FA Cup Final, having played their first game in the competition back in 1881.

West Bromwich Albion, from the Second Division, came through to meet the Blues in the first all-Midlands FA Cup Final for 36 years on 25 April 1931. Albion were going for the double – that of promotion and FA Cup glory in the same season.

It was one of the wettest Cup Final days for years and the *Daily Express* reported: 'As for the players, they were all wet through; they were covered with mud. They were dog-tired, for this had been one of the hardest-played games in the history of modern football.'

The Blues gave every ounce of energy they had yet, on the day, effort was not enough. After an even start, Birmingham thought they had scored in the sixth minute when Bob Gregg darted forward to head Jimmy Cringan's free-kick past a stranded Harold Pearson in the Albion goal. But referee Kingscott ruled that Gregg was offside after a signal from his linesman, Harold Mee of Nottingham.

Albion defended desperately for a time and Pearson had to race out of his area to kick clear from the onrushing Joe Bradford. Then Ernie Curtis skippered past Shaw but his cross was cut out by Magee. Ned Barkas crashed into Joe Carter as Albion counter-attacked and the Blues' skipper was called upon to clear his lines as Glidden and W.G.Richardson raced on to a long ball from Edwards.

After 25 minutes Albion scored. Glidden got in a shot from the right and as the ball zipped across the penalty area it struck Barkas' hand and rebounded to Richardson, whose first-time effort was only parried by Hibbs. Richardson followed up to send the ball into the net.

Birmingham hit back and Bradford and Johnny Crosbie both missed good chances. Three minutes from half-time Bradford's half-hit shot bounced awkwardly and passed narrowly wide of a post with Pearson scrambling along his line.

The start of the second period, Hibbs saved splendidly from Wood and Carter struck the angle with a 20-yarder. The Blues responded with a

snap shot from Crosbie and after 56 minutes they equalised. A long ball by Crosbie found Bradford. With his left shoulder facing the goal, the Blues forward pivoted and sent a right-foot shot past Pearson.

But straight from the restart, a brilliant move ended when W.G.Richardson regained the lead for Albion. Carter, Richardson and Sandford raced at the Blues defence and George Liddell's attempted clearance set-up the centre-forward, who slid the ball past a groping Hibbs from point-blank range.

Hibbs then pulled off a couple of terrific diving saves as Albion took control and lifted the Cup. They achieved that unique double by winning their last two League games.

Birmingham: Hibbs; Liddell, Barkas, Cringan, Morrall, Leslie, Briggs, Crosbie, Bradford, Gregg, Curtis.

West Bromwich Albion: Pearson; Shaw, Trentham, Magee, W.Richardson, Edwards, Glidden, Carter, W.G.Richardson, Sandford, Wood.

Attendance: 90,368
Referee: A.H.Kingscott (Derby)

equalised with a cracking 25-yard volley 12 minutes into the second half, but straight from the kick-off Albion's inside trio stormed upfield and Richardson scrambled the ball past Hibbs for the winner. Albion achieved a unique double of promotion and Cup success in the same season.

At Christmas 1932, manager Knighton signed a new contract, obviously intending to remain at St Andrew's for several more years. But in 1933, Chelsea persuaded him to

Surviving in Style
Leicester City 3 Birmingham 7

THIS was a game the Blues had to win, for they were in a relegation dog-fight with Newcastle, Liverpool, Chelsea, Aston Villa and Middlesbrough.

Sheffield United were already doomed to the Second Division. Birmingham and Newcastle were both on 34 points, Chelsea had 35 and Liverpool and Villa were on 36, with Middlesbrough a point better off. This was the Blues' penultimate League game and two points were imperative on 28 April 1934.

Overnight rain and a heavy downpour an hour or so before the kick-off reduced the Filbert Street pitch to a virtual quagmire. The miserable weather also affected the attendance and there were only 12,000 in the ground at kick-off time.

The Blues got off to a flying start, Sid Moffatt scoring after only four minutes. Charlie Calladine sent Billy Guest racing down the left and from the winger's low cross, Moffatt drove the ball home, right-footed from ten yards.

Leicester fought back and two fine saves from Harry Hibbs prevented the equaliser. But after 25 minutes, Liddle got the better of Harry Booton, allowing Chandler, bursting through the middle, to level the score with a spectacular shot.

The Blues, however, regained their momentum and six minutes later Guest robbed Smith, rounded Black and fired in an unstoppable drive to restore their lead.

Less than a minute later Guest hit the target again. Moffatt produced a dazzling run, centred for Dave Mangnall, who unselfishly allowed the ball to run on for Guest to net with a powerful left-footer.

The Blues might have added to their score before the break, but McLaren saved two long-range efforts from Freddie Roberts and a header from Mangnall. Then Guest struck the outside of the post.

Fifteen minutes into the second half, Chandler reduced the deficit to 3-2, capitalising on a slip by 'Lofty' Morrall, and five minutes later, with

the Blues back-pedalling, Maw nipped in to equalise.

The Blues, though, were not shaken and, straight from the kick-off, a splendid movement involving Mangnall and Joe Bradford resulted in the former edging his side back in front.

On 70 minutes, a misunderstanding in the Leicester defence saw Jones concede an own-goal to give the Blues a 5-3 lead; two minutes later Roberts cracked in number-six and with five minutes remaining, Guest claimed his hat-trick to give the Blues a great victory, and one which kept them in the First Division. Newcastle were relegated with Sheffield United.

Leicester City: McLaren; Black, Jones, Smith, Heywood, Ritchie, Adcock, Maw, Chandler, Lochhead, Liddle.
Birmingham: Hibbs; Booton, Barkas, Stoker, Morrall, Calladine, Moffatt, Roberts, Mangnall, Bradford, Guest.
Attendance: 18,000
Referee: J.S.Brown (Blackburn)

---

go to Stamford Bridge as their manager. Knighton left behind a good squad of players at St Andrew's and his successor was a former Blues player, George Liddell.

His first full season in office (1933-34) was one of experiments rather than a series of success stories and Blues avoided relegation by one point. Liddell introduced new faces, as well as releasing players whom he felt were past their best. He drafted in men like Frank Clack, Billy Horsman, Frank McGurk, Jackie Brown, Charlie Phillips and Ernie Richardson; gambled with the drive and tenacity of centre-forwards Dave Mangnall, Ken Kendrick, Sammy Small and George Haywood. He hoped that the skills would come from half-backs Bob Meacock, Wally Halsall, Ray Devey, Dai Richards, Charlie Calladine, Joey Loughran and George Lea and persevered with Billy Hughes, Don Dearson, Fred Harris, Billy Guest, Joe Devine, Ted Duckhouse, Dennis Jennings, Cyril Trigg and the purposeful Wilson Jones – all within the space of six years.

During his managerial reign, Liddell utilised no fewer than 70 players in Blues' first team in an effort to get a settled, winning side. It was to no avail as Birmingham suffered relegation in the final peacetime season of 1938-39, going down with Leicester City. Of their 42 matches, Blues lost 22, scored 62 goals and conceded 84. They suffered heavy defeats at Aston Villa (5-1), Liverpool (4-0), Preston (5-0), Stoke (6-3) and Manchester United (4-1). In the FA Cup a crowd of 67,341 saw Blues draw 2-2 with Everton in the fifth round – a record for St Andrew's which still stands today.

There were, however, some bright spots on the horizon and of the pre-war players who had broken into Blues' League side, several were to be at St Andrew's after the

hostilities, when Blues once more stormed back into the First Division. These included Dearson, signed from Barry Town and who later established himself in the Welsh national side along with club mate Billy Hughes; Fred Harris, who became club captain; Wilson Jones; Dennis 'Play-anywhere' Jennings; and Cyril Trigg, who proved to be a grand servant to the club, appearing in well over 350 games before retiring in 1954.

League football was abandoned after only three matches at the start of the 1939-40 season and immediately the Government banned all outdoor sporting activities until matters concerning the safety of spectators and players alike could be properly assessed. All contracts between professional clubs and their players were duly cancelled but, within a matter of weeks, the Government decided that competitive football could go ahead, although at first attendances at all grounds had to be restricted to around 5,000.

Friendly matches were arranged and guest players were recruited to fill gaps left by those Blues stars who were drafted into the forces. After three months, however, the Birmingham club ran into new problems. The city's Chief Constable, C.H.H.Moriarty, pronounced that the area directly around the St Andrew's ground constituted a danger zone, thus spectators were banned from watching Blues in action. Local MPs twice raised the matter in Parliament, but the Home Secretary of the day 'regretted' that he could not order a change of decision. While the discussions took place, Blues had to play all their matches on opponent's grounds. Finally, it was decided on 12 March 1940 that Blues could return to St Andrew's.

The Chief Constable was not too pleased, nor were the

Don Dearson (right) scoring for Blues against West Brom at St Andrew's on Good Friday 1938. Blues won 2-1.

Biggest-Ever Blues Attendance
Birmingham 2 Everton 2

IT is unlikely that such a large crowd will ever again assemble inside St Andrew's as the one which witnessed this thrill-a-minute fifth-round FA Cup-tie on 11 February 1939. Everton were on course for a League and Cup double. They led the First Division and were hot favourites to carry all before them on the road to Wembley. The Blues, meanwhile, were struggling desperately and relegation stared them in the face.

As often happens, though, Cup football proved a great leveller and Birmingham played well above themselves, coming so close to producing the shock result of the round.

In the very first attack Jackie Brown, Birmingham's Northern Ireland international, almost put the Blues in front. After 15 minutes Dennis Jennings clipped the outside of a post and shortly afterwards, Charlie Craven headed over from point-blank range.

Everton did their fair share of attacking and Tommy Lawton (twice) and Wally Boyes tested Frank Clack to the full. It was action all the way. On 33 minutes Jennings fired into the sidenetting from ten yards, then the Blues' hefty inside-left, Owen Madden, saw his powerful header brilliantly saved by Ted Sagar.

The Blues, perhaps against the run of play, snatched the lead in the 44th minute when Madden's 25-yard shot was deflected wide of Sagar by Greenhalgh's hip. But straight from the kick-off, Everton went downfield and equalised through their Irish international, Alex Stevenson.

The second half produced a grim struggle. On the hour Everton took the lead through Boyes, the former West Brom winger. The Blues' goalkeeper, Clack, pushed out a corner but the ball fell invitingly for Boyes. His shot appeared to be going out for a goal-kick when it deflected off Lawton and into the net.

Birmingham, though, were still not done for. They took the game to Everton and after some near misses, Madden headed in the equaliser after 80 minutes, following a splendid run by Craven. It was a fair result to a wonderful Cup-tie.

Everton went on to win the replay 2-1 before being knocked out by Wolves (2-0) in the sixth round. The League title found its way to Goodison Park in 1938-39, but the Blues went down after a spell of 18 seasons in the First Division.

Birmingham: Clack; Trigg, Hughes, Dearson, Halsall, Richards, Jennings, Craven, Harris, Madden, Brown.
Everton: Sagar; Cook, Greenhalgh, Mercer, Jones, Thomson, Gillick, Bootham, Lawton, Stevenson, Boyes.
Attendance: 67,341
Referee: W.F.Daly (Orpington)

Gil Merrick punches over the bar from Derby County's Jack Stamps in the 1946 FA Cup semi-final.

eight Council members who backed him, but thousands of fans, many of them working long hours in munitions factories, were delighted that once again they could enjoy their soccer on a Saturday afternoon. For the 'reopening' of St Andrew's on 23 March 1940, there was an attendance of 13,241 to see Blues play Walsall in a Midland Regional League game. At the end of the 1939-40 season, the League introduced a Cup competition and Blues did very well, reaching the last eight before going down to the eventual winners, West Ham United.

In 1940-41, the competitions were better organised with regionalised fixtures being arranged to reduce the travelling. There were, however, even greater difficulties facing Blues when St Andrew's was heavily bombed towards the end of that second wartime season. The German Luftwaffe scored a direct hit on the ground on no fewer than 20 occasions, causing thousands of pounds worth of damage. More was to follow and in January 1942, the Main Stand was destroyed by fire, not from bombs but by a member of the fire service, who mistook petrol for water when attempting to dampen-down a brazier.

With St Andrew's now in a sorry state of twisted steel-work and cratered terraces, Blues sought refuge at Leamington's ground and at unscathed Villa Park for a short while until returning home in season 1943-44. St Andrew's looked a dismal sight with no roof on the 'Spion Kop' and the grandstand badly damaged. Much hard work went into clearing up the wreckage and providing the players with some sort of covered dressing-room accommodation, although on several occasions a nearby factory was utilised, especially in cold weather.

Blues got through seasons 1943-44 and 1944-45 without much trouble although the scars of the fire and the German bombs were still there to be seen. With the war coming to an end, they began to plan for a peacetime future. On 1 June

1945, the Birmingham club named Harry Storer as their manager in succession to George Liddell. Mr W.A.'Bill' Camkin had been appointed honorary managing director and he put a tremendous amount of work into the club which helped keep the soccer flag flying at St Andrew's during a period of uncertainty.

Storer, a former Derbyshire cricketer, was an experienced football man, having played for Grimsby Town, Derby County, Burnley and England (winning two caps). He had managed Coventry City from May 1931 and it was something of a surprise when he decided to leave Highfield Road for St Andrew's.

His methods paid off at St Andrew's and he led Blues to the Football League (South) Championship in his first season at the club. Blues became Birmingham City FC on 1 July 1944 and they became the first club to pay a wartime benefit to a professional player with Harry Hibbs' testimonial against Aston Villa in 1940.

The Football League South was made up of the pre-war First and Second Division clubs from Derby southwards and in winning the title, Blues lost only nine games, recording 28 wins, scoring 98 goals and conceding 45. It was a record good enough to pip Aston Villa for the top prize on goal-average. Also in 1945-46, Birmingham reached the FA Cup semi-finals after a thrilling passage which saw them beat Portsmouth (the Cup holders, 1-0 on aggregate), Watford (6-1 on aggregate with Scotsman 'Jock' Mulraney, signed from Ipswich Town, scoring a splendid hat-trick in the 5-0 win at St Andrew's), Sunderland (3-2 on aggregate after being 2-0 down at one stage) and Bradford (8-2 over two legs, including a 6-0 home win). Blues met Derby County at Hillsborough and in front of a massive 65,000 crowd they held the Rams to a 1-1 draw. In the replay at Maine Road, Blues battled hard to take the game into extra-time but then tragedy struck when Ted Duckhouse broke a leg. Derby took

Blues Christmas Cracker
Birmingham City 6 Leicester City 2

THE transitional season of 1945-46 produced some brilliant performances from the Blues, both at home and away, in League and Cup competitions. They reached the FA Cup semi-finals before losing to Derby County after a replay, but made up for that disappointment by carrying off the League South title, pipping arch-rivals Aston Villa on goal-average.

At St Andrew's, the Blues registered some splendid victories, including 8-0 against Spurs, 5-0 against Swansea, 5-2 over Chelsea and 4-0 against West Brom. On Christmas Day they produced another scintillating display against a useful Leicester City side.

Birmingham had won their previous nine League matches at St Andrew's and an enthusiastic crowd of around 30,000 turned out to see if the Blues could run up ten wins in succession.

Fielding their full-strength line-up, Birmingham did just that, whipping in six goals – and it might have been more, but for Grant, the visiting goalkeeper, pulling off a string of fine saves. Winger Jock Mulraney was the thorn in the Leicester side, having a quite superb game on the right flank. He set up three goals and scored another himself with a wicked cross-shot which flew into the net through a crowd of players. Wilson Jones said that he got a touch on the ball, but Mulraney claimed the goal which gave the Blues an early lead they never relinquished.

The second goal came after a sweet move involving Mulraney and Dougall with Jones finishing off in style. The same player grabbed the third shortly afterwards as Leicester back-pedalled under severe pressure.

The Filbert Street side battled back to reduce the arrears through Dewis on the half-hour. The Blues, however, soon restored their three-goal advantage when Neil Dougall, Fred Harris and Harold Bodle linked up for Dougall to fire hard and low past Grant. Leicester responded again and before the break Dewis made it 4-2, after Frank Mitchell and Ted Duckhouse got into a tangle in front of Gil Merrick.

After the interval, Leicester came out on the attack but the Blues defence held firm and during an excellent second-half, the crowd enjoyed some delightful football played at a frantic pace. Birmingham struck two more goals, from Bodle and the last from Welsh international left winger George Edwards.

Mulraney and Dougall both shaved the woodwork and for Leicester, Mercer, Dewis (twice) and Campbell came near. It was a competent performance by the Blues, who closed the gap at the top of the table, leaving only Charlton Athletic ahead of them. Charlton were gradually overhauled and the Blues went on to lift their first trophy in 25 years.

Birmingham City: Merrick; Duckhouse, Jennings, Harris, Turner, Mitchell, Mulraney, Dougall, Jones, Bodle, Edwards.

Leicester City: Grant; Frame, Howe, Smith, Sheard, Soo, Campbell, Mercer, Dewis, Pimbley, Weatherston.

Attendance: 30,000
Referee: W.E.Wood (Bedford)

---

full of advantage and hammered four goals past Gil Merrick to race through to Wembley, leaving Blues with the League trophy to grace their boardroom. A bumper crowd of 80,480 packed in to see the replay – still a record for a midweek game outside Wembley between two Football League clubs – and the gate receipts amounted to a then record £28,205.

Blues now had Gil Merrick in goal; at full-back were Billy Hughes and Dennis Jennings; the half-back line comprised any three of Ted Duckhouse, Fred Harris, Arthur Turner, Frank Mitchell and Sid Owen; the forward line came from Ambrose 'Jock' Mulraney, Neil Dougall, Harold Bodle, Wilson Jones, George Edwards and Cyril Trigg.

In the first three seasons following World War Two, Blues were not far short of being invincible. They were beaten only eight times at home in 63 matches; they conceded only 102 goals in 126 League games; and they won the Second Division title in 1947-48. New faces had been introduced, with Ken Green stepping in to partner Jennings, who was still playing at the age of 40, at full-back. At outside-right came another Scot, Jackie Stewart, transferred from Raith Rovers, a real bundle of energy who could also play inside-forward.

Blues' record in season 1947-48 was quite brilliant: played 42, won 22, drawn 15, lost five, goals for 65, against 24, points 59. And that magnificent defensive record is still a club record.

Blues set about re-establishing themselves in the top-flight in 1948-49, when they finished 17th, but changes were afoot. After four years as manager, Harry Storer left. So did players Frank Mitchell (sold to Chelsea), Neil Dougall (to Plymouth Argyle) and George Edwards (to Cardiff City). Arthur Turner had earlier moved to Southport.

Bob Brocklebank, the former Aston Villa player, succeeded Storer as manager but could not prevent Birmingham being relegated in 1950. It was Brocklebank, though, who brought together a brand-new team which eventually won back Blues' First Division place in 1954-55. Two years later, with former St Andrew's favourite Arthur Turner as manager, Birmingham City reached their second Wembley FA Cup Final.

Birmingham had initially lasted only two seasons in Division One, dropping back into the Second at the end of 1949-50, when they finished bottom and were relegated, once again with Manchester City. They went out of the FA Cup in the third round, beaten by Swansea, the third time in succession they had fallen at this hurdle.

For one loyal and dedicated clubman it was the old, old story. Veteran Frank Richards, former office-boy, secretary (1925-43) and by now a director at St Andrew's, had seen it all before . . .the joys and disasters, the ups and downs, which had punctuated Blues' fortunes over the years.

Against all the odds, however, in season 1950-51 Birmingham raced through to the FA Cup semi-final for the second time in five years, knocking out, Manchester City, Derby County, Bristol City and high-flying Manchester United, who had won the Cup in 1948. Blackpool, Stan Matthews and all, provided the opposition and after a goalless draw at Maine Road, the Seasiders held the upper hand in the replay at Goodison Park to win 2-1 in a bruising contest. Yet it must be said that Blues were so unlucky not to

Stewart Takes the Glory
Aston Villa 0 Birmingham City 3

THIS game on 4 December 1948 was the first 'Second City' local derby in the League since March 1939 and little wonder there was a bumper crowd packed inside Villa Park. But, as the *Sports Argus* banner headlines proclaimed, it was 'St Andrew's Day at Villa Park'.

It was actually four days after the official day for Scotland's patron saint, but that didn't bother Jackie Stewart, the stocky Scottish winger who netted two of Blues' goals (both from inside-forward) with Harold Bodle claiming the other.

Only four players – two from each side – had survived from the last pre-war derby: goalkeeper Joe Rutherford and full-back George Cummings of Villa and Freddie Harris and Dennis Jennings from Blues, who, in 1939, had formed the right wing but were now right-half and left-back respectively.

Faced by a Villa attack led by the fiery figure of Welsh international Trevor Ford, and with former St Andrew's favourite Jock Mulraney on the right wing, Blues' defence played exceedingly well throughout, restricting the men in claret and blue to only three efforts on goal in the first half (two from George Edwards) and two in the second (both from Ford)

In contrast, Blues themselves, using the long-ball game in contrast to Villa's short-passing approach, attacked with confidence, with the 24-year-old Stewart, signed from Raith Rovers, in devastating form.

He scored the opening goal on 15 minutes, rounding off a flowing move which originated with Ted Duckhouse deep in Blues' territory. Stewart, in the inside-left position, took a clever back-heeler by Neil Dougall before going on to beat Rutherford with a well-placed shot to the goalkeeper's right.

Stewart's second goal arrived on 66 minutes. He popped up in the right place at the right time to hook the ball wide of Rutherford from a set piece involving Harris, who took the free-kick, and Bodle, whose header left Stewart free eight yards from goal.

At this stage Blues were in total control of the game and they added a third goal on 71 minutes when Bodle, who had a fine match, tucked away a chance created by outside-right Johnny Berry, Bodle netting with a cleverly flighted lob over the advancing goalkeeper.

Aston Villa: Rutherford; C.Martin, Cummings, A.Moss, F.Moss, Lowe, Mulraney, Dorsett, Ford, Edwards, L.Smith.

Birmingham City: Merrick; Green, Jennings, Harris, Duckhouse, Mitchell, Berry, Stewart, Dougall, Bodle, Roberts.

Attendance: 61,632
Referee: Capt F.C.Green (Wolverhampton)

have won at Maine Road. With time fast running out, a shot from winger Jackie Stewart struck a goal-post, rebounded to safety and so Blackpool escaped. The Seasiders lost 2-0 in the Final to Newcastle United.

In the League that season, Blues finished a creditable fourth, only three points behind Manchester City, who were runners-up. There were by now several more new faces in the Blues; line-up and, during the course of the season, manager Brocklebank used 22 players. Goalkeeper Merrick was an ever-present , along with Arthur Atkins. The full-backs were usually Ken Green and Jack Badham. Len Boyd was at right-half, Atkins occupied the number-five shirt, with Ray Ferris, Don Dorman and Roy Warhurst filling in at left-half. Jackie Stewart was outside-right with Johnny Berry, whose career was ended after injuries received in the Munich air disaster.

Other members of the Blues' first-team squad around this time included reserve goalkeepers Bill Robertson (ex-Chelsea) and Johnny Schofield, who was to make a name for himself in the years ahead; full-backs Jeff Hall, destined to become an England international but who died of polio at the age of 29, and Roy Martin, who later played under Harry Storer at Derby; half-backs Johnny Watts and Johnny Newman both of whom went on to make the grade with Blues; and forwards Jim Dailey and Ted Purdon. Dailey, the first player signed by manager Brocklebank (from Sheffield Wednesday in 1949) once scored five goals for the Owls against Barnsley in a Second Division match in September 1947; Ted Purdon was a South African who later played for Sunderland.

The man mainly responsible for bringing most of those players to St Andrew's was Walter Taylor, the club's chief scout. Taylor had played as a part-time professional for Atherstone, Leamington and Bournbrook and then joined Coventry City, becoming a 'casual' scout for Blues under Billy Beer in the 1920s. Taylor was born within walking distance of St Andrew's and was an avid supporter of the club. In his time he received several offers to step into management but turned them all down to concentrate on his scouting.

Taylor described goalkeeper Gil Merrick as his 'best signing' for Blues and it was in a friendly match that Taylor first spotted the talents of this fine 'keeper when he was playing for Solihull Town, who were then managed by the former Blues player, Ned Barkas.

Ken Green was another player 'spotted' by eagle-eyed Taylor and so was Jeff Hall. In that 1950-51 season, a youngster who was to become another Blues post-war 'great' captained the Brierley Hill and Sedgley side in the English Schools Trophy Final. His name was Trevor Smith and Taylor's awareness of knowing a fine player when he saw one resulted in him persuading Smith to sign for Blues as an amateur. Five years later, Smith stepped out for Blues at Wembley Stadium for the 1956 FA Cup Final against Manchester City, along with Merrick, Hall and Green.

If season 1950-51 ended in disappointment with the semi-final defeat by Blackpool, there was an even more bitter pill for Blues to swallow the following season when they lost out on promotion by a fraction of a goal, pipped for the runners-up spot in Division Two by Cardiff City. In the Cup, Birmingham got no further than the fourth round, beaten at home by Leyton Orient.

In 1952-53, Blues finished sixth in the Second Division and went out in the quarter-finals of the FA Cup, defeated at the third attempt by Tottenham Hotspur at neutral Molineux. And in 1953-54 they took seventh place in the table and were eliminated by Ipswich Town in the fourth round of the Cup. Further new recruits arrived at St Andrew's. Among them were Noel Kinsey, a Welsh international signed from

Wolves goalkeeper Bert Williams is under pressure against Blues at St Andrew's in September 1949. The game ended 1-1.

Norwich City; wingers Gordon Astall and Alex Govan, both from Plymouth Argyle; Peter 'Spud' Murphy, an ex-Coventry City player who came from Tottenham Hotspur in 1952; Jackie Lane, a robust centre-forward, plucked out of the Army; and Ken Rowley, formerly of Wolves. Ted Purdon, too, was an established member of the side and was leading scorer in 1953-54 with 15 goals, one more than Murphy.

In November 1954, Arthur Turner returned to St Andrew's as manager. When he took over, Blues were lying 12th in the Second Division, promotion seemingly way out

of sight even though there was still half a season to go. Turner set about his task of reviving Blues' sagging fortunes and transformed them almost overnight, driving Birmingham to a promotion side. By the end of the season they were champions. Blues topped the Second Division table for the first time with a 5-1 win at Doncaster in their very last game of the season. They edged Luton into second spot, taking the title by 0.297 of a goal.

Earlier in the season, Blues just could not win away from home, but after Turner's arrival they were virtually unbeatable 'on tour'. Indeed, they had won only one of their

Murphy is Blues Hat-Trick Hero
Doncaster Rovers 0 Birmingham City 5

THIS was Peter Murphy's match. Blues' expensive new inside-left scored a hat-trick in a five-star shooting debut as Doncaster were brushed aside at Belle Vue in this Second Division game on 19 January 1952.

This was only the second time since World War Two that Blues had netted five goals in an away game, but this clash was not nearly as one-sided as the scoreline might suggest, for Rovers had player-manager Peter Doherty back in their side and did as much attacking as Blues. The one telling difference was in the way Blues took their chances, Murphy in particular.

After 11 minutes Blues went ahead with a superb goal. Roy Warhurst started the movement and every member of the attack took part in the build up, pushing the ball around between Rovers players. Murphy was held up near goal, but a neat pass from Wardle found him ready for the return and he hooked the ball past goalkeeper Hardwick from an acute angle. A brilliant finish to an excellent move.

Six minutes before half-time, after Doherty and Harrison had both gone close for Rovers, Murphy was on target again. The home defence was spreadeagled as the result of some good work involving Jack Badham and Warhurst, and when the latter slipped the ball through to Murphy, the newcomer let fly first time, Hardwick being deceived by the speed of the shot.

Tommy Briggs unselfishly set-up Murphy again soon after but this time Hardwick saved his effort on the line.

For the first 20 minutes of the second half, Blues' Gil Merrick was by far the busier of the two goalkeepers, saving well from Harrison, Tindall and Miller.

Blues, though, always looked menacing on the break and on 67 minutes they went 3-0 up with a magnificent goal from Jackie Stewart. Receiving the ball from Badham, the Scotsman fed Smith who in turn beat Miller before laying the ball into Stewart's path 20 yards out. The ball was struck perfectly, and Hardwick was beaten from the time it left the player's boot.

Five minutes later Murphy collected his hat-trick goal, taking a return pass from Stewart before gliding the ball home from 12 yards.

On 82 minutes Blues netted their fifth goal. Stewart centred hard and low from the right and the alert Briggs calmly squeezed the ball between the 'keeper and the post.

Blues had registered their fourth successive away win – then a post-war record – and it saw them leap to the top of the table.

Doncaster Rovers: Hardwick; Makepeace, Graham; Jones, Paterson, Miller; Martin, Doherty, Harrison, Lawler, Tindall.
Birmingham City: Merrick; Green, Martin; Badham, Atkins, Warhurst; Stewart, Smith, Briggs, Murphy, Wardle.

Attendance: 20,000
Referee: F.H.Jerrard (Preston)

Liverpool Hit For Nine
Birmingham City 9 Liverpool 1

LIVERPOOL have established a reputation as one of the finest club sides in the world during the last 20 years as they have taken their League Championship wins to a record number. Back in 1954, however, they were a run-of-the-mill Second Division side, who had just been relegated after 47 seasons in the First Division.

On 11 December 1954, the Blues, against Liverpool, recorded their highest League victory this century.

It was an amazing contest. Admittedly, Liverpool were struggling, but they fielded some fine players, none the less. There was Scottish international Billy Liddell at centre-forward, dashing winger Alan A'Court, classy half-backs Geoff Twentyman and Laurie Hughes, solid full-backs Ray Lambert and Frank Lock, and goalkeeper Doug Rudham, a South African amateur international.

In their previous home game the Blues had beaten Port Vale 7-2 and now it was Liverpool's turn to feel the full force of Birmingham's goalscoring machine.

Playing without injured schemer Noel Kinsey, the Blues got off to a flying start, Jackie Lane scoring after only 48 seconds as the ball took a wicked deflection off Lambert's boot. After 11 minutes, Eddie Brown latched on to Len Boyd's inch-perfect pass to make it 2-0. Five minutes later the nervous Rudham dropped Gordon Astall's corner and Brown was there again to make it 3-0.

Trevor Smith then slipped in midfield and Liddell raced away to reduce the arrears on 19 minutes. But the Blues bounced back and, following two near-misses, Astall was on the spot to make it 4-1, after both Peter Murphy and Brown had seen efforts scrambled away.

The barrage continued up to half-time but the Blues did not hit the target again until the 49th minute, when Lane's presence in the area enabled Astall to chest the ball over the line from a couple of yards for Birmingham's fifth goal. Their sixth came five minutes later, Murphy letting loose a rocket of a shot which Rudham hardly saw.

Astall and Jeff Hall both hit the bar, Brown headed just over and Liverpool could do nothing about the onslaught. The seventh goal arrived in the 77th minute, Alex Govan slamming a sweet left-footer past Rudham from 15 yards. With six minutes remaining, Brown set up Murphy for the eighth goal; and Brown finished off the scoring with a toe-poke at goal a minute later.

Birmingham City: Merrick; Hall, Green, Boyd, Smith, Warhurst, Astall, Lane, Brown, Murphy, Govan.
Liverpool: Rudham; Lambert, Lock, Wilkinson, Hughes, Twentyman, Payne, Anderson, Liddell, Evans, A'Court.
Attendance: 17,514
Referee: G.McCabe (Sheffield)

Eddie Brown scores in the Blues' 5-1 win at Doncaster in May 1955, which sent the Birmingham club back to the old First Division.

first ten away fixtures, yet they finished in magnificent style, losing only one of their remaining 11 games. Into the bargain Birmingham reached the FA Cup quarter-finals before losing to Manchester City by a late goal a St Andrew's.

At one stage in the 1954-55 season Blues had occupied their lowest League position since the war and they literally 'came from nowhere' to clinch promotion with an unbelievable late rush. During the course of the season, they slammed Liverpool 9-1 and Port Vale 7-2 in successive games at home and, overall, they scored more goals (92) than any other Blues side this century. Birmingham were nine points adrift of the leaders going into the final stage of the season; they lay seventh in the table, yet had four games in hand.

Arthur Turner pointed out that games in hand mean, absolutely nothing if they cannot be won and his efforts brought the best out of each player. When he arrived, the air was one of depression but shortly after he had taken charge, Port Vale were thrashed at St Andrew's, Murphy hitting a fine hat-trick, with Kelsey grabbing two and Govan and Eddie Brown one apiece. Brown had been signed the previous month, from Coventry City for £8,000, and he proved to be a great asset this season, hitting 18 goals, two less than top-marksman Peter Murphy. He notched a hat-trick in the rout of Liverpool.

After being knocked out of the FA Cup, morale at St Andrew's needed a boost and that was provided with a 4-1 home win over Doncaster Rovers in mid-March. This left Blues 13 games to play and they had still to get another 18 points to reach the target of 54 set by Turner in November.

With three games remaining, Birmingham required five points to clinch promotion. All three games were away from home but that did not stop high-flying Blues who beat Hull City 3-0, drew 2-2 at Liverpool and then destroyed Doncaster at Belle Vue to regain their First Division place after five years in Division Two.

Injuries crept in towards the end of the season and both goalkeeper Johnny Schofield and defender Jack Badham played important roles in the remaining matches, Schofield doing exceptionally well in the last 15 games. Skipper Len Boyd said afterwards that the turning point was that home win over Doncaster. He recalled: "We had to win that one and by golly we did, in some style too."

He was full of praise when Blues travelled to Doncaster for the crucial last game, which Birmingham had to win to go up. Boyd remembered: "The ground was packed and alive with supporters wearing the colours of Birmingham City. We knew we would win – and so too did those fans – and our performance that day was quite brilliant."

Blues' triumphant team that day was: Schofield; Hall, Badham, Boyd, Smith, Warhurst, Astall, Kinsey, Brown, Murphy and Govan.

Birmingham scored 92 League goals in regaining their First Division place and every member of the attack reached double figures. Twenty-four players turned out in League games, eight of them making less than ten appearances. Skipper Boyd and full-back Green topped the appearances with 39 apiece, Murphy and Govan made 37 and Kinsey 35.

Blues had an excellent season back in Division One, finishing in sixth position – their highest final place in the club's history to date – and they appeared in their second FA Cup Final, 25 years after their first. Blues began the 1955-56 season with a 2-2 home draw against Manchester United and they played steadily throughout the campaign, weighing in with some fine victories, including a 5-0 win at Fratton Park against Portsmouth, 5-2 at Bolton and home successes

Birmingham City in 1955-56. Back row (left to right): J.Newman, J.Watts, J.Hall, E.Plumley, T.Smith, K.Green, R.Shaw (trainer). Front row: Arthur Turner (manager), G.Astall, N.Kinsey, E.Brown, R.Warhurst, P.Murphy, A.Govan.

of 5-0 and 6-2 against Huddersfield and Everton respectively.

In the Cup they began in devastating fashion with a 7-1 win at Torquay, where Brown hit a hat-trick. In the fourth round they hammered Leyton Orient, also away, 4-0; and in an action-packed local derby against West Bromwich Albion at a snow-covered Hawthorns, a goal from Peter Murphy sent Blues into the quarter-finals where they met Arsenal at Highbury – their fourth successive away tie. Birmingham played splendidly against the Gunners and in front of a near-68,000 crowd they raced into the semi-final with a thrilling 3-1 victory, Astall, Murphy and Brown hitting the target.

Just as in 1931, Blues; semi-final opponents were Sunderland, whom they met at Hillsborough. This time they beat the Wearsiders 3-0 – it was 2-0 in 1931 – and a crowd of 65,107 saw Kinsey, Astall and Brown score the goals. Astall afterwards enthused about Blues' performance, saying: "We were magnificent and, honestly, I was surprised we didn't score five – we deserved to."

Blues had several players of international standing in their side in the mid-1950s. Merrick, Hall and Kinsey were all full internationals, Ken Green and Gordon Astall had received 'B' caps, while Smith and Astall later became England players.

Roy Warhurst had a grand season in 1955-56, but missed the Cup Final after being injured at Highbury. Jack Badham took his place in the semi-final and Johnny Newman filled his berth at Wembley.

Blues' opponents in the Final, Manchester City, also had some exceptionally fine players and they fielded this team: Trautmann; Leivers, Little, Barnes, Ewing, Paul (captain), Johnstone, Hayes, Revie, Dyson and Clarke.

The Maine Road club had been beaten by Newcastle United in the previous year's Final and skipper Paul vowed that his team would be back the following season. They made good their boast by defeating Blues 3-1, perhaps against the odds, because most tipsters had forecast a Midlands victory, especially after Blues' extraordinary away form in the previous rounds (18 goals for and only two against in five games).

Don Revie inspired Manchester to victory at Wembley. He found acres of space in his 'deep-lying centre-forward' role and both Johnstone and Hayes were constant threats to a shaky Blues defence. Indeed, there was precious little Blues could do to stop them, yet at half-time the scores were level at 1-1, Hayes having netted early on for City, with Kinsey equalising for Birmingham. In the second half, though, Blues were outplayed and further goals from Lancashire cricketer, Dyson, and Johnstone sealed their fate. It was a dramatic Final, for as well as producing surprise winners, the game saw Wembley's injury 'jinx' strike again. Twenty minutes from time, Bert Trautmann, City's German-born goalkeeper, dived at the feet of Peter Murphy and hurt his neck. He played on in obvious pain and after the game it was disclosed that he had broken his neck.

Birmingham had reached Wembley by playing on rain-saturated pitches, muddy grounds and snow. Their work-rate in the earlier rounds, on these varying surfaces, was tremendous but at sun-bathed Wembley, on a lush pitch, they never got their game together and were beaten by the better team on the day.

The fates did indeed seem to be totally against Blues, for all the winners of the previous six post-war semi-finals which had been staged at Hillsborough had gone on to lift

Eddie Brown watches as Manchester City goalkeeper Bert Trautmann, who broke his neck, dives at the Blues' player's feet in the 1956 FA Cup Final. City's Dave Ewing is the other player.

the trophy at Wembley. And they could not count on the Footballer of the Year 'hoodoo' operating in their favour either.

Since 1948, six current holders of the individual award had played in Wembley Cup Finals and only Joe Mercer (with Arsenal in 1950) had been on the winning side. Stan Matthews and Harry Johnston (both Blackpool, in 1948 and 1951 respectively), Nat Lofthouse (Bolton, 1953), Tom Finney (Preston, 1954) and Don Revie (Manchester City, 1955) all had to be satisfied with runners-up medals. In 1956, however, Footballer of the Year Bert Trautmann received a winners' medal.

Thousands of supporters packed Victoria Square, outside the Council House, to welcome Blues back to Birmingham. Skipper Len Boyd told them: "We feel we have let you down." The roar that greeted that comment was an emphatic 'No', as those dedicated followers demonstrated their loyalty to Birmingham City.

There was hope that Blues would emulate Manchester City's feat and return to Wembley the following year to win the Cup. Birmingham, though, eventually lost 2-0 to Manchester United at Hillsborough in the semi-final.

Blues lost the services of Len Boyd (retired) and Roy Warhurst (sold to Manchester City) for the 1956-57 season, which saw them decline rapidly in the second half of their League programme. It was clear that some team rebuilding had to be done.

The right-half spot, vacated by Boyd, was a constant worry for manager Turner who tried five players – Johnny Watts, Albert Linnecor, Johnny Newman, Bunny Larkin and Graham Sissons. Of these, Watts was the most successful with Larkin showing the most promise. None, however, showed the same drive and urgency as Boyd and, towards the end of that season, Turner signed Dick Neal, an attacking wing-half from Lincoln City. Capped by England at Under-23 level, Neal showed real constructive ability in the few games he played for Blues at the end of 1956-57 and he went on to serve the club splendidly before being transferred to Middlesbrough in October 1961.

It was also clear that reinforcements were required in the forward line. Both Kinsey and Murphy were now finding the pace difficult and too often they faded in the latter stages of

a game. Turner again dug deep into the club's resources and secured the services of winger Mike Hellawell (from Queen's Park Rangers), as well as giving outings to several youngsters, including Bryan Orritt and Keith Neale.

Birmingham finished 12th in the First Division in 1956-57, after an impressive first half of the season which saw them in the top six. They had some exciting home wins, beating Newcastle United 6-1, Leeds United 6-2, Sheffield Wednesday 4-0 and Arsenal 4-2.

In the Cup, Birmingham accounted for Carlisle United in the third round, winning the replay at St Andrew's 4-0 after a 3-3 draw at Brunton Park. In the next round Southend were hammered 6-1 at Roots Hall and Millwall followed, beaten 4-1 at The Den, as Blues continued their superb away form. In the quarter-finals they were drawn at home against Nottingham Forest and, after a goalless draw at St Andrew's, won the City Ground replay with a goal from Peter Murphy.

Then they faced Manchester United, whilst in the other semi-final Aston Villa took on West Bromwich Albion and there was talk of a repeat of the 1931 FA Cup Final when Blues met the Baggies.

Against the 'Busby Babes' Birmingham did their best but it was United who went on to meet Villa. The Villa had knocked out Albion in a replay at St Andrew's and in the Wembley Final the Midlanders won 2-1 to prevent the Old Trafford club achieving the League and Cup double.

Although Blues remained in the First Division until 1965, the seasons following these two great Cup runs were largely undistinguished. In 1957-58 they took 13th place, the following season they finished ninth and were placed 19th in each of the next two campaigns, came 17th in 1961-62, 20th in both 1962-63 and 1963-64 and then, in 1964-65, were relegated after finishing bottom.

They did well in the various Cup competitions and in 1955-58, 1959-60, 1960-61 and 1961-62 they took part in the Inter-Cities Fairs Cup (now the UEFA Cup), reaching the Final in 1960 and 1961 and losing in the semi-final in 1957 (when the competition was carried over to the following season). Blues' first game in this competition was against the crack Italian club, Internazionale, in May 1956 and they produced a fine display to hold the Italians to a 0-0 draw in Milan before winning the return 2-1 at St Andrew's with winger Alex Govan hitting both goals. The Yugoslav side, Zagreb Select, were also beaten 4-0 on aggregate, before Blues took on FC Barcelona in the semi-finals.

At St Andrew's, Birmingham City were quite brilliant and won 4-3, but the Spaniards pulled back to level the scores in the second leg and then beat Blues 2-1 in the replay (away goals did not count double in those days).

Barcelona again opposed City in the 1959-60 competition – this time in the Final. Blues defeated a Cologne Select XI,

Six Goals At Roker
Sunderland 1 Birmingham City 6

THE faithful band of supporters who followed the Blues away from home during the 1957-58 season must have found it a frustrating experience, for it appeared that Birmingham were easy meat for most teams.

They took some real hammerings against Chelsea (5-1), Tottenham (7-1), Sheffield Wednesday (5-3), Preston (8-0), Wolves (5-1) and Blackpool (4-2). They conceded 52 goals in 21 away matches, scoring 33. And six of those came in this splendid victory at Roker Park.

Sunderland, doomed to relegation despite a spirited late rally, were fighting for their First Division lives when the Blues made a 350-mile journey north on 5 April 1958, 24 hours after losing 3-2 at Portsmouth. Everyone in the 34,000 crowd expected a tremendously fierce contest but it turned out to be a massacre as the Blues ripped the home side to shreds to register a quite unexpected win.

Birmingham, who had decided to fly north and were delayed 40 minutes, due to thick cloud, soon got into their stride, Bryan Orritt jumping higher than anyone to nod Harry Hooper's second-minute corner over Fraser's head. Eddie Brown followed up to make sure.

After Brown had missed a 'sitter', Peter Murphy interchanged passes with Hooper and saw his shot rebound off the crossbar. The ball fell invitingly for Hooper, however, who buried the rebound to make it 2-0 after nine minutes. In the 11th minute Trevor Smith ventured upfield and tried a speculative long-range shot. The ball flew off Aitken's boot, straight to Murphy, who made it 3-0.

Three minutes later, Aitken mis-cued his back pass, Orritt nipping in to slip the ball past a stranded Fraser. Sunderland lost Anderson for a time after he had collided with Orritt, but the Blues could not find the net again, although Brown hit the woodwork and both Hooper and Murphy had shots kicked off the line.

Five minutes after the interval, Hooper, Brown and Murphy combined to give Gordon Astall the chance to make it 5-0 and, despite a 74th-minute consolation goal from Don Revie, the Blues finished in style when Brown fired home Hooper's pin-point cross ten minutes from time. With the last kick of the match, Brown, who had a marvellous game, struck the bar with a 20-yard shot.

Sunderland: Fraser; Hedley, Elliott, Anderson, Aitken, Pearce, Fogarty, Revie, Kitchenbrand, O'Neill, Goodchild.

Birmingham City: Schofield; Hall, Green, Larkin, Smith, Neal, Hooper, Orritt, Brown, Murphy, Astall.

Attendance: 34,184
Referee: W.R.Tuck (Chesterfield)

Two-Goal Bunny Blasts Spurs
Tottenham Hotspur 0 Birmingham City 4

GIVING by far their best performance of the season, Blues gave Spurs a real hiding at White Hart Lane in this First Division match on 22 November 1958.

'Bunny' Larkin, whom Blues were hoping was a 'cost nothing' replacement for hot-shot Peter Murphy, was the hero, scoring twice after being switched from wing-half to inside-left. While Larkin collected only two goals, such was his appetite for more that it took a once-in-a-lifetime display by Spurs goalkeeper John Hollowbread to keep him out further.

Larkin took just a quarter of an hour to make his mark. Hollowbread had already turned a vicious drive from Johnny Gordon around a post, but he was left helpless by a stunning right-foot shot from Larkin after he had been set up by full-back Brian Farmer who had robbed Bobby Smith in the centre-circle before feeding a telling pass through to the Blues inside-left.

With Johnny Watts completely outshining Irish international Danny Blanchflower for constructive play, Blues went on to pound Spurs and it became a personal battle between Hollowbread and the Blues' forwards. While Johnny Schofield had only one shot to save in the first 30 minutes, Hollowbread had half-a-dozen including three super stops from Gordon, Brian Taylor and Larkin (again).

On 31 minutes Blues went 2-0 up. Larkin received the ball from Taylor and then switched it quickly to the unmarked Harry Hooper in the centre-forward position. His first shot struck Hollowbread on the knee, but he was first to the rebound and whipped the ball into the net from eight yards. Before half-time Hollowbread again saved splendidly from Eddie Brown and Larkin.

Spurs ran the show for the first ten minutes of the second half but then Blues took over once more. On 58 minutes Trevor Smith, spotting Larkin free, sent a long ball down the middle of the field. Larkin was on to it in a flash and his shot sped past Hollowbread and into the net – 3-0.

Two minutes later it was 4-0 with Hooper making a great goal for Taylor. Hooper weaved his way past three Spurs players before screwing the ball back to Taylor who scored from six yards.

Blues continued to create chances – Larkin, Brown and Taylor all going close – while Smith and Terry Medwin brought good saves out of Schofield at the other end.

Tottenham Hotspur: Hollowbread; Baker, Hopkins, Blanchflower, Norman, Iley, Brookes, Harmer, Dunmore, Smith, Medwin.

Birmingham City: Schofield; Farmer, Allen, Watts, Smith, Neal, Hooper, Gordon, Brown, Larkin, Taylor.

Attendance: 28,708
Referee: G.McCabe (Sheffield)

Blues' Rudd scores with a header against Fulham in September 1960.

Zagreb and the Belgium side, Union St Gilloise, before losing 4-1 on aggregate to the Spanish giants after they had battled to force a 0-0 draw at St Andrew's in the first leg.

The following season Blues raced through to the Final by knocking out the Hungarians, Újpesti Dózsa (5-3 on aggregate), FC Copenhagen (9-4) and Internazionale (4-2) in the semi-final. In the Final they went down to AS Roma, 4-2 on aggregate after a gallant fight. They failed to get past the second hurdle of the 1961-62 competition, losing to Español (Spain) 5-3 on aggregate after receiving a first-round bye.

The Football League Cup was introduced in 1960-61 and Blues were among the top clubs who chose to enter immediately, although many others declined, not considering it a worthwhile proposition. Birmingham had to travel to Bradford in their opening tie and won 1-0 at Park Avenue, with Mike Hellawell netting their goal. In the next round, however, Blues lost 3-1 in a replay at Plymouth.

The following season Swindon Town ended Blues' hopes with a first-round knock-out. Then, in 1962-63, Birmingham City at last won a major trophy when they won the League Cup, beating Aston Villa 3-1 on aggregate in the Final. Former player Gil Merrick was now manager, having taken over from Pat Beasley in 1960. Arthur Turner's reign had ended in September 1958.

Merrick's early years in charge had produced their fair share of problems, both on and off the field, and in early 1962-63, Birmingham found it difficult to win away from home. They played seven away matches from the start of the season until 5 October and had failed to get a goal or a point.

Things began to change following a 1-1 draw at Barrow

in the League Cup. Birmingham's next trip took them to Molineux, where they scored their first victory over Wolves for more than 40 years. Ken Leek netted both goals in their 2-0 victory. In the League Cup, Notts County, Manchester City and Bury (in the semi-final) were all beaten but Blues' League form was still causing concern. Only by winning two of their last three First Division matches – at home to Manchester United and Leicester City – did Birmingham City avoid relegation.

The first leg of the League Cup Final was played at St Andrew's on 23 May 1963, in front of 31,580 spectators. blues gained the initiative with a convincing 3-1 victory. Ken Leek (2) and Jimmy Bloomfield scored for Birmingham and Bobby Thompson replied for Villa. The return leg at Villa Park, four days later, attracted a crowd of 37,921, who saw Blues lift the trophy after a goalless draw.

Only Trevor Smith remained from City's Wembley line-up in 1956. Four others had retired – Merrick (to become manager), Ken Green, Jeff Hall (through polio which caused his premature death) and Peter Murphy. These players had given Birmingham City magnificent service, amassing well over 1,500 senior appearances between them.

Johnny Newman had moved to Leicester City, Gordon Astall to Torquay United, Alex Govan to Portsmouth, Eddie Brown to Leyton Orient, Noel Kinsey to Port Vale, Dick Neal and Bryan Orritt to Middlesbrough and Bunny Larkin to Norwich City. Two players who had come and gone in that period were Harry Hooper (from Wolves in 1957, transferred to Sunderland in 1960) and Johnny Gordon (signed from Portsmouth in 1958 and who went back to Fratton Park three years later).

Super Spurs Checked by Blues
Birmingham City 3 Tottenham Hotspur 3

THIS was the era of the 'Super Spurs'. Tottenham, playing superb football, had swept all before them the previous season to achieve the League Championship and FA Cup double, becoming the first club this century to do so.

They began their defence of the Cup with a visit to St Andrew's in a third-round tie on 6 January 1962. Within half an hour of the kick-off, the Spurs supporters were in full voice, happily singing their battle hymn, 'Glory, Glory, hallelujah', after Tottenham had opened up a three-goal lead.

Ken Leek was foiled early on by Spurs' goalkeeper Bill Brown, but from then until the 32nd minute, it was all Tottenham. On seven minutes Jimmy Greaves darted through the middle, chasing a Maurice Norman clearance. Johnny Schofield half-blocked his first shot but Greaves quickly regained his feet to tuck the ball away.

Schofield saved the day with two breathtaking saves from Greaves and Cliff Jones, but it was the Welsh international who made it 2-0 after 29 minutes. The Tottenham forwards interchanged in bewildering fashion as the ball was passed between the Blues defenders. Then outside-right Terry Medwin popped up on the left wing and his cross was slammed in by Jones. Three minutes later Greaves headed a third after Dave Mackay and Les Allen had interpassed.

Then the complexion of the game started to change. The Blues suddenly began to find space and in the 33rd minute, Jimmy Harris gained possession following a Stan Lynn free-kick. Brown could only watch as the ball flew into the net. Birmingham were on the march.

Four minutes after the interval, the Spurs defence got into a tangle when first Bertie Auld, then Mike Hellawell got in long crosses. When the ball arrived in the middle again, Harris planted a header wide of Brown. The fans invaded the pitch in their delight

and five minutes later they were back again as Leek grabbed a sensational equaliser.

Now it was Tottenham's turn to back-pedal as the Blues looked for a winner. Indeed, Birmingham got the ball in the net a fourth time but the goal was ruled out for offside. Malcolm Beard said afterwards: "Our last goal was the best of the lot – I saw nothing wrong with it at all. We had Spurs on the run after we had drawn level and I thought we could pull off a tremendous victory."

Alas, Spurs won the replay 4-2 and went on to retain the Cup, beating Burnley 3-1 in the Final.

Birmingham City: Schofield; Lynn, Sissons, Hennessey, Smith, Beard, Hellawell, Orritt, Harris, Leek, Auld.
Tottenham Hotspur: Brown; Baker, Henry, Blanchflower, Norman, Mackay, Medwin, White, Allen, Greaves, Jones.
Attendance: 46,096
Referee: K.Howley (Middlesbrough)

Ken Leek (10) and Robin Stubbs (8) in action against Wolves at St Andrew's in March 1963.

League Cup Glory
Birmingham City 3 Aston Villa 1

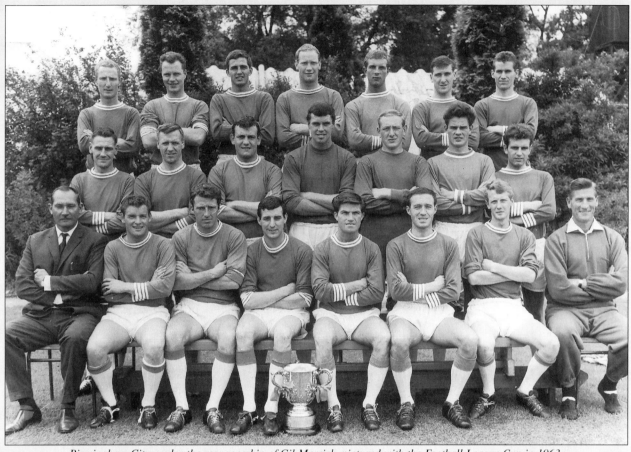

Birmingham City, under the managership of Gil Merrick, pictured with the Football League Cup in 1963.

BIRMINGHAM suffered a dismal 1962-63 League programme which saw them avoid relegation by the skin of their teeth, defeating Leicester City, the FA Cup Finalists, 3-2 in their final game to pull clear by a mere two points. But they made amends by winning the Football League Cup, beating Aston Villa 3-1 on aggregate in the two-legged Final.

The Blues had accounted for Doncaster, Barrow, Notts County, Manchester City and Bury leading up to the Final. Villa had knocked out Peterborough, Stoke, Preston, Norwich and Sunderland.

Villa were clear favourites to lift the trophy for the second time, having hammered the Blues 4-0 at Villa Park two months earlier in a League match. But in the first leg of the Final at St Andrew's on 23 May 1963, Birmingham put on a sparkling team performance and gained the precious two-goal advantage.

The Blues were in irrepressible attacking form, powering forward in quite brilliant style. Early on, Villa goalkeeper Nigel Sims saved twice, from Jimmy Harris and Ken Leek, and then saw a Harris shot deflected on to the crossbar.

In the 14th minute the Blues struck with a breathtaking goal. Malcolm Beard and Terry Hennessey set up Harris, who fed Bertie Auld on the left wing. When the ball was crossed, in came Leek to slam it past Sims. Jimmy Bloomfield then took a knock on the thigh and this disrupted the Blues for a while. Then Villa equalised, against the run of play, through Bobby Thomson, who was soon to sign for Birmingham.

In the 52nd minute the Blues regained the lead, the Harris-Auld-Leek combination working again, with the latter on hand to hit the ball past Sims. Goal number-three came on 66 minutes through Bloomfield, who nipped between the two static Villa defenders to meet Harris' right-wing cross, the ball going in off an upright. Leek (twice) and Auld went close before the end. Four days later, Birmingham held Villa to a goalless draw at Villa Park to lift the League Cup.

Birmingham City: Schofield; Lynn, Green, Hennessey, Smith, Beard, Hellawell, Bloomfield, Harris, Leek, Auld.
Aston Villa: Sims; Fraser, Aitken, Crowe, Sleeuwenhoek, Lee, Baker, Graham, Thomson, Wylie, Burrows.

Attendance: 31,580
Referee: E.Crawford (Doncaster)

On the staff in 1963, Blues had some experienced professionals including Jimmy Bloomfield (formerly of Arsenal), Jimmy Harris (ex-Everton), Stan Lynn (Aston Villa), Bertie Auld (Celtic), Ken Leek (Newcastle United), Ray Martin (Villa) and Colin Green (Everton). Leek and Green were Welsh internationals and Auld had played for Scotland.

There were players, too, who had been groomed by the

Everton goalkeeper Gordon West makes a good catch from Bullock's header at St Andrew's in October 1963.

A Ten-Goal Thriller
Birmingham City 5 Blackburn Rovers 5

THIS was the penultimate League match of the season on 24 April 1965. There was nothing at stake, however. The Blues were already doomed to relegation, whilst Blackburn Rovers would finish in mid-table. But in the event, it turned out to be one of the finest examples of attacking football seen at St Andrew's for some years.

The fans had decided to give the game a miss – under 9,000 paid to enter St Andrew's – but the absentees missed a treat. Those present saw a breathtaking 90 minutes. And for one man, Malcolm Beard, playing out of position, it was a day he would never forget.

Blackburn, fielding many star players, including Bryan Douglas, Keith Newton, Mike England and Ronnie Clayton, were 2-0 ahead inside 20 minutes. Douglas sent Byrom clear down the right and from the centre-forward's pin-point cross, McEvoy headed a simple goal past the Blues' debutant goalkeeper, Len Beel. Three minutes later Ferguson 'nutmegged' Malcolm Page and ran on to beat Beel with a rising shot from 12 yards.

The Blues hit back on the half-hour. Terry Hennessey fed Alec Jackson and the little right winger did the spade-work which was finished off by Geoff Vowden, whose shot on the turn flew past a stranded Fred Else.

Five minutes from half-time, the Blues drew level, thanks to Stan Lynn's penalty after Newton had handled in the area. This gave Lynn ten goals for the season, equalling his own scoring record for a full-back.

Blackburn looked the better all-round side, though, and eight minutes into the second half they regained their two-goal advantage. On 51 minutes England's speculative long-range shot was deflected by Blues' skipper Hennessey into his own net. Two minutes later Ferguson got a free-kick down the right and Douglas headed home his centre. But the Blues hit back quickly and Beard, playing in an unfamiliar number-ten shirt, strode forward to reduce the arrears after some fine work by Jackson and Vowden.

Vowden had a shot charged down and Dennis Thwaites fired over before Rovers went 5-3 in front on 66

minutes, Douglas racing 50 yards past four defenders to slip the ball past Beel.

The game looked to be over until Beard again decided to have a crack at goal, reducing the arrears after 71 minutes. The Blues stormed forward and seven minutes later, Beard completed his first hat-trick to bring the scores level.

The Blues' battle cry of 'Keep Right On To The End Of The Road,' was in full flow throughout this game and the next – their last in the First Division for seven years – as they held Leeds to a 3-3 draw, thus robbing Don Revie's men of the League Championship.

Birmingham City: Beel; Lynn, J.Sharples, Hennessey, Foster, Page, Jackson, Martin, Vowden, Beard, Thwaites.
Blackburn Rovers: Else; Newton, Joyce, Clayton, England, G.Sharples, Ferguson, McEvoy, Byrom, Douglas, Harrison.

Attendance: 8,877
Referee: B.S.Setchell (Luton)

club and who were now establishing themselves in the senior squad. These included Robin Stubbs, Malcolm Beard, Winston Foster, Brian Sharples, Dennis Thwaites, goalkeeper Colin Withers and Terry Hennessey, who in later years was to become an international star with Nottingham Forest and Derby County.

Merrick's managerial career at St Andrew's ended in April 1964, when he was replaced by Joe Mallett, who in turn handed over to the ex-Wolves and England centre-half Stan Cullis. The former Wolves boss of the 1950s was Birmingham City's manager from December 1965 to March 1970.

Birmingham City in 1967-68. Back row (left to right): Pendrey, Green, Thwaites, Page. Middle row: Vowden, Beard, Summerill, Herriot, Sharples, Sleeuwenhoek, Darrell. Front row: Foster, Hockey, Martin, Wylie, Pickering, Murray, Vincent.

In the six years from 1964 to 1970, Blues had their ups and downs. They returned to Division Two in 1965 and in their first two seasons back, finished tenth on each occasion; they came fourth in 1967-68 and reached the semi-finals of the League Cup and FA Cup in 1967 and 1968 respectively. In 1969-70, Birmingham City finished 18th in the Second Division – their lowest League placing for 60 years.

More players arrived, many departed and there were also changes on the board, on the coaching side and on the administrative staff. Secretary Walter Adams, who joined the club in May 1946 as assistant secretary, resigned in February 1966 to be replaced by Alan Instone. Adams, who became secretary in 1953, following the death of Bill Grady, also had a period as general manager.

Clifford Coombes stepped up as chairman in 1965, taking over financial control of the club in succession to Harry Morris. Other new faces appeared on the board and Don Dorman, a former player, was appointed technical adviser and chief scout.

At the start of the 1963-64 season – Gil Merrick's last at the club – centre-forward Alex Harley was signed from Manchester City for £40,000. Harley, though, never reached the heights expected of him and he faded into obscurity before his sudden, tragic death at the age of 33.

Another character, the former Bradford City and Forest player Trevor Hockey, arrived at the club in November 1965 from Newcastle. He spent six years with Blues, appearing in well over 200 games before serving Sheffield United, Norwich City, Aston Villa and Bradford City again. Hockey, too, was to die young, through a heart attack when he was 43.

Geoff Vowden spent seven years at St Andrew's (1964-

71) scoring almost 100 goals in nearly 250 appearances and he, too, later served Villa. Two former West Brom players, Ronnie Fenton, who later worked with Brian Clough at Nottingham Forest, and Alec Jackson, a clever ball-player, were in the team in the mid-1960s, along with Cammie Fraser. Jim Herriot (a goalkeeper signed from Dunfermline), Ron Wylie, who moved from Villa Park in 1965 and skippered Blues in the 1968 FA Cup semi-final against West Brom, and striker Phil Summerill also showed their worth.

So did Barry Bridges and Bert Murray, two former Chelsea players. Graham Leggat, Fulham's Scottish international, and Fred Pickering, an England centre-forward transferred from Everton, also gave good value. The Latchford brothers, Dave and Bob, were now pushing their claims, along with Trevor Francis, a player who was to become a 'superstar' during the 1970s and early 1980s. Garry Pendrey and Johnny Vincent were also on the scene.

Other players who flitted in and out of the side during the later 1960s included Johnny 'Tulip' Sleeuwenhoek, signed from Aston Villa; Jimmy Greenhoff who later gave splendid service to both Stoke City and Manchester United; Tony Hateley, who was by now coming to the end of a fine career which had seen him play for Notts County, Aston Villa, Chelsea, Liverpool and Coventry City; and another striker, George Johnston, secured from Arsenal and sold to Fulham.

In that fine run in the 1966-67 League Cup, Blues – who had fallen at the first hurdle in each of the previous three League Cup competitions – eliminated Nottingham Forest, Ipswich Town, Grimsby Town and Sheffield United, only to lose 7-2 on aggregate to Queen's Park Rangers.

In the following season's FA Cup, after a series of disappointments which had seen them progress beyond the

Greenhoff Hits Four – Misses a Penalty
Birmingham City 5 Fulham 4

THIS game on 5 October 1968 was the sort of match which sends shudders down the spines of managers and coaches, yet thrills the neutrals in the crowd.

It was a real ding-dong tussle, full of attacking football, nine goals, a missed penalty, scores of near misses, action all the way, great value for money and a personal triumph for Blues' Jimmy Greenhoff, who scored four times.

It was action right from the start. After 45 seconds Fulham almost took the lead, but Frank Large's header was well saved by Jim Herriot. On two minutes Blues did score, Johnny Vincent netting after some fine approach work by Ron Wylie and Geoff Vowden.

On 16 minutes it was 2-0. Again Wylie was involved, delivering the perfect through ball for Greenhoff to race on to and score past a static McClelland. Nine minutes later Blues, apparently coasting, went 3-0 up and again Greenhoff was the scorer with Wylie once more deeply involved in the build-up, forcing Dempsey to concede a corner. Vincent's flag-kick was duly converted by Greenhoff.

Then, early in the second half, there came a dramatic turnaround with Fulham taking full control and drawing level with three goals in the space of five minutes. Left winger Les Barrett was the instigator of this incredible recovery, setting up Fulham's first for Large with a header on 48 minutes.

Almost immediately Kerrigan charged forward and his hard, low cross was turned into his own net by the unfortunate Dave Robinson. Straight from the kick-off Fulham surged upfield and Large brought the scores level when he stuck out his right leg to divert the ball past Herriot after some good work done by Malcolm Macdonald and the teasing Barrett.

But Blues bounced back and in the 64th minute Greenhoff, after being brought down by Matthewson, shot wide from the penalty spot. One minute later Greenhoff made amends for that miss by edging Blues back in front, steering the ball through a ruck of players after a mêlée on the edge of the Fulham 18-yard box. Fulham, though, came back with a bang and three minutes later the influential Barrett sent over a looping cross which Macdonald headed into the corner of the net.

Four-all – it was anyone's game and it went Blues' way after an error by the Fulham goalkeeper McClelland in the 71st minute. A long testing ball by Vincent seemed destined to end up in the 'keeper's hands, but McClelland inexplicably dropped it and there waiting to pounce was Greenhoff. He made no mistake, netting his fourth goal of the game and the winner for Blues.

Birmingham City: Herriot; Martin, Page, Wylie, Robinson, Beard, Hockey, Greenhoff, Vowden, Vincent, Summerill.
Fulham: McClelland; Pentecost, Dempsey, Matthewson, Ryan, Brown, Callaghan, Kerrigan, Large, Macdonald, Barrett.
Attendance: 27,318
Referee: J.Finney (Hereford)

Chelsea's Peter Bonetti steadies himself to collect a high ball in an FA Cup tie at St Andrew's in 1968.

Jimmy Greenhoff scoring for Stoke City against Birmingham City, his former club, at the Victoria Ground in November 1972.

fourth round only three times in ten seasons, Birmingham City almost made it to Wembley for a third time in 1968.

They had a tremendous campaign, knocking out Halifax Town 4-2, Orient 3-0, Arsenal 2-1 in a replay and Chelsea 1-0 before taking on West Bromwich Albion in the semi-final at Villa Park. Over 60,000 saw Blues have most of the play and create the better chances, only for the Baggies' goalkeeper John Osborne to put on one of the finest performances of his career to thwart a string of efforts from Fred Pickering, Barry Bridges, Geoff Vowden and Malcolm Beard. Albion won 2-0 with goals from Jeff Astle and Tony Brown and went on to beat Everton 1-0 in the Final. Former Everton star Fred Pickering probably had his finest game for Blues in the 1968 semi-final but he left St Andrew's for Blackpool in June 1969.

Nine months later, Stan Cullis decided to call it a day too and in his place Blues appointed Freddie Goodwin, who had been with Brighton, then in Division Three. Goodwin, a former Manchester United and Leeds wing-half, succeeded in steering Blues back into the First Division at the end of the 1971-72 season.

Goodwin began to make an early impact at St Andrew's, signing four players inside six months: Roger Hynd (from Crystal Palace), Alan Campbell (Charlton), Mike Kelly (Queen's Park Rangers) and Gordon Taylor (Bolton Wanderers). Goodwin introduced teenage star Trevor Francis to League football, as substitute at Cardiff in September 1970, and soon Birmingham were playing with a settled side which possessed skill and aggression.

Blues went 14 games unbeaten from mid-December to the end of March and finished ninth in the Second Division. Goodwin had started the season with the following team: Kelly; Thomson, Pendrey, Hockey, Hynd, Robinson, Murray, Vowden, R.Latchford, Vincent and Summerill. By the end of his first season as Birmingham manager, the regular line-up was: Kelly; Martin, Page, G.Smith, Hynd, Robinson, Campbell, Francis, R.Latchford, Summerill and Taylor. Francis had a terrific first season, scoring 16 League goals including four against Bolton at St Andrew's in February, when he was still only 16 years of age.

Blues' supporters eagerly looked forward to the 1971-72 season, for Goodwin had assembled a side capable of winning promotion and the fans believed he could steer their team back into the First Division. They began confidently, losing only two of their first ten League games. An early League Cup defeat at Loftus Road was soon forgotten as League results remained favourable up to the end of the year, when Birmingham were well positioned in the leading group, although a fair way behind the leaders, Norwich City. Bob Hatton, signed in October from Carlisle United for £82,500, was a new record Blues purchase. Early in January, Portsmouth were slammed 6-3 at St Andrew's and Blues then began a highly successful FA Cup run, which saw them sail through to the semi-finals.

There was now a sense of urgency about the team and home attendances averaged around 28,000, yet manager

Birmingham City in 1972-73. Back row (left to right): R.Hynd, A.Whitehead, T.Carroll, R.Martin, P.Cooper, M.Kelly, S.Harland, A.Want, D.Robinson. Middle row: G.Smith, A.Campbell, G.Pendrey, G.Taylor, R.Hope, M.Page. Front row: S.Phillips, R.Hatton, R.Latchford, T.Francis, P.Summerill, K.Burns.

Goodwin kept his feet on the ground: "There's a long way to go yet – we will take each game as it comes, League or Cup."

From 8 January up to the end of the season, Blues lost only one match – the FA Cup semi-final against Leeds United at Hillsborough – out of a possible 23 and clinched promotion with a last-match win at Orient (1-0), when over 15,000 of their supporters went down to Brisbane Road to cheer Bob Latchford's winner.

It was, indeed, an exceedingly close finish, with only three clubs left in the promotion hunt at the death – Norwich, Blues and Millwall. Norwich went into Division One as champions and neither Blues nor Millwall could overtake them. At one stage it seemed certain that Millwall would go up.

Blues' penultimate game of the season was at Hillsborough and their last at Orient. Millwall had one match to play, at home to Preston. Thus, Birmingham had to win both their fixtures to pip Millwall for second place – and as they had already drawn 12 and lost five of their preceding 19 away matches, supporters were not all that confident that Goodwin's men could manage two away wins on the trot. But they did just that. Millwall beat Preston 2-0, while Blues won 2-1 at Sheffield Wednesday and then took both points at Orient, returning to Division One after a break of seven years.

Blues' average home League attendance in 1971-72 was over 32,000 and they had five 'gates' of over 40,000 at St Andrew's during the second half of the season when, it must be said, that Birmingham City played some quite exceptional football.

Three players were ever-present – Hynd, Campbell and

Latchford – and it was Latchford who also top-scored with 27 goals in League and Cup; Hatton hit 17 and Francis 14. At one stage it looked quite likely that Blues might emulate West Bromwich Albion's feat of winning the FA Cup and promotion from the Second Division in the same season. That dream, however, was destroyed when Don Revie's team won a hard-fought semi-final by 3-0, Mick Jones (2) and Peter Lorimer scoring the Leeds goals.

Back in the top-flight, Blues did themselves proud and took tenth place in the table, losing in the fourth round of the League Cup and in the third round of the FA Cup to Blackpool and Swindon Town respectively. Along with the regulars, Tony Want (from Spurs), Bobby Hope (from West Brom), Kenny Burns, Garry Pendrey, Dave Latchford and John Roberts had all played significant parts in re-establishing Birmingham in the First Division.

Blues were back, but for how long? In 1972-73 they got off to a disastrous start and in mid-November were 21st in the table with only 12 points and only Crystal Palace below them. then another tremendous fight-back saw them shoot up the table, sending neighbours West Brom into Division Two with Palace.

Blues struggled in 1973-74, finishing 19th, and again in 1974-75 (17th). Manager Goodwin left, replaced by the former Leeds United full-back Willie Bell. He soon discovered what a hard task he had on his hands in rejuvenating a team which had lost its confidence.

Goalkeeper Gary Sprake was signed from Leeds in 1973-74, a young defender called Joe Gallagher also signed and he went on to make well over 300 senior appearances for Blues. Perhaps the most frustrating event for the fans was the sale

Birmingham City in 1977-78. Back row (left to right): K.Oliver (chief coach), R.Sbragia, D.Latchford, S.Smith, J.Montgomery, J.Connolly, S.Fox. Middle row: J.Williams (physiotherapist), H.Kendall, J.Calderwood, G.Emmanuel, J.Gallacher, M.Rathbone, K.Broadhurst, R.McDonough, R.Devey (trainer). Front row: M.Page, T.Francis, G.Jones, T.Hibbitt, W.Bell (manager), G.Pendrey, A.Want, A.Styles, K.Bradley.

of striker Bob Latchford in exchange for Everton midfielder Howard Kendall.

Blues might well have made a Wembley appearance in 1975. They had a superb run in the FA Cup, toppling Luton Town, Chelsea, Walsall and Middlesbrough before losing to Second Division Fulham in a semi-final replay. The first game ended 1-1 at Hillsborough and in the Maine Road replay, it was goalless with barely 60 seconds of extra-time remaining. Then Fulham striker John Mitchell chased a hopeful ball into the Blues area and goalkeeper Dave Latchford charged down a shot, only to see the ball rebound from Mitchell's leg and over the line. It was a real blow for the 20,000 Birmingham supporters who made the midweek trip to Manchester and saw a third semi-final defeat for Blues in seven years.

In 1974-75, Blues utilised 26 players, including three left-backs – Pendrey, Archie Styles (signed the season before from Everton) and Steve Bryant. In 1975-76 – Bell's first season in charge – the same number of players turned out in the League.

Eventually there was discontent in the camp, with Blues being unable to field a settled side. Bell brought back former Blues defender, Sid Owen, as senior coach and together they tried to instil some missing fire back into the side. That vital spark was still missing, however, and at the end of the campaign they found themselves saved by the narrowest of margins, finishing 19th with the three clubs below them relegated under the three-up and three-down system.

In 1976-77 and 1977-78, Blues finished in mid-table, although in the former season they were only four points off the relegation zone. They went out of both Cup competitions early in those two campaigns and in 1977 Bell lost his job.

England's 1966 World Cup-winning manager, Sir Alf Ramsey, took over for a while until Jim Smith replaced him in March 1978. Again, players had come and gone in quick succession. Blues secured Terry Hibbitt (from Newcastle), Gary Jones and John Connelly (Everton), Peter Withe (Wolves), Jim Montgomery and Tony Towers (Sunderland), Pat Howard (Arsenal) and Keith Bertschin (Ipswich Town).

Outgoing players included Roger Hynd, Ray Martin, Alan Campbell, Gordon Taylor, Kenny Burns, Stan Harland, Bob Hatton, John Roberts, Gary Sprake and Withe, who was signed by Nottingham Forest boss Brian Clough, after barely a season at St Andrew's. Among the youngsters who had come through the club's junior ranks were Kevan Broadhurst, Gary Emmanuel, Kevin Dillon, Ricky Sbragia and Mike Rathbone.

Jim Smith's first full season in charge was heart-breaking as Blues suffered relegation after six years in the top-flight. They hit rock bottom after the fifth game of their 42-match programme and never got out of the bottom two after that. Scoring goals was the big problem (only 37 in the League) and they lost 18 games by one goal. They failed to hit the net on 17 occasions.

Smith gambled this season by fielding a foreign player in Alberto Tarantini, the Argentinian World Cup star, signed on a one-year contract from Boca Juniors. Tarantini appeared in 23 First Division matches and over 41,000 fans saw his debut at Tottenham in mid-October. Other signings made by Smith included Stewart Barrowclough (from Newcastle), Alan Ainscow (Blackpool), Don Givens (Queen's Park Rangers) and Alan Buckley (Walsall). He took the Derby County and Scottish international midfield player, Bruce Rioch, once of Aston Villa, on loan in December and gave debuts to

Back on Course in Style
Birmingham City 5 Manchester United 1

THIS was the Blues' first win of the 1978-79 season and they achieved it with a style and flourish that made a mockery of their previous record. It is not very often that Manchester United concede five goals in a game, but they crumbled under the Blues' hammer in this First Division match at St Andrew's on 11 November 1978.

Indeed, prior to this confrontation, United had not been hit for five League goals for six years. The Blues, meanwhile, had not scored a nap-hand since hammering Leicester City 6-2 at Filbert Street in December 1976.

Birmingham were struggling. They were bottom of the table, with three points out of 26, and had lost eight of their last nine matches. Earlier in the season Southampton had won 5-2 at St Andrew's.

Manager Jim Smith had utilised 22 players in the first three months of the campaign, recruiting Argentinian World Cup star, Alberto Tarantini, and Walsall striker, Alan Buckley, for £175,000. Six players had been tried at right-back and Smith had attempted to establish a regular midfield division by perming any three from ten players.

Birmingham started well but it was United who took a 13th-minute lead. Malcolm Page was caught in possession by Lou Macari, the ball broke free and Joe Jordan waltzed around Neil Freeman to score with ease.

Ten minutes later, Kevin Dillon netted the first of three goals in the space of 15 minutes which swung the game the Blues' way. Don Givens put the ball inside for Dillon to run forward and hammer a fierce right-footed shot past Paddy Roche. In the 32nd minute, Buckley made it 2-1, leaping at the far post to nod home Givens' looping header following Tarantini's long free-kick.

Then, a determined challenge on Brian Greenhoff by the rampaging Givens set-up Buckley, whose chip went just under the crossbar to send the Blues in at the interval 3-1 ahead.

Givens, who had a sparkling match, got on the score-sheet in the 51st minute, rounding off a movement involving Tony Towers, Mark Dennis and Jimmy Calderwood by heading powerfully past Roche. Another header by Givens in the last minute gave Calderwood the chance to drill in number five.

Three United players were booked – Jordan, Brian Greenhoff and Stewart Houston – all for fouls. And Birmingham's Steve Fox was cautioned for dissent. Tarantini escaped punishment following a heavy tackle on Brian Greenhoff which resulted in the United player being carried off.

Birmingham City: Freeman; Tarantini, Dennis, Towers, Gallagher, Page, Dillon, Buckley, Givens, Calderwood, Fox.

Manchester United: Roche; Nicholl(Albiston), Houston, McCreery, B.Greenhoff, Buchan, Coppell, J.Greenhoff, Jordan, Macari, McIlroy.

Attendance: 23,550
Referee: T.D.Spencer (Swindon)

A goal for Alan Buckley (8) against Manchester United at St Andrew's in November 1978.

Frank Worthington chips the ball over a defensive wall at St Andrew's in 1980.

youngsters Mark Dennis, Pat Van den Hauwe, Trevor Dark and Paul Iley. Later, he signed Steve Lynex from Shamrock Rovers. He also sold Trevor Francis to Nottingham Forest for £1 million.

Smith, a former Sheffield United, Aldershot, Halifax and Lincoln City player, was a disappointed man but was backed all the way by the board of directors, which would soon include comedian Jasper Carrott.

In June 1979, Smith paid £250,000 for West Ham's Alan Curbishley, while at the same time goalkeeper Jim Montgomery went to Nottingham Forest and Alan Buckley returned to Walsall. The following month, after a deal which would have brought Brian Little to St Andrew's from Villa Park foundered on medical grounds Smith signed Terry Lees for £60,000 from the Dutch club, Roda JC and then spent £30,000 on goalkeeper Jeff Wealands from Hull City and Tony Evans from Cardiff.

In early August he made a 'snip' signing when he lured Archie Gemmill to St Andrew's from Nottingham Forest for £150,000, releasing Garry Pendrey to join West Bromwich Albion for £30,000, 24 hours later. Pendrey had given Blues great service as a professional for 13 years, during which time he had amassed in excess of 300 senior appearances.

Blues were quoted at 10-1 to win promotion at the first attempt but they started their programme by losing 4-3 at home to Fulham. After six games, Smith secured the services of Colin Todd (from Everton) and almost immediately he signed Willie Johnston, the former Rangers and West Bromwich Albion Scottish international left winger, from Vancouver Whitecaps. Late in November, Frank Worthington, top-scorer in the First Division the previous season, was bought from Bolton Wanderers for £150,000 and now Blues looked to have just the right blend to make a surge

up the table and challenge for promotion.

Kevan Broadhurst, who was loaned to Walsall earlier in the season, was recalled to play at right-back. At the turn of the year, with 22 games played, Birmingham lay sixth in the table.

In mid-March, after Spurs had knocked them of the FA Cup fifth round, Blues stormed into second place for the first time that season. They were now being regarded as one of the favourites to win promotion, the bookies cutting their price to 3-1. Birmingham had strung together a fine run which had seen them collect 16 points out of a possible 22, winning six home matches on the trot.

Smith had done a fine job and his team now read Wealands; Broadhurst, Dennis, Curbishley, Gallagher, Todd, Ainscow, Worthington, Bertschin, Gemmill and Dillon, with Evans as substitute.

In competition with Blues for the three promotion places were leaders Chelsea, Leicester, Luton, Queen's Park Rangers, Sunderland, Newcastle and West Ham. And in the final run-in, Blues had to take on five of these seven clubs, including two meetings with West Ham. It was a crucial period for both the club and manager.

On April Fool's Day, Blues beat Oldham 2-0 at home and then drew at Queen's Park Rangers and at home to West Ham. They maintained second place but, after a 2-1 defeat at Leicester, they dropped out of the top three. Then successive wins over Luton (1-0) and West Ham (2-1), set Birmingham up for a last-ditch effort. A point at Burnley in their penultimate game, meant that they needed just one more point, at home to Notts County, in their final match to regain First Division status.

Blues won that point, drawing 3-3 in front of a bumper 34,000 gate – the best at St Andrew's since October 1978. They led 2-0 after 20 minutes but County fought back and a

Ian Handysides scores for Blues against Aston Villa at St Andrew's in December 1982.

half-time Blues led 3-2. It was nail-biting stuff in the second half but Blues' determination and will-power, together with fervent support from their fans, saw them through. Wealands made four outstanding saves and he was duly elected Player of the Year by Ladbrokes. The average League attendance at St Andrew's in 1979-80 was 20,420, a slight increase on the previous season.

Back in the top-flight, Blues finished 13th, only five points away from the relegation zone. Smith stuck by the players who had done him proud the season before, bringing in only one new face, David Langan, the Republic of Ireland international full-back signed from Derby County, who was Blues' only League ever-present in 1980-81. That season Blues reached the fifth round of the League Cup (beaten by Liverpool) and the fourth round of the FA Cup (eliminated by Coventry City).

In 1981-82, Jim Smith introduced two Dutchmen – Bud Brocken and Tony Van Mierlo – into the side but, in February 1982, Smith left St Andrew's and became manager of Oxford United two months later. He was replaced at Birmingham by Ron Saunders, who had recently steered Aston Villa to their first League Championship triumph for over 70 years.

Blues finished 16th in Division One in 1981-82 and went out of both Cups at the first stage. In 1982-83 they were 17th in the League and lost in the fourth round of each Cup competition. The following season they nosedived back to Division Two after an abysmal campaign which saw attendances at St Andrew's drop below the 10,000 mark.

Among Saunders' first buys were defender Geoff Scott (from Leicester City), Welsh international Byron Stevenson (Leeds United) and Bristol City striker, Mick Harford.

At the start of 1982-83, Saunders' line-up was Jim Blyth (ex-Coventry City) in goal, Langan and young Phil Hawker, Scott, Van den Hauwe, Broadhurst, Van Mierlo, Frank Carrodus (signed from Wrexham and who had been with Saunders at both Manchester City and Villa), Harford, Curbishley and teenager Carl Francis. As the season wore on, changes were made and during the next eight months Kevin Summerfield (ex-West Bromwich Albion), Noel Blake (ex-Villa), plus three players taken on loan – Kevin Bremner, Mike Ferguson and Howard Gayle – had all been given first-team opportunities.

The disastrous 1983-84 season, when Birmingham City scored only 39 League goals, saw more changes. Billy Wright (Everton), Brian Roberts (Coventry), Tony Rees (Villa) and youngsters like Martin Kuhl, Wayne Mumford, Kevin Rogers and Ivor Linton were called up as Blues fought to avoid relegation. Ferguson (from Everton) and Gayle (Liverpool) signed permanently. It was all to no avail, however and Birmingham dropped into Division Two.

During the summer, Saunders strengthened his squad with the addition of Gerry Daly (from Coventry), Wayne Clarke (an £80,000 capture from Wolves), Ken Armstrong (from Southampton), Paul Gorman (Arsenal) and David Giles (Crystal Palace). He sold Gayle to Sunderland and Blake to Portsmouth to help the finances.

What a difference these new faces made to the team. Aided by some sterling performances from the more experienced players and from the up-and-coming youngsters, and urged on by their fans, Birmingham regained their place in Division One at the first time of asking, just as they had done in 1980.

After 12 games had been played, Blues were lying second in the table and on Boxing Day, at the halfway mark, they were still second and had been knocked out of the League

Blues' Ferguson is sandwiched between two Brighton defenders at St Andrew's in May 1983.

Cup at The Hawthorns. Twenty-one-year-old goalkeeper David Seaman had been transferred from Peterborough United for £100,000 in October and his form between the posts was described as 'bloody marvellous' by his manager. Tony Coton, meanwhile, had been sold to Watford for £300,000. Des Bremner was bought from Villa for £25,000.

As Blues went into 1985 they had Blackburn, Oxford and Portsmouth to contend with at the head of the Second Division. Norwich City knocked Birmingham out of the FA Cup third round at the fourth attempt. Ray Ranson, from Manchester City, was now at right-back and new signing Dave Geddis (Barnsley), Andy Kennedy (Rangers) and Nicky Platnauer (Coventry) figured prominently in the team.

It was tight at the top of the table but gradually Birmingham and Oxford edged themselves away from the pack and, with three games to play, Blues required one point to ensure promotion. In fact they got seven points and finished runners-up behind Oxford, who were managed by former Blues boss, Jim Smith. In third place and also promoted was Ron Saunders' former club Manchester City. Earlier in his career Saunders had been in charge of Oxford.

There were some horrifying scenes at Blues' last League match of the promotion-winning season of 1984-85 when, on 11 May, rioting Leeds United fans caused mayhem at St Andrew's which saw some of the most violent conduct ever witnessed on an English soccer ground. It was reported that 96 police-officers were injured and a young man died from injuries when a wall collapsed on top of him, pushed over by the rampaging supporters. The second half of the game started 31 minutes late. Thus the promotion-winning season

Birmingham City in 1983-84. Back row (left to right): A.Evans, A.Rees, W.Mumford, M.Sturridge, M.Ferguson, P.Shearer, K.Rogers. Middle row: K.Bradley (kit manager), G.Doig (physiotherapist), P.Van den Hauwe, I.Handysides, M.McCarrick, M.Kuhl, J.Blyth, N.Blake, A.Coton, D.Tunnicliffe, R.Hopkins, D.Langan, L.Phillips, I.Ross (reserve-team coach), K.Leonard (first-team coach). Seated: M.Harford, M.Halsall, J.Hagan, R.Saunders (manager), K.Broadhurst, W.Wright, M.Dennis. On ground: J.Tomlinson, A.Greenhalgh, C.Francis, P.Deehan.

ended on a bitter note and the 1985-86 campaign was a disaster for Birmingham City as the team went straight back into Division Two. Everything went wrong from start to finish. Twenty-six players were used, among them Mark Jones (from Brighton), Steve Whitton (on loan from West Ham and who later became a permanent acquisition for Blues), Billy Garton and Mark Smalley (on loan from Manchester United and Nottingham Forest respectively) and youngsters John Frain, Guy Russell and Stuart Storer.

Blues scored only 30 League goals and attendances dropped alarmingly, with only 5,833 present to see Southampton win 2-0 at St Andrew's on 19 April. Towards the end of January – after Blues had suffered a humiliating home defeat at the hands of non-League Altrincham in the FA Cup – manager Saunders left for West Brom. In his place Birmingham appointed John Bond, but there was nothing he could do to prevent the downward slide which looked inevitable from November onwards, when Blues first dropped into the bottom three.

Thee was also a lot of internal discontent and chairman Keith Coombes, who had taken over the position from his father in 1975, resigned in December after a series of crisis meetings of the directors. Mr D.Mortimer resigned as a director. Inside a week Mr Ken Wheldon was elected to the board as chairman and Mr R.Homden elected a director.

Mr Wheldon, who had been chairman of Walsall FC for a number of years, emphasised publicly that Birmingham City Football Club was deeply in debt and that there would be dramatic reductions in staff. It came as no surprise when, at the end of the year, seven employees announced they were leaving the club, among them promotions manager Des Blee,

stadium manager John Clewes and accountant Jim Colledge. A little later, secretary Andrew Waterhouse departed, to be replaced by John Westmancoat who had been secretary of Walsall (under Wheldon) and briefly at West Bromwich Albion. Graham Doig, the club's physiotherapist also left, moving to The Hawthorns to team up with Saunders.

Seasons 1986-87 and 1987-88 were just as bad as 1985-86. In the former, Blues escaped the relegation Play-offs by only two points after a League programme which saw them win only eight of their 42 matches.

Blues lost in the fourth round of both Cups, Walsall beating them in the FA Cup, and their average home League attendance was an all-time low of 7,425, with only 4,457 present at the Grimsby Town fixture on 2 May 1987. In that 1986-87 campaign, Wayne Clarke and Stuart Storer were sold together to Everton in a package deal worth £300,000; Robert Hopkins went to Manchester City, later switching to West Brom; Martin Kuhl joined Sheffield United; and David Geddis threw in his lot with Shrewsbury Town.

Into the club came Roger Hansbury, the former Norwich City, Cambridge United and Burnley goalkeeper; Vince Overson, a big centre-back from Turf Moor; Dennis Mortimer returned to the Midlands after spells with Sheffield United and Brighton (he had won League Championship and European Cup-winners' medals with Aston Villa in 1981 and 1982); Tommy Williams arrived from Leicester City and Steve Wigley was recruited from Sheffield United. Players who had spells on loan in 1986-87 included Richard Cooke, Paul Tomlinson, Mark North and Steve Lynex, who returned 'home' for a second spell at the club.

In December 1986, Blues signed defender Paul Hart for

A Rare Moment to Rejoice
Birmingham City 4 Crystal Palace 1

THE Blues had few reasons to rejoice during the mid-1980s, but occasionally they produced some encouraging performances and this victory against Crystal Palace, lying third in the Second Division on 18 October 1986, was as good as any.

Birmingham were in the lower reaches of the table. They were on the slide, having failed to win any of their previous eight League matches. Attendances at St Andrew's were dwindling and a victory was desperately needed.

The Blues went in front after 20 minutes, when on-loan winger Richard Cooke, playing his last game for the club before returning to Tottenham, weaved in from the right and set up Wayne Clarke, whose pass left Des Bremner in the clear. The former Villa player's right-foot shot flew past George Wood.

Seven minutes later, a corner was only partly cleared and Martin Kuhl delivered an inviting cross from the left which Vince Overson met on the run to glance a perfect side-header beyond the diving Wood for his first goal since joining Birmingham from Burnley.

Taylor's goal for Palace, six minutes into the second half, was the result of a mix-up between Kuhl and Jim Hagan. Taylor was in like a flash and calmly waltzed round Roger Hansbury before slipping the ball into an empty net.

Palace then peppered the Blues' goal and twice came close to equalising before a sensational effort from Steve Whitton brought the house down. Cannon was penalised 30 yards from goal for a foul on Andy Kennedy. The ball was edged sideways to Whitton, who let fly, the

ball hitting the net like a rocket after 65 minutes.

Birmingham always looked more menacing and in the very last minute they went 4-1 in front when Clarke nipped in to net his ninth goal of the season. Alas, there were few performances of the same calibre to come as the Blues avoided the relegation Play-offs by the skin of their teeth.

Birmingham City: Hansbury; Ranson, Williams(Storer), Hagan, Overson, Bremner, Kuhl, Clarke, Whitton, Kennedy, Cooke.
Crystal Palace: Wood; Stebbing, Brush(Higginbottom), Taylor, Droy, Cannon, Finnigan, Ketteridge, Barber, Wright, Otulakowski.

Attendance: 5,987
Referee: D.A.Hedges (Oxford)

Blues' Wayne Clarke tussles with a West Brom defender at a snowy St Andrew's in February 1986.

£35,000 from Sheffield Wednesday but the ex-Leeds United and Nottingham Forest player broke his leg in the first-half of his debut game (against Plymouth Argyle) on New Year's Day and never turned out for Blues again.

Blues started the 1987-88 season with another new

manager, Garry Pendrey, their former defender, who brought with him as coach to St Andrew's, Tony Brown, the former West Brom goalscoring star.

In his programme notes for the first game of the season, against Stoke, Pendrey wrote: "We are not able to lash out a quarter of a million pounds for a striker, we are not able to talk in terms of 26 first-team players. In fact, we are fortunate to be in business at all. However, I can see a little light at the end of what has been a very dark tunnel, thanks to the financial wizardry of the chairman Ken Wheldon.

"I will promise you one thing from everyone at the club 'HONESTY'. No one will be allowed to let you or the club down when they go out on to the pitch. I realise that winning is the only thing that really counts."

As it transpired, Pendrey had an exceedingly tough first season with Blues, who yet again scrambled clear of the relegation zone by the skin of their teeth. He wheeled and dealed in the transfer market, bringing Tony Godden (from Chelsea), John Trewick (Oxford), Gary Childs (Walsall), Kevin Langley (Manchester City) and Ian Atkins (Ipswich) to St Andrew's and selling Julian Dicks (to West Ham) and Tony Rees (to Barnsley). Pendrey also tried to tempt Peter Withe back to Birmingham City. But the side was not good enough to put in any sort of promotion challenge. Joked Pendrey, "We might just have done enough to have stayed in the Third Division."

Twelve months later, Birmingham were a Third Division club. They began the 1988-89 season by losing seven of their first eight League games, including a 5-0 drubbing at Walsall, and that set the pattern for a dreadful season.

Players came and went as Pendrey rang desperate changes in a bid to keep the Blues afloat. Attendances dipped to under 5,000 and the club was beset by financial problems, despite having sold its Elmdon training ground for £350,000 – and 30 per cent share of the development profits – in May 1988.

Time was running out and from mid-January to mid-

Brian Roberts (on ground) and Villa's Mark Walters in Second Division action at Villa Park during the 1987-88 season.

April, the Blues collected only nine points out of 54 and were doomed to relegation well before Easter. They failed to score a single goal in six consecutive matches during that awful spell.

On 25 April 1989, chairman Ken Wheldon announced that he was selling his controlling interest in the club, although he would remain on the board as a consultant. It was also revealed that 54-year-old Dave Mackay, the former Hearts, Spurs, Derby, Swindon and Scotland player, would take over as manager, although Pendrey still had two years of his contract left. Pendrey was offered a coaching position at the club, which he refused.

Before the Mackay deal was secured, Wheldon stated publicly that Pendrey had done a good job at St Andrew's. On paper, at least, Birmingham City had benefited by the fact that incoming transfer fees far outweighed what the club had paid for new players. But the net result was a poor side and Third Division football was to be played at St Andrew's for the first time in the Blues' 114-year history.

The club was sold for approximately £1.6 million to the Kumar brothers. There was also another director introduced – Mr Bryan Slater, company secretary and solicitor to the Kumar brothers' £20 million Manchester-based textile empire. Jack Wiseman and Richard Edmonds remained with Wheldon as directors.

The Kumar brothers – Samesh, Ramesh and Bimal, Manchester clothing kings – moved in and took over control for £400,000, promising to put in 'a fair amount of cash' in an effort to make Blues a big club once again. The atmosphere within the club changed – and, indeed, it had been a long, long time since the start of a new season at St Andrew's had been greeted with so much optimism to that which transpired in August 1989, even though this was

Blues' first-ever season in the Third Division.

The revamped board comprised the three Kumar brothers (Samesh was chairman) along with Mr. H.J.Slater and Jack Wiseman; chief executive was Annie Bassett, who was to introduce the ill-fated membership scheme for supporters in 1990, and Joan Hill (from Peterborough United) was commercial manager. Meanwhile, a new-look team, was created by Dave Mackay, who had previously managed Derby County, Nottingham Forest, Walsall and Doncaster Rovers as well as coaching in Kuwait. Mackay named Bobby Ferguson as his assistant.

By September, the Kumars had taken their promised spending to £430,000 as Mackay brought in the Manchester City midfielder Nigel Gleghorn for £175,000 to go with other new signings Trevor Matthewson (£45,000 from Lincoln City), Phil Sproson (£50,000 from Port Vale), Dennis Bailey (£80,000 from Bristol Rovers) and Colin Gordon (also £80,000 from Fulham). Immediately, supporters everywhere were wondering whether or not this was to be the year that the 'Rebirth of the Blues' was finally about to happen.

Unfortunately it wasn't. Blues missed out on the chance of claiming a Play-off place because of long periods of inconsistency throughout the season.

And to add to the club's woes from time to time, unruly thugs masquerading as Blues fans again caused problems on their travels with a weekend of violence and looting in Blackpool – an incident which was later considered by an FA hearing where the club was cleared of any blame although their away matches thereafter were made all-ticket for travelling supporters.

Back on the field, Blues, after attaining their highest position all season by going third at the end of September, won only one game in October and one in the whole of January and February, once going 12 League and Cup games with only a single victory to show for their efforts. For all that they did not fall below 11th position, and eventually finished in seventh place, a massive 27 points adrift of champions Bristol Rovers and 21 behind third-placed and promoted Notts County.

Occasionally Blues played exceptionally well, beating Northampton Town 4-0 and both Mansfield Town and Rotherham United 4-1, but sometimes they were very poor, struggling against sides battling against relegation at the bottom end of the table. They lost ten and drew five of their 23 away games, crashing 5-2 at Mansfield, 5-1 at both Tranmere and Rotherham, and succumbing 4-0 at Chester City. Their home form was also hit and miss at times and their heaviest defeat at St Andrew's came at the hands of Bristol City (4-0) in mid-January.

The Cup competitions again offered no joy, Blues being knocked out of the Littlewoods Cup and FA Cup by West Ham United (managed by future Blues boss Lou Macari) and Oldham Athletic respectively – the latter after a third-round replay – and it was no consolation that both of these clubs reached the semi-finals.

The Leyland DAF Trophy offered Blues their best chance of reaching Wembley, but even then their hopes perished in the preliminary round due to a disastrous performance at Aldershot who were lingering near the foot of the Fourth Division. The crowd at the Recreation Ground for this tie was a meagre 1,148 – one of the lowest turnouts ever to watch Blues in a competitive match.

On reflection, it took Blues some time to get to grips with football at a lower level but there were some encouraging signs, notably the form of Dennis Bailey (who top-scored with 20 goals), Simon Sturridge up front, and midfielder Nigel Gleghorn who certainly added some grit and determination to that department – a thing which had been sadly lacking for quite a while. Several youngsters also did well, especially Paul Tait.

The defence, although basically sound, with goalkeeper Martyn Thomas doing very well, when under considerable pressure, although he was prone to some horrendous lapses of concentration at times (hence those heavy defeats) and Blues conceded 59 League goals (40 away from home). This typified the way the season went.

Manager Dave Mackay worked hard along with his assistant Ferguson and coaches Fred Davies (the former Wolves goalkeeper) and Tony Brown, but there was clearly something missing; a vital spark was required, whether it be in midfield or attack, and despite the acquisition of Scotsman Dougie Bell (from Shrewsbury Town) to accompany Gleghorn and Langley in the 'engine-room', Blues lacked the creativeness and, indeed, the ability overall to pose a serious threat to those clubs chasing promotion.

At this juncture former St Andrew's favourite, Trevor Francis was approached to become player-manager of Blues, allowing Mackay to act as the club's general manager. But Francis declined the offer, saying that he was still a First Division player and would not drop down into the Third.

It was generally agreed that provided Blues did not follow the well-worn path of selling their promising youngsters and instead make one or two signings to reinforce the squad, perhaps defenders, then promotion could become a reality in 1990-91.

It is common knowledge that Blues have some of the most loyal and dedicated supporters in the country, but the uninspiring form of the team and the mediocre opposition, reduced the average attendance at St Andrew's to 8,000.

Thus it was hoped that such loyalty of the hard core of fans would be rewarded in the not-too-distant future.

In the summer of 1990, manager Mackay secured the services of experienced left-back Greg Downs from Coventry City and immediately made him club captain – Downs was Mackay's only pre-season signing – and the manager began the season by fielding this team at Cambridge United in the opening League game: Thomas; Ashley, Downs; Frain, Overson, Matthewson, Peer, Bailey, Hopkins, Gleghorn, Tait, with Sturridge and Clarkson on the bench.

Blues got off to a good start, winning 1-0 with Gleghorn on target after 61 minutes. But an early exit from the Rumbelows League Cup dented enthusiasm, only for that to be revived after a run of 12 games without defeat, although it must be said that eight were draws, all in succession.

Indeed, this was Blues' best start to a season for 82 years, although it was marred by the tragic death, on 17 August at the age of 27, of former player Ian Handysides, who scored 12 goals in 133 games for Blues in two separate spells with the club.

The fine sequence ended with a crushing 4-1 defeat at Shrewsbury for whom Wayne Clarke scored a hat-trick against his former club, but then Blues started to pick up once more and although their League form was not all that great, they started off well in the Leyland DAF Cup, beating Walsall and Lincoln City during November.

This was to be the competition for Blues who were knocked out of the FA Cup in round two at Brentford after scraping through the opening round at home to Cheltenham Town to the only goal of the game, gifted to them by the hesitancy of a young right-back called Miguel De Souza - later to join Blues as a striker.

All the time the prospect of a Wembley appearance increased, although the Leyland DAF run was intermingled with a mixture of good and bad results in the League, as well as the elimination from the FA Cup plus a change of manager – one Scot replacing another, Lou Macari for Dave Mackay early in the New Year, after terrace protests had forced the latter out of office. In the Leyland DAF competition, meanwhile, Blues accounted, in turn, for Swansea City, Mansfield Town, Cambridge United and then Brentford in the semi-final over two legs.

The second leg against the Bees was the first match beamed 'live' to St Andrew's for a crowd of 6,000 fans who could not obtain tickets to see that exciting 1-0 win at Griffin Park which sent Blues through to the Leyland DAF Final and to Wembley for the first time since 1956.

This was unquestionably the highlight of the 1990-91 season – an appearance at the Empire Stadium – and to celebrate the occasion Blues beat Tranmere Rovers 3-2 to lift the Leyland DAF trophy, much to the delight of their 38,127 fans who 'officially' made the trip down the M1 together with another 3,000 or so who obtained tickets from other sources, to boost the attendance up to 58,756.

It had been 35 years since Blues had graced the home of English football and those fans who were inside the Empire Stadium made the most of a terrific day out!

Despite all this success, it was another inconsistent and disappointing League campaign with Blues finishing in their lowest position ever (12th in Division Three). They mustered only 45 goals (in 46 games) and this is why the team fared badly.

It had all began so very well with Blues stringing together that fine unbeaten run. However, once that run was over, a decline set in and by Christmas it seemed that Division Four was beckoning. It had been obvious that Dave Mackay was

Wembley Glory For Blues
Birmingham City 3 Tranmere Rovers 2

THE 1991 Leyland DAF Trophy Final at Wembley lived up to every expectation of the massed army of Blues followers, with their team dominating virtually the whole of the first half.

Blues went ahead with an excellent opportunist goal from Simon Sturridge on 21 minutes, and four minutes before the interval, with Tranmere pushed back deep in their own half, a blistering 30-yard drive from John Gayle saw Lou Macari's men sweep in to a 2-0 lead.

This scoreline did not flatter the Blues one iota, and but for a magnificent point-blank save by Rovers' excellent goalkeeper Eric Nixon from Dean Peer seconds before the break, after a superb flowing movement involving five men, the lead at the interval may well have been greater. If that had been the case, then the result would have been settled there and then.

However, as always, Blues seemed to decide not to give their fans a relaxing time during the second 45 minutes, restarting the game in a strangely subdued fashion, allowing Tranmere to get right back into the match. Indeed, Tranmere drove forward in numbers and the Merseysiders drew level with two well-taken goals, the first from their Birmingham-born striker Steve Cooper on 61 minutes and the second from Scotsman Jim Steel five minutes later.

The match then ebbed and flowed in a pulsating fashion and could have gone either way, but with extra-time apparently beckoning, Blues made one last surging effort.

In the 86th minute they were awarded a free-kick some 40 yards out on the right-hand touch-line. Ian Clarkson swung the ball into the penalty area where Vince Overson won an important heading duel with Dave Higgins, and as the ball was dropping, big John Gayle, his back to goal, somehow produced an astonishing overhead scissor-kick, sending the ball booming past Nixon's left hand and high into the top corner of the net. What a goal! It was worthy of winning any Cup Final.

This sent the masses of Blues supporters into ecstasy and although the last four minutes seem to take an eternity, frequent renditions of 'Keep Right On To The End Of The Road' carried the team through to the final whistle of one of the most compelling games Blues have ever played in.

Thousands of supporters greeted the players when they brought back the silver trophy to the city for a civic reception – the first major prize won by Blues since they lifted the League Cup in 1963.

Could this storming performance be the springboard for the rebirth of the Blues, hitherto so often an unfulfilled promise in the club's history? Certainly the chances of that were not increased by the shock departure of Macari (following a dispute with the club's directors) only a few weeks after the high point of this tremendous Wembley triumph.

Birmingham City: Thomas; Clarkson, Frain, Peer, Overson, Matthewson, Peer, Gayle, Robinson, Gleghorn, Sturridge(Bailey).
Tranmere Rovers: Nixon; Higgins, Brannan, McNab(Martindale), Hughes, Vickers(Malkin), Morrissey, Irons, Steel, Cooper, Thomas.
Attendance: 58,756
Referee: J.E.Martin (Alton, Hants.)

---

not comfortable as manager and some indecisiveness together with far too many team changes caused unrest in the camp, with the players and even supporters getting annoyed.

The situation could not continue, and following an embarrassing 3-0 home defeat at the hands of Cambridge United in mid-January, Mackay left St Andrew's to be replaced by the former Celtic, Manchester United and Scottish international Lou Macari, who was to be hailed as a messiah after that Wembley triumph.

Macari had previously managed both Swindon Town and West Ham and at the time of his appointment at St Andrew's was facing a charge of alleged tax irregularities.

Immediately Blues started to play with more confidence and commitment, as well as purpose and style. The crowds started to come back (at one stage home League attendances had dropped to around 5,300) and over 16,000 saw Blues' home Leyland DAF Cup semi-final clash with Brentford, although at the end of the season the average attendance at St Andrew's was only just over 7,000, a drop of almost 1,500 on the previous season's figure.

Thirty-one players were utilised in 1990-91, including new signings John Gayle, the Wembley hero, who cost £175,000 from Wimbledon, Ian Rodgerson (£50,000 from Cardiff City), Eamonn Dolan (£30,000 from West Ham) and Trevor Aylott (£40,000 from Bournemouth).

Gayle and Sturridge finished joint leading scorers with ten goals apiece while Trevor Matthewson was the only ever-present.

Twenty-three days after that Wembley triumph, manager Lou Macari dropped a bombshell, quitting Blues to take over as boss of Stoke City, taking with him Chic Bates and Peter Henderson, and as the controversy over his departure raged the Blues Action Group was formed in an effort to oust the Samesh Kumar as chairman of the football club.

Kumar survived the protests but things went from bad to worse when it was learnt that a total of 21 players were out of contract, most of them seemingly reluctant to pledge their future to Birmingham City.

The club was in turmoil, but all credit to caretaker boss Bill Coldwell and coach Ian Atkins who persuaded virtually all of the players to re-sign, and in the end only centre-half Vince Overson refused. He eventually joined Macari at Stoke.

In late July 1991, Blues began a pre-season tour to Ireland and it was whilst on the Emerald Isle that Terry Cooper was named as the club's new manager.

The former Leeds United, Middlesbrough, Bristol City and England full-back was successfully lured away from the hot seat at Exeter City whom he had guided to promotion from Division Four a year earlier.

Cooper, who installed coach Atkins as his assistant, was soon to become a director of the club (appointed in October 1991) quickly got to grips with the situation and things immediately started to happen on the park, Blues suffering only one defeat in their opening 15 games, thus getting off to a flying start.

Cooper quickly signed four new players and introduced two of them in his defence – the skilful Paul Mardon (from

Hicks of Blues (right) and Stein of Stoke battle for the ball during the 1-1 draw at St Andrew's in February 1992.

Bristol City) and the experienced 'stopper' Martin Hicks, a £115,000 buy from Reading, who made 500 League appearances for the Royals. Hicks started off shakily, but finished the season in excellent form, and was duly voted 'Player of the Year' by the supporters.

The other two new faces were Foley Okenla and Eric Hogan and these were followed soon after by Louie Donowa (also from Bristol City) and the manager's son, Mark Cooper (from Exeter City).

Blues bounded along and two more signing were made – strikers Darren Rowbotham and Jason Beckford arriving for a combined fee of £70,000 (most of which was raised by supporters).

Blues sat proudly on top of the Third Division at the start of November following some excellent performances during the first three months of Cooper's reign, including a 3-0 win over Stockport County and a 1-0 triumph in the local derby at The Hawthorns against West Bromwich Albion, which attracted a bumper 26,169 crowd.

At this juncture Blues' line-up usually comprised: Thomas; Clarkson, Matthewson, Peer, Hicks and Mardon, Rodgerson, Frain, Louie Donowa and Gleghorn or Sturridge, with Cooper and Tait also in the reckoning. Kevin Drinkell played five games on loan from Coventry City and was brought in simply because of an injury crisis in attack.

In October 1991, Blues Society started the 'True Blue Club' which gave their supporters the opportunity to subscribe monthly to help buy players with the Canadian World Cup star, Paul Peschisolido being secured from Toronto Blizzard for just £25,000. He was to become a great favourite with the fans but Blues had to do without his services at a crucial time in the season as he was away on World Cup duty. Sadly he was to leave Blues in the summer of 1994,

joining forces with Blues former boss, Lou Macari at Stoke.

As Christmas approached, Blues suffered a few Cup hiccups. They lost badly 3-0 at Torquay in the FA Cup, went out at Crystal Palace in the Rumbelows Cup (rather unluckily in a second replay), and were eliminated at Stoke in the Autoglass Trophy (when fielding a weakened team). In fact, they recorded only three wins in 12 outings and a few rumblings were heard inside St Andrew's.

Nevertheless, once into 1992 and after it was revealed that Blues lost £5,000 a week in 1991 despite winning the Leyland DAF Cup – they perked up again and surged on, only an Autoglass Trophy exit at the hands of Walsall marring their progress.

South African John Paskin (formerly of West Brom) was now in attack and goalkeeper Alan Miller had been taken on loan from Arsenal. But a run of poor results during February (one win in five starts) saw Blues slip down to sixth place.

There was one unsavoury incident in the tense home League game with Stoke City on 29th February when a controversial late equaliser by the visitors sparked off a pitch invasion which turned into a disgraceful riot. The players were taken off the field by referee Roger Wiseman, who had earlier been struck by a fan, and brought back to play out the remaining seconds without any fans inside the ground.

After this incident a distraught Terry Cooper told a six-year-old lad; "Stay at home in future – you don't want to see this at a football match," and he then hinted that he may quit the club because of the violence shown by so-called Blues supporters.

Chairman Kumar claimed the riot was precipitated because of some 'scandalous refereeing decisions' by the match official. He was later asked to explain his comments to the FA and the club were charged with misconduct. He

Gleghorn the Hero as Blues Clinch Promotion
Birmingham City 1 Shrewsbury Town 0

AN almighty roar went out from St Andrew's at 4.47 pm on Saturday 25 April 1992 as the public address system announced that Stoke City had lost at home and, as a result, Blues were sure of promotion.

At that around 4,000 joyous, dancing, banner and flag waving fans invaded the pitch, and then burst into song as manager Terry Cooper thanked them for their great support throughout the season.

It had been six years since Blues had last won promotion and it was Nigel Gleghorn's 34th minute goal against Shrewsbury Town which finally lifted them out of Division Three, to the relief of thousands.

Blues, who had not beaten the Shrews for 12 years, overcame their bogey team in dominant fashion, although the scoreline doesn't really indicate how one-sided the game really was – a game, incidentally, which was rather scrappy, being ruined by a gusty wind which blew straight down the ground from the Railway End.

Shrewsbury, who had lost only one of their previous 15 games, and were battling in vain to avoid relegation, started well enough and should have taken the lead on 20 minutes when former Blues favourite Robert Hopkins deceived on-loan goalkeeper Kevin Dearden with a lob which dipped agonisingly over the bar. Soon after, from a teasing free-kick, Dean Spink's header was just fractionally too high.

The vital goal was down to the resilience of Ian Rodgerson and Simon Sturridge. The latter shook off a challenge from Steve Mackenzie to get a return pass back to Rodgerson. The former Cardiff player then delivered a delicious deep cross to the far post where Gleghorn was waiting to power his header beyond Ken Hughes in the Shrewsbury goal.

After this Hughes was by far the busier of the two goalkeepers, making three excellent saves, one a real beauty from David Rennie's blistering 30-yard drive. He also acrobatically deflected a Rodgerson cross away from his line. Substitute Pat O'Toole headed a Darren Rowbotham effort off the line as Blues tried to add to their score and although Neil Lyne wasted two good chances for the Shrews late on, Blues were deserving winners, with co-defenders Martin Hicks and Trevor Matthewson both outstanding.

Birmingham City: Dearden; Clarkson, Frain, Rennie, Hicks, Matthewson, Rodgerson, Cooper, Rowbotham(Mardon), Gleghorn, Sturridge.
Shrewsbury Town: Hughes; Clark(Henry), Lynch, Mackenzie, Spink, Blake, Taylor, Summerfield, Bremner, Hopkins(O'Toole), Lyne.

Attendance: 19,868
Referee: E.J.Parker (Preston)

---

subsequently apologised for his comments, saying, "My passion got the better of me." Later, an FA Commission looking into that trouble-torn game with Stoke, slapped a £50,000 fine on Blues and ordered them to play at least two games behind closed doors, but these sentences were suspended.

These, though, were the first outward signs of conflict between Cooper and Kumar, and the Blues boss threw up further doubts about his long-term future at St Andrew's by criticising the way the club was run, and following a 1-1 draw with Swansea City (the first game after the riot) he said he'd been 'banging his head against a brick wall'.

Kumar was 'sad and disappointed' with Cooper's attitude, but then tried to retract statements. After a showdown meeting, Cooper agreed to remain at St Andrew's following an *Evening Mail* organised petition, signed more than 4,000 fans, who had pleading him to stay on.

Thankfully, the strained atmosphere between chairman and manager was put to one side, and things soon got back to normal on the pitch as far as Blues were concerned. Following the introduction of Dave Rennie, a £120,000 buy from Bristol City, in defence and Tottenham's Kevin Dearden in goal, Blues raced on to take the runners-up spot in Division Three and so won promotion, which they clinched with a 1-0 win over Shrewsbury Town in their last home game before a near-20,000 crowd, Nigel Gleghorn scoring on 34 minutes, his 22nd goal of the season, which made him Blues' leading marksman (from midfield, too). Rodgerson and Sturridge both hit 11.

The 1991-92 League season ended slightly disappointingly in a way for Blues. They would have taken the championship if they had won one of their last two away games at Wigan and Stockport instead of losing them both.

There is no doubt that manager Cooper had done a splendid job and the fact that Blues had to use 37 players (in all games) including six goalkeepers – Thomas, Carter, Cheesewright, Miller, Dearden and Gleghorn as a substitute – during the season, made his achievement even greater. The diehard St Andrew's faithful backed their team to the hilt and the average home attendance shot up to 12,433, a rise of 5,403 (a staggering 77 per cent) on the previous season including the top attendance in the Third Division, 27,508 for the visit of neighbours West Brom.

The phoenix had risen from the ashes, Blues were on the march again, but could they maintain their form in the higher Division?

That was the question being asked by Brummies everywhere.

Chairman Kumar and Cooper clashed again but after a five-hour meeting, an agreement was forthcoming after assurances were made by Kumar that money would be made available to spend on rebuilding the team.

In the summer of 1992, Cooper recruited goalkeeper Andy Gosney (£35,000 from Portsmouth) and defender Darren Rogers (a free transfer from West Bromwich Albion) these being his only major signings. And he relied on practically the same team which had done the club proud on the run-in to promotion the previous season, fielding this side for the opening League game of the new campaign against Notts County at St Andrew's: Gosney; Clarkson, Frain, Rennie, Rogers, Mardon, Donowa, Tait, Sale, Gleghorn, Sturridge(Rodgerson).

Blues won the game 1-0, Donowa scoring with a superb volley in front of 10,614 fans, rather a low attendance because this was the first ever 'live' televised League match from St Andrew's.

Four successive wins at the start of the season suggested another successful campaign, but this was to prove yet

Ten-Goal Thriller Goes Swindon's Way
Birmingham City 4 Swindon Town 6

THIS was quite a bizarre game – one which certainly caused Blues' manager Terry Cooper to pull his hair out, and for the fans to do likewise. On Monday, 12 April 1993, Blues were searching for every point available in their effort to stave off relegation, while Swindon, under player-manager Glenn Hoddle, were chasing a Play-off spot in Division Two.

However, this wasn't the result Blues wanted or indeed expected – not after being 4-1 in front with half-an-hour remaining.

Right-back Ian Clarkson said in the dressing room afterwards: "This was a real shock. We were cruising along, then Swindon blitzed us. We couldn't believe it." Neither could the manager or the fans.

The game had started rather tamely and neither side created anything which threatened the respective goalkeepers. But then out of the blue, on 25 minutes, Dean Peer gave Blues the lead from Andy Saville's astute pass.

Swindon hit back, came close to equalising but suddenly found themselves 2-0 down. Following a corner on 29 minutes, Blues broke away with left-back John Frain joining the attack. It was Frain, sent through by Paul Moulden, who drove hard and low past Fraser Digby, in the Swindon goal.

Two minutes before the interval, after twice going close, Shaun Taylor, the Swindon centre-back, scored with a header from Micky Hazard's right-wing free-kick.

It was 2-1 to Blues at half-time, but two minutes into the second half Moulden increased the lead, netting with a low cross-shot which flew past Colin Calderwood and Hoddle before deceiving the unsighted Digby.

Before Swindon had reorganised Blues roared into a 4-1 lead, Saville scoring on 51 minutes with a terrific rocket-like shot high into the roof of the net after good work by Peer, Ian Rodgerson and David Smith.

At this point Blues were in complete command of the game, but then Swindon made a dramatic change. They had been playing with a sweeper, but Hoddle decided to utilise only three men at the back, pushing himself further forward into the centre of midfield where he teamed up with Hazard.

Thereafter Blues were under pressure. Swindon surged forward and on 60 minutes Craig Maskell, latching on to Hazard's precise pass, slipped the ball wide of the Blues goalkeeper Andy Gosney to make it 4-2.

Five minutes later Australian international striker Dave Mitchell was on the spot to nod home from close range after Gosney had fingertipped Taylor's looping centre on to his head – 4-3.

Blues, backpedalling, were in complete disarray after 76 minutes when a sweet-flowing move involving Martin Ling and Maskell was finished off in style by Mitchell – 4-4.

Two minutes later full-back Paul Bodin's telling corner-kick was thumped home by Maskell – 4-5 – and Swindon were now rampant.

Blues couldn't raise a gallop and in the very last minute Mitchell completed a fine hat-trick when he ran on to a long pass from Ling to beat both Trevor Matthewson and goalkeeper Gosney before sliding the ball over the line to make it 4-6.

Blues simply didn't know what had hit them from the hour mark onwards. St Andrew's was a cauldron of noise when Blues were leading 4-1. At the final whistle there were boos and jeers as the shell-shocked Blues players trooped off the field, heads bowed, stunned into silence.

Birmingham City: Gosney; Clarkson(Mardon), Frain, Parris, Dryden, Matthewson, Moulden, Rodgerson, Saville, Peer, Smith.
Swindon Town: Digby; Summerbee, Bodin, Hoddle, Calderwood, Taylor, Hazard, MacLaren, Mitchell, Ling, Maskell.
Attendance: 17,903
Referee: J.Lloyd (Wrexham)

---

another false dawn as the next 20 League games provided only two victories, contained a spell of 423 minutes without a League goal and saw Blues spiralling down towards the basement of the Division. It became clear to everyone, players, staff and supporters alike, that the squad was not good enough to compete at a higher grade. And what was alarming was the apparent lack of commitment shown by the players in several matches, especially away from St Andrew's.

Once again the various Cup competitions provided little cheer, Blues being ousted from both the Coca-Cola Cup and FA Cup by clubs from lower divisions (Exeter City and Reading respectively).

The Anglo-Italian tournament saw Blues' first venture into Europe in 30 years, but this poorly supported competition was a failure all round, for it realised more sendings-off than goals, and only a miserly 139 spectators bothered to turn up to watch Blues play Lucchese in Italy, a game which was lost 3-0 and with it interest in the lack-lustre competition.

It was not only on the pitch where the problems lay. Internally there were major problems concerning chairman Samesh Kumar's business which went bankrupt with debts of around £6 million after the BCCI scandal had rocked the

City. Thus on 6 November 1992, the liquidator of collapsed bank BCCI appointed Leonard Curtis as Receiver of the Kumar Brothers' firms and announced that their 84 per cent shareholding in Birmingham City was up for sale. The club was immediately placed in the hands of the Receiver who stated that 12 different groups were interested in buying Birmingham City. This unsatisfactory situation was to last for five months and the club's position, both on and off the field, looked hopeless.

Ian Atkins quit as Cooper's assistant and after the Boxing Day postponement of the Sunderland game, Blues slumped to the foot of the table. In January Cooper again threatened to quit unless the club was saved soon, and the tension within St Andrew's (as well as on the field of play) lingered on right through February.

However, at the beginning of March things started to look up when millionaire publisher David Sullivan, proprietor of the *Sunday Sport* moved in with a successful bid of £1.7 million to take over the club, naming Karren Brady as managing director – and overnight Birmingham City's fortunes soared.

Blues revelled in new-found wealth and manager Terry Cooper, free from constraints imposed by the previous administration, was able to spend money on strengthening the side. In all, six new players were signed for a total of £720,000: West Ham's George Parris for £150,000, full-back Scott Hiley from Exeter City for £100,000, striker Paul Moulden from Oldham Athletic for £150,000 and Coventry City's England Under-21 capped winger David Smith, in a player-exchange deal involving Rennie. Within a fortnight of the buy-out, Richard Dryden arrived from Notts County for £165,000 and Andy Saville was secured from Hartlepool United for £155,000.

This was obviously a difficult time in the season for these new players to come into the team, with relegation staring Blues in the face, but they all responded magnificently, as indeed, did the whole of the Blues side, and the threat of demotion was finally dispelled, although in typical Blues tradition, it took until the final game of the League programme before the problem was resolved.

In the run-in Blues won at Sunderland, were beaten 6-4 at home by Swindon Town in a cracking contest over Easter, lost at Watford, drew with Tranmere Rovers and shared six goals at Twerton Park against Bristol Rovers.

Then came the final match – one which Blues had to win to stay up – and they did just that, beating Charlton Athletic 1-0 in front of a 22,234 St Andrew's crowd. Paul Moulden was the hero and how the fans celebrated. It was reminiscent of that Wembley triumph two years earlier.

Incidentally, League attendances at St Andrew's this term dropped slightly – to 12,255 – but with a winning team that figure would surely increase in vast numbers.

At long last it looked as though Blues had got the right people at the helm: David Sullivan, managing director Karren Brady, directors Peter Day, Alan Jones and Terry Cooper with long-serving Jack Wiseman now chairman.

New owner Sullivan had made it known publicly that he was prepared to spend money in order to bring success to St Andrew's, which had certainly not been the case under the Kumar brothers. But could he – or rather the manager – get the right players for Birmingham City. That remained to be seen.

Cooper strengthened his squad in the summer of 1993 by paying his former club, Exeter City, £250,000 for goalkeeper Kevin Miller, signing Scotsman Ted McMinn, once of Glasgow Rangers, from Derby County for £200,000, recruiting former West Brom and Arsenal defender Chris Whyte from Leeds United for £230,000 and picking up experienced midfielder Keith Downing from Wolves on a free transfer.

In October, Cooper spent another £250,000 on winger Danny Wallace from Manchester United and wrapped up a £40,000 deal with Leeds for striker Carl Shutt. These transactions took Cooper's spending to £1.89 million (on 14 players) under Sullivan.

Wallace headed the winner on his debut against Watford, and victory over Bolton moved Blues up to eighth place in the Division. However, a terrible injury list coupled with a run of five defeats in six games then turned a dissatisfied section of fans against Cooper, who, two days after a 3-0 defeat against Tranmere, decided to quit the club on 29 November 1993, despite Sullivan offering him as much money as he wanted for new players.

After speculation that Steve Coppell was to be the new boss, Sullivan surprised everyone by bringing in the charismatic but relatively unproven Southend United manager Barry Fry to replace Cooper on Friday, 10 December.

Fry, once on the books of Manchester United and previously in charge of Barnet, was immediately told, "You have at least £1 million available to spend on rebuilding the

team," and during his first few weeks in charge, along with his assistant Edwin Stein and coach David Howell, he saw Blues play well and among some encouraging results were successive home wins over Charlton Athletic – 1-0, the goal scored by Kenny Lowe, who had joined the club in a player-exchange deal which sent young defender Graham Potter to Stoke City – and neighbours West Brom 2-0 when Saville (penalty) and Peschisolido were on target.

Despite the snowy conditions, this local derby against the Throstles, which took place three days after Christmas, attracted the season's best crowd in the Division – a bumper 28,228. And a delighted Fry said afterwards: "Forget relegation – we're good enough to win promotion!"

However, after a fiery return to Roots Hall (where Blues lost 3-1) Fry's men then succumbed to non-Leaguers Kidderminster Harriers in the FA Cup, going down 2-1 at home. This was a blow for all concerned at St Andrew's, but Fry and his players tried to get this nightmare out of their system and set about the job in hand of trying to pull clear of the relegation trap-door and edge up the table.

The outcome was that Blues' form nosedived as they slipped deeper and deeper into trouble.

On reflection, Fry's first three months in charge were unbelievable.

He bought several players from clubs he had served in the past and in the February, Blues suffered a fine of £130,000 for 'poaching' Fry from Southend.

At this crucial stage in the campaign Blues went 15 matches without a win – a club record they could have done without.

Blues were struggling as February ran into March and despite an end-of-season run of six wins (including a splendid 4-2 victory at The Hawthorns over fellow relegation candidates Albion) and two draws in their final nine matches, they still went down, finishing below West Brom simply because the Baggies had scored more goals. Some people said that playing their last four games of the season away from home (this because of the scheduled redevelopment plans at St Andrew's) cost Blues their place in Division One, even though they won three of them!

On the very last day of the season any two of three clubs could have been relegated with Peterborough United, who were already doomed. The three involved, reading upwards, were Oxford, Blues and West Brom.

All three won their final matches (Blues at Tranmere, Albion at Portsmouth and Oxford at home to Notts County) and this meant that Blues and Oxford joined Posh in what was now the new Division Two.

An amazing total of 46 players were used during the course of the 1993-94 campaign, a new League record, beating Coventry City's tally of 43 which was set in 1919-20.

Manager Fry signed 19 of them permanently and another three on loan, including midfielder Mark Ward, who later joined the club on a full-time basis. The four players who cost the most money were goalkeeper Ian Bennett (£325,000 from Peterborough United), strikers Steve Claridge (up to £350,000 from Cambridge United) and Steve McGavin (an agreed fee of up to £150,000 from Colchester United) and rugged defender Dave Barnett (£150,000 from Barnet).

Fry released 12 players, among them Ted McMinn to Burnley for £100,000 and David Smith to West Brom for £90,000, and, in fact, during his first 12 months in charge at St Andrew's (December 1993 to December 1994) the manager used 40 players in the first team. Quite astonishing statistics.

Despite that disappointing 1993-94 season, though,

Blues Gun Down Albion
West Bromwich Albion 2 Birmingham City 4

THIS match on 27 April 1994 was a crucial relegation battle for both clubs and it was the never-say-die Blues who shocked Albion with a remarkable victory as their effort to pull off what was now being described as the 'Great Escape' gathered momentum.

Played off the park for half-an-hour and 1-0 down to a fine Kevin Donovan goal on 24 minutes, Barry Fry's men, urged on by an army of 2,500 or so supporters, recovered, more through guts than skill, to thoroughly expose the Baggies' defensive frailties. And in the end they won well. The equaliser came on 38 minutes – Blues' first genuine shot on goal – and the scorer was Steve Claridge, who collected a deflected Scott Hiley cross from the right to drill the ball past the advancing Stuart Naylor.

Blues certainly got an ear-bashing from their manager during the half-time break and they came out for the second period wound up and ready for action. After a couple of chances at either end, Louie Donowa netted a sensational goal to give Blues the lead on 50 minutes.

A long ball downfield towards the edge of the Albion penalty area by Hiley was headed towards the right-hand touch-line by Baggies' goalkeeper Naylor, but Donowa, reacting quickly, controlled the clearance and then delivered a magnificent 40-yard chip which sailed into the unguarded net.

Blues were flying and on 56 minutes, after former Brummie Paul Mardon had fallen over when blocking a shot from Neil Doherty, Naylor presented Andy Saville with an open goal by fumbling the loose ball and it was 3-1 to Barry Fry's men.

Albion were stunned, but they fought back and following the arrival of substitute Gary Strodder, they reduced the deficit in the 64th minute, Strodder made his presence felt inside the area when Lee Ashcroft's free-kick came over, allowing Daryl Burgess to thunder home a header.

Albion were now on the charge, and they should have levelled things up on 67 minutes, but the usually surefooted Bob Taylor, taking Ashcroft's measured pass in his stride, missed what seemed a simple one-on-one with the Blues goalkeeper Ian Bennett.

Three other chances came Albion's way – to Taylor, Andy Hunt and Donovan – and they all went begging.

Blues somehow survived, and went upfield to score another goal to sew up the points with almost the last kick of the game, Steve Claridge racing through unmarked to round Naylor for an easy tap-in.

A joyous Claridge said afterwards: "Albion were by far the better side early on, but we stuck at it and we got what we deserved. Bookings for Albion's defenders Burgess and Mardon shifted the emphasis in the match. They tackled us hard every time we got the ball and in the game today a yellow card or two is sure to be produced on the odd occasion. This time it was Albion men who were penalised and that meant they had to be careful after that."

West Bromwich Albion: Naylor; Parsley, Darton, Ashcroft, Mardon, Burgess, Hunt, Hamilton, Taylor, Donovan, Smith(Strodder).
Birmingham City: Bennett; Hiley, Frain, Donowa, Whyte, Daish, Ward, Saville(Harding), Claridge, Willis, Doherty.

Attendance: 20,316
Referee: J.M.Key (Sheffield)

Blues' average home League attendance was 14,500, up by almost 2,200 on the previous campaign. Saville top-scored in the League with ten goals; Peschisolido hit nine and Steve Claridge seven.

There was a lot of transfer activity during the summer of 1994 and, indeed, just prior to the beginning of the 1994-95 season, Paul Peschisolido's move to Stoke City, in a part-exchange deal involving Dave Regis, was the main one.

For the first three months of the new campaign Blues' form was inconsistent, although they did give Premiership champions-elect Blackburn Rovers a difficult time before losing 3-1 on aggregate in a Coca-Cola Cup tie.

Their best League win was a 4-0 thrashing of Peterborough United at St Andrews. The Posh were also beaten 5-2 at London Road in the Auto Windscreens Shield when Jonathan Hunt, who had joined Blues from Southend United, scored a stunning hat-trick.

The newly-designed all-seater St Andrew's ground was officially opened on 15 November when a near-20,000 crowd witnessed a 1-1 draw with Aston Villa. And it was after this memorable occasion that Blues' form picked up.

They held third spot in the table and then rose to second before taking top spot on the last day of 1994 with a crushing 7-1 home win over Blackpool.

Ricky Otto had now joined Birmingham for a club record £800,000 from Southend United (Regis going to Roots Hall as part of the transaction) and he was soon to be joined by the lanky 6ft 7in striker, Kevin Francis, who joined Blues for

a similar figure from Stockport County.

When Otto arrived, the money involved took manager Fry's spending in his first year at the club to over £2.5 million. Owner David Sullivan told him, "There's a bit more in the kitty if you want it." And so Fry went out and bought Francis.

So Blues saw 1995 in on the back of a resounding win. They were also on top of the Second Division and were well into a record unbeaten run of 23 League and Cup games stretching back to 20 September. Surely even they could not now falter in the run to the championship – or could they?

Never in the history of the club have Blues achieved any success without giving themselves and their supporters a roller-coaster ride and for the next four months this was to be the case yet again.

The first match of 1995, at Bradford, was played on a rock-hard frozen pitch and Blues' fine unbeaten run was maintained only by a last-minute drive by Gary Cooper which equalised an earlier strike from Taylor.

Then the knock-out competitions diverted everyone's attention away from League action with the visit of Liverpool to a packed St Andrew's in the third round of the FA Cup. A crowd of over 25,000 saw battling Blues push their Premiership opponents every inch of the way to earn a goalless draw and a trip to Anfield for the replay.

Following that epic encounter against Liverpool, there was another important game – an Auto Windscreens Shield tie against Hereford United which was played on a muddy

Blues in Seventh Heaven
Birmingham City 7 Blackpool 1

REWRITING the record books was commonplace for Blues during the 1994-95 season and this emphatic win on New Year's Eve was their best in any competition for more than 35 years, since their swashbuckling away performance against Nottingham Forest in the old First Division back in 1959 when they ran up an identical scoreline.

This was Blues' fourth post-World War Two seven-goal haul in a competitive game – falling just two short of the club record victory of 9-1 against Liverpool in 1954.

Blues, though, could have netted double-figures against an enterprising Blackpool side, who themselves may well have netted four or five goals.

Indeed, a final scoreline of 15-5 would have been a truer reflection on how the game went and how many clear-cut chances were created.

All credit to Blackpool who attacked throughout the 90 minutes, contributing greatly to a most enjoyable and enterprising afternoon's entertainment for the 18,000 crowd.

Many sides came to St Andrew's during this season utilising six or seven players, whose basic job it was to frustrate and negate. Blackpool had no such intentions and all credit to their manager Sam Allardyce for his positive approach.

Nevertheless, it was the visitors who stunned the home supporters by taking the lead on eight minutes through Darren Bradshaw, hence the rarity of an opposing player scoring past Ian Bennett.

Blues may well have panicked but urged on by their supporters they took the game by the scruff of the neck and tore into Blackpool. The equaliser, albeit somewhat fortuitous, arrived on 12 minutes when the unfortunate Bradshaw deflected the ball wide of his goalkeeper which brought him the dubious tag of scoring for both sides in the same match – exactly as Ricky Otto had done on his Blues debut a few days earlier.

On 25 minutes – after near misses at both ends – Louie Donowa (the longest serving member of the team on the day) raced away down the left, skinning poor Phil Brown for pace before cutting inside to place his shot into the top corner of the net wide of Capleton.

Then on 37 minutes, Steve Claridge, ever the enigma, brought the ball on to his right foot and buried a sweet drive from all of 30 yards to make it 3-1. Further chances went begging before Ricky Otto delivered the ball from the left for Kenny Lowe to loop a far post header into the net on 53 minutes to put Blues 4-1 in front, and this was stretched to 5-1 on 64 minutes when the unmarked Donowa sidefooted home from close range after Lowe's clever back-heel.

With Blackpool reeling, Blues stormed forward and grabbed a sixth goal on 73 minutes when Claridge chipped delightfully over the advancing goalkeeper, this time after a deft back-heel by substitute Steve McGavin.

The final goal arrived four minutes from time when Blues' other substitute, George Parris, brought back after a loan spell with Bristol City, touched the ball over the line from a yard after good controlled play down the right.

Blues manager Barry Fry, obviously delighted with the result, said afterwards: "We won well, but I was annoyed that we missed so many chances, some of which were far easier than the ones we tucked away. Still, what a way to end 1994. Now for 1995 and all that goes with it – promotion, Wembley and more goals. Yes, I want Blues to score 100."

Birmingham City: Bennett; Poole, Whyte(Parris), Barnett, Daish, Lowe, Cooper, Ward(McGavin), Donowa, Claridge, Otto.

Blackpool: Capleton; Brown (Horner), Burke, Gouck, Murphy, Bradshaw, Quinn, Mellon, Watson, Ellis, Mitchell.

Attendance: 18,025
Referee: J.Rushton (Stoke-on-Trent)

---

surface at St Andrew's. This was negotiated successfully, carrying Blues into their semi-final and a clash with Swansea City. Victory over the Edgar Street side was at a cost, though, with more injuries to dog manager Barry Fry's efforts.

This energy-sapping glut of fixtures duly took its toll on the players and there followed a dismal lack-lustre performance at Bootham Crescent which resulted in defeat at the hands of York City, thus bringing to an end an unbeaten run of 25 matches.

But Blues managed to raise their game once again, for two more important games, against Liverpool in the FA Cup replay at Anfield and against Swansea in the Auto Windscreens Shield semi-final at St Andrew's.

Blues played exceedingly well at Liverpool, eventually losing in a penalty competition, but they squeezed through against Swansea when the team tasted its first experience of a sudden-death extra-time. Paul Tait scored the match-winning goal in Blues' favour in the seventh minute of the first period of added time.

Leyton Orient were to be Blues' next opponents in the Auto Windscreens – one step from Wembley. Blues looked a tired outfit and although they still managed to raise their game at home, on their travels they played well below par with defeats at both Crewe and Bournemouth seeing them knocked down to third place in the table.

Despite vital home wins over Stockport, York and Wrexham, their overall form was disappointing, and, indeed, Blues lost their 22-match unbeaten home record when going down 1-0 to Swansea in a League match, slipping down to fourth spot in the process, but still with a few games in hand.

Was there a crack appearing in Blues' armour? Was the team under pressure? Why had their away form deserted them?

Manager Fry was baffled as the tension within the club manifested itself with open bickering between the boss and the board of directors, and between supporters among themselves.

Strangely, the turning point seemed to come after Blues had demolished Leyton Orient 4-2 to clinch a Wembley day out against runaway leaders of the Third Division, Carlisle United.

After this triumph everything seemed to be geared at winning the championship, yet alone promotion, with David Sullivan leading the challenge.

An inspired eight-match unbeaten run which included two terrific 3-0 wins against fellow promotion-seeking

Blues celebrate victory in the Auto Windscreens Shield Final against Carlisle United with the first-ever 'sudden death' goal in a Wembley Final.

opponents in Wycombe (away) and Oxford United (home) shot Blues up to second place behind Brentford, who themselves were well into a 20-match unbeaten run.

A dismal display by Blues on Easter Monday at Cambridge saw them lose 1-0, only for the team to bounce straight back with a smart 3-1 victory at relegation-haunted Plymouth two days later.

Steve Claridge scored twice against the Pilgrims, one a stunning 25-yarder which clinched the points and took Blues back to the top of the Division.

The match which followed this win at Home Park was the one nobody really wanted at this stage in the season – the Auto Windscreens Shield Final against Carlisle at Wembley, Blues' fifth competitive fixture in 12 days.

But the fans turned out in force, almost 50,000 of them descending on the Empire Stadium to cheer Barry Fry's men on to victory, albeit late on, again in sudden death extra-time with Tait, the man for this sort of occasion, once more coming up trumps with a decisive header from Ricky Otto's chipped pass. It wasn't a good Final, but for Blues supporters it was a great day out.

There were now only four League games left (in ten days) for Blues to do gain automatic promotion, and the most crucial one of all followed three days after that Wembley triumph, at home to League leaders Brentford.

Over 25,000 packed into St Andrew's for the vital 'six-pointer'.

At the time Brentford were one point ahead of Blues. Victory for them would virtually give them the title, but a

win for Blues would put them back in the driving seat – and they had a game in hand.

On a night of high tension it was Blues who came out tops, winning 2-0 with the courageous Kevin Francis (who played with damaged ligaments, suffered at Wembley) and Liam Daish on target. Blues were now in the driving seat. They had to keep on going – and they did.

With two of their last three games at home, their destiny was in their own hands. A dramatic 3-3 draw against Brighton (this after they had led 2-0 and then trailed 3-2 and had Cooper sent off) saw the initiative swing back in Brentford's favour, but then the Londoners failed at home, losing to Plymouth to leave Blues to beat Bradford City at St Andrew's to take the title.

Once more the crowd topped 25,000 as Blues went for glory, but on the night they came up against a brick wall as the visitors shut up shop and stole a point from a goalless draw. Leading scorer Claridge missed two 'sitters' while Blues also had a last-minute claim for a blatant penalty turned down

This placed Blues on a knife-edge with only one match remaining – away at Huddersfield. On the same day Brentford were away to Bristol Rovers.

It was tight: Blues had 86 points, Brentford 84. A defeat at Huddersfield and victory for Brentford would send Blues into the Play-offs. A win, or even a draw, for Blues would see them up automatically.

Around 4,000 fans made the trip north to boost the attendance at the new Sir Alfred McAlpine Stadium to almost 19,000 and after a nervous first half which ended

Blues' First Title for 40 Years
Huddersfield Town 1 Birmingham City 2

BLUES arrived at the splendid Sir Alfred McAlpine Stadium, Huddersfield, for this final League game of the season requiring something to secure their desired future. In this particular case it was even more than crucial than usual in that they probably needed to gain at least a point to win the Second Division championship, which was the only guaranteed way of gaining promotion without taking part in the lottery of the Play-offs.

It came at the end of a cruel schedule of an incredible ten matches in 25 days – including the Wembley Final of the Auto Windscreens Shield against Carlisle – and this had contributed to them having to go into the match against Huddersfield Town without the 'backbone' of the team, namely a central striker (Kevin Francis), a key midfielder (Peter Shearer) and a solid centre-back (Dave Barnett) who were all side-lined through injury.

This forced manager Barry Fry into choosing his first-ever Blues side without a recognised winger and playing a more defensive formation of 4-2-2 against a strong Huddersfield team. who at one time were strong candidates for the title themselves.

There were around 4,000 Blues fans present in the near-19,000 capacity crowd – and the noise they made seemed as if there were 10,000 visiting supporters present, the number who had initially wanted to attend the match.

Blues started this vital match nervously and it was Huddersfield who came closest to scoring early on when Ronnie Jepson's header was brilliantly turned aside by goalkeeper Ian Bennett. After this Blues gained in confidence and they dictated play up to half-time.

The closest they came to scoring was when leading marksman Steve Claridge, the culprit of a couple of missed chances in Blues' previous drawn game against Bradford City which, if they had won, would have clinched the championship, struck the cross-bar from close range.

Blues started the second half as they had ended the first, in control of the general outfield play, and they looked comfortable, knowing that their nearest challengers Brentford were a goal down at Bristol Rovers where they needed to win to stand any chance of pinching the crown off Blues' head.

Blues played the ball around and

creating one or two openings, but they couldn't afford to be too complacent and allow Huddersfield a chance which could prove costly. Then it happened – Blues went in front. Winger Louie Donowa, who had come off the substitutes' bench, combined with Gary Cooper and an opening was set up for Claridge, who found the net on 73 minutes.

The Blues fans behind the goal were ecstatic – and more so when with eight minutes remaining, second substitute Paul Tait poached a second goal which, in effect, clinched the championship. Huddersfield rallied and snatched a last-minute consolation goal through Darren Bullock – but this late response couldn't deny Blues their first League title for 40 years – since they carried off the old Second Division crown in 1955.

Huddersfield Town: Francis; Trevitt, Cowan, Bullock, Scully, Sinnott, Collins(Moulden), Duxbury, Booth, Jepson, Dunn(Billy).

Blues: Bennett; Poole, Frain, Ward, Whyte, Daish, Hunt(Donowa), Claridge, Hendon, Williams(Tait), Cooper.

Attendance: 18,775

Referee: J.Winter (Stockton-on-Tees)

Manager Barry Fry looks pensive as he makes a point to Ed Stein during Blues' crucial game at Huddersfield.

goalless, it was Blues who produced the goods, winning 2-1 to regain their First Division status and also completed the double of League and Auto Windscreens Shield successes.

Manager Fry decided to start without a winger (for the first time since taking over at the club) and following two substitutions, goals arrived from Claridge (72 minutes) and

Tait (85). On the same day Brentford could only draw at Twerton Park and so Blues needn't have worried too much as it turned out. The next step is into the Premiership. And why not? Blues certainly have the support and the ground to be a top flight club. Only time will tell.

Blues' Grounds

Small Heath Alliance played their first matches on a piece of wasteland in Arthur Street, near to the junction with Coventry Road. They occupied this pitch throughout their initial season of 1875-76, moving to their first enclosed ground, in Ladypool Road, Sparkbrook, for season 1876-77, a move designed to gain much needed revenue.

As interest grew, however, they moved back to the Small Heath district of the city in the summer of 1877, occupying a ground in Muntz Street where they were to stay until switching to their present ground at St Andrew's in December 1906.

The Muntz Street ground could initially house around 10,000 spectators. When Blues left there, after 29 years, it was able to accommodate over 30,000 fans. Although it had a well-appointed wooden stand, the pitch left a lot to be desired. It was uneven, rutted and sloped from end to end and from one side to the other.

Some teams were reluctant to play there and Wednesbury Old Athletic offered Blues £5 to reverse their Walsall Cup-tie venue from Muntz Street to their own pitch. Blues obliged, collected the fiver and went on to beat Athletic 4-1. In 1891, The Wednesday (now Sheffield Wednesday) paid Blues £200 to switch their FA Cup-tie from Muntz Street to Olive Grove. Blues again said 'thank you' and banked the money; but this time they were beaten 2-0.

Originally, the Blues paid £5 per annum to rent Muntz Street. In 1905 they paid £300 per annum but the ground was now inadequate as their support grew. In February 1905, an estimated 32,000 crowd packed in to see a First Division derby against Aston Villa. It is said that only 29,000 paid to get in, the others climbing over fences or rushing turnstiles to gain free admittance.

Blues' present ground at St Andrew's was 'discovered' by former player, director and past chairman of the club, Harry Morris, who joined the club as a player in 1884 and later did great work as a member of the board. He showed tremendous foresight when he saw 'a wilderness of stagnant water and muddy slopes' off Garrison Lane, Bordesley Green, and visualised at one glance a footballing arena arising out of that wilderness.

Morris asked a carpenter, not an architect, to draw up the plans for the building and laying out of the St Andrew's ground. The carpenter was Harry Pumfrey, a Blues' supporter from Small Heath. It is recorded that the clerk of the works, Mr T.W.Turley, displayed wonderful enthusiasm, working day after day in the thick of the toil, putting in up to 14 hours work on at least four days of each week. The men worked tirelessly to get the ground ready and asked for no payment in return.

Hundreds of pounds were saved by the dedicated work of Messrs Turley and Pumfrey, the latter being the 'diamond in the rough' whose simple but precise plans and drawings for St Andrew's would have done credit to the most expensive professional architect in the land.

The directors were quick to congratulate these two workers, one just an ordinary 'back-street' carpenter. It was suggested that between them, Turley and Pumfrey saved the club around £2,000 in fees, a great deal of money in those days.

When work began on that 'wasteland' in Garrison Lane, the first consideration was the playing pitch and to make this, two huge pools, which were filled by artesian spring water, had to be drained. This was done satisfactorily and then tons of rubble, including brick-ends and piles of ashes, had to be rolled down into these holes to fill them up.

This was a strenuous job but the volunteers worked furiously under the guidance of Thomas Turley. Some 10,000 square yards of turf were laid by mid-June 1906 and a pitch worthy of staging football matches was there for all to see. The extent of the turfed area was 123 yards by 83 yards, providing a four-yard margin around the actual playing area which measured 115 yards by 75 yards (one of the biggest in the country at that time). It was surrounded by a six-yard wide running track of cinders so that the spectators were at least ten yards clear of the touch-line.

The second major task was to ensure there was a large embankment on one side – the unreserved side – of the ground. So the site was offered as a tip and people from the Bordesley Green, Small Heath and surrounding districts paid Blues money to empty their loads of rubbish there. It is estimated that thousands of tons were dumped there, bringing Blues around £800 in cash. Even in its embryo stage, without any real steps or barriers, this banking was known as the Spion Kop.

Work continued at a fast pace and the Kop gradually took shape. At one point there were 110 tiers, each 13in deep and rising by 5in to a height of 47ft; at the lowest point there were 82 terrace steps. It was said that some 48,000 fans, each paying sixpence (3p), could get a comfortable view of the match from this vantage point.

Once the rubble and rubbish had been firmly bedded into position, the club made clear its intention to erect a roof behind the Tilton Road goal 'to protect at least 12,000 supporters from inclement weather'. The grandstand, which ran for 123 yards along the Garrison Lane side of the ground, had 29 rows of seats installed, each rising nine inches above the one in front. this stand could accommodate 6,000 spectators, all seated, with a further 5,000 being able to stand, undercover, on the 19 terraces in front of it.

The roof, measuring 87ft x 123 yards, was supported by steel stanchions 41ft high, set into between four and ten feet of solid concrete. In its erection, over 450,000 bricks were used, together with some 40 tons of corrugated iron, more than 100 tons of cement and a vast quantity of timber.

In the stand there were six sections for spectators – Block A priced at 1s (5p); Block B at 1s 6d (8p); Block C at 2s (10p); Block D also at 2s; Block E at 1s 6d, and Block F at 1s.

The seats were approached by two flights of stairs with a passageway to each description of seat and all landings, gangways, entrances and exits were illuminated by electric lighting.

The space under the seating was utilised for the club offices, the boardroom, cycle store, four refreshment rooms and a training area which contained a nine-foot square plunge bath, changing-rooms for the players and a spacious billiard room, generously furnished to the extent of 100 guineas by a wealthy Birmingham businessman, Sir John Holder. The whole stand was fitted throughout with apparatus for heating water. Thirty-six turnstiles gave admission to the St Andrew's ground, ten at the Garrison

A big crowd at St Andrew's just after the end of World War Two.

Looking towards the Railway End in the 1950s.

Lane side (also giving access to the unreserved accommodation) and ten more in St Andrew's Street, for the stands and reserved portions of the ground. Behind the goal at the railway end, terrace accommodation was provided for 4,000 spectators (each paying 1s) and it is said that when St Andrew's was completed in late December 1906, it could house 75,000 fans.

The cost of building St Andrew's was £10,000. The ground was initially taken on a 21-year lease and the area on which it was built covered seven and a half acres. St Andrew's was officially opened by Sir John Holder, on 26 December 1906, when Blues played Middlesbrough in a First Division fixture.

It was touch-and-go whether the opening game would go ahead. Thick snow covered the pitch and terraces and scores of volunteers worked throughout the morning of the match to clear the playing area. The game finished goalless in front of 32,000 fans who braved the bitterly cold weather.

Ground developments took effect gradually and by 1939 the rear of the Tilton Road End was covered, as was the Railway End. Part of the latter cover can still be seen. On 11 February 1939, the highest attendance ever to assemble inside St Andrew's – 67,341 – saw Blues play Everton in a

fifth round FA Cup-tie. Shortly after war was declared, the ground was closed because of the danger of air-raids and Blues played away from home or at neutral venues. The matter was raised in Parliament – St Andrew's was the only football ground in the country to be shut down – and the ban lifted in March 1940.

In January 1942, the Main Stand was completely destroyed in the most bizarre circumstances. It was being used as a temporary fire station and someone attempted to put out a brazier with what he thought was water. But his bucket contained petrol and up in flames went all the club records. The club then played at Leamington and Villa Park, returning to their home ground in 1943.

After the war, the Blues set about rebuilding St Andrew's. The construction of the new Main Stand got under way early in the 1950s. Floodlights were used for the first time in October 1956, when Birmingham drew 3-3 with German side, Borussia Dortmund, and after success in the Fairs Cup (now the UEFA Cup), Birmingham covered the Tilton Road End and the Kop. Later, they built a replica of the Main Stand at the Railway End.

In 1988, the St Andrew's ground capacity was given as 38,408, with 10,000 of them seated. There were 2,500 seats in a family enclosure in the City Stand, at the Railway End.

Following the Hillsborough disaster and the subsequent

St Andrew's pictured during the 1957-58 season.

An aerial view of St Andrew's in the 1980s.

Taylor Report, which was to see the fading out of standing areas at leading clubs, the capacity at St Andrew's was slashed even further to 26,000 in 1992, and although this was slightly increased to 28,235 a year later, the need to consider a complete redesign of the whole ground became obvious and indeed desperate.

Under the new regime of David Sullivan, the Gold brothers and Karren Brady, initial plans were drawn up and quickly approved, but just prior to commencement, Miss Brady visited Old Trafford and was so impressed with their cantilever structure with no corner supports (which enables the continuous stands with rounded corners design to be produced, with ultimately the possibility of a horseshoe or even complete 'bowl' stadium) that the plans were rehashed to follow the Manchester United principles.

The first phase of converting the Tilton Road and Kop stands commenced after an emotional home game against Bristol City on 16 April 1994, when mementoes of anything from a bolt to a scoreboard letter, a chunk of concrete to a rivet, were removed as the fans 'helped' with the demolition work.

This was followed by the famous Blues '70s forward-line trio of Trevor Francis, Bob Latchford and Bob Hatton symbolically commencing the new building work.

The £4.5 million development was phased in with the 7,000 all-seater Tilton Road End ready for the opening game of the 1994-95 season on 20 August and the Kop, with its 9,500 seats being handed over in time for the Blackburn Rovers Coca-Cola Cup match in October.

The new all-seater St Andrew's ground was officially opened on 15 November 1994 with a 'friendly' against the old enemy, Aston Villa, when an ecstatic 19,766 crowd showed its appreciation to the club's chief benefactor, David Sullivan and his two fellow directors, David and Ralph Gold. The game ended 1-1.

Work on an independent two or three-tiered stand with some 9-10,000 seats was planned to be erected at the Railway End in 1996, and consequently the now famous 'horseshoe' design stadium with a capacity of over 35,000, would hopefully be completed in time for the 1996-97 season.

Such was the change of atmosphere at the club around that time, that within a matter of weeks of confirming these final plans to complete the stadium, David Sullivan said publicly that really his 'ultimate dream' would be to build a completely new 70,000 all-seater stadium in the city, which would be shared with Aston Villa (Milan' style). That suggestion didn't go down too well with ardent Blues supporters, but in this revised climate, who knows what might transpire in the future?

International Matches Played at St Andrew's

8 April 1922 England 1 v Scotland 1, Att: 20,000
25 October 1941 England 2 v Wales 1, Att: 25,000

Blues Managers

Birmingham City have had 26 team managers and/or secretary-managers over a period of 85 years (1910-95) Seven of them were former players with the club – Bob McRoberts, Billy Beer, Bill Harvey, George Liddell, Arthur Turner, Gil Merrick and Garry Pendrey.

Bob McRoberts
July 1910-May 1915

Born: Coatbridge, Scotland, 12 July 1874.
Died: Birkenhead, 27 February 1959
Until July 1910, Birmingham's team had been selected by a committee, usually comprising five club members, including the captain, secretary and treasurer. Then chairman Walter Hart suggested that a full-time manager should be appointed and former goalscorer Bob McRoberts had the honour of being the first holder of the post of team manager at St Andrew's. He was in office for five years. (*See also Birmingham City Who's Who*).

Frank Richards
(May 1915-May 1923 and August 1927-July 1928)

Born: Birmingham c.1880.
Died: Birmingham c.1963
Career: Hockley Schools; worked in Birmingham's jewellery quarter for two years (1904-06); joined St Andrew's office staff 1906, secretary of club 1911-12; Blues secretary-manager May 1915-May 1923; Blues secretary 1924-25; Preston North End secretary-manager May 1925-July 1927; Blues secretary-manager August 1927-July 1928; Bournemouth & Boscombe Athletic secretary-manager July 1928-June 1930.
Although he acted as secretary-manager at St Andrew's in two spells, Frank Richards was generally regarded as an administration secretary of the club. He let his trainers run the team on a day-to-day basis, not even discussing the signing or selling of players until the paperwork had to be completed, although he did have a say regarding team selection. For 1920-21, Richards forgot to enter the club in the FA Cup. He dispatched his son, Sam, who was then assistant secretary (and who was a long-serving member of the Blues board after World War Two) to

Lancaster Gate to plead for clemency, alas without success.
Honours with Blues: Second Division championship, 1920-21.

Billy Beer
(May 1923-March 1927)

Born: Poolsbrook, near Chesterfield, 4 January 1879
Died: Birmingham, March 1941.
Played 250 games for Blues as a wing-half before retiring.
After a spell working in Australia and then as a licensee he took over as manager of Blues in 1923, acting as secretary-manager for the last two seasons (1925-27) of his four-year spell in charge. (*See also Birmingham City Who's Who*).

Bill Harvey
(March 1927-May 1928)

Born: Netley, Hampshire, 12 April 1896.
Died: South Africa, c.July 1970.
One-time outside-right with the club, he spent only one full season looking after team affairs at St Andrew's. (*See also Birmingham City Who's Who*).

Leslie Knighton
(July 1928-August 1933)

Born: Church Gresley, Derbyshire, near Burton upon Trent, 15 March 1884.
Died: Bournemouth, 10 May 1959.
Career: Local schoolboy football;

Gresley Rovers (1900); Burton United (1901); Fazeley Swifts; Castleford Town

(manager 1904); Huddersfield Town (assistant secretary-manager 1909); Manchester City (assistant secretary-manager August 1912-April 1919); Arsenal (manager May 1919-June 1925); Bournemouth & Boscombe Athletic (manager July 1925-July 1928); Birmingham (manager July 1928-August 1933); Chelsea (manager August 1933-April 1939); Shrewsbury Town (manager August 1945-December 1948); thereafter golf club secretary in Bournemouth in 1950s; Portishead FC (manager 1952-53). Died after short illness.
Leslie Knighton's playing days were cut short by injury, but then he enjoyed a long and fairly successful managerial career, helping develop some fine youngsters at both Huddersfield Town and Manchester City. He struggled to keep Arsenal in the First Division, after being told by his chairman 'not to spend too much money'. Knighton did a reasonable job at St Andrew's and, indeed, his finest moment came with Birmingham when he took them to Wembley in 1931, where they met West Brom in the FA Cup Final. He left St Andrew's for Chelsea after the London club had made him an offer he 'couldn't refuse'.
Honours with Blues FA Cup Final, 1931.

George Liddell
(August 1933-September 1939)

Born: Muirton, County Durham, 14 July 1895
Died: Birmingham.

George Liddell had long wanted to be a Football League manager and Blues obliged him in 1933 after he had made close of 350 appearances as wing-half and full-back for the club. He continued to attend matches at St Andrew's well into the 1950s.

Honours with Blues: FA Cup Final (as a player), 1931.

(See also Birmingham City Who's Who).

Bill Camkin
(September 1939-November1944)

Born: Birmingham c.1890.
Died; Birmingham c.1960.

Throughout World War Two, Bill Camkin was honorary managing director of Birmingham. He looked after team affairs and took charge of running the club, allowing senior trainer George Blackburn, the former Aston Villa player, to organise training sessions and the match-to-match build-up. Camkin did an excellent job, steering Blues through a difficult period when St Andrew's was severely damaged by German bombs. In 1952 ill-health forced his retirement as a Birmingham City director, but he continued to support the club until his death. His son, John Camkin junior, was a well-known sports journalist who later became a director of Coventry City.

Ted Goodier
(November 1944-May 1945)

Born: Farnworth, Lancashire. 15 October 1902.
Died: Farnworth, 4 November 1967.
Career: Brookhouse United (1919); Huddersfield Town (May 1922); Lancaster Town (August 1923); Oldham Athletic (June 1925); Queen's Park Rangers (November 1931); Watford (£1,000, June 1935); Crewe Alexandra (June 1936); Rochdale (June 1937, then player-manager September 1938-November 1944); Birmingham (caretaker manager November 1944-May 1945); Rochdale (manager June 1945-June 1952); Wigan Athletic (manager June 1952-May 1954); Oldham Athletic (manager May 1954-June 1958).

A fair-haired wing-half, 6ft 1in tall, Ted Goodier looked after Blues' team affairs for the second half of that transitional League season after World War Two. In 1949 he guided Rochdale to victory in the Lancashire Cup Final over Blackpool.

Harry Storer
(June 1945-November 1948)

Born: West Derby, Liverpool, 2 February 1898.
Died: Derby, 1 September 1967.
Career: Heanor Secondary Modern School, then inside-forward with Heanor Wesleyians (1913); Marehay FC (1914); Codnor Park; Riddings St James (1916); Eastwood Bible Class; Ripley Town (1917); Eastwood Town; Notts County (amateur 1918); Millwall (trialist); Grimsby Town (February 1919); Derby County (£2,500, March 1921); Burnley (£4,250 February 1929, retiring in May 1931); Coventry City (manager June 1931-June 1945); Birmingham City (manager June 1945-November

1948); Coventry City (manager again November 1948-December 1953); Derby County (manager June 1955-May 1962); Everton (scout mid-1960s). Also played cricket for Derbyshire: 1920-1936, scoring 13,513 runs including 18 centuries (ave. 27.63) and took more than 200 wickets, playing in the county's Championship winning side of 1936.

Harry Storer never won major club honours as a player, but he guided each club he managed to promotion, taking Coventry into Division Two in 1936, Blues to Division One in 1948, and Derby to Division Two in 1957. He also guided Blues to the FA Cup semi-finals in 1946 where they lost to his former club, Derby, in a replay.

A forthright character, he was the personification of traditional qualities of discipline, economy, directness and commonsense. He came from a sporting family – his father kept goal for Arsenal and Liverpool and played cricket for Derbyshire while his uncle was a Derby County footballer and

also played cricket for Derbyshire and for England.

Storer scored 63 goals in 274 appearances for Burnley and as a manager he signed one player, centre-half Martin O'Donnell, on three separate occasions, for Coventry, Blues and Derby. Storer was a sharp-tongued football man with a heart of gold.

Honours with Blues: League South championship, 1946, Division Two championship, 1948.

Bob Brocklebank
(January 1949-October 1954)

Born: Finchley, 23 May 1908.
Died: Brixham, 3 September 1981.
Career: Inside-forward with Finchley Boys; Finchley August (1925); Aston Villa (May 1929); Burnley (March 1936-August 1945, retired as player); Chesterfield (manager September 1945-January 1949); Birmingham City (January 1949-October 1954); West Bromwich Albion (coach-scout October 1954-March 1955); Hull City (manager March 1955-May 1961); Bradford City (manager May 1961-October 1964 when he retired to Brixham).

One of eight brothers, Bob Brocklebank was one of Finchley's most famous players before moving into the Football League. He scored 110 goals in some 300 games for Burnley, including wartime football, and took Blues to the FA Cup semi-finals in 1951, but also saw them relegated from the First Division. Although he did not have the greatest of times as manager of Blues, he did introduce youngsters Trevor Smith, Johnny Schofield and Jeff Hall and secured the services of Eddie Brown, Tommy Briggs, Noel Kinsey, Roy Warhurst, Len Boyd, Gordon Astall and Alex Govan, many of whom formed the basis of Blues' great sides of the mid-1950s. He took Hull to promotion from Division Three in 1959.

Arthur Turner
(November 1954-September 1958)

Born: Chesterton, Staffs. 1 April 1909.
Died: Sheffield, 12 January 1994.

Arthur Turner spent 13 years with Blues, nine as a player and four as manager. He played 312 games for Stoke before joining Blues and took the St Andrew's club back to the First Division in 1955 and to Wembley for the FA Cup Final 12 months later. Malcolm Beard, Winston Foster, Terry Hennessey and Colin Withers were among his best introductions for Blues

whilst his top signings included Dick Neal, Harry Hooper, Mike Hellawell and Bryan Orritt. For the last six months of his managerial career at St Andrew's, Turner was accompanied by Pat Beasley who acted as joint-manager – an appointment which annoyed Turner because he was told by the press and not by the club that Beasley had been taken on. He threatened to resign but chose to stay on for the time being.

As boss of Oxford United, Turner signed the Atkinson brothers, Graham and Ron, and guided the U's into the Football League in 1962 in place of Accrington Stanley. He then saw Oxford climb through the divisions before quitting the Manor Ground in 1969 after ten years' service. He handed over the hot seat to Ron Saunders, who later became manager of Birmingham City. (*See also Birmingham City Who's Who*).

Pat Beasley
(February 1958-May 1960)

Born: Stourbridge, 17 July 1913.
Died: Taunton, 27 February 1986.
Career: Brierley Hill and Brockmoor Schools; Cookley FC; Stourbridge; Arsenal (£550, professional May 1931); Huddersfield Town (May 1936); Fulham (December 1945); Arsenal (guest 1945-46); Bristol City (player-manager July 1950-January 1958, retired from playing May 1952); Birmingham City (joint manager January 1958-May 1960); Fulham (scout 1960-61); Dover (manager June 1961-April 1964). Retired to live in Chard, Somerset.
England international (one cap) Two Football League championship medals with Arsenal in 1934 and 1935; FA Cup runners-up with Huddersfield

1938; Division Two championship medal with Bristol City 1950; (as manager) Division Three South championship 1955.

Pat Beasley was a small, slightly built outside-left or wing-half who was reserve to Joe Hulme and Cliff Bastin at Highbury. He scored well over 75 goals in almost 500 appearances in League and Cup football before going into management. When he first arrived at St Andrew's, Beasley thought he was to be assistant to Arthur Turner but in fact was made joint manager by Blues' chairman Harry Morris, taking over as acting manager in September 1958 and team manager in January 1959. He resigned from his position at St Andrew's in May 1960 after taking Blues to the Fairs Cup Final.

Honours with Blues: Fairs Cup runners-up, 1960.

Gil Merrick
(May 1960-June 1964)

Born: Sparkhill, Birmingham, 26 January 1922.
Gil Merrick joined Blues as a

professional just on the outbreak of World War Two and continued to play for the club throughout the hostilities and afterwards before retiring to become team manager. He spent almost 25 years at St Andrew's, making more than 700 appearances in goal for Blues (over 170 in wartime and 485 in the Football League). He was also capped 23 times by England after modelling himself on his childhood hero, the former Blues and England goalkeeper Harry Hibbs, who was still at St Andrew's when Merrick

first signed for the club. Under Merrick, Blues' victory in the 1963 League Cup Final was the first major honour the club won.

Honours with Blues: Football League Cup winners, 1963.

(*See also Birmingham City Who's Who*).

Joe Mallett
(July 1964-December 1965)

Born: Gateshead, 8 January 1916.
Career: Dunston Colliery Welfare; Charlton Athletic (November 1935); Queen's Park Rangers (on loan May 1937-May 1938); Queen's Park Rangers (£800, February 1939); guested for both Fulham and West Ham United in season 1944-45; Southampton (£5,000, February 1947); Leyton Orient (July 1953); Nottingham Forest (coach, August 1954); Birmingham City (coach, June 1964, manager July 1964-December 1965, then assistant manager until March 1970); Panionios, Athens (manager 1970-1973 and 1973-July 1974); Apollon, Greece (coach, 1973 for six months); New York Cosmos, NASL (coach August 1975); Southampton (scout, late 1970s); San Jose Earthquakes, NASL (coach 1982-83); Southampton (scout again, based in the Midlands, mid-to late 1980s).

Joe Mallet played as a wing-half until he was almost 40 years of age and although his career was disrupted by the war, he still managed over 200 League appearances for Southampton. Mallett made several useful signings for Blues but failed to get the right blend. He did well with Panionios but when the military junta was overthrown in Greece Mallett found himself under arrest for a short while.

Stan Cullis
(December 1965-March 1970)

Born: Ellesmere Port, Cheshire, 25 October 1915.
Career: Ellesmere Port Council School; Bolton Wanderers (amateur 1930); Ellesmere Port Wednesday; Wolverhampton Wanderers (February 1934, retiring as a player in May 1947 to become assistant manager to Ted Vizard at Molineux.) Appointed manager in June 1948-September 1964); Birmingham City (manager December 1965-March 1970); thereafter worked in travel agency and later wrote a weekly column in a local Midlands sports paper, occasionally appearing on commercial radio. He now lives in Malvern.

Won 12 full caps for England and 20 more in wartime; also played for

December 1964-October 1967, retiring as a player in June 1966); New York Generals (coach, November 1967-October 1968); Brighton & Hove Albion (manager, October 1968-May 1970); Birmingham City (manager, May 1970-September 1975); Minnesota Kicks, NASL (coach 1976-79 and 1980-81).

Also played cricket for Lancashire (11 matches, 27 wickets).

One of the Busby Babes, Freddie Goodwin was a talented wing-half, tall with good technique, who came to the fore after the Munich air disaster in 1958 and played in that year's FA Cup

Final defeat at the hands of Bolton Wanderers. He discovered Ray Clemence when boss of Scunthorpe and held a unique post in America, coach of a team (New York Generals) which did not exist and being given an air ticket to travel the world in an effort to assemble a side.

He gave a new meaning to training sessions at St Andrew's, bringing in a yoga expert, and it was he who introduced Trevor Francis to League football as a 16-year-old. When he returned to America in 1976, Goodwin helped form that country's Major Indoor Soccer League which is still flourishing.

Honours with Blues: Division Two runners-up, 1971-72.

Willie Bell
(September 1975-September 1977)
Born: Johnston, Scotland, 3 September 1937.
Career: Neilston Juniors; Queen's

Park, Glasgow (1957); Leeds United (professional July 1960); Leicester City (£40,000, September 1967); Brighton & Hove Albion (player-coach – under Freddie Goodwin – July 1969, retired July 1970); Birmingham City (coach August 1970, manager September 1975-September 1977); Lincoln City (manager December 1977-October 1978); Liberty Baptist College, Virginia, USA. (as soccer coach 1978-80).

Won two amateur caps with Queen's Park and two full Scottish international caps with Leeds United; also with Leeds a Second Division championship medal in 1964, FA Cup runners-up medal in 1965 and Inter-Cities Fairs Cup runners-up medal in 1967.

Willie Bell, who was once a Clydeside apprentice engineer, turned down the chance to join Stoke City before going on to play almost 300 League games as a left-back during his career (204 for Leeds). He achieved nothing of note at St Andrew's and was sacked from his post in September 1977 after Blues' poor start to the season.

He left England to join a religious group in America.

Sir Alf Ramsey
(September 1977-March 1978)
Born: Dagenham, Essex, 22 January 1920.
Career: Essex County and Beacontree High Schools; Five Elms FC (1937); Portsmouth (amateur 1942); Southampton (amateur 1943, professional August 1944); Tottenham Hotspur (£21,000, May 1949 – retired as player May 1955); Ipswich Town (manager, August 1955-January 1963); England (manager January 1963-May 1974); Birmingham City (director, January 1976, taking over as manager from September 1977 to March 1978 when he left the club).
Gained 32 full caps and one 'B' cap

Football League on three occasions; skippered Wolves to 1939 FA Cup Final; as manager saw Wolves win three League championships, in 1954, 1958 and 1959, and the FA Cup twice, in 1949 and 1960.

A hard tackling, dominant centre-half, Stan Cullis played in almost 200 games for Wolves (170 in League and Cup) and as manager at Molineux introduced to League football some of the game's finest players. He did remarkably well during his 16-year reign as boss of Wolves, and to a certain extent he achieved success at Blues, with semi-final appearances in both the League Cup and FA Cup competitions in 1967 and 1968 respectively. In the 1950s, he brought the great European sides over to England to play under the Molineux floodlights – Honvéd, Spartak, Real Madrid and the likes – and it was Cullis who was certainly responsible for laying the foundation stones for Blues' 1972 promotion-winning side. He was an Army physical training instructor during the war, appearing in many representative matches at home and abroad. He was 50 when he took over as manager at St Andrew's.

Freddie Goodwin
(May 1970-September 1975)
Born: Heywood, Lancashire, 28 June 1933.
Career: Chorlton County Secondary School; Manchester United (October 1953); Leeds United (March 1960); Scunthorpe United (player-manager

for England, also made five appearances for Football League side; won Football League championship medal with Spurs in 1951 after gaining a Second Division championship medal in 1950; as manager won Football League championship success with Ipswich Town in 1962 after Second Division championship triumph in 1961 and Third Division South title in 1957; Led England to World Cup glory in 1966.

Sir Alf Ramsey, whose name will always be associated with England winning the World Cup, became the first knight of the realm to manage a Football League club when he took over at St Andrew's in 1977. Ramsey played over 100 games for Saints and 250 for Spurs a skilful right-back before retiring to take over as team manger of Ipswich Town, bringing First Division and European football to Portman Road for the first time in that club's history. A shrewd football tactician (both as a player and manager) he spent only eight months in charge at St Andrew's before ill-health forced him to relinquish his post (the shortest managerial reign in Blues' history). Today he lives in retirement in Ipswich.

Jim Smith
(March 1978-February 1982)
Born: Sheffield, 17 October 1940. Career: Sheffield schoolboy football; Sheffield United (amateur 1957, professional January 1959); Aldershot (July 1961); Halifax Town (July 1963); Lincoln City (March 1968); Boston United (player-manager 1968-72); Colchester United (player-manager October 1972-June 1975, retiring as a

player, 1973); Blackburn Rovers (manager June 1975-March 1978); Birmingham City (manager March 1978-February 1982); Oxford United (manager March 1982-June 1985); Queen's Park Rangers (manager June 1985-December 1988); Newcastle United (manager December 1988-March 1991); Middlesbrough (coach March-June 1991); Portsmouth (manager June 1991 to February 1995).

As manager led Colchester United to promotion from Division Four in 1974; Birmingham City to promotion in 1980 and Oxford United to Division Three championship and then the Division Two title in 1984 and 1985 respectively, and Queen's Park Rangers to runners-up prize in League Cup in 1986.

Known throughout football as 'Bald Eagle', this typically hard-talking but cheerful Yorkshireman, popular with the media, played all his soccer in the Fourth Division as a no-nonsense half-back, amassing a total of 249 League appearances in all after failing though to break into Sheffield United's first team. After retiring he became a shrewd, intelligent manager, doing well with Boston and Colchester initially before reaching a higher standard.

He bought many experienced players to St Andrew's, including Colin Todd, Frank Worthington, Don Givens, Archie Gemmill and Willie Johnston, and he also paid a big fees for the Argentinian World Cup star Alberto Tarantini and Walsall's Alan Buckley. He was sacked by chairman Keith Coombes to make way for Ron

Saunders, himself a former manager of Oxford, Smith's next club.

Smith then secured the services of John Aldridge for Oxford and later he signed David Seaman from Blues when boss of QPR. He had a tough time at both Blackburn and Newcastle, and whilst at Ayresome Park he was coach under Colin Todd, a player he had signed earlier in his career when boss of Blues. He took Pompey to the FA Cup semi-final in 1992, seeing his side lose in a penalty competition to Liverpool.

Jim Smith was the first man to visit all 92 League grounds as a manager for competitive matches.
Honours with Blues: Promotion from Division Two, 1980.

Ron Saunders
(February 1982-January 1986)
Born: Birkenhead, 6 November 1932. Career: Birkenhead & Liverpool Schools; Everton (February 1951); Tonbridge (July 1956); Gillingham (£800, May 1957); Portsmouth (£8,000, September 1958); Watford (£10,000, September 1964); Charlton Athletic (August 1965); Yeovil Town (general manager May 1967-late 1969); Oxford United (manager March-June 1969); Norwich City (manager July 1969-November 1973); Manchester City (manager November 1973-April 1974); Aston Villa (manager June 1974-February 1982); Birmingham City (manager February 1982-January 1986); West Bromwich Albion (manager February 1986-September 1987). Quit football at that stage.

England Youth international; as manager, runners-up in Division Two and Football League championship with Aston Villa in 1975 and 1981 respectively as well as League Cup winners twice, in 1975 and 1977; Division Two championship with Norwich City 1972 and Football League Cup runners-up in 1973; League Cup runners-up with Manchester City in 1974; Division Two runners-up with Birmingham City in 1985.

Ron Saunders was a tough centre-forward who scored over 200 goals in almost 400 League appearances for his five major clubs including 140 in 234 games for Portsmouth. He was the first person to manage three West Midland-based Football League clubs in succession – Villa, Blues and Albion. Saunders enjoyed great success at Villa Park, but thereafter never again reached the heights he had done earlier in his career both as a player and

manager. He briefly took over from former Blues man Arthur Turner at Oxford. A strict disciplinarian, Saunders was in charge when Blues went down to Division Two in 1984 and although he brought them straight back up, after that his career in football dwindled.

Honours with Blues: Division Two runners-up, 1985.

John Bond
(January 1986-May 1987)

Born: Colchester, 17 December 1932. Career: Colchester Schoolboy football; Colchester Casuals (1946-47); Essex Army Cadets; West Ham United (amateur 1949, professional March 1950); Torquay United (January 1966-69 when he retired); Gillingham (coach 1969-70); Bournemouth & Boscombe Athletic (manager May 1970-November 1973); Norwich City (manager November 1973-October 1980); Manchester City (manager (October 1980-February 1983); Burnley (manager June 1983-August 1984); Swansea City (manager (December 1984-December 1985); Birmingham City (manager January 1986-May 1987); Shrewsbury Town (assistant manager 1989, then team manager January 1990); Shrewsbury Town (manager, January 1991-May 1993). Represented Football League XI and toured South Africa with FA in 1956; won Second Division championship and FA Cup winners' medal with West Ham in 1958 and 1964 respectively; as manager won promotion from Division Two and League Cup runners-up prize with Norwich City in 1975; gained promotion from Division Four (as

runners-up) with Bournemouth in 1971 and led Manchester City to FA Cup runners-up in 1981.

A solidly built, resourceful right-back, John Bond scored 35 goals in 428 League and Cup games for West Ham before moving to Plainmoor. He turned down a coaching job at Plymouth to manage Bournemouth, and when he left Dean Court (with his assistant Ken Brown) for Norwich, the Cherries got £10,000 in compensation.

Bond seemed to have lost his touch when he joined Blues and never really settled in at St Andrew's. He quit Gay Meadow in 1993 after the Shrews had failed to make the Play-offs in Division Three.

Garry Pendrey
(May 1987-April 1989)

Born: Winson Green, Birmingham, 9 February 1949.

Garry Pendrey made 360 appearances

in defence for Blues (1966-79) before leaving St Andrew's to play for West Brom immediately after his testimonial match against the Baggies. Eight years later he returned to his first football love as manager and afterwards went into coaching with Wolverhampton Wanderers. (*See Birmingham City Who's Who*).

Dave Mackay
(April 1989-January 1991)

Born: Edinburgh, 14 November 1934. Career: Edinburgh & District Schools; Slateford Athletic, Newtongrange Star FC; Heart of Midlothian (April 1952); Tottenham Hotspur (£32,000 March 1959); Derby County (£5,000 July 1968); Swindon Town (player-manager May 1971-November 1972); Nottingham Forest (manager November 1972-October 1973); Derby County (manager October 1973-December 1976); Walsall (manager March 1977-May 1978); Al-Arabia Sporting Club, Kuwait (manager August 1978-84); Alba Shabab, Dubai (manager season 1986-87); Doncaster Rovers (manager December 1987-March 1989); Birmingham City (manager April 1989-January 1991); Zamalek, Egypt (coach, September 1991-April 1992).

Scottish schoolboy international; 22 full caps plus four at Under-23 level and also represented Scottish League XI on three occasions and later the Football League side twice. Named joint Footballer of the Year in 1969 (with Tony Book). With Hearts twice won Scottish League Cup, in 1955 and 1959, the Scottish Cup in 1956 and the

Scottish League championship in 1958. With Spurs he gained a Football League championship medal in 1961 (the 'double' year) and was again a League championship winner as manager of Derby County in 1975. With Spurs he also collected three FA Cup winners medals – 1961, 1962 and 1967 – and a Second Division championship medal with Derby in 1969.

One of the great wing-halves of his era, Dave Mackay amassed well over 700 senior appearances as a professional, playing 416 games in the English League alone (268 for Spurs). After doing exceedingly well with Hearts and Spurs, he then inspired Derby to the Second Division title and in his first season at the Baseball Ground was voted joint Footballer of the Year. He succeeded Brian Clough as manager at Derby and took the Rams to a second League title. Unfortunately he had a number of heated arguments with the owners of Birmingham City and it was no surprise when he left St Andrew's after less than two years in office.

Lou Macari
(February 1991-June 1991)

Born: Edinburgh, 7 June 1949.
Career: St Michael's Academy; Kilwinning; Kilmarnock Amateurs; Kilwinning Rangers; Glasgow Celtic (June 1966); Manchester United (£200,000 January 1973); Swindon Town (player-manager July 1984-July 1989, retiring as player in June 1986); West Ham United (manager July 1989-

February 1990); Birmingham City (manager February-May 1991); Stoke City (manager May 1991-November 1993), Glasgow Celtic (November 1993-June 1994); Stoke City (October 1994 to date).

Played for Scotland at schoolboy and youth levels before gaining 24 full and two Under-23 caps. With Celtic won two Scottish League championships in 1970 and 1972, Scottish Cup 1971 and 1972, Scottish League Cup in 1972 and 1973. With Manchester United won Second Division championship in 1975 and FA Cup in 1977, taking a runners-up in the latter in 1976; as manager won Division Four championship and then Division Three promotion with Swindon in 1986 and 1987 respectively; Leyland DAF Cup winners with Birmingham in 1991 and Stoke City in 1992 and promotion to Division One in 1993 (with Stoke).

An all-action midfield player who scored his fair share of goals, Lou Macari netted 27 goals in 56 League games for Celtic, 78 in 329 for United and three in 36 for Swindon. In all games for United he netted 88 goals in 391 appearances and notched over 120 goals in more than 500 competitive matches in his career.

He was sacked by Swindon in 1985 after a row with Harry Gregg but was reinstated within a week. When he took charge of West Ham he became only the sixth manager in the London club's history.

In 1990, the FA charged Macari, along with Swindon chairman Brian Hillier, of unauthorised betting on a match involving Swindon Town. He did exceptionally well when in charge at St Andrew's, leading Blues to Wembley for the first time since 1956 but resigned shortly afterwards saying that the club lacked ambition. In his first stint with Stoke he again visited Wembley but then had a rather disappointing stay with Celtic before returning to the Victoria Ground for a second spell, taking over from a fellow Scotsman, Joe Jordan.

Honours with Blues: Leyland DAF Trophy winners, 1991.

Terry Cooper
(August 1991-December 1993)

Born: Castleford, Yorkshire, 12 July 1944.
Career: Brotherton School; Wath Wanderers; Ferrybridge Amateurs; Leeds United (apprentice May 1961, professional July 1962); Middlesbrough (£50,000 March 1975); Bristol City (£20,000, July 1978); Bristol Rovers (player-coach August 1979, then player-manager April 1980-October 1981); Doncaster Rovers (November 1981-May 1982); Bristol City (player-manager May 1982-March 1988, retiring as a player in May 1984 – director of club 1983-

88); Exeter City (manager May 1988-August 1991); Birmingham City (manager August 1991-December 1993, also director of club 1991-93); Exeter City (manager January 1994 to date).
England international (20 caps); with Leeds United won Football League championship medal in 1969, FA Cup runners-up 1970, League Cup winners

1968, Inter-Cities Fairs Cup winners 1968 and 1971 and runners-up in 1967; as manager: with Exeter took Division Four championship in 1990 and Division Three runners-up 1993; with Bristol City won Freight/Rover Trophy in 1986 and runners-up 1987.

Terry Cooper was a fine attacking left-back who amassed some 350 appearances for Leeds before departing for Middlesbrough. He broke his leg at Stoke in April 1972 and it was thought that his career was over but he fought back and was called up again by England in 1974. Under his managership Bristol Rovers were unlucky – relegated and the main stand at Eastville burnt down. He was the first player-manager-director of Bristol City since Vivian Woodward in the early 1900s. Birmingham were lucky not to be relegated in Cooper's first season at St Andrew's and following the takeover by David Sullivan, he duly quit the club after a disappointing start to the 1993-94 campaign.

Barry Fry
(December 1993 to date)

Born: Bedford, 7 April 1945.
Career: Bedford & District Schools; London Boys; Manchester United

(professional April 1962); Bolton Wanderers (May 1964); Luton Town (July 1965); Gravesend & Northfleet (1965-66); Leyton Orient (December 1966); Romford (1968); Bedford Town (July 1969-May 1972); Dunstable Town

(manager c.1973-September 1976); Hillingdon Borough (manager September 1976-August 1977); Bedford Town (manager April 1977-August 1978); Barnet (manager August 1978-January 1985); Maidstone United (manager January 1985-July 1986); Barnet (manager again, July 1986-April 1993); Southend United (manager April-December 1993); Birmingham City (manager December 1993 to date).

England Schoolboy international; as manager took Barnet to GM Vauxhall Conference championship 1992; led Blues to victory in Auto Windscreens Shield Final and to Second Division championship in 1995.

A short and stocky inside-forward, Barry Fry made a total of 21 Football League appearances between 1964 and 1968, failing to make the first team at Old Trafford. He became something of a legend at Bedford Town for being too over elaborate with his free-kicks. Fry took Dunstable to runners-up spot in the Southern League North in 1975. As a non-League boss he signed both Jeff Astle and George Best He clashed several times with his chairman at Barnet, Stan Flashman, but despite internal problems the team continued to do well. Fry had an eventful first 12 months at St Andrew's,

signing and selling players galore, eventually suffering relegation from Division One but then everything went according to plan.

And at the first attempt Fry guided Blues to promotion from the Second Division as well as leading his team to victory at Wembley in the Auto Windscreens Shield Final against Carlisle United.

Yet 1994-95 was a tension-packed season from the word go.

Like he had done in his first six months in charge, Fry bought several new players into the club while releasing very few in comparison. And his dealings proved to be justified at the end of the day.

Fry used over 40 players in his first team in 1994-95, yet his transfer activities, his changes in style of play, his team formations, all worked out for the best. He had his differences with the club's owner, David Sullivan, and the board of directors, but at the end of the day he got his players to do the business where it matters most – out on the field. Yet the glorious end of the season was clouded a little by speculation over the manager's future.

Honours with Blues: Auto Windscreens Shield winners and Division Two championship, 1995.

Birmingham City Who's Who

Appearances and goals statistics include all Football League, FA Cup, League Cup (in all its sponsored forms), European and other senior competitive matches such as the Sherpa Van Trophy etc.

ABBOTT, Walter
Inside-left; Apps 85, Goals 66.
Born: Small Heath, Birmingham, 7 December 1877. Died: Birmingham, 1 February 1941.
Career: Rosewood Victoria, BLUES (April 1896), Everton (July 1899), Burnley (July 1908), BLUES (July 1910). Retired May 1911.
Club honours: Everton: FA Cup winners 1906, runners-up 1907.
Representative honours: England (1 full cap); Football League XI (4).
Walter Abbott holds the Blues' scoring record for most goals in a season – 42 in 1898-99 with 34 coming in 34 League games – and he netted on his debut against Manchester City in a Test Match. A strong running player with a cracking shot, Abbott was converted into a wing-half at Everton, yet still hit 37 goals in over 300 games. Following his return to Birmingham he had only one more game before retiring with a knee injury and thereafter worked for some years in the motor industry at Longbridge. His son, also Walter, played for Grimsby Town in 1920.

ADAMS, Richard
Inside-right; Apps 2, Goals 0.
Born: Quinton, Birmingham, 1866. Deceased.
Quinton Victoria, Wordsley, Calthorpe, BLUES (1887), Calthorpe (1888).
Adams joined Blues for one season from the Calthorpe club in Edgbaston and had a respectable scoring record in friendly matches whilst he remained in the side.

ADEY, George W.
Wing-half/inside-forward; Apps 79, Goals 2.
Born: Handsworth, Birmingham, 1869. Died: Birmingham.
Career: Nineveh Road School, Bournbrook FC, Stourbridge, BLUES (1898), Kettering Town (1902).
Described in the local press as 'not a brilliant player but a willing worker with a reputation for being a hard nut to crack.' Adey was very popular at Kettering after being moved into the half-back line, where he was 'persistent in his efforts and strong in defence'.

ADLINGTON, James H.
Wing-forward; Apps 6, Goals 4.
Born: Shifnal, May 1872. Died: Worcester.
Career: Shifnal Council School, Ironbridge FC (1892), BLUES (August 1895), Berwick Rangers (Worcester, June 1896), Stourport Swifts (1897).
A fast raider with an eye for goal, Adlington was surprisingly released after a fairly successful season with Blues.

AINSCOW, Alan
Midfielder; Apps 121+4, Goals 22.
Born: Bolton, 15 July 1953.
Career: Blackpool (apprentice June 1969, professional July 1971), BLUES (July 1978), Everton (August 1981), Barnsley (loan November 1982), Eastern FC Hong Kong (1983), Wolverhampton Wanderers (August 1984), Blackburn Rovers (December 1985), Rochdale (June 1989), Horwich RMI (August 1990), Flint Town United (cs 1991), Ellesmere Port Town

(coach 1992).
Club honours: Blues: Division Two promotion 1980.
Representative honours: England (Youth caps).
Alan Ainscow was a key figure in Blues' 1980 promotion race, when his low, hard crosses led to many important goals. He made 192 League appearances for Blackpool, and was close to the 500 mark in League appearances when he left Rochdale.

ALLEN, Frederick
Outside-right; Apps 3, Goals 0.
Born: Hockley, Birmingham, July 1860. Died: Birmingham c.1926.
Career: Springhill Methodists, BLUES (1890-92).
Fred Allen is a little-known figure in Birmingham City's history, a fragile forward whose career with Blues seems to have been limited to a brief spell during the club's service in the Football Alliance.

ALLEN, Gary
Forward; Apps 1, Goals 0.
Born: Hillingdon, 1955.
Career: Hillingdon Boys, BLUES (apprentice June 1971, professional 1973), Wimbledon (July 1975), Carshalton Athletic, Dulwich Hamlet, Boreham Wood, Hendon.
Allen was a prolific goalscorer in schools and youth football but his career was hit by injury shortly after he had signed professional forms for Blues. He fought back to earn a first-team outing at Ayr in the Texaco Cup before being given a free transfer and joining Wimbledon, then a non-League club.

ALLEN, George H.
Full-back; Apps 165, Goals 0.
Born: Small Heath, Birmingham, 23 January 1932.
Career: Coventry City (amateur), BLUES (amateur June 1952, professional November 1952), Torquay United (January 1962), Bideford Town (1965).
George Allen was a good, solid defender, whose first-team chances were restricted due to the brilliance of the Hall-Green partnership. After the tragic death of Jeff Hall, Allen made the left-back position his own until he suffered a fractured skull.

ANDERSON, Geoffrey T.
Outside-right; Apps 1, Goals 0.
Born: Sheerness, 26 November 1944.
Career: Canterbury Schools, Ramsgate (July 1960), BLUES (December 1962), Mansfield Town (May 1964), Lincoln City (July 1966), Brentford (August 1967), Hastings United (September 1967).
He was one of a trio of youngsters given their debuts at Manchester United in an attempt to boost the Blues' flagging fortunes. Birmingham won that game but the occasion proved too much for Anderson who was never selected again.

ANDERSON, George Edward ('Nosey')
Outside-left; Apps 80, Goals 10.
Born: Sunderland, 1881. Deceased.
Career: Sunderland Schools, Sunderland Albion (trial), Sunderland Royal Rovers, BLUES (1905), Brentford (August 1909 to May 1912).
'Nosey' Anderson was a winger standing 5ft 8in and weighing 11st 4lb, who supported his home-town club as a boy. Sunderland didn't sign him, however, and usually reserved his best performances for matches against them. After leaving Blues he played 88 games for Brentford, scoring six goals.

ARCHER, Arthur
Full-back; Apps 170, Goals 4.
Born: Derby, 1874. Died: 1940.
Career: Burton St Edmund's (1892), Tutbury Hampton (1893), Swadlincote

Town (January 1895), Burton Wanderers (September 1895), BLUES (£50 August 1897), New Brompton (£40 March 1902), Wingfield House (April 1903), QPR (August 1903), Tottenham Hotspur (guest 1903-05), Norwich City (August 1905), Brighton & Hove Albion (June 1907), Millwall (August 1908). Retired summer 1909. Coached in Germany (1910-12), Ghent (1912-14 & 1920-21), Italy (1921), Belgium (1922-24), Watford (1924).
Club honours: Blues: Division Two runners-up 1901.
Arthur Archer was an imposing figure, one of the toughest defenders of his era. He drew up a fine understanding with first Frank Lester and then William Pratt, and had five excellent seasons with Blues. He made 83 appearances for Norwich before linking up with Brighton.

ARMSTRONG, Kenneth Charles
Centre-half; Apps 69, Goals 1.
Born: Bridgnorth, 31 January 1959.
Career: Beith Juniors, Kilmarnock (June 1977), Southampton (£90,000 June 1983), Notts County (loan March-April 1984), BLUES (£60,000 August 1984), Walsall (£10,000 February 1986). Retired through injury November 1986.
Despite his English birthplace, Ken Armstrong was in every other way a Scot, born whilst his father was working for the Ministry of Defence. Tall and commanding in the air, Armstrong sometimes appeared somewhat clumsy on the ground. He broke an ankle in his first training session with Walsall and never played again. Holder of a degree in marketing and mathematics, he later took employment as a prison social worker.

ASHLEY, Kevin Mark
Right-back; Apps 65+1, Goals 1.
Born: King's Heath, Birmingham, 31 December 1968.
Career: Wheelers Lane School, BLUES (YTS June 1984, apprentice July 1985, professional December 1986), Wolverhampton Wanderers (£500,000 September 1990), Norwich City (loan March 1994), Peterborough United (August 1994).
Kevin Ashley was another in a line of good, young full-backs brought through the youth ranks, only to be sold on reaching maturity. He was a fast, hard-tackling player, particularly strong on the overlap.

ASHURST, Elias A.
Full-back; Apps 70, Goals 1.
Born: Willington, Co Durham, 28

December 1901. Died: Willington, 7 December 1927.
Career: Willington FC, Ashington, Shildon FC (1919), Stanley United (1920), BLUES (January 1922). Retired summer 1926 through illness.
During his heyday Eli Ashurst, who stood

5ft 11in and tipped the scales at 11st 6lb, was as tough a full-back as one could wish to see, although he could also be used in attack to some effect. His declining health led to an early retirement, followed shortly afterwards by his untimely death. Elias's younger brother, William, played for West Bromwich Albion, Notts County and England.

ASTALL, Gordon
Outside-right; Apps 271, Goals 67.
Born: Horwich, 22 September 1927.
Career: Royal Marines, Southampton (amateur), Bolton Wanderers (trial), Plymouth Argyle (professional November

1947), BLUES (£14,000 October 1953), Torquay United (July 1961). Retired May 1963 and settled in the Torbay area, later coaching Upton Vale FC while working for an insurance company.
Club honours: Plymouth Argyle: Division Three South champions 1952; Blues: Division Two champions 1955, FA Cup runners-up 1956, Fairs Cup runners-up 1958.
Representative honours: England (2 full caps, 1 'B' cap); Football League XI (1).
'Sturdy in build and difficult to stop when on the run,' Gordon Astall could play equally well on either wing but usually preferred the right flank. He scored 42 goals in 188 League games for the Pilgrims before settling in quickly at St Andrew's and was a key figure in Blues' promotion-winning side of 1955. Astall scored in each of his two full internationals for England and during a fine career netted over 100 goals, a fine return for a winger.

ASTON, James (Jack) ('Soldier')
Inside-forward; Apps 61, Goals 24.
Born: Walsall, 1877. Died: West Bromwich, February 1934.
Career: Walsall White Star, Fullbrook Saints, Willenhall Pickwick, Bloxwich Strollers, Wednesfield, Walsall, Woolwich Arsenal (May 1899), BLUES (1900), Doncaster Rovers (July 1902), Walsall, Bilston (1904), Blakenhall St Luke's, Walsall Wood.
'Soldier' Aston was an efficient and plucky goalscorer whose elder brother, Jack, played centre-half for Wolves. For Arsenal, 'Soldier' hit three goals in 11 League games before joining Blues.

ATHERSMITH, William Charles
Outside-right or left; Apps 100, Goals 13.
Born: Bloxwich, 10 May 1872. Died: Shifnal, 18 September 1910.
Career: Walsall Road School, Bloxwich Wanderers (1887), Bloxwich Strollers (1888), Unity Gas Depot FC (1890), Aston Villa (February 1891), BLUES (June 1901), Involved in an unsanctioned tour to Germany in 1905 for which he was

suspended. Associated with Bloxwich Strollers (1906) although he was still under ban and did not play, retiring in 1907. Grimsby Town (trainer, June 1907-May 1909).
Club honours: Aston Villa: Division One champions 1894, 1896, 1897, 1899, 1900. FA Cup winners 1895, 1897; runners-up 1892.
Representative honours: England (12 full caps); Football League XI (9).
Charlie Athersmith was one of the game's fastest wingers during the 1890s when he was in his prime playing for Aston Villa and earning the princely sum of £6-a-week. He could centre the ball with unerring precision and could outwit his full-back by sheer ball wizardry as well as pace. He was spotted by Villa whilst starring for Unity Gas Depot FC for whom he once scored seven goals in one game from the wing. He quickly rose to the top, going on to win every honour in the game. Athersmith was a vital cog in the Villa set-up when the League and Cup double was achieved in 1897 and in all he scored 86 goals in 310 appearances in the claret and blue strip. It is reported that in one game when it poured with rain, Charlie ran down the touch-line holding up an umbrella borrowed from a spectator. He died after a short illness. He was the uncle of Ernest Victor Wright, who between the wars played in the forward line for Liverpool.

ATKINS, Arthur Walter
Centre-half; Apps 105, Goals 0.
Born: Tokyo, 21 February 1925. Died: Good Hope Hospital, Sutton Coldfield, 7 January 1988.
Career: Erdington Boys, Paget Rangers, BLUES (August 1948, professional November 1948), Shrewsbury Town (June 1954). Non-League football 1956-58.
Arthur Atkins was an 'old fashioned' centre-half who specialised in goalmouth clearances and he held the number-five spot at St Andrew's prior to the emergence of Trevor Smith. Although born in the Far East (his parents were on business there) he was educated in Erdington and was discovered by Blues playing in the Birmingham Suburban Youth & Old Boys' AFA League. Walsall were keen to acquire him but Blues got in first and he did a fine job during his stay at St Andrew's, especially in 1950-51 when Blues reached the FA Cup semi-finals.

ATKINS, Ian Leslie
Midfielder; Apps 114+3, Goals 9.
Born: Sheldon, Birmingham, 16 January 1957.
Career: Sheldon Heath School, Leafield Athletic (Central Warwickshire Boys' League), Shrewsbury Town (apprentice June 1973, professional January 1975), Sunderland (August 1982), Everton (£70,000 November 1984), Ipswich Town (£100,000 September 1985), BLUES (loan March 1988, signing permanently £50,000

April 1988), Colchester United (player-manager 1990-91), BLUES (assistant manager 1991-92), Cambridge United (player-manager December 1992-May 1993), Sunderland (assistant manager July-November 1993), Doncaster Rovers (manager January 1994-July 1994), Solihull Borough (guest July 1994), Redditch United (August 1994), Northampton Town (manager January 1995).
Club honours: Shrewsbury Town: Division Three champions & Welsh Cup winners 1979.
Ian Atkins was a competitive player with a ferocious tackle who was bought to inject some much needed bite into a lightweight Blues midfield. He enjoyed 15 years in top-class football (1975-90) during which time he served with five different clubs and amassed in excess of 550 League appearances. He made 314 senior appearances and scored 64 goals for Shrewsbury alone. After his return to Blues he turned out against Peterborough before his registration had been completed, an offence for which Blues were fined £10,000.

AULD, Robert ('Bertie')
Outside-left; Apps 147, Goals 31.
Born: Maryhill, Glasgow, 23 March 1938.
Career: Springbrook School, Partick Thistle Boys Club, Panmure Thistle, Maryhill Harp, Celtic (professional March 1955), Dumbarton (loan October 1956-April 1957), BLUES (£15,000 April 1961), Celtic (£12,000 1965), Hibernian (May

1971, coach at Easter Road 1973), Partick Thistle (manager July 1974), Hibernian (manager November 1980-September 1981), Hamilton Academical (manager January 1982-January 1983), Partick Thistle (manager July 1986), Dumbarton (manager January 1988).

Club honours: Celtic: European Cup winners 1967, runners-up 1970, World Club championship 1968, Scottish League Division One champions 1966-67-68 & 1970, Scottish Cup winners 1965, 1967, 1969, runners-up 1970, Scottish League Cup winners 1967-68-60-70; Blues: Football League Cup winners 1963, Fairs Cup runners-up 1961.
Representative honours: Scotland (3 full caps); Scottish League XI (2).
Determined, gritty and sometimes a very fiery player, but one who always thrilled the crowd, Bertie Auld starred in schoolboy and junior football in the Glasgow area before signing for Celtic. He spent a large part of the 1956-57 season on loan to Dumbarton but after returning to Celtic he did well and was chased by a number of clubs before finally agreeing to join Blues. A very skilful player, after returning to Celtic he became part of the great side which became the first British team to win the European Cup and swept the board by capturing all the Scottish domestic honours in the space of five years.

AVEYARD, Walter
Centre-forward; Apps 7, Goals 3.
Born: Thurnscoe, near Wombwell, 11 June 1918.
Career: Denaby United, Sheffield Wednesday (October 1938), BLUES (April 1947), Port Vale (June 1948), Accrington Stanley (March 1952-May 1953).
Walter Aveyard played his early football in and around the Yorkshire coal-mining area, yet made only four appearances for Wednesday (scoring three goals). After his promising start with Blues, a troublesome thigh injury caused him a lengthy absence from action but he later recaptured his old form, scoring 26 goals in 103 games for Vale.

AYLOTT, Trevor Keith Charles
Striker; Apps 31, Goals 1.
Born: Bermondsey, 26 November 1957.
Career: Scott Lidgett School, Downside

Boys Club, Fisher Athletic, Chelsea (apprentice November 1975, professional July 1976), Barnsley (£60,000 November 1979), Millwall (£150,000 August 1982), Luton Town (£55,000 plus Vince Hilaire March 1983), Crystal Palace (July 1984), Barnsley (loan February-March 1986), AFC Bournemouth (£15,000 August 1986), BLUES (October 1990), Oxford United (loan September 1991, signed permanently October 1991), Gillingham (July 1992), Wycombe Wanderers (loan March 1993), Bromley (cs 1993).
Club honours: Bournemouth: Division Three champions 1987.
Trevor Aylott was a tall, heavily built target man, easily recognisable by his head-band. He was particularly adept at holding the ball and laying it off. On his own admission he was not a prolific scorer and he had scored only 82 goals in more than 400 games up the start of the 1991-92 season.

BADHAM, John ('Jack')
Full-back/left-half; Apps 190, Goals 4.
Born: Birmingham, 31 January 1919.
Died: Birmingham, 1 January 1992.
Career: Bordesley Green Schools, Shirley Juniors, Muntz Street Youth Club, BLUES (amateur July 1934, professional May 1946 after service in the Army), Stourbridge

(July 1957), BLUES (junior coach), Moorlands Athletic (player-coach, 1960), Moor Green (manager May 1962).
Club honours: Blues: Division Two champions 1948, 1955.
Jack Badham was a lion-hearted defender and a great favourite with the Birmingham fans. He quickly developed into an adaptable footballer, able to kick strongly with both feet and appeared in eight different positions for the Blues. Badham preferred the full-back position and helped Blues win promotion from the Second Division on two occasions. He also played in the FA Cup semi-finals of 1951 and 1956, but was unfortunate to miss the Final against Manchester City in 1956, John Newman getting the nod after Roy Warhurst had been injured.

BAILEY, Dennis Lincoln
Striker; Apps 80+13, Goals 25.
Born: Lambeth, London, 13 November 1965.
Career: Tulse Hill Comprehensive School, Watford (associate schoolboy forms),

Barking, Fulham (non-contract November 1986), Farnborough Town (July 1987), Crystal Palace £10,000 December 1987), Bristol Rovers (loan February-May 1989), BLUES (£80,000 August 1989), Bristol Rovers (loan March-April 1991), QPR (£150,000 June 1991), Charlton Athletic (loan November 1993), Watford (loan

March 1994), Brentford (loan February 1995).
Club honours: Blues: Leyland DAF Cup winners 1991.
Dennis Bailey was a fast striker who failed to gain a regular place in the Palace line-up but impressed at Bristol with nine goals in 19 games. He started well at Blues (four goals in his first friendly outing) yet found scoring much harder after that. He is a devout Christian.

BAILEY, Edward
Left-back; Apps 1, Goals 0.
Born: Aston, Birmingham, 1860. Died: Birmingham.
Career: Aston Shakespeare, Falling Heath Rangers, BLUES (August 1882), Aston Unity (October 1884), Lea Bank Wanderers.
Young, boyish-looking reserve full-back, Ted Bailey's appearances for Blues were never more than occasional.

BAILEY, Horace Peter
Goalkeeper; Apps 53, Goals 0.
Born: Derby, 3 July 1881. Died: Biggleswade, 1 August 1960.
Career: Derby County (September 1899), Ripley Athletic (1903), Leicester Imperial (to 1905), Leicester Fosse (January 1907), Derby County (April 1909), BLUES (September 1910). Retired cs.1913. Later worked as a rating officer for the Midland Railway Company.
Representative honours: England (5 full caps; 8 Amateur international caps, won gold medal with Great Britain football team in 1908 Olympics.
Although rather small for a goalkeeper (he was only 5ft 8in tall) Horace Bailey was exceptionally agile, bold and confident. He had a big pair of hands and a long, accurate kick. He once conceded 12 goals whilst playing for Leicester Fosse against Nottingham Forest in 1908. Bailey was a railway official by profession and worked for the Derby-based Midland Railway.

BALL, William ('Kosher')
Full-back; Apps 165, Goals 0.
Born: Woodside, Dudley, 9 April 1886. Died: 30 September 1942.
Career: Dudley Welfare, Stourbridge, Leamington, Wellington Town (1909), BLUES (May 1911), Cannock Town (October 1921), Wellington Town. Retired cs 1924.
Club honours: Blues: Division Two champions 1921.
Representative honours: England (1 Victory cap).
Ball was an attacking right-back, fluent and strong, who was a great asset to the side during the four seasons leading up 1915. He was one of only a handful of players to serve Blues before, during and after World War One. He stood 5ft 8in tall and weighed 11st 7lb.

BALLANTYNE, John
Outside-right; Apps 21, Goals 2.
Born: Kilmarnock, 30 June 1892. Died: Scotland.
Career: Kemmuirhill Athletic, Kilmarnock (February 1912), Vale of Leven (July 1912), BLUES (April 1913), Vale of Leven (October 1915), Glasgow Rangers (April 1916), Vale of Leven (May 1916), Dumfries (1918).
Ballantyne was the proverbial 'diminutive winger' with a tremendous burst of speed, often criticised for a tendency to 'overdo the clever stuff'.

BANKS, Francis
Goalkeeper; Apps 3, Goals 0.
Born: Aston, Birmingham, February 1865. Died: Birmingham.
Career: All Saints, BLUES (1889), Warwick County (1890).
Banks, a reserve goalkeeper, was given a

run-out at the end of the 1899-1900 season, conceding 22 goals in his three games.

BANKS, Frederick William ('Sticker')
Outside-left; Apps 1, Goals 0.
Born: Aston, Birmingham, 9 December 1888. Died: Nottingham, 1957.
Career: Park Road FC, Myrtle Villa, BLUES (August 1909), Stourbridge (1910), Wellington Town, Nottingham Forest (September 1911), Stalybridge Celtic (July 1914), Nottingham Forest (1915), Worksop Town (September 1920), Notts County (trainer 1929).
'Sticker' Banks was a good player on his day but had no success with Blues, although he later proved a capable winger with Forest, playing in 73 games and netting five goals during his nine-year association at the City Ground.

BANNISTER, Keith
Half-back; Apps 27, Goals 0.
Born: Sheffield, 13 November 1930.
Career: Rawcliffe Boys (Sheffield), Sheffield United (professional May 1948), BLUES (August 1950), King's Lynn (August 1954), Wrexham (July 1955), Chesterfield (December 1955), Norwich City (July 1956). Peterborough United (July 1957), King's Lynn (July 1958).
Representative honours: England (Youth international caps).
Bannister had to wait two years for his debut due to National Service. Primarily a defender, he found it difficult to hold down a first-team place with any of his League clubs, retiring after nine years in the game with only 65 appearances to his credit.

BARBER Eric
Centre-forward; Apps 5+1, Goals 2.
Born: Dublin, 18 January 1942.
Career: St Finbarr's, Shelbourne (1958), Grimsby Town (trial January 1966), Shelbourne, BLUES (April 1966), Chicago Spurs (June 1967), Kansas City Spurs (franchise change 1968), Shamrock Rovers (loan 1969), Wiener Sportclub (July 1970), Shelbourne (1971-75).
Club honours: Shelbourne: League of Ireland champions 1962, FA of Ireland Cup winners 1960, 1963, runners-up 1962, 1973, 1975.
Representative honours: Republic of Ireland (2 full caps).
Born into a boxing family – his brother Dave was an Irish light-heavyweight champion, Eric Barber arrived at St Andrew's as a full international but proved to be too slow to make any impact on the English scene, although he did win a second cap whilst with Blues. He suffered the indignity of being sent off in the 1973 FA of Ireland Cup Final.

BARKAS, Edward ('Ned')
Full-back; Apps 288, Goals 9.
Born: Wardley, Northumberland, 21 November 1902. Died: Little Bromwich, 24 April 1962.
Career: St Hilda Old Boys, East Boldon, Hebburn Colliery, Bedlington United, South Shields, Wardley Colliery (1919), Norwich City (amateur October 1920), Bedlington United, Huddersfield Town (professional January 1921), BLUES (£4,000 December 1928), Chelsea (May 1937), Solihull Town (player-manager May 1939), Willmott Breedon (1943), Nuffield Mechanics (munitions). Worked as a chargehand during World War Two.
Club honours: Huddersfield Town: Division One champions 1924, 1926, FA Cup runners-up 1928; Blues: FA Cup runners-up 1931.
Representative honours: Toured Canada with FA in 1926.
Ned Barkas started out as a centre-forward but turned into a tough tackling, hard working, strong kicking full-back, never showy or spectacular. Barkas, who worked

as a collier before joining Huddersfield, missed out on a third League championship medal when ousted by Roy Goodall in 1924-25. He was Leslie Knighton's first signing for Blues and was re-signed by

Knighton when he left for Chelsea. Barker had four footballing brothers – Samuel who played for England, Manchester City and Bradford City, Thomas of Bradford City, James, briefly of West Bromwich Albion, and Henry, formerly of Gateshead and Liverpool. His uncle, Thomas Jeffrey, played for Blackpool and he was also cousin to William Felton (Manchester City, Sheffield Wednesday, Spurs and England).

BARLOW, Frederick
Full-back; Apps 3, Goals 0.
Born: King's Heath, Birmingham, 1862. Died: Birmingham.
Career: St Phillips FC (Moseley), Wednesbury Old Athletic, BLUES (1885), Aston Villa (1886), Derby Midland (1887).
Fred Barlow was a regular in Blues' side for two seasons, playing mostly friendly games, until work commitments took him to Derby, where he signed for the local railway company team. He was a rarity for a full-back in Victorian times because of his liking to attack.

BARLOW, Raymond John
Wing-half; Apps 7, Goals 0.
Born: Swindon, 17 August 1926.
Career: Sandford Street School (Swindon), Swindon Town (trial 1942), Garrards FC (1943), West Bromwich Albion (amateur June 1944, professional November 1944), BLUES (June 1960), Stourbridge (August 1961). Retired cs 1962. Guested for Swindon Town 1945-46; played for WBA All Stars 1969-81.
Club honours: WBA: FA Cup winners 1954, Division Two runners-up 1949.
Representative honours: England (1 full cap, 2 'B' caps); Football League XI (4).
A long-legged blond-haired wing-half of undoubted class, Ray Barlow was a strong tackler and a master of the long 40-yard crossfield pass. He was at the veteran stage when signed by Blues and came to the club primarily to give the benefit of his experience to the youngsters. Barlow played in almost 500 competitive games for Albion. He was a useful cricketer who played for local league club West Bromwich Dartmouth.

BARNETT, David K.
Defender; Apps 53 Goals 0.
Born: Birmingham, 16 April 1967.
Career: Wolverhampton Wanderers (apprentice 1983), Alvechurch (1985), Windsor (1986), Colchester United (August 1988), Edmonton Oilers (Canada), West Bromwich Albion (October 1989), Walsall (July 1990), Kidderminster Harriers

(October 1990), Barnet (£10,000 February 1992), BLUES (loan in December 1993, signed for £150,000 February 1994).
Club honours: Blues: Second Division champions 1995, Auto Windscreens Shield winners 1995.
A strong, powerful centre-back, Barnett suffered the indignity of being sent off in his first full game for Blues, against his former club, West Brom on 28 December 1993. He made 30 appearances for Colchester, seven for Walsall and 72 for Barnet, yet failed to make West Brom's first team.

BARRATT, Josiah
Outside-right; Apps 31, Goals 1.
Born: Bulkington, Warwickshire, 21 February 1895. Died: Coventry, April 1968.
Career: Nuneaton Town, Leicester City (December 1916), BLUES (February 1917), Southampton (1918), BLUES (February 1922), Pontypridd (June 1923), Lincoln City (June 1924), Bristol Rovers (May 1926, part-exchange for Harold Armitage), Nuneaton Town, Coventry Colliery (July 1930), Appointed Coventry City Youth-team coach after World War Two. Had trials for Warwickshire CCC.
An experienced winger, dangerous and incisive, with a reputation for speed, 'Joe' Barratt was signed as part of a four-man exchange deal (Elkes & Getgood for Barratt & Foxall). He had a habit of playing with a piece of straw in his mouth. He was the father of Harry Barratt of Coventry City.

BARRETT, James Guy ('Young Jim')
Inside-forward; Apps 13, Goals 5.
Born: West Ham, London, 5 November 1930.
Career: Boleyn Castle, West Ham United (February 1949), Nottingham Forest (December 1954), BLUES (October 1959), West Ham United (as player-manager of 'A' team August 1960), Millwall (coach 1968).
A hard-working if unspectacular player, Jim Barrett scored regularly throughout his career, retiring with a haul of 91 goals in 200 League appearances. Son of former West Ham and England forward, 'Big Jim' Barrett, his first-class career was curtailed by an injury sustained whilst playing for Blues in the Fairs Cup semi-final against Union St Gilloise. He later became landlord of the Napier Arms, Halstead, Essex. He played alongside his father in West Ham's 'A' team in 1945-46.

BARROWCLOUGH, Stewart James
Winger; Apps 27+3, Goals 2.
Born: Barnsley, 29 October 1951.
Career: Barnsley (apprentice March 1967, professional November 1969), Newcastle

United (£33,000 August 1970), BLUES (rated at £150,000 May 1978), Bristol Rovers (£90,000 July 1979), Barnsley (£35,000 February 1981), Mansfield Town (August 1983). Retired 1985; attempted

comeback with Frickley Colliery (September 1991).
Club honours: Newcastle United: Football League Cup runners-up 1976.
Representative honours: England (5 Under-23 caps).
Whilst an automatic first-choice with Newcastle, Stewart Barrowclough earned a reputation as a fast, direct winger who was capable of both attacking and defending. Blues rated him highly enough to exchange him for Terry Hibbitt and John Connolly but, alas, he was disappointing during his spell at St Andrew's.

BARTON, Archibald
Right-back; Apps 1, Goals 0.
Born: Moseley, Birmingham, 1862. Died: Birmingham.
Career: Coles Farm Unity, BLUES (1889-90), King's Heath Comrades.
A tall, enthusiastic full-back, Barton played only one competitive game for Blues, against Birmingham St George in the Football Alliance in September 1889.

BARTON, Percival Harry
Half-back/full-back; Apps 349, Goals 14.
Born: Edmonton, London, 19 August 1895. Died: October 1961.

Career: Montague Road School, Tottenham Thursday, Edmonton Amateurs, Sultan FC, BLUES (January 1914), Stourbridge (August 1929). Retired June 1933. Guested for Spurs during World War One.
Club honours: Blues: Division Two champions 1921.
Representative honours: England (7 full caps).
A dour, industrious player, former butcher's boy, Percy Barton began his career at left-half before being successfully transformed into a full-back. He often fell foul of referees for his over-robust play and was sent off three times as a professional. World War One obviously disrupted his career and he was perhaps a shade unlucky not to have appeared in more than seven internationals. He once headed a goal, against Wolves, from fully 30 yards.

BASS, Jonathan David M.
Midfield; Apps 1, Goals 0.
Born: Weston-Super-Mare, 1 January 1976.
Career: Schoolboy football, BLUES (YTS 1982, professional June 1994).
Son of Tim Bass, a former Bristol City reserve player, he made only one appearance for Blues, in the Coca-Cola Cup-tie against Blackburn Rovers at St Andrew's in October 1994.

BATES, Harry J.
Outside-right; Apps 3, Goals 0.

Born: Sutton Coldfield, July 1890. Died: Birmingham.
Career: Ravensmoor FC, Coventry City (1911), BLUES (August 1912), Walsall (June 1913).
Harry Bates was an amateur who did not make an impact in any of his first-team games, the bulk of his career being spent in Midlands non-League football.

BAYLEY, John Thomas
Full-back; Apps 69, Goals 0.
Born: Walsall, August 1868. Deceased
Career: Walsall Swifts (1887), Walsall Town Swifts (1889), BLUES (May 1890), Walsall Town Swifts (August 1893), Gainsborough Trinity (1895), South Shields (1899).
Club honours: Blues: Division Two champions 1893.
A consistent, sturdy defender, not noted for the power of his kicking, Tom Bayley was once a prominent member of the Blues side but was released after the Test Match failure of 1893.

BAYLEY, Samuel
Forward; Apps 1, Goals 1.
Born: Rugby, November 1878. Died: Coventry.
Career: St Saviour's FC, Rugby, BLUES (July 1899), Leamington (December 1899).
Sam Bayley had a fine game on his debut, scoring a goal and having a hand in two others. Surprisingly, he was never called into action again and left the club shortly afterwards.

BEARD, Malcolm
Wing-half; Apps 403+2, Goals 33.
Born: Cannock, 3 May 1942.
Career: St Chad's School, Cannock & District and Staffordshire Schools XI football, BLUES (amateur June 1957, professional May 1959), Aston Villa (July

1971), Atherstone Town (1973), Saudi Arabia (coach 1974), BLUES (scout 1979), Aston Villa (chief scout 1982), Middlesbrough (coach 1987), Portsmouth (youth coach January-October 1990), Leicester City (chief scout 1993), Aston Villa (chief scout).
Club honours: Blues: Football League Cup winners 1963, Fairs Cup runners-up 1961.
Representative honours: England (Youth caps).
Former Blues wing-half Terry Hennessey once said: "If you had 11 men in your team like Malcolm, you couldn't go wrong." Beard was indeed a tremendous footballer who was held in high esteem by his fellow professionals, He spent 14 years at St Andrew's as a player, appearing in both the 1967 League Cup and 1968 FA Cup semi-finals. He was unfortunately sent off in his last game for Blues (against Millwall in December 1970) after being awarded a deserved testimonial in November 1969.

BEATTIE, John ('Jack') Murdoch
Inside-forward; Apps 36, Goals 9.
Born: Newhills, Scotland, 28 May 1912. Died: Wolverhampton, 15 January 1992.
Career: Hall Russell FC, Aberdeen (professional August 1931), Wolverhampton Wanderers (September 1933), Blackburn Rovers (£2,000 December 1934), BLUES (£2,000 January 1937), Huddersfield Town (£2,500 January 1938), Grimsby Town (£2,500 February 1938). Retired during World War Two after guesting for Walsall.
One of football's wanderers whose services were in constant demand during the 1930s. Clubs were willing to pay considerable sums for Beattie's intelligent positional play and fierce right-foot shooting. A marvellously resourceful footballer, he was always involved in the action.

BECKFORD, Jason Neil
Forward; Apps 6+2, Goals 1.
Born: Manchester, 14 February 1970.
Career: Burnage High School, FA School of Excellence, Manchester City (YTS July 1986, professional June 1987), Blackburn Rovers (loan, March 1991), Port Vale (loan September 1991), BLUES (£50,000 January 1992), Bury (loan April 1994), Stoke City (free transfer August 1994 after month's trial), Millwall (December 1994), Northampton Town assistant manager (May 1995).
Representative honours: England (2 Youth caps).

Brother of Darren (formerly of Port Vale and Norwich City), Jason Beckford signalled his arrival with a goal on his debut but was injured shortly afterwards. This was the first of several, culminating in a leg injury in 1992 which led to an operation to produce a synthetic cartilage. He was released in 1994 to give him a chance to rebuild his career.

BEEL, William John Leonard
Goalkeeper; Apps 1, Goals 0.
Born: Leominster, 23 August 1945.
Career: Shrewsbury Town (apprentice August 1961, professional July 1963), BLUES (January 1965), Shifnal Town (August 1965).
Beel was given his chance late in the 1964-65 season, after Blues had already been relegated, and a harrowing experience it must have been too as Blackburn thumped five goals past him. He was released a couple of weeks later and dropped into minor football.

BEER, William John
Wing-half; Apps 250, Goals 35.
Born: Poolsbrook, nr Chesterfield, 4 January 1879. Died: March 1941.
Career: Staveley Town, Sheffield United (amateur), Chesterfield Town, Sheffield United (professional August 1898), BLUES

(£700 January 1902). Retired May 1910. After leaving football he spent many years sheep-farming in Australia, before returning to England to become a licensee (1920), taking over as manager of BLUES (May 1923-March 1927).
Club honours: Sheffield United: FA Cup winners 1899.
A skilful player of explosive reflexes and subtle imagination, Billy Beer had balance and strength, a fluent body-swerve and booming shot. He joined Blues with Charlie Field, and proved to be a great servant to the club. Beer had made over 100 appearances for Sheffield United and was a penalty expert. Indeed, it is on record that he never missed from the spot). He was also a talented musician and it is said that he was lured south by the promise of a job as a church organist. He is possibly the only footballer to have composed a cantata.

BELL, Douglas K. ('Duggie')
Midfielder; Apps 22, Goals 0.
Born: Paisley, 5 September 1959.
Career: Cumbernauld United, St Mirren, Aberdeen (1979), Rangers (£145,000 May 1985), St Mirren (loan), Hibernian (1986), St Mirren, Shrewsbury Town (£35,000 December 1987), BLUES (£57,500 October 1989), Portadown (loan April 1990), St Mirren (loan January 1991), Released May 1991, joined Partick Thistle (August 1991). Portadown (August 1992), Clyde (July 1993), Elgin City (cs 1994).
Club honours: Aberdeen: Scottish Premier League champions 1980, 1984, 1985, Scottish Cup winners 1982, 1984. Portadown: Irish Cup runners-up 1990; Budweiser and Gold Cup winners 1993.
Representative honours: Scotland (2 Under-21 caps).
Bell made his name as a ball-winning midfielder in the successful Aberdeen side of the 1980s. He proved a big disappointment at Ibrox where he was accused of lack of consistency, a charge that was levelled at him throughout the rest of his career. He was the first Blues player to wear a pair of cycling shorts on a football pitch.

BELLAMY, Samuel Charles
Right-back; Apps 1, Goals 0.
Born: Aston, Birmingham, September 1913. Deceased.
Career: Jenkins Street School, St Andrew's OSL, BLUES (amateur May 1937, professional June 1937), Tamworth (1947).
Bellamy, a young full-back who was born a stone's throw from St Andrew's, saw his career severely disrupted by the war.

BENNETT, Ian Michael
Goalkeeper. Apps 85, Goals 0.
Born: Worksop, 10 October 1970.
Career: QPR (YTS 1988), Newcastle United (professional March 1989),

Peterborough United (free transfer March 1991), BLUES (£325,000 December 1993).
Club honours: Blues: Second Division champions 1995, Auto Windscreens Shield winners 1995.
Bennett has proved an excellent shot-stopper, confident in all aspects of goalkeeping and in 1994-95 kept ten successive clean sheets and was the only ever-present as Blues won the Second Division championship, a remarkable achievement considering that Fry used 37 players in the League campaign alone. He made 89 appearances for Peterborough but failed to make the first team at QPR or Newcastle. He was, though, rated in the £1 million class in 1995.

BENNETT, William Ambrose
Outside-right; Apps 76, Goals 13.
Born: Altrincham, April 1872. Died: Manchester.
Career: Summerfield FC, Crewe Alexandra, BLUES (1896), Stafford Rangers (1901).
Billy Bennett was an injury prone winger but a useful scorer in his heyday. In his first three seasons with Blues his varying knocks meant that he appeared in only 14 games. Nevertheless he had a useful career overall during which time he was described as 'a speedy player, clever at dribbling, who passed and centred at the correct moment'.

BERRY, John James
Outside-right; Apps 114, Goals 6.
Born: Aldershot, 1 June 1926. Died: Farnham, 1995.
Career: St Joseph's School; Aldershot YMCA, BLUES (professional December 1944), Manchester United (£25,000 August 1951). Forced to retire in 1958 following Munich air disaster.

Club honours: Manchester United: Division One champions 1952, 1956, 1957. FA Cup runners-up 1957.
Representative honours: England: (4 full caps, 1 'B' cap); Football League XI (1).
Manchester United had been trying to sign Johnny Berry for over a year before he finally left St Andrew's. A dashing 5ft 5in winger, skilful, with a good shot, he hit 43 goals in 273 outings for the 'Busby Babes' before his career was ended at Munich. A former cinema projectionist he was the brother of Peter Berry (Crystal Palace and Ipswich Town) and after recovering from that tragic air crash, he helped run the family sports shop in Aldershot.

BERTSCHIN, Keith Edwin
Centre-forward; Apps 134+7, Goals 41.
Born: Enfield, 25 August 1956.
Career: Mount Grace School, South

Mimms, Barnet (1972), Ipswich Town (professional October 1973), BLUES (£135,000 July 1977), Norwich City (£200,000 August 1981), Jacksonville Tea Men (loan, summer 1982), Stoke City (£50,000 November 1984), Sunderland (£32,500 March 1987), Walsall (£30,000 July 1988), Chester City (£5,000 November 1990), Aldershot (free transfer August 1991), Solihull Borough (February 1992), Evesham United (October 1993), Barry Town (March 1994), Tamworth (trial August 1994), Worcester City (August 1994), Hednesford Town (March 1995).
Club honours: Ipswich: Youth Cup 1975, Sunderland: Division Three champions 1988, Barry: Welsh Cup 1994.

Representative honours: England (3 Under-21 caps, Youth caps, European Youth champions 1976).
Bertschin scored with his first kick in League football, for Ipswich against Arsenal at Highbury in April 1976. He went on to score over 150 goals in the next 15 years despite breaking the same leg twice whilst at St Andrew's. He is a keen angler.

BIDMEAD, William Harold
Left-back; Apps 3, Goals 0.
Born: West Bromwich, December 1882. Died: Bethnal Green, London, 16 March 1961.
Career: Elwells FC, Walsall, Stourbridge, Brierley Hill Alliance (1902), BLUES (September 1903), Leyton (July 1906), Grimsby Town (May 1908), Brierley Hill Alliance (July 1909). Retired 1911.
Bill Bidmead was the man with the unenviable task of understudying the Glover-Stokes full-back partnership which was generally rated as the best at club level anywhere in the country around the turn of the century. Due to their consistency he hardly managed a first-team outing and, perhaps not surprisingly, was regarded as somewhat disappointing when he did play.

BIRCH, Joseph
Right-back; Apps 1, Goals 0.
Born: Cannock, 6 July 1904. Died: Colchester, 4 December 1980.
Career: Cannock Town (1920), Hednesford Town (August 1926), BLUES (March 1928), Bournemouth & Boscombe Athletic (May 1929), Fulham (October 1931), Colchester United (July 1938).
Club honours: Fulham: Division Three champions 1932. Colchester United: Southern League champions 1939.
Birch was a burly, but exceptionally speedy full-back with a prodigious kick who was unable to secure a regular place in the Blues first team. Later he proved a valuable servant to Fulham and played 195 times for the Cottagers during his seven years with the London club. He was formerly a pit worker.

BIRD, Adrian Lee
Centre-half; Apps 32, Goals 1.

Born: Bristol, 8 July 1969.
Career: Bristol Schools FA, Boco Juniors, BLUES (YTS July 1985, professional July 1987), Moor Green (July 1990). Retired May 1991.
A promising youngster whose career was ruined by a knee injury, Adrian Bird spent a year at the Football Injuries Treatment Centre, Lilleshall, before losing his battle against injury.

BIRD, John ('Jack')
Right-half; Apps 1, Goals 0.
Born: Blackheath, June 1881. Died: Dudley.
Career: Langley St Michael's, Rowley United, BLUES (November 1902), Walsall (1906), Kidderminster Harriers (1913-15).
One of the stalwarts of Birmingham League football before World War One, Jack Bird frequently collected rave reviews for his performances with Walsall, but rather surprisingly was not snapped up by another League club.

BLACK, Simon Anthony
Forward; Apps 3+1, Goals 0.
Born: Birmingham, 9 November 1975.
Career: King's Heath Concorde, Beeches Terriers, Baverstock School, BLUES (YTS June 1991, professional June 1994), Yeovil Town (loan March 1995).
A tall, gangling apprentice who was thrown in at the deep end in the first game of the 1993-94 season. He seemed a little overawed by the experience and was booked in the second half of his debut game.

BLACKMORE, Ritchie
Goalkeeper; Apps 1, Goals 0.
Born: Coleshill, Warwickshire, 1954.
Career: Bristol City (apprentice June 1970), BLUES (professional September 1971), Dundalk (1974), Galway United.
Club honours: Dundalk: Irish League champions 1975, 1976, 1978; Cup winners 1977, 1979, 1981.
Blackmore stole the headlines after saving two penalties in his only game for Blues when Stoke City were beaten in the Texaco Cup.

BLAKE, Anthony J.
Left-back; Apps 2, Goals 0.
Born: Cofton Hill, 26 February 1927.
Career: Rubery Owen FC, BLUES (amateur October 1948, professional January 1949), Gillingham (July 1952).
Blake was a well-built player who joined Blues as a centre-forward, being converted into a defender whilst in the juniors.

BLAKE, Noel Lloyd George
Defender; Apps 96, Goals 5.

Born: Jamaica, 12 January 1962.
Career: Alderlea School, Wilhemena Boys, Sutton Coldfield Town (April 1978), Walsall

(non-contract), Aston Villa (professional August 1979), Shrewsbury Town (loan March 1982), BLUES (£55,000 September 1982), Portsmouth (£150,000 August 1984), Leeds United (£175,000 July 1988), Stoke City (£160,000 February 1990), Bradford City (loan, February-June 1992); Dundee (December 1993).

Fiercely competitive player built like a heavyweight boxer, Noel Blake proved commanding in the air and strong in the tackle. He became a folk hero with the Blues fans and was one of several players sold by manager Ron Saunders after a series of well-publicised off-field misdemeanours.

BLOOMFIELD, James Henry
Inside-forward; Apps 147, Goals 31.
Born: Kensington, 15 February 1934. Died: Chingford, Essex, 3 April 1983.
Career: St Clement's School, Hayes, Brentford (October 1952), Arsenal (July 1954), BLUES (November 1960), Brentford

(June 1964), West Ham United (October 1965), Plymouth Argyle (September 1966), Leyton Orient (player-manager March 1968), Leicester City (manager May 1971-77), Leyton Orient (manager September 1977-August 1981), Luton Town (scout 1981-83).
Club honours: Blues: Football League Cup winners 1963, Fairs Cup runners-up 1961.
Representative honours: England: (2 Under-23 caps); Football League XI (1).
Jimmy Bloomfield was a member of a footballing family, his brother William played for Brentford and his nephew Ray was with Aston Villa. Jimmy was a potent force in the Arsenal attack and after joining Blues became more of a playmaker and less of a goalscorer. Later he proved to be a fine manager, leading both Leicester City and Orient to FA Cup semi-finals.

BLOXHAM, Albert
Defender; Apps 3, Goals 0.
Born: Solihull, 1906. Deceased.
Career: Birmingham Juniors, Overton-on-Dee (cs 1925), Oswestry Town, Torquay United (August 1926), Birmingham (March 1927), Rhyl Athletic (March 1928), Chesterfield (May 1928), Raith Rovers (October 1928), Yeovil & Petters United (September 1929), Millwall (May 1931-May 1933). Later FA coach for Cambridgeshire.
Bloxham was a strong player, 5ft 10in tall and weighing 11st 7lb. He was another of football's great wanderers who found it difficult to claim a first-team place with any of his clubs. Described as a 'touch-line artist, direct and fast as befitted a professional runner'. He was formerly an office clerk.

BLUFF, Edgar Underwood
Inside-forward; Apps 9, Goals 1.
Born: Winchester, March 1880. Died: Northampton, May 1952.

Career: High Hazels FC, Yorkshire Light Infantry, Army Corps, Reading (trial February 1903), Southampton (July 1904), Sheffield United (September 1905), BLUES (December 1907), St Helens Town (May 1908). Representative honours: Sheffield and Yorkshire Select XIs.
Bought out of the Army, Bluff enjoyed a rapid rise to fame culminating in him being named as a reserve for England against Ireland in 1905. However, an equally dramatic loss of form led to him being released by Sheffield United, although, in truth, he never really settled in Yorkshire. He had a short and undistinguished spell with Blues. A turner by trade, his hobby was gardening.

BLYTH, James Anton
Goalkeeper; Apps 16, Goals 0.
Born: Perth, Scotland, 2 February 1955.
Career: Perth Roselea; Preston North End (apprentice June 1971, professional

October 1972), Coventry City (October 1972), Hereford United (loan March 1975), BLUES (August 1982), Nuneaton Borough (August 1985), Coventry City (goalkeeping coach).
Representative honours: Scotland (2 full caps).
Jim Blyth was rated one of the best goalkeepers in the country during his days with Coventry when he earned his Scottish caps. An expensive transfer to Manchester United fell through when he failed a medical on his back, and from then he was constantly troubled by the injury. During his stay with Blues he was prone to making errors. His son was murdered in an incident outside a Hinckley night-club in 1993.

BLYTH, William Naismith
Half-back/inside-forward; Apps 21, Goals 4.
Born: Dalkeith, Scotland, 17 June 1895. Died: Worthing, 1 July 1968.

Career: Wemyss Athletic, Manchester City (June 1913), Arsenal (May 1914), BLUES (May 1929). Retired May 1931. Served in RASC during World War 1.
Club honours: Arsenal: FA Cup runners-up 1927, London Cup winners 1922 & 1924, runners-up 1926.
Representative honours: Scotland (Junior international).
Bill Blyth gave sterling service to Arsenal, making almost 400 first-class appearances for them and skippering the Gunners in the 1927 Cup Final against Cardiff City. Although slight of build he was renowned for his bravery and also for the quality of his left-foot passes. He was also a good golfer and ran a business in Musselburgh, Scotland. Brother-in-law of Provost Inglis of Port Seton.

BODENHAM, John ('Jack')
Goalkeeper; Apps 2, Goals 0.
Born: Perry Barr, Birmingham, 1859. Died: Smethwick.
Career: Aston Manor, BLUES (1881), Birmingham Excelsior (1882).
Bodenham shared the role of goalkeeper with the ageing 'Pouncer' Will Edden for two years before joining the Perry Barr-based Excelsior club. He also opened the batting for Small Heath Alliance cricket team although he rarely scored many runs.

BODLE, Harold
Inside-forward; Apps 110, Goals 36.
Born: Doncaster, 4 October 1920.
Career: Ardwick Junior School, Ridgehill Old Boys, Doncaster Rovers (trial), Bradford (Park Avenue) (trial), Rotherham United (May 1938), BLUES (£2,000, November 1938), Bury (March 1949), Stockport County (October 1952), Accrington Stanley (August 1953-May

1959 returning as manager June 1959 to April 1960), Burton Albion (manager 1962-64), local football manager in Derby. Guested for Doncaster and Rotherham during the war and later ran sub-Post Offices in Burton and Derby.
Club honours: Blues: Football League South winners 1946, Division Two champions 1948.
A former miner, it was not until after the war that Harold Bodle made his name on the soccer field. A real bag of tricks, he claimed that he owed his juggling prowess to practising whilst a child by kicking a small ball against a sideboard. History does not say what his mother thought of that! He once got himself marooned on the cliffs whilst out walking after a Blues game at Plymouth. He was also a useful cricketer and bowls player.

BODLEY, Michael P.
Defender; Apps 3, Goals 0.
Born: Hayes, 14 September 1967.
Career: Chelsea (apprentice June 1983,

professional September 1985), Northampton Town (£50,000 January 1989), Barnet (£15,000 October 1989), Southend United (free transfer July 1993), Gillingham (loan November 1994), BLUES (loan January 1995).
Club honours: Barnet: GMVC champions 1991.
Bodley played only eight games for Chelsea and 22 for Northampton before dropping out of League football to join Barnett with whom he returned (with Barry Fry) in 1991. A strong, competent defender, sure-footed with a positive attitude. He was taken on loan by Blues during a period when injuries and suspensions were disrupting the balance of the defence.

BOND, Benjamin ('Benny')
Winger; Apps 85, Goals 13.
Born: Wolverhampton, 30 August 1904. Died: Wolverhampton, March 1972.

Career: Coseley FC, Pensnett FC, Upper Gornal FC, Wellington, Bilston (1924), Coseley (early 1926), BLUES (amateur March 1926, professional April 1926). Retired May 1932 through injury.
A frail but tricky left-winger, Bond seemed to be the answer to Blues' long-term left-wing problems until laid low by a knee injury that required three cartilage operations.

BONTHRON, Robert Patrick
Right-back; Apps 12, Goals 1.
Born: Dundee, 1883. Deceased.
Career: Raith Athletic, Raith Rovers (July 1900), Dundee (May 1902), Manchester United (1905), Sunderland (May 1907), Northampton Town (June 1908), BLUES (July 1910), Leith Athletic (July 1911).
A no-nonsense defender (5ft 11in and 13st), Bonthron's uncompromising attitude towards the game sometimes led him being attacked by spectators, especially when he was with Manchester United.

BOOTH, Robert
Right-half; Apps 8, Goals 1.
Born: West Hartlepool, 20 December 1890. Died: Durham.
Career: Spennymoor United, Blackpool (May 1912), BLUES (May 1920), Southend United (July 1922), Swansea Town (June 1923), Merthyr Town (March 1925), New Brighton (May 1925).
Guested for Workington during World War One.
Described in contemporary reports as being 'a very quiet hard worker who never becomes ruffled,' Booth spent two years challenging for the right-half position but although he never let the side down, he did not really possess the ability required in the higher divisions.

BOOTON, Harold
Right-back; Apps 162, Goals 2.
Born: Annesley Colliery 2 March 1906.

Died: Denham, Uxbridge, 22 October 1976.
Career: Newstead Evening School, Annesley Colliery FC, Shirebrook FC, BLUES (April 1929, Luton Town (February 1936), Atherstone (May 1938).
A pre-war full-back, solid in the tackle but somewhat haphazard with his distribution, Booton's powerful kicking led to him occasionally taking penalties. In later life he became landlord of the Market Inn at Swadlincote in South Derbyshire. He was renowned in the Blues' dressing-room for having a truly awful singing voice! He was a clerk in the offices at Annesley Colliery and also worked in a tea store before turning to football.

BOSBURY, Charles Edwin
Outside-right; Apps 15, Goals 0.
Born: Newhaven, 5 November 1897. Died: Lincoln, June 1929.
Career: Pemberton Billings (1914), Southampton wartime guest (amateur 1919), Harland & Wolff (1920), Southampton (December 1921), BLUES (August 1922), Preston North End (June 1925), Lincoln City (August 1926-May 1929).
Charlie Bosbury struggled for several years to get regular League action, only to die shortly after achieving his goal. Tall and strongly built, he had pace and resource, being a fine sprinter on the athletics track.

BOWDEN, Frederick
Outside-left; Apps 1, Goals 0.
Born: King's Heath, Birmingham, November 1904.
Career: Darwen (Sparkbrook), Cradley Heath (1923), BLUES (amateur January 1925, professional December 1925). Stourbridge (May 1927), West Ham United (June 1928), Coventry City (May 1929), Evesham Town (1931), Kidderminster Harriers (June 1933), spell in French football (1934), Chesterfield (July 1935). Retired 1942.
Bowden was a fast winger but one who never settled in the professional ranks, dropping back into non-League football quite quickly. He gained little renown after returning to League action either.

BOWKER, Keith
Forward/full-back; Apps 20+3, Goals 5.
Born: West Bromwich, 18 April 1951.
Career: Staffs County FA, BLUES (apprentice 1966, professional August 1968), Exeter City (December 1973), Cambridge United (May 1975), Northampton Town (loan December 1976), Exeter City (August 1977), Torquay United (August 1980), Bideford Town (1982), Taunton Town (player-manager January 1987, resigned cs 1993).
Bowker, a hard working blond-haired player, was overshadowed at St Andrew's by the brilliance of Francis and Latchford. He finished his League career with a useful record of 81 goals in 307 appearances, 66 of them coming in 212 games for Exeter. He had a few First Division outings for Blues at right-back when he replaced the injured Ray Martin. Now a postman.

BOX, Arthur
Goalkeeper; Apps 29, Goals 0.
Born: Hanley, September 1884. Died: Stoke-on-Trent.
Career: Wellington School, Hanley Villa, Northwood Mission, Stoke, Port Vale (August 1904), Stoke (August 1907), BLUES (September 1909), Leek Victoria (April 1910), Croydon Common (August 1910), Crewe Alexandra (November 1911).
A squarely-built goalkeeper, Box was unable to settle with any of his clubs despite a string of capable performances.

BOYD, Leonard A.
Wing-half; Apps 282, Goals 14.

Born: Plaistow, London, 11 November 1923.
Career: Ilford, Royal Navy, Plymouth Argyle (December 1945), BLUES (January 1949). Retired May 1956. Attempted a delayed comeback with Hinckley Athletic (February 1959), later coach and chief scout at Redditch United (1960 onwards).
Club honours: Blues: Division Two champions 1955, FA Cup runners-up 1956.
Representative honours: England (1 'B' cap).

Len Boyd was spotted by Plymouth as a young inside-forward playing in the Navy team but was successfully converted into a fine wing-half, good enough to win a 'B' cap for his country. After signing for Blues he was moved forward again but he struggled and was quickly brought back into the middle-line. With a good footballing brain he developed into a cultured player and assumed the captaincy of Blues, leading the club to promotion and to the FA Cup Final in successive years, although he did carry an injury at Wembley which eventually resulted in him quitting the game.

BRADBURY, William
Inside-forward; Apps 3, Goals 2.
Born: Matlock, 3 April 1933.
Career: Modern Machines FC, Coventry City (professional May 1950), BLUES (November 1954), Hull City (October 1955), Bury (February 1960), Workington (November 1960), Southport (July 1961), Wigan Athletic (player-coach June 1962), Present Cabbies (1963); Kirby Town (March 1964).
Bradbury found it difficult to win a first-team place with Blues due to the form of so many other quality forwards. He had a reputation of playing to the crowd, being particularly fond of the theatrical gesture. His father, George, played for Clapton Orient.

BRADFORD, Joseph
Centre-forward; Apps 445, Goals 267.
Born: Peggs Green, Leicestershire, 22 January 1901. Died: Birmingham, 6 September 1980.
Career: Coalville FC, Peggs Green Victoria (1913), Aston Villa (trial), Derby County (trial), BLUES (£125 professional February 1920), Bristol City (May 1935). A former café owner, he also became a licensee, based initially in Birmingham and then in Stourbridge, and he was a shop proprietor in Sutton Coldfield.
Club honours: Blues: FA Cup runners-up 1931.
Representative honours: England: (12 full caps); Football League XI (5).
The greatest goalscorer in Blues' history, Joe Bradford could so easily have signed for Aston Villa. He was scoring goals

galore in Leicestershire junior football (he once netted 13 times in one game) when Villa invited him for a trial, but Blues were the only club willing to pay his travelling expenses, and consequently he signed on as a professional at St Andrew's in 1920. He was groomed in the reserves and was given an occasional game as Blues headed for the Second Division title in 1921, but it wasn't until the next season that he gained a place in the side. Once in, he stayed put and was a regular performer for the club over the next 14 years, scoring more than ten or more goals in each of 12 of them. He scored Blues' goal in 1931 Cup Final and was given an emotional send-off in his last game at St Andrew's after injuries had begun to affect his overall performances. His brother, William, played for Walsall and his cousin, Hugh Adcock, served both Leicester City and England.

BRAZIER, Colin J.
Defender/wing-half; Apps 16+3, Goals 1.
Born: Solihull, 6 June 1957.
Career: Northfield Town, Wolverhampton

Wanderers (apprentice June 1973, professional August 1975), Jacksonville Tea Men (June 1981), BLUES (October 1982), AP Leamington (March 1983), Lincoln City (April 1983), Walsall (August 1983), Kidderminster Harriers (October 1986), Tamworth (March 1995).
Club honours: Wolves: Football League

Cup winners (sub) 1980.
Representative honours: England (1 Semi-professional cap 1987).
Brazier was a useful squad player at Wolves, being principally a central defender or defensive midfield, but he was never guaranteed a first-team place. Blues bought him to add cover to their defence, but such were the problems at the time that he had a few games at centre-forward, a position that he had an ill-concealed dislike for. After a disagreement with manager Ron Saunders he left St Andrew's and played one game for Leamington (against Blues in a friendly) before rejoining the League with Lincoln as an out-and-out defender.

BREMNER, Desmond George
Midfielder; Apps 195, Goals 5.
Born: Aberchider, Kirkaldy, Scotland, 7 September 1952.
Career: Banks O'Dee, Deveronvale FC, Hibernian (July 1971, professional

November 1972), Aston Villa (£250,000 plus Joe Ward September 1979), BLUES (£25,000 September 1984), Fulham (free transfer August 1989), Walsall (free transfer March 1990), Stafford Rangers (August 1990), Sutton Town (March 1994).
Club honours: Hibernian: Scottish League Cup runners-up 1975, 1979; Aston Villa: Division One champions 1981, European Cup winners 1982, Super Cup winners 1982, World Club championship 1982.
Representative honours: Scotland (1 full cap, 9 Under-23 caps).
Des Bremner first achieved fame north of the border as a highly-rated full-back. Switched successfully to right-side of midfield, he became a star in the successful Villa side of the early 1980s, scoring ten goals in 227 appearances. A tenacious player, Bremner then served Blues in midfield supremely well, proving to be a great servant to the club for five years, sometimes occupying a defensive role.

BREMNER, Kevin Johnston
Striker; Apps 3+1, Goals 1.
Born: Banff, Scotland, 7 October 1957.
Career: Deveronvale FC, Keith, Colchester United (£40,000 October 1980), BLUES (loan October 1982), Wrexham (loan December 1982), Plymouth Argyle (loan January 1983), Millwall (£25,000 February 1983), Reading (£35,000 August 1985), Brighton & HA (£45,000 July 1987), Peterborough United (July 1990) Dundee (September 1991), Shrewsbury Town (loan March 1992), Brora Rangers (player-manager cs 1992); Deveronvale (player-manager cs 1994).
Club honours: Reading: Division Three champions 1986. Peterborough United: Division Four promotion 1991.
Younger brother of Des, Kevin Bremner was a fast, lightweight striker who was one of five players tried by manager Saunders to combat the goal-famine which had set in at St Andrew's in 1982. He set something of a record in season 1982-83 when he played

for five different clubs and scored for each of them.

BRENNAN, Robert Anderson
Inside/outside-left; Apps 40, Goals 7.
Born: in Belfast, 14 March 1925.
Career: Harland & Wolff Welders; Bloomfield United (1943), Distillery, Luton Town (October 1947), BLUES (£20,000 July 1949), Fulham (£19,500 June 1950), Norwich City (£15,000 July 1953), Yarmouth (August 1956), Norwich City (March 1957). Retired April 1960 to become coach at King's Lynn.
Representative honours: Northern Ireland (5 full caps).

Brennan struck over 100 goals in more than 400 senior games during a fine career. He helped Norwich reach the 1959 FA Cup semi-finals, where they lost to his former club, Luton. A good quality footballer, he was unlucky not to have played longer in the First Division.

BRIDGES, Barry John
Utility forward; Apps 104, Goals 46.
Born: Horsford, near Norwich, 29 April 1941.
Career: Norfolk Boys, Chelsea (juniors

July 1956, professional May 1958), BLUES (£55,000 May 1966), QPR (August 1968), Millwall (September 1970), Brighton & Hove Albion (September 1972), Highlands Park (South Africa) (1974), St Patrick's Athletic (Republic of Ireland) (player-manager 1976), Sligo Rovers (manager 1978), Dereham Town (manager), King's Lynn (manager), Horsford (manager). Later a hotelier in Brighton.
Club honours: Chelsea: Youth Cup 1958, Football League Cup winners 1965.
Representative honours: England (4 full caps, 6 Schoolboy and 2 Youth caps). Football League representative honour.
Barry Bridges played with great speed (he was a sprint champion at school) and was responsible for some of the most remarkable goals ever seen at St Andrew's. His over-the-shoulder scissors-kick which knocked Arsenal out of the 1968 FA Cup is still talked about. He became unsettled with Blues and subsequently moved south to facilitate the running of a hotel that he had purchased in Eastbourne. Bridges retired with a total of 215 League goals to his credit in 567 appearances. He appeared in both the 1967 League Cup and 1968 FA Cup semi-finals for Blues.

BRIGGS, George Richard ('Nippy')
Outside-right; Apps 324, Goals 107.
Born: Wombwell, Yorkshire, 23 May 1903.
Died: Yorkshire.
Career: John Street School, Mitchell's Main Colliery FC , Ardsley Athletic, Wombwell (professional 1922), Denaby United, BLUES (£400 with Aubrey Scriven December 1923), Plymouth Argyle (July

1933), St Austell FC (August 1936). Retired 1937.
Club honours: Blues: FA Cup runners-up 1931; Mitchell's Main: Nelson League champions.
After being tried in most forward berths, this stocky, red-headed former coal miner settled down to become a firm favourite on the right wing, the position he occupied in the 1931 Cup Final. He was noted for always chasing an apparently lost cause, sometimes to good effect, most notably on the occasion when he headed his own cross into the net after the ball had been held up in the wind! He stood 5ft 6½in tall, weighed 13st and was brother-in-law to Fred Tunstall (Sheffield United & England). He later worked at Moseley's in Bordesley Green.

BRIGGS, Malcolm D.
Forward; Apps 0+1, Goals 0.
Born: Sunderland, 14 September 1961.
Career: Sunderland & District Schools, BLUES (apprentice 1977, professional August 1979), Durham City (August 1980).
A well-built athlete, Malcolm Briggs was

not even a regular reserve-team player when surprisingly named as substitute at Maine Road at the end of the 1978-79 season. He made a very late entry into the action – three minutes from time – giving him probably the shortest first-team career with Blues of any of the players mentioned in this book.

BRIGGS, Thomas Henry
Centre-forward; Apps 52, Goals 23.
Born: Chesterfield, 27 November 1923.
Died: Grimsby, 10 February 1984.
Career: Plymouth Argyle, Grimsby Town (May 1947), Coventry City (£19,550 January 1951), BLUES (September 1951), Blackburn Rovers (£15,000 December 1952), Grimsby Town (£2,000 March 1958), Glentoran (player-manager May 1959-June 1961). Worked for a radio and TV company in Grimsby after quitting football. Guested for Plymouth during World War Two.

Representative honours: England (1 'B' cap).
A real hefty striker, Tommy Briggs claimed 286 goals in a career record of 390 League games. In one game for Blackburn against Bristol Rovers in February 1955, he scored seven goals.

BROADHURST, Kevan
Defender/wing-half; Apps 167+6, Goals 10.
Born: Dewsbury, 3 June 1959.
Career: Woodkirk School, Morley, Bradford City (trial), BLUES (apprentice August 1975, professional March 1978), Walsall (loan November 1979). Retired through injury March 1986, but later assisted Knowle FC, becoming their general manager in 1991. Sherwood Celtic (January 1992); Knowle (caretaker

manager, September 1993), BLUES (youth coach September 1993; caretaker joint manager December 1994; back to youth coach with appointment of Barry Fry, combining his duties with playing for

Sherwood Celtic from March 1995).
A gritty, hard-tackling player who was given a destructive role, Kevan Broadhurst was good in the air for a small man and spent a season at centre-half after the departure of Joe Gallagher but was dogged by injury throughout his career. He turned down a testimonial in 1985 because he felt that he had not played enough games for Blues to justify one. When it was obvious that he was not going to recover from the knee injury he did, however, accept a benefit match. A fine club man.

BROCKEN, Budde J.P. ('Bud')
Outside-right; Apps 19, Goals 0.
Born: Tilburg, Netherlands, 12 September 1957.
Career: SV Willem II (1975), BLUES (July 1981), FC Groningen (August 1982), SV Willem II (1985), BVV Den Bosch (1990).
Club honours: Den Bosch Dutch Cup runners-up 1991.
Representative honours: Holland: (5 full caps, 2 'B' caps, 8 Under-21 caps, 2 Olympic caps).
Brocken was already a Dutch Under-21 international and had been voted Holland's 'Young Player of the Year' in 1979 when manager Jim Smith signed him during Blues' pre-season tour. He proved to be fast and tricky but his delivery of crosses was somewhat wayward. On returning to Holland his career blossomed and he helped Groningen battle for a place in Europe. He had appeared in more than 450 League games (55 goals scored) in Dutch football up to the start of season 1991-92.

BROWN, Edwin ('Eddie')
Centre-forward; Apps 185, Goals 90.
Born: Preston, 28 February 1926.
Career: Preston North End (professional August 1948), Southampton (September 1950), Coventry City (March 1952), BLUES (October 1954), Leyton Orient (January 1959), Scarborough (1961), Stourbridge (1962), Bedworth Town (player-manager 1963), Wigan Athletic (1964). Retired 1964.
Club honours: Blues: Division Two champions 1955, FA Cup runners-up 1956.
Eddie Brown was almost lost to the game as a youngster when he wanted to enter the priesthood. But he was persuaded out of this by a football-mad clergyman, and developed into a marvellously unorthodox centre-forward, his roaming tactics, designed to pull the centre-half out of position, and playing a crucial part in Blues' success in the mid-1950s. For all his ability Brown is best remembered for his clowning antics, a favourite trick being to 'shake hands' with a corner flag after scoring a goal! He also learnt passages from Shakespeare to quote at press conferences. Brown later returned to his first love as a games teacher at a Roman Catholic College in Preston.

BROWN, Ian
Winger; Apps 0+1, Goals 0.
Born: Ipswich, 11 September 1965.
Career: Luton Town (associate schoolboy), BLUES (non-contract 1984, professional 1985), Felixstowe Town, Sudbury Town, Stowmarket Town, Chelmsford City, Harwich & Parkeston, Chelmsford City, Bristol City (cs 1993), Colchester United (loan March 1994), Northampton Town (loan December 1994).
Ian Brown was a young winger given a run-out for the last 12 minutes of a League Cup-tie against West Brom in November 1985 during an injury crisis. It is believed that he never touched the ball whilst on the pitch.

BROWN, John ('Jackie')
Outside-right; Apps 38, Goals 7.
Born: Belfast, 8 November 1914.
Career: William Ewart & Son, Belfast Celtic (1933), Wolverhampton Wanderers

(December 1934), Coventry City (£3,000 October 1936), BLUES (September 1938), Barry Town (January 1948), Ipswich Town (May 1948). Retired June 1951.
Representative honours: Northern Ireland (10 full caps); Republic of Ireland (2 full caps).
Jackie Brown sprang to fame as a teenager in Ireland whilst serving his apprentice in the linen trade. He failed to impress at Molineux although he did gain the first of his ten caps, adding two Eire caps to his collection with Coventry. On arriving at St Andrew's his direct approach to wing-play created a favourable impression but, try as he might, he was unable to inject much life into a poor attack.

BROWN, Walter Ephraim
Forward; Apps 3, Goals 2.
Born: Handsworth, Birmingham, 1867. Died: Birmingham.
Career: Key Hill School (Hockley), Soho Villa, Grove Hill FC, Hockley Belmont, St James's, BLUES (1891), Crosswells Brewery (1891).
He was a utility forward who spent only two months with Blues, filling three different positions in four outings (one a friendly game).

BRUCE, Daniel
Forward; Apps 10, Goals 2.
Born: Bonhill, Scotland, 20 October 1870. Died: 6 February 1921.
Career: Vale of Leven, Rangers (1891), Notts County (1892), BLUES (£100 November 1895), Perth (1896), Vale of Leven (February 1897), St Mirren (November 1897).
Club honours: Vale of Leven: Scottish Cup runners-up 1890; Notts County: FA Cup winners 1894.
Representative honours: Scotland (1 full cap).
A versatile performer, capable of operating in any forward position or at right-half, Bruce came to Blues with a high reputation, having gained international honours. He was the club's first three-figure transfer but failed to find his true form in Birmingham.

BRUCE, Henry ('Harry')
Full-back; Apps 8, Goals 0.
Born: Coundon, Co Durham, May 1905. Died: Durham.
Career: Durham City, Bishop Auckland, BLUES (amateur January 1925, professional February 1925), Gillingham (May 1928), Torquay United (May 1929), Colwyn Bay United (July 1930), Bankhead Albion, Rochdale (January 1931), Bankhead Albion (April 1931), Reading (May 1931). Retired 1939-40.
He was a strong player who failed to get a Third Division North game for Durham City and was signed by Blues as cover for both full-back berths, staying at St Andrew's for a number of years before leaving to enjoy regular first-team football with the Gills.

BRUETON, Edward M.
Goalkeeper; Apps 1, Goals 0.
Born: Penn, Wolverhampton, 1871. Died: Wolverhampton.
Career: Stafford Rangers, BLUES (September 1894), Willenhall Swifts (December 1894).
Brueton was a trialist who never even tasted reserve-team football with Blues and conceded four goals in his only first-team outing.

BRUNSKILL, Norman H.
Wing-half; Apps 65, Goals 2.
Born: Dipton, Co Durham, 14 June 1912. Died: Boston, 28 February 1988.
Career: South Moor Juniors, Newcastle United (trial), Lintz Colliery, Huddersfield Town (amateur October 1930, professional May 1931), Oldham Athletic (May 1932),

BLUES (£1,300 October 1936), Barnsley (£1,560 November 1938). Released May 1946. Guested for Middlesbrough and Hartlepool in World War One.
Club honours: Barnsley: Division Three North champions 1939.
Brunskill was a tall hard-working wing-half with a voracious appetite for the game and was a grafter with a fierce shot when he chose to let fly. A former coal-miner and son of well-known North-East referee.

BRYANT, Steven Paul
Left-back; Apps 40+2, Goals 1.
Born: Islington, London, 5 September 1953.
Career: Middlesex County Schools, BLUES (apprentice 1970, professional July 1971), Sheffield Wednesday (loan August 1976), Northampton Town (December 1976), Portsmouth (March 1979), Northampton Town (March 1982). Later played in Australia for a time.
Bryant was originally a winger of considerable guile but was converted into a full-back by Blues. Mysteriously omitted (with Calderwood) from the 1975 Cup semi-final team after putting in some promising performances in the earlier rounds, this unsettled the Londoner was never the same player again. He reverted to midfield after leaving St Andrew's.

BUCKLEY, Alan Paul
Forward; Apps 25+4, Goals 8.
Born: Mansfield, 20 April 1951.
Career: Nottingham Forest (apprentice June 1967, professional April 1968), Walsall (August 1973), BLUES (October 1978), Walsall (July 1979, manager at Fellows Park July 1979-July 1981 and May 1982-August 1986), Stourbridge (player, September 1986), Tamworth (October 1986), Kettering Town (manager November 1986), Grimsby Town (manager June 1988), West Bromwich Albion (manager October 1994).
Club honours: (as manager): Grimsby Town: Division Four promotion 1990, Division Three promotion 1991.
Short, stocky forward with an eye for goal, Alan Buckley turned out to be one of Walsall's best-ever signings, scoring over 200 goals in some 500 games for the Saddlers in two spells with the club. He took Walsall to the brink of promotion several times before achieving success with Grimsby and had one good season at St Andrew's. His brother Steve played for Luton Town, Derby County and Lincoln City.

BUCKLEY, Major Franklin Charles
Centre-half; Apps 56, Goals 4.
Born: Urmston, Manchester, 9 November 1882. Died: Walsall, 22 December 1964.
Career: Aston Villa (1903-04), Brighton & Hove Albion (1905), Manchester United (June 1906), Manchester City (September 1907), BLUES (July 1909), Derby County (May 1911), Bradford City (May 1914). Retired 1918 having served as a major in the Footballers' Battalion of the Middlesex Regiment (1916-18), Norwich City (manager March 1919 to 1920); worked as commercial traveller in London until July 1923 when he became manager of Blackpool; Wolverhampton Wanderers (manager May 1927); Notts County (manager March 1944); Hull City (manager May 1946); Leeds United (manager May 1948), Walsall (manager April 1953). Quit football June 1955.
Club honours: Derby County: Division Two champions 1912; (as manager) Wolves: Division Two champions 1932, FA Cup runners-up 1944; League North (War) Cup winners 1942.
Representative honours: England (1 full cap).
Frank Buckley was a tall, heavily built

pivot, hard-working, forceful when attacking, who was better known for his managerial exploits. Always open to ideas, he was a strict disciplinarian and his players were left in no doubt who was in charge. It was the major who called for the numbering of shirts (to help spectators) and he also stepped up fitness procedures, especially at Molineux. Whilst a player he helped run a pig farm at Redditch with his brother, Chris, the former Villa and Arsenal defender.

BULL, Gary William
Striker; Apps 12, Goals 7.
Born: Tipton, 12 June 1966.
Career: Swindon Town, Paget Rangers, Southampton (October 1986), Cambridge United (March 1988), Barnet (March 1989), Nottingham Forest (July 1993), BLUES (loan September 1994).
Club honours: Blues: Second Division champions 1995
Cousin of Wolves' Steve Bull, Gary Bull is also an out-and-out striker. He scored 37 goals in 83 League games for Barnet before joining Forest and had a good loan spell at St Andrew's and would have loved to join Blues permanently but the deal (arranged by manager Fry) was not sanctioned by the club's owner.

BULLOCK, Michael E.
Centre-forward; Apps 31, Goals 11.
Born: Stoke-on-Trent, 2 October 1946.
Career: North Staffs Schools, Stoke Boys, BLUES (apprentice July 1962, professional, October 1963), Oxford United (June 1967), Leyton Orient (October 1968), Halifax Town (player February 1976, manager 1981-84), Goole Town (manager 1986), Ossett Town (manager).
Club honours: Oxford: Division Three champions 1968; Orient: Division Three champions 1970.
Representative honours: England: (Schools international).
Bullock was a star of the Stoke Boys team which won the ESFA Trophy in 1972 and his signing for Blues was obviously influenced by the fact that his brother Peter had recently joined the club. Not particularly tall, he grafted hard and long and acquired a good scoring record during his 15 years in the game at senior level, finishing with 108 goals in 469 League appearances.

BULLOCK, Peter L.
Inside-forward; Apps 28, Goals 3.
Born: Stoke-on-Trent, 17 November 1941.
Career: Stoke City (junior July 1957, professional November 1958), BLUES (March 1962), Southend United (February 1965), Colchester United (October 1965), Exeter City (July 1968), Stafford Rangers (November-December 1968), Walsall (December 1968-May 1970).

Representative honours: England (Schools and Youth international).
Peter Bullock was troubled by injuries throughout his career and found goals hard to come by in the First Division but managed a fair record in the lower sphere. His son, Simon, played a few games for Halifax Town when brother Mick (who also played for Blues) was in charge at The Shay. Elder brother Brian was an amateur with West Brom and on Stoke's books in the 1950s.

BUMPHREY, James
Wing-half; Apps 143, Goals 6.
Born: Morpeth, Northumberland, 1885. Died: Durham.
Career: Ashington Alliance, BLUES (August 1908), Durham City (July 1915).
Not the ideal build for a footballer (5ft 8in tall and 13st in weight) Bumphrey proved a difficult man to beat in the tackle and was also a good header of the ball. He was frequently criticised for being a 'little wild' in his challenges.

BUNCH, Walter
Left-back; Apps 3, Goals 0.
Born: Weston-super-Mare, 1872. Died: Somerset.
Career: Compton Colts, Wolverhampton Wanderers, Bristol Rovers, Walsall (July 1899), BLUES (September 1901). Retired through injury and illness May 1902, and became licensee of the Golden Lion, Chell Street, Dudley.
An experienced full-back, Bunch nevertheless failed to impress during his brief spell with Blues.

BURKINSHAW, Laurence ('Lol')
Outside-right; Apps 75, Goals 12.
Born: Kilnhurst, 2 December 1893. Died: Mexborough, spring 1969.
Career: Kilnhurst Schools, Mexborough Town, Sheffield Wednesday (April 1910), Rotherham Town (June 1914), Kilnhurst FC (August 1918), Stalybridge Celtic (1918-19), BLUES (August 1919), Halifax Town (June 1922), Mexborough Town (August 1923). Guested for Barnsley during World War One.
Club honours: Blues: Division Two champions 1921.

Burkinshaw was a winger who relied more on skill rather than pace but who failed to gain much recognition at top-class level. His brother Jack played for Sheffield Wednesday. Lol Burkinshaw was also a good cricketer.

BURNS, Kenneth
Defender/centre-forward; Apps 195+9, Goals 53.
Born: Glasgow, 23 September 1953.
Career: Glasgow Rangers (schoolboy forms), BLUES (apprentice June 1970, professional July 1971), Nottingham Forest

(£150,000 July 1977), Leeds United (£400,000 October 1981), Derby County (loan March 1983 and February 1984, signing permanently March 1984), Notts County (loan February 1985), Barnsley (August 1985), IF Elfsborg (Sweden) (March 1986), Sutton Town (August 1986, player-manager March 1987), Stafford Rangers (July 1987), Grantham Town (1988), Gainsborough Trinity (1989), Ilkeston Town (player-coach 1990-93); Oakham United (player-coach); Telford United (assistant manager July 1993).
Club honours: Nottingham Forest: European Cup winners 1979, 1980, Division One champions 1978, Football League Cup winners 1978, runners-up 1980; Footballer of the Year 1978.
Representative honours: Scotland (20 full caps, 2 Under-23 caps).

Kenny Burns was a rare talent, a player able and willing to perform in any outfield position with equal effect. Initially a central defender, he was successfully converted into an out-and-out striker after Bob Latchford had departed and his aggressive play and superb heading ability made him a player feared by many. But he always wanted to get back to defending and it was here that he won most of his honours at club and international level. He helped Blues win promotion in 1972 and was with Forest under Brian Clough. Burns totalled in excess of 500 senior appearances as a professional, 424 in the Football League with 170 games for Blues (45 goals) and 137 for Forest.

BURTON, Edward G.
Centre-forward; Apps 1, Goals 0.
Born: Acocks Green, Birmingham, 1869. Died: Birmingham.
Career: Highfield Villa, BLUES (September 1891), Springfield Villa (1892).
Burton was given only one first-team outing (in place of the injured Harry Morris) and did nothing to justify further inclusion in the team.

BURTON, John Henry
Inside-left; Apps 4, Goals 3.
Born: South Bank, 13 August 1875. Died: Derby, 13 May 1949.
Career: Grangetown FC, Blackburn Rovers (March 1906), West Ham United (July 1908), BLUES (September 1909), Nelson (October 1910), Cardiff City (summer 1911), Southend United (May 1914).
He was a rangy scorer with an eye for goal who was at the veteran stage when he joined Blues. He had an impressive record but despite this could not command a regular first-team place at St Andrew's.

BURTON, Michael James
Winger; Apps 0+4, Goals 0.
Born: Birmingham, 5 November 1969.
Career: Tamworth & District Schools,

BLUES (YTS June 1986, professional July 1987), Sheffield Wednesday (January 1991), Shrewsbury Town (March 1991), Moor Green (February 1992), Milton Keynes Borough (May 1992), Moor Green (July 1992), Bromsgrove Rovers, Solihull Borough (January 1994), Redditch United (cs 1994).
He was a stocky, crew-cut winger who favoured pace to beat his opponent but who tended to be a bit wayward with his centres.

BUTLER, Herbert ('Dick')
Centre-half; Apps 11, Goals 0.
Born: Eastwood, Notts, 18 November 1911. Died: Bestwood, Notts, June 1984.
Career: Quarry Road Old Boys, Bestwood Colliery FC (Notts), BLUES (amateur May 1933, professional August 1933), Crewe Alexandra (March 1939). Guested for West Bromwich Albion during World War Two.
Butler was a powerfully built (6ft and 12st 10lb) defender, the star of Blues' Central League side for most of the 1930s, whose first-team outings were limited due to the form and reliability of Morrall and Fillingham. He was also a fine bowls player.

BYE, James Harold
Right-half; Apps 2, Goals 0.
Born: Aston, Birmingham, March 1920.
Career: St Peter's School (Harborne), Bournbrook Alliance, Shirley Juniors, BLUES (junior May 1937, professional August 1937). Retired May 1944. Guested for Nottingham Forest and West Bromwich Albion during World War Two whilst serving in the Army.
Bye served his apprenticeship at St Andrew's but as soon as he had gained a first-team place war broke out and unfortunately he never played again at competitive level after the hostilities had ended.

CALDERWOOD, James
Full-back/midfielder; Apps 147+12, Goals 5.
Born: Glasgow, 28 February 1955.
Career: Glasgow Amateurs, BLUES (apprentice July 1971, professional July 1972), Cambridge United (loan November

1979-January 1980). Contract cancelled by club July 1980 and went to Holland, serving in turn, Willem II (August 1980), Roda JC (1982) and SC Heracles (1988). Den Ham (cs 1990), FC Zwolle (assistant manager January 1992); Cambuur-Leeuwaarden (assistant manager cs 1993).
Representative honours: Scotland (1 Under-23 cap).
Originally a creative midfielder Jimmy Calderwood was converted into a fine, overlapping full-back with a good right foot. Not the strongest in the tackle, he tended to be made the scapegoat when things went wrong but he did very well in Dutch football.

CALLADINE, Charles Frederick
Wing-half; Apps 127, Goals 4.

Born: Wessington, Derbyshire, 24 January 1911. Died: Matlock, Derbyshire, 29 October 1983.
Career: Wessington FC (1927), Ivanhoe FC, Scunthorpe United (1928), BLUES (May 1930), Blackburn Rovers (February 1936), Guildford City (August 1938). Retired during World War Two.
Charlie Calladine was described in 1933, as being 'quick and cunning' and he was also physically strong (at 5ft 9in and 11st) and played with vigour and power, possessing a 'rocket-like' shot. He signed for Blues on the platform of Doncaster railway station. A teetotaller, non-smoker, pigeon-fancier, hiker and a former civil servant.

CAMERON, Edward S.
Inside-forward; Apps 6, Goals 1.
Born: Glasgow, 1895. Died: Stafford.
Career: Clydebank (1919), BLUES (July 1921), Walsall (May 1922), Nelson (March 1924), Stafford Rangers (1926), Exeter City (June 1928), Nelson (trial 1929), Stafford Rangers (August 1929), Cradley Heath (1931), Hednesford Town (1933), Stafford Rangers (July 1934).
Ted Cameron was a burly Scot whose best spell in League football came with Nelson in the Division Three North. He was never a great goalscorer but a player who 'employed direct methods'.

CAMPBELL, Alan James
Midfielder; Apps 204+7, Goals 14.
Born: Arbroath, 21 January 1948.
Career: Hags Head Primary and Arbroath High Schools, Arbroath Lads' Club, Charlton Athletic (apprentice July 1964, professional February 1965), BLUES (October 1970), Cardiff City (March 1976), Carlisle United (November 1980), Redditch United (July 1982), Olton Royale (1986), Highgate United (assistant manager 1989, manager, May 1992); Stratford Town (assistant manager June 1992, manager June 1993-late 1993).
Club honours: Blues: Division Two runners-up 1972.
Representative honours: Scotland (1 Under-23 cap, 4 Youth caps).
There were some adverse comments when Alan Campbell moved to St Andrew's rather than to one of the bigger clubs, but he proved to be a worthy signing and during his five years with Blues his displays were a barometer for the team's performances. When he played well, so too did the rest of the side. Particularly adept at finding space and a fine passer of the ball, Campbell was also a distinctive figure on the field with his long dark hair and a shirt which always looked two sizes too big for him.

CAPEL, Thomas A.
Inside-left; Apps 8, Goals 1.
Born: Chorlton, Manchester, 27 June 1922.
Career: Droylesden, Manchester City (November 1941), Chesterfield (October 1947), BLUES (June 1949), Nottingham Forest (November 1949), Coventry City (June 1954), Halifax Town (October 1955), Heanor Town (July 1956). Served in the Marines during war with Eddie Quigley (Blackburn Rovers and Preston North End) and Ken Oliver (Derby County and Exeter City).
Tommy Capel was a powerful, bustling player who scored plenty of goals elsewhere in a fine career. His brother Fred was a full-back with Chesterfield.

CARR, Derek Henry
Utility-player; Apps 4, Goals 0.
Born: Blidworth, near Mansfield, 1 September 1927.
Career: Oakbrook, Lockheed Leamington, BLUES (amateur December 1947, professional February 1948), Rugby Town (1950), Evesham Town, Boldmere St Michael's.
Derek Carr's appearances were split

between full-back, wing-half and centre-forward, and he had a spell working in the offices at St Andrew's before drifting into non-League football.

CARRIER, William
Right-back; Apps 7, Goals 0.
Born: Ashington, 1887. Died: Co Durham.
Career: Manchester United, Merthyr junior football (1905-09), BLUES (September 1909), Worcester City (August 1912).
A tall, muscular player noted for his heading ability, Carrier was born in the North-East but brought up in South Wales. His spell with Manchester United was unimpressive but he was being touted for Welsh honours before it was discovered that he was an Englishman.

CARRODUS, Frank
Midfielder; Apps 7+2, Goals 0.
Born: Manchester, 31 May 1949.
Career: Altrincham (July 1964), Manchester City (November 1969), Aston Villa (August 1974), Wrexham (December 1979), 'rebel' tour of South Africa (1982), BLUES (August 1982), Bury (October 1983), Witton Albion, Runcorn, Altrincham (1988).
Club honours: Aston Villa: Football League Cup winners 1975, 1977.
Carrodus worked as a civil servant before entering League football and broke through with Villa having been a fringe player at Maine Road. A 'workhorse' in midfield, he lost his place at Villa Park to Des Bremner and was later 'blacklisted' after going to South Africa but Blues gave him another chance. A pigeon fancier, he also enjoyed hiking. He now provides corporate hospitality for sporting events.

CARROLL, Thomas Roger
Right-back; Apps 47, Goals 0.
Born: Dublin, 18 August 1942.
Career: St Finbarr's, Shelbourne (1958), Cambridge City (August 1964), Ipswich Town (July 1966), BLUES (loan October 1971, signed permanently November 1971). Retired from competitive football through injury in October 1973.
Club honours: Shelbourne: Irish Cup winners 1962.
Representative honours: Republic of Ireland (17 full caps).
Carroll starred in both the European Cup and European Cup-winners' Cup competitions in the early 1960s with Shelbourne, for whom he appeared in every outfield position having joined the club as a 15-year-old after he had accompanied his brother, Eddie, to a training session. He always believed in trying to play his way out of difficult situations. After returning to Ireland he served a prison sentence after being found guilty of fraud.

CARTER, Timothy Douglas
Goalkeeper; Apps 3, Goals 0.
Born: Bristol, 5 October 1967.
Career: Bristol Schools, Bristol Rovers (apprentice 1983, professional October 1985), Newport County (loan December 1987), Sunderland (December 1987), Carlisle United (loan March 1988), Bristol City (loan September 1988), BLUES (loan November 1991), Hartlepool United (August 1993), Millwall (January 1994).
Representative honours: England (3 Youth caps).
Carter is a tall 'keeper who played 47 League games for Bristol Rovers and 37 for Sunderland.

CASTLE, Frederick Charles
Centre-forward; Apps 3, Goals 0.
Born: Kings Norton, Birmingham, 29 November 1898. Died: Smethwick, late 1974.
Career: Smethwick Highfield, BLUES (April 1925), Shrewsbury Town (August 1927).

At 5ft 7in, Castle was small for a centre-forward and looked out of his depth in League football.

CATLIN, Robert
Goalkeeper; Apps 8, Goals 0.
Born: London, 22 June 1965.
Career: APIA Leichardt, Marconi Fairfield (Australia), Notts County (August 1992), BLUES (loan March 1993).
Born in England but brought up in Australia after his parents emigrated when he was four years old, Catlin was given an early chance by Notts County but fell from grace after conceding eight goals in his first three games. He was not even a regular in County's reserve team when Blues stepped in during an injury crisis. Catlin kept his first clean sheet in League football on his Blues debut, after which it was announced that they had signed him by mistake. Trevor Morgan had watched Notts' reserves and raved about their goalkeeper so Blues signed the 'reserve' goalkeeper. Unfortunately, their youth goalkeeper was playing in the game Morgan watched. Notts County had been fined £20,000 for irregularities in signing Catlin from Australia.

CHAPLIN, Alfred
Half-back; Apps 4, Goals 0.
Born: Foleshill, 1879, Died: London.
Career: Bablake School, St Paul's Bible Class, Folesworth St Paul's, Folesworth Great Heath, Coventry City (1902), BLUES (May 1903), Woolwich Arsenal (June 1905), Coventry City (1906-12); Longford (1913).
Chaplin was signed by Blues after a promising display for Birmingham Juniors against the Scottish Juniors. He had a reputation as a quality marksman in local football, and once hit 24 goals in one match. He failed to make Arsenal's first team but later enjoyed a good spell with Coventry.

CHAPPLE, Frederick J.
Inside-forward; Apps 53, Goals 16.
Born: Treharris, South Wales, 1880. Died: 1945.
Career: Treharris Boys' Club, Bristol Schools, Aston Villa (August 1906), BLUES (December 1908), Crewe Alexandra (June 1910), Brentford (July 1912), Bristol City (June 1913), Blyth Spartans (1918). Retired cs 1920.
Chapple, a nippy footballer, elusive at times, had only nine games in two-and-a-half years with Villa. He flattered to deceive at St Andrew's where he was a regular if not prolific scorer.

CHARSLEY, Christopher Charles
Goalkeeper; Apps 81, Goals 0.
Born: Leicester, 7 November 1864. Died: Weston-super-Mare, 10 January 1945.
Career: St Patrick's School (Stafford), Stafford Town (1881), Stafford Rangers (from 1883), Aston Villa (guest 1886), BLUES (three separate spells: September 1886, December 1891, December 1893-May 1894) and West Bromwich Albion (August-December 1891). Served in the Birmingham Police Force (from 1884) and later became Chief Constable of Coventry (August 1899), retiring in 1918. He then moved to Weston-super-Mare and was elected to the Town Council, rising to Deputy Mayor in 1939-40 and remaining on the council until his death.
Club honours: Blues: Division Two champions 1893.
Representative honours: England (1 full cap).
Chris Charsley was an amateur goalkeeper who was signed by Blues after putting on a quite brilliant display for Stafford. He was the first player to be capped at full international level whilst a member of the

Blues club. Tall with a safe pair of hands and strong kick. His brother Walter played briefly for Blues.

CHARSLEY, Walter Oscar
Wing-half; Apps 3, Goals 0.
Born: Birmingham, 1865. Died: Birmingham.
Career: BLUES (1890-91 season).
He was overshadowed by his better known brother and made only three first-team appearances when injury took its toll of the regular half-backs.

CHEESEWRIGHT, John Anthony
Goalkeeper; Apps 2, Goals 0.
Born: Romford, 12 January 1973.
Career: Tottenham Hotspur (YTS July 1989), Southend United (March 1991), Kingsbury Town, BLUES (non-contract October 1991), Cobh Ramblers (loan January 1992), Dagenham & Rodbridge (September 1992), Braintree Town, Colchester United (January 1994).
Cheesewright looked a useful prospect early in his career but he never made the grade in League football at Blues.

CHILDS, Gary Paul Colin
Midfielder; Apps 44+18, Goals 2.
Born: King's Heath, Birmingham, 19 April 1964.
Career: Maypole & Brandwood Schools (King's Heath), South Birmingham Boys, West Bromwich Albion (apprentice June 1980, professional February 1982), Walsall (loan October 1983, signing permanently, £15,000 November), BLUES (£21,500 July 1987), Grimsby Town (July 1989).
Club honours: Grimsby: Division Four promotion 1990, Division Three promotion 1991.
Representative honours: England (Youth caps).
Childs played over 150 games for Walsall and helped Grimsby win promotion in two successive seasons under former Blues player Alan Buckley. A ball-playing midfielder, Childs was a firm favourite at Fellows Park but was often criticised for his unwillingness 'to get stuck in' at St Andrew's.

CLACK, Frank E.
Goalkeeper; Apps 66, Goals 0.
Born: Witney, Gloucestershire, 30 March 1912.
Career: Newlands, Witney Town, BLUES (amateur October 1932, professional May 1933), Brentford (July 1939), Bristol City (April 1947), Guildford City (August 1949), Dover (1950). Guest for Mansfield Town and Notts County in World War Two.
Clack was a more than useful goalkeeper who spent his youth as deputy to Harry Hibbs. He did surprisingly well in non-League soccer after the war and on retiring, earned his living as a sawyer in his home town. Clack, who had previously worked in a blanket factory, also enjoyed a game of cricket, tennis and bowls.

CLARIDGE, Stephen E.
Striker; Apps 73 +2, Goals 32.
Born: Portsmouth, 10 April 1966.
Career: Portsmouth (apprentice 1982), Fareham Town (1983), AFC Bournemouth (professional November 1984) Weymouth (£10,000 October 1985), Crystal Palace (August 1988), Aldershot (£14,000 October 1988), Cambridge United (£75,000 February 1990), Luton Town (£160,000 July 1992), Cambridge United (£195,000 November 1992), BLUES (£350,000 January 1994).
Club honours: Cambridge United: Division Three champions 1991. Blues: Second Division champions 1995, Auto Windscreens Shield winners 1995.
Claridge is a good quality marksman, He spent only 48 hours with Crystal Palace before joining Aldershot. Prior to moving

to St Andrew's he had netted 81 goals in just over 260 League and Cup games. He was Blues' leading scorer in 1994-95 with 25 goals which went a long way towards helping the club achieve the Second Division championship and Auto Windscreens Shield double.

CLARK, Wallace
Outside-left; Apps 32.
Born: Jarrow, 14 July 1896. Died: Jarrow, 20 December 1975.
Career: Durham City, Middlesbrough (May 1919), Leeds United (£460 May 1921), BLUES (March 1923), Coventry City (£600, October 1924), Boston Town (August 1925), Barrow (June 1926), Torquay United (July 1927), Connah's Quay, Shotton (January 1930).
Wally Clark was one of those players who simply could not settle down, although he was a regular in the Blues side until injury struck in 1924. Thereafter he began his travels around the country. He stood 5ft 7in tall and weighed 11st.

CLARKE, Albert W.
Inside-forward; Apps 31, Goals 9.
Born: Sheffield, 25 December 1916. Died: 1944 (killed in World War Two whilst serving with the Devonshire Regiment).
Career: Mosborough Trinity, Frickley Colliery, Mexborough Town, Torquay United (September 1934), BLUES (January 1936), Blackburn Rovers (July 1938, in exchange for Walter Hassall). Guest for Torquay United in World War Two.
Club honours: Blackburn Rovers: Division Two champions 1939, War League Cup runners-up 1942.
It is stated that Albert Clarke walked all the way from Sheffield to Devon to sign the appropriate forms which made him a Torquay player in 1934, a plausible story in those days of economic depression when men did indeed walk hundreds of miles around the country to find work. He was a strong, forcing player who had a powerful right-foot shot.

CLARKE, Dennis
Full-back; Apps 20+1, Goals 0.
Born: Stockton-on-Tees, 18 January 1948.
Career: Newtongrange School, Stockton & Durham Boys, BLUES (trial 1963), West Bromwich Albion (apprentice April 1963, professional February 1965), Huddersfield Town (£25,000 January 1969), BLUES (£15,000 September 1973). Retired through injury May 1975.
Club honours: WBA: FA Cup winners 1968, Football League Cup runners-up 1967; Huddersfield Town: Division Two champions 1970.
Dennis Clarke was a capable rather than

brilliant full-back who made history when he became the first substitute to be used in an FA Cup Final when he came on the 1968 Wembley game. He played 26 games for Albion (including two Wembley Finals before he was 21) and over 175 for Huddersfield. Clarke bravely ignored a serious leg injury to continue as a makeshift centre-forward in his last game for Blues and, alas, his courage probably ended his career. After retiring he started a building contractor's business in Huddersfield.

CLARKE, Edward
Left-back; Apps 1, Goals 0.
Born: Stechford, Birmingham, 1871. Died: Birmingham.
Career: Washwood Heath School, BLUES (season 1889-90), Ward End Unity (1885).
He was a young defender who deputised for the injured Frank Speller in his only season with the club.

CLARKE, Edward Oswald
Goalkeeper; Apps 1, Goals 0.
Born: Harborne, Birmingham, 1861. Died: Birmingham.
Career: Harborne, BLUES (1884), Knowle (1885).
He was a local-born goalkeeper who had a poor game against Excelsior in the 1884 FA Cup and was not selected again.

CLARKE, Wayne
Striker; Apps 105, Goals 43.
Born: Willenhall, 28 February 1961.
Career: Wolverhampton Wanderers (apprentice June 1977, professional March 1978), BLUES (£80,000 August 1984), Everton (March 1987), Leicester City (£500,000 July 1989), Manchester City (£500,000 January 1990), Shrewsbury Town (loan October 1990), Stoke City (loan March-May 1991), Wolverhampton Wanderers (loan September-October 1991), Walsall (July 1992); Shrewsbury Town August 1993.
Club honours: Blues: Division Two promotion 1985; Everton: Division One champions 1987, FA Charity Shield winners 1987; Shrewsbury Town: Division Three champions 1994.
Representative honours: England: (Schoolboy and Youth caps).
Wayne Clarke was a fine marksman and the youngest of the famous footballing family, his brothers Frank, Allan, Derek and Kelvin, all having played in League football. He was signed for Blues by Ron Saunders and teamed up well with David Geddis. He later returned to haunt Blues, scoring a hat-trick against them when on loan to Shrewsbury Town.

CLARKSON, Ian Stewart
Defender; Apps 159+13, Goals 0.
Born: Solihull, 4 December 1970.
Career: Chapelfields Primary and Tudor Grange Schools, BLUES (YTS June 1987,

professional December 1988); Stoke City (£50,000 September 1993).

Ian Clarkson is a player who reads the game well and who began as a central defender but was converted into a determined, hard-tackling right-back following Kevin Ashley's departure to Wolves. He has supported Blues since he was ten.

CLAYTON, Harry
Inside-left; Apps 2, Goals 0.
Born: Acocks Green, Birmingham, 1860. Died: Birmingham.
Career: Churchfields, Calthorpe, BLUES (January 1883), Birmingham CFC (1884).
Harry Clayton's stint with Blues was sandwiched between two excellent spells with two of the most prestigious amateur clubs in the city. He was on the winning side in both his outings for Blues.

CLUTTERBUCK, Henry James
Goalkeeper; Apps 66, Goals 0.
Born: Wheatenhurst, June 1873. Died: Gloucester Central Hospital, 19 December 1948.
Career: Hereford Thistle, BLUES (July 1897), QPR (May 1899), Grimsby Town (May 1901), Chesterfield (July 1902), New Brompton (1903), Fulham (August 1904). Retired May 1905.
Clutterbuck was a cool, calculated goalkeeper who in October-November 1898 had possibly the easiest time ever as Blues' last line of defence when their forwards scored 35 goals without reply in only four games.

COCHRANE, James
Inside-right; Apps 3, Goals 1.
Born: Brierley Hill, 26 October 1935.
Career: Brierley Hill Schoolboys, BLUES (June 1951, professional October 1952), Walsall (June 1958 in part-exchange for Brian Taylor), Wellington Town (May 1959), Stourbridge (October 1959).
Great things were expected of Jimmy Cochrane who was the 'playmaker' in the successful Brierley Hill Schoolboys side of 1951. But after his National Service (when he spent two years as a cook) he returned to St Andrew's a stone overweight, out of condition, and he was never the same player again.

COLE, Samuel
Centre-forward; Apps 1, Goals 0.
Born: Smethwick, September 1874. Died: Birmingham.
Career: Stoke (amateur), Smethwick Centaur, BLUES (August 1898), Harborne (1900).
Sammy Cole was used in the reserves as an 'all purpose' forward, scoring regularly. He deputised for Bob McRoberts in his only senior game, after being called out of the crowd to play after Blues' 12th man (Walton) had gone off with the reserves.

CONLIN, James
Outside-left; Apps 23, Goals 2.
Born: Durham, 6 August 1881. Died: Flanders, 23 June 1917.
Career: Captain Colt's Rovers, Cambuslang, Hibernian, Falkirk (January 1900), Albion Rovers (March 1901), Bradford City (August 1904), Broadheath FC, Manchester City (July 1906), BLUES (September 1911), Airdrieonians (1912), Broxburn United (August 1913). Killed during World War One, whilst serving with the Highland Light Infantry.
Club honours: Manchester City: Division Two champions 1910.
Representative honours: England (1 full cap); Football League XI (2 games).
Born in England but brought up in Scotland, Conlin played the traditional Scottish dribbling game and his skills led to him receiving some rough treatment and he was frequently troubled by injury.

CONNOLLY, John
Outside-left; Apps 55+8, Goals 9.
Born: Barrhead, Glasgow, 13 June 1950.
Career: Barrhead High School, Glasgow United (1966), St Johnstone (professional January 1968), Everton (March 1972), BLUES (September 1976), Newcastle United (May 1978), Hibernian (September 1980), Gateshead (January 1982), Blyth Spartans (player-manager November 1982), Gateshead (1984), Ayr United (coach).
Club honours: St Johnstone: Scottish League Cup runners-up 1970. Hibernian: Scottish Division One champions 1981.
Representative honours: Scotland (1 full cap, 2 Under-23 caps).

Clubs were lining up to sign John Connolly after he had been in tip-top form for St Johnstone. A classy ball-playing winger, his career was unfortunately disrupted by injury, especially after he had moved south, although he did have a useful first season at St Andrew's before injury struck again.

COOKE, Richard Edward
Winger; Apps 5, Goals 0.
Born: Islington, London, 4 September 1965.
Career: Albany Comprehensive School, Tottenham Hotspur (apprentice June 1982, professional March 1983), BLUES (loan September 1986), AFC Bournemouth (January 1987), Luton Town (March 1989), AFC Bournemouth (March 1991); Bashley (cs 1993).
Club honours: AFC Bournemouth: Division Three champions 1987.
Representative honours: England (1 Under-21 cap, 14 Youth caps).
Cooke, a stocky winger, had a month on loan at St Andrew's from Spurs.

COOPER, Gary J.
Midfield/Defender; Apps 51+4, Goals 3.
Born: Hammersmith, 20 November 1965.
Career: Stationers' Company School, QPR (apprentice 1981, professional June 1983), Brentford (loan September 1985), Fisher Athletic (1986), Maidstone United (March 1989), Peterborough United (£20,000 March 1991), Birmingham City (free transfer December 1993).
Club honours: Fisher Athletic: Southern League Premiership champions 1987. Blues: Second Division champions 1995, Auto Windscreens Shield winners 1995.
Representative honours: England: (11 Youth caps and Schoolboy caps).
An adaptable footballer, enthusiastic with a superb left foot, Cooper appeared in well over 200 matches before joining Blues, 114 of them coming for Peterborough United.

COOPER, Mark Nicholas
Midfield; Apps 35+9, Goals 5.
Born: Wakefield, Yorkshire, 18 December 1968.
Career: Bristol City (apprentice June 1986, professional September 1987), Exeter City (June 1989), Southend United (loan March-April 1990), BLUES (exchange for Eamonn Dolan September 1991), Liverpool (trial January 1992), Fulham (November 1992), Huddersfield Town (loan March 1993), Wycombe Wanderers (loan January 1994), Exeter City (February 1994).
Cooper, a busy, blond-haired central midfielder, is the son of former Blues manager Terry Cooper. He scored a dramatic late equaliser against Peterborough United when making his home debut as a substitute in September 1991.

COOPER, Paul David
Goalkeeper; Apps 26, Goals 0.
Born: Brierley Hill, 21 December 1953.
Career: Kingswood Secondary Modern School, Staffs County Boys, Boney Hay Juniors, Cannock Athletic, Sutton Coldfield Town, BLUES (apprentice June 1971, professional July 1971), Ipswich Town

(loan March 1974, permanently for £27,000 July 1974), Leicester City (July 1987), Manchester City (March 1989), Stockport County (August 1990).
Club honours: Ipswich: FA Cup winners 1978, UEFA Cup winners 1981; Stockport County: Division Four promotion 1991.
Paul Cooper had a nightmare start with Blues but after leaving St Andrew's he became a stalwart between the posts for Ipswich, for whom he amassed more than 550 senior appearances. A good shot-stopper he also had a magnificent record for saving penalties.

CORBETT, Walter Samuel
Full-back; Apps 48, Goals 0.
Born: Wellington, 26 November 1880. Died: Birmingham, 1955.
Career: Vicarage Road (King's Heath) and King Edward VI Grammar Schools, Thornhill FC (Birmingham), Astbury Richmond, Headingly FC, Soho Villa (Handsworth), Bournbrook, Aston Villa (June 1904), BLUES (July 1907), Wellington Town (June 1911), Wolverhampton Old Church (1913). Also played as a guest for QPR (September 1907) and for Wellington Town (April 1909) whilst with Blues.
Representative honours: England (3 full caps, 18 Amateur caps); Great Britain Olympic soccer gold medalist 1908.
'Watty' Corbett was 'one of the most gentlemanly players one could hope to meet in a long day's march', according to the *Sports Argus* in 1906. Corbett, who remained an amateur throughout his playing career, was indeed a terrific

footballer who, it was said, never did a dirty trick on the field of play. He had a fine turn of speed and helped Villa's reserves win the Birmingham & District League three seasons running. He skippered the Birmingham & District Juniors against Scotland in 1904-05 and was selected to represent a mixed amateur and professional XI on a continental tour in 1906 as partner to the great Blackburn Rovers full-back, Bob Crompton. Corbett, who suffered from polio as a lad, always carried a handkerchief in his withered left hand and whilst a student at grammar school (where he played rugby) he won four scholarships and became such an expert linguist that he was appointed manager of the Birmingham Export House (1922) and was also head of the wages department of Birmingham City Transport until 1945.

CORNAN, Francis
Left-half; Apps 61, Goals 1.
Born: Sunderland, 5 May 1880. Died: Halifax, 31 May 1971.
Career: Sunderland Black Watch, Willington, Barnsley (professional, August 1902), BLUES (April 1905), Aston Villa (May 1908), Spennymoor United (August 1909), Barnsley (September 1909), Nelson (1910), Exeter City (July 1911). Retired May 1915.
Cornan was a tough-tackling, extremely hard-working player who seemed fated to be a perpetual makeweight in transfer dealings. He came to Blues as part of the Benny Green transaction and left as part of a complicated exchange deal with Villa. He suffered recurrences of sciatica which caused him to miss several games with each of his clubs.

COTON, Anthony Philip
Goalkeeper; Apps 114, Goals 0.
Born: Tamworth, 19 May 1961.
Career: Mile Oak Rovers, BLUES (apprentice June 1977, professional October 1978), Watford (£330,000 September 1984), Manchester City (£1 million July 1990).
Representative honours: England (1 'B' cap).

Tony Coton sprang to fame when saving John Halwey's penalty with his first touch in his Football League debut game for Blues against Sunderland in the First Division in 1980-81. A tall man, with strong physique, good reflexes and a safe pair of hands, he had all the assets which combined to make him one of the country's top goalkeepers in the early 1990s. After leaving Watford for Maine Road he quickly established himself in the Manchester side after replacing Andy Dibble, and had a pretty good first season there, making 33 League appearances in all, conceding 46 goals – but saving three penalties in the process.

COX, Geoffrey

Winger; Apps 38, Goals 5.

Born: Stockingford, Warwickshire, 30 November 1934.

Career: Nuneaton Boys, BLUES (amateur June 1950, professional December 1951), Torquay United (December 1957), Plymouth Argyle (September 1967).

Cox's promising career was interrupted by National Service and after he returned to St Andrew's he found Astall and Govan firmly installed as the club's regular wingers. He went on to make 261 League appearances for Torquay (scoring 62 goals) and his son, Maurice, also played for Torquay.

COXFORD, John (Jack)

Centre-half; Apps 16, Goals 0.

Born: North Seaton, 25 July 1904. Died: Bury St Edmunds mid-1978.

Career: North Seaton Colliery, Stakeford United, Sunderland (May 1924), BLUES (April 1927), Bournemouth & Boscombe Athletic (May 1930), Poole Town (May 1934), Northfleet (August 1934).

Coxford, who had a distinctive high forehead, was signed as cover for 'Lofty' Morrall. Following the emergence of Tom Fillingham, he found it difficult to get a place in the first team and departed to the south coast, where he spent four excellent seasons with Bournemouth. Thereafter he had the briefest of spells with Poole (two games), before rounding off his career with Northfleet.

CRAVEN, Charles ('Swerver')

Inside-forward; Apps 21, Goals 2.

Born: Boston, Lincolnshire, 2 December 1909. Died: Solihull, 30 March 1972.

Career: Boston Schools representative,

Boston Trinity, Boston Town, Boston United, Grimsby Town (May 1930), Manchester United (£6,000 June 1938), BLUES (December 1938), Tamworth (June 1939), Sutton Town (August 1951). Guested for Coventry and BLUES during World War Two.

Club honours: Grimsby Town: Division Two champions 1934.

A ball-playing forward with devastating body-swerve, Craven scored 99 goals in 273 League games. He had the misfortune to join Blues at a time when the club had a rather weak attack. A former office clerk, he was also a stylish cricketer and useful at snooker and billiards. He was named as reserve for England against Holland in 1935.

CRAWSHAW, Raymond

Centre-half; Apps 4, Goals 0.

Born: Padiham, Lancashire, February 1908. Died: Burnley.

Career: Great Harwood, Southport (amateur July 1929), Great Harwood (1930), Burnley (July 1931), Great Harwood (1932-33), Accrington Stanley (June 1933), BLUES (£600 April 1934), Bromsgrove Rovers (1935), Burton Town (August 1936), Droitwich Rovers (1937).

Another good, steady defender, Crawshaw's career foundered due to the presence of Morrall and Fillingham. Tall and slimly built, he was useful in the air.

CRINGAN, James Anderson

Wing-half; Apps 285, Goals 12.

Born: Douglas Water, near Lanark, 16 December 1904. Deceased.

Career: Douglas Water Thistle, Sunderland (trial), Bury (trial), South Shields (trial August 1921), BLUES (professional, November 1922), Boston United (player-manager June 1934), Banbury Spencer (manager 1935).

Club honours: Blues: FA Cup runners-up 1931.

A 'bostin' footballer from a footballing family – his brother Willie, playing for Celtic and Scotland – Jimmy Cringan was a tenacious competitor who enjoyed a tough battle in the centre of the park. Essentially a defensive player, he once kept goal for Blues in a friendly, such was his versatility.

CROSBIE, John Anderson

Inside-right; Apps 431, Goals 72.

Born: Gorbals, Glasgow, Scotland, 3 June 1896. Died: February 1982.

Career: Glenbuck Cherrypickers, Muirkirk Athletic, Saltcoats Victoria, Ayr United (August 1913), BLUES (record fee of

£3,700 May 1920), Chesterfield (July 1932), Stourbridge (player-manager November 1932), coached Gothenburg (February-August 1933). A button maker by profession, he was coaching a works team in the Kidderminster area in 1934-35.

Club honours: Blues: Division Two champions 1921, FA Cup runners-up 1931.

Representative honours: Scotland (2 full caps, 1 Victory cap).

Scotsman Johnny Crosbie matured into an exceptionally skilful inside-forward with Blues, a craftsman of the highest class, who provided Joe Bradford with most of his goalscoring openings with some judicious passes. He drew up an uncanny understanding with Bradford, and between them they scored at a prolific rate. Johnny was clever at spotting openings and could send out a 40-yard pass straight to his man.

CROSSTHWAITE, Herbert

Goalkeeper; Apps 49, Goals 0.

Born: Preston, 4 April 1887. Died: Birmingham.

Career: Blackpool, Fulham (August 1907), Exeter City (May 1909), BLUES (December 1910), Stoke (1914). Retired cs 1915 to concentrate on being a constable in the Birmingham Police Force which he joined in 1910. In 1925 he was promoted to Inspector and continued to be a prominent figure in the organisation of the Birmingham Police Charity Sports.

Described as fearless and clever, Bert Crossthwaite was one of a handful of amateurs who served Blues prior to World War One. His cousin, Harold, played for Stockport County.

CURBISHLEY, Llewellyn Charles ('Alan')

Midfield; Apps 153+2, Goals 15.

Born: Forest Gate, London, 8 November 1957.

Career: Forest Gate Boys (1972), West Ham United (apprentice July 1973, professional July 1975), BLUES (£225,000 July 1979), Aston Villa (£100,000, plus Robert Hopkins March 1983), Charlton Athletic (£40,000 December 1984), Brighton & Hove Albion (£32,000 August 1987), Charlton Athletic (£5,000 player-coach July 1990, assistant manager October 1990, joint manager July 1991).

Club honours: Blues: Division Two promotion 1980.

Representative honours: England (Schoolboy, Youth and Under-21 caps).

A determined, all-action competitor with a lovely right foot, Alan Curbishley was on the verge of full international honours when he suffered a serious injury against Brighton. He had amassed well over 600 senior appearances when the 1990-91 season closed.

CURRYER, Leonard

Centre-forward; Apps 2, Goals 0.

Born: Birmingham, 1864. Died: Birmingham.

Career: BLUES (1885-87).

Len Curryer was a reserve forward who was given a couple of run-outs in place of the injured Harry Morris.

CURTIS, Ernest Robert

Outside-left; Apps 180, Goals 53.

Born: Cardiff, 10 June 1907. Died: Cardiff, November 1992.

Career: Severn Road Old Boys, Cardiff Corinthians, Cardiff City (professional November 1925), BLUES (£3,000 March 1928), Cardiff City (November 1933), Coventry City (February 1935), Hartlepool United (July 1937). Retired 1939, later

assistant coach to Cardiff City and also publican in Cardiff.

Club honours: Cardiff: FA Cup winners 1927, FA Charity Shield winners 1927, Welsh Cup winners 1927; Blues: FA Cup runners-up 1931.

Representative honours: Wales (3 full caps, 2 Schoolboy caps)

Switched to the left flank by Blues in order to solve a problem position, Curtis proved a difficult player to knock off the ball and scored his fair share of goals at club level. He was a P-o-W during World War Two.

DAILEY, James

Centre-forward; Apps 42, Goals 14.
Born: Glenboig, Scotland, 8 September 1927.
Career: Wolverhampton Wanderers (amateur 1943), Third Lanark (1945), Sheffield Wednesday (October 1946), BLUES (February 1949), Exeter City (August 1952), Workington (December 1953), Rochdale (October 1957), Weymouth (1959), Bath City, Poole Town, Bridport, Portland Town (manager), Dorchester Town (manager). Later ran sports shop in Weymouth, where he still lives.

A dynamic forward whose time with Blues was hardly an unqualified success, Dailey did, however, finish top scorer in his one full season in the senior side and later proved a prolific marksman in the lower divisions, netting over 100 League goals after leaving St Andrew's, including 74 in 176 games for Workington. He scored five goals for Wednesday against Barnsley in September 1947 to equal Jimmy Trotter's individual scoring record for the Owls.

DAISH, Liam Sean

Defender; Apps 71, Goals 4.
Born: Portsmouth, 23 September 1968.
Career: Portsmouth (apprentice 1984, professional September 1986), Cambridge United (free transfer July 1988), BLUES (£50,000 January 1994).
Club honours: Cambridge United: Division Three champions 1990-91. Blues: Second Division champions 1995, Auto Windscreens Shield winners 1995.
Representative honours: Republic of Ireland (1 full cap, 5 Under-21 caps, 1 'B' cap).

Daish has proved to be one of manager Fry's best signings, being strong in the air, determined and forceful on the ground. He had an excellent 1994-95 campaign in which he skippered Blues to the Second Division championship. The season also saw him booked (and ultimately suspended) for blowing a trumpet in celebration after scoring at Chester! He played in 182 senior games for Cambridge and three for Pompey.

DALE, Richard Armstrong ('Dicky')

Right-half; Apps 150, Goals 0.
Born: Willington, Co Durham, 21 March 1896. Died: c.1970.
Career: Walton School, Walbottle Juniors,

Tow Law Town, North Walbottle FC, Stanley United, BLUES (£250 March 1922), West Bromwich Albion (£1,500 November 1928), Tranmere Rovers (£400 June 1931), Crook Town (October 1932), Tow Law Town. Retired cs 1938.

Dale was a 'chunky' wing-half who was a regular member of the Blues' defence throughout the mid-1920s. Perhaps a shade uncertain at times, he was nevertheless generally regarded as a handy defender, always ready for a battle. He represented the Staffordshire County FA in 1925.

DALY, Gerard Anthony

Midfielder; Apps 74+2, Goals 2.
Born: Cabra, Dublin, 30 April 1954.
Career: Bohemians, Manchester United (£20,000 April 1973), Derby County (£170,000 March 1977), New England Tea Men (NASL) (loan in summers of 1978 & 1979), Coventry City (£310,000 August 1980), Leicester City (loan January 1983), BLUES (August 1984), Shrewsbury Town (October 1985), Stoke City (March 1987), Doncaster Rovers (July 1988), Telford United (player-manager July 1989-October 1993).

Club honours: Manchester United: Division Two champions 1975, FA Cup runners-up 1976; Blues: Division Two promotion 1985.
Representative honours: Republic of Ireland (46 full caps, 1 Under-23 cap).

Gerry Daly was a slim, intelligent and skilful midfield player, whose game came on in leaps and bounds after leaving Ireland. He was never suited to Ron Saunders' long-ball game at Blues and showed an ill-concealed dislike for these tactics, although the team certainly played better when he was in the side. An ace penalty taker, Daly was also a fine snooker player. He scored 23 goals in his 111 League games for Manchester United and 30 from the same number of starts at Derby County.

DARK, Trevor C.

Winger; Apps 2+3, Goals 1.
Born: St Helier, 29 January 1961.
Career: Arsenal (associate schoolboy), Merton Boys, BLUES (apprentice July 1977, professional January 1979), Hendon (1981), Carshalton Athletic, Fisher Athletic, Tooting & Mitcham United.

Dark was principally a reserve at St Andrew's, although his career was affected by him being switched from winger to full-back, a position he showed little aptitude for.

DARRELL, Michael Alan

Inside-forward; Apps 13+5, Goals 2.
Born: Bilston, 14 January 1947.
Career: SE Staffs Schools, BLUES (apprentice April 1962, professional January 1965), Newport County (loan October 1970), Gillingham (loan

December 1970), Peterborough United (May 1971), Bilston (1973), Darlaston (1974).

A great future was predicted for this bow-legged, barrel-chested bundle of energy midfielder after he had put in a series of promising performances as an 18-year-old. His career then seemed to stagnate with only nine League games in the next five season. His brother Brian played for Darlaston.

DAVENPORT, Thomas

Inside-forward; Apps 13, Goals 8.
Born: Kingstanding, Birmingham, 1860. Died: Birmingham.
Career: Hockley Belmont, BLUES (August 1885), St Luke's (1886), BLUES (1888-89); Birmingham St George's.

Davenport was a dashing forward whose goals seemed to be reserved for Cup-ties – seven coming in the FA Cup, plus at least another five in local cup games.

DAVIES, George

Outside-left; Apps 29, Goals 7.
Born: Wellington, Shropshire, February 1900. Deceased.
Career: Wellington St George's, Ironbridge FC, BLUES (April 1918), Southend United (June 1922), Wellington Town (May 1924). Wellington Town (committee member June 1934). Guested for Wrexham in World War One.

Club honours: Blues: Division Two champions 1921.

A short, stubby winger, (5ft 5in tall, 10st 5lb in weight), Davies was recommended to Blues by Jack Elkes. He joined a band of outside-lefts at St Andrew's, none of whom could be described as regular first-teamers. He hit five goals in the last seven League

games of Blues' Second Division championship winning season. Davies was replaced in side by Ted Linley.

DAVIES, Stanley Charles

Inside/centre-forward; Apps 17, Goals 5.
Born: Chirk, near Oswestry, 24 April 1898. Died: Birmingham, 17 January 1972.
Career: Chirk Council Schools, Chirk Schools representative, Chirk FC, Army Signals School (Dunstable), Manchester United (trial), Rochdale (January 1919), Preston North End (April 1919), Everton (£4,000 January 1921), West Bromwich Albion (£3,300 November 1921), BLUES (£1,500 November 1927), Cardiff City (May 1928), Rotherham United (player-manager March 1929), Barnsley (August 1930), Manchester Central (October 1930), Dudley Town (1933), Chelmsford City (trainer April 1938-May 1941), Shorts FC of Rochester (manager during World War Two). Publican in West Bromwich during the 1930s.
Club honours: (as manager) Shorts: Kent Senior Cup winners twice in 1940s.
Representative honours: Wales (18 full caps, 1 'other' cap); toured Canada with Welsh FA June-July 1929.

Stan Davies was a big, strong, forceful player (5ft 10in tall, 12st 12lb in weight) who starred in six different positions for his country (including goalkeeper), an indication of his tremendous versatility. He possessed a cracking shot, could head a ball hard and true, and in his career scored 110 goals in some 250 appearances for his seven major clubs including 83 in 159 games for Albion. During World War One he distinguished himself with the Welsh Fusiliers and was awarded the Military Medal and the Croix de Guerre. His son, John, is now a freelance sports writer based in Bristol.

DAWS, James

Right-half; Apps 47, Goals 1.

Born: *Mansfield Woodhouse,
Nottinghamshire, 27 May 1898. Died:
Birmingham, June 1985.*
Career: *Notts County (amateur May-
November 1919), Mansfield Town
(December 1919), BLUES (January 1920),
Bristol Rovers (amateur March 1924,
professional May 1924 for £250) to June
1925, Mansfield Woodhouse (July 1925),
Poole Town (player-trainer August 1925-
May 1927).*
Daws was a clumsy, somewhat overweight
footballer with a powerful shot, who was
occasionally hot-tempered.

DAYKIN, Thomas
Wing-half; Apps 94, Goals 1.
Born: *Shildon, August 1882. Died: County
Durham.*
Career: *Bishop Auckland (amateur),
Newcastle United (trial), Hobson
Wanderers, Sunderland (1905), BLUES
(December 1908), South Shields (1912).
Retired 1915.*
The local press hailed it as quite a coup
when this powerful player came to Blues.
Basically a reserve at Sunderland, Daykin
had impressed when called into first-team
action but his arrival at St Andrew's
coincided with a period of turmoil both on
and off the field and during his spell at the
club, Blues dropped to the bottom of the
Second Division and found themselves in
severe financial difficulties.

DEACON, Henry ('Harry')
Inside-forward; Apps 3, Goals 0.
Born: *Sheffield, 25 April 1900. Died:
Rotherham, 5 January 1946.*
Career: *Sheffield Boys, Sheffield
Wednesday (amateur), Hallam FC
(Sheffield), BLUES (May 1920), Swansea
Town July (1922), Crewe Alexandra
(August 1931), Southport (June 1934),
Accrington Stanley (December 1934),
Rotherham United (June 1935). Retired
1939.*
Club honours: *Swansea Town: Division
Three South champions 1925.*
Representative honours: *Welsh League v
Irish League May 1931.*
Deacon had Johnny Crosbie to contend
with for the inside-right berth in the Blues'
side but after leaving St Andrew's he gave
Swansea excellent service as both creator
and taker of chances, netting 88 goals in
319 games, all of which made him
extremely popular at Vetch Field, where
9,000 fans saw his benefit match. He stood
5ft 8in tall and weighed 11st 6lb.

DEAKIN, John
Midfield; Apps 3+4, Goals 0.
Born: *Sheffield, 29 September 1966.*
Career: *Barnsley (apprentice July 1983),
Doncaster Rovers (non-contract August
1985), Shepshed Charterhouse (1987),
BLUES (professional September 1989);
Carlisle United (August 1991), Wycombe
Wanderers, Kidderminster Harriers
(August 1992).*
Club honours: *Kidderminster Harriers:
GMVC champions 1994; FA Trophy
runners-up 1995.*
An eager, grafting player who showed no
small degree of skill, Deakin made his
senior debut as a substitute against
Tranmere a few days after joining Blues but
was later hampered by injury.

DEARDEN, Kevin Charles
Goalkeeper; Apps 12, Goals 0.
Born: *Luton, 8 March 1970.*
Career: *Tottenham Hotspur (apprentice
June 1986, professional August 1988),
Farnborough Town (loan September 1988),
Woking (loan January 1989), Cambridge
United (loan March 1989), Hartlepool
United (loan August 1989), Oxford United
(loan December 1989), Swindon Town
(loan March 1990), Peterborough United
(loan August 1990), Hull City (loan*

January 1991), Rochdale (loan August
1991), BLUES (loan, March 1992),
Portsmouth (loan August 1992), Brentford
(November 1993).*
Dearden was taken on loan by Blues after
another loaned goalkeeper, Alan Miller,
had been recalled by Arsenal. Nurtured at
White Hart Lane by both Pat Jennings and
Ray Clemence, Dearden was a competent
performer.

DEARSON, Donald John
Utility player; Apps 136, Goals 17.
Born: *Ynysybwl, 13 May 1914. Died:
Sheldon, Birmingham, 24 December 1990.*
Career: *Llanwit Major Juniors, Barry
(August 1932), BLUES (professional, April
1934), Coventry City (£6,000 February
1947), Walsall (March 1950), Nuneaton
Borough, Bilston United (1952). Retired
1953-54. Guested for Northampton Town,
Nottingham Forest, Wrexham and West
Bromwich Albion during World War Two.*
Club honours: *Blues: Football League
South winners 1946.*
Representative honours: *Wales (3 full caps,
15 Wartime caps, 4 Amateur caps).*
A youngster with an impressive physique,
Don Dearson had already won amateur

caps for his country before joining Blues.
Initially a clever, scheming inside-forward,
with a powerful shot, he was moved into the
half-back line and proved a great success
before rounding off his Blues career at full-
back. A qualified electrical engineer,
Dearson was in a reserved occupation
during the war and this enabled him to
make a total of 166 appearances for Blues
during the hostilities (25 goals scored). At
one time he spent nine weeks in the
Birmingham City Police Force but resigned
to work in the BSA factory, later becoming
an employee of British Leyland, Coventry,
while also running his own grocery
business. A truly grand competitor in every
sense of the word, whether involved in
football or otherwise.

DEELEY, James
Outside-left; Apps 1, Goals 0.
Born: *Evesham, 1871. Died: Worcester.*
Career: *Worcester Rovers, BLUES (August
1895), Hereford Town (July 1896).*
Deeley came in for one game when the
ever-reliable 'Toddy' Hands cried off with a
rare injury.

DENNIS, Mark Earl
Left-back; Apps 145, Goals 1.
Born: *Streatham, London, 2 May 1961.*
Career: *Chelsea Boys, BLUES (apprentice
June 1977, professional August 1978),
Southampton (£100,000, November 1983),
QPR (£250,000 May 1987), Crystal Palace
(August 1988); Brighton & Hove Albion
(trial 1991).*

Representative honours: *England (Youth
caps, 3 Under-21 caps).*
Mark Dennis was a talented player with a
fiery temper who made his debut for Blues
in unusual circumstances. He had travelled
to Norwich with the first team to gain some
experience, but when Jimmy Calderwood
slipped in the dressing-room, cracking his
head, Dennis was called up to play in at
right-back, and soon settled into the side,
taking over his favourite number-three shirt
on a regular basis. It is impossible to talk
about Dennis without reference to his
disciplinary record – sent off 12 times (at
various levels) and booked on numerous
occasions he has been involved in
tempestuous incidents both at home and
away, on the training ground and in one
instance, on New Street Station. At his best,
he was an exciting attacking full-back,
capable of delivering teasing centres, and
with a little more self-discipline would have
surely gained more major honours than the
Under-21 caps he collected whilst with
Blues.

DE SOUZA, Juan Miguel I.
Forward; Apps 8+11, Goals 0.
Born: *Canning Town, 11 February 1970.*
Career: *Newham Schools, Clapton (1987),
Charlton Athletic (July 1989), Bristol City
(free transfer August 1990), Cheltenham
Town (1991), Yeovil Town (1992),
Dorchester Town, Bashley, Dagenham &
Redbridge (1993), BLUES (£25,000
February 1994), Bury (loan November
1994), Wycombe Wanderers (January
1995).*
An enthusiastic player, De Souza was
perhaps out of his depth in League football
after spending quite some time in the lower
reaches of non-League soccer.

DEVEY, Edwin James ('Ted')
Left-half; Apps 94, Goals 6.
Born: *Small Heath, Birmingham, August
1862. Died: Birmingham, 2 September
1946.*
Career: *Bordesley Green Council School,
Birmingham Excelsior, BLUES (April
1888), Burton Wanderers (October 1896).*
Club honours: *Blues: Division Two
champions 1893, Division Two promotion
1894.*
One of the famous set of Birmingham
brothers – Jack, Harry and Bob played for
Aston Villa, Ted for Blues and Will served
with both. Ted Devey was a battling
midfielder with a crunching tackle,
possessing a powerful, if sometimes
inaccurate shot.

DEVEY, Ray
Centre-half; Apps 1, Goals 0.
Born: *Tysley, Birmingham, 19 December
1917.*
Career: *Forman's Road School, Shirley
Juniors, Shirley Old Boys, BLUES (May*

*1937), Mansfield Town (August 1947).
Retired June 1950 when he returned to St
Andrew's, serving as reserve-team trainer,
first-team trainer, physiotherapist and kit-
man before retiring in 1983.*

Ray Devey was a familiar figure to
generations of Blues fans, few of whom
ever saw him play. Devey joined the club as
a teenager, learning his trade in the
reserves, but World War Two put his career
on hold and after serving in the Army he
was forced to take a back seat behind
Turner and Owen. For Mansfield he made
77 League appearances in two seasons.

DEVEY, William
Centre-forward; Apps 13, Goals 18.
Born: *Perry Barr, Birmingham, 12 April
1865. Died: Birmingham, 10 June 1935.*
Career: *Clavendon Montrose, Wellington,
Aston Unity (1884), BLUES (August 1885),
Wolverhampton Wanderers (August 1891),
Aston Villa (December 1892), Walsall Town
Swifts (May 1894), Burton Wanderers
(1895), Notts County (1896), Walsall
(1897), Burton Wanderers (late 1897),
Walsall, Darlaston, BLUES (July 1898).
Retired cs 1900.*
Will Devey was a player who relied on skill
rather than strength and he was one of
Blues' pre-League stars. Not a big man, he
nevertheless had a powerful shot, was
skilful and skippered Blues from 1888 until
his departure in 1891. He was frequently
criticised for a tendency to drop back to
gain possession. Brother of Ted Devey.

DEVINE, Joseph
Wing-half/inside-forward; Apps 56, Goals
2.
Born: *Motherwell, 8 August 1905.*
Career: *Motherwell Watsonians, Cleland
Juniors, Bathgate, Burnley (£250 May
1925), Newcastle United (£5,575 January
1930), Sunderland (£2,599 January 1931),
QPR (£2,500 May 1933), BLUES (£2,000
January 1935), Chesterfield (May 1937).
Later refereed in Highland League football
and worked as a scout for Bristol City.*
After an early career as a goalscorer with
good ball control, Joe Devine had been
converted into a non-stop midfield player
by the time he joined Blues, but despite
some fine displays he often found himself
in the second team, frequently as after
being made the scapegoat for the rest of the

side. He usually reserved his best form for the Arsenal. Red-haired and a dog lover, he was nephew of Joe Cassidy (Scotland) and later in life ran a successful sports outfitters shop in London.

DEVLIN, James Thomas S.
Inside-forward; Apps 2, Goals 1.
Born: Bellshill, Glasgow, October 1904. Died: Scotland.
Career: Vale of Clyde, Shawfield Juniors, Kilsyth Rangers, Third Lanark (April 1922), King's Park, BLUES (September 1924), Preston North End (£362 January 1926), Liverpool (£250 May 1927), Swindon Town (July 1928), Brooklyn Wanderers (USA) (May 1929), Aberdeen (1931), Walsall (August 1932), Zurich (Switzerland, 1933), Fleetwood Town (July 1934), Oldham Athletic (September 1934). Retired 1935-36.
Jim Devlin was one of the game's 'birds of passage', his migrations taking him to four countries. He was a ball-playing forward, direct and forceful in the traditional Scottish mould, but with Crosbie holding down the inside-right berth his chances of first-team action with Blues were limited. His brother, Willie, was also a 'wanderer' appearing for 14 different clubs, most notably Huddersfield and Liverpool.

DICKS, Julian Andrew
Left-back; Apps 95+7, Goals 2.
Born: Bristol, 8 August 1968.
Career: Washwood Heath School (Birmingham), BLUES (YTS, August 1984, professional August 1985), West Ham United (£400,000 March 1988); Liverpool (September 1993), West Ham United (November 1994), both the latter being exchange deals.
Club honours: West Ham United: Division Two promotion 1991.
Representative honours: England (4 Under-21 caps).

Julian Dicks moved from the West Country to Birmingham whilst still at school, thinking he had a better chance of becoming a professional footballer in the Midlands. He was quickly snapped up by Blues and progressed through the ranks before making his senior debut on his 17th birthday. Dicks developed into a fiercely competitive left-back with a penchant for attack. He was, however, subject to occasional rushes of blood and had an unenviable disciplinary record, including a dismissal in his first England Under-21 appearance. He took over as skipper of West Ham.

DILLON, Kevin Paul
Midfielder; Apps 206+6, Goals 19.
Born: Sunderland, 18 December 1959.
Career: Durham Boys, BLUES (apprentice

June 1976, professional July 1977), Portsmouth (£200,000 March 1983), Newcastle United (July 1989), Reading (free transfer August 1991), Newbury Town, Stevenage Borough (October 1994), Yeovil Town (1995).
Club honours: Blues: Division Two promotion 1980.
Representative honours: England (1 Under-21 cap).
A player with silky skills but suspect temperament, the bulk of Kevin Dillon's career with Blues was spent on the left wing, from where he scored some quite stunning goals with curling shots or after a mazy dribble. He had a habit of back-chatting to referees.

DIXON, David P.
Right-back; Apps 4, Goals 0.
Born: North Shields, November 1898. Died: Newcastle upon Tyne.
Career: South Shields, Preston Colliery, BLUES (May 1920), Southend United (May 1925), Rhyl Athletic, Bedlington United (February 1928). Retired 1931.

Dixon was a slim defender (5ft 9in tall, 11st in weight) who was third-choice at Blues behind Womack and Ashurst. He played in only another four games before Southend dropped out of the League.

DIXON, George
Left-back; Apps 1, Goals 0.
Born: Smethwick, April 1859. Died: Birmingham.
Career: Oldbury, BLUES (August 1887), Aston Unity (1888).
Dixon was a capable footballer who deputised for Walter Farley in two games, one being a 6-1 win over Aston Unity, who were so impressed they signed him.

DIXON, Walter
Outside-right; Apps 2, Goals 2.
Born: Perry Barr, Birmingham, 1861. Died: Birmingham.
Career: Brookvale FC, Aston Manor, Excelsior (1886), BLUES (July 1887), Church FC (February 1888).
He was a regular winger for the first part of the 1887-88 season before moving to the North-West ostensibly because he was offered a job there, but there were also rumours of Church offering him a financial inducement.

DOHERTY, Neil
Forward; Apps 16 + 9, Goals 1.
Born: Barrow-in-Furness, 21 February 1969.
Career: Watford (trainee, 1983), Barrow (cs 1988), Leeds United (trial), BLUES (£40,000 February 1994).

Club honours: Barrow: FA Trophy winners 1990.
Doherty entered League soccer at the age of 26, when he made his debut for Blues against Peterborough United. A tricky winger who prefers the left flank, he had been marked down as a possible Premiership player before Barry Fry moved in to bring him to St Andrew's.

DOLAN, Eamonn John
Forward; Apps 10+6, Goals 1.
Born: Chelmsford, 20 September 1967.
Career: Dagenham YC, West Ham United (apprentice August 1983, professional March 1985), Bristol City (loan February 1989), BLUES (£35,000 December 1990), Exeter City (exchange for Mark Cooper September 1991).
Representative honours: Republic of Ireland (Youth and 5 Under-21 caps).
Dolan was an energetic forward whose warming-up and winding-down routines earned him a place in Blues folklore. When named as a substitute he often tended to spend most of his time jogging up and down the touch-line, being escorted from the pitch by police at Exeter and getting himself arrested at the Millmoor ground, Rotherham, on a charge of inciting the crowd, most of whom left at the time. He initially signed for Blues in the summer of 1990 but a dislocated shoulder continued to cause him problems and he was sent back to West Ham. Dolan unfortunately missed the end of the 1990-91 campaign because of yet another arm injury. In May 1993 he underwent an operation for testicular cancer. His twin brother Pat played for Walsall.

DOMINGUEZ, José M.M.
Winger; Apps 20+25, Goals 4.
Born: Lisbon, 16 February 1974.
Career: Benfica, Real Madrid, Benfica (1992), Sport União Sintrense (loan), AD Fafé (loan), BLUES (£50,000 March 1994).
Club honours: Blues: Second Division champions 1995.
Representative honours: Portugal (1 Under-21 cap).

One of the smallest players ever to pull on a Blues shirt at 5ft 3in, Dominguez became a huge favourite with the St Andrew's fans with his tricky runs, neat body-swerve and some cracking shots.

DONOWA, Brian Louis
Winger; Apps. 100+30, Goals 19.
Born: Ipswich, 24 September 1964.
Career: Ipswich Boys, Norwich City (apprentice 1980, professional September 1982), Stoke City (loan December 1985), Real Deportivo de la Coruna (£40,000 February 1986), SV Willem II (1988),

Ipswich Town (1989), Bristol City (£50,000 August 1990), BLUES (£50,000 August 1991); Burnley (loan January 1993), Crystal Palace (loan March 1993), Shrewsbury Town (loan January 1994).
Club honours: Norwich City: FA Youth Cup winners 1983, Milk Cup winners 1985. Blues: Second Division champions 1995, Auto Windscreens Shield winners 1995.
Representative honours: England (3 Under-21 caps).

Donowa made an early impact as a flying winger for Norwich City where he benefited greatly from his experienced forward colleagues. He had a fairly unsuccessful spell abroad before attempting to revive his career in England. Opportunities were rather limited at both Ipswich and Bristol City, however. He is the first Blues substitute to be substituted himself.

DORMAN, Donald J.
Inside-forward; Apps 64, Goals 6.
Born: Hall Green, Birmingham, 18 September 1922.
Career: Shirley Juniors, BLUES (initially in 1945, professional May 1946), Coventry City (September 1951), Walsall (October 1954). Retired May 1957 and returned to BLUES as a scout, rising to chief scout on the death of Walter Taylor. Left Blues, second time round, in 1983, and later took over as chief scout of Aston Villa, before quitting football in 1985.
A paratrooper, wounded and captured at Arnhem, Don Dorman's courage and never-say-die attitude was always evident in his play. He is perhaps best remembered as the head of the scouting network at St Andrew's, which discovered such fine players as Trevor Francis, Kenny Burns, Tony Coton and many others. Dorman left the club as part of manager Ron Saunders' purge of backroom staff.

DORRINGTON, John ('Jack')
Goalkeeper; Apps 111, Goals 0.
Born: Smethwick, May 1881. Died: Handsworth, Birmingham, 9 January 1944.
Career: Langley St Michael's, West Smethwick, West Bromwich Albion (amateur), Bromsgrove Rovers (1899), Kidderminster Harriers, BLUES (July 1901). Retired cs 1913 through injury.
Jock Dorrington was a grand servant to Blues, totally fearless, with a jovial temperament that did wonders for morale, even in difficult times. Jack surprisingly was only first choice in one of his 12 seasons at the club.

DOUGALL, Cornelius ('Neil')
Inside-right; Apps 108, Goals 18.
Born: Falkirk, 7 November 1921.
Career: Burnley (schoolboy forms 1936, professional July 1940), BLUES (£2,750 October 1945), Plymouth Argyle (March 1949). Retired March 1959, became

Plymouth's assistant trainer, moving up to head trainer until March 1968. Guested for Coventry City in World War Two.
Club honours: Blues: Football League South champions 1946, Division Two champions 1948; Plymouth Argyle: Division Three South champions 1952, Division Three champions 1959.
Representative honours: Scotland (1 full cap, 1 Victory cap).

Dougall came from distinguished footballing stock, his father William playing for Falkirk, Burnley and the Scottish League, and his uncle James representing Preston and Scotland. Neil Dougall was a powerful red-headed inside-forward with strong, accurate shot (in both feet but mainly with his right) who made an immediate impact at St Andrew's, scoring a total of ten goals in his first season there. He didn't find the net too often after that but remained a vital cog in the attack mechanism. He went on to score 22 goals in 278 Football League outings for Argyle after leaving the Blues and spent over 20 years at Home Park, becoming a very well respected gentleman in the West Country.

DOUGHERTY, James
Left-half; Apps 136, Goals 3.
Born: New Brighton, 19 November 1878. Died: Liverpool.
Career: New Brighton Old Wanderers, Liskeard YMCA, New Brighton Tower, Chorley, New Brighton Tower, BLUES (September 1901), Coventry City (1908), Stirchley United, Worcester City.
Jim Dougherty was originally a centre-half, but later on in years he became a useful, constructive wing-half with a telling tackle. In those days before the 'stopper' centre-half, of course, all the half-backs linked up with their attack. He was in line for international honours whilst with Blues, but was never selected for duty, although he was penned in as a reserve on two occasions. He was very proud of his magnificent waxed moustache.

DOWNING, Keith G.
Midfield; Apps 2, Goals 0.

Born: Oldbury, 23 July 1965.
Career: Mile Oak Rovers, Notts County (free transfer May 1984), Wolverhampton Wanderers (free transfer August 1987), BLUES (free transfer July 1993), Stoke City (free transfer August 1994).
Club honours: Wolves: Division Three champions 1989, Division Four champions 1988, Sherpa Van Trophy winners 1988.
Downing was a very competitive player, a hard tackler, whose nickname was 'Pyscho'. He gave Wolves excellent service, playing for them in more than 200 games. Injury ruined his stay at St Andrew's.

DOWNS, Gregory
Left-back; Apps 22+1, Goals 1.
Born: Carlton, Nottingham, 13 December 1958.
Career: Weavers School, Norwich City (apprentice March 1975, professional December 1976), Connecticut Bicentennials (loan March-August 1977), Torquay United (loan November-December 1977), Coventry City (£40,000 July 1985), BLUES (free transfer, August 1990), Hereford United (July 1991 as player-coach: manager May 1992 – resigned September 1994); Raunds Town, Kettering Town (November 1994); Redditch United (November 1994), Merthyr Tydfil (November 1994), Worcester City (February 1995), Forest Green Rovers (May 1995).
Club honours: Norwich City: Milk Cup winners 1985; Coventry City: FA Cup winners 1987.
Greg Downs made his League debut on left wing whilst on loan to Torquay but was successfully converted into a fine overlapping left-back, steady under pressure whose crosses were both precise and well struck. He was Norwich's free-kick expert but struggled at Coventry to win over the fans and joined Blues initially as a replacement for Ian Atkins as sweeper but eventually gaining a first-team slot in his accustomed role as left-back.

DRAKE, Alonzo Robson
Inside-forward; Apps 13, Goals 2.
Born: Parkgate, Rotherham, 16 April 1884. Died: Hanley, Huddersfield, 14 February 1919.
Career: Parkgate FC, Rotherham Town (trial), Doncaster Rovers, Sheffield United (professional August 1905), BLUES (£1,000 December 1907), QPR (August 1908), Huddersfield Town (1910).
Drake was a hard-working, dashing player said to have had 'bad luck' with his shooting. Better known as a cricketer, he played as a professional for Yorkshire for five years (1909-14), appearing in 157 matches as a middle-order left-hand batsman and slow left-arm bowler. He did the 'double' in 1913 and followed up by taking 158 wickets in the next season (average 15.30). All told he scored 4,816 runs (average 21.69) and took 480 wickets at 18.00 each for the Tykes. He took 100 wickets and scored 1,000 runs in a season on two occasions, with his best run-return coming in 1911 when he notched 1,487 for an average of 30.97. His best bowling figures were 10-35 for Yorkshire against Somerset. His cricket career was cut short through ill health, leading to his sudden demise at the relatively early age of 34.

DRAPER, Harry
Inside-left; Apps 3, Goals 0.
Born: Chesterfield, 1887. Deceased.
Career: Rotherham Town (April 1909), BLUES (April 1910), Denaby United (September 1911).
Draper was a young 'playmaker' given a run-out with the seniors as Blues struggled in Division Two. He could not settle in Birmingham and made an early return to Yorkshire.

DRINKELL, Kevin Smith
Striker; Apps 5, Goals 2.
Born: Grimsby, 18 June 1960.
Career: Grimsby & District Schools, Grimsby Town (apprentice June 1976, professional June 1978), Norwich City (£105,000 June 1985), Glasgow Rangers (cs 1988), Coventry City (cs 1990), BLUES (loan October 1991), Falkirk (player-coach July 1992), Stirling Albion (player-coach April 1994).
Club honours: Grimsby Town: Division Three champions 1980; Rangers: Scottish League champions and Scottish Cup winners 1989.

Drinkell was a powerful forward taken on loan by Blues following an injury to John Gayle. He scored 102 goals in 309 games for Grimsby before moving to Norwich and did well at Carrow Road and also at Ibrox Park. He made his Football League debut at 17 and scored in his first game for Blues, against Stockport in October 1991.

DRYDEN, Richard Andrew
Defender; Apps 54, Goals 0.
Born: Stroud, 14 June 1969.
Career: Bristol Rovers (trainee 1985, professional July 1987), Exeter City (loan September 1988), Exeter City (March 1989), Notts County (£250,000 August 1991), Manchester City (loan June 1992), Plymouth Argyle (loan, November 1992), BLUES (£165,000 March 1993), Bristol City (£300,000 December 1994).
Club honours: Exeter City: Division Four champions 1989-90.

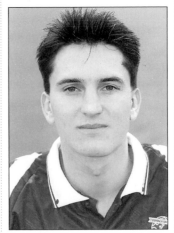

A versatile defender, strong and capable in every department, Dryden passed the milestone of 200 senior appearances in his career during his spell with Blues. He had 105 outings with Exeter, scoring 15 goals.

DUCKHOUSE, Edward ('Ted')
Full-back/centre-half; Apps 139, Goals 4.
Born: Shelfield, Walsall, 9 April 1918. Died: Walsall, 1980.
Career: St Mark's School, Shelfield,

Walsall Wood, Cannock Chase Colliery, Streetly Works, West Bromwich Albion (amateur 1937), BLUES (amateur July 1938, professional August 1938), Northampton Town (August 1950), Rushden Town (July 1952). Retired 1955.
Club honours: Blues: Football League South champions 1946, Division Two champions 1948.
Duckhouse scored on his debut as a centre-forward but thereafter 'big Ted' was a solid, no-nonsense, rock-hard defender who alas broke his leg in the 1946 FA Cup semi-final replay against Derby County when attempting to prevent the first goal – an incident which had a major effect on the outcome of the game when Blues lost 4-0. He recovered well and went on to add 68 League appearances to his tally with Northampton.

DUNCAN, Charles Stanley
Centre-forward; Apps 24, Goals 9.
Born: Kinross, Scotland, 1889. Died: Scotland.
Career: Dunfermline Athletic, BLUES (April 1913), Clyde (September 1915).
Duncan was a short, bustling type of forward, very quick in the box with an eye for goal. He scored over 50 goals for Blues' Central League championship winning side of 1914-15 but despite this form, appeared in only four senior games that season.

DUNLOP, Thomas
Right-back/right-half; Apps 62, Goals 2.
Born: Annbank, Scotland, 7 May 1872. Died: Scotland.
Career: Port Glasgow (trial), Annbank FC, BLUES (April 1896), Dundee Harp (August 1898).
A solidly built defender with a formidable kick, Dunlop was originally a full-back, who developed into a defensive right-half, although when he did make the occasional foray forward, his long range shooting was most effective.

EDMUNDS, William
Half-back; Apps *, Goals *.

Born: Bordesley Green, 8 September 1854.
Died: Birmingham, 1925.
Career: Bordesley Green Council School, BLUES (1875). Retired 1885.
Blues' first official captain, appointed in 1877, Edmunds played in the club's first-ever game in 1875 and remained with Blues until the mid 1880s. An attacking player he once scored a hat-trick in five minutes – two goals for Blues, the other for the opposition. *He never played a League or Cup game in Blues' colours and became a successful businessman after quitting football.

EDWARDS, Ernest Arthur
Half-back; Apps 17, Goals 0.
Born: Stourbridge, 17 February 1892. Died: Kidderminster.
Career: Old Hill Unity, West Bromwich Albion (amateur), Kidderminster Olympic, Leamington Town, Redditch United (August 1911), BLUES (April 1913-1919), Tipton Excelsior, Merthyr Town (1919), Newport County (August 1919), Southend United (June 1923), Dudley Town (1926). Retired 1932. Guested for Newport County (1915).

An all-purpose half-back capable of occupying any of the three positions, Edwards' chances were limited at St Andrew's but after World War One he became a stalwart in the Newport side.

EDWARDS, George
Outside-left; Apps 97, Goals 9.
Born: Kilgetty, Treherbert, South Wales, 2 December 1920.
Career: Narbeth Grammar School, Swansea Town (amateur May 1938), Coventry City (amateur August 1943), BLUES (professional July 1944), Cardiff City (£12,000 December 1948), Retired 1955-56 and later became director of Cardiff City FC (until 1977).

Club honours: Cardiff City: Welsh Cup runners-up 1951. Blues: Football League South champions 1946, Division Two champions 1948.
Representative honours: Wales: (12 full caps, 1 Amateur cap).
George Edwards was spotted by Coventry whilst playing for RAF Wellesbourne and they switched him from inside-left to the left wing, where he became a star performer. Fast and difficult to dispossess, he was a revelation at St Andrew's, becoming a firm favourite with the fans. He went on to make 194 League appearances for Cardiff (34 goals scored). After hanging up his boots, Edwards became a respected broadcaster and regular contributor to BBC Radio Wales and a Sunday newspaper. He was also a qualified teacher and later held a position with an oil company. He was an MA from Birmingham University, his thesis being entitled A History of the Pembrokeshire Coalfields.

EDWARDS, Harry Ross
Inside-forward; Apps 5, Goals 1.
Born: Coventry 1870. Died: Coventry.
Career: Singers FC, BLUES (May 1892), Ryton Rangers (August 1893), Leicester Fosse (October 1893), Derby County (August 1894), Wolverton, London & North-Western Railway Works (1895), Watford (December 1898), Bedford Queens (1899-1900).
Harry Edwards was a talented youngster who was indirectly responsible for the signing of Frank Mobley, his Singers' team-mate. Alas, Harry found it almost impossible to get a first-team game with Blues, due to the terrific form of Walton and Wheldon, and quickly moved on. He failed to settle in the East Midlands but then found quite a niche for himself in the Southern League where he was converted into an attacking centre-half.

EDWARDS, William H.
Outside-left; Apps 5, Goals 1.
Born: Coventry, February 1874. Died: Coventry.
Career: Singers FC, BLUES (September 1896), Rugby (1897).
The defection of 'Toddy' Hands left a considerable gap in the Blues attack and the inexperienced Bill Edwards was given the first chance to plug it. Enthusiastic, he also proved to be rather limited although it is on record that he had the habit of dragging the ball back with the sole of his foot whenever he received a pass. Younger brother of Harry Edwards.

ELKES, Albert John ('Jack')
Inside-right; Apps 35, Goals 15.
Born: Woodhouse Row, Snedshill, Shropshire, 31 December 1894. Died: Rayleigh, Essex, 22 January 1972.
Career: St George's Amateurs, Wellington Town (1911), Stalybridge Celtic (1914),

Shifnal Town, BLUES (January 1918), Southampton (March 1922), Tottenham Hotspur (£1,050 May 1923), Middlesbrough (August 1929), Watford (August 1933), Stafford Rangers (August 1934), Oakengates Town (1935). Retired 1937, became Ford Motor Works FC coach.
Representative honours: Football League XI, FA tour to Australia 1925.
Former miner Jack Elkes was a tall, long-striding player with surprisingly good, close control for such a big man. Very much a playmaker in his wartime appearances, he found it difficult to get a first-team game once the regular players came back. He appeared in three England trials after impressive displays for both Southampton and Spurs (for whom he made over 200 apps). In later years he switched to centre-half, a more suitable position for one who stood 6ft 2in.

ELLIMAN, Richard
Left-back; Apps 4, Goals 0.
Born: West Bromwich, 1859. Died: Wednesbury.
Career: Christ Church, Sandwell (1880), BLUES (August 1882), Smethwick Highfield (Sept 1886).
Elliman was a steady performer who was first-choice for three years, occasionally appearing as a stand-in forward.

ELLIOTT, Anthony Robert
Goalkeeper; Apps 1, Goals 0.
Born: Nuneaton, 30 November 1969.
Career: Park Hall School, from FA School of Excellence to BLUES (YTS June 1986, professional December 1986), Hereford United (December 1988), Huddersfield Town (July 1992), Carlisle United (June 1993).
Club honours: Carlisle: Auto Windscreens Shield runners-up 1995.
Although highly thought of by the staff at the School of Excellence Elliott had to wait for his Blues debut – and when it came, it turned out to be a nightmare. On a wet, slippery surface, Blues crashed 5-0 to rivals Aston Villa in a League Cup-tie at Villa Park. Two months later he was released by the club.

ELLIS, William Thomas
Outside-left; Apps 36, Goals 8.
Born: Wolverhampton, 5 November 1895. Died: Nottingham, October 1971.
Career: Willenhall Swifts, Hickmans Steel Works, Bilston Juniors, Highfield Villa, Bilston Junior Sunderland (May 1919), BLUES (November 1927), Lincoln City (August 1929), York City (November 1930-January 1931). Retired 1932.
Ellis was Sunderland's regular left winger for five years before his transfer back to the Midlands. He earned the reputation as a fine provider of chances in the North-East but failed to capture his best form at St Andrew's. He scored 31 goals in 202 League and FA Cup games for Sunderland.

EMMANUEL, John Gary
Midfielder; Apps 67+11, Goals 6.
Born: Swansea, 1 February 1954.
Career: Swansea Schools, BLUES (apprentice June 1970, professional July 1971), Bristol Rovers (December 1978), Swindon Town (July 1981), Newport County (July 1984), Bristol City (non-contract July 1985), Swansea City (August 1985), Barry Town, Llanelli, Haverfordwest, retired 1993.
Representative honours: Wales (1 Under-23 cap).
Son of Len Emmanuel, formerly Swansea Town, Gary was a willing worker always striving to be in the thick of the action. Perhaps a shade too slow for the top flight, he later carved out a reasonable career in the lower divisions, making well over 300 League appearances after leaving St Andrew's.

ESTEVES, Rui Manuel Guerreiro Nobre
Midfield; Apps 1, Goals 0.
Born: Lisbon, Portugal, 30 January 1967.
Career: Real Benfica, SC Olhanense, Louletano DC, SC Farense (July 1990), SCU Torriense, Vitória Setúbal, SL Benfica (loan), BLUES (loan March 1995 - April 1995).
Slim, blond midfielder who has had little experience of top-flight Portuguese soccer, having spent most of his career in Division Two. Thrown in at the deep end for his Blues debut in the Auto Windscreens Area Final at Orient he showed a nice touch on the ball but is perhaps lacking a bit in physical strength.

EVANS, Anthony ('Tony')
Inside-forward; Apps 71+5, Goals 33.
Born: Liverpool, 11 January 1954.
Career: Formby FC (1971), Blackpool (professional June 1973), Cardiff City (June 1975), BLUES (June 1979), Crystal Palace (August 1983), Wolverhampton Wanderers (April 1984), Bolton Wanderers (loan February 1985), Exeter City (loan March-April 1985), Swindon Town (August 1985), Walsall (non-contract September 1986), Stafford Rangers (November 1986). Football in the Community Officer at Wolverhampton Wanderers (1993).
Club honours: Cardiff City: Welsh Cup winners 1976.
Tony Evans worked as an electrician in Lancashire before joining Blackpool. He never made his mark at Bloomfield Road but after teaming up with Cardiff he became a useful striker. Lack of control let him down at times but generally speaking he did well, finishing up with a League career of 254 games and 87 goals.

EVANS, Hugh
Inside-forward; Apps 14, Goals 0.
Born: Ynysybwl, Wales, 12 December 1919.
Career: St Stephen's School (Luton), Bedford Town (trial), Redditch United, BLUES (December 1947), Bournemouth & Boscombe Athletic (June 1950), Walsall (August 1951), Watford (August 1952), Bedford Town (1954).
Hugh Evans was brought up in Luton and spotted while serving in the Army, Blues signing him only minutes before a scout from Wolves turned up. He was a trier but certainly not good enough to keep a poor Blues side in the First Division. He scored 22 goals in a total of 73 League games, 12 of them coming in in 33 games for Walsall.

EVANS, Robert Owen
Goalkeeper; Apps 3, Goals 0.
Born: Wrexham, August 1881. Died: Coventry, 8 March 1962.
Career: Olympic Juniors (1895), Stansty Villa, Wrexham (August 1898), Blackburn Rovers (£150 April 1903), Croydon Common (May 1908), Coventry City (April 1909), BLUES (June 1913), Nuneaton (May 1914).
Club honours: Wrexham: Welsh Cup winners 1902, runners-up 1903.
Representative honours: Wales (10 full caps).
A star of the Edwardian era, 'R.O.' brought fulsome praise from one contemporary reporter who described him as '…skilful to a degree, quickness personified and rarely indeed does he misjudge the flight of the ball'. His courage led to sundry injuries throughout his career, most notably a dislocated knee early in a Welsh international match. Despite being in obvious pain he bravely saw the game out. He was in the twilight of his career with Blues. He played cricket for Derbyshire and his younger brother, Crad Evans, played for Plymouth Argyle.

EVANS, Sidney John Vivian Leonard
Goalkeeper; Apps 2, Goals 0.
Born: Cardiff, 20 May 1903. Died:

Bournemouth, 26 December 1977.
*Career: Cardiff Corinthians (1922),
Aberdare Athletic (October 1926), Merthyr
Town (July 1927), Cardiff Corinthians
(October 1927), Lovells Athletic, Barry
Town (1928), Cardiff City (amateur April
1930), BLUES (amateur October 1933,
professional October 1933, assistant
trainer at St Andrew's May 1934),
Svenborg (Sweden), 1935), Blackburn
Rovers (trainer, June 1937-39).*
*Club honours: Lovells Athletic: Welsh Cup
winners 1928.*
*Representative honours: Wales (4 full caps,
12 Amateur caps, Schoolboy caps).*
A Barry policeman, Len Evans followed
Chris Charsley, Tom Watson and Bert
Crossthwaite in the line of constables who
have kept goal for Blues. He was something
of a risk-taker, but none the less, was a
classy and reliable 'keeper. His only
weakness was that he tended at times to be
a bit haphazard when clearing the ball.
Evans was capped whilst a Cardiff reserve
when understudying Irishman Tom
Farquharson. This situation was mirrored at
Blues where he spent his time as number-
two to Harry Hibbs. He later worked as a
PT instructor and athletics coach, and was
also good at swimming, boxing, cricket,
baseball and gymnastics. He sung in a choir
and had ambitions to become a clergyman
but in the end chose the roll-necked
goalkeeping jersey instead of a dog collar.

EVANS, Thomas Eli
Right-half; Apps 6, Goals 0.
*Born: Dudley, February 1896. Died:
Stourbridge.*
*Career: Pensnett School, Great Bridge
Celtic, Tipton Parish Church, Bradley
United, Cradley St Luke's, BLUES
(December 1917), Brighton & Hove Albion
(July 1921), Cradley Heath (June 1922-
May 1927).*
One of a host of players to make their debut
for Blues during World War One, this solid
Black Countryman was unable to hold
down a first-team place in peacetime
football. He stood 5ft 7in tall, and weighed
10st 7lb.

EVERS, Albert
Half-back; Apps 2, Goals 0.
*Born: Birmingham, 1868. Died:
Birmingham.*
*Career: Summerfield Tavern, Royal Oak
Rangers, BLUES (January 1891), Yardley
Victoria (October 1891).*
A sturdy defender, Evers played in most of
Blues' friendly games towards the end of
the 1890-91 season whilst Caesar Jenkyns
was under suspension.

EVETTS, Robert
Full-back; Apps 8, Goals 1.
*Born: King's Heath, Birmingham, 1864.
Died: Birmingham.*
*Career: Stirchley Rangers, St Stephen's
Church FC, BLUES (April 1884), Warwick
County (1887).*
Evetts, who demonstrated an ability to play
on either flank, appeared in Blues' 1886 FA
Cup semi-final side.

EYRE, Edmund ('Ninty')
Outside-left; Apps 82, Goals 16.
*Born: Worksop, 2 December 1882. Died:
c.1943.*
*Career: Worksop West End, Worksop Town,
Rotherham Town, BLUES (March 1907),
Aston Villa (December 1908),
Middlesbrough (April 1911), BLUES (April
1914). Retired May 1919.*
A speedy winger and prolific scorer during
his spells with both Worksop clubs and
Rotherham, Eyre favoured the fast,
whipping low cross and was said to have
possessed a fiery temper.

FAIRMAN, Robert
Full-back/half-back; Apps 39, Goals 1.

*Born: Finchley, London, July 1881. Died:
London.*
*Career: Southampton, BLUES (May 1907),
West Ham United (August 1909), BLUES
(June 1912). Retired April 1917.*
A tall well-built defender who had two
spells with Blues, proving a great favourite
each time. A local reporter claimed, "He
covers his position well and kicks strongly
from all angles," ample qualifications for
any full-back of his era.

FALL, Joseph William
Goalkeeper; Apps 2, Goals 0.
*Born: Miles Platting, Manchester, early
1872. Deceased.*
*Career: Leigh Street FC, Middlesbrough
Ironopolis, Newton Heath (August 1893),
Kettering Town (1894), BLUES (May
1895), Altrincham (August 1896).*
Fall had fallen on hard times when Blues
signed him, initially as third-choice behind
Partridge and Roach. He failed to impress
when given his chance, although he had
been a regular with Newton Heath for a
season.

FARLEY, Walter
Wing-half; Apps 1, Goals 0.
*Born: Selly Oak, Birmingham, 1859. Died:
Birmingham.*
*Career: Harborne, Excelsior, BLUES (July
1885), Stourbridge (1887).*
An experienced player by the time he made
his bow for Blues, he held down place in
first team for three months, playing well in
friendly and local Cup-ties, but then his
form deteriorated.

FARMER, Frederick Brian Webb
Full-back; Apps 145, Goals 0.
*Born: Wordsley, Stourbridge, 29 July 1933.
Career: Stourbridge (1949), BLUES
(amateur July 1950, professional May
1954), Bournemouth & Boscombe Athletic
(January 1962). Retired May 1965.*
*Club honours: Blues: Fairs Cup runners-up
1960, 1961.*

A reliable if unspectacular performer,
capable of filling either full-back berth,
Farmer got his chance following the tragic
death of Jeff Hall and held his place for two
years before the emergence of Winston
Foster, coupled with the signing of Stan
Lynn, led to him being relegated to the
reserves and his ultimate departure. He
played almost 250 games in the Football
League, 117 for Blues.

FARMER, Michael C.
Wing-half; Apps 1, Goals 1.
*Born: Leicester, 22 November 1944.
Career: Leicester Schools, BLUES
(apprentice August 1961, professional April
1962), Lincoln City (May 1965); Skegness*

Town (1966), Arnold Town; Skegness Town;
Grantham (1970), Oadby Town (1973),
Grantham Town (February. 1974).
Farmer was a tall, well-built midfielder
with a powerful shot who scored on his
only outing for Blues but was surprisingly
never chosen again despite the team's
persistent relegation battles.

FARNALL, Thomas ('Tot')
Wing-half; Apps 53, Goals 2.
Born: Gloucester, 1871. Died: Gloucester.
*Career: Eastville Rovers, BLUES (April
1895-May 1897), Eastville Rovers, BLUES
(1899), Watford (August 1900), Bristol
Rovers (July 1901), Watford (1902),
Bradford City (July 1903), Barrow (1906),
Gloucester.*
Tot Farnall was a West Countryman with a
fancy for returning to his old clubs. He was
a strong tackler who enjoyed a long-range
shot at goal.

FARRAGE, Thomas Oliver
Outside-left; Apps 7, Goals 2.
*Born: Chopwell, late 1917. Died: Killed in
action, 1944, whilst a pilot in the Army Air
Corps.*
*Career: Walker Celtic, BLUES (November
1937). Guested for Leeds, Luton and
Middlesbrough in World War Two.*
Farrage was a promising young player with
an eye for goal who was a casualty of
World War Two.

FARRELL, Gregory James Philip
Outside-right; Apps 5, Goals 0.
*Born: Motherwell, 19 March 1944.
Career: St Vincent's School, Saltley Boys,
Small Heath Unity, BLUES (amateur June
1969, apprentice January 1960,
professional March 1961), Cardiff City
(March 1964), Bury (March 1967). Retired
May 1970, later assisted Homecare FC in
the Birmingham mid-week League.*
*Club honours: Cardiff City: Welsh Cup
winners 1964.*
Greg was a clever ball player whose
chances were few and far between at St
Andrew's owing to the form of Hellawell
and Auld. In later years he always played
well against Blues. His brother Joe was on
Blues' books as an amateur.

FAULKNER, Kenneth G.
Forward; Apps 2, Goals 0.
*Born: Smethwick, 10 September 1923.
Career: Schools football, Smethwick
Highfield, BLUES (trial 1943, amateur
August 1946), Oldbury United (August
1947).*
*Representative honours: England (Schools
cap).*
Faulkner, a signing as a trialist from local
junior football, made 15 wartime
appearances for Blues but failed to make a
name for himself after the hostilities.

FELTON, Walter Oscar
Half-back; Apps 7, Goals 1.
*Born: Coventry, 1861. Died: Warwick.
Career: The Grove FC, BLUES (September
1884), Walsall Swifts (1886).*
Felton occupied all three half-back
positions during his three years with Blues
and was a very adaptable player.

FENTON, Ronald
Inside-forward; Apps 31+9, Goals 8.
*Born: South Shields, County Durham, 2
September 1940.
Career: South Shields & District Schools,
Durham Boys, West Bromwich Albion (trial
1955), South Shields, Burnley (junior April
1956, professional September 1957), West
Bromwich Albion (£15,000 November
1962), BLUES (£7,500 January 1965),
Brentford (January 1968), Notts County
(July 1970). Retired May 1971, to become
coach at Meadow Lane, later manager
1975-77, moving as assistant trainer-coach
at Nottingham Forest (October 1977).*

Promoted to assistant manager (under
Brian Clough) in 1987 after ten years'
service with Forest. Resigned May 1993,
when Clough also left. Later became an
England scout.
Ronnie Fenton was a battler, a player who
gave his all. He grafted hard and long but
never really repeated his West Brom
performances whilst with Blues. Fenton
netted 52 goals in 212 senior appearances
as a professional, 18 in 66 games for
Albion. Remarkably, half his goals for
Blues came as a substitute.

FENWICK, Paul Joseph
Defender; Apps 13+11, Goals 0.
*Born: Camden, London, 25 August 1969.
Career: Edmonton Oilers, Hamilton
Steelers, Toronto Blizzard, Winnipeg Fury,
(1991), BLUES (professional November
1992-December 1994).*
*Club honours: Winnipeg Fury: Canadian
League champions 1992.*
*Representative honours: Canada (1 full
cap, 8 appearances in Olympic Games).*
Fenwick was a solid defender who was
introduced to first-team football only a
month after joining Blues from Canadian
soccer.

FERGUSON, Michael John
Centre-forward; Apps 25, Goals 9.
*Born: Newcastle upon Tyne, 3 October
1954.
Career: Coventry City (apprentice June
1970, professional December 1971),
Everton (£280,000, August 1981), BLUES
(loan November 1982, signed £60,000 June
1983), Coventry City (loan March 1984),
Brighton & Hove Albion (£40,000, in deal
involving Mark Jones September 1984),
Colchester United (£5,000 March 1986),
Wealdstone United (1987), Football In
Community Officer at Sunderland (1994).*
Ferguson was a powerfully built striker,
good in the air, who scored a combined
total of 54 goals in 128 League games for
Coventry. He top-scored in first season with
Blues but a series of injuries kept him out of
the side for long periods the following year,
but during his loan spell at Highfield Road
he netted some vital goals which helped
keep the Sky Blues in the old First Division,
paradoxically at Blues' expense.

FERRIS, Raymond O.
Half-back; Apps 106, Goals 4.
*Born: Newry, County Down, 22 September
1920.
Career: Distillery (trial), Glentoran (trial),
Newry Town (trial), Brentford (amateur
1938), Cambridge Town (1939), Tottenham
Hotspur and West Ham United (wartime
guest), Crewe Alexandra (professional
March 1945), BLUES (March 1949),
Worcester City (September 1953). Retired
through injury in 1954.*
*Representative honours: Northern Ireland
(3 full caps), toured Canada with Irish FA
(prior to joining Worcester City).*
An industrious, strong-tackling red-head,
son of Jack Ferris, the former Belfast Celtic
and Irish international, he made over 100
appearances for the Alex before
transferring to Blues. He suffered a leg
injury on tour in Canada which eventually
ended his career.

FIELD, Charles William F. ('Oakey')
Outside-left; Apps 89, Goals 15.
*Born: Hanwell, Yorks, December 1879.
Died: Sheffield.
Career: Hanwell, Royal Ordnance
(Southern League), Brentford (August
1896), Sheffield United (1898), BLUES
(January 1902). Retired May 1906.*
*Club honours: Sheffield United: FA Cup
runners-up 1901.*
*Representative honours: Sheffield XI (v
Glasgow).*
On the slight side, but a player who could
hold his own, Charlie Field was a prolific

scorer in junior football, a record he maintained with Brentford, opening his senior career with a hat-trick from the inside-left position. He registered four hat-tricks and a six-timer in 1897-98, and such was his marksmanship that the bigger clubs flocked to see him in action. It was no surprise when he joined Sheffield United, for whom he starred as an inside-right. He was transferred to Blues with teammate Billy Beer, and later fought a lengthy battle against injury. He impressed observers with his pace and dribbling skills as well as his shooting.

FIGURES, William Horace
Inside-left; Apps 9, Goals 2.
Born: Small Heath, Birmingham, 1862. Died: Birmingham.
Career: St John's United, St Andrew's Rovers, BLUES (April 1885), Great Bridge Unity (December 1887), Cradley Heath Welfare.
Figures joined the club from the Sparkbrook church side St John's and became a fixture in the team at inside-left as Blues raced through to the 1886 FA Cup semi-final. He struck up a fine understanding with Teddy Hill but after Hill departed (through injury in 1887) Figures' form slumped and he went off to try his luck in the Black Country.

FILLINGHAM, Thomas ('Tosher')
Centre-half; Apps 192, Goals 9.
Born: Bulwell, Nottinghamshire, 6 September 1904. Died: Bulwell, 1 May 1960.
Career: Bulwell Wesleyan Mission, Butlers Hill Primitives, Daybrook Baptists, Hucknall Colliery FC, Bromley United, BLUES (professional August 1928), Ipswich Town (June 1938). Guested for Mansfield Town and Nottingham Forest in World War Two, retired 1945.

Given his early chance as a forward (he scored twice on his debut) Fillingham later developed into a linchpin of the Blues' defence. Tall, long-legged and strong in the tackle, he was a versatile performer, particularly good in the air, and was seen as the ideal replacement for 'Lofty' Morrall. He retained his forward's instincts throughout his career and could frequently be seen unleashing shots on the opposition goal. Fillingham became Ipswich Town's captain and starred in their first season of League football. Unfortunately he lost an eye in 1950, as a result of an injury sustained playing for Blues against Spurs in April 1934. A one-time dyehouse worker, he had previously been an employee at Hucknall Colliery. He was an excellent cricketer, especially stylish with the bat, and a pretty useful golfer, striking off with a handicap of 14.

FINNEY, Charles William Thomas
Inside-forward; Apps 17, Goals 1.
Born: Stoke-on-Trent, 5 September 1931.
Career: Stoke-on-Trent Schools football,

Edensor Youth Club, Crewe Alexandra (amateur 1947), Stoke City (professional May 1949), BLUES (November 1955), QPR (May 1957), Crewe Alexandra (July 1958), Rochdale (September 1959), Cheltenham Town (November 1959).
He was a capable schemer who was signed to provide cover for the three inside-forward positions.

FIRTH, Jack
Wing-half/inside-forward; Apps 98, Goals 8.
Born: Doncaster, 8 August 1907. Died: Doncaster, 8 December 1987.
Career: Brodsworth Main Colliery, Doncaster Rovers (amateur), BLUES (amateur March 1926, professional August 1926), Swansea Town (August 1933), Bury (May 1936).
Firth was a burly ex-miner who provided excellent cover for both wing-half and two inside-forward positions during his seven seasons with Blues, being first choice for one campaign when Leslie was injured. He played over 100 games for Swansea and was also a useful cricketer with Brodsworth Main. He stood 5ft 9in tall and weighed 11st.

FIRTH, Robert Edwin
Outside-right; Apps 26, Goals 2.
Born: Sheldon, Birmingham, 20 February 1887. Deceased.
Career: Gower Street School (Aston), 6th Battery Royal Field Artillery, Birmingham Corporation Trams, Golders Green, BLUES (April 1909), Wellington Town (May 1911), Nottingham Forest (September 1911), Port Vale (June 1921), Southend United (July 1922). Retired May 1923.

Firth was working as a tram conductor when Blues signed him as a professional in 1909. Mainly a provider of chances, able to centre accurately on the run, his play was little appreciated at St Andrew's and he left with his pal, Fred Banks, for pastures new. The pair remained together, on opposite wings, for nine years before Banks retired. Firth called it a day at the age of 36.

FITZPATRICK, Paul James
Midfield; Apps 7, Goals 0.
Born: Liverpool, 5 October 1965.
Career: Liverpool (apprentice 1981), Tranmere Rovers (apprentice), Preston North End (trial), Bolton Wanderers (March 1985), Bristol City (August 1986), Carlisle United (October 1988), Preston North End (loan December 1988), Leicester City (July 1991), BLUES (January 1993), Bury (loan March 1993), Hamilton Academical (September 1993), Northampton Town (February 1994), Hong Kong, Rushden Diamonds, Leicester United (until May 1995).
Fitzpatrick made over 200 appearances

during his career (109 in the League for Carlisle) before joining Blues. An enterprising player, he always gave 100 per cent out on the park.

FLETCHER, Thomas Wilberforce
Inside-left; Apps 2, Goals 0.
Born: Wednesfield, 1878. Died: Wolverhampton.
Career: Willenhall, BLUES (1900), Cradley St Luke's (1901), Bellswood Rangers (Wolverhampton) (1903).
Fletcher partnered Bob McRoberts in Blues' attack but failed to impress the selection committee.

FOSTER, Arthur Webster
Inside-left; Apps 2, Goals 0.
Born: Deritend, Birmingham, 12 November 1894. Died: Acocks Green, Birmingham, 9 January 1954.
Career: Repton School, Cambridge University. Old Reptonians, Corinthians (Birmingham), BLUES (amateur September 1913), Acocks Green (April 1914), Army football, Old Reptonians (1919).
Arthur Foster was one of the lesser known members of the famous Birmingham sporting family: his brother F.R. 'Bob' Foster played cricket for Warwickshire and England. Arthur was associated with Blues between coming down from University and signing for the Army. He was described as being 'not used to heavy football', although he did score often for the reserves. He played one match for Warwickshire as a wicketkeeper, taking two catches and scoring one run.

FOSTER, Winston Arthur
Full-back/centre-half; Apps 169+1, Goals 2.
Born: South Yardley, Birmingham, 1 November 1941.
Career: Church Road Junior and Cockshutt Secondary Modern Schools, Birmingham County FA Boys, BLUES (junior June 1955, professional November 1958), Crewe Alexandra (loan March 1969), Plymouth Argyle (June 1969), Chelmsford City (1971), Bromsgrove Rovers (player 1972, assistant manager 1973-74).
Club honours: Blues: Fairs Cup runners-up 1961.
Born during the war, hence his patriotic Christian name, Foster began as a long-legged, awkward looking full-back until injuries to Trevor Smith led him to switching to the centre-half position where he looked far more at ease. He performed credibly in this role until laid up with cartilage trouble.

FOUNTAIN, Edwin Joseph ('Joe')
Inside-forward; Apps 3, Goals 0.
Born: Aston, Birmingham, 1871. Deceased.
Career: Calthorpe FC, Small Heath Langley, BLUES (1895), Birmingham St George's (1895); Worcester Rovers (1896), Hereford Town (October 1897), Heath United.
All-action left-sided player who had to bide his time owing to the form and consistency of Wheldon and Hands, Fountain moved to St George's to help boost the flagging fortunes of the Cape Hill club.

FOX, Matthew Christopher
Centre-back; Apps 13+2, Goals 0.
Born: Sheldon, Birmingham, 13 July 1971.
Career: Heathlands and Byng Kendrick Schools, Birmingham Boys, BLUES (YTS June 1987, professional July 1989), Cheltenham Town (loan October 1991), Northampton Town (March 1993), Shrewsbury Town (trial September 1993), Bridgnorth Town (November 1993).
Dogged defender, hard in the tackle and quick to cover, Fox was forced to miss the entire 1989-90 season through injury. He now works in a city centre sports shop.

FOX, Stephen Douglas
Outside-right; Apps 26+3, Goals 1.
Born: Tamworth, 17 February 1958.
Career: Aston Villa (associate schoolboy), Tamworth, BLUES (apprentice June 1975, professional February 1976), Wrexham (December 1978), Port Vale (October 1982), Chester City (July 1984), Llangollen, Tamworth, Rhyl Athletic, Tamworth (1989).
Club honours: Wrexham: Welsh Cup runners-up 1979.
He was a highly combative winger with plenty of flair but seemingly lacking in ambition and consequently most of his career was spent in the lower divisions. He now works as a debt collector.

FOXALL, Frank
Inside-forward; Apps 22, Goals 3.
Born: Sheffield, 1884. Deceased.
Career: All Saints Sunday School, Roundel FC, Wombwell Town (1901), Doncaster Rovers (1902), Gainsborough Trinity (1903), Sheffield Wednesday (April 1907), BLUES (April 1910), Shrewsbury Town (August 1911).
Club honours: Roundel: Hatchard Cup winners.
Frank Foxall did well with Wednesday (scoring nine goals in 45 games) but then after the Hillsborough club had signed Scottish international George Robertson, he was allowed to move to Blues, who at the time were at their lowest ebb, having had to apply for re-election the previous season. He had spent most of his time on the wing but Blues tried him as an inside-forward, an experiment that failed to succeed, and he was quickly switched back to the wing, before changing clubs again.

FOXALL, Frederick Howard
Outside-left; Apps 28, Goals 4.
Born: Stourbridge, 2 April 1898. Died: Smethwick, 17 June 1926.
Career: Saltwells FC, Aston Villa (professional April 1915), Blackheath Town (1916), Southampton (May 1919), Aston Villa (May 1921), BLUES (March 1922), Watford (July 1923). Retired May 1924 through ill health.
Fred Foxall's transfer to Aston Villa in 1921 was annulled by the FA as Southampton had not been consulted about the deal. This did not upset the player, however, and he continued to render sterling service to the Saints as an out-and-out left winger. His 15 months at St Andrew's (when he teamed up with his old colleague Joe Barratt) were fraught with injury and illness, however, and he was grateful to move to Watford. Younger brother to Arthur Foxall, Fred was forced to quit the professional scene in 1924 and died two years later at the age of only 28.

FOY, David Lee
Midfield; Apps 3+1, Goals 0.
Born: Coventry, 20 October 1972.
Career: Allesley Primary and Coundon Court Secondary Schools, BLUES (trainee 1989, professional July 1991), Cobh Ramblers (loan January 1992), Scunthorpe United (March 1993), Weymouth, Stafford Rangers (October 1993), Tamworth (loan January 1994, full transfer October 1994).
Foy was a strong player, a determined lad, but who alas wasn't quite up to League football.

FRAIN, John William
Midfield/left-back; Apps 295+8, Goals 25.
Born: Yardley, Birmingham, 8 October 1968.
Career: Holy Souls Primary & Archbishop Tisley Schools, Birmingham Boys, BLUES (apprentice June 1984, non-contract forms July 1985, professional October 1986).
Club honours: Blues: Leyland DAF Cup winners 1991.
Frain formed an effective youth team full-

back partnership with Julian Dicks but failed to impress in that position when playing in the League side. Lacking in pace, he was then put into midfield where his distribution skills made him a natural, but eventually settled in again at left-back. Frain made his debut at Newcastle in April 1986, scoring a goal to celebrate the occasion, and was Blues' longest-serving player when the 1994-95 season ended. He was also the club's penalty expert.

FRANCIS, Carlos Everton
Wing-forward; Apps 2+3, Goals 0.
Born: West Ham, London, 21 August 1962.
Career: BLUES (apprentice June 1979, professional August 1980), Hereford United (loan December 1983), Enfield (1984).
The first coloured footballer to play for the club, he was very quick but inconsistent and most of his career with Blues was spent in the reserves. Alas, he could not cope with his rejection and Blues were forced to place a restraining order on him after he refused to stay away from the club's training ground. After this sad time he had an unsuccessful spell with Enfield.

FRANCIS, Kevin Derek Michael
Striker; Apps 18, Goals 9.
Born: Moseley, Birmingham, 6 December 1967.
Career: Holy Family & Waverley Schools, Emerald Social, Redditch United, Mile Oak Rovers, Derby County (free transfer, February 1989), Stockport County (£60,000 February 1991), BLUES (£800,000 January 1995).
Club honours: Stockport County: Division Four promotion 1991, Autoglass Trophy runners-up 1992, 1993. Blues: Second Division champions 1995, Auto

Windscreens Shield winners 1995.
At 6ft 7in the tallest player ever to appear in the Football League, Kevin Francis equalled Blues' record signing when he joined the club in mid-January 1995 after an on-off transfer with Stockport which lasted a month owing to a medical report on Francis' knee injury. Nicknamed the 'Inchman' he scored over 120 goals in some 200 senior games for Stockport. He was a Blues' supporter as a lad and had no hesitation in moving to St Andrew's once he was given a clean medical report. Earlier, Everton had shown an interest in taking him into the FA Premiership but that move came to nothing.

FRANCIS, Sean Robert
Forward; Apps 0+6, Goals 0.
Born: Birmingham, 1 August 1972.
Career: Oratory RC School, BLUES (YTS June 1988, professional July 1990), Cobh Ramblers (loan August 1991); Telford United (July 1992), Worcester City (loan January 1992), Northampton Town (August 1993), Cobh Ramblers (October 1993).
A pale looking youngster, Sean Francis was one of the stars of Blues' youth team in 1990-91 with his intelligent off-the-ball runs which created space for his colleagues.

FRANCIS, Trevor John
Inside-forward; Apps 327+2, Goals 133.
Born: Plymouth, 19 April 1954.
Career: Ernesettle Youth Club, Plymouth Boys, BLUES (apprentice June 1969, professional May 1971), Detroit Express (NASL) (loan May-August 1978), Nottingham Forest (£975,000 February 1979), Detroit Express (NASL) (loan June-August 1979), Manchester City (£1,200,000 September 1981), Sampdoria (£800,000 July 1982), Atlanta (£900,000 July 1986), Glasgow Rangers (free transfer September 1987), QPR (March 1988), appointed player-manager December 1988), Sheffield Wednesday (free transfer February 1990, manager June 1991-May 1995).
Club honours: Blues: Division Two promotion 1972; Nottingham Forest: European Cup winners 1979 (scored winning goal), Football League Cup runners-up 1980; Sampdoria: Italian Cup winners 1985; Rangers: Scottish League Cup winners 1988; Sheffield Wednesday: Football League Cup winners and Division Two promotion 1991.
Representative honours: England (52 full caps, 5 Under-23 caps, Youth caps).
With the VAT and levy included, Trevor

Francis became Britain's first £1 million footballer when he moved to Forest in 1979. He had exploded on to the League scene with 15 goals in his first 21 games for Blues, including four in one match against Bolton in February 1971 when he was still 16. He displayed electrifying speed off the mark, intricate dribbling skills, powerful shot and amazing self-confidence that were

to be his trademarks during a long and successful playing career. His impressive total of goals for Blues would have been even better but for two serious injuries. A further lengthy spell of injury whilst with Forest earned him the quite unjustified accusation of being injury prone, but he made his critics eat their words as he was still playing at the age of 39. Throughout the 1970s it seemed as though Francis alone was keeping Blues in the First Division, but with the team destined for the drop in 1979 he was whisked away by Brian Clough after asking to leave St Andrew's. From there he changed clubs regularly, yet always played at the top level, going on to amass a terrific record of more than 700 appearances (with all clubs) and scoring more than 220 goals. He did not have too good a time in his first spell as manager, with QPR, but with Wednesday he did rather better.

FRASER, Adam
Left-back; Apps 24, Goals 0.
Born: Paisley, Scotland, 1871. Deceased.
Career: Glasgow Nomads, Glasgow Northern, BLUES (November 1895), Heart of Midlothian (1896).
Adam Fraser was much hyped on his arrival when it was claimed that he had been a regular player with Celtic. Alas he proved to be something of a let down when it was found that he had actually appeared in only 16 games in the Scottish Second Division for the little known Northern club. He had a reasonable season with Blues but was unable to get into the Hearts side after leaving Birmingham.

FRASER, John Cameron ('Cammie')
Full-back; Apps 41+1, Goals 0.
Born: Blackford, Perthshire, Scotland, 24 May 1941.
Career: Larbert Schools, Gairloch United, Dunfermline Athletic (August 1958), Aston Villa (October 1962), BLUES (February 1965), Falkirk (June 1966).
Club honours: Dunfermline: Scottish Cup winners 1961; Aston Villa: Football League Cup runners-up 1963.
Representative honours: Scotland (2 Under-23 caps).
Fraser was highly rated in Scotland but seemed little more than an average footballer after moving south. After making 40 appearances in the claret and blue strip he walked out on Villa following a contract dispute and joined his wife in a hairdressing business in London before Blues tempted him back into League action. His initial games came as part of Joe Mallett's defensively-minded 'M' formation that failed to keep Blues in the First Division. He was the son of William Fraser, a former Aldershot and Northampton Town player.

FREEMAN, Neil
Goalkeeper; Apps 33, Goals 0.
Born: Northampton, 14 February 1955.
Career: Northampton Town (apprentice

June 1971), Arsenal (professional June 1972), Grimsby Town (March 1974), Southend United (July 1976), BLUES (July 1978), Walsall (loan August 1980), Huddersfield Town (loan January 1981), Peterborough United (September 1981), Northampton Town (non-contract August 1982). Retired February 1983 to become a police constable.
Neil Freeman was nicknamed 'The Hulk' in the Blues dressing-room. Standing 6ft 2in tall and weighing 14st he possessed the necessary physical attributes for a goalkeeper but lapses of concentration tended to cost the team dearly. As a police officer he later patrolled the perimeter of the Northampton pitch he once played on.

FREEMAN, Walter D.
Inside-forward; Apps 37, Goals 11.
Born: Handsworth, Birmingham, June 1887. Died: Birmingham.
Career: Lowestoft, Aston Villa, Fulham (February 1906), BLUES (September 1909), Walsall (April 1911), Wellington (November 1914), Walsall (January 1915). Retired after World War One.
Club honours: Fulham: Southern League champions 1907.
Lesser known brother of Bert Freeman, the former Everton, Burnley and England centre-forward who guested for Blues during wartime football, Walter was an electrician by trade, He proved to be a good, all-round forward able to dribble and shoot with equal effect.

GADSBY, Walter
Inside-right; Apps 4, Goals 3.
Born: Bromsgrove, 1872. Deceased.
Career: Astwood Bank, Redditch Excelsior, BLUES (April 1896), Watford (1898); Redditch Excelsior.
The press hardly went overboard about this hard-shooting forward. After a match in which he scored twice, had one goal disallowed and made another for his partner, the *Birmingham Gazette* announced that he had made '…a promising debut'. A stalwart of the reserves he found it difficult to get first-team football.

GALLAGHER, Joseph Anthony
Centre-half; Apps 330+5, Goals 23.
Born: Liverpool, 11 January 1955.
Career: Lancashire & Merseyside Schools, BLUES (apprentice June 1970, professional January 1972), Wolverhampton Wanderers (£350,000 August 1981), West Ham United (December 1982), Burnley (August 1983), Halifax Town (loan October 1983), Padiham (loan 1984), Coleshill Town (manager 1989).

Retired and became BLUES' Community Liaison Officer (November 1990); Atherstone United (manager June 1991-February 1992); King's Heath (manager

June 1994, making comeback as player September 1994. Resigned February 1995. Representative honours: England (1 'B' cap).

Joe Gallagher's first outings for Blues were at full-back but a lack of manoeuvrability led him being switched to centre-half. Commanding in the air but a little awkward on the ground, he retained the number-five shirt until 1977 when a broken leg sustained in a car crash led to his absence from the game for the first four months of the 1977-78 season. He returned to action with a goal and retained his place in the side until moving to Molineux in a deal which triggered off some rancour between the clubs as Wolves were wound-up still owing most of the transfer money to Blues. His 'B' cap came in 1980 against Australia at St Andrew's.

GALLIMORE, George Arthur

Outside-left; Apps 120, Goals 1.
Born: East Vale, Longton, Stoke-on-Trent, August 1886. Died: Stoke-on-Trent, 1949.
Career: Ashwood Villa, East Vale, Hanley Swifts, Stoke (May 1903), Sheffield United (1908), BLUES (April 1910), Leek Town (September 1911), Est Vale.
Gallimore was a dribbling winger who was among those brought in to help drag Blues up from the bottom of the League in 1910. He lost his first-team place soon after Christmas and rarely looked liked regaining it.

GARD, Alfred

Outside-right; Apps 3, Goals 0.
Born: Reading, 1876. Deceased.
Career: Trowbridge Town (1898), BLUES (July 1900), Maidenhead (August 1901).
Gard was an inexperienced winger whose only season with Blues coincided with one of Billy Bennett's relatively injury-free years. He deputised for Bennett when required but did not impress.

GARDNER, Albert Edward

Wing-half; Apps 120, Goals 4.
Born: King's Heath, Birmingham, April 1887. Died: Birmingham April 1923.
Career: BSA Sports, BLUES (August 1908), King's Heath (loan 1914). Retired 1920.
Albert Gardner, who was profoundly deaf, was discovered playing in the Birmingham Works League. He was a real battler, long on work-rate but short on subtlety. He also had a hard shot but, alas, was rarely on target. He was known as 'The Silent Knight'.

GARDNER, Arthur Edwin

Inside-forward; Apps 19, Goals 11.
Born: West Smethwick, 1878. Deceased.
Career: Smethwick Hall, BLUES (August 1898), Oldbury Town (May 1899), Oldbury Broadwell (1901).
Arthur Gardner was a young forward who had a successful season in Blues' prolific attack of 1898-99 but who fell from grace when Walter Wigmore was signed.

GARRETT, Archibald Campbell E.

Inside-forward; Apps 18, Goals 6.
Born: Lesmahagow, Scotland, 17 June 1919. Died: Bristol, 1994.
Career: Larkhall Saints, Airdrieonians (1935), Preston North End (July 1936), Heart of Midlothian (December 1938), Northampton Town (September 1946), BLUES (November 1947), Northampton Town (December 1948), Wisbech Town (May 1951), Holbeach United (1953). Guested for Northampton and Bristol City in World War Two.
A highly talented and beautifully built goalscorer, son of Archie Garrett, Archie junior played a useful part in Blues' post-war promotion-winning side, his appearances being limited by manager Harry Storer's belief in fielding a settled side. He worked for the GPO in Bristol in the 1960s.

GARTON, William Francis

Centre-half; Apps 5, Goals 0.
Born: Salford, 15 March 1965.
Career: Salford Schools, Manchester United (apprentice June 1981, professional March 1983), BLUES (loan March 1986). Retired May 1990. Made comeback with Salford City (player-manager July 1993); Witton Albion (1993), Hyde United (1994).
Billy Garton came to St Andrew's to gain League experience, but when Blues asked to sign him permanently, Manchester United were not interested. Injuries and illness led to an early retirement.

GAYLE, Howard A.

Outside-right; Apps 58+1, Goals 11.
Born: Liverpool, 18 May 1958.
Career: Liverpool (apprentice June 1974, professional November 1977), Fulham (loan January 1980), Newcastle United (loan November 1982), BLUES (loan January 1983, signed permanently June 1983), Sunderland (£75,000 August 1984), Dallas Sidekicks (NASL) (summer 1986), Stoke City (£125,000 March 1987), Blackburn Rovers (£5,000 August 1987); Halifax Town (July 1992), Accrington Stanley (cs 1993).
Club honours: Sunderland: Milk Cup runners-up 1985.
Representative honours: England (3 Under-21 caps).
Howard Gayle was ready to sign for Newcastle when Blues stepped in, but he proved something of an enigma at St Andrew's. On his day he was fast, aggressive and a potential match-winner, but sometimes he looked sluggish and disinterested. He was transferred to Sunderland after an off-field misdemeanour and topped 200 League appearances before dropping into non-League football.

GAYLE, John

Striker; Apps 49+6, Goals 14.
Born: Turves Green, Birmingham, 30 July 1964.
Career: Turves Green Boys' School, Highgate United, Mile Oak Rovers, Tamworth, Bromsgrove Rovers, Burton Albion (1987), Wimbledon (March 1989), BLUES (November 1990); Walsall (loan August 1993), Coventry City (September 1993), Burnley (September 1994), Stoke City (£70,000 January 1995).
Club honours: Blues: Leyland DAF Cup winners 1991.
John Gayle was a powerfully built striker who had been around the Midlands' non-

League scene before surprisingly linking up with Wimbledon. His time at Plough Lane was acrimonious, culminating in a club suspension following a training ground confrontation with skipper Keith Curle. He struggled to win over the fans at St

Andrew's but his two goals at Wembley earned him the Man of the Match award as Blues carried off the 1991 Leyland DAF Cup.

GEDDIS, David

Striker; Apps 53+3, Goals 21.
Born: Carlisle, 12 March 1958.
Career: Ipswich Town (apprentice June 1973, professional August 1975), Luton Town (loan February 1977), Aston Villa (£300,000 September 1979), Luton Town (loan December 1982), Barnsley (£50,000 September 1983), BLUES (£50,000 December 1984), Brentford (loan November 1986), Shrewsbury Town (£25,000 February 1987), Swindon Town (£25,000 October 1988), Darlington (free transfer March 1990), Football in the Community Officer at Middlesbrough (1993).
Club honours: Ipswich Town: FA Cup winners 1978, FA Youth Cup winners 1975.
Representative honours: England (1 'B' cap, 2 Youth caps).
Dave Geddis sprang to prominence after a fine display in the 1978 FA Cup Final but the predicted rosy future never materialised and he spent most of the 1978-79 season on the subs' bench. He did not really hit it off with Villa yet did well with both Barnsley (24 goals in 50 games) and Blues. After leaving St Andrew's, however, his career went downhill although he did help Darlington regain their Football League status by scoring three goals in nine games during the run-in of the Quakers' GM Vauxhall Conference winning campaign of 1989-90. Geddis was a strong, determined player with good shot.

GEMMILL, Archibald ('Archie')

Midfield; Apps 115, Goals 14.
Born: Paisley, Scotland, 24 March 1947.
Career: Drumchapel Amateurs, St Mirren (1964), Preston North End (£13,000 May 1967), Derby County (£66,000 September 1970), Nottingham Forest (September 1977), BLUES (£150,000 August 1979), Jacksonville Tea Men (March-August 1982), Wigan Athletic (September 1982), Derby County (November 1982-May 1984), Nottingham Forest (coach August 1985-

May 1994), Rotherham United (manager September 1994).
Club honours: Derby County: Division One champions 1972, 1975; Nottingham Forest: Division One champions 1978, Football

League Cup winners 1979, European Cup winners 1979; Blues: Division Two promotion 1980.
Representative honours: Scotland (43 full caps, 1 Under-23 cap).
Despite standing only 5ft 5in tall, Archie Gemmill was an all-action, dynamic, aggressive midfielder who amassed more than 650 League appearances (324 in two spells with Derby) in a marvellous career which spanned 20 years. He did a terrific job with Blues, helping the club regain its First Division status. Gemmill was the first substitute to be used in the Scottish League (St Mirren v Clyde in August 1966). After nine years at Forest as coach he managed Rotherham United when his first game in charge was against Blues.

GEORGE, William

Goalkeeper; Apps 1, Goals 0.
Born: Shrewsbury, 29 June 1874. Died: Birmingham, 4 December 1933.
Career: Woolwich Ramblers (1894), Royal Ordnance & Royal Artillery Plumstead (February 1895), Trowbridge Town (during service with Army), Aston Villa (£50 professional October 1897). Retired and became BLUES trainer (July 1911). After leaving game he worked at the Austin Rover Plant at Longbridge, Birmingham. He played cricket for Warwickshire (1901 & 1902, and 1907), and also served Wiltshire and Shropshire.
Club honours: Aston Villa: Division One champions 1899, 1900, FA Cup winners 1905.
Representative honours: England (3 full caps); Football League XI.
Billy George was a grand servant to Villa whom he served for 14 seasons, accumulating a total of 399 senior appearances. A real heavyweight, he was rather out of condition when called up by Blues during an injury crisis for his only game for the club. He stood almost 6ft 2in tall and tipped the scales at 16st.

GESSEY, Samuel ('Father Sam')

Full-back/centre-half; Apps 4, Goals 0.
Born: Fordhouses, Wolverhampton, February 1858. Deceased.
Career: Wighwick School, Wolverhampton St Luke's, BLUES (September 1877), Willenhall (August 1884). Became director of Small Heath Athletics Club.
Gessey joined Blues on their move to Muntz Street – he owned the land on which the ground was built. He formed a solid full-back partnership with George Edden, Larry Summers and eventually his brother George. He moved to centre-half which he took as a license to roam – and could often be seen chasing the ball all over the pitch. He became part of Small Heath folklore, so much so that a local newspaper referred to him by his nickname in its team-sheets. Gessey was a end batsman and occasional bowler for the Small Heath Alliance cricket team.

GETGOOD, George ('Goodman')

Wing-half; Apps 10, Goals 0.
Born: Coylton, Ayrshire, 15 November 1892. Died: Kidderminster, 22 July 1970.
Career: Ayr United (1912), Reading (July 1914), BLUES (August 1921), Southampton (February 1922), Wolverhampton Wanderers (January 1923), Kidderminster Harriers (March 1925), Aberdare Athletic (July 1926), Shrewsbury Town (November 1926), Bathgate (1927), Bo'ness FC (1928), Nuneaton Town (February 1929), Midland Red Sports (August 1931); Guested for Ayr United (August 1915).
Club honours: Wolves: Division Three North winners 1925.
Getgood was a burly, balding strong-tackling player who was signed to strengthen the team after promotion to Division One, but failed to settle. He made 59 appearances for Wolves whom

he skippered during their Third Division championship-winning season of 1923-24. Later he became a bus conductor and also worked as a porter in Worcester. He stood a shade over 5ft 8in tall and weighed 11st 2lb. Getgood changed his name from Goodman.

GIBSON, Richard Samuel
Outside-right; Apps 120, Goals 19.
Born: Holborn, London, February 1889. Deceased.
Career: Sultan FC, BLUES (September 1911), Manchester United (June 1921-May 1922). Guested for Leicester Fosse in World War One.
Gibson was a diminutive flying winger

with the tendency to overdo the fancy stuff. He played initially as an inside-forward but after switching to the wing he showed great ability, although he had a fiery temper and his longest lasting contribution to the club was to recommend his former junior club colleague, Percy Barton, to St Andrew's.

GILDEA, William Franklyn
Centre-half; Apps 20, Goals 1.
Born: Broxburn, Scotland, 1885. Died: Scotland.
Career: Falkirk (1909), Bradford City (February 1911), BLUES (September 1911), Belfast Celtic (January 1912).
Club honours: Bradford City: FA Cup runners-up 1911 (first game).
A swarthy Scot, Gildea made a rapid rise to fame, appearing in an FA Cup Final after only nine games for Bradford. He was not a success, and was dropped for the replay which City won. He never played for the Yorkshire club again and was not a success with Blues either.

GITTINS, Walter
Full-back; Apps 5, Goals 0.
Born: Aston, Birmingham, 1865. Died: Birmingham.
Career: Lozells Sports Club, BLUES (August 1889), Stafford Rangers (September 1890).
Gittins was a chunky defender with a powerful kick who joined Blues for their first season in the Football Alliance.

GIVENS, Daniel Joseph ('Don')
Forward; Apps 53+11, Goals 10.
Born: Limerick, 9 August 1949.
Career: Dublin Rangers (1964), Manchester United (apprentice June 1965, professional December 1966), Luton Town (April 1970), QPR (£40,000 July 1972), BLUES (£165,000 August 1978), AFC Bournemouth (loan March-April 1980), Sheffield United (March 1981), Neuchâtel Xamax, Switzerland (June 1981). Retired May 1987. Neuchâtel Xamax (youth coach

June 1993, manager November 1993. Now assistant manager).
Club honours: Neuchâtel Xamax: Swiss League champions 1987.
Representative honours: Republic of Ireland (56 full caps).

Don Givens, the son of a champion hurdler, followed the well-trodden path from Ireland to Old Trafford. He suffered badly from home sickness early on but decided to stay in England where he developed into a fine goalscorer, going on to partner Malcolm Macdonald at Luton Town. He won his first cap for the Republic of Ireland (against Denmark in May 1969), whilst still a member of Manchester United's reserve side and did not make his League debut until three months later. It was the first of 408 in the competition (113 goals scored, 76 of them coming in 242 games for QPR). With his very last kick in the Football League – for Sheffield United against Walsall in May 1981 – he missed a penalty which sent the Blades down to the Fourth Division. He was plagued by hip injuries whilst with Blues and it was an arthritic hip which eventually led to his retirement. He scored 19 goals in his 56 full internationals.

GLEGHORN, Nigel William
Midfield; Apps 176, Goals 42.
Born: Seaham, 12 August 1962.
Career: Deneside Junior and Northlea Senior Schools, Seaham Red Star (1977), Ipswich Town (professional August 1985), Manchester City (£47,500 August 1988), BLUES (£175,000 September 1989); Stoke City (October 1992).
Club honours: Blues: Leyland DAF Cup winners 1991. Stoke City: Division Two champions 1993.

Former fireman, Nigel Gleghorn entered League football late, not signing professional forms until he was 23. Surprisingly delicate of touch for such a big man, he possess a powerful left-foot shot

and his unusual surname has led to him being one of the most misspelt of all League players.

GLOVER, John William
Right-back; Apps 124, Goals 2.
Born: West Bromwich, 28 October 1876. Died: Dudley, 20 April 1955.
Career: Christ Church School, West Bromwich Unity, Great Bridge Unity, Halesowen, Rudge-Whitworth FC, West Bromwich Albion (reserves), Blackburn Rovers (May 1897), New Brompton (£100 1899), Liverpool (£350 October 1900), BLUES (£250 January 1904), Brierley Hill Alliance (August 1908). Retired 1910.
Club honours: Liverpool: Division One champions 1901.
Representative honours: Football League XI.
Glover was on the small side for a full-back of his era, and in his younger days was frequently brushed aside by bigger opponents. However, later on he developed into a strong tackler and appeared in international trials for England. He formed a wonderful partnership at Blues with Frank Stokes. On retiring he kept a pub in Brierley Hill and he also represented Shropshire at bowls.

GODDEN, Anthony Leonard
Goalkeeper; Apps 37, Goals 0.
Born: Gillingham, Kent, 2 August 1955.
Career: Napier Secondary Modern School Gillingham, Leonard Star FC, Eastcourt United, Gillingham & District Schools, Gillingham (amateur August 1969), Ashford Town (September 1971), Wolverhampton Wanderers (trial July 1974), West Bromwich Albion (£5,000 August 1975), Preston North End (loan September 1976), Walsall (two loan spells in season 1983-84 – October-December and March-April), Chelsea (loan March 1986, signing permanently May 1986),

BLUES (£35,000 August 1987), Bury (loan December 1988), Sheffield Wednesday (loan March-April 1989), Peterborough United (August 1989), Wivenhoe Town (July 1990), Colchester United (loan March 1991), Warboys Town (manager, August 1991), March Town (manager cs 1993), King's Lynn (coach December 1993, manager February 1994).
Tony Godden was an experienced goalkeeper when he joined Blues, having played 329 games for West Brom. Although he had good reflexes and was a superb shot-stopper he was perhaps a shade suspect when going for high crosses, and during his spell with Blues his performances were sprinkled with errors. He holds West Brom's record of 228 consecutive first-team appearances (to October 1981). He had an indifferent time at Stamford Bridge.

GODFREY, Joseph ('Joby')
Centre-forward; Apps 3, Goals 1.
Born: Walesford, Sheffield, September 1894. Died: Yorkshire.
Career: Kiveton Park, Brighton FC (Sheffield), Nottingham Forest (1916), BLUES (April 1918), Coventry City (October 1919), Manchester United (November 1919), Merthyr Town (May 1920), Rotherham Town (August 1921), Denaby United (March 1922), Beighton Recreational, Mexborough Town, Denaby United (April 1925).
Godfrey was a former miner who leapt to prominence during World War One when he scored a hatful of goals. With the return of first-class football he found things much more difficult, flitting from club to club with alarming speed before returning to a Yorkshire coal-mine. His brother Bruce, a goalkeeper, played several wartime games for Blues.

GOLDIE, Archibald
Right-back; Apps 79, Goals 0.
Born: Hurlford, 5 January 1874. Died: Bordesley Green, 2 April 1953.
Career: Clyde, Liverpool (June 1895), Bootle, New Brighton Tower (August 1900), BLUES (April 1901), Crewe Alexandra (September 1904).
Club honours: Liverpool: Division Two champions 1896.
Unusual amongst Edwardian defenders in that he preferred to pass the ball to his half-backs rather than hoof it upfield, Archie Goldie was a regular in the Liverpool side for five seasons, making 125 League appearances. He teamed up well with the more rumbustious Arthur Archer for two seasons with Blues. After retiring he settled in Birmingham to work at the BSA factory. Brothers William and John were also professional footballers.

GOOCH, Percival George ('Putt')
Centre-forward; Apps 4, Goals 1.
Born: Lowestoft, 1 September 1882. Died: Lothingland, 22 June 1956.
Career: Leiston Road School, Lowestoft Fearnought (1896), Kirkley Juniors, Lowestoft Harriers, Lowestoft IOGT, Lowestoft Town (November 1901), Norwich City (amateur July 1903, professional September 1905), BLUES (March 1907), Notts County (March 1908), Norwich City (August 1909) Lowestoft Town (trainer).
Representative honours: Norfolk County.
Gooch was a tall, impressively moustachio'd forward who was a big favourite in East Anglian football before his transfer to Blues. But he found it difficult to adjust to the higher grade and quickly returned home. His nickname came about from his habit of telling his team-mates to 'put(t)' the ball in front of him when he wanted a pass.

GOOD, Michael
Inside-right; Apps 16, Goals 1.
Born: Airdrie Hill, Scotland, July 1875. Died: Scotland.
Career: Airdrieonians, BLUES (1896), Watford (1898), Bristol City (cs 1902), Reading (1903), Brighton (1904).
A typical Blues forward of the 19th century, Good was short and stocky, although he displayed a fair degree of adaptability, turning out in most forward positions and in the half-back line. He was looked upon primarily as cover for the first team whilst at Blues.

GOODE, Terence Joseph
Winger; Apps 0+2, Goals 0.
Born: Islington, London, 29 October 1961.
Career: Islington & North London Schools, BLUES (apprentice June 1977, professional September 1979), Kettering Town (August 1982).
Blues were already doomed to relegation when this speedy winger was given his

League baptism. The signing of the two Dutchmen – Van Mierlo and Brocken – resulted in Goode leaving St Andrew's. He is a nephew of Charlie George, the former Arsenal, Derby and Southampton striker.

GOODWIN, John ('Jack') William
Outside-right; Apps 33, Goals 8.
Born: Worcester, 29 September 1920. Died: Worcester, 7 May 1995.
Career: Worcester City (1935), BLUES (May 1946), Brentford (April 1949), Dartford (May 1954). Brentford (trainer-coach 1957-63).
Goodwin joined Blues on being demobbed from the Army. A sturdily built player, he was a bustler rather than being tricky and after leaving St Andrew's he scored 22 goals in 131 League games for Brentford before returning to his former club. He represented the Army during World War Two. In 1967 he became chief organiser for the Police Sports Department and toured America coaching soccer. He later worked for Thames Gas.

GORDON, Colin Kenneth
Striker; Apps 22+8, Goals 3.
Born: Stourbridge, 17 January 1963.
Career: Lye Town, Oldbury United, Swindon Town (professional October 1984), Wimbledon (£80,000 July 1986), Gillingham (loan, February 1987), Reading (£80,000 July 1987), Bristol City (loan March 1983), Fulham (£90,000 October 1988), BLUES (£80,000 June 1989), Hereford United (loan September-October 1990), Walsall (loan December-January 1990-91), Bristol Rovers (loan February-March 1991), Leicester City (£100,000 July 1991), Sixes Sports Club (manager 1992).
Gordon was a well-travelled forward who was bought to provide some much needed height to the Blues attack. He struggled with a series of injuries in his first season at St Andrew's and then fell out of favour with manager Dave Mackay when he missed training to take his wife for a medical check-up. Despite both parties declaring that the player would never turn out for Blues again, he was soon to return to the first team. He was the recipient of one of the most unusual injuries ever to strike a Blues player when, in 1989, he missed several matches due to blood poisoning, contracted when a Swansea City player accidentally bit into his arm.

GORDON, John Duncan Sinclair
Inside-forward; Apps 115, Goals 40.
Born: Portsmouth, 11 September 1931.
Career: Portsmouth Civil Service, Hillside Youth Club, Portsmouth (junior July 1947, professional January 1949), BLUES (£10,000 September 1958), Portsmouth (£7,500 March 1961). Retired 1967.
Club honours: Blues: Fairs Cup runners-up 1960; Portsmouth: Division Three

champions 1962.
Gordon was an all-action forward who was very much the Portsmouth fans' favourite, scoring 105 goals in 443 League games for Pompey in two excellent spells at Fratton Park. He netted on his debut for Blues and continued to be a regular marksman for the club, but the lure of his home-town team proved too strong and he duly returned to Portsmouth.

GORMAN, Paul Anthony
Midfield; Apps 7, Goals 0.
Born: Dublin, Ireland, 6 August 1963.
Career: Crumlin Secondary School, Arsenal (apprentice June 1979, professional October 1980), BLUES (June 1984), Carlisle United (£10,000 March 1985), Shrewsbury Town (loan November 1989, signing permanently for £20,000 December 1989), Carlisle United (December 1991), Peterborough United (trial March 1992), Gretna.
Representative honours: Republic of Ireland (1 Under-21 cap, Schoolboy and Youth caps).
Gorman, a successful junior player in Ireland, was spotted by Arsenal's scout in Dublin. His appearances for the Gunners were few and far between and it was little surprise when he was released. Although highly rated by his Blues colleagues, he found it difficult to fit into the team pattern, chiefly because his play was not suited to the long-ball game employed at the time.

GOSNEY, Andrew R.
Goalkeeper; Apps 24, Goals 0.
Born: Southampton, 8 November 1963.
Career: Portsmouth (apprentice 1979, professional November 1981), York City (loan, October 1991), BLUES (£35,000 August 1992). Exeter City (September 1993).
Representative honours: England (5 Youth caps).
Due to the consistency of Alan Knight, Gosney made only 60 appearances in 13 years at Fratton Park. A competent goalkeeper, he would have surely held down a regular first-team place with another club, had he chosen to leave Pompey earlier.

GOVAN, Alexander
Outside-left; Apps 187, Goals 60.
Born: Glasgow, 16 June 1929.
Career: Bridgeton Boys Club, Plymouth

Argyle (juniors June 1944, professional September 1946), BLUES (£6,500 June 1953), Portsmouth (March 1958), Plymouth Argyle (September 1958). Retired 1960.
Club honours: Plymouth Argyle: Division Three South champions 1952, Division Three champions 1959; Blues: Division Two champions 1955, FA Cup runners-up 1956.

Alex Govan was a rattling good left winger, industrious, fast and tricky, and a consistent scorer especially during his first spell with Argyle (30 goals in 117 appearances). His scoring prowess blossomed at St Andrew's, particularly in 1956-57 when he claimed 30 goals in all competitions, the last Blues player to reach this total in a season. His haul included five hat-tricks (three in four games) which was a club record for a winger. His wing play was based upon speed and his preferred manner of taking on an opponent was to push the ball past him and then beat him by sheer speed.

GRAHAM, Harry
Inside-forward; Apps 12, Goals 4.
Born: Edinburgh, 16 December 1887. Died: Scotland.
Career: Granton Oak Vale, St Bernard's (November 1908), Bradford City (April 1910), BLUES (October 1911), Raith Rovers (September 1912), Heart of Midlothian (June 1913), Leicester City (December 1920), St Bernard's (November 1924), Reading (July 1925).
Club honours: Raith Rovers: Scottish FA Cup runners-up 1913.
Representative honours: Scottish League XI.
A qualified dentist whose pre-World War One stay in English soccer was far from successful, Graham was principally a schemer, one of many forwards tried out in the dreadful Blues team of 1911-12. His transfer back to Scotland was held up when St Bernard's claimed that Raith should pay them a fee as they held his Scottish registration. The situation was eventually resolved in Raith's favour. He came back to England later and had four excellent years with Leicester, for whom he scored 16 goals in more than 100 games.

GREEN, Arthur
Right-back; Apps 1, Goals 0.
Born: Grantham, Lincolnshire, 1885. Died: Lincoln.
Career: Seaton Main, Mansfield Town, BLUES (July 1911), Lincoln City (1912), Grantham Town.
Green was a reserve defender whose only appearance for Blues (against Gainsborough Trinity in October 1911) drew the comment that he was 'not strong enough or fast enough for League football'.

GREEN, Benjamin Haigh
Inside-forward; Apps 198, Goals 46.
Born: Penistone, 23 February 1883. Died: Yorkshire.
Career: Oxspring Board School, Penistone Rising Star, Penistone FC, Barnsley (August 1901), BLUES (October 1903), Burnley (May 1909), Preston North End (August 1911), Blackpool (December 1913). Retired during World War One.
A chunky little 'bag of tricks', Green had the distinction of scoring the first goal at St Andrew's, a feat for which he was awarded a piano. In netting that goal (against Preston in December 1905), 'Benny' threw himself headlong at the ball and ended up in a pile of snow behind the goal. He was a consistent marksman throughout his career but had the reputation of being a trouble-maker.

GREEN, Colin Robert
Full-back; Apps 217, Goals 1.
Born: Brynteg, near Wrexham, 10 February 1942.
Career: Wrexham Boys, Everton (amateur July 1957, professional February 1959), BLUES (£12,000 December 1962), Wrexham (loan, January 1971), Tamworth (May 1971), Rhyl FC. On retiring in May 1976, he went into a garage business, and later became a sales representative for a veterinary medicine company.
Club honours: Blues: Football League Cup winners 1963.

Representative honours: Wales (15 full caps, 7 Under-23 caps).
Green made his League debut as a teenager facing Stanley Matthews. He was a barrel-chested defender, speedy on the overlap and particularly quick to recover. His career was hampered by a broken leg, sustained against Bristol City in November 1965. He regained fitness quite quickly and immediately won back his international place. His senior career was eventually ended by a mysterious chest virus which kept him out of League football for two years before his eventual departure from the game. He now lives in Wrexham.

GREEN, Kenneth ('Slasher')
Full-back; Apps 443, Goals 2.
Born: West Ham, London, 27 April 1924.
Career: Millwall (amateur 1940), BLUES (professional November 1943). Retired April 1959. Later ran a sub-post office in Handsworth.
Club honours: Blues: Division Two champions 1948, 1955, FA Cup runners-up 1956.
Representative honours: England (2 'B' caps); Football League XI (2).

One of the most durable of all Blues players, this canny full-back shared in most of the club's triumphs of the post-war period. He joined the St Andrew's staff whilst stationed at Droitwich in the Army, having written in for a trial. He impressed the club's officials so much that he was signed immediately in, of all places, the dressing-room at Villa Park. He was then posted overseas, not returning until 1947 when he was drafted into the Blues' team at right-back. Green held that position for five years until the emergence of Jeff Hall led to him switching over to the left flank, a position he filled to equal effect.

GREEN, Walter Maurice
Forward; Apps 2, Goals 0.
Born: Bordesley Green, Birmingham, 1860. Died: Birmingham.
Career: Coventry Road Congregational Church, BLUES (September 1882), Nichells (November 1883).
Captain of Blues' reserve team, Walter Green had a three-month spell in the first team during 1882-83. He made his debut for the club in an 18-1 win over Elwells of Wednesbury, a match in which Blues had only ten men for all but the first 30 minutes.

GREENHOFF, James
Inside-forward; Apps 36, Goals 15.
Born: Barnsley, 19 June 1946.
Career: Barnsley Schools (English Schools Trophy winners 1961), Yorkshire Boys, Leeds United (apprentice June 1961,

professional August 1963), BLUES (£70,000 August 1968), Stoke City (£100,000 August 1969), Manchester United (£120,000 November 1976), Crewe Alexandra (December 1980, first as player then as player-manager), Toronto Blizzard (NASL) (1981 player-coach), Port Vale (August 1981), Rochdale (player-manager March 1983), Port Vale (player-manager March 1984, later coach at Vale Park). Retired 1985 to concentrate on coaching youngsters at holiday camps which he combined with insurance broking.
Club honours: Leeds United: Fairs Cup runners-up 1967, winners 1968, Football League Cup winners 1968; Stoke City: Football League Cup winners 1972; Manchester United: FA Cup winners 1977, runners-up 1979.
Representative honours: England (5 Under-23 caps); Football League XI.

Jimmy Greenhoff could not command a regular first-team place with Leeds and was signed by Blues' manager Stan Cullis in the middle of the two-legged Fairs Cup Final against Ferencváros, having appeared in the first game. A high quality forward, he scored on his debut for Blues and went on to claim 11 goals in his first ten outings for the club, including a four-timer against Fulham in October 1968, when he also missed a penalty. Very fast, and surprisingly good in the air, Greenhoff soon made it apparent that Blues would be unable to retain his services and after joining Stoke he became one of the most consistent forwards in the Football League. He scored the winning goal for Manchester United in the 1977 FA Cup Final when Lou Macari's shot deflected off him into the net. Greenhoff hit 97 goals in 338 games for Stoke and 36 in 122 outings for United. Brother of Brian (they played together at Old Trafford), Jimmy scored the 'Goal of the Season' for Stoke against Blues at St Andrew's shortly after he left for the Victoria Ground!

GREER, Thomas Gershom
Centre-forward; Apps 2, Goals 0.
Born: Bathgate, Scotland, 1889. Died: Scotland.
Career: Coatbridge Rob Roy, BLUES (December 1910), Reading (August 1912), Swansea Town (August 1913).
Greer was regarded by the local press as rather too lightweight to lead the attack, and after an undistinguished season at Reading he moved to Wales where he achieved the distinction of scoring Swansea Town's first-ever hat-trick.

GREGG, Robert Edmund
Inside-forward; Apps 75, Goals 15.
Born: Ferryhill, Co Durham, 4 February 1904. Deceased.

Career: Ferryhill Athletic, Winlaton Juniors, Spennymoor United, Chilton Colliery, Durham City, Ferryhill Athletic (cs 1926), Darlington (September 1926), Sheffield Wednesday (May 1928), BLUES (£2,200 January 1931), Chelsea (£1,500 September 1933), Boston United (May 1938), Sligo Rovers (1940-44). Retired May 1944.
Club honours: Sheffield Wednesday: Division One champions 1929; Blues: FA Cup runners-up 1931.
After four seasons in the lower reaches, Bob Gregg was signed by Wednesday in time to play a significant part in helping the Owls win the League title in 1929. However, the following year Wednesday bought in the prolific Harry Burgess and Gregg found himself on the side-lines. He stayed at Hillsborough for another two seasons before joining Blues just prior to their FA Cup run. Best remembered by old Blues fans as the man who 'scored' that controversial 'offside goal' at Wembley in 1931. He struggled a lot with injuries whilst at St Andrew's, and was described as being a tricky forward but with the tendency to 'overdo the clever stuff'.

GROSVENOR, Arthur Thomas
Inside-right/wing-half; Apps 115, Goals 18.
Born: Netherton, near Dudley, 22 November 1908. Died: 31 October 1972.
Career: Northfield Road School, Tippity Green Victoria, Vono Works FC, Stourbridge, BLUES (amateur March 1928, professional September 1928), Sheffield Wednesday (February 1936), Bolton Wanderers (May 1937), Dudley Town. Retired 1943.
Representative honours: England (3 full caps); Football League XI (1).
This lanky Black Country man, who was likened to Charlie Buchan, was a brilliant ball-player, being more of a creator of chances than an out-and-out goalscorer. His career was hampered by a series of injuries including two broken legs but he was particularly adept at controlling high balls with his feet. He played only 75 more games after leaving Blues and later worked as a sheet metal worker in Smethwick. He also kept racing pigeons and grew prize-winning tomatoes in his spare time. His brother, Percy, played for West Bromwich Albion and Leicester.

GUEST, William Francis
Outside-left; Apps 84, Goals 17.
Born: Brierley Hill, 8 February 1914. Died: Darwen, 15 November 1994.
Career: Brierley Hill Juniors, Bromley Juniors (Kingswinford), BLUES (juniors August 1928, professional February 1932), Blackburn Rovers (January 1937 in exchange for 'Jack' Beattie), Walsall (August 1947), Peterborough United (1948), Kidderminster Harriers (1949), Lovells Athletic, Hinckley United, Bilston United, Brandwood Rovers (coach). Guested with West Bromwich Albion and Blues during World War Two. Later became a storeman at GEC Witton.
Club honours: Blackburn Rovers: War Cup runners-up 1940.
Guest was an enterprising winger, good on the ball, with a powerful kick. A Black Country man through and through, after the hostilities he came back to the Midlands to sign for Walsall. He was also a good cricketer with Moseley CC and Warwickshire Club & Ground. He joined Blues at the age of 14 and developed rapidly, making his debut whilst still in his teens. His speed and 'fast whipped' centres soon earned him accolades from the press. Although not the most prolific of scorers, he could be relied upon to notch a few each season. He did very well with Blackburn.

HADDON, Harry
Centre-forward; Apps 8, Goals 2.

Born: Pelsall, near Walsall, 1871. Died: Walsall.
Career: Pelsall Villa, Lichfield Barracks (38th Regt) (1894), BLUES (January 1896), Walsall Wood (September 1897).
He was a local player who lost out to the more prolific Jack Jones in the battle to replace Frank Mobley in the Blues attack. Something of a 'bustler', he was criticised before 'not being clever enough to be a centre'.

HAGAN, James
Defender; Apps 150+17, Goals 0.
Born: Monkstown, Northern Ireland, 10 August 1956.
Career: Larne Town (1974), Coventry City (part-time professional January 1977, full-time professional November 1977), Torquay United (loan September-October 1979), Detroit Express (loan March 1980), Seiko FC Hong Kong (loan 1980), BLUES (June 1982), Real Celta Vigo (Spain) (August 1987), Larne (August 1989), Colchester United (October 1989), Larne (January 1990), IFK Oddevold (May 1990), Ballymena United (player-manager June 1991), Carrick Rangers (October 1993), Larne (player-manager March 1994).
Representative honours: Northern Ireland (6 Youth caps); Ulster Young Footballer of the Year 1976.

Jim Hagan was a booking clerk on the Larne-Stranraer ferries when Coventry enticed him over to England. He failed to settle at Highfield Road and was loaned out several times before joining Blues on a free transfer. He proved a reliable player but was prone to the occasional lapse in concentration. After leaving St Andrew's he did well in Europe and has played League football in six different countries.

HAINES, Wilfred Henry
Outside-right; Apps 3, Goals 0.
Born: Stone, Staffs, June 1882. Deceased.
Career: Mount Pleasant Alliance, Newcastle Swifts (1903-04), Stoke (1905-06), Hanley Swifts (1906-07), Stafford Rangers (1907-08), BLUES (£250 July 1908), Leek United (August 1909), Stafford Rangers.
After relegation in 1908, Wilf Haines was one of a group of players signed by Blues to boost the expected promotion run. He failed to establish himself and with the introduction into the ranks of Jack Wilcox it was obvious that his Blues days were numbered and he was released at the end of the season.

HALL, Frederick
Centre-forward; Apps 5, Goals 2.
Born: Worksop, 24 November 1924.
Career: Whitewell Old Boys, BLUES (March 1947), Bedford Town (July 1949).
Fred Hall was a miner in Nottinghamshire when he came to Blues' attention. He was

given an early chance to prove his worth as a centre-forward and although he scored on his debut, his short-comings were evident and consequently his appearances were limited.

HALL, Jeffrey James
Right-back; Apps 264, Goals 1.
Born: Scunthorpe, 7 September 1929. Died: Birmingham, 4 April 1959.
Career: Bingley Schools football, St Anne's FC (Keighley), Wilsden FC, Bank Top FC (1947), Bradford (amateur 1949), REME (during National Service), BLUES (professional May 1950 until his untimely death as a result of polio in 1959).
Club honours: Blues: Division Two champions 1955, FA Cup runners-up 1956.
Representative honours: England (17 full caps, 1 'B' cap); Football League XI (4).

Jeff Hall had been tried in most positions during the early part of his career before eventually developing into an international-class right-back. He earned the reputation throughout the game as a difficult defender to oppose and would surely have won many more caps but for his tragic death. A memorial clock and score-board were erected at the City End of St Andrew's in Jeff Hall's honour.

HALL, John Henry
Inside/centre-forward; Apps 102, Goals 48.
Born: Hucknall, Nottinghamshire, 3 July 1883. Died: Nottingham 1938.
Career: Hucknall Boys' Club, Newark, Nottingham Forest (trial), Mansfield Town (trial), Stoke (professional, October 1904), Brighton & Hove Albion (June 1906), Middlesbrough (April 1908), Leicester Fosse (May 1910), BLUES (December 1910), Hucknall Town (1915). Retired May 1918.
Jack Hall was a terrific marksman who had four and a half excellent seasons at St Andrew's leading up to World War One. He topped the scoring charts for each of his clubs from 1906 to 1913. Hall was signed by Blues for a 'substantial fee' and he immediately set about repaying his way by scoring in each of his first seven games. He was very good in the air despite being only 5ft 9in tall.

HALLAM, John
Outside-right; Apps 151, Goals 62.
Born: Oswestry, February 1869. Died: Swindon, 7 March 1949.
Career: Oswestry Town (1885), Oswestry (1885), Oswestry Crescent (1887), Oswestry Town (1888), BLUES (1890), Swindon Town (1896-May 1901).
Club honours: Blues: Division Two champions 1893, runners-up 1894.
Representative honours: Wales (1 full cap).

Jack Hallam was a pint-sized winger with a devastating burst of speed who was an integral part of the prolific Blues attack of the Victorian era. He later worked for the Great Western Railway based in Swindon.

HALLWORTH, Arthur
Left-half; Apps 1, Goals 0.
Born: Stoke, 1884. Deceased.
Career: Twyford Youth Club, BLUES (September 1906), Leek Alexandra (August 1907), Barlaston Manor FC.
Hallworth was used as cover for all the half-back positions during his one season with Blues but got only one outing, replacing the injured Dougherty. He had a poor game and despite Dougherty's continuing absence Hallworth was not given a second chance

HALSALL, Michael
Midfield; Apps 44+2, Goals 3.
Born: Bootle, Merseyside, 21 July 1961.
Career: Liverpool (apprentice June 1977, professional May 1979), BLUES (March 1983), Carlisle United (£5,000 October 1984), Grimsby Town (£10,000 February 1987), Peterborough United (£25,000 July 1987, coach August 1993).
Club honours: Peterborough United: Division Four promotion 1991.
Representative honours: England (Youth caps).
Halsall never made the first team during his six-year stay at Anfield but he proved to be a willing worker and could never be faulted for his enthusiasm, although he lacked a little skill to shine in the top flight. He was sent off in his last game for Blues. He skippered Peterborough in their promotion campaign of 1990-91.

HALSALL, Walter George ('Salty')
Half-back; Apps 24, Goals 0.
Born: Liverpool, 29 March 1912.
Career: Bootle Celtic, Liverpool (amateur), Marine FC, Burscough Rangers, Bolton Wanderers (amateur December 1931), Blackburn Rovers (amateur November 1932, professional February 1933), BLUES (July 1938), Chesterfield (May 1939). Retired during World War Two.
Club honours: Marine: FA Amateur Cup runners-up 1932.
After a brief but distinguished amateur career, Wally Halsall made his name as an elegant wing-half at Blackburn. But when Rovers signed Charlie Calladine from Blues, the two players, being similar in style, had to contest a first-team place for the best part of three years before both were released, Halsall moving to Blues. He made an immediate impact with the local newspaper critics who described him as a 'tall, stylish player with the heart to do two men's work'. Unfortunately his sterling qualities were not enough to save Blues from relegation and he was released in the summer of 1939. He became a commercial traveller.

HAMPTON, Joseph Henry
Centre-forward; Apps 59, Goals 31.
Born: Wellington, Salop, 21 April 1885.
Died: Rhyl, 15 March 1963.
Career: Wellington Council School, Shifnal Juniors, Wellington Town (1902), Aston Villa (professional April 1904), BLUES (February 1920), Newport County (September 1922 to May 1923 when he prematurely retired), Wellington Town (January 1924), Preston North End (coach from June 1925 to December 1925), BLUES (colts coach, October 1934 to April 1936). Guested for Derby County and Nottingham Forest during World War One.
Club honours: Aston Villa: Division One champions 1910, FA Cup winners 1905, 1913, runners-up 1920; Blues: Division Two champions 1921.
Representative honours: England (4 full caps); Football League XI (3).

Harry Hampton was a fine, thrustful forward with an all-action style which sometimes involved running at full speed and then throwing himself headlong at the goalkeeper. This method was obviously effective as he once managed to charge over the line the legendary 20st giant, Willie Foulke, who was left dangling by his legs from the netting. Known as the 'Wellington Whirlwind', Hampton had scored 242 goals in 376 games for Aston Villa before he was signed by Blues in the twilight of his career. He still turned on the heat, however, and fired home 16 vital goals to help Blues win the Second Division title. After pulling out of football he ran a successful catering business in Rhyl. He discovered that his first name was Joseph quite late in life when there was a query about his birthday and he unearthed his own birth certificate at Somerset House.

HANDLEY, Thomas Henry
Centre-half; Apps 13, Goals 0.
Born: Cotteridge, Birmingham 1882. Deceased.
Career: Kings Norton Metal Works, BLUES (August 1907), Bradford (September 1909).
A tall, muscular defender who looked a useful replacement when called in to substitute for the injured Wigmore, Handley was surprisingly allowed to leave St Andrew's after finishing the 1908-09 campaign as a first-team regular.

HANDS, Thomas ('Toddy')
Outside-left; Apps 149, Goals 43.
Born: Small Heath, 4 January 1870. Deceased.
Career: Green Lane School, Small Heath Langley, Small Heath Unitary Road Methodists, Coventry, Small Heath Unity, BLUES (December 1890), King's Heath (August 1896).
Club honours: Blues: Division Two champions 1893.
Hands did the rounds of the Small Heath clubs, starting with a street side, the site of whose pitch is now the home of one of this book's compilers. Having lived in Langley Road, 'Toddy' is arguably the most local player Blues have ever had, being born within 100 yards of the club's former Muntz Street ground. First choice on the wing for some six years, in keeping with the rest of the 1893 forward line he was small, fast with a great heart, and a Blues man through and through. Surprisingly, he walked out on the club in 1896 because of a dispute about his wages and he never played League football again.

HANDYSIDES, Ian Robert
Midfield; Apps 111+22, Goals 12.
Born: Jarrow, 14 December 1962. Died: Solihull, 17 August 1990.
Career: Durham Boys, BLUES (apprentice June 1978, professional January 1980), Walsall (£17,000 January 1984), BLUES

(March 1986), Wolverhampton Wanderers (loan September-October 1986). Retired through ill health October 1988.
Club honours: Blues: Division Two promotion 1980.
Representative honours: England (Youth caps).

Hailed as the 'new Trevor Francis' on his arrival at St Andrew's, the high expectations proved to be a millstone around Ian Handyside's neck. In fairness he was a different style of player to Francis, being a 'buzzing' midfielder than a striker. He found it hard to cope with First Division football and few people were surprised when Walsall stepped in to sign him. He matured somewhat at Fellows Park but it came as shock when John Bond brought him back to St Andrew's in 1986. He showed far more consistency in his second spell and finally succeeded in gaining a regular first-team spot. In August 1988 he scored a hat-trick in a friendly win over Willenhall. Following this game, however, Handysides complained of a severe headache and shortly afterwards Blues fans were stunned to hear that a brain tumour had been diagnosed. Ian underwent surgery and seemed to be recovering but further tumours developed on his spinal chord, resulting in his tragically early death at the age of 27.

HANSBURY, Roger
Goalkeeper; Apps 68, Goals 0.
Born: Barnsley, 26 January 1955.
Career: Wesborough High School, Yorkshire Youths, Norwich City (apprentice August 1971, professional January 1973), Bolton Wanderers (loan March 1977), Cambridge United (loan November 1977),

Orient (loan December 1978), Eastern Athletic Hong Kong (December 1981), Burnley (August 1983), Cambridge United

(July 1985), BLUES (March 1986), Sheffield United (loan October-November 1987), Wolverhampton Wanderers (loan March-April 1989), Colchester United (loan August 1989), Cardiff City (loan October 1989, signed permanently for £20,000 December 1989). Retired May 1992.
Club honours: Cardiff City: Welsh Cup winners 1992.
Hansbury took a long time to establish himself as a League player due to the consistency of Kevin Keelan at Norwich, and when Keelan finally retired, Hansbury's career was disrupted by a broken leg. Norwich signed Chris Woods and, on recovery, the injured goalkeeper found himself out in the cold again. He arrived at St Andrew's as cover for David Seaman after many travels covering two continents. And when Seaman left, Hansbury once more claimed a regular place in League action. Basically a 'line goalkeeper', he was at his best as a shot-stopper but sometimes was found wanting when asked to deal with crosses.

HARDING, Paul J.
Midfield; Apps 23+3, Goals 1.
Born: Mitcham, 6 March 1964.
Career: Chelsea (apprentice), Wimbledon, Sutton United, Whyteleafe, Epsom & Ewell, Carshalton Athletic, Dulwich Hamlet, Enfield, Barnet (February 1990), Notts County (September 1990), Southend United (loan August 1993), Watford (loan November 1993), BLUES (loan December 1993, £50,000 permanently January 1994).
Club honours: Enfield: FA Trophy winners 1988.
A hard-tackling midfielder, Harding was 26 when he made his Football League debut for Notts County in 1990. He was the only signing by caretaker managers Trevor Morgan and Kevan Broadhurst.

HARDS, Walter Oscar
Outside-left; Apps 5, Goals 2.
Born: Edgbaston, Birmingham, August 1859. Deceased.
Career: Warwick County, Summer Hill Works FC, BLUES (1881), Stourbridge (1884).
A stylish dribbler, Hards was a stalwart of the Blues during the club's early days, being first choice for five seasons. He slowed down a little later and was switched to the inside-forward berth where he proved to be a talented performer although not much of a marksman.

HARE, Charles Boyd
Inside-forward; Apps 45, Goals 14.
Born: Yardley, Birmingham, June 1871.
Died: February 1934.
Career: Warwick County, Birmingham United, Aston Villa (April 1891), Woolwich Arsenal (August 1895), BLUES (November 1896), Watford (July 1898), Plymouth Argyle (1903). Retired 1904.
Club honours: Aston Villa: Division One champions 1894.
Hare was one of a host of fine players produced by Warwick County. At his best he was a clever, incisive footballer whose early career was plagued by injury. He was a great favourite with the Blues fans and it was rather a surprise when he left for Watford. Hare scored 13 goals in 26 games for Villa. Hend served with the Warwickshire Yeomanry in the Boer War. On returning from South Africa he attempted to resume his career in Devon but with limited success.

HARE, Jeremiah
Right-back; Apps 8, Goals 0.
Born: Edgbaston, Birmingham 1860. Deceased.
Career: Pershore Saints, Calthorpe FC, BLUES (August 1884), King's Heath (September 1888).

As Blues' reputation increased locally they were able to attract players from some of the better clubs in the area, and this old-fashioned big kicker was recruited to add stability to the defence. A solid, somewhat limited performer, his star waned after the 1886 FA Cup semi-final when he was given a roasting by West Brom's tricky winger George 'Spry' Woodhall. Jerry Hare remained with the club for another couple of years, playing in the reserves.

HARFORD, Michael Gordon
Striker; Apps 109, Goals 33.
Born: Sunderland, 12 February 1959.
Career: Sunderland Schools & Wearside & District Boys, Lambton Star Boys' Club, Lincoln City (professional July 1977), Newcastle United (£216,000 December 1980), Bristol City (£160,000 August 1981), Newcastle United (£100,000 March 1982), BLUES (£100,000 March 1982), Luton Town (£250,000 December 1984), Derby County (£480,000 January 1990), Luton Town (£325,000 September 1991), Chelsea (August 1992), Sunderland (March 1993), Coventry City (July 1993), Wimbledon (August 1994).
Club honours: Luton Town: Milk Cup winners 1988, runners-up 1989, Simod Cup runners-up 1988.
Representative honours: England (1 full cap, 1 'B' cap).

Mick Harford, a tall target man, powerful in the air but with a nice touch on the ground too, scored regularly throughout his career and each transfer commanded a six-figure fee. His move from Lincoln to Newcastle set a Fourth Division record. Whilst he was at Bristol, the club was on the verge of folding up and he was transferred back to Newcastle to pay off the club's debts – this must surely be rated as one of the shortest stays a player has ever spent with one club as he signed for Blues one hour later. He started off with a debut goal for Blues and maintained a reasonable strike rate that would have been far better had he had more support. Harford turned out to be one of the best strikers in the First Division when with Luton, although during the latter stages of the 1980s he was hampered by injury.

HARLAND, Stanley C.
Wing-half; Apps 51+1, Goals 0.
Born: Liverpool, 19 June 1940.
Career: Liverpool & District Schools, Burnley (amateur 1955), New Brighton (1956), Everton (professional December 1959), Bradford City (July 1961), Carlisle United (June 1964), Swindon Town (August 1966), BLUES (December 1971), Yeovil Town (player-manager May 1973), Portsmouth (assistant manager 1978), Gravesend & Northfleet (manager), Yeovil Town (commercial manager). Later ran a supermarket in Yeovil.
Club honours: Swindon Town: Division Three champions 1969, Football League

Cup winners 1969, Anglo-Italian Cup winners 1970.

Stan Harland was an efficient, hard-working player who had an excellent five-year stint with Swindon, for whom he amassed in excess of 250 senior appearances, this after having failed to make the breakthrough at Goodison Park. He skippered Swindon in their 'double-winning' season of 1968-69. Sadly, his lack of pace was cruelly exposed after promotion. Throughout his career Harland continued to reside in Liverpool and covered literally thousands of miles commuting to his various clubs. In all he accumulated a League record of 471 appearances and scored 33 goals.

HARLEY, Alexander
Centre-forward; Apps 29, Goals 9.
Born: Glasgow, 20 April 1936. Died: Birmingham, 1969.
Career: Third Lanark, Manchester City (August 1962), BLUES (£42,500 August 1963), Dundee (November 1964), Leicester City (May 1965), Toronto City, Newton Unity (Birmingham Works League, late 1960s).
A prolific scorer in both Scotland and Manchester, Alex Harley was the subject of a Blues' record transfer fee when he moved to St Andrew's. Although he finished well up the scoring list he found the going tough in one of Blues' perennial relegation struggles and was soon on his way back to Scotland. At the time of his sudden death he was a croupier in a Birmingham casino.

HARPER, Dennis
Inside-right; Apps 1, Goals 0.
Born: Wednesbury, 12 October 1936.
Career: Darlaston, BLUES (amateur July 1955, professional August 1956), Romford (April 1959), Burton Albion (May 1961), Nuneaton Borough (July 1961-May 1962).
This nicely built youngster was plucked out of West Bromwich junior football, and he received a surprise debut despite not being a reserve-team regular when Kinsey, Orritt, Finney and Linnecor were all injured at the same time. He seemed overawed by the occasion and did not get another chance.

HARPER, Rowland Richard G.
Outside-right; Apps 29, Goals 2.
Born: Lichfield, April 1881. Died: August 1949.
Career: Walsall Wood, BLUES (April 1904), Burton United (April 1907), Aston Villa (August 1907), Notts County (March 1908), Mansfield Invicta (August 1910).
Described as a 'smart footballer', Harper opened his first-class career with a debut goal in Blues' 5-0 thrashing of Forest, and by the end of the season had established himself as the regular right winger. But when Charlie Tickle shrugged off his injury

problems 'Roly' was relegated to the reserves.

HARRIS, Andrew
Utility; Apps 0+2, Goals 0.
Born: Birmingham, 17 November 1972.
Career: BLUES (YTS 1988, professional June 1990), Oxford United (loan October 1991), Exeter City (November 1991), Nuneaton Borough (April 1994).
Harris was an injury-prone youngster who demonstrated a liking for most positions although he looked most comfortable in attack.

HARRIS, Frederick
Inside-forward/wing-half; Apps 312, Goals 68.
Born: Solihull, 2 July 1912.
Career: Formans Road School Sparkbrook, Birmingham City Transport, Osborne Athletic, BLUES (professional March 1933). Retired May 1950.
Club honours: Blues: Division Two champions 1948, Football League South champions 1946.
Representative honours: Football League XI (1).

Fred Harris' career fitted neatly into two sections around the war. At the time of his debut, in front of a Villa Park crowd of 54,000, he was a sharp-shooting inside-forward, and he admitted that when he saw the vast audience that day he wanted to 'disappear'. But it didn't stop him from scoring the opening goal and he continued to find the net regularly right up to the war. The demands of wartime football led to him being converted into a wing-half and it was from here that he found his true metier. His style of hard tackling and clever distribution impressed manager Harry Storer so much that he was made club captain. Harris was almost 38 and still a regular in the Blues side when he retired to set up trade as a chiropodist and physiotherapist in Acocks Green.

HARRIS, James
Forward; Apps 115, Goals 53.
Born: Birkenhead, 18 August 1933.
Career: Birkenhead Schools, Everton (juniors 1948, professional September 1951), BLUES (£20,000 December 1960), Oldham Athletic (July 1964), Tranmere Rovers (August 1966), Rhyl Athletic (October 1966). Retired May 1967 and became steward of the Prenton Golf Club.
Club honours: Blues: Fairs Cup runners-up 1962, Football League Cup winners 1963.
Representative honours: England (1 Under-23 cap); Football League XI (1).
A speedy two-footed striker who was a most difficult player to contain, Jimmy Harris was an individualist who netted over 100 goals in first-class soccer, having by far his best spell as a professional with the

Goodison Park club for whom he served 12 years.

HARRIS, Wallace Norman
Outside-right; Apps 94, Goals 15.
Born: Hockley, Birmingham, 22 February 1900. Died: Davos, Switzerland, 7 September 1933.
Career: Ada Road School, Dudley St James, Burton All Saints, BLUES (November 1922), Walsall (September 1929).
Harris was a frail looking winger with a deceptive change of pace which confused many defenders. He replaced Billy Harvey and made an immediate impression leading to an English trial appearance the following year. He kept his place in the first team for three seasons before increasing health problems led to his release. After a short spell with Walsall his declining health forced him to retire and he died in a sanatorium in Switzerland, aged 33. He was the son-in-law of J.T.Harris, a Blues director.

HARRISON, Arthur
Outside-right; Apps 4, Goals 3.
Born: Stirchley, Birmingham, September 1878. Deceased.
Career: Cotteridge School, Linton FC, BLUES (1902), Brownhills Athletic (1903).
Arthur Harrison, a local winger of considerable goalscoring prowess – he scored twice on his debut – but his career was held back by being deputy to the great Charlie Athersmith.

HARRISON, Michael
Central defender; Apps 3, Goals 0.
Born: Leicester, 21 February 1952.
Career: Mid-Leicester Schools, BLUES (apprentice June 1968, professional October 1970), Southend United (July 1972), Yeovil Town (June 1973).
Mickey Harrison was a fine defender who skippered Blues' Youth team. His senior debut (in his home town) coincided with a remarkable performance by Blues – a 4-1 away win against the eventual champions. Harrison always looked capable but perhaps his lack of height went against him and he dropped out of League football with only 19 games to his credit.

HARRISON, Wilbert ('Fay')
Centre-forward; Apps 1, Goals 2.
Born: Bordesley Green, Birmingham, 1867. Deceased.
Career: Coventry Road FC, Birmingham Excelsior, Birmingham St George's (1886), BLUES (August 1891), Summerfield Saints (1892).
One of the many stars unloaded by the threatened St George's club in 1891, 'Fay' Harrison had been the fulcrum of the Dragons' attack for some time and was tipped to do great things for Blues, but sadly his career faded after his move. He did, though, score twice in his only game for the club.

HART, Paul Anthony

Central defender; Apps 1, Goals 0.
Born: Golborne, Manchester, 4 May 1953.
Career: Stockport County (apprentice June 1969, professional September 1970), Blackpool (June 1973), Leeds United (March 1978), Nottingham Forest (May 1983), Sheffield Wednesday (August 1985), BLUES (December 1986), Notts County (player-coach June 1987), Chesterfield (manager November 1988-January 1991), Grantham Town (player), Nottingham Forest (coach, June 1991); Sheffield Wednesday (coach 1994).

Paul Hart had the terrible misfortune to suffer a broken leg in his debut game for Blues, against Plymouth Argyle in December 1986 when he collided with teammate Tommy Williams, and it turned out to be his only appearance for the club. A solid, uncompromising stopper, generally recognised as one of the hard men of League football, Hart was signed to bolster up a leaky Blues defence but that freak accident brought an end to his career at St Andrew's. He moved to Notts County before fully fit but Blues could hardly be blamed for selling the 34-year-old. He is the brother of Nigel Hart, a former of Wigan, Leicester, Blackburn, Crewe and Bury defender, and son of Johnny Hart, who starred for Manchester City at inside-forward.

HARTWELL, Ambrose Walter

Full-back/centre-half; Apps 51, Goals 1.
Born: Exeter, 28 June 1883. Deceased.
Career: Budleigh Town Schools, Erdington, Feltham, Redditch Excelsior, Erdington, BLUES (August 1901), Bradford (June 1908), QPR (August 1909), Kidderminster Harriers, Shrewsbury Town.

'A thorough trier' seems to be a fair description from Hartwell's contemporaries. In seven seasons with Blues he played in only 51 games in the first team but was always regarded as a 'good man' to have in reserve. The only man in the club's history to have a reserve match as his benefit game, he was renowned for his prodigious kicking, and it was said that he once fired a penalty clean out of the ground.

HARVEY, Charles ('Soldier')

Outside-right; Apps 2, Goals 0.
Born: Small Heath, Birmingham 1879. Deceased.
Career: Dixon Road School, St Phillip's YMCA, BLUES (July 1904), Leek (September 1907), Shrewsbury Town (1909).

Harvey was an Army sergeant stationed at Whittington Barracks near Lichfield when Blues signed him, primarily as a reserve. He failed to make an impact when called into the first team, one critic saying, "He has some notions of football but they are crude as yet."

HARVEY, Edmund ('Martin')

Outside-right; Apps 14, Goals 0.
Born: Kiveton Park, Sheffield, 8 September 1900.
Career: Kiveton Park FC, Huddersfield Town (amateur), BLUES (January 1924), Bradford City (June 1927). Retired through injury February 1930.

Martin Harvey started his career with Blues by alternating with namesake Billy Harvey on the right wing. After a promising opening season a combination of injuries and loss of form took its toll and he was transferred to Bradford City where he showed a goalscoring talent that was never obvious in his Blues days, scoring 16 times in his 47 games for the Valley Parade club before injury struck again.

HARVEY, William ('Billy') Henry Tompkins

Outside-right; Apps 79, Goals 2.
Born: Freemantle, Hampshire, 12 April

1896. Died: South Africa c.July 1970.
Career: Yorkshire Amateurs, 2nd Battalion West Riding Regiment, Sheffield Wednesday (professional October 1919), BLUES (amateur July 1921, professional November 1921), Southend United (August 1925), BLUES (assistant secretary August 1926, manager March 1927-May 1928), Chesterfield (manager June 1932–June 1938), Gillingham (manager June 1938-May 1939).
Club honours (as manager) Chesterfield: Division Three North champions 1936.
Representative honours: England (1 Amateur cap v Ireland); FA Tour to South Africa 1920.

A moustachio'd 'speedster', Harvey was a regular before being superseded by his namesake. A good cricketer, he played for Warwickshire and for Border Province in South Africa.

HASTIE, Ian Scott

Outside-right; Apps 1, Goals 0.
Born: London 1887. Deceased.
Career: Edmonton Royal, BLUES (May 1911), Wycombe Wanderers (April 1912).

The least successful of the trio of players signed from North London junior football prior to World War One (*qv* Barton and Gibson), Hastie was a dribbler with a tendency to 'play by himself'.

HASTINGS, Walter Jesse

Outside-right; Apps 44, Goals 7.
Born: West Hartlepool, 1889. Deceased.
Career: Spennymoor United, West Hartlepool, Brighton & Hove Albion (1908-09 season), BLUES (February 1912), Watford (August 1914), Hartlepool United (1919).
Club honours: Brighton & Hove Albion: Southern League champions 1910.

Hastings was a hard-working winger who liked to cut inside to have a shot at goal. He had to fight off several challengers to retain his position before finally losing out to 'Ninty' Eyre. He later became a referee.

HATELEY, Anthony

Striker; Apps 29+1, Goals 6.
Born: Derby, 13 June 1941.
Career: Normanton Sports Club (April 1954), Derby County (schoolboy forms April 1955), Notts County (amateur May 1956, professional June 1958), Aston Villa (£20,000 August 1963), Chelsea (£100,000 October 1966), Liverpool (£100,000 July 1967), Coventry City (£80,000 September 1968), BLUES (£72,000 August 1969), Notts County (£20,000 November 1970), Oldham Athletic (£5,000 July 1972), Bromsgrove Rovers (May 1974), Prescot Town (July 1975), Keyworth United (December 1978). Retired August 1979. Later worked in the Everton FC lottery

office, then became a free trade representative for a Nottingham brewery.
Club honours: Notts County: Division Three promotion 1960, Division Four champions 1971; Chelsea: FA Cup runners-up 1967.

Tony Hateley was one of the great post-war 'travellers' of League football. A fine header of the ball – he was coached by Tommy Lawton – Hateley scored 211 goals in a total of 434 League games during a splendid career although, in truth, he never really fulfilled the promise he had shown as a youngster. Subject of one of the early six-figure transfers. A tall, muscular player, he probably could have done a lot better with Blues if the team had fielded a quality winger to provide him with the centres which he thrived on. He netted four goals for Villa in an away First Division match at Spurs in 1966, which ended 5-5, and 86 goals in 148 outings for Villa in all. Father of Mark Hateley, the Coventry City, Rangers and England player.

HATTON, Robert John

Forward; Apps 212+6, Goals 73.
Born: Hull, 10 April 1947.
Career: Wath Wanderers (June 1962), Wolverhampton Wanderers (apprentice June 1963, professional November 1964), Bolton Wanderers (March 1967), Northampton Town (October 1968), Carlisle United (July 1969), BLUES (October 1971), Blackpool (July 1976), Luton Town (July 1978), Sheffield United (July 1980), Cardiff City (December 1982). Retired from League football May 1983. Later assisted Lodge Cotterill FC (Birmingham Sunday club).

Like Hateley, Bob Hatton was another terrific nomadic striker who could score

goals from any angle, with either foot and with his head, in all divisions, from almost any distance. Hatton netted 217 goals in 620 League appearances, including 58 in 175 games for Blues. A well built player who preferred to occupy a slot on the left side of the field, he was the final cog in Blues' 1972 promotion attack, Lacking the glamour of Francis and Latchford, he was often the unsung hero but his unselfish work and clinical finishing made him a vital member of the side. He later worked for an insurance company and regularly attends St Andrew's.

HAUSER, Stanley

Goalkeeper; Apps 34, Goals 0.
Born: Handsworth, Sheffield, 20 July 1890.
Died: Handsworth, Birmingham, 10 June 1958.
Career: Handsworth Grammar School Old Boys, Stockton, BLUES (trial 1911), Handsworth Oakhill, BLUES (November 1913), Stourbridge (December 1922), Shrewsbury (1923), Netherton (1924), Cradley St Luke's (1925). Retired May 1927.
Club honours: Blues: Division Two champions 1921.
Representative honours: England (2 Amateur caps in 1914).

Stan Hauser was a capable amateur goalkeeper and dressing-room comic, who served Blues before, during and after World War One. He combined his football with working in the family shop and was spotted by Blues playing in the local Early Closers' League – this after failing a trial with the club two years earlier. He was then given a rapid promotion to the first team, making his debut only four weeks after signing. However, with so many capable 'keepers on the books at the time, he found it nigh on impossible to hold down a first-team place. Like so many 'keepers he had his personal eccentricities, and one particular habit of his was to hang his wrist-watch in the netting behind him during a game.

HAVENGA, William Stephen

Outside-right; Apps 1, Goals 0.
Born: Bloemfontein, South Africa, 6 November 1924.
Career: Bremner Old Boys, BLUES (July 1948), Luton Town (May 1950), Ipswich Town (January 1952), Kettering Town (June 1953), Worcester City (1954), Hinckley Athletic, Halesowen Town. Retired 1962.

During the late 1940s and early '50s, a string of trialists arrived in Birmingham from South Africa. Willie Havenga was one of the earliest and also one of the few to make a Football League appearance. He remained in this country for several years, performing mainly in non-League circles. Havenga hit six goals in 18 League games for Luton and three in 19 for Ipswich.

HAWKER, Philip Nigel
Left-back; Apps 36+1, Goals 1.
Born: Solihull, 7 December 1962.
Career: Langley Secondary School, BLUES (apprentice June 1978, professional June 1980), Walsall (loan December 1982, signed permanently March 1983), West Bromwich Albion (loan September-October 1990), Kidderminster Harriers (December 1990), Solihull Borough (1991). Retired October 1993.
Representative honours: England (2 Youth caps).
Hawker was a tall, long-striding defender whose regular appearances were made during the period when Mark Dennis was absent through suspension. He was thought by many to have a potential as a central defender but rarely was he tried in that role at St Andrew's. He proved a very useful competitor in the lower divisions with Walsall.

HAWLEY, Frederick
Centre-half; Apps 3, Goals 0.
Born: Derby, 28 July 1890. Deceased.
Career: Derby Midland, Shelton United, Leys Recreational, Ripley Town, Sheffield United (January 1913), Coventry City (1919), BLUES (January 1920), Swindon Town (May 1920), Bristol City (March 1923), Brighton & Hove Albion (June 1925), QPR (May 1926), Loughborough Corinthians (April 1928). Retired May 1929. Guested for Derby County, Notts County, Blues and Nottingham Forest during World War One.
Before World War One this powerfully built defender was a First Division regular but he took sometime to settle down after the conflict. Neither of his Midlands clubs received much service from him but he did give a good account of himself with each of his Southern League clubs until the end of his long career.

HAYNES, Harry
Centre-half; Apps 10, Goals 0.
Born: Walsall, 21 April 1873. Died: Southampton, 29 March 1902.
Career: Walsall (1890), Walsall Unity (1891), Wolverhampton Wanderers (February 1893), BLUES (July 1895), Southampton St Mary's (July 1896). Retired 1900 through injury. Was landlord of the Turk's Head and Edinburgh Castle pubs in Southampton.
Haynes signed for Southampton St Mary's (who later became Southampton FC) on a Birmingham railway station with a pen borrowed from the booking office, Blues retaining his League registration. A big, bruising moustachio'd defender, solidly built with legs like tree-trunks, he could withstand the fiercest of challenges and was utterly fearless. His career with Blues coincided with that of Alec Leake, but he became a regular left-back with the Saints, doubling up with a career as a pub landlord.

HAYWOOD, George ('Abie')
Centre-forward; Apps 46, Goals 18.
Born: Coleorton, 11 December 1906. Died: c.1975.
Career: Coleorton Bible Class, Whitwick Imperial (September 1927), Southend United (trial), Chesterfield (November 1927), Gresley Rovers, BLUES (November 1928), Chesterfield (June 1934), Cradley Heath, Southport (December 1935), Cradley Heath (August 1936). Retired 1939.
Although only 5ft 7in in height, this swarthy ex-miner demonstrated exceptional jumping ability, frequently beating much taller men to the ball. Allied to his splendid heading skills, he had good ball control and proved an efficient deputy to Joe Bradford. He hit two goals on his Blues debut. Later he worked as an office clerk at New Lount Colliery.

HEATH, Frederick Sidney

Forward/half-back; Apps 5, Goals 1.
Born: Smethwick, 1865. Deceased.
Career: Smethwick Hall School, Bearwood White Star, Bearwood FC, Cookham, BLUES (August 1889), Stourbridge (1890), Hockley Rose (1891).
Signed for the princely sum of £1.00, this versatile performer understudied six different roles throughout his short career. Later he became a prominent referee.

HEDGES, Thomas
Goalkeeper; Apps 8, Goals 0.
Born: Winson Green, Birmingham 1858. Died: Birmingham, 1941.
Career: Birmingham Heath, Walsall Phoenix, Walsall Swifts, BLUES (September 1883), Darlaston (1887). Later became director of West Bromwich Albion.
Hedges was a competent, squarely built goalkeeper who had four fine seasons with Blues before losing his place to Chris Charsley. When he became a director of West Brom, he formed a link with the club he had played against in the 1886 FA Cup semi-final, when Blues lost 4-0 in a snowstorm.

HELLAWELL, Michael Stephen
Outside-right; Apps 213, Goals 33.
Born: Keighley, Yorkshire, 30 June 1938.
Career: Salts FC, Huddersfield Town (amateur July 1954), QPR (professional August 1955), BLUES (May 1957), Sunderland (January 1965), Huddersfield Town (September 1966), Peterborough United (December 1968), Bromsgrove Rovers (August 1969). Retired May 1971.
Club honours: Blues: Fairs Cup runners-up 1961, Football League Cup winners 1963.
Representative honours: England (2 full apps); played for Division Three South XI 1957.

A red-haired winger with an astonishing turn of speed over 25 yards, Mike Hellawell was exchanged for Bill Finney and went on to score on his Blues debut but then had to wait three seasons before gaining a regular place in the side. However, he impressed sufficiently to win his first England cap two years later. As well as creating chances he also hit his fair share of goals but after leaving Blues he found scoring much more difficult. After retiring he set up in business, running a shop in his home town of Keighley. His brother John played for both Bradford clubs as well as Darlington and Rotherham. Mike was also an exceptionally fine cricketer and played in one county match for Warwickshire.

HENDERSON, Crosbie Gray
Left-back; Apps 6, Goals 0.
Born: Hylton, 12 May 1885. Died: 27 April 1970.
Career: Hylton Rangers, Hylton Star,

Newcastle United (May 1906), Grimsby Town (May 1908), BLUES (August 1910), Brighton & Hove Albion (May 1911), Luton Town (July 1912).

He came to Blues with a reputation of being a good, solid full-back but fell from favour after a short run in the first team at the opening of the 1910-11 season. The consistency of Frank Womack ensured that Crosbie did not break back into the side and at the end of the campaign he was glad to get away to pastures new.

HENDERSON, John Neil
Inside-forward; Apps 4, Goals 0.
Born: Dumfries 1874. Died: Maxwelltown, 30 August 1930.
Career: Fifth King's Rifle Volunteers, Dumfries (1894); Celtic (1895), Victoria United (May 1897), Lincoln City (May 1898), Leicester Fosse (December 1900) BLUES (March 1901), Maxwelltown Volunteers (September 1902); Carlisle United (August 1905), Maxwelltown Volunteers (1906); Annan United (September 1910), Nithsdale Wanderers (November 1910).
John Henderson had just finished an unsuccessful spell at Leicester when Blues signed him to strengthen their promotion bid but he proved disappointing and quickly disappeared back to the junior ranks.

HENDON, Ian Michael
Defender; Apps 4, Goals 0.
Born: Hornchurch, 5 December 1971.
Career: Havering Schools, Essex Schools, London Schools, Tottenham Hotspur (YTS 1988, Professional December 1989), Portsmouth (loan January 1992), Leyton Orient (loan March 1992), Barnsley (loan March 1993), Leyton Orient (August 1993), BLUES (loan March 1995).
Club honours: Tottenham Hotspur: Youth Cup winners 1990, Charity Shield finalist 1991.
Representative honours: England (Schools international, 19 Youth caps, 7 Under-21 caps).
Powerfully-built defender who captained England's Youth side whilst at Spurs. Never given a chance to settle in Tottenham's first team, he was loaned out several times to gain experience before eventually moving on to Orient. There he found himself in a

struggling side and was grateful for a chance at St Andrew's, where he found himself picked immediately following an injury to Dave Barnett.

HENDRIE, Paul F.
Outside-right; Apps 29+3, Goals 1.
Born: Lennoxtown, near Glasgow, 27 March 1954.
Career: St Patrick's High School, Kilsyth Rangers, Celtic (apprentice), Kirkintilloch Rob Roy, BLUES (professional March 1972), Portland Timbers (NASL) (April 1976), Bristol Rovers (September 1977), Halifax Town (July 1979), Stockport County (August 1984), Chelmsley Town (player-coach July 1991), Redditch United (manager March 1992), Tamworth (manager February 1995).
Paul Hendrie was a diminutive long-haired winger, who was often confused at first glance with Steve Phillips. Possessor of plenty of skill and pace, he also had a suspect temperament. After being converted into a midfielder, he went on to chalk up an impressive set of statistics in the lower divisions with Halifax Town and Stockport County despite being suspended many times. His nephew, John, played for several clubs including Coventry, Newcastle, Middlesbrough and still plays for Leeds. His son Lee turned professional with Aston Villa in 1994.

HENNESSEY, William Terrence
Wing-half; Apps 203, Goals 3.
Born: Llay, Mid-Wales, 1 September 1942.
Career: BLUES (juniors June 1958, professional September 1959), Nottingham Forest (November 1965), Derby County (£100,000 February 1970), Tamworth (manager April 1974), Kimberley Town (manager 1977), Tulsa Roughnecks (NASL) (assistant coach 1978), Shepshed Charterhouse (coach 1978-October 1980), Tulsa Roughnecks (assistant coach November 1980, chief coach 1981-83), Vancouver Whitecaps (NASL) (assistant coach), Heidelberg (Australia) (manager 1987-88).
Club honours: Blues: Fairs Cup runners-up 1961, Football League Cup winners 1963; Derby County: Division One champions 1972, Texaco Cup winners 1972.
Representative honours: Wales (39 full caps, 6 Under-23 caps, Schoolboy caps).

One of the finest products to come through the club's youth scheme, Terry Hennessey first sprang to fame in April 1961 when, with only a handful of first-team games behind him, he played a major role in Blues' Fairs semi-final win over Internazionale. A strong tackler, he was able to bring the ball out of defence and then distribute it with telling effect. Throughout the 1960s he was the leading light in Blues' regular battles against relegation. He finally left St Andrew's after the club had been demoted to Division Two. Hennessey spent four good seasons with Forest and became Derby's first six-figure signing when he left the City Ground in 1970 but injury ruined his stay with the Rams. He made 160 League appearances for Forest and 63 for Derby.

HERRIOT, James
Goalkeeper; Apps 212, Goals 0.
Born: Chapelhall, Airdrie, 20 December 1939.
Career: Douglasdale, Dunfermline Athletic (August 1958), BLUES 9 May 1965), Mansfield Town (loan November 1970), Hibernian (August 1971), St Mirren (July 1973), Partick Thistle (February 1975), Morton (loan October 1975), Dunfermline Athletic (1976), Morton (late 1976).
Club honours: Dunfermline: Scottish FA Cup runners-up 1965; Hibernian: Scottish FA Cup runners-up 1972; Scottish League Cup winners 1973.
Representative honours: Scotland (8 full caps); Scottish League XI (2).
Jim Herriot was a distinctive figure on the field owing to his habit of smearing boot polish under his eyes, American Football style, in the belief that this reduced glare from the floodlights etc. He was an infuriating goalkeeper, occasionally brilliant but prone to some spectacular errors of judgment, letting a ball go past him and then turning to see it buried in the back of the net. He enjoyed lasting fame when his name was chosen as a pen-name by the well-known veterinarian author who liked the sound of it.

HIBBITT, Terence Arthur
Midfielder; Apps 122, Goals 11.
Born: Bradford, 1 December 1947. Died: Newcastle upon Tyne, 5 August 1994.
Career: Leeds United (apprentice June 1963, professional December 1964), Newcastle United (£30,000 August 1971), BLUES (rated at £100,000 August 1975), Newcastle United (May 1978-May 1981), Gateshead (July 1982 as player, player-coach January 1983, then as manager August 1986, dismissed October 1986).
Club honours: Leeds United: Fairs Cup runners-up 1968; Newcastle United FA Cup runners-up 1974, Texaco Cup winners 1974.
Terry Hibbitt made a dramatic entry into League football when he scored with his first touch on his debut for Leeds. Most of his time at Elland Road was spent in the 'shadow squad' but there is no doubt he was a highly skilful schemer with a magic left-foot who sadly during his three-year spell at St Andrew's failed to win over the vociferous elements of Blues fans – this after four excellent seasons with Newcastle where he laid on scores of goals for hot-shot Malcolm Macdonald. Brother of Kenny, formerly with Wolves and later Walsall manager, Terry Hibbitt teamed up with Kendall and Campbell in the Blues midfield and it was a niggling knee injury which eventually forced him out of the big time in 1981 after he had amassed close on 430 senior appearances for his three major clubs. He went into a newsagent's business in Newcastle after quitting football.

HIBBS, Henry ('Harry') Edward
Goalkeeper; Apps 389, Goals 0.
Born: Wilnecote, near Tamworth, 27 May 1906. Died: Hatfield, Herts, 23 May 1984.
Career: Wilnecote Holy Trinity FC, Tamworth Castle, BLUES (amateur April 1924, professional May 1924). Retired May 1940 (after appearing in a wartime game against Aston Villa in front of a 15,000 crowd at St Andrew's). Walsall (manager August 1944 to June 1951). Permit player for de Havillands FC (February 1953 to May 1954), Ware Town (manager August

1960), Welwyn Garden City (manager 1962).
Club honours: Blues: FA Cup runners-up 1931.
Representative honours: England (25 full caps); Football League XI (3); FA tour to South Africa 1929.

Although born into a goalkeeping family (his uncle Hubert Pearson and cousin Harold Pearson both kept goal for West Brom, and a further cousin, Horace Pearson for Coventry City) Harry Hibbs was originally a forward. Tamworth Castle FC, however, had a reputation for producing goalkeepers and it was whilst there that he went between the posts for the first time. Quite short, pale and a relative lightweight, Hibbs did not really look the ideal build to be a goalkeeper, but his ability was so obvious that Blues quickly signed him up. After a lengthy apprenticeship under Dan Tremelling, Hibbs finally gained a regular spot in 1929 – and he did not lose it until his retirement. His style of keeping was the exact opposite to Tremelling, Hibbs preferring to rely upon anticipation rather than athleticism to make his saves. That is not to say that he wasn't capable of spectacular efforts when the need arose. A totally unflappable temperament was also part of his make-up, resulting in him being arguably the greatest of all Blues' fine goalkeepers. He was the first footballer to be granted a wartime benefit match.

HICKS, George Wolstenholme
Outside-left; Apps 80, Goals 18.
Born: Weaste, Salford, 30 April 1902.
Career: Salford Lads' Club, Droylesden, Manchester Central, Manchester City (November 1923), BLUES (October 1928), Manchester United (January 1932), Bristol Rovers (September 1932), Swindon Town (August 1933), Rotherham United (November 1933), Manchester North End (September 1934).

Club honours: Manchester City: FA Cup runners-up 1926, Division Two champions 1928.
Blues finally seemed to have ended their long search for a left winger when they signed this slim player in 1928. He had scored over 40 goals in his five years at Maine Road and continued in this vein with 12 goals in his first season at St Andrew's. Goals proved harder to come by the next year as his game was modified to become a provider of chances. Hopes were high as Blues got off to a good start in 1930-31 but after seven games he suffered a severe knee injury.

HICKS, Martin
Central defender; Apps 69+4, Goals 2.
Born: Stratford-upon-Avon, 27 February 1957.
Career: Stratford Town, Charlton Athletic (February 1977), Reading (£20,000 February 1978), BLUES (free transfer August 1991, acting reserve-team manager April 1993); Newbury Town (player-manager July 1993), Worcester City (February 1995).

Club honours: Reading: Division Four champions, 1979, Division Three champions 1986, Simod Cup winners 1988.
Hicks was a vastly experienced professional when he arrived at St Andrew's, having been the linchpin of the Reading defence for many years. He appeared in well over 500 senior games for the Royals and chose Blues to be nearer to his place of birth.

HIGGINS, James
Centre-forward; Apps 6, Goals 3.
Born: Cradley Heath, March 1874. Deceased.
Career: Colley Gate FC, Stourbridge, BLUES (August 1897), Netherton (September 1898), Halesowen Town (1900).
A local youngster who was given a run-out in the absence of Hare and Lewis at the end of his one season with Blues. He repaid the club's faith in him handsomely but with the signing of Bob McRoberts he chose to return to his native Black Country.

HIGGINS, James T.
Centre-forward; Apps 54, Goals 14.
Born: Dublin, 3 February 1926.
Career: Dundalk, BLUES (November 1949), Hereford United (July 1953), Dundalk (1955).
Representative honours: Republic of Ireland (1 full cap).
Higgins was signed along with teammate Eddie O'Hara and was rushed into the first team. A bit of a tearaway with a bustling style, he was best remembered by older Blues fans for his 45-second goal against Manchester United in 1951 which took Blues into the semi-finals of the FA Cup.

HIGGINS, John Bernard
Inside-left; Apps 1, Goals 0.
Born: Harborne, Birmingham, 31 December 1885. Died: Malvern, 3 January 1970.
Career: King Edward VI School (Birmingham), Bournville Excelsior, Bournville Youth, Aston Villa (1906), BLUES (August 1907), Brierley Hill Alliance (September 1908).
Higgins was a true Corinthian, remaining an amateur throughout a long sporting career. He was never particularly prominent on the soccer field, being much better known as a middle-order batsman and slow left-arm spinner in his days with Worcestershire from 1912 to 1930, during which time he amassed 4,149 runs (ave 19.57) in 121 matches (223 innings), with a seasonal best of 1,041 coming in 1928 (ave 30.61). His best bowling return was 5-72 and in all he took 30 wickets (ave 53.46) and held 59 catches. He also represented Staffordshire, and after retiring from the active sport, he was employed at Rugby School as their cricket professional.

HIGGINSON, Jack
Forward; Apps 14, Goals 4.
Born: Dudley 1876. Deceased.
Career: Gornal Wood FC, Dudley Town, BLUES (1900), Stourbridge (1902).
Higginson was a useful utility forward, principally left-sided who had a good run as a stop-gap inside-left in 1900-01. The arrival of Johnny McMillan ended his regular spell and from then on in he was rarely selected.

HILEY, Scott Patrick
Right-back; Apps 52, Goals 0.
Born: Plymouth, 27 September 1968.
Career: Exeter City (apprentice 1984, professional August 1986), BLUES (£100,000, March 1993).
Club honours: Exeter City: Division Four champions 1989-90.

Scott Hiley is a competent full-back who enjoys to overlap. He appeared in 259 League and Cup games for Exeter before joining his former manager, Terry Cooper, at St Andrew's. He suffered with injury in 1994-95.

HILL, Dennis
Outside-left; Apps 4, Goals 0.
Born: Willenhall, 16 August 1929.
Career: Wolverhampton Technical College, Willenhall St Stephens, Willenhall Pickwick, Darlaston, Leicester City (amateur), BLUES (June 1951), Burton Albion (February 1957).
This pacy winger had a wait of two-and-a-half years before getting a run-out in the first team. Although he proved capable at his job, he lacked the goalscoring touch of Alex Govan and hence opportunities were

always going to be limited. Hill showed commendable loyalty to the club before eventually abandoning the full-time game to concentrate on working as a draughtsman.

HILL, Edward Sebastian
Outside-left; Apps 10, Goals 5.
Born: Walsall, July 1860. Deceased.
Career: Walsall Phoenix, BLUES (August 1885), Darlaston (September 1889).
So highly-rated was this goalscoring winger that Blues completely reshuffled their attack to accommodate him. The reshuffle obviously worked as Blues reached their first FA Cup semi-final that year. Ted Hill continued to hold down a place until the formation of the Football Alliance when he decided that regular competitive football was not for him.

HIRONS, John W.
Outside-left; Apps 5, Goals 0.
Born: Erdington, Birmingham, October 1876. Deceased.
Career: Witton Shell Depot FC, Erdington, Pleck Ramblers, Walsall (1901), BLUES (February 1903), Walsall (April 1906).
Hirons was a thorough trier of limited ability, chiefly used to understudy Field, although he did have a run in the left-half position from time to time.

HOCKEY, Trevor J.
Winger/midfield; Apps 231+1, Goals 13.
Born: Keighley, Yorkshire, 1 May 1943. Died: Keighley, 2 April 1987.
Career: Eastwood School (Keighley), West Riding Under 19's, Keighley Central Youth Club (1957-58), (also played rugby for Abertillery (Union) and Keighley (League) as youngster), Bradford City (amateur June 1958, professional May 1960), Nottingham Forest (£15,000 November 1961), Newcastle United (£25,000 November 1963), BLUES (£22,500 November 1965), Sheffield United (£35,000 January 1971), Norwich City (February 1973), Aston Villa (£38,000 June 1973), Bradford City (June 1974), Athlone Town (player-manager March 1976), San Diego Jaws (NASL) (April 1976), Las Vegas Quicksilver (March 1977), San Jose Earthquakes (June 1977), Stalybridge Celtic (manager August 1977). Later attempted to start a soccer section at Keighley Rugby League club; coached the British Army of the Rhine children's team and also coached at Pontins Holiday camps.
Club honours: Newcastle United: Division Two champions 1965.
Representative honours: Wales (9 full caps).

Trevor Hockey was yet another footballing nomad whose professional career spanned close on 16 years, during which time he accumulated well over 600 senior appearances whilst playing on all 92

League club grounds in that time, and having by far his best times with Blues. Initially a winger, Hockey developed into a hard-working, sometimes fiery but very effective midfielder, a player full of Yorkshire grit who always gave 100 per cent. His job was to man-mark an opponent and he often came into conflict with the authorities for his over robust play. Off the field, he was a larger-than-life personality, the proud owner of a pink piano and he made a record entitled *Happy 'cos I'm Blue*, appearing on stage in a concert at Birmingham Town Hall. He was one of the first players to appear for Wales on a parental qualification. He died of a heart attack shortly after playing in a five-a-side tournament in his native Keighley.

HODGES, Frank Charles
Inside-right; Apps 32, Goals 5.
Born: Nechells Green, Birmingham, 26 January 1891. Died: Southport, 5 June 1985.
Career: Alum Rock All Souls, Birmingham Gas FC, BLUES (amateur 1911, professional May 1912), Manchester United (August 1919), Wigan Borough (June 1921), Crewe Alexandra (August 1922), Winsford United (August 1926), Guested for St Mirren during World War One.
Hodges was a local junior who was so impressive partnering Charlie Duncan in the reserves where he notched three hat-tricks, that he was given a prolonged spell in the first team during 1914-15. With Windridge playing his normal striking role Hodges was able to give vent to his normal creative urges. Wounded in the leg during World War One, he decided not to rejoin Blues after the conflict.

HODGETTS, Dennis ('Denny')
Inside-left; Apps 23, Goals 9.
Born: Hockley, Birmingham, 28 November 1863. Died: Aston, Birmingham, 26 March 1945.
Career: Birmingham St George's FC (1878), Great Lever FC (1879), Birmingham St George's (1882), Aston Villa (February 1886), BLUES (October 1896). Retired May 1898 when he returned to Villa Park as coach to the younger players. Became a publican in Birmingham (June 1910), initially taking charge of the Salutation Inn in Summer Lane, Aston. Elected vice-president of Aston Villa in June 1930, a position he held with pride until his death at the age of 81.
Club honours: Aston Villa: Division One champions 1894, 1896, FA Cup winners 1887, 1895, runners-ups 1892.
Representative honours: England (6 full caps); Football League XI (1).
'Denny' Hodges, with his immaculately waxed moustache and smartly greased and parted hair, was a born footballer, a player who was admired by everyone, spectators and fellow professionals alike. He was a clever player, with many ideas. He used both feet with equal effect, was difficult to dispossess (because of his tremendous size and build) and his skilful distribution was so effective, at home and away. He was an uncommonly fine inside-forward (or sometimes outside-left) who in later years turned out to be an admirable coach. In his ten years with Villa he scored 91 goals in 215 appearances.

HOGAN, Thomas Eric
Forward; Apps 0+2, Goals 0.
Born: Cork, 17 December 1971.
Career: FAI School of Excellence, Rockmount FC, Cobh Ramblers (1990), BLUES (£30,000 August 1991), Cobh Ramblers (loan February 1992), Shamrock Rovers (September 1992), Cobh Ramblers (cs 1993), College Corinthians (1994).
Hogan was a slim, red-haired forward who impressed during his trial with Blues on

their Irish tour in the summer of 1991. He left his job in an aluminium factory to become a full-time professional at St Andrew's.

HOLLIS, George
Goalkeeper; Apps 32, Goals 0.
Born: Kenilworth, Warwickshire, 1869. Deceased.
Career: Warwick County, BLUES (1891), reinstated as an amateur and joined Bournbrook (1894). Retired 1897.
Club honours: Blues: Division Two champions 1893.
A swarthy goalkeeper with prominent sideburns, Hollis deputised regularly when Charsley was away on other duties. He kept his shorts up with a decorative cummerbund rather than using a belt.

HOLMES, Ezra
Centre-forward; Apps 2, Goals 0.
Born: West Bromwich 1882. Deceased.
Career: South Staffordshire Regiment, Gainsborough Trinity, BLUES (£400 November 1907), Stamford (March 1908).
Blues made a grave error in judgment when they paid a large fee for this pint-sized forward, who failed to impress on his two appearances. He did not even have time to move home to Birmingham before he found himself on his way back to Lincolnshire.

HOLMES, Paul
Defender; Apps 13, Goals 0.
Born: Stocksbridge, 18 February 1968.
Career: Doncaster Rovers (apprentice June 1984, professional February 1986), Torquay United (£8,000 August 1988), BLUES (June 1992), Everton (£100,000 March 1993).
Paul Holmes proved a speedy footballer, able to occupy the right-back berth as well as that of centre-half. Cool and collected, always looking assured, he might well have become a Liverpool player before joining Blues. He is the son of Albert Holmes, a former Chesterfield defender.

HOLMES, William ('Harry')
Outside-right; Apps 1, Goals 0.
Born: Ambergate, Derbyshire, August 1908.
Career: Milford Ivanhoe, Coventry City (November 1931), Heanor Town (November 1933), Notts County (December 1933), BLUES (November 1934), Heanor Town (August 1935).
Holmes was a capable amateur winger, very popular with the fans during his spell at Coventry. He was reluctant to give up his job as a constructional draughtsman for a career in football, Holmes was the last amateur to play first-team football for Blues.

HOOPER, Harold (Harry)
Winger; Apps 119, Goals 42.

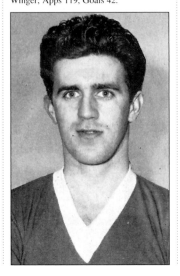

Born: Pittington, Co Durham, 14 June 1933.
Career: Hylton Colliery Juniors, West Ham United (junior 1949, professional November 1950), Wolverhampton Wanderers (£25,000 March 1956), BLUES (£20,000 December 1957), Sunderland (£18,000 September 1960), Kettering Town (May 1963), Dunstable Town (1965), Heanor Town (1967).
Club honours: Blues: Fairs Cup runners-up 1960.
Representative honours: England (6 'B' caps, 2 Under-23 caps); Football League XI (1).
From a footballing family, Harry Hooper's father played for Sheffield United and his brother, Alf, for Halifax Town. Harry junior was Durham sprint champion before turning to football and throughout his career he used his speed to good effect. He signed for the Hammers whilst his father was trainer at Upton Park, and was given an early chance to show his ability, soon making the right-wing position his own and impressing sufficiently to earn a call-up for the full England squad. Wolves were impressed enough to pay a record fee for his services, but despite turning in some fine displays, he did not stay too long at Molineux. On moving to St Andrew's he was switched to the left flank where he continued to perform well and made himself a favourite with the fans. After a few years, when it became obvious that Blues were going nowhere, Hooper moved back to his native North-East.

HOOPER, Lyndon
Midfield; Apps 2+4, Goals 0.
Born: Guyana, 30 May 1966.
Career: Eastern Ontario All Stars, Ottawa Pioneers (1987), Montreal Supra (1988), Toronto Blizzard (NASL) (1989), BLUES (£50,000 October 1993). Released July 1994.
Representative honours: Canada (49 full caps, 1 Olympic Games appearance, Under-21 and Youth caps).
Regarded as the best player in Canada, Lyndon Hooper was the last of the three Canadians brought over by coach Tony Taylor to join Blues. After a trial in the reserves he made an early debut at Villa Park in the League Cup tie, in front of 35,000 spectators. Unfortunately, his arrival coincided with a period of instability at the club and he was unable to convince Barry Fry of his worth. At the end of the season his work permit was not renewed as he had made insufficient appearances. In March 1995 he was apparently still looking for an opening in European soccer. His sister Charmaine is regarded as the star player of Canada's women's soccer team whilst younger brother Ian plays in North Carolina State University's side. His most famous relation, however, is cousin Carl Hooper, the West Indies Test cricketer.

HOPE, Robert
Inside-forward; Apps 42+4, Goals 5.
Born: Bridge of Allan, Scotland, 28 September 1943.
Career: Clydebank High and Dunbartonshire West Schools, Drumchapel Amateurs, Sunderland (trial), Scotland Boys, West Bromwich Albion (amateur August 1959, professional September 1960), BLUES (£66,666 May 1972), Philadelphia Atoms (NASL) (April 1975), Dallas Tornados (NASL) (May-August 1976), Sheffield Wednesday (September 1976), Dallas Tornados (loan April-August 1977 and April-August 1978), Bromsgrove Rovers (player-coach August 1978, appointed manager May 1983), Burton Albion (manager August-October 1988), Bromsgrove Rovers (manager June 1989-September 1994). Played for WBA All Stars (1979-90) and in 1989 was a scout for Wolverhampton Wanderers. After retiring

from football ran a sub-post office in Handsworth Wood, Birmingham, and later at Boldmere, Sutton Coldfield. Also scouted for West Bromwich Albion.
Club honours: WBA: FA Cup winners 1968, Football League Cup winners 1966, runners-up 1967, 1970.
Representative honours: Scotland (2 full caps, 1 Under-23 cap, 2 Schoolboy caps).
Bobby Hope was a player who displayed masterly generalship in midfield for West Brom for whom he scored 42 goals in 403 games. A diminutive performer, Hope was one of the best passers of a ball in the game. He was a surprise signing by Blues to boost their newly-promoted side, but struggled after a bright start and eventually elected to join the exodus to America.

HOPKINS, Robert Arthur ('Hoppy')
Forward/midfield; Apps 195+10, Goals 33.
Born: Hall Green, Birmingham, 25 October 1961.
Career: Pitmaston School, South Birmingham Schools (playing in English Schools Trophy), West Midlands County Boys, Aston Villa (apprentice July 1977, professional July 1979), BLUES (March 1983, in exchange for Alan Curbishley), Manchester City (£130,000 September 1986), West Bromwich Albion (rated at £60,000 March 1989 in exchange deal involving Imre Varadi), BLUES (£25,000 March 1989); Shrewsbury Town (free transfer July 1991), Instant Dictionary FC (Hong Kong) (1992), Solihull Borough (1993), Colchester United (February 1993), Solihull Borough (1994).
Club honours: Aston Villa: FA Youth Cup and Southern Junior Floodlit Cup winners 1980; Blues: Division Two promotion 1985, Leyland DAF Cup winners 1991 (as non-playing sub).

A Blues fanatic all his life, Robert Hopkins' early career was liberally punctured by disciplinary problems before he settled down to become a good professional, turning out at centre-forward, on the right wing, in central midfield and from time to time at full-back. It was unfortunate that the happiest day of his footballing life – when his beloved Birmingham City finally won something at Wembley – turned out to be the last time he was selected for a Blues squad.

HORSMAN, William
Winger; Apps 83, Goals 3.
Born: Doncaster 1902. Deceased.
Career: Selby Town, BLUES (1928), Chester (1935). Retired during World War Two.
A winger who was perpetually on the verge of a breakthrough but never quite made it in Division One, Horsman proved to be a valuable acquisition for Chester, exhibiting goalscoring flair that had never been obvious during his lengthy spell with Blues.

HOUGHTON, Henry Brian ('Bud')
Centre-forward; Apps 4, Goals 1.
Born: Madras, India, 1 September 1936.
Career: St Wilfred's Youth Club, Bradford (amateur 1954, professional October 1955), BLUES (£5,250 October 1957), Southend United (October 1958), Oxford United (£2,000 March 1961), Lincoln City (£6,000 October 1963), Chelmsford City (July 1965), Cambridge United, Wellington Town, Cheltenham Town, Morris Motors.
Club honours: Oxford United: Southern League champions 1961, 1962.
A burly, bustling forward who was always a great favourite with the crowd wherever he went, Houghton was a prolific scorer in the lower divisions, but his style did not suit Blues' game at the time which was built around a more mobile centre-forward.

HOWARD, Henry
Wing-half; Apps 51, Goals 1.
Born: Rotherham, 1871. Deceased.
Career: Yorkshire local football, Rotherham Town (trial), Sheffield Wednesday (trial), Sheffield United, BLUES (April 1902), Wisbech Town (August 1906).
He was a solidly built, defensively minded player who always seemed to promise more than he achieved.

HOWARD, Patrick
Central defender; Apps 43, Goals 0.
Born: Dodworth, 7 October 1947.
Career: Barnsley Boys, Barnsley (apprentice April 1963, professional October 1965), Newcastle United (£21,000 September 1971), Arsenal (£50,000 September 1976), BLUES (£40,000 August 1977), Portland Timbers (loan April-August 1978), Bury (July 1979). Retired 1982 to commence running his own business in Bury.
Club honours: Newcastle United: FA Cup runners-up 1974, Football League Cup runners-up 1976.

An experienced defender who was signed as an emergency replacement for Joe Gallagher after his car crash, Howard gave Blues good service in his first season, helping hold together a rather leaky defence. Injuries suffered during his spell in America restricted his appearances in 1978-79 and he was eventually given a free transfer.

HOWELL, David C.
Defender; Apps 2, Goals 0.
Born: Hammersmith, 10 October 1956.
Career: Fulham (apprentice), Enfield, Hillingdon Borough, Hounslow, Enfield, Barnet (October 1990), Southend United (player-coach July 1993), BLUES (coach December 1993, player September 1994).
Club honours: Barnet: Conference winners 1991; Enfield: Conference winners 1986, FA Trophy winners 1988.
Representative honours: England (15 semi-professional caps).

Howell made his debut for Blues in December 1994, aged 38, as a replacement for the suspended Liam Daish. He had been with Barry Fry since his Hillingdon days, a true professional, totally committed who came to Blues, not as a player but as a coach.

HOWITT, David John
Right-back; Apps 3, Goals 0.
Born: Birmingham, 4 August 1952.
Career: Hodge Hill School, BLUES (apprentice June 1968, professional March 1970), Bury (August 1973), Workington (July 1974), Aldershot (June 1975), Milton Keynes City (August 1981), Milton Keynes Borough (1983), Newport Pagnell Town.
Howitt made close on 200 League appearances during his career, 137 for Aldershot. He was a successful schoolboy midfielder before joining Blues and was converted into a full-back whilst in the reserves. He made his first-team debut after Blues had made a poor start to the 1972-73 campaign but failed to impress and was released at the end of the season. Howitt later acted as player-manager of Milton Keynes City, staying with that club until it folded after failing to record a single win in its last season.

HOYLAND, Frederick
Outside-right; Apps 6, Goals 0.
Born: Pontefract, Yorkshire, March 1898. Deceased.
Career: Swansea Town (February 1921), Bury (1922), Glossop, BLUES (September 1923), Brighton & Hove Albion (May 1924-June 1926).
This well built winger had a brief spell in the team in place of the injured Billy Harvey. He remained a reserve during his time with Brighton in the Third Division South.

HUBBARD, Arthur G.
Left-back; Apps 5, Goals 0.
Born: Erdington, Birmingham, May 1911.
Career: Chester Road School, Moor Green, Wright & Eagle Range Company FC, BLUES (amateur August 1932, professional February 1933), Luton Town (August 1935), Dunstable Town (1939).
Representative honour: FA Amateur XI.
A solid full-back, signed from a works league team, Arthur Hubbard's first-team outings were restricted to only five, as replacement for the injured Ned Barkas.

HUGHES, Jack
Centre-half; Apps 1, Goals 0.
Born: Birmingham 1866. Deceased.
Career: Birmingham Unity, BLUES (August 1890), Lea Hall Constitutionals (1891).
Caesar Jenkyns' deputy in one game – which Blues lost 5-2 – he was never given another chance.

HUGHES, John Norman
Outside-left; Apps 7, Goals 0.
Born: Tamworth, 10 July 1921.
Career: Tamworth Castle, BLUES (June 1947), Tamworth (August 1949), Atherstone Town (1952). Later assistant manager of Tamworth (1955).
He rose to prominence in non-League circles during the war when he impressed with his versatility. Blues used him principally as a winger, a role for which he was not ideally suited and his League chances were restricted accordingly.

HUGHES, William Marshall
Left-back; Apps 110, Goals 0.
Born: Carmarthen, 6 March 1918. Died: Birmingham, 16 June 1981.
Career: Llanelli Boys' School, Swansea Grammar School, Carmarthen, Archer Corinthians, Llanelli, Watchers Celtic, Llanelli Town (1934), Swansea Town (loan, March 1935), BLUES (professional May

1935), Luton Town (July 1947), Chelsea (£12,000 March 1948), Hereford United (August 1951), Flint Town (January 1954). Retired 1955 and later scouted for Chester. Guested for Arsenal, QPR, Tottenham Hotspur and West Ham during World War Two.
Club honours: Flint Town: Welsh Cup winners 1954.
Representative honours: Wales: (10 full caps, 14 Wartime/Victory caps); played for Great Britain v Rest of Europe in 1947.
Billy Hughes matured quickly into a highly skilled full-back, an effective ball-winner who always tried to be constructive, always looking to play his way out of difficulty. He appeared in over 60 games for Blues during World War Two, having been a teenager when he made his senior debut.

HUME, William Sanderson
Wing-half/inside-forward; Apps 10, Goals 2.
Born: Armadale, 18 December 1935.
Career: Dunfermline Athletic, BLUES (February 1958), St Mirren (1960), Berwick Rangers, Bangor City, Hakoah (Melbourne, Australian State League).
A strong man and good ball-player, Billy Hume made his debut for Blues in a friendly against Valencia. It was a problem where to play him, but it eventually settled down at inside-left and had one reasonable run in the first team but met with limited success overall.

HUNT, Jonathan Richard
Midfield; Apps 22+8, Goals 8.
Born: Camden Town, 2 November 1971.
Career: Woking, Barnet, Southend United (July 1993), BLUES (September 1994).
Club honours: Blues: Second Division champions 1995, Auto Windscreens Shield winners 1995.

A very skilful right-sided player, he made a big impact at St Andrew's before injury forced him out of the action early in the 1994-95 season. He scored hat-tricks in Blues' 5-0 League win over Crewe Alexandra in November 1994 and Auto Windscreens Shield game against Peterborough in September (the first Blues hat-trick for over nine years).

HUNTER, William ('Sailor')
Centre-half; Apps 42, Goals 0.
Born: Cardenden, Scotland, 16 August 1900. Deceased.
Career: Bowhill Juniors, BLUES (April 1921), Grimsby Town (January 1927), Coventry City (September 1927), Walsall (1928), Torquay United (December 1929). Retired May 1930.
Rather on the small side for a centre-half at 5ft 8in and 10st 12lb, he was nevertheless one of the mainstays of Blues' reserve side throughout the early 1920s. Hunter could always be relied upon to turn in a solid performance when given a first-team

chance. He gained his nickname from his Naval service during World War One.

HUXFORD, Richard John
Full-back; Apps 5, Goals 0.
Born: Scunthorpe, 25 July 1969.
Career: Scunthorpe United (apprentice), Matlock Town (1987), Burton Albion (1989), Gainsborough Trinity (1989-90), Kettering Town, Barnet (August 1992), Millwall (free transfer July 1993), BLUES (loan February 1994), Bradford City (loan October 1994-January 1995).
Huxford, a no nonsense full-back, was taken on a month's loan after Scott Hiley was injured, ironically at Millwall whence Huxford then came.

HYND, John Roger Shankly
Central defender; Apps 198+8, Goals 5.
Born: Falkirk, 2 February 1942.
Career: Lanark Grammar School, Glasgow Rangers (1961), Crystal Palace (£12,000 July 1969), BLUES (£25,000 July 1970), Oxford United (loan October 1975), Walsall (December 1975), Motherwell (manager June 1978).
Club honours: Rangers: European Cup-winners' Cup runners-up 1967; Blues: Division Two promotion 1972.

Nephew of the great Bill Shankly, Roger Hynd was a defender with the physique of a weightlifter who became a huge favourite with the fans with his refusal to give less than 100 per cent. Although principally a centre-half, he lined-up at centre-forward for Rangers in the 1967 European Cup-winners' Cup Final. Disgusted with the result and his own display, he threw his medal into the crowd after the match. Palace signed him to boost their newly-promoted side but he met with only limited success at Selhurst Park. Freddie Goodwin then enticed him to be the pivot of the Blues defence, and he proved to be a very popular signing, his strong heading, firm tackling and distinctive running style, which involved a very high knee lift, signalling him out above the rest of the team. Possibly the only Blues star to play a trombone, Hynd is currently a PE teacher based in Wishaw (Scotland).

INGLIS, James Allen
Outside-right; Apps 62, Goals 28.
Born: Kirkland, Scotland, 1872. Deceased.
Career: Airdrieonians, BLUES (£40 September 1896), Luton Town (August 1899).
Jimmy Inglis was a fast, direct winger with terrific goalscoring record and he seemed to be the long-term replacement for Jack Hallam until suffering a loss of form which prompted Blues to sign Billy Bennett. Inglis' move to the ailing Luton club was disastrous, for he had only three games before that club dropped out of the Football League.

ISHERWOOD, Dennis
Right-back; Apps 5, Goals 1.

Born: Brierley Hill, 20 January 1947.
Career: Brierley Hill Schools, BLUES (junior June 1962, professional January 1964), Bromsgrove Rovers (1968), Kidderminster Harriers.
Isherwood was a neat, compact full-back who had an eventful first-team career with Blues. He scored on his debut with a 25-yarder and then put through his own goal the following week. He now resides in Kingswinford where he is a prominent figure in junior tennis circles.

ISHERWOOD, Harold
Left-back; Apps 1, Goals 0.
Born: Darwen, Lancashire, May 1905.
Career: Fleetwood, Sunderland (May 1926, BLUES (May 1927), Bournemouth & Boscombe Athletic (June 1928), Worcester City (August 1929).
This stocky defender failed to make the first team with Sunderland. His only game for Blues came in the last match of the 1926-27 season, and after spending the next term in the reserve side he went on to play in 18 matches for Bournemouth before dropping out of the Football League.

ISLIP, Ernest
Inside-forward; Apps 89, Goals 24.
Born: Parkwood Springs, Sheffield, 31 October 1892. Died: Huddersfield, August 1941.
Career: Sheffield Douglas FC (1910), Huddersfield Town (June 1911), BLUES (£1,500 November 1923), Bradford City (£400 May 1927), Kidderminster Harriers (August 1928), Ashton National FC (September 1928), Wrexham (November 1928). Retired February 1929. Guested for Rotherham County, Sheffield Wednesday and West Ham United during World War One.
Club honours: Huddersfield Town: FA Cup winners 1922, runners-up 1920, Division Two runners-up 1920.

An aggressive and wholehearted player who hit 26 goals in 98 League games in four seasons as a centre-forward with Huddersfield before joining Blues, Ernie Islip had been a prolific marksmen in local Yorkshire junior football prior to turning professional. He was left in the cold at St Andrew's following the emergence of George Briggs.

IVEY, Paul Henry Winspeare
Forward; Apps 4+3, Goals 0.
Born: Westminster, London, 1 April 1961.
Career: London & District Schools, BLUES (apprentice June 1977, professional January 1979), Chesterfield (free transfer June 1982), Karlskrona (late 1982), Alvechurch, Kalmar AIK, Vasalund.
As a lad he was described as 'having a lot of skill, a nice touch on the ball and the right potential'. The potential went

unfulfilled in England, but he made a name for himself in the Swedish Second Division where he became a regular goalscorer.

IZON, Charles John
Forward; Apps 26, Goals 8.
Born: Stourbridge, 1870. Deceased.
Career: Old Hill Wanderers, Halesowen, BLUES (September 1893), Walsall (1897).
He was highly rated in local football, and Blues beat several other West Midlands club to land his signature. He announced his arrival at St Andrew's with a hat-trick on his debut, but scored only one more goal that season and thereafter struggled to gain a place in the side, although he also netted in his last game for the club.

JACKSON, Alec
Utility forward; Apps 84+1, Goals 12.
Born: Tipton, 29 May 1937.
Career: Park Lane Secondary Modern School (Tipton), Tipton St John's FC, W.G.Allen's FC, West Bromwich Albion (amateur May 1954, professional September 1954), BLUES (£12,500 June 1964), Walsall (February 1967), Nuneaton Borough (August 1968), Kidderminster Harriers (1970), Warley (1971), Oldbury Town (1972), Warley Borough (early 1973), Darlaston (August 1973), Blakenhall (1974), Lower Gornal (1976), Rushall Olympic (1977), Bush Rangers (1978). Retired 1979. Appeared in charity matches for West Bromwich Albion All Stars (1968-85). Was coach to Coseley Rovers Youth Club (1980-82).
Club honours: WBA: FA Youth Cup runners-up 1955.
Representative honours: Football League XI (1).

Black Country born and bred, Alec Jackson could play well in any forward position and he did just that during his ten-year stay with West Bromwich Albion for whom he scored 52 goals in 208 games. A player with neat footwork, he pulled out of League football with 325 appearances to his name with 60 goals scored. He still lives and works in his beloved Tipton.

JACKSON, Alexander James
Centre-forward; Apps 10, Goals 7.
Born: Glasgow, 28 November 1935.
Career: Shettlestone Juniors, BLUES (£2,000 professional April 1958), Plymouth Argyle (March 1960), Weymouth (1964), later lottery manager of Exeter City.
He was not the tallest of centre-forwards but a hard worker and useful scorer who was surprisingly sold by Blues despite an impressive record. Argyle used him as an inside-forward as well as a number-nine and he proceeded to score 27 goals for them in 75 games. He was badly affected by a broken leg in 1963 and never quite regained his form.

JACKSON, Walter S.
Outside-right; Apps 4, Goals 1.
Born: Northfield, Birmingham, 1870. Deceased.
Career: Selly Park Nomads, Harborne, BLUES (September 1893), Berwick Rangers, Worcester (May 1894).
Given his chance due to an injury to Jack Hallam, Jackson was criticised for having the tendency to 'dally' on the ball, and was generally regarded as not being in Hallam's class. He followed the well trodden road of Blues' rejects to the Worcester side, Berwick Rangers.

JAMES, Arthur
Outside-right; Apps 5, Goals 3.
Born: Longbridge, Birmingham, January 1855. Died: Birmingham June 1911.
Career: Birmingham Carriage Works (1874), BLUES (September 1875). Retired (through injury and illness) 1887.
Representative honours: Birmingham FA XI.
The middle of the three James brothers who were involved in the founding of the Blues, Arthur was unusual in being the only forward amongst the brothers, and a very fine one too. Fast and tricky, with a hard shot, he was a first choice for the Birmingham FA XI in several representative matches.

JAMES, Frederick
Left-back/centre-half; Apps 12, Goals 0.
Born: Bartley Green, Birmingham, February 1853. Deceased.
Career: Northfield Prims, Birmingham Carriage Works FC, BLUES (1875). Retired 1886.
Oldest of the James brothers, Fred was left-back in Blues' first-ever match against Holte Wanderers. A big-hearted player, with little finesse, he later took over captaincy of the team when W.H.Edmunds set up his legal practice in Nottingham. He was still a first-team player when he decided to retire.

JAMES, John Edward ('Jimmy')
Inside-forward; Apps 7, Goals 2.
Born: Harborne, Birmingham, 19 February 1934.
Career: Brighton & Hove Albion (amateur 1949), Paget Rangers, BLUES (junior June 1950, professional March 1951), Torquay United (June 1955).
He combined working in a brass foundry with being a boot boy at Paget Rangers when Blues signed him in 1950. After careful grooming, he was given his senior baptism against Spurs in an FA Cup-tie in 1953 in place of the injured Peter Murphy. But with the side being built up for a push to promotion, Jimmy James' outings after that were limited. He did well after leaving St Andrew's, however, scoring 11 goals in 123 League games for Torquay.

JAMES, Thomas ('Tommy')
Wing-half; Apps 7, Goals 1.
Born: Bartley Green, Birmingham, April 1857. Died: Birmingham, 31 October 1928.
Career: Birmingham Carriage Works FC, BLUES (1875). Retired May 1885.
Youngest of the James brothers and the one who had the shortest career, he was right-half in Blues' inaugural fixture and remained in the side until the start of the 1884-85 season when injuries began to take their toll. More adventurous than Fred, he could frequently be found in the attack. All three brothers were sufficiently well known to be referred to by just their first names in newspaper reports of the day.

JENKINS, James Lindley
Midfield; Apps 3, Goals 0.
Born: West Bromwich, 6 April 1954.
Career: South Staffs Boys, BLUES (apprentice June 1970, professional July

1971), Walsall (free transfer July 1974), Tividale (1975).

Former England Schoolboy trialist, Lindley Jenkins was the work-horse of the Blues youth team in the Francis-Burns era. He made his senior bow during a bad patch for the club and was perhaps a little too sluggish for football at the highest level.

JENKINS, Lee R.
Midfield; Apps 1, Goals 0.
Born: West Bromwich, 17 March 1961.
Career: Barr Beacon School, Aston Villa Boys, Aston Villa (apprentice June 1977, professional January 1979), Port Vale (free transfer November 1980), Rovaniemi Palloseura (Finland) (August 1981), BLUES (October 1985), Finnairin Palloilijat (Finland) (1986).
Club honours: Aston Villa: FA Youth Cup runners-up 1978.
Representative honours: England (Youth caps).
After an unsuccessful spell in England, Lee Jenkins came good in Finland. He returned briefly for a spell with Blues (under Ron Saunders' managership) but broke his ankle in his first game, against West Brom. He never played for Blues again, returning to continue his successful career in Finland.

JENKINSON, Leigh
Forward; Apps 2+1, Goals 0.
Born: Thorne, 9 July 1969.
Career: Hull City (apprentice July 1985, professional June 1987), Rotherham United (loan September 1990), Coventry City (£300,000 March 1993), BLUES (loan November 1993).
A strong-running wide player, 6ft tall with good close control, he managed 14 goals in over 150 games whilst at Boothferry Park.

JENKYNS, Caesar Augustus Llewellyn
Centre-half; Apps 99, Goals 13.
Born: Builth, Wales, 24 August 1866. Died: Birmingham, 23 July 1941.
Career: Southfield, St Andrew's Sunday School, BLUES (1884), Unity Gas, BLUES (July 1888), Newton Heath (May 1896), Walsall (November 1897), Coventry City (coach 1902), Saltley Wednesday FC (guest 1904). Retired cs 1905 and took over the George Inn, Moxley and later joined the police force.
Club honours: Blues: Division Two champions 1893, Division Two promotion 1894.
Representative honours: Wales (8 full caps).
A burly player with a fierce shoulder-charge and shuddering tackle, 'The Mighty Caesar' was the back-bone of the Blues' defence. A born leader, he skippered all the clubs he played for and his country, and was an inspiration to the rest of the team. He could head a ball half the length of the field and once won a competition by sending a dead-ball kick fully 100 yards first bounce. He took great pleasure in thwarting Blues' forwards during later meetings. Controversial to the last, his one game for Saltley led to him receiving a ban as he had not been re-instated as an amateur. He was certainly a tough character and was sent off a few times during his career. He left Blues in 1895 under a cloud, being sacked for brawling with a Derby player whom he alleged had spat at him. His son, Octavius, (classical names ran through the family) had trials with Blues shortly before World War One but was never signed on.

JENNINGS, Dennis Bernard
Outside-right/left-back; Apps 212, Goals 14.
Born: Habberley Valley, near Kidderminster, 20 July 1910.
Career: Franche FC, St Barnabas, Foley Park, Stourport Swifts, Romsley Village, West Bromwich Albion (amateur, early

1928), Kidderminster Harriers (July 1929), Huddersfield Town (October 1930), Grimsby Town (September 1932), BLUES (£1,200 January 1936), Kidderminster Harriers (player-coach March 1951-May 1953), Lockheed Leamington (June 1953). Later retired to live in the village of Little Dinham, near Wadebridge, Cornwall. Guested for Nottingham Forest during World War Two.
Club honours: Grimsby Town: Division Two champions 1934; Blues: Football League South champions 1946, Division Two champions 1948.
He played in every position for Blues except centre-half during his lengthy stay at St Andrew's, making 174 wartime appearances as well as his senior appearances. He produced many calm, unflustered performances in each of his many roles, having started off as an out-and-out winger. Dennis Jennings relied on skill rather than speed and he was almost 41 years of age when he finally left St Andrew's. His speciality was the bicycle kick.

JOHNSON, Arthur
Outside-left; Apps 9, Goals 0.
Born: Atherstone, July 1904.
Career: Atherstone Town, Huddersfield Town (November 1924), Barnsley (October 1925), BLUES (August 1927), Bristol City (May 1928), Coventry City (cs 1931).
A tall winger who returned home after an unhappy spell in Yorkshire, Johnson impressed in practice matches and was given the chance of filling one of Blues' problem positions but had little success.

JOHNSTON, George
Inside-forward; Apps 7+3, Goals 1.
Born: Glasgow, 21 March 1947.
Career: St George Road Youth Cub, Maryhill Boys, Cardiff City (juniors June 1962, professional May 1964), Arsenal (£20,000 March 1967), BLUES (£30,000 May 1969), Walsall (loan September-October 1970), Fulham (£6,000 October 1970), Hereford United (£2,500 August

1972), Newport County (£1,500 September 1973), Caerau (1974).
Club honours: Cardiff City: Welsh Cup winners 1965.
This former Glasgow Corporation tea-boy first caught the eye by scoring regularly for Cardiff whilst still a teenager. Two goals against Arsenal in a charity match led to the Londoners signing him. From there, though, his career took a downward turn, and he was never a first-team regular at Highbury. He moved to Blues as replacement for Fred Pickering but found it difficult to hold down a first-team place and eventually set off on a tour of the lower divisions.

JOHNSTON, William McClure ('Bud')
Outside-left; Apps 18, Goals 0.
Born: Maryhill, Glasgow, 19 December 1946.
Career: Fife County Schools, Bowhill Strollers, Lochore Welfare (1961), Manchester United (trial), Glasgow Rangers (amateur July 1962, professional February 1964), West Bromwich Albion (£138,000 December 1972), Vancouver Whitecaps (NASL) (£190,000 March 1979), BLUES (loan October 1979-February 1980), Vancouver Whitecaps (February 1980), Glasgow Rangers (£40,000 August 1980), Vancouver Whitecaps (May 1982), Heart of Midlothian (September 1982), South China (Hong Kong), Heart of Midlothian (head coach 1983), East Fife (coach 1985), Raith Rovers (coach March-June 1986). Became publican in Glasgow (June 1986) but returned to football in July 1987 as coach to Falkirk. Later acted as scout for West Brom (1991).
Club honours: Rangers: European Cup-winners' Cup winners 1972, runners-up 1967, Scottish FA Cup winners 1966, runners-up 1969, 1971, 1981, Scottish League Cup winners 1965, 1971, runners-up 1966, 1967; Vancouver Whitecaps: NASL Super Bowl winners 1979; Blues: Division Two promotion 1980.
Representative honours: Scotland (22 full caps, 2 Under-23 caps, Youth caps); Scottish League XI (2)
A marvellous, dashing winger, skilful and entertaining, but a player who had a fiery temper, Willie Johnston was sent off no fewer than 15 times during his career (which is probably a record) and was once suspended for 67 days prior to joining West Bromwich Albion in 1972 after falling foul of Ibrox boss, Jock Wallace (a former West Brom goalkeeper). Nevertheless he was a fine winger, although Blues saw him towards the end of his playing days. He scored over 160 goals in more than 400 games as a professional, and once netted a hat-trick of penalties for Rangers against St Johnstone after coming on as a substitute. He also scored two crucial goals to help Rangers win the European Cup-winners' Cup in 1972 against Dinamo Moscow. Johnston was sensationally sent home from the Scottish World Cup party on a drugs charge in 1978.

JOLLY, Edwin ('Teddy')
Centre-half; Apps 21, Goals 2.
Born: Lozells, Birmingham, June 1871. Deceased.
Career: Lozells Street School, Guildford Street FC, Lozells FC, BLUES (August 1893), Berwick Rangers, Worcester (September 1896).
Jolly by name, jolly by nature, 'Teddy' was the life and soul of the Blues' dressing-room, and always willing to try his hand in any position. His two goals came when he made a surprise appearance on the wing. He scored a hat-trick of own-goals in a Birmingham League match in March 1895.

JONES, Aaron
Forward; Apps 5, Goals 0.
Born: Rotherham, 1884. Died: Yorkshire, 1950.

Career: Newstead Byron, Barnsley, BLUES (£170 May 1905), Notts County (August 1907).
A versatile forward, described as 'able, dainty and energetic,' whose five appearances came in three different roles.

JONES, Abraham ('Abe')
Centre-forward; Apps 3, Goals 2.
Born: West Bromwich, April 1899. Deceased.
Career: Bratt Street School, West Bromwich Sandwell, BLUES (September 1919), Reading (August 1921), Brighton & Hove Albion (June 1922), Merthyr Town (August 1923), Stoke City (1924). Also professional boxer (1916).
An enthusiastic, dashing forward who opened his League career with two goals on his Blues debut, but was then kept in the background by Harry Hampton. He remained a reserve for most of his career. Son of 'Abe' Jones, the former West Brom and Middlesbrough centre-half, and nephew of the former Blues star William Henry Jones.

JONES, Charles T.
Outside-left; Apps 1, Goals 0.
Born: Moseley, Birmingham, July 1888. Deceased.
Career: Verity's Works, BLUES (August 1908), Bristol Rovers (1909).
An amateur winger, speedy, but not particularly accurate with his crosses. He made only spasmodic appearances for Bristol Rovers, mainly as deputy for ex-Blues man, Willie Peplow.

JONES, Charles Wilson
Centre-forward; Apps 150, Goals 69.
Born: Pentre Broughton, near Wrexham, 29 April 1914. Died: Birmingham, 9 January 1986.
Career: Brymbo Green (1930), Blackburn Rovers (trial), Bolton Wanderers (trial), Wrexham (professional August 1932), BLUES (£1,500 September 1934), Nottingham Forest (September 1947), Redditch United, Kidderminster Harriers (1948). Retired cs 1950 to go into licensing trade where he stayed until 1978. Guested for Blackpool, Huddersfield Town, West Bromwich Albion and Wrexham during World War Two.
Club honours: Blues: Football League South champions 1946.
Representative honours: Wales (2 full caps).
A pale red-haired, deceptively frail looking forward who had a sterling rise to fame. After two years in Wrexham's reserves, Blues signed him and within six months he was leading his country's attack. He had

two excellent years as Blues' centre-forward before injuries and loss of form affected his overall play. He lost popularity with the fans and was possibly the first Blues player to receive concerted barracking, but despite this he continued to give several years of stalwart service. He scored 45 goals in 75 wartime games for Blues.

JONES, David Wilmott Llewellyn
Inside-forward; Apps 9, Goals 0.
Born: Kingsley, 9 April 1940.
Career: Crewe Alexandra (juniors 1955, amateur May 1956), BLUES (professional April 1957), Millwall (December 1959 to May 1964).
Club honours: Millwall: Division Four champions 1962.
Representative honours: England (Youth caps).
He was a talented young forward who played in 26 League games for Crewe whilst still an amateur. Nurtured carefully for a year at St Andrew's, he was coming along nicely until a major leg injury halted his progress. He did splendidly with Millwall, however, for whom he scored 71 goals in 164 League games in five years at The Den.

JONES, Frederick R.
Inside-left; Apps 1, Goals 0.
Born: Halesowen, 1910.
Career: Old Hill White Star, Halesowen, Huddersfield Town (trial), Leeds United, BLUES (August 1934), Cheltenham Town (September 1935-May 1936).
One of the few mystery men in Blues' history, his only appearance came as a late replacement for Joe Bradford, and in fact it is an appearance credited in some sources to Wilson Jones, who had not signed for Blues at that time. He later played an important part in Cheltenham Town's FA Cup run in 1935-36 when they reached the third round.

JONES, Frederick William
Left-back; Apps 9, Goals 0.
Born: Llandudno, January 1867. Died: Llandudno, 27 December 1910 of apoplectic seizure.
Career: Gloddath Athletic (1886-90), Llandudno Swifts, Bolton Wanderers (trial), West Manchester, Burslem Port Vale (September 1890), Newton Heath, BLUES (August 1892), Lincoln City (1893), Reading, Ellesmere Port, Chirk, Llandudno Swifts (1896-1900), Caernarfon Ironopolis, Llanrwst Major (1903).
Representative honours: Wales (1 full cap).
This lumbering full-back was the first Blues player to be capped for Wales, an honour which crowned a rapid rise to the top. His descent was equally rapid and he was latterly called upon as an emergency goalkeeper rather than as a full-back. He was found dead in a Llandudno street. His brother Arnold played for Blues in 1892-93.

JONES, Gary Kenneth
Outside-right; Apps 36+2, Goals 1.
Born: Whiston, Liverpool, 5 January 1951.
Career: Everton (apprentice June 1966, professional October 1968), BLUES (£110,000 July 1976), Fort Lauderdale Strikers (April 1978).
An aggressive winger, never afraid to run at defences, he was nevertheless plagued by inconsistency throughout his Blues career. His goals tally was a poor return for a player whose primary function was an attacker. On returning from America became landlord of The Albert, one of the trendiest pubs in Liverpool.

JONES, John
Inside-forward; Apps 39, Goals 18.
Born: West Bromwich, October 1874. Died: London, 13 September 1904.

Career: Tantany Rovers, Shaftsbury White Rose, Sandwell Albion, Dudley, Halesowen, BLUES (December 1894), Eastville Rovers (1897), Tottenham Hotspur (July 1902 until his death).
He was a skilful, two-footed player who maintained a respectable strike rate throughout his career and who still holds the Bristol Rovers record for goals in a match (six against Weymouth in the 1900-01 FA Cup). He was known as 'Bristol Jones' during his days with Spurs, to distinguish him from another John Jones. He died of typhoid, aged 29.

JONES, John ('Jack') William ('Cracker')
Left-back; Apps 237, Goals 1.
Born: Rotherham, 8 February 1891. Died: Rotherham, 20 July 1948.
Career: Alma Road School, Allerton Bywater Colliery, Industry FC, Bird-in-Hand FC, Maltby Main Colliery, Army football (RAF), Sunderland (November 1914), BLUES (£2,000 May 1920), Nelson (May 1927), Crewe Alexandra (March 1928), Scarborough (September 1930). Retired 1931.
Club honours: Blues: Division Two champions 1921.
Representative honours: Football League XI (1).
A formidable full-back, well built with a biting tackle, 'Cracker' Jones was something special in the 1920s, being as rough as his partner Frank Womack was fair. Wingers rarely relished a confrontation with this muscular former miner and it was perhaps surprising that he was seldom involved in disciplinary action. He played in dentures until one notable occasion, on a close season tour to Spain, when they were smashed as he took a full-blooded shot in the face, only to have a penalty for handball awarded against him.

JONES, Mark Anthony William
Full-back/utility; Apps 38+2, Goals 0.
Born: Warley, West Midlands, 22 October 1961.
Career: Warley Schools, Aston Villa (apprentice June 1977, professional July 1979), Brighton & Hove Albion (£50,000 March 1984), BLUES (player exchange for Mick Ferguson October 1984), Shrewsbury Town (loan February 1987, permanently March 1987), Hereford United (June 1987), Worcester City (free transfer July 1991), Redditch United (loan October 1992), Merthyr Tydfil (1993).
Club honours: Aston Villa: European Super Cup 1983, World Club Championship 1983, FA Youth Cup and Southern Junior Floodlit Cup winners 1980.
He was a talented full-back at Villa Park and was signed by his former manager, Ron Saunders, for Blues after a short spell with Brighton. His career at St Andrew's was hampered by injury and he was frequently asked to play in positions that he was unsuited.

JONES, Paul Tony
Winger; Apps 0+2, Goals 0.
Born: Solihull, 6 February 1974.
Career: Knowle Juniors, St Peter's School, BLUES (YTS June 1990, professional February 1992), Moor Green (cs 1993).
He was mainly a reserve at St Andrew's, making two appearances as a substitute, coming on both times because of injury to another player.

JONES, Roger
Goalkeeper; Apps 4, Goals 0.
Born: Upton-on-Severn, 8 November 1946.
Career: Portsmouth (apprentice June 1962, professional November 1964), Bournemouth & Boscombe Athletic (May 1965), Blackburn Rovers (£30,000 January 1970), Newcastle United (£20,000 valued but fee not paid March 1976), Stoke City

(February 1977), Derby County (£25,000 July 1980), BLUES (loan February-March 1982), York City (£5,000 August 1982). Retired May 1985, later coach at both York and Sunderland (from 1990).
Club honours: Blackburn Rovers: Division Three champions 1975; York City: Division Four champions 1984.
Representative honours: England (1 Under-23 cap).
Released by Portsmouth when they scrapped their reserve team, Roger Jones developed into a most consistent goalkeeper whilst with Bournemouth and if it had not been for a series of knee injuries he would have surely gone on to greater things. He was a veteran when on loan to Blues, whom he helped out in a crisis, and for whom he was Jim Smith's last signing. He made over 750 appearances (242 in the League for Blackburn) in more than 20 years in the game.

JONES, Thomas ('Prescot')
Inside-forward; Apps 31, Goals 12.
Born: Prescot, 1885. Deceased.
Career: Bootle, Everton (1905), BLUES (September 1910), Southport Central (1912).
A classy forward who found his career hampered by Scottish international Sandy Young although he rarely let Everton down. After 15 games and five goals he left Goodison Park for St Andrew's and proved to be the ideal replacement for Wally Freeman before striking up a fine understanding with Jack Hall. Injury curtailed his appearances in 1911-12 and he eventually joined the ambitious Southport club.

JONES, Thomas Trevellyan
Outside-left; Apps 3, Goals 0.
Born: Shrewsbury, December 1879. Deceased.
Career: Wolverhampton Wanderers (amateur 1898), Shrewsbury Town, BLUES (April 1904), Shifnal Town (1905).
An amateur winger who found League football too much for him. It was said of his debut that he 'lacked confidence and committed a sad error of judgement in persisting in lying offside'.

JONES, Walter
Centre-forward; Apps 4, Goals 0.
Born: Coventry, 1859. Deceased.
Career: The Grove, BLUES (1881), Blackheath (1884).
After a season in the reserves, this dashing forward got his chance in the first team in 1882 and turned out to be one of the most consistent players in the side, the high spot of his career being his four goals in as many

minutes against Darlaston All Saints', a game which was called off after an hour's play with Blues winning 16-0, eight of the goals having arrived in the first 15 minutes of the second-half. He did not do too well in 1883-84, however, and was allowed to move to Blackheath.

JONES, William Henry ('Bullet')
Centre-forward; Apps 253, Goals 102.
Born: Tipton, 12 April 1880. Died: 1957.
Career: Princes End, Smethwick Town, Halesowen (1899), BLUES (professional August 1901), Brighton & Hove Albion (June 1909), BLUES (£225 April 1912), Brighton & Hove Albion (November 1913). Retired after World War One and was Brighton's trainer from 1920 until 1939.
Club honours: Blues: Division Two promotion 1903; Brighton & Hove Albion: Southern League champions 1910.
Representative honours: England (international trialist); Football League XI (1).
Billy Jones ('The Tipton Smasher') was a rip-roaring, all-purpose centre-forward who simply loved to have a crack at goal, with any foot, from almost any distance (hence his nickname). He stood only 5ft 6in tall but weighed 13st 8lb and was all action and feared no one. He spearheaded the Blues attack with great menace and it was noticeable that the decline of the team in the late Edwardian era coincided with a series of injuries to Billy. Blues eventually released him, thinking he was past his best, but the team struggled badly without him and he was re-signed two years later. For a further year he held the front-line together before age and injury caught him with him. Upon the outbreak of World War One, he was one of the first players to sign up with the Footballers' Battalion of the Middlesex Regiment.

JONES, William T.
Right-back; Apps 1, Goals 0.
Born: Bournbrook, Birmingham, 1862. Deceased.
Career: Calthorpe, BLUES (1881), West Bromwich Standard (1883).
Little known full-back whose only first-team game was in an FA Cup-tie against Burton Wanderers in 1885 when he stood in for the 'missing' Jerry Hare.

JORDAN, John William
Forward; Apps 25, Goals 3.
Born: Romford, 8 November 1921.
Career: Bromley, Grays Athletic, West Ham United (amateur 1946), Tottenham Hotspur (professional August 1947), Juventus (August 1948), BLUES (March 1949), Sheffield Wednesday (September 1950), Tonbridge (June 1951), Bedford Town (July 1953).
An energetic footballer, he had one good season with Spurs before throwing in his lot with the Italian giants, Juventus. Unfortunately he had an unhappy time in Turin, and after three weeks' negotiations returned to England to sign for Blues, who at the time were going through a bad patch. They needed Johnny Jordan to score goals, but these never materialised in any great number and shortly after the club had suffered relegation he moved on to Wednesday. Cousin of Clarrie Jordan, the former Doncaster Rovers and Sheffield Wednesday centre-forward.

KEARNS, John H.
Left-back; Apps 64, Goals 1.
Born: Nuneaton, April 1880. Died: Walsall, January 1949.
Career: Brownhills Albion (1898), Hartshill Unity, Coventry City (1903), BLUES (£100 April 1906), Aston Villa (player exchange February 1909), Bristol City (April 1912). Retired cs 1915.
A wonderful positional player who allied a biting tackle with some exciting kicking, he

learned his trade as understudy to Stokes and Glover, both acknowledged masters of the full-back art. He also understudied a fine pair of full-backs at Villa Park (Lyons and Miles) but eventually became first choice with Bristol City, for whom he made almost 100 appearances.

KEATING, Reginald E.
Inside-forward; Apps 5, Goals 1.
Born: Halton, Leeds, 14 May 1904. Died: Northumberland South, 13 October 1961.
Career: Halton Grange, Annfield Plain (1925), Scotswood (1926), Newcastle United (October 1926), Lincoln City (1927), Gainsborough (June 1928), Scarborough (May 1929), Stockport County (May 1930), BLUES (June 1931), Norwich City (June 1932), Cardiff City (June 1933), North Shields (trial August 1933), Bath City (October 1933), Cardiff City (January 1934), Doncaster Rovers (June 1936), Bournemouth & Boscombe Athletic (November 1936), Carlisle United (1937). Retired 1939.
Reg Keating was a pacy footballer, brother of the well-travelled forward Albert Keating (who was principally with Bristol City and Blackburn). Reg lacked his brother's consistency but still managed to score over 50 goals in his League career despite rarely settling in any one place. A contemporary report claimed that he 'works hard and puts across a lot of centres'.

KELLY, John ('Jack')
Inside/centre-forward; Apps 12, Goals 1.
Born: Hetton-le-Hole, 2 March 1913.
Career: Hetton Juniors, Burnley (amateur October 1930, professional November 1930), Newcastle United (player exchange, April 1933), Leeds United (£1,150 February 1935), BLUES (January 1938), Bury (May 1939). Retired during World War Two.
A highly individualistic player, often to the detriment of the team's efforts. His career suffered accordingly and he was a regular first choice in only one of his nine League seasons. He was a butcher by trade and a part-time magician.

KELLY, Michael John
Goalkeeper; Apps 72+2, Goals 0.
Born: Northampton, 18 October 1942.
Career: Islington Boys, Wimbledon (amateur 1958), Queen's Park Rangers (professional March 1966), BLUES (£18,000 August 1970), Minnesota Kicks (player-coach 1976), Plymouth Argyle (reserve- team manager 1976, manager May 1977-February 1978), Fulham (assistant manager February 1978-81), Crystal Palace (assistant manager 1981), Portsmouth (chief coach), West Bromwich Albion (assistant manager-coach September 1982-February 1984), FA School of Excellence (chief coach), England goalkeeping coach (1987-90), Liverpool (goalkeeping coach 1991), Coventry City (reserve coach 1992), Switzerland (coach 1993-94), Middlesbrough (coach November 1994).
Club honours: Wimbledon: FA Amateur Cup winners 1963; Blues: Division Two promotion 1972.
Representative honours: England (3 Amateur caps).
Kelly was a highly competent goalkeeper with a loud voice, who always commanded his penalty area. He had an unusual pre-match ritual which involved kicking the base of both goal-posts and touching the crossbar in the centre.

KENDALL, Howard
Midfield; Apps 134, Goals 18.
Born: Ryton-on-Tyne, 22 May 1946.
Career: Ryton & District Schools, Preston North End (apprentice June 1961, professional May 1963), Everton (£80,000
March 1967), BLUES (£350,000 February 1974 in a deal involving Bob Latchford), Stoke City (£40,000 August 1977), Blackburn Rovers (player-manager June 1979-May 1981), Everton (manager May 1981-June 1987), Athletic Bilbao (manager June 1987-November 1989), Manchester City (manager December 1989-November 1990) Everton manager (November 1990-December 1993), Xanthi (manager May-November 1994), Notts County (manager January-April 1995).*
Club honours: Preston North End: FA Cup runners-up 1964; Everton: FA Cup runners-up 1968, Division One champions 1970; (as manager) Blackburn Rovers: Division Three champions 1980; Everton: Division One champions 1985, 1987, FA Cup winners 1984, runners-up 1985, European Cup-winners' Cup winners 1985, FA Charity Shield winners 1984, 1985, 1986 (shared).
Representative honours: England (6 Under-23 caps, Youth and Schoolboy caps); Football League XI (1).

Howard Kendall rose to prominence when he was the youngest player ever to appear in an FA Cup Final, lining up for Preston against West Ham United in 1964, aged 17 years 345 days, a record he lost to Paul Allen of West Ham in 1980. On 8 May 1981 he became the youngest manager ever appointed by Everton (aged 34 years 351 days) and he also played a few games in his first season back at Goodison. Kendall was voted Manager of the Year for 1984-85 after steering the Merseysiders to the First Division title, the FA Cup Final and success in the European Cup-winners' Cup. The complete midfielder, Kendall teamed up exceedingly well with Colin Harvey and Alan Ball at Everton, where he became a firm favourite with the fans, who also took to him later as a manager. He skippered Blues and helped the club retain its First Division status. During his League career he amassed a total of 613 appearances and scored 65 goals.

KENDALL, Mark Ivan
Goalkeeper; Apps 1, Goals 0.
Born: Nuneaton, 10 December 1961.
Career: Aston Villa (apprentice 1979, professional November 1981), North-ampton Town (July 1982), BLUES (March 1984), Tamworth, Mile Oak Rovers, Hitchin Town, Worcester City, Atherstone Town, Bedworth United, Willenhall, Polesworth North Warwick.
Representative honours: England (Youth caps).
No relation to namesake, formerly of Tottenham, Newport, Wolves and Swansea City, Mark Kendall understudied Tony Coton at St Andrew's and after leaving Blues drew up quite an impressive record on the non-League scene.

KENDRICK, Kenny
Centre-forward; Apps 10, Goals 3.
Born: Bartley Green, Birmingham, May 1913.
Career: Bromsgrove Rovers, Halesowen Town, BLUES (September 1936). Retired June 1944 through injury.
A familiar figure in local non-League circles, Ken Kendrick was quite mature by the time he joined Blues where he linked up with his father, Billy, the club's long-serving trainer. Rather on the small side for a centre-forward (5ft 8in and 10st), he was not ideally suited to the rough and tumble aspects of that position.

KENNEDY, Andrew John
Centre-forward; Apps 62+25, Goals 21.
Born: Stirling, 8 October 1964.
Career: Sauchie Athletic, Glasgow Rangers, Seiko FC of Hong Kong (loan), BLUES (£50,000 March 1985), Sheffield United (loan March 1987), Blackburn Rovers (£50,000 June 1988), Watford (£60,000 August 1990), Bolton Wanderers (loan October 1991), Brighton & Hove Albion (September 1992).
Club honours: Blues: Division Two promotion 1983.
Representative honours: Scotland (Youth caps).

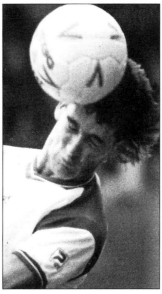

A hard working player, always willing to take on defenders, Andy Kennedy achieved instant popularity with the fans at St Andrew's following several important goals in the 1982-83 promotion campaign. In the long term, however, the faults in his technique (a poor first touch and a tendency to lie too wide) became obvious and he was latterly utilised mainly as substitute in the hope that his pace would unsettle tiring defences.

KERNS, Frederick
Inside-right; Apps 1, Goals 0.
Born: Paddington, London, 1883. Deceased.
Career: Aston Villa (1906), BLUES (December 1908), Bristol Rovers (July 1909).
A forward of limited experience, Fred Kerns arrived at St Andrew's with no League games behind him, being a makeweight in a player-exchange deal. A series of lacklustre reserve appearances did nothing to enhance his reputation and it took an injury crisis to push him into the first team. He failed to make the senior side at Bristol.

KIDD, Jack W.
Inside-forward; Apps 44, Goals 8.
Born: Glasgow, 1884. Deceased.
Career: Glasgow Royal, St Johnstone,
BLUES (November 1910), Brierley Hill Alliance (August 1912).
An agile Scottish ball player who preferred the right side but could turn out on the left if required, Jack Kidd later became one of a group of former Blues players who took pubs in the Brierley Hill area, being landlord of the Star Inn, just down the road from the establishments run by Jack Glover and Walter Wigmore.

KING, Henry Edward
Centre-forward; Apps 30, Goals 7.
Born: Northampton, February 1886. Deceased.
Career: Evesham Star, Worcester City, BLUES (£150 November 1907), Crewe Alexandra (July 1910), Northampton Town (June 1913), Arsenal (April 1914), Leicester City (October 1919), Brentford (September 1920, released in May 1921).

King was a well-built forward signed by Blues whilst still learning his trade. The Blues team of that era was not much of a schooling establishment, but he developed into a marksman of considerable talent, going on to score 67 goals in 99 games for Northampton and 26 in 37 outings for Arsenal, including a four-timer in the Gunners' last game in Division Two to date. He also netted Brentford's first League hat-trick.

KING, Sidney Harvey
Goalkeeper; Apps 2, Goals 0.
Born: Bordesley Green, Birmingham, 1914.
Career: Coventry Road Methodists, Cradley Heath, BLUES (October 1936), Hereford United (1946).
Sid King came to Blues as fourth-choice goalkeeper before World War Two and never looked like earning a first-team place in peacetime. He had very few opportunities during the hostilities and his two games for the club were both in the FA Cup competition as Gil Merrick's deputy.

KINGSTON, Ezekiel
Outside-right; Apps 1, Goals 0.
Born: Walsall, 1858. Deceased.
Career: Wednesbury Old Athletic, BLUES (April 1881), Bloxwich Strollers (1883).
He had only a brief flurry in Blues' first team, playing in the FA Cup-tie against Stafford Road FC and in three friendly matches, including an 18-1 win over Elwell's of Wednesbury.

KINSEY, Noel
Inside-right; Apps 173, Goals 56.
Born: Treorchy, 24 December 1925.
Career: Treorchy Amateurs (1938), Cardiff City (amateur 1941), Norwich City (professional May 1947), BLUES (June 1953), Port Vale (February 1958), King's

Lynn (1961), Lowestoft Town (player-coach June 1962, loan to August 1966). Retired to live in the village of Thorpe, near Norwich. Club honours: Blues: Division Two champions 1955, FA Cup runners-up 1956. Representative honours: Wales (7 full caps).

Noel Kinsey was a scheming inside-forward or occasional wing-half, who earned a great reputation at Norwich before becoming the brains of the Blues attack during the mid-1950s. As well as making goals, he showed a fair ability to take chances, particularly in his first three seasons at St Andrew's when he scored 42 goals.

KIRBY, Conyers
Outside-right; Apps 1, Goals 0.
Born: Bordesley Green, Birmingham, 1884. Died: Spain, c.1945.
Career: Royal Army Medical Corps, Fulham (1905), BLUES (August 1906), Blackpool (July 1907), Kidderminster Harriers (1908), Willenhall Pickwick (1911), Fulham (1913). Retired 1918 and emigrated to Spain.
A sprint champion in the Army, Con Kirby never gained a regular first-team place with either of his major clubs, totalling a mere six games in his League career. He later became a referee in Spain, officiating in a Blues friendly against Barcelona in 1924, when he sent off Alec McClure.

KIRTON, John William
Outside-left; Apps 18, Goals 2.
Born: Pinxton, Derbyshire, 2 November 1873. Died: 27 September 1970.
Career: Glossop North End, Oldham County, Lincoln City (May 1896), BLUES (May 1897), Swindon Town (May 1898), Sunderland (May 1899), Swindon Town (cs 1900), Millwall Athletic (August 1901).
Kirton was an orthodox winger who struck up a good understanding with Wally Abbott in their one season together, when he created a lot of Abbott's 19 goals, although he did not score too many himself. He failed to make Sunderland's first team.

KLONER, Hymie R.
Right-half; Apps 1, Goals 0.
Born: Johannesburg, South Africa, 23 May 1929.
Career: Marist Brothers FC (Transvaal, South Africa), BLUES (November 1950). Returned to South Africa in December 1950.
Another of the string of South African trialists signed by Bob Brocklebank in the early 1950s. He failed to impress but did get one League outing, more than a lot of his colleagues managed. His parents were Polish.

KUHL, Martin
Midfield/defender; Apps 123+9, Goals 6.
Born: Frimley, 10 January 1965.
Career: Schools, BLUES (apprentice June 1981, professional January 1983), Sheffield United (player exchange involving Steve Wigley March 1987), Watford (rated at £300,000 in player exchange deal with Tony Agana February 1988), Portsmouth (£125,000 September 1988), Derby County (£650,000 September 1992), Notts County (loan September 1994), Bristol City (£300,000 December 1994).
Club honours: Blues: Division Two promotion 1985.

Martin Kuhl was an enthusiastic, hard working player who took time to settle before becoming a regular first-teamer with Blues, but his adaptability led to him appearing in all outfield positions for the club in his first two seasons as a professional before he eventually chose to play as a midfield workhorse. He scored the goal against Leeds which led to the infamous riot at St Andrew's. He was set to sign permanently for Notts County but they shipped him back to Derby after he was sent off, eventually departing to Bristol.

LAING, Robert Smith
Outside-left; Apps 19, Goals 2.
Born: Glasgow, 1 February 1925. Died: Birmingham, September 1985.
Career: Falkirk, BLUES (January 1946), Watford (June 1950-May 1952), Worcester City, Halesowen Town, Brierley Hill Alliance, Brush Sports. Retired 1957.

At under 5ft 5in tall and 9st 7lb in weight, Bobby Laing was one of the smallest players ever to pull on a Blues shirt. His first appearance for the club came during

the war when he was stationed at Hednesford, and he made an explosive start to his League career, netting within five minutes of his debut. He remained as second-choice winger for some time before his eventual transfer to Watford, for whom he scored eight goals in 60 League games prior to rounding off his playing days in Midlands non-League football.

LANE, Henry
Outside/inside-right; Apps 2, Goals 0.
Born: Hednesford, 21 March 1909. Died: Cannock, March 1977.
Career: Hednesford Town, Rugeley Villa, Bloxwich Strollers, BLUES (December 1930), Southend United (May 1933), Plymouth Argyle (March 1938), Southend United (May 1946). Retired May 1949, aged 40. Guested for Port Vale during World War Two.
Harry Lane occupied most forward positions during his career, although at 5ft 6in he was a little short for the role as leader of the attack, and with Crosbie and Briggs already well established he did not get much of a look-in. He proved a durable performer in the lower divisions.

LANE, James Charles ('Joe')
Centre-forward; Apps 67, Goals 26.
Born: Watford, 11 July 1892. Died: Abbots Langley, 27 February 1959.
Career: Watford (amateur 1909), Ferencváros Torna (Hungary), Watford (1912), Sunderland (July 1913), Blackpool (November 1913), BLUES (£3,600 March 1920), Millwall (August 1922), Barcelona (coach September 1924), Watford Printing Works FC (1935-36).
Club honours: Blues: Division Two champions 1921.
Representative honours: Football Combination XI (1924).

A printer by trade, Joe Lane started playing football seriously during a two-year attachment to a printing works in Budapest. On his return to England he quickly graduated to League football and became a quality marksman. Blues surprised everyone when they paid a record fee for his services from Blackpool but he immediately proved to be the perfect foil to Harry Hampton, helping the club win promotion from the Second Division. A real sharp-shooter, he was still scoring goals for Watford Printing Works FC when well into his 40s. Lane, who served in the Hertfordshire Yeomanry during World War Two, was a very wealthy man (his father owned a printing company), and he tended to flaunt it, boasting that he never wore the same shirt twice and allowing his teammates to have his cast offs.

LANE, John Geoffrey
Forward; Apps 50, Goals 14.
Born: Selly Oak, Birmingham, 10 November 1931.
Career: Selly Oak Old Blacks, Boldmere St Michael's, BLUES (professional September

1949), Notts County (July 1956), Hinckley Athletic (August 1959), Kidderminster Harriers, Evesham United (June 1961).
Club honours: Blues: Division Two champions 1955.

Lane was a big, strong, sturdily built attacker who was the club's first long-throw expert and who proved a capable understudy for all forward positions but who enjoyed himself most when given an inside berth. He played in contact lenses, which came as a surprise to Notts County's manager who learnt of the fact only when Lane put them in to sign his contract with the Magpies. He went on to score 19 goals in 57 League games for County. His early years spent as a boxer.

LANE, Moses ('Mo') Alexander Edmund
Centre-forward; Apps 15, Goals 4.
Born: Willenhall, 17 February 1895. Died: Cannock, 14 July 1949.
Career: Willenhall Pickwick, Willenhall Town (August 1920), Walsall (December 1920), Willenhall (May 1921), BLUES (April 1922), Derby County (July 1924), Wellington Town (May 1925), Worcester City (cs 1926), Walsall (June 1927), Brierley Hill Alliance (July 1929), Netherton, Dudley. Retired 1933.
Moses Lane served in France and Italy during World War One, when his gallantry earned him the Military Medal. He was a player noted for his speed rather than his general footballing ability.

LANGAN, David Francis
Right-back; Apps 102, Goals 3.
Born: Dublin, 15 February 1957.
Career: Bath Rangers, Cherry Orchard FC, Derby County (apprentice June 1974, professional February 1975), BLUES

(record fee of £350,000 July 1980), Oxford United (free transfer August 1984), Leicester City (loan October 1987), AFC Bournemouth (loan November 1987, signed permanently December 1987), Peterborough United (July 1988), Ramsey Town, Holbeach United, Rothwell Town, Mirlees Blackstone FC (1990).
Club honours: Oxford United: Division Two champions 1985, League Cup winners 1986.
Representative honours: Republic of Ireland (25 full caps, Youth and Schools caps).
David Langan was a very influential attacking right-back who was signed for Blues by manager Jim Smith for a record fee, having previously made 155 senior appearances for the Rams. Langan said he wanted to be with a more successful club – Derby's fortunes were dipping – and he became a firm favourite with the St Andrew's supporters. Alas, a series of knee injuries disrupted his run in the first team and he was eventually freed by manager Ron Saunders in 1984. Langan subsequently rejoined his former boss Smith at Oxford, where he regained some of his earlier form before injuries caught up with him again and he was forced to withdraw from major competition in 1989-90 after totting up in excess of 500 appearances, including games in all four divisions.

LANGLEY, Kevin James
Midfield; Apps 86+2, Goals 2.
Born: St Helens, 24 May 1964.
Career: Wigan Athletic (apprentice June 1980, professional May 1982), Everton (£100,000 July 1986), Manchester City (£150,000 March 1987), Chester City (loan January 1988), BLUES (£100,000 March 1988), Wigan Athletic (£50,000 September 1990), Halifax Town (August 1994), Bangor City.
Club honours: Wigan Athletic: Freight/Rover Trophy runners-up 1986; Everton: FA Charity Shield winners 1986; Bangor City: League of Wales champions 1995.
Kevin Langley was a tall, elegant ball-playing midfielder who earned a high reputation as a youngster with Wigan before his abortive flirtation with First Division football. On his arrival at St Andrew's he was touted as the vital cog in Blues' engine-room, and the man to provide the chances that would take the team back into the First Division. Alas, he never looked comfortable with the Blues' style of play although he later showed flashes of his old form after returning to Springfield Park.

LAPPIN, Hubert Henry
Outside-left; Apps 12, Goals 2.
Born: Manchester, 1879. Died: Liverpool, May 1925.
Career: Springfield FC, Oldham Athletic (October 1900), Newton Heath (April 1901), Grimsby Town (August 1903), Rossendale United (August 1904), Clapton Orient (August 1906), Chester (1907), BLUES (August 1909), Chirk (1910), Hurst, Macclesfield.
Club honours: Chester: Welsh Cup runners-up 1909.
Lappin showed great skill on both wings: Blues and Grimsby used him on the left whilst Newton Heath and Orient played him on the right. He was rarely mentioned in reports of Blues matches, so it appears that he did not have a great impact on the team's overall play.

LARKIN, Bernard Patrick ('Bunny')
Inside-forward/wing-half; Apps 92, Goals 29.
Born: Digbeth, Birmingham, 11 January 1936.
Career: Lea Hall Youth Club, Rockwood

Albion, BLUES (amateur July 1952, professional July 1954), Norwich City (£10,000 March 1960), Doncaster Rovers (£5,000 September 1961), Watford (£4,000 June 1962), Lincoln City (November 1964), Wisbech Town (July 1966), Nuneaton Borough, King's Lynn, Stevenage Athletic, Attleborough Town (coach 1975).
Larkin was a cheerful, fair-haired player who in 1958 was converted from an average wing-half into an exciting forward. He repaid the club's faith in him by netting 23 goals in 1958-59 before a loss of form cost him his place in the side. He was nicknamed 'Rip Van Winkle" after oversleeping and missing the coach on the way to a vital European match.

LATCHFORD, David Barry
Goalkeeper; Apps 239, Goals 0.
Born: King's Heath, Birmingham, 9 April 1949.
Career: Brandwood Secondary Modern School, South Birmingham Schools, BLUES (apprentice June 1964, professional May 1966), Motherwell (July 1977), Bury (March 1979), Barnsley (non-contract 1980), Redditch United (1981), Cheltenham Town (1983), East Worle (1985), Solihull Borough (coach 1992-95).
Club honours: Blues: Division Two promotion 1972, FA Youth Cup runners-up 1967.

He is the eldest of a trio of brothers who all starred in Midlands football in the 1970s, Dave and Bob for Blues and Peter for West Brom. Dave Latchford showed great promise as a youngster and was called up into the England Youth squad but failed to gain a place due to the brilliance of Peter Shilton. He followed his brother into the Blues' first team at the end of the 1968-69 season and made an immediate impression. Despite his bulky appearance, he was surprisingly agile and was also a clean handler of the ball, possessing the ability to make the occasional 'impossible' save, although he conceded eight goals in his own testimonial match. After some years as a funeral director, he became a superintendent of cemeteries for Solihull whilst his son Oliver played for Solihull Borough and West Midlands Police.

LATCHFORD, Robert Dennis
Centre-forward; Apps 190+4, Goals 84.
Born: King's Heath, Birmingham, 18 January 1951.
Career: Brandwood Secondary School, South Birmingham & Warwickshire County Schools, BLUES (apprentice May 1967, professional August 1968), Everton (£350,000 February 1974 in deal involving Howard Kendall and Archie Styles), Swansea City (£125,000 July 1981 (NAC Breda (Holland) (February 1984), Coventry City (June 1984), Lincoln City (July 1985), Newport County (loan January-May 1986), Merthyr Tydfil (August 1986). Later director of Alvechurch FC.
Club honours: Blues: FA Youth Cup runners-up 1967, Division Two promotion 1972; Everton: Football League Cup runners-up 1977; Swansea City: Welsh Cup winners 1982, 1983; Merthyr Tydfil: Welsh Cup winners 1987.
Representative honours: England (12 full caps, 6 Under-23 caps, 4 Youth caps);

Football League XI (1).
Brandwood School has produced several quality players over the years, but few, if any, better than this bearded, swashbuckling target man who, like his elder brother Dave, was highly rated as a youngster. Bob made his League bow for Blues during an injury crisis and quickly figured on the score-sheet, but during the next year or so he found it hard to attune to the top-class game. However, he came good in 1970-71 when he formed a terrific strike-force with Francis and Summerill. The arrival of Bob Hatton strengthened the attack even further and Bob took full advantage of this to net 30 goals in a season for the first time. Tall, well built, good in the air and with a thumping shot, his power and aggression inside the 'box' made him a handful for any defence. Eventually, with Blues facing another relegation battle, his transfer request was granted and he moved to Everton for what was then a League

record fee. At Goodison Park he was an instant success, scoring seven times in his first 13 outings. In 1977-78 he was presented with a cheque for £10,000 by a national newspaper when he became the first player to register 30 goals in Division One since 1972. He stayed with Everton for seven years, during which time he scored 138 goals in 288 games.

LAYTON, George
Left-half/forward; Apps 17, Goals 3.
Born: Stourbridge, 1865. Deceased.
Career: Stourbridge Royal, Cradley St Luke's (1896), Smethwick Wesleyan Rovers (1897), BLUES (September 1898), Dudley Town (1901), Soho Villa (1903).
George Layton was an experienced, long striding half-back who was picked up from local non-League soccer. Layton had a taste for joining in the attack and possessed a cracking good shot, often delivered from well outside the penalty area. He dropped out of the Blues side when Walter Wigmore was switched to defence.

LEA, George Isaac
Right-half; Apps 28, Goals 1.
Born: Donnington Wood, Shropshire, 17 February 1911. Died: Dawley, Shropshire, 24 October 1972.
Career: Oakengates Town, BLUES (September 1932), Millwall (May 1937 to 1943 when he retired). Guested for Wrexham and Wellington Town during World War Two.
Club honours: Millwall: Division Three South champions 1938, Division Three South Cup winners 1937.
Lea was originally a quite a spindly youngster but after joining Blues he put on stones in weight and developed into a powerful half-back with a prodigious shot. His first-team opportunities were always going to be limited with Lew Stoker already established at right-half but Lea remained as a patient and understanding deputy for a number of years. He was a breeder of pigeons and one of his customers was the champion flat-race jockey Sir Gordon Richards.

LEAKE, Alexander
Defender; Apps 221, Goals 23.
Born: Small Heath, Birmingham, 11 July 1871. Died: Birmingham, 29 March 1938.
Career: Jenkins Street and Green Lane Schools (Bordesley Green), Hoskins & Sewell FC, King's Heath Albion, Saltley Gas Works FC, Singers FC, Hopkins & Sewell FC, Old Hill Wanderers (July 1892), BLUES (July 1894), Aston Villa (June 1902), Burnley (December 1907),

Wednesbury Old Athletic (July 1910). Retired as player June 1912, and became Crystal Palace trainer in July 1912, holding office until May 1915. Then Merthyr Town trainer from October 1919 to July 1920 and Walsall's first-team trainer from September

1932 to May 1933. Later coached at schools and colleges around Britain for six years.
Club honours: Aston Villa: FA Cup winners 1905.
Representative honours: England (5 full caps); Football League XI (1).
"With Alex Leake, football is a pleasure. He will crack a joke with an opponent while he robs him of the ball," so said *Rover* in 1906. A genuine 'Brummagem Button,' Leake was a good-tempered, honest worker, whose stamina was unsurpassed. He never played to the gallery, but always battled well for his team. He was as safe as houses, never over doing the fancy stuff, and was always hard to beat in 50-50 situations. A fine tackler, superb at intercepting long passes, his unfamiliar humour made him a great favourite with the fans. He skippered Blues for six years immediately prior to leaving, and during a fine career amassed 464 senior appearances for his three major clubs, including 140 for Villa. Leake was chosen as reserve for England at the age of 41. An excellent swimmer (he could dive to the bottom of the brine baths at Droitwich to retrieve a coin), he was also a fine all-round athletic, specialising in the 400 yards and hurdles events. A keen gardener and a blacksmith by trade, he was cousin of Blues' Jimmy Windridge.

LEATHERBARROW, Charles A. ('Ginger')
Inside-right; Apps 5, Goals 3.
Born: Liverpool, 1869. Deceased.
Career: Northwich Victoria, Rotherham Town, Walsall Town Swifts (December 1893), BLUES (September 1894), Millwall (April 1895), Chatham (September 1896).
Club honours: Millwall: Southern League champions 1896.
Stocky and very quick off the mark, Charlie Leatherbarrow was a regular scorer wherever he went. Although he struggled at Blues he later had several highly successful years in the Southern League.

LEE, John Sebastian
Forward; Apps 7, Goals 3.
Born: Walsall Wood, 1869. Deceased.
Career: Walsall Unity, BLUES (September 1893), Old Hill Wanderers (January 1895), Bilston United (1897), Darlaston (1899).
John Lee, a diminutive sharp-shooter, had a short spell in the first team and did well. It was only due to the ability of Billy Walton that Lee found himself out in the cold for long periods. He remained in his native Midlands rather than join another League club.

LEEK, Kenneth
Centre/inside-forward; Apps 120, Goals 61.
Born: Ynysybwl, near Pontypridd, South Wales, 26 July 1935.

Career: Pontypridd Youth Club, Ynys-y-bwl Boys FC, Northampton Town (professional August 1952), Leicester City (May 1958), Newcastle United (£25,000 June 1961), BLUES (£23,000 November 1961), Northampton Town (£9,000 December 1964), Bradford City (£10,000 November 1965), Rhyl Town (August 1968), Ton Pentre (1970). Retired cs 1970.
Club honours: Blues: Football League Cup winners 1963.
Representative honours: Wales (13 full caps, 1 Under-23 cap).
Ken Leek was born next door to Don Dearson in the same Welsh village but didn't play any sort of soccer until he was 14, having attended two rugby-playing schools. However, he quickly developed into a fine marksman who went on to total 147 goals in 397 League games during a fine career. Leek had a benefit match with Northampton, and being in dispute with Leicester was dropped by manager Matt Gillies on the morning of the 1961 FA Cup Final having scored in all the previous rounds. This inevitably led to his transfer to Newcastle a month later but he failed to settle on Tyneside and soon joined Blues, where his goal touch returned to the team's advantage. His strikes were particularly important during the 1962-63 League Cup run, and he crowned his career at St Andrew's with two goals in the Final against Aston Villa. From then on his playing days moved in a downward spiral.

LEES, Terence
Full-back; Apps 18+1, Goals 0.
Born: Stoke-on-Trent, 30 June 1952.
Career: Stoke City (apprentice June 1968, professional July 1969), Crewe Alexandra (loan March-April 1975), San Jose Earthquakes (loan 1975), Port Vale (August 1975), Sparta Rotterdam (Holland), Roda JC (Holland) (1977-78), BLUES (July 1979), Newport County (August 1981), Altrincham, Morning Star (Hong Kong), DS79 Dordrecht (Holland), Stafford Rangers (1982-83), Scunthorpe United (non-contract September 1984 to May 1985). Macclesfield Town, Kidsgrove Athletic, Hanley Town, Meir KA (coach).
A versatile defender who seemed doomed to being a permanent understudy, Lees was used by Blues principally as a right-back after a trial using him as a sweeper was abandoned. A useful club cricketer, he later became a sports centre manager in his native Potteries.

LEGGAT, Graham
Forward; Apps 17+3, Goals 3.
Born: Aberdeen, 20 June 1934.
Career: Torry Former Pupils FC, Banks O'Dee, Aberdeen (1953), Fulham (£16,000, August 1958), BLUES (£15,000, January 1967), Rotherham United (July 1968), Aston Villa (assistant trainer-coach July 1969), Bromsgrove Rovers (player March 1970), Toronto Star (manager 1971).
Club honours: Aberdeen: Scottish League champions 1955, Scottish FA Cup runners-up 1954, Scottish League Cup winners 1956.
Representative honours: Scotland (18 full caps, 1 Under-23 cap, Youth international); Scottish League XI and Football League XI appearances with Aberdeen (5) & Fulham (1) respectively.
In his heyday, Graham Leggat was a fast goalscoring forward usually found at outside-right. After a successful career in Scotland he moved to Fulham and in his first season at the Cottage played a vital part in helping the London club win promotion to Division One. He continued to score at a fair rate – averaging a goal every two games – until his move to Blues. By this time he had lost most of his speed and looked rather out of condition, but he remained a prolific marksman at Football

Combination level. During his days with Blues he earned some extra money as a male model. He is now a prominent sports commentator on Canadian television. Leggat scored 127 goals in 254 League games whilst at Craven Cottage.

LEONARD, Arthur Ralph ('Bamford')
Inside-right; Apps 75, Goals 26.
Born: Leicester, 1874. Deceased.
Career: 17th Leicestershire Regiment, Leicester Fosse (1895), Rushden Town, Sheppey United, Glentoran, BLUES (£120 November 1901), Stoke (January 1904), St Bernard, Clapton Orient, Plymouth Argyle, Reading (1909).
This player appeared under a pseudonym for the latter half of his career, his real name being Arthur Leonard Bamford. He joined the club in bizarre circumstances: Blues saw 'Leonard' play with his Irish side and were so impressed that they immediately signed him for £120. Leicester were also represented at the match and recognised him as their absentee player, Bamford. After being accused of this he disappeared for several days, sending a telegram to his wife saying that he had fled to America. He later resurfaced in Bristol and was persuaded to return to Birmingham to face the music. He admitted that he was indeed Bamford and the case was settled when Blues paid Leicester a further £20. It proved to be money well spent for 'Leonard' became a big hit with the Blues supporters, a real bag of tricks, capable of both scoring and making goals. Indeed, he was regarded as the star forward in the side.

LEONARD, John ('Jack')
Outside-right; Apps 9, Goals 1.
Born: Gloucester, 1876. Deceased.
Career: Bedminster, Bristol City (August 1899), BLUES (November 1899), Cheltenham Town (May 1900).
An intricate dribbler who had one fine season with Bedminster in the Southern League, but when they merged with the Bristol City club he fell from favour. His face never really fitted at Birmingham either and he quickly moved back to the West Country.

LESLIE, Alexander ('Alec') James
Left-half; Apps 143, Goals 0.
Born: Greenock, Scotland, April 1902. Died: Greenock, 1974.
Career: Greenock Wayfarers, Port Glasgow Juniors, St Mirren (1919), Houghton-le-Spring (1921), Morton (1923), St Mirren (1924), Torquay United (£100 August 1925), BLUES (£750 April 1927). Retired May 1932.
Club honours: Blues: FA Cup runners-up 1931.
Leslie was primarily a defensive half-back, solid in the tackle despite his relatively slight build (5ft 7in tall and 10st 3lb in weight). He rarely shot at goal and scored

only once during his career – a 35-yarder which crept through the goalkeeper's legs. He had a great influence in midfield and was a player who loved to 'push-pass' the ball through to his forwards, using his toe-end rather than the instep of his boot. He became a regular in the Blues side in 1927-28 and after a niggling knee injury ended his career he became landlord of the Freemason's Arms in Hawkes Street and later worked for the Inland Revenue before returning to his native Scotland.

LESTER, Frank
Full-back; Apps 78, Goals 0.
Born: Wednesbury, 1870. Deceased.
Career: Walsall Unity, BLUES (1895), Walsall (1901).
A sturdy, reliable back who demonstrated more power then finesse in his play. His partnership with Billy Pratt was regarded as one of the finest in the League.

LEWIS, William Jasper
Outside-right; Apps 3, Goals 2.
Born: Bordesley Green, Birmingham, 1871. Deceased.
Career: Windsor Street Gas Depot FC, BLUES (February 1894), Hereford Town (1896), Stourbridge, Leicester Fosse (May 1902).
Bill Lewis was a winger with a goalscoring bent who was perhaps unlucky to have played so few games for Blues. He later resurfaced with Leicester as a centre-forward but managed only three goals in 31 appearances before drifting out of League football.

LEWIS, Wilson Arnold
Centre-forward; Apps 21, Goals 7.
Born: Evesham, 1873. Deceased.
Career: Hereford Thistle (1895), BLUES (August 1897), Bromyard (May 1898).
Wilson Lewis swapped the chocolate and yellow of Thistle for the blue of Small Heath, and Blues kept faith in this rather slow forward for most of his one season with the club. He did well in the early part of the year but his form dropped off after Christmas and the arrival of Bob McRoberts left him surplus to requirements, so he moved back to Herefordshire.

LIDDELL, George M.
Wing-half, later full-back; Apps 345, Goals 6.
Born: Durham, 14 July 1895. Deceased.
Career: Johnstone Grammar School, City of Leeds Training College, the Honourable Artillery Company XI, Duke of Wellington FC, the Army (played rugby), Yorkshire Amateurs, South Shields (amateur 1916), BLUES (professional May 1920). Retired April 1932, and became manager at St

Andrew's (June 1933 to May 1939) in succession to Leslie Knighton who had moved to Chelsea.
Club honours: Blues: FA Cup runners-up

1931.
George Liddell was a dapper, moustachio'd defender, cool under pressure, a fine positional player possessing a healthy kick and strong tackle, who could always be relied upon to give a solid performance. Began as a wing-half where he prompted his forwards well and notched a few goals with his powerful long-range shooting. He switched to full-back after the departure of Frank Womack, and his skills shone above the average player in that position, being a defender who preferred to pass the ball rather than lash it blindly downfield. In later years he combined football with his career as a teacher with the result that he frequently missed midweek away matches. Not the most popular of players with his teammates, it was a surprise when he was elected manager and there was considerable dressing-room rancour throughout his managerial career. He later taught at Leigh Road School, Washwood Heath and at Cotteridge Infants' School.

LINDON, Albert Edward
Goalkeeper; Apps 7, Goals 0.
Born: Aston, Birmingham, 24 January 1891. Died: Dowlais, Wales, 1 October 1976.
Career: Vaughan United, Delta Metal

Works FC (1907), Birmingham Fruiterers FC, BLUES (June 1910), Aston Villa (August 1911), Barnsley (May 1912), Coventry City (£1,000, May 1919), Merthyr

Town (August 1920, becoming player-manager August 1924), Charlton Athletic (December 1927, then player-manager January 1928, player-assistant manager June 1928). Retired as player in 1931 and became caretaker manager at The Valley in December 1932, becoming assistant manager May 1933-March 1934, Arsenal (scout 1947-December 1949), Cardiff City (scout January 1950), Merthyr Tydfil (manager June 1958-May 1959, and August-November 1959), Swindon Town (scout 1960), Newport County (scout October 1961).
Club honours: Merthyr Town: Welsh Cup runners-up 1924; Charlton Athletic: Division Three South Champions 1928-29.
Albert Lindon's long career in football began as a youngster fresh from works soccer. A tall, well-built goalkeeper, he was unable to make his mark in his home town, his best years coming probably with Charlton, a club he served in most capacities throughout the years. He put on quite a bit of weight late on in life and at 16st is the heaviest man ever to play for Charlton.

LINES, Wilton
Forward; Apps 7, Goals 1.
Born: Birmingham 1874. Deceased.
Career: BLUES (1898-99).
Lines was given a run-out in most forward positions but proved unable to replace any of the regulars.

LINFORD, John Russell
Centre-forward; Apps 1+1, Goals 0.
Born: Norwich, 6 February 1957.
Career: Gorleston, Ipswich Town (August 1981), Colchester United (loan January 1983), Southend United (loan March 1983), DS 79 Dordrecht (Holland), FC Den Haag (Holland), Ipswich Town, BLUES (loan November 1984), NAC Breda (Holland), Fortuna Sittard (Holland) (1985), FC Zurich (Switzerland) (1988), FC Utrecht (Holland) (1988), Bury Town (1989), Go Ahead Eagles (Holland) (January 1990), Fortuna Sittard (Holland) (July 1990), Wroxham, King's Lynn.
He was a lanky striker whose brief spell with Blues was far from impressive, although he proved more successful on the continent and scored 76 goals for his six Dutch clubs up to 1991.

LINLEY, Edward A.
Outside-left; Apps 118, Goals 11.
Born: East Retford, 26 September 1894. Deceased.
Career: Worksop Town, BLUES (£800 plus Tom Pike December 1920), Nottingham Forest (1926), Sutton Town (1927), Mansfield Town (March 1928).
Club honours: Blues: Division Two champions 1920-21.
Balding and knock-kneed, Ted Linley was not an obvious choice as a professional footballer. Appearances can be deceptive, however, and he showed himself a guileful

performer for several years, fighting off the challenges of a host of players who were bought to replace him. He had only a short spell at Forest before moving back to the mining area.

LINNECOR, Albert R.
Wing-half/inside-forward; Apps 18, Goals 0.
Born: Nechells, Birmingham, 30 November 1933.
Career: Lea Village School, Brookhill Juniors, BLUES (amateur February 1950, professional May 1952), Boston United (August 1954), Lincoln City (April 1957 to May 1964), Grantham Town (July 1967), Worksop Town (June 1969), Bourne Town (January 1970), Lincoln City (youth coach 1973), Ruston Sports (manager 1974).
A local youngster who had been a star in schoolboy football before joining Blues, Albert Linnecor made his debut in the run-in to the 1955-56 Cup Final when he replaced the injured Roy Warhurst, but lost out in the scramble for the position at Wembley. He was used regularly as a forward and proved a good marksman, netting five goals in one game against Swindon in 1955. He had a successful period at Lincoln for whom he scored 52 goals in 264 League appearances before moving into non-League circles in 1964.

LINNEY, David William
Midfield; Apps 0+1, Goals 0.
Born: King's Heath, Birmingham, 5 September, 1961.
Career: Schoolboy football, BLUES (apprentice June 1977, professional September 1979), Oxford United (August 1982), Yeovil, Basingstoke Town, Weymouth, Chard Town.
He showed a fair degree of versatility in Blues' reserves side but was not given a chance in the first team. Discarded by Ron Saunders in his first clear-out as manager, Linney teamed up again with his former boss, Jim Smith, at Oxford and spent one season at the Manor Ground.

LINTON, Ivor
Right-back/midfield; Apps 3+1, Goals 0.
Born: West Bromwich, 20 November 1959.
Career: West Bromwich & District Schools, Staffordshire Boys, Aston Villa (trial April 1976, apprentice May 1976, professional September 1977), Peterborough United (free transfer July 1982), BLUES (trial December 1983-February 1984), Bilston Town (May 1984), Kasko IK (Finland), IF Kraft Narpes (Finland).
Club honours: Aston Villa: FA Youth Cup runners-up 1978.
He was highly rated as a midfielder when with Aston Villa, but failed to make the breakthrough and moved to Peterborough United after only 17 games (plus 11 as a substitute) in six seasons at Villa Park. Released by Posh, he had an unsuccessful trial with Blues before going to Finland where he became a forward.

LITTLEFORD, Arthur George
Right-back; Apps 3, Goals 0.
Born: Wellington, 1868. Deceased.
Career: South Yardley FC, BLUES (1893), Berwick Rangers (Worcester) (1895).
Littleford was a regular reserve full-back with Blues and although given plenty of outings in friendlies and County Cup matches he was rarely tried in League competition, and generally disappointed when he did play.

LODGE, Lewis Vaughan
Right-back; Apps 1, Goals 0.
Born: Darlington, 21 December 1872. Died: Buxton, 21 October 1916.
Career: Durham School (played for the rugby XV), Magdalene College at Cambridge, Casuals (1893-94), Corinthians (1894-98), BLUES (1896),

Newbury Town, Durham Town.
Club honours: Casuals: FA Amateur Cup runners-up 1894.
Representative honours: England (5 full caps 1894-96), Cambridge University Blue (3 times).
Blues appeared to have pulled off a coup when this great Corinthian agreed to play for them. Pressure of work, however, prevented Lewis Lodge from being able to turn out on a regular basis. He was employed as a master at Harris Hill School, Newbury. A powerfully built back of the old school brigade, he was reliable in his tackling and kicking. He also played three cricket matches for Hampshire, scoring only six runs (average 1.5) and taking 0 for 6. He died in mysterious circumstances, being found drowned in a pool.

LOGAN, John Theodore
Outside-left; Apps 1, Goals 0.
Born: Edinburgh, 1871. Deceased.
Career: Edinburgh Emmett, Partick Thistle, BLUES (1896), Musselburgh (1897).
Logan was a disappointing Scottish signing whose outings, whether in League or friendly games, rarely threatened the opposition.

LOUGHRAN, Joseph Lane
Wing-half; Apps 34, Goals 2.
Born: Consett, Co Durham, 12 August 1915.
Career: Medomsley Juniors, Consett FC, Dudley College, BLUES (August 1933), Luton Town (May 1937), Burnley (July 1939), Southend United (September 1949-May 1953), Newhaven (permit player).
Joe Loughran was a short, energetic wing-half who was physical education student at college when he came to the notice of Blues. He was able to play equally as well on either side of the field. After retiring he was employed as the organiser of physical education for East Sussex Schools.

LOVESEY, James
Left-back; Apps 1, Goals 0.
Born: Smethwick, 1864. Deceased.
Career: Hockley Hill Transport FC, BLUES (1886), Birmingham Belmont (1887).
Lovesey was employed in the jewellery trade in Birmingham. He was a regular at full-back for just half a season, making his last appearance on Christmas Day 1886 against Mitchell St George's.

LOWE, C.Bernard
Inside-left; Apps 16, Goals 3.
Born: Cradley Heath, 1885. Deceased.
Career: Lye Cross Parish, Harborne Lynwood, Halesowen, BLUES (1908), Darlaston (1911), Netherton (1913). Retired during World War One.
Lowe was a skilful forward, often asked to play wider than he liked, who was a star of Birmingham League football for several years. He was not a prolific scorer and it was stated that his greatest forte was the 'manoeuvring of the ball in midfield'.

LOWE, Kenneth
Midfield; Apps 19+8, Goals 3.
Born: Sedgefield, 6 November 1961.
Career: Hartlepool United (apprentice 1977, professional 1979), Billingham Town, Gateshead, Spearwood Dalmatic (Australia), Gateshead, Morecambe, Barrow, Sarborough United (free transfer January 1988), Barrow, Barnet (£40,000 March 1991), Stoke City (free transfer August 1993), BLUES (£75,000 December 1993), Carlisle United (loan September 1994).
Club honours: Barrow: Northern Premier League champions 1986, 1989, FA Trophy winners 1990.
Ken Lowe, who was quite tall for a midfield player at 6ft 1in, was a useful squad member at St Andrew's. He made 59

appearances for Hartlepool, four for Scarborough, 84 for Barnet and 13 for Stoke. He gained a BSc in engineering.

LYNEX, Stephen Charles
Winger; Apps 45+21, Goals 13.
Born: West Bromwich, 23 January 1958.
Career: All Saints Junior and Churchfields Comprehensive Schools West Bromwich, West Bromwich Town Boys, Charlemont Farm Boys Club, Sandwell Rangers, Aston Villa (trial), Wolverhampton Wanderers (trial), West Bromwich Albion (apprentice July 1974, professional January 1977), Sligo Rovers (trial), Shamrock Rovers (free transfer July 1977), QPR (trial), BLUES (April 1979), Leicester City (£60,000 February 1981), BLUES (loan October-December 1986), West Bromwich Albion (£5,000 March 1987), Cardiff City (free transfer June 1988), Telford United (March 1990), Trafford Park FC (August 1990), Mitchells & Butlers FC (March 1991). After retiring from competitive football (1990) he became a publican in Birmingham, playing for Ansells FC (1992-93).
Club honours: WBA: FA Youth Cup winners 1976; Shamrock Rovers: FA of Ireland Cup winners 1978; Blues: Division Two promotion 1980; Leicester City: Division Two promotion 1983.
Representative honours: League of Ireland XI (1978).

Unable to gain a place in the Baggies' first team, Steve Lynex went to Ireland where he gained valuable experience including European competition, but was happy to return to England when the opportunity presented itself. He made his debut for Blues after the club had already been condemned to relegation. The following year he earned a 'semi-regular' place in the side and scored some vital goals in the promotion campaign where he

demonstrated a happy knack of being in the right place at the right time. Lynex proved a highly successful signing for Leicester, playing principally on the right-wing. He was less successful after leaving Filbert Street. In a useful career in League football he amassed well over 400 senior appearances and netted more than 70 goals.

LYNN, Stanley
Right-back; Apps 148, Goals 30.
Born: Bolton, 18 June 1928.
Career: Whitecroft Road School, Whitworth's FC (April 1944), Accrington Stanley (amateur August 1945, professional July 1947), Aston Villa (£10,000 March 1950), BLUES (October 1961), Stourbridge (August 1966). Retired May 1968 but assisted Aston Villa All Stars (1970 to 1985). Keen golfer and later a storeman with the Lucas Industries Group, residing in Shirley.
Club honours: Aston Villa: FA Cup winners 1957, FA Charity Shield runners-up 1957, Division Two champions 1960, Football League Cup winners 1961; Blues: Football League Cup winners 1963.

Stan Lynn was a well built full-back who could kick like a mule, especially from dead-ball situations and he once scored a hat-trick – two goals coming from the from the penalty-spot – for Villa against Sunderland in January 1958 to become the first full-back to achieve this feat in Division One. Lynn lost a lot of his speed and was considered 'over the hill' when he joined Blues but he still gave an excellent account of himself during his four-year spell at St Andrew's. Lynn finished as Blues' top-scorer in 1964-65 – from right-back. He appeared in 446 League games during his career (64 goals scored), and hit 38 goals in 324 senior outings for Villa. His League Cup winners' award with Blues was won against Villa, his old club.

McCAFFERTY, William
Inside-forward; Apps 4, Goals 0.
Born: Rutherglen, 9 December 1882. Deceased.
Career: Rutherglen Glencairn, Celtic (March 1902), Bolton Wanderers (loan November 1902), Stenhousemuir (November 1903), Bathgate (July 1905), Reading (November 1905), BLUES (£350 December 1906), Bathgate, Portsmouth (February 1908), Brentford (November 1909).
A forward of Scottish extraction who made his name at Reading, McCaffery signed for Blues on a free transfer plus the gate receipts of a friendly between the clubs. He scored in the friendly but that was, in fact, his only goal for Blues as Benny Green kept him out of the side. He was not a great success with his later clubs either.

McCARRICK, Mark Bernard
Right-back; Apps 15+5, Goals 0.
Born: Liverpool, 4 February 1962.

Career: Winsford Verdin Comprehensive School, West Bromwich Albion (apprentice 1977), Caroline Hill FC, Christchurch United, Witton Albion (1982), BLUES (professional May 1983), Lincoln City (£4,000 July 1984), Crewe Alexandra (non-contract February 1986), Koparit (March 1986), Runcorn (October 1986), Tranmere Rovers (£5,000 August 1987), Altrincham (March 1991), Northwich Victoria (August 1991), Marine, Winsford Town. Emigrated to Spain January 1992 to run bar in Magaluf, returning to play for Bangor City (1993).
Club honours: Tranmere Rovers: Division Four promotion 1990, Division Three promotion 1991, Leyland DAF Cup winners 1990.
He was regarded as something of a lucky mascot as his appearance in the first team coincided with a lengthy unbeaten spell. His lack of pace was cruelly exposed by Watford's John Barnes in the 1984 FA Cup quarter-final and he found himself 'freed' at the end of the season. He did exceedingly well with Tranmere, though.

McCLURE, Alexander
Centre-half; Apps 198, Goals 4.
Born: Workington, 3 April 1892. Died: Birmingham, August 1973.
Career: Grangetown Juniors, BLUES (January 1912), Aston Villa (December 1923), Stoke (October 1924), Coventry City (September 1926), Walsall (March 1928), Luton Town (colts trainer late 1927), Bromsgrove Rovers, Market Harborough Town, BLUES (colts manager 1928-32, later assistant manager May 1932-34). After leaving football worked for Rudge Motor Cycles and later ran a successful haulage company in Small Heath.
Club honours: Blues: Division Two champions 1921.
International honours: Football League XI (2).

Possessor of a fine physique and excellent positional sense, Alec McClure was the fulcrum of the Blues' defence for 12 years, injuries permitting. Few forwards relished a run-in with the powerful northerner who delivered a terrific shoulder-charge but who also had a suspect temperament. He skippered Blues' reserve side to victory in three competitions before establishing himself in the first team at St Andrew's. After returning to St Andrew's as colts manager he earned the reputation as a hard taskmaster. His brother Sam played for Blackburn Rovers and his nephew Joe for Everton, Brentford and Exeter City.

McCOURTY, William
Left-half; Apps 1, Goals 0.
Born: Morpeth, 1884. Deceased.
Career: North Seaton, BLUES (May 1909), Ryton FC (1910).
A former miner from the North-East, his

career in League football was brief. He enjoyed an early debut due to an injury to Tommy Daykin, but had a poor game as Blues struggled against Glossop. He never got a second chance!

McDONAGH, James Martin ('Seamus')
Goalkeeper; Apps 1, Goals 0.
Born: Rotherham, 6 October 1962.
Career: Rotherham United (apprentice November 1968, professional October 1970), Bolton Wanderers (£10,000 August 1976), Everton (£250,000 July 1980), Bolton Wanderers (£90,000 August 1981, player exchange deal), Notts County

(£50,000 July 1983), BLUES (loan September 1984), Gillingham (loan March-April 1985), Sunderland (loan August-September 1985), Wichita Wings (NASL) (October 1985), Scarborough (free transfer November 1987), Huddersfield Town (loan February-March 1988), Charlton Athletic (free transfer March 1988), Galway United (player-manager 1988), Spalding United (1989), Grantham Town (early 1990), Telford United (player-reserve team manager 1990-91), Arnold Town (1993).
Club honours: Bolton Wanderers: Division Two champions 1978.
Representative honours: Republic of Ireland (24 full caps); England Youth caps.
A burly 'keeper of great experience, he was signed by Blues after the departure of Tony Coton. His career at St Andrew's was limited to only one match as two more goalkeepers, Prudhoe and Seaman, were signed in rapid succession. Unusually he was capped by two countries. He played over 270 games for Bolton (in two spells) and 135 for Rotherham.

McDONNELL, Martin
Centre-half; Apps 32, Goals 0.
Born: Newton-le-Willows, 27 April 1924. Died: Coventry, 13 April 1988.
Career: Everton (August 1942), Southport (August 1946), BLUES (May 1947), Coventry City (October 1949), Derby County (July 1955), Crewe Alexandra (July 1958). Retired 1961.
Club honours: Derby County: Third Division North champions 1957.
Principally deputy to Ted Duckhouse, tough guy Martin McDonnell was an uncompromising defender, not surprising for a former paratrooper. He was a great favourite of manager Harry Storer who signed him three times – for Blues, Coventry and Derby. He played in 250 games whilst at Highfield Road. McDonnell bred Alsatian dogs in his spare time.

McDONOUGH, Roy
Striker; Apps 2, Goals 1.
Born: Solihull, 16 October 1958.
Career: Warwickshire Schools, Aston Villa

Boys, BLUES *(apprentice October 1974, professional October 1976), Walsall (£15,000 September 1978), Chelsea (£15,000 October 1980), Colchester United (£15,000 February 1981), Southend United (£5,000 August 1983), Exeter City (£2,000 January 1984), Cambridge United (free transfer October 1984), Southend United (free transfer August 1985), Colchester United (player-manager 1990-May 1994), Braintree Town (August 1994), Dagenham & Redbridge (October 1994).*
Club honours: Southend United: Division Four promotion, 1990, Division Three promotion 1991; Colchester United: GM Vauxhall Conference champions 1992.
A tall, long-haired youngster, he was given a try out in the Blues' first team at the end of the 1976-77 season. He spent the next term in the reserves before beginning a tour of the lower divisions, never playing again in the top flight. But he proved a good, honest professional who always gave his all at whatever level he played. He scored 15 goals in 82 League games for Walsall, 24 in 93 for Colchester and 35 in 201 for Southend. He was occasionally used as a goalkeeper in Blues' youth side. Sacked as Colchester's manager by his father-in-law, chairman George Parker, his wife Jackie continued as lottery manager.

MacDOWELL, Duncan John
Centre-forward; Apps 2, Goals 0.
Born: Paddington, London, 18 December 1963.
Career: BLUES (apprentice June 1980, professional August 1981), Leatherhead (non-contract 1982-83).
A series of promising games in the reserves led to an early call-up for this pacy strong-running forward, but the following season he left to join Willie Bell's touring Christian missionary football team.

McGAVIN, Stephen James
Striker; Apps 21+12, Goals 7.
Born: North Walsham, 24 January 1969.
Career: Ipswich Town (trainee June 1985, professional 1987), Thetford (1988), Sudbury (free transfer 1989), Colchester United (£10,000, March 1991), BLUES (£150,000, January 1994), Wycombe Wanderers (March 1995).
Club honours: Colchester United: GM Vauxhall Conference champions 1992, FA Trophy winners 1992. Blues: Second Division champions 1995.
McGavin scored 19 goals in 70 games for Colchester before joining Blues a fortnight before his 25th birthday. A workmanlike footballer with good skills. At Blues he failed to score the goals his general play deserved.

McGURK, Francis Reynolds
Outside-right; Apps 19, Goals 2.
Born: Hamilton, Scotland, 15 January 1909. Died: Birmingham, 2 March 1978.
Career: Blantyre Celtic, Clyde (1931), BLUES (June 1933), Bristol City (May 1935), Whittaker Ellis (1936).
Representative honours: Scotland (1 full cap).
McGurk came south with a reputation as a goalscorer, something he never lived up to at St Andrew's. His dribbling skills, however, created such a favourable impression that he was rapidly promoted to the national team after only two years as a professional. His decline was just as rapid, though, and inside three years he was playing in the Birmingham Works League.

McINTOSH, Alexander
Inside-forward; Apps 23, Goals 4.
Born: Dunfermline, 14 April 1916.
Career: Hearts of Beath FC, Folkestone Town, Wolverhampton Wanderers (May 1937), BLUES (January 1947), Coventry City (February 1948), Kidderminster Harriers (1949), Hednesford Town (1950),
Bilston (1951). Retired 1953.
Club honours: Wolverhampton Wanderers: FA Cup runners-up 1939, Wartime Cup winners 1942; Blues: Division Two runners-up 1948.
A skilful, two-footed inside-forward with a powerful shot in both feet, Alex McIntosh had been a regular in the Wolves side before the war, but during the hostilities he spent some time inside a prisoner-of-war camp, and it was hardly surprising that on his return to League action, he never really regained his earlier form. His time with Blues was spent mainly as cover for Bodle and Dougall.

McKAY, John (Jack)
Forward; Apps 21, Goals 2.
Born: Hebburn, County Durham, 1885. Deceased.
Career: Hebburn, BLUES (1910), Blyth (1912).
A dribbling forward whose appearances were split between inside and outside-left, he opened his Blues career with a debut goal but was primarily a supplier of chances.

McKEE, Frank
Left-half; Apps 24, Goals 0.
Born: Cowdenbeath, 25 January 1923. Died: Birmingham, 1988.
Career: Lochgelly Albert, Dundee United (October 1947), BLUES (February 1948), Gillingham (July 1952), Gloucester City (August 1956), Kidderminster Harriers (1957).
McKee was a versatile Scotsman who was at home in most midfield roles. At his best prompting his forwards, he was rarely given much of a first-team run as Blues' tactics demanded a more defensive wing-half. He worked for South Staffordshire Water Company until his retirement.

McMILLAN, John Stuart
Inside-forward; Apps 52, Goals 25.
Born: Port Glasgow, 16 February 1871. Died: Derby, 4 November 1941.
Career: Port Glasgow Athletic, St Bernard's, Derby County (December 1890), Leicester Fosse (May 1896), BLUES (January 1901), Bradford City (May 1903), Glossop North End (May 1906), BLUES (trainer August 1909), Gillingham (manager 1919- August 1922).
A regular Scottish junior whilst only 14 years old, Johnny McMillan nevertheless had only a brief spell in Scottish League football, leaving St Bernard's after a row about professionalism. A classy left-footed forward who had the knack of complementing every centre-forward he played alongside, he is the holder of the Blues' record for most goals in a game – five against Blackpool on 2 March 1901 – a feat he also achieved with Derby. In his later days at Blues he was slowed down by injuries and it was no great surprise when Bradford City took him on as their captain during their first League season. His son Stuart managed Derby County when they won the FA Cup in 1946, beating Blues in the semi-final.

McMINN, Kevin Clifton 'Ted'
Winger; Apps 22+4, Goals 0.
Born: Castle Douglas, 28 September 1962.
Career: Glenafton Athletic (1980), Queen of the South (January 1982), Glasgow Rangers (£50,000 October 1984), Sevilla (Spain) (£225,000 January 1987), Derby County (£300,000 February 1988), BLUES (£115,000 July 1993), Burnley (loan February, signed full-time March 1994).
Club honours: Rangers: Scottish League Cup winners 1986;
Burnley: Division Two promotion 1994.
Known affectionately as the 'Tinman', Ted McMinn was a strong player, good on the ball who enjoyed to occupy a position wide on the right. He played well over 140

games in Scotland before trying his luck in Spain. At Derby he proved an exciting player who often threatened to turn the game his side's way.

McROBERTS, Roberts
Centre-forward; Apps 187, Goals 82.
Born: Coatbridge, near Motherwell, Scotland, 12 July 1874. Died: Birkenhead, 27 February 1959.
Career: Coatbridge FC (1892), Airdrieonians, Albion Rovers, Gainsborough Trinity (August 1896), BLUES (£150 August 1898), Chelsea (£100 August 1905). Retired May 1909 and returned to BLUES as team manager in July 1910, holding the position for five years, up to August 1915.
Club honours: Blues: Division Two champions 1901.
Bob McRoberts was an elegant, ball-juggling forward who preferred to score his goals with finesse rather than using hurly-burly tactics. He was signed by Blues after a short spell at Gainsborough where he stood out in a poor side. At Blues he rapidly made a name for himself, although he once declared that he didn't 'give a tinker's cuss' what people thought of his play. After seven seasons at Blues he moved to London and was Chelsea's first-ever signing. He played for the Londoners in their initial League game in September 1905, against Stockport County, and whilst at Stamford Bridge he was used as both a centre-forward and a centre-half. On retiring he became Blues' first full-time paid manager.

MADDEN, David John
Midfield; Apps 5, Goals 1.
Born: London, 6 January 1963.
Career: Southampton (apprentice 1979, professional January 1981), AFC Bournemouth (loan January 1983), Arsenal (free transfer August 1983), Charlton Athletic (free transfer June 1984), Los Angeles Lazers (1985), Reading (November 1987), Crystal Palace (August 1988), BLUES (loan January 1990), Maidstone United (free transfer July 1990-coach January 1992).
Club honours: Crystal Palace: FA Cup runners-up 1990.
This stylish midfielder had had his fair share of ups and downs before he moved to St Andrew's and his brief spell with Blues was a microcosm of his career as a whole. Voted 'Man of the Match' on his debut, he gave a goal away in his second game with an awful back-pass, only to bounce back in his next outing with a quite brilliant strike. Manager Dave Mackay wanted to sign him permanently, but the money was not available and three months later he appeared at Wembley in the FA Cup Final,
only to be freed by Palace shortly afterwards! He returned from his honeymoon in 1992 suffering from malaria.

MADDEN, Owen
Inside/outside-left; Apps 15, Goals 5.
Born: Cork, 5 December 1916. Died: Cork, 20 January 1991.
Career: Cork High School, Cork Southern Rovers, Cork Hibernians, Norwich City (May 1936), BLUES (£2,000 February 1938), Cork City (May 1939), Cork United, Cork Athletic (1948, manager 1953). Sligo Rovers (guest 1939-44).
Club honours: Cork United: League of Ireland champions 1941, 1942, 1943, 1945 & 1946, Irish Cup winners 1941, 1947, runners-up 1942, 1943; Cork Hibs: Irish Cup runners-up 1936.
Representative honours: Republic of Ireland (2 full caps).
Madden was highly rated in Ireland and there were accusations of 'poaching' when Norwich signed him. He was unable to gain a regular place with either of his English clubs, but his place in Blues' history is earned by virtue of his goal against Everton in the 1939 FA Cup-tie, a game watched by St Andrews' record crowd. After his return to his native country he enjoyed a phenomenally successful career as a goalscorer.

MAIN, Walter Seymour
Inside-left; Apps 41, Goals 14.
Born: Motherwell, 1875. Deceased.
Career: Airdrieonians, BLUES (1899), St Bernard's FC (1901).
A Scottish ball artist who took over the second striker's role when Walter Wigmore switched to centre-half. He had two years in and out of the team before being replaced by Johnny McMillan.

MANGNALL, David
Centre-forward, Apps 39, Goals 15.
Born: Wigan, 21 September 1907. Died: Penzance, 10 April 1962.
Career: Maltby New Church FC, Maltby Colliery, Rotherham United (trial), Huddersfield Town (trial), Doncaster Rovers (amateur 1926), Leeds United (professional November 1927), Huddersfield Town (£3,000 December 1929), BLUES (February 1934), West Ham United (£2,950 March 1935), Millwall (May 1936), QPR (May 1939). Guested for Fulham, Millwall and Southend United during World War Two. Appointed QPR manager 1944, retiring in June 1952.
Club honours: Millwall: Division Three South champions 1937, Division Three (South) Cup winners 1937.

In a career spanning some 25 years (first as a goalscorer and then as a manager) Dave Mangnall set foot on practically every ground in the country. He scored 52 goals for Maltby New Church in one season and 35 for Maltby Colliery in another. And he netted ten goals in a single reserve match for Leeds. Whilst at Huddersfield he had the unusual experience of scoring 42 goals in the 1931-32 season and then finding himself dropped the next year. His spell with Blues was blighted by injury problems but he soon found his touch again after his departure to West Ham. He gave up his job as a miner to turn professional with Leeds United. Mangnall hit 61 goals in only 79 League games for Huddersfield, and all told scored more then 120 goals in less than 200 appearances as a professional. After leaving the game he went into business in Cornwall.

MARDON, Paul Jonathan
Defender; Apps 54+9, Goals 0.
Born: Bristol, 14 September 1969.
Career: Boco Juniors, Bristol City (YTS June 1985, professional September 1987), Doncaster Rovers (loan September 1990), BLUES (tribunal set fee of £115,000 July 1991), Liverpool (trial January 1992), West Bromwich Albion (£450,000 November 1993).

A strong, forceful defender, 6ft, 11st 10lb, Mardon has the ability to judge a last-minute tackle to perfection. He joined Blues after failing to earn a regular place in the Bristol City team, and came from same junior side as Adrian Bird and Julian Dicks.

MARTIN, Raymond B.
Full-back; Apps 364+10, Goals 1.
Born: Wolverhampton, 23 January 1945.
Career: South-East Staffs Boys, Aston Villa (junior 1960), BLUES (apprentice June 1961, professional May 1962), Portland Timbers (NASL) (loan May 1975, full-time May 1976), Minnesota Kicks (1979). Retired 1979 and was later soccer coach at Oregon State University.
Club honours: Blues: Division Two promotion 1972.
Whilst a youngster at Villa Park, Martin broke manager Joe Mercer's toe in a training session. Within a few weeks he was released, although the two incidents were probably not related! Carefully nurtured at St Andrew's before being given his League baptism shortly before his 19th birthday, he impressed sufficiently to retain his place for most of that season and was a regular member of the first-team squad for the next 12 years. During his time, Martin was the victim of much abuse from the terraces but to his credit he persevered and eventually won over his critics to become a much-loved character. A player who always gave the impression of thoroughly enjoying his football, his trademark was his amazing slide tackle. His only goal for Blues came

against Hull City in a home Division Two game in April 1970. Blues' Player of the Year in 1969-70 and 1970-71, he was given a deserved testimonial by the club in 1971.

MARTIN, Robert ('Roy')
Full-back; Apps 74, Goals 0.
Born: Glengarnock Village, Kilwinning, Scotland, 16 May 1929.
Career: Glengarnock Schools, Kilwinning Rangers, BLUES (professional March 1950), Derby County (March 1956), Chesterfield (July 1960), Burton Albion (July 1961), Long Eaton United (1963).
Club honours: Derby County: Division Three North champions 1957.
A polished full-back who provided highly capable cover for the Hall-Green partnership and tended to be rather overshadowed because of this. In his entire League career he was only once regarded as an indisputable first choice and that was in Derby's Third Division North championship winning season under former Blues manager Harry Storer and alongside another former Blues player, Martin McDonnell. Martin, who suffered a broken leg during his time a the Baseball Ground, was employed as a butcher after retiring from the game.

MASSART, David L.
Inside/centre-forward; Apps 3, Goals 0.
Born: Yardley, Birmingham, 2 November 1919.
Career: Bells Athletic, BLUES (amateur 1938, professional February 1939), Walsall (June 1947), Bury (March 1948), Chesterfield (February 1951), Weymouth (August 1951). Later hotelier in Weymouth where he now lives.
Club honours: Blues: Football League South champions 1946.
Dave Massart was a bold, strong, determined, never-say-die goalscorer who grabbed a hat-trick in each of his first three home games for Walsall at the start of 1947-48 and ended up with 23 goals in 27 games for the Saddlers that season. He later netted 45 goals in 85 League matches for Chesterfield. A real old fashioned number-nine, Massart could not wrest a regular place in the Blues side from Cyril Trigg.

MATTHEWSON, Trevor
Central defender; Apps 202+1, Goals 13.
Born: Sheffield, 12 February 1963.
Career: Pye Bank Junior School, Herries Comprehensive School, Sheffield Wednesday (apprentice June 1979, professional February 1981), Newport County (October 1983), Stockport County (September 1985), Lincoln City (£13,000 August 1987), BLUES (£45,000 August 1989), Preston North End (September 1993), Bury (August 1994).
Club honours: Lincoln City: GM Vauxhall Conference champions 1988; Blues: Leyland DAF Cup winners 1991.
Matthewson, a tall, well-built defender, skippered Lincoln back into the Football

League in 1988 and indeed the Imps were somewhat put out when the tribunal valued him at only £45,000. He has played occasionally as a full-back where he showed a flair for overlapping. His uncle Reg played Sheffield United, Fulham and Chester.

MEACOCK, William Robert
Centre-half; Apps 14, Goals 0.
Born: Hoole, 26 July 1910.
Career: Hoole and Newton FC, Blackpool (May 1930), Torquay United (August 1931), Tranmere Rovers (July 1933), Lincoln City (May 1935), BLUES (June 1938), Bristol City (May 1939).
An experienced defender who was amongst a group of new players signed by Blues to boost the club's flagging fortunes in 1938. Not the tallest of centre-halves, Bob Meacock was a solid tackler but he was not quite up to top-class football.

MEATES, William Percival
Goalkeeper; Apps 17, Goals 0.
Born: Bournemouth, 1871. Deceased.
Career: Eastbourne, BLUES (1895), Warmley FC (1897), Nottingham Forest (trial 1898).
Meates, a tall, long-legged 'keeper, battled with Jimmy Roach for two years for the green jersey. He left to join West Country Southern Leaguers Warmley.

MERRICK, Gilbert Harold
Goalkeeper; Apps 551, Goals 0.
Born: Sparkhill, Birmingham, 26 January 1922.
Career: Acocks Green School, Fenton Rovers, Olton Sports, Shirley Juniors, Solihull Town (July 1939), BLUES (amateur August 1938, professional August 1939). Retired 1960 and became manager of BLUES (June 1960-April 1964). Bromsgrove Rovers (manager 1967), Atherstone Town (manager 1970). Guested for several clubs during World War Two including Northampton Town, Nottingham Forest and West Bromwich Albion.
Club honours: Blues: Football League South champions 1946, Division Two champions 1948, 1955, FA Cup runners-up 1956; (as manager): Blues: Inner-Cities Fairs Cup runners-up 1961, Football League Cup winners 1963.
Representative honours: England (23 full caps); Football League XI (11).

Probably the best goalkeeper in Britain during the early to mid- 1950s, Gil Merrick was powerfully built with a dapper moustache and huge hands, one of the long line of great Blues 'keepers, who modelled his style upon that of his predecessor, Harry Hibbs, although he was perhaps a touch more 'showier' than H.H. Superbly athletic, Merrick was a brilliant handler of the ball but had the misfortune to be England's 'last line of defence' for both of those thrashings

by the Hungarians in 1953-54. He was nicknamed 'Mister thirteen' in Hungary after the return game in Budapest. He played 170 games for Blues during World War Two, making over 700 appearances for the club overall. He now lives in retirement in Birmingham. His son Neil played for AFC Bournemouth.

METCALFE, John
Outside-left; Apps 2, Goals 0.
Born: Acocks Green, Birmingham, 2 June 1935.
Career: Yardley Boys, BLUES (amateur June 1951, professional October 1952), York City (June 1957), Walsall (July 1958-May 1959).
A short, sturdily built winger whose entire professional career was spent almost exclusively in reserve-team football, for he made only seven senior appearances for these three clubs.

MILLARD, Albert Alexander
Centre-forward/centre-half; Apps 33, Goals 15.
Born: West Bromwich, 1 October 1898. Deceased.
Career: Bratt Street School (West Bromwich), Swan Village, Coseley, Cardiff City, BLUES (1919), Coventry City (November 1920), Crystal Palace (July 1922), Charlton Athletic (October 1924), Leamington Town (1925). Retired 1926.
Millard was a highly versatile player, equally adept in defence or attack, and Blues' top scorer in 1919-20. He was the club's regular centre-forward until Hampton and Lane arrived on the scene, and then he moved back into defence where he continued to exhibit his great all round ability.

MILLARD, Arthur Arnold
Forward; Apps 4, Goals 3.
Born: Birmingham, 1869. Deceased.
Career: Smethwick Centaur, BLUES (1891), Lea Hall (1892).
A player with a fine scoring record who perhaps deserved more than four first-team games.

MILLER, Alan John
Goalkeeper; Apps 16, Goals 0.
Born: Epping, 29 March 1970.
Career: Epping Forest School, FA School of Excellence, Arsenal (YTS June 1986, professional May 1988), Plymouth Argyle (loan November 1988), West Bromwich Albion (loan August 1991), BLUES (loan December 1991), Middlesbrough (£500,000 August 1994).
Club honours: Arsenal: FA Youth Cup winners 1988, European Cup-winners' Cup winners 1994. Middlesbrough: Division Two promotion 1995.
Representative honours: England (4 Under-21 caps, Youth caps) Miller made only eight League appearances in six years as a professional at Highbury. He was one of Bryan Robson's first signings for Middlesbrough. He stands 6ft 2in and has good reflexes.

MILLER, Kevin
Goalkeeper; Apps 30, Goals 0.

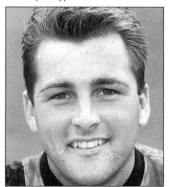

Born: Falmouth, 15 March 1969.
Career: Falmouth Town (1985), Newquay United, Exeter City (free transfer March 1989), BLUES (£250,000 May 1993), Watford (£250,000 August 1994).
Club honours: Exeter: Division Four champions 1990.
Kevin Miller was bought by his former boss, Terry Cooper, to replace Andy Gosney but spent only one season at St Andrew's before new boss Barry Fry replaced him with Ian Bennett. He made exactly 200 appearances for Exeter. He stands 6ft 1in tall.

MILLINGTON, Charles J.H.
Outside-right; Apps 87, Goals 13.
Born: Lincoln, 25 April 1884. Died: Lincoln, 13 June 1955.
Career: Grantham Town (1901), Ripley Athletic (January 1905), Aston Villa (September 1905), Fulham (£400 October 1907), BLUES (£600 August 1909), Wellington Town (August 1912), Brierley Hill Alliance (March 1913), Stourbridge (April 1914). Retired May 1920 and went to work as an iron moulder in a Lincoln factory.
Charlie Millington was quick and strong with plenty of courage, who proved a revelation on the wing for Blues. Never a great goalscorer, he had a turn of speed second to none. Millington spent 20 years in football and hit 14 goals in 38 games for the Villa, and 21 in 63 for Fulham. He was also a very capable cricketer on the Minor Counties circuit with Lincolnshire. His cousin, Ben, played for Fulham and his son, Charlie junior, was a Blues trialist.

MILLS, Bertie Reginald ('Paddy')
Inside-forward; Apps 13, Goals 3.
Born: Multan, India, 23 February 1900.
Career: Barton Town, Hull City (September 1920), Notts County (£3,750 March 1926), BLUES (February 1929), Hull City (December 1929), Scunthorpe United (1933), Gainsborough Trinity (1935).
Mills was a direct, strong, hard-working forward who never knew the meaning of surrender. A prolific marksman with his other clubs, he had difficulty settling into Blues' style of play. He earned the nickname 'Paddy' because of his fiery temper. His brothers, Percy and Arthur, were also professional footballers. After retiring he earned his living as a security man at a Scunthorpe steelworks.

MITCHELL, Frank Rollason
Left-back; Apps 106, Goals 8.
Born: Goulborn, New South Wales, Australia, 3 June 1922. Died: Lapworth, Warwickshire, 2 April 1984.
Career: Coventry City (amateur), BLUES

(professional September 1943), Chelsea (January 1949), Watford (August 1952). Retired 1958. Guested for Arsenal, Northampton Town and Portsmouth whilst serving in the Royal Navy during World War Two.
Club honours: Blues: Football League South champions 1946, Division Two champions 1948.
Representative honours: FA XI.
Although born in Australia, Frank Mitchell moved to England whilst in his teens. He originally regarded cricket his major sport and joined Warwickshire's ground staff at the age of 15. He guested for Blues in 1942-43 and so impressed the club that he was signed as a full-timer soon afterwards. He gained a regular place in the side in 1945-46 and developed into a cool, classy wing-half. His calm temperament led to him getting the job of penalty-taker and his method of taking spot-kicks is well chronicled: at the start of his run-up he would always hitch up his shorts before striding forward and aiming a low shot into the corner of the net. On the cricket field he was a medium-pace bowler for Warwickshire (17 matches in 1946-48) taking 22 wickets at an average of 38.9. He also had trials for Kent and assisted Cornwall and Hertfordshire, as well as Knowle & Dorridge CC (Warwicks), becoming secretary of the latter club, for whom he scored a century at the age of 47. He was in charge of the sports grounds and coaching facilities at Kynoch's for many years after hanging up his boots.

MITTELL, James Lyons
Goalkeeper; Apps 6, Goals 0.
Born: Merthyr Tydfil, 1908.
Career: Wigan Borough (1929), BLUES (1931), Luton Town (1933).
Mittell was an experienced reserve 'keeper who joined Blues when the Wigan club folded. He was more spectacular than Harry Hibbs but had few chances to show off his skills at St Andrew's.

MOBLEY, Frank
Centre-half; Apps 103, Goals 64.
Born: Handsworth, Birmingham, 21 November 1868. Died: 1940.
Career: Hockley Belmont, Cape Hill, Singers FC of Coventry (May 1886), BLUES (April 1892), Bury (May 1896), Warmley (Bristol), Coventry City (1900). Retired April 1902 and returned to Birmingham where he went into business.
Club honours: Blues: Division Two champions 1893.
Although at 5ft 8in he was on the small side for a centre-forward Frank Mobley was fast and fearless and possessed a terrific shot. A lot of his goals came about when he charged the 'keeper and the ball over the line together. In 1892 Blues' directors sent a scout to watch Harry Edwards in action for Singers. He impressed and was duly signed by the club, along with Mobley who impressed even more.

MOFFATT, Sidney Hugh
Outside-right; Apps 17, Goals 3.
Born: Congleton, Cheshire, 16 September 1910. Died: Macclesfield, 20 September 1981.
Career: Congleton Town (1930), BLUES (December 1933), Millwall (June 1936-May 1937).
Son of England wing-half Hugh Moffatt (Burnley and Oldham), Sid was something of a sprinter with a good body-swerve and a liking for cutting inside his full-back and trying a shot at goal. He could not settle in at Millwall and played only twice for the Lions.

MOLES, James R.
Wing-half; Apps 33, Goals 0.
Born: Leyton, London, 1885. Deceased.
Career: Leyton, BLUES (1909), Edmonton (1911).
An enthusiastic half-back whose aggressive instincts were sometimes regarded as a liability. He had been a prominent player in London non-League circles when Blues

signed him to understudy Buckley. He spent most of his career at left-half.

MONTGOMERY, James
Goalkeeper; Apps 73, Goals 0.
Born: Sunderland, 9 October 1943.
Career: St Hilda's School (Sunderland),

Sunderland (amateur June 1958, professional October 1960), Southampton (loan October 1976), BLUES (February 1977), Nottingham Forest (August 1979), BLUES (temporary coach July-August 1980), Sunderland (player-coach and reserve-team player, August 1980-July 1982). Returned to Sunderland as youth coach in 1993.
Club honours: Sunderland: FA Cup winners 1973.
Representative honours: England (6 Under-23 caps, Youth international).
Jim Montgomery was a superb goalkeeper who made more than 700 appearances during a career which spanned over 20 years. He made a record 537 League appearances for Sunderland and it was undoubtedly his terrific 'double-save' which saw off Leeds United in the 1973 Cup Final. He went to Nottingham Forest as cover for Peter Shilton, and was surely kept out of the senior England side only by the great Gordon Banks. Montgomery proved to be an inspired signing by Blues and produced some quite marvellous saves during his spell at St Andrew's.

MOORE, Ernest W.
Left-back; Apps 1, Goals 0.
Born: Birmingham, 1869. Deceased.
Career: Sparkhill Alliance, BLUES (1893), Hockley Hill (1895).
Ernie Moore was given a try out in the United Counties League in 1893, a late-season competition designed to fill gaps in the fixture list He played in two games and seemed to have a promising future, but when Blues signed 'Dowk' Oliver, Moore was pushed out. He made his Football League debut the following season when Oliver was injured on Boxing Day but that was the end of his career with Blues.

MOORE, George S. ('Kid')
Inside-forward; Apps 3, Goals 0.
Born: Coventry, 1884. Deceased.
Career: Nuneaton Borough, BLUES (1908), Leamington Town (1909).
George Moore was a highly popular youngster when with Nuneaton but his transfer to Blues didn't go down too well with the fans. He failed to settle in League football and was soon back in Warwickshire junior soccer.

MORAN, Richard ('Whoopie')
Centre-forward; Apps 2+7, Goals 1.
Born: Maidstone, 9 September 1963.
Career: Fareham Town, Gosport Borough (1987), Fujita (Japan) (1988), BLUES (trial August 1990, taken on full-time September 1990), Kettering Town (loan

March 1991), Bashley Town (July 1991), Waterlooville (September 1991).
Moran was a big, awkward-looking forward who was signed by Blues after his return from a two-year spell in Japan. He was a prolific scorer in non-League soccer and was on the verge of having trials with Leeds until injury intervened. He had the unusual distinction of being substituted at half-time during his initial first-team trial with Blues because he had to dash off to be best man at a friend's wedding that afternoon. He scored on his debut for Blues but failed to show that he was good enough for League competition.

MORELAND, A.Geoffrey
Centre-forward; Apps 3, Goals 0.
Born: Wolverhampton, June 1912.
Career: Prestwood Amateurs, Stafford Rangers, Swindon Town (1937), BLUES (May 1938), Port Vale (November 1938).
A tall, well built target man, Moreland was a prominent figure in non-League football before his move to Swindon. His League career was transient as he switched clubs rapidly with little success.

MORFITT, John William
Centre-forward; Apps 1, Goals 0.
Born: Sheffield, 28 September 1908. Deceased.
Career: Sheffield Heeley, Mansfield Town, BLUES (March 1928), Blackpool (1931), Bradford March 1932), Southend United (September 1932). Retired June 1936.
Morfitt was yet another footballing rover who failed to make his mark with any of his clubs. He relied on speed rather than muscle power and consequently was easily knocked off the ball.

MORGAN, John
Centre-half; Apps 1, Goals 0.
Born: Penicuik, Scotland, 17 March 1900. Deceased.
Career: Edinburgh Emmett, BLUES (August 1924), Doncaster Rovers (1926), Bristol City (1930), Barrow (June 1931), Walsall (1933), Worcester City, (Ireland), Atherstone Town (1938).
A strongly built player whose only game for Blues came when both Cringan and Hunter were injured. He was never called up again.

MORGAN, Thomas
Centre-half; Apps 2, Goals 0.
Born: Walsall, 1860. Deceased.
Career: Darlaston Road Council School, Walsall Town Swifts, BLUES (August 1882), Darlaston (June 1883).
A youngster who alternated with the more experienced Sam Gessey throughout his one term at Muntz Street, Morgan lost the struggle and had dropped out of contention by February, moving on to Darlaston at the end of the season.

MORGAN, Trevor J.
Forward/defender; Apps 1+1, Goals 0.
Born: Forest Gate, London, 30 September 1956.
Career: Tonbridge (July 1977), Sydney St George, Dartford, Leytonstone, AFC Bournemouth (September 1980), Mansfield Town (November 1981), AFC Bournemouth (March 1982), Bristol City (March 1984), Exeter City (November 1984), Bristol Rovers (September 1985), Bristol City (January 1987), Bolton Wanderers (June 1987), Colchester United (October 1989), Happy Valley (Hong Kong), Exeter City (November 1990), South China (Hong Kong), BLUES (assistant manager January 1993), Solihull Borough (December 1993), Exeter City (assistant manager February 1994).
Morgan had a long and interesting career before joining Blues as assistant manager to Terry Cooper. He had amassed well over 600 senior appearances (481 in the Football

League) as a professional before moving to St Andrew's.

MORGAN, William Albert L. ('Mollie')
Outside-left; Apps 68, Goals 13.
Born: Old Hill, 3 November 1891. Deceased.
Career: Cradley St Luke's, BLUES (November 1912), Coventry City (1920), Crystal Palace (July 1922), Cradley St Luke's (June 1925), Shrewsbury Town (1927).

Rather on the plump side for a winger, Bill Morgan was one of the 'bulldozer' type who moved to inside-forward after leaving Blues. He maintained a respectable strike rate throughout his career.

MORLEY, William Anthony
Outside-left; Apps 4, Goals 3.
Born: Ormskirk, 26 August 1954.
Career: Ormskirk & Burscough Schools, Skelmersdale Boys, Preston North End (apprentice June 1970, professional September 1972), Burnley (record £100,000 February 1976), Aston Villa (£200,000 June 1979), West Bromwich Albion (£75,000 December 1983), BLUES (loan November-December 1984), FC Seiko (Hong Kong) (loan August 1985), FC Den Haag (Holland) (£25,000 July 1986),

Walsall (trial June 1987), Notts County (trial early 1987), West Bromwich Albion (late July 1987), Burnley (loan October-November 1988), Tampa Bay Rowdies (USA) (March 1989), Hamrun Spartans (Malta) (1990), New Zealand League football (1990-91), Sutton Coldfield Town (1993), Bromsgrove Rovers (assistant manager 1993), Stratford Town (April 1995).
Club honours: Aston Villa: Division One champions 1981, European Cup winners

1982, European Super Cup winners 1983, World Club championship runners-up 1983; Den Haag: Dutch Cup runners-up 1987.
Representative honours: England (6 full caps, 1 'B' cap, 1 Under-23 cap, 7 Youth caps).
A top-class winger whilst with Burnley and Villa, Tony Morley was a player who hugged the touch-line, had pace, dribbling ability and a telling shot. He first came to Blues' notice when he scored a quite stunning goal against them when playing for Burnley. The club never made an offer and Morley moved to Villa instead. He was in the doldrums when he finally arrived at St Andrew's on loan in 1984 and he subsequently became only the second player ever to turn out for Blues, Villa and Albion in League football. Blues could not sign him simply because they had no money.

MORRALL, George Richard ('Lofty')
Centre-half; Apps 266, Goals 7.
Born: Smethwick, 4 October 1905. Died: Birmingham, 15 November 1955.
Career: Gorse Street Primitive Methodists, Chance's Glass Works FC, Littleton Harriers, Allen Everitt's Sports, West Bromwich Albion (trial), BLUES (professional March 1927), Swindon Town (June 1936). Retired 1940.
Club honours: Blues: FA Cup runners-up 1931.
George Morrall was a tall, commanding figure in the heart of the Blues defence. He dominated in the air was reliable on the ground and possessed a ferocious tackle. He gained a regular place in the side in 1928-29 and went on to put in some sterling performances for the club, being tipped at one stage for England honours. Uncle of Terry Morrall (formerly of Aston Villa).

MORRIS, Arthur ('Hetty')
Inside-left; Apps 4, Goals 2.
Born: Market Drayton, Shropshire, 1882. Died: Shrewsbury, 1945.
Career: Shrewsbury Town, BLUES (1906), Shrewsbury Town (1908).
A ball-playing midfielder who scored on his debut for Blues but who did not impress sufficiently to gain an automatic place in the side. Both his goals earned Blues points.

MORRIS, David J.
Inside-left; Apps 3, Goals 0.
Born: Walsall, 1888. Deceased.
Career: Walsall Conduits FC, Darlaston, BLUES (1910), Tipton Town (1912).
This inexperienced forward from the Black Country who was given his chance by Blues in 1911-12 after the team had got off to an atrocious start. He looked lost in League competition, however, and was soon on his way back to junior circles.

MORRIS, Harry
Wing-half/centre-forward; Apps 69, Goals 4.
Born: Birmingham, 11 April 1886. Died: Birmingham, June 1931.
Career: Small Heath Council School, BLUES (August 1883). Retired May 1893.
Few men gave Blues better service than Harry Morris, who joined the club as a 17-year-old centre-forward, at a time when he was also an apprentice plumber. He eventually became an accomplished right-half, skippering the side many times, and was indeed a grand leader, showing immense determination and sportsmanship. After retiring it was Harry Morris who 'found' the St Andrew's Ground, having become a director of the club in 1903. His two sons (Harry junior and Len) followed him on to the board, with the former attaining directorship in 1929, and taking over as chairman in 1933. He was president in 1967, the year of his death. Harry senior

died in 1931, having attended that season's FA Cup Final when Blues lost 2-1 to West Bromwich Albion, 45 years after he had

played for Small Heath against the Baggies in the 1886 FA Cup semi-final at Aston. A shrewd businessman, Harry Morris was one of the first people in Birmingham to see the potential in talking pictures and at the time of his death he was on the board of several local cinemas in the district. His brother Charles played for Blues in their pre-League days.

MORRIS, Ronald
Outside-left; Apps 5+10, Goals 0.
Born: Birmingham, 25 September 1970.
Career: FA School of Excellence, BLUES (YTS June 1986, professional September 1988, contract cancelled 1989), Nuovo Pistoiese (Italian Interregionale League), Redditch United (1990), Kings Norton Ex-service, Sandwell Borough, West Bromwich Albion (trial), Shrewsbury Town (trial February 1994).
One of the first intake of youngsters from the School of Excellence, Ronnie Morris soon fell foul of the authorities for a series of misdemeanours. Undeterred by this, Blues took him on and he impressed in the youth team, showing good pace and aggression. At the end of 1987-88 he was given a run-out as substitute and looked a fair prospect. But he had a problem with his attitude and after some training ground incidents, Blues sacked him. He played a few games in Italy before he was sent back to England when it was found that his signing was void as it had occurred after the Italian transfer deadline. He has since had occasional forays into non-League football with limited success.

MORRIS, Seymour
Winger; Apps 83, Goals 31.
Born: Ynyshir, South Wales, 15 February 1908.
Career: Ynyshir, School, Cathay's FC, Lovells Athletic, Aberaman, Huddersfield Town (March 1933), BLUES (March 1935). Retired 1944.
Representative honours: Wales (5 full caps).
Fast and tricky but somewhat frail, Seymour Morris' career at Blues was blighted by injuries. At Huddersfield he had been regarded primarily as an inside-forward but had made only six appearances for them, scoring three goals, when Blues stepped in. He switched to the left wing – his more natural position – but it took him two years to establish himself as a regular in the side at St Andrew's. Then injuries and international call-ups saw him absent. He was one of five Welsh internationals on

Blues' books in 1938-39, although only four ever appeared on the international scene together. Seymour Morris still lives in South Wales.

MORTIMER, Dennis George
Midfield; Apps 37, Goals 6.
Born: Liverpool, 5 April 1952.
Career: Kirby Boys, Coventry City (apprentice July 1967, professional September 1969), Aston Villa (£175,000 December 1975), Sheffield United (loan December 1984), Brighton & Hove Albion (August 1985), BLUES (August 1986), Kettering Town (non-contract August 1987), Redditch United (player-manager late 1987-October 1988), West Bromwich Albion (community officer August 1989, youth-team manager 1992, assistant manager June 1993-October 1994).
Club honours: Coventry City: FA Youth Cup runners-up 1970; Aston Villa: Football League Cup winners 1977, Division One champions 1981, European Cup winners 1982, European Super Cup winners 1983, World Club Championship runner-up 1982.
Representative honours: England (3 'B' caps, 6 Under-23 caps, Youth caps); toured Australia with FA in 1971.

A driving force in midfield, Dennis Mortimore first rose to prominence with Coventry when his hair was so long that the fans called him 'Doris'. He moved to Villa Park and became an instant success, his hard running style making him the archetypal 'Ron Saunders player', although his game contained much more than sheer athleticism. His career was coming to an end when he joined Blues and after a promising start at St Andrew's he fell out of favour with the fans and left after only one season. He played over 400 games for Villa and during his League career amassed a total of 590 appearances.

MORTON, Roy Steven
Midfield; Apps 6, Goals 1.
Born: Birmingham, 29 October 1955.
Career: Warley Boys, Manchester United (apprentice June 1971, professional November 1972), BLUES (free transfer September 1973), AP Leamington (June 1977).
Representative honours: England (Youth caps, Schoolboy caps).
Morton was a star of Midlands schools football for whom big things were predicted, but he struggled at Old Trafford and was freed when it became obvious that he was not going to break through. A chunky midfield workhorse with a terrific shot, he was restricted to a few games as Howard Kendall's understudy at St Andrew's.

MOULDEN, Paul Anthony
Striker; Apps 20+3, Goals 6.
Born: Farnworth, 6 September 1967.
Career: Bolton Boys' Club (1980-82),

Manchester City (apprentice June 1984, professional September 1984), AFC Bournemouth (£160,000 August 1989), Oldham Athletic (£225,000 March 1990), Brighton & Hove Albion (loan August 1992), BLUES (£150,000 March 1993), Huddersfield Town (free transfer March 1995).

Club honours: Manchester City: FA Youth Cup winners 1986; Oldham Athletic: Division Two champions 1991.

Representative honours: England (15 Youth caps, Schoolboy caps).

As a teenager with Bolton Boys' Club, Paul Moulden once scored 289 goals in a season (1981-82). He continued his good work with Manchester City's intermediate and reserve teams and also did well in the senior side, scoring 26 times in 79 games. Thereafter his form see-sawed and he struggled with injury during his first full season at St Andrew's. He is the son of Tony Moulden, the former Bury, Rochdale, Peterborough and Notts County player.

MOUNTENEY, Arthur ('Pecker')
Inside-forward; Apps 97, Goals 30.
Born: Belgrave, Leicester, 11 February 1883. Died: Leicester, 1 June 1933.
Career: Leicester Imperial, Leicester Fosse (November 1903), BLUES (April 1905), Preston North End (April 1909), Grimsby Town (July 1911), Portsmouth (December 1912), Hinckley Athletic (September 1914).
Although he was a big, burly forward, Arthur Mounteney was not the 'battering ram' that one might expect. Indeed, during his stay at Blues, he was frequently criticised for not using his weight enough. Surprisingly quick for his size, he preferred to beat opponents with a short, sharp passing manoeuvres. He also played cricket and was an attractive middle-order batsman, representing Leicestershire for 13 years, scoring 5,306 runs (six centuries) at an average of 20.8.

MUIR, Ian James
Inside-forward; Apps 2, Goals 0.
Born: Coventry, 5 May 1963.
Career: Caludon Castle School, Stockingford Scholars, Bedworth Juniors, QPR (apprentice June 1979, professional September 1980), Burnley (loan November 1982), BLUES (free transfer August 1983), Brighton & Hove Albion (free transfer February 1984), Swindon Town (loan January 1985), Tranmere Rovers (July 1985).
Club honours: Tranmere Rovers: Leyland DAF Cup winners 1990, Division Three promotion 1991.
Representative honours: England (1 Youth caps, Schoolboy caps).
Ian Muir is a goalpoaching striker whose abilities were misjudged by a string of managers until his profitable association

with Tranmere where he holds the overall club goalscoring record. Although a regular marksman in Blues' reserves, he was never given the extended run in the first team that perhaps he deserved.

MULLETT, Joseph
Left-half/full-back; Apps 3, Goals 0.
Born: Blackheath, 2 October. 1936. Died: Cradley Heath.
Career: Malt Mill United, BLUES (amateur February 1955, professional July 1955), Norwich City (£2,000 February 1959), King's Lynn (August 1968), Lowestoft Town (July 1970), Yarmouth Town (October 1971).
Club honours: Norwich City League Cup winners 1962.
This powerfully built wing-half who was given a run in the Blues' first team shortly after returning from his National Service in the far East. He was never assured of a senior place due to the consistency of Dick Neal. Converted to full-back at Norwich, he proved a great favourite with the Carrow Road fans. He later became a market trader and then shopkeeper in Old Hill, West Midlands.

MULRANEY, Ambrose ('Jock')
Outside-right/left; Apps 41, Goals 16.
Born: Wishaw, near Motherwell, 18 May 1916.
Career: Wishaw White Rose, Carluke Rovers, Hearts (trial), Celtic (August 1933), Hamilton Academical (trial), Sligo Rovers (trial), Blackpool (trial), Clapton Orient (trial), Dartford (1935), Ipswich Town (August 1936), BLUES (£3,750 October 1945), Shrewsbury Town (July 1947), Kidderminster Harriers (July 1948), Aston Villa (September 1948), Cradley Heath (player-manager August 1949), Brierley Hill (manager 1952-53). Retired May 1954. Assisted several clubs during war whilst serving in the RAF, including BLUES (118 apps, 41 goals), Blackburn Rovers, Brentford, Charlton Athletic, Chelsea, Hibernian, Leicester City, Manchester City, Millwall, Third Lanark and Wolverhampton Wanderers.
Club honours: Ipswich: Southern League champions 1937; Blues: Football League South champions 1946.
Representative honours: Scotland (Schoolboy trialist); Scottish Alliance XI 1934.
A fast raiding Scottish winger who could

occupy either flank, 'Jock' Mulraney joined Blues after demobilisation from five years' RAF service. He joined Celtic after turning down Hearts but failed to break into the first team at Parkhead. He scored Ipswich Town's first-ever Football League hat-trick (against Bristol City in April 1939). Mulraney went into the RAF in March 1940 and he rose to the rank of flight-sergeant as a PT instructor. He suffered a

heart attack in 1968 and has since undergone two eye operations. He now resides in Kinver.

MUMFORD, Wayne E.
Right-back; Apps 6+2, Goals 0.
Born: Rhymney, 3 November 1964.
Career: Coventry Boys, Manchester City (apprentice 1980), BLUES (professional September 1982), Worcester City (1984), Coventry Sporting (1985), Leamington Town (April 1986), Bedworth United (December 1986). Retired 1987.
Representative honours: Wales (Youth caps).
Welsh-born but brought up in Coventry, Wayne Mumford came to Blues when Manchester City decided not to offer him a professional contract. He proved a competent deputy without really doing enough to justify a regular first-team place and spent a few years playing in the Southern League until a knee injury ended his career.

MUMFORD, William Richard
Right-back; Apps 3, Goals 0.
Born: Stirchley, Birmingham, 3 March 1894. Died: Birmingham 1971.
Career: Bournville, BLUES (1920), Brighton & Hove Albion (April 1921), Redditch (September 1921).
He was picked up from Birmingham Combination football and given a trial run in the first team at the end of 1919-20. With the arrival of Jack Jones the next season, though, he found himself pushed down the queue for a first-team place and was released in the summer of 1921.

MURPHY, Peter ('Spud')
Inside-left; Apps 278, Goals 127.
Born: West Hartlepool, 7 March 1922. Died: 7 April 1975.
Career: Dunlop, Coventry City (amateur), BLUES (amateur), Millwall (guest 1945-46), Coventry City (professional May 1946), Tottenham Hotspur (£18,500 June 1950), BLUES (£20,000 January 1952), Rugby Town. Retired May 1961 and went into licensing trade.
Club honours: Tottenham Hotspur: Division Two champions 1951; Blues: Division Two champions 1955, FA Cup runners-up 1956.
Born in the North-East but moved to

Coventry with his family at the age of four, Peter Murphy had been on Blues' books as an amateur before Coventry signed him as a professional. He was initially a schemer and it was as such that he joined Arthur Rowe's 'Push and Run' side at Spurs, and played as an inside-forward in their 1950-51 championship winning season, deputising for Les Bennett. With Bennett fit again, Murphy found himself playing out of position on the left wing and he was grateful of a chance to move to St

Andrew's. He switched to a more attacking role when Tommy Briggs left, and thereafter his career blossomed. His phenomenal left-foot shooting from anywhere within 30-40 yards took many goalkeepers by surprise and he topped the Blues' scoring lists four times. In 1959 he was given the job of coaching the youngsters but at the end of the season was called back into the first team as Blues struggled against relegation. He repaid Blues' faith in him with four vital goals in seven games as relegation was avoided. He is perhaps best remembered as the Blues player involved in the incident with Manchester City's goalkeeper, Bert Trautmann, in the 1956 FA Cup Final, when the German broke his neck. Murphy had boundless energy and was always in the thick of the action. A magnificent marksman he netted a total of 158 goals in 399 League appearances for his three clubs.

MURRAY, Albert George ('Ruby')
Outside-right/right-back; Apps 151+9, Goals 23.
Born: Shoreditch, near Hoxton, 22 September 1942.
Career: Chelsea (junior June 1958, professional May 1961), BLUES (£25,000 August 1966), Brighton & Hove Albion (February 1971), Peterborough United (September 1973). Retired May 1977.
Club honours: Chelsea: Football League Cup winners 1965.
Representative honours: England (Youth caps, 6 Under-23 caps).

Bert Murray turned out in just about every position whilst with Chelsea including emergency goalkeeper (a role he also performed for Blues). Lightly built and quick, Murray was originally a winger and it was in this role that he shone for Chelsea, being particularly adept at finding scoring positions. It was as a winger that Blues initially played him and he got off to a fine start, scoring two goals on his debut. In November 1966, Ray Martin was injured and Murray took over the right-back berth, doing such a fine job that he held the position for the next 18 months. In 1969 he was switched back to a forward role and impressed, holding down the slot as a striker wide on the right until he was ousted by a promising youngster called Trevor Francis. Murray made 595 League appearances and scored 108 goals for his four major clubs. He later became landlord of the White Horse in Market Deeping, Lincolnshire.

MURRAY, James Arthur
Inside-right; Apps 1, Goals 1.
Born: Benwhat, February 1879. Died: Glasgow, June 1933.
Career: St Augustine's, Ayr United (1897), Aston Villa (March 1901), BLUES

(November 1901), Watford (1902), Kettering Town (May 1903), King's Heath Albion (1905).

Jim Murray had a brief and unsuccessful spell at Villa Park, but drew fulsome praise after a goalscoring debut for Blues, one critic saying: "He is fairly fast, has capital command of the ball and can shoot excellently." Despite this, his only other first-team outings came in friendlies.

NEAL, Richard Marshall ('Ticker')
Left-half; Apps 197, Goals 18.
Born: Dinnington, 1 October 1933.
Career: Wath Wanderers (1948), Wolverhampton Wanderers (juniors August 1949, professional March 1951), Lincoln City (July 1954), BLUES (£18,000 plus Albert Linnecor April 1957), Middlesbrough (October 1961), Lincoln City (August 1963), Rugby Town (July 1964), Hednesford Town (player-manager May 1965). Brierley Hill Alliance (player-manager December 1967), Blakenhall (player-manager February 1968). Later a publican in Birmingham and Penkridge (Staffs).
Club honours: Blues: Inter Cities Fairs Cup runners-up 1960.
Representative honours: England (4 Under-23 caps); Young England XI.

Dick Neal was effective in both defence and attack. Powerfully built he failed to make a first-team appearance with Wolves but developed quickly at Lincoln. Blues signed him for what was then a considerable fee and gave him the job of prompting his forwards. As befitted a man of over 6ft tall and weighing in excess of 12st, Neal was also a fearsome tackler. He lost his place to Terry Hennessey before moving to Ayresome Park. He totalled 415 League appearances in his career, and skippered Blues in 1960-61. His father, Richard Neal senior, played for Blackpool, Derby County, Southampton, Bristol City and Accrington Stanley before World War Two.

NEALE, Keith Ivan
Inside-forward; Apps 5, Goals 1.
Born: Yardley, Birmingham, 19 January 1935.
Career: Metropolitan FC, BLUES (amateur August 1953, professional February 1954), Lincoln City (November 1957-May 1959), Kettering Town (July 1959), Boston United (September 1960), Gainsborough (August 1963)
A cheerful, fair-haired forward who was plucked out of the Works League, Keith Neale was groomed in the juniors for three years before being given his League debut. Always regarded as a reserve, his chances were few and he fared little better at Lincoln before dropping out of the League. He went to live in the village of Chaddesley Corbett, Worcestershire.

NEEDHAM, Andrew Paul
Forward; Apps 2+1, Goals 1.
Born: Oldham, 13 September 1955.
Career: Harlow & Essex Boys, BLUES (apprentice June 1971, professional August 1973), Blackburn Rovers (July 1976), Aldershot (March 1977).
Needham was a tall forward whose aggressive attitude made him look a good prospect in junior football. But when given his chance by Blues, he looked out of place and although he scored in his second game he was quickly discarded. It was very much the same story at Blackburn but he scored over 30 goals in more than 100 games for Aldershot.

NEEDHAM, John ('Jack')
Inside-forward; Apps 20, Goals 5.
Born: Newstead, Nottinghamshire, 1891. Deceased.
Career: Mansfield Wesleyans, Mansfield Town (July 1907). BLUES (June 1909), Wolverhampton Wanderers (April 1910), Hull City (March 1920). Retired May 1921.
Jack Needham was a promising youngster with an eye for goal but was mysteriously allowed to leave Blues after a good first season. However, he made Blues pay dearly by scoring against them regularly in later years. Needham became known as 'Mr Consistency' at Molineux where he formed a marvellous left-wing partnership with Sammy Brooks while scoring 61 goals in 206 games for the Wanderers.

NEIL, Peter W.H.
Outside-right; Apps 5, Goals 0.
Born: Methil, Fife, Scotland, 1898. Deceased.
Career: East Fife, BLUES (April 1921), Heart of Midlothian (September 1922).
Peter Neil had only a handful of games (as deputy for W.H.Harvey) before returning to Scotland.

NEILSON, Peter M.
Outside-left; Apps 3, Goals 1.
Born: Glasgow, 1890. Deceased.
Career: Airdrieonians, BLUES (August 1913), Wallyford (March 1914).
Another of the long line of Scottish ball players who came south to try their luck in England, Neilson had a tendency to 'play the dribbling game,' which met with some criticism from the local Press. His one goal did earn Blues a victory, though.

NEWMAN, John Henry George
Half-back; Apps 65, Goals 0.
Born: Hereford, 13 December 1933.
Career: Hereford United Juniors, St Andrew's Athletic (July 1949), BLUES (professional March 1951), Leicester City (£12,000 November 1957), Plymouth Argyle (January 1960), Exeter City (£8,000 plus player, November 1967). In April 1969 was appointed manager of Exeter (after a spell as player-manager at St James' Park) and held the position until December 1976; Grimsby Town (manager January 1977), Derby County (assistant manager July 1979, manager January-November 1982), Hereford United (manager March 1983-July 1987), Notts County (assistant manager July 1988), Mansfield Town (chief scout 1990-93), Burton Albion (assistant manager 1994).
Club honours: Blues: Division Two champions 1955, FA Cup runners-up 1956.
Representative honours: Wales (Junior international).
John Newman attended a Welsh school hence his incongruous international record. He was a boot boy at non-League Hereford United when Blues signed him in 1949 and he came through the ranks at St Andrew's to develop into a solid, no-nonsense defender, able to deputise in all three half-back positions. He was surprisingly chosen to play in the 1956 FA Cup Final ahead of far more experienced teammates, but

eventually left the club when it became obvious that he was never going to become a regular in the first team, despite the departure of both Len Boyd and Roy Warhurst. He did remarkably well after leaving Blues, altogether accumulating well over 600 senior appearances (in major League and Cup competitions) during his 20 years in the professional game. In November 1964 he gained note by passing a penalty-kick a yard forward for his colleague Mike Trebilcock to run on to and score from less than 12 yards range.

NORTH, Marc Victor
Forward; Apps 4+1, Goals 1.
Born: Ware, Herts, 29 May 1966.
Career: Hertfordshire Boys, Luton Town (apprentice June 1982, professional April 1984), Lincoln City (loan March 1985), Scunthorpe United (loan January 1987), BLUES (loan March 1987), Grimsby Town (£40,000 August 1987), Leicester City (March 1989), Luton Town (monthly contract July 1991), Grimsby Town (September 1991), Leicester United (October 1991), Shepshed Albion, Walsall (trial), Kettering Town (April 1992), St Andrew's Social Club, Corby Town, St Andrew's Social Club.
Marc North was signed by Luton as a schoolboy goalkeeper but made his League bow for the Hatters as a central defender. By the time he arrived at St Andrew's he had completed the transformation and had become a forward. North showed a fair degree of skill during his short spell with Blues, although no attempt was made to sign him permanently. Played for Lincoln in the match when Bradford City's stand burned down.

OAKES, Alfred William
Inside-left; Apps 1, Goals 0.
Born: Bewdley, Worcs, 22 July 1901. Died: Bristol, 25 December 1967.
Career: RAF (Uxbridge), Chesham United (1922), Millwall (July 1923), Reading (May 1925), Rhyl Athletic (June 1926), Worcester City, BLUES (£300 February 1927), Rhyl Athletic (June 1928), New Brighton (August 1929), Wigan Borough (June 1931), Frickley Colliery (November 1931), Stalybridge Celtic (August 1932). Retired through injury May 1933.
Alf Oakes was a tall, red-haired forward who was a regular scorer in non-League circles but proved a big disappointment at St Andrew's. He was Wigan's top marksman with four goals when they withdrew from the League in October 1931. His son, Don Oakes, played for Arsenal.

OAKES, Thomas Frank
Forward; Apps 38, Goals 8.
Born: Cheltenham, 1874. Deceased.
Career: Hereford Thistle, BLUES (August 1896), Gloucester City (1900).
The *Birmingham Gazette* reported that this talented striker had a promising debut and announced that he had scored a hat-trick. The former is true; the latter false, as he failed to score at all. He played in three different forward positions for Blues but was perhaps best at inside-right. He slipped out of the first-team reckoning for two years before moving back to the non-League game.

O'GRADY, Michael
Winger/midfield; Apps 2+1, Goals 0.
Born: Leeds, 11 October 1942.
Career: Huddersfield Town (juniors June 1958, professional November 1959), Leeds United (£30,000 October 1965), Wolverhampton Wanderers (£80,000 September 1969), BLUES (loan February 1972), Rotherham United (November 1972). Retired through injury May 1974.
Club honours: Leeds United: Fairs Cup runners-up 1967, winners 1968, Division One champions 1969.

Representative honours: England (2 full caps, 3 Under-23 caps); Football League XI (3).

Originally a pacy left-winger, Mike O'Grady gained his first full cap when only 20 and, wishing to play at a higher grade of football, he joined Don Revie's great Leeds side of the 1960s where, despite frequent injuries, he played his part in their quest for honours. Further injuries disrupted his spell at Molineux and it was while recuperating from one of these knocks that he joined Blues, becoming the first loan player to make a League appearance for the club.

O'HARA, Edward Patrick
Outside-left; Apps 6, Goals 0.
Born: Dalkey, near Dublin, 22 February 1927. Died: 8 March 1987.
Career: Dundalk, BLUES (November 1949), Hereford United (1951), Sligo Rovers, Drumcondra, Lockheed Leamington, Hereford United.
He was rated higher than Jimmy Higgins when they were transferred together to Blues. Things proved otherwise as his first-team opportunities were limited owing to the presence at St Andrew's of so many other good wingers.

OKENLA, Folorunso ('Foley')
Winger; Apps 4+9, Goals 1.
Born: Ibadan, 9 October 1967.
Career: Leventis United (Nigeria), Julius Berger (Nigeria), Wimbledon (trial), Brighton & Hove Albion (trial), Blackburn Rovers (trial), Burnley (trial), Exeter City BLUES (non-contract August 1991), Montreal Impact, Kingstonian.
Representative honours: Nigeria (19 full caps); African Nations Cup runners-up 1988.
The most unusual of Blues' 1991 signings, this fast and tricky winger had been over in Britain for two years, trying his luck with a number of clubs. He made a devastating entry into League soccer with a goal in his first game, which led to the most spectacular display of celebration ever witnessed at St Andrew's. He played under his first name in Nigeria.

OLIVER, John ('Dowk')
Left-back; Apps 62, Goals 0.
Born: Southwick, 1867. Deceased.
Career: Southwick, Sunderland (August 1887), Middlesbrough Ironopolis (June 1892), BLUES (April 1894), Durham (1896).
John Oliver was a star of Sunderland's pre-League days but was soon discarded as Roker men began their golden era in the 1890s. He spent two years with the Ironopolis club, as they tried to bring professional football to Middlesbrough, and proved a settling influence to Blues' defence when they struggled to establish themselves in the First Division. He drew appreciative comment for the power of his kicking.

OLLIS, William
Right-half; Apps 112, Goals 2.

Born: Bordesley Green Birmingham, 12 August 1871. Died: Birmingham, May 1940.
Career: Newall Juniors, Southfield FC, Warwick County, BLUES (April 1891), Hereford Thistle (February 1896). Retired through injury 1899.
Club honours: Blues: Division Two champions 1893.

He was a solid, hard-grafting player who came to Blues' attention in friendly matches against them, taking over the captaincy when Caesar Jenkyns was sacked. He held the job for a only short while, however, and moved on halfway through the season.

OLNEY, James Fulford
Centre-half; Apps 3, Goals 0.
Born: Greet, Birmingham, February 1910. Died: 1944 whilst serving with Grenadier Guards.
Career: Tyseley Rangers, Newbridge Albion, Redditch United (1935), BLUES (May 1936), Swindon Town (December 1938). Retired c.1943.

He was a very tall, slim centre-half who was the nephew of the Aston Villa and Derby County goalkeeper, Ben Olney. Extremely powerful in the air as might be expected from a man topping 6ft 3in, he was too similar in style to 'Tosher' Fillingham to be able to gain a regular first-team place.

O'NEILL, Alan
Forward; Apps 2+2, Goals 0.
Born: Cork, 27 August 1973.
Career: Cork City (1990), Cobh Ramblers (1991), BLUES (£15,000 February 1992), Cobh Ramblers (1993).
Representative honours: Republic of Ireland (18 Schools caps).

O'Neill stayed at St Andrew's for less than a year. Perhaps too much was expected of him after Irish football.

O'REILLY, Gary Mills
Centre-half; Apps 1, Goals 0.
Born: Isleworth, Middlesex, 21 March 1961.
Career: Tottenham Hotspur (apprentice June 1977, professional September 1979), Brighton & Hove Albion (£45,000 August 1984), Crystal Palace (£40,000 January 1987), BLUES (loan March 1991), Brighton & Hove Albion (July 1991).
Club honours: Crystal Palace: FA Cup runners-up 1990.
Representative honours: Republic of Ireland (Youth caps).

An experienced defender, O'Reilly joined Blues as cover on the transfer deadline. He scored for Palace in the 1990 FA Cup Final but the following season found it impossible to hold down a regular place in their line-up. Sadly he broke his nose early in the second half of his one and only game in Blues' colours and failed to recover from the injury before his loan period expired.

ORRITT, Bryan ('Orrible')
Inside-forward/wing-half; Apps 119, Goals 27.
Born: Caernarfon, North Wales, 22 February 1937.
Career: Caernarfon Grammar School (played rugby and soccer), Llanfair PG FC, Bangor City (1955), BLUES (1956), Middlesbrough (March 1962), Johannesburg Rangers (South Africa) (1966).
Club honours: Blues: Fairs Cup runners-up 1960, 1961.
Representative honours: Wales (3 Under-23 caps).

Bryan Orritt was an enterprising footballer who appeared in all 11 positions during his playing career. Primarily a winger or inside-forward whilst with Blues, his best spell in the first team came in 1957-58 when he replaced Noel Kinsey. He was not

really the playmaker Blues were looking for and when Johnny Gordon was signed, Orritt was forced to take a back seat. He was one of the few Welsh-speaking footballers in the League. Later became a prominent coach in South Africa, working with black youngsters in Soweto.

OSBORNE, Ian L.
Right-back; Apps 11, Goals 0.
Born: Leicester, 28 October 1952.
Career: Mid-Leicester Boys, BLUES (apprentice 1968, professional October 1970), Port Vale (June 1976).

A nippy, overlapping full-back who showed considerable promise as a youngster, his spell in Blues' reserve side was rather longer than usual, however, and on stepping up to the first team he proved disappointing, his defensive skills not being as strong as his attacking ones. He made his League debut in his home town.

OTTEWELL, Sidney
Inside-forward; Apps 5, Goals 2.
Born: Horsley, Derbyshire, 23 October 1919.
Career: Holbrook Miners' Welfare, Chesterfield (November 1936), BLUES (June 1947), Luton Town (December 1947), Nottingham Forest (July 1948), Mansfield Town (January 1950), Scunthorpe United (March 1952), Lockheed Leamington (manager 1960-January 1969).

After a successful spell with Chesterfield, Sid Ottewell was signed by Blues as a utility forward to help with the push for promotion. Although impressing with his purposeful shooting, he did not stay long at St Andrew's. He appeared in a total of 188 League games (52 goals) during his career.

OTTO Ricky Junior
Forward; Apps 25+6, Goals 6.
Born: Hackney, 9 November 1967.

Career: Haringey Borough, Dartford, Leyton Orient (free transfer November 1990), Southend United (£100,000 July 1993), BLUES (£800,000 December 1994).
Club honour: Blues: Second Division champions 1995, Auto Windscreens Shield winners 1995.

A record signing for Blues, Ricky Otto had the dubious honour of scoring for both sides on his debut, in the 1-1 draw against Cambridge United at St Andrew's on 17 December 1994. A dreadlocked winger, skilful, enterprising and a big favourite with the fans, he hit 15 goals in 68 games for Orient and 20 in 70 for Southend. Came into League football late after serving a prison sentence for armed robbery.

OVERSON, Vincent David
Central defender; Apps 209+3, Goals 5.
Born: Kettering, 15 May 1952.
Career: Exeter Primary School, Kingswood Grammar School, Kingswood Boys, Corby Town, Long Buckby FC, Burnley (apprentice June 1968, professional November 1979), BLUES (£235,000 June 1986), Stoke City (tribunal set fee of £55,000 August 1991).
Club honours: Burnley: Division Three champions 1982; Blues: Leyland DAF Cup winners 1991; Stoke City: Autoglass Trophy winners 1992, Division Two champions 1993.
Representative honours: England (Youth cap).

Vince Overson was a powerfully built defender who was on the verge of joining the Army when Burnley took him under their wing. His wholehearted approach to the game made him a great favourite with the fans but his relations with the St Andrew's club were not always amicable. His wife failed to settle in the Midlands and eventually returned to Burnley. Overson twice went on the transfer list in the hope of moving back north and when his contract expired in 1991 he walked out on Blues and joined his former manager, Lou Macari, at Stoke. He made 247 appearances for Burnley before transferring to St Andrew's. Vince's brother, Richard, was also a professional footballer, turning out for Burnley and Hereford.

OWEN, Sidney William
Centre-half; Apps 5, Goals 0.
Born: Birmingham, 29 February 1922.
Career: Birmingham YMCA, BLUES (professional October 1945), Luton Town (player June 1947-May 1959, manager at Kenilworth Road April 1959 to April 1960), Leeds United (coach May 1960), BLUES (assistant manager October 1975-September 1977), Hull City (coach December 1977-February 1978), Manchester United (youth-team coach May 1978-April 1981).

Club honours: Blues: Football League South champions 1945-46; Luton Town: FA Cup runners-up 1959.
Representative honours: England (3 full caps); Football League XI (2).

Sid Owen was a commanding defender, particularly strong in the air. His chances of success with Blues were baulked by the consistency of Ted Duckhouse but he proved to be an excellent signing for Luton, for whom he played over 400 games (388 in the League) during his 12 years at Kenilworth Road. He later made a name for himself as a coach, playing major role in Leeds' success in the 1960s and 1970s. Owen appeared in in five war games for Blues. He was voted 'Footballer of the Year' in 1959 after leading Luton to the FA Cup Final, where they were beaten 2-1 by Nottingham Forest.

OWEN, William
Goalkeeper; Apps 6, Goals 0.
Born: Coventry, April 1903.
Career: Nuneaton Borough, BLUES (April 1926), Fulham (August 1929), Coventry City (1930), Stourbridge (1931), Nuneaton Town (1934).

A spectacular goalkeeper who had a short period in the first team whilst Hibbs was injured. This run coincided with four Blues' defeats and when Hibbs was fit again, Bill Owen went back into the reserves.

PAGE, Malcolm Edward
Defender/wing-half; Apps 382+9, Goals 10.
Born: Knucklas, Radnorshire, mid-Wales, 5 February 1947.
Career: Radnorshire & District Boys, BLUES (apprentice July 1964, professional September 1964), Oxford United (February 1981). Retired March 1982.
Club honours: Blues: Division Two promotion 1971-72.
Representative honours: Wales (28 full caps, 6 Under-23 caps, 4 Schoolboy caps).

Blues' most capped player (whilst with club), Malcolm Page spent 17 seasons at St Andrew's and during that time played in every position for the club except goal. He skippered both club and country and was perhaps best equipped as a full-back or defensive midfielder, although he did have a lengthy run in the side as a centre-half, but at 5ft 9in was a little small for this role. Not a great creative player, Page was more of a 'man marker' and he could also unleash a powerful shot, once booming in a terrific goal against Huddersfield in the FA Cup of 1972. A grand servant to the club, he never asked for a transfer during his long association with St Andrew's. Currently he works in Birmingham for a large insurance company.

PARR, Harold
Right-half; Apps 1, Goals 0.
Born: Newcastle upon Tyne, 1914.
Career: Wellington High School, Dawley Rovers, Wrockwardine Wood, Donnington Wood, Sankey's, Wellington Town, BLUES (October 1937), Dawley Rovers (October 1939), Stafford Rangers (1939-40).
He was a forceful player who did the tour of Shropshire junior clubs before arriving at St Andrew's. His brief spell in League football was cut short by the war.

PARRIS, George Michael R.
Defender/midfield; Apps 49+3, Goals 2.
Born: Ilford, 11 September 1964.
Career: Redbridge Schools, West Ham United (apprentice July 1981, professional September 1982), BLUES (£150,000 March 1993), Brentford (loan August 1994), Bristol City (loan December 1994), Brighton & HA (loan March 1995).
Representative honours: England Schoolboys.

George Parris has proved a hardworking, consistent and competitive midfielder who can also play in defence. In more than ten years as a professional at Upton Park, he appeared in almost 300 senior games for the Hammers, scoring 18 goals. He added bite to the Blues' engine-room before being loaned out in late 1994 after losing his place in the first team.

PARTRIDGE, Charles
Goalkeeper; Apps 30, Goals 0.
Born: Wednesbury 1867. Deceased.
Career: Park Street School, Wednesbury Old Athletic, BLUES (September 1890), Willenhall Town (1896), Sparkhill, Park Mills (1897), Redditch Town, Headless Cross (January 1898).
Although signed from the prestigious Black Country club, The Old 'Uns, Partridge quickly earned the reputation as an erratic performer, as likely to lose a game on his own as save his team. In only one of his five seasons with Blues was he allowed to give full vein to his talents, and in that campaign he earned the distinction as the goalkeeper who conceded nine goals in Blues' record defeat.

PASKIN, William John
Striker; Apps 8+3, Goals 3.
Born: Capetown, South Africa, 1 February 1962.
Career: Hellenic (Australia) (July 1980), Toronto Blizzard (Canada) (May 1983), South China (Hong Kong) (August 1984), Seiko (Hong Kong) (August 1985), KV Kortrijk (Belgium) August 1986), Dundee United (trial July 1987), West Bromwich Albion (non-contract March 1988, professional August 1988), Wolverhampton Wanderers (£75,000 June 1989), Stockport County (loan September 1991), BLUES

(loan November 1991), Shrewsbury Town (loan February 1992), Wrexham (free transfer February 1992), Bury (free transfer July 1994).
Paskin was a tall striker, taken on loan by Blues at a time when a goalscorer was desperately required. He failed to make much impression but later scored 14 goals in 60 games for Wrexham.

PEART, John ('Jack') George
Centre-forward; Apps 3, Goals 0.
Born: South Shields, 3 October 1888. Died: Paddington, London, 3 September 1948.
Career: South Shields Adelaide (1905), Sheffield United (May 1907), Stoke (July 1910), Newcastle United (£600 March 1912), Notts County (February 1913), BLUES (November 1919), Derby County (January 1920), Ebbw Vale (player-manager August 1920), Port Vale (player January 1922), Norwich City (July 1922), Rochdale (player-manager March 1923, retiring as player May 1924), Bradford City (manager July 1930), Fulham (manager May 1935 until death).
Club honours: Notts County: Division Two champions 1914.
Representative honours: Football League XI (1), Southern League XI (3).

One of the great travellers of football, Jack Peart was a fine opportunist goalscorer although this facet of his game was missing at St Andrew's. He had a reputation for being 'the most injured man in football'. He proved to be a reasonably successful manager, taking Fulham to an FA Cup semi-final.

PEER, Dean
Midfield; Apps 133+17, Goals 12.
Born: Wordsley, Stourbridge, 8 August 1969.
Career: Ashwood Park and Buckpool School, Lye Town, Stourbridge Falcons, BLUES (YTS July 1985, professional July 1987), Mansfield Town (loan December 1992), Walsall (loan, then full transfer November 1993).
Club honours: Blues: Leyland DAF Cup winners 1991.
Dean Peer was a distinctive gangling figure – 6ft 2in tall and 12st 6lb in weight – who initially played wide on the right side of midfield. Not the fastest of players but a genuine trier, he was then moved into a central midfield position where he looked far more comfortable although he had to take his fair share of abuse from the St Andrew's terraces. He displayed a hitherto unsuspected scoring ability at Walsall, scoring a hat-trick shortly after his move.

PENDREY, Garry James Sidney ('Gazzer')
Full-back/defender; Apps 337+23, Goals 5.
Born: Lozells, Birmingham, 9 February 1949.

Career: Lozells Junior School, Handsworth Technical College Birmingham, Aston Schools, Stanley Star, Harborne Lynwood, BLUES (apprentice July 1965, professional October 1966), West Bromwich Albion (£30,000 August 1979), Torquay United (August 1981), Bristol Rovers (December 1981), Walsall (player-coach July 1982, later assistant manager May 1983-August 1986), Wolverhampton Wanderers (coach November 1986), BLUES (manager June 1987-April 1989), Wolverhampton Wanderers (coach July 1989-March 1994), Coventry City (coach February 1995), WBA All Stars 1982-91.
Club honours: Blues: FA Youth Cup runners-up 1967, Division Two promotion 1972.

Garry Pendrey skippered the successful Blues youth side of 1967 and later captained both the reserve and senior teams. A player who always believed in leading by example, Pendrey was not the most naturally talented of footballers but he was a tenacious tackler and whole-hearted grafter. He was the youngest-ever Blues captain in 1969, at 20 years 6 months, the honour perhaps coming a little too early for him to appreciate it. He became a cult hero with the St Andrew's fans, known as 'Gazzer' when a certain Geordie was still a child. He was surprisingly sold to West Brom shortly after his testimonial game against the Baggies. After a promising start to his coaching career, he came back to Blues as manager but he was not a success, and the advent of the Kumar brothers proved to be the end of his managerial exploits, and he returned to his coaching duties. He was assistant at Walsall under former Blues player Alan Buckley.

PENTLAND, Frederick Beaconsfield
Inside-left; Apps 1, Goals 0.
Born: Wolverhampton, 18 September 1883. Died: Poole, 16 March 1962.
Career: Willenhall Swifts, Avondale Juniors, BLUES (August 1900), Blackpool (June 1903), Blackburn Rovers (October 1903), Brentford (May 1906), QPR (May 1907), Middlesbrough (June 1908), Halifax Town (February 1913), Stoke (May 1913). Coached in Germany at outbreak of World War One and was interned for the duration. Coached in France (1920), Athletic Bilbao (coach 1921-36), Brentford (coach 1936-37), Barrow (manager January 1938-September 1939).
Club honours: Brentford: Southern League champions 1908.
Representative honours: England (5 full caps).
Fred Pentland's father, a former Lord Mayor of Birmingham, was such an admirer of Benjamin Disraeli, Earl of Beaconsfield, that he named his son

accordingly. During his career at Blues, Pentland was regarded as a reserve wing-half but was called up for a game as an inside-forward due to an injury crisis. Later he developed into an international class winger, and subsequently became a respected coach. He seemed to be unlucky with choice of jobs, being in Germany at the outbreak of World War One and in Spain when the Civil War started. In Germany he started a football league with fellow internees and England internationals Steve Bloomer and Sam Wolstenholme.

PEPLOW, William Watling
Outside-right; Apps 17, Goals 0.
Born: Derby, 1885. Deceased.
Career: Redditch, BLUES (April 1907), Bristol Rovers (August 1908 to May 1915).
Peplow had a patchy season with Blues, during which time his speed was not always matched by the quality of his crosses. He blossomed at Bristol, though, and became a regular scorer for Rovers, his performances catching the eye of the England selectors although he failed to reproduce his best form in an international trial and full recognition never came.

PESCHISOLIDO, Paolo P. ('Paul')
Striker; Apps 40+8, Goals 17.
Born: Scarborough Ontario, Canada, 25 May 1971.
Career: Toronto Blizzard (Canada), Kansas City Comets (USA) (1990), Toronto Blizzard (Canada), BLUES (£25,000 November 1992), Stoke City (£400,000 in deal involving Regis, August 1994).
Representative honours: Canada (15 full caps, 9 Olympic Games appearances).

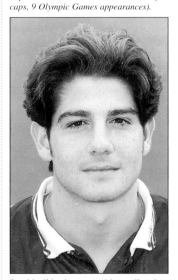

Peschisolido is an exciting, all-action, industrious utility forward, eager inside the penalty area. He made a big impact at St Andrew's and then did likewise at Stoke, where he was reunited with his former boss, Lou Macari. In 1990 he was voted the USA Major Indoor Soccer League's Newcomer of the Year.

PHILLIPS, Cuthbert ('Charlie')
Outside-right/centre-forward; Apps 25, Goals 10.
Born: Victoria, Monmouthshire, June 1910. Died: Lichfield, Staffs, 15 October 1969.
Career: Victoria Council School, Ebbw Vale (1925-26), Plymouth Argyle (trial), Wolverhampton Wanderers (professional August 1929), Aston Villa (£9,000 January 1936), BLUES (March 1938), Chelmsford City (May 1939). Retired during war.
Club honours: Wolverhampton Wanderers: Division Two champions 1932; Aston Villa: Division Two champions 1938.
Representative honours: Wales (13 full caps, 2 Schoolboy caps).
Charlie Phillips was something of a rough

and tumble character but a clever ball-playing utility forward for all that. He was coming to the end of a fine career when he arrived at St Andrew's. He also had quite a temper and was sent off twice as a professional. He scored 65 goals in 202 games for Wolves and five in 22 outings for Villa. He was also a useful cricketer, a fine tennis player, did well at golf and also participated at rugby union and on the athletics track as a young lad. After leaving football he became a licensee, first at the Butler's Arms at Bushbury in Wolverhampton, and later in Lichfield.

PHILLIPS, Leslie Michael
Midfield; Apps 45+9, Goals 4.
Born: Lambeth, London, 7 January 1963.
Career: London Schools, BLUES (apprentice June 1979, professional August 1980), Oxford United (March 1984), Northampton Town (August 1993), Marlow (cs 1994).
Club honours: Oxford United: Division Two promotion 1985, Milk Cup winners 1986.
Representative honours: England (3 Youth caps).

Phillips was a busy little player who had all the makings of a useful midfield linchpin, fearless in the tackle and a good passer of the ball. However, his style was not ideally suited to the role he was asked to do at St Andrew's and he was rarely given a decent run in the first team. Jim Smith took him to Oxford where he proved more successful despite injuries and occasional bouts of indiscipline.

PHILLIPS, Steven Edward
Forward; Apps 19+7, Goals 1.
Born: Edmonton, London, 4 August 1954.
Career: BLUES (apprentice June 1970, professional August 1971), Torquay United (loan December 1974), Northampton Town (£5,000 October 1975), Brentford (February 1977), Northampton Town (£40,000 August 1980), Southend United (March 1982), Torquay United (loan January 1986), Peterborough United (November 1986), Exeter City (loan September 1987), Chesterfield (loan January 1988), Stamford, British Timken Duston (player-manager).
Representative honours: England (2 Youth caps).
A pint-size long-haired forward who had a marvellous career in the lower divisions, Steve Phillips scored over 250 goals in more than 700 senior appearances (560 in the League) before moving into non-League football in 1988. He always looked out of his depth in the First Division, but Blues must have regretted selling him.

PHOENIX, Arthur Frederick ('Ginger')
Inside-forward; Apps 3, Goals 0.
Born: Hadfield, 5 July 1897. Deceased.
Career: Urmston & District Schools, Hadfield, Glossop (1922), BLUES (May 1923), Aston Villa (May 1924), Barnsley (May 1925), Exeter City (July 1926), Wigan Borough (July 1929), Bath City (June 1930), Torquay United (November 1930), Mansfield Town (July 1931), Racing Club de Paris (August 1932), Sandbach Ramblers (October 1933), Dublin Shelbourne (January 1934), Colwyn Bay United (August 1934), Brierley Hill Alliance (January 1935). Retired May 1937.
Phoenix was yet another soccer nomad who never really settled in one place, yet always gave a good account of himself on the field of play.

PICKERING, Frederick
Centre-forward; Apps 88, Goals 32.
Born: Blackburn, 19 January 1941.
Career: Blackburn amateur football, Blackburn Rovers (junior August 1956, professional January 1958), Everton (£85,000 March 1964), BLUES (£50,000 August 1967), Blackpool (June 1969), Blackburn Rovers (March 1971), Brighton & Hove Albion (trial, February 1972).
Club honours: Blackburn Rovers: FA Youth Cup winners 1959.
Representative honours: England (3 full caps, 3 Under-23 caps); Football League XI (1).

Originally a right-back, Fred Pickering developed into one of the country's leading strikers. Fast, skilful and brilliant in the air, he scored a hat-trick on his international debut in a 10-0 win over the United States, and hit over 30 goals in each of two successive seasons in the 1960s, but missed the 1966 FA Cup Final through injury. With the emergence at Goodison Park of Joe Royle, Pickering was deemed surplus to requirements and Cullis brought him to St Andrew's, hoping that he would lead Blues back into the First Division. Indeed, the fans were treated to two seasons of classic centre-forward play but although Pickering and his fellow attackers scored plenty of goals, the defence was leaky and promotion was missed. He returned to Division One with Blackpool, and later went back to his first club, Blackburn. But he had a few disputes with Rovers manager Ken Furphy and was eventually sacked from Ewood Park. He later worked as a fork-lift truck driver.

PIKE, Theophilus ('Tot') Enos
Outside-left; Apps 17, Goals 4.
Born: Sunderland, 25 March 1907. Died: Bury St Edmunds, 26 October 1967.
Career: Sunderland Co-op Wednesday, Fulham (1925), Bournemouth & Boscombe Athletic (June 1927), BLUES (February 1928), Southend United (June 1930), Norwich City (June 1933), Bury Town (player-coach 1935 to May 1937), Norfolk & Suffolk FA (coach 1938-39).
Pike was a ball-juggling but somewhat frail forward whose career was hampered by a string of serious injuries, culminating in him missing the entire 1929-30 season prior to his release from St Andrew's. Pike later became a publican in East Anglia.

PIMBLEY, Douglas William
Outside-left; Apps 2, Goals 0.
Born: King's Norton, Birmingham, 19 June 1917.
Career: King's Norton YMCA, Northfield, Stourbridge, Leicester City (amateur), BLUES (July 1946), Notts County (March 1948).
Pimbley was a powerful forward who had spent four and a half years abroad in the Army prior to joining Blues. He was signed in anticipation that his strength would assist the rest of the front line, but it was not to be and he spent most of his time in the reserves.

PLATNAUER, Nicholas R.
Full-back/midfield; Apps 31+5, Goals 2.
Born: Leicester, 10 June 1961.
Career: Bedford Town, Bristol Rovers (August 1981), Coventry City (£50,000 August 1983), BLUES (£55,000 December 1984), Reading (loan January-February 1986), Cardiff City (free transfer September 1986), Notts County (£50,000 August 1989), Port Vale (loan January-April 1991), Leicester City (free transfer July 1991), Kettering Town, Scunthorpe United (March 1993), Mansfield Town (August 1993), Lincoln City (February 1994).
Club honours: Notts Co: Division Three promotion 1990, Division Two promotion 1991.
Nicky Platnauer was working as bank clerk when Bedford Town folded and he was

surprisingly signed by Bristol Rovers. He so impressed that Rovers' boss Bobby Gould took him to Coventry when he became boss at Highfield Road. Platnauer, though, proved a disappointment in the First Division but Ron Saunders bought him to Blues to play wide on the left in the promotion bid. After a promising start he dropped out of the reckoning but in later years did well at full-back.

POINTER, Ernest
Goalkeeper; Apps 29, Goals 0.
Born: Sparkbrook, Birmingham, 1872. Deceased.
Career: Redditch Town, BLUES (1896), Berwick Rangers (Worcester, 1898), BLUES (September 1900), Kidderminster Harriers (May 1901).
A very erratic goalkeeper but capable enough to keep Blues in the promotion picture in 1896-97, Pointer's only season in the League side. He came back for a second spell with the club but failed to gain a regular place, even in the reserve side.

POINTON, Thomas Seth
Outside-left; Apps 4, Goals 1.
Born: Coventry, 1890. Deceased.
Career: Coventry City (amateur), Redditch Town, BLUES (amateur August 1913), Redditch Town (April 1914), Walsall (June 1914), Nuneaton Town (1919), Coventry City (1920), Redditch, Tamworth Castle (1925).
Blues were so eager to sign this promising winger that they were fined £5 for playing him in the reserves before the transfer was completed. He impressed in the second XI, earning an amateur international trial, but was not selected for his country. In League football he was thought to be a little slow 'to work out what he had to do when he had the ball'.

POOLE, Gary John
Defender; Apps 46, Goals 2.
Born: Stratford, London, 11 September 1967.
Career: Tottenham Hotspur (junior 1983, professional July 1985), Cambridge United (free transfer August 1987), Barnet (£3,000 March 1989), Plymouth Argyle (free transfer June 1992), Southend United (£350,000 July 1993), BLUES (player exchange deal) September 1994).
Club honours: Barnet: GMVC winners 1991. Blues: Second Division champions 1995, Auto Windscreens Shield winners 1995.
Poole, a solid, tough-tackling right-back, was with Barry Fry at Barnet and Southend

before joining Blues. He had made around 200 senior appearances as a professional prior to his move to St Andrew's in the move where no fee changed hands but he and Jonmathan Hunt came to Blues whilst Dave Regis and Roger Willis went to Southend.

POTTER, Graham Stephen
Midfield/defender; Apps 30+2, Goals 2.

Born: Solihull, 20 May 1975.
Career: BLUES (YTS June 1991, professional July 1992), Wycombe Wanderers (loan September 1993), Stoke City (£75,000 December 1993).
Representative honour: England (1 Youth cap).
Potter was a teenage defender whose great strength was in overlapping. A shade naïve at times, he had a tendency to get sucked inside from time to time, leaving his flank unprotected. All the same it was still a surprise when he was traded to Stoke in part-exchange for Kenny Lowe.

POWELL, Aubrey
Inside-forward; Apps 15, Goals 1.
Born: Cynlais, near Swansea, 19 April 1918.
Career: Cwm Wanderers, Swansea Town (amateur), Leeds United (November 1935), Everton (£10,000 July 1948), BLUES (August 1950), Wellington Town (August 1951). Retired May 1952.
Representative honours: Wales (8 full apps, 4 Victory internationals).
Aubrey Powell was a neat if somewhat fragile footballer who fought back after his career was written off by doctors following a broken leg in 1937. He missed an extra season but regained his place before the war, during which he served in Belgium before returning to pick up the first of his eight Welsh caps. Further injuries curtailed his career, both at Everton and at Blues. He hit 19 goals in 73 League games for Leeds and five in 35 for Everton. He later opened a confectioner's shop.

POWELL, Herbert
Inside-forward; Apps 5, Goals 1.
Born: Maidstone, Kent, 1880. Deceased.
Career: Treharris, Nottingham Forest (1904), Gresley Rovers (1905), Grantham Avenue (February 1906), Chesterfield (1906), Barnsley (February 1907); Carlisle United (1907), New Brompton (1908), Coventry City (1909), BLUES (December 1910), Rotherham Town (1911), Portsmouth (1913), Bournemouth & Boscombe Athletic (1914), Brentford (1915), Worksop Town (1919), Grantham (March 1922), Retford (1922), Sutton Town (1923).
A hard shooting forward who had 'been about a bit' before joining Blues, Herbert Powell scored on his debut but quickly fell from favour and soon continued on his travels around football.

PRATT, William
Outside-left; Apps 27, Goals 1.
Born: Highgate, Birmingham, 1872. Deceased.
Career: St John's (Deritend), BLUES (1889), Small Heath Unity (1892), Worcester Rovers (1898).
Billy Pratt was a local winger whose talents were more given to providing chances rather than taking them. A grand dribbler and crosser of the ball he was nevertheless somewhat on the slow side. He is frequently confused with his namesake who didn't join Blues until four years after the first Billy Pratt had left.

PRATT, William
Left-back; Apps 139, Goals 0.
Born: Birmingham, 1874. Deceased.
Career: Hoskins & Sewell FC, BLUES (August 1894). Retired May 1902 through injury.
This Billy Pratt joined Blues as a youngster fresh from Birmingham Works League soccer. By the time he left eight years later, he had earned the reputation as a powerful, uncompromising full-back with a terrific kick in both feet.

PRESTON, Josiah
Right-back; Apps 7, Goals 0.
Born: Derby, 1885. Deceased.

Career: Derby Midland, Burton Wanderers, Burton United (1905), BLUES (1908), Halesowen (May 1910).
Preston was a sturdy player who was one of a group of backs who struggled to replace the ageing Stokes and Corbett. Not such a classy performer as either of his predecessors, he was a strong and solid reserve nevertheless.

PRICE, George ('Jack')
Right-back; Apps 1, Goals 1.
Born: Sparkbrook, Birmingham, 1863. Deceased.
Career: Hockley Brook (1883), Aston Villa (1884), BLUES (August 1885), St Luke's FC (September 1888).
One of a cluster of players from the Belmont club, Jack Price was a good prompting half-back who was a virtual ever-present in his only season at Muntz Street. He left after a poor performance in the Derby Charity Cup Final when Blues lost 3-0 to Derby County.

PRICE, John Lester
Inside-right; Apps 1, Goals 0.
Born: Lichfield, 1879. Deceased.
Career: Shenstone BC, BLUES (August 1897), Watford (1900), Doncaster Rovers (October 1901).
John Price was a young forward who gave sterling service to the Birmingham League side for several years. He left Blues under a cloud after being charged with assault upon a ticket collector at Small Heath Railway Station.

PRICE, Ryan
Goalkeeper; Apps 1, Goals 0.
Born: Coven, nr Wolverhampton, 13 March 1970.
Career: Bolton Wanderers (YTS 1986-87), Stafford Rangers, BLUES (£20,000 August 1994).
Club honour: Blues: Auto Windscreens Shield winners 1995.
Ryan Price made his debut for Blues in the Auto Windscreens game at Peterborough in September 1994, conceding a goal in the first minute. He is, though, a good, reliable 'keeper with safe pair of hands.

PRITCHARD, Tilson
Right-back; Apps 1, Goals 0.
Born: Walsall Wood, 1872. Deceased.
Career: Burntwood Swifts, BLUES (April 1894), Lichfield Town (August 1895).
Pritchard was given a try-out by Blues in the United Counties League at the end of 1893-94 when he had a poor game. He resurfaced in the next January when 'Dowk' Oliver was injured, but was totally out of his class as Blues crashed 9-1.

PRUDHOE, Mark
Goalkeeper; Apps 5, Goals 0.
Born: Washington, Co Durham, 8 November 1963.
Career: Washington Youths, Sunderland

(apprentice June 1980, professional September 1981), Hartlepool United (loan November 1983), BLUES (£22,000 September 1984), Walsall (£22,000 February 1986), Doncaster Rovers (loan December 1986), Grimsby Town (loan March 1987), Hartlepool United (loan August 1987), Bristol City (loan November 1987), Carlisle United (£10,000 December 1987), Darlington (March 1989), Stoke City (June 1993), Peterborough United (loan October 1994), Liverpool (loan November-December 1994).
Club honours: Darlington: GM Vauxhall Conference champions 1990, Division Four champions 1991.
Squarely built goalkeeper Mark Prudhoe was signed three days before Jim McDonagh and 11 days before David Seaman, to became the second of four Blues goalies in four games in September 1984. With Seaman eventually settling in as first choice, Prudhoe was restricted almost entirely to League Cup games. He travelled around a bit after leaving St Andrew's before eventually settling at Darlington.

PUMFREY, Bernard
Left-back; Apps 13, Goals 1.
Born: Stirchley, Birmingham, May 1873. Died: Gainsborough, 18 July 1930.
Career: Birmingham St Mark's, BLUES (1892), Gainsborough Trinity (1894).
This slim, clean-cut defender was not really built like a Victorian full-back. Although born in Birmingham he came from a well-known Upton-on-Severn family who had owned land in the town since the 15th century. On signing for Gainsborough he set up as a joiner, building up his trade until he had established a large company which still exists in the town. Although not a footballer, his brother, Harry, played a major part in Blues' history as the designer of the St Andrew's ground.

PURDON, Edward John
Centre-forward; Apps 70, Goals 30.
Born: Johannesburg, South Africa, 1 March 1930.
Career: Maritz Brothers (South Africa), BLUES (professional August 1950), Sunderland (January 1954), Workington (March 1957), Barrow (March 1958), Bath City (August 1959), Bristol Rovers (August 1960), Toronto City, Polish White Eagles (Toronto) (1961).

A powerhouse, thrustful blond centre-forward, Ted Purdon was never afraid to go in where it hurt and was by far the most successful of Blues' signings from South Africa. At 6ft tall and 13st in weight he possessed all the physical attributes necessary for a striker and his physique allied to a total lack of fear made him a handful for any centre-half. A useful cricketer, he was once selected as 12th man by Warwickshire. Purdon scored 87 goals in 228 League games with his five English clubs.

PURVES, William Michael
Right-back; Apps 43, Goals 0.
Born: Belfast 1870. Deceased.
Career: Glentoran, BLUES (April 1893), Glentoran (May 1897). Later trainer with Glentoran (from 1900).
A hot-headed Irishman with a crunching tackle, he was surprisingly free from disciplinary problems during his career, despite being the sort of player opposition fans love to hate. He was one of the few successes in Blues' first season in Division One.

QUINN, Stephen James
Striker; Apps 1+3, Goals 0.
Born: Coventry, 15 December 1974.
Career: Cardinal Wiseman School, BLUES (YTS July 1991), Blackpool (July 1993), Stockport County (loan March 1994).
Representative honours: Northern Ireland (1 'B' cap, Youth caps).
Steve Quinn proved a talented young forward who was a prolific scorer in Blues' youth teams. He was given an occasional run-out whilst still a YTS player and great things were predicted for him. Surprisingly he refused to sign a professional contract and moved after a considerable wrangle to Blackpool where he considered there was a greater chance of first-team action. Once there, however, he had difficulty establishing himself in their team.

QUINTON, Walter
Left-back; Apps 9, Goals 0.
Born: Anston, near Rotherham, 3 December 1917.
Career: Dinnington Athletic (1934), Rotherham United (July 1937), BLUES (July 1939), Brentford (April 1949), Southend United (August 1952), Shrewsbury Town (October 1952).
A short, squat defender, Quinton was fated to be a reserve throughout his career. He was at his best when dogging wingers and denying them space. He joined Brentford in a double-deal with Jackie Goodwin, spending one year in their first team before dropping back into the Football Combination. He later worked at Bulpitts and was a keen singer.

RANDLE, Jack
Left-back; Apps 116, Goals 1.
Born: Bedworth, Warwickshire, 23 August 1902. Died: Bournemouth 1990.
Career: Exhall Colliery, Bedworth Boys' Club, Coventry City 1922, BLUES (November 1927), Southend United (April 1933), Bournemouth & Boscombe Athletic (June 1933), Guildford City (1934).
Like so many pre-war full-backs this burly defender was an ex-miner. Not the fastest of players but very strong, in the latter part of his Blues career he played principally in midweek matches when George Liddell's evening classes would not allow him to appear. He later became groundsman at Newdegate Colliery, Nuneaton. Randle once scored a hat-trick of own-goals during his Coventry days.

RANSON, Raymond
Right-back; Apps 157+1, Goals 0.
Born: St Helens, 12 June 1960.
Career: Sutton High School, St Helens Schoolboy football and District Boys teams, Manchester City (apprentice June 1976, professional June 1977), BLUES (£15,000 November 1984), Newcastle United (£175,000 December 1988), Manchester City (loan January 1993), Reading (July 1993).
Club honours: Manchester City: FA Cup runners-up 1981.
Representative honours: England (11 Under-21 caps, 2 Youth caps, Schoolboy caps).
An attacking right-back with a good turn of speed and the ability to hit pin-point crosses, Ray Ranson gained a regular first-

team place with Manchester City whilst still in his teens and progressed quickly to the England Under-21 side. He had a disagreement with the management at Maine Road and with his career at a crossroads, Blues stepped in to sign him. He proved an immediate success at St Andrew's but then tended to struggle towards the end of his spell when his defensive shortcomings were more noticeable, especially when he was up against a fast-raiding or tricky winger.

RATHBONE, Michael John

Right-back; Apps 22+3, Goals 0.
Born: Sheldon, Birmingham, 6 November 1958.
Career: Sir Wilfred Martineau School, Aston Villa Boys, BLUES (apprentice December 1974, professional November 1976), Blackburn Rovers (loan February 1979, signing permanently for £40,000 March 1979), Preston North End (£20,000 August 1987 to May 1991), Darwen (commercial manager, August 1991), Halifax Town (physiotherapist 1992, then manager-physiotherapist, sacked March 1995)).
Representative honours: England (2 Youth caps).
Mike Rathbone was a steady player who was always keen to support his forwards when possible, sometimes to the detriment of his defensive duties. Never an automatic choice at Blues, he later did an excellent job with his two Lancashire clubs, making over 300 senior appearances for Blackburn Rovers during his eight-year stay at Ewood Park and more than 100 for Preston North End.

RAWSON, Albert Norman

Centre-forward; Apps 19, Goals 9.
Born: West Melton, October 1900. Died: Yorkshire, c.1980.
Career: Sheffield United, BLUES (February 1923), Barnsley (1924).
Signed to boost Blues' flagging fortunes after they had lost seven games in a row and were heading towards relegation, Albert Rawson's arrival seemed to boost Blues as he scored in each of his first five games and the club survived. He missed the start of the 1923-24 campaign and was unable to command a first-team place thereafter. In later years he went into business in Yorkshire, working for a mining concern.

REED, Arthur

Inside-forward; Apps 29, Goals 13.
Born: Sheffield, 1883. Deceased.
Career: Leadhill St Mary's, Doncaster Rovers, BLUES (April 1912). Retired 1917 through injury.
An unlikely looking footballer being 5ft 5in tall with a 'roly-poly' physique, he was nevertheless quite a useful forward and the local Press described him as 'quick, eager and never afraid to let fly'. His Doncaster career was limited to one reserve and one first-team game, a cup final in which Reed scored the winning goal only for Doncaster to be disqualified as he was an unregistered player.

REES, Anthony Andrew

Forward; Apps 88+23, Goals 16.
Born: Merthyr Tydfil, 1 August 1964.
Career: Aston Villa (apprentice August 1980, professional August 1982), BLUES (free transfer July 1983), Peterborough United (loan October 1985), Shrewsbury Town (loan March 1986), Barnsley (March 1988), Grimsby Town (August 1989), West Bromwich Albion (£30,000 November 1994).
Club honours: Aston Villa: FA Youth Cup winners 1980; Grimsby Town: Division Four promotion 1990, Division Three promotion 1991.
Representative honours: Wales (1 full cap, 1 Under-21 cap, Youth caps, Schoolboy caps).

Tony Rees built up a considerable reputation in Villa's youth side until a broken leg halted his progress, causing him to miss a complete season. On recovering he chose to join Blues and stepped straight into the first team. He played initially wide on the right where he displayed an ability to take on defenders, but he also seemed a little lacking in stamina. His career stagnated for a while but after joining Alan Buckley at Grimsby his fortunes improved.

REGAN, Matthew John

Centre-forward; Apps 7, Goals 2.
Born: Worcester, 18 June 1944.
Career: Sacred Heart College, Worcester Royal Grammar School, Claines FC, BLUES (amateur June 1959, professional September 1961), Shrewsbury Town (October 1964), Brentford (March 1966), Crewe Alexandra (November 1966), Doncaster Rovers (September 1968).
Although he attended a rugby playing school John Regan did enough with his junior club to impress Blues' scouts. Given an early first-team try out, he responded by scoring on his debut but with Jimmy Harris playing so well, first-team chances were always at a premium. He left the club whilst still very young and plied his trade around the lower divisions before dropping out of League football at the age of 27. He scored 53 League goals in 181 games after leaving Blues.

REGIS, David R.

Striker; Apps 5+2, Goals 2.
Born: Paddington, 3 March 1964.
Career: Dunstable, Fisher Athletic, Windsor & Eton, Barnet, Notts County (£25,000 September 1990), Plymouth Argyle (£200,000 November 1991), AFC Bournemouth (loan August 1992), Stoke City (£100,000 October 1992), BLUES (£200,000 & player August 1994), Southend United (September 1994).
Club honours: Barnet: Clubcall Cup 1989; Stoke City: Division Two champions 1993.
Dave Regis came from a sporting family, being the brother of former England centre-forward Cyrille Regis, and the cousin of international sprinter John Regis. He made his name as a prominent member of Barnet's Conference side and was signed along with Paul Harding by Notts County. He got off to a good start with Notts and his value spiralled upwards, increasing eightfold in only 14 months when Plymouth signed him. He struggled in Devon, however, and it wasn't until joining Stoke that he regained some of his form. Barry Fry battled hard to sign him, eventually allowing Paul Peschisolido to go in exchange. On arriving at Blues he struggled to find his touch but it was something of a surprise when Fry transferred him again so quickly. Regis broke his leg shortly after joining Southend.

RENNIE, David

Defender/Midfield; Apps 34+3, Goals 4.
Born: Edinburgh, 29 August 1964.
Career: Leicester City (apprentice July 1980, professional May 1982), Leeds United (£50,000 January 1986), Bristol City (£175,000 July 1989), BLUES (£120,000 February 1992), Coventry City (£100,000 March 1993).
Representative honours: Scotland (Youth caps).
Dave Rennie, an experienced defender, was 28 when he joined Blues, and had already made over 250 senior appearances. He added stability to the Blues rearguard.

REYNOLDS, William Thomas

Left-back; Apps 13, Goals 0.
Born: Tewkesbury, 1870. Deceased.
Career: St Luke's, BLUES (April 1893), Berwick Rangers (Worcester 1894).
Blues used six left-backs on their way to promotion in 1893-94 and this stocky defender was the most regular choice. But he was not considered good enough for First Division football and was released at the end of the season.

RICHARDS, Carroll L. ('Carl')

Centre-forward; Apps 18+1, Goals 2.
Born: St Mary's, Jamaica, 12 January 1960.
Career: Dulwich Hamlet, Enfield, AFC Bournemouth (£10,000 July 1986), BLUES (£70,000 October 1988), Peterborough United (£37,000 July 1989), Blackpool (£60,000 January 1990), Enfield, Bromley (loan then full transfer).
Club honours: Enfield: Gola League champions 1986; AFC Bournemouth: Division Three champions 1987.
Representative honours: England (1 semi-professional cap).
Bournemouth fought off several other clubs to land this highly-rated non-League striker. He was an immediate success at Dean Court where he formed an effective partnership with Trevor Aylott as the Cherries ran away with the Third Division title. Garry Pendrey paid a large amount of money to bring 'Carl' to St Andrew's but he proved a great disappointment. Being unable to settle off the field, he took his troubles on to the pitch and after a series of poor performances the crowd got on his back, his morale suffered, and in the end was grateful to move to Peterborough.

RICHARDS, David ('Dai') Thomas

Left-half; Apps 66, Goals 2.
Born: Abercanaid, South Wales, 31 October 1906. Died: Yardley, Birmingham, 1 October 1969.
Career: Abercanaid Council School, Riverfield FC, Belingoed, Merthyr Town (1925), Wolverhampton Wanderers (£300 August 1927), Brentford (November 1935), BLUES (March 1937), Walsall (August 1939), Sedgley (1945).
Club honours: Wolverhampton Wanderers: Division Two champions 1932.
Representative honours: Wales (21 full caps).
A goalscorer at school, Dai Richards developed into a first-class tactical wing-half, an effective passer of the ball and a good covering player with a strong tackle. He became a building contractor after retiring from the game. His brother, Billy, also played for Wolves in the late 1920s.

RICHARDSON, Ernest William

Outside-right; Apps 3, Goals 0.
Born: Bishops Burton, 1910.
Career: Leven FC, BLUES (February 1936), Swansea Town (November 1938).
A short, lightweight, but very fast winger, Ernie Richardson was third choice behind White and Jennings at St Andrew's. His spell with Swansea was not a great success either, lasting barely a season in which he appeared 18 times.

RILEY, Harold

Outside-right; Apps 1, Goals 0.
Born: Oldham, 22 November 1909. Died: Lincoln, 12 April 1982.
Career: Altrincham (1927), Hunt, BLUES (April 1928), Ashton National (1929), Accrington Stanley (July 1930), Lincoln City (August 1931), Notts County (April 1933), Cardiff City (July 1934), Northampton Town (July 1936), Exeter City (May 1938), Rushton Bucyrus (1945-46). Retired 1947.
Club honours: Lincoln City: Division Three North champions 1932.
Starting his League career on the last day of the 1928-29 season, Harry Riley was an odd choice for a right winger, being naturally left-footed and normally an inside-forward 'link man'. He was described as 'small and clever' but was said to reserve his best performances 'until the retained list was under review'.

RIOCH, Bruce David

Midfield; Apps 3, Goals 0.
Born: Aldershot, 6 September 1947.
Career: Stapsley High School, Dynamoes Boys Club, Cambridge & District and London Borough Schools, Luton Town (apprentice July 1963, professional September 1964), Aston Villa (£100,000 with brother Neil July 1969), Derby County (£200,000 February 1974), Everton (£180,000 December 1976), Derby County (£150,000 November 1977), BLUES (loan December 1978), Sheffield United (loan March 1979), Seattle Sounders (NASL) (March 1980) Torquay United (October 1980, player-manager July 1982-January 1984), Seattle Sounders (NASL) (coach July 1985-January 1986), Middlesbrough (assistant manager February 1986, manager March 1986-March 1990), Millwall (manager April 1990-March 1992), Bolton Wanderers (manager May 1992).
Club honours: Luton Town: Division Four champions 1968; Aston Villa: Division Two champions 1972, Football League Cup runners-up 1971; Derby County: Division One champions 1975; Middlesbrough: (as manager) Division Two promotion 1988; Bolton Wanderers: (as manager) Division One promotion 1995.

Representative honours: Scotland: (24 full caps); toured with FA party in 1969.
The first English-born player to captain Scotland, Bruce Rioch, the son of a Scottish army sergeant-major, was a grand attacking midfielder with cannonball shot and was one of the first English players to represent Scotland on a parental qualification. Rioch joined Aston Villa from Luton but had his best days at Derby from where Blues took him on loan in December 1978. Rioch scored 160 goals in 530 League games before launching a successful career in management, recently steering Bolton to the Premiership via the Play-offs, following some memorable cup victories in the last

few seasons. His father represented Great Britain at athletics, and his brother Daniel (Neil) also played for Luton and Villa, as well as York City, Northampton and Plymouth.

ROACH, James
Goalkeeper; Apps 17, Goals 0.
Born: West Bromwich, 12 January 1864. Died: Birmingham c.1955.
Career: Small Heath Royal, 2nd Dragoon Guards, Saltley Gas Works FC, Hereford Thistle, BLUES (August 1895), Hereford Town (1896), Eastville (Bristol Rovers (1897).
Jim Roach was already an experienced goalkeeper when he arrived in Birmingham and had a nerve-racking season when Blues were relegated. He reappeared in 1950, as an entrant in a *Sports Argus* 'oldest reader' competition. He lost. His grandson James, was a Blues junior and England youth international.

ROBB, William R.
Goalkeeper; Apps 45, Goals 0.
Born: Rutherglen, near Glasgow, 20 March 1895. Died: Aldershot, 18 February 1976.
Career: Rutherglen Welfare, Lanarkshire Boys' Club, Kirkintilloch Rob Roy, BLUES (professional January 1914), Armadale (1915), Third Lanark (guest 1916-17), Glasgow Rangers (April 1920), Hibernian (June 1926), Aldershot (£100 June 1930), Guildford City (August 1937). Retired May 1939.
Club honours: Glasgow Rangers: Scottish Division One champions 1921, 1923, 1924, 1925, Scottish Cup runners-up 1921, 1922; Guildford City: Southern League champions 1938.
Representative honours: Scotland (2 full caps); Scottish League XI (2).
Robb was a fine Scottish goalkeeper who enjoyed 27 years in the game before retiring at the age of 44. Big and weighty, he played all his early football in Lanarkshire before moving to the Midlands. He returned to Scotland during World War One and spent six years at Ibrox before trying his luck with Hibernian. He holds the record for the longest gap between Football League appearances: over 17 years, from 1915 (with Blues) to August 1932 (with Aldershot).

ROBERTS, Brian Leslie Ford ('Harry')
Full-back/defender; Apps 206+7, Goals 0.
Born: Manchester, 6 November 1955.
Career: Coventry City (apprentice June 1972, professional May 1974), Hereford United (loan February 1975), BLUES (£10,000 March 1984), Wolverhampton Wanderers (free transfer June 1990), Coventry City (reserve coach July 1992). Coach at Knightlow School, Stretton-on-Dunsmore.
Signed by Blues as a result of a 'Buy a Player Fund' amongst the fans, Roberts was

a determined full-back who had made 215 League appearances for Coventry, in close on 12 years at Highfield Road. And when he scored his first goal, some supporters were so shocked that they had special badges made proclaiming: 'I saw Harry score a goal'. A cheerful, likeable chap with a great sense of humour, he had to work hard to overcome the boo-boys at St Andrew's but when he left for Molineux he had become a cult hero, and passed the 500-mark in first-team outings whilst with Wolves.

ROBERTS, Frederick
Inside-left; Apps 32, Goals 10.
Born: Greets Green, West Bromwich, 9 October 1909. Died: Luton, January 1979.
Career: Smethwick Highfield, Thomas Pigott's Works FC, BLUES (September 1933), Luton Town (December 1934), Kettering Town (August 1945). Retired May 1948.
Spotted playing in the Birmingham Works League, Fred Roberts made an immediate impression at St Andrew's, earning his debut after only one month with Blues. He continued to hold down a regular place for most of the season as a scheming inside-forward, although he was occasionally tried in the centre. He struggled early on in 1934-35 and was quickly transferred to Luton where he proved an extremely popular player. His brother, Bill, played for Cardiff City.

ROBERTS, Harold
Outside-left; Apps 38, Goals 3.
Born: Liverpool, 12 January 1920.
Career: Harrowby Juniors, Chesterfield (September 1939), BLUES (£12,000 November 1948), Shrewsbury Town (June 1951), Scunthorpe United (July 1953), Gresley Rovers (1956).
Former commando Harry Roberts was a hard-working winger who provided a plentiful supply of good quality crosses to his fellow forwards. He tended to be a little injury-prone and so missed a large proportion of matches during his two-and-a-half year stay at St Andrew's. Altogether, though, he made over 200 appearances in the Football League with his four clubs, scoring 27 goals.

ROBERTS, John Griffith
Centre-half; Apps 79, Goals 1.
Born: Abercynon, near Swansea, 11 September 1946.
Career: Abercynon Town (1961), Swansea Town (apprentice June 1963, professional July 1964), Northampton Town (November 1967), Arsenal (£35,000 May 1969), BLUES (£140,000 October 1972), Wrexham (August 1976), Hull City (August 1980), Oswestry Town (player-manager

July 1981). Retired 1983.
Club honours: Arsenal: Division One champions 1971; Wrexham: Division Three champions 1978, Welsh Cup winners 1978, runners-up 1979.
Representative honours: Wales (22 full caps, 1 Under-21, 5 Under-23 caps).
John Roberts was working as a railway fireman when he joined Swansea Town. At first no one really knew his best position, but he eventually took to the centre-half berth and remained there practically throughout his career, scoring his fair share of goals for Northampton, mostly from set pieces. He spent close on four years with Blues after being signed by manager Freddie Goodwin. After retiring Roberts became a salesman for a North Wales-based stationery company and later was a driving instructor. In his career he amassed in excess of 400 League appearances (145 for Wrexham) and he notched 38 goals.

ROBERTS, Josiah Edmund
Right-back; Apps 1, Goals 0.
Born: West Smethwick, 1871. Deceased.
Career: Mitchell St George's, BLUES (1892), Walsall Wood (1893).
Josiah Roberts played his one game for Blues in the aftermath of Fred Speller's broken leg, but he lacked the ability needed to succeed in League football.

ROBERTSON, George
Inside-forward/wing-half; Apps 87, Goals 17.
Born: Glasgow, 1883. Deceased.
Career: Rutherglen Glencairn, Clyde (August 1901), Rangers (August 1902), Clyde (August 1902), Blackburn Rovers (September 1902), Clyde (August 1903), BLUES (December 1910), Bloxwich Strollers (May 1914), Brierley Hill Alliance (1921).
George Robertson was a hard working schemer whose first spell in England was short-lived. He was primarily a left-half until Blackburn moved him further forward in 1902. He took to his new role quickly and his strong shooting proved profitable to the club. Robertson disappeared from the local football scene in September 1914, but a few weeks later it transpired that he had signed up for the Army and he served in World War One.

ROBERTSON, James
Inside-right; Apps 7, Goals 2.
Born: Glasgow, 1880. Deceased.
Career: Glasgow United, Crewe Alexandra (1901), BLUES (£25 April 1903), Chelsea (£50 August 1905), Glossop North End (1907), Partick Thistle, Ayr United, Barrow (1912), Leeds City (July 1912), Gateshead (1913). Retired 1915.
This slim goal poacher was highly rated at Crewe but took some time to settle into League football. One of three Blues players signed by Chelsea in the London club's first League season, he became a regular marksman during his two years at Stamford Bridge, as he did with his later teams. Described as 'speedy with a deadly shot'.

ROBERTSON, James E.
Centre-forward; Apps 8, Goals 2.
Born: Dundee, 1910.
Career: Lochee United, Logie Thistle, Dundee (June 1928), BLUES (£1,250 December 1933), Kilmarnock (£1,000 July 1934). Retired 1938.
Representative honours: Scotland (2 full caps).
A prolific scorer north of the border, Jimmy Robertson had difficulty settling in the Midlands. His homesickness badly affected his play and Blues were only too glad to recoup most of the money paid for him. At Kilmarnock he was unpopular with the fans but still maintained a record

of a goal every two games. The Killies supporters criticised him for lacking 'thrust and initiative'.

ROBERTSON, William
Left-half/inside-right; Apps 103, Goals 15.
Born: Pontypool, 1873. Deceased.
Career: Abercorn FC (1894), BLUES (February 1896), Eastville (Bristol) Rovers (April 1899), BLUES (July 1902), Bristol Rovers (1903).
Here was a two-footed grafter whose career was the opposite to his namesake George. He joined Blues as an inside-forward but did not find his true metier until switching to wing-half. Unusually, he scored a hat-trick from left-half against Luton in 1898 but he was unable to break into the team during his second spell in Birmingham.

ROBERTSON, William Harold
Goalkeeper; Apps 3, Goals 0.
Born: Crowthorne, 25 March 1923.
Career: Crowthorne Boys' Club, Camberley ATC, RAF Lossiemouth, Chelsea (October 1945), BLUES (December 1948), Stoke City (£8,000 June 1952). Retired May 1960.
Bill Robertson started off as centre-forward in junior football in his native Crowthorne, and was top scorer for Camberley ATC whom he helped win the Aldershot Minor League championship (his only medal during his entire playing career). At the age of 20 he turned to goalkeeping in the RAF and quickly developed into a capable last line of defence. He had difficulties, however, in establishing himself at Stamford Bridge, and after moving to St Andrew's his career came to a complete standstill when the brilliance of Gil Merrick restricted him to only three games in three and a half years. His move to Stoke, however, resurrected his flagging fortunes and he settled in to become one of the League's most consistent performers, appearing in 250 League and Cup games for the Potters. On retirement he took a newsagent's shop in Bucknell, Staffs, but in 1963 he moved back to the south of England.

ROBINSON, Arthur Charles ('Nat')
Goalkeeper; Apps 306, Goals 0.
Born: Coventry, 28 February 1878. Died: Coventry, 15 May 1929.
Career: Allesley FC, Coventry Stars, Singers FC, BLUES (professional August 1898), Chelsea (July 1908), Coventry City (May 1910). Retired to become a publican at the Red House Inn, Barrass Green, Coventry.
Club honours: Blues: Division Two promotion 1901, 1903.
Representative honours: England (2 trials); Football League XI (2).
He always donned two jerseys when keeping goal, irrespective of the weather and it is said that Nat Robinson wore only two pairs of boots throughout his lengthy career. He often used to whistle when annoyed, and he also had a pet dog called 'Ninety' after the number of minutes in a game. He was described by a contemporary as being 'all arms and legs' due to the way he used to 'windmill' his arms round in 'Catherine Wheel style' to put off his opponents. Nevertheless he was a brilliant, if somewhat eccentric custodian, a real character, who was one of the first practitioners of the art of rushing out of the penalty area to clear the ball.

ROBINSON, Colin R.
Forward; Apps 39+3, Goals 6.
Born: Birmingham, 15 May 1960.
Career: Mile Oak Rovers, Shrewsbury Town (professional November 1982), BLUES (January 1988), Hereford United (August 1989), Worcester City (July 1991),

Bridgnorth Town (March 1994), Halesowen Town (cs 1994), Shifnal Town.
Club honours: Shrewsbury: Welsh Cup winners 1984.

Colin Robinson was a swarthy, bearded striker who had been a regular if not prolific scorer at Gay Meadow for some years before Garry Pendrey recruited him to St Andrew's to boost Blues' mediocre attack. He scored in his second full game for Blues but was injured the next week and missed the rest of the season. The following term he earned a regular place in the side but rarely looked likely to provide the goals the club desperately needed to halt their slide into Division Three.

ROBINSON, David ('Sugar')
Central defender; Apps 125+2, Goals 4.
Born: Bartley Green, Birmingham, 14 July 1948.
Career: Woodgate Valley Junior & Bartley Green Senior Schools, Birmingham District Boy & Warwickshire Schools, England Schoolboy trialist, BLUES (apprentice June 1964, professional July 1966), Walsall (February 1973), Chelmsley Town (manager 1976), Tamworth (September 1978), Oldbury United (manager 1980).

An England Schoolboy trialist and West Brom fan as a youngster, Dave Robinson came to Blues as an inside-forward and struck up a fine partnership with Phil Summerill in the youth side. He was then moved back into the defence and after a good run in the reserves he was given his League debut against Aston Villa in September 1968. He always looked impressive, and was entrusted with the job of taking penalties. When he signed Robinson, Blues' manager Stan Cullis said: "He's saved us £80,000." After leaving Blues, Robinson added almost 200 more appearances to his tally with Walsall.

ROBINSON, Philip John
Midfield; Apps 12, Goals 0.
Born: Stafford, 6 January 1967.
Career: Stafford & District Schools, Aston Villa (apprentice June 1983, professional January 1985), Wolverhampton Wanderers (June 1987), Notts County (£67,500 August 1989), BLUES (loan March-May 1991), Huddersfield Town (September 1992), Northampton Town (loan August 1994), Chesterfield (December 1994).
Club honours: Wolverhampton Wanderers: Division Four champions 1988, Division Three champions 1989, Sherpa Van Trophy winners 1988; Notts County: Division Three Play-off winners 1990, promotion to Division One in 1991; Blues: Leyland DAF Cup winners 1991; Huddersfield Town: Autoglass Trophy runners-up 1994.

Villa were undecided as to whether this busy redhead was better in defence or midfield, and his career with them suffered from constant changes of position. Graham

Turner took him to Wolves where he blossomed as a ball-winner in their meteoric rise through the divisions, and a further transfer to Meadow Lane led him to the unusual feat of winning promotion four seasons running. Lou Macari would have liked to sign him permanently but the money was not available.

ROBINSON, Steven Eli
Midfield; Apps 6+2, Goals 0.
Born: Nottingham, 17 January 1975.
Career: BLUES (trainee June 1991, professional June 1993).
Steve Robinson is a thoughtful footballer, aggressive and eager to participate.

ROBINSON, Thomas Edward
Inside-left; Apps 10, Goals 1.
Born: Coalville, Leicestershire, 11 February 1909.
Career: Coalville YMCA, Gresley Rovers (1926), BLUES (November 1928), Blackpool (May 1933), Chesterfield (October 1933), Lincoln City (June 1934), Northampton Town (July 1935), Gillingham (May 1936), Walsall (1937), Tunbridge Wells Rovers, Nuneaton Borough. Retired during war.
He was an inside-forward of limited ability whose wanderings took him through all four divisions of the Football League. A collier by trade.

RODGERSON, Ian
Right-back/midfield; Apps 116, Goals 6.
Born: Hereford, 9 April 1966.
Career: Aylestone School, Hereford United (associate schoolboy), Pegasus Juniors, Hereford United (June 1985), Cardiff City (£7,000 August 1988), BLUES (loan December 1990, signed permanently January 1991), Sunderland (July 1993).

Ian Rodgerson suffered an early setback when he was not taken on as an apprentice at Edgar Street because the club axed its youth team. But he was eventually given a second chance by Hereford and developed into a useful midfielder, playing wide on the right, ever eager to support his forwards. He was unlucky to miss the 1991 Leyland DAF Cup Final triumph through injury. The son of Alan Rodgerson, the former Middlesbrough inside-forward, he was injured in car crash before the 1993-94 season.

ROE, Arthur ('Archie')
Inside-forward; Apps 3, Goals 0.
Born: Newcastle-on-Tyne, 1892. Deceased.
Career: South Shields (1918), BLUES (1919), Gillingham (1920).
Roe was one of a string of inside-forwards Blues tried out in the first post-war season of 1919-20, but who met with no success.

ROGERS, Darren J.
Defender; Apps 22+4, Goals 0.
Born: Birmingham, 9 April 1970.

Career: Bartley Green School, West Bromwich Albion (YTS June 1986, professional July 1988), BLUES (free transfer July 1992), Kidderminster Harriers (loan March 1993), Lincoln City (trial July 1994), Wycombe Wanderers (loan November 1993, Walsall (free transfer July 1994).
Darren Rogers is a utility defender, fast and mobile with a good strong tackle.

ROGERS, Kevin Penry
Midfield; Apps 8+1, Goals 1.
Born: Merthyr Tydfil, 23 September 1963.
Career: Merthyr Schools, Aston Villa (apprentice September 1979, professional September 1981), BLUES (free transfer April 1983), Wrexham (July 1984), Rhyl Athletic (1985), Merthyr Tydfil (October 1986).
Club honours: Merthyr Tydfil: Welsh Cup winners 1987.
Representative honours: Wales (Semi-professional caps, Youth caps, Schoolboy caps).

Kevin Rogers was primarily a 'grafter' who was a regular member of Blues' reserve side but who did little to impress during his rare first-team outings. A school colleague of Tony Rees.

RONSON, William
Midfield; Apps 2, Goals 0.
Born: Fleetwood, 22 January 1957.
Career: Blackpool Boys, Blackpool (apprentice June 1973, professional February 1974), Cardiff City (£125,000 July 1979), Wrexham (£100,000 October 1981), Barnsley (£50,000 August 1982), BLUES (loan November 1985), Blackpool (non-contract January 1986), Baltimore Blast (USA) (summer 1986), Detroit Rockers (USA) (1992), Tampa Bay Rowdies (USA) (1992).
Ronson was a tigerish midfielder whose talents were highly rated by all his clubs. He came to Blues following a disagreement with Barnsley manager, Allan Clarke, which had left him out of favour at Oakwell. Ronson was one of the most successful performers on the American indoor circuit. In England he accumulated a total of 368 League appearances as a professional, scoring 20 goals.

ROTHERHAM, Walter
Inside-left; Apps 3, Goals 0.
Born: Stafford, 1859. Deceased.
Career: Wolverhampton St Luke's FC, BLUES (1880), Leabrook FC (1883).
Work commitments prevented this exceptionally useful goalscorer from making many appearances for Blues.

ROULSON, Joseph
Right-half; Apps 125, Goals 4.
Born: Sheffield, 1890. Deceased.

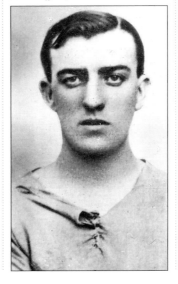

Career: Cammel Laird FC (1910), BLUES (August 1912), Swansea Town (April 1923-25).
Club honours: BLUES: Division Two champions 1921.
Roulson was a 'hard as nails' wing-half, similar in style to his partner, Percy Barton. A former steelworker, he was picked up from the Sheffield Workers' League and after a brief spell with Swansea he returned to work in that city.

ROWBOTHAM, Darren
Striker; Apps 34+7, Goals 6.
Born: Cardiff, 22 October 1966.
Career: St Cogan's School; Plymouth Argyle (junior July 1983, professional November 1984), Exeter City (October 1987), Torquay United (£25,000 September 1991), BLUES (£20,000 January 1992), Mansfield Town (loan December 1992), Hereford United (loan March 1993), Crewe Alexandra (free transfer July 1993).
Club honours: Exeter City: Division Four champions 1990.

Representative honours: Wales (Youth cap).
Rowbotham scored plenty of goals in the lower divisions, always gave 100 per cent effort and was dangerous both in the air and on the ground. He netted 58 goals in 142 games for Exeter.

ROWLEY, Kenneth Frank
Inside-forward; Apps 42, Goals 20.
Born: Pelsall, 29 August 1926.
Career: Pelsall Juniors, Elkingtons FC, Wolverhampton Wanderers (professional October 1947), BLUES (January 1951), Coventry City (November 1954). Retired through injury April 1955, Bromsgrove Rovers (1957).
This pint-sized forward with a tremendous shot signed for Blues after a lengthy spell in Wolves' reserve side. He had a marvellous strike rate until suffering a serious injury in November 1952. Doctors said he would never play again but he defied them and played another 14 games, scoring eight goals, before he was transferred to Coventry where he had only three more outings before he was forced to hang up his boots at the age of 28.

RUDD, William Thomas
Forward; Apps 26, Goals 4.
Born: Manchester, 13 December 1941.
Career: Manchester Schools, Manchester United (amateur 1956), Stalybridge Celtic (1958), BLUES (professional October 1959), New York All Stars (loan summer 1961), York City (November 1961), Grimsby Town (July 1966), Rochdale (£1,500 February 1968), Bury (£5,000 June 1970).
After leaving Blues, Billy Rudd certainly came good and scored 68 goals in 574 League games for his next four clubs, including 34 in 193 outings for York and 18

in 189 for Bury. A former cabinet maker he was never a popular player with the fans at St Andrew's and failed to gain a regular place in the side. His career with Blues was effectively over when Bertie Auld arrived from Celtic. His uncle Jack played for Manchester City.

RUSHTON, Brian William Eric
Right-back; Apps 15, Goals 0.
Born: Sedgley, 21 October 1943.
Career: Brierley Hill Schools, Dudley Boys, BLUES (amateur 1959, professional October 1960), Notts County (June 1967).
Rushton captained the successful Brierley Hill Schools team before linking up with Blues. Although a fine player as a lad, his coltish physique was hardly ideal for the role of full-back and latterly efforts were made, unsuccessfully, to convert him into a wing-half.

RUSSELL, Cecil John ('Jack')
Forward; Apps 27, Goals 2.
Born: Northfield, 19 June 1904.
Career: Northfield, Bournville, Bromsgrove Rovers, BLUES (February 1924), Bristol Rovers (June 1927), Worcester City (June 1928), Bournemouth & Boscombe Athletic (June 1930), Luton Town (May 1934), Norwich City (October 1934), Worcester City (May 1936), Shirley Town (August 1937), Solihull Town (August 1939).
Russell made his debut as a promising inside-forward during an injury crisis at St Andrew's. The promise was largely unfulfilled and the remainder of his career with Blues was spent as a utility reserve. He later had a successful spell at Dean Court, scoring four goals in a game on two separate occasions.

RUSSELL, Guy Robert
Centre-forward; Apps 7+5, Goals 0.
Born: Shirley, 28 September 1967.
Career: Knowle North Star, BLUES (YTS June 1984, professional May 1986), Carlisle United (loan March 1987), Kemin Palloseura (Finland) (April 1989), Moor Green (October 1989).
He was a regular scorer for Blues at both youth and reserve-team levels but looked out of his depth in the senior side. His brief excursion in Finland ended with 'KePs' being relegated. He returned to England and scored regularly in the Southern League.

RUSSELL, Martin Christopher
Midfield; Apps 4+2, Goals 0.
Born: Dublin, 27 April 1967.
Career: Belvedere Youth Club, Manchester United (apprentice June 1973, professional May 1984), BLUES (loan October 1986), Norwich City (loan January 1987), Leicester City (£25,000 March 1987), Scarborough (£105,000 February 1989),

Middlesbrough (£175,000 March 1990), Portadown (August 1991).
Club honours: Portadown Gold Cup winners 1992, Budweiser Cup winners 1992, Mid-Ulster Cup winners 1992, 1993, 1994. Northern Ireland PFA Player of the Year 1992.
Representative honours: Republic of Ireland (4 Under-21 caps, Youth caps).
Russell was a skilful midfielder who was particularly adept at quick changes of direction and short passes. He did not seem to relish a hard fight, however, and had the tendency to disappear when the boots were flying. He did, though, possess a good shot when he decided to use it.

RUTHERFORD, Mark Robin
Winger; Apps 1+4, Goals 0.
Born: Birmingham, 25 March 1972.
Career: BLUES (YTS June 1988, professional July 1990), Shelbourne (October 1991), Shrewsbury Town (loan February 1994).
Club honours: Shelbourne: Irish League champions 1992, Irish Cup winners 1993, Football League Cup runners-up 1994; Shrewsbury: Division Four champions 1994.
Mark Rutherford proved a fast, tricky player who graduated through the YTS scheme. He enjoyed a good scoring record for Blues' third team, but his League career was arrested by series of niggling injuries. However, he still looked to have a fine future ahead of him.

SABIN, Alfred
Right-half; Apps 2, Goals 0.
Born: Oldbury 1904. Deceased.
Career: Accles & Pollocks Works FC, BLUES (March 1930), Oldbury United (August 1930), Leamington Town (1932).
An attacking wing-half who was given a trial by Blues at the end of the 1929-30 season, but who was not offered a contract.

SALE, Mark David
Striker; Apps 16+11, Goals 3.
Born: Rugeley, Staffs, 27 February 1972.
Career: Stoke City (July 1990), Yeovil Town (loan 1991), Cambridge United (July 1991), Stafford Rangers (trial), Rocester (1991-92), BLUES (March 1992), Torquay United (March 1993), Preston North End (August 1994).
This 6ft 5in striker was a good squad player, often appearing on the substitutes' bench.

SAMSON, Ambrose Arthur
Goalkeeper; Apps 2, Goals 0.
Born: Measham, 1897. Deceased.
Career: Measham Town, BLUES (1922), Burton Town (1923).
Samson was a tall, bulky 'keeper, rather flashy at times, whose outings were restricted due to the form of Dan Tremelling.

SAVILLE, Andrew V.
Striker; Apps 57+8, Goals 18.
Born: Hull, 12 December 1964.
Career: Malet Lambert School, Hull City Minors (1979); Hull City (professional

September 1983), Walsall (£100,000 March 1989), Barnsley (£90,000 March 1990), Hartlepool United (£60,000 March 1992), BLUES (£155,000 March 1993), Burnley (loan December 1994).
Saville was a strongly built, 6ft striker whose scoring record was not all that impressive when Blues paid out £155,000 for his services on the transfer deadline of 1993. He had managed 65 goals in 303 outings in League and Cup competition, but had a good first full season at St Andrew's, being joint leading scorer with Peschisolido (ten goals).

SBRAGIA, Richard ('Ricky')
Defender; Apps 15+2, Goals 1.
Born: Lennoxtown, Scotland, 26 May 1956.
Career: Glasgow Amateurs, BLUES (apprentice June 1972, professional May 1974), Morton (loan), Walsall (£15,000 October 1978), Blackpool (£35,000 July 1980), York City (August 1982), Darlington (loan August-September 1985), York City (youth-team coach 1989-94).
Of Italian descent, hence his surname, Sbragia was a tall, slimly built defender particularly strong in the air but a little ungainly on the ground. He made 275 League appearances after leaving Blues, including 77 for Walsall and 149 for York.

SCHOFIELD, John Reginald
Goalkeeper; Apps 237, Goals 0.
Born: Atherstone, Warwickshire, 8 February 1931.
Career: Nuneaton Borough Reserves, BLUES (professional February 1950), Wrexham (July 1966-May 1968), Atherstone Town (player-manager August 1968), Bromsgrove Rovers (1969), Tamworth (1970), Atherstone Town (manager July 1972).
Club honours: Blues: Division Two champions 1955, Inter Cities Fairs Cup runners-up 1960, 1961, Football League Cup winners 1963.

Big-hearted and brave, Johnny Schofield survived a pit explosion (at Baddesley Colliery, Warwickshire, in November 1957) and a fractured skull (playing for Blues against Manchester United in 1960, diving at Alex Dawson's feet) and still came up smiling. A dedicated footballer he understudied Gil Merrick for quite a while before taking over in 1960. In 1962 he broke some fingers but this was his last major injury and he then held his place until the combination of advancing years and the signing of Jim Herriot led to him leaving the club. After retiring he became the proprietor of a wines and spirits business in Atherstone as well as being a season-ticket holder at St Andrew's.

SCOTT, Geoffrey Samuel
Defender; Apps 18+1, Goals 0.
Born: Birmingham, 31 October 1956.
Career: Solihull Borough, Highgate

United, Stoke City (professional April 1977), Leicester City (February 1980), BLUES (February 1982), Charlton Athletic (October 1982), Middlesbrough (June 1984), Northampton Town (September 1984), Cambridge United (May 1985), Solihull Borough (1986), Moor Green (January 1987), Highgate United (manager July 1988, resigning in August 1989).

Signed in the midst of an injury crisis, Geoff Scott's career at St Andrew's was characterised by a series of errors which accounts for his short spell in the first team. He is one of a select band of players (George Smith and William Wragg are the others) to sign for Blues immediately after scoring a goal for them (an own-goal). Scott spent his best time with Stoke for whom he played in 78 League games.

SCOTT, Richard Paul
Defender; Apps 17+2, Goals 0.
Born: Dudley, 29 September 1974.
Career: BLUES (YTS July 1991, professional May 1993); Shrewsbury (March 1995).

His senior debut, at right-back, came against Derby County at St Andrew's in April 1993 before a 15,400 crowd.

SCRIVEN, Aubrey
Outside-left; Apps 52, Goals 9.
Born: Highley, Shropshire, 7 July 1903. Deceased.
Career: Highley Boys' Club, Denaby United, BLUES (December 1923), Bradford City (£400 May 1927), Bristol City (May 1932), Worcester City (July 1934), Brierley Hill Alliance (August 1935). Retired 1940.
Club honours: Bradford City Division

Three North champions 1929; Worcester Welsh Cup winners 1934.

Aubrey Scriven was a talented but inconsistent player, one of the men tried to solve the perennial left-wing problem. He proved more successful than most but still could not establish himself in the side. He had a useful five-year spell at Bradford.

SCRIVENS, Thomas
Inside-forward; Apps 16, Goals 9.
Born: Walsall, 1876. Deceased.
Career: Walsall Star, Smethwick Rovers, BLUES (January 1897), Wellingborough (June 1898), BLUES (August 1898), Willenhall (August 1900).
He was a hard-shooting forward who was an effective partner for Bob McRoberts during his second spell with Blues. He was then mysteriously released in the summer of 1900.

SEALEY, Leslie Jesse
Goalkeeper; Apps 15, Goals 0.
Born: Bethnal Green, 29 September 1957.
Career: Leyton High School, Interwood; Bethnal Green Boys' Club, Coventry City (apprentice April 1974, professional March 1976), Luton Town (£100,000 August 1983), Plymouth Argyle (loan October 1984), Manchester United (loan December 1989, full May 1990), Aston Villa (July 1991), Coventry City (loan March 1992), BLUES (loan October 1992), Manchester United (January 1993), Blackpool (June 1994), West Ham United (December 1994).
Club honours: Manchester United: FA Cup winners 1990, European Cup-winners' Cup winners 1991, Football League Cup runners-up 1991, 1994; Luton Town: Full Members' Cup runners-up 1988, Football League Cup runners-up 1989.
Les Sealey, a vastly experienced goalkeeper, accumulated well over 500 senior appearances prior to joining Blues for a three-month loan period in 1992.

SEAMAN, David Andrew
Goalkeeper; Apps 84, Goals 0.
Born: Rotherham, 19 September 1963.
Career: Leeds United (apprentice September 1979, professional September 1981), Peterborough United (£4,000 August 1982), BLUES (£100,000 October 1984), QPR (£225,000 August 1986), Arsenal (£1.3 million May 1990).
Club honours: Arsenal: Division One champions 1991, FA Cup winners 1993, Football League Cup winners 1993, European Cup-winners' Cup winners 1994, European Cup-winners' Cup runners-up 1995.
Representative honours: England (14 full caps, 10 Under-21 caps, 6 'B' caps); Football League XI (1).
A brilliant goalkeeper, with fine reactions and safe pair of hands, David Seaman was

rated third best in the world in 1990-91 after helping Arsenal win the First Division title. He was released by Leeds without ever appearing in their first team but proved a shrewd buy for Peterborough and it was something of a coup when Blues signed him in 1984. Indeed, he was one of the few successes in season 1985-86, during which he played a 'blinder' at Highbury.

SELLMAN, Alfred
Centre-half; Apps 1, Goals 0.
Born: Exeter, 1881. Deceased.
Career: Bridgetown Amateurs, BLUES (January 1904), Leyton (1905), Newton Abbott.
Sellman was a powerful player who made a big impression on his debut, one critic describing him as 'very strong and his tackling and feeding give promise of his being a class half-back in the near future'. Alas, he never lived up to that promise. A useful cricketer, he had a trial with Kent as a wicketkeeper.

SHARP, Frank
Inside-left; Apps 5, Goals 0.
Born: Burton upon Trent, 1900. Deceased.
Career: Barton BSC, BLUES (1922), Chesterfield (1923).
Sharp, a former steel worker, earned a few games as a replacement for Jack Whitehouse shortly after turning professional. Principally a playmaker, he did not fit in when asked to play a more attacking role.

SHARPLES, Brian
Centre-half; Apps 71+1, Goals 2.
Born: Bradford, 6 September 1944.
Career: Henry Parkes Junior School, Woodlands Comprehensive School, BLUES (amateur September 1959, professional December 1961), Exeter City (December 1968). Retired 1971.
Brought up in Coventry, this awkward looking defender was tried in most positions before finally settling down in the centre-half spot after he had acted as sweeper in manager Joe Mallett's controversial 'M' plan. Never really a first-team regular at Blues, he fell from favour when Stan Cullis took over but came back into the side when Winston Foster underwent a cartilage operation. A rather limited player, Sharp was somewhat cumbersome when the ball was on the ground. He now owns a chain of shoe shops in Bristol. Sharples came from a sporting family, his sister was a county netball player and his father a champion sprinter, he is also a distant relative of Sam Cowan (Manchester City and England).

SHAW, Frederick
Inside-forward; Apps 5, Goals 0.
Born: Hucknall, 1909. Deceased.

Career: Annesley Colliery FC, BLUES (amateur September 1932, professional October 1932), Notts County (December 1934), Mansfield Town (July 1937). Retired c.1943.
A shade on the small side for the role of target man he was often asked to play, Shaw was a lightweight, highly mobile, with an eye for goal. He proved far more successful after moving back to his native Nottinghamshire.

SHAW, John ('Jack')
Left-half; Apps 11, Goals 0.
Born: Oldham, 2 October 1916. Died: 22 October 1973.
Career: South Shore Wesleyans, Lytham (December 1933), Oldham Athletic (March 1934), Mossley (July 1936), Grimsby Town (May 1937), BLUES (March 1939), Watford (October 1945). Retired May 1948.
A tall, muscular player, more destructive than constructive, whose arrival at St Andrew's found him pitched into the vain struggle against relegation. He had little chance to show his prowess with Blues owing to the outbreak of war. His uncle, George Tyson, played Rugby League football for Oldham.

SHAW, Raymond
Wing-half; Apps 13, Goals 0.
Born: Walsall, 18 May 1913. Died: 1980.
Career: Walsall (amateur), Streetly Works, Darlaston, BLUES (May 1937), BLUES May 1947 to become BLUES' coach, Walsall (manager October 1964 - March 1968).
Ray Shaw was a constructive player but who seldom shone, although he did appear in 111 first-team games during the war. He became a top-class coach, though, a role he played at St Andrew's for many years before taking over as boss at Fellows Park.

SHEARER, Peter A.
Forward; Apps 33+5, Goals 13.
Born: Birmingham, 4 February 1967.
Career: Coventry City (associate schoolboy), BLUES (apprentice June 1983, professional February 1985), Rochdale (July 1986), Nuneaton Borough (1987), Cheltenham Town (1988), AFC Bournemouth (February 1989), Coventry City (trial 1993), Dundee (trial 1993), BLUES (January 1994).
Club honour: Blues: Second Division champions 1995, Auto Windscreens Shield winners 1995.
Representative honour: England (semi-professional caps).

As a youngster Peter Shearer tended to be a bit lazy off the ball. In his first spell at St Andrew's he was played chiefly as a forward or attacking midfielder in the first team but as a centre-half in the reserves. Released whilst still a teenager he failed to make the grade at Rochdale either but a

spell in non-League football seemed to do him good and he was a much better player by the time Bournemouth signed him. Nevertheless it was still a surprise when Barr Fry brought him back to St Andrew's. Again he struggled to establish himself and he was soon placed on the open to transfer list. The 1994-95 season brought about an amazing transformation as he emerged as a star of the team. His tenacious tackling coupled with the ability to score priceless goals made him the most improved player in the club although his aggression sometimes brought him problems with referees.

SHORT, Charles
Inside/centre-forward; Apps 19, Goals 12.
Born: Birmingham Excelsior, BLUES (August 1889), Unity Gas Depot (1890), BLUES (October 1890), Bloxwich Strollers (1892).
Short was a fine goalpoacher who gained a certain notoriety as the player who got Blues kicked out of the FA Cup. He had played for the club in season 1889-90 but his registration had been allowed to lapse. He returned to Blues after a few games with Unity Gas, but no one had bothered to re-register him for the competition. He scored in a 2-0 win over Wednesbury Old Athletic, who protested that Blues had fielded an ineligible player. Their protest was upheld and consequently Blues were thrown out of the tournament.

SHORT, George Frederick
Utility; Apps 30, Goals 2.
Born: Birmingham 1866. Deceased.
Career: Unity Gas Company FC, BLUES (1887), Oldbury Town (1895).
Club honours: Blues: Division Two champions 1893.
An elder brother of Charlie and the first genuine utility player the club ever had, George Short began as a winger, but worked his way through most positions before settling down as full-back He was Fred Speller's replacement for two years.

SHORT, John ('James')
Inside-forward; Apps 17, Goals 10.
Born: Hucknall, Nottinghamshire, April 1896. Deceased.
Career: Arnold St Mary's, South Notts Hussars Yeomanry, Lincoln City (1916), Notts County (1917), BLUES (October 1919), Watford (May 1920), Ilkeston United (May 1922), Norwich City (May 1923), Newark Town (September 1924), Grantham Town, Lewison FC (September 1927).

He was another fine goalscorer whose stay at St Andrew's was short but explosive. He kept up his fine marksmanship record throughout his career which was seriously affected by wounds received during World War One.

SHUFFLEBOTTOM, John ('Jack')
Centre-half; Apps 1, Goals 0.

Born: Macclesfield, February 1888. Died: Crewe, 1954.
Career: Old Mill FC, BLUES (March 1905), Oldham Athletic (August 1907), Portsmouth (May 1909), Southport Central (£150 July 1911). Retired October 1914.
Jack Shufflebottom was a long striding, raven-haired defender with strong kick who was basically a reserve with most of his clubs. Oldham Athletic retained his registration from 1907 until 1911, when he played outside the Football League. He worked as a timber merchant's agent in the Birmingham area for a number of years either side of World War One.

SHUTT, Carl Steven
Striker; Apps 21+8, Goals 4.
Born: Sheffield, 10 October 1961.
Career: Sheffield Wednesday (associate schoolboy April 1976), Spalding United (1982), Sheffield Wednesday (free May 1985), Bristol City (£55,000 October 1987), Leeds United (£50,000 March 1989), BLUES (£50,000 August 1993), Manchester City (loan January 1994), Bradford City (loan August 1994, full transfer September 1994).
Club honours: Leeds United: Division One champions 1992, Division Two champions 1990.
Carl Shutt had a useful record – 68 goals in 226 appearances – before transferring to Blues, but he never settled at St Andrew's, injury plaguing him in 1994. He played in same side as Chris Whyte at Elland Road.

SIMMS, Charles ('Bowie')
Centre-half; Apps 14, Goals 0.
Born: Birmingham, 12 February 1859. Died: Birmingham, 20 July 1935.
Career: Calthorpe, Mitchell's St George, BLUES (first as a player from August 1884 to May 1892, then as first-team trainer until 1905 and thereafter as head groundsman at St Andrew's until January 1914, when he retired from football).
Simms was a real heavyweight who served Blues for close on 30 years. Weighing almost 14st, with his bandy legs and walrus moustache, he looked the very epitome of a Victorian footballer. He joined Blues at the age of 25 and was a regular performer in defence from 1884 until 1892, although from time to time he was dogged by injury. He made his League debut when he was almost ready to quit the game as a player, taking over from Caesar Jenkyns who missed the train to Lincoln. He also turned out in goal a few times in various friendly matches. A grand club man, on retiring as a player he was immediately offered the job as 'spongeman', a position he held for more than a decade before taking up his duties as groundsman. His brother, Arnie, was on Blues' books in the pre-League era. Simms played cricket for Small Heath Langley.

SINGER, Dennis James
Inside-forward; Apps 31, Goals 15.
Born: Cefn Hengoed, 30 August 1937.
Career: Fleur de Lys FC, Hengoed FDL, Newport County (amateur 1954, professional May 1956), BLUES (September 1960), Bournemouth & Boscombe Athletic (£7,000 September 1962), Newport County (July 1964).
Club honours: Blues: Fairs Cup runners-up 1961.
Jimmy Singer had an excellent strike record as a League player – 62 goals in a total of 138 games – but was never very popular with the fans, especially those at St Andrew's, despite his happy knack of being in the right place when chances appeared. He later owned a restaurant in Caerleon.

SISSONS, John Graham
Centre-half/full-back; Apps 106, Goals 0.
Born: Chester-le-Street, Co Durham, 20 May 1934.
Career: Kiveton Boys, Erdington Juniors,

Country Girl FC, BLUES (professional July 1954), Peterborough United (December 1962), Walsall (November 1964).
A dark haired, swarthy and honest worker, Sissons joined Blues prior to his National Service. After demob he settled into the reserve team as deputy to Trevor Smith, before finally taking over in the left-back position following George Allen's departure. A capable defender, if limited in his distribution, he played exactly 100 League games for Walsall and 68 for Posh.

SLATER, Frederick
Centre-forward; Apps 5, Goals 1.
Born: Burton upon Trent, 25 September 1925.
Career: Burton Albion, BLUES (professional November 1947), York City (June 1951), Corby Town (1952), Nuneaton Borough (1954).
A 'rough and tumble' striker, spotted in non-League football, After a year in the reserves Fred Slater was given his chance as Blues attempted to replace Cyril Trigg. Sadly after only ten minutes of his debut, Slater was stretchered off with a broken leg. He recovered before the end of the season but could not permanently depose Jimmy Dailey.

SLATER, William
Centre-forward; Apps 5, Goals 4.
Born: Birmingham, 1858. Deceased.
Career: Calthorpe, BLUES (September 1879), Brades Heath (1884).
A goalscoring star of the early 1880s, Billy Slater claimed Blues' first ever competitive goal – in the FA Cup-tie against Derby Town in 1879. He was also a useful cricketer, being a middle-order batsman and star bowler for the Small Heath Alliance CC.

SLEEUWENHOEK, John Cornelius ('Slogger' & 'Tulip')
Centre-half; Apps 29+3, Goals 0.
Born: Wednesfield, 26 February 1944. Died: Birmingham, July 1989.
Career: Wood End County and Wandsbridge Secondary Schools, Aston Villa (juniors, June 1959, professional February 1961), BLUES (£45,000 November 1967), Torquay United (loan March 1971), Oldham Athletic (July 1971 to May 1972). Retired with knee injury in July 1974 after a brief spell in the Cheshire County League. Played for Villa Old Stars (1970s) and later worked for Aston Villa on the lottery department.
Club honours: Aston Villa: Football League Cup runners-up 1963.
Representative honours: England (2 Under-23 caps, Youth caps, Schoolboy caps); Football League XI (1).

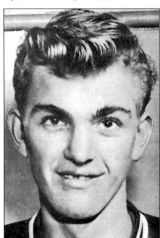

Son of a Dutch parachute instructor, Johnny Sleeuwenhoek was fed on cheese and stout as a lad to build him up, but late in his career had to fight the flab. At his peak this

blond defender was a solid performer who played 260 times for the Villa. Blues signed him in an attempt to boost their promotion chances but a troublesome knee curtailed his career at St Andrew's. He wore spectacles off the field and his son, Kris, was once a junior with both Wolves and Derby County. His League Cup runners-up prize came against Blues in the 1963 Final.

SMALL, Bryan
Full-back; Apps 3, Goals 0.
Born: Birmingham, 15 November 1971.
Career: Aston Villa (YTS July 1988, professional July 1990), BLUES (loan, September 1994).
Representative honours: England (8 Youth caps, 7 Under-21, 8 youth caps).
Bryan Small signed for Villa from the same junior club that produced Paul Tait and Matthew Fox A highly-rated youngster, he could not displace Earl Barratt or Steve Staunton at Villa Park and so was loaned out to Blues to give him some first-team action. After a useful debut he found it difficult to adjust to life in Division Two and by the end of his loan spell was out of the Blues team as well.

SMALL, Samuel John
Centre-forward; Apps 6, Goals 0.
Born: Birmingham, 15 May 1912. Died: Birmingham, 19 December 1993.
Career: Bromsgrove Rovers, BLUES (March 1934), West Ham United (January 1937), Brighton & Hove Albion (March 1948).
Club honours: West Ham United: League War Cup winners 1940.
An unselfish, hard working forward, Small was never able to force his way into regular contention with Blues but he proved a shrewd signing for West Ham, scoring 40 goals in 107 League games despite having his career disrupted by the war. He assumed a more creative role as his career wound down.

SMALLEY, Mark Anthony
Central defender; Apps 7, Goals 0.
Born: Newark, Notts, 2 January 1965.
Career: Nottingham Forest (apprentice June 1981, professional January 1983), BLUES (loan March 1986), Bristol Rovers (loan August 1986), Leyton Orient (February 1987), Mansfield Town (loan November 1989, signed for £15,000 January 1990), Maidstone United (May 1991), Kettering Town (cs 1992), Ilkeston Town (cs 1993).
Representative honours: England (1 Youth cap).
Smalley was a constructive centre-half who looked promising during his short spell at St Andrew's, but there was never any question of Blues signing him permanently.

SMITH, Andrew Walter
Centre-forward; Apps 59, Goals 34.
Born: Camberwell, London, April 1896. Died: March 1968.
Career: Camberwell & Southwark School, Langley Green Juniors, Crosswell's Brewery FC, BLUES (amateur August 1912, professional August 1914), Manchester City (guest 1914-18), West Bromwich Albion (£100 July 1919), Stoke (£1,500 March 1923), Wigan Borough, Bournemouth & Boscombe Athletic. Retired May 1925.
Club honours: West Bromwich Albion: Division One champions 1920, FA Charity Shield winners 1920 (2 goals scored v Spurs).
Andy Smith was a strong forward, well built, who could also perform well at centre-half. A good header of the ball, he became an even more effective force with the advent of Jack Hall. He was one of four Smiths on Blues' books in 1914, although no more than two ever played together in the same team. He scored 22 goals in 81 games for West Brom.

SMITH, Arthur R. ('Nipper')
Outside-left; Apps 52, Goals 4.
Born: Stourbridge, 1887. Deceased.
Career: Brierley Hill Alliance, QPR (1911), BLUES (June 1912), Brierley Hill Alliance (1914). Later secretary of Brierley Hill Alliance, retiring from office in May 1934.
Nipper Smith was a short, very fast winger who was a master of the early ball into the middle. He was a teacher at St Peter's College, Saltley, Birmingham, during his stay with Blues and later became a respected administrator in local non-League football.

SMITH, Austin
Centre-forward; Apps 2, Goals 2.
Born: Birmingham, 1865. Deceased.
Career: St Phillip's College, Saltley, Aston Unity, Walsall Town (1886), BLUES (August 1887), Bournville FC (May 1888).
Austin Smith was a prolific marksman with the knack of being able to score goals in twos and threes rather than in singles. He hit over 30 in various matches during 1887-88 but was then surprisingly released by the club. He emigrated in late 1888 for business reasons.

SMITH, Bernard
Left-back; Apps 12, Goals 0.
Born: Sileby, 1908. Deceased.
Career: Loughborough College, Loughborough Corinthians, BLUES (February 1932), Coventry City (August 1935). Retired 1939.
Club honours: Coventry City: Division Three South champions 1936.
A well built defender whose appearances were restricted due to the continued good form of Ned Barkas, Smith was little more than an average player with a solid tackle.

SMITH, David
Midfield/winger; Apps 40+4, Goals 3.
Born: Stonehouse, Gloucestershire. 29 March 1968.
Career: Coventry City (YTS June 1984, professional July 1986), AFC Bournemouth (loan January 1993), Dundee United (trial February 1993), BLUES (March 1993), West Bromwich Albion (£90,000 January 1994).
Representative honours: England (10 Under-21 caps).

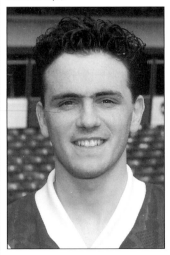

A good attacking midfielder who preferred to left flank, he scored 19 goals in 182 outings for Coventry with whom he won England Under-21 recognition.

SMITH, George
Left-half; Apps 1, Goals 0.
Born: Birmingham, 1868. Deceased.
Career: BLUES (season 1890-91).
He played only once in Blues' League side, at Sunderland in April 1891 when Ted Devey missed the train.

SMITH, George

Midfielder; Apps 41+4, Goals 0.
Born: Newcastle upon Tyne, 7 October 1945.
Career: Newcastle United (apprentice June 1961, professional September 1963), Barrow (March 1965), Portsmouth (May 1967), Middlesbrough (January 1969), BLUES (March 1971), Cardiff City (June 1973), Swansea City (May 1975), Hartlepool United (October 1977). Later manager of Gateshead, making a short return to playing before becoming coach at Queen's Park Rangers and later Doncaster Rovers.
Club honours: Blues: Division Two promotion 1972; Cardiff City: Welsh Cup winners 1974.

George Smith was a stocky, blond-haired bulldozer-type midfielder, able to perform no matter what the conditions, as was demonstrated by his brilliant display against Norwich in March 1972 on one of the most atrocious playing surfaces ever seen at St Andrew's. A boyhood fan of Newcastle, it was his greatest regret that he never made the first team during his spell at St James's Park. He once scored for Blues whilst he was a Middlesbrough player. In all he accumulated a grand total of 487 League appearances in his career.

SMITH, Gilbert

Right-back; Apps 14, Goals 0.
Born: Oldbury, 1869. Deceased.
Career: Causeway Green Villa, BLUES (1893), Berwick Rangers (Worcester) 1894).
The Oldbury area was certainly productive for Blues scouts in the Victorian era, and this cumbersome defender was recommended to the club by his friend, Fred Wheldon, and was given an early chance to show his worth when Teddy Jolly was considered too slow to play at full-back. Gilbert Smith was no better and by Christmas 1893, three months after his debut, he was in the reserves.

SMITH, John

Inside-left; Apps 6, Goals 1.
Born: Wednesfield, 1882. Deceased.
Career: Cannock, Stafford Road, Wolverhampton Wanderers (1902), BLUES (April 1906), Bristol Rovers (March 1907), Norwich City (May 1908), Luton Town (July 1909), Millwall Athletic (March 1911), Coventry City (May 1912).
John Smith was a short, stocky Black Countryman who had been a useful player at Molineux before joining Blues, with whom he struggled, finding it difficult to replace Arthur Mounteney, whose greater bulk was more suited to Blues' style of play at the time.

SMITH, Joseph

Right-back; Apps 50, Goals 0.
Born: Darby End, Dudley, 17 April 1890. Died: Royal Hospital, Wolverhampton, 9 June 1956.
Career: Halesowen Road Council School (Netherton), Netherton St Andrew's, Darby End Victoria, Cradley Heath St Luke's, West Bromwich Albion (professional May 1910), guested for Everton (1915-18) and Notts County (1917-18), BLUES (May 1926), Worcester City (player-manager May 1929-July 1932 when he retired).
Club honours: West Bromwich Albion: Division Two champions 1911, Division One champions 1920, FA Charity Shield winners 1920.
Representative honours: England (2 full caps, 1 Victory international, Junior international).
Right-back Joe Smith was a strategist, strong kicker and an excellent positional player, who amassed 471 appearances during his 16 years with West Brom before switching to St Andrew's, as cover for Womack and Jones. Despite his declining powers he continued to fill in at right-back effectively for a further three years. After leaving football he became a publican, taking the Red Lion (Darby End), and later worked at Lloyds Proving House, eventually becoming chief tester. A very well-respected local figure in the Netherton and Dudley area, he is Netherton's only international footballer.

SMITH, Joseph Enoch

Left-half; Apps 8, Goals 0.
Born: Barnard Castle, Co Durham, 1888. Deceased.
Career: Hickleton Main Colliery, BLUES (1912), Richmond FC (1915).
Former miner Joe Smith is the least known of the Smiths of 1914. He was apparently always at his best when defending, the press declaring that 'he held his opponents in check effectively but should show more discretion putting the ball forward'.

SMITH, Samuel James

Centre-forward; Apps 33, Goals 13.
Born: Pelsall, 7 September 1909.
Career: Pleck Old Boys, Walsall (trial 1927), Walsall LMS, BLUES (December 1930), Chelsea (July 1934), Norwich City (May 1935), Walsall (January 1936), Stourbridge (August 1936).
A dashing, tearaway striker who became an instant hit by scoring two goals on his debut for Blues at Aston Villa, he saw his career founder after leaving the Midlands, failing to make a single appearance for Chelsea and playing only once for Norwich.

SMITH, Stephen John

Goalkeeper; Apps 3, Goals 0.
Born: Lydney, Gloucestershire, 12 June 1957.
Career: Gloucester Boys, Cardiff City (associate schoolboy), BLUES (apprentice June 1973, professional July 1975), Bradford City (£5,000 March 1978), Crewe Alexandra (August 1982), Trowbridge Town (November 1983, manager January 1984).
Representative honours: England youth international.
Steve Smith was a reserve goalkeeper at St Andrew's who, if he was inconsistent and made some embarrassing awful mistakes, saved Kenny Dalglish's penalty in Blues' centenary match. He holds Bradford City's club record for most clean sheets in a season and made 105 League appearances for Bradford in his four-year spell at Valley Parade, following on with 54 for Crewe.

SMITH, Trevor

Centre-half; Apps 430, Goals 3.
Born: Brierley Hill, 13 April 1936.
Career: Quarry Bank Secondary Modern School, Brierley Hill & Sedgley Schoolboys (English Schools Trophy), BLUES (amateur

July 1951, professional April 1953), Walsall (£18,000 October 1964). Retired February 1966. Later a permit player in the Lichfield Sunday League (1967-68) and was manager of Mile Oak Rovers in 1970-71.
Club honours: Blues: Youth tournament winners (Switzerland) 1952, Division Two champions 1955, FA Cup runners-up 1956, Fairs Cup runners-up 1960, Football League Cup winners 1963.
Representative honours: England (2 full caps, 2 'B' caps, 15 Under-23 caps, Youth caps, Schoolboy caps); Football League XI (2).

Trevor Smith was a skinny defender when he played alongside the great Duncan Edwards in the Brierley Hill Schools side, but thereafter he developed into a muscular centre-half weighing 13st 7lb. A commanding figure in the number-five shirt, Smith skippered Blues many times and put in several fine performances in the heart of the defence. He made his Blues debut at the age of 17 and conceded an own goal in his first match. When Billy Wright retired in 1959 it was Smith who succeeded him in the England team. He broke down shortly after leaving St Andrew's for Walsall and there were rumours that Blues had 'cheated' their neighbours in allowing an injured player to join the ranks at Fellows Park. Smith became a licensee in Tamworth and thereafter was manager of Thresher's wine store in the Bull Ring Shopping Centre, Birmingham, before moving in the same line to Dagenham, Essex.

SMITH, Walter

Inside-forward; Apps 26, Goals 6.
Born: Bootle, 1885. Deceased.
Career: Liverpool (trial), Southend United, Chester, Bury (November 1911), BLUES (April 1914), Altrincham (1916).
This experienced, ball playing inside-forward was signed by Blues to create the chances for main strikers, Andy Smith and Jack Hall. He eventually lost out, however, to the more talented Jimmy Windridge for this role, and had to be content with reserve-team football with only an occasional first-team outing coming his way, and then mainly due to injuries received by other forwards.

SMITH, William Alfred

Inside-right; Apps 17, Goals 5.
Born: West Bromwich, April 1882. Deceased.
Career: West Bromwich Baptists, Worcester City, West Bromwich Albion (1902), Brierley Hill Alliance (May 1905), Coventry City (1907), BLUES (1908), Coventry City (1909), Nuneaton Town (1912), Coventry City (September 1913).
Billy Smith was another excellent maker of chances, but a player who was also capable of scoring his fair share of goals. He formed a useful wing partnership with Benny Green, but eventually he lost his place in

the first team when the skilful Jack Wilcox joined the ranks at St Andrew's.

SMITH, William Henry

Wing-half/inside-forward; Apps 62, Goals 23.
Born: Plymouth, 7 September 1926.
Career: Royal Marines, Plymouth United (1944), Plymouth Argyle (August 1945), Reading (August 1947), Northampton Town (July 1948), BLUES (February 1950), Blackburn Rovers (December 1952), Accrington Stanley (player-coach July 1960-62, caretaker manager December 1961 - March 1962).
This Billy Smith had a good career in the game, totalling 237 League appearances and scoring 42 goals, before drifting out of the top grade in 1962 when Accrington Stanley lost their Football League status. He played Rugby Union at school but took up soccer after the war. He began as a utility forward but reverted to the wing-half berth after leaving St Andrew's.

SMITHIES, George Herbert

Centre-forward; Apps 1, Goals 0.
Born: Ribchester, 1907. Deceased.
Career: Bangor College, Northern Nomads, Preston North End (1929), BLUES (1931), Darley Dale FC (1932), Measham Motors.
Representative honours: England (Amateur caps).
George Smithies was a late arrival into League football after a successful amateur career whilst he was busy completing his teaching studies. Despite being somewhat undersized for a striker (5ft 8in), he met with early success at Deepdale with Preston North End, top-scoring in his debut season. Thereafter, however, his career went into decline, leading to an early return to non-League action.

SOUTHALL, George ('Sconnie')

Outside-left; Apps 14, Goals 0.
Born: Cradley Heath, 1880. Deceased.
Career: Quarry Bank Celtic, Halesowen Royal, Redditch Excelsior, Stourbridge, BLUES (December 1905), Halesowen (August 1907), Dudley Town, Lye Town.
The hero of Stourbridge fans and for several seasons one of the stars in the Birmingham League, at local non-League level George Southall looked quite brilliant both as a chance-maker and goal-taker, but he was unable to reproduce this form with Blues. After leaving St Andrew's, he again did well on the non-League scene, especially with Halesowen.

SOUTHAM, James Henry

Left-back; Apps 3, Goals 0.
Born: Willenhall, 19 August 1917. Died: Birmingham, 1982.
Career: Stowheath Junior & Senior Schools, Shornhill Recreational Centre FC, West Bromwich Albion (amateur March 1939, professional November 1942), Newport County (£300 May 1946), BLUES (November 1946), Northampton Town (June 1949). Retired May 1955, to become assistant trainer with Walsall. Guested for Aberaman, Arsenal, Colchester United, Ipswich Town and Newport County during World War Two.
A steady, reliable full-back who was rarely given a look-in due to the consistency of the Green-Jennings combination, Southam later established himself at Northampton for whom he made 144 League appearances before hanging up his boots. He was denied a testimonial match with the Cobblers because they 'couldn't find time to fit one in'.

SPEEDIE, David Robert

Striker; Apps 12, Goals 2.
Born: Glenrothes, 20 February 1960.
Career: Adwick School, Barnsley (apprentice August 1977, professional

October 1978), Darlington (£5,000 June 1980), Chelsea (£70,000 June 1982), Coventry City (£780,000 July 1987), Liverpool (£675,000 February 1991), Blackburn Rovers (£450,000 August 1991), Southampton (£400,000 July 1992), BLUES (loan October 1992), West Bromwich Albion (loan January 1993), West Ham United (loan March 1993), Leicester City (free transfer July 1993). Forced to retire January 1995 and joined coaching staff at Filbert Street.

Club honours: Chelsea: Division Two champions 1984, Full Members' Cup winners 1986; Blackburn Rovers: Division Two promotion 1992; Leicester City: Division One promotion 1994.

Representative honours: Scotland (10 full caps, 1 Under-21 cap).

David Speedie was one of the game's characters – very skilful, occasionally brilliant, sometimes very fiery. He had scored 175 goals in 611 senior games up to 1994 when injury caused him to miss out on Leicester's return to the top flight.

SPELLER, Frederick
Full-back; Apps 93, Goals 0.
Born: Marlow, 1864. Died: Birmingham, 1940.
Career: Great Marlow FC, BLUES (1888). Retired May 1894.
Not the muscular type one associates with Victorian full-backs but a player who preferred to pass the ball to his half-backs, Speller was the undisputed first-choice left-back until a broken leg sustained against Darwen in October 1892 effectively ended his career. He attempted a comeback in late 1893 but called it a day at the end of that season.

SPRAKE, Gareth
Goalkeeper; Apps 22+2, Goals 0.
Born: Swansea, 3 April 1945.
Career: Llansamlet School, Leeds United (apprentice June 1960, professional May 1962), BLUES (£100,000 October 1973). Retired through ill health 1975.
Club honours: Leeds United: Division Two champions 1964, Division One champions 1969, FA Cup runners-up 1965, 1970, Football League Cup winners 1968, Fairs Cup winners 1968, 1971, runners-up 1967, FA Charity Shield winners 1969.
Representative honours: Wales (37 full caps, 5 Under-23 caps, Schoolboy caps).

Gary Sprake was a well-built goalkeeper who made a big impression whilst still a youngster culminating in an international debut at the age of 18 years and seven

months, the youngest Welsh goalkeeper ever. He continued to star for Leeds, winning domestic and European honours under Don Revie's managership. At his best Sprake was a spectacular, athletic 'keeper, capable of pulling off seemingly impossible saves, but a series of well publicised errors led to him becoming something of a joke among opposition fans. He had been dropped by Leeds and was going through a bad patch when Blues signed him and he soon showed his new club both aspects of his game, saving a penalty on his debut and scoring an own-goal in his next match. Keeping behind the Blues defence in the mid-1970s was not the ideal way of rebuilding one's confidence and Sprake struggled before succumbing to a chest virus. He later worked as a local government official in Solihull.

SPRIGG, Charles
Outside-left; Apps 16, Goals 0.
Born: Smethwick, 1889. Deceased.
Career: Smethwick Centaur, Bilston United, BLUES (November 1912), Redditch (1913), BLUES (1914), Moor Green (1915).
Sprigg had two spells with Blues but never really looked the part, although he did reasonably well in the Birmingham League. He was the first active Blues player to enlist during World War One, joining the Royal Field Artillery in July 1915.

SPROSON, Philip Jesse
Centre-half; Apps 16, Goals 1.
Born: Trent Vale, Stoke-on-Trent, 13 October 1959.
Career: Port Vale (apprentice 1975, professional December 1977). Retired through injury May 1989, BLUES (£50,000 August 1989). Retired again September 1990, but has since played for Stafford Rangers and Northwich Victoria.
Phil Sproson is a member of a family that has been involved with Port Vale for many years and for whom his uncle Roy holds the club appearance record. Phil was a solid, no-nonsense pivot and had worn the centre-half shirt for 11 years until injury ruined his career. Doctors advised him to retire but after a short respite he tried to get back into League soccer and Blues were ordered to pay Port Vale £50,000 for his services in lieu of insurance money. At St Andrew's he looked slow and overweight but remained in the team until further knee trouble struck him down again.

SPROSTON, Neil Robert
Centre-forward; Apps 0+1, Goals 0.
Born: Dudley, 20 November 1970.
Career: BLUES (YTS June 1986, professional July 1988), Alvechurch (August 1990), Armitage 90 (November 1990), Oldswinford (August 1991), Dudley Town (1992), Gornal Sports, Lye Town (1993-94).
In the absence of Kennedy, Rees and Whitton, this powerfully built youngster was called up for his League debut a month before his 17th birthday. Perhaps not surprisingly he looked overawed by the occasion and things were not made easier when he received a head wound which required stitches. On his return to the youth team he was shuffled around from attack to defence before settling into a midfield role, prior to his release.

SQUIRES, Barrie
Outside-left; Apps 1, Goals 0.
Born: Sparkhill, Birmingham, 29 July, 1931.
Career: Golden Hillock Road School, BSA Air Training Cadets, Wycombe Wanderers (amateur), Portsmouth (trial April 1952), Bristol City (trial July 1952), BLUES (professional May 1953), Bradford City (June 1954), Yeovil Town (July 1955).

This young ex-airman eventually got his chance of League action with his fourth club. He never really had a look-in with Blues due to the consistency of Alex Govan and wasn't too successful either at Bradford, making only nine appearances for the Bantams.

STAINTON, Ronald George ('Mick')
Left-back; Apps 1, Goals 0.
Born: Bournville, Birmingham, 1909.
Career: Kings Norton Schools, Bournville, BLUES (August 1927), Worcester City (July 1932), Shirley Town (1934).
Representative honours: England (1 Schools cap).
A stocky full-back of great loyalty, Mick Stainton spent five seasons playing in Blues' reserve team without ever looking likely to make the first team.

STANLEY, Alfred ('Eddy')
Forward; Apps 30, Goals 17.
Born: Edgbaston, Birmingham, 1860.
Died: Birmingham c.1930.
Career: Calthorpe, BLUES (September 1881). Retired 1891 through injury.
A brilliant dribbler who was the idol of the Blues fans throughout his career, Stanley was capable of playing in the all forward positions but was most comfortable at inside-right. Universally known as 'Eddy,' he was frequently referred to as just that in team lists.

STANLEY, Wilson
Outside-right; Apps 1, Goals 0.
Born: Hockley, Birmingham, 1863. Deceased.
Career: Hockley Belmont, BLUES (1886), Oldbury Broadwell (1887), Warwick County (1888).
The younger brother of 'Eddy', Wilson was a capable winger, fast and tricky with a good scoring record. He had to share that position with Arthur Jones, but although near the end of his career, was still good enough to hold down the place.

STANTON, Arthur
Right-back; Apps 6, Goals 0.
Born: Bloxwich, 1892. Deceased.
Career: Bloxwich Strollers, BLUES (April 1913), Oldbury (1918).
A solid defender who understudied both full-backs roles capably for two seasons. Although somewhat limited with a lack of pace, he had a powerful kick and a strong tackle.

STARBUCK, Philip Michael
Forward; Apps 3, Goals 0.
Born: Nottingham, 24 November 1968.
Career: Nottingham Forest (apprentice June 1984, professional August 1986), BLUES (loan March 1988), Hereford United (loan February 1990), Blackburn Rovers (loan September 1990), Huddersfield Town (August 1991), Sheffield United (loan October 1994, full transfer January 1995).
Club honours: Huddersfield Town: Autoglass Trophy runners-up 1994.
Starbuck was one of several youngsters Forest allowed to be loaned out to gain experience. He signed for Blues when they were struggling in the lower reaches of Division Two and although impressing with his speed and ball control, he seemed to lack the killer touch in front of goal.

STEEL, William Gilbert
Left-back; Apps 91, Goals 0.
Born: Blantyre, Scotland, 6 February 1908.
Career: Bridgtown Waverley, St Johnstone (1926), Liverpool (August 1931), BLUES (£5,000 March 1935), Derby County (February 1939-40), Airdrieonians (trainer April 1950, manager April 1954), Third Lanark (manager January 1963-June 1964).
Billy Steel was a footballing full-back who

received more than his fair share of criticism during his early days at St Andrew's for his reluctance to rely on the 'big boot'. He had, however, succeeded in winning over most of his hecklers by the time he left Blues. His move to Derby but his career was curtailed by World War Two. Steel later qualified as a masseur and assisted the Scottish national team in this capacity during the 1950s.

STEVENSON, William Byron
Defender; Apps 85+6, Goals 3.
Born: Llanelli, 7 September 1956.
Career: Leeds United (apprentice, April 1972, professional September 1973), BLUES (March 1982 in exchange for Frank Worthington), Bristol Rovers (July 1985), Garforth Miners Welfare (1988, later manager to 1990).
Representative honours: Wales (15 full caps, 3 Under-21 caps, Youth caps).
Leeds were grooming this tall defender to take over from Norman Hunter, but circumstances meant that he found himself playing at left-back more often than not. He was never an automatic choice at Elland Road, although he was regularly called up for duty with Wales until he was sent off for violent conduct, against Turkey in November 1979, and was banned from international football for four years. In 1982 he became Ron Saunders' first signing and fitted nicely into the heart of the Blues' defence, using his anticipatory skills to good effect. He later switched to midfield where his form became patchy, his lack of pace being sometimes exploited. He took charge of the Angel Hotel, Rothwell, Yorkshire after retiring from football.

STEWART, John ('Jackie') G.
Outside-right; Apps 218, Goals 55.
Born: Lochgelly, Fife, 4 September 1921.
Career: Lochgelly Welfare, Donibristle Youth Club, Raith Rovers (August 1939), BLUES (January 1948), Raith Rovers (February 1955). Later became trainer at Stark's Park, and remained in football until 1963 before going into business in Cowdenbeath.
Club honours: Blues: Division Two champions 1948.
Early in 1948 Blues manager Harry Storer announced that he was trying to sign a Scottish winger who would 'enable the team to gain promotion'. A week later he returned from Fife with all-action bag of tricks, Jackie Stewart. Fast, direct and a big favourite with the St Andrew's fans, Stewart was only 5ft 5in tall but he was tough and feared no one. A former miner, he possessed a terrific shot and once scored four goals in a match against Manchester City in September 1948. He returned to Scotland after suffering injury problems.

STOKER, Lewis
Right-half; Apps 246, Goals 2.
Born: Wheatley Hill, Co Durham, 31

March 1910. Died: Birmingham, May 1979.
Career: Bearpark School, Brandon Juniors, Esh Winning Juniors, Bearpark FC, West Stanley, BLUES (trial June 1930, professional September 1930), Nottingham Forest (May 1938). Retired during World War Two.
Representative honours: England (3 full caps); Football League XI (1).
Lew Stoker was an excellent 'feeder of the attack', a marvellously effective player who enjoyed to drive forward from centre-field whenever he could, often trying a shot at goal. After retiring he worked as a chargehand at Wimbush's Bakery, just around the corner from St Andrew's. His younger brother, Bob Stoker, played for Bolton and Huddersfield during the 1930s.

STOKES, Frank
Full-back; Apps 213, Goals 1.
Born: Burslem, Stoke, 7 June 1881. Died: 1945.
Career: Burslem Park Boys, Burslem Port Vale, Reading, BLUES (October 1903). Retired August 1910 following serious knee injury.
Representative honours: England trialist 1902, 1903, 1905, 1906.

Frank Stokes was a magnificent full-back, all muscle, yet extremely mobile and safe under pressure. He and his partner Glover were perhaps the best pair of full-backs ever to play together for Blues. The reliable Stokes had the bitter experience of not being selected for his own benefit match (he was in the reserves that day). His only goal for Blues was a 25-yard crackerjack, fired in left-footed against Notts County in October 1906. He was easily recognisable on the pitch by the ungainly way he carried his arms.

STORER, Stuart John
Outside-right; Apps 7+3, Goals 0.
Born: Harborough Magna, 16 January 1967.
Career: Rugby Schools, Wolverhampton Wanderers (associate schoolboy), Mansfield Town (YTS August 1983), VS Rugby (March 1984), BLUES (apprentice June 1984, professional January 1985), Everton (£200,000 March 1987), Wigan Athletic (loan August 1987), Bolton Wanderers (December 1987, signed permanently January 1988), Exeter City (March 1993).
Club honours: Bolton Wanderers: Sherpa Van Trophy winners 1989.
Stuart Storer was a steady player during his stay with Blues and showed himself capable of winning a game on his own, especially in the reserves, but rarely reproduced this form in the first team. His transfer to Everton (with Wayne Clarke)

was highly controversial. The inflated valuation of Storer was looked upon by Wolves as a way of denying them money for Clarke (they were entitled to 50 per cent of any profit Blues made on him). Blues, however, apparently decided that it was the only way of getting some of the money Wolves had not paid them for Joe Gallagher.

STUBBS, Robin Gregory
Centre-forward; Apps 70, Goals 20.
Born: Quinton, 22 April 1941.
Career: Castle Road Primary School, Oldbury Grammar School, Oldbury Boys, BLUES (amateur June 1956, professional April 1958), Torquay United (August 1963), Bristol Rovers (July 1969), Torquay United (February 1972). Retired 1974.

Robin Stubbs was a slim, fair-haired goalscorer who was tipped for great things at St Andrew's but never quite had the temperament to sustain his position. Nevertheless he was a player Blues should never have sold, for he went on to become a prolific scorer after leaving St Andrew's, netting 122 League goals in 238 games in his two spells with Torquay and 32 in 93 outings for Bristol Rovers. He made the national newspapers when his wife, Anthea Redfern, a television personality, left him to marry comedian Bruce Forsyth. He now works as a salesman in Torquay.

STURRIDGE, Simon Andrew ('Studger')
Forward; Apps 161+25, Goals 38.
Born: Birmingham, 9 December 1969.
Career: William Cowper and Duddeston Manor and St George's Schools (Birmingham), BLUES (YTS June 1985, professional July 1988), Stoke City (September 1993).
Club honours: Blues: Leyland DAF Cup winners 1991.
A terrific marksman in the Birmingham

Boys League, Simon Sturridge followed his elder brother, Michael, to St Andrew's. His goalscoring exploits continued at youth level, leading to an early call-up for the first team. His speed, ball-control and alertness in the box, combined to make him a firm favourite with the fans. Sturridge netted the vital goal at Brentford which sealed Blues' return to Wembley for the first time in 35 years, and he then scored the opening goal in that 1991 Leyland DAF Cup Final against Tranmere. His younger brother Dean plays for Derby County and was on loan to Torquay in 1994-95.

STYLES, Arthur ('Archie')
Left-back; Apps 79+3, Goals 4.
Born: Liverpool, 3 September 1949.
Career: Liverpool Boys, Everton (apprentice August 1965, professional August 1967), BLUES (February 1974 in part exchange for Bob Latchford), Peterborough United (July 1978), Portsmouth (July 1979).
Representative honours: England (Youth caps, Schoolboy caps).
Styles looked a good prospect at Goodison Park but his career stagnated as he was restricted to only 23 appearances in seven years with Everton. He came to Blues as a makeweight in the Latchford deal but had a few problems establishing himself in the side. His major asset was his speed off the mark and he was usually at his best when going forward, but was not very strong in the tackle.

SUMMERFIELD, Kevin J.
Forward; Apps 4+4, Goals 2.
Born: Walsall, 7 January 1959.
Career: Alma Street & Joseph Leckie Schools (Walsall), Walsall Town Boys, West Bromwich Albion (apprentice July 1975, professional January 1977), BLUES (free transfer May 1982), Walsall (loan December 1982, signed permanently on free transfer February 1983), Cardiff City (free transfer July 1984), Plymouth Argyle (£5,000 December 1984), Exeter City (loan March 1990), Shrewsbury Town (October 1990).
Club honours: West Bromwich Albion: FA Youth Cup winners 1976; Shrewsbury Town: Division Three champions 1994.
Representative honours: England (Youth caps).
A reserve striker at West Brom, Kevin Summerfield still achieved a respectable scoring record of five goals in 13 appearances when called into the first team. He came to Blues but failed to establish himself in the senior side and went on loan to Walsall. That was the signal for a fairytale: when the teams were drawn together in the FA Cup, Summerfield was recalled to St Andrew's and after coming on as a substitute he scored the winning goal. In later years he took up a midfield role.

SUMMERILL, Philip Ernest
Forward; Apps 118+13, Goals 52.
Born: Erdington, 20 November 1947.
Career: King's Rise School, Aston Boys, BLUES (apprentice June 1963, professional December 1964), Huddersfield Town (January 1973), Millwall (November 1974), Wimbledon (September 1977), Highgate United (May 1979), Atherstone Town, Redditch United, Highgate United to 1985.
Club honours: Blues: Division Two promotion 1972.
Representative honours: England (Youth caps).
Phil Summerill was a tall, spindly striker who started off as a winger and after moving into the centre became an instant success. He had three excellent seasons from 1968-71 at St Andrew's when he scored 52 goals in 118 games, some of his efforts being quite spectacular. During a fine career he netted 81 goals in 289

appearances. After his second spell with Highgate United he took up coaching at a youth centre in Sparkhill, Birmingham, which he did between working as a painter and decorator. In later years he worked for the City Council's Football Development and Coaching Department, and is a regular visitor to St Andrew's.

SUMMERS, Lawrence A.
Left-back/wing-half; Apps 2, Goals 0.
Born: Birmingham, 1859. Died: Birmingham, 1940.
Career: The Grove, BLUES (1880), Hockley Hill FC (1882).
After an impressive display for Blues against Derby Town in the FA Cup in November 1881, Summers held his place in the side, until injuries to the James brothers led to him switching to the half-back line, a role which did not suit him. When the James men returned he found that the Gesseys had settled in at full-back and therefore he was allowed to leave the club.

SYKES, E.Albert A.
Left-half; Apps 1, Goals 0.
Born: Maltby Victory, Maltby, Yorkshire, 1900. Deceased.
Career: Maltby Miners' Welfare, Maltby Town, BLUES (August 1924), Brighton & Hove Albion (May 1926), Lincoln City (June 1928), Peterborough & Fletton United (cs 1931), Luton Town, Grantham (1932-33).
Sykes was a chunky former miner whose play was in the Percy Barton mould and with Barton and Dickie Dale on the books at the same time he was regarded as surplus to requirements and was not given the chance to show off his talents.

SYKES, Ernest Arthur
Right-back; Apps 10, Goals 0.
Born: Temple Normanton, 1912.
Career: Temple Normanton Old Boys, Sutton Town, BLUES (March 1936), Cardiff City (June 1939). Retired 1944.
Ernie Sykes was a tall, powerful defender who was a useful squad player. Frustrated by the lack of first-team action he moved to South Wales but after he had made only three appearances for Cardiff, his career was curtailed by World War Two.

SYKES, John ('Jack') George
Left-back; Apps 34, Goals 0.
Born: Wombwell, Yorkshire, 1915.
Career: Wombwell FC, BLUES (August 1932), Millwall (May 1937).
Jack Sykes was a defensive half-back who spent three years in Blues' reserves before making his League debut. He was an immediate success with his strong-running and clever covering but a loss of form late in 1936 led to him being dropped. He was rarely selected again and left at the end of the season. Later he was a licensee at the Park Tavern, Dudley Road, Birmingham.

TAIT, Paul Ronald
Forward/midfield; Apps 121+27, Goals 15.
Born: Sutton Coldfield, 31 July 1971.
Career: Hodge Hill Junior and Byng Kendrick Senior Schools, Hurley Colts, BLUES (YTS June 1987, professional August 1988), Millwall (loan February 1994), Bolton Wanderers (trial July 1994).
Club honour: Blues: Second Division champions 1995, Auto Windscreens Shield winners 1995.

Few people could look less like a professional footballer than the pale-faced, frail Paul Tait. Looks can deceive, however, and Tait possesses excellent ball skills and was a prolific scorer in youth-team football. Later encouraged to play in midfield, he developed a telling pass and the ability to ghost past an opponent in the penalty area. A serious injury received against Leyton Orient in January 1991 led to him being fitted with a synthetic knee ligament and his career was in jeopardy, but he kept fighting back. In the Auto Windscreens Shield Final he came on as substitute and scored the winner, a feat marred by his controversial celebration of the goal, and a fortnight later, also as a substitute, scored the Blues' second goal at Huddersfield which effectively sealed the Second Division championship.

TARANTINI, Alberto Cesar
Full-back/centre-half; Apps 24, Goals 1.
Born: Buenos Aires, Argentina, 3 December 1955.
Career: Boca Juniors (Argentina), BLUES (£295,000 October 1978), Talleres Cordoba (Spain) (May 1979), River Plate (Argentina) (1980), Bastia (Corsica), Toulouse (France), Urania Geneva (Switzerland) (1988), Platense (Argentina) (1989).
Representative honours: Argentina (59 full caps, World Cup winners 1978).
On 25 June 1978, Alberto Tarantini, a stylish, attacking full-back, proudly showed off his World Cup winners' medal after Argentina had beaten Holland in the Final in Buenos Aires. Four months later he made his Football League debut for Blues at Tottenham when he lined up opposite his Argentinian colleague Ossie Ardiles, with Ricardo Villa watching from the stand. He took time to settle into the team and once even jumped into the crowd to deal with a heckler. After meeting with limited success in Europe and he returned home when Urania were relegated into Swiss non-League football in 1989. He now runs coaching schools for youngsters in Argentina.

TATTON, Joseph
Centre-half; Apps 1, Goals 0.
Born: Handsworth, Birmingham, 1859. Died: Birmingham, 1933.
Career: St Mark's FC, BLUES (1880), Nechells (1882), Aston Manor. Became a director of BLUES in 1898.
Tatton was a solid, no-nonsense pivot, who

was probably more successful as a committee man than he was a footballer. He helped mastermind the signing of Bob McRoberts and several other players around the turn of the century. He opened the batting for the Small Heath Alliance cricket team but his top score was only five runs. His brother Harry was also associated with Blues.

TAYLOR, Brian Joseph
Outside-left; Apps 67, Goals 9.
Born: Walsall, 24 March 1937.
Career: Walsall (amateur July 1952, professional September 1954), BLUES (£10,000 plus Jimmy Cochrane, June 1958), Rotherham United (October 1961), Shrewsbury Town (August 1963), Port Vale (August 1965), Barnsley (June 1967), Kidderminster Harriers (July 1968), Bromsgrove Rovers (1970).
A sprightly winger with terrific pace and ability, Brian Taylor's career received a major setback when he fractured his leg playing against Union St Gilloise in the Fairs Cup semi-final. He returned to action a year later, but by then had lost a lot of the speed which had characterised his game. Altogether he scored 43 goals in 316 League appearances (19 in 75 for Walsall).

TAYLOR, Gordon
Outside-right or left; Apps 189+14, Goals 10.
Born: Ashton-under-Lyne, 28 December 1944.
Career: Mossley Road County Primary School, Ashton-under-Lyne Grammar School, Curzon Ashton FC (1959-60), Bolton Wanderers (amateur June 1960, professional January 1962), BLUES (£18,000 December 1970), Blackburn Rovers (March 1976), Vancouver Whitecaps (NASL) (loan June-August 1977), Bury (June 1978). Retired in 1980 and became secretary of the PFA having served on the committee while a player at Bury.
Club honours: Blues: Division Two promotion 1972.

Gordon Taylor was an orthodox winger, quick, with good skills, who was mainly used on the right flank. His direct, all-action style and his ability to deliver high quality crosses made him a favourite with the Blues fans. One of several graduates to play for Blues, Taylor possesses a BSc in Economics, gained through part-time studies at Bolton Technical College. He made 622 League appearances in a career which, by coincidence, saw him serve with four clubs whose names all began with the letter 'B'. He is now chief executive of the players' union and one of the most influential men in football.

TAYLOR, Joseph
Left-back; Apps 3, Goals 0.
Born: Aston, Birmingham, 1857. Died: Sutton 1950.
Career: Britannia Victoria, Aston Shakespeare, Witton White Star, Hockley Belmont (1880), BLUES (August 1881), Brookvale (1884).
Joe Taylor was a heavily-built defender whose initial spell in the first team coincided with Elliman's move forward. He later linked up with Elliman to form a fine partnership.

TAYLOR, William
Utility; Apps 4, Goals 1.
Born: Smethwick, 1869. Deceased.
Career: Langley Green Victoria, BLUES (1891), Quinton (1892).
Bill Taylor was another friend of Fred Wheldon who recommended him to Blues, but who the club didn't know where to play. He was tried on both wings, at right-back and in two half-back positions before he was released.

TAYLOR-SMITH, Dr Ian L. (also known as Ian Smith)
Centre-forward; Apps 0+2, Goals 0.
Born: Edinburgh, 2 April 1952.
Career: Queen's Park (amateur 1969-70), BLUES (semi-professional March 1975), Heart of Midlothian (August 1977), Queen of the South (1979), Bromsgrove Rovers (1984). Played also for WBA All Stars (1982-87). Retired and became a qualified doctor of medicine.
A big, strong player who scored regularly for Blues in reserve-team soccer and always looked a good prospect. He was, however, unwilling to commit himself to being a full-time footballer as he always regarded a medical career as his chief priority. He spent some time working at the Queen Elizabeth Medical Centre in Birmingham and later at a maternity clinic in Barbados.

TEBBS, James T.
Outside-left; Apps 4, Goals 1.
Born: Melton Mowbray, May 1878. Deceased.
Career: Loughborough Town, BLUES (1900), Leicester United (1902).
Jimmy Tebbs was Loughborough Town's top-scorer in their last season in the Football League (four goals out of 18 scored by the club), but with Sid Wharton showing outstanding form, he was forced to switch to the right to get a game with Blues. He failed to impress and his stay with the club was restricted chiefly to Birmingham League action.

TEWKESBURY, Kenneth Cyril
Goalkeeper; Apps 5, Goals 0.
Born: Brighton, 10 April 1909. Died: 20 November 1970.
Career: Birmingham University, BLUES (amateur October 1929), Aston Villa (December 1931), Notts County (1932), Aston Villa (professional January 1933), Bradford (July 1935), Walsall (May 1936). Retired August 1939
Representative honours: England (6 Amateur caps).
Tewkesbury joined Blues whilst studying for his BSc at Birmingham University. A quiet, bespectacled man, he was not the obvious choice as a goalkeeper but at 6ft 3in and 12st he possessed the necessary physical attributes. Despite poor eyesight he still proved to be a capable 'keeper but he resisted all efforts to sign professional until 1933. He married the daughter of Blues director, W.H.Bull and worked for many years in Birmingham's Jewellery Quarter.

TEYCHENNE, Victor
Half-back; Apps 2, Goals 0.
Born: Wednesbury, July 1859. Died: West Bromwich, 1934.

Career: Wednesbury Town, Wednesbury Old Athletic, BLUES (1880), Smethwick Centaur (1882), Wednesbury Swifts.
Teychenne was a tough Black Countryman who usually played at centre-half, although the club sometimes lined up with two half-backs and six forwards, and therefore his role was not always easy to define. He kept wicket with great success for Small Heath Alliance CC and once he took off his pads and took four wickets. He was also a sprinter for Small Heath AC, of which he was a founder member.

THIRLAWAY, William J.
Outside-left; Apps 23, Goals 1.
Born: New Washington, Co Durham, 1 October 1896. Died: Sunderland, 1983.
Career: Usworth Colliery, West Ham United (1921), Southend United (June 1924), Luton Town (May 1925), South Shields (1925), BLUES (May 1926), Cardiff City (March 1927), Tunbridge Wells Rangers (1930), Washington Colliery (1932). Retired 1934.
Club honours: Cardiff City: Welsh Cup winners 1928, runners-up 1929.
Thirlaway was a former miner who had a rapid rise to West Ham's first team. There followed a dramatic loss of form, however, and for two years he was out in the cold. He then travelled around the League, apparently unable to settle in any one place. At Blues it was the same story and after a good start he again faded badly. Only at Cardiff did he manage any sort of consistency and there he was unfortunate enough to miss the 1927 FA Cup Final because he was Cup-tied (whilst at Blues). Hardly the ideal build for a winger, being short and stocky, yet on his day he was a great crowd-pleaser.

THOMAS, Martin Richard
Goalkeeper; Apps 176, Goals 0.
Born: Senghenydd, Wales, 28 November 1959.
Career: St Helen's and Cardinal Newman Schools, Bristol Rovers (apprentice June 1975, professional September 1977), Cardiff City (loan July-September 1982), Southend United (loan February-March 1983), Newcastle United (loan March 1983, signed for £35,000 July 1983), Middlesbrough (loan October 1984), BLUES (£75,000 October 1988), Cheltenham Town (August 1993).
Club honours: Blues: Leyland DAF Cup winners 1991.
Representative honours: Wales (1 full cap, 2 Under-21 caps, Youth cap).

Thomas was an erratic but sometimes brilliant 'keeper who always seemed more comfortable making reaction saves rather than taking crosses. His penalty saves against Swansea City in 1991 were a major contribution in Blues' Leyland DAF Cup success. He has also been responsible for one of the most unusual goals ever scored at St Andrew's, when, against Shrewsbury

Town in March 1989, he caught the ball and then stepped back over his own line with it. He made over 400 League appearances.

THOMPSON, Horace
Outside-left; Apps 1, Goals 0.
Born: Birmingham: 1900.
Career: BLUES (August 1922 to May 1923).
Horace Thompson was a little known winger who made only one League appearance for Blues, against Oldham on 3 February 1923. In some reports he is mistaken for Len Thompson, the former Swansea player. Described as 'a youngster who has been doing well in the reserves', he was freed at the end of the season.

THOMPSON, Leonard
Inside-left; Apps 2, Goals 0.
Born: Sheffield, 18 February 1901. Deceased.
Career: Hallam FC, Barnsley (amateur 1917), BLUES (1918), Swansea Town (1922), Arsenal (March 1928), Crystal Palace (June 1933). Retired 1934. Later re-instated as an amateur and assisted Islington Corinthians. Also had a spell as Tottenham Hotspur's reserve-team manager.
Len Thompson did well as a winger during the latter part of the war but met with greater success when he switched inside. He earned a reputation as a penalty-taker, but later in his career he was dogged by injuries.

THOMPSON, Thomas
Outside-left; Apps 1, Goals 0.
Born: Smethwick, 1879. Died: Birmingham, 1939.
Career: Nettlefolds FC, BLUES (1902), Oldbury Town (1903).
With Sid Wharton nearing the end of his career, Blues were desperate for a new left winger and they went for this speedy performer who had been playing for the works team of a well-known local factory. The local press were far from impressed, however, claiming that Thompson would be lucky ever to play in the League; they were almost right, for he was released after only one game.

THOMSON, Robert Anthony
Full-back; Apps 69, Goals 0.
Born: Smethwick, 5 December 1943.
Career: Lyndon High School, Wolverhampton Wanderers (apprentice June 1959, professional July 1961), BLUES (£40,000 March 1969), Walsall (loan November-December 1971), Luton Town (July 1972), Hartford Bicentennials (NASL) (April

1976), Port Vale (October 1976), Connecticut Bicentennials (NASL) (player-coach April 1977), Memphis Rogues

(NASL) (March 1979), Stafford Rangers (player-manager August 1979), brief spells with Brewood, Solihull Borough and Tipton Town. Retired May 1987.
Club honours: Wolverhampton Wanderers: FA Youth Cup runners-up 1962.
Representative honours: England (8 full caps, 15 Under-23 caps); Football League XI (4).
All the local Midland clubs tried to sign this elegant, speedy full-back who had starred in schoolboy football. Wolves won the chase and Thomson quickly developed into an international player, gaining all his caps before he was 22, after which he suffered a loss of form and was omitted from the England squad. During a splendid club career, though, he played in a total of 477 Football League games for his five different clubs. He made close on 300 appearances for Wolves and added another 100 or so outings to his tally with the Hatters. After retiring, he concentrated on running his successful sports shop in Sedgley, near Dudley, although he occasionally turned out in local charity matches up to 1990.

THOMSON, Robert G.N.
Inside-forward/wing-half; Apps 125+4, Goals 25.
Born: Dundee, 21 March 1937.
Career: Dundee & Dunblane Schools, Albion Rovers (amateur 1951), Airdrieonians (amateur August 1952), Wolverhampton Wanderers (trials, then professional August 1954), Aston Villa (June 1959), BLUES (September 1963), Stockport County (December 1967), Bromsgrove Rovers (May 1968), Retired 1970.
Club honours: Aston Villa: Division Two champions 1960, Football League Cup winners 1961, runners-up 1963.
This chunky, wavy-haired Scot, with an aggressive approach, tired of waiting for his chance at Molineux after making only one League appearance in his five years there. Instead, he became an instant hit with Villa and was top scorer in their promotion season of 1959-60. He netted 70 goals in 171 games for Villa before moving to St Andrew's, four months after playing against Blues in his second League Cup Final, when he scored against his future club. He gave Blues good service early on and proved an excellent replacement for Ron Wylie, when Wylie suffered a broken leg in 1966. Thomson now lives close to the centre of Birmingham and keeps fit by playing squash and tennis.

THOROGOOD, Jack
Outside-left; Apps 24, Goals 2.
Born: Dinnington, Yorks, 4 April 1911. Died: Bridlington, late 1970.
Career: Owston Park Rangers, Frickley Colliery, Manchester City (trial), BLUES (November 1930), Millwall (June 1934), Doncaster Rovers. Guested for several clubs during World War Two.
He looked promising when he arrived at St Andrew's, but although highly praised for both his speed and the quality of his crosses, he was never able to establish himself in the first team. His move to London brought him more regular League football and he scored his fair share of goals.

THRELFALL, Wilfred
Outside-left; Apps 5, Goals 0.
Born: Morecambe, 1901.
Career: Sunderland, BLUES (July 1927), Bournemouth & Boscombe Athletic (June 1928), Morecambe (March 1928).
Threlfall was an inexperienced winger who had failed to make a League appearance for Sunderland. Nevertheless, he started as first choice for Blues in 1927-28 but quickly dropped from favour. He made only three appearances for Bournemouth.

THWAITES, Dennis
Outside-left; Apps 91+4, Goals 21.
Born: Stockton-on-Tees, 14 December 1944.
Career: Stockton Council School, BLUES (amateur June 1960, professional May 1962). Retired in 1972 but played for Rover FC (Solihull) in the Birmingham Works League.
Representative honours: England (Youth caps, Schoolboy caps).

Dennis Thwaites was something of a teenage prodigy who broke into the Blues' first team as a 17-year-old in 1962, but who then spent a further ten seasons at St Andrew's without ever holding down a regular first-team place. Thwaites suffered badly from nerves which materially affected his play. He is currently working as a hospital porter in Blackpool. He is the uncle of Steve Lilwall (West Brom).

TICKLE, Charles Howard
Inside-forward; Apps 91, Goals 15.
Born: Northfield, Birmingham, 1884. Deceased.
Career: Selly Oak St Mary's, Bournbrook, BLUES (January 1902), Coventry City (1908), Worcester City (free transfer June 1913), Birmingham Trams, Redditch Town, Birmingham Trams. Later became Birmingham City Trams FC secretary.

Described as 'fast, clever in footwork and able to centre accurately', this talented but rather inconsistent player struggled to make an impact during his six years with Blues. It was quite a surprise, though, when he was released just after enjoying his best-ever season.

TINKLER, Alfred
Centre-half; Apps 103, Goals 3.
Born: Manchester, 1887. Died: Croydon, 1950.
Career: Ilkeston Town (amateur 1907), Derby County (January 1909), Heanor United, Ilkeston Town (May 1911), BLUES (December 1911), Burton United (1915). Retired 1917.
Alf Tinkler was a teacher who arrived at St Andrew's with the reputation as a trouble-maker having previously walked out on Derby County. Fortunately this side of his character was never in evidence during his spell with Blues and his robust style made him very popular with the fans. One report stated that he 'tackles with sureness and assists his forwards well'.

TODD, Colin
Defender; Apps 107+1, Goals 0.
Born: Chester-le-Street, 12 December 1948.
Career: Chester-le-Street Boys, Sunderland (apprentice July 1964, professional December 1966), Derby County (£180,000 February 1971), Everton (£330,000 September 1978), BLUES (£300,000

September 1979), Nottingham Forest (£70,000 August 1982), Oxford United (February 1984), Vancouver Whitecaps (NASL) (May 1984), Luton Town (October 1984). Retired 1985 and became manager of Whitley Bay, moving to Middlesbrough (as youth coach May 1986, then became assistant manager to Bruce Rioch at Ayresome Park in May 1986, taking over as manager in March 1990 to June 1991), Bradford City (assistant manager January 1992), Bolton Wanderers (assistant manager May 1992).
Club honours: Sunderland: FA Youth Cup winners 1967; Derby County: Division One champions 1972, 1975, Texaco Cup winners 1972; Blues: Division Two promotion 1980. Voted PFA Footballer of the Year in 1975.
Representative honours: England (27 full caps, 14 Under-23 caps, Youth caps); Football League XI(3).
Colin Todd was one of the finest defenders in the Football League during the 1970s, always elegant, poised, scrupulously fair and a brilliant reader of the game. Indeed, that was what inspired Brian Clough to pay what was then a record fee for a defender when he signed Todd for Derby. Todd always looked comfortable on the ball and in an exceptionally fine career he made over 800 senior appearances, chalking up his 500th game in the Football League (out of a total of 641) for Blues shirt against Swansea City in October 1979. His current managerial partnership with Bruce Rioch is one of the most highly-rated in soccer.

TOMLINSON, Paul
Goalkeeper; Apps 11, Goals 0.

Born: Brierley Hill, 22 February 1964.
Career: Middlewood Rangers, Sheffield United (professional June 1983), BLUES (loan March-April 1987), Bradford City (£47,500 June 1987).

Tomlinson was a tall, athletic goalkeeper whose spell with Blues coincided with troubled times, when he had to play behind a rather uneasy and leaky defence, but still produced some excellent performances.

TOWERS, Mark Anthony

Midfielder/sweeper; Apps 100+3, Goals 4.
Born: Manchester, 13 April 1952.
Career: Manchester City (apprentice July 1967, professional April 1969), Sunderland (£100,000 plus Mick Horswill March 1974), BLUES (£140,000 July 1977). Montreal Manic (NASL) (March 1981), Tampa Bay Rowdies (NASL), Vancouver Whitecaps (NASL) (August 1984), Rochdale (non-contract player February-May 1985). Retired 1986.
Club honours: Manchester City: European Cup-winners' Cup winners 1970, FA Charity Shield winners 1972, Football League Cup runners-up 1974; Sunderland: Division Two champions 1976.
Representative honours: England (3 full caps, 8 Under-23 caps, Youth caps, Schoolboy caps).

Tony Towers proved a huge disappointment at Blues after having built up a fine reputation as a midfielder with his two previous clubs. On his day he displayed fine ball skills, good passing ability and was very consistent, but his better performances were at the tail end of his spell at St Andrew's when he was acting as a sweeper.

TRAVERS, James Edward ('George')

Centre-forward; Apps 2, Goals 0.
Born: Newtown, Birmingham.
Died: Smethwick, 31 August 1946.
Career: Birchfield Road School (Aston), Bilston United (1904), Rowley United (1905), Wolverhampton Wanderers (July 1906), BLUES (August 1907), Aston Villa (December 1908), QPR (May 1909), Leicester Fosse (August 1910), Barnsley (January 1911), Manchester United (February 1914), Swindon Town (1919), Millwall (June 1920), Norwich City (October 1920), Gillingham (July 1921), Nuneaton Town (September 1921), Cradley St Luke's (November 1922), Bilston United (1929). Retired May 1931.
Club honours: Barnsley: FA Cup winners 1912.

Travers was a real footballing 'wanderer' who served with 15 different clubs in 21 years (1904-29) scoring for virtually every single one at some sort of level, including a hat-trick on his debut for Villa against Bury on Boxing Day 1908. Powerfully built, he was a grand header of the ball and packed a ferocious right-foot shot, but sadly he never really fitted in at St Andrew's or indeed at Villa Park, despite that sensational debut.

TREMELLING, Richard Daniel

Goalkeeper; Apps 395, Goals 0.
Born: Mansfield Woodhouse, 12 November 1897. Died: Birmingham, 15 August 1978.
Career: Langwith Junction Wagon Works FC (as a full-back), Shirebrook Juniors (goal), Lincoln City (professional August 1918), BLUES (May 1919), Bury (May 1932, assistant trainer January 1936), BLUES (assistant trainer June 1936-September 1941).
Club Honours: Blues: Division Two champions 1921.
Representative honours: England (1 full cap); Football League XI (3).

Affectionately known as the 'India Rubber Man' (apparently because he 'bounced' around on his line) Dan Tremelling joined Blues on the 13th of the month and left also on the 13th; he spent 13 years at St Andrew's and played in 13 FA Cup-ties – but 13 was not an unlucky number for this utterly reliable, sometimes absolutely brilliant goalkeeper, who was a great catcher of the ball. He took up goalkeeping by accident after being placed there during an injury crisis at Langwith. After retiring he became landlord of the Old Lodge pub near St Andrew's. His brother, William, played for Blackpool and Preston.

TREWICK, John ('Tucker')

Midfield/left-back; Apps 39+3, Goals 0.
Born: Stakeford, near Bedlington, Northumberland, 3 June 1957.
Career: Bedlington Grammar School, Northumberland Boys, West Bromwich Albion (apprentice July 1972, professional July 1974), Newcastle United (£234,000 December 1980), Oxford United (loan January 1984, signing permanently May 1984), BLUES (£30,000 September 1987-June 1989), Bromsgrove Rovers (August-October 1989), Hartlepool United (October 1989), Bromsgrove Rovers, Gateshead (October 1990), Tamworth. Coached Birmingham Festival League side. West Bromwich Albion youth coach 1993.
Club honours: Oxford United: Division Two champions 1985, Milk Cup winners 1986.
Representative honours: England (Youth caps, Schoolboy caps).

Trewick was a determined midfield grafter whose arrival at St Andrew's coincided with Blues' heaviest home defeat for 27 years (6-0 against Crystal Palace on 5 September 1987). Not the most naturally gifted of players, he was the target of persistent heckling from the fans throughout his days at Blues, probably because of his preference for the short pass rather than anything more ambitious. In later years he performed well at left-back and amassed over 300 League appearances altogether.

TRIGG, Cyril

Centre-forward/right-back; Apps 291, Goals 72.

Born: Measham, Leicestershire, 8 April 1917. Died: Birmingham, 9 April 1993.
Career: Leicester & District Schools, Binley Welfare, Coventry City (trials), Bedworth Town, BLUES (junior August 1935, professional November 1935), Stourbridge United (player-coach May 1954). Retired 1957. Guested for Blackpool and Nottingham Forest during World War Two when he served with the RAF in India and Burma.
Club honours: Blues: Football League South champions 1946, Division Two champions 1948.

Cyril Trigg played through three generations of Blues' teams, witnessing relegation, promotion, success and failure. He saw many changes at the club, played under four managers, occupied several positions yet still came up trumps, especially when he was at his peak, scoring goals from centre-forward. A terrific club man, 'Triggy' was at one stage simultaneously the best full-back and best centre-forward inside St Andrew's. During the war he appeared in 95 games yet rattled in no fewer than 88 goals.

TURNER, Arthur Samuel

Inside-right; Apps 1, Goals 0.
Born: Birmingham 1867. Deceased.
Career: Aston Villa, BLUES (September 1890-April 1891).
Released by Aston Villa without making a first-team appearance, although given a trial by Blues he was not taken on as a full-time player.

TURNER, Arthur Owen

Centre-half; Apps 53, Goals 0.
Born: Chesterton, Staffs, 1 April 1909. Died: Sheffield, 12 January 1994.
Career: Downing Tileries FC, Woolstanton PSA, West Bromwich Albion (amateur 1929), Stoke City (professional November 1930), BLUES (£6,000 January 1939), Southport (February 1948). Retired May 1949. Crewe Alexandra (manager August 1949-1950), Stoke City (assistant manager 1950-53), BLUES (manager November 1954 to September 1958), Oxford United (manager January 1959-69), Rotherham United (chief scout). Played cricket regularly for Silverdale CC for whom he

scored five centuries.
Club honours: Stoke City: Division Two champions 1933, Blues: Football League South champions 1946; (as manager), Blues: Division Two champions 1955, FA Cup runners-up 1956; Oxford United: Division Four promotion 1965, Division Three champions 1968.
Arthur Turner served Blues for 13 years, in

two excellent spells with the club, first as a player and then as manager. A resolute, no-nonsense defender, he was good in the air and strong on the ground but his career was badly affected by the war. He appeared in 186 games for Blues during the hostilities, after he had made 312 appearances for Stoke City. He was manager of Oxford United when they joined the Football League

TWELL, Terence K.

Goalkeeper; Apps 2, Goals 0.
Born: Doncaster, 21 February 1947.
Career: Bourne Town, BLUES (professional October 1964), Stamford Town (1968).
Great things were expected of this acrobatic young goalkeeper, and a series of fine displays led him into the first team in October 1967, in attempt to help a defence which had given away a number of 'bad' goals. However, on his debut he was beaten by a 30-yard lob and in the next game he could do nothing to hold a rampant Norwich attack which hit four past him. He returned to the second team and was released at the end of that season after being reduced to playing centre-forward for the youth side.

VALE, Archibald

Goalkeeper; Apps 2, Goals 0.
Born: Aston, Birmingham, July 1861. Died: Birmingham, 18 February 1904.
Career: Erdington Rugby Club, BLUES (September 1882), Aston Villa (August 1883), Erdington LC (September 1884), Walsall Royal Star (1888). Retired 1902 through ill health.
A convert from the oval ball game, Archie Vale used his handling skills to good effect and was described as 'little but very active and nimble'.

VAN DEN HAUWE, Patrick William Roger

Full-back/defender; Apps 138+5, Goals 1.
Born: Dendermonde, Belgium, 16 December 1960.
Career: BLUES (apprentice July 1977, professional August 1978), Everton (£100,000 September 1984), Tottenham Hotspur (£575,000, August 1989), Millwall (September 1993), Notts County (February 1995).
Club honours: Everton: Division One champions 1985, 1987, FA Cup runners-up 1985, 1989, European Cup-winners' Cup winners 1985; Tottenham Hotspur: FA Cup winners 1991.
Representative honours: Wales (13 full caps).

Pat Van den Hauwe moved to London with his parents as a young boy and was snapped up by Blues, but although given his League baptism in 1978, he had to wait three years

before establishing himself in the first team. He became a cult figure at Goodison Park and played 135 League games for the Merseysiders prior to his move to White Hart Lane. Van den Hauwe forfeited his birthright (as a Belgium) by opting out of National Service and eventually he was capped by Wales, who were always on the lookout for players no matter how tenuous their links with that country. His father, Rene, was a former Belgian League goalkeeper.

VAN MIERLO, Antonius Wilhelmus Matthias Theodore
Outside-left; Apps 47, Goals 4.
Born: Soarandonk, Netherlands, 24 August 1957.
Career: (In Holland) Kraanvogals, SV Eindhoven (1976), SV Willem II (1979), BLUES (June 1981), (In Holland) SV Willem II (1982), Racing White Daring Molenbeek (1983), MVV Maastricht (1985), AA Gent (1986), Racing Club Harelbeke (1988), VVV Venlo (loan 1989), SV Willem II (youth team trainer 1990).
Club honours: Molenbeek: Belgium Division Two champions 1985.
Representative honours: Holland (3 full caps).
Van Mierlo first sprang to the attention of Blues' fans with a brilliant display for Willem II in a pre-season friendly at St Andrew's in 1980. He had electrifying pace but found it difficult to cope with the physical demands of the English game. He was used to playing in centre of the attack, and perhaps his talents could have been better utilised there, rather than on the left wing which is where Blues played him. Now works behind the scenes at Willem II.

VINCENT, John Victor
Midfield; Apps 190+4, Goals 44.
Born: West Bromwich, 8 February 1947.
Career: Brierley Hill Schools, BLUES (apprentice June 1962, professional February 1964), Middlesbrough (£40,000 March 1971), Cardiff City (£35,000 October 1972), Atherstone Town (August 1975), Connecticut Bicentennials (NASL) (1977).
Representative honours: England (5 Youth caps).

Johnny Vincent played the old-fashioned game as he simply glided past challengers with style and grace. He triggered off many attacks and possessed a hard shot. Vincent was a star in schools and junior football and made his League debut shortly after his 17th birthday, gaining a regular place in the Blues first team in 1966. As his career progressed he showed a distinct dislike of the physical aspects of the game and Blues manager Freddie Goodwin eventually traded him for the more robust style of George Smith. Vincent later became a publican, in Northfield, Birmingham, at The Travellers Rest, and later still in Oldbury and Warley.

VOWDEN, Geoffrey Alan
Forward; Apps 245+8, Goals 94.
Born: Barnsley, 27 April 1941.
Career: Jersey DM (1957), Nottingham Forest (amateur 1958, professional January 1960), BLUES (£25,000 October 1964), Aston Villa (£12,500 March 1971), Kettering Town (player and assistant manager 1974), New York Cosmos (NASL) (June-August 1974). Coached in Saudi Arabia in mid-1970s as well as at local youth centres in the Nottingham area, and was appointed reserve-team coach at Sheffield United (1980-81).
Club honours: Villa: Division Three champions 1972.

Born in Yorkshire but brought up in the Channel Islands, Geoff Vowden developed into a fine goalscorer who found the net over 150 times in more than 450 competitive matches between 1960 and 1974. He netted 40 goals in 90 League outings for Forest and on 7 September 1968, he wrote his name into the history books when he became the first substitute to score a hat-trick in a League game, in Division Two, for Blues against Huddersfield at St Andrew's.

WADDELL, George Barr
Right-half; Apps 2, Goals 0.
Born: Lesmahagow, Lanarkshire, 13 July 1889. Died: Sible Headingham, Essex, 17 September 1966.
Career: Dalziel Rovers (Motherwell), Burnbank Athletic, Larkhill United, Glasgow

Rangers, Kilmarnock (loan 1912-13), Bradford City (£1,000 June 1914), Preston North End (£1,750 September 1920), Oldham Athletic (£250 July 1922), BLUES (£325 October 1922), Hamilton Academical (July 1923), New Brighton (week's trial November 1923), Wolverhampton Wanderers (November 1923), Aberaman Athletic (player-coach season 1924-25), Chorley (November 1925), Fraserburgh (player-coach), Preston North End (assistant trainer/reserve-team coach), Dick Kerr's XI (women's team trainer season 1930-31), Ribble Motors FC (August 1931- December 1933).
George Waddell had a varied career and kicked his last ball at the age of 43. A man of many clubs but principally a reserve with most of them, he was a heavily built midfielder with a powerful if not always accurate shot.

WALKER, William Baird
Centre-forward; Apps 30, Goals 10.
Born: New Cummock, 1893. Deceased.
Career: Lugar Boswell, Bradford City (August 1911), Lanemark (March 1913), BLUES (November 1913), Coventry City (November 1919), Merthyr Town (1920), Bristol City (October 1922), Sheffield Wednesday (October 1923), Weymouth (player-manager 1924), Leamington Town (1925).

Bill Walker suffered from homesickness during first spell in England but Blues gave him a second chance and he repaid them with eight goals in 12 games in his first season at St Andrew's. He never found scoring quite so easy after that, but he did manage six hat-tricks in the reserves in 1914-15.

WALLACE, Alexander
Outside-left; Apps 2, Goals 1.
Born: Darwen, Lancashire, 1872. Died: Bolton, 1950.
Career: Blackpool, Manchester City (June 1894), Baltimore (USA) (October 1894), BLUES (November 1897), Hereford Thistle (January 1898).
Alex Wallace was suspended *sine die* after his departure to America in 1894, along with Manchester City's Tom Little and Mitchell Calvey. Little returned almost immediately and was pardoned by his former employees, but Wallace had to wait a shade longer before he was allowed back into the game. A talented ball player, his three years of inactivity showed after he joined Blues.

WALLACE, David Lloyd 'Danny'
Forward; Apps 13+6, Goals 2.
Born: Greenwich, 21 January 1964.
Career: West Greenwich School, Southampton (apprentice June 1980, professional January 1982), Manchester United (£1.2 million September 1989), Millwall (loan March 1993), BLUES (£250,000 October 1993), Wycombe

Wanderers (March 1995).
Club honours: Manchester United: European Cup-winners' Cup winners 1991, FA Charity Shield winners 1990.
Representative honours: England (1 full cap, 14 Under-21 caps, 9 Youth caps); UEFA Under-21 tournament winners 1984.
Danny Wallace enjoyed a tremendous career at The Dell – 79 goals in 321 appearances – where he played in same team as his brothers, Ray and Rodney. A fast, skilful winger who also performs through the middle, Wallace joined Blues after losing his place at Old Trafford, after scoring ten goals in 71 outings for the Reds. He had barely played for two years when he joined Blues and it was quickly obvious that he was still unfit during his spell at St Andrew's.

WALLINGTON, Sidney Percy
Left-half; Apps 2, Goals 0.
Born: Small Heath, Birmingham, 15 October 1908. Died: Birmingham, December 1989.
Career: Ada Road School, Birmingham Schools, Wolseley Sports FC, BLUES (April 1928), Bristol Rovers (October 1933), Worcester City (1937), Cradley St Luke's (1939). Retired 1935.
Club honours: Bristol Rovers: Division Three South Cup winners 1935.
Representative honours: Birmingham Schools; English Schools FA Trophy runners-up 1923.
Wallington spent four patient years in Blues' reserves before getting his chance in the senior side, but by then it was obvious that he had no future in the First Division. He switched to right-half with Bristol Rovers and did well in the lower divisions. His son was on Blues' books in the 1950s.

WALTON, William Howard T. ('Mother')
Inside-forward/wing-half; Apps 200, Goals 63.
Born: Hockley Brook, Birmingham, 6 August 1871. Died: Dudley Road Hospital, Winson Green, Birmingham, 10 February 1963.
Career: Hockley Belmont, BLUES (August 1888), Dudley (May 1903). Club honours: Blues: Division Two champions 1893, Division Two runners-up 1894, 1901.
A clever ball-player with smart movement and strong shot, Walton served up some scintillating entertainment for the spectators during his 15 years service with Blues. Initially a dashing inside-forward, he later switched to half-back where his encouragement of the younger members of the team earned him the epithet of 'Mother'. Walton watched Small Heath play in the 1886 FA Cup semi-final against West Brom after he had cleared snow off the pitch before kick-off; he was present when St Andrew's was officially opened in 1905; and he attended the Wembley Cup Finals of 1931 and 1956. Indeed, he was a regular attender at St Andrew's until shortly before his death at the age of 91. Always a part-time footballer, he continued to work as a silversmith in Hockley throughout his playing days.

WANT, Anthony George
Full-back/defender; Apps 122+5, Goals 2.
Born: Hackney, North London, 13 December 1948.
Career: Hackney Schools, London Borough Boys, Tottenham Hotspur (apprentice June 1964, professional December 1965), BLUES (£60,000 June 1972). Contract cancelled by mutual consent, February 1978, when he moved to the NASL, playing first with Minnesota Kicks and later with Philadelphia Fury.
Representative honours: England (Youth caps).
Tony Want made over 50 appearances for Spurs before signing for Blues as a full-

back to strengthen their 1971-72 promotion side. His best performances, however, came after he had been successfully converted into a central defender. He was hampered by injuries throughout his career, and suffered a severe fracture of his leg in a Texaco Cup-tie against Newcastle. But he battled back to fitness and regained a first-team place. After his NASL career he returned to England in 1982 and became a successful businessman, living in Solihull. He played in several charity games with WBA All Stars during mid-1980s.

WARD, Mark William
Midfield; Apps 64, Goals 5.
Born: Huyton, 10 October 1962.
Career: Everton (apprentice 1978, professional September 1980), Northwich Victoria (free transfer 1981), Oldham Athletic (£10,000 July 1983), West Ham United (£250,000 August 1985), Manchester City (£1 million December 1989), Everton (£1.1 million August 1991), BLUES (loan March 1994, signed for £500,000 August 1994).
Club honour: Blues: Second Division champions 1995, Auto Windscreens Shield winners 1995.
Representative honours: England (semi-professional cap).

Inspirational midfielder Mark Ward returned to Goodison Park for £1 million in 1991, ten years after Everton had released him on a free transfer. He played 92 games for Oldham, 209 for West Ham, 67 for Manchester City and 94 for Everton (all in his second spell). Whilst on loan to the Blues he was an inspirational figure their abortive effort to avoid relegation in 1994, so much so that he was signed before the next season to orchestrate the battle for promotion.

WARD, Walter
Goalkeeper; Apps 5, Goals 0.
Born: Birmingham 1869. Deceased.
Career: BLUES (season 1890-91)
Walter Ward was a big, strong goalkeeper who occasionally deputised for Chris Charsley when the England man was absent from Blues' side.

WARDLE, William
Outside-left; Apps 68, Goals 7.
Born: Hetton-le-Hole, Co Durham, 20 January 1918. Died: January 1989.
Career: Fatfield Juniors, Houghton Colliery Welfare, Southport (October 1936), Manchester City (£2,200 October 1937), Grimsby Town (July 1939), Blackpool (August 1948), BLUES (£8,000 September 1951), Barnsley (November 1953), Skegness Town (1955). Retired cs 1957.
A lightweight ball-playing winger with a reputation for being one of the cleverest dribblers of his day, as is so often the case with dribblers, Wardle was frequently

criticised for a tendency to over-elaborate. Despite this, his talents were much in demand throughout his career. His brother, George Wardle, was also a 'wanderer' playing for Middlesbrough, Cardiff, QPR and Darlington.

WARHURST, Roy
Wing-half; Apps 239, Goals 10.
Born: Handsworth, Sheffield, 18 September 1926.
Career: Atlas & Norfolk FC, Huddersfield Town (amateur 1943), Sheffield United (amateur May 1944, professional September 1944), BLUES (£8,000 March 1950), Manchester City (£10,000 June 1957), Crewe Alexandra (March 1959), Oldham Athletic (August 1960), Banbury Spencer (August 1961). Retired 1964.
Club honours: Blues: Division Two champions 1955.

Roy Warhurst was a stocky wing-half with a bone-crunching tackle and it is hard to believe that such a fine 'destroying' player could have begun his career as a winger. That, though, was the role he was asked to play in his early days at St Andrew's. He lined up in the attack alongside Len Boyd, but it was not until these two fine players dropped back to fill the respective wing-half positions that the Blues' revival began, Warhurst's hard grafting style being the ideal complement to the more artistic Boyd. Warhurst missed the 1956 Cup Final through injury, his absence being considered a crucial factor in the club's defeat. Unpopular with opposition fans and in particular those at Maine Road, it was indeed a surprise when he eventually moved to Manchester City. He was appointed captain on his arrival at Oldham, after having amassed in excess of 300 League appearances prior to that, including 216 for Blues, 40 for Manchester City and 51 for Crewe. He rounded off his playing days with Banbury Spencer, a club that rejoiced in the nickname of the Gay Puritans. Later he became a scrap metal dealer in Birmingham, while residing in Lichfield.

WARMINGTON, Peter
Inside-forward; Apps 9, Goals 3.
Born: Wythal, near Birmingham, 8 April 1934.

Career: Redditch Boys' Club, Redditch Juniors, BLUES (junior August 1949, amateur December 1951, professional February 1952), Bromsgrove Rovers (June 1957), Redditch United, Droitwich Town.
Talented goalscorer Peter Warmington was a player who was unlucky with injuries throughout his career. He scored on his debut and found the net again two games later. Usually deputy for any of the regular inside trio, he occasionally filled in at half-back.

WASSALL, Harold
Left-back; Apps 60, Goals 1.
Born: Stourbridge, 21 September 1879. Died: Dudley, March 1951.
Career: Brierley Hill Alliance, BLUES (£75 January 1902), Bristol Rovers (1904).
Wassall was a powerfully built defender with a terrific kick who often cleared the ball first time without taking time to get it under control.

WATKINS, Ernest Thomas
Inside-forward; Apps 8, Goals 1.
Born: Finchley, 3 April 1898. Died: Finchley, 10 October 1976.
Career: Army Football (World War One), Barnet (August 1920), Finchley, BLUES (October 1922), Southend United (February 1924), Brentford (January 1926), Millwall (February 1930), Thames (June 1930), Fulham (August 1930), Gillingham (trial August 1931), Charlton Athletic (November 1931). Retired through injury May 1932.
Blues were the odd stop in this much-travelled striker's tour of the south-east. They were also the only club for whom he did not score regularly. A goal poacher whose best work was done inside the area, his career was ended by a knee injury sustained in February 1932.

WATSON, John ('Jack') S.
Right-back; Apps 2, Goals 0.
Born: Bulwell, Nottinghamshire, September 1892. Died: Nottingham, 1957.
Career: Bulwell FC, Manchester City, Oldham Athletic (1916), Bloxwich Strollers (1918), BLUES (July 1919), Measham Town (1920).
This tall, balding full-back had tried his luck with two other League clubs before coming to Blues. He deputised in a couple of games for Ball but made very little impression and was quickly released.

WATSON, Thomas
Left-back/goalkeeper; Apps 4, Goals 0.
Born: Yardley Wood, Birmingham, 1870. Died: Birmingham, April 1902.
Career: Yardley Victoria, BLUES (1894).
Another of the group of policemen who have kept goal for the Blues as an amateur, Tom Watson was a fine all-round athlete and a prominent figure in organising athletics meetings in the Small Heath area. He joined Birmingham police in 1895, rose to the rank of sergeant in 'E' Division and could be seen policing Blues home games until his early death. Watson initially played as a full-back but was switched to 'keeper in the reserves due to an injury crisis. He did sufficiently well to play twice for the first team in this role.

WATTS, Ernest
Inside-right; Apps 2, Goals 0.
Born: Birmingham, 1875. Deceased.
Career: BLUES (season 1899-90).
Ernie Watts was a local inside-forward who was given his chance in the mass shake-up following Blues' 9-1 defeat at Sheffield Wednesday. The team's form did not improve and both games in which he appeared were lost. All the new men, Watts included, were then dropped.

WATTS, John William
Right-half; Apps 248, Goals 3.

Born: Vauxhall, Birmingham, 13 April 1931.
Career: Saltley Old Boys, BLUES (junior August 1948, professional August 1951), Nuneaton Borough (July 1963), Bromsgrove Rovers (1964). Retired 1969.
Club honours: Blues: Division Two champions 1955, Inter Cities Fairs Cup runners-up 1960.

Johnny Watts was a versatile wing-half who could also fill in at centre-half. A tireless worker who was ever-reliable, he possessed a terrific sliding tackle which sometimes brought him into conflict with European referees during Blues' exploits in the Fairs Cup. He was spotted by Blues' chief scout Walter Taylor whilst playing on Glebe Farm Recreation Ground, and after returning from his National Service he quickly settled down at St Andrew's. With the retirement of Len Boyd, Watts gained a regular place in the side until Terry Hennessey appeared on the scene.

WEALANDS, Jeffrey Andrew
Goalkeeper; Apps 118+1, Goals 0.
Born: Darlington, 26 August 1951.
Career: Darlington Cleveland Bridge FC, Wolverhampton Wanderers (apprentice June 1968, professional October 1968), Northampton Town (loan February 1970), Darlington (July 1970), Hull City (£10,000 March 1972), BLUES (£30,000 July 1979), Manchester United (loan February 1983, signed later in year on full-time basis), Oldham Athletic (loan March 1984), Preston North End (loan December 1984), Altrincham (May 1985 to May 1987), Barrow (August 1987), Altrincham (1988, director March 1995).
Club honours: Blues: Division Two promotion 1980.

A capable if unspectacular goalkeeper, Jeff Wealands was voted Blues' player of the year in their promotion season of 1979-80, but fell into dispute with manager Ron Saunders in 1982 and found himself out of favour. He gained revenge on Saunders, however, when after bravely battling back after injury, he helped non-Leaguers Altrincham knock Blues out of the FA Cup in 1985. Wealands appeared in a total of 391 League games during a fine career, 240 coming at Hull and 102 with Blues. His days at Old Trafford were marred by a recurring back injury, but was still playing in the GM Vauxhall Conference at the age of 40.

WEBB, Isaac ('Ike')
Goalkeeper; Apps 6, Goals 0.
Born: Worcester, 1 October 1874. Died: Dudley Road Hospital, Winson Green, Birmingham, March 1950.
Career: Worcester Park School, St Clement's Rangers, Berwick Rangers (Worcester), Worcester Olympic, Evesham Town, Mansfield Town, Lincoln City, Mansfield Town, Wellington Town, BLUES (1898), West Bromwich Albion (May 1901), Sunderland (£250 December 1904), QPR (1907). Retired May 1910 and joined the West Yorkshire Regiment as a catering orderly. Made a comeback with WBA as a guest in August 1918, aged 43.
Club honours: WBA: Division Two champions 1902.
Webb was employed as a salmon fisherman at Evesham before becoming a professional footballer. A big, burly goalkeeper with outstanding reflexes, he was quick off his line, besides being spectacularly agile at times. He always wore a cap and at one stage in his eventful career he fractured his skull and played on for quite sometime afterwards before realising what had happened.

WEBB, Matthew Leslie
Winger; Apps 1, Goals 0.
Born: Bristol, 1976.
Career: BLUES (YTS July 1993, professional May 1995).
A promising youngster, Webb had an early call-up to the first team after only one Pontin's League match. He is pacy and a useful crosser of the ball and high hopes are held for him.

WEBB, Sidney
Inside-forward; Apps 3, Goals 0.
Born: Coventry, February 1884. Died: Leamington, 1956.
Career: St Saviour's FC, Stourbridge, Aston Villa, Burton United, Wednesbury Old Athletic, BLUES (April 1911), Worcester City (August 1912).
Sid Webb was a rotund little schemer who had a very short League career but who was always regarded as one of the leading stars of the Birmingham League.

WESTON, Donald Patrick
Centre-forward; Apps 25, Goals 3.
Born: New Houghton, 6 March 1936.
Career: East Derbyshire Boys, 31st Training Regiment Royal Artillery, Wrexham (amateur July 1957, professional June 1959), BLUES (£5,000 January 1960), Rotherham United (£5,000 December 1960), Leeds United (£7,500 December 1962), Huddersfield Town (£3,500 October 1965), Wrexham (December 1966), Chester (August 1968), Altrincham, Bethesda.
Club honours: Rotherham United: Football League Cup runners-up 1961; Leeds United: Division Two champions 1964; Blues: Fairs Cup runners-up 1960.
Fast, direct, incisive and likely striker who acquired a useful record as a marksmen, Weston netted a total of 95 goals in his 275 League games for seven different clubs. Although he had difficulty hitting the target for Blues, he was top-scorer for Leeds in 1963-64.

WHARTON, Sidney Emmanuel
Outside-left; Apps 167, Goals 25.
Born: Birmingham, June 1876. Died:

Birmingham, 1951.
Career: Smethwick Wesleyan Rovers, BLUES (November 1897). Retired May 1903, but remained with the club for a short time acting as coach.
Club honours: Blues: Division Two runners-up 1901, 1903.
Representative honours: England (unofficial international cap); Football League XI.
A sprightly winger, rather rotund but with great speed, good ball-control and fine shot, Sid Wharton was a creator of chances rather than a taker, but he was forever in the thick of the action, loved a battle, and was always highly regarded. In later years he became a turf accountant in Smethwick, the company surviving to this day, and he was also an accomplished MC especially in the boxing ring.

WHATMORE, Neil
Forward; Apps 25+2, Goals 7.
Born: Ellesmere Port, Cheshire, 17 May 1955.
Career: Bolton Wanderers (apprentice June 1971, professional May 1973), BLUES (£350,000 August 1981), Oxford United (loan October 1982), Bolton Wanderers (loan December 1982), Oxford United (£25,000 February 1983), Bolton Wanderers (loan March-April 1984), Burnley (part-exchange deal involving Billy Hamilton August 1984), Mansfield Town (November 1984) Bolton Wanderers (August 1987), Mansfield Town (player-reserve team coach December 1987), Worksop Town (August 1988), coached Manning Rangers (South Africa) (from March 1992).
Club honours: Bolton Wanderers: Division Two champions 1978; Mansfield Town: Freight/Rover Trophy winners 1987.

A sharp, incisive striker, Neil Whatmore was top marksman for Bolton in five of the previous six seasons before joining Blues where he teamed up again with his old teammate from Burnden Park, Frank Worthington. Alas, the pair could not reproduce the form they had shown with the Trotters and Whatmore found himself selected only spasmodically. When Ron Saunders arrived, both players found themselves surplus to requirements, although Whatmore remained at St Andrew's for a further year but was rarely selected.

WHEELER, William John ('Jack')
Goalkeeper; Apps 13, Goals 0.
Born: North Littleton, nr Evesham, 13 July 1919.
Career: Littleton Juniors, Evesham Early Closers FC, Cheltenham Town, BLUES (professional March 1938), Huddersfield Town (August 1948), Kettering Town (July 1956), Evesham Town, Notts County (trainer June 1957, caretaker manager September 1968 to November 1969). Retired 1982.

Club honours: Huddersfield Town: Division Two runners-up 1953.
A goalkeeper who dominated his area, Jack Wheeler was signed by Blues as the eventual successor to Harry Hibbs, but with Gil Merrick emerging, he was sold to Huddersfield after the war and after a brief spell in the reserves at Leeds Road he went on to make over 165 League appearances for Huddersfield up to 1956. When they won promotion in 1952-53, Wheeler was part of a six-man defence which played in every game.

WHELDON, George Frederick ('Diamond')
Inside-left; Apps 129, Goals 82.
Born: Langley Green, Oldbury, 1 November 1869. Died: Worcester, 13 January 1924.
Career: Chance's Infants and Langley St Michael's Senior Schools, Rood End White Star, Langley Green Victoria, West Bromwich Albion (trial 1888), BLUES (February 1890), Aston Villa (£350 June 1896), West Bromwich Albion (£100 August 1900), QPR (December 1901), Portsmouth (August 1902), Worcester City (July 1904), Coventry City (May 1905). Retired January 1907. Played county cricket for Worcestershire from 1899 to 1926, scoring 4,938 runs in 138 matches at an average of 22.54. He hit three centuries, took 95 catches (some as wicketkeeper and was a very occasional slow right-arm spin bowler. He also played cricket for Carmarthenshire and was later a publican in Worcester.
Club honours: Blues: Division Two champions 1893, Division Two runners-up 1894; Aston Villa: Division One champions 1897, 1899, 1900, FA Cup winners 1897.
Representative honours: England (4 full caps); Football League XI (4).
The youngest in a family of ten, 'Diamond' Freddie Wheldon was a brilliant footballer, an exceptional talent, a great goalscorer, who simply enjoyed playing the game. His intricate footwork often bemused the best defenders in the country and he developed the art of the 'daisy cutter' shot. On the bumpy pitches of the 19th century such a shot was a goalkeeper's nightmare and a high proportion of Wheldon's goals were scored in this way. He scored two goals on his debut for Blues – a game in which the local press got his name wrong. He was also the scorer of Blues' first-ever Football League goal in 1892. After leaving Blues, Wheldon was instrumental in helping Villa achieve the League and Cup double and when he joined Albion he became the first player ever to represent the three big Midland clubs. He was involved in an unusual incident early on his career when one of his shots struck the referee in the pocket where he kept his matches for his pipe. The matches set alight and the official's jacket went up in flames. Wheldon often played wearing a pair of golfing stockings and his brother, Sam, also served with West Brom.

WHITE, Frank Robert Harvey
Outside-right; Apps 156, Goals 50.
Born: Wilnecote, near Tamworth, 14 November 1911. Died: 1985.
Career: Stoneware Ltd FC (Tamworth), Tamworth (1930), BLUES (September 1931), Preston North End (December 1938), Redditch United (August 1946). Retired 1950, and later coached his former club, Tamworth. Guested for Aldershot, Mansfield Town, Sheffield United and Wrexham during World War Two
Frank White was a fine goalscoring outside-left, fast, a good dribbler with telling shot, who was recommended to Blues by Harry Hibbs. He had been a prolific marksman in junior circles before moving to St Andrew's but surprisingly his early days with Blues were spent in the left

wing berth. The management soon realised their mistake and thereafter he obliged with some sparkling performances and match-winning goals. He teamed up with Wilson Jones at Redditch after the war.

WHITE, Thomas Wilson
Right-back; Apps 15, Goals 0.
Born: West Bromwich, September 1896. Died: Wednesbury, 1960.
Career: Notts County, BLUES (March 1918), Worksop Town (January 1921), Newport County (September 1922), Kidderminster Harriers (1925).
Tom White was a slow, cumbersome defender who relied on the big clearance. Initially he understudied Billy Ball but then after winning his place in the side he lost out to Jack Whitehouse who had been converted from inside-forward.

WHITE, Vincent Harry
Left-half; Apps 2, Goals 0.
Born: Walsall, December 1899. Deceased.
Career: Erdington, Wednesbury Old Athletic, BLUES (May 1921), Redditch Town (loan 1922), Ellesmere Port (1924), Oswestry.
A stocky, defensive wing-half whose appearances were restricted due to the fine form of Percy Barton. White's greatest strength was his tackling ability.

WHITEHEAD, Alan James
Central defender; Apps 5+1, Goals 0.
Born: Bordesley Green, Birmingham, 3 September 1951.
Career: Erdington & Saltley Schools, BLUES (apprentice September 1967, professional August 1970), Kettering Town (free transfer July 1974).
A promising winger when he joined Blues, Whitehead appeared in almost every position before eventually settling at the back. He played some important games in Blues' run-in to promotion in 1972, when he replaced the injured Stan Harland, but appeared only once in the First Division. His brother Clive had a lengthy career, most notably with Bristol City and West Brom.

WHITEHEAD, James Gilbert
Inside-left; Apps 2, Goals 0.
Born: Birmingham, May 1858. Deceased.
Career: King's Norton Boys' Club, BLUES (August 1881), Lea Hall (September 1882).
He was a utility forward who was switched around all the inside positions with little success.

WHITEHOUSE, John ('Jackie') Charles
Forward; Apps 115, Goals 35.
Born: Smethwick, 4 March 1897. Died: Halesowen, 3 January 1948.
Career: Smethwick Hall, Blackheath Town,

Redditch, BLUES (August 1916), Derby County (May 1923), Sheffield Wednesday (February 1929), Bournemouth &

Boscombe Athletic (August 1930), Folkestone Town (May 1933), Worcester City (player-manager 1934). Retired August 1935, later scouted for Derby County.

Club honours: Blues: Division Two champions 1921.

Jackie Whitehouse rose to prominence as one of the local youngsters given their chance during World War One. A pugnacious forward with a reputation for being one of the game's hard men, he was never averse to 'mixing it' with a defender.

WHITTON, Stephen Paul

Striker; Apps 117+2, Goals 35.
Born: East Ham, London, 4 December 1960.
Career: Coventry City (apprentice June 1977, professional September 1978), West Ham United (£175,000 July 1983), BLUES (loan January 1986, signing permanently for £75,000 August 1986), Sheffield Wednesday (£275,000 March 1989), Halmstads BK (Sweden) (loan 1990), Ipswich Town (£120,000 January 1991), Colchester United (player-coach March 1994, caretaker manager May 1994).

Blues made a profit of £200,000 on Steve Whitton, which was very good business. Although a Londoner, he began his career in the Midlands where he developed into a strong, hard-running striker, with surprisingly delicate ball-control. He loved to run at defenders before letting fly with a powerful right-foot shot. He was among the Swedish League's top scorers during his spell with Halmstads.

WHYTE, Christopher Anderson

Defender; Apps 79+1, Goals 1.
Born: Islington, 2 September 1961.
Career: Highbury Grove School, Arsenal

(apprentice 1976, professional December 1979), Crystal Palace (loan August 1984), Los Angeles Lazers (USA), West Bromwich Albion (free transfer August 1988), Leeds United (£400,000 June 1990), BLUES (£250,000 August 1993).
Club honours: Leeds United: Division One champions 1992. Blues: Second Division champions 1995.
Representative honours: England (4 Under-21 caps).

Chris Whyte came to St Andrew's with some 350 games under his belt and has done an excellent job in Blues' defence. He was switched to left-back with great success by manager Fry in 1994-95.

WIGLEY, Stephen

Winger; Apps 98, Goals 5.
Born: Ashton-under-Lyne, 15 October 1961.
Career: Curzon Ashton, Nottingham Forest (March 1981), Sheffield United (October 1985), BLUES (player-exchange deal involving Martin Kuhl March 1987), Portsmouth (£350,000 March 1989), Exeter City (August 1993), Bognor Regis Town (1994), Aldershot Town March 1995.

A speedy, winger, good on the ball, Steve Wigley made over 100 appearances under Brian Clough before transferring to Bramall Lane. He teamed up at Fratton Park with former Blues player, Kevin Dillon. A good crosser of the ball, a lot of his work at St Andrew's went to waste because of the lack of a true centre-forward in the side. He did much better at Pompey with the likes of Whittingham and Clarke around.

WIGMORE, Walter

Inside-forward/centre-half; Apps 355, Goals 25.
Born: Chipping Sodbury, 25 February 1873. Died: Worksop, 8 September 1931.
Career: Kiveton Park, Worksop, (1889), Sheffield United (1895), Worksop Town (March 1896), Gainsborough Trinity (August 1896, BLUES (£180 March 1899), Brierley Hill Alliance (August 1912). Retired May 1913.
Club honours: Blues: Division Two runners-up 1901, 1903.
Representative honours: Players Union XI (1); Football League XI (1).

Walter Wigmore was a powerful inside-forward who was signed by Blues to renew his partnership with Bob McRoberts, his former Gainsborough teammate. Wigmore fulfilled these duties adequately until an injury to Alec Leake led to him being switched to centre-half where his form was a revelation, Leake being moved to wing-

half on his recovery. Wigmore remained first-choice pivot for nine years, helping Blues to two promotions, before a lengthy series of injuries ended his League career. He was then tempted to Brierley Hill with the offer of a pub tenancy. Renowned throughout the footballing community as 'the man who would never head the ball', he always attempted to bring the ball to foot, no matter how high it was, and was therefore often in trouble with referees for 'dangerous play'. But most officials tended to be lenient with him, regarding his actions as clumsy rather than malicious.

WILCOX, Frederick Jeremiah

Inside-left; Apps 84, Goals 32.
Born: Bristol, 7 July 1880. Died: Bristol, 1954.
Career: Glendale FC, Bristol Rovers (August 1901), BLUES (£125 plus a friendly, March 1903), Middlesbrough (March 1906). Retired 1910.
Representative honours: England trialist.

A dashing forward, regarded by some critics as the finest dribbler of his day, such was his ability that Middlesbrough saw him as the perfect foil for Steve Bloomer – and they were not at all disappointed as Wilcox managed 20 goals to Bloomer's 31 over the next two years. A damaged knee, suffered after colliding with a goal-post, caused him to retire in 1910. He returned to Bristol where he set up his own business.

WILCOX, Harold Melbourne

Inside-forward; Apps 17, Goals 3.
Born: Hockley, Birmingham, 7 January 1878. Died: Plymouth, 21 July 1937.
Career: King's Parish School (Bromsgrove), St David's YC, Selly Oak St Mary's, BLUES (September 1898), Watford (July 1900), Preston North End (1901), Plymouth Argyle (1905), Leicester Fosse (August 1906), West Bromwich Albion (November 1907), Plymouth Argyle (May 1908). Retired May 1920.
Club honours: Preston North End: Division Two champions 1904; Plymouth Argyle: Southern League champions 1913.
Representative honours: Southern League XI (2).

A fine inside-forward, with heavy moustache, Harry Wilcox amassed some 400 appearances during his lengthy career which finally ended when he was 42. He later switched to the centre-half position, albeit one with an attacking bent in those pre-stopper days.

WILCOX, John Mitchell

Winger; Apps 48, Goals 2.
Born: Stourbridge, January 1886. Died: Lichfield, August 1940.
Career: Stourbridge Standard, Cradley St

Luke's, Dudley, Halesowen, Aston Villa (July 1908), BLUES (player-exchange deal involving George Travers, November 1908), Southampton (June 1911), Wellington Town (May 1912). Retired 1916.

Wilcox was the most recent of the four unrelated Wilcoxes to play for Blues before World War One. He was a winger of fitful brilliance who loved to take on defenders. He was never a great goalscorer but he was a regular supplier of chances for his teammates.

WILCOX, Leslie

Outside-left; Apps 4, Goals 2.
Born: West Bromwich, 1865. Deceased.
Career: West Bromwich Highfield, BLUES (September 1889-April 1890).

Wilcox made his debut with Fred Wheldon and Jack Hallam as Blues tried a new-look forward-line in 1899-90. All three newcomers scored but whilst two went on to become stalwarts of the club, Wilcox found himself out in the cold. It is still quite a mystery as to why such a useful winger suddenly disappeared after only a few games.

WILKES, Frederick

Centre-forward; Apps 5, Goals 4.
Born: Handsworth, Birmingham, 1869. Deceased.
Career: Handsworth Boys Club, BLUES (April 1891), Brownhills (September 1892).

Wilkes played in several friendly matches for Blues at the end of the 1890-91 season and looked a good acquisition but, despite Blues having a centre-forward problem during the next campaign, he was overlooked. He scored a hat-trick in his only FA Cup-tie, against Brierley Hill Alliance in 1891.

WILLETTS, Walter ('Wally')

Outside-left; Apps 1, Goals 0.
Born: Smethwick, 1860. Deceased.
Career: Langley Victoria, BLUES (April 1884), Oldbury (1885).

Willetts took quite sometime to bed into the first team but when he had settled down he proved to be a useful footballer, being quick and a fair provider of chances. His finest game came against Excelsior in the Birmingham Senior Cup in November 1884, a match which had to be replayed when Excelsior claimed that the ball was 'insufficiently inflated during the last 25 minutes'.

WILLIAMS, Dean

Goalkeeper; Apps 5, Goals 0.
Born: Lichfield, 5 January 1972.
Career: Hansbury Farm Junior and Glascote Comprehensive Schools, BLUES (YTS June 1988, professional January 1990), Cobh Ramblers (loan August 1991), Tamworth (March 1992), Newcastle United (trial July 1993), Brentford (August 1993), Doncaster Rovers (August 1994).

Williams is on the slim side for a 'keeper but showed abundant talent in his first few senior outings, being a fine handler of high crosses.

WILLIAMS, Harry

Left-back; Apps 1, Goals 0.
Born: Aston, Birmingham, 1875. Deceased.
Career: Aston Unity, Aston Manor, BLUES (April 1896), Nechells (1897).

Not much can be gleaned about this man's style of play. He came in for the indisposed Billy Pratt in a game at Blackpool in 1897 but the match itself was barely covered in the Birmingham press, and his contribution was not mentioned at all!

WILLIAMS, James William ('Ginger')

Inside-forward; Apps 12, Goals 3.
Born: Buckley, mid-Wales, 1888. Died: France, 5 June 1916.
Career: Bury, Accrington Stanley (1907), BLUES (August 1908), Accrington

(February 1909), Crystal Palace (June 1909), Millwall (February 1914).
Representative honours: Wales (2 full caps).
He scored plenty of goals in junior football before joining Blues, but although he impressed in pre-season trials he had to wait for his debut. When he did get his chance he failed to impress but later made a big impact with Palace. He was killed whilst serving with the Footballer's Battalion.

WILLIAMS, Paul Anthony
Forward; Apps 9+3, Goals 1.
Born: Stratford, London, 16 August 1965.
Career: Aveley, Clapton, Woodford Town, Charlton Athletic (£12,000 August 1986), Brentford (loan October-December 1987), Sheffield Wednesday (£600,000 August 1990), Crystal Palace (September 1992), BLUES (loan March 1995).
Club honours: Sheffield Wednesday: Football League Cup winners 1991; Crystal Palace: Division One champions 1994. Blues: Second Division champions 1995.
Fast forward who had maintained a respectable strike record throughout his career but found himself out in the cold at Selhurst Park after Palace's promotion. Joined Blues in time to make his debut against Orient in the Auto Windscreens Area Final and marked his presence with a goal. At first he seemed a useful acquisition but later he struggled to show his best form.

WILLIAMS, Thomas Edward
Central-defender; Apps 73+1, Goals 2.
Born: Winchburgh, Scotland, 18 December 1957.
Career: Hazel St School, Leicester Beavers (1972), Leicester City (apprentice June 1974, professional December 1975), BLUES (free transfer July 1986), Grimsby Town (August 1988).
Club honours: Leicester City: Division Two champions 1980.

Tom Williams was a solid, no-nonsense defender, who played in 241 League games for Leicester, initially as a full-back and latterly as a centre-half, before moving to St Andrew's. He overcame two broken legs during his stay at Filbert Street and put in some splendid performances for Blues, so it was something of a surprise when he was given a free transfer in 1988. He is now a police officer in Leicestershire.

WILLIS, Roger C. ('Harry')
Midfield; Apps 12+8, Goals 5.
Born: Sheffield, 17 June 1967.
Career: Dunkirk (1987), Grimsby Town (professional July 1989), Barnet (£10,000 August 1990), Watford (£175,000 October 1992), BLUES (£150,000 December 1993),

Southend United (September 1994).
Club honours: Barnet: GMVC winners 1991.
Willis was a striker who did well at Barnet, scoring 17 goals in just over 50 games in their first season as a Football League club, but who never settled at St Andrew's.

WILSON, Alfred Richmond
Right-back; Apps 2, Goals 0.
Born: Sothall, Sheffield 1895. Deceased.
Career: Sheffield Wednesday (1915), BLUES (April 1919), Rotherham County (1920).
After failing to make the first team at Sheffield, Alf Wilson moved to Blues as cover for the regular full-back pairing, but alas he was restricted to only two outings on successive days over Christmas 1919. He did not break into Rotherham's team either.

WINDRIDGE, James Edwin
Inside-forward; Apps 61, Goals 19.
Born: Small Heath, 21 October 1882. Died: Small Heath, 23 September 1939.
Career: Small Heath Alma, BLUES (junior 1899, professional 1901), Chelsea (£190 April 1905), Middlesbrough (November 1911), BLUES (April 1914). Retired 1916.
Representative honours: England (8 full caps).

A highly effective but individualistic forward, Jimmy Windridge of the best dribblers of his day. Although obviously skilful he seemed lazy during his first spell with Blues and was off-loaded to Chelsea with his colleague Robertson in time for the London club's first-ever League season. The move south was perhaps the best thing he could have done, for he thrived in his new surroundings, gained England honours (scoring seven goals in eight internationals) and hit 58 goals in 152 games for the Pensioners before going to Middlesbrough. He was well past his best when he returned to Blues but still managed to score five goals in a League game against Glossop in 1915. During World War One he organised a scratch Blues team to play in local charity matches. A useful cricketer he had seven games for Warwickshire, scoring 161 runs at an average of 14.64. He also took one for 13 with the ball. Cousin of Alec Leake.

WITHE, Peter
Centre-forward; Apps 48, Goals 11.
Born: Liverpool, 30 August 1951.
Career: All Hallows' School Speke, Smith Coggins FC, Skelmersdale, Southport (August 1971), Barrow (December 1971), Port Elizabeth City and Arcadia Shepherds (South Africa) (1972-73), Wolverhampton Wanderers (£13,500 November 1973), Portland Timbers (NASL) (1975), BLUES

(£50,000 August 1975), Nottingham Forest (£42,000 September 1976), Newcastle United (£200,000 August 1978), Aston Villa (record £500,000 May 1980), Sheffield United (July 1985), BLUES (loan September-November 1987), Huddersfield Town (July 1988, initially as assistant manager and player-coach), Aston Villa (assistant manager and coach to Josef Venglos January 1991, reserve-team coach under Ron Atkinson July 1991), Wimbledon (manager October 1991-January 1992), Evesham United (player February 1992), community liaison officer West Midlands and Blues (1993), Aston Villa (youth development officer August 1994).
Club honours: Nottingham Forest: Division One champions 1978, Football League Cup winners 1978; Aston Villa: Division One champions 1981, European Cup winners, Super Cup winners 1982, FA Charity Shield winners 1981 (2 goals scored v Spurs).
Representative honours: England (11 full caps).
One of soccer's goalscoring nomads, Peter Withe served with 11 different Football League clubs during his 17 years as a striker, during which time he chalked up a fine record: 232 goals in 640 games (all competitions). Big, strong and fearless, he never really established himself at St Andrew's where his power in the air seemed to be counterbalanced by his clumsiness on the ground. Under the guidance of Brian Clough he developed into a splendid target man, being a fine exponent of the chest pass. He played a major role in both Forest's and later Villa's glory years, netting the winning goal for the latter in the 1982 European Cup Final. His brother, Chris, has played for several League clubs, while his son, Jason, who started off with West Brom and later served Burnley is currently Blues' Football in the Community officer.

WITHERS, Colin Charles ('Tiny')
Goalkeeper; Apps 116, Goals 0.
Born: Erdington, Birmingham, 21 March 1940.

Career: Paget Road School, West Bromwich Albion (amateur 1956), BLUES (professional May 1957), Aston Villa (£18,000 November 1964), Lincoln City (June 1969), Go-Ahead Eagles Deventer (Holland) (1970), Atherstone Town (1972-73). Retired 1974.
Representative honours: England (Schoolboy cap).
Colin Withers conceded six goals when making his League debut for Blues at White Hart Lane in November 1960. But after that heart-breaking baptism he settled down to give the club great service and later made 163 appearances for rivals Aston Villa. Standing 6ft 3in tall and weighing 13st, he was an imposing figure between the posts, often producing some sterling performances. After retiring he ran a hotel in Blackpool and was later a publican in Bridgnorth.

WOLLASTON, James
Right-half; Apps 1, Goals 0.
Born: Hall Green, Birmingham 1873. Died: King's Norton, December 1918.
Career: Yardley Vics, BLUES (April 1891), Stechford Royal Unity (August 1891).
Wollaston was a local man whose career with Blues seems to have been confined to just a month (April 1891) when he played in three friendlies and one Alliance match. Normally a centre-half, he replaced Harry Morris at right-half in that Alliance fixture.

WOLSTENHOLME, Trevor John
Wing-half/inside-forward; Apps 2, Goals 1.
Born: Prestbury, 18 June 1943.
Career: Prestwick & Whitfield Boys, Chloride FC, BLUES (junior July 1959, professional September 1960), Torquay United (August 1963), York City (July 1966).
Wolstenholme made a dramatic entry into senior football when he replaced Welsh international Ken Leek for a League Cup-tie at Barrow, scoring Blues' goal in the 1-1 draw. He was switched to wing-half for the replay which was his last outing for the club. As a defender he played 82 League games for Torquay and 11 for York later in his career.

WOMACK, Francis ('Frank')
Full-back; Apps 515, Goals 0.
Born: Wortley, near Attercliffe, Sheffield, 16 September 1888. Died: Caistor, Lincolnshire, 8 October 1968.
Career: Rawmarsh FC, BLUES (professional July 1908), Worcester City

(player-manager May 1928), Torquay United (manager July 1930), Grimsby Town (manager May 1932 to May 1936), Leicester City (manager October 1936-September 1939), Notts County (manager July 1942-March 1944), Oldham Athletic (manager February 1945-April 1947), Grimsby Town (caretaker manager January-May 1951).
Club honours: Blues: Division Two champions 1921.
Representative honours: England trialist (3); Football League XI (1)

Frank Womack skippered Blues for 17 consecutive seasons in a 20-year association with the St Andrew's club, subsequently becoming the first player-manager to be appointed in the Birmingham League (May 1928) and leading Worcester City to that championship in his very first season in charge at St George's Lane. According to fellow professionals, Womack was on par with West Brom's England international Jesse Pennington as being the best full-back in the Midlands in the five years leading up to World War One. He was involved in a bribery scandal in 1913, being offered 55 guineas to 'fix' the Blues v Grimsby match so that it would end in a draw. He reported the matter to officials, a trap was set and the culprit duly arrested, charged and found guilty. One of Blues' greatest-ever players, Womack was obviously annoyed and very unhappy when he was released in 1928. At 39 years, 207 days old, he is the oldest player ever to appear for Blues in a first-class match and still holds the club appearance record.

WOOD, Edmund Eli
Centre-half; Apps 1, Goals 0.
Born: King's Norton, Birmingham, 10 February 1903. Deceased.
Career: Redditch, Rhyl Athletic, Northampton Town (March 1923), BLUES (May 1925), Rhyl Athletic (1928), Newcastle United (May 1928), Rhyl Athletic, Wellington Town.
A powerful half-back whose career was restricted by the consistency of Morrall, Eli Wood seems to have had a great liking for the seaside town of Rhyl.

WORTHINGTON, Frank Stewart
Centre-forward; Apps 84+4, Goals 33.
Born: Halifax, 23 November 1948.
Career: Huddersfield Town (apprentice July 1964, professional November 1966), Leicester City (£70,000 August 1972), Bolton Wanderers (£87,000 September 1977), Philadelphia Fury (NASL) (loan May 1979), BLUES (£150,000 November 1979), Tampa Bay Rowdies (NASL) (loan April 1981), Leeds United (exchange for Byron Stevenson March 1982), Southampton (£30,000 June 1983), Brighton & Hove Albion (May 1984), Tranmere Rovers (player-manager July 1985), Preston North End (February 1987), Stockport County (loan November 1987, signed permanently March 1988, Capetown

Spurs (South Africa) (April 1988), Chorley (October 1988), Stalybridge Celtic (December 1988), Galway United (February 1989), Weymouth, Radcliffe Borough, Guiseley, Hinckley Town (player-manager September 1990-May 1991), Halifax Town (part-time coach October 1991).
Club honours: Huddersfield: Division Two champions 1970; Bolton: Division Two champions 1978; Blues: Division Two promotion 1980.
Representative honours: England (8 full caps, 2 Under-23 caps); Football League XI (1).
Anyone who saw Frank Worthington play will have their own thoughts and memories of this immensely skilful footballer. He had the ability to control the ball with one touch and always seemed casual in his approach, even arrogant at times, but he was a class player. Always a larger than life character, both on and off the field, his ill-concealed disdain of the regimented tactics employed during the 1970s probably cost him a hatful of caps. His cavalier approach earned him the nickname of 'swash-buckling hero', and as one of soccer's great nomads his lengthy League career saw him score 236 goals in a total of 757 appearances. His best period was with Leicester (72 goals in 210 games), but he also did well with Huddersfield, Bolton, Blues and Tranmere. His brothers – Dave and Bob – also played League football, while his nephew, Gary, was carrying on the family tradition with Wigan Athletic in 1991. Worthington still plays in charity matches and was granted a benefit by the PFA in 1991, having a game arranged for him at St Andrew's which attracted a near-7,000 crowd.

WRAGG, William A.
Right-back; Apps 1, Goals 0.
Born: Knebworth, 1877. Deceased.
Career: Nottingham Forest (April 1896), Leicester Fosse (March 1899, BLUES January 1901), Watford (August 1901), Hinckley Town (1902), Chesterfield (August 1903), Brighton & Hove Albion (September 1905).
Club honours: Nottingham Forest: FA Cup winners 1898.
Principally a constructive wing-half in his early days at Forest, Wragg engineered their first goal in the 1898 Cup Final. He switched to full-back shortly before moving to Leicester and he was their free-kick expert. He was kept in reserve at Blues by the tigerish tackling of George Adey. Wragg was another player signed by Blues shortly after he had scored an own-goal for them.

WRATTEN, Adam Philip
Defender; Apps 0+1, Goals 2.
Born: Coventry, 30 November 1974.
Career: BLUES (YTS 1991, professional May 1993), Yeovil Town (loan April 1995).
Wratten made a superb start to his Blues' career – scoring twice against Wolverhampton Wanderers at St Andrew's in the Anglo-Italian Cup in September 1993 after coming on as a substitute.

WRIGHT, Patrick Daniel Joseph
Full-back; Apps 3, Goals 0.
Born: Oldbury, 17 November 1940.
Career: St Chad's School, Springfield Boys' Club, BLUES (professional November 1959), Shrewsbury Town (September 1962), Derby County (October 1967), Southend United (loan March 1970),

Rotherham United (player-coach September 1970), Waterlooville (player-manager 1971), Portsmouth (reserve-team coach 1972, chief coach 1974), Zambia (national team coach 1976), Saudi Arabia (national coach 1978, youth-team manager 1979), United Arab Emirates (assistant manager 1979), Al Nasr of Dubai (chief coach 1980-84).
Rarely called up by Blues, Pat Wright later developed into a useful full-back with the Shrews, making over 200 appearances of the Gay Meadow club. He passed his preliminary coaching certificate in 1964 and since then has coached in over 70 different countries. Currently runs his own company which organises coaching courses. He is also on the Planning Committee of the FA School of Excellence.

WRIGHT, William ('Billy')
Centre-half/; Apps 135+2, Goals 14.
Born: Liverpool, 28 April 1958.
Career: Everton (apprentice June 1974, professional January 1977), BLUES (free transfer June 1983), Chester City (loan February-March 1986), Carlisle United (free transfer August 1986), Morecambe (August 1988).
Club honours: Blues: Division Two promotion 1985.
Representative honours: England (2 'B' caps, 6 Under-21 caps).
A stocky performer and an ace penalty-taker, who was an ever-present in Blues' promotion winning side of 1984-85, Wright played in 198 games for the Merseysiders

and accumulated more than 400 senior appearances overall whilst roaming around all Four Divisions of the League in a comparatively short period of time. His uncle, Tommy, is the former Everton and England right-back. Billy Wright skippered Blues and was very popular with the fans. He was released by the club after developing weight problems.

WYLIE, Ronald M.
Right-half/inside-forward; Apps 146+3, Goals 2.
Born: Glasgow, 6 August 1933.
Career: Clydesdale Juniors (1946-47), Notts County (amateur April 1948, professional September 1950), Aston Villa (£9,250 November 1958), BLUES (July 1965), Aston Villa (coach May 1970), Coventry City (coach, then assistant manager), Cyprus FA (adviser) West Bromwich Albion (manager July 1982-February 1984), Aston Villa (reserve-team coach-manager February 1984-May 1987). Scouted for several clubs until becoming Football in the Community Officer at Villa Park in August 1990.
Club honours: Aston Villa: Division Two champions 1960, Football League Cup winners 1961; Midlands 'Footballer of The Year' 1965.
Representative honours: Scotland (2 Schoolboy caps).

Ron Wylie was a midfielder who scored 77 goals in more than 700 games as a professional footballer, of which 51 came in 551 League appearances. Stylish, cultured, skilful and very constructive, he was signed for Notts County by former Villa star and later manager, Eric Houghton. Said to be well past his best when he joined Blues, he proved everyone wrong by appearing in almost 150 games before announcing his retirement when almost 37 years of age.

YATES, Mark Jason
Utility player; Apps 48+17, Goals 7.
Born: Birmingham, 24 January 1970.
Career: Heybridge School, Stourbridge & District Boys, Forest Falcons FC, BLUES (YTS June 1986, professional July 1988), Colchester United (loan August 1990-February 1991), Burnley (£40,000 August 1991), Lincoln City (loan February 1993), Doncaster Rovers (August 1993), Kidderminster Harriers (August 1994).
Club honours: Blues: Leyland DAF Cup winners 1991. Kidderminster Harriers: FA Trophy runners-up 1995.
Representative honours: FA XI 1994-95.
Mark Yates' career was hampered by injury as well as him being asked to play in a number of positions, including that of targetman. Lack of inches prevented him from prospering up front, but he put in some sterling performances in midfield.

Blues in the Football League
1892 to 1995

	P	W	D	L	F	A	Pts	Pos		P	W	D	L	F	A	Pts	Pos
DIVISION TWO										**DIVISION TWO**							
1892-93	22	17	2	3	90	35	36	1st	1950-51	42	20	9	13	64	53	49	4th
1893-94	28	21	0	7	103	44	42	2nd	1951-52	42	21	9	12	67	56	51	3rd
DIVISION ONE									1952-53	42	19	10	13	71	66	48	6th
1894-95	30	9	7	14	50	74	25	12th	1953-54	42	18	11	13	78	58	47	7th
1895-96	30	8	4	18	39	79	20	15th	1954-55	42	22	10	10	92	47	54	1st
DIVISION TWO										**DIVISION ONE**							
1896-97	30	16	5	9	69	47	37	4th	1955-56	42	18	9	15	75	57	45	6th
1897-98	30	16	4	10	58	50	36	6th	1956-57	42	15	9	18	69	69	39	12th
1898-99	34	17	7	10	85	50	41	8th	1957-58	42	14	11	17	76	89	39	13th
1899-1900	34	20	6	8	78	38	46	3rd	1958-59	42	20	6	16	84	68	46	9th
1900-01	34	19	10	5	57	24	48	2nd	1959-60	42	13	10	19	63	80	36	19th
DIVISION ONE									1960-61	42	14	6	22	62	84	34	19th
1901-02	34	11	8	15	47	45	30	17th	1961-62	42	14	10	18	65	81	38	17th
DIVISION TWO									1962-63	42	10	13	19	63	90	33	20th
1902-03	34	24	3	7	74	36	51	2nd	1963-64	42	11	7	24	54	92	29	20th
DIVISION ONE									1964-65	42	8	11	23	64	96	27	22nd
1903-04	34	11	8	15	39	52	30	11th	**DIVISION TWO**							
1904-05	34	17	5	12	54	38	39	7th	1965-66	42	16	9	17	70	75	41	10th
1905-06	38	17	7	14	65	59	41	7th	1966-67	42	16	8	18	70	66	40	10th
1906-07	38	15	8	15	52	52	38	9th	1967-68	42	19	14	9	83	51	52	4th
1907-08	38	9	12	17	40	60	30	20th	1968-69	42	18	8	16	73	59	44	7th
DIVISION TWO									1969-70	42	11	11	20	51	78	33	18th
1908-09	38	14	9	15	58	61	37	11th	1970-71	42	17	12	13	58	48	46	9th
1909-10	38	8	7	23	42	78	23	20th	1971-72	42	19	18	5	60	31	56	2nd
1910-11	38	12	8	18	42	64	32	16th	**DIVISION ONE**							
1911-12	38	14	6	18	55	59	34	12th	1972-73	42	15	12	15	53	54	42	10th
1912-13	38	18	10	10	59	44	46	3rd	1973-74	42	12	13	17	52	64	37	19th
1913-14	38	12	10	16	48	60	34	14th	1974-75	42	14	9	19	53	61	37	17th
1914-15	38	17	9	12	62	39	43	5th	1975-76	42	13	7	22	57	75	33	19th
1919-20	42	24	8	10	85	34	56	3rd	1976-77	42	13	12	17	63	61	38	13th
1920-21	42	24	10	8	79	38	58	1st	1977-78	42	16	9	17	55	60	41	11th
DIVISION ONE									1978-79	42	6	10	26	37	64	2	21st
1921-22	42	15	7	20	48	60	37	18th	**DIVISION TWO**							
1922-23	42	13	11	18	41	57	37	17th	1979-80	42	21	11	10	58	38	53	3rd
1923-24	42	13	13	16	41	49	39	14th	**DIVISION ONE**							
1924-25	42	17	12	13	49	53	46	8th	1980-81	42	13	12	17	50	61	38	13th
1925-26	42	16	8	18	66	81	40	14th	1981-82	42	10	14	18	53	61	44	16th
1926-27	42	17	4	21	64	73	38	17th	1982-83	42	12	14	16	40	55	50	17th
1927-28	42	13	15	14	70	75	41	11th	1983-84	42	12	12	18	39	50	48	20th
1928-29	42	15	10	17	68	77	40	15th	**DIVISION TWO**							
1929-30	42	16	9	17	67	62	41	11th	1984-85	42	25	7	10	59	33	82	2nd
1930-31	42	13	10	19	55	70	36	19th	**DIVISION ONE**							
1931-32	42	18	8	16	78	67	44	9th	1985-86	42	8	5	29	30	73	29	21st
1932-33	42	14	11	17	57	57	39	13th	**DIVISION TWO**							
1933-34	42	12	12	18	54	56	36	20th	1986-87	42	11	17	14	47	59	50	19th
1934-35	42	13	10	19	63	81	36	19th	1987-88	44	11	15	18	41	66	48	19th
1935-36	42	15	11	16	61	63	41	12th	1988-89	46	8	11	27	31	76	35	23rd
1936-37	42	13	15	14	64	60	41	12th	**DIVISION THREE**							
1937-38	42	10	18	14	58	62	38	18th	1989-90	46	18	12	16	60	59	66	7th
1938-39	42	12	8	22	62	84	32	21st	1990-91	46	16	17	13	45	49	65	12th
DIVISION TWO									1991-92	46	23	12	11	69	52	81	2nd
1946-47	42	25	5	12	74	33	55	3rd	**DIVISION TWO/ONE**							
1947-48	42	22	15	5	55	24	59	1st	1992-93	46	13	12	21	42	52	40	19th
DIVISION ONE									1993-94	46	13	12	21	52	69	51	22nd
1948-49	42	11	15	16	36	38	37	17th	**DIVISION THREE/TWO**							
1949-50	42	7	14	21	31	67	28	22nd	1994-95	46	25	14	7	84	37	89	1st

Three points awarded for a win since the 1981-82 season.

Blues Against Other League Clubs

Birmingham City (Small Heath) have played 99 clubs in the Football League since 1892. Below is the Blues' record against each club. Some clubs modified their names (eg Leicester Fosse became Leicester City) but in all cases the current name used by each club cover all games under previous names.

		HOME					AWAY				
	P	W	D	L	F	A	W	D	L	F	A
AFC BOURNEMOUTH	10	0	3	2	1	3	2	0	3	7	9
ARSENAL	110	29	13	13	108	66	4	16	35	37	109
ASTON VILLA	96	20	12	16	74	68	12	13	23	60	82
BARNSLEY	48	14	4	6	44	27	9	6	9	35	40
BLACKBURN ROVERS	88	27	13	4	84	40	7	8	29	61	117
BLACKPOOL	74	20	8	9	88	50	7	8	22	31	62
BOLTON WANDERERS	94	24	12	11	85	55	6	14	27	42	100
BOOTLE	2	1	0	0	6	2	1	0	0	4	1
BRADFORD	16	4	1	3	16	11	2	2	4	7	19
BRADFORD CITY	14	4	3	0	8	3	2	3	2	7	11
BRENTFORD	28	7	3	4	25	13	8	2	4	19	15
BRIGHTON & HA	14	3	3	1	11	8	1	2	4	4	12
BRISTOL CITY	44	10	8	4	36	23	6	5	11	18	29
BRISTOL ROVERS	12	3	3	0	10	6	0	5	1	6	7
BURNLEY	74	20	6	11	63	44	4	9	24	36	76
BURTON SWIFTS	14	6	0	1	20	7	6	1	0	20	6
BURTON UNITED	2	1	0	0	2	0	1	0	0	1	0
BURTON WANDERERS	2	1	0	0	3	2	1	0	0	6	2
BURY	60	15	5	10	48	36	9	4	17	31	51
CAMBRIDGE UNITED	8	1	1	2	2	6	2	0	2	5	3
CARDIFF CITY	54	15	8	4	42	23	9	2	16	30	43
CARLISLE UNITED	18	6	1	2	16	9	2	2	5	13	15
CHARLTON ATHLETIC	36	12	4	2	39	14	2	6	10	15	28
CHELSEA	68	13	9	12	62	57	6	10	18	39	63
CHESTER CITY	8	3	1	0	5	2	3	0	1	6	4
CHESTERFIELD	14	4	3	0	12	5	2	4	1	9	7
COVENTRY CITY	40	9	7	4	33	20	7	5	8	27	28
CREWE ALEXANDRA	10	4	0	1	20	3	3	1	1	12	7
CRYSTAL PALACE	22	6	1	4	17	16	1	2	8	8	24
DARLINGTON	2	1	0	0	1	0	0	1	0	1	1
DARWEN	8	4	0	0	21	4	0	2	2	5	8
DERBY COUNTY	86	22	10	11	81	60	6	15	22	44	86
DONCASTER ROVERS	14	4	1	2	23	7	3	1	3	12	6
EVERTON	104	17	15	20	74	77	6	12	34	60	123
EXETER CITY	4	1	1	0	2	1	1	0	1	3	2
FULHAM	56	14	8	6	52	41	8	8	12	34	48
GAINSBOROUGH TRINITY	20	6	4	0	37	12	4	3	3	13	8
GATESHEAD	4	1	1	0	5	1	0	0	2	0	4
GLOSSOP	20	5	3	2	28	9	3	1	6	12	21
GRIMSBY TOWN	58	15	7	7	62	38	5	7	17	28	42
HARTLEPOOL UNITED	2	1	0	0	2	1	0	0	1	0	1
HUDDERSFIELD TOWN	80	20	6	14	72	50	7	16	17	32	62
HULL CITY	50	13	9	3	55	31	8	6	11	21	38
IPSWICH TOWN	44	8	7	7	28	23	5	0	17	27	55
LEEDS CITY	14	4	1	2	16	13	0	2	5	4	14
LEEDS UNITED	76	21	11	6	71	35	6	12	20	23	56
LEICESTER CITY	112	31	8	17	103	71	16	11	29	93	115

		HOME					AWAY				
	P	W	D	L	F	A	W	D	L	F	A
LEYTON ORIENT	36	10	6	2	29	13	4	7	7	22	26
LINCOLN CITY	34	13	2	2	51	12	9	6	2	29	20
LIVERPOOL	86	19	10	14	68	42	6	7	30	53	102
LOUGHBOROUGH TOWN	8	4	0	0	16	0	2	1	1	5	4
LUTON TOWN	48	13	7	4	49	24	11	7	6	32	29
MANCHESTER CITY	110	34	10	11	126	68	8	10	37	52	109
MANCHESTER UNITED	80	15	15	10	62	53	9	8	23	34	60
MANSFIELD TOWN	4	1	1	0	4	1	1	0	1	4	6
MIDDLESBROUGH	80	21	12	7	73	44	10	15	15	46	56
MIDDLESBROUGH IRON	2	1	0	0	2	1	0	0	1	0	3
MILLWALL	24	8	2	2	19	7	3	3	6	14	21
NEW BRIGHTON	6	3	0	0	9	2	0	2	1	2	6
NEWCASTLE UNITED	82	21	7	13	73	53	7	14	20	44	80
NEWPORT COUNTY	2	0	1	0	1	1	1	0	0	3	0
NORTHAMPTON TOWN	4	2	0	0	7	0	0	1	1	3	4
NORTHWICH VICTORIA	4	2	0	0	14	2	2	0	0	13	0
NORWICH CITY	32	10	3	3	30	17	1	7	8	19	38
NOTTINGHAM FOREST	76	16	9	13	68	52	11	12	15	45	51
NOTTS COUNTY	52	15	6	5	44	25	5	8	13	26	48
OLDHAM ATHLETIC	20	4	2	4	15	13	4	2	4	10	15
OXFORD UNITED	20	3	5	2	10	7	4	2	4	8	10
PETERBOROUGH UNITED	8	2	2	0	7	1	1	1	2	5	6
PLYMOUTH ARGYLE	24	7	3	2	27	11	5	4	3	17	15
PORTSMOUTH	60	18	6	6	63	34	9	7	14	43	47
PORT VALE	18	8	0	1	35	8	3	2	4	12	16
PRESTON NORTH END	72	22	8	6	70	36	4	11	21	32	74
QUEEN'S PARK RANGERS	30	11	3	1	29	10	3	4	8	17	25
READING	10	1	3	1	6	5	1	4	0	8	6
ROTHERHAM UNITED	26	10	1	2	39	18	5	5	3	22	20
SHEFFIELD UNITED	82	23	8	10	78	43	9	5	27	53	94
SHEFFIELD WEDNESDAY	70	17	14	4	53	25	8	6	21	49	94
SHREWSBURY TOWN	18	3	2	4	5	6	1	3	5	4	10
SOUTHAMPTON	28	4	6	4	16	15	4	1	9	10	18
SOUTHEND UNITED	6	2	1	0	6	2	0	0	3	2	9
STOCKPORT COUNTY	26	9	2	2	28	10	4	2	7	13	19
STOKE CITY	74	18	8	11	48	40	5	8	24	34	69
SUNDERLAND	88	22	10	12	66	51	7	6	31	47	96
SWANSEA CITY	26	8	3	2	28	10	6	3	4	14	11
SWINDON TOWN	12	3	1	2	14	11	2	2	2	7	8
TORQUAY UNITED	2	1	0	0	3	0	1	0	0	2	1
TOTTENHAM HOTSPUR	68	16	6	12	46	37	7	6	21	30	73
TRANMERE ROVERS	8	2	1	1	3	4	1	0	3	3	11
WALSALL	18	8	1	0	35	7	5	1	3	17	14
WATFORD	20	5	3	2	17	9	2	0	8	8	18
WEST BROMWICH ALBION	92	14	12	20	51	65	11	15	20	47	67
WEST HAM UNITED	74	22	7	8	68	36	13	9	15	49	70
WIGAN ATHLETIC	6	0	3	0	3	3	0	1	2	1	5
WIMBLEDON	2	1	0	0	4	2	1	0	0	2	1
WOLVERHAMPTON W	96	17	16	15	70	70	9	6	33	45	94
WREXHAM	4	2	0	0	7	2	0	1	1	1	2
WYCOMBE WANDERERS	2	0	0	1	0	1	1	0	0	3	0
YORK CITY	2	1	0	0	4	2	0	0	1	0	2

Birmingham Season-by-Season

1889-90

Football Alliance

Player columns: Banks F, Barton J, Charsley C, Clark E, Davenport E, Devey EJ, Devey W, Gittins W, Hallam J, Heath F, Jenkyns CAL, Lines W, Morgan A, Morris H, Pratt W, Short C, Short GF, Simms C, Speller F, Stanley AE, Walton WH, Watts C, Wheldon GF, Wilcox L

#	Date		Opponent	Res	Scorers	Att	Banks F	Barton J	Charsley C	Clark E	Davenport E	Devey EJ	Devey W	Gittins W	Hallam J	Heath F	Jenkyns CAL	Lines W	Morgan A	Morris H	Pratt W	Short C	Short GF	Simms C	Speller F	Stanley AE	Walton WH	Watts C	Wheldon GF	Wilcox L
1	Sep	7 (h)	Birmingham St	GW 3-2	Short, Stanley, W.Devey	2,000		2	1		11	6	9				10	5			4			7		3	8			
2		14 (h)	Bootle	D 2-2	W.Devey, Stanley	2,000			1		11	6	9	3				5	8		4			7		2	10			
3		21 (a)	Walsall TS	D 1-1	W.Devey	1,500			1		11	6	9	3					10		4			7	5	2	8			
4	Oct	12 (a)	Sunderland A	L 1-6	Davenport	1,000			1		11	6	9	3				5	8		4			7		2	10			
5		19 (h)	Sheffield W	D 2-2	W.Devey 2	3,000			1		8	6	9	3			11	5			4	10		7		2				
6	Nov	2 (a)	Nottingham F	D 0-0		1,000			1			6	9	3			11	5			4			7		2	10	8		
7		9 (h)	Walsall TS	L 0-2		3,000			1			6	9	3			10	5			4			7		2	11	8		
8		23 (h)	Grimsby T	W 3-1	W.Devey 2, Heath	3,000			1			6	9	3			10	5			4			7		2	11	8		
*9	Dec	21 (a)	Sheffield W	L 1-9	Brayshaw (og)	1,500	1					6					10	5	8		4	9				2	7			
10		25 (a)	Birmingham St	GL 1-4	Heath	5,000			1			6		3			9	5			4	11		7		2			10	8
11		26 (a)	Grimsby T	L 0-4		3,000			1			6		3			9	5			4	11		7		2	10		8	
12		28 (h)	Long Eaton R	W 3-1	Stanley 2, Pratt	2,000			1			6		3			10	5	7		4	11				2	9		8	
13	Jan	4 (h)	Crewe A	L 0-2		3,000			1				9	3			11			6	4	10		7	5	2	8			
14	Feb	15 (h)	Darwen	W 6-2	Jenkyns, Hallam, W.Devey, Wheldon 2, Wilcox	500			1	3			9	2	7	6	5				4						8		10	11
15		22 (a)	Crewe A	L 2-6	W.Devey, Stanley	600			1			6	9	2	3			5	7			11			4		10	8		
16		25 (a)	Long Eaton R	W 2-0	W.Devey, Lines	500			1			6	9	3			5	7			4	11				2	10	8		
17	Mar	8 (h)	Nottingham F	W12-0	W.Devey 6, G.Short 3, Hallam, E.Devey 2	1,000			1			6	9	3	7	4	5						11	10	8					
18		15 (h)	Newton Heath	D 1-1	Wilcox	2,000			1			6	9	3	7	10	5				4					2	8			11
19		29 (h)	Sunderland A	L 1-3	W.Devey	2,000			1			6	9	3	7	4	5							7	8	2	10			
20	Apr	4 (a)	Bootle	L 0-6		1,000				1		6	9	3	7	4	5								8	2			10	11
21		5 (a)	Darwen	L 2-4	Hallam, Morris	1,000	1					6	9	3	8	4				7					5	2	10			11
22		7 (a)	Newton Heath	L 1-9	W.Devey	4,000	1						9	3			4	5			7	11			6	2	8	10		
	FINAL LEAGUE POSITION: 10th in Division One. Average home League attendance: 1,068						Appearances	3	1	18	2	5	19	18	21	7	7	19	17	7	1	18	10	1	13	7	20	13	13	2	2	4
	*Match 9 played with only ten players						Goals					1	2	18		3	2	1	1			1	1		4			5			2	2

1 own-goal

FA Cup

	Date		Opponent	Res	Scorers	Att	Charsley C	Davenport E	Devey EJ	Devey W	Gittins W	Jenkyns CAL	Lines W	Pratt W	Short C	Simms C	Speller F	Stanley AE	Walton WH	Watts C
Q2	Oct	26 (a)	Oldbury T	W 3-1	W.Devey 2, Davenport	1,000	1	8	6	9	3	10	5	4	11		7	2		
Q3	Nov	16 (a)	Wednesbury OA	W 5-1	Walton 2, W.Devey 2, Heath	2,000	1		6	9	3	10	5	4			7	2	11	8
Q4	Dec	7 (h)	Walsall TS	W 4-0	W.Devey 3, Stanley	2,000	1		6	9	3	10	5	4			7	2	11	8
1	Jan	18 (h)	Clapton O	W 3-1	W.Devey, Stanley 2	2,000	1			9	3	10	5	4	11		6	2	7	8
2	Feb	1 (a)	Wolves	L 1-2	W.Devey	3,000	1	10		9	3	6	5	4	11			2	7	8
						Appearances	5	2	3	5	5	5	5	5	3		3	1	5	4	4
						Goals		1		9			1					3	2	

1890-91

Football Alliance

Player columns: Bayley JT, Charsley C, Charsley W, Devey EJ, Devey W, Evers G, Hallam J, Hands T, Heath F, Hughes J, Jenkyns CAL, Morris H, Partridge C, Pratt W, Short C, Simms C, Speller F, Smith G, Turner AS, Walton WH, Ward W, Wheldon GF, Wollaston J

#	Date		Opponent	Res	Scorers	Att	Bayley JT	Charsley C	Charsley W	Devey EJ	Devey W	Evers G	Hallam J	Hands T	Heath F	Hughes J	Jenkyns CAL	Morris H	Partridge C	Pratt W	Short C	Simms C	Speller F	Smith G	Turner AS	Walton WH	Ward W	Wheldon GF	Wollaston J
1	Sep	6 (a)	Walsall TS	L 2-5	W.Devey, Reynolds (og)	5,000	3			6	9		7			5		4	1	11		2			8		10		
2		13 (h)	Sunderland A	L 0-3		5,000	3	1		6	9		7				5	4		11		2			8		10		
3		27 (a)	Grimsby T	L 1-3	Jenkyns	2,000	3	1		6	9		7				5	4		11		2			8		10		
4	Oct	11 (a)	Sheffield W	D 3-3	Walton, W.Devey, Hallam	7,000	3	1		6	9		7				5	4		11		2			8		10		
5		18 (h)	Walsall TS	L 0-1		5,000	3	1		6	9		7				5	4		11	8	2					10		
6	Nov	1 (h)	Stoke	W 5-1	Short 3, Wheldon, W.Devey	2,500	3	1		6	9		7				5	4		11	8	2					10		
7		8 (a)	Bootle	D 1-1	W.Devey	1,000	3			6	9		7				5	4		11	8	2				1	10		
8		22 (h)	Darwen	L 3-4	Hallam 2, Wheldon	2,000	3	1		6	9		7				5	4		11		2		8			10		
9		29 (a)	Birmingham St	L 4-5	Hallam 2, W.Devey 2	2,000	3			6	9		7				5	4		11	8	2				1	10		
10	Dec	13 (a)	Newton Heath	L 1-3	Hallam	1,000	3			6	9		7		4		5		1	11	8	2					10		
11		27 (a)	Stoke	L 2-4	Short 2	3,000	3		6		9		7	11			5	4			8	2					10		
12	Jan	3 (a)	Darwen	L 3-5	W.Devey, Hallam, Wheldon	3,000	3	1	4	6	9		7	11			5				8	2					10		
13		10 (h)	Sheffield W	W 7-1	Wheldon, Short 2, Jenkyns 2, W.Devey 2	500	3	1		6	8		7	11			5	4			9	2					10		
14	Feb	7 (h)	Crewe A	W 4-3	W.Devey 3, Wheldon	2,000	3	1		6	8		7	11			5	4			9	2					10		
15		21 (h)	Grimsby T	L 1-2	Hallam	2,000	3	1		6	9		7	11				4			8	5	2				10		
16		26 (a)	Nottingham F	W 5-4	Jenkyns 2, Short, W.Devey, Hands	2,500	3	1		6	8		7	11	4		5				9	2					10		
17		28 (h)	Nottingham F	W 4-2	Short 3, Wheldon	5,000	3	1		6	8		7	11	4		5				9	2					10		
18	Mar	7 (h)	Newton Heath	W 2-1	Wheldon 2	2,000	3	1		6	8		7	11	4		5				9	2					10		
19		16 (h)	Birmingham St	L 1-4	Hands	1,000	3	1		6			7	11	5			4			9	2					10		
20		21 (h)	Bootle	W 7-1	Hands 2, W.Devey 2, Wheldon 3	1,000	3		4	6	8	5	7	11							9	2				1	10		
21		31 (a)	Sunderland A	L 0-4		3,000	3				8	4	7	11			5				9	2	6			1	10		
22	Apr	11 (a)	Crewe A	L 2-6	W.Devey 2	2,000	3	1		6	8		7		5						11	9	2				10	4	
	FINAL LEAGUE POSITION: 10th. Average home League attendance: 2,545.						Appearances	22	15	3	20	22	2	22	11	6	1	17	14	2	11	17	22	1	1	4	5	22	1	
							Goals					17		8	4			5				11					1		11	

1 own-goal

FA Cup

	Date		Opponent	Res	Scorers	Att	Bayley JT	Charsley C	Devey EJ	Devey W	Hallam J	Jenkyns CAL	Morris H	Pratt W	Short C	Simms C	Walton WH	Wheldon GF
Q1	Oct	4 (h)	Hednesford T	W 8-0	Wheldon 3, Hallam, W.Devey 2, Jenkyns, Webster (og)	1,500	2	1	6	9	7	5	4	11	8	3	8	10
Q2	Dec	6 (a)	Wednesbury OA	W2-0*	Short, Hallam	2,000	2	1	6	9	7	5	4	11	1	3		10
	*Small Heath disqualified for fielding an unregistered player.						Appearances	2	2	2	2	2	2	2	2	1	2	1	2
							Goals			3	2		1						3

1 own-goal

1891-92

Football Alliance

#		Date	Opponent	Result	Scorers	Att.	Allen F	Bayley JT	Brown W	Burton EG	Charsley C	Currier L	Devey EJ	Hallam J	Hands T	Harrison W	Hollis G	Jenkyns CAL	Kendrick W	Millard A	Morris H	Ollis W	Pratt W	Short J	Simms C	Speller F	Taylor W	Walton WH	Wheldon GF	Wilkes F
1	Sep	5 (h)	Burton S	W 3-1	Hallam 2, Wilkes	2,000		2	11				6	8			1	5				4				3	7		10	9
2		12 (h)	Birmingham St	D 2-2	Brown, Hands	3,000		2	8				6	7	11		1	5				4				3		9	10	
3		19 (a)	Burton S	L 3-6	E.Devey, Wheldon 2	2,000		2					8	9	11		1	5		6		4				3	7		10	
4		26 (h)	Lincoln C	W 4-0	Wheldon 3, Brown	2,000		2	8		1		6	7				5				4				3		11	10	9
5	Oct	8 (a)	Nottingham F	L 0-2		2,000					1		6	7	11			5		8	9	4				3	2		10	
6		10 (h)	Sheffield	D 1-1	Millard	1,000					1		6	7	11			5		8	9	4				3	2		10	
7		17 (h)	Walsall TS	W 4-1	Hands 2, Morris, Wheldon	2,000		2					6	7	11		1	5			9	4				3		8	10	
8	Nov	21 (a)	Bootle	W 1-0	Jenkyns	3,000	7	2					6	9	11		1	5				4				3		8	10	
9		28 (a)	Birmingham St	L 0-1		500	7	2					6	9			1	5				4	11			3		8	10	
10	Dec	12 (h)	Crewe A	W 3-1	Hallam 2, Jenkyns	600	7	2					6	8	11		1	5				4				3			10	9
11		19 (a)	Grimsby T	W 2-1	Lundie (og), Hallam	1,000		2					6	7	11		1	5				4				3		8	10	9
12		26 (a)	Newton Heath	D 3-3	Walton, Wheldon 2	7,000		2					6	7	11		1	5			9	4				3		8	10	
13	Jan	2 (a)	Ardwick	D 2-2	Harrison 2	3,000		2		1			6	7	11	9		5				4				3		8	10	
14		9 (a)	Sheffield W	L 3-6	Hallam, Walton, McConnachie (og)	5,000		2					6	7	11		1	5			9	4				3		8	10	
15	Feb	13 (a)	Lincoln C	D 1-1	Wheldon	2,000		2					6	7	11			5				4		8	1	3	9		10	
16		20 (a)	Ardwick	W 4-0	Wheldon 2, Hallam, Walton	2,000		2					6	7	11		1	5			9	4				3		8	10	
17		27 (h)	Newton Heath	W 3-2	Walton, Hallam, Wheldon	3,000		2					6	7	11		1	5			9	4				3		8	10	
18	Mar	26 (h)	Bootle	W 4-1	Walton 2, Wheldon 2	2,000		2				9	6	7	11		1		5			4				3		8	10	
19	Apr	2 (h)	Grimsby T	W 3-0	Hallam, Wheldon 2	2,000		2					6	7	11		1	5			9	4				3		8	10	
20		9 (a)	Walsall TS	W 4-3	Hallam, Wheldon 2, Hands	4,000		2					6	7	11		1	5			9	4				3		8	10	
21		16 (h)	Nottingham F	L 1-2	Walton	3,500		2					6	7	11		1	5			9	4				3		8	10	
*22		20 (a)	Crewe A	W 2-0	Wheldon 2	1,000		2				9	6	7	11		1	5				4				3			10	

FINAL LEAGUE POSITION: 3rd. Average home League attendance: 2,100.
*Match 22 played with only ten players

	Appearances	3	20	3	1	4	2	22	22	19	1	17	20	1	3	9	22	1	1	1	22	6	15	22	4
	Goals			2				1	10	4	2		2		1	1							6	21	1

2 own-goals

FA Cup

		Date	Opponent	Result	Scorers	Att.	Allen F	Bayley JT	Brown W	Burton EG	Charsley C	Currier L	Devey EJ	Hallam J	Hands T	Harrison W	Hollis G	Jenkyns CAL	Kendrick W	Millard A	Morris H	Ollis W	Pratt W	Short J	Simms C	Speller F	Taylor W	Walton WH	Wheldon GF	Wilkes F
Q1	Oct	3 (a)	Leicester F	W 6-2	Hands, Millard 2, Hallam, Wheldon	1,000				1			6	9	11			5		8	7	4				3	2		10	
Q2		24 (a)	Burton W	D 1-1	Wheldon	4,000				1			6	7	11			5			9	4				3	2	8	10	
R		31 (h)	Burton W	W 2-1	Taylor, Wheldon	2,000		2		1			6	7				5			9	4				3	11	8	10	
Q3	Nov	14 (h)	Burton S	W 4-2	Hands, Walton 2, Wheldon	3,000		2		1			6	7	11			5			9	4				3		8	10	
Q4	Dec	5 (h)	Brierley Hill A	W 6-2	Wheldon, Wilkes 3, Walton, Hands	1,000				1			6	7	11			5				4				3	2	8	10	9
1	Jan	16 (h)	Royal Arsenal	W 5-1	Hallam 2, Wheldon 2, Walton	4,000		2		1			6	7	11			5			9	4				3		8	10	
2		30 (a†)	Sheffield W	L 0-2		4,000		2		1			6	7	11			5			9	4				3		8	10	

†Small Heath forfeited home advantage.

	Appearances		4		7			7	7	6			7		1	6	7				7	4	6	7	1
	Goals								3	3					2							1	4	8	3

1892-93

Manager: Committee

#		Date	Opponent	Result	Scorers	Att.	Charsley C	Bayley JT	Speller F	Ollis W	Jenkyns CAL	Devey EJ	Hallam J	Walton WH	Mobley F	Wheldon GF	Hands T	Short GF	Edwards HR	Hollis G	Roberts JE	Pumfrey B	Jones FW	Simms C	Morris H
1	Sep	3 (h)	Burslem PV	W 5-1	Wheldon 2, Short, Hallam, Edwards	2,500	1	2	3	4	5	6	7			10	11	9	8						
2		10 (a)	Walsall TS	W 3-1	Wheldon, Jenkyns, Pinches (og)	2,500	1	2	3	4	5	6	7			10	11	9	8						
3		17 (a)	Sheffield U	L 0-2		3,500	1		3	4	5	6	7		9	10	11	2	8						
4		24 (h)	Lincoln C	W 4-1	Wheldon 2, Jenkyns, Mobley	2,500			3	4	5	6	7		9	10	11	2	8	1					
5	Oct	1 (a)	Grimsby T	L 2-3	Wheldon 2	3,000		2	3	4	5	6		8	9	10	11		7	1					
6		3 (a)	Burton S	W 3-2	Wheldon, Lawrence (og), Mobley	2,000	1	2	3	4	5	6	7	8	9	10	11								
7		8 (h)	Crewe A	W 6-0	Walton, Wheldon, Hallam, Devey, Mobley, Hands	2,500	1		3	4	5	6	7	8	9	10	11	2							
8		22 (a)	Ardwick	D 2-2	Wheldon 2	6,000		2	3	4	5	6	7	8	9	10	11			1					
9		29 (a)	Darwen	W 3-2	Mobley, Hallam, Hands	2,000	1	2	3	4	5	6	7	8	9	10	11								
10	Nov	5 (a)	Bootle	W 4-1	Walton, Mobley, Wheldon, Hands	1,500	1	3		4	5	6	7	8	9	10	11				2				
11		12 (h)	Burton S	W 3-2	Mobley, Walton, Jenkyns	3,000	1	2		4	5	6	7	8	9	10	11					3			
12	Dec	3 (h)	Sheffield U	D 1-1	Wheldon	2,000	1	2		4	5	6	7	8	9	10	11					3			
13		10 (a)	Darwen	L 3-4	Hallam 2, Hands	3,000	1	2		4	5	6	7	8	9	10	11					3			
14		17 (h)	Walsall TS	W 12-0	Wheldon 2, Walton 3, Hallam 2, Mobley 3, Hands 2	2,000	1	2		4	5	6	7	8	9	10	11					3			
15		24 (a)	Northwich V	W 6-0	Mobley 2, Wheldon 2, Walton, Hands	1,000		2		4	5	6	7	8	9	10	11				1	3			
16		31 (a)	Crewe A	W 3-1	Mobley, Hands, Hallam	1,500	1	2		4	5	6	7	8	9	10	11					3			
17	Jan	7 (a)	Lincoln C	W 4-3	Wheldon 3, Hands	1,500				4		6	7	8	9	10	11	2				3	5		
18		14 (a)	Northwich V	W 6-2	Ollis, Wheldon 3, Walton, Hallam	2,000		2		4	5		7	8	9	10	11	2		1		3			
19	Feb	18 (h)	Bootle	W 6-2	Hallam 3, Mobley 2, Wheldon	2,000		2		4	5		7	8	9	10	11	3		1					6
20		25 (h)	Grimsby T	W 8-3	Hands 2, Hallam 2, Wheldon, Walton 3	2,500		2		4	5		7	8	9	10	11	6				3			
21	Mar	25 (a)	Burslem PV	W 3-0	Walton 2, Hallam	1,000	1	2		4	5		7	8	9	10	11	6				3			
22	Apr	1 (h)	Ardwick	W 3-2	Hallam 2, Walton	1,000	1	2		4	5		7	8	9	10	11	6				3			

FINAL LEAGUE POSITION: 1st in Division Two. Average home League attendance: 2,181.

	Appearances	14	18	9	22	21	18	21	19	19	22	22	10	5	8	1	3	8	1	1
	Goals				1	3	1	17	14	14	25	11	1	1						

2 own-goals

Test Matches

		Date	Opponent	Result	Scorers	Att.	Charsley C	Bayley JT	Speller F	Ollis W	Jenkyns CAL	Devey EJ	Hallam J	Walton WH	Mobley F	Wheldon GF	Hands T	Short GF	Edwards HR	Hollis G	Roberts JE	Pumfrey B	Jones FW	Simms C	Morris H
T	Apr	22 (n*)	Newton Heath	D 1-1	Wheldon	4,000	1	2		4	5		7	8	9	10	11	6					3		
R		27 (n†)	Newton Heath	L 2-5	Walton, Mobley	6,000	1	2		4	5		7	8	9	10		6					3	11	

*Played at the Victoria Ground, Stoke-on-Trent. †Played at Bramall Lane, Sheffield.

	Appearances	2	2		2	2		2	2	2	2	1	2					2	1	
	Goals								1	1	1									

FA Cup

		Date	Opponent	Result	Att.	Charsley C	Bayley JT	Speller F	Ollis W	Jenkyns CAL	Devey EJ	Hallam J	Walton WH	Mobley F	Wheldon GF	Hands T	Short GF	Edwards HR	Hollis G	Roberts JE	Pumfrey B	Jones FW	Simms C	Morris H
1	Jan	21 (a)	Burnley	L 0-2	6,500	1	2		4	5		7	8	9	10	11	6					3		

	Appearances	1	1		1	1		1	1	1	1	1	1					1		
	Goals																			

1893-94

Manager: Committee

No	Date		Opponents	Result	Scorers	Att	Hollis G	Smith G	Pumfrey B	Ollis W	Jenkyns CAL	Devey EJ	Hallam J	Walton WH	Mobley F	Wheldon GF	Hands T	Jolley E	Lee J	Short GF	Izon CJ	Spiller F	Reynolds WT	Jackson W	Littleford AG	Purves W	Partridge C	Charsley C	Watson P
1	Sep	2 (a)	Walsall TS	W 3-1	Lee 2, Wheldon	5,000	1		3	4	5	6	7		9	10	11	2	8										
2		4 (h)	Rotherham T	W 4-3	Wheldon, Hands, Mobley, Hallam	3,000	1		3	4	5	6	7		9	10	11	2	8										
3		9 (h)	Burton S	W 6-1	Wheldon 2, Jolley 2, Hands, Lee	2,000	1	2	3	4	5	6			9	10	11	7	8										
4		16 (h)	Walsall TS	W 4-0	Jenkyns, Izon 3	2,000	1		3	4	5	6	7			10	11			8	2	9							
5		23 (a)	Liverpool	L 1-3	Jenkyns	8,000	1	2	3	4	5	6	7			10	11			8		9							
6		25 (a)	Burslem PV	L 0-5		1,000	1	2	3	4	5	6	7			10	11			8		9							
7		30 (a)	Ardwick	W 1-0	Wheldon	5,000	1	2		4	5	6	7			10	11			8		9	3						
8	Oct	7 (h)	Grimsby T	W 5-2	Walton 3, Izon, Hallam	3,000	1	2		4	5	6	7	8		10	11					9	3						
9		4 (h)	Liverpool	L 3-4	Wheldon, Jenkyns, Hands	5,000	1	2		4	5	6	7	8	9	10	11						3						
10		21 (h)	W Arsenal	W 4-1	Wheldon 2, Hallam, Hands	3,000	1	2		4	5	6	7	8		10	11			9			3						
11		28 (h)	Newcastle U	W 2-0	Mobley, Wheldon	3,000	1	2		4	5	6	7	8	9	10	11						3						
12	Nov	11 (a)	Lincoln C	W 5-2	Wheldon, Mobley 3, Walton	1,000	1	2		4		6	7	8	9	10	11		5				3						
13		25 (a)	Middlesbro' I	L 0-3		200	1	2		4		6	7	8	9	10	11		5				3						
14	Dec	2 (h)	Northwich V	W 8-0	Wheldon 4, Mobley 3, Walton	1,500	1	2		4	5	6	7	8	9	10	11						3						
15		6 (h)	Crewe A	W 6-1	Hallam, Mobley 2, Hands, Walton, Jenkyns	500	1	2		4	5	6	7	8	9	10	11						3						
16		9 (a)	Burton S	W 2-0	Mobley, Hands	1,500	1	2		4	5	6		8	9	10	11						3	7					
17		16 (h)	Newcastle U	L 1-4	Hallam	2,500	1	2		4	5	6	7	8	9	10	11						3						
18		23 (h)	Middlesbro' I	W 2-1	Pumfrey, Walton	2,000	1		8	4	5	6	7			10	11			9			3	2					
19		30 (h)	Lincoln C	W 6-0	Devey, Wheldon 2, Mobley, Hands, Walton	1,000	1			4	5	6		8	9	10	11						3	7	2				
20	Jan	6 (a)	Northwich V	W 7-0	Walton, Mobley 3, Hands 2, Wheldon	500	1		3	4	5	6		8	9	10	11							7	2				
21		13 (a)	Crewe A	W 5-3	Jackson, Walton 2, Mobley, Hands	1,000	1			4	5	6		8	9	10	11						3	7	2				
22	Feb	3 (a)	Notts C	L 1-3		6,000				4	5	6	7	8	9	10	11	6		3						1			
23	Mar	3 (a)	Grimsby T	L 1-2	Mobley	5,000	1			4	5	6	7		9	10	11	6		3	8								
24		17 (h)	Ardwick	W10-2	Wheldon 2, Hallam 2, Hands, Jenkyns, Walton, Mobley 3	2,500				4	5	6	7	8	9	10	11			2								1	3
25		23 (a)	Rotherham T	W 3-2	Walton, Hallam, Wheldon	1,000	1			4	5	6	7	8	9	10	11			2									3
26		24 (h)	Burslem PV	W 6-0	Hands, Walton 2, Mobley 2, Wheldon	4,000				4	5	6	7	8	9	10	11			3						2	1		
27		31 (a)	W Arsenal	W 4-1	Jenkyns, Wheldon, Mobley, Hallam	6,000				4	5	6	7	8	9	10	11			3						2	1		
28	Apr	7 (h)	Notts C	W 3-0	Hands 2, Walton	8,500				4	5	6	7	8	9	10	11			3						2			
			Appearances				23	14	8	28	26	28	22	20	21	28	28	7	7	8	8	2	12	4	3	4	1	4	2
			Goals						1		6	1	9	16	24	22	14	2	3		4			1					

FINAL LEAGUE POSITION: 2nd in Division Two. Average home League attendance: 2,928

Test Match

	Date		Opponents	Result	Scorers	Att	Ollis W	Jenkyns CAL	Devey EJ	Hallam J	Walton WH	Mobley F	Wheldon GF	Hands T	Short GF	Purves W	Partridge C
T	Apr	28(n*)	Darwen	W 3-1	Hallam, Walton, Wheldon	3,000	4	5	6	7	8	9	10	11	3	2	1
			Appearances				1	1	1	1	1	1	1	1	1	1	1
			Goals							1	1		1				

*Played at the Victoria Ground, Stoke-on-Trent.

FA Cup

	Date		Opponents	Result	Scorers	Att	Hollis G	Ollis W	Jenkyns CAL	Devey EJ	Hallam J	Walton WH	Mobley F	Wheldon GF	Hands T	Reynolds WT	Jackson W
1	Jan	27 (h)	Bolton W	L 3-4	Hallam, Mobley, Wheldon	7,000	1	4	5	6	7	8	9	10	11	3	2
			Appearances				1	1	1	1	1	1	1	1	1	1	1
			Goals								1		1	1			

1894-95

Manager: Committee

No	Date		Opponents	Result	Scorers	Att	Partridge C	Purves W	Oliver JHS	Ollis W	Jenkyns CAL	Devey EJ	Hallam J	Walton WH	Mobley F	Wheldon GF	Hands T	Brueton EM	Izon CJ	Leatherbarrow C	Jolley E	Lewis WJ	Moore E	Pritchard T	Fountain EJ	Jones J	Watson T
1	Sep	1 (a)	Aston Villa	L 1-2	Hands	20,000	1	2	3	4	5	6	7	8	9	10	11										
2		3 (a)	Everton	L 0-5		8,000	1	2	3	4	5	6	7	8	9	10	11										
3		8 (h)	Bolton W	W 2-0	Wheldon 2	5,000	1	2	3	4	5	6	7	8	9	10	11										
4		15 (a)	Wolves	L 1-2	Wheldon	4,000	1	2	3	4	5	6	7	8	9	10	11										
5		22 (a)	Preston NE	W 1-0	Hands	5,000	1	2	3	4	5	6	7	8	9	10	11										
6		29 (h)	Preston NE	D 4-4	Hands, Wheldon, Mobley 2	4,000		2	3	4	5	6	7	8	9	10	11	1									
7	Oct	6 (h)	Wolves	W 4-3	Walton 2, Mobley, Wheldon	5,000	1	2	3	4	5	6	7	8	9	10	11										
8		13 (a)	Burnley	L 1-3	Mobley	5,000	1	2	3	4	5	6	7	8	9	10	11										
9		20 (h)	Aston Villa	D 2-2	Wheldon (pen), Hallam	14,000	1	2	3	4	5	6	7	8	9	10	11										
10		27 (a)	Stoke	D 2-2	Mobley, Hands	1,500	1	2	3	4	5	6	7	8	9	10	11										
11	Nov	3 (h)	Everton	D 4-4	Wheldon, Izon, Hallam, Jenkyns	10,000	1	2	3	4	5	6	7	8		10	11		9								
12		10 (a)	West Brom A	L 1-4	Hands	4,523	1	2	3	4	5	6	7	8	9	10	11										
13		17 (h)	Stoke	W 4-2	Walton, Hallam, Mobley, Wheldon	3,000	1	2	3	4	5	6	7	8	9	10	11										
14		24 (a)	Bolton W	W 2-1	Hallam, Wheldon	5,000	1	2	3	4	5	6	7		9	10	11			8							
15	Dec	1 (h)	Sheffield U	W 4-2	Leatherbarrow 3, Wheldon (pen)	5,000	1	2	3	4	5	6	7		9	10	11			8							
16		8 (a)	Sunderland	L 1-7	Hallam	6,000	1	2	3	4	5	6	7		9	10	11			8							
17		15 (a)	Liverpool	L 1-3	Mobley	7,000	1	2	3	4	5	6	7		9	10	11			8							
18		22 (h)	Nottingham F	L 1-2	Mobley	3,000	1	2	3	4	5		7	8	9	10	11				6						
19		26 (a)	Sheffield W	L 0-2		14,000	1	2	3	4	5	6	7	8	9	10	11										
20		29 (h)	Liverpool	W 3-0	Mobley, Lewis, Walton	5,000	1	2		4	5			8	9	10	11				6	7	3				
21	Jan	5 (a)	Blackburn R	L 1-9	Walton	4,000	1	3		4		6		8	9	5	11			10		7	2				
22		26 (h)	Nottingham F	L 0-2		5,500	1	2	3	4	5	6	7		9	10	11							8			
23	Feb	9 (h)	Sunderland	D 1-1	Hands	15,000	1	2	3	4	5	6	7	8	9		11								10		
24		23 (h)	West Brom A	L 1-2	Mobley	8,100	1	2	3	4	5	6		8	9	10	11								7		
25	Mar	2 (h)	Blackburn R	D 1-1	Mobley	5,000		2	3	4	5	6	7	8	9	10	11									1	
26		16 (h)	Derby C	L 3-5	Jenkyns, Hallam, Walton	6,000	1	2	3	4	5	6	7	8		10	11				9						
27		23 (h)	Burnley	W 1-0	Wheldon	5,500	1	2	3	4	5	6	7	8	9	10											11
28		28 (h)	Sheffield W	D 0-0		3,000	1	2	3	4	5	6	7	8	9	10	11										
29		30 (a)	Derby C	L 1-4	Mobley	1,500	1	2	3	4	5	6	7	8	9	10	11										
30	Apr	13 (a)	Sheffield U	W 2-0	Mobley, Hill (og)	5,000	1	2	3	4		6	7	8	9	10	11			5							
			Appearances				27	30	28	30	28	28	27	26	28	29	29	1	2	5	3	2	1	1	2	1	2
			Goals								2		6	6	13	11	6		1	3		1					

FINAL LEAGUE POSITION: 12th in Division One.   Average home League attendance: 6,440

1 own-goal

FA Cup

	Date		Opponents	Result	Scorers	Att	Partridge C	Purves W	Oliver JHS	Ollis W	Jenkyns CAL	Devey EJ	Hallam J	Walton WH	Mobley F	Wheldon GF	Hands T
1	Feb	2 (h)	West Brom A	L 1-2	Walton	10,203	1	2	3	4	5	6	7	8	9	10	11
			Appearances				1	1	1	1	1	1	1	1	1	1	1
			Goals											1			

1895-96

Manager: Committee

No	Date	Opponent	Res	Scorers	Att	Roach J	Purves W	Oliver JHS	Ollis W	Jolley E	Fraser A	Hallam J	Walton WH	Mobley F	Wheldon GF	Hands T	Partridge C	Devey DJ	Fall JW	Haynes H	Jones J	Izon CJ	Meates WP	Lester F	Leake A	Adlington JH	Bruce D	Farnall T	Haddon H	Lodge LV	Robertson W	Pratt W	Fountain EJ	Dunlop T	Deeley J	Abbott WA	Lewis WJ
1	Sep 2	(a) Sheffield U	L 0-2		6,000		2	3	4	5		7	8	9	10	11	1	6																			
2	7	(a) Aston Villa	L 3-7	Walton, Mobley, Hands	13,000	1	2	3	4	5		7	8	9	10	11		6																			
3	14	(h) Stoke	L 1-2	Hallam	7,500		2	3	4	5		7	8	9	10	11		6	1																		
4	21	(a) Nottingham F	L 0-3		6,000	1	2	3	4	5		7			10	11			6	8	9																
5	28	(h) Bolton W	L 1-2	Mobley	4,500	1	2	3	4	5		7		9	10	11				8		6															
6	Oct 5	(a) Preston NE	L 2-3	Mobley 2	2,000	1		3	4	5		7		9	10	11				8		2	6														
7	12	(a) Bury	W 5-4	Wheldon 2, Mobley, Jones 2	6,000	1		3	4	5		7		9	10	11				8		2	6														
8	19	(a) Stoke	L 1-6	Jones	8,000		2	3	4	5		7		9	10				1	8	11		6														
9	26	(h) Aston Villa	L 1-4	Jones	10,000		2	3	4	6		7			10	11					9	5	8							1							
10	Nov 9	(h) Nottingham F	W 1-0	Mobley	5,000	1		3	4	6		7		9	10	11						5	8	2													
11	23	(h) Preston NE	W 5-2	Wheldon 2, Jones 2, Mobley	5,000	1		3	4	6				9	10	11							8	2	5		7										
12	30	(a) Derby C	L 0-8		8,000	1		3	4		6		8		10	11							7	2	5			9									
13	Dec 7	(h) Everton	L 0-3		3,000	1		3	4		6	7	8		10	11								2	5			9									
14	14	(a) Sunderland	L 1-2	Wheldon	4,000	1		3	4		6	7	8		10	11								2	5			9									
15	21	(a) West Brom A	D 2-2	Bruce, Adlington	6,000	1		3	4		6		8		10	11								2	5	9	7										
16	26	(h) Burnley	W 1-0	Adlington	5,500	1		3	4		6			9	10	11							8	2	5		7										
17	Jan 4	(h) Derby C	L 1-3	Adlington	10,000	1		3	4		6		8		10	11								2	5	9	7										
18	18	(h) Wolves	W 3-2	Adlington, Bruce, Ollis	6,000	1		3	4		6		8			11							9	2	5	10	7										
19	25	(a) Wolves	L 2-7	Wheldon, Mobley	4,000	1		3	4		6		8	9		11								2	5	10	7										
20	Feb 3	(a) Everton	L 0-3		8,000			3			6	7			10	11							9	2	5			1	4		8						
21	8	(h) Sheffield W	D 1-1	Leake	5,000			3			6	7			10	11							9	2	5			1	4		8						
22	22	(a) Bolton W	L 1-4	Mobley	7,000			3			6	7		9	10	11							8	2	5			1	4								
23	29	(h) Blackburn R	W 2-1	Robertson, Wheldon	7,000			3			6	7			10	11								2	5		9	1	4		8						
24	Mar 7	(h) Bury	W 1-0	Haddon	5,000			3			6	7			10	11								2	5		9	1	4		8						
25	21	(a) Blackburn R	L 1-2	Haddon	5,000			3			6	7			10	11								2	5		9	1	4		8						
26	Apr 3	(a) Burnley	D 1-1	Robertson	8,000			3			6	7			10	11								2	5		9	1	4		8						
27	4	(h) Sheffield W	L 0-3		6,000			3			6	7			10								9		5			1	4		8			2	11		
28	6	(a) West Brom A	D 0-0		3,750			3			6	7	8					1					9		5						8		10	2			
29	7	(h) Sheffield U	W 2-1	Mobley 2	6,000			3			6	7		9	10	11								2	5			1	4		8						
30	11	(h) Sunderland	L 0-1		8,000			3			6	7			10	11							9	2	5			1	4		8						
		Appearances				15	7	29	19	11	19	12	9	28	30	25	1	3	2	9	14	6	12	20	14	6	9	11	5	1	8	1	1	2	1		
		Goals							1			1	1	11	7	1					6				1	4	2		2		2						

FINAL LEAGUE POSITION: 15th in Division One.   Average home League attendance: 6,233

Test Matches

No	Date	Opponent	Res	Scorers	Att	Roach J	Purves W	Oliver JHS	Ollis W	Jolley E	Fraser A	Hallam J	Walton WH	Mobley F	Wheldon GF	Hands T	Partridge C	Devey DJ	Fall JW	Haynes H	Jones J	Izon CJ	Meates WP	Lester F	Leake A	Adlington JH	Bruce D	Farnall T	Haddon H	Lodge LV	Robertson W	Pratt W	Fountain EJ	Dunlop T	Deeley J	Abbott WA	Lewis WJ
T1	Apr 18	(a) Liverpool	L 0-4		20,000			3			6	7			10	11							9	2	5			1	4		8						
	20	(h) Liverpool	D 0-0		5,000			3			6	7	4		10	11							9	2	5			1			8						
T2	25	(a) Manchester C	L 0-3		9,500			3			6	7			10	11							9	2	5			1	4		8						
	27	(h) Manchester C	W 8-0	Jones 3, Wheldon 3, Abbott, Hallam	2,000	1					6	7			10	11					9			2	5				4		8					3	10
		Appearances				1		3			4	3	1	1	4	3					4		3	4	4			3	4		1					1	1
		Goals										1			3						3														1	

FA Cup

No	Date	Opponent	Res	Scorers	Att	Roach J	Purves W	Oliver JHS	Ollis W	Jolley E	Fraser A	Hallam J	Walton WH	Mobley F	Wheldon GF	Hands T	Partridge C	Devey DJ	Fall JW	Haynes H	Jones J	Izon CJ	Meates WP	Lester F	Leake A	Adlington JH	Bruce D	Farnall T	Haddon H	Lodge LV	Robertson W	Pratt W	Fountain EJ	Dunlop T	Deeley J	Abbott WA	Lewis WJ
1	Feb 1	(h) Bury	L 1-4	Lewis	15,000	1		3			6		8	9		11								5			2	10	4								7
		Appearances				1		1			1		1	1		1								1			1	1	1								1
		Goals																																		1

1896-97

Manager: Committee

Player columns: Pointer E, Lester F, Pratt W, Farnall T, Leake A, Walton WH, Inglis J, Robertson W, Jones J, Abbott WA, Edwards W, Dunlop T, Bennett WA, Hodgetts D, Izon CJ, Haddon H, Logan J, Meates WP, Hare CB, Good M, Oakes TF, Gadsby W, Williams H

#		Date		Opponent	Result	Scorers	Att	P E	L F	P W	F T	L A	W WH	I J	R W	J J	A WA	E W	D T	B WA	H D	I CJ	H H	L J	M WP	H CB	G M	O TF	G W	W H
1	Sep	5	(h)	Newcastle U	W 3-1	Leake, Inglis, Jones	4,000		3		4	5	6	7	8	9	10	11	2							1				
2		12	(a)	Newcastle U	L 3-4	Jones 2, Inglis	10,853	1	3		4	5	6	7	8	9	10	11	2											
3		14	(h)	Darwen	W 5-1	Inglis, Walton, Robertson 2, Nixon (og)	800	1		3	4	5	6	7	8	9	10	11	2											
4		19	(h)	Lincoln C	L 1-2	Edwards	6,500	1		3	4	5	6	7	8	9	10	11	2											
5		26	(a)	Burton S	D 1-1	Inglis	2,000	1	3		4	5	6	11	8	9	10		2	7										
6	Oct	3	(h)	Burton S	L 1-2	Inglis	4,000	1	2	3	4	5	6	7	10	9	11			8										
7		10	(a)	Newton Heath	D 1-1	Jones	7,000	1	2	3	4	5	6	7	8	9			11			10								
8		17	(h)	Gainsboro' T	D 2-2	Inglis, Leake	6,000	1	2	3		5	6	7	8	9			4		10	11								
9		24	(a)	Walsall	W 6-1	Izon, Inglis 2, Walton 2, Jones	4,000		2	3		4	5	6	7		8				10	11	9		1					
10		31	(h)	Grimsby T	L 0-1		7,500	1	2	3		4	5	6	7		8				10		9	11						
11	Nov	14	(h)	W Arsenal	W 5-2	Hodgetts, Farnall, Walton, Hare, Robertson	2,000	1	2	3	4	5	6	7	9						10	11				8				
12		21	(a)	Darwen	L 0-2		3,000	1	2	3	4	5	6	7	9		11				10					8				
13		28	(h)	Newton Heath	W 1-0	Jones	4,000	1	2	3	4	5	6	7		9					10	11				8				
14	Dec	12	(a)	Grimsby T	L 1-2	Inglis	2,000	1	2	3	4	5	6	7	9		11				10					8				
15		19	(a)	Loughboro' T	L 0-2		1,000	1	2	3		5	6	7							10	11	9			8	4			
16		25	(h)	Walsall	D 3-3	Inglis, Hare, Izon	7,500	1	2	3		5	6	7		8					10	11				9	4			
17	Jan	1	(a)	Manchester C	L 0-3		16,000	1	2	3		5	6	7	8						10	11				9				
18		2	(a)	Gainsboro' T	W 3-1	Hodgetts 2, Izon	1,500	1	2	3	4	5	8		10						11	9				7	6			
19		23	(a)	Blackpool	W 3-1	Inglis 2, Hare	1,000	1	2	3		5	6	7	8				4		10					9		11		
20	Feb	13	(a)	Burton W	W 6-2	Gadsby 2, Inglis, Hare, Hodgetts, Walton	2,000	1	2	3		5	6	7					4		10					9		11	8	
21		27	(h)	Burton W	W 3-2	Hodgetts, Hare, Oakes	6,000	1	2	3		5	6	7					4		10					9		11	8	
22	Mar	6	(h)	Blackpool	L 1-3	Hodgetts	5,000	1	2	3		5		7	6				4		10					9		11	8	
23		13	(a)	Lincoln C	W 3-1	Inglis, Oakes, Jones	2,000	1		3		5		7	6	8			4		10					9		11		2
24		20	(a)	Loughboro' T	W 3-0	Jones 2, Leake	4,000	1	2	3		5		7	6	8			4		10					9		11		
25		27	(h)	Leicester F	W 1-0	Hodgetts	5,500	1	2	3		5		7	6	8			4		10					9		11		
26		29	(a)	W Arsenal	W 3-2	Hodgetts 2, Hare	3,000	1	2	3		5		7	6	8			4		10					9		11		
27	Apr	3	(a)	Notts C	W 2-1	Abbott 2	4,000	1	2	3		5		7	6	8	10		4							9		11		
28		10	(h)	Notts C	W 3-1	Abbott 2, Inglis	7,000	1	2	3		5		7	6	8	10		4		11					9				
29		16	(h)	Leicester F	D 2-2	Hare, Inglis	2,000	1	2	3		5		7	6	8	10		4		11					9				
30		19	(h)	Manchester C	W 3-1	Leake 2, Hare	600	1	2	3		5		7	6	8	10		4		11					9				

FINAL LEAGUE POSITION: 4th in Division Two.   Average home League attendance: 4,526

	Appearances	28	27	27	15	30	21	29	23	20	12	5	18	2	22	9	3	1	2	20	3	9	3	1
	Goals			1	5	5	16	3	9	4	1				9	3				8		2	2	

1 own-goal

FA Cup

#		Date		Opponent	Result	Scorers	Att																							
1	Jan	30	(h)	Notts C	L 1-2	Walton	10,000	1	2	3		5	6	7	8				4		10					9		11		
						Appearances		1	1	1		1	1	1	1				1		1					1		1		
						Goals								1																

1897-98

Manager: Committee

Player columns: Clutterbuck HJ, Archer A, Lester F, Dunlop T, Leake A, Robertson W, Inglis JA, Lewis W, Hare CB, Abbott WA, Kirton JW, Oakes TF, Gadsby W, Walton WH, Good M, Wallace A, Pratt W, Wharton SE, Webb I, Higgins J

#		Date		Opponent	Result	Scorers	Att	C HJ	A A	L F	D T	L A	R W	I JA	L W	H CB	A WA	K JW	O TF	G W	W WH	G M	W A	P W	W SE	W I	H J
1	Sep	4	(a)	Burton S	W 3-1	Inglis 2, Abbott	1,500	1	2	3	4	5	6	7	8	9	10	11									
2		11	(h)	Leicester F	W 2-1	Abbott, Gadsby	3,000	1	2	3	4	5	6			9	10	11	7	8							
3		18	(a)	Loughboro' T	W 2-0	Walton 2	2,000	1	2	3	4	5	6	7		9	10	11		8							
4		25	(h)	Burton S	W 2-1	Hare 2	7,500	1	2	3	4	5	6	7		9	10	11		8							
5	Oct	2	(a)	Darwen	D 1-1	Walton	3,000	1	2	3	4	5	6	7		9	10	11		8							
6		9	(h)	Gainsboro' T	W 4-3	Abbott 2, Robertson, Hare	4,500	1	2	3	4	5	6	7	8	9	10	11									
7		16	(a)	Blackpool	L 1-4	Hare	1,500	1	2	3	4	5	6		10	11	8		7		9						
8		23	(a)	Newton Heath	W 2-1	Lewis 2	3,000		3	4	5	11		8	2	10		7	6	9							
9	Nov	6	(h)	Loughboro' T	W 1-0	Abbott	5,000	1	2	3	4	5		8	9	10		7	6				11				
10		13	(a)	Grimsby T	L 1-3	Wallace	2,000	1	2	3	4	5		8	9	10		7	6				11				
11		27	(a)	Newcastle U	L 0-4		11,000	1	2		4	5		7	8	9	10		6				3	11			
12	Dec	4	(h)	Walsall	W 6-0	Hare, Oakes 2, Abbott 2 (1 pen), Kirton	3,000	1	2		4	5	6		9	7	10	11	8				3				
13		18	(h)	Walsall	W 2-1	Lewis 2	3,000	1	2		4	5	6		9	7	10	11	8				3				
14		25	(h)	Darwen	W 5-1	Lewis, Abbott 3, Kirton	6,500	1	2		4	5	6		9	7	10	11	8				3				
15		27	(h)	Manchester C	L 0-1		10,000	1	2		4	5	6		9	7	10	11	8				3				
16	Jan	8	(h)	Burnley	D 2-2	Abbott, Leake	12,000	1	2		4	5	6		9	7	10	11	8				3				
17		15	(a)	Lincoln C	W 2-1	Abbott, Lewis	2,500	1	2		4	5	6		9	7	10	11	8				3				
18		29	(a)	Blackpool	L 2-3	Lewis, Robertson	6,000	1	2		4	5	6		9	7	10	11	8				3				
19	Feb	5	(a)	Burnley	L 1-4	Oakes	4,000	1	2		4	5	6	7	9		10	11	8				3				
20		12	(h)	Luton T	W 4-2	Oakes, Abbott 2 (1 pen), McEwan (og)	4,000	1	2		4	5	6		9	7	10		8				3	11			
21		19	(a)	Gainsboro' T	D 0-0		2,000	1	2		4	5	6		9	7	10		8				3	11			
22	Mar	5	(a)	W Arsenal	L 2-4	Hare, Oakes	8,000	1	2		4		6		9	7	10	11	8		5		3				
23		12	(h)	Grimsby T	L 0-2		6,500	1	2		4	5	6		9	7	10	11	8				3				
24		26	(a)	Leicester F	L 0-2		2,000	1	2		4		6	7	8	9	10	11			5		3				
25	Apr	2	(a)	Luton T	W 2-1	Dunlop, Inglis	3,000		2		4	5	6	7		10		11		8			3		1	9	
26		9	(a)	Newton Heath	L 1-3	Higgins	3,000		2		4	5	6	7		10	11			8			3		1	9	
27		11	(a)	Manchester C	D 3-3	Abbott, Leake, Good	2,000	1	2		4	5	6			10		7		8			3	11		9	
28		12	(h)	Newcastle U	W 1-0	Higgins	5,000		2		4	5	6			10		7		8			3	11	1	9	
29		16	(h)	Lincoln C	W 4-0	Oakes, Abbott 2, Higgins	4,000		2		4	5	6			10		7		8			3	11	1	9	
30		23	(h)	W Arsenal	W 2-1	Abbott 2	4,500	1	2		4	5	6			10		7		8			3	11		9	

FINAL LEAGUE POSITION: 6th in Division Two.   Average home League attendance: 5,633

	Appearances	26	29	10	30	28	28	10	20	23	30	18	22	1	8	8	2	20	7	4	6
	Goals				1	2	2	3	7	6	19	2	6	1	3	1	1			3	

1 own-goal

FA Cup

#		Date		Opponent	Result	Scorers	Att	C HJ	A A	L F	D T	L A	R W	I JA	L W	H CB	A WA	K JW	O TF	G W	W WH	G M	W A	P W	W SE	W I	H J
Q3	Oct	3	(a)	Port Vale	L 1-2	Walton	2,000	1	2	3		5	11		8	9	10		7		6	4					
						Appearances		1	1	1		1	1		1	1	1		1		1	1					
						Goals													1								

1898-99

Manager: Committee

#	Date		Opponent	Result	Scorers	Att.	Clutterbuck HR	Archer A	Pratt W	Dunlop T	Leake A	Robertson W	Bennett WA	Good M	McRoberts R	Abbott WA	Wharton SE	Webb I	Wilcox HM	Oakes TF	Inglis JA	Walton WH	Gardner A	Lester F	Layton G	Devey W	Wigmore W	Adey G	Price JL
1	Sep	3 (a)	Burton S	W 6-2	Abbott 2, McRoberts 2, Dunlop, Leake	3,000	1	2	3	4	5	6	7	8	9	10	11												
2		5 (h)	Lincoln C	W 4-1	Bennett, Leake, Abbott 2	3,000	1	2	3	4	5	6	7	8	9	10	11												
3		10 (h)	Burslem PV	L 1-2	Abbott	10,000	1	2	3	4	5	6	7	8	9	10	11												
4		17 (h)	Barnsley	W 3-1	McRoberts, Abbott, Wharton	3,000		2	3	4	5	6	7		9	10	11	1	8										
5		24 (a)	Loughboro' T	D 1-1	McRoberts	2,000	1	2	3	4	5	6	7		9	10	11		8										
6	Oct	8 (a)	Grimsby T	L 0-2		2,000	1	2	3	4	5	6		10	9	8	11			7									
7		15 (h)	Newton Heath	W 4-1	Abbott, Walton, Robertson, Inglis	5,000	1	2	3	4	5	6			9	10	11				7	8							
8		22 (a)	New Brighton T	L 0-4		3,000	1	2	3	4	5	6			9	10	11				7	8							
9	Nov	5 (a)	W Arsenal	L 0-2		7,000	1	2	3	4	5	6			9	10	11				7	8							
10		12 (h)	Luton T	W 9-0	Gardner 2, McRoberts, Wharton, Inglis, Robertson 3, Abbott	4,000	1	2	3		5	6			9	10	11				7	4	8						
11		26 (h)	Darwen	W 8-0	Gardner 2, Abbott 5 (1 pen), Robertson	2,000	1	2	3		5	6			9	10	11				7	4	8						
12	Dec	3 (a)	Gainsboro' T	D 1-1	Gardner	1,500	1	2	3		5	6			9	10	11				7	4	8						
13		17 (a)	Glossop NE	W 2-1	Abbott, Inglis	1,000	1	2	3		5	6			9	10	11				7	4	8						
14		24 (a)	Walsall	W 2-1	Gardner, McRoberts	6,500	1	2	3		5	6			9	10	11				7	4	8						
15		26 (h)	Blackpool	W 5-0	Inglis, Walton, Abbott 2, McRoberts	4,000	1	2	3		5	6			9	10	11				7	4	8						
16		27 (h)	Manchester C	W 4-1	Abbott 2, Inglis, McRoberts	10,000	1	2	3		5	6			9	10	11				7	4	8						
17		31 (h)	Burton S	W 4-1	Robertson, Gardner 2, Abbott	4,000	1	2	3		5	6			9	10	11				7	4	8						
18	Jan	7 (a)	Burslem PV	L 0-1		4,000	1	2	3		5	6			9	10	11				7	4	8						
19		14 (a)	Barnsley	L 2-7	Gardner, Walton	2,000	1	2	3		5	6			9	10	11				7	4	8						
20		21 (a)	Loughboro' T	W 6-0	Abbott 3, Wharton 2, Wilcox	3,000	1	2	3		5	6			9	10	11		8		7	4							
21	Feb	4 (h)	Grimsby T	W 2-1	Abbott, Robertson	6,000	1	2	3		5	6			9	10	11				7	4							
22		18 (h)	New Brighton T	W 3-2	Abbott 2, Wilcox	9,500	1		3		5				9	10	11		8		7	4		2	6				
23		25 (a)	Newton Heath	L 0-2		2,000	1	2	3		5	6				10	11		9		7	4	8						
24	Mar	4 (a)	W Arsenal	W 4-1	Abbott 3, Wharton	3,000	1	2	3		5	6	7			10	11				9	4	8						
25		8 (a)	Blackpool	D 1-1	Devey	2,000	1	2	3		5	6	7			10	11					4	8			9			
26		11 (a)	Luton T	W 3-2	Abbott 3 (1 pen)	1,000	1	2	3		5	6	7			10	11				9	4	8						
27		18 (h)	Leicester F	L 0-3		10,000	1	2	3		5	6	7			10	11				9	4	8						
28		25 (a)	Darwen	D 1-1	McRoberts	2,000	1	2	3		5	6	7		8	10	11					4					9		
29		31 (a)	Lincoln C	D 2-2	Wigmore, Bennett	5,000	1	2	3		5	6	7		8	10	11					4					9		
30	Apr	1 (h)	Gainsboro' T	W 6-1	Abbott 3, Wigmore 2, Bennett	6,000	1	2	3		5	6	7		8	10	11					4					9		
31		8 (a)	Manchester C	L 0-2		20,000	1	2			5	6	7		8	10	11					4			3		9		
32		15 (h)	Glossop NE	D 1-1	McRoberts	6,000	1	2	3		5	6	7		8	10	11					4				7	9		
33		22 (a)	Walsall	L 0-2		4,000	1	2	3		5	6			8	10	11					4					9	7	
34		29 (a)	Leicester F	D 0-0		4,000	1	2	3		5					10	11					4					9	7	8
			Appearances				33	33	30	9	34	32	13	4	26	34	34	1	9	2	17	28	16	5	2	2	7	2	1
			Goals							1	2	7	3		10	34	6		2		5	2	9			1	3		

FINAL LEAGUE POSITION: 8th in Division Two. Average home League attendance: 5,588.

FA Cup

Rd	Date		Opponent	Result	Scorers	Att.	Clutterbuck HR	Archer A	Pratt W	Dunlop T	Leake A	Robertson W	McRoberts R	Abbott WA	Wharton SE	Wilcox HM	Oakes TF	Inglis JA	Walton WH	Gardner A
Q3	Oct	29 (h)	Chirk	W 8-0	Walton 3, Inglis 2, Abbott 2, Leake	3,000	1	2	3	4	5	6	9	10	11			7	8	
Q4	Nov	19 (h)	Druids	W 10-0	Abbott 2, McRoberts 3, Gardner, Inglis 2, Leake, Hughes (og)	4,000	1	2	3		5	6	9	10	11			7	4	8
Q5	Dec	10 (h)	Burslem PV	W 7-0	Gardner, McRoberts, Abbott 3, Wharton, Inglis	7,000	1	2	3		5	6	9	10	11			7	4	8
1	Jan	28 (h)	Manchester C	W 3-2	Abbott, McRoberts 2	15,399	1	2	3		5	6	9	10	11			7	4	8
2	Feb	11 (a)	Stoke	D 2-2	Robertson, Wharton	16,000	1	2	3		5	6	9	10	11		8	7	4	
R		15 (h)	Stoke	L 1-2	Inglis	14,379	1	2	3		5	6		10	11	9	8	7	4	
			Appearances				6	6	6	1	6	6	5	6	6	2	1	6	6	3
			Goals								2	1	6	8	2			6	3	2

1 own-goal

1899-1900

Manager: Committee

Player columns: Robinson AC · Archer A · Pratt W · Adey G · Leake A · Farnell T · Bennett WA · Wigmore W · McRoberts R · Main W · Wharton SE · Walton WH · Wilcox HM · Oakes TF · Scrivens T · Leonard J · Lester F · Layton G · Bayley JT · Aston J · Cole S

#	Date	Venue/Opponent	Result	Scorers	Att	Rob	Arch	Pratt	Adey	Leake	Farn	Benn	Wigm	McR	Main	Whar	Walt	Wilc	Oake	Scri	Leon	Lest	Layt	Bayl	Asto	Cole
1	Sep 2	(h) Walsall	W 3-2	Wigmore 2, Wharton	8,000	1	2	3		5	6	7	8	9	10	11	4									
2	9	(a) Middlesbrough	W 3-1	McRoberts 3	10,000	1	2	3	4	5	6	7	8	9	10	11										
3	16	(h) Chesterfield	W 5-3	McRoberts, Bennett 2, Main, Wilcox	8,000	1	2	3	4	5	6	7		9	10	11		8								
4	23	(a) Gainsboro' T	W 4-1	McRoberts, Wharton, Bennett 2	2,000	1	2	3	4	5	6	7		9	10	11		8								
5	30	(h) Bolton W	D 0-0		12,000	1	2	3	4	5	6	7		9	10	11		8								
6	Oct 2	(h) Lincoln C	W 5-0	Wigmore 2, McRoberts 3	4,000	1	2	3	7		6		5	9	10	11		8	4							
7	7	(a) Loughboro' T	W 2-1	Main, Farnell	2,500	1	2	3	7		6		5	9	10	11			4	8						
8	14	(h) Newton Heath	W 1-0	Main	9,000	1	2	3		5	6		4	9	10	11	7			8						
9	21	(a) Sheffield W	L 0-4		9,000	1	2	3	4	5	6		8	9	10	11	7									
10	Nov 4	(a) Burton S	W 3-0	Archer (pen), Wharton, McRoberts	1,500	1	2	3	7		6	4	5	9	10	11				8						
11	11	(a) New Brighton T	D 2-2	Scrivens, Leake	1,500	1	2	3	4	5	6			9	10	11		7		8						
12	25	(a) W Arsenal	L 0-3		4,000	1	2	3	4	5	6			9	10	11		7		8						
13	Dec 2	(h) Barnsley	W 5-0	Main, McRoberts, Wigmore 2, Leonard	4,000	1	2	3	4	5	6		8	9	10	11					7					
14	16	(h) Luton T	W 3-0	Bennett 2, Scrivens	2,000	1	2		4	5	6	7		9	10	11				8		3				
15	23	(a) Burslem PV	L 0-3		1,500	1	2		4	5	6	7		9	10	11				8		3				
16	30	(a) Walsall	L 0-1		3,000	1	2		4	5	6	7		9	10	11				8			3			
17	Jan 6	(h) Middlesbrough	W 5-1	McRoberts 2, Scrivens, Bennett, Bayley	1,000	1	2	3	4	5		7		9		11				8			6	10		
18	13	(a) Chesterfield	D 0-0		1,500	1	2	3	4	5				9	10	11				8	7		6			
19	20	(a) Gainsboro' T	W 8-1	Wharton, McRoberts 3, Layton 2, Bennett, Main	4,000	1	2	3	4	5		7		9	10	11				8			6			
20	27	(h) Burslem PV	W 2-1	Aston, Leake	4,000	1	2	3	4	5	6	7		9	10	11									8	
21	Feb 3	(h) Bolton W	D 1-1	McRoberts	6,000	1	2	3	4	5	6	7		9	10	11									8	
22	10	(a) Loughboro' T	W 6-0	Aston 3, Leake 2, Adey	2,000	1	2	3	7	5	6	4		9	10	11									8	
23	12	(h) Grimsby T	L 0-1		2,000	1	2	3	7	5	6	4		9	10	11									8	
24	17	(a) Newton Heath	L 2-3	Aston, Wharton	6,000	1	2	3	4	5	6	7		9	10	11									8	
25	24	(h) Sheffield W	W 4-1	Layton, Wharton, Leake, Bennett	9,000	1	2	3	4	5		7		9	10	11							6		8	
26	Mar 10	(h) Burton S	W 2-0	Leake, Aston	5,000	1	2	3	4	5		7		9	10	11							6		8	
27	17	(h) New Brighton T	W 2-0	Scrivens 2	5,000	1	2	3	4	5		7		9	10	11				6					8	
28	24	(a) Grimsby T	L 0-2		5,000	1	2	3	4	5		7		9	10	11				6					8	
29	31	(h) W Arsenal	W 3-1	Leake, McRoberts, Aston	3,000	1	2	3	4	5		7		9	10	11				6					8	
30	Apr 7	(a) Barnsley	D 1-1	Leake	2,000	1	2	3	4	5	6	7		9	10	11									8	
31	13	(a) Lincoln C	D 0-0		5,000	1	2	3	4	5	6	7		9	10	11									8	
32	14	(h) Leicester F	W 4-1	McRoberts, Wharton, Main, Wragg (og)	6,000	1	2	3	4	5	6	7		9	10	11									8	
33	17	(a) Leicester F	L 0-2		6,000	1	2	3	4	5	6	7		9	10	11									8	
34	21	(a) Luton T	W 2-1	Main, McRoberts	1,000	1	2	3	4	5	6	7		9	10	11									8	
		Appearances				34	34	31	32	29	19	24	26	30	20	34	3	6	2	13	7	2	11	1	15	1
		Goals					1		1	8	1	9	6	19	7	7		1		5	1		3	1	7	

FINAL LEAGUE POSITION: 3rd in Division Two. Average home League attendance: 5,176

1 own-goal

FA Cup

#	Date	Venue/Opponent	Result	Scorers	Att	Rob	Arch	Pratt	Adey	Leake	Farn	Benn	Wigm	McR	Main	Whar	Walt	Wilc	Oake	Scri	Leon	Lest	Layt	Bayl	Asto	Cole
Q3	Oct 28	(h) Oswestry U	W 10-2	Scrivens 2, Wharton 2, Main 2, Wigmore, McRoberts 2, Adey	1,000	1	2	3	7		6	4	5	9	10	11				8						
Q4	Nov 22	(h) Wrexham	W 6-1	McRoberts 3, Scrivens 2, Wigmore	1,500	1	2	3	6		4	7	5	9	10	11				8						
Q5	Dec 9	(h) Walsall	D 0-0		4,000	1	2	3	4	5	6		8	9	10	11					7					
R	14	(a) Walsall	L 0-2		1,000	1	2	3	4	5	6		8	9	10	11				7						
		Appearances				4	4	4	3	4	4	1	3	4	4	4				3	2					
		Goals							1				2	5	2	2				4						

1900-01

Manager: Committee

#		Date		Opponent	Result	Scorers	Att	Robinson AC	Archer A	Pratt W	Adey G	Wigmore W	Leake A	Bennett WA	Aston J	McRoberts R	Main W	Wharton SE	Tebbs J	Layton G	Webb I	Walton WH	Lester F	Higginson J	Fletcher F	Wragg W	Gard A	McMillan JS	Henderson J
1	Sep	1	(a)	Burslem PV	D 2-2	Aston, Main	3,000	1	2	3	4	5	6		8	9	10	11	7										
2		8	(h)	Leicester F	D 0-0		7,000	1	2	3	4	5		7	8	9	10	11		6									
3		15	(a)	New Brighton T	D 0-0		4,000		2	3	4	5	6	7	8	9	10	11			1								
4		22	(h)	Gainsboro' T	W 6-0	Leake 2, McRoberts 2, Walton, Thornley (og)	2,000	1	2	3	4	5	10	7		9		11		6		8							
5		29	(a)	Walsall	D 2-2	McRoberts, Wigmore	3,000	1	2			5	10	7	8	9		11		6		4	3						
6	Oct	6	(h)	Burton S	W 2-0	Walton, Higginson	2,000	1	2		4	5	6	7		9		11				8	3	10					
7		13	(a)	Barnsley	W 2-1	Higginson, Aston	4,000	1	2	3		5	6	7	8	9		11				4		10					
8		20	(h)	W Arsenal	W 2-1	Aston, Higginson	8,000	1	2	3		5	6	7	8	9		11				4		10					
9		27	(a)	Blackpool	D 0-0		3,000	1	2	3		5	6	7	8	9		11				4		10					
10	Nov	10	(h)	Chesterfield	D 0-0		6,000	1	2			5	6	7	8	9		11				4	3	10					
11		17	(a)	Grimsby T	D 1-1	Higginson	4,000	1	2	3		5	6	7	8	9		11				4		10					
12		24	(h)	Lincoln C	W 2-0	McRoberts, Leake	4,000	1	2	3		5	6	7	8	9		11				4		10					
13	Dec	1	(a)	Newton Heath	W 1-0	McRoberts	5,000	1	2			5	6	7	8	9		11				4	3	10					
14		8	(h)	Glossop	W 1-0	Aston (pen)	7,000	1	2			5	6	7	8	9		11				4	3	10					
15		15	(a)	Middlesbrough	W 1-0	Archer	10,000	1	2		4	5	6	7	8	9		11					3	10					
16		22	(h)	Burnley	L 0-1		10,000	1	2		4	5		7	8	9		11		6			3	10					
17		26	(h)	Stockport C	W 2-0	Aston, McRoberts	7,000	1	2	3	4	5		7	8	9	10	11	6										
18		29	(h)	Burslem PV	W 2-1	McRoberts 2	4,000	1	2	3	4	5	6	7	8	9		11							10				
19	Jan	5	(a)	Leicester F	D 1-1	Aston	6,000	1	3		4	5	2	7	8	9		11					6	10					
20		12	(h)	New Brighton T	W 4-0	McRoberts 2, Main 2	3,000	1	3		2	5	6	7	8	9	10	11				4							
21		19	(a)	Gainsboro' T	W 2-1	Aston, McRoberts	2,000	1	3		4	5	6	7	8	9		11							2				
22	Feb	16	(h)	Barnsley	W 3-1	McRoberts, Aston, Tebbs	5,000	1	3		2	5	6		8	9		11	7			4						10	
23	Mar	2	(h)	Blackpool	W 10-1	Archer, Aston 2, McRoberts 5, McMillan 2	5,000	1	3		2	5	6	7	8	9		11				4						10	
24		9	(a)	Stockport C	D 0-0		2,000	1	3		2	5	6	7	8	9		11				4						10	
25		16	(a)	Chesterfield	D 1-1	McMillan	3,000	1	3		2	5	6		8	9	7	11				4						10	
26		30	(a)	Lincoln C	L 1-3	McMillan	3,000	1	2	3		5	6	7	8			11				4						9	10
27	Apr	1	(h)	Grimsby T	W 2-1	Aston, McMillan	3,500	1	2	3	4	5			8		10	11									7	9	
28		6	(h)	Newton Heath	W 1-0	McMillan	6,000	1	2	3	7	5	6		8		10	11				4						9	
29		8	(h)	Walsall	W 2-1	Aston, Main	7,000	1	2	3	4	5	6		8		10	11									7	9	
30		13	(a)	Glossop	L 0-2		2,000	1	2	3	4	5	6	7	8		10	11										9	
31		15	(a)	Burton S	W 2-0	McMillan 2	2,000	1	3		2	5	6	7	8	9		11				4						10	
32		20	(h)	Middlesbrough	W 2-1	McMillan 2	8,000	1	3		2	5	6		8	9		11				4						10	8
33		22	(a)	W Arsenal	L 0-1		3,500	1	3		2	5	6	7		9		11				4						10	8
34		27	(a)	Burnley	L 0-1		5,000	1	3		2	5	6	7			10	11				4						9	8
						Appearances		33	34	16	24	34	31	28	29	26	13	33	3	4	1	24	7	11	2	1	3	13	4
						Goals			2			1	3		12	13	4	1	1			2		4				10	

FINAL LEAGUE POSITION: 2nd in Division Two.   Average home League attendance: 5,558

1 own-goal

FA Cup

#		Date		Opponent	Result	Scorers	Att	Robinson AC	Archer A	Pratt W	Adey G	Wigmore W	Leake A	Bennett WA	Aston J	McRoberts R	Main W	Wharton SE	Tebbs J	Layton G	Webb I	Walton WH	Lester F	Higginson J	Fletcher F	Wragg W	Gard A	McMillan JS	Henderson J
1	Feb	9	(a)	Stoke	D 1-1	Main	13,000	1	3		2	5	6	7	8	9	10	11				4							
R		13	(a)	Stoke	W 2-1*	Bennett, Wharton	10,000	1	3		2	5	6	7	8	9	10	11				4							
2		23	(h)	Burnley	W 1-0	McMillan	11,000	1	3		2	5	6	7	8	9		11				4						10	
3	Mar	23	(h)	Aston Villa	D 0-0		18,000	1	2	3	4	5	6	7	8		10	11										9	
R		27	(a)	Aston Villa	L 0-1		15,000	1	2	3		5	6	7	8		10	11				4						9	
						Appearances		5	5	2	4	5	5	5	5	3	4	5				4						3	
						Goals								1			1	1										1	

*After extra-time

1901-02

Manager: Committee

FINAL LEAGUE POSITION: 17th in Division One. Average home League attendance: 13,058

#	Mon	Date	Opponent	Res	Scorers	Att	Robinson AC	Goldie A	Archer A	Walton WH	Wigmore W	Leake A	Athersmith WC	Aston J	McRoberts R	McMillan JS	Wharton SE	Bennett WA	Higginson J	Adey G	Jones WH	Tebbs J	Murray J	Leonard A	Bunch W	Pratt W	Dougherty J	Wassall H	Beer WJ	Field CWF	Hartwell A	Pentland F
1	Sep	2 (h) Liverpool		D 0-0		10,000	1	2	3	4	5	6		8	9	10	11	7														
2		7 (h) Bolton W		W 2-0	Aston, McRoberts	12,000	1	2	3	4	5	6		8	9	10	11		7													
3		14 (a) Manchester C		W 4-1	Aston 2, McRoberts, McMillan	18,000	1	2	3	4	5	6	7	8	9	10	11															
4		21 (h) Wolves		L 1-2	Aston	17,000	1	2	3	4	5	6	7	8	9	10	11															
5		28 (a) Liverpool		L 1-3	McMillan	20,000	1	2	3	4	5	6	7	8	9	10	11															
6	Oct	5 (h) Newcastle U		W 3-1	Aston, McMillan, McRoberts	12,000	1	2	3	6	5		7	8	9	10	11			4												
7		12 (h) Aston Villa		L 0-2		23,000	1	2	3	4	5	6	7	8	9	10	11															
8		19 (h) Sheffield U		W 5-1	McMillan 2, Athersmith, Jones, McRoberts	15,000	1	2	3		5	6	7		9	10		11		4	8											
9		26 (a) Nottingham F		D 1-1	Jones	11,000	1	2	3		5	6	7		9	10		11		4	8											
10	Nov	2 (h) Bury		W 1-0	Wigmore	15,000	1	2	3	4	5	6	7	8	9	10	11															
11		9 (a) Blackburn R		L 1-3	Archer (pen)	6,000	1	2	3	4	5	6	7		9	10						8		11								
12		23 (a) Everton		L 0-1		20,000	1	2	3		5	6	7		9	10	11		8	4												
13		30 (h) Sunderland		L 2-3	McMillan, Murray	16,000	1	2	3	4	5	6	7		9	10	11						8									
14	Dec	7 (a) Grimsby T		L 0-1		6,000	1	2	3		5	6	7		9	10	11		8	4												
15		21 (h) Sheffield W		D 1-1	Leonard	8,000	1	2	3		5	6	7		9	10	11			4				8								
16		26 (a) Aston Villa		L 0-1		40,000	1	2			5	6	7		9	10	11			4				8	3							
17		28 (a) Notts C		L 1-6	Leonard	6,000	1				5	6	7		9	10	11			4				8	2	3						
18	Jan	4 (a) Bolton W		L 0-4		5,000	1	2		5		3	7		9	10	11			4				8			6					
19		11 (h) Manchester C		W 1-0	McRoberts (pen)	12,000	1	2	3		5	6	7		9	10	11			4				8								
20		18 (a) Wolves		L 1-2	McRoberts	9,000	1	2			5		7	8	9	10				4				11			6	3				
21	Feb	1 (a) Newcastle U		L 0-2		13,000	1	2	3		5	6	7	8	9					4	10			11								
22		15 (a) Sheffield U		W 4-1	McRoberts, Field, Leonard, Wharton	8,000	1	2	3		5	6	7		9		11							8					4	10		
23		17 (h) Stoke		D 1-1	Athersmith	8,000	1	2	3		5	6	7		9		11							8					4	10		
24		22 (h) Grimsby T		W 6-0	Field 2, Leonard, McRoberts, Wigmore, McConnell (og)	12,000	1	2	3		5	6	7		9		11							8					4	10		
25	Mar	1 (a) Bury		L 0-2		5,000	1	2	3		5	6	7		9		11							8					4	10		
26		8 (h) Blackburn R		W 2-0	Wharton 2	15,000	1	2	3		5	6	7		9		11							8					4	10		
27		15 (a) Stoke		L 0-1		4,000	1	2	3		5	6	7		9		11							8					4	10		
28		22 (h) Everton		L 0-1		16,000	1	2	3		5		7		9		11				6			8					4	10		
29		29 (a) Sunderland		D 1-1	Athersmith	8,600	1	2				6	7		9		11							8				3	4	10	5	
30		31 (a) Derby C		D 0-0		6,000	1	2				6	7		9		11							8				3	4	10	5	
31	Apr	5 (h) Nottingham F		D 1-1	Athersmith	6,000	1	2				6	7		9	10	11							8				3	4		5	
32		12 (h) Derby C		W 5-1	Leonard 2, McMillan, McRoberts, Wharton	5,000	1	2		4		6	7		9	10	11							8				3			5	
33		19 (a) Sheffield W		W 2-1	McRoberts, Wharton	10,000	1	2			5	6	7		9	10	11							8				3	4			
34		26 (h) Notts C		D 0-0		20,000	1	2			5	6	7		9		11							8				3	4	10		
		Appearances					34	33	24	11	28	33	32	11	32	24	29	3	3	13	4	1	1	20	2	1	2	7	12	10	4	
		Goals							1		2		4	5	10	7	5				2		1	6						3		

1 own-goal

FA Cup

#	Mon	Date	Opponent	Res	Scorers	Att	Robinson AC	Goldie A	Archer A	Walton WH	Wigmore W	Leake A	Athersmith WC	Aston J	McRoberts R	McMillan JS	Wharton SE	Bennett WA	Higginson J	Adey G	Jones WH	Tebbs J	Murray J	Leonard A	Bunch W	Pratt W	Dougherty J	Wassall H	Beer WJ	Field CWF	Hartwell A	Pentland F
1	Feb	7 (a) Portsmouth		L 1-2	McRoberts	15,000	1	2			5	6	7	8	9		11			4					3					10		
		Appearances					1	1			1	1	1	1	1		1			1					1					1		
		Goals													1																	

1902-03

Manager: Committee

#		Date	Opponent	Result	Scorers	Att	Robinson AC	Goldie A	Wassell H	Beer WJ	Wigmore W	Dougherty J	Athersmith WC	Leonard A	McRoberts R	McMillan JS	Wharton SE	Field CWF	Jones WH	Hartwell A	Dorrington J	Tickle CH	Harrison A	Howard H	Thompson T	Windridge JE	Hirons JW	Wilcox FJ
1	Sep	6 (a)	Leicester F	W 3-1	Field 2, McRoberts	5,000	1	2	3	4	5	6	7	8	9			10	11									
2		13 (h)	Manchester C	W 4-0	Jones, McMillan, Leonard 2	12,000	1	2	3	4	5	6	7	8	9	10			11									
3		20 (a)	Burnley	L 1-2	McMillan	3,000	1	2	3	4	5	6	7	8	9	10			11									
4		27 (h)	Preston NE	W 3-1	Leonard, McMillan, Wigmore	10,000	1	2	3	4	9	6	7	8		10	11				5							
5	Oct	4 (a)	Burslem PV	D 2-2	McMillan, Athersmith	3,000		2	3	9	5	6	7	8		10	11			4		1						
6		11 (h)	Barnsley	W 2-1	Athersmith, Leonard	7,000	1	2		4	5	3	7	8	9		11	10	6									
7		18 (a)	Gainsboro' T	L 0-1		3,000	1	2	3	4			7	8	9			11		6	5		10					
8		25 (h)	Burton U	W 2-0	Field, Athersmith	7,000	1	2	3	4	5	6	7	8	9			10	11									
9	Nov	1 (a)	Bristol C	D 1-1	McRoberts	12,000	1	2	3	4	5	6	7	8	9	10		11										
10		8 (h)	Glossop	W 3-1	McRoberts 2, Beer	5,000	1	2	3	4	5	6	7	11	9				10			8						
11		15 (a)	Manchester U	W 1-0	Beer	25,000	1	2	3	4	5	6	7	8	9	10	11											
12		22 (h)	Stockport C	W 2-0	Beer, McRoberts	4,000	1	2	3	4	5	6	7	8	9	10	11											
13		29 (a)	Blackpool	W 1-0	Leonard	3,000	1	2	3	4	5	6	7	8	9	10	11											
14	Dec	6 (h)	W Arsenal	W 2-0	Leonard, Wigmore	10,000	1	2	3	4	5	6	7	8	9	10	11											
15		13 (a)	Doncaster R	L 0-2		3,000	1	2	3	4	5	6	7	8	9	10	11											
16		20 (h)	Lincoln C	W 3-1	Harrison 2, Leonard	6,000	1	2	3	4	5	6		8	9			11		10			7					
17		26 (h)	Chesterfield	W 2-1	Athersmith, Beer	11,000	1	2	3	4	5	6	7	8	9		11	10										
18		27 (a)	Chesterfield	D 1-1	McRoberts	6,000	1	2	3	4		5	7	8	9	11		10						6				
19	Jan	3 (h)	Leicester F	W 4-3	Leonard 2, Field, McRoberts	6,000	1	2	3	4	5	6	7	8	9		11	10										
20		17 (h)	Burnley	W 3-0	Leonard, Field, Athersmith	6,000	1	2	3	4	5		7	8	9		11	10						6				
21		24 (a)	Preston NE	L 1-2	Beer	5,000	1	2	3	4	5	6	7		9		10	8							11			
22		31 (a)	Burslem PV	W 5-1	McRoberts, Jones, Beer, Windridge 2	6,000	1	2	3	4	5	6	7		9		11	8								10		
23	Feb	14 (h)	Gainsboro' T	W 1-0	McRoberts	5,000	1	2	3		5	6	7	8	9		11	4								10		
24		21 (a)	Burton U	W 1-0	McRoberts	3,750	1	2	3	4	5	6	7	8	9											10	11	
25		23 (a)	Manchester C	L 0-4		20,000	1	2	3	4	5	6	7	8	9			11								10		
26		28 (h)	Bristol C	W 2-0	Windridge 2	12,000	1	2	3	4		6	7	8	9		11				5					10		
27	Mar	7 (a)	Glossop	W 1-0	Windridge	2,000	1	2	3	4			8	9			11						7			10		
28		21 (a)	Stockport C	W 2-1	McRoberts, Harrison	5,000	1	2	3	4		6		8	9		11				5		7			10		
29		28 (h)	Blackpool	W 5-1	Wilcox 2, McRoberts, Beer (pen), Wolstenholme (og)	7,000	1	2	3	4		6	7	8	9						5						11	10
30	Apr	4 (a)	W Arsenal	L 1-6	McRoberts	15,000	1	2	3	4		6	7	8	9						5						11	10
31		10 (a)	Lincoln C	W 1-0	Leonard	5,000		2	3	4	5	6	7	8	9		11					1						10
32		11 (h)	Doncaster R	W 12-0	Leonard 4, Wilcox 4, Athersmith, Field, McRoberts, Dougherty	8,000		2	3	4		5	7	8	9		11					1		6				10
33		13 (a)	Barnsley	L 0-3		5,000		2	3	4		6	7	8	9		11	5				1						10
34		20 (h)	Manchester U	W 2-1	Leonard, Wilcox	4,000		2	3	4	5		8		9		11					1		7	6			10

FINAL LEAGUE POSITION: 2nd in Division Two. Average home League attendance: 7,411

| | | Appearances | 29 | 34 | 33 | 33 | 26 | 31 | 30 | 32 | 31 | 12 | 14 | 17 | 14 | 6 | 5 | 2 | 4 | 4 | 1 | 7 | 3 | 6 |
| | | Goals | | | | 7 | 2 | 1 | 6 | 16 | 14 | 4 | | 6 | 2 | | | | 3 | | | 5 | | 7 |

1 own-goal

FA Cup

#		Date	Opponent	Result	Scorers	Att	Robinson AC	Goldie A	Wassell H	Beer WJ	Wigmore W	Dougherty J	Athersmith WC	Leonard A	McRoberts R	McMillan JS	Wharton SE	Field CWF	Jones WH	Hartwell A	Dorrington J	Tickle CH	Harrison A	Howard H	Thompson T	Windridge JE	Hirons JW	Wilcox FJ
1	Feb	7 (a)	Derby C	L 1-2	Windridge	17,000	1	2	3		5	6	7	8	9			11	4							10		
		Appearances			1	1	1		1	1	1	1	1			1	1						1		
		Goals																					1		

1903-04

Manager: Committee

League — Division One

#	Mon	Date	V	Opponent	Result	Scorers	Att
1	Sep	1	(a)	Derby C	L 1-4	Leonard	7,000
2		5	(h)	Sheffield U	L 1-3	Wilcox	15,000
3		7	(h)	Nottingham F	D 3-3	Leonard, Wilcox, Athersmith	10,000
4		12	(a)	Newcastle U	L 1-3	Wilcox	17,000
5		19	(h)	Aston Villa	D 2-2	Wilcox, Robertson	25,000
6		26	(a)	Middlesbrough	L 1-3	Howard	20,000
7	Oct	3	(h)	Liverpool	L 1-2	Wigmore	10,000
8		10	(a)	Bury	L 0-1		7,000
9		17	(h)	Blackburn R	W 2-1	Windridge 2	11,000
10		24	(a)	Nottingham F	W 1-0	Wilcox	7,000
11		31	(h)	Sheffield W	D 0-0		13,000
12	Nov	7	(a)	Sunderland	L 1-3	Wigmore	12,000
13		14	(h)	West Brom A	L 0-1		12,563
14		21	(a)	Wolves	L 0-1		6,000
15		28	(a)	Everton	L 1-5	Leonard	10,000
16	Dec	5	(h)	Stoke	W 1-0	Robertson	6,000
17		19	(h)	Manchester C	L 0-3		12,000
18		26	(a)	Notts C	L 0-2		12,000
19	Jan	2	(a)	Sheffield U	D 1-1	Jones	15,000
20		9	(h)	Newcastle U	W 3-0	Beer 2, Jones	8,000
21		16	(a)	Aston Villa	D 1-1	Green	20,000
22		23	(h)	Middlesbrough	D 2-2	Athersmith, Field	11,000
23		30	(a)	Liverpool	W 2-0	Jones, Wilcox	15,000
24	Feb	13	(a)	Blackburn R	D 1-1	Jones	2,000
25		27	(a)	Sheffield W	L 2-3	Jones 2	6,000
26	Mar	5	(h)	Sunderland	W 2-1	Beer 2	12,000
27		12	(a)	West Brom A	W 1-0	Green	22,760
28		19	(h)	Wolves	W 3-0	Green, Beer, Wilcox	8,000
29		26	(h)	Everton	D 1-1	Beer	10,000
30	Apr	2	(a)	Stoke	L 0-1		6,000
31		4	(h)	Bury	W 1-0	Wilcox	15,000
32		9	(h)	Derby C	W 1-0	Jones	7,000
33		16	(a)	Manchester C	L 0-4	·	15,000
34		23	(h)	Notts C	W 2-0	Green, Jones	8,000

FINAL LEAGUE POSITION: 11th in Division One. Average home League attendance: 11,386

League — appearances (shirt numbers)

#	Robinson AC	Goldie A	Stokes F	Beer WJ	Wigmore W	Howard H	Athersmith WC	Green BH	McRoberts R	Wilcox FJ	Field CWF	Dorrington J	Wassell H	Dougherty J	Leonard A	Hartwell A	Jones WH	Robertson J	Bidmead WT	Windridge JE	Hirons JW	Glover J	Chaplin A
1		2			5	6	7		9	10	11	1	3	4	8								
2		2			5	6	7		9	10	11	1	3	4	8								
3		2			5		7		9	10		1	3	6	11	4	8						
4	1	2			5	6	7		9	10			3	4	11			8					
5	1	2			5	6	7		9	10			3	4	11			8					
6	1	2			5	6	7		9	10	11		3	4	8								
7	1	2			5		7		9	10			3	6	11	4	8						
8	1			4	5		7		9				3	6	11			8	2	10			
9	1		3	4	5	6	7	8	9				2		11					10			
10	1		3	4	5	6	7		11	9			2				8			10			
11	1		3	4		6	7		5	9	11		2				8			10			
12	1	2	3	4	5		7	11	6	9							8			10			
13	1	2	3	4	5		7	8	9						11					10	6		
14	1		3	4	5	6	7	8	10				2					9			11		
15	1		3	4	5	6	7	8					2		11	10		9					
16	1		3	4	5	6	7	8			11		2			10		9					
17	1		3	4	5	6	7			9	11		2				8			10			
18	1		3	4	5	6		8		9	11		2				7			10			
19	1		3	4	5	6	7	8		10	11					2	9						
20	1		3	4	5	6	7	8		10	11					2	9						
21	1	4	3			6	7	8			11				10		9					2	5
22	1		3				7	8		10	11			4	5		9					2	6
23	1		3		5	6	7	8		10	11						9					2	4
24	1		3		5	6	7	8			11						9			10		2	4
25	1		3	4	5	6	7	8		10	11						9					2	
26	1		3	4	5	6	7	8		10	11						9					2	
27	1		3	4	5	6	7	8		10	11						9					2	
28	1		3	4	5	6	7	8		10	11						9					2	
29	1		3	4	5	6	7	8		10	11						9					2	
30	1		3	4	5	6	7	8		10	11						9					2	
31	1		3	4	5	6	7	8		10	11						9					2	
32	1		3	4	5	6	7	8		10	11						9					2	
33	1		3	4	5	6	7	8	10		11						9					2	
34	1		3	4	5	6	7	8	10		11						9					2	
Appearances	31	10	26	23	31	28	33	23	14	28	22	3	16	9	16	4	21	6	1	9	2	14	4
Goals				6	2	1	2	4		8	1				3		8	2		2			

FA Cup

#	Mon	Date	V	Opponent	Result	Scorers	Att	Robinson AC	Goldie A	Stokes F	Beer WJ	Wigmore W	Howard H	Athersmith WC	Green BH	McRoberts R	Wilcox FJ	Field CWF	Dorrington J	Wassell H	Dougherty J	Leonard A	Hartwell A	Jones WH	Robertson J	Bidmead WT	Windridge JE	Hirons JW	Glover J	Chaplin A
1	Dec	12	(a)	Manchester U	D 1-1	Wassell	10,000	1		3	4	5	6	7	8			11		2			10		9					
R		16	(h)	Manchester U	D 1-1*	Leonard	4,000	1		3	4	5	6	7	9			11		2		8					10			
2R		21	(n†)	Manchester U	D 1-1*	Field	5,000	1		3	4	5		7		9	11			2	6				8		10			
3R	Jan	11	(n§)	Manchester U	L 1-3	Athersmtih	10,000	1		3	4	5	6	7	8		10	11							2	9				
						Appearances		4		4	4	4	3	4	3			4	2	3	1	2	1	2	1		2			
						Goals								1				1		1		1								

*After extra-time. †Played at Bramall Lane, Sheffield. §Played at Hyde Park, Manchester.

1904-05

Manager: Committee

No	Date	Opponent	Result	Scorers	Att	Robinson AC	Glover J	Stokes F	Beer WJ	Wigmore W	Dougherty J	Tickle CH	Green BH	Jones WH	Wilcox FJ	Field CWF	Howard H	Athersmith WC	McRoberts R	Hartwell A	Windridge JE	Jones T	Harvey C	Sellman A	Bird J
1	Sep 3	(a) Manchester C	L 1-2	Green (pen)	30,000	1	2	3	4	5		7	8	9	10	11	6								
2	10	(h) Notts C	L 1-2	Beer (pen)	12,500	1	2	3	4	5			8	9	10	11	6	7							
3	17	(a) Sheffield U	L 1-2	Beer (pen)	12,000	1	2	3	4	5			8	9	10	11	6	7							
4	24	(h) Newcastle U	W 2-1	Jones 2	15,000	1	2	3	4	5	6		8	9	10	11			7						
5	Oct 1	(a) Preston NE	D 2-2	Wilcox, McRoberts	8,000	1	2	3	4	5	6		8	9	10	11			7						
6	8	(h) Middlesbrough	W 2-1	Field, Beer (pen)	14,000	1	2	3	4		6		8	9	10	11			7	5					
7	15	(a) Wolves	W 1-0	Wilcox	8,000	1	2	3	4		6		8		9	11			7	5	10				
8	22	(h) Bury	W 5-0	Wilcox, Field, Green 2, McRoberts	12,000	1		3	4	5	6		8	9	10	11			7	2					
9	29	(a) Aston Villa	L 1-2	Wilcox	40,000	1	2	3	4	5	6		8	9	10	11			7						
10	Nov 5	(a) Blackburn R	W 2-0	Wigmore, Green	12,000	1	2	3	4	5	6	7	8	9		11					10				
11	12	(a) Nottingham F	W 2-0	McRoberts, Jones	10,000	1	2	3	4	5	6		8	9	10	11			7						
12	19	(h) Sheffield W	W 2-1	Jones, Green	10,000	1	2	3	4	5	6		8	9	10	11			7						
13	26	(a) Sunderland	W 4-1	Wilcox, Jones 2, Green	12,000	1		3	4	5	6	8	7	9	10	11					2				
14	Dec 3	(h) W Arsenal	W 2-1	Dougherty, Jones	20,000	1		3	4	5	6		8	9	10	11			7		2				
15	10	(a) Derby C	L 0-3		6,000	1		3	4	5	6	7	8	9	10						2	11			
16	17	(h) Everton	L 1-2	Jones	15,000	1		3	4	5	6		8	9	10	11					2				
17	26	(a) Middlesbrough	W 1-0	McRoberts	10,000	1		3	4	5			8	9	10	11	6		7		2				
18	31	(h) Manchester C	W 3-1	Jones 2, Wilcox	11,000	1		3	4	5			8	9	10	11	6		7		2				
19	Jan 2	(a) Bury	D 1-1	Green	10,000	1		3	4	5			8	9	10	11	6	7			2				
20	7	(a) Notts C	D 0-0		6,000	1		3	4	5	6		8		9	11	7	10			2				
21	14	(h) Sheffield U	W 2-0	Jones, Wilcox	15,000	1		3	4	5	6	7	8	9	10	11					2				
22	21	(a) Newcastle U	W 1-0	Tickle	24,000	1	2	3	4	5	6	7	8	9	10	11									
23	28	(h) Preston NE	W 2-0	Wilcox 2	20,000	1	2	3		5	4	7	8	9	10		6				11				
24	Feb 11	(h) Wolves	W 4-1	Wilcox 3, Green	15,500	1	2	3	4	5	6	7	8	9	10						11				
25	25	(h) Aston Villa	L 0-3		32,000	1	2	3	4	5	6	7	8	9	10	11									
26	Mar 4	(a) Blackburn R	W 4-1	Jones 2 (1 pen), Field, Beer	5,000	1	2	3	4	5	6	7	8	10		11					9				
27	11	(h) Nottingham F	L 1-2	Field	8,500	1	2	3	4	5	6	7	8	9		11					10				
28	18	(a) Sheffield W	L 1-3	Green	12,000	1	2	3	4	5	6		8	9		11			7		10				
29	25	(h) Sunderland	D 1-1	Jones	8,000	1	2	3	4	5			8	9		11	6				10	7			
30	Apr 1	(a) W Arsenal	D 1-1	Jones	20,000	1	2	3	4	5		7	8	9		11	6				10				
31	8	(h) Derby C	W 2-0	Green, Jones	12,000	1	2	3			6	7	8	9	10	11	4			5					
32	15	(a) Everton	L 1-2	Hartwell	20,000	1	2	3			6	7	8	9	10		4			5	11				
33	22	(h) Stoke	L 0-1		10,000	1	2	3	4		5	7	8		10	11	6		9						
34	29	(a) Stoke	L 0-1		10,000	1	2	3	4			7	8			11	6			9	10			5	
		Appearances				34	24	34	31	28	25	16	34	30	27	30	13	5	14	15	10	2	1	1	
		Goals							4	1	1	1	10	16	12	4			4	1					

FINAL LEAGUE POSITION: 7th in Division One. Average home League attendance: 14,441

FA Cup

No	Date	Opponent	Result	Att	Robinson AC	Glover J	Stokes F	Beer WJ	Wigmore W	Dougherty J	Tickle CH	Green BH	Jones WH	Wilcox FJ	Field CWF	Howard H	Athersmith WC	McRoberts R	Hartwell A	Windridge JE	Jones T	Harvey C	Sellman A	Bird J
1	Feb 4	(h) Portsmouth	L 0-2	25,000	1	2	3		5	6	7	8	9	10						11		4		
		Appearances			1	1	1		1	1	1	1	1	1						1		1		
		Goals																						

1905-06

Manager: Committee

No.	Date	Opponent	Res	Score	Scorers	Att	Robinson AC	Glover J	Stokes F	Beer WJ	Wigmore W	Dougherty J	Tickle CH	Green BH	Jones WH	Wilcox FJ	Field CWF	Mounteney A	Hartwell A	Anderson GE	Cornan F	Howard H	Harper A	Jones A	Bidmead T	Southall G	Shuttlebotham J	Smith J	Kearns J
1	Sep 2 (h)	Preston NE	D	1-1	Jones	18,000	1	2	3	4	5	6	7	8	9	10	11												
2	9 (a)	Newcastle U	D	2-2	Green, Wilcox	28,000	1	2	3	4	5	6	7	8	9	10	11												
3	16 (h)	Aston Villa	W	2-0	Jones, Mounteney	30,000	1	2	3	4	5	6	7		9	10	11	8											
4	23 (a)	Liverpool	L	0-2		15,000	1	2	3	4	5	6	7		9	10	11	8											
5	30 (h)	Sheffield U	W	2-0	Wilcox, Mounteney	15,000	1	2	3	4	5	6	7		9	10	11	8											
6	Oct 7 (a)	Notts C	D	0-0		12,000	1	2	3	4	5	6	7			10	11	8				9							
7	14 (h)	Stoke	W	2-0	Jones 2	12,000	1		3	4	5	6	7		9	10	11	8	2										
8	21 (a)	Bolton W	W	1-0	Jones	18,000	1	2	3	4	5	6	7		9	10		8		11									
9	28 (h)	W Arsenal	W	2-1	Beer, Jones	16,000	1	2	3	4	5	6	7		9			8		11	10								
10	Nov 4 (a)	Blackburn R	L	1-5	Cornan	10,000	1	2	3	4	5	6	7		9			8		11	10								
11	11 (h)	Sunderland	W	3-0	Anderson, Jones, Tickle	11,000	1	2	3	4	5	6	7	8	9					11	10								
12	18 (a)	Wolves	D	0-0		5,000	1	2	3		5	6	7	8	9					11	10	4							
13	25 (a)	Everton	W	2-1	Jones, Anderson	15,000	1	2	3	4	5	6	7	8	9					11	10								
14	Dec 2 (h)	Derby C	W	3-1	Tickle, Mounteney, Wigmore	12,000	1	2	3	4	5	6	7	8	9			10		11									
15	9 (a)	Sheffield W	L	2-4	Tickle, Jones	12,000	1	2	3	4	5	6	7	8	9	10				11									
16	16 (h)	Nottingham F	W	5-0	Wilcox 3, Harper, Jones	10,000	1	2	3	4	5	6		8	9	10				11			7						
17	23 (a)	Manchester C	L	1-4	Green	15,000	1	2	3	4	5	6	7	8	9	10				11									
18	25 (a)	Middlesbrough	L	0-1		10,000	1	2		4	5	6	7	8	9			10	3	11									
19	26 (h)	Middlesbrough	W	7-0	Green 5, Jones, Williamson (og)	10,000	1	2		4	5	6		8	9			10	3	11			7						
20	28 (a)	Sheffield U	L	0-3		15,000	1	2		4	5	6		8	9			10	3	11			7						
21	30 (a)	Preston NE	L	0-3		15,000	1		3	4	5			8				10	2	11	6		7	9					
22	Jan 1 (a)	Bury	L	0-1		10,000	1		2	4	5		7	8	9	10			3	11	6								
23	6 (h)	Newcastle U	L	0-1		8,000	1		3	4	5			8	10	9			2	11	6		7						
24	20 (a)	Aston Villa	W	3-1	Mounteney, Jones, Dougherty	40,000	1	2			5	6		8	9			10	3	11	4		7						
25	27 (h)	Liverpool	W	1-0	Mounteney	20,000	1	2		4	5	6		8	9			10	3	11			7						
26	Feb 10 (h)	Notts C	W	4-2	Mounteney, Green, Jones 2	6,500	1	2	3	4				8	9			10	5	11	6		7						
27	17 (a)	Stoke	D	2-2	Jones 2	5,000	1	2	3	4		6		8	9	10			5	11			7						
28	Mar 3 (a)	W Arsenal	L	0-5		25,000	1	2				6			9	10		5		11	4		7	8	3				
29	17 (a)	Sunderland	L	1-3	Anderson	15,000	1		3	4	5			8	9			10	2	11	6		7						
30	24 (h)	Wolves	D	3-3	Mounteney, Jones 2	5,000	1		3		5		7	8	9			10	2	11	6	4							
31	26 (h)	Bolton W	L	2-5	Mounteney, Tickle	10,000	1	2	3		5		7	8	9			10			6	4	11						
32	Apr 7 (a)	Derby C	D	0-0		5,000	1	2	3			6		8	9			10	5	11	4		7						
33	9 (h)	Everton	W	1-0	Mounteney	10,000	1	2	3			6		8	9			10	5	11	4		7						
34	14 (h)	Sheffield W	W	5-1	Tickle 3, Jones 2	7,000	1	2	3			6		8	9			10	5	11	4		7						
35	16 (h)	Bury	L	0-3		10,000	1	2	3			6		8	9			10		11	4		7			5			
36	21 (a)	Nottingham F	L	1-2	Jones	8,000	1	2				6	7		9			10	5	11	4				3			8	
37	23 (a)	Blackburn R	W	3-0	Mounteney, Smith, Green	10,000	1	2	3			6	7	8	9			11	5									10	4
38	28 (h)	Manchester C	W	3-2	Green, Jones, Edmondson (og)	5,000	1	2	3			6	7	8	9			11	5									10	4
		Appearances					38	32	31	26	28	31	20	36	35	17	7	25	19	23	15	3	15	4	2	5	1	3	2
		Goals								1	1	1	7	10	22	5		10		3	1		1					1	

FINAL LEAGUE POSITION: 7th in Division One. Average home League attendance: 11,868.

2 own-goals

FA Cup

No.	Date	Opponent	Res	Score	Scorers	Att	Robinson AC	Glover J	Stokes F	Beer WJ	Wigmore W	Dougherty J	Tickle CH	Green BH	Jones WH	Wilcox FJ	Field CWF	Mounteney A	Hartwell A	Anderson GE	Cornan F	Howard H	Harper A	Jones A	Bidmead T	Southall G	Shuttlebotham J	Smith J	Kearns J
1	Jan 13 (h)	Preston NE	W	1-0	Beer	10,000	1	2	3	4	5	6		8	9					11	10		7						
2	Feb 3 (a)	Stoke	W	1-0	W.H.Jones	15,000	1	2	3	4	5			8	9			10		11	6		7						
3	24 (a)	Tottenham H	D	1-1	Harper	28,000	1	2	3	4	5	6		8	9			10		11			7						
R	28 (h)	Tottenham H	W	2-0*	Green, Mounteney	34,000	1	2	3	4	5			8	9	11		10			6		7						
4	Mar 10 (h)	Newcastle U	D	2-2	Green, W.H.Jones	27,000	1	2	3	4	5			8	9			10		11	6		7						
R	14 (a)	Newcastle U	L	0-3		39,059	1	2	3	4	5			8	9			10		11	6		7						
		Appearances					6	6	6	6	6	2		6	6	1		5		5	5		6						
		Goals								1				2	2			1					1						

*After extra-time

1906-07

Manager: Committee

League players (columns, left to right): Robinson AC, Glover J, Stokes F, Beer WJ, Wigmore W, Dougherty J, Tickle CH, Green BH, Jones WH, Mounteney A, Anderson GE, Kirby C, Harper A, Kearns J, Dorrington J, Smith J, Hallworth A, McCafferty W, Jones A, Southall G, Coman F, Hartwell A, Morris A, Eyre E, Gooch PG, Harvey C

#	Date		Opponent	Res	Scorers	Att	Rob	Glo	Sto	Bee	Wig	Dou	Tic	Gre	JoW	Mou	And	Kir	Har	Kea	Dor	Smi	Hal	McC	JoA	Sou	Com	Hwl	Mor	Eyr	Goo	Hvy
1	Sep 1	(a)	Preston NE	L 0-2		10,000	1	2	3	4	5	6	7	8	9	10	11															
2	3	(h)	Bristol C	D 2-2	Green, Mounteney	10,000	1	2	3	4	5	6	7	8	9	10	11															
3	8	(h)	Newcastle U	L 2-4	Jones, Beer	17,000	1	2	3	4	5	6		8	9	10	11	7														
4	15	(a)	Aston Villa	L 1-4	Mounteney	45,000	1	2	3	4	5	6		8	9	10	11		7													
5	22	(h)	Liverpool	W 2-1	Jones, Mounteney	10,000	1	2	3	4	5	6		8	9	10	11		7													
6	29	(a)	Bristol C	W 0-0		17,000	1		3	4	5	6		8	9	10	11		7	2												
7	Oct 6	(h)	Notts C	W 2-0	Stokes, Kearns	10,000	1		3	4	5	6		8	9	10	11		7	2												
8	13	(a)	Sheffield U	L 0-2		8,000		2		6	5	4		8	9	10	11		7	3	1											
9	20	(h)	Bolton W	W 4-2	Jones, Beer (pen), Anderson	12,000	1	2	3	4	5	6	8	7	9	10	11															
10	27	(a)	Manchester U	L 1-2	Jones	14,000	1	2	3	4	5	6	8	7	9		11							10								
11	Nov 3	(h)	Stoke	W 2-1	Jones 2	10,000	1	2	3	4	5		8	7	9	10	11							6								
12	10	(a)	Blackburn R	L 0-1		10,000	1	2	3	4	5		8	7	9	10	11		6													
13	17	(h)	Sunderland	W 2-0	Jones, Tickle	10,000	1	2	3	4	5		8	7	9	10	11		6													
14	24	(h)	Derby C	W 2-1	Anderson, Wigmore	10,000	1	2	3	4	5			7	9	10	11		6						8							
15	Dec 1	(a)	Everton	L 0-3		12,000	1	2	3	4	5			8	9	10			7									11				
16	8	(h)	W Arsenal	W 5-1	Green 2, Jones 2, Beer	19,000	1	2	3	4	5	6		8	9	10			7									11				
17	15	(a)	Sheffield W	W 1-0	Beer	10,000	1	2	3	4	5	6		8	9	10			7									11				
18	22	(h)	Bury	W 3-1	Mounteney 2, Wigmore	10,000	1	2	3	4	5	6		8	9	10			7									11				
19	25	(a)	Manchester C	L 0-1		24,000	1	2	3	4	5	6		8	9	10										7		11				
20	26	(h)	Middlesbrough	D 0-0		32,000	1	2	3	4	5	6		8	9	10			7									11				
21	29	(h)	Preston NE	W 3-0	Green 2, Jones	20,000	1	2	3	4	5	6	7		9	10	11							8								
22	Jan 1	(a)	Middlesbrough	L 0-1		10,000	1	2	3	4	5	6	7		9	10	11							8								
23	5	(a)	Newcastle U	L 0-2		26,000	1	2	3	6	5	4		10	9	8	7			11												
24	19	(h)	Aston Villa	W 3-2	Glover, Mounteney, Green	50,000	1	2	3	4	5			8	9	10	11		7								6					
25	26	(a)	Liverpool	L 0-2		15,000	1	2		4	5			7	9	10					3		8			11	6					
26	Feb 9	(a)	Notts C	D 2-2	Jones 2	8,000	1		2	3	4		8	7	9					5		10				11	6					
27	16	(h)	Sheffield U	D 0-0		10,000	1			3	4		8	7	9	11				2		10				5	6					
28	Mar 2	(h)	Manchester U	D 1-1	Morris	20,000		2	3	4	5		7	8	9							1					6		10	11		
29	9	(a)	Stoke	L 0-3		10,000	1	2	3	4	5		7	8	9											11	6		10			
30	11	(a)	Bolton W	W 3-2	Tickle, Green, Anderson	10,000	1	2	3	4	5	6	7	8	9		11									10						
31	16	(h)	Blackburn R	W 2-0	Jones, Tickle	10,000	1	2	3	4	5	6	7	8	9		11									10						
32	23	(a)	Sunderland	L 1-4	Anderson	18,000	1	2	3	4	5	6	7	8	9		11									10						
33	29	(h)	Manchester C	W 4-0	Green, Gooch, Anderson, Jones	10,000	1	2	3	4	5	6	7	8	10		11														9	
34	30	(a)	Derby C	D 1-1	Wigmore	5,000	1	2	3	4	5	6	10	8	9		11															7
35	Apr 6	(h)	Everton	W 1-0	Green	11,000	1	2	3	4	5	6	7	8	9		11									10						
36	13	(a)	W Arsenal	L 1-2	Glover	18,000	1	2	3	4	5		7	8	10											6				11	9	
37	25	(h)	Sheffield W	D 1-1	Morris	10,000	1	2	3	4	5		7	8	9		11									6			10			
38	27	(a)	Bury	L 0-1		10,000	1		2	6	5	4		11	10	9			7	3						8						
					Appearances		36	33	37	38	37	26	19	38	38	25	31	1	7	9	2	3	1	4	1	9	13	1	3	2	3	1
					Goals			2	1	4	3		3	9	15	6	5			1									2		1	

FINAL LEAGUE POSITION: 9th in Division One. Average home League attendance: 15,315

FA Cup

#	Date		Opponent	Res	Scorers	Att	Rob	Glo	Sto	Bee	Wig	Dou	Tic	Gre	JoW	Mou	And	Kir	Har
1	Jan 12	(a)	Liverpool	L 1-2	Green (pen)	20,000	1	2	3	4	5	6		8	9	10	11		7
					Appearances		1	1	1	1	1	1		1	1	1	1		1
					Goals									1					

1907-08

Manager: Committee

#	Date	Opponent	Result	Scorers	Att.	Robinson AC	Glover J	Stokes F	Beer WJ	Wigmore W	Cornan F	Peplow W	Green BH	Jones WH	Mounteney A	Eyre E	Tickle CH	Anderson GE	Dougherty J	Corbett WS	Gooch PG	Morris AS	Higgins JB	Travers W	Dorrington J	Holmes E	Kearns J	Hartwell A	King H	Bluff EW	Drake A	Fairman R	Handley TH	Moore G
1	Sep 4	(a) Middlesbrough	L 0-1		10,000	1	2	3	4	5	6		8	9	10	7	11																	
2	7	(h) Preston NE	W 2-0	Mounteney	10,000	1	2	3	4	5	6		8	9	10	11	7																	
3	14	(a) Bury	L 0-1		12,000	1	2	3	4	5	6		8	9	10	11	7																	
4	16	(h) Bury	L 0-1		10,000	1	2	3	4	5		7		9	10	11	8	6																
5	21	(h) Aston Villa	L 2-3	Eyre, Tickle	45,000	1	2	3	4	5	10		8		9	11	7	6																
6	28	(a) Liverpool	W 4-3	Green, Mounteney 2, Eyre	20,000	1		3	4	5	10		8		9	11	7	6	2															
7	Oct 5	(h) Middlesbrough	L 1-4	Green	20,000	1		3	4	5	10		8		9		11	6	2	7														
8	12	(a) Sheffield U	L 0-1		12,000	1	2	3	4	5	6	7	9			11	8					10												
9	19	(h) Chelsea	D 1-1	Green	20,000	1	2	3	4	5	6	7	9			11	8						10											
10	26	(a) Nottingham F	D 1-1	Green	10,000	1	2	3		5	6	7	8			11	10		4		9													
11	Nov 2	(h) Manchester U	L 3-4	Jones, Eyre 2	20,000	1	2	3	4	5	6	7	8	9		11	10																	
12	9	(a) Blackburn R	L 0-1		14,000		2	3	4	5	6	7	8	9		11	10							1										
13	16	(h) Bolton W	W 2-1	Green, Eyre	10,000		2	3	4	5	6	7	8			11	10							1					9					
14	23	(a) Newcastle U	L 0-8		16,000		2		4		6	7	8			11	10							1			3	5	9					
15	Dec 7	(h) Sunderland	L 0-2		10,000		2	3		5	6	7	4		10	11	8							1					9					
16	14	(a) W Arsenal	D 1-1	Green	3,000			3	4	5	6		9			11								1		2			8	10				
17	21	(h) Sheffield W	W 2-1	Drake, Jones	5,000			3	4	5	6	7	4	9		11								1		2				10				
18	25	(h) Manchester C	W 2-1	Eyre, Bluff	20,000			3	4	5	6		7	9		11								1		2			8	10				
19	26	(h) Notts C	D 0-0		28,000			3	4	5	6	7		9		11	8				2			1						10				
20	27	(a) Notts C	D 0-0		5,000				4			7	9		8	11		6						1		3			10			2	5	
21	28	(a) Bristol C	D 0-0		12,000				4	5		7		9		11	8		6	3				1		2				10				
22	Jan 4	(a) Preston NE	D 1-1	Jones	8,000			3	4	5	6		8	9		11	7							1		2				10				
23	18	(a) Aston Villa	W 3-2	Eyre, Green, Drake	39,500				4	5		6		9		11	7				2			1		3			8	10				
24	25	(h) Liverpool	D 1-1	Mounteney	15,000				4	5		6		9		11	7				2			1		3			8	10				
25	Feb 8	(h) Sheffield U	D 0-0		15,000			3	4	5		6	9			11	7							1		2			8	10				
26	15	(a) Chelsea	D 2-2	Jones, Eyre	30,000			3	4	5		6	9	10		11	7							1		2			8					
27	29	(a) Manchester U	L 0-1		12,000			3		5	6	7	4	9	8		11							1		2				10				
28	Mar 7	(h) Blackburn R	D 1-1	Mounteney	5,000					5	6		4	9	8	11	7				2			1		3				10				
29	14	(a) Bolton W	L 0-1		5,000			3	4	5		6	9	10		11	7							1		2			8					
30	18	(a) Everton	L 1-4	Tickle	10,000			3	4	5	6		8	9	10	11	7							1		2								
31	21	(h) Newcastle U	D 1-1	Tickle	20,000	1		3	5		6	7	4	10	9	11	8									2								
32	28	(h) Everton	W 2-1	Jones, Beer	12,000				4	5		7	6	9	10		8	11			2			1		3								
33	30	(h) Nottingham F	W 1-0	Jones	10,000				4	5		7	6	9	10		8	11			2			1		3								
34	Apr 4	(a) Sunderland	L 0-1		15,000				4	5		6	9	8	10	7	11							1		3						2		
35	11	(h) W Arsenal	L 1-2	Beer	15,000			3	8	5		6	9	10		11	7			4				1		2								
36	17	(a) Manchester C	L 1-2	Mounteney	27,000	1		3	4	5		6	8	9	10	1	7									2								
37	18	(a) Sheffield W	W 4-1	Jones, Beer, Anderson, Green	10,000	1		3	4	5	6		7	9	10			11									3			8		2		8
38	25	(h) Bristol C	L 0-4		4,000			3	4	5	6		7	9	10			11						1		2								8

FINAL LEAGUE POSITION: 18th in Division One. Average home League attendance: 15,473.

| Appearances | 14 | 13 | 28 | 34 | 35 | 26 | 17 | 36 | 23 | 25 | 31 | 31 | 8 | 6 | 11 | 1 | 1 | 1 | 24 | 2 | 23 | 1 | 1 | 9 | 11 | 3 | 1 | 1 | |
| Goals | | | | 3 | 1 | | | 8 | 7 | 6 | 8 | 3 | 1 | | | | | | | | | | | | 1 | 2 | | | |

FA Cup

#	Date	Opponent	Result	Scorers	Att.	Robinson AC	Glover J	Stokes F	Beer WJ	Wigmore W	Cornan F	Peplow W	Green BH	Jones WH	Mounteney A	Eyre E	Tickle CH	Anderson GE	Dougherty J	Corbett WS	Gooch PG	Morris AS	Higgins JB	Travers W	Dorrington J	Holmes E	Kearns J	Hartwell A	King H	Bluff EW	Drake A	Fairman R	Handley TH	Moore G
1	Jan 11	(a) West Brom A	D 1-1	W.H.Jones	36,727			3	4	5	6		8	9		11	7							1		2				10				
R	15	(h) West Brom A	L 1-2	Eyre	24,895				4	5	6		8	9		11	7				2			1		3				10				

| Appearances | | 1 | 2 | 2 | 2 | | 2 | 2 | | 2 | 2 | | | | 1 | | | 2 | | 2 | | | | 2 | | | | | |
| Goals | | | | | | | | 1 | | 1 | | | | | | | | | | | | | | | | | | | |

1908-09

Manager: Committee

No	Date	Opponent	Res	Scorers	Att	Dorrington J	Corbett WS	Kearns J	Beer WJ	Wigmore W	Fairman R	Green BH	Smith W	Jones WH	Mounteney A	Eyre E	Womack F	Williams JW	Stokes F	Haynes WH	Travers GE	Wilcox J	Lowe CB	Moore G	Chapple FJ	Anderson GE	Daykin T	King H	Kerns F	Handley T	Box A	Bumphrey J	Jones CJ	Gardner AE
1	Sep 2 (h)	Bolton W	W 2-0	Eyre 2	8,000	1	2	3	4	5	6	7	8	9	10	11																		
2	5 (a)	Gainsboro' T	W 3-1	Eyre 2, W.H.Jones	5,000	1		2	4	5	6	7	8	9	10	11	3																	
3	7 (h)	Bradford	W 3-1	Smith, Fairman, W.H.Jones	15,000	1	2	3	4	5	6	7	8	9		11		10																
4	12 (h)	Grimsby T	W 3-1	W.H.Jones, Green (pen), Smith	15,000	1	2	3	4	5	6	7	8	9		11		10																
5	19 (a)	Fulham	D 1-1	Green	38,000	1	2	3	4	5	6	7	8	9	10	11																		
6	26 (h)	Burnley	W 2-0	Fairman, W.H.Jones	20,000	1	2	3	4	5	6	7	8	9		11		10																
7	Oct 6 (a)	Bradford	W 2-1	Beer, Baddeley (og)	8,000	1		3	4	5	6	7	8	9		11		10	2															
8	10 (h)	Wolves	D 1-1	Smith	20,000	1	2	3	4		6	5	8	9		11		10		7														
9	17 (a)	Oldham A	L 0-2		20,000	1		2	4		6	7	9	8	5	11		10	3															
10	24 (h)	Clapton O	W 1-0	Williams	10,000	1		2	4		6	7	8	9	5	11		10	3															
11	31 (a)	Leeds C	L 0-2		15,000	1		2	5			6	4	8	10	11	3			7	9													
12	Nov 7 (h)	Barnsley	W 2-1	Green, W.H.Jones	10,000	1		2	4	5		6	8	9		11	3					7	10											
13	14 (a)	Tottenham H	L 0-4		25,000	1	2	3	4	5	6		8	9		11						7	10											
14	21 (h)	Hull C	L 1-2	Beer	5,000	1		2	5			4	8			11	3			9	6	7	10											
15	28 (a)	Derby C	W 2-1	Moore, Mounteney	10,000	1	2	3	5		6	4			9	11		10				7		8										
16	Dec 5 (h)	Blackpool	D 2-2	Chapple, Smith	6,000	1	2	3	5		6	4	9				8					7			10	11								
17	12 (a)	Chesterfield	L 2-4	Mounteney, Anderson	5,000	1		2	5			4			9		3					7	8		10	11	6							
18	19 (h)	Glossop	L 1-2	Smith	5,000	1	2	3	4	5			8	9								7			10	11	6							
19	25 (h)	Stockport C	W 4-2	Chapple 4	10,000	1		2	4	5					9		3					7			10	11	6	8						
20	26 (a)	West Brom A	D 1-1	King	38,049	1	2	3	4	5					9							7			10	11	6	8						
21	28 (h)	West Brom A	D 0-0		30,035	1	2	3	4	5					9							7			10	11	6	8						
22	Jan 1 (a)	Bolton W	L 1-2	Beer	25,000	1		2	4	5					9		3					7			10	11	6	8						
23	2 (a)	Gainsboro' T	D 2-2	King, Beer	5,000	1		2	4	5	6						3								10	11	9	7	8					
24	9 (a)	Grimsby T	W 3-0	Williams 2, Chapple	5,000	1		2	4			7					3	9							10	11	6	8		5				
25	23 (h)	Fulham	L 1-3	Beer	9,000	1	2		4			7					3	9							10	11	6	8		5				
26	30 (a)	Burnley	D 1-1	Beer	8,000			2	9	4							3					7			10		6			5	1	8	11	
27	Feb 13 (a)	Wolves	L 0-2		10,000			2	4							11	3					7			10		6	9		5	1	8		
28	20 (h)	Oldham A	W 2-0	Beer 2	10,000			2	9	4							3					7			11		6	10		5	1	8		
29	27 (a)	Clapton O	L 2-3	King, Bumphrey	7,000				9	4							3		2			7			11		6	10		5	1	8		
30	Mar 13 (a)	Barnsley	L 1-3	King	4,000	1			5	4							3		2						7	10	6	9				8		
31	20 (h)	Tottenham H	D 3-3	King, Mounteney, Daykin	14,000	1	4		5						10		3		2						7		6	9				8		
32	27 (h)	Hull C	L 1-4	Bumphrey	8,000	1			4	5		7		11			3		2						10		6	9				8		
33	Apr 3 (h)	Derby C	D 1-1	King	5,000	1			4	5					6		3		2						7	10	9	11				8		
34	9 (a)	Stockport C	L 2-3	Chapple, Lowe	6,000	1			4			6				11	3		2				8		10		9	7		5				
35	10 (a)	Blackpool	L 0-2		4,000	1			4			6				11	3		2				8		10		9	7		5				
36	12 (h)	Leeds C	W 1-0	Bumphrey	3,000	1			4			6				11	3		2						10		9	7		5		8		
37	17 (h)	Chesterfield	W 3-0	Mounteney 3	1,500	1									9	11	3		2				8			10	6	7		5				4
38	24 (a)	Glossop	L 1-3	Mounteney	500	1									9	11	3		2							10	6	8		5		7		4
				Appearances		34	15	27	33	23	19	18	17	18	16	15	14	12	23	3	1	18	11	2	19	12	17	19	1	12	4	12	1	2
				Goals					8		2	3	5	5	7	4		3					1	1	7	1	1	6				3		

FINAL LEAGUE POSITION: 11th in Division Two. Average home League attendance: 10,607.

1 own-goal

FA Cup

No	Date	Opponent	Res	Scorers	Att	Dorrington J	Corbett WS	Kearns J	Beer WJ	Wigmore W	Fairman R	Green BH	Smith W	Jones WH	Mounteney A	Eyre E	Womack F	Williams JW	Stokes F	Haynes WH	Travers GE	Wilcox J	Lowe CB	Moore G	Chapple FJ	Anderson GE	Daykin T	King H	Kerns F	Handley T	Box A	Bumphrey J	Jones CJ	Gardner AE
1	Jan 16 (h)	Portsmouth	L 2-5	Chapple (pen), King	18,813	1	2	3	4	5					9							7			10	11	6	8						
				Appearances		1	1	1	1	1					1							1			1	1	1	1						
				Goals																					1			1						

1909-10

Manager: Committee

#	Date	Opponent	Res	Scorers	Att	Dorrington J	Womack F	Stokes F	Beer WJ	Buckley F	Daykin T	Wilcox J	Millington C	Freeman W	Chapple FJ	Lappin H	King H	Corbett WS	Moles J	Bumphrey J	Gardner AE	McGourty AE	Lowe CB	Wigmore W	Box A	Needham J	Banks F	Preston J	Frith RE	Burton JH	Carrier W
1	Sep 4 (h)	Oldham A	D 2-2	Millington, Beer	20,000	1	2	3	4	5	6	7	8		10	11	9														
2	11 (a)	Barnsley	L 1-5	Chapple	3,000	1		3	4		6	7	9		10	11		2	5	8											
3	13 (h)	Glossop	D 2-2	Lowe, Millington	3,000	1		3	9			7	8		11			2	5		4	6	10								
4	18 (h)	Fulham	D 1-1	Chapple	12,000	1		3	5		6	7	8	9		11		2			4		10								
5	25 (a)	Burnley	L 0-2		5,000	1		3	4	5	6	7	8	9	10	11									2						
6	Oct 2 (h)	Leeds C	L 1-2	Freeman	14,000			3		5	6	7	8	9		11		2			4				1	10					
7	9 (a)	Wolves	L 2-4	Buckley, Chapple	10,000	1	3			4	5	6	7	8	9	11									2	10					
8	16 (h)	Gainsboro' T	W 5-0	Millington 2, Needham 3	10,000	1	3			5	6	7	8	9	11			2			4					10					
9	23 (a)	Grimsby T	W 2-0	Freeman, Wilcox	5,000	1	3			5	6	7	8	9	11						4				2	10					
10	30 (h)	Manchester C	D 1-1	Freeman	18,000	1	3			5	6	7	8	9	11			2			4					10					
11	Nov 6 (a)	Leicester F	L 1-3	Freeman	10,000	1	2	3			6	7	8	9	11				5		4					10					
12	13 (h)	Lincoln C	W 1-0	Needham	5,000	1	3				6	7	8	9				2	5		4					10	11				
13	20 (a)	Clapton O	L 0-3		6,000	1	3				6	7	8	9		11			5		4					10		2			
14	27 (h)	Blackpool	L 1-2	Chapple	1,000		3				6	7	8	9	11		5				4				1	10		2			
15	Dec 4 (a)	Hull C	L 0-7		6,000		3				6		8	9	11		5				4				1	10		2	7		
16	11 (h)	Derby C	L 1-3	Freeman	5,000		3				6	7	8	9	11		5				4				1	10		2			
17	18 (a)	Stockport C	D 1-1	Lappin	4,000		3		5			7	8	9	11	10			6		4				1			2			
18	25 (a)	Glossop	L 1-4	Chapple	3,000		3				6	7	8	9	11	10	5				4				1			2			
19	27 (a)	West Brom A	L 1-3	Millington	12,104		3				6		8	9	11		5				4				1	10		2	7		
20	28 (h)	Bradford	L 0-1		15,000		3				6		8	9	11		5				4				1	10		2	7		
21	Jan 1 (h)	West Brom A	L 0-1		15,500		3				6	9	8		11		5				4				1	10		2	7		
22	8 (a)	Oldham A	D 1-1	Lappin	8,000		3				6	9	8			11	5				4				1	10			7		2
23	22 (h)	Barnsley	W 2-1	Freeman, Chapple	5,000		3	2			6	7	8	9	11		5				4				1	10					
24	29 (a)	Fulham	D 0-0		10,000		3	2	5		6	7	8	9	11						4				1	10					
25	Feb 12 (a)	Leeds C	L 1-2	Freeman	10,000		3	2	5	11	6	7	8	9							4				1	10					
26	19 (h)	Wolves	W 1-0	Freeman	2,000		3		5	11	6	7	8	9							4			2	1	10					
27	26 (a)	Gainsboro' T	L 0-1		3,000		3		5	11	6	7	8	9							4			2	1	10					
28	28 (h)	Burnley	W 2-1	Chapple, Freeman	1,000		3		5			7	8	9	11		6	2			4				1	10					
29	Mar 5 (h)	Grimsby T	L 2-4	Needham, Chapple	14,000		3		5			7	8	9	11		6	2			4				1	10					
30	12 (a)	Manchester C	L 0-3		15,000		2	3	5			7	8	9	11		6				4				1	10					
31	19 (h)	Leicester F	W 2-1	Burton, Buckley	10,000		3		5	11		7	8	9			6				4				1					10	2
32	26 (a)	Lincoln C	L 2-3	Burton, Millington	5,000		3		5	11		7	8	9			6				4				1					10	2
33	28 (a)	Bradford	L 0-5		8,000		3		5	11		7	8	9			6				4			2	1	10					
34	Apr 2 (h)	Clapton O	L 1-2	Burton	8,000		3		5	11		7	8	9			6				4				1					10	2
35	9 (a)	Blackpool	L 0-2		3,000	1	2		5	11			8	9			6				4					10			7		3
36	16 (h)	Hull C	L 0-2		8,000	1	2		5	11			8	9			6				4					10			7		3
37	23 (a)	Derby C	L 1-3	Millington	5,000		2		5	11		7	8	9			6				4					10			7		3
38	30 (h)	Stockport C	W 3-0	Freeman, Millington, Lowe	3,000		2	3		11		7	8	9			6				4		5		1	10					
		Appearances				14	22	20	6	25	23	27	36	33	31	11	9	9	27	7	34	1	3	9	24	20	1	7	8	4	7
		Goals							1	2		1	8	10	8	2							2			5				3	

FINAL LEAGUE POSITION: 20th in Division Two. Average home League attendance: 8,921

FA Cup

#	Date	Opponent	Res	Scorers	Att	Womack F	Stokes F	Buckley F	Daykin T	Millington C	Chapple FJ	Lappin H	Bumphrey J	Gardner AE	Box A	Preston J
1	Jan 15 (h)	Leicester F	L 1-4	Lappin	15,119	2	3	5	6	8	10	11	9	4	1	7
		Appearances				1	1	1	1	1	1	1	1	1	1	1
		Goals										1				

1910-11

Manager: Bob McRoberts

#	Date	Venue / Opponent	Result	Scorers	Att	Dorrington J	Bonthron RP	Henderson CG	Corbett WS	Buckley F	Daykin T	Firth RE	Millington C	Jones T	Foxall F	Gallimore G	Abbott WA	McKay J	Gardner AE	Freeman W	Bumphrey J	Draper H	Womack F	Lowe CB	Kidd J	Lindon AE	Moles J	Wigmore W	Hall JH	Robertson E	Greer T	Bailey HP	Powell M	Wilcox J
1	Sep 3	(a) Fulham	L 0-3		25,000	1	2	3	4	5	6	7	8		10	11	9																	
2	Sep 10	(h) Bradford	W 1-0	McKay	18,000	1	2	3	4	5	6	7	8	9		11		10																
3	Sep 17	(a) Burnley	D 2-2	Millington, Jones	10,000	1	2	3		5	6	7	8	9	10	11			4															
4	Sep 24	(h) Gainsboro' T	D 1-1	Jones	12,000	1	2	3	4	5	6	7	8	9	10					11														
5	Oct 1	(a) Leeds C	D 1-1	Bonthron (pen)	8,000	1	2	3	4	5	6	7	10	9						11	8													
6	Oct 8	(h) Stockport C	L 1-3	Jones	14,000	1	2	3	4	5	6		8	9		11						7	10											
7	Oct 15	(a) Derby C	L 0-1		10,000	1	2		4	5	6		7	9									8	10	3	11								
8	Oct 22	(h) Barnsley	W 1-0	Freeman	10,000	1	2		4	5	6	7			9								8	11	3	10								
9	Oct 29	(a) Leicester F	L 0-2		10,000	1	2		4	5	6		8	9	10	11								7	3									
10	Nov 5	(h) Wolves	L 1-3	Foxall	20,000	1	2			5	6			9	10	11			4				7	3	8									
11	Nov 12	(a) Chelsea	D 2-2	Jones, Wigmore	17,000						2	7		9	10	11			4				3		8		1	5	6					
12	Nov 19	(h) Clapton O	L 0-1		12,000						2	7			10	11			4		9		3		8		1	6	5					
13	Nov 26	(a) Blackpool	L 1-3	Kidd	4,000						2	7		9	10	11			4				3		8		1	6	5					
14	Dec 3	(h) Glossop	L 1-2	Jones	2,000	1			2	5	6	7		9	10	11			4				3		8									
15	Dec 10	(a) Lincoln C	W 1-0	Firth	6,000	1				5	6	7	10	9		11			4				3		8	2								
16	Dec 17	(h) Huddersfield T	W 2-1	Gallimore, Hall	4,000	1				5	2	7			10	11			4				3		8			6	9					
17	Dec 24	(a) Bolton W	L 1-5	Hall	6,000	1				5	2	7			10	11			4				3		8			6	9					
18	Dec 26	(a) Hull C	L 1-4	Hall	9,000	1			2	5	6	7				11		10	4				3		8				9					
19	Dec 27	(h) West Brom A	D 1-1	Hall	37,520	1				5	6	7				11		10	4				3		8			2	9					
20	Dec 31	(h) Fulham	D 1-1	Hall	14,000	1				5		7			10	11			4				3		8			2	9	6				
21	Jan 7	(a) Bradford	D 2-2	Firth, Hall	10,000	1				5	2	7				11		10	4				3		8				9	6				
22	Jan 21	(h) Burnley	D 1-1	Jones	6,000		2					7		10		11			4		8		3				1	5		6	9			
23	Jan 28	(a) Gainsboro' T	L 0-1		3,000							7		10		11			4				3		8	2	1	5	9	6				
24	Feb 4	(h) Leeds C	W 2-1	Foxall, Powell	15,000					5	4	7				11							3					2	9	6		1	8	10
25	Feb 13	(a) Stockport C	L 1-3	Buckley	2,000					5	4	7				11							3					2	9	6		1	8	10
26	Feb 18	(h) Derby C	W 2-0	Jones, Foxall	16,000				2	5		7		9		11			4				3		8					6		1	10	
27	Feb 25	(a) Barnsley	W 3-2	Jones, Hall 2	2,500					5	2	7		10		11			4				3		8				9	6		1		
28	Mar 4	(h) Leicester F	W 1-0	Buckley	8,000					5	2	7		10		11			4				3		8				9	6		1		
29	Mar 11	(a) Wolves	L 1-3	Hall	8,000					5	2	7		10		11			4				3		8				9	6		1		
30	Mar 18	(h) Chelsea	W 2-1	Hall, Kidd	25,000					5	2	7		10				11	4				3		8				9	6		1		
31	Mar 25	(a) Clapton O	L 1-2	Hall	6,000					5	2	7		10				11	4				3		8		1		9	6				
32	Apr 1	(h) Blackpool	W 2-0	McKay, Hall	13,000						2	7		10				11	4				3		8			5	9	6		1		
33	Apr 8	(a) Glossop	L 1-2	Jones	2,000						2	7		9		11		10	4				3		8			5		6		1		
34	Apr 14	(h) Hull C	W 1-0	Hall	10,000					5	4	7		10				11					3		8			2	9	6		1		
35	Apr 15	(h) Lincoln C	L 0-1		10,000					5	4	7		10				11					3		8			2		6		1	9	
36	Apr 17	(a) West Brom A	L 0-1		27,042					5	2	7		10				11	4				3		8				9	6		1		
37	Apr 22	(a) Huddersfield T	L 1-7	Jones	9,000					5	2	7		10				11	4				3		8				9	6		1		
38	Apr 29	(h) Bolton W	W 2-1	Millington, Jones	15,000	1				5	2	7		10				11	4				3		8				9	6				
		Appearances				19	11	6	11	30	35	17	25	28	21	18	1	15	18	4	12	3	32	2	26	7	6	14	19	19	1	12	4	2
		Goals					1			2		2	2	11	3	1		2		1			2		2			1	13				1	

FINAL LEAGUE POSITION: 16th in Division Two. Average home League attendance: 13,764

FA Cup

#	Date	Venue / Opponent	Result	Scorers	Att	Dorrington J	Bonthron RP	Henderson CG	Corbett WS	Buckley F	Daykin T	Firth RE	Millington C	Jones T	Foxall F	Gallimore G	Abbott WA	McKay J	Gardner AE	Freeman W	Bumphrey J	Draper H	Womack F	Lowe CB	Kidd J	Lindon AE	Moles J	Wigmore W	Hall JH	Robertson E	Greer T	Bailey HP	Powell M	Wilcox J
1	Jan 14	(h) Oldham A	D 1-1	Hall (pen)	28,827	1	2			5		7				11		10	4				3		8				9	6				
R	Jan 17	(a) Oldham A	L 0-2		6,400	1			2			7				11			4				3		8			5	9	6				10
		Appearances				2	1		1	1		2				2		1	2				2		2			1	2	2				1
		Goals																											1				

1911-12

Manager: Bob McRoberts

Player columns (left to right): Bailey HP, Ball W, Womack F, Bumphrey J, Gildea W, Daykin T, Millington C, Kidd J, Hall JH, Webb S, McKay J, Dorrington J, Gardner AE, Morris DJ, Robertson E, Wigmore W, Gibson A, Jones T, Conlin J, Graham H, Green A, Crossthwaite H, Hastie I, Tinkler A, George W, Greer T, McClure A, Bates HK, Hastings W, Reed A, Jones WH

No	Date	Venue/Opponent	Result	Scorers	Att	Bai	Ball	Wom	Bum	Gil	Day	Mil	Kidd	Hall	Webb	McK	Dor	Gar	Mor	Rob	Wig	Gib	JoT	Con	Gra	Gre	Cro	Has	Tin	Geo	Gre	McC	Bat	Hst	Reed	JoW
1	Sep 2	(h) Bradford	L 2-3	Kidd 2 (1 pen)	20,000		2	3	4		6	7	8	9	10	11	1			5																
2	Sep 9	(a) Fulham	L 1-2	Hall	12,000	1		3		5	2	7	8	9	6	11			4	10																
3	Sep 11	(a) Barnsley	L 1-3	Millington	5,000			3		5	6	7	8		10				4	10	2									1	9					
4	Sep 16	(h) Derby C	L 0-4		12,000	1	2	3		5		7	8	9		11			4	10		6														
5	Sep 23	(a) Stockport C	L 0-2		5,000	1	2	3	8	5	4	7	10	9		11						6														
6	Sep 30	(h) Leeds C	W 4-3	Hall 4	10,000	1	2	3				7		9				4				6	8	10	11											
7	Oct 7	(a) Wolves	L 0-1		12,000	1	2	3	4	5		7		9								6		8	11				10							
8	Oct 14	(h) Leicester F	W 4-0	Hall 2, Graham 2	15,000	1	2	3	4	5		7		9								6		8	11				10							
9	Oct 21	(a) Gainsboro' T	D 0-0		2,000	1		2	4	5		7		9								6		8	11		3		10							
10	Oct 28	(h) Grimsby T	D 2-2	Hall (pen), Gildea	15,000	1	2	3	4	5		7		9								6		8	11				10							
11	Nov 4	(a) Nottingham F	W 1-0	Graham	7,000	1	2	3	4	5		7	8									6		9	11				10							
12	Nov 11	(h) Chelsea	L 1-4	Gibson	25,000		2	3	4	5		7		9								6		8	11			1	10							
13	Nov 18	(a) Clapton O	L 0-2		2,000	1		3	4	5	2			9								6		8	11		7		10							
14	Nov 25	(h) Bristol C	D 0-0		12,000	1		3	4	5	2	7		9								6		8	10	11										
15	Dec 2	(a) Burnley	D 1-1	Jones	13,000			3	4	5	2	7		9				1				6		8	10	11										
16	Dec 9	(a) Huddersfield T	L 2-3	Kidd, Millington	2,000			3	4	5	2	7	10	9				1				6		8					11							
17	Dec 16	(h) Blackpool	W 2-1	Hall, Kidd	5,000	1		3	4	5	2	7	10	9								6		8			1									
18	Dec 23	(a) Glossop	L 0-2		1,000	1	2	3	4	5		7	10	9											11				8		6					
19	Dec 25	(a) Hull C	L 0-4		12,000	1		3	4	5	2	7	10	9											11				8		6					
20	Dec 26	(h) Hull C	W 5-1	Kidd 2, Millington, Hall, Graham	10,000	1		3		5	2	7	10	9				4							11				8		6					
21	Dec 30	(a) Bradford	L 0-3		14,000			3		5	2	7	10	9			1	4							11				8		6					
22	Jan 6	(h) Fulham	L 1-3	Tinkler	7,000	1		3		5	2	7	10					4							11				8		9					
23	Jan 27	(a) Stockport C	W 2-0	Conlin, Robertson	12,000	1	2	3						9				4		10					11						6	5	7			8
24	Feb 3	(a) Gainsboro' T	D 2-2	Jones, Hall	10,000	1	2	3				7		9				4		10					11						6	5				8
25	Feb 10	(h) Wolves	W 3-1	Hall 3 (1 pen)	25,000	1	2	3				7		9						10	4										6	5		11		8
26	Feb 17	(a) Leicester F	L 2-5	Conlin, Jones (pen)	10,000		2	3	6					9				4		10					11							5	7			8
27	Feb 21	(h) Derby C	W 1-0	Gardner	6,000		2	3	6					9				4		10								1				5	7	11		8
28	Mar 2	(a) Grimsby T	L 0-1		5,000		2	3	6					9				4		10					11		5		1				7			8
29	Mar 9	(h) Nottingham F	W 4-2	Jones 2, Hastings, Hall	8,000	1	2	3	6					9				4		10		7					5							11		8
30	Mar 16	(h) Chelsea	W 2-0	Hall, Robertson	27,000	1	2	3	6					9				4		10		7					5							11		8
31	Mar 23	(h) Clapton O	W 4-0	Hall 3, Jones (pen)	6,000	1	2	3	6					9				4		10		7					5							11		8
32	Mar 30	(a) Bristol C	L 1-2	Hastings	8,000	1	2	3	6					9				4		10		7					5		1					11		8
33	Apr 5	(a) Leeds C	D 0-0		5,000	1	2	3	6					9				4		10		7					5							11		8
34	Apr 6	(h) Burnley	W 4-0	Hall, Reed 2, Hastings	35,000	1	2	3	6					8				4		10		7					5							11	9	
35	Apr 8	(a) Barnsley	L 0-1		4,000	1	2	3	6							10		4		8		7					9				5			11		
36	Apr 13	(h) Huddersfield T	W 1-0	Hall	10,000	1	2	3	6					8				4				7					5							11	9	
37	Apr 20	(a) Blackpool	L 0-1		2,000	1	2	3	6					8				4				7					5						10	11	9	
38	Apr 27	(h) Glossop	W 2-0	Robertson 2	6,000	1	2	3	6					8				4		10		7					5							11	9	
		Appearances				29	26	38	31	18	13	22	14	35	3	4	4	22	3	30	3	22	3	21	12	1	4	1	19	1	1	7	2	14	4	11
		Goals								1		3	6	21				1		4		1		1	2				4			1		3	2	5

FINAL LEAGUE POSITION: 12th in Division Two. Average home League attendance: 13,052

FA Cup

No	Date	Venue/Opponent	Result	Att	Bai	Ball	Wom	Gil	Day	Mil	Kidd	Hall	Gar	Wig	Gra	JoW
1	Jan 13	(h) Barnsley	F 0-0	19,500	1	2	3	5	6	7	10	9	4		11	8
R	Jan 22	(a) Barnsley	L 0-3	11,900	1	2	3	5	6	7	10	9	4	8	11	
		Appearances			2	2	2	2	2	2	2	2	2	1	2	1
		Goals														

1912-13

Manager: Bob McRoberts

Player columns (left→right): Bailey HP · Ball W · Womack F · Gardner AE · Tinkler A · Bumphrey J · Gibson A · Jones WH · Hall JH · Robertson E · Smith AR · Dorrington J · Reed A · Hastings W · Crosthwaite H · McClure A · Fairman R · Smith AW · Bates JHK · Sprigg C · Roulson C · Smith J · Morgan WA · Duncan C · Ballantyne J

#	Date		Opponent	Result	Scorers	Att	Bai	Bal	Wom	Gar	Tin	Bum	Gib	Jon	Hal	Rob	SmAR	Dor	Ree	Has	Cro	McC	Fai	SmAW	Bat	Spr	Rou	SmJ	Mor	Dun	Blt
1	Sep 7	(a)	Bradford	D 0-0		12,000	1	2	3	4	5	6	7	8	9	10	11														
2	9	(h)	Fulham	W 2-1	Robertson, Hall	7,000		2	3	4	5	6	7	8	9	10	11	1													
3	14	(h)	Wolves	D 0-0		3,000	1	2	3	4	5	6	7	8	9	10	11														
4	21	(a)	Leicester F	W 2-1	Jones, Robertson	14,000	1	2	3	4	5	6	7	8	9	10	11														
5	28	(h)	Stockport C	D 1-1	Hall	20,000	1	2	3	4	5	6	7	8	9	10	11														
6	Oct 5	(a)	Preston NE	L 0-1		8,000	1	2	3	4	5	6			9	10			7	8	11										
7	12	(h)	Burnley	W 3-0	Jones, Hastings, Hall	15,000	1	2	3	4	5	6		8	9				7	10	11										
8	19	(a)	Hull C	W 2-1	Jones, Robertson	10,000		2	3	4	5	6		8	9	10			7		11	1									
9	26	(h)	Glossop	D 0-0		5,000	1	2	3	4		6		8	9	10			7		11		5								
10	Nov 2	(a)	Clapton O	W 2-0	Bumphrey, Jones	10,000		2	3	4		6		8	9	10			7		11	1	5								
11	9	(h)	Lincoln C	W 4-1	Hall 2, Jones, Bumphrey	35,000		2	3	4		6		8	9	10			7		11	1	5								
12	16	(a)	Nottingham F	L 1-3	Jones	10,000		2		4		6		8	9	10	11		7			1	5	3							
13	23	(h)	Bristol C	W 3-0	Hastings, Robertson, A.R.Smith	20,000		2		4	5	6		8	9	10	11		7			1		3							
14	30	(h)	Blackpool	W 3-2	Hall, Gardner, Robertson	10,000		2		4	5	6	8		9	10	11		7			1		3							
15	Dec 7	(a)	Huddersfield T	D 0-0		6,000		2		4	5	6			9	10	11		7	8		1		3							
16	14	(h)	Leeds C	D 2-2	A.W.Smith, Tinkler	20,000	1	2	3	4	5	6		8		10	11		7					9							
17	21	(a)	Grimsby T	D 2-2	Robertson, Jones	5,000		2	3	4	5	6		8		10	11					1		9	7						
18	25	(h)	Barnsley	W 3-1	Gardner, Robertson 2	35,000		2	3	4	5	6		8		10	11		7			1		9							
19	26	(h)	Bury	L 1-2	A.W.Smith	8,000		2	3	4	5	6		8		10	11		7			1		9							
20	28	(h)	Bradford	D 1-1	Jones	20,000		2		4	5	6		8		10			7			1		3		9		11			
21	Jan 1	(a)	Bury	L 0-3		10,000		2		4		6		8		10			7			1	5	3		9		11			
22	4	(a)	Wolves	D 2-2	Jones 2	7,000	1	2		9				8									5	3		11	4	6	10		
23	18	(h)	Leicester F	W 5-1	A.R.Smith, Hall 2, Jones, King (og)	12,000		2			6			8	9						7	1	5	3		11	4		10		
24	25	(a)	Stockport C	W 1-0	Jones	4,000		2	3	4	5			8	9				7			1				11		6	10		
25	Feb 8	(h)	Preston NE	L 0-1		35,000		2	3	4	5		7	8	9						11	1						6	10		
26	15	(a)	Barnsley	L 0-3		2,000		2	3					8	9	10	11		7			1	5			4	6				
27	22	(h)	Hull C	W 3-1	Duncan, Robertson, Jones	10,000		2	3			6		8		7	10	11				1	5			4				9	
28	Mar 1	(a)	Glossop	W 2-0	Jones, Robertson	3,000		2	3			6		8		7	10	11				1	5			4				9	
29	8	(h)	Clapton O	D 1-1	Duncan	14,000		2	3			6		8		7	10	11				1	5			4				9	
30	15	(a)	Lincoln C	W 1-0	Duncan	5,000		2	3			6	7				10	11		8		1	5			4				9	
31	22	(h)	Nottingham F	W 2-0	Reed 2	6,000			3		4	6	7				10	11		8		1	5	2						9	
32	24	(a)	Fulham	L 2-3	Robertson, Duncan	8,000			3		4	6	7				10	11		8		1	5	2						9	
33	25	(a)	Barnsley	L 0-1		10,000		2	3		5	6	7		9			11		8		1				4			10		
34	29	(a)	Bristol C	W 3-0	Reed 2, Robertson	6,000		2	3		4	6	7		9	10	11			8		1	5								
35	Apr 5	(a)	Blackpool	L 0-2		5,000		2	3		4	6	7		9	10	11			8		1	5								
36	12	(h)	Huddersfield T	W 3-2	Jones 2, Robertson	10,000		2	3		4	6	7	9		10	11			8		1	5								
37	19	(a)	Leeds C	L 0-4		8,000		2	3		4	6	7		9	10	11			8		1	5								
38	26	(h)	Grimsby T	W 2-1	Reed 2	3,000		2	3		4	6			9	10	11			8		1	5						7		
	Appearances						9	36	30	23	27	34	15	33	22	30	37	1	13	15	28	19	10	6	1	5	8	4	5	6	1
	Goals									2	1	2		16	8	13	2		6	2				2						4	

FINAL LEAGUE POSITION: 3rd in Division Two. Average home League attendance: 15,157

1 own-goal

FA Cup

#	Date		Opponent	Result	Att	Bai	Bal	Gar	Tin	Bum	Jon	Hal	Rob	Ree	Cro	SmAW
1	Jan 11	(a)	Manchester C	L 0-4	17,442	1	2	4	5	6	8	9	10	7	11	3
	Appearances					1	1	1	1	1	1	1	1	1	1	1
	Goals															

1913-14

Manager: Bob McRoberts

#		Date (venue)	Result	Scorers	Att.	Evans RD	Ball W	Womack F	Edwards EA	McClure A	Bumphrey J	Ballantyne J	Duncan C	Hall JH	Reed A	Hastings W	Tinkler A	Jones WH	Smith AW	Smith AR	Crossthwaite H	Roulson J	Robertson E	Gibson A	Foster AW	Neilson PA	Hodges FC	Walker WB	Fairman R	Smith J	Morgan WA	Hauser S	Pointon TS	Stanton A	Barton PH	Robb WR	Gardner AE
1	Sep	3 (h) Stockport C	W 3-2	Reed 2, Hastings	15,000	1	2	3	4	5	6	7	8	9	10	11																					
2		6 (h) Bradford	L 1-2	W.H.Jones	25,000	1	2	3	4		6	7		9	10	11	5	8																			
3		13 (a) Notts C	L 1-5	A.W.Smith	12,000	1	2	3	4		6	7	10				5	8	9	11																	
4		20 (h) Leicester F	W 1-0	Ballantyne	20,000		2	3	5		6	7				11	4		8	9		1		10													
5		27 (a) Wolves	L 0-1		16,000		2	3	5		6	7				11	4		8	9		1		10													
6	Oct	4 (h) Hull C	D 1-1	Hastings	14,000		2	3	5		6					11	4		8	9		1		7	10												
7		11 (a) Barnsley	D 1-1	Gibson	8,800		2	3	5		6		8				4		9			1		10		11	7										
8		18 (h) Bury	W 1-0	Neilson	20,000		2	3	5		6		8				4		9			1		10		11	7										
9		25 (a) Huddersfield T	L 0-7		10,000		2	3	5		6		8				4		9			1		10		11	7										
10	Nov	1 (h) Lincoln C	W 2-0	A.W.Smith, Hodges	20,000		2	3	5		6		8				4		9			1		7		11	10										
11		8 (a) Blackpool	D 2-2		5,000		2	3	5		6		8				4		9			1		7		11	10										
12		15 (h) Nottingham F	W 2-0	Bumphrey, Walker	15,000		2	3	5		6		8				4		9			1		7			10	11									
13		22 (a) W Arsenal	L 0-1		23,500		2	3	5		6		8				4		9			1		7			10	11									
14		29 (h) Grimsby T	L 1-2	Walker	18,000		2	3	5		6		8				4		9			1		7			10	11									
15	Dec	6 (a) Fulham	L 0-1		10,000		2	3	5		6		8				4		9			1		7			10	11									
16		13 (a) Bristol C	W 2-1	Gibson, Walker	10,000		2	3	5		6		8				4		9		1			7			10	11									
17		20 (h) Leeds C	L 0-2		15,000		2	3	5		6		8				4		9		1			7			10	11									
18		25 (h) Glossop	W 6-0	Walker 2, Foster, Hall 2, Bumphrey	25,000		2	3	5		6		8				4		9		1			7	10			11									
19		26 (a) Glossop	L 1-4	Walker	5,000		2	3	5		6		8				4		9		1			7			10	11									
20		27 (a) Bradford	L 1-5	Morgan	8,000		2	3	4	5	6		8						9		1			7				11			10						
21	Jan	1 (a) Stockport C	L 0-2		6,000		2	3	5		6		8	9			4				1			7							10		11				
22		3 (h) Notts C	W 2-1	Morgan, Pointon	10,000		2		5		6	7	8	9			4				1							11			10	3					
23		17 (a) Leicester F	D 0-0		6,000		2	3	5	4			8	9		11					1			7							10	6					
24		24 (h) Wolves	W 4-1	Reed, Duncan, Ballantyne, Morgan	25,000		2	3		4		7	9		8	11	5				1										10	6					
25	Feb	7 (h) Hull C	D 0-0		9,000		2	3		4		7	9		8	11	5				1										10	6					
26		14 (h) Barnsley	D 0-0		15,000		2	3		4		7	8			11	5				1			9							10	6					
27		24 (a) Bury	L 1-3	Gibson	6,000			3	5	4			9			11					1			7							10	6			2		
28		28 (h) Huddersfield T	L 1-4	A.R.Smith	7,000		2	3	5	4		7	9			11					1										10	6					
29	Mar	7 (a) Lincoln C	D 1-1	Morgan	8,000		2	3	5	4		7	9	8		11					1										10	6					
30		14 (h) Blackpool	D 0-0		7,000			3	5	4		7	9	8	10						1								2		1	6	11				
31		21 (a) Nottingham F	L 1-3	Hall	5,000		2	3	5	4		7	8	9	10						1										1	6	11				
32		28 (h) W Arsenal	W 2-0	A.W.Smith 2	17,810		2	3				7	8	10	9				11		1		6									5		4			
33	Apr	4 (a) Grimsby T	W 2-0	A.W.Smith 2	10,000		2	3				7	8		9				6		1										5			4			
34		10 (h) Clapton O	W 2-0	Hall, A.W.Smith	25,000		2	3			6	7	8		5				9		1												4				
35		11 (h) Fulham	L 0-1		20,000		2	3				7			5				9		1							10					6	4			
36		13 (a) Clapton O	D 2-2	Walker, Hall	10,000			3				7	8		5				6		1			9								2	5	4			
37		18 (h) Bristol C	D 2-2	W.Smith, A.W.Smith	17,000		2	3				7	8		9				6		1												5	4			
38		25 (a) Leeds C	L 2-3	A.W.Smith, Gardner	10,000		2		5			7			9				9		1												3	6	4		
		Appearances				3	30	36	15	16	23	19	12	17	8	11	22	9	18	14	17	12	5	18	2	3	10	12	6	4	14	16	4	4	16	2	7
		Goals									2	2	1	5	3	2		1	10	1				3	1	1	1	8			4		1				1

FINAL LEAGUE POSITION: 14th in Division Two. Average home League attendance: 17,411.

W.Smith played number-10 in Matches 33 & 34 ; number-8 in Matches 35, 37,38 scoring 1 goal; **E.Eyre** played number-11 in Matches 33-38; **J.E.Windridge** played number-10 in Matches 36-38.

FA Cup

#		Date (venue)	Result	Scorers	Att.	Evans RD	Ball W	Womack F	Edwards EA	McClure A	Bumphrey J	Ballantyne J	Duncan C	Hall JH	Reed A	Hastings W	Tinkler A	Jones WH	Smith AW	Smith AR	Crossthwaite H	Roulson J	Robertson E	Gibson A	Foster AW	Neilson PA	Hodges FC	Walker WB	Fairman R	Smith J	Morgan WA	Hauser S	Pointon TS	Stanton A	Barton PH	Robb WR	Gardner AE
1	Jan	10 (h) Southend U	W 2-1	Duncan 2	18,000		2	3	5	4			9	8		11					1			7							10	6					
2		31 (h) Huddersfield T	W 1-0	Morgan	45,000		2	3		4			8	11	5						1			7			9				10	6					
3	Feb	23 (h) Queen's Park R	L 1-2	Duncan	35,000		2	3	5	4	7	8			11						1						9				10	6					
		Appearances					3	3	2	3	1	2	1	1	3	1					2			2							3	3					3
		Goals											3																		1					

1914-15

Manager: Bob McRoberts

#	Date	Opponent	Res	Scorers	Att	Robb WR	Ball W	Womack F	Bumphrey J	Tinkler A	Barton PH	Gibson A	Smith W	Walker WB	Windridge JE	Eyre E	Edwards EA	Smith AW	Morgan WA	Reed A	Gardner AE	Hall JH	McClure A	Duncan C	Roulson J	Hodges FC	Sprigg C	Stanton A
1	Sep 2 (a)	Nottingham F	D 1-1	W.Smith	4,000	1	2	3	4	5	6	7	8	9	10	11												
2	Sep 5 (a)	Leicester F	L 0-1		4,000	1	2	3	4	5	6	7	8	9	10	11												
3	12 (h)	Barnsley	W 2-0	Eyre, A.W.Smith	10,000	1	2	3	4	5		7	8		10	11	6	9										
4	19 (a)	Glossop	D 3-3	Tinkler, A.W.Smith (pen), Gibson	500	1	2	3	4	5	6	7	8			11		9	10									
5	26 (h)	Wolves	L 1-2	Gibson	20,000	1	2	3	4	5	6	7	8			11		9	10									
6	Oct 3 (a)	Fulham	W 3-2	Windridge, A.W.Smith 2	12,000	1	2	3	4	5	6	7	8		10	11		9										
7	10 (h)	Stockport C	L 0-1		12,000	1	2	3	4	5	6	7	8		10	11		9										
8	17 (a)	Hull C	D 0-0		7,000	1	2	3	4	5	6	7			10	11		9	8									
9	24 (h)	Leeds C	W 6-3	A.W.Smith 3, Barton, Windridge, Gibson	8,000	1	2	3		5	6	7	8		10	11		9			4							
10	31 (a)	Clapton O	D 1-1	Gibson	8,000	1	2	3		5	6	7			10	11		9			4	8						
11	Nov 7 (h)	Arsenal	W 3-0	A.W.Smith 2, Gibson	15,000	1	2	3		5	6	7			10	11		9			4	8						
12	14 (a)	Derby C	L 0-1		4,000	1	2	3		5	6	7			10	11		9			4	8						
13	21 (h)	Lincoln C	W 2-0	Gibson, A.W.Smith (pen)	5,000	1	2	3			6	7			10	11		9			4	8	5					
14	28 (h)	Blackpool	W 3-0	Gibson, W.Smith, A.W.Smith (pen)	5,000	1	2	3			6	7	8		10	11		9			4		5					
15	Dec 5 (a)	Grimsby T	L 0-1		5,000	1	2	3	4		6	7	8		10	11		9					5					
16	12 (h)	Huddersfield T	W 1-0	Duncan	9,000	1	2	3	4	5	6	7	8		10	11								9				
17	19 (a)	Bristol C	W 3-2	Barton, A.W.Smith, Gibson	4,000	1	2	3	4	5	6	7	8		10	11		9										
18	25 (h)	Bury	W 1-0	Gibson	20,000	1	2	3		5	6	7	8		10	11		9							4			
19	26 (a)	Bury	W 3-1	Roulson 2, Windridge	9,000	1	2	3		5	6	7			10			9							4	8	11	
20	28 (h)	Nottingham F	W 3-0	A.W.Smith 2 (1 pen), Hodges	15,000	1	2	3		5	6	7			10			9							4	8	11	
21	Jan 2 (h)	Leicester F	W 2-0	Gibson, Windridge	15,000	1		3		5	6	7			10			9							4	8	11	2
22	6 (h)	Glossop	W 11-1	A.W.Smith 4, Windridge 5 (1 pen), Eyre, Hodges	8,000	1	2	3		5	6	7			10	11		9							4	8		
23	Feb 13 (a)	Stockport C	L 1-3	A.W.Smith	3,000	1		3		5	6	7						9	10						4	8	11	2
24	27 (a)	Leeds C	L 0-2		7,000	1	2	3		5	6	7						9	10						4	8	11	
25	Mar 1 (h)	Fulham	W 1-0	Barton	5,000	1	2	3		5	6	7		8		11			10					9	4			
26	6 (h)	Clapton O	W 1-0	A.W.Smith	10,000	1	2	3		5	6	7		8				9	10						4		11	
27	8 (a)	Barnsley	L 1-2	Roulson (pen)	10,000	1	2	3		5	6	7		8					10					9	4		11	
28	13 (a)	Arsenal	L 0-1		19,067	1	2	3		5	6	7			10	11		9							4	8		
29	20 (h)	Derby C	L 0-2		18,000	1	2	3		5	6	7			10			9							4	8	11	
30	24 (h)	Hull C	D 2-2	Reed, A.W.Smith	10,000	1	2	3		5		7			10		6	9		11					4	8		
31	27 (a)	Lincoln C	W 1-0	Morgan	3,000	1	2		6	5	3	7						9	10						4	8	11	
32	Apr 2 (a)	Preston NE	L 0-2		10,000	1	2	3		5	6	7			10	11		9							4	8		
33	5 (h)	Preston NE	D 1-1	Hodges	10,000	1	2	3		5	6	7			10			9	11						4	8		
34	10 (h)	Grimsby T	W 3-0	Windridge, Barton, Roulson (pen)	10,000	1	2	3	6	5	9	7			11				10						4	8		
35	14 (a)	Blackpool	L 1-3	W.Smith	5,000	1	2	3	6			7	9		11				10				5		4	8		
36	17 (a)	Huddersfield T	D 0-0		4,000	1	2	3		5	6	7			10	11		9							4	8		
37	19 (a)	Wolves	D 0-0		8,000	1	2	3	6	5		7			10	11		9							4	8		
38	24 (h)	Bristol C	D 1-1	Windridge	10,000	1	2	3	6	5		7			11			9	10						4	8		
		Appearances				38	36	37	18	29	37	38	21	5	26	23	2	30	8	3	6	4	4	4	21	17	9	2
		Goals								1	4	10	3		11	2		21	1	1				1	4	3		

FINAL LEAGUE POSITION: 6th in Division Two. Average home League attendance: 11,315.

FA Cup

#	Date	Opponent	Res	Scorers	Att	Robb WR	Ball W	Womack F	Bumphrey J	Tinkler A	Barton PH	Gibson A	Smith W	Walker WB	Windridge JE	Eyre E	Edwards EA	Smith AW	Morgan WA	Reed A	Gardner AE	Hall JH	McClure A	Duncan C	Roulson J	Hodges FC	Sprigg C	Stanton A
1	Jan 9 (h)	Crystal P	D 2-2	A.W.Smith (pen), Eyre	18,000	1	2	3		5	6	7			10	11		9							4	8		
R	(a†) Crystal P		W 3-0*	Gibson, Tinkler, A.W.Smith	17,000	1	2	3		5	6	7			10	11		9							4	8		
2	30 (a)	Brighton & HA	D 0-0*		9,000	1	2	3		5	6	7			10	11		9							4	8		
R	Feb 6 (h)	Brighton & HA	W 3-0	Gibson, Morgan, A.W.Smith	28,000	1	2	3		5	6	7						9	10						4	8	11	
3	20 (h)	Oldham A	L 2-3	Gibson, Hodges	45,000	1		3		5	6	7						9	10				2		4	8	11	
		Appearances				5	4	5		5	5	5			3	3		5	2				1		5	5	2	
		Goals								1		3				1		3	1							1		

†Played at St Andrew's, Birmingham.　*After extra-time.

1919-20

Secretary/Manager: Frank Richards

#	Date		Venue/Opponent	Result	Scorers	Att	Tremelling DR	Ball W	Womack F	Roulson J	McClure A	Barton P	Burkinshaw L	Walker WB	Millard B	Whitehouse J	Morgan WA	Gibson R	Godfrey J	Evans T	Elkes J	Gardner A	Watson J	White VT	Short J	Roe A	Davies G	Pearl J	Wilson A	Hawley F	Hampton H	Lane J	Jones A	Mumford WR
1	Aug	30 (h)	Hull C	W 4-1	Gibson, Walker, Godfrey, Whitehouse	16,000	1	2	3	4	5	6		8		10	11	7	9															
2	Sep	1 (a)	South Shields	L 0-1		12,000	1	2	3	4	5	6		8		10	11	7	9															
3		6 (a)	Hull C	D 0-0		10,000	1	2	3	4	5	6		8		10	11	7	9															
4		10 (h)	South Shields	W 4-0	Millard 2, Morgan 2	12,000	1	2	3	4	5	6	7	8	9	10	11																	
5		13 (h)	Coventry C	W 4-1	Morgan, Whitehouse, Millard 2	18,000	1	2	3	4	5	6	7	8	9	10	11																	
6		20 (a)	Coventry C	W 3-1	Millard 2, Whitehouse	15,000	1	2	3	4	5	6	7	8	9	10	11																	
7		27 (h)	Huddersfield T	W 4-2	Elkes 2, Whitehouse, Burkinshaw	16,000	1	2	3		5	6	7		9	10	11			4	8													
8	Oct	4 (a)	Huddersfield T	D 0-0		5,000	1	2	3	6		5	7		9	10	11				8	4												
9		11 (h)	Blackpool	W 4-2	Walker, Whitehouse, Jones (og), Elkes	16,000	1		3	4	5	6	7		9	10	11				8		2											
10		18 (a)	Blackpool	L 0-3		8,000	1		3	4	5	6	7		9	10	11				8		2											
11		25 (h)	West Ham U	L 0-1		25,000	1		3	4	5	6	7		9	10	11				8			2										
12	Nov	1 (a)	West Ham U	W 2-1	Short, Millard	20,000	1		3	4	5	6			9	10	11	7						2	8									
13		8 (h)	Wolves	W 2-0	Short 2	30,000	1		3	4	5	6				10	11	7						2	8	9								
14		15 (a)	Wolves	W 2-0	Millard, Short	12,000	1		3	4	5	6			9		11							2	8	10	7							
15		22 (h)	Rotherham C	D 2-2	Morgan, Barton	15,000	1		3	4	5	6				10	11							2	8	7	9							
16		29 (a)	Rotherham C	W 3-0	Short, Millard 2	12,000	1	2	3	4	5	6	7		9		11				10				8									
17	Dec	6 (a)	Stoke	W 1-0	Short	15,000	1	2	3	4	5	6	7		9		11				10				8									
18		13 (h)	Stoke	W 2-1	Short 2	30,000	1	2	3	4	5	6	7				11				10				8	9								
19		20 (a)	Grimsby T	W 3-0	Millard 2, Morgan	4,000	1	2	3	4	5	6	7		9	10	11								8									
20		25 (a)	Leicester C	L 0-1		20,000	1		3	4	5	6	7		9	10	11								8				2					
21		26 (a)	Leicester C	L 0-1		20,000	1		3	4		6	7		5	10	11								8			9	2					
22		27 (h)	Grimsby T	W 4-0	Morgan, Elkes, Burkinshaw, Millard (pen)	25,000	1	2	3	4		6	7		5	10	11				9				8									
23	Jan	3 (a)	Bristol C	D 1-1	Millard	14,000	1	2	3	4		6	7		9	10	11				8									5				
24		17 (h)	Bristol C	W 1-0	Davies	29,500	1	2	3	4		6	7		9	10									8		11			5				
25		24 (h)	Stockport C	D 1-1	Elkes	30,000	1	2	3	4	5	6	7		9	10	11				8													
26	Feb	7 (h)	Barnsley	D 0-0		30,000	1	2	3	4	5	6	7		9	10	11	8																
27		14 (a)	Barnsley	W 5-0	Barton, Hampton 2, Gibson, Whitehouse	9,000	1	2	3	4	5	6	7			10	11	8													9			
28		28 (h)	Nottingham F	W 2-1	Hampton	8,000	1		3			6	7			10	11	8		4				2						5	9			
29	Mar	6 (a)	Lincoln C	D 2-2	Hampton, Lane (pen)	8,000	1		3	4		6	7		5		11	8						2							9	10		
30		10 (h)	Nottingham F	W 8-0	Hampton 4, Lane 2, Burkinshaw 2	15,000	1		3	6			7		5	10				4				2			11				8	9		
31		13 (h)	Lincoln C	W 7-0	Davies, Lane 3, Atkin (og), Hampton, Whitehouse	28,000	1		3	4		6	7		5	10								2			11				8	9		
32		15 (a)	Stockport C	L 1-2	Robson (og)	4,000	1		3	4		6	7		5	10								2			11				8	9		
33		20 (a)	Bury	L 0-1		18,000	1		3			6	7		5	10				4				2			11				8	9		
34		27 (h)	Bury	L 0-2		25,000	1		3	4	5	6				10		7						2			11				8	9		
35	Apr	3 (a)	Port Vale	W 3-1	Hampton, Lane, Elkes	15,000	1		3	4		6			5		2				10				7		11				8	9		
36		5 (a)	Fulham	W 2-1	Russell (og), Short	18,000	1		3			6			5		2			4	10				7		11				8	9		
37		6 (h)	Fulham	W 2-0	Jones 2	20,000	1		3			6	7		5		2			4	10						11					9	8	
38		10 (h)	Port Vale	W 3-0	Lane, Elkes 2	30,000	1		3	4		6	7		5		2				10						11					9	8	
39		17 (a)	Clapton O	L 1-2	Lane	12,000	1		3	4		6	7		5		2				10						11					9	8	
40		24 (h)	Clapton O	W 2-1	Short, Lane	20,000	1		3	4		6	7		5	10									8		11					9		2
41		26 (a)	Tottenham H	D 0-0		35,000	1		3	4		6	7		5	10									8		11					9		2
42	May	1 (h)	Tottenham H	L 0-1		39,000	1		3	4	5	6	7		8	10											11					9		2
				Appearances			42	20	39	38	24	41	32	11	29	36	28	10	3	6	16	1	2	11	16	3	16	3	2	3	10	14	3	3
				Goals								2	4	2	14	7	6	2	1		8				10		2				11	10	2	

FINAL LEAGUE POSITION: 3rd in Division Two. Average home League attendance: 22,880.

4 own-goals

FA Cup

#	Date		Venue/Opponent	Result	Scorers	Att	Tremelling DR	Ball W	Womack F	Roulson J	McClure A	Barton P	Burkinshaw L	Walker WB	Millard B	Whitehouse J	Morgan WA	Gibson R	Godfrey J	Evans T	Elkes J	Gardner A	Watson J	White VT	Short J	Roe A	Davies G	Pearl J	Wilson A	Hawley F	Hampton H	Lane J	Jones A	Mumford WR
1	Jan	10 (h)	Everton	W 2-0	Burkinshaw, Whitehouse	44,000	1	2	3	4		6	7		5	10	11					9		8										
2		31 (h)	Darlington	W 4-0	Millard, Whitehouse 3	47,000	1	2	3	4	5	6	7		9	10	11								8									
3	Feb	21 (a)	Liverpool	L 1-2	Barton	50,000	1	2	3	4	5	6	7			10	11					8									9			
				Appearances			3	3	3	3	2	3	3		2	3	3					2		1	1						1			
				Goals								1	1		1	4																		

1920-21

Secretary/Manager: Frank Richards

#	Date	Result	Scorers	Att	Tremelling DR	Womack F	Jones JW	Roulson J	McClure A	Barton P	Burkinshaw L	Crosbie J	Lane J	Hampton H	Whitehouse J	Ball W	Liddell G	Millard B	Morgan WA	Davies G	Booth R	White VT	Gibson R	Elkes G	Daws J	Bradford J	Linley E	Hauser S
1	Aug 28 (a) South Shields	L 0-3		15,000	1	3				6	7	8	9	10	2	4	5	11										
2	31 (h) Hull C	W 5-1	Crosbie 2, Barton, Lane 2	30,000	1	3	2	4	5	6	7	8	9	10				11										
3	Sep 4 (h) South Shields	D 1-1	Whitehouse	30,000	1	3	2	4	5	6	7	8	9	10				11										
4	6 (a) Hull C	L 0-1		14,000	1	3	2	4	5	6	7	8	9	10				11										
5	11 (a) Cardiff C	L 1-2	Crosbie	30,000	1	3	2	4	5	6	7	8	9	10						11								
6	18 (h) Cardiff C	D 1-1	Whitehouse	35,000	1	3	2		5	6	7	8	9	10						11	4							
7	25 (a) Leicester C	L 0-3		17,000	1	3		4	5	6		8	9	10	7					11		2						
8	Oct 2 (h) Leicester C	W 5-0	Lane 2, Hampton 3	18,000	1	3		4	5	6		8	9	10	11							2	7					
9	9 (a) Blackpool	L 0-3		10,000	1			4	5	3		8	9	10	11		6					2	7					
10	16 (h) Blackpool	W 3-0	Whitehouse 2 (1 pen), Lane	20,000	1		3	4	5	6		8	9	10	11							2	7					
11	23 (a) Sheffield W	W 2-1	Whitehouse 2	30,000	1	2	3	4	5	6	7	8	9	10	11													
12	30 (h) Sheffield W	W 4-0	Crosbie, Whitehouse, Hampton, Lane	30,000	1	2	3	4	5	6	7	8	9	10	11													
13	Nov 6 (a) Wolves	W 3-0	Burkinshaw, Crosbie, McClure	30,000	1	2	3	4	5	6	7	8	9		11					10								
14	13 (h) Wolves	W 4-1	Hampton 2, Barton, Lane	40,000	1	2	3	4	5	6	7	8	9	10	11													
15	20 (a) Stoke	W 2-1	Hampton 2	15,000	1	2	3		5	6		8	9	10	11									4				
16	27 (h) Stoke	W 3-0	Lane, Burkinshaw, Crosbie	30,000	1	2	3		5	6	7	8	9	10	11									4				
17	Dec 4 (h) Coventry C	W 3-2	Whitehouse 2, Lawrence (og)	30,000	1	2	3	4	5	6	7	8	9	10	11													
18	11 (a) Coventry C	W 4-0	Burkinshaw, Lane, Hampton 2	22,000	1	2	3	4	5	6	7	8	9	10	11													
19	18 (h) Leeds U	W 1-0	McClure	20,000	1	2	3	4	5	6		8		9	11							7	10					
20	25 (a) West Ham U	D 1-1	Bradford	37,000	1	2	3	4	5	6	7	8		10	11											9		
21	27 (h) West Ham U	W 2-1	Hampton 2	60,000	1	2	3	4	5	6	7	8		10	11											9		
22	Jan 1 (a) Leeds U	L 0-1		24,000	1	2	3	4	5	6	7	8		10	11											9		
23	15 (a) Stockport C	W 3-0	Crosbie, Lane, Whitehouse	10,000	1	2	3	4		6	7	8	9		10										5		11	
24	22 (h) Stockport C	W 5-0	Lane 2, Crosbie, Whitehouse, Linley	30,000	1	2	3		5	6	7	8	9		10										4		11	
25	Feb 5 (h) Notts C	W 2-1	Burkinshaw 2	35,000	1	2	3		5	6	7	8	9		10										4		11	
26	12 (a) Clapton O	D 1-1	Burkinshaw	15,000	1	2	3		5	6	7	8	9		10										4		11	
27	16 (a) Notts C	D 0-0		14,000		2	3		5	6	7	8	9		10										4		11	1
28	19 (h) Clapton O	D 0-0		20,000		2	3		5	6	7	8	9	10											4		11	1
29	26 (a) Bury	W 1-0	Hampton	25,000		2	3		5	6		8	9	10									7		4		11	1
30	Mar 5 (h) Bury	W 4-0	Crosbie 2, Linley, Barton	35,000		2	3		5	6	7	8	9	10											4		11	1
31	12 (a) Bristol C	W 1-0	Lane	26,000			3		5	6	7	8	9	10					2						4		11	1
32	19 (h) Bristol C	D 0-0		35,000			3	4	5	6	7	8	9	10					2								11	1
33	25 (a) Fulham	L 0-5		40,000			3	4	5	6	7	8	9	10					2								11	1
34	26 (h) Barnsley	L 1-3	Hampton	40,000		2	3		5	6	7	8		10						9	4						11	1
35	29 (h) Fulham	W 1-0	Booth	25,000		2	3		5	6	7	8		9	10					11	4							1
36	Apr 2 (a) Barnsley	D 1-1	Davies (pen)	20,000		2	3		5	6		8	9	10						11	4		7					1
37	9 (h) Nottingham F	W 3-0	Crosbie, Lane 2	30,000		2	3		5		7	8	9	10			6			11	4							1
38	16 (h) Nottingham F	D 1-1	Crosbie	8,000	1	2	3		5	6	7	8	9	10						11	4							
39	23 (h) Rotherham C	W 3-2	Crosbie 2, Davies	35,127	1	2	3	4	5	6	7	8	9	10						11								
40	30 (a) Rotherham C	D 1-1	Barton	12,000	1	2	3		5	6	7	8	9	10		4				11								
41	May 2 (h) Port Vale	W 4-0	Hampton, Davies 2 (1 pen), Barton	28,000	1	2	3		5	6	7	8	9	10		4				11								
42	7 (a) Port Vale	W 2-0	Hampton, Davies	10,000		2	3		5	6	7	8		10		4				11						9		1
	FINAL LEAGUE POSITION: 1st in Division Two. Average home League attendance: 31,244.			**Appearances**	30	38	37	22	40	41	35	42	34	29	33	4	2	2	5	10	6	4	7	2	11	4	12	12
				Goals					2	5	6	14	15	16	11					5	1					1	2	

1 own-goal

FA Cup

#	Date	Result	Scorers	Att	Tremelling DR	Womack F	Jones JW	Roulson J	McClure A	Barton P	Burkinshaw L	Crosbie J	Lane J	Hampton H	Whitehouse J	Ball W	Liddell G	Millard B	Morgan WA	Davies G	Booth R	White VT	Gibson R	Elkes G	Daws J	Bradford J	Linley E	Hauser S
1	Jan 8 (a) Luton T	L 1-2	Barton	12,700	1	2	3	4	5	6	7	8		10	11											9		
				Appearances	1	1	1	1	1	1	1	1		1	1											1		
				Goals						1																		

1921-22

Secretary/Manager: Frank Richards

Match results

#	Date		Opponent	Result	Scorers	Attendance
1	Aug	27 (h)	Burnley	L 2-3	Elkes 2	40,000
2		29 (a)	Chelsea	W 2-1	Elkes, Hampton	30,000
3	Sep	3 (a)	Burnley	L 1-3	Elkes	30,000
4		5 (h)	Chelsea	W 5-1	Whitehouse 2, Elkes 2, Crosbie	35,000
5		10 (a)	Everton	L 1-2	Crosbie	30,000
6		17 (h)	Everton	D 1-1	Whitehouse	30,000
7		24 (a)	Sunderland	L 1-2	Whitehouse	30,000
8	Oct	1 (h)	Sunderland	W 1-0	Whitehouse	30,000
9		8 (h)	Huddersfield T	L 0-2		40,000
10		15 (a)	Huddersfield T	L 0-1		15,000
11		22 (h)	Bolton W	D 1-1	Crosbie	20,000
12		29 (a)	Bolton W	W 2-1	Bradford 2	19,140
13	Nov	5 (h)	Arsenal	L 0-1		28,620
14		12 (a)	Arsenal	L 2-5	Whitehouse, Bradford	30,000
15		19 (a)	Blackburn R	D 1-1	Bradford	15,000
16		26 (h)	Blackburn R	W 1-0	Burkinshaw	20,000
17	Dec	3 (a)	Oldham A	W 1-0	Cameron	12,973
18		10 (h)	Oldham A	W 3-0	Whitehouse, Liddle, Crosbie	18,000
19		17 (h)	Sheffield U	W 2-1	Elkes, Whitehouse	25,000
20		24 (a)	Sheffield U	W 2-1	Whitehouse, Lane	15,000
21		26 (a)	West Brom A	L 0-1		49,488
22		27 (h)	West Brom A	L 0-2		44,500
23		31 (h)	Cardiff C	L 0-1		35,000
24	Jan	14 (a)	Cardiff C	L 1-3	Crosbie	35,000
25		21 (h)	Newcastle U	L 0-4		20,000
26	Feb	4 (h)	Liverpool	L 0-2		15,000
27		8 (a)	Newcastle U	W 1-0	Harvey	25,000
28		11 (a)	Liverpool	L 0-1		30,000
29		18 (h)	Manchester U	L 0-1		20,000
30		25 (a)	Manchester U	D 1-1	Bradford	35,000
31	Mar	11 (a)	Aston Villa	D 1-1	Liddell	52,000
32		15 (a)	Aston Villa	W 1-0	Crosbie	34,190
33		18 (a)	Middlesbrough	D 1-1	Crosbie	15,000
34		25 (h)	Middlesbrough	W 4-3	Bradford 2, Crosbie, Hampton	20,000
35	Apr	1 (h)	Tottenham H	L 0-3		34,000
36		8 (a)	Tottenham H	L 1-2	Hampton	19,638
37		14 (a)	Manchester C	L 0-1		35,000
38		15 (a)	Bradford C	W 2-1	Bradford 2	25,000
39		18 (h)	Manchester C	W 3-1	McClure, Bradford, Hampton	39,000
40		22 (h)	Bradford C	W 1-0	Foxall	20,000
41	May	1 (a)	Preston NE	D 2-2	Crosbie 2	20,000
42		6 (h)	Preston NE	L 0-2		19,000

Player appearances — part 1

#	Tremelling DR	Womack F	Hunter W	Getgood G	McClure A	Barton P	Harvey WH	Crosbie J	Bradford J	Elkes JE	Linley E	Dixon D	Hauser S	Jones JW	Hampton H
1		2		4	5	6	7			10	11		1	3	8
2				4	5	6	7			10	11	2	1	3	8
3	1	2	3	4	5	6	7	8		10	11				
4	1	2	3	4	5	6	7	8		10	11				
5	1	2	3	4	5	6		8		10	11				
6	1	2			5	6		8		10	11			3	
7	1	2			5	6		8		10	11			3	
8	1	2		5		6	7	8		10	11			3	
9	1	2		4	5	6	7	8		10	11			3	
10	1	2			5	6		8		10	11			3	4
11	1	2			5			8		10	11			3	4
12	1	2		4	5	6	7	8	9	10	11			3	
13	1			4	5	6		8	9	10	11	2		3	
14	1	2		4	5	6	7		9					3	8
15	1	2			5		7		9					3	8
16	1	2			5									3	8
17	1	2			5									3	8
18	1	2			5		7	8	9					3	
19	1	2			5		7	8		10				3	
20	1	2	3		5	6	7	8							
21	1	2	3					8		10					
22	1	2	3		5			8							
23	1	2	3		5		7	8							
24	1	2	3		5		7	8			11				
25	1	2	3		5	6	7	8			11				
26	1	2				6	7		9					3	
27	1	2				6	7	8	9					3	
28	1	2				6	7	8	9					3	
29	1	2				6	7	8	9		11			3	
30	1	2			5	6	7	10	9		11			3	
31	1				5	6		8	9					3	
32	1				5	6		8	9					3	10
33	1				5	6		8	9					3	
34	1				5	6		8	9					3	4
35	1				5	6		8	9					3	
36	1				5				9					3	8
37	1	5							8					3	9
38	1				5	6		8	9					3	10
39	1				5	6		8	9					3	10
40	1				5	6		8						3	9
41	1				5	6		8						3	9
42		2			5	6		8					1	3	10
Appearances	39	30	9	10	35	29	21	34	17	16	17	2	3	33	18
Goals					1			10	10	7					4

Player appearances — part 2

#	Lane J	Cameron E	Whitehouse J	Burkinshaw L	Booth R	Neil WH	Liddell G	Daws J	Roulson J	Thompson L	Deacon H	Davies G	Barratt J	Foxall F	Ashurst E	White VH
1	9															
2			9													
3			9													
4				9												
5				9	7											
6				9		4	7									
7				9		4		6								
8				9				4								
9				9												
10				9			7									
11				9			7	6								
12																
13					7											
14	10		11													
15	10		11				6	4								
16	10	9	11	7			6	4								
17	10	9	11	7			6	4								
18	10		11				6	4								
19		9	11				6	4								
20	9	10	11					4								
21	9		11			7	6	5	4							
22	9		11			7	6	4		10						
23	10	9	11				6	4								
24	9						6	4		10						
25	9	10						4								
26	10						5	4				8	11			
27	10						5		4				11			
28	10						5		4				11			
29							5		4		10					
30							4	8								
31	10						4	2					7	11		
32							4	2					7	11		
33	10						4						7	11	2	
34	10						4						7	11	2	
35	10						4						7	11	2	
36	10						4						7	11	2	6
37			10				4						7	11	2	6
38			11				4						7		2	
39							4						7	11	2	
40	10						4						7	11	2	
41	10						4						7	11	2	
42	9						4							7	11	
Appearances	19	6	25	4	2	5	20	12	15	2	2	3	12	11	9	2
Goals	1	1	9	1			2							1		

FINAL LEAGUE POSITION: 18th in Division One. Average home League attendance: 27,967.

FA Cup

Failed to enter in 1921-22.

1922-23

Secretary/Manager: Frank Richards

#		Date	Venue/Opponent	Result	Scorers	Att	Tremelling DR	Womack F	Jones JW	Liddell G	McClure A	Barton P	Barratt J	Crosbie J	Bradford J	Whitehouse J	Foxall F	Daws J	Dale RA	Sharp J	Linley E	Waddell G	Watkins ET	Bosbury CE	Ashurst E	Thompson L	Rawson AN	Samson AA	Clarke W	Harvey WH	Lane MA	Hunter W
1	Aug	26 (a) Chelsea	D 1-1	Bradford	40,000	1	2	3	4	5	6	7	8	9	10	11															
2		28 (h) Newcastle U	L 0-2		35,000	1	2	3	4	5	6	7	8	9	10	11															
3	Sep	2 (h) Chelsea	L 0-1		35,000	1	2	3	6	5		7	8	9	10	11	4														
4		6 (a) Newcastle U	D 0-0		20,000	1	2	3		5		7	8	9			4	6	10	11											
5		9 (a) Manchester C	W 1-0	Bradford	22,000	1	2	3	4	5		7	8	9				6	10	11											
6		13 (h) Stoke	W 2-0	Bradford 2	20,000	1	2	3	4	5		7	8	9				6	10	11											
7		16 (h) Manchester C	L 0-1		30,000	1	2	3	4	5	6	7	8	9					10	11											
8		23 (a) Bolton W	L 0-3		15,000	1	2	3	4	5	6	7	8	9					10	11											
9		30 (h) Bolton W	W 2-0	Bradford 2	25,000	1	2	3	4	5	6	7	8	9	10	11															
10	Oct	7 (a) Blackburn R	D 1-1	Bradford	25,000	1	2	3	4	5	6	7	8	9	10	11															
11		14 (h) Blackburn R	D 1-1	Whitehouse	28,000	1	2	3	6	5		7	8	9	10	11					4										
12		21 (a) Middlesbrough	L 1-2	Whitehouse	15,000	1	2	3	6	5		7	8	9	10	11					4										
13		28 (h) Middlesbrough	W 2-0	Bradford, Foxall	28,000	1	2	3	6	5		7	8	9	10	11		4													
14	Nov	4 (h) Cardiff C	D 0-0		25,000	1	2	3	6	5		7	8	9	10			4		11											
15		11 (a) Cardiff C	D 1-1	Watkins	20,000	1	2	3		5	6		8	9	10			4		11		7									
16		18 (h) Nottingham F	W 2-0	Bradford, Linley	16,000	1	2	3		5	6		8	9	10			4		11		7									
17		25 (a) Nottingham F	D 1-1	Bradford	12,000	1	2	3		5	6		8	9	10			4		11		7									
18	Dec	2 (h) Arsenal	W 3-2	Foxall, Linley 2 (1 pen)	29,772	1	2	3		5	6		8	9		11		4		10		7									
19		9 (a) Arsenal	L 0-1		30,000	1	2	3		5	6		8	9		11		4		10		7									
20		16 (h) Everton	D 1-1	Foxall	25,000	1	2	3		5	6		8	9		11		4		10		7									
21		23 (a) Everton	L 1-2	Bradford	12,000	1	2	3		5	6		8	9		11		4		10		7									
22		25 (h) Huddersfield T	D 0-0		20,000	1	2	3			6		8	9	10	11	5	4				7									
23		26 (a) Huddersfield T	L 0-4		15,000	1	2	3			6		8	9	10	11	5					7									4
24		30 (a) Sunderland	L 3-5	Bradford, Whitehouse 2	10,000	1	2	3			6	7	8	9	10	11	5	4													
25	Jan	6 (h) Sunderland	L 1-2	Barratt	25,000	1		3		5	6	7	8	9		11		4		10			2								
26		20 (a) West Brom A	L 0-2		32,180	1		3	6	5			8	9		11		4		10			2	7							
27		27 (a) West Brom A	L 0-1		25,123	1		3	6	5			8	9		11		4		10			2	7							
28	Feb	3 (a) Oldham A	L 0-2		20,000	1		3		5	6		8	9				4		10			2	7	11						
29		10 (h) Oldham A	L 2-3	Bradford 2	8,542	1	2	3	6	5			8	9	10		4			11		7									
30		17 (a) Sheffield U	L 1-7	Rawson	10,000	1	2	3		5	6		8	10				4		11				7		9					
31	Mar	3 (a) Preston NE	W 3-2	Rawson, Bradford, Crosbie	14,000			3		5	6		8	10		11		4					2	7		9	1				
32		10 (h) Preston NE	W 1-0	Rawson	20,000			3		5	6		8	10		11		4					2	7		9	1				
33		12 (h) Sheffield U	W 4-2	Rawson 2, Daws, Bradford	15,000	1		3		5	6		8	10			4						2			9		11	7		
34		17 (h) Aston Villa	W 1-0	Rawson	50,000	1		3		5	6		8	10			4						2			9		11	7		
35		24 (a) Aston Villa	L 0-3		40,000	1		3		5	6	7	8	10			4						2			9		11			
36		31 (h) Liverpool	L 0-1		30,000	1		3		5	6		8	10				4					2			9		11	7		
37	Apr	2 (a) Stoke	D 0-0		20,000	1		3	5		6		8	10				4					2			9		11	7		
38		7 (a) Liverpool	D 0-0		30,000	1		3		5	6		8	10				4					2			9		11	7		
39		14 (h) Tottenham H	W 2-1	Rawson, McClure	15,000	1		3	6	5			8	10				4		11			2			9			7		
40		21 (a) Tottenham H	L 0-2		16,355	1		3	4	5	6		8	10						11			2			9			7		
41		28 (h) Burnley	W 1-0	Bradford	19,400	1		3		5	6		8	9				4					2					11	7	10	
42	May	5 (h) Burnley	W 2-0	Bradford, Rawson	8,000	1		3		5	6			9				4					2			8		11	7	10	
		Appearances				40	27	41	19	38	31	18	32	39	16	17	15	22	5	26	2	8	15	16	1	13	2	7	9	2	1
		Goals								1		1	1	18	4	3	1			3		1				8					

FINAL LEAGUE POSITION: 17th in Division One. Average home League attendance: 25,328

FA Cup

#		Date	Venue/Opponent	Result	Scorers	Att	Tremelling DR	Womack F	Jones JW	Liddell G	McClure A	Barton P	Barratt J	Crosbie J	Bradford J	Whitehouse J	Foxall F	Daws J	Dale RA	Sharp J	Linley E	Waddell G	Watkins ET	Bosbury CE	Ashurst E	Thompson L	Rawson AN	Samson AA	Clarke W	Harvey WH	Lane MA	Hunter W
1	Jan	13 (a) Huddersfield T	L 1-2	Bradford	27,200	1		3		5	6	11	8	9		7		4		10			2								
		Appearances				1		1		1	1	1	1	1		1		1		1			1								
		Goals												1																	

1923-24

Manager: Billy Beer

No	Date	Venue/Opponent	Result	Scorers	Att	Tremelling DR	Ashurst E	Jones JW	Dale RA	Cringan J	Barton P	Harvey WH	Crosbie J	Bradford J	Islip E	Clarke W	McClure A	Lane M	Womack F	Daws J	Rawson AN	Pheonix F	Linley F	Liddell G	Briggs G	Hoyland W	Hunter W	Russell JC	Dixon D	Harris WJ
1	Aug 25 (h) Aston Villa	W 3-0	Bradford 2, Lane	41,300	1	2	3	4		6	7	8	9		11	5	10												
2	29 (a) Liverpool	L 2-6	Bradford 2	16,000	1	2	3	4		6	7	8	9		11	5	10												
3	Sep 1 (a) Aston Villa	D 0-0		59,147	1		3	4		6	7	8	9		11	5	10	2											
4	5 (h) Liverpool	W 2-1	Bradford, Lane	25,000	1		3	4		6	7	8	9		11	5	10	2											
5	8 (h) Sunderland	L 0-2		25,000	1		3	4		6	7	8	9		11	5	10	2											
6	10 (h) Bolton W	L 0-3		15,000	1		3	4		6	7	8	9		11	5	10	2											
7	15 (a) Sunderland	D 1-1	Rawson	25,000	1		3	5	10	6	7		9		11			2	4	8									
8	22 (h) Arsenal	L 0-2		20,000	1		3	4	10	6	7		9		11	5		2		8									
9	29 (a) Arsenal	D 0-0		35,000	1		3	5		6	7	8			11			2	4	9	10								
10	Oct 6 (h) Blackburn R	D 1-1	Bradford	19,000	1		3	5		6	7		9		11			2	4	8	10								
11	13 (a) Blackburn R	L 1-4	Bradford	20,000	1	2	3			6	7		9		11	5			4	8	10								
12	20 (h) Huddersfield T	L 0-1		18,000	1	2	3			6	7	8			11	5	10			9		4							
13	27 (a) Huddersfield T	L 0-1		10,000	1	2			5	6	7	8	9		11		10	3				4							
14	Nov 3 (a) West Ham U	L 1-4	Bradford	22,000	1	2		4		6	7	8	9		11		10	3				5							
15	10 (h) West Ham U	W 2-0	Bradford, Islip	20,000	1	2			5	6	7	8	9	10	11			3	4										
16	17 (h) Notts C	D 0-0		12,000	1	2			5	6	7	8	9	10	11			3	4										
17	24 (a) Notts C	D 1-1	Bradford	8,000	1	2			5	6	7	8	9	10	11			3	4										
18	Dec 1 (a) Everton	L 0-2		15,000	1	2			5	6	7	8	9	10	11			3	4										
19	8 (h) Everton	L 0-1		10,000	1	2		4	5	6	7		9	10	11			3				8							
20	15 (a) West Brom A	D 0-0		24,786	1	2		4	5	6	7	8	9	10	11			3											
21	22 (h) West Brom A	D 0-0		32,000	1	2		4	5	6	7	8	9	10	11			3											
22	26 (h) Manchester C	W 3-0	Lane, Bradford, Harvey	30,000	1	2		4	5	6	7		9		11		10	3	8										
23	29 (a) Tottenham H	D 1-1	Bradford (pen)	25,000	1	2	3	4	5	6	7		9		11		10		8										
24	Jan 1 (a) Bolton W	D 1-1	Cringan	30,000	1	2		4	5	6	7		9		11		10	3	8										
25	5 (a) Tottenham H	W 3-2	Bradford, Cringan, Lane	19,500	1	2		4	5	6	7		9		11		10	3	8										
26	19 (h) Nottingham F	L 0-2		15,000	1	2		4	5	6	7	8	9	10	11			3											
27	26 (a) Nottingham F	D 1-1	Islip	10,000	1	2	3	4	5	6	7	8	9	10	11														
28	Feb 9 (a) Burnley	W 2-1	Cringan, Bradford	8,000	1	2		4	5	6		8	9	10	11			3					7						
29	16 (h) Middlesbrough	W 2-1	Bradford 2	11,000	1	2		4	5	6		8	9	10	11			3					7						
30	23 (a) Middlesbrough	W 1-0	Islip	10,000	1	2		4	5	6		8	9	10	11			3					7						
31	27 (h) Burnley	W 2-1	Bradford 2	14,500	1	2		4	5	6		8	9	10	11			3					7						
32	Mar 1 (h) Preston NE	W 2-0	Bradford 2	12,000	1		3	4	5	6	7	8	9	10	11			2											
33	8 (a) Preston NE	L 0-1		15,000	1		3	4	5	6	7	8	9	10	11			2											
34	15 (a) Chelsea	D 1-1	Ashurst	25,000	1	9	3	4	5	6	7	8		10	11			2											
35	22 (h) Chelsea	W 1-0	Briggs	20,000	1	2	3	4	5	6	7	8		10	11									9					
36	Apr 5 (h) Newcastle U	W 4-1	Linley, Bradford 2, Crosbie	20,000	1	2	3	4	5	6	7	8	9	10								11							
37	9 (a) Newcastle U	L 1-2	Bradford	8,000	1	2					7	8	9	10				3				11	4	5	6				
38	12 (a) Sheffield U	W 2-0	Bradford, Linley	8,000	1	2	3	4	5	6	7	8	9	10								11							
39	18 (a) Manchester C	L 0-1		30,000	1	2	3	4	5		7	8	9	10								11		6					
40	19 (h) Sheffield U	L 0-1		16,000	1	2		4	5		7	8	9	10				3				11		6					
41	26 (a) Cardiff C	L 0-2		15,000	1	2			5	6		8	9	10				3				11	4				7		
42	May 3 (h) Cardiff C	D 0-0		33,000	1	2	3	4	5	6		8	9	10	11												7		
		Appearances				42	31	22	34	31	39	35	31	37	27	25	9	13	31	8	6	3	18	6	3	6	1	2	1	1
		Goals					1			3		1	1	24	3			4			1		2		1					

FINAL LEAGUE POSITION: 14th in Division One. Average home League attendance: 20,395.

FA Cup

No	Date	Venue/Opponent	Result	Att	Tremelling DR	Ashurst E	Jones JW	Dale RA	Cringan J	Barton P	Harvey WH	Crosbie J	Bradford J	Islip E	Clarke W	McClure A	Lane M	Womack F	Daws J	Rawson AN	Pheonix F	Linley F	Liddell G	Briggs G	Hoyland W	Hunter W	Russell JC	Dixon D	Harris WJ
1	Jan 12 (a) Huddersfield T	L 0-1		31,000	1	2		4	5	6	7		9	10				3	8			11							
		Appearances			1	1		1	1	1	1		1	1				1	1			1							
		Goals																											

1924-25

Manager: Billy Beer

No	Date	Opponent	Result	Scorers	Att	Tremelling DR	Womack F	Jones JW	Liddell G	Cringan J	Barton P	Harvey W	Crosbie J	Bradford J	Islip E	Linley E	Ashurst E	Dale R	Morgan J	Devlin T	Russell J	Scriven A	Harris WJ	Harvey E	Briggs G	Dixon D	Hunter W	Sykes A	Bruce H
1	Aug 30 (h)	Everton	D 2-2	Linley, Crosbie	30,000	1		3		5	6	7	8	9	10	11	2	4											
2	Sep 3 (h)	Tottenham H	L 0-2		20,000	1		3		5	6	7	8	9	10	11	2	4											
3	6 (a)	Sunderland	L 0-4		30,000	1	2	3			6	7	8	9	10	11		4	5										
4	8 (h)	Bolton W	W 1-0	Howarth (og)	15,000	1	2	3	4	5	6	7		9								8	10	11					
5	13 (h)	Cardiff C	W 2-1	Bradford 2	18,500	1	2	3	4	5	6	7	8	9									10	11					
6	15 (h)	Notts C	W 1-0	Bradford	20,000	1		3	4	5	6	7	8	9				2					10	11					
7	20 (a)	Preston NE	L 0-1		15,000	1	2	3	4	5	6		8		10			9					11	7					
8	27 (h)	Burnley	W 1-0	Cringan	20,000	1	2	3	4	5	6	7	8	9	10									11					
9	Oct 4 (a)	Leeds U	W 1-0	Islip	24,000	1	2	3	4	5	6	7	8	9	10									11					
10	11 (h)	Aston Villa	W 1-0	Islip	48,000	1	2	3	4	5	6	7	8	9	10									11					
11	18 (a)	West Brom A	D 1-1	Islip	35,617	1	2	3	4	5	6	7	8	9	10									11					
12	25 (h)	Huddersfield T	W 1-0	Bradford	15,000	1	2	3	4	5	6	7	8	9	10									11					
13	Nov 1 (h)	Blackburn R	D 1-1	Bradford	15,000	1	2	3	4	5	6	7	8	9	10									11					
14	8 (a)	West Ham U	W 1-0	Bradford (pen)	28,000	1	2	3	4	5	6		8	9	10								11	7					
15	15 (h)	Sheffield U	D 1-1	Crosbie	20,000	1	2	3	4	5	6		8	9	10								11	7					
16	22 (a)	Newcastle U	L 0-4		18,000	1	2	3	4	5	6		8	9	10	11						7							
17	29 (h)	Liverpool	W 5-2	Bradford 3 (1 pen), Barton, Islip	25,000	1	2	3	4	5	6		8	9	10	11						7							
18	Dec 6 (a)	Nottingham F	D 1-1	Bradford (pen)	10,000	1	2	3	4	5	6		8	9	10	11						7							
19	13 (h)	Bury	L 0-1		20,000	1		3	6	5			8	9		11	2	4			10	7							
20	20 (a)	Manchester C	D 2-2	Bradford, Islip	40,000	1	2	3	4	5	6		8	9	10	11						7							
21	25 (h)	Arsenal	W 2-1	Crosbie, Islip	36,000	1	2	3	4	5	6		8	9	10	11						7							
22	26 (a)	Arsenal	W 1-0	Islip	40,000	1	2	3	4	5	6		8		10	11						7			9				
23	27 (a)	Everton	L 1-2	Islip	30,000	1	2	3	4	5	6		8		10	11						7			9				
24	Jan 1 (a)	Bolton W	L 0-3		20,000	1	2	3	4		6		8	9	10	11					5	7							
25	3 (h)	Sunderland	W 2-1	Crosbie, Barton	25,000	1	2	3	4		6		8	9	10	11					5	7							
26	17 (a)	Cardiff C	L 0-1		10,000	1	2	3	4	5			8		10	11		6			10	7		9					
27	24 (h)	Preston NE	W 3-0	Linley, Briggs 2	15,000	1	2	3	4	5			8		10	11		6				7			9				
28	Feb 2 (a)	Burnley	L 2-3	Briggs, Devlin	25,000	1	2	3		5			8			11		6		10		7			9				4
29	7 (h)	Leeds U	D 0-0		20,000	1	2	3	4	5		7	8		10	11		6							9				
30	14 (a)	Aston Villa	L 0-1		60,000	1	2	3	4	5			8		10	11		6					7		9				
31	28 (h)	Huddersfield T	L 0-1		12,000	1		3	4	5			8		10	11	2	6					7		9				
32	Mar 14 (h)	West Ham U	D 1-1	Crosbie	20,000	1	3		4	5			8		10	11		6					7		9	2			
33	16 (h)	West Brom A	D 0-0		30,000	1	2	3	4	5			8		10	11		6					7	9					
34	21 (a)	Sheffield U	L 3-4	Islip, Briggs, Liddell	15,000	1	2	3	4	5			8		10	11		6					7	9					
35	28 (h)	Newcastle U	D 1-1	Cringan	36,000	1	2	3	4	5			8		10	11		6					7	9					
36	Apr 2 (a)	Blackburn R	L 1-7	Islip	3,000	1	2	3		5	6		8		10	11		4					7	9					
37	4 (a)	Liverpool	D 1-1	Briggs	28,000	1	2	3	4				8		10			6				11	7	9			5		
38	10 (a)	Tottenham H	W 1-0	Crosbie	30,411	1	2	3	4				8		10			6				11	7	9			5		
39	11 (h)	Nottingham F	D 1-1	Briggs	15,000	1	2	3	4				8		10			6				11	7	9			5		
40	18 (a)	Bury	W 4-1	Briggs 2, Scriven, Crosbie	12,000	1	2	3	4				8		10			6				11	7	9			5		
41	25 (h)	Manchester C	W 2-1	Scriven, Crosbie	13,000	1	2	3	4				8		10			6				11	7	9			5		
42	May 2 (a)	Notts C	W 1-0	Islip	8,000	1	2	3	4				8		10							11	7	9			5	6	
		Appearances				42	37	41	37	33	25	13	40	24	34	24	7	22	1	2	5	19	16	12	19	1	6	1	1
		Goals							1	2	2		8	11	11	2				1		2			8				

FINAL LEAGUE POSITION: 8th in Division One. Average home League attendance: 22,547.

1 own-goal

FA Cup

No	Date	Opponent	Result	Scorers	Att	Tremelling DR	Womack F	Jones JW	Liddell G	Cringan J	Barton P	Harvey W	Crosbie J	Bradford J	Islip E	Linley E	Ashurst E	Dale R	Morgan J	Devlin T	Russell J	Scriven A	Harris WJ	Harvey E	Briggs G	Dixon D	Hunter W	Sykes A	Bruce H
1	Jan 10 (h)	Chelsea	W 2-0	Briggs 2	32,000	1	2	3	4	5	6		8		10	11							7	9					
2	31 (h)	Stockport C	W 1-0	Harris	36,000	1	2	3	4	5	6		8		10						11		7	9					
3	Feb 21 (a)	Liverpool	L 1-2	Briggs	44,064	1	2	3	4	5			8	10	11			6					7	9					
		Appearances				3	3	3	3	3	2		2	1	2	3		1			1		3	3					
		Goals																					1	3					

1925-26

Manager: Billy Beer

No	Date	Opponent	Result	Scorers	Att	Tremelling DR	Womack F	Jones JW	Liddell G	Cringan J	Barton P	Harris WJ	Crosbie J	Bradford J	Briggs G	Islip E	Linley E	Hunter W	Dale R	Scriven A	Bowden F	Russell JC	Ashurst E	Bruce H	Castle FC	Hibbs H
1	Aug 29 (a)	Sunderland	L 1-3	Bradford	25,000	1	2	3	4	5	6		8	9	7	10	11									
2	31 (h)	Manchester C	W 1-0	Bradford	20,000	1	2	3	4	5	6		8	9	7	10	11									
3	Sep 5 (h)	Blackburn R	W 2-0	Islip, Bradford	16,000	1	2	3	4				8	9	7	10		5	6	11						
4	9 (a)	Everton	D 2-2	Harris, Islip	25,000	1	2	3			6	7	8	9		10		5	4	11						
5	12 (a)	Bury	L 1-2	Bradford	16,000	1	2	3	4			7	8	9		10		5	6	11						
6	16 (h)	Huddersfield T	L 1-3	Scriven	25,000	1	2	3	4	5	6	7	8		9	10				11						
7	19 (h)	Notts C	L 0-1		5,000	1	2	3	4	5	6	7	8	10	9					11						
8	21 (h)	Everton	W 3-1	Bradford 2, Briggs	15,000	1	2	3	4	5	6	7	8	9	10					11						
9	26 (h)	West Brom A	W 3-0	Islip 2, Briggs	34,850	1	2	3	4	5	6	7	8	9	10	11										
10	Oct 3 (a)	Sheffield U	L 1-4	Bradford	12,000	1	2	3	4	5	6	7	8	9	10	11										
11	10 (h)	Cardiff C	W 3-2	Crosbie, Bradford, Briggs	30,000	1	2	3	4	5	6	7	8	9	10	11										
12	17 (a)	Aston Villa	D 3-3	Bradford 2, Spiers (og)	55,000	1	2	3	4	5	6	7	8	9	10	11										
13	24 (a)	Leicester C	D 1-1	Islip	30,000	1	2	3	4	5	6	7	8	9	10	11										
14	31 (a)	Newcastle U	W 3-1	Islip 2, Crosbie	30,000	1	2	3	4	5		7	8	9	11	10			6							
15	Nov 7 (h)	Bolton W	L 0-1		25,000	1	2	3	4	5		7	8	9	11	10			6							
16	14 (a)	Manchester U	L 1-3	Crosbie	23,559	1	2	3	4	5		7	8	9	11	10			6							
17	21 (h)	Liverpool	W 2-0	Briggs, Crosbie	12,000	1	2	3	4	5		7	8	9	10				6	11						
18	Dec 5 (h)	Leeds U	W 2-1	Scriven, Crosbie	13,435	1	2	3	4	5		7	8	9					6	11						
19	7 (a)	Burnley	L 1-3	Briggs	15,000	1	2	3		5	6	7	8	9					4	11						
20	12 (a)	West Ham U	D 2-2	Cringan (pen), Bradford	18,000	1	2	3	4	5		7	8	9	10				6	11						
21	19 (h)	Arsenal	W 1-0	Briggs	26,843	1	2	3	4	5		7	8	9	10				6	11						
22	25 (h)	Tottenham H	W 3-1	Bradford 3	29,568	1	2	3	4	5		7	8	9	10				6	11						
23	26 (a)	Tottenham H	L 1-2	Bradford	44,429	1	2	3	4	5		7	8	9				10	6	11						
24	28 (a)	Huddersfield T	L 1-4	Bradford	25,000	1	2	3	4		6	7	8	9	10				5		11					
25	Jan 1 (a)	Bolton W	L 3-5	Bradford 2, Harris	25,000	1			4	3		7		9	8	10	5	6		11		2				
26	2 (h)	Sunderland	W 2-1	Briggs, Russell	20,000	1		3	4		6	7	8	9	10		5			11		2				
27	16 (a)	Blackburn R	D 4-4	Bradford 3, Harris	20,000	1	2	3	4		6	7	8	9	10					11						
28	23 (h)	Bury	L 2-3	Briggs, Crosbie	15,000	1	2	3	4	5	6	7	8	9	10					11						
29	Feb 6 (a)	West Brom A	L 1-5	Harris	23,104	1		3	4	5		7	8	9	10			6		11		2				
30	13 (h)	Sheffield U	W 2-0	Linley, Briggs	18,000	1	2	3	4			7	8	9	10		5		6	11						
31	20 (a)	Cardiff C	L 0-2		20,000	1	2	3	4		6	7	8	9	10			5		11						
32	27 (h)	Aston Villa	W 2-1	Briggs 2	45,000	1	2	3	4			7	8	9	10			5	6	11						
33	Mar 3 (a)	Notts C	L 0-3		15,000	1	2	3			6	7	8	9	10			5	4	11						
34	6 (a)	Leicester C	L 0-1		20,000	1	2	3	4			7	8	9	10			5	6	11						
35	13 (h)	Newcastle U	D 1-1	Crosbie	30,000	1	2	3	4	9		7	8		10			5	6	11						
36	Apr 2 (a)	Manchester C	W 4-2	Briggs 2, Linley, Crosbie	60,000	1	2	3	4			7	8	10	9		11	5	6							
37	3 (a)	Liverpool	D 2-2	Bradford 2 (1 pen)	35,000	1	2	3	4	8		7		10	9		11	5	6							
38	10 (h)	Burnley	L 1-7	Bradford	20,000	1	2	3	4			7	8	10	9		11	5	6							
39	17 (a)	Leeds U	D 0-0		12,186	1	2	3	4	5		7	8	9					6	11		10				
40	19 (h)	Manchester U	W 2-1	Bradford, Jones	8,948	1	2	3	4			7	8	9				5				11	10	6		
41	24 (h)	West Ham U	W 1-0	Bradford	15,000	1	2	3	4	5		7	8	10					6						9	
42	May 1 (a)	Arsenal	L 0-3		22,240		2	3	4	5		7	8	10					11	6					9	1
		Appearances				41	39	40	39	27	21	39	40	32	34	15	16	18	24	16	1	13	3	1	2	1
		Goals						1		1		4	8	26	13	7	2			2		1				

FINAL LEAGUE POSITION: 14th in Division One. Average home League attendance: 21,649.

1 own-goal

FA Cup

No	Date	Opponent	Result	Scorers	Att	Tremelling DR	Womack F	Jones JW	Liddell G	Cringan J	Barton P	Harris WJ	Crosbie J	Bradford J	Briggs G	Islip E	Linley E	Hunter W	Dale R	Scriven A	Bowden F	Russell JC	Ashurst E	Bruce H	Castle FC	Hibbs H
3	Jan 9 (h)	Grimsby T	W 2-0	Russell, Briggs	36,000	1		3	4		6	7	8	9	10			5		11		2				
4	30 (a)	South Shields	L 1-2	Bradford (pen)	20,000	1		3	4	5		7	8	9	11	10			6			2				
		Appearances				2		2	2	1	1	2	2	2	2	1		1	1	1		2				
		Goals												1	1							1				

1926-27

Manager: Billy Beer to March 1927 then Bill Harvey

Player columns (left to right): Tremelling DR, Womack F, Jones JW, Liddell G, Cringan J, Dale R, Harris WJ, Crosbie J, Briggs G, Bradford J, Thirlaway W, Barton P, Castle FC, Smith J, Russell J, Hibbs H, Hunter W, Scriven A, Islip E, Bond B, Owen W, Harvey E, Bruce H, Oakes AW, Leslie A, Wood E, Isherwood H

No	Date	Opponent	Result	Scorers	Att	Tre	Wom	Jon	Lid	Cri	Dal	Har	Cro	Bri	Bra	Thi	Bar	Cas	Smi	Rus	Hib	Hun	Scr	Isl	Bon	Owe	Hvy	Bru	Oak	Les	Woo	Ish
1	Aug 28 (h)	Blackburn R	W 3-1	Briggs, Bradford 2	30,000	1	2	3	4	5		7	8	9	10	11	6															
2	30 (a)	Leicester C	L 2-5	Bradford, Harris	25,000	1	2	3	4	5		7	8		10	11	6	9														
3	Sep 4 (a)	Huddersfield T	W 2-0	Bradford 2	20,000	1	2	3	4	5	6	7	8	9	10	11																
4	11 (h)	Sunderland	W 2-0	Briggs 2	40,000	1	2	3	4	5	6	7	8	9	10	11																
5	13 (h)	Sheffield W	D 0-0		13,376	1	2	3	4	5	6	7	8	9	10	11																
6	18 (a)	West Brom A	W 2-1	Briggs 2	26,803	1	2	3	4	5	6	7	8	9	10	11																
7	20 (h)	Everton	W 1-0	Briggs	15,000	1		3	4	5	6	7	8	9		11			2	10												
8	25 (h)	Bury	D 2-2	Briggs 2	23,984	1		3	4	5	6	7	8	9		11			2	10												
9	Oct 2 (a)	Bolton W	L 0-1		15,000	1		3	4	5	6	7	8	9		11			2	10												
10	9 (a)	Tottenham H	L 1-6	Bradford	29,392			3	4	5	6	7	8	9		11			2	10	1											
11	16 (h)	Derby C	W 1-0	Harris	25,000	1			4	5	6	7	8	9	10	11	3		2													
12	23 (a)	Manchester U	W 1-0	Harris	32,010	1			4	5	6	7	8	9	10	11	3		2													
13	30 (h)	Aston Villa	L 1-2	Crosbie	48,500	1			4	5	6	7	8	9	10	11	3		2													
14	Nov 6 (a)	Cardiff C	L 0-1		10,000	1			4	5	6	7	8	9	10	11	3		2													
15	13 (h)	Burnley	W 1-0	Bradford	10,000	1			4		6	7	8	9	10	11	3		2			5										
16	20 (a)	Newcastle U	L 1-5	Briggs	20,000	1			4		6	7	8	9	10	11	3		2			5										
17	27 (h)	Leeds U	W 2-0	Harris, Bradford	19,707	1			4		6	7	8	9	10	11	3		2			5										
18	Dec 4 (a)	Liverpool	L 1-2	Briggs	35,000	1			4		6	7	8	9	10	11	3		2			5										
19	11 (h)	Arsenal	D 0-0		22,982	1			4	5	6	7	8	9	10		3		2				11									
20	18 (a)	Sheffield U	L 3-4	Briggs, Harris, Bradford	20,000	1			4	5	6	7	8	9	10		3		2				11									
21	25 (a)	West Ham U	L 0-1		30,000	1	3		4			7	8	9	10		6		2				5	11								
22	27 (h)	West Ham U	L 0-2		35,000	1	3		4				8	9		7	6		2				5	10	11							
23	Jan 1 (h)	Leicester C	W 2-1	Bradford 2	34,500	1	2	3	4	5			8	9	10		6						11	7								
24	15 (a)	Blackburn R	L 2-3	Islip, Scriven	9,000		2	3	4	5			8	9			6						11	10	7	1						
25	22 (h)	Huddersfield T	L 1-3	Thirlaway	15,000		2	3	4	5			8	9		11	6							10		1	7					
26	Feb 5 (h)	West Brom A	W 1-0	Bradford	34,000		2		4	5	6		8	10	9		3							11	7	1						
27	12 (a)	Bury	L 1-3	Islip	12,000		2		4	5	6		8	10	9		3							11	7	1						
28	16 (a)	Sunderland	L 1-4	Briggs	8,000		2			5	6		8	10	9		3							11	7	1		4				
29	26 (h)	Tottenham H	W 1-0	Cringan	21,145	1	2		4	5	6		8	9		11	3								7				10			
30	Mar 5 (a)	Derby C	L 1-4	Crosbie	12,000	1	2		4	5	6		8	10	9	11	3								7							
31	12 (h)	Manchester U	W 4-0	Bradford 2, Crosbie, Scriven	14,392	1	2		4	5	6		8	10	9		3						11		7							
32	19 (a)	Aston Villa	L 2-4	Bond, Scriven	51,000	1	2		4	5	6		8	10	9		3						11		7							
33	Apr 2 (a)	Burnley	W 2-0	Bradford, Crosbie	8,000	1	2		4	5	6		8	10	9		3						11		7							
34	4 (h)	Bolton W	W 6-1	Crosbie 2, Bradford, Briggs, Scriven, Cringan	20,000	1	2		4	5	6		8	10	9		3						11		7							
35	9 (h)	Newcastle U	W 2-0	Bradford, Bond	30,000	1	2		4	5	6		8	10	9		3						11		7							
36	16 (a)	Leeds U	L 1-2	Bradford	18,703	1		3	4	5			8	10	9				2				11		7					6		
37	18 (a)	Everton	L 1-3	Opp own-goal	20,000	1	2		4	5			8	10	9		3						11		7					6		
38	19 (h)	Sheffield W	D 4-4	Scriven, Bradford, Liddell, Briggs	17,720	1	2		4	5		8		10	9		3						11		7					6		
39	23 (h)	Liverpool	W 3-0	Briggs, Bradford, Bond	25,000	1	2		4	5			8	10	9		3						11		7					6		
40	27 (h)	Cardiff C	L 1-2	Bradford	20,000	1	2		4	5	3		8	10	9								11		7					6		
41	30 (a)	Arsenal	L 0-3		22,619	1	3		4				8	10	9								11		7			2		6	5	
42	May 7 (a)	Sheffield U	L 2-3	Bradford, Briggs	14,226	1			4	5			8	10	9								11		7			2		6		3
		Appearances				36	26	14	41	35	29	22	39	41	34	22	30	1	17	6	1	6	17	7	19	5	1	3	1	7	1	1
		Goals					1	2			5	6	16	22	1								5	2	3							

FINAL LEAGUE POSITION: 17th in Division One. Average home League attendance: 24,372.

1 own-goal

FA Cup

No	Date	Opponent	Result	Scorers	Att	Tre	Wom	Jon	Lid	Cri	Dal	Har	Cro	Bri	Bra	Thi	Bar	Cas	Smi	Rus	Hib	Hun	Scr	Isl	Bon	Owe	Hvy	Bru	Oak	Les	Woo	Ish
3	Jan 8 (h)	Manchester C	W 4-1	Bradford, Islip, Crosbie, Briggs	39,503	1	2	3	4	5			8	10	9		6							11	7							
4	29 (a)	Southampton	L 1-4	Briggs	15,804		2	3	4	5	6		8	7	9	11								10		1						
		Appearances				1	2	2	2	2	1		2	2	2	1	1							2	1	1						
		Goals											1	2	1									1								

1927-28

Secretary/Manager: Bill Harvey

#	Date	Opponent	Result	Scorers	Att.	Tremelling DR	Smith J	Randle J	Liddell G	Cringan JA	Leslie A	Bond B	Crosbie J	Bradford J	Briggs GR	Ellis WT	Womack F	Barton P	Harris F	Threlfall W	Dale R	Johnson A	Bruce H	Coxford J	Stainton RG	Bloxham A	Firth J	Davies SC	Hibbs H	Morrall GR	Curtis ER	Pike T
1	Aug 27 (a)	Tottenham H	L 0-1		37,408	1			4	5	6	7		9	10		2	3	8	11												
2	29 (h)	Huddersfield T	W 3-1	Bradford 2, Harris	20,000	1	2		4	5	6	7		9	10			3	8	11												
3	Sep 3 (h)	Manchester U	D 0-0		25,863	1	2		4	5	6	7		9	10			3	8	11												
4	7 (a)	Sunderland	L 2-4	Bond, Bradford	15,000	1	2				6	7		9	10			3	8		5	11	4									
5	10 (a)	Everton	L 2-5	Bradford, Briggs	35,000	1	2		4		6	7		9	10			3	8		5	11										
6	17 (h)	Cardiff C	L 1-3	Bond	30,000	1	2		4		6	7	8	9	10						10	5	3									
7	24 (a)	Blackburn R	D 4-4	Bradford 4	10,000	1	2		4		6	7		9	10				8	11			3	5								
8	Oct 1 (h)	Bolton W	D 1-1	Harris	12,000	1	2		4		6	7		9	10				8	11				5	3							
9	8 (a)	Sheffield W	W 3-2	Briggs 2, Bradford	19,974	1	2		4		6			9	10			3	8			11		5		7						
10	15 (h)	Middlesbrough	W 3-2	Bradford, Bloxham, Briggs	20,000	1	2		3		6			9	10				8		4	11		5		7						
11	22 (h)	Bury	D 2-2	Harris, Bradford	15,000	1	2			5	6	7		9	10			3	8		4	11										
12	29 (a)	Sheffield U	L 1-3	Bond	15,000	1	2				6	7		9	10			3	5		4	11						8				
13	Nov 5 (h)	Aston Villa	D 1-1	Crosbie	50,000	1	2			5	6	7	8	9	10			3			4	11										
14	12 (a)	Burnley	L 1-2	Bradford	12,000	1	2	3		5	6	7	8	9	10						4	11										
15	19 (h)	Arsenal	D 1-1	Crosbie	10,030	1	2	3		5	6	7	8	9	10							11									4	
16	26 (a)	Portsmouth	D 2-2	Crosbie 2	14,000	1	2	3	4		6	7	8		10	11								5				9				
17	Dec 3 (h)	Leicester C	L 0-2		15,000		2	3		5	6		8	9		11					4				7			10	1			
18	10 (a)	Liverpool	W 3-2	Davies, Briggs 2	30,000	1	2	3	4	5	6	7	8	9		11												10				
19	17 (h)	West Ham U	L 1-2	Bradford	30,000	1	2	3	4	5	6	7	8	9		11												10				
20	24 (a)	Derby C	L 1-4	Bradford	8,000	1		3		5	6	7	8	9		11	2											10		4		
21	26 (h)	Sunderland	D 1-1	Davies	20,000			3		5	6	7	8	9		11	2	4										10	1			
22	31 (h)	Tottenham H	W 3-2	Bradford 2, Briggs	11,603			3		5	6	7	8	9		11	2	4										10	1			
23	Jan 2 (h)	Newcastle U	D 1-1	Briggs	40,000			3		5	6	7	8	9		11	2											10	1	4		
24	7 (a)	Manchester U	D 1-1	Briggs	16,853			3		5	6	7	8	9		11	2											10	1	4		
25	21 (h)	Everton	D 2-2	Ellis, Briggs	30,000	1		3		5	6	7	8	9		11	2											10			4	
26	Feb 4 (h)	Blackburn R	W 2-1	Bradford 2	20,000		2	3		5	6	7	8	9		11												10	1	4		
27	11 (a)	Bolton W	L 2-3	Bradford, Crosbie	10,000		2	3	4	5	6	7	8	9		11												10	1			
28	22 (a)	Cardiff C	L 1-2	Briggs	10,000		2	3		5	6	7	8	9		11												10	1	4		
29	25 (a)	Middlesbrough	D 1-1	Firth	20,000	1		3	2	5	6	7	8	9		11											10			4		
30	Mar 3 (a)	Bury	W 3-2	Bradford 2, Briggs	10,000	1		3	2		6	7	8	9		11	5											10			4	
31	7 (h)	Sheffield W	W 1-0	Ellis	12,076	1		3	2		6	7	8	9		11	5											10			4	
32	10 (h)	Sheffield U	W 4-1	Briggs 3, Bond	20,000	1	2	3	4		6	7	8	9		11	5													10		
33	17 (a)	Aston Villa	D 1-1	Bradford	60,000	1		3	2	4	6	7	8	9		11	5													10		
34	24 (h)	Burnley	W 4-0	Bradford 3, Crosbie	20,000	1		3	2	4	6	7	8	9		11	5													10		
35	31 (a)	Arsenal	D 2-2	Crosbie, Ellis	13,990	1		3	2	4	6	7	8			11	5										9			10		
36	Apr 7 (h)	Portsmouth	W 2-0	Bond, Ellis	30,000	1	2	3	4		6	7	8	9		11	5													10		
37	9 (a)	Huddersfield T	L 0-2		15,000	1	2	3	4		6	7	8	9		11	5										5			10		
38	10 (h)	Newcastle U	L 0-2		25,000	1		3	4		6	7		9		11	2	5								8				10		
39	14 (a)	Leicester C	L 0-3		15,000	1		3	2		6	7	8	9		11											5			10	4	
40	21 (h)	Liverpool	W 2-0	Bradford 2	18,000	1	2	3	4		6	7	8	9			5													10		11
41	28 (a)	West Ham U	D 3-3	Bradford 2, Briggs	16,000	1	2	3	4		6	7	8	9			5													10		11
42	May 5 (h)	Derby C	W 2-1	Curtis, Carr (og)	20,000	1	2	3	4		6			9	10		5														8	11
		Appearances				34	27	29	25	25	42	24	28	37	40	20	15	16	11	5	8	9	3	8	1	3	6	14	8	10	11	3
		Goals										5	7	29	16	4			3							1	1	2			1	

FINAL LEAGUE POSITION: 11th in Division One. Average home League attendance: 21,646.

1 own-goal

FA Cup

Rd	Date	Opponent	Result	Scorers	Att.	Tremelling DR	Smith J	Randle J	Liddell G	Cringan JA	Leslie A	Bond B	Crosbie J	Bradford J	Briggs GR	Ellis WT	Womack F	Barton P	Harris F	Threlfall W	Dale R	Johnson A	Bruce H	Coxford J	Stainton RG	Bloxham A	Firth J	Davies SC	Hibbs H	Morrall GR	Curtis ER	Pike T
3	Jan 14 (h)	Peterboro' &F U	W 4-3	Davies, Bradford 3	38,128	1		3		5	6	7	8	9		11	2											10		4		
4	28 (a)	Wrexham	W 3-1	Randle (pen), Davies 2	16,000		2	3		5	6		8	9	7	11												10	1	4		
5	Feb 18 (a)	Manchester U	L 0-1		52,568		2	3	4	5	6		8	9	7	11												10	1			
		Appearances				1	2	3	1	3	3	1	3	3	2	3	1											3	2	2		
		Goals						1						3														3				

1928-29

Manager: Leslie Knighton

Player columns (left → right): Tremelling DR · Liddell G · Randall J · Cringan J · Barton P · Leslie A · Bond B · Crosbie J · Briggs G · Bradford J · Ellis W · Curtis E · Firth J · Dale R · Hibbs H · Pike T · Hicks GW · Coxford J · Smith J · Morrall G · Barkas E · Mills BR · Horsman W · Riley H · Birch J

No	Date	V	Opponent	Result	Scorers	Att.	Trm	Lid	Ran	Cri	Bar	Les	Bon	Cro	Bri	Bra	Ell	Cur	Fir	Dal	Hib	Pik	Hks	Cox	Smi	Mor	Brk	Mil	Hor	Ril	Bir
1	Aug 25	h	Manchester C	W 4-1	Bond, Bradford, Ellis, Briggs	45,000	1	2	3	4	5	6	7	8	9	10	11														
2	27	a	Leicester C	L 3-5	Briggs, Crosbie, Ellis	20,000	1	2	3	4	5	6	7	8	9		11		10												
3	Sep 1	a	Huddersfield T	D 0-0		25,000	1	2	3	4	5	6	7	8	9	10	11														
4	8	h	Everton	L 1-3	Briggs	30,000	1	2	3	4	5	6	7	8	9		11		10												
5	10	h	Leicester C	W 1-0	Briggs	20,000	1	2	3	4	5	6	7	8	9		11	10													
6	15	a	Arsenal	D 0-0		30,118	1	2	3		5	6	7	8	9		11	10	4												
7	22	h	Blackburn R	W 4-0	Bradford 2, Briggs 2	30,000		2	3		5	6	7	8	9	10	11		4		1										
8	29	a	Sunderland	W 4-3	Bradford 3, Bond	25,000	1	2	3		5	6	7	8	9	10	11		4												
9	Oct 6	h	Derby C	L 1-4	Bond (pen)	30,000	1	2	3		5	6	7	8	9	10	11		4												
10	13	a	Sheffield W	L 0-3		21,677	1	2	3		5	6	7	8	9		11	10	4												
11	20	a	Manchester U	L 0-1		17,522		2	3		5	6	7	8	9				4	1		11									
12	27	h	Aston Villa	L 2-4	Cringan, Bradford	40,000		2	3		5	6	7	8	9	10			4	1		11									
13	Nov 3	a	Liverpool	W 2-1	Curtis, Bradford	35,000		2	3	4		6	8	7	9	10					1		11	5							
14	10	h	West Ham U	D 2-2	Bradford, Hicks	25,000		2	3	4		6	8	7	9	10					1		11	5							
15	17	a	Newcastle U	L 0-1		30,000		2	3	4		6	7		9			10	8		1		11	5							
16	24	h	Burnley	L 3-6	Briggs, Bradford, Hicks	10,000		2	3	4		6	7		10	9			8				11	5							
17	Dec 1	a	Cardiff C	W 4-1	Hicks 2, Firth, Crosbie	12,000	1		4	3	5	6	8	7	9	10							11			2					
18	8	h	Sheffield U	D 2-2	Bradford 2	15,000	1		4	3	5	6	8	7	9	10							11			2					
19	22	h	Leeds U	W 5-1	Bradford 3, Liddell, Hicks	16,057	1		4	3	5	6	8	7	9							10	11			2					
20	25	h	Bolton W	L 0-2		40,000	1		4	3	5	6	8	7	9							10	11			2					
21	26	a	Bolton W	L 2-6	Pike, Bradford	20,000	1		4	3		6	8	7	9							10	11			5			2		
22	29	a	Manchester C	W 3-2	Pike 2, Bradford	35,000	1		4	3		6	8	7	9							10	11			5	2				
23	Jan 5	h	Huddersfield T	L 1-2	Barkas (pen)	20,000	1		4	3	5	6	11	8	7	9						10				2					
24	19	a	Everton	W 2-0	Hicks 2	20,000			4	3	5		8	7	9						1	10	11			6	2				
25	Feb 2	a	Blackburn R	L 1-4	Ellis	30,000			4	3			7	8			10				1	9	11	6		5	2				
26	9	h	Sunderland	W 1-0	Pike	16,000			4	3		6	7	8							1	10	11			5	2	9			
27	16	a	Derby C	D 2-2	Bond, Mills	15,000			4	3		6	7	8							1	10	11			5	2	9			
28	23	h	Sheffield W	W 4-1	Bond, Mills, Hicks, Bradford	28,599			4	3		6	7	8		10					1		11			5	2	9			
29	Mar 2	h	Manchester U	D 1-1	Hicks	16,738			4	3		6	7	8		10					1		11			5	2	9			
30	9	a	Aston Villa	W 2-1	Mills, Crosbie	59,322			4	3		6		8	7	10					1		11			5	2	9			
31	13	h	Arsenal	D 1-1	Hicks	11,001			3				8	7	10		6	4			1		11			5	2	9			
32	16	h	Liverpool	D 0-0		20,000			4	3		6		8		10	7						11			5	2	9			
33	20	a	Bury	L 1-3	Bradford	10,000	1		3			6		8		10		4					11			5	2	9	7		
34	23	a	West Ham U	L 1-2	Firth	20,000	1	2	3			6		8	7	9		4				10	11			5					
35	29	a	Portsmouth	L 1-3	Ellis	30,000		3					8				10	6	4		1		11	5			2	9	7		
36	30	h	Newcastle U	D 0-0		30,000	1		4	3		6	7	8	9	10							11	5			2				
37	Apr 1	h	Portsmouth	W 1-0	Bradford	15,000	1	2	3			6		8	7	10		4					11			5		9			
38	6	a	Burnley	L 0-4		12,000		2	3			6		8	9	10		4			1		11			5		7			
39	13	h	Cardiff C	D 0-0		15,000		4	3			6		8	7	9		10			1		11			5	2				
40	20	a	Sheffield U	L 2-3	Hicks 2	15,000		4	3			6		8	7	9					1	10	11			5	2				
41	27	h	Bury	W 3-2	Crosbie, Bradford 2	18,140	1	4	3			6		8	10	9							11			5	2		7		
42	May 4	a	Leeds U	W 1-0	Briggs	8,151	1	4	3			6		8	10	9							11			5	2			7	
	Appearances						24	40	41	22	5	38	22	38	35	32	12	10	12	7	18	12	30	7	4	19	18	11	3	1	1
	Goals						1		1				5	4	8	22	4	1	2			4	12				1	3			

FINAL LEAGUE POSITION: 15th in Division One. Average home League attendance: 23,406.

FA Cup

Rd	Date	V	Opponent	Result	Scorers	Att.	Trm	Lid	Ran	Cri	Bar	Les	Bon	Cro	Bri	Bra	Hib	Pik	Hks	Mor	Mil
3	Jan 12	h	Manchester C	W 3-1	Briggs, Bradford 2	25,005		4	3	5		6	8	7	9		1	10	11		2
4	26	a	Chelsea	L 0-1		56,953		4	3	5			7	8	9		1	10	11	6	2
	Appearances						2	2	2	1	1	2	1	2	2		2	2	2	1	2
	Goals														1	2					

1929-30

Manager: Leslie Knighton

#	Date	Opponent	Result	Scorers	Att.	Hibbs H	Barkas E	Randle J	Liddell G	Cringan J	Blyth W	Bond B	Crosbie J	Bradford J	Briggs GR	Hicks GW	Curtis E	Firth J	Morrall GR	Leslie A	Tremelling DR	Mills BR	Horsman W	Haywood G	Coxford J	Robinson T	Tewkesbury KC	Booton H	Fillingham T	Sabin A
1	Aug 31 (a) Aston Villa	L 1-2	Bradford	38,000	1	2	3	4	5	6	7	8	9	10	11														
2	Sep 4 (h) West Ham U	W 4-2	Bradford 3, Barkas	20,000	1	2	3	4	5	6	7	8	9		11	10													
3	7 (h) Huddersfield T	W 4-1	Bradford 2, Curtis, Liddell	25,000	1	2	3	4	5	6	7	8	9		11	10													
4	14 (a) Sheffield U	L 2-4	Curtis, Barkas (pen)	15,000	1	2	3	4	5	6	7	8	9		11	10													
5	16 (a) West Ham U	W 1-0	Bradford	16,000	1	2	3				7	8	9		11	10	4	5	6										
6	21 (h) Newcastle U	W 5-1	Bradford 3, Curtis, Crosbie	35,000	1	2	3				7	8	9		11	10	4	5	6										
7	28 (a) Blackburn R	L 5-7	Bradford 3, Crosbie 2	25,000	1	2	3			6	7	8	9		11	10	4	5											
8	Oct 5 (h) Middlesbrough	D 1-1	Bradford	15,000		2	3			6	7	8	9		11	10	4	5		1									
9	12 (a) Liverpool	D 1-1	Curtis	28,000		2	3			6	7	8	9		11	10	4	5		1									
10	17 (a) Leicester C	L 1-2	Curtis	20,000		2	3			6	7	8			11	10	4	5		1	9								
11	19 (a) Leeds U	L 0-1		20,067		2	3			6	7	8			11	10	4	5		1	9								
12	26 (h) Sheffield W	W 1-0	Hicks	27,221	1	2	3			6		8	9		11	10	4	5				7							
13	Nov 2 (a) Burnley	L 1-3	Crosbie	15,000		2	3			6		8	9		11	10	4	5		1		7							
14	9 (h) Arsenal	L 2-3	Bradford, Crosbie	33,904	1	2	3		6			8	9	7	11	10	4	5											
15	16 (a) Bolton W	D 0-0		15,000	1	2	3		6			8	9	7	11	10	4	5											
16	23 (h) Everton	D 0-0		20,000	1	2	3				7	8	9		11	10	4	5	6										
17	30 (a) Derby C	L 1-3	Curtis	12,000	1	2	3		6		7	8	9		11	10	4	5											
18	Dec 7 (h) Manchester C	W 3-0	Curtis, Haywood 2	18,000	1	2	3					8		10	11	7	4	5	6				9						
19	14 (a) Portsmouth	L 1-2	Barkas (pen)	20,000	1	2		3				8		10	11	7	4	5	6				9						
20	21 (h) Sunderland	W 3-1	Hicks, Haywood, Briggs	14,223	1	2		3				8		10	11	7	4	5	6				9						
21	25 (a) Manchester U	D 0-0		18,626	1	2		3				8		10	11	7	4	5	6				9						
22	26 (h) Manchester U	L 0-1		35,682	1	2		3	6			8		10	11	7	4	5					9						
23	28 (h) Aston Villa	D 1-1	Crosbie	40,000	1	2		3				8		10	11	7	4	5	6				9						
24	Jan 4 (a) Huddersfield T	D 1-1	Hicks	15,000	1	2		3	6			8		10	11	7	4						9	5					
25	18 (h) Sheffield U	W 2-1	Curtis, Bradford	25,000	1	2		3	6			8	9	10	11	7	4	5											
26	Feb 1 (h) Blackburn R	L 1-2	Bradford	20,000		2		3	6			8	9	7	11	10	4	5		1									
27	8 (a) Middlesbrough	L 1-5	Haywood	15,000		2		3	6		7	8		10	11		4	5		1			9						
28	15 (h) Liverpool	W 1-0	Haywood	20,000	1	2		3	6			8		10	7	11	4	5					9						
29	22 (h) Leeds U	W 1-0	Haywood	17,703	1	2		3	6			8		10	7	11	4	5					9						
30	Mar 8 (h) Burnley	W 2-0	Bradford, Cringan	20,000	1	2		3	6			8		10	7	11	4	5					9						
31	15 (a) Arsenal	L 0-1		32,174	1	2		3		6		8	9		7	11	4	5											
32	22 (h) Bolton W	W 3-1	Blyth 2, Bradford	15,000	1	2		3		11		8	9		7		4	5											
33	29 (a) Everton	W 4-2	Crosbie, Bradford, Blyth, Briggs	25,000	1	2		3		11		8	9	10	7		4	5	6										
34	Apr 2 (a) Newcastle U	D 1-1	Morrall	30,000				3				8		9	11		4	5	6			7			10	1	2		
35	5 (h) Derby C	L 2-4	Briggs, Robinson	20,000				3				8		9	11		4	5	6			7			10	1	2		
36	12 (a) Manchester C	W 4-1	Fillingham 2, Hicks, Briggs	25,000	1	2		3				8			7	11	4	5	6						10			9	
37	18 (a) Grimsby T	L 1-2	Morrall	10,000	1	2		3				8			7	11	4	5	6						10			9	
38	19 (h) Portsmouth	W 1-0	Fillingham	20,000	1	2		3		11		8	9	10	7		4	5	6									9	
39	22 (h) Grimsby T	L 0-2		15,000	1	2		3		11		8	9		7		4	5	6						10				
40	26 (a) Sunderland	L 0-2		10,000	1	2		3						10	8	11	4	5	6			7						9	
41	28 (a) Sheffield W	D 1-1	Blyth	9,310	1			3		10			9		8	11		5	6			7					2		4
42	May 3 (h) Leicester C	W 3-0	Bradford 3	9,340	1			3		10			9		8	11		5	6			7					2		4
	Appearances				33	38	18	28	15	19	14	39	27	29	38	25	36	37	18	7	2	7	12	1	7	2	4	4	2
	Goals					3		1	1	4		7	23	4	4	8		2					6		1			3	

FINAL LEAGUE POSITION: 11th in Division One. Average home League attendance: 22,193.

FA Cup

#	Date	Opponent	Result	Scorers	Att.	Hibbs H	Barkas E	Randle J	Liddell G	Cringan J	Blyth W	Bond B	Crosbie J	Bradford J	Briggs GR	Hicks GW	Curtis E	Firth J	Morrall GR
3	Jan 11 (h) Bolton W	W 1-0	Morrall	35,000	1			3		6		8	9	10	11	7	4	5
4	25 (a) Arsenal	D 2-2	Briggs 2	50,000	1			3		6		8	9	10	11	7	4	5
5	29 (h) Arsenal	L 0-1		47,521	1			3		6		8	9	7	11	10	4	5
	Appearances				3			3		3		3	3	3	3	3	3	3
	Goals													2				1

1930-31

Manager: Leslie Knighton

No	Date	Venue	Opponent	Result	Scorers	Att	Hibbs H	Liddell G	Barkas E	Firth J	Morrall G	Cringan J	Briggs GR	Crosbie J	Bradford J	Blythe W	Hicks GW	Haywood G	Fillingham T	Curtis E	Horsman W	Booton H	Tewkesbury KC	Leslie A	Tremelling DR	Randle J	Lane H	Stoker L	Thorogood J	Gregg R	Morfitt J	Bond B	Robinson T	Calladine CF
1	Aug 30	(h)	Sheffield U	W 3-1	Morrall, Briggs, Bradford	27,576	1	2	3	4	5	6	7	8	9	10	11																	
2	Sep 1	(a)	Leicester C	L 1-2	Briggs	15,000	1	2	3	4	5	6	7	8			11	9		10														
3	6	(a)	Derby C	D 0-0		15,000	1	2	3	4		6	7	8	9		11		5	10														
4	10	(h)	Newcastle U	D 1-1	Bradford	19,862	1	2	3	4		6	7	8	9		11		5	10														
5	13	(h)	Manchester C	W 3-2	Briggs 2, Bradford	17,705	1	2	3	4		6	9	8	10		11		5		7													
6	17	(a)	Newcastle U	D 2-2	Briggs, Morrall	30,000	1		3	4	5	6	9	8			11			10	7	2												
7	20	(a)	Portsmouth	D 2-2	Hicks, Briggs	15,000	1		3	4	5		9	8			11		6	10	7	2												
8	27	(h)	Arsenal	L 2-4	Briggs, Roberts (og)	31,693			3	4	5		9	8		11			6	10	7	2	1											
9	Oct 4	(a)	Blackburn R	L 1-2	Horsman	15,000	1		3	4	5		9	8	10					11	7	2		6										
10	11	(h)	Blackpool	D 1-1	Curtis	29,650	1	2	3		5	4	9	8	10					11	7			6										
11	18	(a)	Aston Villa	D 1-1	Briggs	59,787	1	2	3		5	4	9	8	10					11	7			6										
12	25	(h)	Chelsea	W 6-2	Bradford 2, Curtis, Briggs 2, Crosbie	18,000	1	2	3		5	4	9	8	10					11	7			6										
13	Nov 1	(a)	Manchester C	L 0-2		11,479	1	2	3		5	4	9	8	10					11	7			6										
14	8	(h)	West Ham U	L 0-2		25,000	1	2	3		5	4	9	8	10					11	7			6										
15	15	(a)	Middlesbrough	D 1-1	Curtis	8,000	1	2	3		5	4		8	10			9		11	7			6										
16	22	(h)	Grimsby T	W 4-1	Fillingham, Firth 3	14,767		2		10	5	4		8					9	11	7			6	1	3								
17	29	(a)	Bolton W	L 0-2		12,000	1	2			5	4			10				9	11	7			6		3	8							
18	Dec 6	(h)	Huddersfield T	W 2-0	Bradford, Curtis	13,885	1	2			5	6			8				9	10	7					3		4	11					
19	13	(a)	Sheffield W	L 1-9	Briggs	21,226	1	2			5	6	10	8					9	11	7	3						4						
20	20	(h)	Liverpool	W 2-0	Briggs 2	18,000	1	2			5	4	9	8						10	7			6		3			11					
21	25	(h)	Leeds U	L 0-1		24,991	1	2		4	5	6	9	8						10	7					3			11					
22	26	(a)	Leeds U	L 1-3	Curtis	12,381	1	2		4	5	6	8					9		10	7					3			11					
23	27	(a)	Sheffield U	L 1-3	Cringan	20,000			2		5	6	9	8					4	10	7				1	3			11					
24	Jan 3	(h)	Derby C	L 1-2	Curtis	15,000		2	5			6		8						9					1	3	7	4	11	10				
25	17	(a)	Manchester C	L 2-4	Briggs, Gregg	18,000	1	2	3		5	4	7	8	9					11				6						10				
26	28	(h)	Portsmouth	W 2-1	Briggs, Bradford	15,000	1		3		5	4	7	8	9					11		2		6						10				
27	31	(a)	Arsenal	D 1-1	Bradford	30,913	1	2	3	10	5	4	7	8	9					11				6										
28	Feb 7	(h)	Blackburn R	W 4-1	Bradford 4	30,000	1	2	3		5	4		8	9					11	7			6						10				
29	18	(a)	Blackpool	W 1-0	Crosbie	10,000	1		3	6	5	4		8	9					11	7	2								10				
30	21	(h)	Aston Villa	L 0-4		50,000	1	2		6		4	8		9				5	11	7					3				10				
31	Mar 7	(h)	Manchester U	D 0-0		17,678	1	2		10		4	7		9				5	11				6		3				8				
32	16	(a)	West Ham U	W 2-1	Firth, Bradford	12,000	1		3	10	5	4	7		9				6	11		2								8				
33	21	(h)	Middlesbrough	L 1-2	Jarvis (og)	19,467	1	2	3	10	5	4	7							11				6						8	9			
34	25	(a)	Chelsea	L 0-1		30,000			3	10	5	6	9						4	11	7	2			1					8				
35	28	(a)	Grimsby T	L 1-4	Fillingham	12,000		2	3	10	5	4	7	8					9	11				6	1									
36	Apr 3	(a)	Sunderland	L 0-1		15,000	1	2	3	10		4	9	8					5	11	7			6										
37	4	(h)	Bolton W	L 0-2		13,700	1		3	4			9	8					5	11		2		6								7	10	
38	6	(h)	Sunderland	W 1-0	Gregg	18,000	1		3	10			7						5	9				6		2		4	11	8				
39	11	(a)	Huddersfield T	L 0-1		15,000	1		3	10									5	11	7			6		2		4		8				9
40	15	(a)	Liverpool	D 0-0		28,000	1		3					8				9	5	11				6		2		4		10		7		
41	18	(h)	Sheffield W	W 2-0	Gregg, Curtis	16,441	1	2	3	8	5								5	11				6				4		10		7		
42	May 2	(h)	Leicester C	W 2-1	Curtis, Bradford	10,365	1	2	3		5	4	7	8	9					11				6						10				
						Appearances	36	29	34	25	31	34	32	31	22	2	7	4	21	40	24	10	1	24	5	13	2	7	7	15	1	3	1	1
						Goals				4	2	1	15	2	14		1		2	8	1									3				

FINAL LEAGUE POSITION: 19th in Division One. Average home League attendance: 21,275.

2 own-goals

FA Cup

Round	Date	Venue	Opponent	Result	Scorers	Att	Hibbs H	Liddell G	Barkas E	Firth J	Morrall G	Cringan J	Briggs GR	Crosbie J	Bradford J	Blythe W	Hicks GW	Haywood G	Fillingham T	Curtis E	Horsman W	Booton H	Tewkesbury KC	Leslie A	Tremelling DR	Randle J	Lane H	Stoker L	Thorogood J	Gregg R	Morfitt J	Bond B	Robinson T	Calladine CF
3	Jan 10	(a)	Liverpool	W 2-0	Curtis, Bradford	43,907	1	2	3		5	4	10	8	9					11	7			6										
4	24	(h)	Port Vale	W 2-0	Bradford 2	39,885	1	2	3		5	4	7	8	9					11				6						10				
5	Feb 14	(h)	Watford	W 3-0	Bradford, Curtis 2	49,729	1	2	3		5	4		8	9					11	7			6						10				
6	28	(h)	Chelsea	D 2-2	Bradford, Curtis	55,298	1	2	3		5	4	7	8	9					11				6						10				
R	Mar 4	(a)	Chelsea	W 3-0	Firth, Bradford 2	74,365	1	2	3	10	5	4	7	8	9					11				6										
SF	14	(n*)	Sunderland	W 2-0	Curtis 2	43,570	1	2	3	10	5	4	7	8	9					11				6										
F	Apr 25	(n†)	West Brom A	L 1-2	Bradford	90,368	1	2	3		5	4	7	8	9					11				6						10				
						Appearances	7	7	7	2	7	7	6	7	7					7	2			7						4				
						Goals				1					8					6														

*Played at Elland Road, Leeds. †Played at Wembley Stadium.

1931-32

Manager: Leslie Knighton

#	Date		Opponent	Res	Scorers	Att	Hibbs H	Liddell G	Barkas E	Stoker L	Morrall GR	Leslie A	Briggs GR	Crosbie J	Smithies GH	Bradford J	Curtis E	Randle J	Gregg RE	Fillingham T	Hicks GW	Cringan J	Horsman W	Calladine C	Keating R	Tewkesbury KC	Grosvenor T	Thorogood J	Smith SJ	Firth J	Booton H	Haywood G	Mittell JL	Wallington SP
1	Aug	29 (a)	Everton	L 2-3	Briggs, Curtis	30,000	1	2	3	4	5	6	7	8	9	10	11																	
2	Sep	2 (h)	Newcastle U	W 4-1	Briggs 2, Curtis, Bradford	20,000	1	2		4	5	6	7	8		9	11	3	10															
3		5 (h)	Arsenal	D 2-2	Bradford 2 (1 pen)	26,810	1	2		4	5	6	7	8		9	11	3	10															
4		12 (a)	Blackpool	D 1-1	Hicks	25,000	1	2	3	4	5		7	8		9			10	6	11													
5		16 (a)	Sunderland	W 3-2	Crosbie, Bradford, Briggs	20,000	1		3	4	5		7	8		9	11	2	10	6														
6		19 (h)	Sheffield U	L 1-3	Crosbie	30,000	1		3	4	5		7	8		9	11	2	10	6														
7		23 (h)	Sunderland	D 0-0		15,000	1	2	3	4	5		7	8		9	10			6						11								
8		26 (a)	Blackburn R	W 2-1	Bradford, Jones (og)	10,000	1	2	3	4				8		9	11		10	6			5	7										
9	Oct	3 (h)	Portsmouth	W 2-1	Bradford 2	20,000	1	2	3	4				8		9	11		10	6			5	7										
10		10 (a)	Derby C	L 1-2	Morrall	10,000	1	2	3	4	5			8			7		10	6					9	11								
11		17 (h)	Grimsby T	W 2-1	Gregg, Bradford	18,000		2	3	4	5		7	8		9			10	6						11		1						
12		24 (a)	Middlesbrough	L 0-2		12,000	1	2	3	4	5		7			9			10	6							8		11					
13		31 (h)	Bolton W	D 2-2	Bradford 2	20,000	1	2	3	4	5		7			9			10		6						8		11					
14	Nov	7 (a)	Sheffield W	L 1-5	Bradford	17,438		2	3	4	5		7	8		9			10		6							1	11					
15		14 (h)	Leicester C	W 2-0	Grosvenor, Bradford	16,000	1	2	3	4	5		7			9	11		10		6						8							
16		21 (a)	Aston Villa	L 2-3	Smith 2	49,900	1	2	3	4	5		7				11		10		6						8		9					
17		28 (h)	Huddersfield T	W 5-0	Smith 2, Curtis, Briggs, Bradford	20,000	1	2	3	4	5		7			10	11				6						8		9					
18	Dec	5 (a)	Liverpool	L 3-4	Briggs, Grosvenor, Smith	25,000	1	2		4	5		7			10	11	3			6						8		9					
19		12 (h)	West Ham U	W 4-1	Bradford 2, Curtis 2	30,000	1	2	3	4	5		7			10	11				6						8		9					
20		19 (a)	Chelsea	L 1-2	Bradford	20,000	1	2	3		5		7			9	11		10	6							8			4				
21		25 (a)	West Brom A	W 1-0	Curtis	38,053	1	2	3		5		7	8		10	11				6								9	4				
22		26 (h)	West Brom A	W 1-0	Bradford	57,806	1	2	3	4	5		7			10	11				6						8		9					
23	Jan	2 (h)	Everton	W 4-0	Haywood 2, Curtis, Bradford	30,000	1		3	4						10	11			5	6						8				2	9		
24		16 (a)	Arsenal	L 0-3		37,843	1	3		4	5		7			10	11				6						8				2	9		
25		30 (a)	Sheffield U	L 0-1		15,000	1	3		4	5					10	11			6	7						8		9		2			
26	Feb	3 (h)	Blackpool	W 3-0	Curtis, Grosvenor, Bradford	19,540	1			4	5					10	11			3	7						8		6		2	9		
27		6 (h)	Blackburn R	W 2-1	Bradford, Curtis	20,000	1	3		4	5					10	11				7						8		6		2	9		
28		17 (h)	Portsmouth	L 1-2	Haywood	10,000	1			4	5					10	11	3		6	7						8				2	9		
29		20 (h)	Derby C	D 1-1	Curtis	18,721	1	3		4	5					10	11			6	7						8				2	9		
30		27 (a)	Grimsby T	D 1-1	Horsman	7,000	1	3		4	5						11	10		6	7						8				2	9		
31	Mar	5 (h)	Middlesbrough	W 3-0	Curtis 2 (2 pens), Crosbie	22,000	1	3		4	5			8			11			6	7	9					10		2					
32		12 (a)	Bolton W	L 1-5	Keating	8,000	1	3		4	5			8			11			6	7	9					10		2					
33		19 (h)	Sheffield W	L 1-2	Grosvenor	17,271	1	3		4	5					9	11			6	7						8		10	2			1	
34		26 (a)	Leicester C	L 1-3	Smith	20,000		3		4	5		7			10	11			6							8		9	2			1	
35		28 (a)	Manchester C	L 1-2	Briggs	20,000		3		4			7			10	11		5	6							8		9	2			1	
36		29 (h)	Manchester C	L 1-5	Bradford	12,000		3		4			7			9	11		5	6							8		10	2			1	
37	Apr	2 (h)	Aston Villa	D 1-1	Smith	48,000	1	2		4	5		7			10	11			6							3		8	9				
38		9 (a)	Huddersfield T	D 1-1	Briggs	7,000	1	2		4	5		7			10	11			6							3		8	9	4			
39		16 (h)	Liverpool	W 3-1	Bradford 2, Grosvenor	9,848	1	2		4	5		7			10	11			6							3		8	9				
40		23 (a)	West Ham U	W 4-2	Briggs 2, Curtis, Smith	12,000	1	2		4	5		7			10	11			6							3		8	9				
41		30 (h)	Chelsea	W 4-0	Grosvenor, Smith, Briggs, Bradford	20,000	1	2		4	5		7			10											3		8	11	9			6
42	May	7 (a)	Newcastle U	W 3-0	Bradford 2, Smith	10,000	1			4	5		7			10											3		8	11	9	2		6
			Appearances				36	37	19	39	37	3	30	15	1	37	35	6	16	17	1	30	11	2	5	2	26	5	15	9	15	7	4	2
			Goals							1			11	3		26	13		1	1	1		1				6		10			3		

FINAL LEAGUE POSITION: 9th in Division One. Average home League attendance: 23,380.

1 own-goal

FA Cup

#	Date		Opponent	Res	Scorers	Att	Hibbs H	Liddell G	Barkas E	Stoker L	Morrall GR	Briggs GR	Bradford J	Curtis E	Cringan J	Grosvenor T	Smith SJ	Booton H
3	Jan	9 (h)	Bradford C	W 1-0	Bradford	37,749	1		3	4	5	7	10	11	6	8	9	2
4		23 (a)	Grimsby T	L 1-2	Bradford	18,000	1	2	3	4	5	7	10	11	6	8	9	
			Appearances				2	2	1	2	2	2	2	2	2	2	2	1
			Goals										2					

1932-33

Manager: Leslie Knighton

Player columns (left to right): Hibbs H, Booton H, Cringan J, Stoker L, Morrall GR, Fillingham T, Briggs G, Grosvenor T, Smith SJ, Bradford J, Curtis E, Randle J, Firth J, Horsman W, Gregg RE, Smith B, Thorogood J, Lea G, Haywood G, Robinson T, Barkas E, Calladine CF, Mittell JL, White FR

#	Date	Opponent	Res	Scorers	Att	Hibbs H	Booton H	Cringan J	Stoker L	Morrall GR	Fillingham T	Briggs G	Grosvenor T	Smith SJ	Bradford J	Curtis E	Randle J	Firth J	Horsman W	Gregg RE	Smith B	Thorogood J	Lea G	Haywood G	Robinson T	Barkas E	Calladine CF	Mittell JL	White FR
1	Aug 27 (h)	Arsenal	L 0-1		31,952	1	2	3	4	5	6	7	8	9	10	11													
2	31 (a)	Manchester C	L 0-1		26,000	1	2		4	5	6	7	8	9	10	11	3												
3	Sep 3 (a)	Everton	L 1-4	Grosvenor	30,000	1	2		4	5			8	9	10	11	3	6	7										
4	7 (h)	Manchester C	W 3-0	Briggs, Bradford 2	20,000	1	2		4	5		7	8		9	11	3	6		10									
5	10 (h)	Blackpool	W 2-1	Curtis (pen), Bradford	19,148	1	2		4	5		7	8		9	11	3	6		10									
6	17 (a)	Derby C	D 2-2	Bradford, Briggs	16,000	1	2		4	5		7	8		9	11				10	3								
7	24 (a)	Blackburn R	W 3-1	Grosvenor, Curtis, Gregg	25,000	1	2		4	5	6	7	8		9	11				10	3								
8	Oct 1 (a)	Leeds U	D 1-1	Thorogood	14,193	1	2			5	6	7	8		9				4	10	3	11							
9	8 (h)	Sheffield W	W 2-1	Thorogood, Grosvenor	14,999	1	2		4	5		7	8							10	3	11	6	9					
10	15 (a)	West Brom A	L 0-1		29,145	1	2		4	5		7	8	9						10	3	11	6						
11	22 (a)	Aston Villa	L 0-1		54,000	1	2		4	5		7	8	9						10	3	11							
12	29 (h)	Middlesbrough	L 1-4	Bradford	7,558	1	2		4	5	6	7	8	9						10	3	11							
13	Nov 5 (a)	Chelsea	L 2-4	Grosvenor, Curtis (pen)	30,000	1	2		4	5	6		8					7		10	3	11		9					
14	12 (h)	Huddersfield T	L 0-2		10,000	1	2		4	5	6	7	8							10		11			3	6			
15	19 (a)	Sheffield U	L 1-2	Briggs	10,000	1	2		4	5	6	7	8	9						10		11			3				
16	26 (h)	Wolves	D 0-0		24,168	1	2		4	5	6	7	8	9	10							11			3				
17	Dec 3 (a)	Bolton W	D 2-2	Bradford, Briggs	8,000	1	2	6	4	5		7	8		9	11				10					3				
18	10 (h)	Liverpool	W 3-0	Gregg 3	12,000	1	2	6	4	5		7	8		9	11				10					3				
19	17 (a)	Leicester C	D 2-2	Cringan, Gregg	10,000	1	2	6	4	5		7	8		9	11				10					3				
20	24 (h)	Portsmouth	W 4-0	Grosvenor 2, Bradford, Gregg	10,000	1	2		4	5		7	8		9	11				10					3	6			
21	26 (a)	Newcastle U	L 1-2	Curtis	43,000	1	2		4		6	7	8			11				10	3			9		6			
22	27 (h)	Newcastle U	L 1-2	Richardson (og)	40,000	1	2		4	5		7	8		9	11				10					3	6			
23	31 (a)	Arsenal	L 0-3		37,800	1	2		4		6	7	8			11				10				9	3	6			
24	Jan 7 (h)	Everton	W 4-0	Haywood 3, Grosvenor	20,000	1	2		4		6	7	8			11				10				9	3	6			
25	21 (a)	Blackpool	W 1-0	Calladine	10,000	1	2		4	5		7	8			11								9	10	3	6		
26	Feb 1 (h)	Derby C	W 3-1	Gregg, Haywood, Curtis	19,687	1	2		4	5		7	8			11				10				9	3	6			
27	4 (a)	Blackburn R	L 0-2		10,000	1	2		4	5		7	8			11				10				9	3	6			
28	11 (h)	Leeds U	W 2-1	Haywood, Curtis (pen)	22,157	1	2		4	5		7	8			11				10				9	3	6			
29	Mar 8 (h)	Aston Villa	W 3-2	Briggs, Bradford, Grosvenor	50,000	1	2		4	5		7	8		9	11				10					3	6			
30	11 (a)	Middlesbrough	D 2-2	Bradford, Curtis	12,000	1	2		4	5		7	8		9	11				10					3	6			
31	18 (h)	Chelsea	D 0-0		20,000	1	2		4	5		7	8		9	11				10					3	6			
32	25 (a)	Huddersfield T	D 0-0		10,000		2			5		7	8		9	11				10	4				3	6		1	
33	Apr 1 (h)	Sheffield U	W 4-1	Bradford 2, Curtis 2	10,000		2			5		7	8		9	11				10	4				3	6		1	
34	5 (a)	Sheffield W	D 1-1	Curtis	6,088	1	2			5			8	9		11			7	10	4				3	6			
35	8 (a)	Wolves	L 0-1		25,000	1	2		4	5			8			11			7	10				9	3	6			
36	14 (a)	Sunderland	L 0-1		15,000	1	2		4	5			8			11			7	10				9	3	6			
37	15 (h)	Bolton W	W 2-1	Bradford 2	18,000	1	2		4	5		7	8		9	11				10					3	6			
38	17 (a)	Sunderland	W 2-0	Curtis, Bradford	9,722	1	2	6	4	5			8		9	11			7	10					3				
39	22 (a)	Liverpool	L 0-1		15,000	1	2		4	5			8		9	11			7						3	6			10
40	26 (h)	West Brom A	D 1-1	Briggs	27,000	1	2		4	5		7	8			11				10				9	3	6			
41	29 (h)	Leicester C	L 0-4		9,894	1	2		4	5		7	8		9	11				10					3	6			
42	May 6 (a)	Portsmouth	D 1-1	Grosvenor	10,000	1	2		4	5		7	8		9	11				10					3	6			
		Appearances				40	42	5	38	38	15	35	42	6	26	36	4	5	6	34	9	9	5	11	28	23	2	2	1
		Goals					1					6	9		14	11				7		2		5			1		

FINAL LEAGUE POSITION: 13th in Division One. Average home League attendance: 20,044.

1 own-goal

FA Cup

#	Date	Opponent	Res	Scorers	Att	Hibbs H	Booton H	Stoker L	Morrall GR	Briggs G	Grosvenor T	Curtis E	Gregg RE	Haywood G	Robinson T	Barkas E
3	Jan 14 (h)	Preston NE	W 2-1	Gregg, Grosvenor	29,497	1	2	4	5	7	8	11	10	9	3	6
4	28 (h)	Blackburn R	W 3-0	Curtis 2, Haywood	25,617	1	2	4	5	7	8	11	10	9	3	6
5	Feb 18 (a)	Middlesbrough	D 0-0		25,000	1	2	4	5	7	8	11	10	9	3	6
R	22 (h)	Middlesbrough	W 3-0	Gregg, Haywood, Curtis	29,191	1	2	4	5	7	8	11	10	9	3	6
6	Mar 4 (a)	West Ham U	L 0-4		44,233	1	2	4	5	7	8	11	10	9	3	6
		Appearances				5	5	5	5	5	5	5	5	5	5	5
		Goals									1	3	2	2		

1933-34

Manager: George Liddell

No	Date	Opponent	Result	Scorers	Att	Hibbs H	Booton H	Barkas E	Stoker L	Morrall GR	Calladine CF	McGurk FR	Grosvenor T	Bradford J	Smith SJ	Guest WF	Haywood G	Curtis ER	Fillingham T	Horsman W	Gregg RE	Evans L	Roberts F	White F	Lea G	Robertson J	Thorogood J	Smith B	Shaw F	Clack F	Mangnall D	Moffatt S	Cringan JA	Sykes J
1	Aug 26 (a)	Arsenal	D 1-1	Bradford	44,662	1	2	3	4	5	6	7	8	9	10	11																		
2	30 (h)	Manchester C	L 0-1		30,000	1	2	3	4	5	6	7	8	9	10	11																		
3	Sep 2 (h)	Everton	D 2-2	Haywood, Grosvenor	34,029	1	2	3	4	5	6	7	8	10			9	11																
4	6 (a)	Manchester C	L 0-1		20,000	1	2	3	4	5	6		8	9					11	7	10												
5	9 (a)	Middlesbrough	W 3-0	Horsman, Bradford 2	5,000	1	2	3	4		6		8	10			9	11	5	7													
6	16 (h)	Blackburn R	W 2-0	S.J.Smith, Curtis (pen)	20,000	1	2	3	4		6		8	10	9			11	5	7													
7	23 (a)	Newcastle U	D 0-0		22,000	1	2	3	4		6	7	8	10	9			11	5														
8	30 (h)	Leeds U	W 4-0	Bradford, Grosvenor, S.J.Smith, Curtis	21,566	1	2	3	4		6	7	8	10	9			11	5														
9	Oct 7 (a)	Derby C	L 0-4		15,000	1	2	3	4		6	7	8	10	9			11	5														
10	14 (h)	West Brom A	L 0-1		29,103		2	3	4		6	7	10	8			9	11	5							1							
11	21 (h)	Wolves	D 0-0		33,166	1	2	3	4		6	7	8	10					5				9	11									
12	28 (a)	Stoke C	D 1-1	Roberts	20,000	1	2	3	4		6	7	8	10					5				9	11									
13	Nov 4 (h)	Liverpool	L 1-2	Roberts	18,000	1	2	3	4		6	7	8	10					5				9	11									
14	11 (a)	Portsmouth	W 2-0	White, Fillingham	15,000	1	2	3	4		6		8						9	7			10	11	5								
15	15 (h)	Sunderland	D 1-1	Lea	15,000	1	2	3	4		6		8						9	7			10	11	5								
16	25 (a)	Chelsea	D 1-1	White	18,000		2	3	4		6								5	7		1	10	11	9								
17	Dec 2 (h)	Aston Villa	D 0-0		35,000	1	2		4	5	6		8	9					3	7			10	11									
18	9 (a)	Tottenham H	L 2-3	Roberts, White	18,000	1	2		4	5	6		8	9					3	7			10	11									
19	23 (a)	Huddersfield T	D 0-0		6,000	1	2	3	4	5	6		8							7			10	11	9								
20	25 (a)	Sheffield U	L 1-2	Roberts	20,000	1	2	3		5	6		8							7			10	11	4	9							
21	26 (h)	Sheffield U	W 4-2	White, Robertson, Roberts, Bradford	30,000	1	2	3	4	5	6		8							7			10	11		9							
22	30 (h)	Arsenal	D 0-0		34,771	1	2	3	4	5	6		8							7			10	11		9							
23	Jan 2 (a)	Sheffield W	L 1-2	McGurk	12,754	1	2	3	4	5	6	8								7			10	11		9							
24	6 (a)	Everton	L 0-2		18,000	1	2	3	4	5					10			6	7				8	11		9							
25	20 (h)	Middlesbrough	D 0-0		20,000	1	2	3	8	5					10	11	9	6	7								4						
26	29 (a)	Blackburn R	L 1-3	McGurk	20,000	1			4	5	6	7		9		11		2					10					3	8					
27	Feb 3 (h)	Newcastle U	L 1-2	McGurk	18,000	1			4	5	6	7		10		11		2					9					3	8					
28	10 (a)	Leeds U	L 0-1		14,753		2	3	4	5	6	7	8			11							10							1	9			
29	21 (h)	Derby C	W 2-1	S.J.Smith, Mangnall	20,000		2	3	4	5	6	7	8		10	11														1	9			
30	24 (a)	West Brom A	W 2-1	Roberts, White	24,525		2	3	4	5	6	7	8										10	11						1	9			
31	Mar 3 (a)	Wolves	L 0-2		30,000	1	2		4	5	6	7	8										10	11				3			9			
32	10 (h)	Stoke C	L 0-1		25,000	1	2	3	4	5	6	7	8										10	11							9			
33	17 (a)	Liverpool	L 1-4	Moffatt	40,000	1	2		4	5	6		8										10	11							9	7		
34	24 (h)	Portsmouth	W 3-1	Barkas (pen), Guest, Mangnall	12,000		2	3	4	5	6		8			11							10							1	9	7		
35	28 (h)	Leicester C	W 3-0	Sharman (og), Moffatt, Mangnall	20,000		2		4	5	6		8			11							10							1	9	7	3	
36	26 (a)	Sunderland	L 1-4	Booton (pen)	18,000		2		4	5	6		8			11							10							1	9	7	3	
37	Apr 3 (h)	Sheffield W	W 3-0	Catlin (og), Roberts, Guest	24,021		2	3	4		6					11			5	7			10							1	9			
38	7 (h)	Chelsea	L 0-3		30,000			3	4		6		8	9		11			5	7			10							1			2	
39	14 (a)	Aston Villa	D 1-1	Calladine	40,000		2	3		5	6		8	10		11			9					4						1		7		
40	21 (h)	Tottenham H	W 2-0	Whateley (og), Calladine	30,000	1	2	3	4	5	6		8	10		11			9													7		
41	28 (a)	Leicester C	W 7-3	Moffatt, Guest 3, Mangnall, Roberts, Jones (og)	18,000	1	2	3	4	5	6		8	10		11															9	7		
42	May 5 (h)	Huddersfield T	L 1-3	Barkas (pen)	19,442	1	2	3		5	6		8	10		11															9	7		4
	Appearances					31	39	36	39	28	42	18	18	31	10	16	4	8	22	17	1	2	28	17	6	6	2	2	6	9	12	8	3	1
	Goals						1	2			2	3	2	5	3	5	1	2	1	1			8	5	1	1					4	3		

FINAL LEAGUE POSITION: 20th in Division One. Average home League attendance: 24,718.

4 own-goals

FA Cup

No	Round/Date	Opponent	Result	Scorers	Att	Hibbs H	Booton H	Barkas E	Stoker L	Morrall GR	Calladine CF	Grosvenor T	Bradford J	Guest WF	Haywood G	Fillingham T	Horsman W	Roberts F	White F	Robertson J	Clack F
3	Jan 13 (h)	Sheffield U	W 2-1	Robertson, Haywood	33,177	1	2	3	4	5	6			11	9	7		10		8	
4	27 (h)	Charlton A	W 1-0	Morrall	30,203	1	2	3	4	5	6	8		11		7		10		9	
5	Feb 17 (h)	Leicester C	L 1-2	Haywood	48,561		2	3	4	5	6	8			9	7		10	11		1
	Appearances					2	3	3	3	3	3	2		2	2	3		3	1	2	1
	Goals									1					2					1	

1934-35

Manager: George Liddell

#	Date	Venue / Opponent	Result	Scorers	Att.	Hibbs H	Booton H	Barkas E	Stoker L	Morrall GR	Calladine CF	Moffatt S	Harris F	Mangnall D	Bradford J	Guest WF	Hubbard A	Clack F	Jones CW	White F	McGurk FR	Fillingham T	Lea G	Small S	Grosvenor T	Crawshaw R	Holmes H	Horsman W	Roberts F	Dearson D	Devine J	Smith B	Steel W	Morris S
1	Aug 25 (h)	Aston Villa	W 2-1	Harris, Guest	54,200	1	2	4	5	6	7	8	9	10	11	3																		
2	29 (a)	West Brom A	W 2-1	Sandford (og), Bradford	22,025		2	4	5	6	7	8	9	10	11	3	1																	
3	Sep 1 (a)	Stoke C	L 0-2		25,000	1	2	4	5	6	7	8	9		11	3		10																
4	3 (h)	West Brom A	L 1-2	White	25,000	1	2	4	5	6	7	8	9		11	3				10														
5	8 (h)	Manchester C	L 1-3	Mangnall	20,000	1	2	4	5	6		8	9	10		3				11	7													
6	15 (a)	Middlesbrough	W 1-0	Bradford	15,000	1	2		5	6	7	8	9	10	11							3	4											
7	22 (h)	Blackburn R	W 1-0	White	15,000	1	2		5	6	7	8		10	11					9		3	4											
8	29 (a)	Arsenal	L 1-5	White	47,868		2		5	6	7	8		10	11		1			9		3	4											
9	Oct 6 (h)	Portsmouth	W 2-1	Mangnall 2	25,000	1	2	3	4	5	6	7	10	9	11										8									
10	13 (a)	Liverpool	L 4-5	Booton (pen), Mangnall 3	20,000	1	2	3	4	5	6	7	10	9	11										8									
11	20 (a)	Chelsea	L 0-1		20,000	1	2	3	4		6	7	10	9	11									5	8									
12	27 (a)	Wolves	L 1-3	Mangnall	30,000	1	2	3	4	5	6	7	8	10					9	11														
13	Nov 3 (h)	Leicester C	L 2-3	Jones 2	15,000		2	3	4	5	6			10	8		1		9	11								7						
14	10 (a)	Derby C	D 1-1	Guest	20,077	1	2	3	4	5	6			10		11			9						8			7						
15	17 (h)	Grimsby T	W 3-2	Jones 2, Guest	20,000	1	2	3	4	5	10					11			9			6			8			7						
16	24 (a)	Preston NE	W 1-0	Roberts	15,000	1	2	3	4	5	6								9	11					8			7	10					
17	Dec 1 (h)	Tottenham H	W 2-1	Jones, Guest	20,546	1	2	3	4	5	6			10		11			9						8			7						
18	8 (a)	Sunderland	L 1-5	Barkas (pen)	20,000	1	2	3	4	5	6			10		11			9						8			7						
19	15 (h)	Huddersfield T	L 0-4		15,000	1	2	3	4	5	6			10		11			9									7		8				
20	22 (a)	Everton	L 0-2		20,148	1	2	3	4		6			10	8				9	11								7		5				
21	25 (h)	Sheffield W	L 1-2	Mangnall	23,496	1	2	3	4		6			9	10					11								7		5	8			
22	26 (h)	Sheffield W	L 0-4		24,499	1	2		4					10		11			9			3	6					7		5	8			
23	29 (a)	Aston Villa	D 2-2	Mangnall 2	42,000	1	2	3			6	8		9	10	11			7			5	4											
24	Jan 5 (h)	Stoke C	D 0-0		20,000		2	3	4		6		8	9		11	1		7			5									10			
25	19 (a)	Manchester C	D 0-0		25,000	1	2	3	4		6		8	9		11			7			5									10			
26	Feb 2 (a)	Blackburn R	L 1-3	Harris	20,000	1	2				6		8	9		11			7			5	4								10	3		
27	6 (h)	Middlesbrough	W 4-2	Jones 2, White 2	15,000		2	3	4		6		8		10	11	1		9	7		5												
28	9 (h)	Arsenal	W 3-0	Jones, Bradford, Harris	50,188	1	2	3	4				8		10	11			9	7		5								6				
29	23 (h)	Liverpool	L 1-3	Harris	25,000	1	2	3	4		6		8						9	7		5						11			10			
30	Mar 6 (a)	Chelsea	D 2-2	Guest, Harris	18,000	1	2	3	4	5	6		8	9		11			7												10			
31	9 (h)	Wolves	D 1-1	Jones	25,000		2	3	4		6		8			11	1		9	7		5									10			
32	16 (a)	Leicester C	L 1-2	Stoker	20,000		2		4		6		8			11	1		9	7		5									10	3		
33	23 (h)	Derby C	W 3-2	Jones 3	11,627	1		3	4		6	7	8			11			9			5									10	2		
34	30 (a)	Grimsby T	L 3-4	White 2 (1 pen), Bradford	10,000			3	4	5	6		8		10	11	1		9	7													2	
35	Apr 6 (h)	Preston NE	W 3-0	White 3 (1 pen)	18,000			3	4	5	6		8		10		1		9	7													2	11
36	10 (a)	Portsmouth	L 1-2	White	15,000	1		3	4	5			8		10	11			9	7											6	2		
37	13 (a)	Tottenham H	D 1-1	Jones	27,190	1		3	4	5			8		10				9	7												2		11
38	19 (a)	Leeds U	D 1-1	Jones	14,786	1		3	4	5	6		8			11			9	7											10	2		
39	20 (h)	Sunderland	D 2-2	White, Jones	25,000	1	2			5	6					11			9	7			4						8		10	3		
40	22 (h)	Leeds U	W 3-1	Calladine, Harris 2	18,008	1		3			5	6	8			11			9	7			4								10	2		
41	27 (a)	Huddersfield T	D 2-2	Harris 2	10,000	1					6		8			10			9	7		5	4									2		11
42	May 4 (h)	Everton	L 2-3	White, Jones	16,634	1		3	4		6		8			10	11		9	7												2		
		Appearances				33	33	30	37	26	38	10	30	25	15	27	5	9	26	32	1	17	9	2	8	4	1	10	1	4	14	1	11	3
		Goals					1	1	1		1		9	10	4	5			16	13											1			

FINAL LEAGUE POSITION: 19th in Division One. Average home League attendance: 22,795.

1 own-goal

FA Cup

#	Date	Venue / Opponent	Result	Scorers	Att.	Hibbs H	Booton H	Barkas E	Stoker L	Morrall GR	Calladine CF	Moffatt S	Harris F	Mangnall D	Bradford J	Guest WF	Hubbard A	Clack F	Jones CW	White F	Fillingham T	Grosvenor T
3	Jan 12 (h)	Coventry C	W 5-1	Harris 3, Mangnall, Guest	40,349	1	2	3	4		6		8	9	10	11					7	5
4	26 (a)	Southampton	W 3-0	White, Fillingham, Guest	28,291	1	2	3	4		6		8	9	10	11					7	5
5	Feb 21 (a)	Blackburn R	W 2-1	Whiteside (og), White	35,000	1	2	3	4		6		8		10	11			9		7	5
6	Mar 6 (a)	Burnley	L 2-3	Jones, White	47,670	1	2	3	4		6		8		10	11			9		7	5
		Appearances				4	4	4	4		4		4	2	4	4			2		4	4
		Goals											3	1		2			1	3	1	

1 own-goal

1935-36

Manager: George Liddell

#	Date		Opponent	Result	Scorers	Att	Hibbs H	Barkas E	Steel W	Stoker L	Morrall GR	Calladine CF	White F	Harris F	Jones CW	Devine J	Guest WF	Booton H	Morris S	Lea G	Fillingham T	Dearson D	Loughran J	Grosvenor T	Clack F	Hughes WM	Sykes J	Jennings D	Clarke A	Trigg C	Richardson E	Olney JNF	Small F
1	Aug 31	(a)	Wolves	L 1-3	Harris	35,000	1	2	3	4	5	6	7	8	9	10	11																
2	Sep 4	(a)	Leeds U	D 0-0		13,271	1	2	3	4	5	6	7	8	9	10	11																
3	7	(h)	Arsenal	D 1-1	Devine	42,804	1		3	4	5	6	7	8	9	10	11	2															
4	11	(a)	Leeds U	W 2-0	Jones, White	14,298	1		3	4	5	6	7	8	9	10	11	2															
5	14	(a)	Manchester C	L 1-3	Guest	30,000	1		3	4	5	6	7	8	9	10	11	2															
6	18	(a)	West Brom A	D 0-0		18,083	1		3	4	5	6	7	8	9	10	11	2															
7	21	(h)	Stoke C	L 0-5		15,000	1		3	4	5	6	7	8	9	10		2	11														
8	28	(a)	Blackburn R	W 2-1	Jones, Harris	12,000	1	2	3				7	10	9	6	11			4	5	8											
9	Oct 5	(h)	Chelsea	W 2-1	Harris, Craig (og)	20,000	1	2	3	4			7	10	9		11				5		6	8									
10	12	(a)	Liverpool	W 2-1	Harris, Jones	30,000	1	2	3	4			7	10	9		11				5		6	8									
11	19	(a)	Sheffield W	L 1-3	White	13,479	1	2	3	4			7	10	9		11				5		6	8									
12	26	(h)	Portsmouth	W 4-0	White, Harris 2, Jones	30,000	1	2	3	4			7	10	9		11				5		6	8									
13	Nov 2	(a)	Preston NE	L 1-3	Harris	10,000	1	2	3	4			7	10	9		11				5		6	8									
14	9	(h)	Brentford	W 2-1	Jones, Stoker	25,000	1	2	3	4		11	7	10	9	8					5		6										
15	16	(a)	Derby C	D 2-2	Calladine, Harris	23,893	1	2	3	4		11	7	10	9						5		6	8									
16	23	(h)	Aston Villa	D 2-2	Jones 2	60,250	1	3		4			7	10	9		11	2			5		6	8									
17	30	(a)	Bolton W	L 0-2		12,000	1		3	4			7	10	9		11	2			5		6	8									
18	Dec 7	(h)	Huddersfield T	W 4-1	Jones 2, White, Guest	15,000	1	2	3	4			7	10	9		11				5		6	8									
19	14	(a)	Middlesbrough	W 2-0	Jones 2	10,000		2	3	4			7	10	9		11				5		6	8	1								
20	21	(h)	Everton	W 4-2	Jones (og), Harris, White, Loughran	16,994	1	2	3	4			7	10	9		11				5		6	8									
21	25	(a)	Grimsby T	L 0-1		15,000	1	2	3	4			7	10	9	8	11				5		6										
22	26	(h)	Grimsby T	D 1-1	Guest	20,000	1	2	3	4			7	10	9		11				5		6	8									
23	28	(h)	Wolves	D 0-0		35,000	1	2	3	4				10	9		11				5	7	6	8									
24	Jan 4	(a)	Arsenal	D 1-1	Jones	44,534	1	2	3	4				10	9	7	11				5		6	8									
25	18	(h)	Manchester C	L 0-1		20,000	1	2						10	9	8	11				5		6			3	4	7					
26	Feb 1	(h)	Blackburn R	W 4-2	Guest, Harris 2, Jennings	25,000	1	2	3	4				10	9	8	11				5		6					7					
27	6	(a)	Stoke C	L 1-3	Jones	10,000	1	2	3	4				10	9		11				5	8						6	7				
28	8	(a)	Chelsea	D 0-0		30,000	1	2	3	4	5			10	9	8	11											6	7				
29	15	(h)	Liverpool	W 2-0	Jones, Harris	18,000	1	2	3	4	5			10	9	8			11									6	7				
30	29	(a)	Brentford	W 1-0	Harris	20,000	1	2	3	4	5			10	9	8			11									6	7				
31	Mar 7	(h)	Bolton W	D 0-0		12,000	1	2	3	4	5			10	9				11									6	7	8			
32	14	(a)	Portsmouth	W 3-0	Harris, Morris 2	15,000	1	2	3	4				10	9	8			11		5		6					7					
33	21	(h)	Derby C	L 2-3	Jones, Barkas (pen)	25,509	1	2	3	4				10	9	8			11		5		6					7					
34	28	(a)	Aston Villa	L 1-2	Fillingham	50,000	1			4				10	9	8	11				5					3	6	7		2			
35	Apr 4	(h)	Preston NE	D 0-0		15,000				4	5			10		8	11				3				1		6	7	9	2			
36	10	(a)	Sunderland	L 1-2	Harris	41,000	1	2	3	4	5			10	9	8	11										6	7					
37	11	(a)	Huddersfield T	L 0-1		5,000	1		3	4	5			10	9	8											6	7		2			
38	13	(h)	Sunderland	L 2-7	Loughran, Clarke	15,000		2	3	4				10		8			11				6		1		6	7	9				
39	18	(h)	Middlesbrough	W 1-0	Harris	20,000		2	3	4	5			10	9	8			11						1		6	7					
40	22	(h)	Sheffield W	W 4-1	Jones 3, Harris	9,089			3		5			10	9								8	4	1		6	7		2	11		
41	25	(a)	Everton	L 3-4	Jones, Guest, Dearson	18,323		2			5			10	9		11						8	4	1	3	6	7					
42	May 2	(h)	West Brom A	L 1-3	Barkas (pen)	28,124		2		4				10			11				8					1	3	6	7			5	9

FINAL LEAGUE POSITION: 12th in Division One. Average home League attendance: 22,955.

	Hibbs H	Barkas E	Steel W	Stoker L	Morrall GR	Calladine CF	White F	Harris F	Jones CW	Devine J	Guest WF	Booton H	Morris S	Lea G	Fillingham T	Dearson D	Loughran J	Grosvenor T	Clack F	Hughes WM	Sykes J	Jennings D	Clarke A	Trigg C	Richardson E	Olney JNF	Small F
Appearances	35	32	36	38	17	9	22	42	39	24	30	7	9	1	24	6	23	14	7	4	15	18	3	4	1	1	1
Goals		2		1			5	17	19	1	5		2			1	1	2				1	1				

2 own-goals

FA Cup

#	Date		Opponent	Result	Scorers	Att	Barkas E	Steel W	Stoker L	White F	Harris F	Jones CW	Devine J	Guest WF	Fillingham T	Loughran J	Grosvenor T	Clack F	Hughes WM
3	Jan 11	(a)	Barnsley	D 3-3	White, Jones, Harris	29,330	2	3	4	7	10	9	8	11	5	6		1	
R	15	(h)	Barnsley	L 0-2		34,000	2		4	7	10	9		11	5	6	8		3
	Appearances						1	2	1	2	2	2	1	2	2		2	1	1	1
	Goals									1	1	1							

1936-37

Manager: George Liddell

No	Date	Opponent	Res	Scorers	Att	Hibbs H	Trigg C	Steel W	Stoker L	Fillingham T	Sykes J	Jennings D	Dearson D	Jones CW	Harris F	Morris S	Small S	Devine J	Butler H	Barkas E	Clack F	Lea G	Richardson E	White F	Loughran J	Brunskill N	Clarke A	Guest WF	Olney JF	Beattie JM	Kendrick K	Richards D	Hughes WM	Sykes EA
1	Aug 29 (h)	Portsmouth	W 2-1	Dearson, Morris	30,000	1	2	3	4	5	6	7	8	9	10	11																		
2	Sep 2 (a)	West Brom A	L 2-3	Morris, Jones	26,013	1	2	3	4	5	6	7	8	9	10	11																		
3	5 (a)	Chelsea	W 3-1	Morris, Harris, Dearson	30,000	1	2	3	4	5	6	7	8		10	11	9																	
4	9 (h)	West Brom A	D 1-1	Harris	34,135	1	2	3		5	6	7	8		10	11	9	4																
5	12 (h)	Stoke C	L 2-4	Jennings, Harris	10,000	1	2	3			6	7	8	9	10	11		4	5															
6	16 (h)	Manchester C	D 1-1	Morris	20,000	1	2				6	7	8	9	10	11		4	5	3														
7	19 (a)	Charlton A	D 2-2	Jones, Morris	35,000	1	2				6	7	8	9	10	11		4	5	3														
8	26 (h)	Grimsby T	L 2-3	Jones, Harris	20,000		2				6	7	8	9	10	11		4		3	1	5												
9	Oct 3 (a)	Liverpool	L 0-2		25,000	1	2		4	5			8	9	10	11		6		3				7										
10	10 (h)	Leeds U	W 2-1	Jones, Harris	23,833	1	2		4	5			8	9	10	11		6		3				7										
11	17 (h)	Huddersfield T	W 4-2	Fillingham, Jones, White 2 (1 pen)	26,172	1	2		4	5		11		9	10					3				7	6	8								
12	24 (a)	Everton	D 3-3	Brunskill, Harris, Morris	26,995	1	2	3	4					9	10	11						5		7	6	8								
13	31 (h)	Bolton W	D 1-1	Morris	25,000	1	2	3	4	5				9	10	11								7	6	8								
14	Nov 7 (a)	Brentford	L 1-2	Dearson	25,000	1	2	3		5			8	9	10	11		4						7	6									
15	14 (h)	Arsenal	L 1-3	Devine	39,940	1	2	3	4	5			8	9		11		10						7	6									
16	21 (a)	Preston NE	D 2-2	White 2 (1 pen)	15,000	1	2	3	4	5	6		8	9	10	11								7										
17	28 (a)	Sheffield W	D 1-1	Millership (og)	17,993	1	2	3	4	5	6		8	9	10	11								7										
18	Dec 5 (a)	Manchester U	W 2-1	White, Jones	16,544	1	2		4	5	6		8	9		11				3				7	10									
19	12 (h)	Derby C	L 0-1		8,892	1	2		4	5	6		8	9		11				3				7	10									
20	19 (a)	Wolves	L 1-2	Clarke	15,000	1	2		4		6		8	9		11				3	5			7	10									
21	25 (h)	Sunderland	W 2-0	Harris, Jones	15,000	1	2		4		6		8	9	10					3	5			7			11							
22	26 (h)	Portsmouth	L 1-2	Jones	33,000	1	2		4		6		8	9	10	11				3	5			7										
23	28 (a)	Sunderland	L 0-4		15,000	1	2		4	5	6		8	9	10	11				3				7										
24	Jan 2 (h)	Chelsea	D 0-0		16,000	1	2	3		5			10	9			8							7	6	4	11							
25	9 (a)	Stoke C	L 0-2		15,000		2			5	6					8				3	1	4		7	10	9	11							
26	23 (h)	Charlton A	L 1-2	White	15,000	1	2		4						10	11				3				7	6			5	8	9				
27	Feb 2 (a)	Grimsby T	D 1-1	Harris	6,000	1	2			5		8			10	11				3				7		4				9				
28	6 (h)	Liverpool	W 5-0	Morris, Beattie, Jennings, Harris, White	20,000	1	2			5		8			10	11				3				7		4				9				
29	13 (a)	Leeds U	W 2-0	Beattie, Morris	13,674	1	2			5		8			10	11				3				7		4				9				
30	20 (a)	Huddersfield T	D 1-1	Beattie	10,000	1	2			5		8			10	11				3				7		4				9				
31	27 (h)	Everton	W 2-0	Beattie, White	21,150	1	2	3		5		8			10	11				3				7		4				9				
32	Mar 6 (a)	Bolton W	D 0-0		15,000	1	2	3		5		8			10	11				3				7		4				9				
33	13 (h)	Brentford	W 4-0	Morris 2, White, Harris	25,000	1	2			5		8			10	11				3				7		4				9		6		
34	20 (a)	Arsenal	D 1-1	Beattie	46,086	1	2			5					10			8		3				7		4	11			9		6		
35	26 (a)	Middlesbrough	L 1-3	Clarke	10,000	1	2			5		8			10					3		7				4	11			9		6		
36	27 (h)	Preston NE	W 1-0	Harris	33,828	1	2			5		7	8		10											4	11			9		6	3	
37	29 (h)	Middlesbrough	D 0-0		15,000	1	2			5		7	8		10	11										4				9		6	3	
38	Apr 3 (a)	Sheffield W	W 3-0	Morris 2, Richards	20,804	1	2			5		8			10	11								7		4				9		6	3	
39	10 (h)	Manchester U	D 2-2	Clarke, Beattie	19,130							8			10	11							1			4	7	5		9		6	3	2
40	17 (a)	Derby C	L 1-3	Morris	10,802	1	2			5		8			10	11										4	7			9		6	3	
41	24 (h)	Wolves	W 1-0	Jennings (pen)	30,000	1		2		5		8				11		6		3				7		4	10			9				
42	May 1 (h)	Manchester C	D 2-2	Morris, Clarke	25,000	1		2	6	5		8				11				3				7		4	10			9			3	
					Appearances	39	38	17	19	32	17	25	22	22	35	35	3	17	3	22	3	6	2	27	8	21	11	3	2	17	1	8	6	1
					Goals					1		3	3	8	11	15		1						9	1		4			6		1		

FINAL LEAGUE POSITION: 12th in Division One. Average home League attendance: 22,432.

1 own-goal

FA Cup

Rd	Date	Opponent	Res	Scorers	Att	Hibbs H	Trigg C	Steel W	Stoker L	Fillingham T	Sykes J	Jennings D	Dearson D	Jones CW	Harris F	Morris S	Small S	Devine J	Butler H	Barkas E	Clack F	Lea G	Richardson E	White F	Loughran J	Brunskill N	Clarke A	Guest WF	Olney JF	Beattie JM	Kendrick K	Richards D	Hughes WM	Sykes EA
3	Jan 16 (a)	Stoke C	L 1-4	Morris	26,155	1	2				6	7			10	11				3	5			9	4	8								
					Appearances	1	1				1	1			1	1				1	1			1	1	1								
					Goals											1																		

1937-38

Manager: George Liddell

FINAL LEAGUE POSITION: 18th in Division One. Average home League attendance: 25,452.

No	Date	Opponent	Res	Scorers	Att	Hibbs H	Trigg C	Hughes WM	Brunskill N	Fillingham T	Richards D	White F	Jennings D	Beattie JM	Dearson D	Morris S	Clarke A	Clack F	Jones CW	Steel W	Shaw R	Stoker L	Kendrick K	Bellamy SC	Harris F	Butler H	Kelly J	Madden O	Phillips C	Parr H
1	Aug 28	(a) Stoke C	D 2-2	Richards, Morris	30,000	1	2	3	4	5	6	7	8	9	10	11														
2	Sep 1	(h) Middlesbrough	W 3-1	Beattie 3	30,000	1	2	3	4	5	6	7	8	9	10	11														
3	Sep 4	(h) Portsmouth	D 2-2	Morris, White	40,000	1	2	3	4	5	6	7	8	9		11	10													
4	Sep 8	(a) Middlesbrough	D 1-1	Jones	15,000		2	3	4	5	6	7	8		10		11	1	9											
5	Sep 11	(a) Chelsea	L 0-2		35,000		2	3	4	5	6	7	8	9		11		1	10											
6	Sep 15	(h) Leicester C	W 4-1	Jones 3, White	25,000	1	2		4	5	6	7		8	10	11			9	3										
7	Sep 18	(h) Charlton A	D 1-1	Jones	35,000	1	2		4	5	6	7		8	10	11			9	3										
8	Sep 25	(a) Preston NE	L 1-2	White	25,000	1	2		4	5	6	7		8	10	11				3	9									
9	Oct 2	(h) Grimsby T	D 2-2	Jones, Morris	30,000	1		3	4	5	6	7		8		11	10		9	2										
10	Oct 9	(a) Leeds U	L 0-1		20,698	1	2	3	4	5	6	7		8		11	10		9											
11	Oct 16	(a) Sunderland	L 0-1		18,000	1	2	3	4	5	6	10	7	8		11			9											
12	Oct 23	(h) Derby C	W 1-0	Brunskill	23,992	1	2	3	4	5	6	10	8	9		11	7													
13	Oct 30	(a) Manchester C	L 0-2		20,000	1	2		4	5		7	11	9	8		10			3		6								
14	Nov 6	(h) Huddersfield T	D 2-2	Dearson 2	25,000	1	2	3	4	5	6	7		10	8	11			9											
15	Nov 13	(a) Blackpool	W 3-0	Clarke 2, Morris	12,000	1		3	4	5	6			8	10	11	7		9	2										
16	Nov 20	(h) Wolves	W 2-0	Dearson, Kendrick	40,000		2	3	4	5	6			8	10	11	7	1	9											
17	Nov 27	(a) Bolton W	D 1-1	Clarke	20,000		2	3	4		6			8	10	11	7	1				4	9							
18	Dec 4	(h) Arsenal	L 1-2	Morris	18,440	1	2	3	4	5	6			8	10	11	7		9											
19	Dec 11	(a) Everton	D 1-1	Morris	17,018	1	2	3	4	5	6			9	8	11	7								10					
20	Dec 18	(h) Brentford	D 0-0		20,000	1	2	3	4	5	6				8	11	7		9						10					
21	Dec 27	(h) Liverpool	D 2-2	Morris, Kendrick	35,000	1	2	3	4	5	6				8	11	7		9						10					
22	Jan 1	(h) Stoke C	D 1-1	Jones	25,000	1	2	3	4		6	7	11	8					9						10	5				
23	Jan 15	(a) Portsmouth	D 1-1	Beattie	20,000	1	2	3	4		6		11		10		7		9						5					
24	Jan 22	(h) Chelsea	D 1-1	Jones	15,000	1	2	3	4		6		11		10		7		9							5	8			
25	Jan 29	(a) Charlton A	L 0-2		20,000		2	3	4	5	6		11		10		7	1	9								8			
26	Feb 5	(h) Preston NE	L 0-2		25,000	1	2	3	4		6	7			10				9						5		8		11	
27	Feb 12	(a) Grimsby T	L 0-4		10,000	1	2	3			6	7			10				9			4			8	5	11			
28	Feb 19	(h) Leeds U	W 3-2	Dearson 2, White (pen)	20,403	1	2	3		5	6	7			8							4			10			9	11	
29	Feb 26	(h) Sunderland	D 2-2	Madden, Harris	25,000	1	2	3		5	6	7			8							4			10			9	11	
30	Mar 5	(a) Derby C	D 0-0		14,533	1	2	3		5	6	7			8							4			10			9	11	
31	Mar 12	(h) Manchester C	D 2-2	Harris 2	25,000	1	2	3		5	6	7			8	11						4			10			9		
32	Mar 19	(a) Huddersfield T	L 1-2	Dearson	12,000	1		3		5	6	7	8		10					2		4						9		11
33	Mar 26	(h) Blackpool	D 1-1	Harris	9,440			3	4	5	6	7	8		11					2		4			10			9		
34	Apr 2	(a) Wolves	L 2-3	Jones, Phillips	30,000			3	4	5	6	11			8			1	9	2					10				7	
35	Apr 6	(a) Liverpool	L 2-3	Harris, Jennings	15,000			3		5		11	6		8			1	9	2		4			10				7	
36	Apr 9	(h) Bolton W	W 2-0	Harris, Phillips	20,000	1		3		5		11	6		8				9	2		4			10				7	
37	Apr 15	(h) West Brom A	W 2-1	Dearson 2	25,008	1	2			5	11		7	6	8					3		4			10				9	
38	Apr 16	(a) Arsenal	D 0-0		35,161	1	2			5	9		11	6	8		7			3		4			10					
39	Apr 18	(a) West Brom A	L 3-4	Jennings, Phillips 2	34,406	1	2			5	6	7	4		8					3					10			11	9	
40	Apr 23	(h) Everton	L 0-3		22,224	1	2			5			7	6	8					3					10			11	9	4
41	Apr 30	(a) Brentford	W 2-1	Harris, Jennings (pen)	25,000	1	2			5		6	11	4	8				9	3					10				7	
42	May 7	(a) Leicester C	W 4-1	Dearson, Clarke, White 2	15,000	1	2			5		11	4		8		7		9	3	6				10					
		Appearances				34	35	32	35	31	35	35	18	19	35	22	17	8	18	16	2	13	7	1	19	5	8	7	9	1
		Goals							1		1	6	3	4	9	7	4		9	2					7			1	4	

FA Cup

No	Date	Opponent	Res	Att	Hibbs H	Trigg C	Hughes WM	Brunskill N	Fillingham T	Richards D	White F	Jennings D	Beattie JM	Dearson D	Morris S	Clarke A	Clack F	Jones CW	Steel W	Shaw R	Stoker L	Kendrick K	Bellamy SC	Harris F	Butler H	Kelly J	Madden O	Phillips C	Parr H
3	Jan 8	(h) Blackpool	L 0-1	40,321	1	2	3	4		6	7	11		8				9						10	5				
		Appearances			1	1	1	1		1	1	1		1				1						1	1				
		Goals																											

1938-39

Manager: George Liddell

No	Date	Opponent	Result	Scorers	Att	Hibbs H	Trigg C	Steel W	Jennings D	Meacock RW	Halsall WG	Phillips C	Dearson D	Moreland G	Harris F	Morris S	Hughes WM	Brunskill N	Brown J	Jones CW	Kelly J	Farrage TO	Richards D	White F	Duckhouse E	Madden O	Wheeler WJ	Shaw R	Clack F	Butler H	Craven C	Sykes EA	Bye J	Turner A	Bodle H	Shaw J	Kendrick K
1	Aug 27	(h) Sunderland	L 1-2	Jennings (pen)	25,000	1	2	3	4	5	6	7	8	9	10	11																					
2	31	(a) Leeds U	L 0-2		13,578	1	2	3	4	5	6	7	8	9	10	11																					
3	Sep 3	(a) Manchester U	L 1-4	Harris	22,228	1	2	3	4	5	6	7	8	9	10	11																					
4	7	(h) Leicester C	W 2-1	Kelly, Jones	25,000	1		2		5	6		8				3	4		9	10	11		7													
5	10	(h) Stoke C	L 1-2	Harris	30,000	1		2		5			6		8		3	4	7	9	10	11															
6	12	(a) Leicester C	L 1-2	Farrage	9,000	1		2		5			6		8		3	4	7	9		11		10													
7	17	(a) Chelsea	D 2-2	Brown (pen), Jones	38,000	1		2		5	6		8				3	4	7	9	10	11															
8	24	(h) Preston NE	L 1-3	Farrage	20,000	1		2		5	6		8				3	4	7	9	10	11															
9	Oct 1	(a) Charlton A	D 4-4	Harris 2, Duckhouse, White	20,000	1	2						4		8		3	5	11				6	7	9	10											
10	8	(h) Bolton W	L 0-2		25,000		2				5		4		8		3			9		11	6	7			1	10									
11	15	(h) Derby C	W 3-0	White 2, Brown	27,858		2		8		5	9	4		10		3		11				6	7					1								
12	22	(a) Grimsby T	L 0-1		12,000		2	3	8		5	9	6		10			4	11					7					1								
13	29	(h) Aston Villa	W 3-0	Harris 2, Brown	55,301		2		8		5	9	4		10		3		11				6	7					1								
14	Nov 5	(a) Wolves	L 1-2	Phillips	25,000		2		8	5		9	4		10		3		11				6	7					1								
15	12	(h) Everton	W 1-0	Phillips	27,548		2		7		5	9	4		10		3		11	8			6						1								
16	19	(a) Huddersfield T	L 1-3	Morris	12,000		2		8			9	4		10	11	3						6	7					1	5							
17	26	(h) Portsmouth	W 2-0	Jennings (pen), Dearson	18,862		2		8				4	9	10		3		11				6	7					1	5							
18	Dec 3	(a) Arsenal	L 1-3	Jennings (pen)	33,710		2		8		5		4		10		3		11	9			6	7					1								
19	10	(h) Brentford	W 5-1	White 4, Phillips	25,000		2				5	9	4		10		3		11				6	7					1		8						
20	17	(a) Blackpool	L 1-2	White	10,000		2	3			5	9	4		10				11				6	7					1		8						
21	24	(a) Sunderland	L 0-1		12,000		2		7		5	9	4		10		3		11				6						1		8						
22	26	(h) Middlesbrough	W 2-1	Morris, Trigg	22,000		2			5			4			7	3		11				6		9	10			1		8						
23	27	(a) Middlesbrough	D 2-2	Harris, Phillips	33,000					5		8	4		10		3		7				6		9				1		11	2					
24	31	(h) Manchester U	D 3-3	Jennings, Phillips, Dearson	20,787			3	7	5		9	4		10				11				6						1		8	2					
25	Jan 14	(a) Stoke C	L 3-6	Jennings (pen), Harris, Duckhouse	18,000				7	5			4		10		3		11						9			6	1		8	2					
26	28	(a) Preston NE	L 0-5		15,000				7		5						3		11	9						10		6	1		8	2	4				
27	Feb 4	(h) Charlton A	L 3-4	Harris 3	30,000		2		7		4	9	8		10		3		11									6	1					5			
28	18	(a) Derby C	W 1-0	Brown	15,411		2		7		5		4		9		3		11				6			10			1		8						
29	22	(a) Bolton W	L 0-3		10,000		2		4		5				9	11	3		7				6			10			1		8						
30	25	(h) Grimsby T	D 1-1	Craven	25,000		2		4		5				9	11	3		7				6						1		8				10		
31	Mar 4	(a) Aston Villa	L 1-5	Dearson	40,874		2		7		5		4		10		3		11	9									1		8					6	
32	11	(h) Wolves	W 3-2	Harris, Morris, Jones	45,000		2		8				4		10	11	3		7	9									1					5		6	
33	18	(a) Everton	L 2-4	Harris, Jones	29,687		2		8				4		10	11	3		7	9									1					5		6	
34	29	(h) Huddersfield T	D 1-1	Jones	12,000		2		8				4		10		3		7	9		11							1					5		6	
35	Apr 1	(a) Portsmouth	L 0-2		20,000				7				8		10	11	3			9			6				1					2		5		4	
36	7	(a) Liverpool	L 0-4		30,000				8				4		10		3		11	9							1					2		5		6	7
37	8	(h) Arsenal	L 1-2	Kendrick	33,250								4		10		3		11	9							1				8	2		5		6	7
38	10	(h) Liverpool	D 0-0		20,000		2		8				4		10	11	3		7	9							1							5		6	
39	15	(a) Brentford	W 1-0	Jones	18,000	1	2		7				4		10		3		11	9											8			5		6	
40	22	(h) Blackpool	W 2-1	Craven, Harris	25,000	1	2		7				4		10	11	3			9											8			5		6	
41	26	(h) Chelsea	D 1-1	Brown	30,000	1	2						4		10	11	3		7	9											8			5		6	
42	29	(h) Leeds U	W 4-0	Brown, Scaife (og), Morris 2	12,522	1	2		3				4		10	11			7	9								6			8			5			
					Appearances	13	30	12	29	13	21	15	39	4	37	14	34	7	34	21	4	7	19	13	4	5	5	5	24	2	17	7	1	12	1	11	2
					Goals		1		5			5	3		14	5			6	6	1	2		8	2						2						1

FINAL LEAGUE POSITION: 21st in Division One. Average home League attendance: 26,434.

1 own-goal

FA Cup

Rd	Date	Opponent	Result	Scorers	Att	Hibbs H	Trigg C	Steel W	Jennings D	Meacock RW	Halsall WG	Phillips C	Dearson D	Moreland G	Harris F	Morris S	Hughes WM	Brunskill N	Brown J	Jones CW	Kelly J	Farrage TO	Richards D	White F	Duckhouse E	Madden O	Wheeler WJ	Shaw R	Clack F	Butler H	Craven C	Sykes EA	Bye J	Turner A	Bodle H	Shaw J	Kendrick K
3	Jan 7	(h) Halifax T	W 2-0	Jennings, Phillips	23,522				7	5		9			10		3		11				6						1		8	2	4				
4	21	(h) Chelmsford C	W 6-0	Harris 2, Brown, Jennings, Madden 2	44,494				7	5			4		9		3		11							10		6	1		8	2					
5	Feb 11	(h) Everton	D 2-2	Madden 2	67,341		2		7		5		4		9		3		11				6			10			1		8						
R	15	(a) Everton	L 1-2	Harris	64,796		2		7		5		4		9		3		11				6			10			1		8						
					Appearances		2		4	2	2	1	3		4		4		4				3			3		1	4		4	2	1				
					Goals				2			1			3				1							4											

1946-47

Manager: Harry Storer

#		Date / Opponent	Result	Scorers	Att.	Merrick G	Dearson D	Hughes W	Harris F	Duckhouse E	Mitchell F	Mulraney A	Dougall N	Jones CW	Bodle H	Edwards G	Owen S	Massart D	Jennings D	Turner A	Trigg C	Goodwin JW	Devey R	Shaw R	Dorman D	McIntosh A	Hall F	Pimbley D	Wheeler WJ	Faulkner KG
1	Aug 31 (a)	Tottenham H	W 2-1	Jones 2	51,256	1	2	3	4	5	6	7	8	9	10	11														
2	Sep 4 (h)	Leicester C	W 4-0	Jones 2, Mulraney, Dougall	35,000	1	2	3		5	6	7	8	9	10	11	4													
3	7 (h)	Burnley	L 0-2		53,000	1	2	3		5	6	7	8		10	11	4	9												
4	12 (a)	Leicester C	L 1-2	Mulraney	20,000	1				2	6	7	8	9	10	11	4			3	5									
5	14 (a)	Barnsley	L 1-3	Mulraney	28,000	1	4	3		9	6	7	8		10	11					5	2								
6	18 (a)	West Brom A	L 0-3		42,031	1	2	3			6	7		9	10	11	4				5	8								
7	21 (h)	Newport C	D 1-1	Bodle	20,000	1	2	3			6	7		9	10	11	4					8	5							
8	25 (h)	West Brom A	W 1-0	Dearson	50,535	1	4	3		2	6		8	9	10	11					5	7								
9	28 (a)	Southampton	L 0-1		24,920	1	4	3			6		8	9	10	11					5	2	7							
10	Oct 5 (h)	Nottingham F	W 4-0	Bodle, Trigg, Edwards 2	35,000	1	2	3			6	7	8		10	11					5	9		4						
11	12 (a)	Coventry C	D 0-0		35,000	1	2	3			6		8		10	11					5	9	9	7	4					
12	19 (a)	Chesterfield	W 1-0	Jones	15,000	1		3			6		8	9	10	11		9			5	2	7	4						
13	26 (h)	Millwall	W 4-0	Bodle, Trigg 2, Dougall	25,000	1	2	3			6	7	8		10	11					5	9		4						
14	Nov 2 (a)	Bradford	L 0-2		21,638	1	2	3			6	11	8		10						5	9	7	4						
15	9 (h)	Manchester C	W 3-1	Dougall, Mulraney, Trigg	30,000	1	2	3	4		6	7	8		10	11					5	9								
16	16 (a)	West Ham U	W 4-0	Bodle, Edwards 2, Trigg	25,000	1	2	3	4		6	7	8		10	11					5	9								
17	23 (h)	Sheffield W	W 3-1	Trigg 2, Dougall	32,425	1	2	3	4		6	7	8		10	11					5	9								
18	30 (a)	Fulham	W 1-0	Trigg	25,000	1	2	3	4		6	7	8		10	11					5	9								
19	Dec 7 (h)	Bury	W 3-0	Duckhouse, Dougall, Edwards	20,000	1	2	3	4	9	6	7	8		10	11					5									
20	14 (h)	Luton T	W 3-1	Trigg 3	25,000	1	2	3	4		6	7	8		10	11					5	9								
21	21 (a)	Plymouth A	W 6-1	Bodle 3, Mulraney 2, Edwards	26,000	1		3	4	2	6	7	8		10	11					5	9								
22	25 (h)	Swansea T	W 3-1	Dougall, Bodle, Feeney (og)	33,000	1		3	4	2	6	7	8		10	11					5	9								
23	26 (a)	Swansea T	L 0-1		20,000	1		3	4		6	7	8		10	11			2		5	9								
24	28 (h)	Tottenham H	W 1-0	Mulraney	44,171	1	2		4		6	7	8		10	11			3		5	9								
25	Jan 4 (a)	Burnley	L 0-1		45,000	1	2		4		6	7	8			11			3		5	9				10				
26	18 (h)	Barnsley	L 1-2	Duckhouse	35,000	1	6		4	9		7			10				3		5	2				8				
27	Feb 1 (h)	Southampton	W 3-1	Trigg 2, Mulraney	32,878	1			4	2	6	7			10	11			3		5	9				8				
28	15 (h)	Coventry C	W 2-0	Trigg 2	30,000	1			4	2	6	7	8		10	11			3		5	9								
29	22 (h)	Chesterfield	D 0-0		27,000	1			4	2	6		8		10	11			3		5	9	7							
30	Mar 15 (a)	Manchester C	L 0-1		59,535	1		3	4	9	6	7	8			11			2		5					10				
31	22 (h)	West Ham U	W 3-0	McIntosh, Mitchell (pen), Trigg	26,629	1		3	4	5	6	7	8			11			2			9				10				
32	29 (a)	Sheffield W	L 0-1		27,500	1		3	4	5	6	7	8			11			2			9				10				
33	Apr 4 (a)	Newcastle U	D 2-2	McIntosh, Bodle	57,259	1		3	4	5	6	7			10	11	9		2							8				
34	5 (h)	Fulham	W 2-1	Hall, Goodwin	30,000	1		3	4	5	6				10	11			2			7				8	9			
35	7 (h)	Newcastle U	W 2-0	Bodle, Trigg	43,000	1		3	4	5	6				10				2			7				8	9	11		
36	12 (a)	Bury	L 0-2		18,882	1		3	4	5	6				10				2			7				8	9	11		
37	19 (h)	Luton T	W 1-0	Goodwin	30,000	1		3	4		6			9	10	11			2		5	7				8				
38	26 (a)	Plymouth A	W 2-0	Edwards, Bodle	25,000	1		3	4	5	6			9	10	11			2			7				8				
39	May 3 (h)	Bradford	W 4-0	Dougall, Bodle 2, Mitchell (pen)	23,083	1		3	4	5	6			9	10	11			2			7				8				
40	10 (a)	Nottingham F	D 1-1	Harris	14,000	1			4	5	6			9	10	11			3			2			7	8				
41	17 (a)	Millwall	W 2-0	McIntosh, Dougall	15,000	1			4	5	6			9	10	11			3			2				8			1	7
42	26 (a)	Newport C	W 3-0	Bodle 2, Dougall	14,000	1			4	5	6			9	10	11			3			2				8				7
		Appearances				41	25	28	29	25	41	27	35	9	36	39	5	3	18	27	29	15	1	5	2	14	3	2	1	2
		Goals					1		1	2	2	8	9	5	15	7					17	2				3	1			

FINAL LEAGUE POSITION: 3rd in Division Two. Average home League attendance: 32,462.

1 own-goal

FA Cup

Rd	Date / Opponent	Result	Scorers	Att.	Merrick G	Dearson D	Hughes W	Harris F	Duckhouse E	Mitchell F	Mulraney A	Dougall N	Jones CW	Bodle H	Edwards G	Jennings D	Turner A	Trigg C	Goodwin JW	Dorman D
3	Jan 11 (a) Fulham	W 2-1	Jones, Dorman	30,000	1	6		4	9		7			10	11	3	5	2		8
4	25 (h) Portsmouth	W 1-0	Harris	30,000	1	6		4	2		7	8		10	11	3	5	9		
5	Feb 8 (h) Manchester C	W 5-0	Bodle, Trigg 2, Mitchell (pen), Mulraney	50,000	1			4	2	6	7	8		10	11	3	5	9		
6	Mar 1 (a) Liverpool	L 1-4	Mitchell (pen)	51,911	1			4	2	6	7	8		10	11	3	5	9		
	Appearances				4	2		4	4	2	4	3	1	3	4	4	4	4		1
	Goals					1		2	1		1	1			2			1		

1947-48

Manager: Harry Storer

Player columns (left to right): Merrick G, Trigg C, Southam JH, Harris F, Duckhouse E, Mitchell F, Goodwin JW, McIntosh A, Dougall N, Bodle H, Edwards G, Quinton W, Aveyard W, McDonnell M, Hughes JN, Green K, Berry J, Jennings D, Ottewell S, Garrett AC, Wheeler WJ, Stewart JG, Dorman D, Laing R, Badham J

#	Date	Venue / Opponent	Result	Scorers	Att	Mer	Tri	Sou	Har	Duc	Mit	Goo	McI	Dou	Bod	Edw	Qui	Ave	McD	Hug	Gre	Ber	Jen	Ott	Gar	Whe	Ste	Dor	Lai	Bad
1	Aug 23	(h) Barnsley	L 2-3	Bodle, Mitchell (pen)	39,000	1	2	3	4	5	6	7	8	9	10	11														
2		(a) Coventry C	W 1-0	Aveyard	30,000	1	2		4	5	6	7		8	10	11	3	9												
3	30	(a) Plymouth A	W 3-0	Dougall, Bodle, Aveyard	20,000	1	2		4	5	6	7		8	10	11	3	9												
4	Sep 3	(h) Coventry C	D 1-1	Bodle	30,000	1	2		4	5	6	7		8	10	11	3	9												
5	6	(h) Luton T	W 2-1	Bodle, Aveyard	25,000	1	2		4		6			8	10	11	3	9	5	7										
6	10	(h) Newcastle U	D 0-0		35,000	1	2		4		6			8	10	11	3	9	5	7										
7	13	(a) Brentford	W 2-1	Trigg, Edwards	10,000	1	9		4		6			8	10	11	3		5	7	2									
8	17	(a) Newcastle U	L 0-1		51,704	1	9		4		6			8	10	11	3		5		2	7								
9	20	(h) Leicester C	W 1-0	Dougall	30,000	1			4		6			8	10	11	3	9	5		2	7								
10	27	(a) Leeds U	W 1-0	Trigg	37,135	1	9		4	2	6	7	8		10	11			5		3									
11	Oct 4	(h) Fulham	W 3-1	Bodle, Trigg 2	40,000	1	9		4	2	6	8	7		10	11			5		3									
12	11	(h) Chesterfield	D 0-0		30,000	1			4	5	6	8	7		10	11		9			2		3							
13	18	(a) West Ham U	D 0-0		32,000	1			4	2	6	8		9	10	11			5		3	7								
14	25	(h) Bury	W 2-0	Bodle, Dougall	35,000	1	9		4	2	6	7		8	10	11			5				3							
15	Nov 1	(a) Southampton	L 0-2		27,000	1			4		6	7	9	8	10	11			5		2		3							
16	8	(h) Doncaster R	W 3-0	Goodwin 2, Bodle	25,000	1			4			7	9	8	10	11			5		2		3	6						
17	15	(a) Nottingham F	W 2-0	McIntosh, Goodwin	30,000	1			4		6	7	10	9		11			5		2		3	8						
18	22	(h) Bradford	W 4-3	Ottewell 2, Goodwin, Mitchell (pen)	29,020	1			4		6	7	10	9		11			5		2		3	8						
19	29	(a) Cardiff C	L 0-2		35,000	1	2		4	5	6	7	9	8		11							3	10						
20	Dec 6	(h) Sheffield W	W 1-0	Westlake (og)	31,217				4	5	6	7		8	10	11					2		3		9	1				
21	13	(a) Tottenham H	W 2-1	Garrett, Dougall	53,730				4	5	6	7		8	10	11					2		3		9	1				
22	20	(h) Barnsley	W 1-0	Bodle	20,000				4	5	6	7		8	10	11					2		3		9	1				
23	25	(a) Millwall	D 0-0		25,560				4	5	6	7		8	10	11					2		3		9	1				
24	27	(h) Millwall	W 1-0	Goodwin	46,000				4	5	6	7		8	10	11					2		3		9	1				
25	Jan 3	(h) Plymouth A	D 1-1	Goodwin	36,000				4	5	6	7		8	10	11					2		3		9	1				
26	17	(a) Luton T	W 1-0	Bodle	20,000	1	9		4	5	6			8	10	11					2		3				7			
27	31	(h) Brentford	D 0-0		37,000	1	9		4	5	6				10	11					2		3				7	8		
28	Feb 14	(h) Leeds U	W 5-1	Laing 2, Stewart 2, Dorman	39,955	1	9		4	5	6				10						2		3				7	8	11	
29	21	(a) Fulham	D 1-1	Bodle	13,000	1	9		4	5	6				10						2		3				7	8	11	
30	28	(a) Chesterfield	W 3-0	Stewart, Dougall, Bodle	10,000	1				5	6			9	10						2		3				7	8	11	4
31	Mar 6	(h) West Ham U	L 0-1		44,000	1				5	6			9	10						2		3				7	8	11	4
32	13	(a) Bury	D 1-1	Edwards	23,420	1			4	5	6			8	10	11					2		3		9		7			
33	20	(h) Southampton	D 0-0		42,000	1			4	5	6			8	10	11					2		3		9		7			
34	27	(a) Doncaster R	D 0-0		25,000	1	9		4	5	6				10	11					2		3				7	8		
35	29	(h) West Brom A	W 4-0	Stewart 2, Bodle, Trigg	43,168	1	9		4	5	6				10	11					2		3				7	8		
36	30	(a) West Brom A	D 1-1	Bodle	51,945	1	9		4	5	6				10	11					2		3				7	8		
37	Apr 3	(h) Nottingham F	W 2-1	Stewart, Mitchell (pen)	40,000	1	9		4	5	6			8	10	11					2		3				7			
38	10	(a) Bradford	W 2-1	Mitchell (pen), Stewart	16,782	1	9		4	5	6			8	10	11					2		3				7			
39	17	(h) Cardiff C	W 2-0	Trigg, Bodle	52,880	1	9		4	5	6			8	10	11					2		3				7			
40	19	(a) Leicester C	D 0-0		20,000	1	9		4	5	6			8	10	11					2		3				7			
41	24	(a) Sheffield W	D 0-0		25,990	1	9		4	5	6			8	10	11					2		3				7			
42	May 1	(h) Tottenham H	D 0-0		35,569	1	9		4	5	6			8	10	11					2		3				7			
		Appearances				36	25	1	40	36	41	16	9	34	39	37	8	7	13	3	35	3	29	5	8	6	17	8	4	2
		Goals					6				4	6	1	5	14	2		3						2	1		7	1	2	

FINAL LEAGUE POSITION: 1st in Division Two. Average home League attendance: 36,467.

1 own-goal

FA Cup

Rd	Date	Venue / Opponent	Result	Att	Mer	Tri	Sou	Har	Duc	Mit	Goo	McI	Dou	Bod	Edw	Qui	Ave	McD	Hug	Gre	Ber	Jen	Ott	Gar	Whe	Ste	Dor	Lai	Bad
3	Jan 10	(h) Notts C	L 0-2	53,000	1	9		6	5	10	7		8		11					2		3						4	
		Appearances			1	1		1	1	1	1		1		1					1		1						1	
		Goals																											

1948-49

Manager: Harry Storer until November 1948 then Bob Brocklebank from January 1949

#	Date	Opponent	Result	Scorers	Att	Merrick G	Green K	Jennings D	Harris F	Duckhouse E	Badham J	Stewart JG	Dougall N	Trigg C	Bodle H	Edwards G	Garrett AC	McKee F	Hughes J	Laing R	Mitchell FR	Dorman D	McDonnell M	Slater F	Hall F	Roberts H	Berry J	Goodwin JW	Boyd L	Evans H	Dailey J	Ferris R	Jordan JW	Robertson W	Quinton W	Southam WJH
1	Aug 22 (a)	Wolves	D 2-2	Bodle, Trigg	54,361	1	2	3	4	5	6	7	8	9	10	11																				
2	25 (h)	Middlesbrough	D 0-0		37,000	1	2	3	4	5	6	7	8	9	10	11																				
3	28 (h)	Chelsea	W 1-0	Stewart	48,000	1	2	3	4	5	6	7	8	9	10	11																				
4	Sep 1 (a)	Middlesbrough	D 1-1	Garrett	37,000	1	2	3	4	5	6	7	8	9		11	10																			
5	4 (a)	Everton	W 5-0	Trigg 2, Stewart 2, Garrett	49,199	1	2	3	4	5		7	8	9			10	6	11																	
6	8 (a)	Manchester C	L 0-1		26,841	1	2	3	4	5		7	8	9			10	6	11																	
7	11 (h)	Preston NE	W 1-0	Garrett	44,000	1	2	3	4	5		7	8	9			10	6	11																	
8	15 (h)	Manchester C	W 4-1	Stewart 4	40,000	1	2	3	4	5		7	8	9			10	6		11																
9	18 (a)	Burnley	D 2-2	Trigg, Bodle	40,000	1	2	3	4	5		7	8	9			10	6		11																
10	25 (h)	Stoke C	W 2-1	Harris, Dougall	49,800	1	2	3	4	5		7	8	9		11	10	6																		
11	Oct 2 (a)	Charlton A	D 1-1	Garrett	56,000	1	2	3	4	5		7	8	9		11	10	6																		
12	9 (a)	Bolton W	D 0-0		43,376	1	2	3	4	5		7	8	9		11	10	6																		
13	16 (h)	Liverpool	L 0-1		43,000	1	2	3	4	5		7	8	9		11	10	6																		
14	23 (a)	Blackpool	L 0-1		30,000	1	2	3	4	5		7		9	10			6		11	8															
15	30 (h)	Derby C	L 0-1		52,129	1	2	3	4	5		7	8		10			6		11	9															
16	Nov 6 (a)	Arsenal	L 0-2		62,000	1	2	3	4	5		7		9	10			6		11	8															
17	13 (h)	Huddersfield T	W 1-0	Hepplewhite (og)	35,000	1	2	3	4	5	6	7			10					8	11	9														
18	20 (a)	Manchester U	L 0-3		45,482	1	2	3	4			7			10		9	8		11	6		5													
19	27 (h)	Sheffield U	L 1-2	Hall	25,000	1	2	3		5		7			10						6	8	4		9	11										
20	Dec 4 (a)	Aston Villa	W 3-0	Stewart 2, Bodle	61,632	1	2	3	4	5		8	9		10						6					11	7									
21	11 (h)	Sunderland	D 0-0		29,000	1	2	3	4	5		8			10						6					11	7	9								
22	18 (h)	Wolves	L 0-1		48,000	1	2	3	4	5		8	9		10						6					11	7									
23	25 (h)	Newcastle U	W 2-0	Trigg, Roberts	42,000	1	2	3	4	5			8	9	10						6					11	7									
24	27 (a)	Newcastle U	L 0-1		49,457	1	2	3	4	5			8	9	10						6					11	7									
25	Jan 1 (a)	Chelsea	L 0-2		28,850	1	2	3	4	5			10	9							6					11	7		8							
26	22 (a)	Preston NE	D 0-0		27,000	1		3	6	5		9	2	8												11	7		4	10						
27	Feb 5 (h)	Burnley	D 0-0		35,000	1		3	6	5		9	2	8												11	7		4	10						
28	12 (h)	Everton	D 0-0		35,000	1		3	6	5		7	8	2	10											11			4			9				
29	19 (a)	Stoke C	L 1-2	Harris	28,000	1		3	6	5		7	8	2	10											11			4			9				
30	26 (h)	Charlton A	W 1-0	Stewart	36,000	1		3	10	5	4	8		2												11	7		6			9				
31	Mar 5 (h)	Bolton W	D 0-0		21,000	1		3	10	5	4	8		2												11	7		6			9				
32	12 (a)	Liverpool	L 0-1		43,763	1		3	10	5	2	8									9					11	7		4			6				
33	19 (h)	Manchester U	W 1-0	Boyd	46,819	1		3	10		2	8											5	9		11	7		4			6				
34	26 (a)	Sheffield U	L 0-4		26,000	1		3	4		2	8											5	9		11	7					6	10			
35	Apr 2 (h)	Arsenal	D 1-1	Jordan	38,503	1	2	3	10	5	4	7								11											9	6	8			
36	9 (a)	Huddersfield T	D 0-0		18,856		2	3	10	5	4	7								11											9	6	8			1
37	15 (a)	Portsmouth	L 1-3	Dorman	38,000	1	2	3		5	4	7								11		10									9	6	8			
38	16 (h)	Blackpool	D 1-1	Jordan	35,000	1	2	3		5	9	8								11		4					7					6	10			
39	18 (h)	Portsmouth	W 3-0	Badham, Stewart, Hindmarsh (og)	30,000	1		3		5	9	10								11		4	2				7					6	8			
40	23 (a)	Derby C	L 0-1		25,548	1		3		5	9	10								11		4	2				7					6	8			
41	30 (h)	Aston Villa	L 0-1		45,000	1		3	10	5	9	7								11		4	2									6	8			
42	May 7 (a)	Sunderland	D 1-1	Roberts	28,007	1		3		5	9	7										4	2			11			6				10			8
				Appearances		41	41	30	36	39	18	37	24	23	19	8	10	11	3	14	11	10	9	3	2	17	16	1	9	2	7	11	9	1		
				Goals					2		1	11	1	5	3		4					1			1	2		1				2			

FINAL LEAGUE POSITION: 17th in Division One. Average home League attendance: 38,821

2 own-goals

FA Cup

Rd	Date	Opponent	Result	Scorers	Att	Merrick G	Green K	Jennings D	Harris F	Duckhouse E	Badham J	Stewart JG	Dougall N	Trigg C	Bodle H	Edwards G	Garrett AC	McKee F	Hughes J	Laing R	Mitchell FR	Dorman D	McDonnell M	Slater F	Hall F	Roberts H	Berry J	Goodwin JW	Boyd L	Evans H	Dailey J	Ferris R	Jordan JW	Robertson W	Quinton W	Southam WJH
3	Jan 8 (h)	Leicester C	D 1-1	Roberts	14,000	1	2		4	5	6		8	9	10											11	7							3		
R	15 (a)	Leicester C	D 1-1*	Bodle	37,000	1		3		4	5			9			6					8				11	7		10							2
2R	17 (h)	Leicester C	L 1-2	Dorman	31,609			3		4	5			9			6					8				11	7		10				1			2
				Appearances		2	3	3		3	1		1	2	2		2					2				3	3		2				1		1	2
				Goals										1								1				1										

*After extra-time

1949-50

Manager: Bob Brocklebank

#	Date		Opponent	Result	Scorers	Att.	Merrick G	Trigg C	Green K	Dorman D	Duckhouse E	Harris F	Stewart JG	Brennan RA	Dailey J	Capel T	McKee F	McDonnell M	Boyd L	Ferris R	Berry J	Badham J	Atkins A	Jordan JW	Laing RS	Evans H	Jennings D	Carr DH	Havenga W	Slater F	Roberts H	Higgins J	O'Hara E	Blake A	Warhurst R
1	Aug 20	(h)	Chelsea	L 0-3		45,000	1	2	3	4	5	6	7	8	9	10	11																		
2	24	(h)	West Brom A	W 2-0	Dailey 2	50,027	1		3		5		7	8	9	10			2	4	6	11													
3	27	(a)	Stoke C	L 1-3	Capel	30,000	1		3		5		7	8	9	10			2	4	6	11													
4	31	(a)	West Brom A	L 0-3		50,299	1		3		5		7	8	9	10			2	4	6	11													
5	Sep 3	(h)	Burnley	L 0-1		37,000	1		3				7		9		10	4			6		2	5	8	11									
6	10	(a)	Sunderland	D 1-1	Dailey	48,552	1		3				7	8	9		10	5	4	6	11	2													
7	14	(h)	Wolves	D 1-1	Dailey	47,000	1		3	4			7	8	9		10	5		6	11	2													
8	17	(h)	Liverpool	L 2-3	Brennan, Dailey	40,000	1		3	4			7	8	9		10	5		6	11	2													
9	24	(a)	Arsenal	L 2-4	Berry 2	53,000	1		3	4			7	8	9	10		5		6	11	2													
10	Oct 1	(h)	Bolton W	D 0-0		25,000	1	2	3			4	8			9	10		5		7	6				11									
11	8	(h)	Portsmouth	L 0-3		38,000	1	2	3			4				8	9	10		5	11	7	6												
12	15	(a)	Huddersfield T	L 0-1		22,872	1	2								10	9		6	5	11	7	4		8			3							
13	22	(h)	Everton	D 0-0		30,000	1						11	10	9				4		8	6	5				3	2	7						
14	29	(a)	Middlesbrough	L 0-1		35,000	1		2			6	7	10			11		4		8	9	5				3								
15	Nov 5	(h)	Blackpool	L 0-2		35,000	1		2			6		10					4		7		5	8			3			9	11				
16	12	(a)	Newcastle U	L 1-3	Slater	30,113	1		2		5	6		10							7		4	8		11	3			9					
17	19	(h)	Fulham	D 1-1	Brennan	20,995	1		2		5	6		10							7		4	8			3					9	11		
18	26	(a)	Manchester C	L 0-4		30,501	1		2		5	6		10							7		4	8			3					9	11		
19	Dec 3	(h)	Charlton A	W 2-0	Stewart, Berry	29,000	1					6	7	10						11	2	5	8				3	4		9					
20	10	(a)	Aston Villa	D 1-1	Brennan	44,520	1			6			7	10				4		11	2	5	8				3			9					
21	17	(a)	Chelsea	L 0-3		40,000	1		3				7	10				4	6	11	2	5	8							9					
22	24	(h)	Stoke C	W 1-0	Higgins	30,000	1		3	6			7	10				4		11	2	5	8							9					
23	26	(h)	Derby C	D 2-2	Capel, Stewart	45,477	1		3				7	10				4	6	11	2	5	8							9					
24	27	(a)	Derby C	L 1-4	Brennan	37,459	1		2				7	10					6	11	4	5	8				3			9					
25	31	(a)	Burnley	D 1-1	Dailey	25,362	1		5	6					9				8		7	2				10	3	4		11					
26	Jan 14	(h)	Sunderland	L 1-2	Dailey	32,000	1	2		6			7	8	9				4		11	5				10	3								
27	21	(a)	Liverpool	L 0-2		37,668	1		2	6			7	8	9				4		11	5				10	3								
28	Feb 4	(h)	Arsenal	W 2-1	Dailey, Brennan	35,000	1		2	6			7	10	9				4		11	5	8				3								
29	18	(a)	Bolton W	L 0-1		25,000	1			6	2		7	10	9				4		11	5	8										3		
30	25	(a)	Portsmouth	L 0-2		30,000	1		3	4	2	10	8		9			6			7	5					11								
31	Mar 4	(h)	Huddersfield T	W 2-1	Dailey, Brennan	27,000	1		2	8				10	9			4	6	7	5						11					3			
32	11	(a)	Fulham	D 0-0		25,000	1			8			7	10	9			4	6			2	5				11								
33	18	(h)	Manchester C	W 1-0	Brennan	30,000	1			4			7	10	9				6	8	2	5					3								11
34	25	(a)	Blackpool	D 1-1	Stewart	20,000	1			8			7	10	9			4	6	11	2	5					3								
35	Apr 1	(h)	Newcastle U	L 0-1		30,000	1			8			7	10	9			4	6	8	2	5					3			11					
36	7	(a)	Manchester U	W 2-0	Stewart, Berry	47,170	1	9					7	8				4	6	11	2	5					10	3							
37	8	(a)	Everton	D 0-0		46,828	1	9			2			8				4	6	7							10	3			11				
38	10	(a)	Manchester U	D 0-0		35,863	1	9			2			8				4	6	7		5					10	3							11
39	15	(h)	Middlesbrough	D 0-0		32,000	1	9	2		5			8				4	6	7							10	3							11
40	22	(a)	Charlton A	L 0-2		43,000	1	9	2		5		7	10				4	6	11			8					3							
41	29	(h)	Aston Villa	D 2-2	Trigg 2	26,144	1	9	2		5	10	7	8				4	6	11								3							
42	May 6	(a)	Wolves	L 1-6	Trigg	42,935	1	9	2		5	10	7	8				4	6	11								3							
			Appearances				42	12	29	16	15	12	31	39	23	8	8	10	27	25	39	28	20	15	1	9	25	3	1	2	7	8	2	2	3
			Goals					3					4	7	9	2					4									1		1			

FINAL LEAGUE POSITION: 22nd in Division One. Average home League attendance: 34,310.

FA Cup

#	Date		Opponent	Result	Att.	Merrick G	Green K	Dorman D	Brennan RA	Dailey J	Ferris R	Berry J	Evans H	Jennings D	Carr DH	Slater F
3	Jan 7	(a)	Swansea T	L 0-3	10,000	1	5	6	8	9	7	2	10	3	4	11
			Appearances			1	1	1	1	1	1	1	1	1	1	1
			Goals													

1950-51

Manager: Bob Brocklebank

No	Date	Opponent	Res	Scorers	Att	Merrick G	Badham J	Green K	Boyd L	Atkins A	Dorman D	Berry J	Powell A	Trigg C	Smith WH	Roberts H	Stewart JG	Higgins J	McKee F	Warhurst R	Kloner H	Martin R	Ferris R	Hall J	Rowley KF	Dailey J	O'Hara E
1	Aug 19 (a)	Swansea T	W 1-0	Boyd	28,000	1	2	3	4	5	6	7	8	9	10	11											
2	23 (h)	Leicester C	W 2-0	Trigg, Smith	28,000	1	2	3	4	5	6	7	8	9	10	11											
3	26 (h)	Grimsby T	D 1-1	Powell	32,000	1	2	3	4	5	6	7	8	9	10	11											
4	28 (a)	Leicester C	W 3-1	Trigg, Smith, Stewart	31,000	1	2	3	4	5	6	11	8	9	10		7										
5	Sep 2 (a)	Notts C	W 1-0	Smith	34,648	1	2	3	4	5	6	11	8		10		7	9									
6	6 (h)	Coventry C	D 1-1	Higgins	25,000	1	2	3	4	5	6	11	8		10		7	9									
7	9 (h)	Preston NE	W 1-0	Smith	33,000	1	2	3	4	5		7	8		10	11		9	6								
8	11 (h)	Coventry C	L 1-3	Berry	30,453	1	2	3	4	5		7	8		10	11		9	6								
9	16 (a)	Bury	L 1-4	Dorman	16,809	1	2	3	4	5	8	11	7		10			9	6								
10	23 (h)	Queen's Park R	D 1-1	Heath (og)	27,000	1	2	3	4	5	6	7	8		10	11		9									
11	30 (a)	Chesterfield	D 1-1	Trigg	12,309	1	2	3	4	5	6	7	8	9	10	11											
12	Oct 7 (a)	Southampton	W 2-0	Smith, Green	25,499	1	2	3	4	5	6	7	8	9	10	11											
13	14 (h)	Barnsley	W 2-0	Smith, Boyd	27,000	1	2	3	4	5	6	7		9	10	11		8									
14	21 (a)	Brentford	L 1-2	Trigg	19,207	1	2	3	4	5	6	7		9	10	11		8									
15	28 (h)	Blackburn R	W 3-2	Trigg, Smith, Stewart	25,000	1	2	3	4	5	6	11	8	9	10		7										
16	Nov 4 (a)	Hull C	L 2-3	Trigg 2	30,000	1	2	3	4	5	6	11	8	9	10		7										
17	11 (h)	Doncaster R	L 0-2		27,000	1	2	3	4	5	6	11	8	9	10		7										
18	18 (a)	Sheffield U	L 2-3	Smith, Stewart	20,000	1	2	3	4	5	6	11		9	8		7			10							
19	25 (h)	Luton T	W 3-0	Higgins 2, Smith	20,000	1	2	3	4	5		11		9	10		7	8					6				
20	Dec 2 (a)	Leeds U	L 0-3		23,355	1	2	3		5		11		9	10		7	8					6	4			
21	9 (h)	West Ham U	W 3-1	Higgins, Stewart, Smith	18,000	1		2	4	5		11		9	10		7	8				3	6				
22	16 (h)	Swansea T	W 5-0	Trigg 3, Stewart, Berry	16,000	1		2	4	5		11		9	10		7	8				3	6				
23	23 (a)	Grimsby T	D 1-1	Smith	14,000	1		2	4	5		11		9	10		7	8				3	6				
24	25 (a)	Manchester C	L 1-3	Trigg	40,064	1		2	4	5		11		9	10		7	8				3	6				
25	26 (h)	Manchester C	W 1-0	Trigg	32,000	1	3	2	4	5		11		9	10		7	8					6				
26	30 (h)	Notts C	L 1-4	Stewart	33,000	1	3	2	4	5		11		9	10		7	8					6				
27	Jan 13 (a)	Preston NE	L 0-1		32,000	1	2		4	5	8	11		9			7	10				3	6				
28	20 (a)	Bury	D 3-3	Trigg 2, Stewart	26,000	1			4	5		11		9	10		7					3	6		2	8	
29	Feb 3 (a)	Queen's Park R	L 0-2		12,071	1	2			5	4	11		9	10		7	8				3	6				
30	17 (h)	Chesterfield	W 2-1	Trigg, Higgins	34,980	1		2	4	5		11		9	10		7	8				3	6				
31	28 (h)	Southampton	W 2-1	Trigg, Stewart	12,593	1	2	3	4	5		11		9	10		7	8					6				
32	Mar 3 (a)	Barnsley	W 2-0	Dailey, Stewart	15,381	1	2	3	4	5		11			10		7	8					6			9	
33	17 (a)	Blackburn R	W 3-2	Dailey 2, Higgins	25,000	1	2	3	4	5		7			10			8					6			9	11
34	23 (h)	Cardiff C	D 0-0		15,000	1	2	3	4	5		7			10			8					6			9	11
35	24 (h)	Hull C	W 2-1	Dailey, Boyd	28,000	1	2	3	4	5		7						8			6				10	9	11
36	26 (a)	Cardiff C	L 1-2	Rowley	20,000	1	2	3	4	5		7						8					6		10	9	11
37	31 (a)	Doncaster R	W 1-0	Trigg	17,000	1	2	3	4	5		7						8		11			6		10		
38	Apr 7 (h)	Sheffield U	W 3-0	Higgins, Rowley, Warhurst	22,000	1	3	2		5	4	7		9				8		11			6		10		
39	14 (a)	Luton T	D 1-1	Warhurst	16,324	1	3	2		5	4	7		9				8		11			6		10		
40	21 (h)	Leeds U	L 0-1		23,809	1		2		5	4	7		9				8		11		3	6		10		
41	25 (h)	Brentford	D 1-1	Smith	14,000	1	4	2		5		11		9	10		7	8				3	6				
42	28 (a)	West Ham U	W 2-1	Rowley, Ferris	16,500	1	3	2	4	5		11		9	10		7						6		8	9	
				Appearances		42	35	39	36	42	21	42	15	30	35	10	25	28	3	9	1	10	20	1	8	6	4
				Goals				1	3		1	2	1	17	12		9	7		2			1		3	4	

1 own-goal

FINAL LEAGUE POSITION: 4th in Division Two. Average home League attendance: 24,728.

FA Cup

Rd	Date	Opponent	Res	Scorers	Att	Merrick G	Badham J	Green K	Boyd L	Atkins A	Dorman D	Berry J	Powell A	Trigg C	Smith WH	Roberts H	Stewart JG	Higgins J	McKee F	Warhurst R	Kloner H	Martin R	Ferris R	Hall J	Rowley KF	Dailey J	O'Hara E
3	Jan 6 (h)	Manchester C	W 2-0	Stewart, Higgins	30,057	1		2	4	5	8	11		9			7	10				3	6				
4	27 (a)	Derby C	W 3-1	Stewart, Trigg, Smith	37,384	1	2		4	5		11		9	10		7	8				3	6				
5	Feb 10 (h)	Bristol C	W 2-0	Stewart, Trigg	47,831	1	2		4	5		11		9	10		7	8				3	6				
6	24 (h)	Manchester U	W 1-0	Higgins	50,000	1	2	3	4	5		11		9	10		7	8					6				
SF	Mar 10 (n†)	Blackpool	D 0-0		70,000	1	3	2	4	5		11		9	10		7	8					6				
R	14 (n§)	Blackpool	L 1-2	Smith	70,114	1	3	2	4	5		11		9	10		7	8					6				
				Appearances		6	5	4	6	6	1	6		6	5		6	6				3	6				
				Goals										2	2		3	2									

†Played at Maine Road, Manchester. §Played at Goodison Park, Liverpool.

1951-52

Manager: Bob Brocklebank

#	Date	Opponent	Result	Scorers	Att.
1	Aug 18 (h)	Bury	W 2-1	Trigg, Higgins	24,000
2	22 (h)	Leeds U	D 1-1	Ferris	17,081
3	25 (a)	Leicester C	L 0-4		20,000
4	29 (a)	Leeds U	D 1-1	Purdon	15,008
5	Sep 1 (h)	Nottingham F	L 0-2		24,000
6	3 (a)	Sheffield W	D 1-1	Higgins	32,490
7	8 (a)	Brentford	L 0-1		25,000
8	12 (h)	Sheffield W	D 0-0		13,894
9	15 (h)	Doncaster R	D 2-2	Badham, Dorman	17,000
10	22 (h)	Everton	W 3-1	Briggs, Purdon, Wardle	27,138
11	29 (h)	Southampton	D 1-1	Briggs	26,000
12	Oct 6 (h)	Swansea T	D 1-1	Higgins	28,000
13	13 (a)	Coventry C	D 1-1	Rowley	20,000
14	20 (h)	West Ham U	W 2-1	Stewart, Briggs	21,000
15	27 (a)	Sheffield U	L 2-4	Rowley, Stewart	31,528
16	Nov 3 (h)	Barnsley	W 2-1	Briggs, Stewart	20,000
17	10 (a)	Hull C	W 1-0	Briggs	27,482
18	17 (h)	Blackburn R	L 0-1		22,000
19	24 (a)	Queen's Park R	W 2-0	Briggs, Smith	14,836
20	Dec 1 (h)	Notts C	W 2-0	Smith 2	27,000
21	8 (a)	Luton T	W 4-2	Purdon, Smith, Stewart, Warhurst	17,000
22	15 (a)	Bury	L 0-3		12,347
23	22 (h)	Leicester C	W 2-0	Briggs, Wardle	22,500
24	25 (h)	Rotherham U	W 4-0	Smith 3, Purdon	28,000
25	26 (a)	Rotherham U	W 2-1	Briggs, Badham	22,000
26	29 (a)	Nottingham F	W 1-0	Briggs	24,166
27	Jan 5 (h)	Brentford	L 1-2	Wardle	28,500
28	19 (a)	Doncaster R	W 5-0	Murphy 3, Briggs, Stewart	20,000
29	26 (h)	Everton	L 1-2	Stewart	33,000
30	Feb 9 (a)	Southampton	L 0-2		18,688
31	16 (a)	Swansea T	L 0-4		22,000
32	Mar 1 (h)	Coventry C	W 3-1	Briggs, Stewart, Murphy	33,000
33	8 (a)	West Ham U	W 1-0	Briggs	24,000
34	15 (h)	Sheffield U	W 3-0	Trigg, Murphy 2	28,000
35	22 (a)	Barnsley	W 2-1	Murphy, Stewart	14,305
36	29 (h)	Hull C	D 2-2	Smith, Briggs	15,000
37	Apr 5 (a)	Blackburn R	W 4-1	Smith, Briggs 2, Dailey	19,000
38	11 (h)	Cardiff C	W 3-2	Briggs, Green, Sherwood (og)	31,000
39	12 (h)	Queen's Park R	W 1-0	Trigg	28,000
40	14 (a)	Cardiff C	L 1-3	Briggs	30,000
41	19 (a)	Notts C	L 0-5		24,360
42	26 (h)	Luton T	W 3-1	Briggs, Purdon, Stewart	29,000

FINAL LEAGUE POSITION: 3rd in Division Two. Average home League attendance: 24,570.

Player grid (shirt numbers by match):

#	Merrick G	Hall J	Green K	Boyd L	Badham J	Ferris R	Stewart JG	Higgins J	Trigg C	Rowley K	Berry J	Atkins A	Purdon E	Dailey J	Smith WH	Warhurst R	Wardle W	Martin R	Dorman D	Briggs TH	Murphy P	Watts JW	Newman J	Robertson W
1	1	2	3	4	5	6	7	8	9	10	11													
2	1	2	3	4	5	6	7	8	9	10	11													
3	1		3	4	2	6	7	8	9	10	11	5												
4	1		3	4	2	6	7				11	5	8	9	10									
5	1		3	4	2	6	7					5	8	9		11								
6	1		3	4	2	6	7	10	9	11		5	8											
7	1		3	4	2		7	8	9			5			10	6	11							
8	1			4	2		7		9			5			10	6	11	3	8					
9	1			4	2		7		9	10		5				6	11	3	8					
10	1			4	2		7			10		5	8			6	11	3		9				
11	1	2		4	5		7			10			8			6	11	3		9				
12	1	2		4			7	8		10		5				6	11	3		9				
13	1			4	2		7	8		10		5				6	11	3		9				
14	1			4	2		7	8		10		5				6	11	3		9				
15	1			4	2		7	8		10		5				6	11	3		9				
16	1			4	2		7	8		10		5				6	11	3		9				
17	1	2		4	5		7			10			8			6	11	3		9				
18	1	2		4	5		7			10			8			6	11	3		9				
19	1			4	2		7					5	8		10	6	11	3		9				
20	1			4	2		7					5	8		10	6	11	3		9				
21	1			4	2		7					5	8		10	6	11	3		9				
22	1			4	2		7					5	8		10	6	11	3		9				
23	1			4	2		7					5	8		10	6	11	3		9				
24	1			4	2		7					5	8		10	6	11	3		9				
25	1			4	2		7					5	8		10	6	11	3		9				
26	1			4	2		7					5	8		10	6	11	3		9				
27	1			4	2		7					5	8		10	6	11	3		9				
28	1			4	2		7					5			8	6	11	3		9	10			
29	1			4	2		7					5			8	6	11	3		9	10			
30	1			4	2	6	7					5			8		11	3		9	10			
31	1				2		7					5			8	6	11	3		9	10	4		
32	1			4	2		7								8	6	11	3		9	10		5	
33	1			4	2		7					5			8	6	11	3		9	10			
34	1			4	2		7		9			5			8	6	11	3			10			
35	1			4	2		7					5			8	6	11	3		9	10			
36	1			4	2		7					5			8	6	11	3		9	10			
37			2	4			7					5		10	8	6	11	3		9				1
38	1		2	4			7					5			8	6	11	3		9	10			
39	1		2	4			7		9			5			8	6	11	3			10			
40	1		2	4			7					5			8	6	11	3		9	10			
41	1		2	4			7					5			8	6	11	3		9	10			
42	1		2	4			7			10		5	8			6	11	3		9				
Appearances	41	6	33	37	39	14	37	10	12	12	4	31	19	5	19	36	35	19	2	33	15	1	1	1
Goals			1		2	1	9	3	3	2			5	1	9	1	3		1	18	7			

1 own-goal

FA Cup

Rd	Date	Opponent	Result	Scorers	Att.	Merrick G	Hall J	Green K	Boyd L	Badham J	Ferris R	Stewart JG	Higgins J	Trigg C	Rowley K	Berry J	Atkins A	Purdon E	Dailey J	Smith WH	Warhurst R	Wardle W	Martin R	Dorman D	Briggs TH	Murphy P	Watts JW	Newman J	Robertson W
3	Jan 12 (a)	Fulham	W 1-0	Briggs	26,000	1			4	2		7	9				5			10	6	11	3		8				
4	Feb 2 (h)	Leyton O	L 0-1		49,000	1			4	2		7					5			8	6	11	3		9	10			
Appearances						2			2	2		2	1				2			2	2	2	2		2	1			
Goals																									1				

1952-53

Manager: Bob Brocklebank

#		Date		Opponent	Result	Scorers	Att.	Merrick G	Green K	Martin R	Boyd L	Badham J	Warhurst R	Stewart J	Purdon E	Briggs TH	Murphy P	Wardle W	Cox G	Watts JW	Newman J	Higgins J	Ferris R	Rowley K	Smith WH	Schofield J	Trigg C	Atkins A	Bannister K	Metcalf J	Hall J	Cochrane J	James J	Lane JG
1	Aug	23	(a)	Rotherham U	D 1-1	Purdon	15,000	1	2	3	4	5	6	7	8	9	10	11																
2		27	(a)	Luton T	W 1-0	Briggs	20,893	1	2	3	4	5	6	7	8	9	10		11															
3		30	(h)	Fulham	L 1-4	Briggs	30,000	1	2	3	4	5		7	8	9	10		11	6														
4	Sep	3	(h)	Luton T	D 2-2	Briggs, Murphy	17,500	1	2	3	4			7		9	10		11	6	5	8												
5		6	(a)	West Ham U	W 2-1	Higgins, Murphy	25,000	1	2	3	4		6			9	11			7	5	8		10										
6		10	(h)	Leeds U	W 1-0	Rowley	14,133	1	2	3	4		6	7		9	8				5			11			10							
7		13	(h)	Leicester C	W 3-1	Briggs, Murphy, Rowley	30,000	1	2	3	4		6	7	11	9	8									5	10							
8		17	(h)	Leeds U	D 2-2	Rowley 2	18,371	1	2	3	4		6	7	11	9	8									5	10							
9		20	(a)	Notts C	L 0-2		24,538	1	2	3	4		6	7	10	9					11		5			8								
10		27	(h)	Southampton	W 2-0	Rowley 2	22,000	1	2	3	4	5	6			9	8	11	7					10										
11	Oct	4	(a)	Bury	L 0-3		16,069		2	3	4	5	6			9	8	11	7					10				1						
12		11	(a)	Swansea T	D 1-1	Purdon	24,800	1	2	3	4	5	6		10	9	8	11	7															
13		18	(h)	Huddersfield T	L 0-2		27,000	1	2	3	4	5	6	7	10	9	8		11															
14		25	(a)	Sheffield U	D 2-2	Murphy, Wardle	30,000	1	2	3	4	5	6	7		9	8	11						10										
15	Nov	1	(h)	Barnsley	W 3-1	Murphy, Rowley (pen), Stewart	20,000	1	2	3	4	5	6	7			8	11						10			9							
16		8	(a)	Lincoln C	D 1-1	Trigg	16,220	1	2	3	4	5	6	7		8	10										9							
17		15	(h)	Hull C	W 4-3	Trigg (pen), Murphy, Stewart, Cox	18,000		2	3	4	5	6	7		8	10		11						1		9							
18		22	(a)	Blackburn R	W 2-1	Murphy 2	18,400	1	2	3	4		6	7		8	10		11								9	5						
19		29	(h)	Nottingham F	L 0-5		17,000	1	2	3			6	7			10		11			8					9	5	4					
20	Dec	6	(a)	Everton	D 1-1	Murphy	23,858	1	2	3	4		6	7	8		10	11					5				9							
21		13	(h)	Brentford	W 3-1	Trigg, Murphy 2	10,000	1	2	3	4		6	7	8		10	11					5				9							
22		20	(a)	Rotherham U	W 4-0	Trigg (pen), Purdon, Murphy, Wardle	12,000	1	2	3	4		6	7	8		10	11					5				9							
23		25	(h)	Plymouth A	W 4-0	Purdon, Murphy 2, Stewart	31,703	1	2	3	4		6	7	8		10	11					5				9							
24		27	(a)	Plymouth A	L 1-2	Trigg (pen)	25,050	1	2	3	4		6	7	8		10	11					5				9							
25	Jan	3	(a)	Fulham	L 1-3	Purdon	20,000	1	2		4	3	6	7	8		10						5				9			11				
26		17	(h)	West Ham U	W 2-0	Trigg, Purdon	22,000	1	3				6	7	8		10	11					5				9		4		2			
27		24	(a)	Leicester C	W 4-3	Murphy 3, Trigg	27,478	1	3				6	7	8		10	11					5				9		4		2			
28	Feb	7	(h)	Notts C	W 3-2	Trigg 2 (2 pens), Murphy	24,500	1	3				6	7	8		10	11					5				9		4		2			
29		21	(h)	Bury	L 0-2		26,000	1	3				6	7	8		10	11					5				9		4		2			
30	Mar	7	(a)	Huddersfield T	D 1-1	Ferris	28,636	1	3				5	6	7			11					10				9		4		2	8		
31		11	(h)	Swansea T	L 1-4	Purdon	8,820	1	3				6		7	9				5								2	4	11		8	10	
32		14	(h)	Sheffield U	L 1-2	Cox	22,500	1	3		4	5					11	8			6					9					2		10	
33		21	(a)	Barnsley	W 3-1	Badham, James 2	7,406	1	3		6	9					11	7		5			10						4		2	8		
34		28	(h)	Lincoln C	D 2-2	Trigg (pen), Stewart	14,000	1	3		6	5		7			10	11					8				9		4		2			
35	Apr	3	(a)	Doncaster R	L 0-1		20,000		3		6	9		7			10	11	5				8		1				4		2			
36		4	(a)	Hull C	L 0-2		23,484		3		4			6	7	10		11	8	5					1	9					2			
37		6	(h)	Doncaster R	W 2-1	Lane, Boyd	12,500		3		4			6	7			11	8	5			1								2			9
38		11	(h)	Blackburn R	L 1-2	Cox	20,000	1	3		4			6	7	10		11	8	5											2			9
39		15	(a)	Southampton	D 1-1	Warhurst	18,387		3		8	7	6				10	11					5						1		4	2		9
40		18	(a)	Nottingham F	W 2-0	Lane, Boyd	16,203		3		8			6	7		10				11		5						1		4	2		9
41		25	(h)	Everton	W 4-2	Boyd 2, Murphy, Stewart	17,083	1	3		8			6	7		10				11		5								4	2		9
42	May	1	(a)	Brentford	L 1-4	Lane, Murphy	9,000	1	3		8			6	7		10	11					5								4	2		9
				FINAL LEAGUE POSITION: 6th in Division Two. Average home League attendance: 20,046.			Appearances	35	42	24	40	18	31	33	22	17	34	25	23	3	7	4	23	8	1	7	19	3	14	2	16	2	3	6
							Goals				4	1	1	5	7	4	20	2	3			1	1	7			10						2	3

FA Cup

#		Date		Opponent	Result	Scorers	Att.	Merrick G	Green K	Martin R	Boyd L	Badham J	Warhurst R	Stewart J	Purdon E	Briggs TH	Murphy P	Wardle W	Cox G	Watts JW	Newman J	Higgins J	Ferris R	Rowley K	Smith WH	Schofield J	Trigg C	Atkins A	Bannister K	Metcalf J	Hall J	Cochrane J	James J	Lane JG
3	Jan	14	(a)	Oldham A	W 3-1	Murphy 3	26,580	1	3		4		6	7	8		10	11					5				9				2			
4		31	(a)	Sheffield U	D 1-1	Purdon	43,104	1	3		6			8	7	9	10	11					5						4		2			
R	Feb	4	(h)	Sheffield U	W 3-1	Murphy 2, Wardle	29,500	1	3		6			8	7	9	10	11					5						4		2			
5		14	(a)	Chelsea	W 4-0	Purdon 2, Trigg, Murphy	45,872	1	3		6			11	7	8	10						5				9		4		2			
6		28	(h)	Tottenham H	D 1-1	Wardle	52,348	1	3		6			10	7	8		11					5				9		4		2			
R	Mar	4	(h)	Tottenham H	D 2-2*	Ferris, Boyd	59,543	1	3		6	4		10	7			11					5				9				2	8		
2R		9	(n†)	Tottenham H	L 0-1		50,801	1	3		6	5			7	8		11					10				9		4		2			
				*After extra-time. †Played at the Molineux Grounds, Wolverhampton.			Appearances	7	7		7	2	6	7	6		4	6					7				5		5		7	1		
							Goals				1				3		6	2					1				1							

1953-54

Manager: Bob Brocklebank

#	Date		Opponent	Result	Scorers	Att	Merrick G	Hall J	Green K	Boyd L	Badham J	Warhurst R	Stewart J	Kinsey N	Purdon E	Murphy P	Govan A	Martin R	Bannister K	Newman J	Schofield J	Astall G	Smith T	Watts JW	Trigg C	Rowley K	Lane JG	Cox G	Cochrane J	James J	Hill D	Atkins A	Squires B	Allen G
1	Aug 19	(h)	Hull C	W 2-0	Murphy, Govan	25,000	1	2	3	4	5	6	7	8	9	10	11																	
2	22	(h)	Swansea T	W 6-0	Purdon 2, Murphy 3, Kinsey	27,000	1	2			5	6	7	8	9	10	11	3	4															
3	24	(a)	Plymouth A	D 2-2	Kinsey, Govan	20,800	1	2			5	6	7	8	9	10	11	3	4															
4	29	(a)	Rotherham U	L 0-1		14,000	1	2		4	5	6	7	8	9	10	11	3																
5	Sep 2	(h)	Plymouth A	W 3-0	Purdon, Kinsey, Stewart	22,000	1		2	5		6	7	8	9	10	11	3	4															
6	5	(h)	Leicester C	L 1-2	Stewart	30,885	1		2	5		6	7	8	9	10	11	3	4															
7	9	(h)	Luton T	W 5-1	Murphy 3, Purdon 2	19,000	1		2	5		6	7	8	9	10	11	3	4															
8	12	(a)	Stoke C	L 2-3	Purdon, Hall	22,953	1	7	2	5		6		8	9	10	11	3	4															
9	16	(a)	Luton T	L 0-2		12,227	1		2	5		6	7	8	9	10	11	3	4															
10	19	(h)	Fulham	D 2-2	Purdon 2	22,000	1		2	6			7	8	9	10	11	3	4	5														
11	26	(a)	West Ham U	W 2-1	Purdon, Kinsey	30,000	1	2	3	4		6	7	8	9	10	11			5														
12	Oct 3	(h)	Leeds U	D 3-3	Kinsey, Murphy, Govan	26,434	1	2	3	4		6	7	8	9	10	11			5														
13	10	(h)	Lincoln C	W 1-0	Stewart	23,000		2	3	4		6	7	8	9	10	11			5	1													
14	17	(a)	Bristol R	D 1-1	Purdon	35,164	1	2	3	4	5	6		8	9	10	11					7												
15	24	(h)	Brentford	W 5-1	Purdon, Kinsey, Murphy, Govan, Bragg (og)	24,000	1	2	3	4	5	6		8	9	10	11					7												
16	31	(a)	Derby C	W 4-2	Purdon, Stewart, Murphy, Astall	18,278	1	2	3	4		6	8		9	10	11					7	5											
17	Nov 7	(h)	Blackburn R	D 0-0		25,000	1	2	3	4		6	8		9	10	11					7	5											
18	14	(a)	Doncaster R	L 1-3	Kinsey	16,000	1	2	3	4		6		8	9	10	11			5		7												
19	21	(h)	Bury	D 0-0		21,000	1		2	4		6		8	9	10	11	3				7	5											
20	28	(a)	Oldham A	W 3-2	Kinsey, Astall, Govan	18,264	1	2	3			6		8		10	11					7	5	4	9									
21	Dec 5	(h)	Everton	W 5-1	Trigg, Murphy, Astall 2, Clinton (og)	23,557	1	2	3			6		8		10	11					7	5	4	9									
22	12	(a)	Hull C	L 0-3		19,752	1	2	3			6		8		10	11					7	5	4	9									
23	19	(a)	Swansea T	W 3-1	Rowley 2, Purdon	18,000	1	2	3	4		6		8	9		11					7	5			10								
24	25	(h)	Notts C	W 3-0	Rowley 2, Govan	30,489	1	2	3	4		6		8	9		11					7	5			10								
25	26	(a)	Notts C	L 1-2	Astall	21,000		2	3	4		6		8	9		11				1	7	5			10								
26	Jan 2	(h)	Rotherham U	L 2-3	Purdon 2	17,000	1	2	3	4		6		8	9		11					7	5			10								
27	16	(a)	Leicester C	W 4-3	Murphy, Rowley, Govan 2	34,604	1	2	3	4		6		8		9	11			5		7				10								
28	28	(h)	Stoke C	W 1-0	Kinsey	26,233	1	2	3	4		6		8			11					7	5					9	10					
29	Feb 6	(h)	Fulham	L 2-5	Trigg 2	21,500	1	2	3	4		6	7	10		8	11						5		9									
30	13	(h)	West Ham U	W 2-0	Cochrane, Astall	22,704	1	2	3	4		6				10						7	5						8	9	11			
31	20	(a)	Leeds U	D 1-1	Rowley	22,803	1	2	3			6		8			11					7	5	4		10								
32	27	(a)	Lincoln C	W 1-0	Lane	13,853	1	2	3	8		6			10		11					7	5	4			9							
33	Mar 6	(h)	Bristol R	D 1-1	Boyd	25,300	1	2	3	8		6			10		11					7	5	4			9							
34	13	(a)	Brentford	L 0-2		12,600	1	2	3	6	4		8		10							7	5									11	9	
35	20	(h)	Derby C	W 3-0	Trigg 2, Stewart	18,219	1	2	3	6			7	4	8							11	5		9	10								
36	27	(a)	Bury	D 1-1	Stewart	11,293		2	3	6			7	4	8						1	11	5		9	10								
37	Apr 3	(h)	Oldham A	W 2-1	Murphy, Boyd	15,848		2	3				7	4		10	11				1	8	5		9									
38	10	(a)	Blackburn R	L 0-3		32,100	1	2	3	4		6		8		10	11					7	5				9							
39	16	(a)	Nottingham F	D 1-1	Kinsey	25,135	1		2	4		6	7	8			11	3					5		9		10							
40	17	(h)	Doncaster R	L 0-1		15,270	1		2	4		6	7	8			11	3					5		9		10							
41	19	(h)	Nottingham F	D 2-2	Lane, Stewart	14,540	1		2	4		6	7	8			11						5		9		10							3
42	24	(a)	Everton	L 0-1		62,865	1		2			6	7	8			11	3		5		4			9		10							
					Appearances		38	32	39	35	7	37	22	37	23	33	37	13	8	7	4	24	24	7	11	8	8	1	1	2	1	1	1	1
					Goals			1		2			7	10	15	13	8					6			5	6	2		1					

FINAL LEAGUE POSITION: 7th in Division Two. Average home League attendance: 22,594.

2 own-goals

FA Cup

#	Date		Opponent	Result	Scorers	Att	Merrick G	Hall J	Green K	Boyd L	Badham J	Warhurst R	Stewart J	Kinsey N	Purdon E	Murphy P	Govan A	Martin R	Bannister K	Newman J	Schofield J	Astall G	Smith T	Watts JW	Trigg C	Rowley K	Lane JG
3	Jan 9	(a)	Wolves	W 2-1	Murphy, Rowley	36,784	1	2	3	6				4		8	11			5		7				10	9
4	30	(a)	Ipswich T	L 0-1		25,000	1	2	3	4		6		8	9		11					7	5			10	
					Appearances		2	2	2	2		1		2	1	2	2			1		2	1			2	1
					Goals											1										1	

1954-55

Manager: Bob Brocklebank until October then Arthur Turner from November 1954

Player columns (left to right): Merrick G, Green K, Allen G, Boyd L, Newman J, Warhurst R, Astall G, Kinsey N, Lane J, Rowley K, Govan A, Smith T, Murphy P, Warmington P, Cox G, Hill D, Badham J, Watts J, Martin R, Hall J, Stewart J, Schofield J, Brown E, Bradbury W, James J

#	Date		Opponents	Result	Scorers	Att	Mer	Grn	All	Boy	New	War	Ast	Kin	Lan	Row	Gov	Smi	Mur	Wmg	Cox	Hil	Bad	Wat	Mar	Hal	Ste	Sch	Bro	Bra	Jam
1	Aug 21	(a)	Stoke C	L 1-2	Warhurst	27,984	1	2	3	4	5	6	7	8	9	10	11														
2	25	(h)	Bristol R	W 2-1	Kinsey, Rowley	26,000	1	2	3	4	5	6	7	8	9	10	11														
3	28	(a)	Rotherham U	W 3-1	Govan 2, Warhurst	27,000	1	2	3	4	5	6	7	8	9	10	11														
4	30	(a)	Bristol R	D 1-1	Warhurst	26,191	1	2	3	4	5	6	7	8	9		11		10												
5	Sep 4	(a)	Luton T	L 0-1		16,347	1	2	3	4		6	7	8	9		11	5		10											
6	8	(h)	Ipswich T	W 4-0	Kinsey 2, Warmington, Astall	21,238	1	2	3	4		6	7	8				5		9	10	11									
7	11	(h)	Hull C	D 0-0		25,000	1	2	3	4		6	7	8				5		9	10	11									
8	15	(h)	Ipswich T	W 2-1	Warmington, Murphy	16,783	1	2	3	4			7	8			11		10	9			5	6							
9	18	(a)	Lincoln C	D 1-1	Kinsey	14,537	1	2	3	4			7	8			11	5	10	9				6							
10	25	(h)	Bury	L 1-3	Lane	22,000	1	2					7	8	9		11	5	10				4	6	3						
11	Oct 2	(a)	Leeds U	L 0-1		21,200	1		3	4	5	6		8		10	11		9							2	7				
12	9	(a)	Fulham	L 1-2	Astall	31,500			3	4	5	6	7	8	9		11		10							2		1			
13	16	(a)	Swansea T	W 2-0	Murphy 2	20,000			3	4	5	6	7	8			11		10							2		1	9		
14	30	(h)	Derby C	D 1-1	Brown	20,568			3	4	5	6	7	8			11		10							2		1	9		
15	Nov 6	(a)	West Ham U	D 2-2	Murphy 2	25,500	1	3		4	5	6	7	8			11		10							2			9		
16	13	(h)	Blackburn R	W 3-1	Brown, Astall, Govan	24,000	1	3		4	5	6	7	8			11		10							2			9		
17	20	(a)	Plymouth A	L 0-1		19,184	1	3		4	5	6	7	8			11		10							2			9		
18	27	(h)	Port Vale	W 7-2	Brown, Murphy 3, Kinsey 2, Govan	16,500	1	3		4		6	7	8			11	5	10							2			9		
19	Dec 4	(a)	Notts C	L 2-3	Murphy, Govan	14,000	1	3		4		6	7	8			11	5	10							2			9		
20	11	(h)	Liverpool	W 9-1	Brown 3, Lane, Murphy 2, Astall 2, Govan	17,514	1	3		4		6	7	8			11	5	10							2			9		
21	18	(h)	Stoke C	W 2-0	Brown, Govan	22,100	1	3		4		6	7	8			11	5	10							2			9		
22	25	(h)	Nottingham F	L 0-1		33,500	1	3		4		6	7	8			11	5	10							2			9		
23	27	(h)	Nottingham F	W 2-0	Murphy, Burkitt (og)	25,725	1	3		4			7	8			11	5	10					6		2			9		
24	Jan 1	(a)	Rotherham U	W 2-0	Kinsey, Govan	17,000	1	3		4			7	8			11	5	10					6		2			9		
25	Feb 5	(h)	Lincoln C	D 3-3	Murphy 2, Kinsey	20,500		3		4	5	6	7	8					10		11					2		1	9		
26	12	(a)	Bury	W 1-0	Brown	12,547	1	3		4		6	7	8			11	5	10							2			9		
27	Mar 2	(h)	Leeds U	W 2-0	Lane, Govan	10,774	1	3		4		6	7	8	9		11	5	10							2					
28	5	(a)	Swansea T	W 3-0	Lane, Kinsey, Boyd	25,000	1	3		4	5	6	7	8	9		11		10							2					
29	16	(h)	Doncaster R	W 4-1	Kinsey, Murphy, Astall, Warhurst	5,621	1	3		4	5	6	7	8			11		10							2			9		
30	19	(a)	Derby C	D 0-0		19,489	1	3		4		6	7	8			11	5	10							2			9		
31	26	(h)	West Ham U	L 1-2	Brown	9,200		3				6	7	8			11	5	10					4		2		1	9		
32	30	(h)	Fulham	W 3-2	Lane, Astall 2	7,000		3				6	7		8		11	5	10					4		2		1	9		
33	Apr 2	(a)	Blackburn R	D 3-3	Lane, Murphy, Kinsey	27,800		3		4		6	7	8	9		11	5	10							2		1			
34	8	(a)	Middlesbrough	W 5-2	Lane, Brown 2, Govan 2	35,000	1		3	4		6	7		8		11	5	10							2			9		
35	9	(h)	Plymouth A	W 3-1	Kinsey, Lane, Govan	25,078			3	4		6	7	8	9		11	5	10							2		1			
36	11	(h)	Middlesbrough	W 3-0	Kinsey, Murphy, Govan	23,675			3	4		6	7	8			11	5	10							2		1	9		
37	16	(a)	Port Vale	L 0-2		24,936			3	4		6	7	8			11	5	10							2		1	9		
38	20	(h)	Luton T	W 2-1	Murphy 2	35,790			3	4			7	8			11	5	10					6		2		1	9		
39	23	(h)	Notts C	D 1-1	Brown	28,016			3	4			7	8			11	5	10					6		2		1	9		
40	25	(a)	Hull C	W 3-0	Bradbury 2, Govan	12,848			3	4			7				11	5	10					6		2		1	9	8	
41	30	(a)	Liverpool	D 2-2	Brown, Astall	38,392			3	4		6	7	8			11	5	10							2		1	9		
42	May 4	(a)	Doncaster R	W 5-1	Brown, Murphy, Astall 2, Govan	21,303			3	4		6	7	8			11	5	10							2		1	9		
			Appearances				27	29	13	39	17	34	33	35	22	4	37	24	37	5	4	2	11	10	1	32	1	15	28	2	
			Goals							1		4	11	13	8	1	15		20	2									14	2	

FINAL LEAGUE POSITION: 1st in Division Two. Average home League attendance: 21,002.

1 own-goal

FA Cup

Rnd	Date		Opponents	Result	Scorers	Att	Mer	Grn	All	Boy	New	War	Ast	Kin	Lan	Row	Gov	Smi	Mur	Wmg	Cox	Hil	Bad	Wat	Mar	Hal	Ste	Sch	Bro	Bra	Jam
3	Jan 8	(a)	Hull C	W 2-0	Kinsey, Brown	25,920	1	3		4			7	8			11	5	10							2			9	6	
4	29	(h)	Bolton W	W 2-1	Govan, Wheeler (og)	56,800	1	3		4		6	7	8			11	5	10							2			9		
5	Feb 19	(a)	Doncaster R	W 2-1	Brown 2	57,800	1	3		4		6	7	8			11	5	10							2			9		
6	Mar 12	(h)	Manchester C	L 0-1		58,000	1	3		4		6	7	8			11	5	10							2			9		
			Appearances				4	4		4	3	4	4	4			4	4	4							4		1	4		
			Goals											1			1												3		

1 own-goal

1955-56

Manager: Arthur Turner

No	Date	Opponent	Result	Scorers	Att	Merrick G	Hall J	Green K	Boyd L	Smith T	Warhurst R	Astall G	Kinsey N	Brown E	Murphy P	Govan A	Newman J	Badham J	Lane J	Bradbury W	Warmington P	Schofield J	Martin R	Watts J	Hill D	Finney W	Linnecor A	Cox G	Allen G
1	Aug 20 (h)	Manchester U	D 2-2	Kinsey, Astall	37,994	1	2	3	4	5	6	7	8	9	10	11													
2	24 (a)	Newcastle U	D 2-2	Murphy, Astall	34,390	1	2	3	4		6	7	8	9	10	11	5												
3	27 (a)	Sheffield U	W 3-0	Brown, Kinsey, Murphy	27,000	1	2	3	4	5	6	7	8	9	10	11													
4	31 (h)	Newcastle U	W 3-1	Brown, Murphy, Warhurst	38,690	1	2	3	4	5	6	7	8	9	10	11													
5	Sep 3 (h)	Preston NE	L 0-3		48,000	1	2	3	4	5	6	7	8	9	10	11													
6	5 (a)	Aston Villa	D 0-0		57,690	1	2	3	4		6	7	8	9	10	11	5												
7	10 (a)	Burnley	L 2-3	Kinsey, Astall	22,549	1	2	3	4		6	7	8	9	10	11	5												
8	17 (h)	Luton T	D 0-0		31,000	1	2		4		6	7	8	9	10	11	5	3											
9	21 (h)	Aston Villa	D 2-2	Brown, Astall	32,642	1	2		4	5	6	7	8	9	10	11		3											
10	24 (a)	Charlton A	L 0-2		21,193	1	2		4	5	6	7		9		11		3	8	10									
11	Oct 1 (h)	Tottenham H	W 3-0	Brown, Murphy, Clarke (og)	31,320	1	2		4	5	6	7		9	10	11		3	8										
12	8 (h)	Sunderland	L 1-2	Hudgell (og)	38,000	1	2		4	5	6	7	8	9	10	11		3											
13	15 (a)	Portsmouth	W 5-0	Brown 3, Kinsey, Govan	29,357	1	2		4	5	6	7	8	9	10	11		3											
14	22 (h)	Manchester C	W 4-3	Lane, Murphy, Govan, Boyd	28,500	1	2		4	5		7		9	10	11		3	8		6								
15	29 (a)	Wolves	L 0-1		47,006	1	2		4		6	7	8	9	10	11	5	3											
16	Nov 5 (h)	Chelsea	W 3-0	Astall 2, Boyd	30,499	1	2		4	5	6	7	8	9	10	11		3											
17	12 (a)	Blackpool	L 0-2		22,967	1	2		4	5	6	7	8	9		11		3	10										
18	19 (h)	Huddersfield T	W 5-0	Brown 2, Murphy, Astall, Warhurst	24,900	1	2		4	5	6	7	8	9	10	11		3											
19	26 (a)	Cardiff C	L 1-2	Brown	28,000	1	2		4	5	6	7	8	9	10	11		3											
20	Dec 3 (h)	Arsenal	W 4-0	Kinsey 2, Brown, Astall	35,765	1	2		4	5	6	7	8	9	10	11		3											
21	10 (a)	Bolton W	L 0-6		12,081	1	2		4	5	6	7	8	9	10	11		3											
22	17 (a)	Manchester U	L 1-2	Brown	27,704		2			5	6	7	8	9	10							1	3	4	11				
23	24 (h)	Sheffield U	L 0-2		23,800		2		4	5	6	7	8	9	10	11						1	3						
24	26 (h)	Everton	W 6-2	Brown 2, Kinsey 3, Govan	26,541		2	3		5	6	7	8	9	10	11						1		4					
25	27 (a)	Everton	L 1-5	Astall	42,366		2	3		5	6	7	8	9	10	11						1		4					
26	31 (a)	Preston NE	D 1-1	Astall	21,000	1	2	3		5	6	7	8	9		11			10					4					
27	Jan 14 (h)	Burnley	L 1-2	Kinsey	27,200	1	2	3	4	5	6	7	8	9		11			10										
28	21 (a)	Luton T	W 1-0	Brown	20,000	1	2	3	4	5	6	7	10	9		11										8			
29	Feb 4 (a)	Charlton A	W 4-0	Brown 3, Kinsey	24,611	1	2	3	4	5	6	7	10	9		11										8			
30	11 (a)	Tottenham H	W 1-0	Astall	26,160	1	2	3	4		6	7	10	9		11	5									8			
31	25 (h)	Portsmouth	W 3-2	Kinsey 2, Boyd	32,159	1	2	3	4	5	6	7	10	9		11										8			
32	Mar 7 (a)	Huddersfield T	D 1-1	Brown	9,224	1	2	3	4			7	10	9	8	11	5										6		
33	10 (h)	Wolves	D 0-0		45,161	1	2	3				7		9	10	11	5							4		8	6		
34	21 (a)	Chelsea	W 2-1	Kinsey, Govan	12,637	1	2	3	4			7	8	9	10	11	5										6		
35	24 (h)	Blackpool	L 1-2	Murphy	47,933	1	2	3	4	5			8	9	10	11					6					7			
36	31 (a)	Manchester C	D 1-1	Murphy	44,799	1		3		5		7			10	11					9			4		8	6	3	
37	Apr 2 (h)	West Brom A	W 2-0	Brown, Murphy	38,892	1	2	3		5		7		9	10	11								4		8	6		
38	3 (a)	West Brom A	W 2-0	Murphy 2	35,780	1	2	3		5					10	11	4				9					8	6	7	
39	7 (h)	Cardiff C	W 2-1	Brown, Baker (og)	37,154	1	2	3	4					9	10	11	5									8	6	7	
40	14 (a)	Arsenal	L 0-1		31,733	1	2		4			7	4	9	10	11	5									8	6		3
41	18 (a)	Sunderland	L 0-1		14,824	1	2	3	6			7	8		10	11	4			5	9								
42	21 (h)	Bolton W	W 5-2	Kinsey, Warmington, Astall, Wheeler 2 (og's)	29,640	1	2	3		5		7	8		10	11	4				9						6		
		Appearances				38	38	28	32	30	30	39	34	38	38	36	14	16	10	1	2	4	2	10	1	10	6	3	2
		Goals							3		2	12	14	21	12	4			1		1								

FINAL LEAGUE POSITION: 6th in Division One. Average home League attendance: 33,828.

5 own-goals

FA Cup

Rd	Date	Opponent	Result	Scorers	Att	Merrick G	Hall J	Green K	Boyd L	Smith T	Warhurst R	Astall G	Kinsey N	Brown E	Murphy P	Govan A	Newman J	Badham J	Lane J	Bradbury W	Warmington P	Schofield J	Martin R	Watts J	Hill D	Finney W	Linnecor A	Cox G	Allen G
3	Jan 7 (a)	Torquay U	W 7-1	Astall, Brown 3, Kinsey, Murphy 2	18,739	1	2	3	4	5	6	7	8	9	11				10										
4	28 (a)	Leyton O	W 4-0	Brown 2, Murphy, Finney	24,727	1	2	3	4	5	6	7	10	9	11											8			
5	Feb 18 (a)	West Brom A	W 1-0	Murphy	57,381	1	2	3	4	5	6	7	10	9	11											8			
6	Mar 3 (a)	Arsenal	W 3-1	Astall, Murphy, Brown	67,872	1	2	3	4	5	6	7	8	9	10	11													
SF	17 (n†)	Sunderland	W 3-0	Kinsey, Astall, Brown	65,107	1	2	3	4	5		7	8	9	10	11	6												
F	May 5 (n§)	Manchester C	L 1-3	Kinsey	98,982	1	2	3	6	5		7	8	9	10	11	4												
		Appearances				6	6	6	6	6	4	6	6	6	6	3	2		1							2			
		Goals										3	3	7	5											1			

†Played at Hillsborough, Sheffield. §Played at Wembley Stadium.

1956-57

Manager: Arthur Turner

Player columns (left to right): Merrick G, Hall J, Green K, Linnecor A, Smith T, Warhurst R, Astall G, Kinsey N, Brown E, Murphy P, Govan A, Watts J, Finney W, Farmer B, Warmington P, Cox G, Orritt B, Larkin B, Badham J, Schofield J, Newman J, Allen G, Harper D, Sissons G, Neale K, Neal R

No	Date	Opponent	Res	Scorers	Att	Mer	Hal	Gre	Lin	Smi	War	Ast	Kin	Bro	Mur	Gov	Wat	Fin	Far	Wmg	Cox	Orr	Lar	Bad	Sch	New	All	Har	Sis	Nea	Nel
1	Aug 18 (a) Manchester U	D 2-2	Govan, Jones (og)	32,752	1	2	3	4	5	6	7	8	9	10	11															
2	22 (h) Portsmouth	W 3-1	Astall, Govan 2	30,000	1	2	3	4	5	6	7	8	9	10	11															
3	25 (h) Arsenal	W 4-2	Brown, Murphy 2, Govan	37,200	1	2	3		5	6	7	8	9	10	11	4														
4	29 (a) Portsmouth	W 4-3	Govan 3, Astall	25,000	1	2	3		5	6	7	8	9	10	11	4														
5	Sep 1 (a) Burnley	L 0-2		25,531	1	2	3		5	6	7	8	9	10	11	4														
6	5 (h) Newcastle U	W 6-1	Kinsey, Murphy, Murphy 2, Govan 3	32,506	1	2	3		5	6	7	8	9	10	11	4														
7	8 (h) Preston NE	W 3-0	Govan 3	44,500	1	2	3		5	6	7	8	9	10	11	4														
8	15 (a) Chelsea	L 0-1		40,530	1	2	3		5	6	7	8	9	10	11	4														
9	22 (h) Cardiff C	W 2-1	Kinsey, Govan	39,931	1	2	3		5	6	7	8	9	10	11	4														
10	29 (a) Wolves	L 0-3		44,191	1	2	3		5	6	7	8	9		11	4	10													
11	Oct 6 (h) Bolton W	D 0-0		30,000	1				5	6	7	8	9			4		2	10	11										
12	13 (a) Leeds U	D 1-1	Larkin	34,460	1	2	3		5	6	7		9		11	4				8		10								
13	20 (h) Luton T	W 3-0	Brown 2, Orritt	32,000	1	2	3		5	6	7		9	10	11	4				8										
14	27 (a) Aston Villa	L 1-3	Kinsey	54,862	1	2			5	6	7	8	9	10	11	4								3						
15	Nov 3 (h) Blackpool	D 2-2	Astall, Govan	35,595	1	2	3		5	6	7		9		11	4				8		10								
16	10 (a) Manchester C	L 1-3	Kinsey	21,005	1	2	3		5	6	7	8	9		11	4	10													
17	17 (a) Charlton A	W 4-2	Brown, Kinsey, Astall, Murphy	29,000		2	3		5	6	7	10	9		11						8			1	4					
18	24 (a) Sunderland	W 1-0	Orritt	33,807	1	2	3		5	6	7	10	9		11						8					4				
19	Dec 1 (h) Tottenham H	D 0-0		39,036	1	2	3		5	6	7	10	9		11						8					4				
20	8 (a) Everton	L 0-2		29,529	1		3			6		10	9		11	4	2	7		8							3			
21	15 (h) Manchester U	W 3-1	Brown 2, Orritt	36,146	1	2	3	4	5	6	7		9	10	11						8									
22	22 (a) Arsenal	L 0-4		28,644	1	2	3		5	6	7		9	10	11	4					8									
23	25 (h) Sheffield W	W 4-0	Brown, Murphy, Astall, Govan	24,380	1	2	3		5	6	7		9	10	11	4					8									
24	29 (h) Burnley	W 2-0	Brown, Govan	32,000	1	2	3		5	6	7		9	10	11	4					8									
25	Jan 1 (a) Newcastle U	L 2-3	Brown, Govan	29,383	1	2	3		5	6	7	8	9	10	11	4														
26	12 (a) Preston NE	L 0-1		19,430	1	2		4	5	6	7	10	9		11						8				3					
27	19 (h) Chelsea	L 0-1		30,157	1	2	3	4	5	6	7	8	9	10	11															
28	Feb 2 (a) Cardiff C	W 2-1	Brown, Astall	18,000	1	2	3		5		7		9	10	11	6					8					4				
29	9 (h) Wolves	D 2-2	Astall, Govan	45,915	1	2	3		5		7		9	10	11	6					8					4				
30	20 (a) Bolton W	L 1-3	Astall	20,000		2	3		5	6	7	10	9		11	4							8	1						
31	Mar 9 (h) Everton	L 1-3	Brown	23,781	1	2	3		5	6	7		9		11		10				8					4				
32	16 (a) Blackpool	L 1-3	Brown	17,610	1	2	3		5	6	7	8	9	10	11													4		
33	30 (a) Charlton A	L 0-1		17,830	1	2	3		5	6		9	8	10	11	4				7										
34	Apr 3 (a) Luton T	D 0-0		15,000	1		2	8	5	6	7		9	10	11										3					
35	6 (h) Sunderland	L 1-2	Brown	24,548	1		2	8		6	7		9	10	11										5	3				
36	10 (h) Aston Villa	L 1-2	Murphy	29,893	1	2	3		5	6		8	9	10	11											4	7			
37	13 (a) Tottenham H	L 1-5	Astall	33,512	1	2	3		5	6	7	8			11		9			10	4									
38	20 (h) Leeds U	W 6-2	Brown 2, Govan 3, Astall	30,642	1	2	3		5	6	7	8	9	10	11	4														
39	22 (a) West Brom A	D 0-0		18,828	1		5			6	7	8		10	11	4	2								3			9		
40	23 (h) West Brom A	W 2-0	Kinsey, Govan	33,301	1	2	5				7	8	9	10	11	4									3					6
41	27 (h) Manchester C	D 3-3	Brown, Govan, Phoenix (og)	23,700	1	2	5				7	8	9	10	11	4									3					6
42	29 (a) Sheffield W	L 0-3		15,307	1	2			5		7		9	10	11	4					8	6			3	4				
	Appearances				40	36	40	11	37	33	40	28	38	35	35	27	4	3	1	4	18	7	1	2	8	8	1	1	2	2
	Goals										10	6	16	7	24						3	1								

FINAL LEAGUE POSITION: 12th in Division One. Average home League attendance: 32,582.

2 own-goals

FA Cup

Rd	Date	Opponent	Res	Scorers	Att	Mer	Hal	Gre	Lin	Smi	War	Ast	Kin	Bro	Mur	Gov	Wat	Fin	Far	Wmg	Cox	Orr	Lar	Bad	Sch	New	All	Har	Sis	Nea	Nel
3	Jan 5 (a) Carlisle U	D 3-3	Murphy 2, Astall	27,445	1	2	3		5	6	7	8	9	10	11	4														
R	9 (h) Carlisle U	W 4-0	Brown 2, Kinsey, Astall	56,000	1	2		4	5	6	7	8	9	10	11										3					
4	26 (a) Southend U	W 6-1	Murphy, Govan 3, Cox, Lawler (og)	30,000	1	2			5	6		8	9	10	11					7					4	3				
5	Feb 16 (a) Millwall	W 4-1	Kinsey 2, Govan, Brown	41,000	1	2	3		5	6	7	8	9	10	11	4														
6	Mar 2 (h) Nottingham F	D 0-0		58,000	1	2	3		5	6	7	8	9		11	4					10									
R	6 (a) Nottingham F	W 1-0	Murphy	36,486	1	2	3		5	6	7	8	9	10	11	4														
SF	23 (n†) Manchester U	L 0-2		65,107	1	2	3		5	6	7	8	9	10	11	4														
	Appearances				7	7	5	1	7	7	6	7	7	6	7	5				1	1				1	2				
	Goals										2	3	3	4	4					1									

†Played at Hillsborough, Sheffield.

1 own-goal

1957-58

Manager: Arthur Turner until February 1958 then joint with Pat Beasley

#	Date	Opponents	Result	Scorers	Att	Schofield J	Hall J	Green K	Watts J	Smith T	Neal R	Astall G	Kinsey N	Brown E	Murphy P	Govan A	Merrick G	Hellawell M	Mullett J	Neale K	Larkin B	Allen G	Newman J	Orritt B	Farmer B	Houghton B	Hooper H	Jones D	Sissons G
1	Aug 24 (h)	Aston Villa	W 3-1	Brown, Kinsey, Murphy	50,807	1	2	3	4	5	6	7	8	9	10	11													
2	28 (a)	Nottingham F	D 1-1	Brown	28,555		2	3	4	5	6	7	8	9	10	11	1												
3	31 (a)	Chelsea	L 1-5	Brown	43,806		2	3	4	5	6	7	8	9	10	11	1												
4	Sep 4 (h)	Nottingham F	L 0-2		26,772	1	2	3	4	5	6	7	8	9	10	11													
5	7 (a)	Newcastle U	L 1-4	Hellawell	29,784	1	2	3	4	5	6		8	9	10	11		7											
6	11 (h)	Tottenham H	D 0-0		26,484		2	3	4	5	10	7		9		11	1			6	8								
7	14 (a)	Burnley	L 1-3	R.Neal	20,422		2	3	4	5	10	7		9		11	1			6	8								
8	18 (a)	Tottenham H	L 1-7	Brown	35,192		2	3		5	10	7	8	9		11	1		6			4							
9	21 (h)	Preston NE	W 3-1	K.Neale, Murphy, Govan (pen)	24,848		2	7				8		3	10	11	1			6		4	9	5					
10	28 (a)	Sheffield W	L 3-5	Orritt 2, Murphy	20,311		2			5	6	7	8		10	11	1				3	4		9					
11	Oct 1 (a)	West Brom A	D 0-0		39,909		2	3	4		6	7		9	10	11	1				8			5					
12	5 (h)	Manchester C	W 4-0	Murphy 3, Brown	28,500		2	3	4		6	7		9	10	11	1				8			5					
13	12 (h)	Wolves	L 1-5	Astall	43,005		2	3	4		6	7		9	10	11	1				8			5					
14	19 (a)	Arsenal	W 3-1	Orritt, R.Neal 2	39,006			3	4	5	6	7		9	10	11	1						2	8					
15	26 (h)	Bolton W	W 5-1	Brown 2, Orritt, Murphy, Watts	26,225	1		3	4	5	6	7		9	10	11							2	8					
16	Nov 2 (a)	Luton T	L 0-3		17,000			3	4	5	6	7		9	10	11	1						2	8					
17	9 (h)	Sunderland	L 2-3	Murphy, Govan	25,800			3	4	5	6	7		9	10	11	1						2	8					
18	16 (a)	Everton	W 2-0	Murphy 2	34,875		2		4	5	6	7		9	10	11	1							8	3				
19	23 (h)	Blackpool	D 0-0		32,168		2		4	5	6	7		9	10	11	1							8	3				
20	30 (a)	Leeds U	D 1-1	Orritt	21,358		2		4	5	6			9	10	11	1						8	3	9				
21	Dec 7 (h)	Manchester U	D 3-3	Kinsey, Murphy, Astall	35,791		2			5	6	11	8	9	10		1				4				3		7		
22	14 (a)	Leicester C	D 2-2	Kinsey, Astall	28,610		2			5	6	11	8	9	10		1				4				3		7		
23	21 (a)	Aston Villa	W 2-0	Brown, Kinsey	39,889		2			5	6	11	8	9	10		1				4				3		7		
24	26 (h)	West Brom A	L 3-5	Brown, Hooper (pen), R.Neal	48,396		2			5	6	11	8	9	10		1				4				3		7		
25	28 (h)	Chelsea	D 3-3	Brown, Murphy 2	37,976		2			5	6	11	8	9	10		1				4				3		7		
26	Jan 11 (a)	Newcastle U	W 2-1	Brown, Kinsey	34,825		2	3		5	6		8	9	10	11	1				4						7		
27	18 (h)	Burnley	L 2-3	Murphy, Hooper	22,281	1	2			5	6	11	8		10						4		9		3		7		
28	Feb 1 (a)	Preston NE	L 0-8		21,373		2		4	5	6		8	9		11	1								3		7	10	
29	22 (a)	Wolves	L 1-5	Murphy	36,941		2			5	6			9	10	11	1				4			8	3		7		
30	Mar 1 (h)	Arsenal	W 4-1	Brown 2, Murphy, Hooper	26,824		2	3		5	6	7		9	10		1				4			8			11		
31	5 (a)	Manchester C	D 1-1	Murphy	27,812		2	3		5	6	7		9	10		1				4			8			11		
32	8 (a)	Bolton W	L 0-1		18,309		2	3			6	7		9	10		1				4			8			11		5
33	12 (h)	Sheffield W	W 1-0	Orritt	14,937		2	3		5	6	7		9			1				4			8			11	10	
34	15 (h)	Luton T	D 1-1	Orritt	25,225	1	2	3		5	6	7		8							4			9			11	10	
35	22 (a)	Blackpool	L 2-4	Astall, Hooper (pen)	11,549	1	2	3	4	5	6	7		9	10									8			11		
36	29 (h)	Everton	W 2-1	Hooper 2	21,628	1	2	3	4	5	6	7		9									8	10			11		
37	Apr 4 (a)	Portsmouth	L 2-3	Murphy, Hooper	33,072	1	2	3	4	5	6	7		9	10									8			11		
38	5 (a)	Sunderland	W 6-1	Murphy, Astall, Brown, Hooper, Orritt 2	34,184	1	2	3		5	6	8		9	10						4			7			11		
39	7 (h)	Portsmouth	W 4-1	Brown, Orritt, Murphy, Hooper	23,380	1	2	3		5	6	11		9	10						4			8			7		
40	12 (h)	Leeds U	D 1-1	Orritt	23,102	1	2	3		5	6	11		9	10						4			8			7		
41	19 (a)	Manchester U	W 2-0	Hooper, Green	38,991	1	2	3			6	11			10						4			9			7	8	5
42	26 (h)	Leicester C	L 0-1		27,614	1	2	3		5	6	11			10						4			9			7	8	
				Appearances		14	37	31	22	37	40	37	15	37	36	20	28	1	3	3	22	4	6	25	13	2	22	5	2
				Goals				1	1		4	5	5	15	20	2		1		1				11			10		

FINAL LEAGUE POSITION: 13th in Division One. Average home League attendance: 29,647.

FA Cup

Rd	Date	Opponents	Result	Att	Schofield J	Hall J	Green K	Watts J	Smith T	Neal R	Astall G	Kinsey N	Brown E	Murphy P	Govan A	Merrick G	Hellawell M	Mullett J	Neale K	Larkin B	Allen G	Newman J	Orritt B	Farmer B	Houghton B	Hooper H	Jones D	Sissons G
3	Jan 8 (a) York C		L 0-3	24,000		2		4	5	6	11	8	9	10		1							3			7		
			Appearances			1		1	1	1	1	1	1	1		1							1			1		
			Goals																									

1958-59

Manager: Arthur Turner and Pat Beasley until September then only Beasley

No	Date	V	Opponent	Res	Scorers	Att	Merrick G	Hall J	Green K	Larkin B	Smith T	Neal R	Hooper H	Orritt B	Brown E	Murphy P	Taylor B	Sissons G	Houghton B	Watts J	Jones D	Schofield J	Gordon J	Astall G	Hellawell M	Farmer B	Allen G	Jackson AJ	Stubbs R	Hume W
1	Aug 23	(a)	Aston Villa	D 1-1	Murphy	53,028	1	2	3	4	5	6	7	8	9	10	11													
2	27	(a)	West Brom A	D 2-2	Brown, Houghton	46,468	1	2	3	4		6	7	10	9			11	5	8										
3	30	(h)	Luton T	L 0-1		32,000	1	2	3	4		6	7	10	9			11	5	8										
4	Sep 3	(h)	West Brom A	L 0-6		35,915	1	2	3	4		6	7	8	9	10	11			5										
5	6	(a)	Bolton W	L 0-2		24,707	1	2	3	4	9	10	7	8				11		5		6								
6	10	(a)	Leeds U	D 0-0		25,228	1	2	3			6	7		9	10	11	5		4		8								
7	13	(h)	Burnley	W 2-1	Brown, Murphy	24,004	1	2	3			6	7		9	10	11	5		4		8								
8	17	(h)	Leeds U	W 4-1	Brown 4	24,051	1	2	3			6	7		9	10	11	5		4		8								
9	20	(a)	Preston NE	L 0-3		20,000		2	3			6	7		9	10	11	5		4	1	8								
10	27	(h)	Leicester C	W 4-2	Gordon, Murphy, Hooper, Astall (pen)	33,291	1	2	3			6	7		9	10		5		4			8	11						
11	Oct 4	(a)	Everton	L 1-3	Murphy	26,408	1	2	3			6			9	10		5		4			8	11	7					
12	11	(a)	West Ham U	W 2-1	Hooper, Neal	29,500	1	2	3			6	7	10	9	11		5		4			8							
13	18	(h)	Nottingham F	L 0-3		31,571	1	2	3			6	7	10	9	11		5		4			8							
14	25	(a)	Wolves	L 1-3	Astall	36,156	1		3	6		10			9		11	5		4			8	7						2
15	Nov 1	(h)	Portsmouth	D 2-2	Brown, Taylor	23,695	1	2	3	6			7		9	10	11	5		4			8							
16	8	(a)	Blackburn R	L 2-3	Brown, Larkin	28,800	1	2		10	5	6	7		9		11			4			8				3			
17	15	(h)	Newcastle U	W 1-0	Larkin	28,720	1	2		10	5	6	7				11			4			8				3	9		
18	22	(h)	Tottenham H	W 4-0	Larkin 2, Hooper, Taylor	28,708				10	5	6	7		9		11			4		1	8			2	3			
19	29	(h)	Manchester U	L 0-4		28,618				10	5	6	7		9		11			4		1	8			2	3			
20	Dec 6	(a)	Chelsea	L 0-1		27,773	1	2		10	5	6			9		11			4			8	7			3			
21	13	(h)	Blackpool	W 4-2	Jackson, Gordon, Larkin, Astall	16,231	1	2		10	5	6					11			4			8	7			3	9		
22	20	(a)	Aston Villa	W 4-1	Jackson 2, Astall (pen), Neal	31,827	1	2		10	5	6					11			4			8	7			3	9		
23	26	(h)	Manchester C	W 6-1	Jackson 2, Gordon, Larkin 2, Taylor	34,263	1	2		10	5	6					11			4			8	7			3	9		
24	27	(a)	Manchester C	L 1-4	Jackson	29,276	1	2		10	5	6					11			4			8	7			3	9		
25	Jan 3	(a)	Luton T	W 1-0	Neal	15,538	1			10	5	6					11			4			8	7		2	3	9		
26	31	(a)	Burnley	W 1-0	Gordon	22,151	1	2		10	5	6			11					4			8	7			3	9		
27	Feb 7	(h)	Preston NE	W 5-1	Orritt, Gordon, Larkin 2, Astall	21,252	1	2		10	5	6		9	11					4			8	7			3			
28	21	(h)	Everton	W 2-1	Larkin, Hooper	22,660	1	2		10	5	6	11	9						4			8	7			3			
29	28	(h)	West Ham U	W 3-0	Larkin 2, Neal	21,001	1	2		10		6			11			5		4			8	7			3	9		
30	Mar 7	(a)	Nottingham F	W 7-1	Stubbs 2, Gordon, Astall 2, Hooper, Watts	18,827	1	2		10	5	6	11							4			8	7			3		9	
31	14	(h)	Wolves	L 0-3		37,222	1	2		10	5	6	11							4			8	7			3		9	
32	18	(a)	Leicester C	W 4-2	Stubbs 3, Gordon	15,413	1	2		10	5	6			11					4			8	7			3		9	
33	21	(h)	Portsmouth	D 1-1	Larkin	18,149	1	2		10	5	6			11					4			8	7			3		9	
34	Apr 8	(a)	Bolton W	L 1-3	Stubbs	29,600	1			10	5	6			11					4			8	7		2	3		9	
35	11	(h)	Tottenham H	W 5-1	Stubbs, Gordon, Larkin, Hooper (pen), Baker (og)	20,534	1			10	5	6	11							4			8	7		2	3		9	
36	14	(h)	Arsenal	W 4-1	Stubbs, Larkin 2, Astall	25,791	1			10	5	6			11					4			8	7		2	3		9	
37	18	(a)	Manchester U	L 0-1		42,827	1			10	5	6			11					4			8	7		2	3		9	
38	20	(a)	Blackpool	L 0-2		12,260				9	5	6			10		11			4		1	8	7		2	3			
39	22	(a)	Blackburn R	W 3-0	Larkin 2, Taylor	22,941				9	5	6			10		11			4		1	8	7		2	3			
40	25	(h)	Chelsea	W 4-1	Gordon 2, Hooper, Taylor	19,571					5	6	11				10			4		1	8	7		2	3		9	
41	29	(a)	Newcastle U	D 1-1	Hooper	19,776					5	6	11		10					4		1	8	7		2	3		9	
42	May 4	(a)	Arsenal	L 1-2	Stubbs	26,129						6			10		11	5		4		1	8	7		2	3		9	
			Appearances				34	29	15	31	27	39	34	12	17	10	26	16	2	38	4	8	33	26	1	13	27	6	12	2
			Goals							18		4	8	1	8	4	5		1	1			10	8				6	9	

FINAL LEAGUE POSITION: 9th in Division One. Average home League attendance: 26,893.

1 own-goal

FA Cup

Rd	Date	V	Opponent	Res	Scorers	Att	Merrick G	Hall J	Green K	Larkin B	Smith T	Neal R	Hooper H	Orritt B	Brown E	Murphy P	Taylor B	Sissons G	Houghton B	Watts J	Jones D	Schofield J	Gordon J	Astall G	Hellawell M	Farmer B	Allen G	Jackson AJ	Stubbs R	Hume W
3	Jan 25	(a)	Middlesbrough	W 1-0	Harris (og)	36,587	1	2		10	5	6			11					4			8	7			3	9		
4	28	(h)	Fulham	D 1-1	Jackson	42,677	1	2		10	5	6			11					4			8	7			3	9		
R	Feb 4	(a)	Fulham	W 3-2	Hooper 2, Larkin	27,521	1	2		10	5	6	11							4			8	7			3	9		
5	14	(h)	Nottingham F	D 1-1	Astall	55,300	1	2		10	5	6	11	9						4			8	7			3			
R	18	(a)	Nottingham F	D 1-1	Gordon	39,431	1	2		10	5	6	11	7						4			8				3	9		
2R	23	(n†)	Nottingham F	L 0-5		34,458	1	2		10	5	6	11	9						4			8	7			3			
			Appearances				6	6		6	6	6	4	3	2					6			6	5			6	4		
			Goals							1			2										1	1				1		

†Played at Filbert Street, Leicester.

1 own-goal

1959-60

Manager: Pat Beasley

No	Date		Opponent	Result	Scorers	Att	Schofield J	Farmer B	Allen G	Watts J	Smith T	Neal R	Astall G	Gordon J	Stubbs R	Orritt B	Hooper H	Taylor B	Larkin B	Hellawell M	Sissons G	Merrick G	Barrett J	Wright P	Weston D	Hume W	Rudd W	Murphy P
1	Aug 22	(h)	Wolves	L 0-1		41,260	1	2	3	4	5	6	7	8	9	10	11											
2	26	(h)	Newcastle U	W 4-3	Stubbs, Gordon, Orritt, Hooper (pen)	26,981	1	2	3	4	5	6	7	8	9	10	11											
3	29	(a)	Tottenham H	D 0-0		45,243	1	2	3	4	5	6		8	9	10		7	11									
4	Sep 2	(a)	Newcastle U	L 0-1		35,395	1	2	3	4	5	6		8	9	10		7	11									
5	5	(h)	Manchester U	D 1-1	Watts	38,220	1	2	3	4	5	6		8	9		11		7	10								
6	9	(h)	Chelsea	D 1-1	Larkin	28,101	1	2	3	4	5	6		8	9		11		7	10								
7	12	(a)	Preston NE	L 2-3	Stubbs, Neal	19,134	1	2	3	4	5	6		8	9		11		7	10								
8	16	(a)	Chelsea	L 2-4	Hooper (pen), Scott (og)	31,651	1	2	3	4	5	6		8	9	10	11			7								
9	19	(h)	Leicester C	L 3-4	Hooper 2 (1 pen), Smith	25,003	1	2		4	5	6		8	9	10	11		7	3								
10	26	(a)	Burnley	L 1-3	Orritt	23,471		2	3	4	5	6		8		10	11	9	7			1						
11	Oct 3	(h)	Leeds U	W 2-0	Barrett, Taylor	25,298		2	3	4	5	6	7	8	9		11					1	10					
12	10	(h)	Sheffield W	D 0-0		21,769	1	2	3	4	5	6		8	9		11	10	7									
13	17	(a)	Nottingham F	W 2-0	Stubbs, Gordon	24,754	1	2	3	4			7	8	9		11			6	5		10					
14	24	(a)	Fulham	L 2-4	Gordon 2	26,698	1		3	4	5	6		8	9		11		7	2			10					
15	31	(a)	Arsenal	L 0-3		34,605	1	2	3	4	5	6		8	9		11	7					10					
16	Nov 7	(h)	Luton T	D 1-1	Barrett	19,007	1	2	3	4	5	6		8	9		11	7					10					
17	14	(a)	Everton	L 0-4		19,172	1	2	3	4	5			8	9	10	11	6	7									
18	21	(h)	Blackpool	W 2-1	Larkin, Hooper	24,782	1	2	3	4	5	6		8	9		11	10	7									
19	28	(a)	Blackburn R	L 1-2	Barrett	20,600	1		3	4	5	6		9			11	10	7				8	2				
20	Dec 5	(h)	Manchester C	W 4-2	Gordon 2, Barrett, Hooper	18,678	1	2	3	4	5	6		9			11	10	7				8					
21	12	(a)	Bolton W	L 1-4	Hooper	16,074	1	2	3	4	5	6		9			11	10	7				8					
22	19	(a)	Wolves	L 0-2		22,363	1	2	3	4	5	6		9			11	10	7				8					
23	26	(h)	West Ham U	W 2-0	Astall, Hooper	29,745	1	2	3	4	5		7	10	9		11	6					8					
24	28	(a)	West Ham U	L 1-3	Astall	26,500	1	2	3	4	5	6	7	8	9		11	10										
25	Jan 2	(a)	Tottenham H	L 0-1		27,525	1	2	3	4	5	6	7	8	9		11	10										
26	16	(a)	Manchester U	L 1-2	Larkin	47,361	1	2	3	4	5	6	7						8						9	10	11	
27	23	(h)	Preston NE	W 2-1	Larkin, Neal	24,137	1	2	3	4	5	6	7						8						9	10	11	
28	Feb 6	(a)	Leicester C	W 3-1	Weston, Hume, Hooper	25,946	1	2	3	4	5	6					11	7	8						9	10		
29	27	(a)	Manchester C	L 0-3		23,479	1	2	3	4	5	6		8			11	7		10					9			
30	Mar 5	(h)	Nottingham F	W 4-1	Gordon 2, Neal, Hooper	24,820	1	2	3	4	5	6	7	8	9		11								10			
31	9	(a)	Leeds U	D 3-3	Hume, Hooper, McConnell (og)	8,557	1	2	3	4	5	6	7	8			11								9	10		
32	12	(a)	Fulham	D 2-2	Gordon, Hooper	25,100	1	2	3	4	5	6	7	8			11								9	10		
33	19	(h)	Bolton W	L 2-5	Weston, Gordon	24,183	1	2	3	4	5	6		8			11				7				9	10		
34	26	(h)	Luton T	D 1-1	Weston	19,620	1	2	3	4	5	6	7	8			11								9	10		
35	Apr 2	(h)	Everton	D 2-2	Gordon, Astall	24,872	1	2	3	4	5	6	7	8	10		11								9			
36	9	(a)	Blackpool	W 1-0	Gordon	13,595	1	2	3	4	5	6	7	8			11								9			10
37	16	(h)	Arsenal	W 3-0	Murphy 2, Gordon	27,216	1	2	3	4	5	6	7	8			11								9			10
38	18	(h)	West Brom A	L 1-7		28,685	1	2	3	4	5	6	7	8			11								9			10
39	19	(a)	West Brom A	D 1-1	Gordon	37,937	1	2	3	4	5	6	7	8			11								9			10
40	23	(a)	Sheffield W	W 4-2	Murphy 2, Astall, Hooper	26,248	1	2	3	4	5	6	7	8			11								9			10
41	27	(h)	Burnley	L 0-1		37,014	1		3	4	5	6	7	8			11						2		9			10
42	30	(h)	Blackburn R	W 1-0	Gordon	24,487	1		3	4	5	6	7	8			11						2		9			10
			Appearances				40	40	36	41	41	39	19	39	18	16	39	8	19	11	8	2	10	1	16	8	4	7
			Goals							1	1	3	4	16	3	2	13	1	4				4		3	2		4

FINAL LEAGUE POSITION: 19th in Division One. Average home League attendance: 26,880.

2 own-goals

FA Cup

No	Date		Opponent	Result	Scorers	Att	Schofield J	Farmer B	Allen G	Watts J	Smith T	Neal R	Astall G	Gordon J	Stubbs R	Orritt B	Hooper H	Taylor B	Larkin B	Hellawell M	Sissons G	Merrick G	Barrett J	Wright P	Weston D	Hume W	Rudd W	Murphy P
3	Jan 9	(a)	Watford	L 1-2	Hooper	31,500	1	2	3	4	5	10	7	9			11	6					8					
			Appearances				1	1	1	1	1	1	1	1			1	1					1					
			Goals														1											

1960-61

Manager: Gil Merrick

Player columns (left to right): Schofield J, Farmer B, Allen G, Watts J, Smith T, Neal R, Astall G, Gordon J, Weston D, Rudd W, Hooper H, Stubbs R, Beard M, Singer DJ, Sissons G, Hellawell M, Barlow R, Orritt B, Taylor B, Withers C, Bloomfield J, Harris J, Hennessey T, Foster W

#	Date		Opponent	Result	Scorers	Att	Sc	Fa	Al	Wa	Sm	Ne	As	Go	We	Ru	Ho	St	Be	Si	Sis	He	Ba	Or	Ta	Wi	Bl	Ha	Hn	Fo
1	Aug 20	(a)	Bolton W	D 2-2	Gordon, Hooper	20,543	1	2	3	4	5	6	7	8	9	10	11													
2	24	(a)	West Brom A	W 2-1	Rudd, Hooper	22,102	1	2	3	4	5	6	7	8	9	10	11													
3	27	(h)	Sheffield W	D 1-1	Hooper	27,180	1	2	3	4	5	6	7	8	9	10	11													
4	31	(h)	West Brom A	W 3-1	Gordon, Astall, Williams (og)	37,740	1	2	3	4	5	6	7	8	9	10	11													
5	Sep 3	(a)	Fulham	L 1-2	Rudd	19,297	1	2	3	4	5	6	7	8	9	10	11													
6	6	(a)	Arsenal	L 0-2		20,285	1	2	3	4	5	6	7	8	9	10	11													
7	10	(h)	Preston NE	L 1-3	Gordon	24,410	1	2	3	4	5	6	7	8		10	11	9												
8	14	(h)	Arsenal	W 2-0	Stubbs 2	22,904	1	2	3	4	5	6	11	8		10	7	9												
9	17	(a)	Burnley	L 1-2	Cummings (og)	20,749	1	2	3	4	5		11	8		10	7	9	6											
10	24	(h)	Nottingham F	W 3-1	Gordon, Singer, Astall	26,615	1	2	3	4	5		11	8			7	9	6	10										
11	Oct 1	(a)	Manchester C	L 1-2	Singer	27,665	1	2	3	4	5		11	8			9	6		10	5	7								
12	8	(a)	West Ham U	L 3-4	Rudd, Hellawell 2	16,000	1	2	3	4		6	11	8		10		9			5	7								
13	15	(h)	Chelsea	W 1-0	Hellawell	23,337	1	2	3	4		6	11	8					8	9	5	7								
14	22	(a)	Aston Villa	L 2-6	Hellawell, Thompson (og)	46,306	1	2	3	4		6	11	9				8		10	5	7								
15	29	(h)	Wolves	L 1-2	Showell (og)	32,273	1	2	3	4		6		9			11			10	5	7	8							
16	Nov 5	(a)	Blackburn R	L 0-2		13,400	1	2	3	4		6			9		11			10	5	7	8							
17	12	(h)	Manchester U	W 3-1	Gordon, Taylor, Neal	31,549	1	2	3	4	5	6		8						10		7			9		11			
18	19	(a)	Tottenham H	L 0-6		46,010			3	4	5	6		8						9	2	7			11	1	10			
19	26	(h)	Leicester C	L 0-2		25,583		2	3	4	5	6		8						9		7			11	1	10			
20	Dec 3	(a)	Blackpool	W 2-1	Hellawell 2	27,691		2	3	4	5	6						8		9		7			11	1	10			
21	10	(h)	Everton	L 2-4	Neal, Stubbs	27,691		2	3	4	5	6						8				7			11	1	10	9		
22	17	(h)	Bolton W	D 2-2	Harris 2	19,050		2	3	4	5	6						8				7			11	1	10	9		
23	24	(a)	Newcastle U	D 2-2	Hellawell, Neal	20,354		2	3		5	6		8								7	4		11	1	10	9		
24	26	(h)	Newcastle U	W 2-1	Bloomfield, Hellawell	29,435		2	3		5	6		8								7	4		11	1	10	9		
25	31	(a)	Sheffield W	L 0-2		24,496		2	3		5	6		8								7	4		11	1	10	9		
26	Jan 14	(h)	Fulham	W 1-0	Singer	23,290		2	3	4		6								10	5	7			11	1	8	9		
27	21	(a)	Preston NE	W 3-2	Bloomfield, Hellawell, Singer	7,644		2	3	4		6								10	5	7			11	1	8	9		
28	Feb 11	(a)	Nottingham F	L 0-1		23,407		2	3	4	5	6		9						10		7			11	1	8			
29	25	(h)	West Ham U	W 4-2	Harris 2 (1 pen), Bloomfield, Neal	16,850		2	3	4		6	7	8							5				11	1	10	9		
30	Mar 4	(a)	Chelsea	L 2-3	Gordon, Astall	27,727		2	3	4	5	6	7	8											11	1	10	9		
31	11	(h)	Aston Villa	D 1-1	Singer	41,645		2		4	5	6	7							10	3				11	1	8	9		
32	18	(a)	Wolves	L 1-5	Singer	23,384		2		4	5	6						11		9	3				7		8	10		
33	22	(h)	Manchester C	W 3-2	Harris (pen), Bloomfield 2	18,092		2			5	6								10	3	7			11	1	8	9	4	
34	25	(h)	Blackburn R	D 1-1	Hellawell	19,288		2	3		5	6								10		7			11	1	8	9	4	
35	31	(a)	Cardiff C	W 2-0	Harris (pen), Orritt	18,000		2	3		5	6						11				7		8		1	10	9	4	
36	Apr 1	(a)	Everton	L 0-1		31,872		2	3		5	6						11				7		8		1	10	9	4	
37	3	(h)	Cardiff C	W 2-1	Harris, Orritt	20,047		2	3		5	6						11				7		8		1	10	9	4	
38	8	(h)	Tottenham H	L 2-3	Harris 2 (1 pen)	40,960		2	3		5	6										7		8	11	1	10	9	4	
39	15	(a)	Manchester U	L 1-4	Foulkes (og)	28,376		2	3		5	6			9							7		8	11	1	10		4	
40	22	(h)	Blackpool	L 0-2		17,834	1	2	3		5	6						8				7			11		10	9	4	
41	27	(h)	Burnley	L 0-1		15,011		2	3			6								10		7			11	1	8	9	4	5
42	29	(a)	Leicester C	L 2-3	Harris, Singer	19,920		2	3			6								10		7			11	1	8	9	4	5
			Appearances				18	41	39	29	31	39	17	24	7	18	10	12	3	18	13	28	5	12	17	24	25	20	10	2
			Goals									4	3	6		3	3	3		7		10		2	1		5	10		

FINAL LEAGUE POSITION: 19th in Division One. Average home League attendance: 25,751.

5 own-goals

FA Cup

#	Date		Opponent	Result	Scorers	Att	Fa	Al	Wa	Sm	Ne	As	St	Si	Sis	He	Ta	Wi	Bl	Ha
3	Jan 7	(a)	Nottingham F	W 2-0	Singer 2	29,905	2		4	5	6			10	3	7	11	1	8	9
4	28	(h)	Rotherham U	W 4-0	Singer 2, Neal, Harris	31,931	2	3	4	5	6			10		7	11	1	8	9
5	Feb 18	(h)	Leicester C	D 1-1	Harris (pen)	53,589	2	3	4	5	6	11		10		7		1	8	9
R	22	(a)	Leicester C	L 1-2	Harris	41,916	2	3	4	5	6	7		10			11	1	8	9
			Appearances				4	3	4	4	4	2		4	1	3	3	4	4	4
			Goals								1			4						3

League Cup

#	Date		Opponent	Result	Scorers	Att	Sc	Fa	Al	Wa	Sm	Ne	As	Go	Ru	Ho	Si	Sis	He	Ba	Or	Ta	Wi	Bl
2	Oct 31	(a)	Bradford	W 1-0	Hellawell	4,736	1	2	3	4		6	11				10	5	7	8	9			
3	Nov 14	(h)	Plymouth A	D 0-0		15,300		2	3	4	5	6		8					7		9	11	1	10
R	16	(a)	Plymouth A	L 1-3	Wyatt (og)	14,132		2	3	4	5	6		8	9	10			7			11	1	
			Appearances				1	3	3	3	2	3	1	2	1	1	1	1	3	1	2	2	2	1
			Goals																1					

1 own-goal

1961-62

Manager: Gil Merrick

No	Date		Opponent	Result	Scorers	Att	Withers C	Farmer B	Beard M	Watts J	Smith T	Neal R	Hellawell M	Bloomfield J	Harris J	Rudd W	Auld R	Foster W	Hennessey T	Orritt B	Allen G	Stubbs R	Singer DJ	Taylor B	Schofield J	Sissons G	Lynn S	Leek K	Wright P	Bullock P	Thwaites D
1	Aug 19	(h) Fulham	W 2-1	Harris, Bloomfield	25,371	1	2	3	4	5	6	7	8	9	10	11														
2	22	(a) Nottingham F	L 1-2	Harris	19,436	1		3	4	5	6	7	8	9	10	11	2													
3	26	(a) Sheffield W	L 1-5	Bloomfield	30,595	1		3		5	6	7	8	9		11	2	4		10										
4	30	(h) Nottingham F	D 1-1	Harris	21,079	1		6		5	4	7	8	9		11	2	3		10										
5	Sep 2	(h) Leicester C	L 1-5	Bloomfield	21,950	1		6		5	4	7	8	9		11	2	3		10										
6	6	(a) West Brom A	D 0-0		20,541	1		6	4	5		7	8	9		11	2	3		10										
7	9	(a) Ipswich T	L 1-4	Singer	20,017	1		6	4	5		7	8	9			2	3		10		11								
8	16	(h) Burnley	L 2-6	Bloomfield, Hellawell	18,742		2	6		5	4	7	10	9							3	8	11	1						
9	20	(h) West Brom A	L 1-2	Hellawell	22,902		2	6		5		7	10	9		11		4	8					1	3					
10	23	(a) Arsenal	D 1-1	Harris (pen)	31,749		2	6		5		7	8	9		11		4	10					1	3					
11	30	(h) Bolton W	W 2-1	Bloomfield, Auld	17,192		2	6		5		7	8	9		11		4	10					1	3					
12	Oct 7	(h) Wolves	L 3-6	Harris 2 (1 pen), Bloomfield	29,122		2	6		5		7	10	9				4	8				11	1	3					
13	14	(a) Manchester U	W 2-0	Orritt, Hellawell	30,674		2	6				7	8	9		11	5	4	10					1	3					
14	21	(h) Chelsea	W 3-2	Harris, Bloomfield 2	20,079			6				7	8	9		11	5	4	10					1	3	2				
15	28	(a) Aston Villa	W 3-1	Harris 2, Orritt	39,790			6		5		7	8	9		11		4	10					1	3	2				
16	Nov 4	(h) Blackpool	D 1-1	Orritt	21,450			6		5		7	8	9		11		4	10					1	3	2				
17	11	(a) Blackburn R	L 0-2		12,080			6		5		7		9		11		4	10		8			1	3	2				
18	18	(h) West Ham U	W 4-0	Harris (pen), Bloomfield, Orritt, Auld	20,645			6		5		7	8	9		11		4	10					1	3	2				
19	25	(a) Sheffield U	L 1-3	Harris	16,838			6		5		7		9		11		4	8					1	3	2	10			
20	Dec 2	(h) Cardiff C	W 3-0	Leek 2, Hellawell	20,939			6		5		7		9		11		4	8					1	3	2	10			
21	9	(a) Tottenham H	L 1-3	Leek	32,509			6		5		7		9		11		4	8					1	3	2	10			
22	16	(h) Fulham	W 1-0	Leek	12,630			6		5		7		9		11		4	8					1	3	2	10			
23	23	(h) Sheffield W	D 1-1	Leek	19,078			6		5		7		9		11		4	8					1	3	2	10			
24	26	(h) Manchester C	D 1-1	Leek	21,902			6		5		7		9		11		4	8					1	3	2	10			
25	Jan 13	(a) Leicester C	W 2-1	Harris, Auld	22,681			6		5		7	8	9		11		4						1	3	2	10			
26	20	(a) Ipswich T	W 3-1	Leek 2, Baker (og)	26,968			6		5		7	8	9		11		4						1	3	2	10			
27	Feb 3	(a) Burnley	L 1-7	Auld	24,246			6		5		7	8	9		11		4						1	3	2	10			
28	10	(h) Arsenal	W 1-0	Harris	27,797			6		5		7	8	9		11	2	4						1	3		10			
29	17	(a) Bolton W	L 2-3	Leek, Auld	13,308			6		5		7	8	9		11	2	4						1	3		10			
30	24	(a) Wolves	L 1-2	Leek	29,662			6		5		7	8			11		4			9			1	3	2	10			
31	Mar 3	(h) Manchester U	D 1-1	Leek	25,817			6		5		7	8			11		4			9			1	3	2	10			
32	9	(a) Chelsea	D 1-1	Leek	23,959			6		5		7	8	9		11		4						1	3	2	10			
33	17	(h) Aston Villa	L 0-2		45,885			6		5		7	8	9		11		4						1	3	2	10			
34	24	(a) Blackpool	L 0-1		11,854			6		5		7	8	9		11		4						1	3	2	10			
35	30	(h) Blackburn R	W 2-1	Leek, Hellawell	17,430			6		5		7	8	9		11		4						1	3	2	10			
36	Apr 6	(a) West Ham U	D 2-2	Bloomfield, Lynn	22,548			6		5		7	8	9		11		4						1	3	2	10			
37	11	(a) Manchester C	W 4-1	Harris, Bloomfield, Leek, Hellawell	21,941			6	4	5		7	8	9		11	2							1	3		10			
38	14	(h) Sheffield U	W 3-0	Harris 2 (1 pen), Hellawell	19,476			6		5		7	8	9		11	2	4						1	3		10			
39	20	(a) Everton	L 1-4	Leek	47,506		2	6		5		7	8	9		11		4						1	3		10			
40	21	(a) Cardiff C	L 2-3	Leek 2	8,800			6		5		7	8	9		11	2	4						1			10	3		
41	24	(h) Everton	D 0-0		21,910			6				7	8			11	5	4						1	3		10	2	9	
42	28	(h) Tottenham H	L 2-3	Leek, Beard	29,614			6		5		7	8	9		11	2	4						1	3		10			
		Appearances				7	8	42	5	39	6	42	35	39	2	39	15	34	16	5	7	2	3	35	33	21	24	2	1	
		Goals						1				7	11	16		5			4			1				1	18			

FINAL LEAGUE POSITION: 17th in Division One.   Average home League attendance: 23,587.

1 own-goal

FA Cup

Rd	Date		Opponent	Result	Scorers	Att	Beard M	Smith T	Hellawell M	Harris J	Auld R	Hennessey T	Orritt B	Schofield J	Sissons G	Lynn S	Leek K
3	Jan 6	(h) Tottenham H	D 3-3	Harris 2, Leek	46,096	6	5	7	9	11	4	8	1	3	2	10
R	10	(a) Tottenham H	L 2-4	Harris, Leek	62,917	6	5	7	9	11	4	8	1	3	2	10
		Appearances					2	2	2	2	2	2	2	2	2	2	2
		Goals								3							2

League Cup

Rd	Date		Opponent	Result	Scorers	Att	Farmer B	Beard M	Smith T	Neal R	Hellawell M	Bloomfield J	Harris J	Hennessey T	Orritt B	Allen G	Stubbs R	Singer DJ	Taylor B	Schofield J	Sissons G	Wright P
1	Sep 13	(h) Swindon T	D 1-1	Neal	11,584	2	6	5	4	7	8				3	9	10	11	1		
R	25	(a) Swindon T	L 0-2		13,063	2	6	5		7	10	9	4	8					1	3	11
		Appearances				2	2	2	1	2	2	1	1	1	1	1	1	1	2	1	1
		Goals							1												

1962-63

Manager: Gil Merrick

#	Date	Opponent	Res	Scorers	Att	Schofield J	Lynn S	Sissons G	Hennessey T	Smith T	Beard M	Hellawell M	Bullock P	Harris J	Leek K	Auld R	Thwaites D	Stubbs R	Bloomfield J	Watts J	Withers C	Sharples B	Foster W	Regan MJ	Farrell G	Green C	Rushton B	Wolstenholme T
1	Aug 18 (a)	Tottenham H	L 0-3		51,140	1	2	3	4	5	6	7	8	9	10	11												
2	21 (a)	Arsenal	L 0-2		34,004	1	2	3	4	5	6	7	8	9	10		11											
3	25 (h)	Leyton O	D 2-2	Bullock, Hellawell	23,500	1	2	3	4	5	6	7	8		10		11	9										
4	29 (h)	Arsenal	D 2-2	Leek, Lynn (pen)	27,135	1	2	3	4	5	6	7			10		11	9	8									
5	Sep 1 (a)	Manchester U	L 0-2		39,847	1	2	3	4	5	6	7		9	10	11			8									
6	8 (h)	Burnley	W 5-1	Hellawell 2, Leek, Bloomfield, Bullock	24,423	1	2	3	4	5	6	7	10		9		11		8									
7	12 (a)	West Brom A	L 0-1		25,499	1	2	3	4	5	6	7	10		9		11		8									
8	15 (a)	Sheffield W	L 0-5		22,255	1	2	3	4	5		7	10		9		11		8		6							
9	19 (h)	West Brom A	D 0-0		28,625		2		4		6	7		9	10	11			8		1	3	5					
10	22 (h)	Fulham	W 4-1	Harris, Leek, Auld, Lynn (pen)	20,477		2		4		6	7		9	10	11			8		1	3	5					
11	29 (a)	Leicester C	L 0-3		22,110		2		4		6	7		9	10	11			8		1	3	5					
12	Oct 6 (a)	West Ham U	L 0-5		21,039			3	4	5	6	7	8	9	10	11					1		2					
13	13 (h)	Manchester C	D 2-2	Regan, Stubbs	21,114		2	3	4	5	6	7	10				11		8		1			9				
14	24 (a)	Wolves	W 2-0	Leek 2	26,226		2	3	4	5	6	7		9	10	11			8		1							
15	27 (h)	Aston Villa	W 3-2	Leek 2, Lynn (pen)	42,207		2	3	6	5		7		9	10	11			8	4	1							
16	Nov 3 (a)	Sheffield U	W 2-0	Stubbs, Hellawell	19,188		2	3	6	5		7		9	10	11			8	4	1							
17	10 (h)	Nottingham F	D 2-2	Harris, Leek	22,024		2	3	6	5		7		9	10	11			8	4	1							
18	17 (a)	Ipswich T	W 5-1	Harris 2, Leek 2, Auld	16,775		2	3	5	6		7		9	10	11			8	4	1							
19	24 (h)	Liverpool	L 0-2		27,050		2	3	6	5		7		9	10	11			8	4	1							
20	Dec 1 (a)	Blackpool	D 1-1	Leek	12,955		2	3	6	5			8	9	10	11				4	1				7			
21	8 (h)	Blackburn R	D 3-3	Bloomfield, Leek 2	16,089		2	3	6	5				9	10	11			8	4	1				7			
22	15 (h)	Tottenham H	L 0-2		36,623		2		4	5	6	7		9	10	11			8		1					3		
23	22 (a)	Leyton O	D 2-2	Bloomfield 2	11,646		2		4		6	7		9	10	11			8		1		5			3		
24	Mar 21 (a)	Manchester C	L 1-2	Harris	28,798		2		4	5	6	7		9	10	11			8		1					3		
25	9 (h)	Wolves	L 3-4	Auld, Lynn 2 (2 pens)	18,217		2		4	5	6	7		9	10	11			8		1					3		
26	16 (a)	Aston Villa	L 0-4		46,680	1	2		4	5	6	7		9	10	11			8							3		
27	23 (h)	Sheffield U	L 0-1		18,032	1	2		4	5	6	7		9	10	11			8							3		
28	30 (h)	Sheffield W	D 1-1	Auld (pen)	12,800	1			6	5	3	7		9	10	11			8	4							2	
29	Apr 3 (h)	Bolton W	D 2-2	Leek 2	13,190	1			6	5	3	7		9	10	11			8	4							2	
30	6 (h)	Ipswich T	L 0-1		17,013	1			6	5	3	7		9	10	11			8	4							2	
31	13 (a)	Nottingham F	W 2-0	Leek 2	15,575	1			6	5	3	7			10	11			8	4				9			2	
32	15 (a)	Everton	D 2-2	Bloomfield, Leek	50,122	1			4	5	6	7		9	10	11			8							3	2	
33	16 (h)	Everton	L 0-1		29,719	1			4	5	6	7		9	10	11			8		5					3	2	
34	20 (h)	Blackpool	L 3-6	Bloomfield, Leek, Auld	15,372	1			4	5	6	7		9	10	11			8							3	2	
35	24 (a)	Bolton W	D 0-0		12,860				4	5	6	7			10	11		9	8		1					3	2	
36	27 (a)	Blackburn R	L 1-6	Auld	9,500				4	5	6	7		9	10	11			8		1					3	2	
37	May 1 (h)	West Ham U	W 3-2	Harris, Auld, Hennessey	14,392		2		4	5	6	7		9	10	11			8		1					3		
38	4 (a)	Fulham	D 3-3	Harris, Hellawell, Auld	20,279		2		4	5	6	7		9	10	11			8		1					3		
39	8 (a)	Liverpool	L 1-5	Leek	23,684		2		4	5	6	7		9	10	11			8		1					3		
40	10 (h)	Manchester U	W 2-1	Bloomfield 2	21,814		2		4	5	6	7		9	10	11			8		1					3		
41	14 (a)	Burnley	L 1-3	Bloomfield	14,340		2		4	5	6	7		9	10	11			8		1					3		
42	18 (h)	Leicester C	W 3-2	Harris, Auld, Lynn (pen)	23,931	1	2		4	5	6	7		9	10	11			8							3		

FINAL LEAGUE POSITION: 20th in Division One.   Average home League attendance: 22,559.

	Schofield J	Lynn S	Sissons G	Hennessey T	Smith T	Beard M	Hellawell M	Bullock P	Harris J	Leek K	Auld R	Thwaites D	Stubbs R	Bloomfield J	Watts J	Withers C	Sharples B	Foster W	Regan MJ	Farrell G	Green C	Rushton B	Wolstenholme T
Appearances	18	33	17	42	37	34	40	14	29	41	36	6	12	28	13	24	3	5	2	2	17	9	
Goals		6		1			5	2	8	20	9		2	9					1				

FA Cup

#	Date	Opponent	Res	Scorers	Att	Lynn S	Hennessey T	Smith T	Beard M	Hellawell M	Harris J	Leek K	Auld R	Bloomfield J	Withers C	Green C
3	Mar 5 (h)	Bury	D 3-3	Leek, Harris, Lynn (pen)	11,361	2	4	5	6	7	9	10	11	8	1	3
R	7 (a)	Bury	L 0-2		16,625	2	4	5	6	7	9	10	11	8	1	3
	Appearances					2	2	2	2	2	2	2	2	2	2	2
	Goals					1					1	1				

League Cup

#	Date	Opponent	Res	Scorers	Att	Schofield J	Lynn S	Sissons G	Hennessey T	Smith T	Beard M	Hellawell M	Bullock P	Harris J	Leek K	Auld R	Thwaites D	Stubbs R	Bloomfield J	Watts J	Withers C	Sharples B	Foster W	Regan MJ	Farrell G	Green C	Rushton B	Wolstenholme T
2	Sep 26 (h)	Doncaster R	W 5-0	Leek 2, Bloomfield, Harris, Auld	11,361		2		4		6	7		9	10	11			8		1	3	5					
3	Oct 15 (a)	Barrow	D 1-1	Wolstenholme	6,289		2	3	4	5	6	7			11		8					9					10	6
R	29 (h)	Barrow	W 5-1	Harris 2, Stubbs, Leek, Arrowsmith (og)	11,765		2	3		5		7		9	10	11	8		4	1								
4	Nov 14 (h)	Notts C	W 3-2	Lynn (pen), Harris, Auld	13,187		2	3	6	5		7		9	10	11	8		4	1								
5	Dec 11 (h)	Manchester C	W 6-0	Lynn 2 (1 pen), Leek, Auld, Leivers (og), Sear (og)	18,010		2		6	5	3	7		9	10	11	8		4	1								
SF	Mar 27 (h)	Bury	W 3-2	Bullock, Leek, Auld	11,266	1			6	5	3	7	9		10	11		8	4					2				
	Apr 8 (a)	Bury	D 1-1	Leek	9,177	1			4	5	6	7			10	11		8	5				9	3	2			
F	May 23 (h)	Aston Villa	W 3-1	Leek 2, Bloomfield	31,580	1	2		4	5	6	7		9	10	11		8							3			
	27 (a)	Aston Villa	D 0-0		37,921	1	2		4	5	6	7		9	10	11		8							3			
	Appearances					4	7	3	8	7	7	9	1	6	8	9	3	6	5	5	5	1	1	2	3	2	2	1
	Goals						3						1	4	8	4		1	2								1

3 own-goals

1963-64

Manager: Gil Merrick

No	Date	Venue & Opponents	Result	Scorers	Att	Withers C	Lynn S	Green C	Foster W	Smith T	Hennessey T	Hellawell M	Bloomfield J	Harley A	Leek K	Auld R	Beard M	Bullock P	Harris J	Rushton B	Farrell G	Thomson RG	Schofield J	Thwaites D	Martin Ray	Anderson G	Bullock M	Farmer B	Regan MJ	Vincent J
1	Aug 24 (h)	Bolton W	W 2-1	Lynn (pen), Hellawell	24,817	1	2	3	4	5	6	7	8	9	10	11														
2	28 (a)	Leicester C	L 0-1		27,661	1	2	3	4	5	6	7	8	9	10	11														
3	31 (a)	Fulham	L 1-2	Lynn (pen)	21,260	1	2	3		5	4	7	8	9		11	6					10								
4	Sep 4 (h)	Leicester C	W 2-0	Leek, Hellawell	23,851	1	2	3		5	4	7	8	9	10	11	6													
5	7 (a)	Manchester U	D 1-1	Harley	36,874	1	2	3		5	4	7	8	9	10	11	6													
6	11 (h)	West Brom A	L 0-1		34,666	1	2	3		5	4	7	8	9	10	11	6													
7	14 (a)	Burnley	L 1-2	Harris	20,550	1	2	3	4	5		7	10			11	6	8	9											
8	18 (a)	West Brom A	L 1-3	Harris	29,662	1		3		5	4	7	8	9	10		6		11		2									
9	21 (h)	Ipswich T	W 1-0	Beard	19,095	1		3		5	4	7	8	9	10		6			2	11									
10	28 (a)	Sheffield W	L 1-2	Thomson	18,903	1		3		5	4	7	8	9		11	6			2		10								
11	Oct 2 (a)	Tottenham H	L 1-6	Auld	37,649		2	3		5	4	7		9		11	6					10	1	8						
12	5 (h)	Everton	L 0-2		23,593		2	3		5	4	7	8	9		11	6					10	1							
13	19 (a)	Sheffield U	L 0-3		18,974	1	2	3		5	4	7	8	9	10	11	6													
14	26 (h)	Wolves	D 2-2	Harley, Woodfield (og)	24,804	1	2	3		5	4	7	8	9			6				11	10								
15	Nov 2 (a)	Chelsea	W 3-2	Harley, P.Bullock, Auld	22,974	1	2	3		5	4	7	8	9		11	6	10												
16	5 (a)	Arsenal	L 1-4	Bloomfield	33,908	1	2	3		5	4	7	8	9		11	6	10												
17	9 (h)	Blackpool	W 3-2	Bloomfield, Auld, Lynn	17,516	1	2	3		5	4	7	8	9		11	6	10												
18	16 (a)	Blackburn R	L 0-3		14,800	1	2	3		5	4	7	8		10	11	6		9											
19	23 (h)	Nottingham F	D 3-3	Auld 2, Smith	18,158	1	2	3		5	4	7	8		10	11	6		9											
20	30 (a)	Stoke C	L 1-4	Auld	27,308	1	2	3		5		7	8	9	10	11	6					4								
21	Dec 7 (h)	West Ham U	W 2-1	Auld, Lynn (pen)	15,357	1	2	3		5	4	7	8		10	11	6		9											
22	14 (a)	Bolton W	W 2-0	Leek, Hellawell	9,517	1	2	3		5	4	7	8		10	11	6		9											
23	21 (h)	Fulham	D 0-0		13,092	1	2	3		5	4	7	8		10	11	6		9											
24	28 (h)	Arsenal	L 1-4	Harley	23,329	1	2	3		5		7	8	9	10	11	6					4								
25	Jan 11 (a)	Manchester U	W 2-1	M.Bullock, Harley	44,695	1	2			5	4		8	9		11	6					10			3		7			
26	18 (h)	Burnley	D 0-0		15,871	1	2			5	4	7	8			11	6					10			3		9			
27	Feb 1 (a)	Ipswich T	L 2-3	Regan, Farmer	13,349	1	2			5	4	7	8									10		11	3			6	9	
28	8 (h)	Sheffield W	L 1-2	Harley	15,460	1	2			5	4	7	8	9			6					10		11	3					
29	18 (a)	Everton	L 0-3		36,252	1	2			5	4	7	8	9	10		6							11	3					
30	22 (h)	Liverpool	L 1-2	Leek	41,823	1		3		5	4	7	8		10		6				9			11						2
31	29 (h)	Tottenham H	L 1-2	Thomson	28,433	1		3		5	4	7	8	9			6					10		11						2
32	Mar 7 (a)	Wolves	L 1-5	Harley	16,421	1		3		5	4	7	8	9		11	6					10			2					
33	13 (h)	Blackburn R	D 2-2	Leek, Auld	15,780	1		3		5	4	7			10	11	6							9	2				8	
34	20 (a)	Blackpool	L 0-3		10,201	1		3		5	4	7			10	11	6							9	2				8	
35	28 (h)	Chelsea	L 3-4	Thwaites 2, Auld	14,482	1		3		5	4	7	8			11	6							10	2				9	
36	30 (a)	Aston Villa	W 3-0	Harris, Hellawell, Lynn (pen)	25,890	1	2	3		5	4	7	8		10	11	6		9											
37	31 (h)	Aston Villa	D 3-3	Bloomfield, Leek, Lynn (pen)	28,048	1	2	3		5	4	7	8		10	11	6		9											
38	Apr 4 (a)	Nottingham F	L 0-4		13,888	1	2	3		5	4	7	8		10	11	6		9											
39	11 (h)	Stoke C	L 0-1		19,890	1	2		9	5	4	7	8			11	6					10			3					
40	17 (a)	West Ham U	L 0-5		22,106		2			5	4	7	8			11	6				9	10	1		3					
41	22 (h)	Liverpool	W 3-1	Leek, Hellawell, Lynn (pen)	22,623	1	2		6	5	4	7	8		10	11								9	3					
42	25 (h)	Sheffield U	W 3-0	Auld, Smith, Lynn (pen)	26,191		2		6	5	4	7	8	9		11						10	1		3					
				Appearances		38	33	33	14	34	39	39	34	23	26	34	36	11	5	3	2	21	4	10	14	1	2	1	3	2
				Goals			8			2		5	3	7	6	10	1	1	3			2		2			1	1	1	

FINAL LEAGUE POSITION: 20th in Division One. Average home League attendance: 21,996.

1 own-goal

FA Cup

No	Date	Venue & Opponents	Result	Scorers	Att	Withers C	Lynn S	Green C	Foster W	Smith T	Hennessey T	Hellawell M	Bloomfield J	Harley A	Leek K	Auld R	Beard M	Bullock P	Harris J	Rushton B	Farrell G	Thomson RG	Schofield J	Thwaites D	Martin Ray	Anderson G	Bullock M	Farmer B	Regan MJ	Vincent J
3	Jan 4 (h)	Port Vale	L 1-2	Beard	21,615	1	2	3		5	4	7	8		10	11	6		9											
				Appearances		1	1	1		1	1	1	1		1	1	1		1											
				Goals													1													

League Cup

No	Date	Venue & Opponents	Result	Scorers	Att	Withers C	Lynn S	Green C	Foster W	Smith T	Hennessey T	Hellawell M	Bloomfield J	Harley A	Leek K	Auld R	Beard M	Bullock P	Harris J	Rushton B	Farrell G	Thomson RG	Schofield J	Thwaites D	Martin Ray	Anderson G	Bullock M	Farmer B	Regan MJ	Vincent J
2	Sep 25 (a)	Norwich C	L 0-2		16,714	1		3		5	4	7	8	9	10		6			2	11									
				Appearances		1		1		1	1	1	1	1	1		1			1	1									
				Goals																										

1964-65

Manager: Joe Mallett

#	Date	Opponent	Res	Scorers	Att	Withers C	Lynn S	Green C	Foster W	Smith T	Beard M	Hellawell M	Jackson A	Harley A	Leek K	Thwaites D	Hennessey T	Thomson RG	Auld R	Schofield J	Martin R	Vincent J	Vowden G	Sharples B	Bullock P	Fenton R	Page M	Fraser C	Beel W	Bullock M
1	Aug 22 (a)	Nottingham F	L 3-4	Harley, Hellawell, Lynn (pen)	26,019	1	2	3	4	5	6	7	8	9	10	11														
2	26 (h)	Fulham	D 2-2	Leek, Lynn (pen)	20,678	1	2	3	4	5	6	7	8	9	10	11														
3	29 (h)	Stoke C	L 1-2	Lynn (pen)	20,692	1	2	3	4	5	6		7	9			11	8	10											
4	Sep 2 (a)	Fulham	L 1-3	Beard	13,100	1	2	3	4	5	6	7		9				8	10	11										
5	5 (a)	Tottenham H	L 1-4	Thomson	34,809	1	2	3	5		6	7	8		10			4	9	11										
6	9 (h)	West Brom A	D 1-1	Thomson	26,485		2		5		6	7	8		10			4	9	11	1	3								
7	12 (h)	Burnley	W 2-1	Thomson, Lynn (pen)	16,856		2		5		6	7	8		10			4	9	11	1	3								
8	16 (a)	West Brom A	W 2-0	Auld, Williams (og)	26,013		2		5		6	7	8		10			4	9	11	1	3								
9	19 (a)	Sheffield U	L 1-3	Thomson	16,390		2		5		6	7	8		10			4	9	11	1	3								
10	26 (h)	Everton	L 3-5	Leek, Hellawell, Hennessey	21,240		2		5		6	7	8		10			4	9	11	1	3								
11	30 (h)	Wolves	W 2-0	Leek, Lynn	22,000		2		5		6	7	8		10			4	9	11	1	3								
12	Oct 10 (h)	Liverpool	D 0-0		19,850		2		5		6	7	8		10			4	9	11	1	3								
13	17 (a)	Sheffield W	L 2-5	Auld, Hennessey	16,161		2		5		6	7	8					4	9	11	1	3	10							
14	24 (a)	Blackpool	W 3-0	Vowden, Leek, Lynn (pen)	15,800		2		5		6	7			10			4	9	11	1	3	8							
15	31 (a)	Blackburn R	L 1-3	Harley	13,721		2		5		6	7		10				4	9	11	1	3	8							
16	Nov 7 (a)	Arsenal	L 2-3	Vowden, Leek	20,219		2		5		6				10		7	4	9	11	1	3	8							
17	14 (a)	Leeds U	L 1-4	Thomson	32,030		2		5		6	7			10			4	9	11	1	3	8							
18	22 (h)	Chelsea	L 1-6	Jackson	18,003		2		5		6	7	10					4	9	11	1	3	8							
19	28 (a)	Leicester C	D 4-4	Thomson 2 (1 pen), Vowden, Thwaites	15,848		2		5		6		7			11		4	9		1	3	10	8						
20	Dec 5 (h)	Sunderland	W 4-3	Thomson, Sharples, Jackson, Thwaites	13,565		2		5		6		7		10	11		4	9		1	3		8						
21	12 (h)	Nottingham F	D 1-1	Thomson	14,396		2		5		6		7			11		4	9		1	3	10	8						
22	16 (a)	Manchester U	D 1-1	Thwaites	25,271		2	3	5		6		7			11		4	9		1		10	8						
23	26 (h)	West Ham U	W 2-1	Thwaites, Lynn	23,324		2	3	5		6		7			11		4	9		1		10	8						
24	28 (a)	West Ham U	L 1-2	Sharples	23,800		2		5		6		7			11		4		10	1	3	9	8						
25	Jan 2 (h)	Tottenham H	W 1-0	Beard	33,833		2	3	5		6		7			11		4		10	1		9		8					
26	16 (a)	Burnley	L 0-2		9,959		2	3	5		6		7			11		4			1		10	8		9				
27	23 (h)	Sheffield U	D 1-1	Foster	16,680		2	3	5		6		7			11		4			1		10	8		9				
28	Feb 6 (a)	Everton	D 1-1	Fenton	34,043		2	3	5		6		7			11					1		10	4		9	8			
29	13 (a)	Aston Villa	L 0-1		32,491		2	3	5		6		7			11					1		10	8		9	4			
30	24 (h)	Liverpool	L 3-4	Vowden, Fenton, Thwaites	39,253		2	3	5		6					11		4	9		1		10			7	8			
31	27 (h)	Sheffield W	D 0-0		12,138		2	3	5		6					11		4	9		1		10			7	8			
32	Mar 6 (a)	Blackpool	L 1-3	Vowden	11,464		2	3	5		6					11		4	9		1		10				8			7
33	13 (h)	Wolves	L 0-1		18,860		2	3	5		6		7			11		4	9		1		10				8			
34	17 (a)	Stoke C	L 1-2	Vowden	12,899		2		5		6		7			11		4			1	8	10	3						9
35	Apr 3 (a)	Chelsea	L 1-3	Lynn (pen)	28,975		2		5		6		7			11		4			1	8	10	3						9
36	6 (a)	Arsenal	L 0-3		16,048		2		5		6		7			11		4			1	8	10	3						9
37	10 (h)	Leicester C	W 2-0	Vowden, Jackson	12,460		2	3	5				7			11		4			1	8	10	6						9
38	12 (a)	Aston Villa	L 0-3		37,003		2	3	5				7			11		4			1		9	6			10			8
39	17 (a)	Sunderland	L 1-2	Lynn (pen)	31,958		2		5				7			11		4			1		10	3			6	8		9
40	19 (h)	Manchester U	L 2-4	Vowden, Thwaites	38,907		2		5		10		7			11		4			1		9	3			6	8		
41	24 (h)	Blackburn R	D 5-5	Vowden, Beard 3, Lynn (pen)	8,877		2		5		10		7			11		4			1		9	3			6	8		
42	26 (h)	Leeds U	D 3-3	Vowden, Beard, Thwaites	16,644		2	3	5		10		7			11		4			1		9	3			6			
	Appearances					5	39	22	42	4	39	16	36	5	14	26	38	25	17	36	19	5	27	19	1	6	8	5	1	7
	Goals						10		1		6	2	3	2	5	7	2	9	2				10	2		2				

1 own-goal

FA Cup

#	Date	Opponent	Res	Scorers	Att	Lynn S	Green C	Foster W	Beard M	Jackson A	Thwaites D	Thomson RG	Schofield J	Martin R	Vowden G	Sharples B
3	Jan 9 (a)	West Ham U	L 2-4	Jackson, Thwaites	31,056	2	3	5	6	7	11	4	10	1	9	8
	Appearances					1	1	1	1	1	1	1	1	1	1	1
	Goals									1	1					

League Cup

#	Date	Opponent	Res	Scorers	Att	Lynn S	Foster W	Beard M	Hellawell M	Jackson A	Leek K	Thomson RG	Auld R	Schofield J	Martin R	Vincent J
2	Sep 23 (h)	Chelsea	L 0-3		15,300	2	5	6	7	8	10	4	9	11	1	3
	Appearances					1	1	1	1	1	1	1	1	1	1	1
	Goals															

FINAL LEAGUE POSITION: 22nd in Division One. Average home League attendance: 19,714.

1965-66

Manager: Joe Mallett until December 1965 then Stan Cullis

No	Date	Opponent	Result	Scorers	Att	Heriot J	Martin Ray	Green C	Wylie R	Foster W	Hennessey T	Jackson A	Vowden G	Beard M	Thomson RG	Thwaites D	Sharples B	Fraser C	Page M	Schofield J	Vincent J	Fenton R	Lynn S	Darrell M	Bullock M	Hockey T	Barber E
1	Aug 21	(h) Crystal P	W 2-1	Thwaites 2	19,205	1	2	3	4	5	6	7	8	9	10	11											
2	25	(h) Middlesbrough	D 1-1	Beard	16,764	1	2	3	4	5	6	7	9	8	10	11											
3	28	(a) Preston NE	D 3-3	Vowden, Beard 2	16,397	1	2	3	**4**	5	6	7	9	8	10	11	12										
4	31	(a) Middlesbrough	D 1-1	Vowden	17,300	1		3		5	4	7	9	8	10	11	6	2									
5	Sep 4	(h) Charlton A	D 2-2	Beard, Jackson (pen)	15,331	1		3		5	4	7	9	8	10	11	6	2									
6	8	(h) Leyton O	D 2-2	Thomson, Vowden	7,598	1		3		5	6	7	8	10	9	11		2	4								
7	11	(a) Plymouth A	L 1-6	Vowden	10,606	1		3	4	5	6	7	8	10	9	11		2									
8	13	(a) Leyton O	L 1-2	Thomson	7,114			3	10	5	6	7	9		8			2	4	1	11						
9	18	(h) Portsmouth	L 1-3	Beard	11,793			3	10		6		9	8		11	5	2	4	1	7						
10	25	(a) Bolton W	W 2-1	Thomson, Vowden	11,925		3	2	4		6	11	8	10	9					1	7	5					
11	Oct 9	(h) Norwich C	W 1-0	Jackson	11,622		3	2	4		6	11	8	10	9					1	7	5					
12	16	(a) Bury	L 1-5	Darrell	8,814		3	2	4		6	11	9	10						1	7	5		8			
13	23	(h) Southampton	L 0-1		11,861			3	4	5		7				11		2	6	1	8			10	9		
14	30	(a) Derby C	L 3-5	Bullock, Vincent, Page	12,465			3	4	5		7				11		2	6	1	8			10	9		
15	Nov 6	(h) Cardiff C	W 4-2	Bullock, Thomson, Lynn (pen), Jackson	10,743	1			4	5		7	8			11		2	6				3	10	9		
16	13	(a) Carlisle U	L 0-1		10,243	1			4	5	6	7	8			11		2					3	10	9		
17	20	(h) Coventry C	L 0-1		25,950	1	3	2	4	5		8	9	6		11								10		7	
18	27	(a) Bristol C	L 0-2		13,727	1	3	**2**	4	5		8	10	6		11			12		9					7	
19	Dec 4	(h) Manchester C	W 3-1	Jackson, Vowden, Thwaites	10,442	1	3		4	5		8	10	6	9	11		2								7	
20	11	(a) Rotherham U	W 4-3	Vowden 3, Jackson	10,404	1	3		4	5		8	10	6	9	11		2								7	
21	18	(h) Bury	W 4-0	Thomson, Thwaites 2, Fenton	10,811	**1**	3		4	5		8	10	6	9	11		2				12				7	
22	28	(h) Huddersfield T	W 2-1	Vowden, Thwaites	19,750	1	3		4	5		8	10	6	9	11		2								7	
23	Jan 1	(a) Norwich C	D 2-2	Vowden, Fenton	15,829	1	3		4	5		8	10	6	**9**	11		2				12				7	
24	8	(h) Carlisle U	W 2-1	Vowden, Beard	14,989	1	3		4	5		8	10	6		11		2			9					7	
25	29	(a) Crystal P	L 0-1		14,190	1	3		4	5		8	10	6	9	11		2								7	
26	Feb 5	(h) Preston NE	D 1-1	Jackson	14,600	1	3			5		8	10	6	9	11		2	4							7	
27	19	(a) Charlton A	L 1-2	Thwaites	13,722	1	3		4	5		8	10	6	9	11		2								7	
28	26	(h) Plymouth A	W 1-0	Thomson	13,115	1	3		4	5		8	10	6	9	11		2								7	
29	Mar 5	(a) Southampton	W 1-0	Thwaites	18,295	1	3		4	5		8	10	6	9	11		2								7	
30	12	(a) Portsmouth	W 1-0	Vowden	12,367	1	3		4	5		8	10	6	9	11		2								7	
31	15	(a) Huddersfield T	L 0-2		19,156	1	3		4	5		8	10	6	9	11		2								7	
32	19	(h) Bolton W	L 0-1		13,766	1	3		4	5		8	10	6	9	11		2								7	
33	26	(h) Ipswich T	W 1-0	Beard	9,375	1	3		4	5		7	10	6		11		2			8	9					
34	Apr 2	(a) Cardiff C	W 3-1	Vowden 2, Carver (og)	8,290	1	3		4	5		7	10	6		**11**		2			8	9			12		
35	9	(h) Derby C	D 5-5	Vowden, Hockey, Beard 2 (1 pen), Saxton (og)	13,083	1	3		4	5		7	10	6	12			2			8	**9**				11	
36	11	(h) Wolves	D 2-2	Vincent, Vowden	28,880	1	3		4	5		7	10	6				2			8	9				11	
37	12	(a) Wolves	L 0-2		27,500	1	3		4	5		7	10	6	9			2			8					11	
38	16	(a) Coventry C	L 3-4	Fenton, Vowden, Jackson	27,063	1	3		4	5		7	10	6				2			8	9				11	
39	22	(h) Bristol C	L 1-3	Beard (pen)	11,677	1	3		4	5		7	10	6				2			8	9				11	
40	30	(a) Manchester C	L 1-3	Vowden	28,409	1	3	2	4	5		7	10	6							8	9				11	
41	May 3	(h) Ipswich T	W 4-1	Fenton 2, Vowden, Jackson	9,115	1	3		4	5		11	10	6				2				9				7	8
42	17	(h) Rotherham U	W 3-0	Barber, Vowden, Hockey	11,453	1	3		4	5		11	10	6				2				9				7	8
		Appearances				35	34	15	38	36	15	40	38	36	27	30	3	33	8	7	11	15	5	6	4	24	2
		Substitutes													1		1		1			2			1		
		Goals										8	21	10	6	8			1		2	5	1	1	2	2	1

FINAL LEAGUE POSITION: 10th in Division Two. Average home League attendance: 14,398.

2 own-goals

FA Cup

Rd	Date	Opponent	Result	Scorers	Att	Heriot J	Martin Ray	Green C	Wylie R	Foster W	Hennessey T	Jackson A	Vowden G	Beard M	Thomson RG	Thwaites D	Sharples B	Fraser C	Page M	Schofield J	Vincent J	Fenton R	Lynn S	Darrell M	Bullock M	Hockey T	Barber E
3	Jan 22	(h) Bristol C	W 3-2	Vowden 2, Thomson	24,340	1	3		4	5		8	10	6	9	11		2								7	
4	Feb 12	(h) Leicester C	L 1-2	Thwaites	46,680	1	3		4	5		8	10	6	9	11		2								7	
		Appearances				2	2		2	2		2	2	2	2	2		2								2	
		Goals											2		1	1											

League Cup

Rd	Date	Opponent	Result	Scorers	Att	Heriot J	Martin Ray	Green C	Wylie R	Foster W	Hennessey T	Jackson A	Vowden G	Beard M	Thomson RG	Thwaites D	Sharples B	Fraser C	Page M	Schofield J	Vincent J	Fenton R	Lynn S	Darrell M	Bullock M	Hockey T	Barber E
2	Sep 22	(a) Mansfield T	L 1-2	Beard	9,344		3	4	10		6	11		9				2		1	8	7	5				
		Appearances					1	1	1		1	1		1				1		1	1	1	1				
		Goals												1													

1966-67

Manager: Stan Cullis

#	Date		Opponent	Result	Scorers	Att	Herriot J	Martin, Ray	Green C	Wylie R	Foster W	Beard M	Hockey T	Thomson RG	Bridges B	Vowden G	Murray A	Fenton R	Thwaites D	Sharples B	Jackson A	Vincent J	Bullock M	Isherwood D	Leggat G	Barber E	Summerill P	Darrell M	Page M
1	Aug 20	(a)	Wolves	W 2-1	Murray 2	26,800	1	2	3	4	5	6	7	8	9	10	11												
2	24	(a)	Portsmouth	W 5-4	Bridges, Vowden 2, Murray, Beard	16,934	1	2	3	4	5	6	7	8	9	10	11												
3	27	(h)	Norwich C	W 2-1	Vowden, Murray	25,516	1	2	3	4	5	6	7	8	9	10	11												
4	30	(h)	Portsmouth	W 3-0	Thomson, Vowden, Pack (og)	23,493	1	2	3	4	5	6	7	8	9	10	11												
5	Sep 3	(a)	Coventry C	D 1-1	Vowden	36,339	1	2	3	**4**	5	6	7	8	9	10	11	12											
6	7	(a)	Plymouth A	D 1-1	Murray	18,820	1	2			5	6	7	4	9	10	11	8											
7	10	(h)	Bury	L 1-3	Thomson	22,345	1	2	3	4	5	6	7	8	9	10	11												
8	17	(a)	Preston NE	L 0-3		13,577	1	2	3	4	5	6	7	8	9	10	**11**	12											
9	24	(h)	Rotherham U	L 2-3	Bridges, Thomson	19,515	1	2	3	4	5	6	**7**	8	9	10	12		11										
10	27	(h)	Plymouth A	D 0-0		18,313	1	2	3	4	5	6	**7**	8	9	10	12		11										
11	Oct 1	(a)	Millwall	L 1-3	Vowden	15,776	1	2	3	4	5	6	7	8	9	10	11												
12	8	(a)	Ipswich T	L 2-3	Thomson, Vowden	15,120	1	2	3	4	5	6	11	9	7	10	8												
13	15	(h)	Bristol C	W 4-0	Vowden, Murray, Thwaites, Ford (og)	15,358	1	2	3	4	5	6		8	7	**10**	11	9	12										
14	22	(a)	Carlisle U	L 0-2		10,900	1		3	4	2	6		9	7	10	8	12	11	5									
15	29	(h)	Blackburn R	D 1-1	Beard	17,626	1	2	3			6	7		9	10	11	**4**	12	5	8								
16	Nov 5	(a)	Bolton W	L 1-3	Hockey	9,875	1	2	3			6	11	4	9	10	7			5	8								
17	12	(h)	Charlton A	W 4-0	Bullock, Vincent, Vowden 2	14,023	1	2	3			6	11	4	7	10				5		8	9						
18	19	(a)	Derby C	W 2-1	Beard, Thomson	17,382	1	2	3			6	11	4	7	10				5		8	9						
19	26	(h)	Crystal P	W 3-1	Bullock, Vincent, Vowden	16,820	1	**2**	3			6	11	4	7	10	12			5		8	9						
20	Dec 3	(a)	Huddersfield T	L 1-3	Bullock	14,930	1		3			6	11	4	7	10	2			5		8	9						
21	10	(h)	Cardiff C	L 1-2	Bullock	17,046	1		3			6	7	4	11	10	2			5		8	9						
22	17	(h)	Wolves	W 3-2	Bullock, Vowden, Bridges	27,527	1		3			6	7	4	11	10	2			5		8	9						
23	26	(h)	Northampton T	W 3-0	Vincent 2, Vowden	24,302	1		3			6	7	4	11	10	2			5		8	9						
24	27	(a)	Northampton T	L 1-2	Bridges	15,433	1		3			6	7	4	11	10	2			5		8	9						
25	31	(a)	Norwich C	D 3-3	Bullock, Vowden, Bridges	15,773	1					6	7	4	11	10	3			5		8	9	2					
26	Jan 7	(h)	Coventry C	D 1-1	Curtis (og)	36,317	1		3			6	7	4	11	10	2			5			9	8					
27	14	(a)	Bury	W 2-0	Bridges 2	6,960	1		3			6	7	4	11	10	2			5			9	8					
28	21	(h)	Preston NE	W 3-1	Vowden, Bridges 2	18,486	1		3			6		4	11	10	2			5		8	9	7					
29	Feb 4	(a)	Rotherham U	L 2-3	Leggat, Hockey	10,934	1		3			6	7	4	11	10	2			5		8		9					
30	11	(h)	Millwall	W 2-0	Bullock, Bridges	18,008	1		3			6	**7**	4	11	10	2			5			9		8	12			
31	25	(h)	Ipswich T	D 2-2	Vincent, Thomson	18,491	1		3			6	7	4	11		2			5		10			8	9			
32	Mar 4	(a)	Blackburn R	L 0-1		14,908	1		3			6	7	4	11	8	2	9		5		10							
33	18	(h)	Carlisle U	L 1-2	Vincent	17,613	1		3		5	6	7	4		8	2	9				10					11		
34	25	(a)	Bristol C	L 1-3	Vincent	20,579	1		3	8		6	7	4	11	9	2			5		10							
35	27	(h)	Hull C	W 2-1	Beard, Isherwood	17,056	1		3		5	6	8	4	11	9	7				2	10							
36	28	(a)	Hull C	W 2-0	Murray 2	23,122	1		3	4		**6**	8	12		10	7	9			2	11							
37	Apr 1	(a)	Bolton W	D 2-2	Vowden, Murray	18,187	1		3	4			8	6	9	10	7				2	11							
38	15	(h)	Derby C	W 2-0	Bridges 2	15,332	1			**4**		6	8		7	10	3				2	11	9			12			
39	22	(a)	Crystal P	L 1-2	Bridges	13,064	1		3	4		6	8		7	10	2			5		11	**9**					12	
40	28	(h)	Huddersfield T	L 0-1		14,385	1		3	4		6	8		7	9	2			5		10		11					
41	May 6	(a)	Cardiff C	L 0-3		12,872	1		3	4		6	8		7	9	2			5		10				11			
42	12	(a)	Charlton A	L 0-1		10,102	1	2	3	4	12	6	8			10	7			**5**		9			11				
			Appearances				42	19	40	21	16	41	39	35	39	41	37	6	3	27	2	22	14	5	9	1	3		
			Substitutes								1		1					3	3	2					1		1	1	
			Goals									4	2	6	13	16	9		1			7	7	1	1				

FINAL LEAGUE POSITION: 10th in Division Two. Average home League attendance: 19,798.

3 own-goals

FA Cup

#	Date		Opponent	Result	Scorers	Att	Herriot J	Martin, Ray	Green C	Wylie R	Foster W	Beard M	Hockey T	Thomson RG	Bridges B	Vowden G	Murray A	Fenton R	Thwaites D	Sharples B	Jackson A	Vincent J	Bullock M	Isherwood D	Leggat G
3	Jan 28	(h)	Blackpool	W 2-1	Vowden, Thomson	27,603	1		3			6	7	4	11	10	2			5		8			9
4	Feb 18	(a)	Rotherham U	D 0-0		15,723	1		**3**			6	7	4	11	10	2			5	12		9		8
R	21	(h)	Rotherham U	W 2-1	Hockey, Bridges	35,482	1	3				6	7	4	11	10	2			5		8			9
5	Mar 11	(a)	Arsenal	W 1-0	Vowden	40,665	1		3		5	6	7	4	11	8	2					10			9
6	Apr 8	(h)	Tottenham H	D 0-0		51,467	1		3	4		6	7	8	11	10	2	9		5					
R	12	(a)	Tottenham H	L 0-6		52,304	1		3	4		6	7	**8**	11	10	2	12		5					9
			Appearances				6	1	5	2	1	6	6	6	6	6	6	1		5		3	1		3 2
			Substitutes															1			1				
			Goals										1	1	1	2									

League Cup

#	Date		Opponent	Result	Scorers	Att	Herriot J	Martin, Ray	Green C	Wylie R	Foster W	Beard M	Hockey T	Thomson RG	Bridges B	Vowden G	Murray A	Fenton R	Thwaites D	Sharples B	Jackson A	Vincent J	Bullock M	Isherwood D	Leggat G	Barber E
2	Sep 13	(a)	Nottingham F	D 1-1	Vowden	19,271	1	2	3	4	5	6	7	8	9	10	11									
R	20	(h)	Nottingham F	W 2-1	Bridges, Vowden	21,510	1	2	3	4	5	6	7	8	9	10		11								
3	Oct 4	(h)	Ipswich T	W 2-1	Beard (pen), Hockey	15,116	1	2	3	4	5	6	11	9	7	10	8									
4	26	(a)	Grimsby T	W 4-2	Bridges 2, Fenton, Vowden	11,298	1	2	3	**4**		6	7		9	10	11	12		5	8					
5	Dec 7	(a)	Sheffield U	W 3-2	Vincent, Bullock, Hockey	15,023	1		3			6	11	4	7	10	2			5		8	9			
SF	Jan 17	(h)	Queen's Park R	L 1-4	Bridges	34,295	1	8	3			6	7	4	11	10	2			5			9			
	Feb 7	(a)	Queen's Park R	L 1-3	Barber	24,604	1		3			6	7	4	11	10	2			5			9			8
			Appearances				7	5	7	4	3	7	7	6	7	7	6	1		4	1	1	3			1
			Substitutes															1								
			Goals									1	2		4	3		1				1	1			1

1967-68

Manager: Stan Cullis

						Herriot J	Murray A	Martin, Ray	Wylie R	Sharples B	Beard M	Bridges B	Vincent J	Pickering F	Vowden G	Hockey T	Green C	Thomson RG	Page M	Twell T	Fenton R	Leggat G	Sleeuwenhoek JC	Foster W	Summerill P	Darrell M	Thwaites D
1	Aug 19 (h)	Bolton W	W 4-0	Vincent, Bridges 2, Hockey	23,537	1	2	3	4	5	6	7	8	9	10	11											
2	26 (a)	Huddersfield T	W 3-2	Vincent, Vowden 2	14,228	1	2	3	4	5	6	7	8	9	10	11											
3	29 (a)	Middlesbrough	D 1-1	Vincent	25,814	1	2	3	4	5	6	7	8	9	10	11											
4	Sep 2 (h)	Ipswich T	D 0-0		25,463	1	2	3	4	5	6	7	8	9	10	11											
5	4 (h)	Hull C	W 6-2	Pickering, Vincent, Vowden, Bridges, Beard (pen), Murray	25,913	1	2	12	4	5	6	7	8	9	10	11	3										
6	9 (a)	Carlisle U	D 1-1	Vowden	11,200	1	2		4	5	6	7	8	9	10	11	3	12									
7	16 (h)	Blackburn R	D 1-1	Bridges	28,972	1	2	12	4		6	7	8	9	10	11	3		5								
8	23 (a)	Blackpool	L 0-1		25,572	1	2	12	4		6	7	8	9	10	11	3		5								
9	26 (h)	Middlesbrough	W 6-1	Pickering 2, Vincent, Bridges 2, Vowden	28,885	1	2	3	4		6	7	8	9	10	11			5								
10	30 (h)	Millwall	L 2-3	Pickering, Vincent	30,576	1	2	3	4		6	7	8	9	10	11			5								
11	Oct 7 (a)	Aston Villa	W 4-2	Bridges 2, Beard (pen), Vowden	49,984	1	2		4		6	7	8	9	10	11	3		5								
12	14 (a)	Portsmouth	D 2-2	Pickering, Vowden	26,243		2		4		6	7	8	9	10	11	3		5	1							
13	21 (a)	Norwich C	L 2-4	Vowden, Bridges	16,963		2	3			6	7	8	9	10	11			5	1	4						
14	28 (h)	Rotherham U	W 4-1	Bridges 3, Vowden	21,478	1		2	4	5	6	7	8	9	10	**11**	3						12				
15	Nov 4 (a)	Derby C	D 2-2	Vincent, Bridges	25,484	1	2				6	7	8	9	10	11	3	4					5				
16	11 (h)	Preston NE	W 3-0	Vincent 2, Bridges	27,664	1	2		4		6	7	8	9	10	11	3						5				
17	18 (a)	Cardiff C	W 3-1	Vincent, Bridges, Murray	13,817	1	2		4		6	7	8	9	10	11	3						5				
18	25 (h)	Crystal P	W 1-0	Vincent	27,538	1	2		4		6	7	8	9	10	11	3						5				
19	Dec 2 (a)	Charlton A	L 1-3	Bridges	18,855	1	2		4		6	7	8	9	10	11	3						5				
20	9 (a)	Queen's Park R	W 2-0	Pickering, Hazell (og)	25,281	1	2		4		6	7	8	9	10	11	3						5				
21	16 (a)	Bolton W	D 1-1	Farrimond (og)	10,258	1	2		4		6	7	8	9	10	11	3						5				
22	23 (h)	Huddersfield T	W 6-1	Pickering 2, Vincent, Vowden, Bridges, Leggat	26,163	1	2		4		6	7	8	9	10	**11**	3					12	5				
23	26 (h)	Bristol C	W 4-1	Bridges, Vowden, Leggat, Briggs (og)	40,429	1	2		4		6	7	8	9	10		3					11	5				
24	30 (a)	Bristol C	L 1-3	Vincent	23,493	1	2	3	4		6	7	8	9	10							11	5				
25	Jan 6 (a)	Ipswich T	L 1-2	Vowden	16,681	1	2	3	4		6	7	8	9	10	11							5				
26	13 (h)	Carlisle U	L 1-3	Vowden	21,686	1	2		4		6	7	8	9	10	11	3						5				
27	20 (a)	Blackburn R	W 2-0	Pickering, Vowden	17,934	1	2		4		6	11	8	9	10	7	3							5			
28	Feb 3 (h)	Blackpool	L 1-2	Wylie	28,008	1	2		4		6	11	8	9	10	7	3							5			
29	10 (a)	Millwall	D 1-1	Vowden	13,961	1	**2**		4		6	11	8	9	10	7	3		12					5			
30	24 (h)	Aston Villa	W 2-1	Bridges 2	45,283	1		2	4		6	7	8	9	10		3		11					5			
31	Mar 2 (a)	Portsmouth	W 2-1	Pickering, Foster	27,836	1	2	3	4		6	7		9	8	11			10					5			
32	16 (h)	Norwich C	D 0-0		28,951	1	2	3				7	8	9		6			4					5	11		
33	23 (a)	Rotherham U	D 1-1	Pickering	15,711	1	2	3	**4**		6	7		9	8	11			10					5		12	
34	Apr 2 (h)	Derby C	W 3-1	Vowden, Bridges, Richardson (og)	29,327	1	2	12	4		6	11		9	7	**8**	3		10					5			
35	6 (h)	Preston NE	D 0-0		16,872	1	8	**3**	4		6	11	7	9			2		10				12	5			
36	13 (h)	Cardiff C	D 0-0		29,044	1	8	3	4		6	11	12	9	7		**2**		10					5			
37	15 (a)	Plymouth A	W 2-1	Pickering, Vowden	13,886	1	2	3	4		6	11		9	8				10			7		5			
38	16 (h)	Plymouth A	D 2-2	Page, Wylie	29,359	1	2	3	4		6	11		9	8				10			7		5			
39	20 (a)	Crystal P	D 0-0		14,949	1	2	3	4		6	11	8	9					10					5		7	
40	May 4 (a)	Queen's Park R	L 0-2		25,985	1	2	12	4		6	11	8	9	**7**		3		10					5			
41	7 (a)	Charlton A	W 4-0	Pickering, Bridges 2, Vincent	19,916	1	2	3	4		6	7	11	9	8				10					5			
42	11 (a)	Hull C	W 1-0	Wilson (og)	10,346	1	2	3	4		6	7	11	9	8				10					5			
	FINAL LEAGUE POSITION: 4th in Division Two. Average home League attendance: 28,083.				**Appearances**	40	40	21	39	7	41	42	36	42	40	30	26	1	20	2	1	4	12	16	1	1	
					Substitutes			5					1						1	1			3			1	
					Goals		2		2		2	23	14	13	17	1			1			2		1			

5 own-goals

FA Cup

						Herriot J	Murray A	Martin, Ray	Wylie R	Sharples B	Beard M	Bridges B	Vincent J	Pickering F	Vowden G	Hockey T	Green C	Thomson RG	Page M	Twell T	Fenton R	Leggat G	Sleeuwenhoek JC	Foster W
3	Jan 27 (a)	Halifax T	W 4-2	Pickering, Vowden, Bridges, Beard	18,119	1	2		4		6	11	8	9	10	7	3							5
4	Feb 17 (h)	Leyton O	W 3-0	Vowden 2, Bridges	29,320	1		2	4		6	7	8	9	10		3		11					5
5	Mar 9 (a)	Arsenal	D 1-1	Vowden	45,526	1	2	3	4		6	7	8	9	10		11							5
R	12 (h)	Arsenal	W 2-1	Bridges 2	51,586	1	2	3	4		6	7		9	10	11			8					5
6	30 (h)	Chelsea	W 1-0	Pickering	51,576	1	2	12	4		6	11		9	7	8	3		10					5
SF	Apr 27 (n†)	West Brom A	L 0-2		60,831	1	2	3	4		6	11		9	7				8					5
†Played at Villa Park, Birmingham.					**Appearances**	6	5	4	6		6	6	3	6	6	3	5		4					6
					Substitutes			1																
					Goals						1	4		2	4									

League Cup

						Herriot J	Murray A	Martin, Ray	Wylie R	Sharples B	Beard M	Bridges B	Vincent J	Pickering F	Vowden G	Hockey T	Green C	Thomson RG	Page M
2	Sep 13 (a)	Plymouth A	W 2-0	Vowden, Hockey	10,038	1	2		4		6	7	8	9	10	11	3		5
3	Oct 11 (a)	Derby C	L 1-3	Bridges	24,827	1	2	3	4		6	7	8	9	10	11			5
					Appearances	2	2	1	2		2	2	2	2	2	2	1		2
					Substitutes														
					Goals							1			1	1			

1968-69

Manager: Stan Cullis

#	Date		Opponent	Result	Scorers	Att	Herriot J	Murray A	Green C	Wylie R	Sharples B	Beard M	Hockey T	Vincent J	Pickering F	Page M	Bridges B	Sleeuwenhoek J	Vowden G	Martin, Ray	Darrell M	Summerill P	Foster W	Greenhoff J	Robinson D	Thwaites D	Pendrey G	Thomson RA	Latchford RA	Latchford D
1	Aug 10	(h)	Norwich C	L 1-2	Pickering	27,515	1	2	3	4	5	6	7	8	9	10	11													
2	17	(a)	Crystal P	L 2-3	Vowden, Vincent	17,679	1	2	**3**	4		6	7	12	9	8	11	5	10											
3	20	(a)	Charlton A	L 1-3	Vincent	14,220	1	2	3	4		6	7	11	9	10		5	8											
4	24	(h)	Portsmouth	W 5-2	Pickering 2, Vowden, Summerill, Tindall (og)	23,915	1		3			6		8	9	4			5	7	2	10	11							
5	28	(a)	Cardiff C	L 0-4		15,008	1		3			6		8	9	4			5	7	2	10	11							
6	31	(a)	Preston NE	L 1-4	Greenhoff	13,112	1	2	3			6	7	11	9	4				10	12		5	8						
7	Sep 7	(h)	Huddersfield T	W 5-1	Greenhoff, Pickering, Vowden 3	25,001	1	2	3	4		6		8	10	7			12				11	5	9					
8	14	(a)	Middlesbrough	L 1-3	Vincent	17,398	1	2	3	4		**6**		7	9	10			12				11	5	8					
9	17	(h)	Bury	L 1-3	Greenhoff	24,178	1	2	3	4			7	9		6			10				11	5	8					
10	21	(a)	Aston Villa	W 4-0	Vowden, Greenhoff, Vincent, Summerill	40,527	1			4		6	7	10		3			9	2		11		8	5					
11	28	(a)	Carlisle U	W 3-2	Greenhoff, Summerill, Green	7,623	1		3			6	7	10		4			9	2		11		8	5					
12	Oct 5	(h)	Fulham	W 5-4	Summerill 4, Vincent	27,318	1			4		6	7	8					10	2		11		9	5					
13	8	(h)	Cardiff C	W 2-0	Greenhoff, Vincent	28,238	1		3			6	**7**	11		10			9	2		12		8	5					
14	12	(a)	Bristol C	D 0-0		19,478	1		3			6	7	11		10			9	2				8	5					
15	19	(h)	Millwall	L 1-2	Greenhoff (pen)	29,770	1		3	4		6	**7**	11	9	12			10	2				8	5					
16	26	(a)	Derby C	L 0-1		34,218	1	12				6	7	10		4			9	2		11	3	8	5					
17	Nov 2	(h)	Oxford U	L 0-1		23,466	1	**7**	3			6	11	10	9	4			8	2		12			5					
18	9	(a)	Blackburn R	L 2-3	Pickering 2	11,721	1		3	4		6	11	10	9				7	2				8	5					
19	16	(h)	Blackpool	W 1-0	Summerill	22,206	1		3			6	7	10		4			9	2		11		8	5					
20	23	(a)	Bolton W	D 0-0		7,005	1		3	4			7	10	9	6				2		11		8	5					
21	30	(h)	Hull C	W 5-2	Pickering, Greenhoff, Summerill 3	21,077	1		3	4			7	10	9	6				2		11		8	5					
22	Dec 7	(a)	Sheffield U	L 0-2		14,369	1		3	4			7	10	9	6				2		11		8	5					
23	14	(h)	Bristol C	W 2-0	Pickering 2	18,749	1	12	3	4			7	**10**	9	6				2		11		8	5					
24	21	(a)	Millwall	W 3-1	Pickering, Vincent, Darrell	11,921	1		3	4			7	10	9	6					2	11		8	5					
25	26	(a)	Fulham	L 0-2		13,192	1		3	4			7	10	9	6				2		11		8	5					
26	Jan 11	(a)	Oxford U	W 2-1	Pickering, Summerill	11,492	1		**3**	4		6	7	10	9			12		2		11		8	5					
27	14	(h)	Derby C	D 1-1	Pickering	39,977	1		3	4			7	10	9			5		2		11		8	6					
28	18	(h)	Blackburn R	W 3-1	Pickering, Robinson (pen), Coddington (og)	27,160	1			4		3	7	10	9			5		2				8	6	11				
29	Feb 1	(a)	Blackpool	L 1-2	Jones (og)	11,294	1		3			6	7	10	9	4				2				8	5	11				
30	Mar 1	(a)	Norwich C	D 1-1	Vowden	16,429	1		3	8		6	7	11	9	4			10	2					5					
31	4	(h)	Sheffield U	D 2-2	Pickering, Beard	25,123	1		3	8		6	7	11	9			5	10	2				4						
32	8	(h)	Crystal P	L 0-1		25,298	1		**3**			6	4	10	9				7	2		11		8	5		12			
33	15	(a)	Portsmouth	D 0-0		15,550	1					6	10	7	9	4			12	2		11		8	5		3			
34	22	(h)	Preston NE	W 3-1	R.Latchford 2, Summerill	22,020	1			4		6	10	8	9					2		11		7				3	9	
35	25	(h)	Bolton W	W 5-0	Vincent, Summerill 3, Beard	20,454	1					4	10	8	5					2		11		7	5		6	3		
36	29	(a)	Huddersfield T	D 0-0		8,105	1					6	10		9	5				2	12	11		7			4	3	8	
37	Apr 5	(h)	Carlisle U	W 3-0	Greenhoff 2, Hockey	22,397	1					3	10	8	9	4						11		7	5		6	2		
38	7	(h)	Charlton A	D 0-0		25,894	1					3	10	8	9	4						11		**7**	5		6	2		
39	8	(a)	Bury	W 2-1	Summerill 2	5,819	1			4			8	9	2				7			10	11		5		6	3		1
40	12	(a)	Aston Villa	L 0-1		53,584	1			4			10	8	9	2			7				11		5		6	3		1
41	15	(a)	Hull C	W 2-1	Vincent, Hockey	8,702	1					4	10	8		5				2		11		7			6	3	9	1
42	19	(h)	Middlesbrough	W 3-1	Summerill 2, G.Smith (og)	25,899	1					6	10	8		5			7	2		11		7			4	3	9	1
			Appearances				38	8	28	26	1	32	37	40	32	33	2	7	22	31	4	28	5	31	29	2	8	10	4	4
			Substitutes					2						1				1	3		2	2					1			
			Goals						1			2	2	9	14				7		1	16		14	1			2		

FINAL LEAGUE POSITION: 7th in Division Two. Average home League attendance: 26,008.

4 own-goals

FA Cup

#	Date		Opponent	Result	Scorers	Att	Herriot J	Green C	Wylie R	Beard M	Hockey T	Vincent J	Pickering F	Page M	Sleeuwenhoek J	Martin, Ray	Darrell M	Summerill P	Foster W	Greenhoff J	Robinson D	Thwaites D
3	Jan 4	(h)	Lincoln C	W 2-1	Pickering, Robinson	31,429	1	3	4		7		9	6		2		10	11	8	5	
4	25	(a)	Sheffield W	D 2-2	Pickering, Thwaites	52,062	1	3		6	7	10	9	4	12	2				**8**	5	11
R	28	(h)	Sheffield W	W 2-1	Pickering, Beard	51,463	1	3		6	10	7	9	4		2				8	5	11
5	Feb 11	(h)	Manchester U	D 2-2	Beard, Robinson (pen)	51,685	1	3	6	12	10	7	9	4		2				8	5	**11**
R	24	(a)	Manchester U	L 2-6	Greenhoff, Summerill	61,934	1	3	6	11	10	7	9	4		2		12		**8**	5	
			Appearances				5	5	3	3	5	4	5	5		5	1	1		5	5	3
			Substitutes							1					1			1				
			Goals							2			3					1		1	2	1

League Cup

#	Date		Opponent	Result		Att	Herriot J	Murray A	Green C	Wylie R	Beard M	Vincent J	Pickering F	Page M	Vowden G	Martin, Ray	Foster W	Greenhoff J
2	Sep 3	(h)	Chelsea	L 0-1		31,560	1	2	3	**4**	6	8	9	10	7	12	11	5
			Appearances				1	1	1	1	1	1	1	1	1		1	1
			Substitutes													1		
			Goals															

1969-70

Manager: Stan Cullis until March 1970

Player columns (left→right): Herriot J · Martin, Ray · Thomson RA · Page M · Robinson D · Pendrey G · Vowden G · Hockey T · Latchford R · Beard M · Vincent J · Summerill P · Wylie R · Murray A · Hateley A · Johnston G · Steeuwenhoek JC · Latchford D · Darrell M · Thwaites D

#	Date	V	Opponent	Res	Scorers	Att	Her	Mar	Tho	Pag	Rob	Pen	Vow	Hoc	LaR	Bea	Vin	Sum	Wyl	Mur	Hat	Joh	Ste	LaD	Dar	Thw
1	Aug 9	(a)	Leicester C	L 1-3	Summerill	35,168	1	2	3	4	5	6	7	8	9	10	**11**	12								
2	16	(h)	Oxford U	L 1-3	Summerill	27,067	1	2	3	6	**5**	4	7		9	8	10	11	12							
3	19	(h)	Portsmouth	D 1-1	Summerill	24,936	1	2	3		5	6	10	8	9	4		11		7						
4	23	(a)	Blackpool	L 0-2		17,495	1	2	3	4	5	6	**8**	10				11	12	7	9					
5	27	(a)	Hull C	D 0-0		12,242	1	2	3		5	6	8			4	10	11		7	9					
6	30	(h)	Queen's Park R	W 3-0	Murray 3	32,660	1	2	3		5	6	8			4	10	11		7	9					
7	Sep 6	(a)	Bolton W	L 0-2		10,998	1	2	3		5	6	12	8		4	10	**11**		7	9					
8	13	(h)	Sheffield U	W 2-1	Vincent, Murray	27,201	1	2	3		5	6	8			4	10	11		7	9					
9	16	(h)	Norwich C	W 3-1	Murray, Summerill 2	26,408	1	2	3		5	6	12	8		4	10	11		**7**	9					
10	20	(a)	Charlton A	W 1-0	Hateley	13,988	1	2	3		5	6	8			4	10	11		7	9					
11	27	(h)	Carlisle U	D 1-1	Summerill	28,765	1	2	3		5	6	8			4	10	11		7	9					
12	Oct 4	(a)	Bristol C	L 0-2		18,706	1	2	3		5	6	8			4	10	11		7	9					
13	8	(a)	Oxford U	L 0-2		12,476	1	2	3		5	6	11	8		4	10				9	7				
14	11	(h)	Blackburn R	W 3-0	Vowden 2, Summerill	25,602	1	2	3			6	8	10		4		11		7	9	5				
15	18	(a)	Aston Villa	D 0-0		54,470	1	2	3			6	8	10		4		11		7	9	5				
16	25	(h)	Cardiff C	D 1-1	Hateley	28,385	1	2	3			6	8	10		4		**11**	12	7	9	5				
17	Nov 1	(a)	Watford	W 3-2	Vincent, Vowden, Murray	17,440	1	2	3		5	6	10	11		4	8			7	9					
18	8	(h)	Swindon T	W 2-0	Vowden, Murray	28,167	1	2	3		5	6	8	10		4		11		7	9					
19	12	(a)	Portsmouth	D 1-1	Murray	16,508	1	2	3		5	6	8	10		4		11		7	9					
20	15	(a)	Preston NE	L 1-4	Hateley	22,564	1	2	3		5	6	8	**10**		4		11	12	7	9					
21	22	(h)	Millwall	W 2-0	Hateley, Vincent	22,564	1	2	3		5	6	10	11		4	8			7	9	12				
22	Dec 6	(a)	Huddersfield T	D 2-2	Vowden, Murray	24,956	1	2	3	4	5	6	8	10				11	12	7	**9**					
23	13	(a)	Sheffield U	L 0-6		17,332	1	2	3	4	5	6	8	10				11	12	7	**9**					
24	16	(a)	Middlesbrough	L 2-4	Hateley, Murray	17,020		2	3	4				8		6	10	11		7	9	5	1			
25	26	(h)	Blackpool	L 2-3	James (og), Hateley	29,540		**2**	3	4			12	8		6	10	11		7	9	5	1			
26	27	(a)	Queen's Park R	L 1-2	Page	15,688		2	3	4				8	10	6		11		7	9	5	1			
27	Jan 10	(a)	Charlton A	W 3-0	Vincent, Beard, Johnston	18,031	1	2	3	4	5			10		6	8	11		7	**9**	12				
28	17	(a)	Carlisle U	L 3-4	Summerill 3	7,912	1	2	3	4	5			10		6	8	11		7	9					
29	31	(a)	Bristol C	D 2-2	Vincent, Summerill	20,421	1	2	3	4	5			10		6	8	11		7	9					
30	Feb 14	(h)	Leicester C	L 0-1		25,990		2	3	4	5		12	10		6	8	11			9	**7**	1			
31	21	(a)	Cardiff C	L 1-3	Bell (og)	21,910		2	3	4	5		7	10		8	6	11			9	12	1			
32	24	(h)	Bolton W	W 2-0	Vincent, Summerill	19,489		2	3	4	5		9	10		6	8	11		7			1			
33	28	(h)	Watford	D 0-0		22,766		2	3	4	5		9	10		6	8	11		7			1			
34	Mar 4	(a)	Blackburn R	D 1-1	Mulraney (og)	8,639		2	3		5	4	9	10		6	8	11		7			1			
35	11	(a)	Millwall	L 2-6	Hockey, Murray	7,825		2	3		5	4	9	10		6	8	11		7			1			
36	14	(h)	Middlesbrough	D 0-0		17,984		2	3		5	4	9	7	10	6	8	11					1			
37	21	(a)	Huddersfield T	L 0-2		18,502		2	3		5	4	8	9		6	10	11					1			
38	28	(h)	Preston NE	W 1-0	Vowden	16,469		2	3	12	**5**		10	9		4	6	8		7			1			
39	30	(h)	Aston Villa	L 0-2		41,696		2	3	8				6		4	10	11		7	9	5	1	12		
40	31	(a)	Swindon T	L 1-4	Summerill	20,835		2	3				7	9	10	4	6	11			8	5		1		
41	Apr 4	(h)	Hull C	L 2-4	R.Latchford, Martin	13,530		2	3				7	4	9	6	10	**11**		12	8	5		1		
42	15	(a)	Norwich C	L 0-6		12,994		2	3	10	5	4	9	7		6	8	11						1		
			Appearances				26	42	42	17	33	27	29	41	10	38	36	30	1	33	26	6	9	16		
			Substitutes									1		3				4	3	1		3		1		
			Goals					1		1			6	1	1	1	6	13		11	6	1				

FINAL LEAGUE POSITION: 18th in Division Two. Average home League attendance: 24,028.

3 own-goals

FA Cup

#	Date	V	Opponent	Res	Att	Her	Mar	Tho	Pag	Rob	Vow	Hoc	Bea	Vin	Sum	Mur	Hat
3	Jan 3	(a)	Chelsea	L 0-3	45,088	1	2	3	4	5		10	6	8	11	7	9
			Appearances			1	1	1	1	1		1	1	1	1	1	1
			Substitutes														
			Goals														

League Cup

#	Date	V	Opponent	Res	Att	Her	Mar	Tho	Rob	Pen	Vow	LaR	Bea	Vin	Sum	Mur
2	Sep 3	(a)	Brighton & HA	L 0-2	24,232	1	2	3	5	6	8	9	4	10	11	7
			Appearances			1	1	1	1	1	1	1	1	1	1	1
			Substitutes													
			Goals													

1970-71

Manager: Freddie Goodwin

Player columns (left to right): Kelly M · Thomson RA · Pendrey G · Hockey T · Hynd JRS · Robinson D · Murray A · Vowden G · Latchford R · Vincent J · Summerill P · Hateley A · Francis T · Martin, Ray · Page M · Green C · Sleeuwenhoek JC · Bowker K · Beard M · Campbell A · Latchford D · Thwaites D · Taylor G · Harrison M · Smith G · Johnson G · Darrell M

League

#		Date	V	Opponent	Result	Scorers	Att
1	Aug	15	(h)	Queen's Park R	W 2-1	Summerill, Vowden	30,785
2		22	(a)	Carlisle U	W 3-0	Vincent, R.Latchford 2	9,244
3		29	(h)	Luton T	D 1-1	Vowden	30,141
4	Sep	1	(h)	Middlesbrough	L 0-1		27,769
5		5	(a)	Cardiff C	L 0-2		22,081
6		12	(h)	Oxford U	D 1-1	Francis	22,346
7		19	(a)	Portsmouth	L 0-1		18,037
8		26	(h)	Charlton A	D 1-1	Summerill	20,767
9		29	(a)	Bristol C	L 1-2	Summerill	15,975
10	Oct	3	(a)	Hull C	W 1-0	R.Latchford	17,882
11		10	(h)	Sheffield U	L 0-1		22,350
12		17	(a)	Queen's Park R	L 2-5	R.Latchford 2	13,074
13		20	(h)	Leicester C	D 0-0		25,381
14		24	(a)	Watford	L 1-2	Vowden	14,707
15		31	(h)	Swindon T	W 2-1	Vincent, Robinson	18,502
16	Nov	7	(a)	Sunderland	L 1-2	Summerill	15,994
17		14	(h)	Orient	W 1-0	Page	14,137
18		21	(a)	Bolton W	L 0-3		7,141
19		28	(h)	Norwich C	D 2-2	Vincent, Summerill	13,630
20	Dec	5	(a)	Millwall	L 1-2	Summerill	8,489
21		12	(h)	Sheffield W	W 1-0	R.Latchford	14,239
22		19	(a)	Carlisle U	W 1-0	Francis	15,670
23		26	(a)	Blackburn R	D 2-2	Bowker, Francis	8,787
24	Jan	9	(h)	Bristol C	W 2-0	Taylor, R.Latchford	15,292
25		16	(a)	Leicester C	W 4-1	R.Latchford 2, Bowker, Summerill	25,657
26		30	(a)	Norwich C	D 2-2	Summerill 2	11,964
27	Feb	6	(h)	Millwall	W 3-1	Page, Summerill (pen), Francis	21,893
28		13	(a)	Sheffield W	D 3-3	Francis 2, R.Latchford	13,138
29		20	(h)	Bolton W	W 4-0	Francis 4	25,600
30		27	(a)	Swindon T	W 2-1	Francis 2	19,860
31	Mar	6	(h)	Watford	W 2-0	Summerill, Francis	27,605
32		13	(a)	Orient	W 2-0	Summerill, Francis	11,167
33		20	(h)	Sunderland	W 3-1	Summerill 2 (1 pen), Francis	34,194
34		27	(h)	Cardiff C	W 2-0	Francis, Summerill	49,025
35	Apr	3	(a)	Luton T	L 2-3	R.Latchford, Summerill	25,172
36		9	(a)	Oxford U	L 0-1		16,196
37		10	(h)	Blackburn R	W 1-0	Campbell	25,572
38		13	(h)	Hull C	D 0-0		33,109
39		17	(a)	Sheffield U	L 0-3		29,364
40		24	(h)	Portsmouth	D 1-1	R.Latchford	19,440
41		27	(a)	Middlesbrough	D 0-0		12,802
42	May	1	(a)	Charlton A	D 1-1	R.Latchford	10,723

FINAL LEAGUE POSITION: 9th in Division Two. Average home League attendance: 24,164.

League player grid (match no. against shirt numbers worn):

#	Kelly	Thmn	Pndry	Hock	Hynd	Robn	Murr	Vwdn	Ltch R	Vinc	Smrl	Htly	Frcs	Martn	Page	Grn	Slwk	Bwkr	Brd	Cmpl	Ltch D	Thwt	Tylr	Harr	Smth
1	1	2	3	4	5	6	7	8	9	10	11														
2	1	2	3	4	5	6	7	8	9	10		11													
3	1	2	3	4	5	6	7	8	9	10	11														
4	1	2	3	4	5	6	7	8	9	10	11														
5	1	2	3	4	5	6	7	8	**9**	10	11	12													
6	1		3	7	5	6		8	9		11	10	2	4											
7	1		10	4	9	6		8			11		7	2		3	5								
8	1		12	4	5	6		8		10	11	9	7	2				**3**							
9	1		3	4	5	6		8	9	10	11		7	2											
10	1		3	4	5	6		8	9	10	11			2			7								
11	1	2	3	4	5	6	**7**	8	9	10	11							12							
12	1	2		8	5	4		12	9	10	11		3					6	7						
13	3			8	5			4	9	10	11		2					6	7	1					
14		3			5			4	**9**	10	11		2	12				6	8	1	7				
15	1		3	4	5	6	7	9			10	11	2					8							
16	1		3	4	5	6	7				**10**	11	2	9				12	8						
17	1		3	8	5	6				9			2	4				10	7						
18	1	3		8	5	6			**9**	12	11		2	4				10	7						
19	1	3		8		5		9			10	11	2	4				6	7						
20	1	3		8	5			**9**	12	10	11		2	4				6	7						
21	1		3		5	6		9				12	8	2	4			10		**7**			11		
22	1		3		5	6		9					8	2	4			10					11	7	
23	1		3		5	6		9					8	2	4			10					11	7	
24			3		5	6		9		10			2	4				8		**7**	1	12	11		
25		12	3		5			9		10			2	4				8		7	1		11		6
26		3			5			9		10			2	4				8		7	1		11		6
27		3		5	6			9		10			8	2	4					7	1		11		
28		3		5	6			9		10			8	2	4					7	1		11		
29	1	3		5	6			9		10			**8**	2	4				12	7	1		11		
30	1	3		5	6			9		10			8	2	4					7			11		
31	1	3		5	6			9		10			8	2	4					7			11		
32	1	3		5	6			9		10			8	2						7			11	4	
33	1			5	6			9		10			8	2	3					7			11	4	
34	1			5	6			9		10			8	2	3					7			11	4	
35	1	12		5	6			9		10			**8**	2	3					7			11		
36	1	12		5	6			9		10			**8**	2	3					7			11		
37	1			5	6			9		10			8	2	3					7			11		
38	1			5	6			9		10			8	2	3					7			11		
39	1			5	6			9		10			8	2	3					7			11		
40	1	4		5	6			9		10			8	2	3					7			11		
41	1	10		5	6					9				2	3			8		7			11	4	
42	1			5	6			9		10				2	3					7			8	11	

	Kelly	Thmn	Pndry	Hock	Hynd	Robn	Murr	Vwdn	Ltch R	Vinc	Smrl	Htly	Frcs	Martn	Page	Grn	Slwk	Bwkr	Brd	Cmpl	Ltch D	Thwt	Tylr	Harr	Smth
Appearances	34	11	24	24	40	38	8	16	35	16	38	2	21	36	27	2	1	8	7	29	8	5	21	2	9
Substitutes		4						1	1	1		1						2	1			1			
Goals						1		3	13	3	16		16		2			2		1			1		

FA Cup

#		Date	V	Opponent	Result	Scorers	Att
3	Jan	2	(a)	Huddersfield T	D 1-1	Summerill (pen)	26,486
R		5	(h)	Huddersfield T	L 0-2		26,558

#	Kelly	Thmn	Pndry	Hock	Hynd	Robn	Murr	Vwdn	Ltch R	Vinc	Smrl	Htly	Frcs	Martn	Page	Grn	Slwk	Bwkr	Brd	Cmpl	Ltch D	Thwt	Tylr	Harr	Smth
3	1			3	5	6			9		12		8	2	4			**10**		7			11		
R				3	5	6	12		9				**8**	2	4					7	1		11		
Appearances	1			2	2	2			2		1		2	2	2			1		2	1		2		
Substitutes							1				1														
Goals											1														

League Cup

#		Date	V	Opponent	Result	Scorers	Att
1	Aug	18	(h)	Wrexham	D 3-3	Murray, Vowden, Vincent	21,623
R		26	(a)	Wrexham	W 3-2	Vowden, Vincent, Hockey	17,019
2	Sep	9	(a)	Colchester U	D 1-1	Summerill	8,085
R		15	(h)	Colchester U	W 2-1	Vowden, Summerill	17,606
3	Oct	6	(h)	Nottingham F	W 2-1	Summerill 2	23,015
4		27	(a)	Bristol R	L 0-3		21,426

#	Kelly	Thmn	Pndry	Hock	Hynd	Robn	Murr	Vwdn	Ltch R	Vinc	Smrl	Htly	Frcs	Martn	Page	Grn	Slwk	Bwkr	Brd	Cmpl	Ltch D	Thwt	Tylr	Harr	Smth	Jhn
1	1	3		4	5	6	7	8	9	10		12		2												11
R	1		3	4	5	6	7	8	9	10	11			2												
2	1		3	7	5	6		8	9	10	11			2	4											
R	1	2	6	7	5	4		8					9		10	3		12								11
3	1	2	3	4	5	6	7	8	9	10	11															
4	1	3		8	5			9		10	11		7	2	4			12		6						
Appearances	6	4	4	6	6	5	3	6	4	5	5		2	4	2	1		1		1					1	1
Substitutes												1						1		1						
Goals			1				1	3		2	4															

1971-72

Manager: Freddie Goodwin

League Results

No	Date	V	Opponent	Result	Scorers	Att
1	Aug 14	(a)	Sunderland	D 1-1	Bowker	9,749
2	21	(h)	Carlisle U	W 3-2	Summerill, Bowker, Campbell	26,245
3	28	(a)	Portsmouth	L 0-1		14,729
4	Sep 1	(a)	Hull C	L 0-1		16,746
5	4	(h)	Charlton A	W 4-1	Francis, R.Latchford 3	25,231
6	11	(a)	Luton T	D 0-0		14,678
7	18	(a)	Bristol C	W 1-0	R.Latchford	28,745
8	25	(a)	Blackpool	D 1-1	Francis	22,160
9	28	(h)	Watford	W 4-1	R.Latchford 3, Francis	28,095
10	Oct 2	(h)	Oxford U	D 0-0		31,759
11	9	(a)	Queen's Park R	L 0-1		16,039
12	16	(h)	Sunderland	D 1-1	R.Latchford	27,341
13	19	(a)	Swindon T	D 1-1	R.Latchford	14,024
14	23	(h)	Preston NE	D 2-2	R.Latchford, Francis	28,956
15	30	(a)	Burnley	D 1-1	R.Latchford	17,137
16	Nov 6	(h)	Orient	W 2-0	Hatton, R.Latchford	27,349
17	13	(a)	Norwich C	D 2-2	Campbell (pen), R.Latchford	24,262
18	20	(a)	Millwall	L 0-3		15,123
19	27	(h)	Fulham	W 3-1	R.Latchford, Hatton 2	25,545
20	Dec 4	(a)	Middlesbrough	D 0-0		15,761
21	11	(h)	Sheffield W	D 0-0		29,272
22	18	(a)	Charlton A	D 1-1	Hatton	8,289
23	27	(h)	Cardiff C	W 3-0	Pendrey, Hatton, Francis	40,793
24	Jan 1	(a)	Bristol C	L 0-1		17,457
25	8	(h)	Portsmouth	W 6-3	Hatton 2, R.Latchford 2, Campbell (pen), Francis	22,410
26	22	(a)	Watford	W 1-0	Francis	10,884
27	29	(h)	Swindon T	W 4-1	Francis, R.Latchford 2, Hatton	27,824
28	Feb 12	(h)	Preston NE	D 0-0		17,794
29	19	(h)	Burnley	W 2-0	Taylor, Hatton	32,035
30	Mar 4	(h)	Norwich C	W 4-0	Hatton 2, R.Latchford, Hynd	40,899
31	11	(a)	Queen's Park R	D 0-0		35,557
32	21	(a)	Carlisle U	D 2-2	Hatton, R.Latchford	12,281
33	25	(h)	Luton T	W 1-0		34,395
34	31	(a)	Oxford U	W 1-0	Hatton	18,740
35	Apr 1	(a)	Cardiff C	D 0-0		23,692
36	4	(h)	Blackpool	W 2-1	R.Latchford, Francis	45,181
37	8	(h)	Millwall	W 1-0	R.Latchford	43,483
38	18	(a)	Fulham	D 0-0		16,533
39	22	(h)	Middlesbrough	D 1-1	Francis	37,202
40	25	(h)	Hull C	W 2-0	Campbell (pen), Francis	40,749
41	29	(a)	Sheffield W	W 2-1	Hatton, Francis	28,132
42	May 2	(a)	Orient	W 1-0	R.Latchford	33,383

FINAL LEAGUE POSITION: 2nd in Division Two. Average home League attendance: 32,337.

League appearances (shirt numbers per match)

No	Kelly M	Martin R	Page M	Smith G	Hynd JRS	Pendrey G	Campbell A	Bowker K	Latchford R	Summerill P	Taylor G	Phillips S	Latchford D	Robinson D	Francis T	Burns K	Carroll T	Hatton R	Harland S	Cooper P	Harrison M	O'Grady M	Whitehead A
1	1	2	3	4	5	6	7	8	9	10	11		12										
2	1	2	3	4	5	6	7	8	9	10	11	12											
3		2	3	4	5	6	7	8	9	10	11		1	12									
4	1	2	3	4	5	11	7		9	10					6	8	12						
5	1	2	3	4	5	6	7		9	10	11				8								
6		2	3	4	5	10	7		9		11		1		6	8							
7	1	2	4	12	5	3	7		9	10	11				6	8							
8	1	2	4	12	5	3	7		9	10	11				6	8							
9	1	2	4		5	3	7		9	10	11				6	8							
10	1	2	4		5	3	7		9	10	11				6	8							
11	1	2	4	11	5	3	7		9	12	**10**				6	8							
12	1	2	4		5	3	7		9	10	11				6	8							
13	1	2	4	10	5	**3**	7		9	12	11				6	8							
14	1	2	4	10	5	3	7		9		11				6	8							
15	1		4	11	5	3	7		9						8	6	2	10					
16	1			4	5	3	7		9		11				8	6	2	10					
17	1	6			5	3	7		9		11				8	4	2	10					
18	1		4	11	5	3	7		9						8	6	2	10					
19	1			4	5	3	7	11	9						8	6	2	10					
20	1			4	5	3	7	11	9						8	10	2			6			
21	1			4	5	3	7	11	9						8	10	2			6			
22				4	5	3	7		9		11		1		8		2	10	6				
23				4	5	3	7		9		11		1		8		2	10	6				
24				4	5	3	7		9	11			1		8		2	10	6				
25				4	12	5	**3**	7	9		11				8		2	10		1	6		
26				4	5	3	7		9		11				8		2	10	6	1			
27	12	4			5	3	7		9		11				8		2	10	6	1			
28				4	5	3	7		9		11				8		2	10	6	1			
29				4	5	3	7		9		11				8		2	10	6	1			
30				4	5	3	7		9		11		1		8		2	10	6			12	
31				4	5	3	7		9		11		1		8		2	10	6				
32				4	5	3	7		9		11		1		8		2	10	6				
33		2	4		5	3	7		9		11		1		8			10	6				
34			4	11	5	3	7		**9**		12		1		8		2	10	6				
35			4	11	5	3	7		9				1		8		2	10	6				
36			4	11	5	3	7		9						8		2	10	6	1			
37			4	11	5	**3**	7		9		12				8		2	10	6	1			
38		2	4	5		7			9						8		3	10	6	1		11	
39		2	4	5		7			9		12				8		3	10		1		**11**	6
40		12	4	5	3	7			9		11				8		2	10	**6**	1			
41			4	5	3	7			9		11				8		2	10		1			6
42			4	5	3	7			9		11				8		2	10		1			6
Appearances	19	14	38	22	42	40	42	6	42	7	27	6	11	10	39	7	27	26	19	12	1	2	3
Substitutes		1	1	3							2	3	1			2		1				1	
Goals					1	1	4	2	23	1	1				12			15					

FA Cup

No	Date	V	Opponent	Result	Scorers	Att
3	Jan 15	(h)	Port Vale	W 3-0	Hynd, Francis 2	32,937
4	Feb 5	(a)	Ipswich T	W 1-0	R.Latchford	40,709
5	26	(h)	Portsmouth	W 3-1	Hatton, R.Latchford 2	43,886
6	Mar 18	(a)	Huddersfield T	W 3-1	Page, R.Latchford, Hatton	52,470
SF	Apr 15	(n†)	Leeds U	L 0-3		54,723

†Played at Hillsborough, Sheffield.

No	Kelly M	Martin R	Page M	Smith G	Hynd JRS	Pendrey G	Campbell A	Bowker K	Latchford R	Summerill P	Taylor G	Phillips S	Latchford D	Robinson D	Francis T	Burns K	Carroll T	Hatton R	Harland S	Cooper P	Harrison M	O'Grady M	Whitehead A
3				4	5	3	7		9		11				8		2	10	6	1			
4				4	5	3	7		9		11				8		2	10	6	1			
5				**4**	12	5	3	7	9		11		1		8		2	10	6				
6				4	5	3	7		9		11		1		8		2	10	6				
SF			4	11	5	3	7		**9**		12				8		2	10	6	1			
Appearances				5	1	5	5	5	5		4	2			5		5	5	5	3			
Substitutes					1							1											
Goals			1		1				4						2			2					

League Cup

No	Date	V	Opponent	Result	Att
2	Sep 7	(a)	Queen's Park R	L 0-2	15,032

No	Kelly M	Martin R	Page M	Smith G	Hynd JRS	Pendrey G	Campbell A	Bowker K	Latchford R	Summerill P	Taylor G	Phillips S	Latchford D	Robinson D	Francis T	Burns K	Carroll T	Hatton R
2		2	3	4	5	6	7		9	10	11		1		8			
Appearances		1	1	1	1	1	1		1	1	1		1		1			
Substitutes																		
Goals																		

1972-73

Manager: Freddie Goodwin

Player columns (left→right): Cooper P, Carroll T, Want A, Campbell A, Hynd JRS, Harland S, Hope R, Francis T, Latchford R, Hatton R, Taylor G, Pendrey G, Page M, Kelly M, Whitehead A, Summerill P, Howitt D, Burns K, Latchford D, Martin Ray, Roberts J, Calderwood J, Bowker K, Smith G, Phillips S, Hendrie P, Robinson D

#	Date		Opponent	Result	Scorers	Att.	CoP	CaT	WaA	CmA	HyJ	HaS	HoR	FrT	LaR	HtR	TaG	PeG	PgM	KeM	WhA	SuP	HwD	BuK	LaD	MrR	RoJ	CaJ	BoK	SmG	PhS
1	Aug 12	(h)	Sheffield U	L 1-2	R.Latchford	37,045	1	2	3	4	5	6	7	8	9	10	11														
2	15	(h)	Newcastle U	W 3-2	McFaul (og), Hope, R.Latchford	35,831	1	2	3	4	5	6	7	8	9	10	11	12													
3	19	(a)	Ipswich T	L 0-2		17,855	1	2	3	4	5	6		8	9	10	11	7	12												
4	23	(a)	Tottenham H	L 0-2		30,798		2	3	4	5	6		8	9		11	7	10	1											
5	26	(h)	Crystal P	D 1-1	Francis	31,066			3	4	5	6	10	8	9		11	7		1	2	12									
6	30	(a)	West Brom A	D 2-2	Hatton, R.Latchford	37,252			3	4	5	6	10		9	8	11	7		1						2					
7	Sep 2	(a)	Wolves	L 2-3	Hope, Burns	32,599			3	4	5	6	10		9	8	11	7		1				12		2					
8	9	(h)	Manchester C	W 4-1	R.Latchford 3, Campbell	32,983		2	3	4	5	6	10	8	9		11	7	12	1											
9	16	(a)	Derby C	L 0-1		23,753		2		4	5		10	8	9		11	3	6						1		7				
10	23	(h)	Everton	W 2-1	R.Latchford, Francis	37,133		2		4	5		10	8	9		11	12	3					6	1		7				
11	26	(a)	Arsenal	L 0-2		30,003				4	5		10	8	9		11	12	3					6	1	2	7				
12	30	(a)	West Ham U	L 0-2		26,482				4	5		12	10	8		11		3					6	1	2	7				
13	Oct 7	(h)	Chelsea	D 2-2	Hope, R.Latchford	38,756		2	3	12	5		7	8	9		11	10	6				11		1		4				
14	14	(a)	Manchester U	L 0-1		52,104		2	3	12	5			10	8	9	11	4	7				11		1		6				
15	21	(a)	Southampton	D 1-1	Roberts	30,757		2			5		7	8	9	10	11	3	4				1				6				
16	28	(h)	Coventry C	D 0-0		35,161		2			5	6	7	8	9	10	11	3	4						1						
17	Nov 4	(h)	Tottenham H	D 0-0		38,504						6	7	8	9	10	11	3	4						1	2	5				
18	11	(a)	Newcastle U	L 0-3		26,010			3	8		6	7		9	10	11	4						12	1	2	5				
19	18	(a)	Stoke C	W 2-1	R.Latchford 2	23,040			3		5	6	7		9	10	11	4							1	2			8		
20	25	(h)	Norwich C	W 4-1	Pendrey, Hope, Want, Hatton	32,890			3		5	6	7		9	10	11	4							1	2			8		
21	Dec 2	(a)	Liverpool	L 3-4	Taylor, Hope, R.Latchford	45,407			3		5	6	7		9	10	11	4						1		2			8		
22	9	(h)	Leicester C	D 1-1	Calderwood	32,481			3	7	5	6			9	10	11	4						1				8	2		
23	16	(a)	Leeds U	L 0-4		25,285			3		5				9	10	11	4						1		6	8	2	7		
24	23	(h)	Arsenal	D 1-1	Bowker	32,721			3		5	6	11	8	9		4							1			2	7	10		
25	26	(a)	Everton	D 1-1	R.Latchford	39,363			3		5	6	8		9		11	4						1			2	7	10		
26	30	(h)	Ipswich T	L 1-2	Hatton	32,705			3		5	6	8		9	12	11	4						1			2	7	10		
27	Jan 27	(a)	Manchester C	L 0-1		31,882			3	12	5			10	9	8	11	4						1		2	6		7		
28	Feb 10	(h)	Derby C	W 2-0	R.Latchford, Francis	38,096				7	5			8	9	10	11	3	4					12	1	2	6				
29	17	(a)	Sheffield U	W 1-0	Francis	22,220				7	5			8	9	10	11	3	4						1	2	6				
30	27	(h)	Wolves	L 0-1		43,759				7	5			8	9	10	11	3	4					12	1	2	6				
31	Mar 3	(a)	Chelsea	D 0-0		26,259				7	5			8	9	10	11	3	4						1	2	6				
32	6	(a)	Crystal P	D 0-0		26,014				7	5			8	9	10	11	3	4						1	2	6				
33	10	(h)	Manchester U	W 3-1	R.Latchford, Hatton, Campbell (pen)	51,278				7	5			8	9	10	11	3	4						1	2	6				
34	17	(a)	Southampton	L 0-2		14,674				7	5			8	9	10	11	3	4						1	2	6				
35	24	(h)	Coventry C	W 3-0	Hatton, R.Latchford, Taylor	34,775				7	5			8	9	10	11	3	4						1	2	6				
36	31	(a)	Norwich C	W 2-1	R.Latchford 2	24,209				7	5			8	9	10	11	3	4						1	2	6				
37	Apr 7	(h)	Liverpool	W 2-1	R.Latchford, Hatton	48,114				7	5			8	9	10	11	3	4						1	2	6				
38	14	(a)	Leicester C	W 1-0	Campbell	27,652				7	5			8	9	10	11	3	4						1	2	6				
39	21	(h)	Stoke C	W 3-1	Page, Francis, Hatton	32,513				7	5			8	9	10	11	3	4						1	2	6				
40	23	(h)	West Ham U	D 0-0		36,942				7	5			8	9		11	3	4					10	1	2	6				
41	28	(a)	West Brom A	W 3-2	R.Latchford, Hynd, Burns	36,784				7	5			8	9	12	11	3	4					10	1	2	6				
42	30	(h)	Leeds U	W 2-1	Francis, Burns	34,449				7	5			11	8	9		3	4					10	1	2	6				12

FINAL LEAGUE POSITION: 10th in Division One. Average home League attendance: 36,663.

	CoP	CaT	WaA	CmA	HyJ	HaS	HoR	FrT	LaR	HtR	TaG	PeG	PgM	KeM	WhA	SuP	HwD	BuK	LaD	MrR	RoJ	CaJ	BoK	SmG	PhS
Appearances	3	11	20	29	40	18	24	31	42	31	34	39	26	7	1	1	2	9	32	23	21	5	5	5	3
Substitutes			3		1	1				1	2	1	1			1		5			1	1	1		1
Goals			1	3	1		5	6	19	7	2	1	1					3			1	1	1		

1 own-goal

FA Cup

Rd	Date		Opponent	Result	Scorers	Att.	CaT	HyJ	HaS	HoR	FrT	LaR	HtR	TaG	PeG	PgM	LaD	RoJ
3	Jan 13	(a)	Swindon T	L 0-2		17,373	3	5	6	10	8	9	12	11	4	2	1	7
Appearances							1	1	1	1	1	1		1	1	1	1	1
Substitutes													1					
Goals																		

League Cup

Rd	Date		Opponent	Result	Scorers	Att.
2	Sep 5	(h)	Luton T	D 1-1	R.Latchford	20,962
R	13	(h)	Luton T	D 1-1*	Campbell	13,806
2R	19	(n†)	Luton T	W 1-0	Francis	11,451
3	Oct 3	(h)	Coventry C	W 2-1	Francis, Barry (og)	27,803
4	31	(a)	Blackpool	L 0-2		13,332

†Played at the County Ground, Northampton. *After extra-time.

	CoP	CaT	WaA	CmA	HyJ	HaS	HoR	FrT	LaR	HtR	TaG	PeG	PgM	KeM	BuK	LaD	MrR
Appearances	1	3	2	4	4	3	4	5	5	3	2	5	3	1	1	3	4
Substitutes				1						2	1				1	2	
Goals				1				2	1								

1 own-goal

FA Cup 3rd/4th Play-off (1972)

Date		Opponent	Result	Att.	CoP	CaT	WaA	CmA	HyJ	HaS	HoR	FrT	LaR	HtR	TaG
Aug 5	(h)	Stoke C	D 0-0*	25,841	1	2	3	4	5	6	7	8	9	10	11
Appearances					1	1	1	1	1	1	1	1	1	1	1
Substitutes															
Goals															

*Birmingham won 4-3 with penalties from Campbell, Francis, Hope and Harland.

1973-74

Manager: Freddie Goodwin

#	Date	Opponent	Res	Scorers	Att	Latchford D	Martin Ray	Pendrey G	Page M	Hynd JRS	Burns K	Campbell A	Francis T	Latchford R	Hatton R	Taylor G	Roberts J	Cooper P	Calderwood J	Phillips S	Hope R	Want A	Clarke D	Sprake G	Gallagher J	Kelly M	Hendrie P	Jenkins L	Kendall H	Styles A
1	Aug 25 (a)	Manchester C	L 1-3	Hatton	34,178	1	2	3	4	5	6	7	8	9	10	11														
2	8 (h)	Tottenham H	L 1-2	Hatton	37,754	1	2	3	4	5	6	7	8	9	10	11														
3	Sep 1 (h)	Derby C	D 0-0		34,596	1	2	3	4	5	6	7	8	9	10	11	12													
4	5 (a)	Chelsea	L 1-3	Page	25,660	1	2	3	4	5	10	7	8	9		11	6													
5	8 (a)	Leeds U	L 0-3		39,736		2	3	4	5	6		8	9		12		1	7	10	11									
6	11 (a)	Chelsea	L 2-4	Hatton, Taylor	30,252		2	3	4	5	6	12		9	10	11		1	7		8									
7	15 (h)	Liverpool	D 1-1	R.Latchford	35,719	1		3			4	12		9	10	11	6		8		7	2								
8	22 (a)	Queen's Park R	D 2-2	R.Latchford, Burns	18,701	1		12			5	4		9	10	11	6		7		8	3	2							
9	29 (a)	Ipswich T	L 0-3		26,919	1					5	4	12	9	10	11	6		7		8	3	2							
10	Oct 6 (a)	Arsenal	L 0-1		23,915		12				4	8	9		10	11	6		7			3	2	1	5					
11	13 (h)	Wolves	W 2-1	Francis (pen), Burns	34,977			4	12	5	7	8	9	10	11	6						3	2	1						
12	20 (a)	Manchester U	L 0-1		48,937			4		5	9	7	8	12	10	11	6					3	2							
13	27 (h)	Everton	L 0-2		31,181			4		12	7	8	9	10	11	6						3	2	1	5					
14	Nov 3 (a)	Sheffield U	D 1-1	Hynd	19,339			4		5	11	8	9	10			6					3		1	2		7			
15	10 (h)	Southampton	D 1-1	Hatton	25,297			4		5		8	9	10	11	6					12	3		1	2		7			
16	17 (h)	Stoke C	L 2-5	Hynd, R.Latchford	19,179			6		5	4	8	9	10	11							3	2	1			7			
17	24 (a)	Leicester C	W 3-0	R.Latchford 3	27,719			5			6	7	8	9	10	11						3	2	1				11		
18	Dec 8 (h)	Newcastle U	W 1-0	Burns	25,428	1	2	4		5	7	8	9	12	10		6								3			11		
19	15 (a)	West Ham U	W 3-1	Burns 2, Hatton	23,767	1	2	4		5	7	8	9		10		6								3			11		
20	22 (a)	Ipswich T	L 0-3		15,289	1	2	4		5	6	7	8	9	10		12								3			**11**		
21	26 (h)	Coventry C	W 1-0	R.Latchford	33,423		2	4			6	7	8	9	10	11	5							1	3					
22	29 (h)	Leeds U	D 1-1	R.Latchford	50,451		2	4			6	7	8	9	10	11	5							1	3					
23	Jan 1 (a)	Derby C	D 1-1	Hatton	31,189	1	2	4		12	6	7	8	9	10	11	5								3					
24	12 (a)	Liverpool	L 2-3	R.Latchford	39,094		2	4			6	7	8	9	10	11	5							1	3					
25	19 (h)	Manchester C	D 1-1	R.Latchford	31,401		2	4			6	7	8	9	10	11	5	12						1	3					
26	Feb 2 (a)	West Ham U	D 0-0		27,948		2	4			6	8	7	9	10						11	3		1	5					
27	6 (a)	Tottenham H	L 2-4	England (og), Phillips	14,345		2	4			6	8	7	9	10					12	11	3		1	5					
28	16 (a)	Wolves	L 0-1		33,821		2	7			6		9	8	11					12	10	3		1	5				4	
29	23 (h)	Arsenal	W 3-1	Gallagher, Hatton, Francis	29,822	1	2	3			6	9	7	8	10	11					12				5				4	
30	Mar 2 (a)	Coventry C	W 1-0	Hatton	27,825	1	2	3			6	9	7	8	10	11									5				4	
31	9 (h)	Everton	L 1-4	Hatton	33,944	1	2	3			6	9	7	8	10	11									5				4	12
32	16 (h)	Manchester U	W 1-0	Gallagher	37,768	1	2				6	9	7	8	10	11	5								12				4	3
33	20 (a)	Norwich C	L 1-2	Styles	19,094	1	2			5		9	7	8	10	11	6								12				4	3
34	23 (a)	Southampton	W 2-0	Burns, Francis	23,349	1	2	3			5	9	7	8	10	11	6								12				4	
35	30 (h)	Sheffield U	W 1-0	Hatton	27,877	1	2	3		5		9	7	8	10	11	6												4	
36	Apr 6 (a)	Leicester C	D 3-3	Burns 3	28,486	1	2	3			5	9	7	8	10	11	6								12				4	
37	12 (a)	Burnley	L 1-2	Campbell	16,991	1	2	3		5		9	7	8	10	11	6								12				4	
38	13 (h)	Stoke C	D 0-0		20,467	1	2	3		5		7	8		10	11	6								9				4	
39	16 (h)	Burnley	D 2-2	Hatton 2	36,548	1	2	4		5		7	8		10	11	6								9				4	12
40	20 (a)	Newcastle U	D 1-1	Francis	32,102	1	2		11	5		7	8		10		6								9				4	3
41	23 (a)	Queen's Park R	W 4-0	Taylor, Francis 2, Kendall	39,160	1	2	3		5		9	7	8	10	11	6								12				4	
42	27 (h)	Norwich C	W 2-1	Hatton, Burns	44,182	1	2	3			5	9	7	8	10	11	6												4	
	Appearances					25	29	38	7	34	36	32	37	25	39	33	28	2	7	1	6	11	11	14	21	1	5	2	15	3
	Substitutes						2	1	2	1	3	1	2	2	2		2	3		2	3				5			1	2	1
	Goals								1	2	10	1	6	10	14	2									1				1	1

FINAL LEAGUE POSITION: 19th in Division One. Average home League attendance: 33,048.

1 own-goal

FA Cup

#	Date	Opponent	Res	Scorers	Att	Latchford D	Martin Ray	Pendrey G	Page M	Hynd JRS	Burns K	Campbell A	Francis T	Latchford R	Hatton R	Taylor G	Roberts J	Cooper P	Calderwood J	Phillips S	Hope R	Want A	Clarke D	Sprake G	Gallagher J	Kelly M	Hendrie P	Jenkins L	Kendall H	Styles A
3	Jan 5 (h)	Cardiff C	W 5-2	Francis, R.Latchford 2, Hatton 2	22,435		2	4		5		7	8	9	10	11	6							1	3					
4	26 (a)	Queen's Park R	L 0-2		23,367		2	4			6	7	8	9	10	11						3		1	5					
	Appearances						2	2		1	1	2	2	2	2	2	1					1		2	2					
	Substitutes																													
	Goals												1	2	2															

League Cup

#	Date	Opponent	Res	Scorers	Att	Latchford D	Martin Ray	Pendrey G	Page M	Hynd JRS	Burns K	Campbell A	Francis T	Latchford R	Hatton R	Taylor G	Roberts J	Cooper P	Calderwood J	Phillips S	Hope R	Want A	Clarke D	Sprake G	Gallagher J	Kelly M	Hendrie P	Jenkins L	Kendall H	Styles A
2	Oct 9 (a)	Blackpool	D 1-1	Burns	7,943		4					9	7	8	10	11	6					3	2	1	5					
R	16 (h)	Blackpool	W 4-2	Burns, Hatton 3	16,880		4			5	9	7		12	10	11	6					3	2	1		8				
3	30 (a)	Newcastle U	D 2-2	R.Latchford 2	13,025		4			5	7	8	9	10	11	6			12			3	2	1						
R	Nov 7 (a)	Newcastle U	W 1-0*	Francis (pen)	19,276		4			5	7	8	9	10	11	6						3	2	1						
4	21 (a)	Ipswich T	W 3-1	R.Latchford 3	12,241		4			5	6	7	8	9	10				12			3	2	1				11		
5	Dec 19 (h)	Plymouth A	L 1-2	Hatton	15,273	1	2	4		5	7	8	9	12	10		6								3			11		
	Appearances					1	6			5	6	3	5	4	6	4	5					5	3	4	4	1		3		
	Substitutes												1	1					2											
	Goals									2		1	5	4																

*After extra-time.

1974-75

Manager: Freddie Goodwin

Player columns (left → right): Latchford D · Martin Ray · Pendrey G · Kendall H · Hynd JRS · Roberts J · Campbell A · Francis T · Burns K · Hatton R · Page M · Taylor G · Styles A · Gallagher J · Stragia R · Bryant S · Calderwood J · Phillips S · Hendrie P · Emmanuel G · Clarke D · Morton R · Sprake G · Want A · Kelly M · Smith I

#	Date		Opponent	Res	Scorers	Att	Latch	Mart	Pend	Kend	Hynd	Robe	Camp	Fran	Burn	Hatt	Page	Tayl	Styl	Gall	Stra	Brya	Cald	Phil	Hend	Emma	Clar	Mort	Spra	Want	Kell	Smit
1	Aug 17	(h)	Middlesbrough	L 0-3		32,019	1	**2**	3	4	5	6	7	8	9	10	11	12														
2	20	(h)	Leicester C	L 3-4	Burns, Francis 2 (1 pen)	27,961	1	12	3	4	5	6	7	8	9	10	2	11														
3	24	(a)	Leeds U	L 0-1		30,820	1			4			7	8	9	10	2	11	3	5	6											
4	28	(a)	Leicester C	D 1-1	Francis	24,018	1	2		4			7	8	9	10	6	11	3	5												
5	31	(h)	Wolves	D 1-1	Burns	33,785	1	2	7	4				8	9	10	6	11	3	5												
6	Sep 7	(a)	Queen's Park R	W 1-0	Gallagher	16,058	1	2		4				8	9	10	6	11	3	5												
7	14	(h)	Derby C	W 3-2	Hatton, Francis 2 (2 pens)	27,795	1			4	12		7	8	9	10	6	11	3	5												
8	21	(a)	Carlisle U	L 0-1		12,691	1	2		4	12		7	8	9	10	6	11	3	5												
9	25	(a)	West Ham U	L 0-3		29,495	1	2		4	12		7	8	9	10	6	11	3	5												
10	28	(h)	Arsenal	W 3-1	Burns, Hatton 2	25,584	1	2	6	4	12		7	8	9	10		11	3	5												
11	Oct 5	(h)	Coventry C	L 1-2	Francis (pen)	30,282	1	2	6	4			7	8	9	10		11		5		3										
12	12	(a)	Luton T	W 3-1	Francis 3	15,097	1	2	6	4			7	8	9	10				5		3	11									
13	15	(h)	Leeds U	W 1-0	Francis	36,513	1	2	6	4			7	8	9	10			3	5			11									
14	19	(h)	Newcastle U	W 3-0	Burns, Styles, Hatton	33,339	1	2	6	4			7	8	9	10			3	5			11									
15	26	(a)	Sheffield U	L 2-3	Hatton, Styles	21,639	1	2	6	4	12		7	**8**	9	10			3	5			11									
16	Nov 2	(h)	Chelsea	W 2-0	Hatton, Kendall	30,364	1	2	6	4			7		9	10			3	5			11	8								
17	9	(a)	Burnley	D 2-2	Rodaway (og), Taylor	15,835	1	2	3	4	5		7		**9**			6	8				11	12	10							
18	16	(h)	Manchester C	W 4-0	Kendall, Hatton 2, Burns	35,143	1	2	12	4			7		9	10		6	8	3		5	11									
19	23	(a)	Tottenham H	D 0-0		27,761	1	2		4			7		9	10		6	8	3		5	11									
20	30	(a)	Everton	L 1-4	Calderwood	38,369	1	2	**9**	4	12		7			10		6	8	3		5	11									
21	Dec 7	(h)	Stoke C	L 0-3		33,999	1	**2**	12	4			7		9	10		6	8	3		5										
22	14	(a)	Middlesbrough	L 0-3		23,737	1	2	12	4			7		9	10		6	8	3		5										
23	21	(h)	Liverpool	W 3-1	Taylor, Kendall (pen), Hatton	26,608	1		6	4	5		7		9	10		2	8	3			11			12						
24	26	(a)	Derby C	L 1-2	Hatton	26,121	1		6	4			7		9	10		2	8	3		5	11									
25	28	(h)	Ipswich T	L 0-1		30,266	1		6	4			**7**		9	10		2	8	3		5	11			12						
26	Jan 11	(a)	Stoke C	D 0-0		26,157	1		6	4	12				9	**10**		2	8	3		5	11					7				
27	18	(a)	Everton	L 0-3		32,284	1		6	4			7		9	10		2	8	3		5	11									
28	Feb 1	(h)	Burnley	D 1-1	Emmanuel	24,990	1	2		4	6				9	10			8	3		5	11			7						
29	8	(a)	Chelsea	L 1-2	Hatton	18,144	1			4	6		7		9	10		2	8	5		3										
30	18	(h)	Tottenham H	W 1-0	Hatton	24,240	1		6	4					9	10		7	8	5		3	11			2						
31	22	(a)	Manchester C	L 1-3	Taylor	33,240	1		6	4					9	10		7	8	5		3	11			2						
32	Mar 1	(a)	Wolves	W 1-0	Hendrie	28,256	1		6	4					9	10		3	8	5	12		11		7	2						
33	15	(a)	Arsenal	D 1-1	Burns	17,845	1			4		6			9	10			8	5		3			7		11					
34	18	(h)	West Ham U	D 1-1	Bryant	33,998	1			4		6		8		10	11			5		3	2		9	7	12					
35	22	(h)	Queen's Park R	W 4-1	Francis, Campbell, Hatton, Calderwood	32,832	1			4		6	7	8		10	11			5		3	2		9				1		12	
36	25	(h)	Carlisle U	W 2-0	Francis, Burns	33,761	1			4		6	7	8	9	10	11			5		3	2							1		
37	29	(a)	Liverpool	L 0-1		49,454	1			4		6		8	9	10				5		3	2		7			11				
38	Apr 1	(a)	Ipswich T	L 2-3	Burns, Hatton	27,401	1		6	4				8	9	10	11			5		3	2			7						
39	12	(a)	Coventry C	L 0-1		24,180	1		6	4				8	9	10	11	2		5		3				7	12					
40	19	(h)	Luton T	L 1-4	Francis	28,755	1		6	4				8	9	10	11	2	7			3					12					
41	26	(a)	Newcastle U	W 2-1	Kendall, Pendrey	23,471	1		7	4				8	6	10	11	9		5		3	2									
42	29	(h)	Sheffield U	D 0-0		33,677	1		10	4				8	6	9	11			5		3	2									
	Appearances						39	21	27	39	6	7	28	23	39	41	28	34	23	38	1	15	25	1	9	9	3	3	2	1		
	Substitutes							1		3	6	1								1			1		1	2					2	2
	Goals								1	4			1	13	8	14		3	2	1		1	2		1	1						

FINAL LEAGUE POSITION: 17th in Division One. Average home League attendance: 30,854.

1 own-goal

FA Cup

Rd	Date		Opponent	Res	Scorers	Att	Latch	Pend	Kend	Hynd	Robe	Camp	Fran	Burn	Hatt	Page	Tayl	Styl	Gall	Brya	Cald	Hend	Emma
3	Jan 4	(a)	Luton T	W 1-0	Kendall	17,543	1	6	4					9	10		2	8	3	5	11	7	
4	25	(a)	Chelsea	W 1-0	Burns	36,650	1	6	4	10				9			2	8	3	5	11	7	
5	Feb 15	(h)	Walsall	W 2-1	Hatton, Burns	45,881	1	6	4					9	10		7	8	5	3	11		2
6	Mar 8	(h)	Middlesbrough	W 1-0	Hatton	47,260	1		4	12				9	10		2	8	5	3	11	7	
SF	Apr 5(nt)		Fulham	D 1-1	Gallagher	54,166	1	3	4		6	7	8	9	10		2		5		11		
R	9(ns)		Fulham	L 0-1*		35,205	1	6	4				8	9	10		2		5	3	11	7	
	Appearances						6	5	6	1	2	1	2	6	5	6	6	2	6	3	1	3	4
	Substitutes												1										
	Goals								1					2	2				1				

†Played at Hillsborough, Sheffield. §Played at Maine Road, Manchester. *After extra-time.

League Cup

Rd	Date		Opponent	Res	Scorers	Att	Latch	Mart	Pend	Kend	Hynd	Camp	Fran	Burn	Tayl	Styl	Gall	Cald
2	Sep 11	(a)	Crewe A	L 1-2	Gallagher	7,194	1	2	12	4	6	7	8	9	11	3	5	**10**
	Appearances						1	1		1	1	1	1	1	1	1	1	1
	Substitutes								1									
	Goals																1	

1975-76

Manager: Freddie Goodwin until September 1975 then Willie Bell

#	Date		Opponent	Res	Scorers	Att	Latchford D	Osborne I	Bryant S	Kendall H	Gallagher J	Roberts J	Calderwood J	Phillips S	Hendrie P	Hatton R	Taylor G	Want A	Hynd JRS	Burns K	Francis T	Pendrey G	Martin Ray	Hope R	Withe P	Hibbitt T	Campbell A	Page M	Styles A	Emmanuel G	Smith S	Needham A	Morton R
1	Aug	16 (a)	Leicester C	D 3-3	Hatton, Kendall 2 (1 pen)	25,547	1	2	3	4	5	6	7	8	9	10	11																
2		19 (h)	Manchester U	L 0-2		33,177	1	2	3	4	5			8	9	7	10	11	6	12													
3		23 (h)	Everton	L 0-1		26,795	1		3	4	5	12	9		7	10		2		6	8	11											
4		26 (a)	Middlesbrough	L 0-2		22,423	1		3	4	5	12	9		7	10	8	2		6		11											
5		30 (a)	Ipswich T	L 2-4	Hatton 2	22,649	1		3	4	5					10				6	8	11	2	7	9								
6	Sep	6 (h)	Queen's Park R	D 1-1	Kendall	27,305	1		3	4	5					10				6	8		2	7	9	11							
7		13 (a)	Wolves	L 0-2		25,142	1		3	4	5	6				10					8		2	7	9	11							
8		20 (h)	Burnley	W 4-0	Campbell, Withe, Kendall, Francis	25,830	1		3	4	5					10				6	8		2		9	11	7						
9		23 (h)	Newcastle U	W 3-2	Withe 2, Francis (pen)	31,166	1		3	4	5					10				6	8	12	2		9	11	7						
10		27 (a)	Aston Villa	L 1-2	Francis	53,782	1	2		4	5					10	3			6	8	12			9	11	7						
11	Oct	4 (h)	Sheffield U	W 2-0	Hatton, Francis	26,121	1		3	4	5					10				6	8		2		9	11	7						
12		11 (a)	Liverpool	L 1-3	Hatton	36,532	1		3		5					10	11	12		6	8	4	2		9		7						
13		18 (h)	Leeds U	D 2-2	Francis, Gallagher	33,775	1			4	5					10	12			6	8	3	2		9	11	7						
14		25 (a)	Norwich C	L 0-1		20,178	1			4	5	6				10	11				8	3	2		9		7						
15	Nov	1 (h)	West Ham U	L 1-5	Francis	28,474	1			4	5	6				10	12			9	8	3	2			11	7						
16		8 (a)	Manchester C	L 0-2		28,329	1			4	5									6	8	3	2		9	11	7						
17		15 (h)	Arsenal	W 3-1	Francis (pen), Withe, Hatton	21,652	1	2	3	4	5					10	11			6	8	7			9								
18		22 (a)	Leeds U	L 0-3		26,640	1	2	3	4	5			8		10			11	6		7			9								
19		29 (a)	Coventry C	L 2-3	Burns, Kendall (pen)	21,687	1		8	4	5				7	10			3	6			2		9	11							
20	Dec	6 (h)	Derby C	W 2-1	Burns, Page	30,620	1	2		4	5					10			3	6	8				9	11		7					
21		13 (a)	Everton	L 2-5	Kendall, Withe	20,188	1	2	12	4	5					10			3	6	8				9	11		7					
22		20 (h)	Leicester C	W 2-1	Francis (pen), Withe	21,890	1	2		4	5					10			3	6	8	7			9	11							
23		26 (a)	Tottenham H	W 3-1	Francis 2, Withe	21,657	1	2	7	4	5					10			3	6	8				9	11							
24		27 (h)	Stoke C	D 1-1	Hatton	37,166	1	2	7	4	5					10			3	6	8				9	11							
25	Jan	10 (h)	Wolves	L 0-1		28,552	1			5	4					10			3	6	8		2		9		7	11					
26		17 (a)	Queen's Park R	L 1-2	Francis	16,759	1			4	5				12	10			3	6	8		2		9		7	11					
27		31 (a)	Manchester C	L 1-3	Withe	50,274	1			4	5					10		12		6	8		2		9	11	7	3					
28	Feb	7 (h)	Middlesbrough	W 2-1	Kendall, Hatton	18,599	1		3	4	5					10	11			6	8		2				9	7					
29		14 (h)	Manchester C	W 2-1	Gallagher, Kendall	22,445	1			4	5		11			10				6	8		2		9		7	3					
30		21 (a)	Arsenal	L 0-1		20,907	1			4	5		11			9				6	8		2			10	7	3	12				
31		28 (h)	Norwich C	D 1-1	Francis (pen)	22,359	1			4	5		11			10				6	8				9		2	3	7				
32	Mar	6 (h)	West Ham U	W 2-1	Withe, Emmanuel	19,868	1			4	5		12							6	8		2		9	11	10	3	7				
33		13 (h)	Liverpool	L 0-1		31,797				4	5		7					12	3	8	6		2		9	11	10				1		
34		20 (h)	Coventry C	D 1-1	Francis (pen)	22,956				4	5					10			3	8	6		2			11	7	3			1	9	
35		27 (a)	Derby C	L 2-4	Francis, Needham	28,161	1			4	5				9				3	8	6		2			11	7	10				12	
36	Apr	3 (h)	Aston Villa	W 3-2	Hibbitt, Burns, Francis	46,251	1			4	5							2	12	6	9	8				11	7		3			10	
37		7 (a)	Newcastle U	L 0-4		18,547	1			4		6	9				5		10	12		8					2	7	3				
38		10 (a)	Burnley	L 0-1		13,668	1	10		5			2							6	8				9	11	4	3	7				
39		13 (h)	Ipswich T	W 3-0	Francis (pen), Hibbitt, Burns	20,497	1			5			2							6	9	8			10	11	4	3	7				
40		17 (h)	Tottenham H	W 3-1	Gallagher, Francis, Burns	30,616	1			5			2					12		6	9	8			10	11	4	3	7				
41		19 (a)	Stoke C	L 0-1		19,918	1	11		5			2							6	9	8			10		4	3	7				
42	May	4 (h)	Sheffield U	D 1-1	Hibbitt	28,782	1			4	5		12							6	9	8			10	11	2	3	7				
			Appearances				40	10	19	36	41	5	15	4	5	33	7	20		36	35	14	22	3	32	27	9	19	16	10	2	2	
			Substitutes					1			2	3				4	2	1	1			3								1		1	
			Goals							8	3					8				5	17				9	3	1	1		1		1	

FINAL LEAGUE POSITION: 19th in Division One. Average home League attendance: 28,002.

FA Cup

R	Date		Opponent	Res	Scorers	Att	Latchford D	Osborne I	Bryant S	Kendall H	Gallagher J	Roberts J	Calderwood J	Phillips S	Hendrie P	Hatton R	Taylor G	Want A	Hynd JRS	Burns K	Francis T	Pendrey G	Martin Ray	Hope R	Withe P	Hibbitt T	Campbell A	Page M	Styles A
3	Jan	3 (a)	Portsmouth	D 1-1	Francis	19,414	1	2		4	5					10	3			6	8	12			9	11		7	
R		6 (h)	Portsmouth	L 0-1		26,106	1	11		5	12					10	3			6	8	4	2		9			7	
			Appearances				2	1	1	1	2					2	2			2	2	1	1		2	1		2	
			Substitutes										1									1							
			Goals																		1								

League Cup

R	Date		Opponent	Res	Scorers	Att	Latchford D	Osborne I	Bryant S	Kendall H	Gallagher J	Roberts J	Calderwood J	Phillips S	Hendrie P	Hatton R	Taylor G	Want A	Hynd JRS	Burns K	Francis T	Pendrey G	Martin Ray	Hope R	Withe P	Hibbitt T	Campbell A	Page M	Styles A	Morton R
2	Sep	9 (h)	Orient	W 4-0	Gallagher, Morton, Hatton, Want	18,238	1			4	5					10		12		6	8	3	2		9	11				7
3	Oct	7 (h)	Wolves	L 0-2		29,822	1		3	4	5					10				6	8	12	2		9	11	7			
			Appearances				2		1	2	2					2				2	2	1	2		2	2	1			1
			Substitutes															1				1								
			Goals								1					1		1												1

1976-77

Manager: Willie Bell

Player columns (left to right): Latchford D, Page M, Styles A, Kendall H, Gallagher J, Want A, Pendrey G, Francis T, Burns K, Hibbitt T, Jones G, Calderwood J, Emmanuel G, Withe P, Connolly J, Rathbone M, Sbragia R, Broadhurst K, Fox S, Montgomery J, McDonough R

#	Date		Opponent	Result	Scorers	Att	Lat	Pag	Sty	Ken	Gal	Wan	Pen	Fra	Bur	Hib	Jon	Cal	Emm	Wit	Con	Rat	Sbr	Bro	Fox	Mon	McD
1	Aug 21	(a)	Manchester U	D 2-2	Burns, Styles	58,898	1	2	3	4	5	6	7	8	9	10	11	12									
2	24	(h)	Leeds U	D 0-0		35,399	1	2	3		5	6	4	8	9	10	11	7	12								
3	28	(h)	Liverpool	W 2-1	Francis, Gallagher	33,228	1	2	3	4	5	6	7	8		10	11				9						
4	Sep 4	(a)	Norwich C	L 0-1		19,271	1	2	3	4	5	6	7	8		10	11				9						
5	11	(h)	West Brom A	L 0-1		38,448	1	2	3	4	5	6		8		10	7				9	11					
6	18	(a)	Aston Villa	W 2-1	Burns, Connolly	50,084	1	2	3	4	5	6		8	9	10	7	12			11						
7	25	(a)	Coventry C	L 1-2	Burns	25,989	1	2	3		5	6		8	9	4	10	7			11						
8	Oct 2	(h)	Derby C	W 5-1	Burns 4, Connolly	29,190	1	2	3		5	6	12	8	9	4	10	7			11						
9	16	(h)	Middlesbrough	W 3-1	Gallagher, Burns, Francis (pen)	27,740	1	2	3		5	**6**	12	8	9	4	10	7			11						
10	20	(a)	Tottenham H	L 0-1		20,193	1	2	**3**		5		6	8		10	7	4		9	11	12					
11	23	(a)	Newcastle U	L 2-3	Gallagher, Francis (pen)	30,898	1		3		5		6	8	9	10	7		**4**	12	11	2					
12	26	(a)	Bristol C	W 1-0	Burns	21,927	1		3		5		6	8	9	10	7			4	11	2					
13	30	(h)	Queen's Park R	W 2-1	Burns, Francis	31,471	1	2	3		5		6	8	9	10	7	4			11						
14	Nov 6	(a)	Arsenal	L 0-4		23,603	1	2	3		5	6		8	9	10	7	4			11						
15	20	(a)	Stoke C	L 0-1		21,486	1	2	3		5	6	4	8	9	10	**7**	12			11						
16	27	(h)	Manchester C	D 0-0		29,722	1	2	3		5	6	7	8	9	10			4		11						
17	Dec 4	(a)	Leicester C	W 6-2	Emmanuel, Francis, Burns 3, Rofe (og)	20,388	1	2	3		5	6	4	8	9	10				7	11						
18	7	(h)	Ipswich T	L 2-4	Connolly, Burns	31,161	1	2	3		5	6	**4**	8	9	10				7	11	12					
19	11	(h)	Sunderland	W 2-0	Jones, Francis	24,597	1	4	3		5	6		8	9	10	7				11	2					
20	18	(a)	Everton	D 2-2	Francis, Hibbitt	32,541	1	2	3	4	5	6		8	9	10	7				11						
21	27	(h)	West Ham U	D 0-0		39,978	1	6	3	4	5			8	9	10	7				11	2					
22	Jan 18	(a)	Arsenal	D 3-3	Francis 3	23,247	1	2		4	5			8		10	7			9	11	3					
23	22	(h)	Manchester U	L 2-3	Francis, Emmanuel	35,316	1		3	4	5	6		8		10	7			9	11	2					
24	Feb 2	(a)	Leeds U	L 0-1		22,805	1	2		4	5			8	9	10	7				11	3	6				
25	5	(a)	Liverpool	L 1-4	Burns	41,073	1	6	3	4	5			8	9	10	7				11	2					
26	12	(h)	Norwich C	W 3-2	Burns 2, Broadhurst	21,809	1	2	3	4	5	6		8	9	10					11			7			
27	28	(a)	West Brom A	L 1-2	Francis	27,393	1	2			5	6		8	9	10					3			**7**	12		
28	Mar 5	(h)	Coventry C	W 3-1	Francis, Connolly, Emmanuel	22,607	1	2			**5**	6		8	9	10	7		4	12	11	3					
29	12	(a)	Derby C	D 0-0		24,523			3	**4**		6	12	8	5	10				9	11	2			7	1	
30	19	(h)	Tottenham H	L 1-2	Connolly	23,398				4	5		3	8	6	10	9	7			11	2				1	
31	22	(a)	Middlesbrough	D 2-2	Francis 2	15,884				4	5	6	**3**	8		10		2		7	9	12			11	1	
32	Apr 2	(h)	Newcastle U	L 1-2	Fox	20,283		2	3	4	5	**6**	3	8		10	11				9				7	1	
33	8	(a)	West Ham U	D 2-2	Gallagher, Francis	28,167				4	5	6	3	8	9	10		2		7	11					1	
34	9	(h)	Bristol C	W 3-0	Francis 3 (2 pens)	19,626				4	5	6	3	8	9	10	7	2			11					1	
35	11	(a)	Ipswich T	L 0-1		29,025				4		6	3	**8**	9	10	7	12			11	2	5			1	
36	16	(h)	Stoke C	W 2-0	Francis, Burns	19,554				4	5	6	3	8	9	10	7	2			11					1	
37	19	(a)	Manchester C	L 1-2	Burns	36,203				4		6	3	8	9	10	7	2	12		11		5			1	
38	30	(h)	Leicester C	D 1-1	Kendall	20,836				**4**	**5**		3	8	9	10	7	2			11	12	6			1	
39	May 7	(a)	Sunderland	L 0-1		34,193				4			3	8	9	10	7	2			11		5			1	6
40	10	(h)	Aston Villa	W 2-1	Hibbitt, Francis (pen)	43,721	1	4			5		3	8	9	10	7	2			11		6				
41	14	(h)	Everton	D 1-1	Kendall	22,436	1	5		4			3	8	9	10	7	2			11		6				
42	23	(a)	Queen's Park R	D 2-2	Kendall, McDonough	14,976		2		**4**	**5**		3	8	9	10	7	12			11		6			1	9
			Appearances				30	31	24	25	37	29	24	42	36	42	30	22	10	3	37	13	8	2	3	12	2
			Substitutes										3						4	6		3	1				
			Goals						1	3	4			21	19	2	1		3		5		1	1	1		1

FINAL LEAGUE POSITION: 13th in Division One. Average home League attendance: 28,338.

1 own-goal

FA Cup

#	Date		Opponent	Result	Scorers	Att	Lat	Pag	Sty	Ken	Gal	Wan	Pen	Fra	Bur	Hib	Jon	Cal	Emm	Wit	Con	Rat
3	Jan 8	(h)	Portsmouth	W 1-0	Kendall	31,598	1	6	**3**	4	5	12		8	9	10	7				11	2
4	29	(h)	Leeds U	L 1-2	Burns	38,663	1	6	3	4	5			8	9	10	7				11	2
			Appearances				2	2	2	2	2			2	2	2	2				2	2
			Substitutes									1										
			Goals							1					1							

League Cup

#	Date		Opponent	Result	Scorers	Att	Lat	Pag	Sty	Ken	Gal	Wan	Pen	Fra	Bur	Hib	Jon	Cal	Emm	Wit	Con	Rat
2	Aug 31	(a)	Blackpool	L 1-2	Pendrey	12,203	1	2		4	5	6	7	8		10	11				9	3
			Appearances				1	1		1	1	1	1	1		1	1				1	1
			Substitutes																			
			Goals										1									

1977-78

Manager: Wille Bell until September 1977, Sir Alf Ramsey until March 1978 then Jim Smith.

Column key (left→right): Montgomery J, Calderwood J, Pendrey G, Towers A, Howard P, Page M, Jones G, Francis T, Bertschin K, Hibbitt T, Connolly J, Want A, Styles A, Rathbone M, Broadhurst K, Emmanuel G, Fox S, Sbragia R, Dillon K, Gallagher J, Latchford D, Smith S

#	Date	Opponent	Res	Scorers	Att	Mon	Cal	Pen	Tow	How	Pag	Jon	Fra	Ber	Hib	Con	Wan	Sty	Rat	Bro	Emm	Fox	Sbr	Dil	Gal	Lat	Smi
1	Aug 20 (h)	Manchester U	L 1-4	Hibbitt	28,005	1	2	3	4	5	6	7	8	9	10	11											
2	24 (a)	Chelsea	L 0-2		18,008	1	2	3	4	5		7	8	9	10	11	6										
3	27 (a)	Leeds U	L 0-1		24,551	1	2	3	4	5		7	8	9	10	11	6	12									
4	Sep 3 (h)	Liverpool	L 0-1		26,239	1		3	4	5	11		8	9	10				2	6	12	7					
5	10 (a)	Middlesbrough	W 2-1	Francis 2	19,242	1		3		4			8	9	10		6		2	7	11		5				
6	17 (a)	Newcastle U	W 3-0	Connolly, Bertschin 2	18,953	1		3	4	5	2		8	9	10	12	6			7	11						
7	24 (a)	West Brom A	L 1-3	Connolly	29,160	1			4	5	2		8	9	10	7		3		6	11						
8	Oct 1 (a)	Aston Villa	W 1-0	Bertchin	45,436	1	2	3	4	5			8	9	10		6			7	11						
9	4 (h)	Queen's Park R	W 2-1	Francis 2	21,304	1	2	3		5	4		8	9	10	7	6				11						
10	8 (h)	Coventry C	D 1-1	Francis (pen)	27,414	1	2	3		5	4	12	8	9	10	7	6				11						
11	15 (a)	Ipswich T	L 2-5	Francis 2	21,250	1	2	3	7	5	4		8	9	10		6				11						
12	22 (h)	Derby C	W 3-1	Hibbitt 2, Towers	23,108	1	2	3	4	5	7		8	9	10		6				11						
13	29 (a)	Arsenal	D 1-1	Bertschin	31,355	1	2	3	4	5	7		8	9	10	12	6				11						
14	Nov 5 (h)	Wolves	W 2-1	Francis, Hibbitt	28,103	1	2	3	4		7		8	9	10		6				11		5				
15	12 (a)	Everton	L 1-2	Bertschin	37,793	1	2	3	4		7		8	9	10	12	6				11		5				
16	19 (a)	Leicester C	D 1-1	Francis	21,208	1	2	3	4		7	12	8	9	10		6						5	11			
17	26 (a)	Norwich C	L 0-1		17,161	1	2	3			5	7	8	9	10		6				11			4			
18	Dec 3 (h)	Nottingham F	L 0-2		29,925	1	2	3	12	5	7		8	9	10		6				11			4			
19	10 (a)	Manchester C	L 0-3		36,671	1	2	3	4	5	7		8	9	10		6				11			12			
20	17 (h)	Everton	D 0-0		22,177	1	2	3	4	5	7		8	9	10		6				11						
21	26 (a)	West Ham U	L 0-1		25,572	1	2	3	4	5	7		8	9	10		6				11						
22	27 (h)	Bristol C	W 3-0	Gallagher, Towers, Francis	24,110	1	2	3	4	5	7		8	9	10	12								11	6		
23	31 (h)	Chelsea	L 4-5	Bertschin, Francis 2, Hibbitt	19,876	1	2	3	4	5	7		8	9	10	12								11	6		
24	Jan 2 (a)	Manchester U	W 2-1	Dillon, Francis	53,501	1	2		4	5			8	9	10	7		3						11	6		
25	14 (a)	Leeds U	L 2-3	Bertschin, Connolly	23,703	1		3		4	6	2	8	9	10	7							5	11			
26	21 (a)	Liverpool	W 3-2	Emmanuel, Bertschin, Francis (pen)	48,401	1	2	3	4		6		8	9	10						7			11	5		
27	Feb 4 (a)	Middlesbrough	L 1-2	Gallagher	14,302	1	2	3	4		6		8	9	10						7			11	5		
28	25 (h)	Aston Villa	W 1-0	Francis	33,679	1	2			4	6	12	8	9	10			3				7		11	5		
29	28 (h)	West Brom A	L 1-2	Francis	26,633		2			4	6		8	9	10			3		7				11	5	1	
30	Mar 4 (a)	Coventry C	L 0-4		22,925	1	2			4	6		8	9	10			3		7	12			11	5		
31	15 (a)	Newcastle U	D 1-1	Francis	18,146	1	2	3	4	6	7		8	9	10	11									5		
32	18 (h)	Derby C	W 3-1	Connolly, Francis, Bertschin	19,843	1	2	3	4	6	7		8	9	10	11									5		
33	21 (h)	Arsenal	D 1-1		22,087	1	2	3	4	6	7		8	9	10	11									5		
34	25 (a)	Bristol C	W 1-0	Francis	21,884	1	2	3	4	6	7		8	9	10	11				12					5		
35	28 (h)	West Ham U	W 3-0	Francis 2 (1 pen), Bertschin	23,554	1	2	3	4	6	7		8	9	10						11				5		
36	Apr 1 (a)	Wolves	W 1-0	Francis	19,926	1	2	3	4	6	7		8	9	10					12	11				5		
37	8 (h)	Norwich C	W 2-1	Gallagher, Francis	20,858	1	2	3	4	6	7		8	9	10		12				11				5		
38	11 (h)	Ipswich T	D 0-0		19,289	1	2	3	4	6	7		8	9	10		12				11				5		
39	15 (a)	Leicester C	W 4-1	Hibbitt, Pendrey, Bertschin, Francis	15,431	1	2	3	4	6			8	9	10		12				11		7		5		
40	22 (h)	Manchester C	L 1-4	Sbragia	25,294	1	2	3	4				8	9	10						11	6	7		5		
41	25 (a)	Queen's Park R	D 0-0		16,049	1		3	4		2		8	9						6	10	11		7	5		
42	29 (a)	Nottingham F	D 0-0		37,625	1	2	3					8	9	10					6	4	11	7		5		
		Appearances				41	36	37	37	35	29	3	42	42	41	12	18	5	2	9	20	10	5	16	21	1	
		Substitutes						1				1	2			8				1	2	1		1			
		Goals						1	2				25	11	6	4					1		1	1	3		

FINAL LEAGUE POSITION: 11th in Division One. Average home League attendance: 23,910.

FA Cup

#	Date	Opponent	Res	Scorers	Att	Mon	Cal	Pen	Tow	How	Pag	Jon	Fra	Ber	Hib	Con	Wan	Sty	Rat	Bro	Emm	Fox	Sbr	Dil	Gal	Lat	Smi
3	Jan 7 (h)	Wigan A	W 4-0	Francis 2, Bertschin 2	29,202	1	2		4	5			8	9	10	7		3						11	6		
4	Feb 1 (a)	Derby C	L 1-2	Bertschin	31,955		2	3	4	6			8	9	10							7		11	5		1
		Appearances				1	2	1	2	2			2	2	2	1		1				1		2	2		1
		Substitutes																									
		Goals											2	3													

League Cup

#	Date	Opponent	Res	Att	Mon	Cal	Pen	Tow	How	Pag	Jon	Fra	Ber	Hib	Con	Wan	Sty	Rat	Bro	Emm	Fox	Sbr	Dil	Gal	Lat	Smi
2	Aug 30 (h)	Notts C	L 0-2	14,993	1	2	3	4	5	11	7	8	9	10					6							
		Appearances			1	1	1	1	1	1	1	1	1	1					1							
		Substitutes																								
		Goals																								

1978-79

Manager: Jim Smith

FINAL LEAGUE POSITION: 21st in Division One. Average home League attendance: 20,164.

No	Date	Venue	Opponent	Res	Scorers	Att
1	Aug 19	(a)	Manchester U	L 0-1		56,136
2	22	(h)	Middlesbrough	L 1-3	Bertschin	24,182
3	26	(h)	Derby C	D 1-1	Givens	21,963
4	Sep 2	(a)	Bolton W	D 2-2	Francis 2	20,284
5	9	(h)	Liverpool	L 0-3		31,740
6	16	(a)	Norwich C	L 0-4		16,407
7	23	(h)	Chelsea	D 1-1	Givens	18,458
8	30	(a)	Leeds U	L 0-3		23,331
9	Oct 7	(h)	Manchester C	L 1-2	Ainscow	18,378
10	14	(a)	Tottenham H	L 0-1		41,230
11	21	(a)	Aston Villa	L 0-1		36,145
12	28	(a)	Coventry C	L 1-2	Givens	25,446
13	Nov 4	(a)	West Brom A	L 0-1		31,988
14	11	(h)	Manchester U	W 5-1	Dillon, Buckley 2, Givens, Calderwood	23,550
15	18	(a)	Derby C	L 1-2	Givens	24,720
16	21	(h)	Bolton W	W 3-0	Dillon, Buckley, P.Jones (og)	21,643
17	25	(h)	Bristol C	D 1-1	Tarantini	21,552
18	Dec 2	(a)	Southampton	L 0-1		23,391
19	9	(h)	Everton	L 1-3	Buckley	23,391
20	16	(a)	Nottingham F	L 0-1		25,224
21	26	(a)	Wolves	L 1-2	Buckley	26,315
22	30	(a)	Arsenal	L 1-3	Francis (pen)	27,877
23	Feb 3	(a)	Chelsea	L 1-2	Bertschin	22,129
24	10	(h)	Leeds U	L 0-1		17,620
25	13	(a)	Liverpool	L 0-1		35,207
26	24	(h)	Tottenham H	W 1-0	Towers	20,980
27	Mar 3	(a)	Aston Villa	L 0-1		42,419
28	6	(h)	Queen's Park R	W 3-1	Buckley, Towers (pen), Broadhurst	12,650
29	10	(h)	Coventry C	D 0-0		17,311
30	24	(a)	Middlesbrough	L 1-2	Givens	15,013
31	27	(h)	Norwich C	W 1-0	Givens	12,168
32	31	(a)	Bristol C	L 1-2	Gallagher	15,584
33	Apr 3	(h)	Ipswich T	D 1-1	Gallagher	12,499
34	7	(h)	Southampton	D 2-2	Barrowclough 2 (1 pen)	12,125
35	14	(h)	Wolves	D 1-1	Ainscow	20,556
36	17	(a)	Ipswich T	L 0-3		17,676
37	21	(h)	Nottingham F	L 0-2		22,189
38	24	(h)	West Brom A	D 1-1	Gallagher	19,897
39	28	(a)	Everton	L 0-1		22,958
40	May 1	(a)	Manchester C	L 1-3	Lynex	27,366
41	5	(h)	Arsenal	D 0-0		14,015
42	7	(a)	Queen's Park R	W 3-1	Buckley 2, Dark	9,600

Appearances grid (League)

Player columns: Montgomery J, Calderwood J, Emmanuel G, Towers A, Gallagher J, Broadhurst K, Barrowclough S, Ainscow A, Bertschin K, Givens D, Fox S, Francis T, Page M, Pendrey G, Freeman N, Rathbone M, Howard P, Dillon K, Dennis M, Van den Hauwe P, Tarantini A, Buckley A, Rioch BD, Dark T, Ivey P, Lynex S, Briggs M

No	Mont	Cald	Emm	Tow	Gal	Bro	Barr	Ain	Bert	Giv	Fox	Fran	Page	Pen	Free	Rath	How	Dill	Den	Van	Tar	Buck	Rio	Dark	Ivey	Lyn	Bri
1	1	2	3	4	5	6	7	8	9	10	11	12															
2	1	2	3	4	5	6	7	12	9	11	10	8															
3	1			7	5	6	4		11	9	10		8	2	3												
4		2	12	4	5		7	10		9		8			1	3		6	11								
5		2	10	8	5		7	12		9	11			3	1			6	4								
6		10	8	5	6		12	7		9	11				1		3	2	4								
7	1	10		6	5	2		11	7	9		8			3				4								
8	1	10		6	5	2			8	9	11		7						4	3							
9	1	10		6	5	2			11	8			9	12					4	3	2						
10	1	10			5	12	11	8		9			7	6					4	3	2						
11		8	10		5	2				9	11		7	6					3	4							
12		2	10	4	5			11		9			7	6	1				3		8						
13		2	10	4	5			11		9			7		1			12	3		6	8					
14		10		4	5					9	11		6		1			7	3		2	8					
15		10		4	5			12		9	11		6		1			7	3		2	8					
16		10		4	5					9	11		6		1			7	3		2	8					
17				4	5			12		9	11		6		1			7	3		2	10					
18		7		4	5					9	11		6	12	1			8	3		2	10					
19		2		4	5			12		9	11	8	6		1			7	3			10					
20	1	2			5			11	12	9			8	6				7	3			10	4				
21	1			4	5			11		9			8	6				10	3		2	12	7				
22	1			7		5				9			8	6				11	3		2	10	4				
23	1		12	5	4			7	9				8	6	3			11			2	10					
24				4	5		7	8	9				2		1			11	3		6	10		12			
25				4	5			8	9	12			2		1			11	3		6	10		7			
26				4	5			7	8	9			2		1			10	3		6	12		11			
27				4	5	11		7	8	9			2		1			10	3		6						
28				4	5	12		7	8	9			2	3	1			10			6	11					
29	3			4	5			11	7	9			2		1			10			6	8					
30				4	5			11	7	9			2		1		6	10	3			8					
31				4	5	12		10	7	9			2	6	1			11	3			8					
32		12		4	5	8		11	7	9			2		1			10	3		6						
33	9			4	5			11	7				2		1			10	3		6	8					
34	8				5	4	11	7					2		1			10	3		6			12			
35				4	5	2	7	8		9					1			11	3	12	6	10					
36	2			4	5			11	7	9			10		1				6	3	8			12			
37	1	2		4	5			10	8	9			7					11	3		6	12					
38	2				5			11	7	9			4		1			10	3	6		10					
39	2				5			11	8	9			4		1			7	3	6		10			12		
40	2				5			10	7						1	3		6		4		8			9	11	12
41	2				5			10	7	9					1	6		11	3	4		12				8	
42																		10	3	6		8		12	11	4	
Appearances	13	24	12	31	41	13	26	27	9	38	13	8	32	9	29	2	5	35	31	7	23	24	3	2	3	2	
Substitutes		1	1	1				3	3	4		1	1	1				1			1	4		3	2	1	
Goals		1		2	3	1	2	2	2	7		3						2			1	8		1		1	

1 own-goal

FA Cup

No	Date	Venue	Opponent	Res	Att
3	Jan 6	(h)	Burnley	L 0-2	19,034

	Mont	Tow	Gal	Bro	Ain	Ber	Page	Pen	Dill	Den	Buc	Rio
Team	1	4	5	2	12	11	8	6	7	3	10	9
Appearances	1	1	1	1		1	1	1	1	1	1	1
Substitutes					1							
Goals												

League Cup

No	Date	Venue	Opponent	Res	Scorers	Att
2	Aug 30	(h)	Southampton	L 2-5	Gallagher, Francis	18,464

	Mont	Tow	Gal	Bro	Barr	Ain	Ber	Giv	Fox	Page	Pen	Free
Team	1	4	12	5	6	7	10	9	11	8	2	3
Appearances	1	1		1	1	1	1	1	1	1	1	1
Substitutes			1									
Goals			1							1		

1979-80

Manager: Jim Smith

#	Date	Opponent	Result	Scorers	Att.	Freeman N	Calderwood J	Dennis M	Curbishley L	Van den Hauwe P	Page M	Ainscow A	Evans A	Bertschin K	Gemmill A	Dillon K	Wealands J	Gallagher J	Towers A	Lees T	Lynex S	Todd C	Givens D	Johnston W	Worthington F	Broadhurst K
1	Aug 18 (h)	Fulham	L 3-4	Evans, Dillon, Bertschin	19,179	1	2	3	4	5	6	7	8	9	10	11										
2	22 (a)	Sunderland	L 0-2		25,877			3	4		2	7	8	9	10	11	1	5	6							
3	25 (a)	Cardiff C	W 2-1	Evans 2	11,314			3	4		2	7	8	9	10	11	1	5	6	12						
4	Sep 1 (h)	Bristol R	D 1-1	Dillon	15,330			3	4			7	8	9	10	11	1	5	6			2				
5	8 (a)	Chelsea	W 2-1	Lynex, Curbishley	17,182			3	4			7	8		10	11	1	5	6		9	2				
6	15 (h)	Charlton A	W 1-0	Lynex	16,156			3	4			7	10	9	8	11	1	5	6		12	2				
7	22 (a)	Orient	D 2-2	Lynex, Curbishley	5,550			3	4			7		9	10	11	1	5	6		8	2	12			
8	29 (h)	Newcastle U	D 0-0		19,967			3	4			7			10	11	1	5	6		8	2	9			
9	Oct 6 (a)	Preston NE	D 0-0		10,740			3	4			7	9		10	11	1	5	6		8	2	12			
10	9 (h)	Sunderland	W 1-0	Lynex	18,960			3	4			7	12		10		1	5	6		8	2	9	11		
11	13 (a)	Wrexham	L 0-1		13,693			3	4			7		9	10		1	5	6		8	2	12	11		
12	20 (a)	Swansea C	W 2-0	Lynex, Gemmill	18,624			3	4			7		9	10		1	5	6		8	2	12	11		
13	27 (h)	Shrewsbury T	W 1-0	Ainscow	17,869			3	4			7	12		10		1	5	6		8	2	9	11		
14	Nov 3 (a)	Fulham	W 4-2	Gemmill (pen), Givens 2, Lock (og)	8,243			3	4			7	8	3	10		1	5	6			2	9	11		
15	10 (h)	Cambridge U	W 1-0	Lynex	17,120			3	4			7	8		10		1	5	6		12	2	9	11		
16	17 (a)	Watford	L 0-1		14,378			3	4				8	12		10	1	5	6		7	2	9	11		
17	24 (a)	Luton T	W 3-2	Bertschin 3	13,720			3	4					9		10	1	5	8	2	7	6		11		
18	Dec 1 (h)	Leicester C	L 1-2	Gallagher	25,748			3	4					9		10	1	5	7	2	12	6		11	8	
19	8 (a)	Notts C	D 1-1	Lynex	11,381			3	4			8			10	7	1	5		11	6			9		2
20	15 (h)	Burnley	W 2-0	Worthington 2	13,997			3	12				9		4	10	1	5		7	6			11	8	2
21	21 (a)	Oldham A	L 0-1		6,652			3	12				9		4	10	1	5		7	6			11	8	2
22	29 (h)	Cardiff C	W 2-1	Worthington, Bertschin	16,682			3	4			7		9	10		1	5		6				11	8	2
23	Jan 1 (h)	Queen's Park R	W 2-1	Ainscow, Gemmill	25,963	1		3	4			7		9	10			5		6				11	8	2
24	12 (a)	Bristol R	L 0-1		9,351			3	4			7		9	10	12	1	5		11	6				8	2
25	Feb 2 (a)	Charlton A	W 1-0	Gemmill	6,821				4			7		9	10		1	5	2	12	6			11	8	3
26	9 (h)	Orient	W 3-1	Bertschin 3	17,474			3	4			7		9	10		1	5	6		12			11	8	2
27	20 (a)	Newcastle U	D 0-0		28,038			3	4			7		9	10		1	5		11	6				8	2
28	23 (a)	Wrexham	W 2-0	Dillon, Evans	19,306			3	4			7	12	9	8	11	1	5		10	6					2
29	29 (a)	Swansea C	W 1-0	Lynex	16,363			3	4			7	12	9		11	1	5	10	8	6					2
30	Mar 8 (a)	Shrewsbury T	L 0-1		14,801			3	4			7		9	10	11	1	5		8	6			12		2
31	11 (h)	Chelsea	W 5-1	Broadhurst, Borota (og), Dillon, Ainscow 2	27,297			3	4			7		9	10	11	1	5			6				8	2
32	15 (h)	Preston NE	D 2-2	Gemmill (pen), Worthington	19,548			3	4			7		9	10	11	1	5			6				8	2
33	22 (a)	Cambridge U	L 1-2	Smith (og)	6,805			3	4			7		9	10	11	1	5		12	6				8	2
34	29 (h)	Watford	W 2-0	Bertschin, Gemmill (pen)	16,582			3	4			7	12	9	10	11	1	5			6				8	2
35	Apr 1 (h)	Oldham A	W 2-0	Gemmill, Ainscow	17,118			3	4			7		9	10	11	1	5			6				8	2
36	5 (a)	Queen's Park R	D 1-1	Dillon	16,609			3	4			7		9	10	11	1	5	8	12	6					2
37	7 (h)	West Ham U	D 0-0		28,377			3	4			8		9	10	11	1	5	6	12	7					2
38	12 (a)	Leicester C	L 1-2	Gemmill (pen)	26,075			3	4			7		9	10	11	1	5	6	12	2			8		
39	19 (h)	Luton T	W 1-0	Bertschin	23,662			3	4			7		9	10	11	1	5		12	6			8		2
40	22 (a)	West Ham U	W 2-1	Ainscow, Bertschin	36,167			3	4			7		9	10	11	1	5	8	6						2
41	26 (a)	Burnley	D 0-0		10,314			3	4			7		9	10	11	1	5		6	8			12		2
42	May 3 (h)	Notts C	D 3-3	Bertschin, Curbishley, Dillon	33,863				4			7		9	10	11	1	5		3	6	8				2
	Appearances					2	1	40	40	1	3	37	10	34	37	30	40	41	22	9	20	33	7	15	17	23
	Substitutes							2					3	3		1		1		10	1	3		2		
	Goals								3			6	4	12	8	6		1			8		2		4	1

FINAL LEAGUE POSITION: 3rd in Division Two. Average home League attendance: 20,427.

3 own-goals

FA Cup

#	Date	Opponent	Result	Scorers	Att.	Freeman N	Calderwood J	Dennis M	Curbishley L	Van den Hauwe P	Page M	Ainscow A	Evans A	Bertschin K	Gemmill A	Dillon K	Wealands J	Gallagher J	Towers A	Lees T	Lynex S	Todd C	Givens D	Johnston W	Worthington F	Broadhurst K
3	Jan 5 (h)	Southampton	W 2-1	Bertschin, Gallagher	24,648	1		3	4			7		9	10			5			12	6		11	8	2
4	26 (h)	Middlesbrough	W 2-1	Gemmill (pen), Bertschin	29,152				4			7		9	10		1	5			2	6		11	8	3
5	Feb 16 (a)	Tottenham H	L 1-3	Bertschin	49,936			3	4			7		9	10		1	5			12	6		11	8	2
	Appearances					1		2	3			3		3	3		2	3			1	3		3	3	3
	Substitutes																				3					
	Goals													3	1			1								

League Cup

#	Date	Opponent	Result	Scorers	Att.	Freeman N	Calderwood J	Dennis M	Curbishley L	Van den Hauwe P	Page M	Ainscow A	Evans A	Bertschin K	Gemmill A	Dillon K	Wealands J	Gallagher J	Towers A	Lees T	Lynex S	Todd C	Givens D	Johnston W	Worthington F	Broadhurst K
2	Aug 28 (h)	Preston NE	W 2-1	Ainscow, Dillon	13,660			3	4		2	7	8	9	10	11	1	5	6							
	Sep 4 (a)	Preston NE	W 1-0	Lynex	11,043			3	4			7	8		10	11	1	5	6		2	9				
3	26 (h)	Exeter C	L 1-2	Ainscow	13,669			3	4			7		12	10	11	1	5	6		8	2	9			
	Appearances							3	3		1	3	2	1	3	3	3	3	3		1	2	1	1		
	Substitutes													1												
	Goals											2				1					1					

1980-81

Manager: Jim Smith

#	Date		Opponent	Result	Scorers	Att.	Wealands J	Langan D	Dennis M	Curbishley L	Gallagher J	Givens D	Ainscow A	Bertschin K	Worthington F	Gemmill A	Dillon K	Todd C	Page M	Lynex S	Evans A	Hawker P	Lees T	Coton A	Handysides I	Broadhurst K	Van den Hauwe P	Ivey P	Goode T
1	Aug	16 (h)	Coventry C	W 3-1	Curbishley 2, Dillon	21,907	1	2	3	4	5	6	7	8	9	10	11												
2		20 (a)	Nottingham F	L 1-2	Worthington	26,561	1	2	3	4	5	12	7	8	9	10	11	6											
3		23 (h)	Manchester U	D 0-0		28,661	1	2		4	5		7	9	8	10	11	6	3										
4		30 (a)	Southampton	L 1-3	Worthington	21,683	1	2	3	**4**	5		7	8	9	10	11	6		12									
5	Sep	6 (h)	Liverpool	D 1-1	Worthington	27,042	1	2	3	4	5		7	8	9	10	11	6											
6		13 (a)	Brighton & HA	D 2-2	Curbishley, Bertschin	15,788	1	2		4	5	12	7	8	**9**	10	11	6	3										
7		20 (h)	West Brom A	D 1-1	Givens	22,016	1	2	3	4	5	12	7	**8**	9	10	11	6											
8		27 (a)	Norwich C	D 2-2	Ainscow, Worthington	13,801	1	2	3	4	5	8	7		9	10	11	6		12									
9	Oct	4 (a)	Wolves	L 0-1		22,777	1	2	3	4	5	8	7		9	10	11	6		12									
10		7 (h)	Arsenal	W 3-1	Lynex, Worthington, Dillon	15,511	1	2	3	4	5		7		9	10	11	6		8									
11		11 (a)	Aston Villa	L 1-2	Worthington (pen)	33,879	1	2	3	4	5		7		9	10	11	6		8									
12		18 (a)	Manchester C	W 1-0	Gemmill (pen)	30,041	1	2	3	4	5	12	7		9	10	11	6		8									
13		25 (h)	Stoke C	D 1-1	Bertschin	16,535	1	2	3	4	5			8	9	10	11	6	7										
14	Nov	1 (a)	Middlesbrough	W 2-1	Worthington 2	14,061	1	2	3	4	5		7	8	9	10	11	6											
15		8 (h)	Crystal P	W 1-0	Bertschin	16,910	1	2	**3**	4	5		7	8	9	10	11	6			12								
16		11 (h)	Nottingham F	W 2-0	Worthington 2	22,433	1	2		4	5		7	8	9	10	11	6				3							
17		15 (a)	Coventry C	L 1-2	Curbishley	18,758	1	2		4	5		7	8	9	10	**11**	6		12		3							
18		22 (h)	Tottenham H	W 2-1	Curbishley, Ainscow	24,817	1	2		4	5		7	8	9	10	11	6				3							
19		29 (a)	Everton	D 1-1	Ainscow	22,258	1	2		4	5		7	8	9	10	11	6				3							
20	Dec	6 (h)	Leicester C	L 1-2	Scott (og)	18,479	1	2		**4**	5		7	8	9	10	11	6		12		3							
21		13 (a)	Aston Villa	L 0-3		41,101	1	2		4	5		7	8	9	10	11	6		12		3							
22		20 (h)	Ipswich T	L 1-3	Ainscow	16,161	1	2		4	5	11	7	8	9	10	12	6				3							
23		26 (a)	Leeds U	D 0-0		19,214	1	2		4	5		7	8	9	10	11	6					3						
24		27 (h)	Sunderland	W 3-2	Gemmill, Bertschin, Worthington	19,005		2		4	5		7	8	9	10	11	6					3	1					
25	Jan	10 (a)	Tottenham H	L 0-1		24,909	1	2		4	5		7	8	9	10		6		11	3								
26		13 (a)	Ipswich T	L 1-5	Worthington	21,158	1	2		4	5		7	8	9	10		6		12	11	3							
27		17 (h)	Southampton	L 0-3		16,491		2		4	5		7	8	9	10	11	6			3			1	12				
28		31 (a)	Manchester U	L 0-2		39,081	1	2		4	5		7	8	9	10	11	6		12						3			
29	Feb	7 (h)	Brighton & HA	W 2-1	Evans, Curbishley	13,691	1	2		**4**	5		7	12	9	10		6	11		8					3			
30		14 (a)	Liverpool	D 2-2	Evans, Ainscow	32,199	1	2			5	12	7		9	10	4	6			8					11	3		
31		20 (h)	Norwich C	W 4-0	Ainscow, Evans 2, Gemmill	14,686	1	2			5		7		9	10	4	6			8					11	3		
32		28 (a)	West Brom A	D 2-2	Worthington, Ainscow	24,853	1	2			5	12	7		9		4	6			8	**10**				11	3		
33	Mar	17 (h)	Wolves	W 1-0	Worthington	20,005	1	2	3		5		7		9	10	4	6			8					11			
34		21 (h)	Manchester C	W 2-0	Worthington, Evans	16,160	1	2	3		5		7		9	10	4	6			8				12	11			
35		28 (a)	Stoke C	D 0-0		14,624	1	2	3		5		7		9	10	4	6			8					11			
36		31 (a)	Arsenal	L 1-2	Worthington	17,431	1	2	3		5		7	12	9	10	4	6			8					11			
37	Apr	4 (a)	Middlesbrough	W 2-1	Evans, Broadhurst	12,472	1	2	3		5		7	9		10	4	6			8					11			
38		11 (a)	Crystal P	L 1-3	Ainscow	9,820	1	2			5		7	9		10	4	6			8	3				11	12		
39		18 (a)	Sunderland	L 0-3		20,158	1	2					7	9		10	4	6			8				11	3	5		
40		21 (a)	Leeds U	L 0-2		14,505		2			5		7		9		10	4			8			1	11	3	6	12	
41		25 (a)	Leicester C	L 0-1		13,666		2			5		7		9		10	4			8				3	11	6		12
42	May	2 (h)	Everton	D 1-1	Evans	12,863	1	2	3		5					10	4	6			8				7	11		**9**	12
			Appearances				39	42	19	29	41	4	40	28	36	41	38	40	2	6	16	11	2	3	6	15	3	1	
			Substitutes									6						2		8	1				2			1	1	2
			Goals							6		1	8	4	16	3	2			1	7					1			

FINAL LEAGUE POSITION: 13th in Division One. Average home League attendance: 19,248.

1 own-goal

FA Cup

#	Date		Opponent	Result	Scorers	Att.	Wealands J	Langan D	Dennis M	Curbishley L	Gallagher J	Givens D	Ainscow A	Bertschin K	Worthington F	Gemmill A	Dillon K	Todd C	Page M	Lynex S	Evans A	Hawker P	Coton A
3	Jan	3 (h)	Sunderland	D 1-1	Bertschin	23,098	1	2		4	5		7	8	9	10	11	6				3	
R		7 (a)	Sunderland	W 2-1	Bertschin, Evans	27,793	1	2		4	**5**		7	8	9	10		6	11	12		3	
4		24 (a)	Coventry C	L 2-3	Worthington (pen), Ainscow	29,492		2		4	5		7	8	9	10	11	6			1	3	1
			Appearances				2	3		3	3		3	3	3	3	2	3	1			3	1
			Substitutes																	1			
			Goals										1	2	1						1		

League Cup

#	Date		Opponent	Result	Scorers	Att.	Wealands J	Langan D	Dennis M	Curbishley L	Gallagher J	Givens D	Ainscow A	Bertschin K	Worthington F	Gemmill A	Dillon K	Todd C	Page M	Lynex S	Hawker P
2	Aug	26 (h)	Bristol C	W 2-1	Ainscow, Gemmill (pen)	12,163	1	2	3	4	5		7	9	8	10	11	6			
	Sep	2 (a)	Bristol C	D 0-0		6,958	1	2	3	4	5		7	8	9	10	11	6			
3		23 (h)	Blackburn R	W 1-0	Gallagher	14,580	1	2	3	4	5	8	7		9	10	11	6			
4	Oct	28 (h)	Ipswich T	W 2-1	Worthington (pen), Ainscow	18,968	1		3	4	5	11	7	8	9	10		6	2		
5	Dec	2 (a)	Liverpool	L 1-3	Bertschin	30,236	1	2		4	5	12	7	8		10	11	6		9	3
			Appearances				5	4	4	5	5	2	5	4	4	5	4	5	1	1	1
			Substitutes									1									
			Goals								1		2	1	1	1					

1981-82

Manager: Jim Smith to February 1982 then Ron Saunders

Player columns (left to right): Wealands J, Langan D, Dennis M, Broadhurst K, Hawker P, Todd C, Brocken B, Dillon K, Evans A, Gemmill A, Van Mierlo A, Handysides I, Whatmore N, Worthington F, Van den Hauwe P, Curbishley L, Coton A, Scott G, Jones R, Phillips L, Stevenson B, Linney D, MacDowall D, Harford M

#	Date	V	Opponent	Res	Scorers	Att	Wea	Lan	Den	Bro	Haw	Tod	Brk	Dil	Eva	Gem	VMi	Han	Wha	Wor	VdH	Cur	Cot	Sco	Jon	Phi	Ste	Lin	Mac	Har
1	Aug 29	(a)	Everton	L 1-3	Van Mierlo	33,045	1	2	3	4	5	6	7	8	9	10	11	12												
2	Sep 1	(h)	Ipswich T	D 1-1	Evans	17,328	1	2	3	5		6	7	4	9	10	11		8											
3	5	(h)	Nottingham F	W 4-3	Broadhurst, Evans, Whatmore 2	19,035	1	2	3	5		6	7	4	9	10	11	12	8											
4	12	(a)	Middlesbrough	L 1-2	Whatmore	13,189	1	2	3	5		6	7	4	9	10	11	12	8											
5	19	(h)	Manchester C	W 3-0	Evans 3	20,109	1	2	3	5		6	7	4	9	10	11	12	8											
6	22	(a)	Arsenal	L 0-1		19,504	1	2	3	5		6	7	4	9	10	11	12	8											
7	26	(a)	Aston Villa	D 0-0		40,763	1	2	3	5		6	7	4	9	10	11	12	8											
8	Oct 3	(h)	West Ham U	D 2-2	Langan, Dillon	22,290	1	2	3	5		6	7	4	9	10	11	12	8											
9	10	(h)	Southampton	W 4-0	Worthington 2, Whatmore 2	16,938	1	2	3	5		6	7	4		10	11		8	9										
10	17	(a)	Manchester U	D 1-1	Worthington (pen)	48,514	1	2	3	5		6	7	4		10	11	12	8	9										
11	24	(a)	Stoke C	L 0-1		15,399	1	2	3	5		6	7	4	9	10	11		8											
12	31	(h)	West Brom A	D 3-3	Gemmill, Evans, Worthington (pen)	21,301	1	2	3	5		6	7	4	9	10	11		8	12										
13	Nov 7	(a)	Brighton & HA	D 1-1	Evans	18,292		2		5		6	7	8	9	10	11				3	4	1							
14	21	(h)	Wolves	L 0-3		18,223		2		5		6	7	8	9	10	11	12			3	4	1							
15	28	(a)	Swansea C	L 0-1		15,097		2		5		6	7	8	9	10	11	12			3	4	1							
16	Dec 5	(h)	Notts C	W 2-1	Evans 2 (1 pen)	11,914		2		5		6	7	8	9	10	11				3	4	1							
17	Jan 5	(a)	Ipswich T	L 2-3	Van Mierlo, Broadhurst	19,188		2		5		6	7	8	9	10	11				3	4	1							
18	9	(a)	Nottingham F	L 1-2	Worthington	15,906		2		5		6	7	8		10	11			9	3	4	1							
19	26	(h)	Coventry C	D 3-3	Broadhurst, Evans 2	13,023		2		5		6	7	8	9	10	11				3	4	1							
20	30	(h)	Manchester C	L 2-4	Worthington 2	28,438		2		5		6	7	8		10	11			9	3	4	1							
21	Feb 6	(h)	Middlesbrough	D 0-0		10,715	1	2	3	5		6		8		10	11		9	7		4								
22	13	(a)	West Ham U	D 2-2	Whatmore, Van Mierlo	22,512		2	3			6		8			11	12	9	7	5	4	1		10					
23	16	(h)	Sunderland	W 2-0	Van Mierlo, Worthington	10,776		2	3			6		8			11		9	7	5	4	1		10					
24	20	(h)	Aston Villa	L 0-1		32,779		2	3			6		8			11		9	7	5	4	1		10					
25	27	(a)	Southampton	L 1-3	Worthington (pen)	20,620		2	3			6		8			11		9	7	5	4	1		12					
26	Mar 6	(a)	Manchester U	L 0-1		19,637	1	2	3					10	8		11	12	9	7	5	6					4			
27	13	(h)	Stoke C	W 2-1	Curbishley, Hawker	12,018	1	2	3	4	5			10	8		11		9	7		6					12			
28	20	(a)	West Brom A	D 1-1	Evans	21,160	1	2	3					10	8		11	12	9	7	5	6					4			
29	23	(h)	Tottenham H	D 0-0		17,708	1	2	3					10	8		11		9	7	5	6					4			
30	27	(h)	Brighton & HA	W 1-0	Harford	13,234	1	2	3					10	8		11			7	5	6					4			9
31	30	(a)	Liverpool	L 1-3	Harford	24,224	1	2	3					10	8		11	12		7	5	6					4			9
32	Apr 6	(a)	Everton	L 0-2		12,273	1	2	3					10	8		11			7	5	6		12			4			9
33	10	(h)	Leeds U	L 0-1		14,497	1	2	3					10	8		11				5	6		12		7	4			9
34	12	(a)	Sunderland	L 0-2		14,821	1	2	3					10	8		11				5	6		12		7	4			9
35	17	(a)	Wolves	D 1-1	Harford	18,964		2	3					10	8		11				5	6	1	12		7	4			9
36	24	(h)	Swansea C	W 2-1	Broadhurst, Harford	14,973		2	3	4				10	8		11		12		5	6	1			7				9
37	28	(a)	Tottenham H	D 1-1	Harford	25,470		2	3	4				10	8		11		12		5	6	1			7				9
38	May 1	(a)	Notts C	W 4-1	Phillips, Evans 2, Harford	10,710		2	3	4				10	8		11				5	6	1			7				9
39	4	(h)	Arsenal	L 0-1		13,133		2	3	4				10	8		11		12		5	6	1			7				9
40	8	(h)	Liverpool	L 0-1		25,381		2	3	4				10	8		11				5	6	1			7				9
41	12	(a)	Leeds U	D 3-3	Harford 2, Evans	18,583		2	3	4				10	8		11				5	6	1			7				9
42	15	(a)	Coventry C	W 1-0	Harford	15,905		2	3	4				10	8		11		12		5	6	1			7				9
			Appearances				23	36	17	35	19	19	17	35	29	19	40	8	22	18	30	29	15	14	4	7	12		2	12
			Substitutes						1						1			12		2	2	1		1		4	1			
			Goals					1		4	1			1	15	1	4		6	9		1				1				9

FINAL LEAGUE POSITION: 16th in Division One. Average home League attendance: 17,116.

FA Cup

Rd	Date	V	Opponent	Res	Scorers	Att	Wea	Lan	Den	Bro	Haw	Tod	Brk	Dil	Eva	Gem	VMi	Han	Wha	Wor	VdH	Cur	Cot	Sco	Jon	Phi	Ste	Lin	Mac	Har
3	Jan 2	(h)	Ipswich T	L 2-3	Worthington (pen), Curbishley	17,236		2	3	5		6	7		9	10	11	12				4	1							
			Appearances					1	1	1		1	1		1	1	1					1	1							
			Substitutes															1												
			Goals																	1		1								

League Cup

Rd	Date	V	Opponent	Res	Scorers	Att	Wea	Lan	Den	Bro	Haw	Tod	Brk	Dil	Eva	Gem	VMi	Han	Wha	Wor	VdH	Cur	Cot	Sco	Jon	Phi	Ste	Lin	Mac	Har
2	Oct 6	(h)	Nottingham F	L 2-3	Whatmore, Worthington	14,330	1	2	3	5		6	7	4		10	11		8	9										
	28	(a)	Nottingham F	L 1-2	Evans	16,316	1			5	3	6	7	4	8	10	11	12		9	2									
			Appearances				2	1	1	2	1	2	2	2	1	2	2	1	2	1										
			Substitutes															1												
			Goals												1				1	1										

1982-83

Manager: Ron Saunders

Player columns (left to right): Blyth J · Langan D · Hawker P · Scott G · Van den Hauwe P · Broadhurst K · Van Merlo A · Carrodus F · Harford M · Curbishley L · Francis C · Hagan J · Evans A · Dillon K · Dennis M · Summerfield K · Phillips L · Stevenson B · Blake N · Handysides I · Brazier C · Bremner K · Coton A · Ferguson M · Gayle H · Halsall M · Hopkins R · Whatmore N · Mumford W · Kuhl M

#	Date		Opponent	Result	Scorers	Att	Bly	Lan	Haw	Sco	VdH	Bro	VMe	Car	Har	Cur	Fra	Hag	Eva	Dil	Den	Sum	Phi	Ste	Bla	Han	Bra	Bre	Cot	Fer	Gay	Hal	Hop	Wha	Mum	Kuh
1	Aug 28	(a)	Manchester U	L 0-3		48,673	1	2	3	4	5	6	7	8	9	10	11																			
2	31	(h)	Liverpool	D 0-0		20,176	1	2	3	4	5	6	7	11	9	10		12	8																	
3	Sep 4	(a)	Stoke C	L 1-4	Curbishley	14,412	1	2	3	4	5	6	7	11	9	10						8														
4	8	(a)	Norwich C	L 1-5	Broadhurst	13,860	1	2		4	5	6		11	9	10		12				8	3	7												
5	11	(a)	West Ham U	L 0-5		18,754	1		4		5		7	11	9	10						8	3	12	6											
6	18	(h)	Coventry C	W 1-0	Evans	11,681	1	2								10		12	7	8		3		6	4	5	11			9						
7	25	(a)	Brighton & HA	L 0-1		9,845	1	2					7			10		12	3	8				6	4	5	11			9						
8	Oct 2	(h)	Watford	D 1-1	Summerfield	13,870	1	2		3	6		7			10						8	12	4	5	11				9						
9	9	(h)	Luton T	L 2-3	Langan (pen), Brazier	13,772	1	2		3	6					10						8		4	5	11	7			9						
10	16	(a)	Nottingham F	D 1-1	Bremner	14,548	1				6			12		10			3		7			4	5	11	9	8						2		
11	23	(h)	Ipswich T	D 0-0		12,051	1			3	6					10			7					4	5	11	9	8						2		
12	30	(a)	Arsenal	D 0-0		20,699				3	6					10			2	8	7			4	5	11	9	12	1							
13	Nov 6	(a)	West Brom A	W 2-1	Dillon (pen), Blake	18,520				3	6					10			2	7				4	5	11	8		1	9						
14	13	(a)	Notts C	D 0-0		9,118				3	6					10		8	2	7				4	5	11			1	9						
15	20	(a)	Manchester C	D 0-0		23,174				3	6					10	12		2	7				4	5	11	8		1	9						
16	27	(h)	Sunderland	W 2-1	Ferguson, Evans	12,375	1				6					10			2	8	7	3		4	5	11				9						
17	Dec 4	(a)	Everton	D 0-0		13,703				3	6					10				8	7			4	5	11	2		1	9						
18	11	(h)	Southampton	L 0-2		11,199				3	6					10			2	8	7			4	5	11	12		1	9						
19	18	(a)	Tottenham H	L 1-2	Langan	20,546		10		3	6			8					2	7	11			4	5	11			1	9						
20	27	(h)	Aston Villa	W 3-0	Blake, Handysides, Ferguson	43,864		2		3	6				9	10				7				4	5	11			1	8						
21	29	(a)	Swansea	D 0-0		11,840		2		3	6			8	10					7				4	5	11			1	9						
22	Jan 1	(h)	Manchester C	D 2-2	Ferguson 2	16,362		2			6			8	10			4		7	3				5	11			1	9						
23	3	(a)	Stoke C	D 1-1	Phillips	15,428		2			6				9	10				7	3		8	4	5	11			1							
24	15	(h)	Manchester U	L 1-2	Dillon (pen)	19,333					6				9	10			2	7	3	8		4	5	11			1							
25	22	(a)	Liverpool	L 0-1		30,986					6				9	10			2	7	3	12		5	11	4			1	8						
26	Feb 5	(h)	West Ham U	W 3-0	Harford, Ferguson, Gayle	12,539		2			6				9	10					11		3	4	5				1	8	7					
27	26	(h)	Nottingham F	D 1-1	Harford	12,987					6				9	10			2		11		3	4	5				1	8	7					
28	Mar 5	(a)	Ipswich T	L 1-3	Dennis	16,436					12	6			9	10			2		11		3	4	5				1	8	7					
29	15	(h)	Arsenal	W 2-1	Van den Hauwe, Dillon	11,276					6				9	10			2		11		3	4	5	8			1	7						
30	19	(a)	West Brom A	L 0-2		20,794					6				9	10			2		11			4	5				1	7			8			3
31	22	(a)	Watford	L 1-2	Ferguson	14,229									9	10			2		11		3	4	5				1	8		7	6			
32	26	(h)	Notts C	W 3-0	Ferguson 2 (1 pen), Harford	11,744					6				9				2				3	4	5				1	8		7	10	11		
33	Apr 2	(a)	Swansea C	D 1-1	Stevenson (pen)	13,591					6				9				2		3		8	4	5	12			1			7	10	11		
34	4	(a)	Aston Villa	L 0-1		40,897					6				9				2		3			4	5				1	8		7	10	11		
35	9	(h)	Norwich C	L 0-4		11,733					6	2			9					3		12		4	5	7			1	8			10	11		
36	12	(a)	Luton T	L 1-3	Hopkins	12,868					2	6			9					3		12		4	5				1	8		7	10	11		
37	16	(a)	Coventry C	W 1-0	Phillips	10,420					2				9					4			3		5	12			1	8		7	10	11		
38	23	(h)	Everton	W 1-0	Hopkins	11,045	1				2	12			9					4			3		5	8						7	10	11		
39	30	(a)	Sunderland	W 2-1	Blake (pen), Harford	14,818					2	7			9					4			3		5	8							10	11		
40	May 2	(h)	Brighton & HA	D 1-1	Handysides	15,977	1				2				9					4			3	5	6	12	7					8	10	11		
41	7	(h)	Tottenham H	W 2-0	Halsall, Harford	18,947					7				9					4			3	5	6	8			1				10	11		
42	14	(a)	Southampton	W 1-0	Harford	20,327					7				9					2			3	5	6	8			1				11			10
	Appearances						14	14	4	4	30	28	4	7	29	30	2	30	7	27	23	2	11	30	37	26	10	3	28	20	13	12	11	2	2	2
	Substitutes										1	1		1				3	2				3	2	1			3	1	1						
	Goals							2			1	1			6	1			2	3	1	1	2	1	3	2	1	1		8	1	1	2			

FINAL LEAGUE POSITION: 17th in Division One. Average home League attendance: 15,880.

FA Cup

#	Date		Opponent	Result	Scorers	Att	VdH	Bro	Har	Cur	Eva	Dil	Den	Sum	Phi	Ste	Bla	Han	Bra	Bre	Cot	Fer
3	Jan 8	(a)	Walsall	D 0-0		12,697	6		9	10	2		7	3		8	4	5	11	12	1	
R	11	(h)	Walsall	W 1-0*	Summerfield	14,774	6			10	2		7	3	12	4	5	11	8		1	9
4	29	(a)	Crystal P	L 0-1		12,327	6		9	10	2		7	3	11		5	12	4		1	8
	Appearances						3		2	3	3		3	3	1	1	2	3	2	2	3	1
	Substitutes														1			1	1			
	Goals													1								

*After extra-time

League Cup

#	Date		Opponent	Result	Scorers	Att	Bly	Lan	Sco	Bro	VMe	Cur	Eva	Dil	Den	Sum	Phi	Ste	Bla	Han	Bra	Cot	Fer	Wha
2	Oct 5	(a)	Shrewsbury T	D 1-1	Handysides	5,003	1	2	3	6	12	10				8	7	4	5	11	9			
	26	(h)	Shrewsbury T	W 4-1	Evans, Curbishley 2, Dillon	7,861	1		3	6		10	8	7				4	5	11	9			2
3	Nov 9	(h)	Derby C	W 3-1	Handysides, Dillon (pen), Curbishley	12,475			3	6		10	2	7				4	5	11	8	1	9	
4	30	(a)	Burnley	L 2-3	Evans, Handysides	10,405				6		10	2	8	7		12	4	5	11	3	1	9	
	Appearances						2	1	3	4		4		2	2	4		1	4	4	4	4	2	2	1
	Substitutes										1						1							
	Goals											3	2	2						3				

1983-84

Manager: Ron Saunders

Player columns (left to right): Coton A, Hagan J, Stevenson B, Blake N, Wright W, Broadhurst K, Handysides I, Phillips L, Harford M, Van den Hauwe P, Hopkins R, Rees A, Halsall M, McCarrick M, Gayle H, Mumford W, Rogers K, Kuhl M, Muir I, Linton I, Kendall M, Roberts B

#	Date		Opponent	Result	Scorers	Att.	Cot	Hag	Ste	Bla	Wri	Bro	Han	Phi	Har	VdH	Hop	Ree	Hal	McC	Gay	Mum	Rog	Kuh	Mui	Lin	Ken	Rob
1	Aug 27	(a)	West Ham U	L 0-4		19,729	1	2	3	4	5	6	**7**	8	9	10	11	12										
2	30	(a)	Notts C	L 1-2	Harford	11,031	1	2		4	5	6	12	8	9	3	11	7	10									
3	Sep 3	(h)	Watford	W 2-0	Hopkins, Halsall	11,931	1	2		4	5	6		8	9	3	11	7	10									
4	6	(h)	Stoke C	W 1-0	Blake (pen)	13,728	1	2		4	5	6		8	9	3	11	**7**	10	12								
5	10	(a)	Wolves	D 1-1	Wright (pen)	15,933	1	2		4	5	6		8	9	3	11	7	10		12							
6	17	(h)	Ipswich T	W 1-0	Gayle	13,159	1		12	4	5	6		8	9	3	**11**	7			2							
7	24	(a)	Everton	D 1-1	Gayle	15,253	1		12	4	5	**6**		8	9	3	11	7	10		2							
8	Oct 1	(h)	Leicester C	W 2-1	Rees, Harford	15,212	1	2		4	5			8	9	3	11	6	10		7							
9	15	(a)	Aston Villa	L 0-1		39,318	1	2	12	4	5	**6**			9	3	11	8	10		7							
10	22	(h)	Tottenham H	L 0-1		19,016	1	2		6	4	5		12	9	3	11	**8**	10		7							
11	29	(a)	West Brom A	W 2-1	Gayle, Harford	20,224	1	2		6	4	5		8	9	3	11		10		7							
12	Nov 5	(h)	Coventry C	L 1-2	Blake	16,169	1	2		6	4	5		8	**9**	3	11		10		7	12						
13	12	(a)	Luton T	D 1-1	Hopkins	11,111	1	2		6	4	5		10	8	3	11				7	9						
14	19	(a)	Queen's Park R	L 1-2	Harford	10,824	1	2		6	4	5		10	8	9	3	11			7							
15	26	(h)	Sunderland	L 0-1		11,948	1	2		6	4	5		10	8	9	3	11			7							
16	Dec 3	(a)	Liverpool	L 0-1		24,791	1	2			5			8	9	3	11	6			7		4	10				
17	10	(a)	Norwich C	L 0-1		9,971	1	2		6	4	5		8	9	3		10			7	11						
18	17	(a)	Southampton	L 1-2	Stevenson	15,248	1	2		6	4	5		8	9	3		10		**7**		11		12				
19	26	(h)	Nottingham F	L 1-2	Rogers	14,482	1	2			4	5			9	3	11	7			12	10	**8**	6				
20	27	(a)	Arsenal	D 1-1	Hopkins	25,642	1	**2**	8		4	5			9	3	11	7			12	10		6				
21	31	(a)	Watford	L 0-1		14,359	1		6		4	5	3		9	8	11	7		10				2				
22	Jan 2	(h)	Everton	L 0-2		10,004	1		8		4	5	6		12	9	3	11	7		2	**10**						
23	14	(a)	West Ham U	W 3-0	Hopkins, Halsall, Harford	10,334	1		2		4	5	6		9	3	11		10		7		8					
24	21	(a)	Ipswich T	W 2-1	Harford, Butcher (og)	12,900	1			4	5	6			9	3	**11**	12	10	2	7		8					
25	Feb 4	(a)	Leicester C	W 3-2	Peake (og), Gayle, Wright (pen)	13,770	1			4	5	6			9	3	11		10	2	7		8					
26	7	(h)	Manchester U	D 2-2	Hopkins, Wright (pen)	19,957	1		12	4	5	6			9	3	11		10	2	7		**8**					
27	11	(h)	Wolves	D 0-0		14,319	1		8	4	5	6			9	3	11	7		2								
28	25	(h)	Tottenham H	W 1-0	Harford	23,564	1	6	10	4	5			11	9	3		7		2			8					
29	28	(h)	West Brom A	W 2-1	Rees, Broadhurst	16,780	1	12	10	4	5	6			9	3		**11**		2	7		8					
30	Mar 3	(a)	Coventry C	W 1-0	Gayle	13,705	1	12	10	4	5	6			9	3	11			2	7		8					
31	17	(a)	Stoke C	L 1-2	Gayle	13,506	1	3		4	5	6			9	10	11			12	7		8			2		
32	20	(h)	Luton T	D 1-1	Wright (pen)	9,592	1	3		4	5	6			9	8	11	10			7					2		
33	24	(h)	Notts C	D 0-0		9,040	1	3		4		6			9	5	11	10		12	7		8			2		
34	31	(h)	Aston Villa	W 2-1	Stevenson, Gayle	23,993	1	3	6	4					8	11		10	9	7	5					2		
35	Apr 7	(a)	Manchester U	L 0-1		39,891	1	3	6	4	5				9	8		10	**11**	7	12					2		
36	14	(h)	Queen's Park R	L 0-2		10,255	1	12	8	4	5	**6**			9	3	11	10		7						2		
37	21	(h)	Nottingham F	L 1-5	Harford	15,323	1	11	8	4	5	12			9	3		**10**	7		6					2		
38	23	(h)	Arsenal	D 1-1	Kuhl	11,164		4			5	6			9	3	11		2	7		10	12		1	8		
39	28	(a)	Sunderland	L 1-2	Wright (pen)	13,061	1	4			5				9	3		2	7		11	10	8			6		
40	May 5	(h)	Liverpool	D 0-0		18,809	1	2		4	5				9	3	11	7			10	8				6		
41	7	(a)	Norwich C	D 1-1	Gayle	13,601	1	2		4	5				9	3	11	12	7		10	**8**				6		
42	12	(h)	Southampton	D 0-0		16,455	1	2		4	5				9	3	11	9	6	7	10	8						

FINAL LEAGUE POSITION: 20th in Division One. Average home League attendance: 14,106.

	Cot	Hag	Ste	Bla	Wri	Bro	Han	Phi	Har	VdH	Hop	Ree	Hal	McC	Gay	Mum	Rog	Kuh	Mui	Lin	Ken	Rob
Appearances	41	30	21	39	40	22	4	18	39	42	32	22	21	12	32	3	8	20	1	3	1	11
Substitutes		3	4			1	1	2				3		3	1	2	1	2		1		
Goals			2	2	5	1			8		5	2	2		8		1	1				

2 own-goals

FA Cup

Rnd	Date		Opponent	Result	Scorers	Att.	Cot	Hag	Ste	Bla	Wri	Bro	Han	Phi	Har	VdH	Hop	Ree	Hal	McC	Gay	Mum	Rog	Kuh
3	Jan 7	(a)	Sheffield U	D 1-1	Wright (pen)	17,202	1		2	4	5	6			9	3	11		10		7			8
R	10	(h)	Sheffield U	W 2-0	Harford, Wright (pen)	10,888	1		2	4	5	6			9	3	11		10		7			8
4	28	(a)	Sunderland	W 2-1	Kuhl, Harford	21,226	1			4	5	6			9	3	11		10	2	7			8
5	Feb 18	(h)	West Ham U	W 3-0	Hopkins, Rees, Wright (pen)	29,570	1		10	4	5	6			9	3	11	7		2	7			8
6	Mar 10	(h)	Watford	L 1-3	Terry (og)	40,220	1		10	4	5	6			9	3	11			2	7			8

	Cot	Ste	Bla	Wri	Bro	Har	VdH	Hop	Ree	Hal	McC	Gay	Kuh
Appearances	5	4	5	5	5	5	5	5	1	3	3	4	5
Goals		3				2		1	1				1

1 own-goal

League Cup

Rnd	Date		Opponent	Result	Scorers	Att.	Cot	Hag	Ste	Bla	Wri	Bro	Han	Phi	Har	VdH	Hop	Ree	Hal	Gay	Rog	Kuh
2	Oct 5	(a)	Derby C	W 3-0	Watson (og), Rees, Gayle	13,114	1	2	12	4	5			8	9	3	11	**6**	10	7		
	25	(h)	Derby C	W 4-0	Harford 3, Gayle	7,786	1	2	6	4	5			8	9	3	11		10	7		
3	Nov 8	(h)	Notts C	D 2-2	Handysides, Phillips	10,484	1	2	6	4	5	9	8			3	11		10	7		
R	22	(a)	Notts C	D 0-0*		8,268	1	2	6	4	5		**8**	9	3	11		12		7		10
2R	29	(a)	Notts C	D 0-0*		9,678	1	2	6	4	5		8	9	3	11				7		10
3R	Dec 5	(a)	Notts C	W 3-1	Hopkins 2, Harford	7,361	1	2		4	5		8	9	3	11	6			7		10
4	20	(h)	Liverpool	D 1-1	Harford	17,405	1	2	6	4	5		8	9	3	**11**		12	7			10
R	22	(a)	Liverpool	L 0-3		11,638	1	2	6	4	5		8	9	3	11	10			7		

*After extra-time

	Cot	Hag	Ste	Bla	Wri	Bro	Han	Phi	Har	VdH	Hop	Ree	McC	Gay	Rog	Kuh
Appearances	8	8	6	8	8	1	8	7	8	7	3	4		8	3	1
Substitutes		1											1	1		
Goals				1	1	5		2	1			2				

1 own-goal

1984-85

Manager: Ron Saunders

Player columns (left to right): Coton A, Roberts B, Van den Hauwe P, Wright W, Hagan J, Daly G, Stevenson B, Clarke W, Ferguson M, Gorman P, Hopkins R, Kuhl M, Armstrong K, Harford M, Halsall M, McDonagh J, Bremner D, Seaman D, Jones M, Rees A, Ranson R, Linford J, Morley A, Platnauer N, Geddis D, Shearer P, Russell G, Kennedy A, Prudhoe M, Storer S, Brown I

#	Date		Opponent	Result	Scorers	Att.
1	Aug 25	(a)	Oldham A	W 1-0	Clements (og)	5,309
2	Sep 1	(h)	Wimbledon	W 4-2	Clarke 2, Ferguson, Hopkins	10,445
3	4	(a)	Fulham	W 1-0	Clarke	6,031
4	8	(a)	Crystal P	W 2-0	Clarke, Hopkins	6,519
5	15	(h)	Carlisle U	W 2-0	Clarke, Harford	11,740
6	18	(h)	Portsmouth	L 0-1		18,012
7	22	(a)	Wolves	W 2-0	Hopkins, Kuhl	12,698
8	29	(a)	Huddersfield T	W 1-0	Hopkins	11,480
9	Oct 6	(a)	Brighton & HA	L 0-2		13,697
10	13	(h)	Blackburn R	L 0-2		12,754
11	20	(a)	Notts C	W 3-1	Clarke 2, Harford	5,790
12	27	(h)	Oxford U	D 0-0		20,416
13	Nov 3	(h)	Shrewsbury T	D 0-0		9,807
14	10	(a)	Manchester C	L 0-1		25,369
15	17	(a)	Charlton A	L 1-2	Morley	4,841
16	24	(h)	Barnsley	D 0-0		9,505
17	Dec 1	(a)	Cardiff C	W 2-1	Morley 2	5,057
18	8	(h)	Middlesbrough	W 3-2	Saxby (og), Rees, Wright (pen)	8,004
19	15	(a)	Leeds U	W 1-0	Clarke	15,854
20	22	(a)	Wimbledon	W 2-1	Geddis 2	3,674
21	26	(h)	Grimsby T	W 2-1	Geddis, Platnauer	14,168
22	29	(h)	Fulham	D 2-2	Clarke, Hopkins	11,827
23	Jan 1	(a)	Sheffield U	W 4-3	Hopkins, Geddis, Clarke, West (og)	16,571
24	Feb 2	(a)	Huddersfield T	W 1-0	Geddis	7,460
25	23	(a)	Shrewsbury T	L 0-1		7,177
26	Mar 2	(a)	Oxford U	W 3-0	Clarke 2, Geddis	11,584
27	5	(h)	Oldham A	L 0-1		10,489
28	9	(h)	Notts C	W 2-1	Clarke, Hopkins	9,046
29	12	(a)	Carlisle U	L 1-2	Clarke	4,099
30	16	(a)	Blackburn R	L 1-2	Rees	10,596
31	19	(h)	Manchester C	D 0-0		18,004
32	23	(h)	Brighton & HA	D 1-1	Hopkins	8,983
33	30	(h)	Wolves	W 1-0	Geddis	10,230
34	Apr 5	(a)	Grimsby T	L 0-1		6,926
35	8	(h)	Sheffield U	W 4-1	Clarke 2, Daly, Kennedy	10,234
36	13	(a)	Portsmouth	W 3-1	Geddis 3	23,983
37	16	(h)	Crystal P	W 3-0	Clarke, Geddis, Kennedy	10,721
38	20	(a)	Charlton A	W 2-1	Kennedy, Wright (pen)	10,697
39	27	(h)	Barnsley	W 1-0	Geddis	6,757
40	May 4	(h)	Cardiff C	W 2-0	Hopkins, Kennedy	15,570
41	6	(a)	Middlesbrough	D 0-0		7,840
42	11	(h)	Leeds U	W 1-0	Kuhl	24,847

FINAL LEAGUE POSITION: 2nd in Division Two. Average home League attendance: 12,522.

Summary (league):

	Coton	Roberts	VdHauwe	Wright	Hagan	Daly	Stevenson	Clarke	Ferguson	Gorman	Hopkins	Kuhl	Armstrong	Harford	Halsall	McDonagh	Bremner	Seaman	Jones	Rees	Ranson	Linford	Morley	Platnauer	Geddis	Shearer	Russell	Kennedy	Prudhoe
Appearances	7	41	6	42	21	29	6	40	2	6	39	25	36	12	2	1	30	33	9	5	28	1	4	11	18	2	1	4	1
Substitutes					8	1						2	2											1	4	1			
Goals				2		1		17	1		9	2		2						2			3	1	12			4	

3 own-goals

FA Cup

Rd	Date		Opponent	Result	Scorers	Att.
3	Jan 5	(h)	Norwich C	D 0-0		12,941
R	23	(a)	Norwich C	D 1-1*	Wright	11,883
2R	26	(a)	Norwich C	D 1-1*	Geddis	11,755
3R	28	(a)	Norwich C	L 0-1		12,396

*After extra-time

	Roberts	Wright	Hagan	Daly	Clarke	Kuhl	Armstrong	Seaman	Ranson	Hopkins	Geddis
Appearances	4	4	1	4	4	4	3	4	4	4	4
Substitutes			2								
Goals		1									1

League Cup

Rd	Date		Opponent	Result	Scorers	Att.
2	Sep 25	(h)	Plymouth A	W 4-1	Clarke, Hopkins, Harford, Rees	7,964
	Oct 9	(a)	Plymouth A	W 1-0	Clarke	4,650
3	30	(h)	West Brom A	D 0-0		17,616
R	Nov 7	(a)	West Brom A	L 1-3	Shearer	16,717

	Roberts	Wright	VdHauwe	Daly	Clarke	Kuhl	Armstrong	Harford	Hopkins	Geddis	Seaman	Shearer	Others
Appearances	4	4	4	2	3	1	2	4	4	3	2	1	—
Substitutes									1	1		1	
Goals					2			1		1		1	

1985-86

Manager: Ron Saunders to January 1986 then John Bond

Player columns (left to right): Seaman D, Ranson R, Roberts B, Wright W, Armstrong K, Daly G, Bremner D, Clarke W, Jones M, Geddis D, Hopkins R, Kuhl M, Hagan J, Kennedy A, Dicks J, Platnauer N, Jenkins L, Ronson W, Rees A, Russell G, Whitton S, Garton W, Smalley M, Handysides I, Frain J, Storer S

No	Date		Venue/Opponent	Result	Scorers	Att.
1	Aug	17	(h) West Ham U	W 1-0	Hopkins	11,164
2		20	(a) Watford	L 0-3		14,278
3		24	(a) Chelsea	L 0-2		16,534
4		26	(h) Oxford U	W 3-1	Kennedy, Briggs (og), Hopkins	10,568
5		31	(a) Everton	L 1-4	Kennedy	28,066
6	Sep	3	(h) Manchester C	W 1-0	Geddis	11,706
7		7	(h) Aston Villa	D 0-0		24,971
8		14	(a) Ipswich T	W 1-0	Geddis	11,616
9		21	(h) Leicester C	W 2-1	Geddis 2	9,834
10		28	(a) Queen's Park R	L 1-3	Armstrong	10,911
11	Oct	5	(h) Sheffield W	L 0-2		11,708
12		19	(a) West Brom A	L 1-2	Kennedy	14,576
13		26	(h) Coventry C	L 0-1		9,267
14	Nov	2	(a) Luton T	L 0-2		8,550
15		9	(h) Newcastle U	L 0-1		8,162
16		16	(a) Southampton	L 0-1		13,167
17		23	(h) Liverpool	L 0-2		15,062
18		30	(a) Arsenal	D 0-0		16,673
19	Dec	7	(h) Watford	L 1-2	Wright (pen)	7,043
20		14	(a) West Ham U	L 0-2		17,481
21		21	(h) Chelsea	L 1-2	Platnauer	10,594
22		26	(h) Nottingham F	L 0-1		10,378
23		28	(a) Manchester C	D 1-1	Geddis	24,055
24	Jan	1	(a) Manchester U	L 0-1		43,095
25		11	(h) Ipswich T	L 0-1		6,856
26		18	(h) Everton	L 0-2		10,502
27	Feb	1	(a) Oxford U	W 1-0	Clarke	9,086
28		8	(h) West Brom A	L 0-1		11,514
29		16	(a) Coventry C	D 4-4	Kennedy 2, Whitton, Kuhl	14,271
30	Mar	1	(h) Queen's Park R	W 2-0	Clarke (pen), Hopkins	7,093
31		8	(a) Sheffield W	L 1-5	Geddis	17,491
32		12	(a) Leicester C	L 2-4	Clarke, Kennedy	8,458
33		15	(h) Tottenham H	L 1-2	Kennedy	9,394
34		22	(a) Aston Villa	W 3-0	Clarke 2, Whitton	26,294
35		29	(h) Manchester U	D 1-1	Handysides	22,551
36		31	(a) Nottingham F	L 0-3		13,134
37	Apr	6	(h) Luton T	L 0-2		8,836
38		12	(a) Newcastle U	L 1-4	Hopkins	19,981
39		16	(a) Tottenham H	L 0-2		9,359
40		19	(h) Southampton	L 0-2		5,833
41		26	(a) Liverpool	L 0-5		42,021
42	May	3	(h) Arsenal	L 0-1		6,234

FINAL LEAGUE POSITION: 21st in Division One. Average home League attendance: 10,899.

Player appearance grid (shirt numbers; columns as listed above):

No	Sea	Ran	Rob	Wri	Arm	Dal	Bre	Cla	Jon	Ged	Hop	Kuh	Hag	Ken	Dic	Pla	Jen	Ron	Ree	Rus	Whi	Gar	Sma	Han	Fra	Sto
1	1	2	3	4	5	6	7	8	9	10	11	12														
2	1	2	3	4		6	7	8	9	10	11	12	5													
3	1	2		4	5		7	8	3	10	11	6		9	12											
4	1	2		4	5		7	8	3	10	11	6		9												
5	1	2		4	5		7	8	3	10	11	6		9												
6	1	2	12	4	5		7	8	3	10	11	6		9												
7	1		2	4	5			8	3	10	11	6		9	7											
8	1	2	8	4					3	10	11	6	5	9	7	12										
9	1	2	8	4	5		7		3	10	11			9		6										
10	1		2	4	5		7	8	3	10	11			9	6	12										
11	1		2	4	5		7		3	10	11	8	6	9		12										
12	1	2		4	5		7		3		11	6		9	12	10	8									
13	1	2	7		4	5			3	10	11	6	8	9		12										
14	1	2	8		5		7		3	10	11	6	4	9												
15	1	2	3		5		7	8		10			4	9	6		11									
16	1	2	3	7	5			8		10			6	4	9	12	11									
17	1	2	3	8	5		7			10	11	6	4	9					12							
18	1	2	3	6	5		7	8	9		11		4	12	10											
19	1	2	3	6	5		7		10		11	12	4	9	8											
20	1	2	3	6			7		10				5	4		8	11		9							
21	1	2	3	4			7				11		6	5	9	10	12		8							
22	1	2	3	4			7				11	6	5	9		8	10		12							
23	1	2		4			7		10	11	6	5		9	3	8			12							
24	1	2	12	4	5			8			11	6	7	9	3	10										
25	1	2			5		7		10		11	6	4	9	3	8					12					
26	1	2	3	6	5		7	8			11		4	12		10		9								
27	1	2	3		5		7	8		10	11	6	4	12							9					
28	1	2	3		5		7	8		10	11	6	4								9					
29	1	2	3				7	8		10	11	6	4	9							5					
30	1	2	3				7	8		10	11	6	4	9						12	5					
31	1	2	3				7	8		10	11	6	4			12				9	5					
32	1	2	3				7	8		12	11	6	4								10	5				
33	1	2	3				7	8			11	6	4	9	12						10	5				
34	1	2	3	9			7	8			11	6	4								10	5				
35	1	2	3	9			7	8			11	6	4									5		10		
36	1	2	3	9			7	8			11	6				12						4	5	10		
37	1	2			5			8			11	6		9	3							4		10		
38	1	2			5			8			11	6	7		3							4	10	9		
39	1		2					8	9		11	6	4	12	3	7						5	10			
40	1		2					8	9		11	6	4			3	7					5	10	12		
41	1		6	2	10			8			11	12	5		3	9						4				7
42	1							8			11	6	4	10	3	9						5			12	7
Appearances	42	37	31	29	22	2	32	28	19	25	38	33	31	27	18	12	1	2	4		8	5	7	6	1	2
Substitutes		2										1		4	5	5	5		4	1				2		
Goals				1	1			5		6	4	1		7		1					2			1		

1 own-goal

FA Cup

No	Date		Venue/Opponent	Result	Scorers	Att.
3	Jan	14	(h) Altrincham	L 1-2	Hopkins	6,636

	Sea	Ran	Rob	Wri	Arm	Dal	Bre	Cla	Jon	Ged	Hop	Kuh	Hag	Ken	Dic	Pla
	1	2	8	12	5		7				11	6	4	9	3	10
Appearances	1	1	1		1		1				1	1	1	1	1	1
Substitutes				1												
Goals														1		

League Cup

No	Date		Venue/Opponent	Result	Scorers	Att.
2	Sep	24	(a) Bristol R	W 3-2	Wright 2 (2 pens), Geddis	4,332
	Oct	7	(h) Bristol R	W 2-1	Kennedy, Tanner (og)	3,686
3		29	(h) Southampton	D 1-1	Kennedy	4,832
R	Nov	6	(a) Southampton	L 0-3		9,085

	Sea	Ran	Rob	Wri	Arm	Dal	Bre	Cla	Jon	Ged	Hop	Kuh	Hag	Ken	Dic	Pla
	1	2	8	4	5		7			3	10	11		12	9	6
	1		2	4	5		7				11	6	3	9	8	10
	1	2	7	4					3	10	11	6	5	9	12	8
	1	2	8	12	5		7			3	10	11	6	4	9	
Appearances	4	3	4	3	3		3			3	3	4	3	3	4	1
Substitutes			1											1		1
Goals			2							1				2		

1 own-goal

1986-87

Manager: John Bond

FINAL LEAGUE POSITION: 19th in Division Two. Average home League attendance: 7,426.

#		Date	Venue/Opponent	Result	Scorers	Att.	Hansbury R	Jones M	Dicks J	Hagan J	Overson V	Kuhl M	Bremner D	Rees A	Whitton S	Mortimer D	Hopkins R	Clarke W	Handysides I	Roberts B	Storer S	Peer D	Cooke R	Ranson R	Kennedy A	Williams T	Russell G	Geddis D	Lynex S	Bird A	Hart P	Tomlinson P	North M	Wigley S	Ashley K	Frain J
1	Aug	23 (a) Stoke C	W 2-0	Hemming (og), Whitton	11,541	1	2	3	4	5	6	7	8	9	10	11																			
2		25 (h) Bradford C	W 2-1	Mortimer 2	7,003	1	2	3	4	5	6	7	8	9	10	11																			
3		30 (h) Derby C	D 1-1	Clarke	12,209	1	2	3	4	5	6	7	12	9	10	11	8																		
4	Sep	3 (a) Brighton & HA	L 0-2		9,750	1	2	3	4	5	6	7	12	9	10		8	11																	
5		6 (a) Sheffield U	D 1-1	Bremner	10,297	1		3	4	5	6	7		9	10		8		2			11													
6		13 (h) Huddersfield T	D 1-1		6,934	1		3	4	5	6	7		9	10		8		2			11													
7		20 (a) Hull C	L 2-3	Clarke 2	6,851	1		3	4	5	6			9	10		8		2			7	11												
8		27 (h) Ipswich T	D 2-2	Clarke 2	7,227	1		3	4	5	6	7	12	9	10		8		2			11													
9	Oct	4 (h) Barnsley	D 1-1	Kennedy	6,427	1		3	4	5	6	7		10	9		8						11	2			12								
10		11 (a) Portsmouth	L 0-2		11,252	1			4	5	6	7		9			8						11	2	10			3							
11		18 (h) Crystal P	W 4-1	Bremner, Overson, Whitton, Clarke	5,987	1			4	5	6	7		9			8	12					11	2	10			3							
12		25 (a) Sunderland	L 0-2		15,553	1		3	4	5	6	7	11	9			8	12						2	10										
13	Nov	1 (a) West Brom A	L 2-3	Lynex, Clarke	15,029	1	2	3		5	6	7		9	10		8								4			11							
14		8 (h) Oldham A	L 1-3	Clarke (pen)	6,082	1		3	4	5	6	7	12	9	10		8		2									11							
15		15 (a) Millwall	W 2-0	Clarke, Rees	4,795	1		3		5	6	7	10	9			8	2							4			12					11			
16		21 (h) Leeds U	W 2-1	Clarke, Bremner	7,836	1		3		5	6	7	10	9			8	2							4			12					11			
17		29 (h) Grimsby T	W 1-0	Whitton	4,734	1		3		5	6	7		9			8	2	12						4			10					11			
18	Dec	6 (h) Blackburn R	D 1-1	Clarke	6,428	1		3		5	6	7	10	9			8	2							4								11			
19		13 (a) Shrewsbury T	L 0-1		4,797	1		3		5	6	7	10	9			8	2							4								11			
20		19 (h) Sheffield U	W 2-1	Clarke 2 (1 pen)	5,007	1		3		5	6	7	10	9			8	2							4								11			
21		26 (a) Reading	D 2-2	Lynex, Clarke	7,442	1		3	4	5	6	7	10	9			8	2		12								11								
22		29 (h) Millwall	D 1-1	Mortimer	8,008	1		3	4	5	6	7		10					2	3	8		9	4				11	5						
23	Jan	1 (h) Plymouth A	W 3-2	Kuhl, Clarke, Mortimer	8,696	1				10	7	9			6		8	11	3				2	12	4				5						
24		3 (a) Bradford C	D 0-0		8,679	1				11	7	10	9	6			8	5	3				2		4										
25		24 (h) Stoke C	D 0-0		10,641	1		5		11	7	10	9	6			8		3				2		4										
26	Feb	7 (a) Derby C	D 2-2	Bremner, Whitton	16,834	1		6		5	11	7	10	9			8		3				2		4										
27		14 (h) Brighton & HA	W 2-0	Rees 2	6,439	1		5		11	7	10	9	6			8	3					2	12	4										
28		21 (a) Ipswich T	L 0-3		10,005	1		5		11	7		9	6			10	3					2	8	4										
29		28 (h) Hull C	D 0-0		6,858	1				11	7	10	9	6			8	5	3				2		4										
30	Mar	3 (a) Huddersfield T	D 2-2	Whitton, Rees	5,177	1	12		5		7	11	9	6			8	10	3				2		4										
31		14 (a) Crystal P	L 0-6		6,201	1		5		11	7	8	9	6			10	3					2		4										
32		21 (h) Portsmouth	L 0-1		9,823			3		5	7	10	9	6			12		2				4								1	8	11		
33		28 (a) Barnsley	D 2-2	Whitton, Wigley	4,688			3		5	7	10	9	6			8		2				4					4			1	12	11		
34		31 (h) Sunderland	W 2-0	North, Whitton	5,563			3		5	7		9	6			8	12	2									4			1	10	11		
35	Apr	4 (a) Oldham A	D 2-2	Whitton, Linighan (og)	6,555			3		5	7		9	6			8	2										4			1	10	11		
36		11 (h) West Brom A	L 0-1		11,158						7		9	6			8	2							4			5			1	10	11	3	12
37		18 (a) Plymouth A	D 0-0		13,372			3		5	7	10	9				8								4				6		1		11	2	7
38		20 (h) Reading	D 1-1	Frain	5,427			3		5	7	10	9				8								4				1			11	2		6
39		25 (a) Leeds U	L 0-4		19,100			3		5	7	10	9	6			8								4				1			11	2		
40	May	2 (h) Grimsby T	W 1-0	Whitton	4,457			3		5	7	10	9	6			8								4				1			11	2		
41		5 (a) Blackburn R	L 0-1		5,624			3		5	7		9	6			8								4				1	10		11	2		
42		9 (h) Shrewsbury T	L 0-2		7,724			3		5	7	10	9	6			8				12				4				1			11	2		
		Appearances				31	5	33	12	34	23	40	27	39	33	3	24	19	23	3	1	5	16	5	29	3	2	10	6	1	11	4	11	7	2
		Substitutes					1						3					1	1	3	1		1	4			2							
		Goals							1	1	4	4	9	4			16							1			2				1	1		1

2 own-goals

FA Cup

#		Date	Venue/Opponent	Result	Scorers	Att.	Hansbury R	Jones M	Dicks J	Hagan J	Overson V	Kuhl M	Bremner D	Rees A	Whitton S	Mortimer D	Hopkins R	Clarke W	Handysides I	Roberts B	Storer S	Peer D	Cooke R	Ranson R	Kennedy A	Williams T
3	Jan	10 (a) Ipswich T	W 1-0	Mortimer	11,616	1		5		11	7	10	9	6			8	3					2		4
4		31 (a) Walsall	L 0-1		14,810	1				11	7	10	9	6			8	5	3				2		4
		Appearances				2		1		2	2	2	2	2			1	2	2				2		2
		Substitutes																							
		Goals												1											

League Cup

#		Date	Venue/Opponent	Result	Scorers	Att.	Hansbury R	Jones M	Dicks J	Hagan J	Overson V	Kuhl M	Bremner D	Rees A	Whitton S	Mortimer D	Hopkins R	Clarke W	Handysides I	Roberts B	Storer S	Peer D	Cooke R	Ranson R	Kennedy A	Williams T	Russell G	Geddis D	Lynex S
2	Sep	23 (a) Middlesbrough	D 2-2	Whitton, Mortimer	9,412	1		3	4	5	6	7	11	9	10		8		2									
	Oct	7 (h) Middlesbrough	W 3-2*	Clarke 2, Whitton	4,978	1			4	5	6	7		9			8					11			2	10	3	12
3		29 (a) Tottenham H	L 0-5		15,542	1		3	4	5	6	7		9			8						2	10	11			12
		Appearances				3		2	3	3	3	3	1	3	1		3		1			1	2	2	2			
		Substitutes																										2
		Goals												2	1		2											

*After extra-time

1987-88

Manager: John Bond

No	Date	Opponent	Result	Scorers	Att	Godden A	Ranson R	Dicks J	Williams T	Overson V	Handysides I	Bremner D	Kennedy A	Whitton S	Rees A	Wigley S	Roberts B	Bird A	Trewick J	Childs G	Hansbury R	Frain J	Withe P	Sproston N	Russell G	Robinson C	Yates M	Starbuck P	Langley K	Atkins I	Morris R	Tait P	Ashley K
1	Aug 15	(h) Stoke C	W 2-0	Rees 2	13,137	1	2	3	4	5	6	7	8	9	10	11																	
2	22	(a) Aston Villa	W 2-0	Handysides, Rees	30,870	1		3	4	5	6	7	8	9	10	11	2																
3	29	(h) Bournemouth	D 1-1	Kennedy	8,284	1		3	4		6	7	8	9	**10**	11	2	5		12													
4	Sep 1	(a) Millwall	L 1-3	Rees	6,758	1		3	**4**	5	6	7	8	9	10	11	2	12															
5	5	(h) Crystal P	L 0-6		7,011	1		3		5		7	**8**	9	10	11	2	4	6	12													
6	12	(a) Swindon T	W 2-0	Handysides, Whitton	9,128	1	2	**3**	4	5	8	7		9	10	11			6	12													
7	15	(h) Blackburn R	W 1-0	Whitton	6,032		2	3	4	5	8	7	14	9	**10**	11			**6**	12	1												
8	19	(h) Shrewsbury T	D 0-0		7,183		2	3	4	5	8	7	12	9		11					1	6	**10**										
9	26	(a) Plymouth A	D 1-1	McElhinney (og)	8,912		2	3	4	5	8	7	12	**9**	10	11			6		1												
10	30	(a) West Brom A	L 1-2	Kennedy	15,399		**2**	3	4		8	7	12	**9**	10	11		5	6	12	1												
11	Oct 3	(h) Huddersfield T	W 2-0	Whitton 2	6,282	1		3	4	5	8	7	12	9	**10**	11	2		6														
12	10	(h) Reading	D 2-1	Whitton, Kennedy	6,147	1	2	3	4	5	8	7	12	9	**10**	11			6														
13	17	(a) Bradford C	L 0-4		12,256	1	2	3	4	5	8	7			10	11			6				9										
14	20	(a) Sheffield U	W 2-0	Withe 2	9,287	1	2	3	4	5	8				**10**	11			6	7		12	9										
15	24	(h) Middlesbrough	D 0-0		7,404	1	2	3	4	5	8	7				11			**6**	**10**		12	9	14									
16	31	(a) Oldham A	W 2-1	Frain, Whitton (pen)	5,486	1	2	3	**4**	5		7		9		11	12			8		6	**10**										
17	Nov 3	(h) Barnsley	W 2-0	Whitton 2	6,622	1	2	3		5		7		9	12	11	4			8		6	**10**										
18	7	(a) Hull C	L 0-2		7,901	1	2	3		**5**		7		9	12	11	4	14		8		6	**10**										
19	14	(h) Leicester C	D 2-2	Whitton 2	8,666	1	2	3		5		7		9	12	11	4		6	8			**10**										
20	21	(a) Manchester C	L 0-3		22,690	1	2	**3**	5			7	12	9	10	11	4		6	8													
21	28	(h) Ipswich T	W 1-0	Frain	6,718	1	2		5		12	7	10	**9**	14	11	**4**		3	8		6											
22	Dec 5	(a) Leeds U	L 1-4	Kennedy	15,977	1	2			5	10	7	9		**4**	11		12	3	**8**		6			14								
23	12	(h) Aston Villa	L 1-2	Kennedy	22,789	1	2			5	10	7	9			11	4		3	8		**6**			12								
24	19	(a) Blackburn R	L 0-2		8,542	1	2	3		5	4	7	9			11			6	8					10								
25	26	(h) Plymouth A	L 0-1		9,166	1	2	3		5		7	**9**	12	10	11	4		6	8													
26	28	(a) Shrewsbury T	D 0-0		6,397		2	3		5			10	9		11	4		6	8	1	7											
27	Jan 1	(a) Bournemouth	L 2-4	Dicks, Wigley	8,500		2	3	5			7	12	9		11	4		**6**	8	1				10								
28	2	(h) Swindon T	D 1-1	Childs	7,829	1	2	3	5			7	10	9		11	4			8		6											
29	16	(a) Stoke C	L 1-3	Kennedy	10,076		2	3	6	5	11	7	**9**		12		4		10	8	1												
30	Feb 6	(a) Crystal P	L 0-3		8,809		2	3	4	5	14	7		9	10	11			**6**	**8**	1					12							
31	9	(h) Millwall	W 1-0	Whitton	5,819		2	3	4	5	6	7		9		11				8	1					10							
32	27	(a) Huddersfield T	D 2-2	Robinson, Whitton	5,441		2	3	4	5	6	7		9	12	11				**8**	1					10							
33	Mar 5	(h) Bradford C	D 1-1	Whitton	8,101		2	3	4	5		7		9		11				8	1	6				**10**	12						
34	8	(h) West Brom A	L 0-1		12,331		2	3	4	5		7		**9**		11				8	1	6					12	10					
35	12	(a) Reading	D 1-1	Handysides	6,285		2	3	4	5	10	7				11	8		6		1							9					
36	19	(h) Oldham A	L 1-3	Wigley	6,012		2		4	5	10	7	12			11	3		6	8	1							**9**					
37	27	(a) Middlesbrough	D 1-1	Atkins	15,456		2		4	5	10	7	12			11	3				**1**				9				8	6			
38	Apr 2	(h) Hull C	D 1-1	Williams	7,059		2		4	5	**10**	**7**		9		11	3		14		1				12				8	6			
39	5	(a) Leicester C	L 0-2		13,541		2		4	5			12	9		11	3		**7**	14	1				**10**				8	6			
40	9	(h) Sheffield U	W 1-0	Kennedy	7,046		2		4	5			10	9		11	3			7	1								8	6			
41	23	(a) Barnsley	D 2-2	Whitton (pen), Jeffels (og)	4,949		2		**4**	5	10	**7**	12	9		11	3			14	1								8	6			
42	30	(h) Manchester C	L 0-3		8,014		**2**			5	7		10	**9**		11	3	4		12	1								8	6			14
43	May 2	(a) Ipswich T	L 0-1		11,067		2			5	10		12			11	3	4	7	14	1				**9**		**8**			6			
44	6	(h) Leeds U	D 0-0		6,024				**4**		7			9		11	3	5			1	2			**10**				8	6	12	14	
FINAL LEAGUE POSITION: 19th in Division Two. Average home League attendance: 8,576.					Appearances	22	38	32	33	37	28	37	15	32	17	43	26	6	25	23	22	12	8		6	3	1	3	7	8			
					Substitutes						2		13	1	6		1	3	1	9		2		1	3	1	2				1	1	1
					Goals			1	1		3		7	14	4	2				1		2	2			1				1			

2 own-goals

FA Cup

Rd	Date	Opponent	Result	Scorers	Att	Godden A	Ranson R	Dicks J	Williams T	Overson V	Handysides I	Bremner D	Kennedy A	Whitton S	Rees A	Wigley S	Roberts B	Bird A	Trewick J	Childs G	Hansbury R	Frain J	Withe P	Sproston N	Russell G	Robinson C	Yates M	Starbuck P	Langley K	Atkins I	Morris R	Tait P	Ashley K
3	Jan 9	(a) Gillingham	W 3-0	Greenall (og), Williams, Handysides	9,267		2	3	5		7		10	9		11	4			8	1	6											
4	30	(a) Barnsley	W 2-0	Rees, Wigley	13,219		2	3	4	5	10	7			9	11			6	8	1												
5	Feb 20	(h) Nottingham F	L 0-1		34,494		2	3	4	5	6	7		9	**10**	11			12	8	1												
					Appearances		3	3	3	2	3	2	1	2	2	3	1		1	3	3	1											
					Substitutes														1														
					Goals				1		1				1	1																	

1 own-goal

League Cup

Rd	Date	Opponent	Result	Scorers	Att	Godden A	Ranson R	Dicks J	Williams T	Overson V	Handysides I	Bremner D	Kennedy A	Whitton S	Rees A	Wigley S	Roberts B	Bird A	Trewick J	Childs G	Hansbury R	Frain J	Withe P	Sproston N	Russell G	Robinson C	Yates M	Starbuck P	Langley K	Atkins I	Morris R	Tait P	Ashley K
1	Aug 18	(a) Mansfield T	D 2-2	Whitton, Handysides	4,425	1		3	4	5	6	7	8	9	10	11	2																
	25	(h) Mansfield T	L 0-1		6,054	1		3	4		6	7	**8**	9	10	11	2	5		12													
					Appearances	2		2	2	1	2	2	2	2	2	2	2	1															
					Substitutes															1													
					Goals						1			1																			

1988-89

Manager: Garry Pendrey

#	Date	Opponent	Result	Scorers	Att.
1	Aug 27 (a)	Watford	L 0-1		12,656
2	Sep 3 (h)	Leicester C	L 2-3	Walsh (og), Robinson	7,932
3	10 (a)	Oldham A	L 0-4		5,796
4	17 (h)	Sunderland	W 3-2	Childs, Atkins, Robinson	6,871
5	20 (a)	Walsall	L 0-5		8,780
6	24 (a)	Blackburn R	L 0-3		7,562
7	Oct 1 (h)	Barnsley	L 3-5	Atkins, Robinson, Langley	4,892
8	4 (h)	Plymouth A	L 0-1		4,921
9	8 (a)	Bournemouth	W 1-0	Frain	6,186
10	15 (h)	West Brom A	L 1-4	Bremner	10,453
11	22 (a)	Manchester C	D 0-0		20,205
12	25 (h)	Stoke C	L 0-1		6,262
13	29 (a)	Swindon T	L 1-2	Atkins (pen)	6,937
14	Nov 5 (h)	Portsmouth	D 0-0		5,866
15	12 (a)	Oxford U	L 0-3		5,589
16	19 (a)	Hull C	D 1-1	Langley	5,134
17	22 (h)	Leeds U	D 0-0		6,168
18	26 (h)	Ipswich T	W 1-0	Witton	5,932
19	Dec 3 (a)	Bradford C	D 2-2	Whitton, Richards	9,503
20	10 (h)	Crystal P	L 0-1		6,523
21	16 (h)	Chelsea	L 1-4	Whitton	7,987
22	26 (a)	Shrewsbury T	D 0-0		7,347
23	31 (a)	Brighton & HA	L 0-4		9,324
24	Jan 2 (a)	Oldham A	D 0-0		5,998
25	14 (a)	Leeds U	L 0-1		21,838
26	21 (h)	Watford	L 2-3	Whitton 2 (1 pen)	6,396
27	Feb 4 (a)	Plymouth A	W 1-0	Robinson	7,721
28	11 (h)	Bournemouth	L 0-1		6,444
29	18 (h)	Manchester C	L 0-2		11,707
30	25 (a)	West Brom A	D 0-0		16,148
31	28 (a)	Stoke C	L 0-1		7,904
32	Mar 4 (h)	Oxford U	D 0-0		4,954
33	11 (a)	Portsmouth	L 0-1		8,078
34	18 (h)	Walsall	W 1-0	Wigley	6,558
35	25 (a)	Leicester C	L 0-2		9,564
36	27 (h)	Shrewsbury T	L 1-2	Sturridge	4,964
37	Apr 1 (a)	Sunderland	D 2-2	Frain, Yates	10,969
38	4 (a)	Chelsea	L 1-3	Richards	14,796
39	8 (h)	Brighton & HA	L 1-2	Sturridge	4,579
40	15 (a)	Barnsley	D 0-0		6,464
41	18 (h)	Swindon T	L 1-2	Peer	4,026
42	22 (h)	Blackburn R	W 2-0	Robinson, Yates	5,813
43	29 (a)	Ipswich T	L 0-4		9,975
44	May 1 (h)	Bradford C	W 1-0	Frain	4,735
45	6 (h)	Hull C	W 1-0	Yates	4,686
46	13 (a)	Crystal P	L 1-4	Sturridge	17,581

FINAL LEAGUE POSITION: 23rd in Division Two. Average home League attendance: 6,289.

Player line-ups (shirt numbers worn):

#	Godden A	Ranson R	Roberts B	Atkins I	Bird A	Trewick J	Bremner D	Langley K	Whitton S	Robinson C	Wigley S	Overson V	Frain J	Childs G	Morris R	Clarkson P	Tait P	Thomas M	Peer D	Yates M	Richards C	Sturridge S	Ashley K	Hansbury R	Fox M	Hopkins R	Burton M	Russell G	Elliott A
1	1	2	3	4	5	6	7	8	9	10	11																		
2	1	2	3	4	6			8	9	10	11	5	7																
3	1	2	3	4	6			8	9	10	11	5	7	12	14														
4	1	2	3	4			7		9	10	11	5	6	8															
5	1	2	3	4		8	7		9	10	11	5	6	12															
6	1	2	3	4	6	8	7		9	10	11	5																	
7	1	2	**3**	4			14	**8**	9	10	11	5		12			7	6											
8	1	2	3	4	6		7	8	9	10	11	5		12	14			1											
9		2		4	6		7		9	10	11	5	3					1		8	12								
10				4	6		7		**10**	11	5	3	8	12				1	2	9	14								
11		2		4			7		10	11	5	3	8					1	6	9	12								
12		2		4	12		7		10	11	5	3	8					1	6	9	14								
13		2	3	4			7	8	**10**	11		5		12	5			1	6	14	9								
14		2	3	4	5		7	6		11		8				12	1			9	**10**								
15			3	4			7	6		11	5	8				1				9	10	12	2						
16		2		4	8		7	6		11	5	3				1				9	10								
17		2	3	4			7	6	9	11	5		8			1				12	10								
18		2	3	4			7	6	9	11	5		8			12	14			**10**			1						
19		2	3	4	8		7	6	9	11	5										10		1						
20		2	3	4			7	6	9	11	5		8								10		1						
21		2	3	4			7	6	9	14	11	5	12	8				1			**10**								
22			3	4	8	12	7	6	9		11	5						1			**10**	2							
23			3	4		8	7	6	9	12	11	5						1			**10**	2							
24		2		4	3		7	6	9		5		11				8	1			10								
25				4	3		7	6	9	10	11	5		12			8	1			2								
26				4	3		7	6	9	10	11	5					8	1		12	2								
27		7		4	3			6		10	11	5	9				8	1			2								
28		7		4	3			6	9	10	11	5	8			**12**	14	1			2								
29		6		4	3	7			9	10	11	5		8				1		12	2								
30		6		4		7			9	10	11	3		12			8	1		14	2	5							
31				4		7	12	9	10	11	5	3	6				8	1		14	2								
32		6		4	7				10	11	5	3	12					1	9		**8**	2							
33		6		4	7	12			10	11	5	3						1	9	8	2								
34				4	7				10	11	5	3	8					1	9	12	2		6						
35		6		4	7				10		5	3	8					1	9	2					11	12			
36		6		4	7				9		5	3	8	12				1	10	2					**11**				
37		6		4	7						5	3	8			1	2		11	10	9								
38		6		4	7						5	3	8			1	2		11	10	9								
39		6		4	7				9		5	3	8			1	2			10					11	12			
40		6		4	7						10	5	3	8		9	1	2	11										
41		6		4	7						3	9	1	2	11		10		5	8									
42		6			7			8			5	3		2	1	4	9		10						11				
43		6			7			8			5	3	12	2	1	4	9		10						11	14			
44		6			7			8			5	3	9	2	1	4			10						11				
45		6			7			8			5	3	12	2	1	9	4		10						11				
46		6	4		7						5	3	12	2	1	8	9		10						11				
Appearances	7	17	41	40	11	10	28	34	23	31	33	41	28	16	3	9	6	36	15	16	18	13	15	3	3	9			
Substitutes					1	1	1	2					2	7		7	1		4	2	3	1	8			3			
Goals				3			1	2	5	5	1		3	1					1	3	2	3							

1 own-goal

FA Cup

#	Date	Opponent	Result	Att.
3	Jan 7 (h)	Wimbledon	L 0-1	10,431

	Atkins I	Bird A	Trewick J	Bremner D	Langley K	Whitton S	Robinson C	Wigley S	Thomas M	Yates M	Richards C	Sturridge S
Line-up	4	3	7	6	9	**10**	11	5	8	12	2	1
Appearances	1	1	1	1	1	1	1	1	1		1	1
Substitutes										1		
Goals												

League Cup

#	Date	Opponent	Result	Scorers	Att.
1	Aug 30 (a)	Wolves	L 2-3	Thompson (og), Bird	11,007
	Sep 6 (h)	Wolves	W 1-0	Whitton	8,981
2	27 (h)	Aston Villa	L 0-2		21,177
	Oct 12 (a)	Aston Villa	L 0-5		19,753

	Godden A	Ranson R	Roberts B	Atkins I	Bird A	Trewick J	Bremner D	Langley K	Whitton S	Robinson C	Wigley S	Overson V	Frain J	Childs G	Clarkson P	Tait P	Peer D	Yates M	Richards C	Fox M	Russell G
1a	1	2	3	4	5	6	12	**8**	9	10	11		7								
1b	1	2	3	4	6			8	**9**	10	11	5	7	12						14	
2a	1	**2**	3	4			12	8	14	10	11	5				7			9		
2b		**2**		4			7			10	11	5	3	14	**9**	6		8		12	1
Appearances	3	4	3	4	2	1	1	3	2	4	4	3	3		2	2		1	1		1
Substitutes							2		1					1	1					1	
Goals					1				1												

1 own-goal

1989-90

Manager: Dave Mackay

Players (left to right): Thomas M, Clarkson I, Frain J, Atkins I, Sproson P, Matthewson T, Peer D, Bailey D, Yates M, Langley K, Sturridge S, Ashley K, Overson V, Gordon C, Hopkins R, Tait P, Gleghorn N, Deakin J, Hansbury R, Roberts B, Bell D, Harris A, Madden D, Rutherford M, Williams D

#	Date		Opponent	Result	Scorers	Att.
1	Aug	19 (h)	Crewe A	W 3-0	Yates, Sturridge, Bailey	10,447
2		26 (a)	Bristol C	L 0-1		8,938
3	Sep	2 (h)	Swansea C	W 2-0	Bailey, Hopkins	8,071
4		9 (a)	Shrewsbury T	L 0-2		4,714
5		16 (h)	Tranmere R	W 2-1	Gordon, Bailey	8,604
6		23 (a)	Brentford	W 1-0	Sturridge	5,386
7		26 (h)	Walsall	W 2-0	Bailey (pen), Tait	10,834
8		30 (a)	Blackpool	L 2-3	Sturridge, Gleghorn	5,737
9	Oct	7 (a)	Rotherham U	L 1-5	Sturridge	4,450
10		14 (h)	Northampton T	W 4-0	Gleghorn 2, Bailey 2 (1 pen)	8,731
11		17 (a)	Chester C	L 0-4		1,882
12		21 (h)	Huddersfield T	L 0-1		7,951
13		28 (a)	Bury	D 0-0		3,383
14		31 (h)	Cardiff C	D 1-1	Sturridge	7,468
15	Nov	4 (a)	Reading	W 2-0	Sturridge, Hicks (og)	3,527
16		11 (h)	Leyton O	D 0-0		7,491
17		25 (h)	Bolton W	W 1-0	Bailey (pen)	8,081
18	Dec	1 (a)	Wigan A	L 0-1		2,600
19		16 (h)	Preston NE	W 3-1	Yates, Bailey, Frain	6,391
20		26 (a)	Bristol R	D 0-0		6,573
21		30 (a)	Notts C	L 2-3	Atkins (pen), Bailey	7,786
22	Jan	1 (h)	Fulham	D 1-1	Gleghorn	8,932
23		13 (a)	Bristol C	L 0-4		11,277
24		20 (a)	Crewe A	W 2-0	Sturridge, Bailey	4,681
25		27 (h)	Shrewsbury T	L 0-1		7,461
26	Feb	9 (a)	Tranmere R	L 1-5	Bailey (pen)	6,033
27		13 (a)	Swansea C	D 1-1	Madden	3,603
28		17 (h)	Wigan	D 0-0		5,473
29		24 (a)	Bolton W	L 1-3	Gordon	7,618
30	Mar	3 (h)	Mansfield T	W 4-1	Sturridge, Bailey 2, Ashley	5,746
31		6 (h)	Blackpool	W 3-1	Peer, Sturridge, Bailey (pen)	7,085
32		10 (a)	Walsall	W 1-0	Gleghorn	6,036
33		13 (h)	Brentford	L 0-1		8,169
34		17 (a)	Rotherham U	W 4-1	Tait, Atkins, Gordon, Sturridge	6,985
35		20 (a)	Northampton T	D 2-2	Peer, Gleghorn	4,346
36		24 (h)	Chester C	D 0-0		7,584
37		31 (a)	Huddersfield T	W 2-1	Bailey, Gleghorn	5,837
38	Apr	3 (a)	Mansfield T	L 2-5	Gleghorn, Bailey	4,163
39		7 (h)	Bury	D 0-0		6,808
40		10 (a)	Cardiff C	W 1-0	Hopkins	3,322
41		14 (a)	Fulham	W 2-1	Hopkins, Gleghorn	4,568
42		16 (h)	Bristol R	D 2-2	Hopkins, Matthewson	12,438
43		21 (a)	Preston NE	D 2-2	Bailey 2	7,680
44		24 (h)	Notts C	L 1-2	Hopkins	10,533
45		28 (h)	Leyton O	W 2-1	Hopkins, Peer	5,691
46	May	5 (h)	Reading	L 0-1		14,278

FINAL LEAGUE POSITION: 7th in Division Three. Average home League attendance: 8,558.

League appearances / goals summary

	Thomas	Clarkson	Frain	Atkins	Sproson	Matthewson	Peer	Bailey	Yates	Langley	Sturridge	Ashley	Overson	Gordon	Hopkins	Tait	Gleghorn	Deakin	Hansbury	Roberts	Bell	Harris	Madden
Appearances	42	15	36	45	12	46	22	40	12	33	30	31	27	14	16	7	43	3	1	9	14	5	3
Substitutes		5	2				5	3	8		1			3	7	2	7	4		1	1	1	2
Goals			1	2		1	3	18	2		10	1		3	6	2	9						1

1 own-goal

FA Cup

#	Date		Opponent	Result	Scorers	Att.
1	Nov	17 (a)	Leyton O	W 1-0	Sturridge	4,063
2	Dec	9 (a)	Colchester U	W 2-0	Gleghorn 2	3,858
3	Jan	6 (h)	Oldham A	D 1-1	Gleghorn	13,131
R		10 (a)	Oldham A	L 0-1		9,982

FA Cup — Appearances: Thomas 4, Clarkson 3, Frain 4, Atkins 4, Matthewson 4, Bailey 4, Sturridge 4, Overson 2, Gordon 3, Hopkins 4, Gleghorn 4, Bell 4. Substitutes: 1, 2, 1. Goals: Sturridge 1, Gleghorn 3.

League Cup

#	Date		Opponent	Result	Scorers	Att.
1	Aug	22 (h)	Chesterfield	W 2-1	Atkins, Bailey	6,722
		28 (a)	Chesterfield	D 1-1	Bailey	3,313
2	Sep	19 (h)	West Ham U	L 1-2	Sproson	10,987
	Oct	4 (a)	West Ham U	D 1-1	Atkins	12,187

League Cup — Appearances: Thomas 4, Clarkson 1, Frain 2, Atkins 4, Sproson 4, Matthewson 4, Peer 3, Bailey 4, Yates 2, Langley 1, Sturridge 2, Ashley 3, Overson 3, Gordon 2, Hopkins 2, Tait 1, Gleghorn 2. Substitutes: 1, 1, 1, 1, 1, 1. Goals: Atkins 2, Sproson 1, Bailey 2.

1990-91

Manager: Dave Mackay until January 1991 then Lou Macari

Player columns (left to right): Thomas M · Ashley K · Downs G · Frain J · Overson V · Matthewson T · Peer D · Bailey D · Hopkins R · Gleghorn N · Tait P · Sturridge S · Fox S · Moran R · Clarkson I · Rutherford M · Aylott T · Gordon C · Gayle J · Rodgerson I · Dolan E · Francis S · Bell D · Yates M · O'Reilly G · Robinson P · Williams D

#	Date	Venue & Opponent	Result	Scorers	Att	Tho	Ash	Dow	Fra	Ove	Mat	Pee	Bai	Hop	Gle	Tai	Stu	Fox	Mor	Cla	Rut	Ayl	Gor	Gay	Rod	Dol	Fra	Bel	Yat	ORe	Rob	Wil
1	Aug 25	(a) Cambridge U	W 1-0	Gleghorn	6,338	1	2	3	4	5	6	7	8	9	10	11	12															
2	Sep 1	(h) Leyton O	W 3-1	Bailey, Hopkins, Moran	5,847	1	2	3	4		6	7	8	9	10	11	12	5	14													
3	8	(a) Stoke C	W 1-0	Gleghorn	16,009	1	2	3	4		6	7	8		10	11	12	5	9													
4	15	(h) Bury	W 1-0	Peer	7,344	1		3	4	5	6	7	8		10	11	12		9	2												
5	18	(h) Exeter C	D 1-1	Bailey	7,703	1		3	4	5	6	7	8	12	10	11	9		14	2												
6	22	(a) Wigan A	D 1-1	Tait	3,907	1			4	5	3		8	7	10	11	9	6		2	12											
7	29	(h) Preston NE	D 1-1	Bailey	7,154	1	12		4	5	3	7	8	9		11		6		2	10											
8	Oct 2	(a) Fulham	D 2-2	Matthewson, Overson	4,011	1	10		4	5	3	7	8	11	9			6		2	12											
9	6	(a) Reading	D 2-2	Matthewson, Sturridge	5,695	1		3	4	5	6	7	8	11	10		9			2												
10	13	(h) Southend U	D 1-1	Sturridge	9,333	1		3	4	5	6	7	8	11	10		9			2												
11	20	(h) Grimsby T	D 0-0		10,123	1		3	4	5	6	7	8	2	10	11	9	12														
12	23	(a) Crewe A	D 1-1	Gleghorn	4,449	1		3	4	5	6	7	12	2	10	11	8					9										
13	27	(a) Shrewsbury T	L 1-4	Bailey	6,050	1			4	5	3		12	7	10	11	8	6		2	14	9										
14	Nov 3	(h) Huddersfield T	L 1-2	Tait	7,412	1		3	4	5	6	7	12	2	10	11	8					9										
15	10	(a) Chester C	W 1-0	Hopkins	2,273	1		3	4	5	6	7	8	2	10	11	12					9										
16	24	(h) Bournemouth	D 0-0		7,416	1		3	4	5	6	7	8	2	10	11	12					9										
17	Dec 1	(a) Swansea C	L 0-2		4,896	1		3	4	5	6	7	12		10	11				2		9										
18	15	(h) Rotherham U	W 2-1	Tait, Overson	4,734	1		3	4	5	6	14	12		10	11				2		9	7		8							
19	21	(a) Tranmere R	L 0-1		5,034	1			3	5	6	7	8	4	10	11	12			2		9										
20	26	(h) Brentford	L 0-2		6,612	1			3	5	6	7	8	4	10	11	12		14	2		9										
21	29	(h) Bolton W	L 1-3	Bailey	7,318	1			3	5		7	12	4	10	11		6		2		9			8							
22	Jan 1	(a) Mansfield T	W 2-1	Gayle 2	3,652	1			4	5	3	7	8		10			6				9	2	11								
23	5	(h) Bradford C	D 1-1	Frain (pen)	6,315	1			4	5	3	7	8		10		12	6				9	2	11								
24	12	(a) Leyton O	D 1-1	Sturridge	4,708	1			4	5	3	7	8		10		12	6				9	2	11								
25	19	(h) Cambridge U	L 0-3		5,859	1			4	5	3	14	8		10			6		2		9		7	11	12						
26	26	(a) Bury	W 1-0	Sturridge	3,009	1			3	5	6	7	4		10	11				2		9			8							
27	Feb 2	(a) Exeter C	W 2-0	Gayle 2	5,154	1			3	5	6	7	4		10	11				2		9			8							
28	5	(h) Wigan A	D 0-0		5,319	1			3	5	6	7	4		10	11				2		9		14	8	12						
29	13	(a) Bradford C	L 0-2		4,776	1			3	5	6	7	8	4	10	11				2		9							12			
30	16	(a) Bournemouth	W 2-1	Sturridge, Mundee (og)	6,330	1			3	5	6	7	8		10	11				2		9			4	12						
31	23	(h) Chester C	W 1-0	Dolan	6,702	1			3	5	6	7			10	11				2		9			4	8						
32	Mar 2	(h) Swansea C	W 2-0	Sturridge, Rodgerson	6,903	1			3	5	6	7	12		10	11				2		9			8	4			14			
33	9	(a) Rotherham U	D 1-1	Frain (pen)	5,015	1			3	5	6	7	12		10	11				2		9			8	4			14			
34	12	(h) Fulham	W 2-0	Peer, Gleghorn	8,083	1			3	5	6	7		4	10	11				2		9			8							
35	16	(a) Preston NE	L 0-2		5,334	1			3	5	6	7	9		10	11	12			2					8				4			
36	18	(a) Southend U	L 1-2	Gleghorn	6,328	1			3	5	6	7		11	10	12				2		9			8				4			
37	23	(h) Reading	D 1-1	Rodgerson	6,795	1			3	5	6	7			10	11	12			2				9	8				4			
38	34	(a) Brentford	D 2-2	Frain, Gleghorn	6,757	1			3	5	6				10	11				2		12	7	9	8			4	14			
39	Apr 2	(a) Tranmere R	W 1-0	Yates	7,675	1			3	5	6	7			10	11				2				9				4	8			
40	7	(a) Bolton W	L 1-3	Gayle	11,280	1			3	5	6	7		11	10					2		12		9	8			4				
41	13	(h) Mansfield T	D 0-0		7,635	1			3	5	6	7		12	10	11				2				9	8			4	14			
42	16	(h) Stoke C	W 2-1	Matthewson, Hopkins	6,729	1			3	5	6			11	10					2			12	9	8	7		4				
43	20	(a) Grimsby T	D 0-0		8,842	1			3		6	7		12	11	10				2				9	8	4		5				1
44	27	(h) Crewe A	L 0-2		6,429	1			3		6	7		11	10					2			12	9	8			5				1
45	May 4	(h) Shrewsbury T	L 0-1		6,256	1			3	5	6	14	12	11	10					2				9	7			4				
46	11	(a) Huddersfield T	W 1-0	Gayle	5,195	1			3	5	6	4		11	10					2				9	7			8				

FINAL LEAGUE POSITION: 12th in Division Three. Average home League attendance: 7,030.

	Tho	Ash	Dow	Fra	Ove	Mat	Pee	Bai	Hop	Gle	Tai	Stu	Fox	Mor	Cla	Rut	Ayl	Gor	Gay	Rod	Dol	Fra	Bel	Yat	ORe	Rob	Wil
Appearances	45	3	16	42	40	46	37	25	18	42	17	33	9	2	34	1	23	3	20	25	5		1	8	1	9	1
Substitutes		1					3	7	5		5	2	6			3	2	2	2		5		3	1			
Goals				3	2	3	2	5	3	6	3	6		1					6	2	1			1			

1 own-goal

FA Cup

#	Date	Venue & Opponent	Result	Scorers	Att	Tho	Ash	Dow	Fra	Ove	Mat	Pee	Bai	Hop	Gle	Tai	Stu	Fox	Mor	Cla	Rut	Ayl	Gor	Gay	Rod	Dol	Fra	Bel	Yat	ORe	Rob	Wil
1	Nov 17	(h) Cheltenham T	W 1-0	Sturridge	7,942			3	4	5	6	7	8	2	10	11	9					12									1	
2	Dec 12	(h) Brentford	L 1-3	Aylott	5,072	1		3	4	5	6	7	8		10	11				2		12		9							1	

	Tho	Ash	Dow	Fra	Ove	Mat	Pee	Bai	Hop	Gle	Tai	Stu			Cla		Ayl		Gay							Rob	
Appearances	1		2	2	2	2	2	2	1	2	1	2			1		1		1							1	
Substitutes																	1	1									
Goals												1					1										

League Cup

#	Date	Venue & Opponent	Result	Scorers	Att	Tho	Ash	Dow	Fra	Ove	Mat	Pee	Bai	Hop	Gle	Tai	Stu	Fox	Mor	Cla	Rut	Ayl	Gor	Gay	Rod	Dol	Fra	Bel	Yat	ORe	Rob	Wil
1	Aug 28	(h) Bournemouth	L 0-1		5,110	1	2	3	4	5	6	7	8	9	10	11	12															
2	Sep 4	(a) Bournemouth	D 1-1	Downs (pen)	4,490	1	2	3	4		6	7	8	9	10	11	12	5	14													

	Tho	Ash	Dow	Fra	Ove	Mat	Pee	Bai	Hop	Gle	Tai	Stu	Fox	Mor
Appearances	2	2	2	2	1	2	2	2	2	2	2	1		
Substitutes													2	1
Goals			1											

1991-92

Manager: Terry Cooper

Player columns (left to right): Thomas M, Clarkson I, Matthewson T, Frain J, Hicks M, Mardon P, Rodgerson I, Gayle J, Peer D, Gleghorn N, Sturridge S, Yates M, Okenla F, Dolan E, Donowa L, Cooper M, Jones P, Atkins I, Tait P, Drinkell K, Carter T, Paskin J, Cheesewright JA, Hogan E, Miller K, Rowbotham D, Beckford J, Francis S, Rennie D, Dearden K, Foy D

#	Date	Venue/Opponent	Res	Scorers	Att.	Shirt numbers (in player-column order)
1	Aug 17 (h) Bury	W 3-2	Gleghorn, Gayle, Okenla	9,033	Tho 1, Cla 2, Mat **3**, Fra 4, Hic 5, Mar 6, Rod 7, Gay **8**, Pee 9, Gle 10, Stu 11, Yat 12, Oke 14
2	24 (a) Fulham	W 1-0	Rodgerson	4,762	1, 2, 3, 5, 6, 7, 9, 10, 11, Yat 4, Oke 12, Dol **8**
3	31 (h) Darlington	W 1-0	Sturridge	8,768	1, 2, 3, 5, 6, 7, **8**, 9, 10, 11, 12, 4
4	Sep 3 (a) Hull C	W 2-1	Sturridge, Rodgerson	4,801	1, 2, 3, 5, 6, 7, 9, 10, 11, 4, 8
5	7 (a) Reading	D 1-1	Sturridge	6,649	1, 2, 3, 5, 6, **7**, 9, 10, 11, 4, 8, 12
6	14 (h) Peterboro' U	D 1-1	Cooper	9,408	1, 2, 3, 5, **6**, 9, 10, 11, 7, 4, 8, 12, 14
7	17 (h) Chester C	W 3-2	Sturridge, Frain (pen), Gleghorn	9,154	1, 2, 3, 5, 6, 7, 9, 10, 11, 4, 8
8	21 (a) Hartlepool U	L 0-1		4,643	1, 2, 8, 5, 6, 7, 9, 10, 11, 4, 8
9	28 (h) Preston NE	W 3-1	Matthewson, Gleghorn, Rodgerson	8,760	1, 2, 3, 8, 5, 6, 7, 10, 11, 4, 9
10	Oct 5 (a) Shrewsbury T	D 1-1	Gleghorn	7,035	1, 2, 3, 8, 5, 6, 7, 14, 10, 11, 4, 9, 12
11	12 (h) Stockport C	W 3-0	Cooper, Drinkell, Donowa	12,634	1, 2, 3, 8, 5, 6, 7, 10, 11, 12, 4, 9
12	19 (a) Wigan A	D 3-3	Sturridge, Gleghorn, Rodgerson	9,662	1, 2, 3, 8, 5, 6, 7, 14, 10, 11, 12, 4, 9
13	26 (a) West Brom A	W 1-0	Drinkell	26,168	1, 2, 3, 8, 5, 6, 10, 11, 7, 4, 9
14	Nov 2 (h) Torquay U	W 3-0	Gleghorn (pen), Sturridge, Donowa	9,478	1, 2, 3, 8, 5, 6, 4, 10, 11, 7, 9
15	6 (h) Brentford	D 2-2	Sturridge, Cooper	8,798	1, 2, 3, 8, 5, 6, 14, 12, 10, 11, 7, 4, 9
16	9 (a) Huddersfield T	L 2-3	Gleghorn, Matthewson	11,688	1, 2, 3, 8, 5, 6, 7, 4, 10, 11, 9, 12
17	23 (a) Exeter C	W 1-0	Gleghorn	11,319	2, 5, 3, 6, 7, 4, 10, 11, 9, 8, 1, 12
18	30 (h) Bradford C	W 2-0	Peer, Gleghorn	10,468	2, 5, 3, 6, 7, 4, 10, **11**, 9, 8, 1, 12
19	Dec 14 (a) Bournemouth	L 1-2	Paskin	6,048	2, 5, 3, 12, 6, 7, 4, 10, **9**, 8, 11, 1, 14
20	21 (h) Fulham	W 3-1	Gleghorn, Rodgerson 2	8,877	2, 5, 3, 6, 7, 4, 10, 11, 8, 9, 1
21	26 (a) Darlington	D 1-1	Rodgerson	4,421	2, 5, 3, 6, 7, 4, 10, 11, 12, 8, 9, 1
22	28 (a) Bury	L 0-1		4,254	2, 12, 3, 5, 6, 7, 4, 10, 11, 8, 9, 1
23	Jan 1 (h) Hull C	D 2-2	Paskin, Gleghorn	12,983	3, 2, 5, 6, 7, 10, **11**, 12, 8, 4, 14, 9, 1
24	4 (a) Stoke C	L 1-2	Beckford	18,914	3, 2, 5, 6, 7, 10, 12, 4, 9, 1, 8, 11
25	11 (h) Leyton O	D 2-2	Cooper, Paskin	10,445	2, 6, 3, 5, 7, 8, 10, 12, 4, 9, 1, **11**
26	18 (a) Swansea C	W 2-0	Rodgerson, Rowbotham	4,147	2, 6, 3, 5, 7, 8, 10, 4, 9, 1, 11, 12
27	Feb 8 (h) West Brom A	L 0-3		27,508	2, 6, 3, 5, 7, 14, 10, 12, 9, 4, 1, 8, 11
28	11 (a) Bradford C	W 2-1	Gleghorn, Sturridge	7,008	2, 6, 5, 7, 10, **11**, 9, 4, 3, 1, 8, 12
29	15 (h) Bournemouth	L 0-1		10,898	2, 6, 5, 7, 10, 11, 9, 4, **3**, 14, 1, 8, 12
30	22 (a) Leyton O	D 0-0		5,995	2, 11, 5, 7, 10, 4, 9, 3, 8, 1, 6
31	29 (a) Stoke C	D 1-1	Frain (pen)	22,162	2, 3, 5, 6, 7, 10, **11**, **12**, 8, 1, 9, 4
32	Mar 3 (h) Swansea C	D 1-1	Rowbotham	9,475	2, 3, 5, 6, 7, 10, **12**, 8, 1, 9, 14, 4
33	10 (h) Brentford	W 1-0	Matthewson	13,290	2, 6, 3, 5, 7, 10, **11**, **12**, 14, 8, 1, 9, 4
34	17 (a) Bolton W	D 1-1	Rodgerson	7,329	6, 3, 5, 2, 7, 10, 12, 11, 8, 1, 9
35	21 (h) Huddersfield T	W 2-0	Sturridge, Gleghorn	12,482	2, 3, 8, 5, 6, 7, 10, **11**, 12, 9, 4, 1
36	24 (a) Torquay U	W 2-1	Rowbotham, Matthewson	2,446	3, 8, 5, 6, 7, 10, 11, 2, 9, 4, 1
37	28 (a) Exeter C	L 1-2	Hicks	5,479	2, 3, 8, 5, **6**, 7, 10, 11, 12, **9**, 4, 1
38	31 (a) Peterboro' U	W 3-2	Frain (pen), Sturridge, Matthewson	12,081	2, 6, 3, 5, 7, 10, 11, 8, 9, 4, 1
39	Apr 4 (h) Reading	W 2-0	Rowbotham, Frain (pen)	12,229	2, 6, 3, 5, 10, **11**, 8, 9, 12, 4, 1
40	11 (a) Chester C	W 1-0	Gleghorn	4,895	2, 6, 3, 5, 10, 11, 8, **9**, 4, 1
41	14 (h) Bolton W	W 2-1	Frain (pen), Rennie	14,440	2, 6, 3, 5, 14, **7**, 10, 11, 8, 9, 4, 1
42	18 (h) Hartlepool U	W 2-1	Matthewson, Gleghorn	13,698	2, 6, 3, 5, 10, 11, 7, 8, 9, 4, 1
43	21 (a) Preston NE	L 2-3	Gleghorn, Rennie	7,738	2, 6, 3, 5, 12, 10, 11, 14, 8, 9, 4, 1
44	25 (h) Shrewsbury T	W 1-0	Gleghorn	19,868	2, 6, 3, 5, 12, 7, 10, 11, 8, 9, 4, 1
45	28 (a) Wigan A	L 0-3		5,950	2, 6, 3, 5, 9, 7, 10, **11**, 8, 12, 4, 1
46	May 2 (a) Stockport C	L 0-2		7,840	2, 6, 3, 5, 14, 7, 10, 12, 8, 9, 4, 1

FINAL LEAGUE POSITION: 2nd in Division Three. Average home League attendance: 12,399.

	Tho	Cla	Mat	Fra	Hic	Mar	Rod	Gay	Pee	Gle	Stu	Yat	Oke	Dol	Don	Coo	Jon	Atk	Tai	Dri	Car	Pas	Che	Hog	Mil	Row	Bec	Fra	Ren	Dea	Foy
Appearances	16	42	35	44	41	31	38	2	18	46	38	1	2	1	20	2	27			5	10	5	2	8	1	15	21	2	17	12	
Substitutes		1		1	4	1	3		2		1	5	1	6		6	1	3	2			2		1		1	2	3			
Goals		6	5	1			9	1	1	17	10		1		2	4				2		3				4	1		2		

A.O'Neill played number-14 in Match 31, number-11 in Match 32, number-7 in Match 39 and number-12 in Match 40; **M.Sale** played number-14 in Matches 37 & 45, number-12 in Matches 38 & 41, number-7 in Match 40 and number-11 in Match 46.

FA Cup

#	Date	Venue/Opponent	Res	Scorers	Att.	Numbers
1	Nov 16 (a) Torquay U	L 0-3		4,123	1, 2, 3, 8, 5, 6, 7, 12, 10, 11, 9, 4

	Appearances	Substitutes	Goals
	1 1 1 1 1 1 1 1 1 1 1 (with sub 1)		

League Cup

#	Date	Venue/Opponent	Res	Scorers	Att.	Numbers
1	Aug 20 (a) Exeter C	W 1-0	Rodgerson	4,071	1, 2, 3, 5, 6, 7, 9, 10, 11, 4, 8
	27 (h) Exeter C	W 4-0	Hicks, Yates, Peer, Gleghorn	6,179	1, 2, 3, 5, 6, 7, 9, 10, 11, 4, 8
2	Sep 25 (a) Luton T	D 2-2	Rodgerson, Gleghorn	6,315	1, 2, 3, 8, 5, 6, 7, 9, 10, 11, 4
	Oct 8 (h) Luton T	W 3-2	Peer, Gleghorn 2	13,252	1, 2, 3, 8, 5, 6, 7, 9, 10, 11, 4
3	29 (h) Crystal P	D 1-1	Sturridge	17,270	1, 2, 3, 8, 5, 6, 4, 10, 11, **7**, 9, 14
R	Nov 19 (a) Crystal P	D 1-1*	Gleghorn	10,698	1, 2, 5, 3, 6, 7, 4, 10, 11, 9, 8, 12
2R	Dec 3 (a) Crystal P	L 1-2	Peer	11,384	2, 5, 3, 12, 6, 7, 4, 10, **11**, 9, 8, 1, 14

*After extra-time

	Appearances		Substitutes		Goals
	6 7 5 7 5 7 6　7 7 7 2 1 2 5	(subs) 1　1　1　1	1 2　3 5 1 1		

1992-93

Manager: Terry Cooper

Player columns (left to right): Gosney A, Clarkson I, Frain J, Rennie D, Rogers D, Mardon P, Donowa L, Tait P, Sale M, Gleghorn N, Sturridge S, Rodgerson I, Hicks M, Cooper M, Beckford J, Rowbotham D, Matthewson T, Peer D, Sealey L, Holmes P, Gayle J, Speedie D, Potter G, Peschisolido P, Fenwick P, Fitzpatrick P, Quinn S, Foy D, Thomas M, Catlin R, Hiley S, Parris G

#	Date	Venue	Opponent	Result	Scorers	Att.
1	Aug 16	(h)	Notts C	W 1-0	Donowa	10,614
2	22	(a)	Cambridge U	W 3-0	Rennie 2, Donowa	5,015
3	30	(h)	Grimsby T	W 2-1	Gleghorn, Rowbotham	6,807
4	Sep 1	(h)	Southend U	W 2-0	Tait, Beckford	8,234
5	5	(a)	Portsmouth	L 0-4		12,152
6	12	(a)	Millwall	D 0-0		8,581
7	19	(a)	Luton T	D 1-1	Rowbotham	8,481
8	27	(h)	Wolves	L 0-4		14,391
9	Oct 3	(a)	Oxford U	D 0-0		7,096
10	10	(h)	Leicester C	L 0-2		13,443
11	17	(a)	Tranmere R	L 0-4		7,901
12	24	(h)	Bristol R	W 2-1	Matthewson, Frain (pen)	9,874
13	Nov 1	(a)	Charlton A	D 0-0		4,445
14	4	(h)	Newcastle U	L 2-3	Speedie, Potter	14,376
15	7	(a)	Bristol C	L 0-3		10,008
16	21	(a)	Barnsley	L 0-1		5,603
17	28	(a)	West Ham U	L 1-3	Rodgerson	15,004
18	Dec 5	(h)	Brentford	L 1-3	Frain	8,582
19	12	(a)	Derby C	L 1-3	Speedie	16,662
20	19	(h)	Watford	D 2-2	Peschisolido, Frain	7,182
21	Jan 9	(h)	Luton T	W 2-1	Frain (pen), Gayle	9,601
22	12	(a)	Swindon T	D 0-0		14,398
23	17	(a)	Wolves	L 1-2	Tait	13,560
24	22	(h)	Peterboro' U	W 2-0	Gayle, Frain (pen)	10,277
25	27	(a)	Southend U	L 0-4		4,065
26	30	(h)	Cambridge U	L 0-2		9,425
27	Feb 6	(a)	Notts C	L 1-3	Potter	8,550
28	9	(h)	Millwall	D 0-0		8,504
29	13	(a)	Portsmouth	L 2-3	Sturridge, Peschisolido	10,935
30	20	(h)	Grimsby T	D 1-1	Gayle	5,237
31	28	(a)	Leicester C	L 1-2	Matthewson	10,284
32	Mar 6	(h)	Oxford U	W 1-0	Peschisolido	11,104
33	9	(a)	Peterboro' U	L 1-2	Peschisolido	7,600
34	13	(a)	Bristol C	L 0-1		15,611
35	16	(h)	Sunderland	W 1-0	Peschisolido	10,934
36	20	(a)	Brentford	W 2-0	Peschisolido 2	7,532
37	23	(h)	Barnsley	W 3-0	Saville 2, Moulden	12,664
38	28	(a)	Newcastle U	D 2-2	Saville, Rodgerson	27,087
39	Apr 3	(h)	West Ham U	L 1-2	Saville	19,053
40	6	(h)	Derby C	D 1-1	Moulden	15,424
41	10	(a)	Sunderland	W 2-1	Moulden, Saville	16,382
42	12	(h)	Swindon T	L 4-6	Peer, Frain, Moulden, Saville	17,903
43	17	(a)	Watford	L 0-1		9,186
44	24	(h)	Tranmere R	D 0-0		14,600
45	May 1	(a)	Bristol R	D 3-3	Saville, Mardon, Smith	5,150
46	8	(h)	Charlton A	W 1-0	Moulden	22,234

FINAL LEAGUE POSITION: 19th in Division Two. Average home League attendance: 12,328.

Appearances: 21 25 45 15 14 18 18 28 9 11 15 24 16 3 3 10 40 13 12 12 17 10 16 16 3 7 1 3 5 8 7 13
Substitutes: 3 3 3 3 6 5 7 2 3 4 2 2 3 7 3
Goals: 1 2 2 1 1 2 1 2 2 1 3 2 2 7

P.Moulden played number-7 in Matches 34-46, was substituted in Matches 36 & 39 and scored 5 goals; D.Smith played number-11 in Matches 34-46 and scored 1 goal; R.Dryden played number-5 in Matches 36-46; A.Saville played number-9 in Matches 37-46 and scored 7 goals; R.Scott played number-2 in Match 40.   2 own-goals

FA Cup

#	Date	Venue	Opponent	Result	Att.
1	Nov 15	(a)	Reading	L 0-1	7,667

Appearances / Substitutes / Goals

League Cup

#	Date	Venue	Opponent	Result	Scorers	Att.
1	Aug 18	(a)	Exeter C	D 0-0		3,030
	25	(h)	Exeter C	L 1-4	Sale	5,175

Appearances: 2 2 2 1 2 2 2 2 2 2 1 1 1
Substitutes: 1 1
Goals: 1

1993-94

Manager: Terry Cooper until December then Barry Fry

No	Date		Opponent	Result	Scorers	Att
1	Aug	14 (a)	Charlton A	L 0-1		7,708
2		22 (h)	Wolves	D 2-2	Peschisolido, Saville	15,117
3		28 (a)	Barnsley	W 3-2	Smith 2, Shutt	7,241
4		31 (h)	Crystal P	L 2-4	Peschisolido 2	13,856
5	Sep	4 (h)	Derby C	W 3-0	Saville 2, Frain	14,582
6		12 (a)	Leicester C	D 1-1	Peschisolido	10,366
7		18 (h)	Grimsby T	D 1-1	Donowa	11,302
8		25 (h)	Luton T	D 1-1	Shutt	11,081
9	Oct	2 (a)	Middlesbrough	D 2-2	Peschisolido 2	13,801
10		9 (a)	Sunderland	L 0-1		19,265
11		16 (h)	Watford	W 1-0	Wallace	12,823
12		19 (h)	Bolton W	W 2-1	Shutt, Phillips (og)	12,071
13		23 (a)	Peterboro' U	L 0-1		7,575
14		31 (h)	Millwall	W 1-0	Shutt	9,377
15	Nov	2 (a)	Bristol C	L 0-3		9,192
16		6 (h)	Nottingham F	L 0-3		16,996
17		20 (h)	Portsmouth	L 0-1		11,896
18		27 (h)	Tranmere R	L 0-3		9,915
19	Dec	4 (a)	Nottingham F	L 0-1		22,061
20		11 (a)	Crystal P	L 1-2	Saville	11,295
21		18 (h)	Charlton A	W 1-0	Lowe	13,714
22		26 (a)	Stoke C	L 1-2	Peschisolido	16,584
23		28 (h)	West Brom A	W 2-0	Saville (pen), Peschisolido	28,228
24	Jan	1 (a)	Southend U	L 1-3	Peschisolido	10,729
25		3 (h)	Oxford U	D 1-1	Donowa	15,142
26		11 (a)	Notts C	L 1-2	Cooper	7,212
27		15 (a)	Watford	L 2-5	Willis, McGavin	7,636
28		22 (h)	Sunderland	D 0-0		15,884
29	Feb	5 (h)	Peterboro' U	D 0-0		15,140
30		12 (a)	Millwall	L 1-2	Saville	9,438
31		19 (h)	Notts C	L 2-3	Frain (pen), Saville	12,913
32		22 (a)	Wolves	L 0-3		24,931
33		25 (a)	Derby C	D 1-1	Claridge	16,624
34	Mar	5 (h)	Barnsley	L 0-2		15,382
35		12 (a)	Grimsby T	L 0-1		5,405
36		15 (h)	Leicester C	L 0-3		14,681
37		19 (a)	Luton T	D 1-1	Claridge	7,690
38		26 (h)	Middlesbrough	W 1-0	Saville	12,409
39		29 (a)	Oxford U	L 0-2		8,344
40	Apr	2 (h)	Stoke C	W 3-1	Claridge, Ward, Willis	13,568
41		9 (h)	Southend U	W 3-1	Doherty, Saville, Willis	14,307
42		16 (a)	Bristol C	D 2-2	Claridge (pen), Donowa	20,316
43		23 (a)	Portsmouth	W 2-0	Willis, Claridge (pen)	11,101
44		27 (a)	West Brom A	W 4-2	Claridge 2, Donowa, Saville	20,316
45		30 (a)	Bolton W	D 1-1	Willis	13,602
46	May	8 (a)	Tranmere R	W 2-1	Donowa, Garnett (og)	15,210

FINAL LEAGUE POSITION: 22nd in Division One. Average home League attendance: 14,378.

	Miller K	Hiley S	Frain J	Parris G	Dryden R	Downing K	Marsden P	Black S	Saville A	Smith D	McMinn E	Donowa L	Fenwick P	Whyte C	Peschisolido P	Moulden P	Shutt C	Tait P	Scott R	Hooper L	Wallace D	Jenkinson L	Harding P	Cooper G	Lowe K	Bennett I	Willis R	Daish L	Claridge S	McGavin S	De Souza M	Doherty N
Appearances	24	28	26	22	34	1	5	2	38	22	19	14	6	33	21	5	18	9	5	1	8	2	14	16	10	22	11	19	17	6	1	12
Substitutes			2				3			1	3	3	7	3		3	2	8	1	1	4	2	1	2	2	2		5		1	2	6	1
Goals			2						10	2		5			9		4				1		1	1	1		5		7	1		1

M.Ward played number-7 in Matches 38-46, scoring once; D.Rogers played number-3 in Match 42; G.Potter played number-3 in Matches 11-17 and was substituted in Match 16; T.Morgan played number-14 in Match 13; D.Barnett played number-4 in Matches 23, 24 & 32, number-6 in Matches 33 & 34, number-5 in Matches 40-42 and number-14 in Match 22 and was substituted in Match 34; P.Shearer played number-6 in Match 29 and number-4 in Match 30; R.Huxford played number-2 in Matches 32-36; J.Dominguez played number-11 in Matches 35-37 and number-14 in Matches 38 & 39 and was substituted in Match 37.

2 own-goals

FA Cup

No	Date		Opponent	Result	Scorers	Att
3	Jan	8 (h)	Kidderminster H	L 1-2	Harding	19,668

	Miller K	Frain J	Parris G	Saville A	Smith D	McMinn E	Donowa L	Peschisolido P	Harding P	Lowe K	Willis R	Daish L	Claridge S	McGavin S
Appearances	1	1	1	1	1	1	1	1	1	1	1	1	1	
Substitutes							1							1
Goals									1					

League Cup

No	Date		Opponent	Result	Scorers	Att
1	Aug	17 (h)	Plymouth A	W 3-0	Parris, Frain, Peschisolido	9,304
		24 (a)	Plymouth A	L 0-2		3,659
2	Sep	21 (h)	Aston Villa	L 0-1		27,815
	Oct	6 (a)	Aston Villa	L 0-1		35,856

	Miller K	Hiley S	Frain J	Parris G	Dryden R	Downing K	Marsden P	Saville A	Smith D	McMinn E	Donowa L	Fenwick P	Whyte C	Peschisolido P	Moulden P	Shutt C	Tait P	Scott R	Wallace D
Appearances	4	4	4	2	4	1	2	3	4	1	2	1	4	2	1	3	1		1
Substitutes							1			1	1	1					1		
Goals			1	1										1					

1994-95

Manager: Barry Fry

#	Date	Opponent	Result	Scorers	Att	Bennett I	Hiley S	Dryden R	Williams P	Ward M	Shearer C	Whyte C	Lowe K	Claridge S	Willis R	Robinson S	Donowa L	Frain J	Daish L	Harding J	Hendon J	Doherty N	Scott R	De Souza J	Tait P	Wallace D	Small B	Bodley M	Webb M	Bull G	Francis K	Poole K	Hunt J	McGavin S
1	Aug 13	(a) Leyton O	L 1-2	Claridge	7,578	1	2	3		4	5	6	7	8	9	10	11	12	14															
2	20	(h) Chester C	W 1-0	Donowa	12,188	1	2			4	5	6	7	8	9	11	12	3	6	10														
3	27	(a) Swansea C	W 2-0	Claridge 2	5,797	1	2			4	5	8		9		11	14	12	6	10				3	7									
4	30	(h) Wycombe W	L 0-1		14,305	1	2			4	5	8		9		14	9	11	6					3	7	10									
5	Sep 3	(h) Plymouth A	W 4-2	Regis 2, Wallace, Tait	13,202	1	2			4	5			12		14	9	12	6	7				3	10	11									
6	10	(a) Oxford U	D 1-1	Claridge	8,077	1				4									6	7				3	10	11	3								
7	13	(a) Rotherham U	D 1-1	Bull	3,799	1		4			5			12				9	6						10	11			6						
8	18	(h) Peterboro' U	W 4-0	Bull 2, Tait, Dominguez	10,800	1	6			4	5							9	14	3					10	11			9					2	7
9	24	(h) Hull C	D 2-2	Claridge (pen), Dominguez	12,192	1				4	5							12							10	12	3		9					2	7
10	Oct 1	(a) Wrexham	D 1-1	Claridge	6,002	1				4								11	6					14	10	12			9					2	7
11	8	(h) Huddersfield T	D 1-1	Bull	15,265	1				4	11					14		11	3	6					12				9					2	7
12	15	(a) Brighton & HA	W 1-0	Donowa	11,004	1				4	11							10	3	6					12				9					2	7
13	22	(h) Brentford	W 2-1	Shearer, Ward	7,779	1				4	11	3						12	3	6					12	10			9					2	7
14	29	(h) Bristol R	W 2-0	Bull, Claridge	15,886	1				4	11	3		8				10	3	6					12				9					2	14
15	Nov 1	(h) Crewe A	W 5-0	Hunt 3, Donowa, Claridge	14,212	1				4	11	3		8				10	3	6					14				9					2	14
16	5	(a) Shrewsbury T	W 2-0	Bull, Hunt	5,942	1				4	11	3	8					8	3	6									9					2	14
17	19	(h) Bournemouth	D 0-0		15,477	1				4	11	3						10	6						12				9					2	7
18	26	(a) Stockport C	W 1-0	Hunt	5,577	1				4	11							14	6		12				12				9					2	7
19	Dec 10	(a) Chester C	W 4-0	Daish, Claridge, McGavin, Lowe	3,946	1						3	14	8				10	6						14				9					2	9
20	17	(h) Leyton O	W 2-0	Donowa 2	20,022	1				4		3	14	8				10	6	11									9					2	9
21	26	(h) Cambridge U	D 1-1	Otto	20,098	1				4		3	14	8		7			6	11		7							9					2	9
22	28	(a) Cardiff C	W 1-0	Otto	7,420	1						3		8		7						9							9					2	
23	31	(h) Blackpool	W 7-1	Claridge 2, Donowa 2, Lowe, Parris, Bradshaw (og)	18,025	1				4		3	9	8					6						12	14			9					2	14
24	Jan 2	(a) Bradford C	D 1-1	Cooper	10,539	1				4		3	10	8					6			12			14				9					2	9
25	14	(a) York C	L 0-2		6,828	1				4		3	11	8		7			6	14		12			12				9					2	
26	Feb 4	(h) Stockport C	W 1-0	Dinning (og)	17,160	1				4		2				7			6						11				9					2	
27	11	(a) Crewe A	L 1-2	Donowa	6,359	1				4	14	3				7			6	12					11			6	9					2	
28	18	(h) York C	W 4-2	Francis 2, Otto, Shearer	14,846	1			10	4	11					7			6						11				9					2	8
29	21	(h) Oxford U	W 3-0	Francis, Claridge, Daish	19,781	1			10	4	11					7			6			14			11				9					2	8
30	25	(a) Peterboro' U	W 5-2	Francis 2, Shearer, Otto, Donowa	18,884	1			7	4	11					7			6			14		12	11				9					2	
31	Mar 4	(h) Hull C	D 0-0		9,845	1			8	4	11	6		8	14				6			4	9						9					2	
32	11	(h) Swansea C	L 0-1		16,191	1	2		14	4	11	3		7		7			6			11			7				9			14		2	9
33	18	(a) Wycombe W	W 3-0	Shearer, Claridge, Poole	7,289	1			10	4	11	3		8					6			6			12				9					2	
34	21	(h) Oxford U	W 3-0	Francis, Claridge, Daish	19,781																	14													
35	21	(a) Bournemouth	L 1-2	Francis	6,024	1			7	4	11	3		8		7			6			14		12	9				9					2	
36	25	(h) Wrexham	W 5-2	Francis 2, Shearer, Otto, Donowa	18,884	1			8	4	11	6	14	8					6						12				9					2	
37	29	(a) Bristol R	D 1-1	Claridge	8,010	1			14	4	11	3				7			6			12		7	11				9					2	
38	Apr 1	(h) Rotherham U	W 2-1	Francis, Shearer	16,077	1	2		14	4	11	3				7			6			12			11				9			14		2	7
39	4	(a) Blackpool	D 1-1	Claridge	4,944	1			10	4		3				7			6					4					9					2	7
40	11	(h) Shrewsbury T	D 1-1	Claridge 2	18,366	1	2		12	4	11					7			6			14			14				9					2	7
41	15	(a) Cardiff C	W 2-1	Tait, Ward (pen)	17,455	1			9	4		3		8					6						11				9					2	12
42	17	(a) Cambridge U	L 0-1		5,317	1	2		9	4		3		8				5							14				9			11		2	12
43	19	(h) Plymouth A	W 3-1	Claridge 2, Whyte	8,550	1			4			5						12	3										9					2	7
44	26	(h) Brentford	W 2-0	Francis, Daish	25,081	1				4	11	5				7			6						14				9					2	7
45	29	(a) Brighton & HA	D 3-3	Dominguez, Shearer, Ward	19,056	1	2		12	4	11	5				7		2	6						11					2				2	7
46	May 2	(h) Bradford C	D 0-0		25,139	1				4		5				7			6						11									2	7
47	6	(a) Huddersfield T	W 2-1	Claridge, Tait	18,775	1			10	4		8				7		9	6						12									2	7

FINAL LEAGUE POSITION: 1st in Division Two. Average home League attendance: 16,941.

	Bennett I	Hiley S	Dryden R	Williams P	Ward M	Shearer C	Whyte C	Lowe K	Claridge S	Willis R	Robinson S	Donowa L	Frain J	Daish L	Harding J	Hendon J	Doherty N	Scott R	De Souza J	Tait P	Wallace D	Small B	Bodley M	Webb M	Bull G	Francis K	Poole K	Hunt J	McGavin S
Appearances	46	9	3	8	41	20	31	4	41	1	5	21	4	37	9	3	6	4	18	34	4	3	3	10	15	34	18	10
Substitutes			3			3	7		3		1		5		9	2	18	1	4	2	12	3	3			6	8	1	5
Goals				3	7	1	2	20			9	2		3					4	11							6	8	1

D.Barnett played number-5 in Matches 10-35, 38-41, 43. **G.Cooper** played number-3 in Match 12, number-4 in Match 19, number-10 in Match 20 & 21, number-11 in Match 22 & 23, number-24-26, number-8 in Match number-27, number-3 in Match 28 & 29, number-8 in Match 30, number-3 in Match 33-36, 38-41, number-10 in Match 42, number-3 in Match 43-45, number-11 in Match 46. Goals 1. **D.Howell** played number-6 in Matches 21 & 22. **R.Otto** played number-11 in Matches 22 & 23, 25-29, number-12 in Match 30, number-10 in Matches 31 & 32, number-12 in Matches 33 & 34, number-10 in Matches 35-37, number-14 in Match 38, number-10 in Matches 39-41, number-14 in Match 42, number-10 in Matches 43-44, number-14 in Match 45. Sub appearances 6. Goals 4. **G.Parris** played number-12 in Match 23, number-11 in Match 24. Sub appearances 1. Goals 1.
2 own-goals

FA Cup

#	Date	Opponent	Result	Scorers	Att	Bennett I	Whyte C	Poole K	Barnett D	Ward M	Shearer C	Hunt J	McGavin S	Claridge S	Donowa L	Daish L	Tait P	De Souza J	Shearer P	Lowe K	Dominguez J	Cooper G	Otto R	Doherty N	Frain J
1	Nov 12	(a*) Slough Town	W 4-0	Shearer 2, McGavin 2	13,394	1	2	3	4	5	6	7	8	9	10	11	12	14							
2	Dec 12	(h) Scunthorpe U	D 0-0		13,832	1	2	3	4	5	6		9	7		11	12	14							
R	14	(a) Scunthorpe U	W 2-1	McGavin, Cooper	6,280	1	2	3	4	5	6		9	7		11		11		10	4	12			
3	Jan 7	(h) Liverpool	D 0-0		25,326	1	2	3	4	5	6		8	7		11		9	7	11		10			
R	18	(a) Liverpool	D 1-1†	Otto	36,275	1	2		4	5	6	8	14	7		11	3	9	12	11		3	10	3	

	Bennett I	Whyte C	Poole K	Barnett D	Ward M	Shearer C	Hunt J	McGavin S	Claridge S	Donowa L	Daish L	Tait P	De Souza J	Shearer P	Lowe K	Dominguez J	Cooper G	Otto R	Doherty N	Frain J
Appearances	5	5	3	5	5	5	1	5	5		5	2	5	2	2	2	3	1	1	1
Substitutes								1				1	1	1			1			1
Goals						2		2					1				1	1		

*Played at St Andrew's, Birmingham.
†After extra-time. Liverpool won 2-0 on penalties.

League Cup

#	Date	Opponent	Result	Scorers	Att	Bennett I	Hiley S	Scott R	Whyte C	Shearer P	Ward M	Claridge S	Donowa L	Daish L	Harding P	Lowe K	Dominguez J	Ward M	Saville A	De Souza J	Doherty N	Dryden R	Frain J	Tait P	Wallace D	McGavin S	Cooper G	Bass J	Barrett D	Moulden P
1	Aug 16	(a) Shrewsbury T	L 1-2	Daish	5,049	1	2	3	4	5	6	7	8	9	10	11	12	14												
R	23	(h) Shrewsbury T	W 2-0	Saville, Claridge (pen)	9,847	1	2	3	4	5	6	11	8		10			4	9	7				5	3	10	11	14	9	
2	Sep 20	(a) Blackburn R	L 0-2		14,517	1	2	6	4	7	8				7	11	8		5	12	4		7	11		5	3	10	11	14
R	Oct 4	(h) Blackburn R	D 1-1	McGavin	16,275	1	2		8	6	11				7	10	4			12	9					3	12	9	2	5	14

	Bennett I	Hiley S	Scott R	Whyte C	Shearer P	Ward M	Claridge S	Donowa L	Daish L	Harding P	Lowe K	Dominguez J	Ward M	Saville A	De Souza J	Doherty N	Dryden R	Frain J	Tait P	Wallace D	McGavin S	Cooper G	Bass J	Barrett D	Moulden P
Appearances	4	2	3	4	3	4	2	1	2	3	2	3	1	1	1	2	1	1	2	1	2	5	1	1	
Substitutes												1	2		1										
Goals							1		1					1							1				

Blues' Pre-League FA Cup Record

1881-82

No	Date	V	Opponent	Result	Scorers	Att
1	Oct 17	(h)	Derby Town	W 4-1	Slater 2, Hards, A.James	1,000
2	Dec 3	(a)	Wednesbury OAL	0-6		3,000

	Bodenham J	Gessey S	Summers L	James T	Teychenne V	James F	Hards W	Rotherham W	James A	Whitehead J	Slater W	Tatton J
1	1	2	3	4	5	6	7	8	9	10	11	
2	1	2	3	4	9	6	7	8		10	11	5
Appearances	2	2	2	2	2	2	2	2	1	2	2	1
Goals							1		1		2	

1882-83

No	Date	V	Opponent	Result	Scorers	Att
Pr1			Bye			
1	Nov 11	(h)	Stafford Rd Wks	D 3-3	Slater 2, T.James	2,000
R	18	(a)	Stafford Rd Wks	L 2-6	Stanley, Hards	1,000

	Gessey S	James T	James F	Hards W	Slater W	Vale A	Elliman R	Morgan T	Jones W	Stanley AE	Green E	Kingston E	Bailey E	Taylor J
1	3	5	7		11	1	2	4	6	8	9	10		
R	4	7	6		11	1		5	9	8	10		2	3
Appearances	2	1	2	1	2	2	1	2	2	2	2	1	1	1
Goals		1		1	2					1				

1883-84

No	Date	V	Opponent	Result	Scorers	Att
1	Oct 20	(h)	Birmingham Ex	D 1-1	A.James	1,500
R	Nov 11	(n*)	Birmingham Ex	L 2-3	A.James, Stanley	2,000

*Played at Aston Lower Grounds.

	Bodenham J	Gessey S	James T	Teychenne V	James F	James A	Vale A	Stanley AE	Green E	Hedges T	Clayton H	Clarke E
1	5	6	4		7	11	2	9	8	3	1	10
R	5	6	4	11	7		2	8	9	3	1	10
Appearances	2	2	2	1	2	1	2	2	2	2	2	2
Goals						2		1				

1884-85

No	Date	V	Opponent	Result	Scorers	Att
1	Nov 8	(a)	Birmingham Ex	L 0-2		2,000

	Summers L	James F	James A	Vale A	Stanley AE	Clarke E	Hare J	Felton W	Morris H	Simms C	Willetts W
1	4	6	7	2	10	1	3	5	8	9	11
Appearances	1	1	1	1	1	1	1	1	1	1	1
Goals											

1885-86

No	Date	V	Opponent	Result	Scorers	Att
1	Oct 31	(h)	Burton	W 9-2	Stanley 4, Davenport 2, Evetts, A.James, Morris	1,000
2	Nov 14	(h)	Darwen	W 3-1	Felton, Morris, Stanley	2,000
3	Dec 12	(h)	Derby C	W 4-2	Hill, Stanley 2, Davenport	3,000
4			Bye			
5	Jan 16	(h)	Davenham	W 2-1	Figures, Davenport	6,000
6	Feb 13	(h)	Redcar	W 2-0	Davenport 2	6,000
SF	Mar 6	(n*)	West Brom A	L 0-4		4,100

*Played at Aston Lower Grounds.

	Hedges T	Jones W	Evetts R	James F	Simms C	Felton W	James A	Davenport T	Stanley AE	Figures W	Morris H	Hare J	Hill E
1	1	2	3	4	5	6	7	8	9	10	11		
2	1		3	4	5	6		8	9	11	7	2	10
3	1		3	4	5	6		8	9	11	7	2	10
5	1		3	4	5	6		8	9	11	7	2	10
6	1		3	4	5	6		8	9	11	7	2	10
SF	1		3	4	5	6		8	9	11	7	2	10
Appearances	6	1	6	6	6	6	1	6	6	6	6	5	5
Goals			1			1	1	6	7	1	2		1

1886-87

No	Date	V	Opponent	Result	Scorers	Att
1	Oct 30	(a)	Mitchell's St G	L 1-3	Price	5,000

	Evetts R	Stanley AE	Figures W	Morris H	Hare J	Hill E	Charsley C	Lovesey J	Price J	Barlow F	Stanley W
1	5	9	11	7	2	10	1	3	4	6	8
Appearances	1	1	1	1	1	1	1	1	1	1	1
Goals									1		

1887-88

No	Date	V	Opponent	Result	Scorers	Att
1	Oct 15	(h)	Aston Unity	W 6-1	Smith 2, Figures, W.Dixon 2, Stanley	2,000
2	Nov 5	(h)	Aston Villa	L 0-4		12,000

	Jones W	Simms C	Davenport T	Stanley AE	Figures W	Morris H	Hill E	Barlow F	Dixon G	Dixon W	Adams R	Smith A	Farley W
1	2		10	11	6	5	1	3	4	7	8	9	
2	2	5	10	11	6		1	3		7	8	9	4
Appearances	2	1	2	2	2	1	2	2	1	2	2	2	1
Goals				1	1					2		2	

1888-89

No	Date	V	Opponent	Result	Scorers	Att
Pr1			Bye			
Pr2	Oct 27	(h)	Burslem PV	W 3-2	Watson 2, Hill	2,000
Pr3	Nov 17	(h)	Leek	W 4-0	Hill, Jenkyns, Devey, Stanley	3,000
Pr4	Dec 8	(h)	Burton W	W 9-0	E.Devey 4, W.Devey 4, Short	2,000
1	Feb 2	(h)	West Brom A	L 2-3	Hill 2	3,034

	Charsley C	Morris A	Speller F	Morris H	Jenkyns C	Simms C	Short G	Stanley AE	Devey W	Hill E	Watson T	Devey E
Pr2	1	2	3	4	5	6	7	8	9	10	11	
Pr3	1	2	3	4	5	6	7	8	9	10	11	
Pr4	1	2	3	4	5	6	7	8	9	10		11
1	1	2	3	4	5		7	8	9	11	10	6
Appearances	4	4	4	4	4	3	4	4	4	4	3	2
Goals					1		1	1	5	4	2	4

Blues in Wartime

BIRMINGHAM did not play competitive soccer in the first wartime season of 1915-16, but they took part in 106 competitive matches in the period 1916 to 1919, appearing in the Midland Section's Principal and Subsidiary Tournaments. Attendances were good throughout the wartime period and in 1917-18, the Blues averaged 13,000 for each home game, with a wartime best of 26,000 for the visit of Leeds City in November 1917.

Like most clubs they called upon guest players and these included Pearson, Pennington, Bowser, Jephcott and Richardson (all West Brom) and Hampton, Edgley, Wallace and Weston (Aston Villa). Wolves helped out with players like Arthur and Sammy Brooks and Peers. Other famous names to turn out included Charlie Buchan of Sunderland. The Blues' best season was 1918-19, when they won the Subsidiary Tournament and finished runners-up to Nottingham Forest in the Principal Tournament.

After three games of the 1939-40 Football League season, the game was again severely disrupted by war. Once the Government's ban on soccer was lifted, Birmingham's secretary-manager Bill Camkin arranged some attractive friendly matches before regional competition again became the order of the day.

The Blues finished third in the Football League Midland Section in 1939-40, despite having to play all their games away from St Andrew's from October to March, when the ground as closed because of the dangers of air-raids.

These were difficult times for all clubs and Birmingham were no exception. Travelling home from Luton, their team coach crashed into a traffic-island during the black-out, though thankfully, no one was injured. Walsall provided the opposition when St Andrew's reopened on 23 March 1940 and a crowd of 12,000 saw the Blues win 2-1.

In 1940-41, the Blues competed in the Football League South but were able to manage only 16 games, due to bomb damage at St Andrew's. The 1941 close season saw further enemy action and the club announced that they would be able to stage matches only at the beginning and end of the 1941-42 season, when the weather was likely to be at its best. Reluctantly, Birmingham decided to play only friendly games that season.

On 21 January 1942 came the now well-known accident when a fireman threw what he thought was water on to a brazier. The bucket contained petrol and the Main Stand went up in flames. With it perished the club's entire records and playing kit. In 1942-43, playing all their home games at Villa Park, the Blues managed to compete in the Football League North. The following season they returned to St Andrew's, which was still in a dreadful state. Players changed in local factory premises and spectators braved the elements, for there was no covered accommodation to speak of.

Repair work was carried out in the summer of 1944 and throughout the next two seasons. The Blues, meanwhile, soldiered on in the regional competition and in June 1945, just after the end of the war in Europe, Birmingham appointed Harry Storer as manager.

The 1945-46 season saw brighter days for the club which was now known as Birmingham City, City was added in 1944. The Blues won the Football League South championship and reached the FA Cup semi-finals before losing to Derby in a replay. They produced some quite scintillating football in this last season under wartime conditions and many Blues fans today harbour special memories of those times.

Wartime Record 1916-19

	P	W	D	L	F	A
1916-17	36	17	11	8	73	50
1917-18	34	15	8	11	65	49
1918-19	36	25	1	10	85	43
Total	106	57	20	29	221	142

Top Appearances

F.Womack	92
J.Whitehouse	87
W.Ball	84
A.Gardner	68
E.Edwards	50
A.McClure	48
S.Bowser	42
A.Smith	40
J.Roulson	34
J.Wootton	31
W.Walker	31

Top Goalscorers

J.Whitehouse	48
J.Godfrey	27
W.Walker	17
S.Stevens	12
T.Butler	12
S.Bowser	9

Wartime Record 1939-46

	P	W	D	L	F	A
1939-40	37	18	7	12	76	76
1940-41	18	7	2	9	43	49
1941-42	Did not compete in any competition					
1942-43	38	17	4	17	59	59
1943-44	38	20	9	9	86	50
1944-45	42	17	12	13	68	56
1945-46 (League)	42	28	5	9	96	45
1945-46 (FA Cup)	10	4	4	2	19	10
Total	225	111	43	71	447	345

Top Appearances

A.Turner	186
D.Jennings	174
G.Merrick	172
D.Dearson	166
A.Mulraney	118
R.Shaw	111
F.Harris	104
C.Trigg	95
H.Bodle	83
C.W.Jones	75
F.Mitchell	70
G.R.Edwards	58
W.Hughes	55
R.L.Bright	46
E.Duckhouse	45

Top Goalscorers

C.Trigg	88
C.W.Jones	45
A.Mulraney	41
H.Bodle	35
D.Dearson	25
D.Massart	18
G.R.Edwards	17
R.L.Bright	14
N.Dougall	13
J.Acquaroff	10

1916-17

			1	2	3	4	5	6	7	8	9	10	11
1 Sep 2 (h) Huddersfield T	W 2-1	Roulson (pen), Whitehouse	Hauser	Ball	Womack	Roulson	McClure	Edwards	Wallace	Mercer	Walker	Whitehouse	Morgan
2 9 (a) Lincoln C	L 2-3	Roulson (pen), Morgan	..	..	..	..	..	..	..	..	..	..	..
3 16 (h) Sheffield W	W 4-1	Whitehouse 2, Freeman, Wallace	..	..	..	Gardner	..	..	..	..	Freeman	..	..
4 23 (a) Bradford	W 3-2	Montgomery, Whitehouse, Jephcott	..	..	..	Roulson	..	..	Jephcott	..	Montgomery	..	..
5 30 (a) Chesterfield T	W 3-0	Montgomery, Mercer, Roulson (pen)	Anstey	..	..	..	..	..	..	..	..	..	..
6 Oct 7 (h) Hull C	W 4-2	Walker 2, Ball (pen), Whitehouse	Pearson	..	..	Gardner	..	..	..	..	..	..	S.Brooks
7 14 (a) Nottingham F	W 4-0	Lowe (og), Jephcott, Mercer, Whitehouse	..	..	..	Roulson	..	..	..	..	..	..	..
8 21 (h) Barnsley	W 2-0	Morgan, Rounds (og)	..	..	..	Gardner	..	..	..	..	..	..	..
9 28 (a) Leeds C	D 1-1	Hopkins	..	..	..	..	..	..	..	..	Hopkins	..	..
10 Nov 4 (h) Sheffield U	W 5-0	Whitehouse 3, Montgomery, Mercer	..	..	..	..	..	..	..	..	Montgomery	..	..
11 11 (a) Bradford C	D 1-1	Whitehouse	..	..	..	..	..	..	..	Wild	..	..	Middlemiss
12 18 (h) Leicester F	W 2-1	S.Brooks, Gardner	..	..	..	McCourty	..	..	..	Gardner	..	..	S.Brooks
13 25 (a) Grimsby T	L 0-3		Anstey	..	..	Gardner	..	..	..	Hooton	..	..	Best
14 Dec 2 (h) Notts C	W 4-0	Whitehouse 2, S.Brooks, Montgomery	..	..	..	..	..	..	..	Montgomery	Hampton	..	S.Brooks
15 9 (a) Huddersfield T	L 1-2	Jephcott	Pearson	..	..	Roulson	..	..	..	Turner	Hopkins	..	Best
16 23 (a) Sheffield W	W 2-0	Whitehouse, Edwards	..	..	..	..	..	..	..	..	Griffiths	..	Best
17 25 (a) Rotherham C	L 2-8	Turner 2	Yarnall	..	..	..	..	..	Smith	..	..	..	..
18 26 (h) Rotherham C	L 1-3	Turner	Pearson	..	Roulson	Gardner	..	..	..	..	..	..	..
19 30 (h) Bradford	L 1-2	Bell	..	..	Womack	Brooks	..	..	Jephcott	..	Bell	..	..
20 Jan 6 (h) Chesterfield T	D 2-2	Arrowsmith (og), Whitehouse (pen)	..	..	..	..	..	..	Smith	..	Freeman	..	S.Brooks
21 13 (a) Hull C	W 1-0	Montgomery	Peers	..	..	Roulson	..	..	..	..	Montgomery	..	Edgley
22 20 (h) Nottingham F	W 1-0	Buckley	..	..	..	..	..	..	..	Mercer	Buckley	..	..
23 27 (a) Barnsley	L 1-2	Bell	..	..	..	..	Bowser	A.Brooks	..	Turner	Bell	..	..
24 Feb 3 (h) Leeds C	D 1-1	Edwards	..	..	Weston	Gardner	..	Edwards	Jephcott	..	..	..	..
25 10 (a) Sheffield U	D 0-0		..	Gardner	Womack	Charles	..	Brelsford	Barratt	Dobson	..	..	..
26 17 (h) Bradford C	D 1-1	Whitehouse	Pearson	Ball	..	Gardner	McClure	Edwards	Gibson	Bowser	..	..	..
27 24 (h) Leicester F	D 1-1	Turner	Peers	Gardner	..	Bowser	Newman	..	Smith	Turner	Hubbard	..	..
28 Mar 3 (h) Grimsby T	W 3-0	Bowser 2, Whitehouse	..	Ball	..	Gardner	McClure	..	Jephcott	Bowser	Duncan	..	Best
29 10 (a) Notts C	D 1-1	Whitehouse	..	..	..	..	Foxall	Newman	..	..	Bell	..	..
30 Apr 28 (h) Lincoln C	D 0-0		Westwood	..	..	..	McClure	Edwards	Smith	Bell	Montgomery	..	Wooton

FINAL LEAGUE POSITION: 3rd in Midland Section: Principal Competition

Midland Section: Subsidiary Competition

31 Mar24 (a) Leicester F	W 5-1	Bowser, Moore, Bell, McClure, Whitehouse	Peers	Ball	Womack	Bowser	McClure	Edwards	Smith	Moore	Bell	Whitehouse	Wootton
32 31 (h) Notts C	D 1-1	Edwards	..	..	..	..	..	..	..	..	Whent	Clarke	..
33 Apr 6 (a) Nottingham F	D 3-3	Bowser 2, Montgomery	..	..	..	Osborne	..	..	..	Bowser	Montgomery	Whitehouse	Best
34 9 (h) Nottingham F	W 4-3	Whitehouse 3, Bell	Lindon	..	..	Gardner	..	..	..	..	Bell	..	..
35 14 (a) Leicester F	L 2-4	Whitehouse, Bell	Peers	..	..	Osborne	..	..	..	..	..	..	..
36 21 (a) Notts C	W 2-0	Crowe, Whitehouse	Westwood	..	..	Gardner	..	..	..	Whitehouse	Bowser	Crowe	Wooton

Appearances: Anstey B.* 3, Ball W. 34, Barratt J. 1, Bell J.* 10, Best E. 10, Bowser S.* 13, Brelsford W.* 1, Brooks A.* 3, Brooks S.* 9, Buckley C.* 1, Charles W. 1, Dobson H.* 1, Clarke W. 1, Crowe F. 1, Duncan C. 1, Edgley H.* 7, Edwards E. 33, Foxall H. 1, Freeman B.* 2, Gardner A. 19, Gibson R. 1, Griffiths J. 3, Hampton H.* 1, Hauser S. 4, Hooton W. 1, Hopkins J.* 2, Hubbard J. 1, Jephcott C. 17, Lindon A.* 1, McClure A. 31, McCourty W. 1, Mercer A. 11, Middlemiss H.* 1, Montgomery H.* 13, Moore T. 1, Morgan W. 5, Newman A. 2, Osborne A.* 2, Pearson H. 13, Peers E.* 12, Roulson J. 12, Smith A. 14, Turner A. 10, Walker W. 2, Wallace C.* 3, Weston T.* 1, Westwood R. 2, Whent G. 1, Whitehouse J. 35, Wild G. 1, Womack F. 34, Wootton J.* 4, Yarnall G. 1.
Total: 396.

Goalscorers: Ball W. 1, Bell J. 5, Bowser S. 5, Brooks S. 2, Buckley C. 1, Crowe F. 1, Edwards E. 3, Freeman B. 1, Gardner A. 1, Hopkins J. 1, Jephcott C. 3, McClure A. 1, Mercer A. 3, Montgomery H. 6, Moore T. 1, Morgan W. 2, Roulson J. 3, Turner A. 4, Walker W. 2, Wallace C. 1, Whitehouse J. 23, Opponents own-goal 3.
Total: 73.

*Denotes guest players

1915-16

No official first-team matches played during this season.

1917-18

		1	2	3	4	5	6	7	8	9	10	11
1 Sep 1 (h) Hull C	W 2-1 Montgomery, Whitehouse	Lindon	Ball	Womack	Gardner	Bowser	Edwards	Jephcott	Bell	Montgomery	Whitehouse	Wootton
2　8 (a) Hull C	W 2-1 Montgomery, Boxley	..	..	..	..	..	Barton	..	Whitehouse	..	Boxley	..
3　29 (h) Barnsley	W 3-1 Stevens 2, Butler	..	..	..	..	..	Edwards	..	..	Stevens	Butler	Best
4 Oct 6 (a) Barnsley	D 3-3 Boxley 2, Jephcott	..	..	..	Roulson	..	Newman	..	..	Boxley	..	..
5　13 (a) Bradford	L 0-1	..	Barton	..	..	..	Edwards	..	..	..	..	Wootton
6　20 (h) Bradford	W 2-0 Wootton, Whitehouse	..	Ball	..	Gardner	..	..	..	..	Stevens	..	..
7　27 (a) Sheffield U	L 1-3 Bowser	..	..	..	Roulson	..	..	..	..	..	..	..
8 Nov 3 (h) Sheffield U	W 4-1 Stevens 2, Whitehouse, Wootton	..	..	..	Gardner	..	..	..	..	..	..	..
9　10 (a) Leeds C	L 0-1	..	..	..	Roulson	..	Barton	..	..	Sambrooke	..	Sheldon
10　17 (h) Leeds C	W 3-1 Mercer, Stevens 2	..	..	..	Gardner	..	Edwards	..	Mercer	Stevens	Whitehouse	Wootton
11　24 (a) Nottingham F	L 1-2 Boxley	..	..	..	..	..	..	Smith	Whitehouse	Boxley	Butler	..
12 Dec 1 (h) Nottingham F	D 1-1 Butler	..	..	..	..	..	..	Jephcott	Boxley	Stevens	..	..
13　8 (h) Grimsby T	L 0-1	..	Gardner	..	Evans	..	..	Wallace	..	..	..	..
14　15 (a) Grimsby T	D 2-2 Richardson, Stevens	..	Crump	..	Gardner	Robinson	Barton	Smith	Richardson	..	..	..
15　22 (h) Bradford C	W 2-1 McClure, Bowser	..	Pennington	..	..	McClure	Crowe	..	Bowser	..	Whitehouse	..
16　25 (h) Leicester F	D 0-0	..	Wilson	..	..	..	Edwards	Jephcott	Mercer	..	..	Sheldon
17　26 (a) Leicester F	L 0-3	..	..	..	Evans	..	Crowe	Smith	..	..	..	Wootton
18　29 (a) Bradford C	W 3-0 Morgan 2, Stevens	..	Newman	..	Gardner	Bowser	..	..	Whitehouse	..	Morgan	Scorgie
19 Jan 5 (a) Notts C	D 3-3 Shea, Roulson, Butler	..	Wilson	..	Roulson	..	..	..	Shea	Johnson	Butler	Wootton
20　12 (h) Notts C	W 7-2 Stevens 3, Smith, Butler, Whitehouse, Wootton	..	Ball	..	Gardner	..	Edwards	..	Whitehouse	Stevens	..	..
21　19 (a) Huddersfield T	L 2-4 Whitehouse 2	..	..	..	Roulson	Hawley	..	..	..	Montgomery	..	..
22　26 (h) Huddersfield T	W 2-1 Butler 2	..	..	..	Gardner	..	Hunter	..	..	Stevens	..	..
23 Feb 2 (h) Sheffield W	W 4-1 Smith, Butler 2, Stevens	..	..	..	..	Bowser	Edwards	..	Butler	..	Elkes	..
24　9 (a) Sheffield W	W 2-0 Bowser, Whitehouse	..	Wilson	..	Roulson	Hunter	Crowe	..	Bowser	Bell	Whitehouse	..
25　16 (h) Rotherham C	W 2-0 Bell, Whitehouse	..	Ball	Pennington	Gardner	Bowser	Hunter	..	Whitehouse	..	Butler	..
26　23 (a) Rotherham C	L 0-1	Cooper	Wilson	Womack	Roulson	Hunter	Crowe	Gibson	Bowser	Johnson	..	..
27 Mar 2 (h) Lincoln C	W 5-0 Butler 2, Gibson 2, Bell	Whitehouse	Ball	..	Gardner	Bowser	Hunter	Smith	Gibson	Bell	..	..
28　9 (a) Lincoln C	D 3-3 Smith, Lees, Bell	Beard	White	Wilson	..	..	..	..	Butler	..	Lees	..

FINAL LEAGUE POSITION: 3rd in Midland Section: Principal Competition.

Subsidiary Competition

		1	2	3	4	5	6	7	8	9	10	11
29 Mar16 (h) Nottingham F	D 0-0	Cooper	Ball	White	Gardner	Bowser	Hunter	Smith	Butler	Bell	Elkes	Wootton
30　23 (a) Nottingham F	L 0-1	..	Wilson	..	..	..	Harper	..	Elkes	..	Butler	..
31　30 (a) Notts C	L 1-5 Tinsley	..	Whitehouse	..	Roulson	..	Edwards	..	Butler	..	Tinsley	..
32 Apr 6 (h) Notts C	W 3-2 Bowser, Wootton, Butler	..	Ball	Williams	Gardner	..	Hunter	..	Whitehouse	..	Butler	..
33　13 (a) Leicester F	D 1-1 Butler	..	Wilson	Womack	Crowe	..	Harper	..	Short	..	..	Barnes
34　20 (h) Leicester F	W 1-0 Godfrey	B.Godfrey	Ball	..	Gardner	..	Bell	..	Howell	J.Godfrey	..	Davies

Appearances: Ball W. 20, Baines A. 1, Barton P. 4, Beard J. 1, Bell J.* 11, Best E. 2, Bowser S.* 29, Boxley D. 6, Butler T. 26, Cooper A.* 6, Crowe F. 7, Crump A. 1, Davies G. 1, Edwards E. 15, Elkes J. 3, Evans T. 2, Gardner A. 23, Gibson R. 2, Godfrey B. 1, Godfrey J. 1, Harper J. 2, Hawley F.* 2, Howell H.* 1, Hunter G.* 8, Jephcott H.* 12, Johnson H.* 2, Lees J.* 1, Lindon A. 25, McClure A. 3, Mercer A.* 3, Morgan W. 1, Montgomery H.* 3, Newman A. 2, Pennington J.* 2, Richardson S.* 1, Robinson A. 1, Roulson J. 9, Sambrooke C. 1, Scorgie J. 1, Shea D.* 1, Sheldon A. 2, Short J. 1, Smith A. 20, Stevens S.* 15, Tinsley R.* 1, Wallace C.* 1, Whitehouse J. 23, White T. 4, Williams W. 1, Wilson A.* 8, Womack F. 28, Wootton J. 27. Total: 374.

Goalscorers: Bell J. 3, Bowser S. 4, Boxley D. 4, Butler T. 12, Gibson R. 2, Godfrey J. 1, Jephcott C. 1, Lees J. 1, McClure A. 1, Mercer A. 1, Morgan W. 2, Montgomery H. 2, Richardson S. 1, Roulson J. 1, Shea D. 1, Smith A. 3, Stevens S. 12, Tinsley R. 1, Whitehouse J. 8, Wootton J. 4. Total: 65.

*Denotes guest players.

1918-19

#	Date/Opponent	Result	1	2	3	4	5	6	7	8	9	10	11
1	Sep 7 (a) Nottingham F	L 0-1	Cooper	Jones	Womack	Gardner	Hawley	Osborne	A.Smith	Walker	J.Godfrey	Whitehouse	Davies
2	14 (h) Nottingham F	L 2-3 Whitehouse, Walker	..	Ball	Pennington	..	..	Edwards	..	..	..	..	..
3	21 (a) Leeds C	L 1-3 J.Godfrey	..	Jones	Womack	..	..	Hunter	..	Buchan	..	..	..
4	28 (h) Leeds C	W 4-2 J.Godfrey 2, Davies, Whitehouse	B.Godfrey	Ball	..	..	..	..	..	Walker	..	..	..
5	Oct 5 (a) Sheffield U	W 3-1 J.Godfrey 3	..	Jones	..	..	..	Crowe	Hill	..	..	..	..
6	12 (h) Sheffield U	W 4-1 Brown 3, Walker	..	Ball	..	..	..	..	A.Smith	..	Brown	..	..
7	19 (h) Bradford	W 2-0 Hawley, Walker	Cooper	..	..	..	..	Hunter	..	..	..	..	..
8	26 (a) Bradford	D 1-1 J.Godfrey	..	Jones	..	..	..	Harper	Newman	..	J.Godfrey	Bennett	Scorgie
9	Nov 2 (h) Hull C	W 5-1 J.Godfrey 2, Whitehouse, Walker 2	..	Ball	..	..	..	Crowe	Brown	..	..	Whitehouse	Sheldon
10	9 (a) Hull C	W 3-0 Brown 2, Whitehouse	..	Jones	..	..	..	Kay	..	..	..	..	Scorgie
11	16 (h) Coventry C	W 3-1 Walker 2, J.Godfrey	Robb	Ball	..	..	..	Hunter	..	..	..	..	Davies
12	23 (a) Coventry C	W 3-1 Whitehouse, J.Godfrey, Davies	Cooper	..	..	..	..	Edwards	Davies	..	..	..	Morgan
13	30 (h) Barnsley	W 7-0 J.Godfrey 3, Whitehouse, Walker 2, Hunter	..	..	..	..	..	Hunter	..	..	..	..	..
14	Dec 7 (a) Barnsley	L 1-2 Morgan	..	..	..	..	..	Kay	..	..	..	..	..
15	14 (a) Rotherham C	W 2-0 J.Godfrey, Whitehouse	..	..	Milsom	..	..	..	..	..	..	..	..
16	21 (h) Rotherham C	W 2-0 Whitehouse, Walker	..	..	Womack	..	..	..	..	..	..	..	..
17	25 (h) Leicester F	L 0-2	..	..	..	..	..	..	..	..	..	..	..
18	26 (a) Leicester F	W 4-0 Whitehouse 2, J.Godfrey 2	..	..	..	..	..	..	..	..	..	..	..
19	29 (a) Bradford C	W 3-2 Whitehouse, Morgan, J.Godfrey	B.Godfrey	..	..	Roulson	Crowe	MacKenzie	..	..	..	..	..
20	Jan 4 (h) Bradford C	W 5-1 J.Godfrey 3, Walker, Whitehouse	..	..	..	Gardner	McClure	Roulson	..	..	..	..	..
21	11 (h) Notts C	L 0-7	Cooper	..	..	..	Hawley	Crowe	..	..	..	..	..
22	18 (a) Notts C	L 0-2	B.Godfrey	..	..	Roulson	..	Barton	..	..	..	..	..
23	25 (h) Huddersfield T	W 1-0 Davies	Robb	..	..	Gardner	Hunter	..	..	..	..	..	..
24	Feb 2 (h) Huddersfield T	L 0-1	B.Godfrey	..	..	Roulson	McClure	..	..	..	Gillott	..	..
25	8 (a) Sheffield W	W 1-0 Walker	..	..	..	..	..	..	..	..	J.Godfrey	..	..
26	15 (h) Sheffield W	W 4-2 A.W.Smith, Whitehouse 2, Davies	..	..	..	Hunter	..	..	Gibson	..	A.W.Smith	..	Davies
27	22 (a) Grimsby T	W 4-1 J.Godfrey 2, Davies, Walker	..	..	Wilson	..	..	Roulson	..	..	J.Godfrey	..	..
28	Mar 1 (h) Grimsby T	W 4-0 Whitehouse 2, A.W.Smith 2	..	..	Womack	Roulson	..	Hunter	..	Whitehouse	A.W.Smith	Morgan	..
29	8 (a) Lincoln C	L 0-1	..	..	White	..	..	..	..	..	J.Godfrey	..	..
30	15 (h) Lincoln C	W 3-0 Short, McClure, Whitehouse	..	..	..	Gardner	..	..	..	Short	Duncan	Whitehouse	..

FINAL LEAGUE POSITION: 2nd in Midland Section: Principal Competition

Subsidiary Competition

#	Date/Opponent	Result	1	2	3	4	5	6	7	8	9	10	11
31	Mar 22 (a) Nottingham F	W 3-1 Hunter, Short, Gibson	B.Godfrey	Ball	Womack	Roulson	McClure	Hunter	Gibson	Short	Walker	Elkes	Morgan
32	29 (h) Nottingham F	W 1-0 Walker	..	..	..	..	..	..	..	Walker	Johnson	Butler	Scorgie
33	Apr 5 (h) Notts C	L 0-3	..	..	White	Gardner	..	Sheldon	..	Short	J.Godfrey	Elkes	Morgan
34	12 (a) Notts C	W 2-1 Gardner, Elkes	..	..	Womack	..	..	Roulson	..	Walker	..	..	..
35	19 (h) Leicester F	W 3-0 Short, Walker, Morgan	Tremelling	Wilson	..	..	..	..	..	Short	..	Walker	..
36	26 (a) Leicester F	W 4-2 Crowe, J.Godfrey 3	..	Ball	..	..	..	..	..	..	..	Crowe	..

Appearances: Ball W. 30, Barton P. 5, Bennett R. 1, Brown D.* 5, Buchan C.* 2, Butler T. 1, Cooper A.* 15, Crowe F. 6, Davies G. 27,. Duncan C. 1, Edwards E. 2, Elkes J. 3, Gardner A. 26, Gibson R. 11, Gillott F. 1, Godfrey B. 17, Godfrey J. 28, Harper J.* 1, Hawley F.* 21, Hill A. 1, Hunter G.* 13, Johnson H.* 1, Jones G. 5, Kay A. 6, McClure A. 14, Mackenzie A. 1, Milsom R. 1, Morgan W. 21, Newman A. 1, Osborne F. 1, Pennington J.* 1, Robb W. 1, Roulson J. 13, Scorgie J. 3, Sheldon A. 2, Short J. 5, Smith A.W. 2, Smith A. 6, Tremelling D. 2, Walker W. 29, White T. 3, Whitehouse J. 29, Wilson A.* 2, Womack F. 30. Total: 396.

Goalscorers: Brown D. 5, Crowe F. 1, Davies G. 5, Elkes J. 1, Gardner A. 1, Gibson R. 1, Godfrey J. 26, Hawley F. 1, Hunter G. 2, McClure A. 1, Morgan W. 3, Short J. 3, Smith A.W. 3, Walker W. 15, Whitehouse J. 17. Total: 85.

*Denotes guest players.

1939-40

Match	1	2	3	4	5	6	7	8	9	10	11
1 Aug26 (a) Tottenham H D 1-1 Brown	Hibbs	Trigg	Hughes	Bye	Turner	Shaw	Brown	Dearson	Duckhouse	Harris	Farrage
2 30 (h) Leicester C W 2-0 Farrage, Sharman (og)	..	..	..	..	..	..	..	..	..	..	..
3 Sep 2 (h) Burnley W 2-0 Dearson, Duckhouse	..	..	..	..	..	..	..	..	..	..	..
4 Oct 21 (a) Wolves W 3-2 Broome, Edwards, Dearson	..	..	..	..	..	Iverson	Edwards	..	Broome	..	Brown
5 28 (a) Walsall W 2-1 Jennings, Dearson	..	..	..	Massie	..	..	Jennings	..	..	..	..
6 Nov 4 (h) Luton T W 2-1 Duckhouse, Dearson	..	..	..	Bye	Devey	Shaw	..	..	Duckhouse	..	Guest
7 11 (a) Coventry C L 1-3 Brown	Wheeler	..	..	..	Allen	..	..	Craven	..	..	J.Brown
8 18 (a) West Brom A D 2-2 Brown 2	Hibbs	Quinton	Cummings	Massie	Turner	Iverson	Edwards	..	Broome	..	..
9 25 (a) Leicester C W 3-1 Jones, Bye, Edwards	..	..	Jennings	Bye	..	..	..	..	Jones	Bodle	Bate
10 Dec 2 (a) Northampton T D 1-1 Jones	..	..	..	..	..	..	..	Martin	..	..	Guest
11 9 (a) Wolves L 2-6 Broome 2	..	..	..	..	..	..	..	Dearson	Broome	Craven	J.Brown
12 16 (a) Walsall W 2-1 Edwards, Broome	Wheeler	Hughes	Cummings	..	..	Shaw	..	..	..	Harris	..
13 27 (a) West Brom A L 0-3	..	Trigg	Hughes	Massie	Devey	..	Kernick	Bye	Jones	..	Guest
14 30(n*)Coventry C L 2-4 Broome, Bodle	Hibbs	Hughes	Cummings	Bye	Turner	..	Edwards	Dearson	Broome	..	Bodle
15 Jan 13(n*)Leicester C D 3-3 Guest 2, Duckhouse	Wheeler	Trigg	..	Massie	..	..	Broome	..	Duckhouse	Bodle	Guest
16 20 (a) Northampton T L 0-3	Hibbs	..	Quinton	Bye	..	Iverson	Edwards	..	Bodle	Craven	..
17 Feb10 (a) Luton T L 2-4 Harris (pen), Roberts (og)	Wheeler	Quinton	Hughes	..	F.W.Moss	Shaw	..	..	Jones	Harris	..
18 24 (a) West Brom A L 1-6 Edwards	..	Trigg	..	..	Dearson	..	..	Martin	..	..	Bodle
19 Mar 2 (a) Leicester C L 1-2 Jones	..	Quinton	..	Dearson	Turner	Bye	Jones	Craven	Rowley	..	J.Brown
20 9 (a) Northampton T W 2-1 Turner (pen), Brown, Bodle	..	..	Bellamy	Bye	..	Deakin	..	..	Dearson	Bodle	..
21 16 (a) Wolves L 1-3 Bodle	..	..	..	Foulkes	..	..	..	..	..	..	..
22 23 (h) Walsall W 2-1 Jones 2	..	..	Hughes	Bye	..	Foulkes	J.Brown	Duckhouse	Jones	..	Jennings
23 25 (a) West Brom A L 1-4 Duckhouse	..	Trigg	Bellamy	..	..	Deakin	..	Craven	Duckhouse	..	Shaw
24 26 (h) Luton T W 5-4 Bodle 2, Jones 2, Godden	..	..	Quinton	Deakin	Foulkes	Shaw	Jones	E.Brown	Harris	..	Godden
25 30 (h) Luton T W 4-1 Jones, Trigg 2, Bodle	..	Quinton	Bellamy	Dearson	..	Jennings	J.Brown	Jones	Trigg	..	..
26 Apr 6 (h) Coventry C W 2-0 Trigg 2	..	..	Hughes	..	Turner	Harris	..	..	..	Harris	..
27 10 (h) Wolves L 0-1	..	..	..	..	..	..	..	..	..	Bodle	..
28 20 (a) Newport C D 2-2 Godden 2	..	..	..	Bye	..	..	..	Dearson	..	..	..
29 27 (h) Newport C W 5-2 Trigg 2, Bodle 2, Godden	..	..	..	Dearson	..	..	..	Jones	..	..	..
30 May 1 (h) Northampton T W 3-1 Gardner, Bodle, Trigg	..	..	..	..	Foulkes	..	Jones	Gardner	..	..	Morris
31 4 (h) Reading W 2-0 Trigg, Jones	..	..	..	..	Turner	..	J.Brown	Jones	..	..	Godden
32 11 (h) Reading W 2-0 Godden, Bodle	..	..	..	Bye	..	..	Jones	Dearson	..	..	..
33 18(n†)Arsenal W 2-1 Trigg, Turner	..	..	..	..	..	..	J.Brown	..	..	..	..
34 20 (h) Leicester C D 0-0	Merrick	..	..	..	Foulkes	..	Jones	Gardner	..	..	F.Moss
35 25 (a) West Ham U L 2-4 Trigg 2	Wheeler	..	..	..	Turner	..	J.Brown	Dearson	..	..	Godden
36 Jun 5 (a) Coventry C D 0-0	..	..	..	..	Foulkes	..	Jones	..	..	..	..
37 8 (h) Walsall W 8-1 Bodle 2, Duckworth 2, Jones 2, Brown, Godfrey (og)	..	..	..	..	Devey	..	J.Brown	Jones	Duckhouse	..	F.Moss

*Played at Leamington. †Played at White Hart Lane, London. Matches 1-3 were played in the abandoned Football League Division Two. Matches 4-37 were in the Midland Regional League. Matches 28, 29, 31, 32, 33 & 35 were in the League Cup competition.

Appearances: Allen J.P.1, Bate J. 1, Bellamy S.C. 4, Bodle H. 23, Broome F.H.7, Brown E. 1, Brown J. 23, Bye J.H. 26, Craven C. 9, Cummings G. 4, Deakin F.A. 4, Dearson D.J. 27, Devey R. 3, Duckhouse E. 9, Edwards G.R. 10, Farrage T.O. 3, Foulkes R.E.7, Gardner F.C. 2, Godden A.E. 11, Guest F. 6, Harris F. 28, Hibbs H.E. 12, Hughes W.M. 26, Iverson R.T. 7, Jennings D.B. 8, Jones C.W. 20, Kernick D.H.G. 1, Martin J.R. 2, Massie A. 4, Merrick G.H. 1, Morris S. 1, Moss F. 2, Moss F.W. 1, Quinton W. 24, Rowley S. 1, Shaw R. 13, Trigg C. 25, Turner A. 26, Wheeler W.J. 24. Total: 407.

Goalscorers: Bodle 12, Jones 11, Trigg 11, Brown J. 6, Duckhouse 6, Broome 5, Godden 5, Dearson , Edwards 4, Guest 2, Turner 2, Bye 1, Farrage 1, Gardner 1, Harris 1, Jennings 1, Opponents own-goals 3. Total: 76.

1940-41

Match	1	2	3	4	5	6	7	8	9	10	11
1 Aug31 (a) Nottingham F W 3-2 Jones, Bodle, Godden	Merrick	Quinton	Hughes	Bye	Foulkes	Deakin	Pearce	Kernick	Jones	Bodle	Godden
2 Sep 7 (h) Nottingham F W 2-1 Trigg, Bye	Wheeler	..	..	Bye	..	..	Jones	Dearson	Trigg	Harris	Gardner
3 14 (a) Cardiff C L 2-5 Trigg 2	..	..	Jennings	..	Bye	Pearce	..	..	..	Kernick	..
4 21 (h) Cardiff C W 3-2 Harris (pen), Trigg 2	Merrick	..	..	Dearson	..	Harris	Jones	Gardner	..	Bye	Godden
5 28 (a) West Brom A W 2-1 Dearson, Eastham	..	..	..	..	..	..	Jennings	..	..	Eastham	..
6 Oct 5 (h) West Brom A L 1-3 Jones	..	..	Deakin	..	..	..	..	..	Jones	..	..
7 12 (a) Mansfield T L 1-4 Jennings	..	..	Galley	..	..	..	..	..	Kernick	..	Moss
8 19 (a) Mansfield T W 4-1 Trigg 2, Jones, Harris (pen)	Wheeler	..	Hughes	Jennings	Deakin	..	Jones	Dearson	Trigg	..	Morris
9 26 (a) Leicester C L 1-2 Gardner	Merrick	..	..	..	Foulkes	..	..	..	..	..	Gardner
10 Nov 2 (h) Leicester C L 1-2 Trigg	..	..	Jennings	Dearson	..	..	..	Gardner	..	..	Godden
11 9 (a) Stoke C L 0-5	Wheeler	..	Hughes	Bye	Turner	..	Brown	..	..	Jones	Craven
12 16 (h) Stoke C W 6-2 Trigg 5, Craven	..	..	..	Devey	..	..	..	Jennings	..	..	..
13 30 (a) Notts C D 3-3 Trigg 3	Merrick	..	..	..	..	Deakin	..	..	..	..	..
14 Dec 7 (a) Northampton T L 1-2 Trigg	..	..	..	Dearson	Foulkes	R.Shaw	Jennings	Gill	..	..	..
15 25 (a) Walsall L 3-6 Trigg 3	..	Batty	Bye	..	..	..	Brown	..	..	..	Thayne
16 Feb15 (a) Leicester C D 3-3 Dearson, Shaw, Gardner	..	Quinton	Deakin	..	..	Harris	..	Gardner	R.Shaw	Gill	Godden
17 22 (a) Leicester C L 2-3 Gardner, Dearson	..	Jennings	..	Devey	..	..	Kernick	..	Dearson	..	Brown
18 Mar 1 (a) Luton T W 5-2 Dearson 3, Gill, Forsyth (og)	..	Quinton	Hughes	..	..	..	Jennings	..	..	..	..

Other Matches

19 Aug31 (h) RAF XI	D 1-1
20 Sep14 (h) Services XI	D 3-3

Appearances: Batty S.G. 1, Bodle H. 1, Brown J. 7, Bye J.H. 6, Craven C. 4, Deakin F.A. 7, Dearson D.J. 14, Devey R. 4, Eastham G.R. 6, Foulkes R.E. 14, Galley D.S. 1, Gardner F.C.12, Gill J. 5, Godden A.E. 6, Harris F. 13, Hughes W.M. 12, Jennings D.B. 12, Jones C.W. 12, Kernick D.H.G. 4, Merrick G.H. 13, Morris S. 1, Moss F.W. 1, Pearce H. 2, Quinton W. 16, Shaw R. 3, Thayne W. 1, Trigg C. 12, Turner A. 3, Wheeler W.J. 5. Total: 198.

Goalscorers: Trigg 20, Dearson 6, Gardner 3, Jones 3, Harris 2, Bye 1, Bodle 1, Eastham 1, Craven 1, Godden 1, Gill 1, Jennings 1, Shaw 1, Opponent own-goal 1. Tota:l 43.

1941-42

Friendlies

1 Aug20 (h) RAF XI	W 3-1	
2 Sep 6 (h) Czech Army XI	W 3-2	
3 13 (h) Wolves	W 4-0	
4 20 (a) Wolves	W 4-2	
5 27 (h) RAF XI	W 2-0	
6 Oct 4 (h) Aldershot Army XI	L 2-4	
7 11 (h) Northampton T	W 4-1	
8 Nov 1 (h) Birmingham Wks AFD	W 7-0	
9 8 (h) All Welsh XI	L 2-3	
10 15 (a) Aston Villa	L 0-7	
11 22 (h) Czech Army XI	W 4-0	
12 Dec 6 (h) British Army	L 3-6	
13 20 (a) West Brom A	L 1-4	
14 Mar14 (a) Aston Villa	L 0-4	
15 21 (a) Derby C	D 2-2	
16 28 (a) Wolves	W 3-0	
17 Apr 4 (n*)RAF XI	D 1-1	
18 6 (h) Aston Villa	W 2-1	
19 18 (a) Chester	D 3-3	
20 25 (a) Walsall	D 0-0	
21 May 2(n*)Leicester C	L 0-3	
22 9 (a) Leicester C	L 2-4	
23 25 (a) Coventry C	L 2-4	
24 30 (a) West Brom A	L 1-4	

*Played at Villa Park.

1942-43

Match	1	2	3	4	5	6	7	8	9	10	11
1 Aug29 (a) Leicester C W 1-0 McCormick	Merrick	Quinton	Jennings	R.Shaw	Devey	Harris	McCormick	Dearson	Acquaroff	Finian	Batty
2 Sep 5 (h) Leicester C W 2-1 Brown, R.Shaw	..	..	..	Tranter	..	R.Shaw	Brown	McCormick	..	Dearson	Guest
3 12 (h) Derby C L 0-5	..	..	..	Dearson	Deakin	..	McCormick	Vause	Trigg	Acquaroff	Brown
4 19 (a) Derby C L 1-3 Ottewell	..	Hardwick	..	..	Turner	..	..	Craven	Pears	..	Ottewell
5 26 (a) Northampton T L 1-4 Ottewell	..	Quinton	Bellamy	Jennings	Chapman	..	Batty	..	..	Ottewell	Eden
6 Oct 3 (h) Northampton T L 0-2	..	Sibley	Jennings	R.Shaw	Dearson	Mitchell	McCormick	..	Acquaroff	..	Guest
7 10 (h) Stoke C W 1-0 Acquaroff	..	Quinton	..	..	Turner	..	..	Acquaroff	Dearson	..	Pearson
8 17 (a) Stoke C W 3-1 Bate, Craven, Gill	..	..	..	Bate	..	R.Shaw	..	Gill	Ottewell	Craven	..
9 24 (h) Coventry C D 2-2 Acquaroff 2	..	..	..	Bye	..	Mitchell	Acquaroff	Craven	R.Shaw	Robinson	Ottewell
10 31 (h) Coventry C W 1-0 Harris	Bartram	..	..	Dearson	..	R.Shaw	McCormick	Harris	Acquaroff	..	..
11 Nov 7 (h) Walsall W 4-3 Watton, Dearson 3	Merrick	..	..	R.Shaw	..	Mitchell	..	Dearson	Watton	Craven	..
12 14 (a) Walsall L 0-1	..	..	..	..	..	..	..	..	Acquaroff	..	..
13 21 (a) Aston Villa L 1-2 Cummings (og)	..	..	..	..	..	..	..	..	..	Bray	Craven
14 28 (h) Aston Villa W 2-1 Callaghan (og), Watton	..	..	..	..	..	..	J.Collins	McCormick	Watton	Acquaroff	Ottewell
15 Dec 5 (h) West Brom A W 3-0 Dearson, Ottewell 2	..	..	..	..	..	..	..	..	Dearson	..	..
16 12 (a) West Brom A L 3-4 McCormick 2, Craven	..	..	Hughes	Bye	..	..	McCormick	Craven	..	..	..
17 19 (a) Wolves D 1-1 Jones	King	..	Jennings	R.Shaw	..	..	Buttens	McCormick	..	Jones	Moss
18 25 (h) Wolves W 1-0 Jones	Merrick	Trigg	..	Smith	..	..	McCormick	Acquaroff	Dearson	..	Ford
19 26 (a) Northampton T L 1-5 McCormick	..	..	..	R.Shaw	..	..	..	Dearson	Acquaroff	Craven	Gill
20 Jan 2 (h) Northampton T L 2-4 Dearson, Jones	..	Quinton	..	Harris	Tranter	Bye	Watton	McCormick	Dearson	Acquaroff	Jones
21 9 (h) Leicester C W 5-0 McCormick, Howe (og), Jones 2, Craven	..	..	..	Dearson	Turner	Mitchell	McCormick	Craven	Watton	Jones	Acquaroff
22 16 (a) Leicester C L 1-2 Acquaroff	..	..	..	..	..	..	..	..	..	..	..
23 23 (a) Walsall D 1-1 Jones	..	..	..	..	..	R.Shaw	..	..	..	..	..
24 30 (h) Walsall W 1-0 Acquaroff	..	..	..	..	..	..	..	Gill	Acquaroff	Craven	Brown
25 Feb 6 (h) West Brom A L 0-1	..	..	..	..	..	..	..	..	Watton	..	Goffin
26 13 (a) West Brom A L 1-2 McEwan	..	..	..	Acquaroff	..	..	..	McEwan	Dearson	..	Gill
27 20 (a) Coventry C L 0-1	..	..	..	..	..	..	..	Ainsley	McEwan	..	..
28 27 (h) Coventry C W 3-1 Craven, Watton, McEwan	..	..	..	R.Shaw	..	Sweeney	Millichap	McEwan	Watton	..	..
29 Mar 6 (a) Walsall W 2-1 Watton, Trickett	..	..	..	..	..	Middleton	..	Craven	..	Trickett	Davy
30 13 (h) Walsall W 2-1 Romp, Turner	..	..	..	Watts	..	Mitchell	Lewis	G.Collins	Romp	Acquaroff	..
31 20 (h) Coventry C L 1-2 Acquaroff	..	Trigg	..	Acquaroff	..	Middleton	..	Craven	Watton	J.Shaw	..
32 27 (a) Coventry C L 1-2 Acquaroff	..	Quinton	..	R.Shaw	..	Mitchell	Acquaroff	Richards	Trigg	Craven	Lewis
33 Apr 3 (h) West Brom A W 5-3 Ottewell 3, Watton, Dearson	Jenkins	..	..	Acquaroff	..	R.Shaw	Eden	Dearson	Ottewell	Watton	Davy
34 10 (a) West Brom A W 4-0 Craven, Dearson, Lewis, Richards	Merrick	..	..	..	..	..	Lewis	Richards	Dearson	Craven	Eden
35 17 (h) Northampton T W 1-0 Eden	..	..	..	..	..	..	..	..	Watton	..	..
36 24 (a) Northampton T L 0-1	..	Turner	..	..	Dolphin	..	McCormick	Pope	..	..	..
37 26 (a) Aston Villa L 0-1	..	Jennings	Hapgood	..	Turner	..	G.Collins	..	Dearson	Harris	..
38 May 1 (a) Chesterfield D 1-1 Acquaroff	..	Shelton	Jennings	..	..	..	Webber	..	Dolphin	Bodle	..

Matches 19-28 were League Cup Qualifying games.

Appearances: Acquaroff J. 31, Ainsley G.E. 1, Bartram S. 1, Bate J. 1, Batty S.G. 2, Bellamy S.C.1, Bodle H. 1, Bray J. 1, Brown J. 3, Buttens D.J. 1, Bye J.H. 3, Chapman S. 1, Collins G.E. 2, Collins J.F. 2, Craven C. 24, Davy H. 4, Deakin F.A. 1, Dearson D.J. 23, Devey R. 2, Dolphin L.G. 2, Eden E. 7, Finian R.J. 1, Ford R. 1, Gill J.D. 7, Goffin W.C. 1, Guest W.F. 2, Hapgood E.A. 1, Hardwick G.F.M. 1, Harris F. 4, Hughes W.M. 1, Jenkins P.J. 1, Jennings D.B. 37, Jones C.W. 6, King S.H. 1, Lewis C.J. 6, McCormick J. 28, McEwan W. 3, Merrick G.H. 35, Middleton N. 2, Millichap E. 2, Mitchell F. 16, Moss F.W. 1, Ottewell S. 13, Pears W.T. 2, Pearson T.U. 2, Pope J. 1, Quinton W. 30, Richards E. 3, Robinson G.H. 2, Romp L.W. 1, Shaw J. 1, Shaw R. 31, Shelton J.B.T. 1, Sibley E. 1, Smith T.W. 1, Sweeney F. 1, Tranter G. 2, Trickett J.E. 1, Trigg C. 5, Turner A. 32, Vause P.G. 1, Watton G.D. 14, Watts F. 1, Webber W. 1, Total: 418.

Goalscorers: Acquaroff 8, Dearson 7, Ottewell 7, Jones 6, Craven 5, McCormick 5, Watton 5, McEwan 2, Bate 1, Brown 1, Eden 1, Gill 1, Harris 1, Lewis 1, Richards 1, Romp 1, R.Shaw 1, Trickett 1, Turner 1, Opponent own-goals 3. Total: 59.

1943-44

			1	2	3	4	5	6	7	8	9	10	11
1 Aug28 (a) Coventry C	D 0-0		Merrick	H.Turner	Hughes	Dearson	Hayward	Shaw	Mulraney	Harris	Hinsley	Doherty	Sibley
2 Sep 4 (h) Coventry C	L 1-2 Revell		..	..	Quinton	Shaw	..	Mitchell	..	Dearson	Revell	Acquaroff	Redwood
3 11 (h) Leicester C	W 3-0 Hinsley 2 (1 pen), Acquaroff		..	..	Jennings	Acquaroff	A.Turner	..	..	..	Hinsley	Peacock	Ottewell
4 18 (a) Leicester C	D 2-2 Hinsley, Bright		..	..	..	Bye	Acquaroff	Shaw	..	..	..	S..Stanton	Bright
5 25 (h) Northampton T	L 1-3 Gee		..	..	..	Shaw	..	Sinclair	Gee	Harris	..	Doherty	..
6 Oct 2 (a) Northampton T	L 1-2 Shaw		..	Quinton	..	Dearson	A.Turner	Shaw	..	Jones	..	Day	N.Roberts
7 9 (a) Derby C	L 3-5 Mulraney, Trigg 2		..	..	..	Acquaroff	..	..	Mulraney	Dearson	Trigg	Craven	Bright
8 16 (h) Derby C	D 3-3 Trigg, Bright, Bye		..	..	..	Bye	Acquaroff	..	..	..	..	..	..
9 23 (a) Stoke C	D 1-1 Dearson		..	H.Turner	Quinton	Acquaroff	A.Turner	Bye	..	..	..	Shaw	..
10 30 (h) Stoke C	W 2-0 Trigg, Mulraney		..	..	..	Shaw	..	Mitchell	..	..	..	Jennings	Sibley
11 Nov 6 (a) Walsall	W 4-2 Trigg 2, Bright, Dearson		..	..	..	Bye	..	Jennings	N.Roberts	..	..	Shaw	Bright
12 13 (h) Walsall	W 5-1 Trigg 2 (1 pen), Mulraney 2, Bright		..	..	..	Dolphin	..	..	Mulraney	T.Roberts	..	..	..
13 20 (h) Aston Villa	W 2-1 Mulraney, Dearson		..	..	..	Jennings	..	Mitchell	..	Dearson	..	..	..
14 27 (a) Aston Villa	L 0-3		..	..	..	Shaw	..	Jennings	..	..	..	Acquaroff	..
15 Dec 4 (a) West Brom A	W 3-1 Mulraney 2, Trigg		..	..	Jennings	Dearson	..	Shaw	..	T.Roberts	..	T.Stanton	..
16 11 (h) West Brom A	W 3-0 Roberts, Trigg 2 (1 pen)		..	Green	..	..	..	Middleton	..	..	..	Shaw	..
17 18 (h) Wolves	W 4-2 Trigg 2, Doherty, Bright		..	H.Turner	Quinton	..	..	Shaw	..	..	..	Doherty	..
18 25 (a) Wolves	L 0-3		..	..	Jennings	Harris	..	Middleton	..	Acquaroff	..	Trickett	Godden
19 26 (a) West Brom A	D 1-1 Shaw		..	..	..	..	..	Mitchell	..	Dearson	..	R.Shaw	Bright
20 Jan 1 (h) West Brom A	W 4-0 Bright 2, Trigg, Mulraney		..	Green	..	Acquaroff	..	..	..	T.Roberts	..	..	..
21 8 (h) Northampton T	W 5-1 Trigg, Roberts, Mulraney 2, Dearson		..	H.Turner	Hughes	Dearson	..	Shaw	..	..	..	Doherty	..
22 22 (h) Stoke C	W 4-1 Mitchell, Acquaroff, Mulraney, Bright		..	..	Jennings	..	..	Mitchell	..	..	Acquaroff	R.Shaw	..
23 29 (a) Stoke C	L 1-4 Trigg		..	..	..	..	..	Shaw	..	Quinton	Trigg	T.Roberts	..
24 Feb 5 (a) Wolves	W 2-0 Trigg 2		..	Green	Quinton	H.Turner	..	Dearson	..	T.Roberts	..	Shaw	..
25 12 (h) Wolves	W 2-1 Trigg (pen), Bright		..	Quinton	Green	McKillop	..	Jennings	..	Dearson	..	..	..
26 19 (h) Aston Villa	D 1-1 Trigg		..	H.Turner	Quinton	Dearson	..	Acquaroff	..	Jennings	..	..	..
27 26 (a) Aston Villa	W 2-1 Trigg 2		..	..	..	..	..	Mitchell	..	T.Roberts	..	..	..
28 Mar 4 (h) Leicester C	W 3-1 Mulraney, Trigg 2		..	..	..	..	..	..	..	..	..	..	..
29 11 (a) Leicester C	L 1-2* Bright		..	..	..	..	..	Acquaroff	..	..	..	..	..
30 18 (h) Manchester U	W 3-1 Bodle, Shaw, Trigg		..	..	..	..	..	Shaw	..	..	..	Bodle	..
31 25 (a†) Manchester U	D 1-1 Trigg		..	Quinton	Hughes	..	..	Mitchell	..	Bodle	..	Shaw	..
32 Apr 1 (h) Manchester C	L 0-1		..	..	..	Shaw	..	..	..	Craven	..	Bodle	Jennings
33 8 (h) Manchester C	D 0-0		..	..	..	Dearson	..	S.Stanton	..	T.Roberts	..	Shaw	Bodle
34 10 (a) Coventry C	W 3-0 Trigg 2, Godden		..	Green	Jennings	Craven	..	..	Hackett	Dearson	..	Barnett	Godden
35 15 (a) Walsall	D 2-2 Trigg 2		..	H.Turner	Quinton	Green	..	..	Jennings	T.Roberts	..	..	Bright
36 22 (h) Walsall	W 5-0 Jennings, Trigg 4		..	Green	..	Shaw	..	..	..	Mulraney	..	..	Morris
37 29 (h) Northampton T	W 3-1 Morris, Trigg (pen), Dearson		..	H.Turner	Jennings	Dearson	..	Montgomery	Mulraney	Craven	..	S.Stanton	..
38 May 6 (a) Northampton T	W 5-0 Roberts 2, Mulraney 2, Faulkner		..	..	..	Craven	Morgan	S.Stanton	Faulkner	Mulraney	Barnett	T.Roberts	Bright

*After extra-time. †Played at Maine Road, Manchester. Matches 19-27 were League North Cup Qualifying games. Matches 28-33 were League North Cup proper.

Appearances: Acquaroff J. 13, Barnett R.H. 4, Bodle H. 4, Bright R.L. 27, Bye J.H. 4, Craven C. 6, Day E.F. 1, Dearson D.J. 30, Doherty P.D. 4, Dolphin L.G. 1, Faulkner R. 1, Gee H. 2, Godden A.E. 2, Green K. 7, Hackett J. 1, Harris F. 4, Hayward L.E. 2, Hinsley G. 5, Hughes W.M. 5, Jennings D.B. 26, Jones W.V.A. 1, McKillop T. 1, Merrick G.H. 38, Middleton N. 2, Mitchell F.R. 11, Montgomery J.D. 1, Morgan L.D. 1, Morris S. 2, Mulraney A. 33, Ottewell S. 1, Peacock T. 1, Quinton W. 24, Redwood H. 1, Revell C. 1, Roberts N.E. 2, Roberts T.D. 16, Shaw R. 32, Sibley T. 2, Sinclair M. 1, Stanton S.H. 7, Stanton T. 1, Trickett J.E. 1, Trigg C. 30, Turner A. 32, Turner H. 27. Total: 418.

Goalscorers: Acquaroff 2, Bodle 1, Bright 10, Bye 1, Dearson 5, Doherty 1, Faulkner 1, Gee 1, Godden 1, Hinsley 3, Jennings 1, Mitchell 1, Morris 1, Mulraney 14, Revell 1, T.Roberts 4, Shaw 3, Trigg 35. Total: 86.

1944-45

		1	2	3	4	5	6	7	8	9	10	11
1	Aug 26 (a) Port Vale L 0-3	Merrick	H.Turner	Jennings	Dearson	A.Turner	Stanton	Mulraney	Small	Trigg	Shaw	Morris
2	Sep 2 (h) Port Vale W 4-0 Trigg 4	..	Jennings	Stanton	Small	..	Shaw	..	Roberts	..	Craven	Bright
3	9 (h) Coventry C L 1-2 Craven	..	..	..	Dearson	..	Mitchell	..	..	..	..	Sibley
4	16 (a) Coventry C W 1-0 Faulkner	..	..	Quinton	Small	..	Stanton	Faulkner	Mulraney	..	Shaw	Bright
5	23 (a) Leicester C W 1-0 Shaw	..	Quinton	Jennings	..	..	Dearson	..	..	..	..	..
6	30 (h) Leicester C D 3-3 Mulraney 2, Trigg	..	Jennings	Stanton	..	..	..	..	..	..	..	Morris
7	Oct 7 (h) Aston Villa W 3-2 Mulraney, Trigg 2	..	..	Shaw	Dearson	..	Stanton	..	..	..	Small	Bright
8	14 (a) Aston Villa D 1-1 Bright	..	..	Hughes	..	..	Shaw	..	..	..	..	..
9	21 (a) Stoke C D 0-0	..	..	Craven	Shaw	..	Stanton	Mulraney	Faulkner	Dearson	Barnett	..
10	28 (h) Stoke C D 1-1 Bright	..	..	Jenks	Small	..	Hicklin	Faulkner	Mulraney	..	Shaw	..
11	Nov 4 (h) Wolves W 1-0 Small	..	..	Hughes	Dearson	..	F.Harris	Mulraney	Small	Martin	..	..
12	11 (a) Wolves W 4-0 Trigg 3, Faulkner	..	..	..	..	..	Shaw	Faulkner	Mulraney	Trigg	Hicklin	Sibley
13	18 (a) Walsall L 1-4 Small	Adams	..	Mitchell	..	..	..	..	..	..	Small	Bright
14	25 (a) Walsall D 2-2 Mulligan (og), Shelton (og)	Merrick	..	Dearson	Hicklin	..	Stanton	..	Craven	..	Shaw	Mulraney
15	Dec 2 (h) Northampton T D 0-0	..	..	..	Shaw	..	Small	..	Hicklin	..	Craven	Trentham
16	9 (a) Northampton T L 1-2 Small	..	..	Trigg	Dearson	..	Greatrix	..	Small	Hikins	Shaw	White
17	16 (h) West Brom A W 2-0 Tranter (og), Trigg	..	Pope	Quinton	..	..	Shaw	Mulraney	Hilkins	Trigg	Small	..
18	23 (a) West Brom A W 4-1 Trigg 2, White 2	..	Jennings	..	..	..	..	..	..	..	..	..
19	26 (h) Wolves D 0-0	King	..	Stanton	Hicklin	W.Harris	Small	Faulkner	..	Dearson	Bodle	..
20	30 (h) Walsall W 3-1 Trigg 3	..	..	Hughes	Dearson	A.Turner	Shaw	Mulraney	Small	Trigg	..	Bright
21	Jan 6 (h) Coventry C W 5-1 Hikins, Trigg 3, White	Merrick	..	Quinton	..	..	Hughes	..	Hikins	..	Small	White
22	13 (a) Coventry C W 2-1 White, Trigg	..	..	Shaw	..	..	Mitchell	..	Small	..	Craven	..
23	20 (a) Aston Villa L 1-3 Harris	King	..	Quinton	..	..	..	..	F.Harris	..	Shaw	Small
24	27 (h) Aston Villa L 0-1	Merrick	Quinton	Hughes	..	..	F.Harris	..	Hikins	..	Small	White
25	Feb 3 (h) Northampton T W 4-0 Bodle 2, Trigg 2	..	Jennings	Quinton	..	..	Small	..	..	..	Bodle	..
26	10 (a) Northampton T L 1-2 Mulraney	..	..	Jenks	..	..	Mitchell	..	Small	..	Marriott	Bright
27	17 (a) West Brom A L 0-4	..	..	Quinton	Craven	..	Hicklin	..	Hikins	Hughes	Small	O'Donnell
28	24 (h) West Brom A D 1-1 Dearson	..	..	..	..	..	Shaw	..	Micheson	Dearson	F.Harris	..
29	Mar 3 (a) Walsall W 2-0 Kernick 2	..	..	Metcalf	..	..	..	..	Kernick	..	White	..
30	10 (a) Aston Villa L 0-5	..	..	..	..	..	..	Berry	Dearson	Clements	F.Harris	Mulraney
31	17 (h) Aston Villa L 0-3	..	Metcalf	Jennings	Dearson	Booth	..	Mulraney	Kernick	Jordan	Craven	Bright
32	24 (a) Northampton T W 2-0 Mulraney, Massart	..	Jennings	Metcalf	Booth	A.Turner	Dearson	..	F.Harris	Massart	Shaw	..
33	31 (h) Northampton T D 2-2 Massart, Mulraney	..	..	..	..	..	..	..	Small	..	..	White
34	Apr 2 (a) Wolves L 1-2 Turner (pen)	..	..	Stanton	..	..	..	Morris	Kennick	..	Fenton	Bright
35	7 (h) Wolves D 0-0	..	..	Quinton	Dearson	..	Mitchell	Mulraney	Massart	Garrett	Shaw	..
36	14 (a) Wolves L 0-1*	..	..	..	Booth	..	..	..	Hikins	Dearson	..	..
37	21 (h) Coventry C L 1-2 Bright	..	Williams	Jennings	Hicklin	..	Dearson	Berry	Mulraney	Stanton	Lewis	..
38	28 (a) Coventry C D 2-2 Lewis, Bright	..	Jennings	Shaw	Booth	..	..	Mulraney	Craven	Massatt	..	..
39	May 5 (h) West Brom A W 4-1 Massart 3, Lewis	..	.. ..	Stanton	Hicklin	..	Shaw	..	Elliott	..	Marriott	Lewis
40	12 (a) West Brom A W 3-2 Massart 3	..	..	..	..	..	Dearson	..	Bodle	..	..	Bright
41	19 (h) Nottingham F W 4-1 Mulraney, Massart, Dearson, Matthews	..	..	..	..	Ball	..	..	Hikins	..	Murrell	Matthews
42	26 (a) Nottingham F D 0-0	..	..	Smith	Dearson	A.Turner	Hicklin	Faulkner	Murrell	..	Marriott	..

*After extra-time. Matches 20-29 were League North Cup Qualifying games. Matches 32, 33, & 36 were League Cup North proper. Matches 37 & 38 were in the Midland League Cup.

Appearances: Adams H.S. 1, Ball R.T. 1, Barnett R.H. 1, Berry J.R. 2, Bodle H. 4, Booth W.S. 6, Bright R.L. 19, Clements A.B. 1, Craven C. 12, Dearson D.J. 38, Elliott J.M. 1, Faulkner K.G. 14, Fenton J.W. 1, Garrett A.A.1, Greatrix J. 1, Harris F. 6, Harris W. 1, Hicklin W.A. 11, Hikins D., 10, Hughes W.M. 7, Jenks N. 2, Jennings D.B. 40, Jordan C. 1, Kernick D.H.G. 3, King S.H. 3, Lewis R. 3, Marriott A.H.P. 4, Martin G.B.H. 1, Massart D.L. 9, Matthews J.B.2, Merrick G.H. 38, Metcalf W.F. 5, Mitchell F.R.7, Micheson F. 1, Morris S. 3, Mulraney A. 37, Murrell R.E. 2, O'Donnell H. 3, Pope A.L. 1, Quinton W. 12, Roberts T.D. 2, Shaw R. 30, Sibley T. 2, Small S.J. 24, Smith S.R. 1, Stanton S. 14, Trentham D.H. 1, Trigg C. 22, Turner A. 39, Turner H. 1, White F.R.H. 10, Williams I. 1. Total: 462.

Goalscorers: Trigg 22, Massart 9, Mulraney 7, Bright 4, White 4, Small 3, Bodle 2, Dearson 2, Faulkner 2, Lewis 2, Kernick 2, Craven 1, Harris 1, Hikins 1, Matthews 1, Shaw 1, Turner 1, Opponents own-goals 3. Total: 68.

1945-46

		1	2	3	4	5	6	7	8	9	10	11
1 Aug25 (h) West Ham U	L 0-1	Merrick	Duckhouse	Jennings	Dearson	Turner	Mitchell	White	Dougall	Massart	Bodle	Edwards
2 Sep 1 (a) West Ham U	L 2-3 Massart, Edwards	..	Jennings	Jenks	..	..	Harris	Mulraney	..	..	..	..
3 3 (h) Luton T	W 3-2 Dougall 2, Bodle	..	..	..	..	..	..	..	..	..	..	..
4 8 (h) West Brom A	W 4-0 Edwards, Mulraney, Duckhouse, Jones	..	..	Shaw	..	..	..	..	..	Duckhouse	Jones	..
5 15 (a) West Brom A	D 0-0	..	..	Hughes	..	..	..	..	..	..	..	..
6 17 (a) Coventry C	W 3-2 Bodle, Duckhouse, Mulraney	..	..	..	..	..	Mitchell	..	..	..	Bodle	..
7 22 (a) Swansea T	W 4-2 Mulraney, Dougall, Massart 2	..	..	..	..	..	Harris	..	..	Massart	..	..
8 29 (a) Swansea T	W 5-0 Bodle 2, Duckhouse, Jones, Mulraney	..	..	Stanton	..	..	..	..	Jones	Duckhouse	..	..
9 Oct 6 (h) Tottenham H	W 8-0 Duckhouse, Massart 2, Dougall, Bodle, Edwards, Mulraney 2	..	Duckhouse	Jennings	..	..	owen	..	Dougall	Massart	..	..
10 13 (a) Tottenham H	W 1-0 Mulraney	..	..	..	Dearson	..	Harris	..	..	..	..	..
11 20 (a) Brentford	L 1-2 White	..	..	..	Harris	Shaw	Mitchell	Jones	..	..	..	White
12 27 (h) Brentford	W 1-0 Massart	..	..	..	Dearson	Turner	Harris	Mulraney	..	..	..	Edwards
13 Nov 3 (h) Chelsea	W 5-2 Bodle 2, Jones, Turner (pen), Edwards	..	..	..	..	..	..	..	..	Jones	..	..
14 10 (a) Chelsea	W 3-2 Jones 2, Turner (pen)	..	..	..	Harris	..	Mitchell	..	..	..	..	White
15 17 (a) Millwall	L 1-5 Jones	..	..	..	Dearson	..	Harris	..	..	..	..	Edwards
16 24 (h) Millwall	W 4-0 Bodle, Jones, Edwards 2	..	..	..	Harris	..	Mitchell	..	..	..	..	..
17 Dec 1 (a) Southampton	D 1-1 Duckhouse	..	Dearson	..	..	..	..	..	..	Duckhouse	..	..
18 8 (h) Southampton	W 4-0 Bodle 2, Duckhouse, Edwards	..	..	..	..	..	..	..	..	..	..	..
19 15 (a) Derby C	W 2-0 Edwards, Jones	..	Duckhouse	..	..	..	..	..	..	Jones	..	..
20 22 (h) Derby C	W 1-0 Bodle	..	..	..	..	..	..	..	..	..	..	..
21 25 (h) Leicester C	W 6-2 Jones 2, Dougall, Bodle, Edwards, Mulraney	..	..	..	..	..	..	..	..	..	..	..
22 26 (a) Leicester C	W 1-0 Mulraney	..	..	..	..	..	Dearson	..	..	..	..	..
23 29 (h) Coventry C	W 2-0 Edwards, Dougall	..	..	..	..	..	..	..	..	..	..	..
24 Jan 12 (a) Aston Villa	D 2-2 Dearson, Dougall	..	..	..	..	..	Mitchell	..	..	Dearson	..	..
25 19 (h) Aston Villa	W 3-1 Jones 2, Mulraney	..	..	Hughes	..	..	Dearson	..	..	Jones	..	..
26 Feb 2 (a) Arsenal	W 3-0 Jones, Edwards 2	..	..	Jennings	..	..	Mitchell	..	..	..	..	..
27 16 (h) Charlton A	W 1-0 Jones	..	..	..	..	..	..	..	Dearson	..	..	..
28 23 (h) Fulham	W 2-0 Laing, White	..	Dearson	..	..	..	..	White	Dougall	..	..	Laing
29 Mar13 (h) Arsenal	L 0-1	King	Duckhouse	..	Dearson	..	..	Mulraney	McPherson	..	..	Edwards
30 16 (h) Plymouth A	L 0-1	Merrick	..	..	Harris	..	Dearson	..	Dougall	..	..	..
31 30 (a) Portsmouth	W 4-3 Mulraney, Jones, Dougall, Bodle	..	Dearson	..	..	..	Mitchell	..	..	..	..	..
32 Apr 1 (a) Plymouth A	W 3-2 Jones 3	..	..	..	..	..	..	..	..	..	..	..
33 6 (a) Nottingham F	L 0-1	King	..	..	..	..	Owen	..	..	..	..	..
34 10 (h) Portsmouth	W 1-0 Jones	Merrick	..	..	..	..	Mitchell	..	..	..	..	..
35 13 (h) Nottingham F	W 3-1 Bodle, Jones, Harris	..	..	..	Owen	..	..	..	Harris	..	..	..
36 15 (a) Fulham	L 2-3 Dougall 2	..	..	..	..	..	..	Dougall	..	..	..	..
37 19 (h) Newport C	W 3-2 Mulraney, Massart 2	..	..	..	Harris	Owen	..	Mulraney	Dougall	Massart	..	Laing
38 20 (a) Wolves	D 3-3 Bodle, Edwards, Harris	..	..	..	..	Turner	..	..	..	Jones	..	Edwards
39 22 (a) Newport C	W 1-0 Massart	..	..	..	..	..	..	..	..	Massart	..	..
40 27 (h) Wolves	L 0-1	..	..	..	..	..	..	..	..	Jones	..	..
41 29 (a) Charlton A	D 0-0	Ditchburn	..	..	..	..	..	..	..	Massart	..	..
42 May 4 (a) Luton T	W 3-0 Bodle, Mitchell (pen), Mulraney	Merrick	..	..	..	..	..	..	..	Trigg	..	..

FINAL LEAGUE POSITION: 1st in Football League South

FA Cup

				1	2	3	4	5	6	7	8	9	10	11
3 Jan 5 (h) Portsmouth	W 1-0 Flewin (og)		33,845	Merrick	Duckhouse	Jennings	Harris	Turner	Mitchell	Mulraney	Dougall	Jones	Bodle	Edwards
9 (a) Portsmouth	D 0-0		23,716	..	..	..	..	..	..	..	..	..	..	..
4 26 (h) Watford	W 5-0 Mulraney 3, Jones, Bodle		25,000	..	..	..	..	..	..	..	..	..	..	..
30 (a) Watford	D 1-1 Jones		6,000	King	..	..	..	..	..	..	..	..	..	..
5 Feb 9 (a) Sunderland	L 0-1		45,000	Merrick	..	..	..	..	..	..	..	..	..	..
13 (h) Sunderland	W 3-1 Jones 2, Mulraney		40,000	King	..	..	..	..	..	..	..	..	..	..
6 Mar 2 (a) Bradford	D 2-2 Dougall, Jones		19,732	Merrick	..	..	..	..	..	..	..	..	..	..
9 (h) Bradford	W 6-0 Dougall 2, Bodle 2, Mulraney 2		49,858	..	..	..	..	..	..	..	..	..	..	..
SF 23(n†)Derby C	D 1-1 Mulraney		65,013	..	..	..	..	..	..	..	..	..	..	..
R 27(n†)Derby C	L 0-4*		80,407	..	..	..	..	..	..	..	..	..	..	..

†Played at Hillsborough, Sheffield. ‡Played at Maine Road, Manchester. *After extra-time.

League Appearances: Bodle H. 40, Dearson D.J. 34, Ditchburn E.G. 1, Dougall C. 38, Duckhouse E. 26, Edwards G.R. 38, Harris F. 39, Hughes W.M. 4, Jenks N. 2, Jennings D.B. 41, Jones C.W. 27, King S.H. 2, Laing R.S. 2, Massart D.L. 11, McPherson I. 1, Merrick G.H. 39, Mitchell F.R. 26, Mulraney A. 38, Owen S.W. 5, Shaw R. 2, Stanton S. 1, Trigg C. 1, Turner A. 40, White F.R.H. 4. Total: 462.

League Goalscorers: Jones 20, Bodle 16, Edwards 13, Mulraney 13, Dougall 10, Massart 9, Duckhouse 6, Harris 2, Turner 2, White 2, Dearson 1, Laing 1, Mitchell 1. Total: 96.

Blues in Europe

Inter-Cities Fairs Cup

1956-58
Played in four groups, the top club in each group qualifying for the semi-finals)
Group 'B'
15 May 1956 v Internazionale (Italy) (a) 0-0
Merrick; Badham, Green, Watts, Newman, Warmington, Cox, Kinsey, Brown, Murphy, Govan.
Att: 8,000
21 May 1956 v Zagreb Select (Yugoslavia) (a) 1-0
Brown
Merrick; Badham, Allen, Boyd, Newman, Warhurst, Lane(Cox), Finney, Brown, Kinsey, Murphy.
Att: 12,000
3 Dec 1956 v Zagreb Select (h) 3-0
Orritt, Brown, Murphy
Merrick; Farmer, Allen, Watts, Green, Warhurst, Cox, Orritt, Brown, Murphy, Govan.
Att: 40,144
17 Apr 1957 v Internazionale (h) 2-1
Govan 2
Merrick; Hall, Green, Watts, Smith, Warhurst, Astall, Kinsey, Brown, Murphy, Govan.
Att: 34,461

Final Group 'B' Table

	P	W	D	L	F	A	Pts
Birmingham C	4	3	1	0	6	1	7
Internazionale	4	2	1	1	6	2	5
Dinamo Zagreb	4	0	0	4	0	9	0

Semi-final (1st leg)
23 Oct 1957 v Barcelona (Spain) (h) 4-3
Murphy 2, Brown, Orritt
Merrick; Farmer, Allen, Larkin, Smith, Watts, Astall, Orritt, Brown, Neal, Murphy.
Att: 30,791
Semi-final (2nd leg)
13 Nov 1957 v Barcelona (a) 0-1 (aggregate 4-4)
Merrick; Hall, Allen, Larkin, Smith, Neal, Astall, Kinsey, Brown, Murphy, Govan.
Att: 60,000
Replay
26 Nov 1957 v Barcelona (n*) 1-2
Murphy
Merrick; Hall, Farmer, Watts, Smith, Neal, Astall, Orritt, Brown, Murphy, Govan.
Att: 20,000
*Played at the St Jacob Stadium, Basle, Switzerland.

1958-60
Round 1 (1st leg)
14 Oct 1958 v Cologne Select (West Germany) (a) 2-2
Neal, Hooper
Merrick; Hall, Green, Watts, Sissons, Neal, Hooper, Gordon, Brown, Orritt, Murphy.
Att: 12,000
Round 1 (2nd leg)
11 Nov 1958 v Cologne Select (h) 2-0 (aggregate 4-2)
Larkin, Taylor
Merrick; Hall, Allen, Watts, Smith, Neal, Hooper, Gordon, Brown, Larkin, Taylor.
Att: 20,266

Round 2 (1st leg)
6 May 1959 v Dinamo Zagreb (Yugoslavia) (h) 1-0
Larkin
Schofield; Farmer, Allen, Watts, Sissons, Neal, Hooper, Gordon, Stubbs, Larkin, Taylor.
Att: 21,411
Round 2 (2nd leg)
24 May 1959 v Dinamo Zagreb (a) 3-3 (aggregate 4-3)
Larkin 2, Hooper
Schofield; Farmer, Allen, Watts, Smith, Neal, Astall, Gordon, Stubbs, Larkin, Hooper.
Att: 50,000
Semi-final (1st leg)
Oct 7 v Union St Gilloise (Belgium) (a) 4-2
Hooper, Gordon, Barrett, Orritt
Merrick; Sissons, Farmer, Watts, Smith, Neal, Hooper, Gordon, Orritt, Barrett, Taylor.
Att: 20,000
Semi-final (2nd leg)
11 Nov 1959 v Union St Gilloise (h) 4-2 (aggregate 8-4)
Gordon 2, Larkin, Hooper (pen)
Schofield; Farmer, Allen, Watts, Smith, Larkin, Hellawell, Barrett, Gordon, Hooper, Taylor.
Att: 14,152
Final (1st leg)
29 Mar 1960 v Barcelona (Spain) (h) 0-0
Schofield; Farmer, Allen, Watts, Smith, Neal, Astall, Gordon, Weston, Orritt, Hooper.
Att: 40,524

Jimmy Harris breaks through the Internazionale defence in the Fairs Cup semi-final leg in Italy in April 1961.

Blues manager Gil Merrick (centre, in dark suit) tries to calm things down in Rome in October 1961 after the second leg of the Fairs Cup Final between Birmingham and Roma erupted.

Final (2nd leg)
4 May 1960 v Barcelona (a) 1-4 (aggregate 1-4)
Hooper
Schofield; Farmer, Allen, Watts, Smith, Neal, Astall, Gordon, Weston, Murphy, Hooper.
Att: 75,000

1960-61
Round 1 (1st leg)
Oct 19 v Újpesti Dózsa (Hungary) (h) 3-2
Gordon 2, Astall
Schofield; Farmer, Allen, Watts, Sissons, Neal, Hellawell, Rudd, Gordon, Singer, Astall.
Att: 23,381
Round 1 (2nd leg)
Oct 26 v Újpesti Dózsa (a) 2-1 (aggregate 5-3)
Rudd, Singer
Schofield; Farmer, Allen, Watts, Smith, Neal, Hellawell, Barlow, Gordon, Singer, Rudd.
Att: 25,000
Round 2 (1st leg)
Nov 23 v Boldklub Copenhagen (Denmark) (a) 4-4
Gordon 2, Singer 2
Withers; Farmer, Allen, Watts, Smith, Neal, Hellawell, Gordon, Singer, Bloomfield, Taylor.
Att: 2,500

Round 2 (2nd leg)
Dec 7 v Boldklub Copenhagen (h) 5-0 (aggregate 9-4)
Stubbs 2, Harris, Bloomfield, Hellawell
Withers; Farmer, Allen, Watts, Smith, Neal, Hellawell, Stubbs, Harris, Bloomfield, Taylor.
Att: 22,486
Semi-final (1st leg)
Apr 19 v Internazionale (Italy) (a) 2-1
Harris, Balleri (og)
Withers; Farmer, Allen, Hennessey, Smith, Neal, Hellawell, Stubbs, Harris, Bloomfield, Orritt.
Att: 20,000
Semi-final (2nd leg)
May 3 v Internazionale (h) 2-1 (aggregate 4-2)
Harris 2
Schofield; Farmer, Allen, Hennessey, Smith, Neal, Hellawell, Orritt, Harris, Bloomfield, Auld.
Att: 29,530
Final (1st leg)
Sep 27 v AS Roma (Italy) (h) 2-2
Hellawell, Orritt
Schofield; Farmer, Sissons, Hennessey, Foster, Beard, Hellawell, Bloomfield, Harris, Orritt, Auld.
Att: 21,005

Final (2nd leg)
Oct 11 v AS Roma (a) 0-2 (aggregate 2-4)
Schofield; Farmer, Sissons, Hennessey, Smith, Beard, Hellawell, Bloomfield, Harris, Singer, Orritt.
Att: 50,000

1961-62
Round 1
Birmingham City received a bye
Round 2 (1st leg)
Nov 15 v RCD Español (Spain) (a) 2-5
Bloomfield, Harris (pen)
Schofield; Lynn, Sissons, Hennessey, Smith, Beard, Hellawell, Bloomfield, Harris, Orritt, Auld.
Att: 60,000
Round 2 (2nd leg)
Dec 7 v RCD Español (h) 1-0 (aggregate 3-5)
Auld
Schofield; Lynn, Sissons, Hennessey, Smith, Beard, Hellawell, Orritt, Harris, Leek, Auld.
Att: 16,874

Blues in Other Competitions

Football League Jubilee

1938-39
Aug 20 v Coventry City (a) 0-2
Hibbs; Trigg, Steel, Brunskill, Meacock, Halsall, White, Phillips, Dearson, Harris, Farrage.
Att: 12,133

1939-40
Aug 19 v Coventry City (a) 2-3
Turner, Morris
Hibbs; Trigg, Hughes, Bye, Turner, Shaw, Brown, Dearson, Jones, Harris, Morris.
Att: 7,979

Festival of Britain

1950-51
May 7 v Airdrieonians (h) 3-5
Berry 2, Kelly (og)
Merrick; Green, Martin, Boyd, Newman, Ferris, Stewart, Higgins, Dailey, Rowley, Berry.
Att: 7,985
May 12 v Dinamo Yugoslavia (h) 0-2
Merrick; Green, Martin, Boyd, Newman, Dorman, Stewart(James), Dailey, Trigg, Rowley, Berry.
Att: 12,058
May 18 v Home Farm (Dublin) (a) 2-1
Stewart, Berry
Merrick; Green, Martin, Boyd, Newman, Ferris, Stewart, Dailey, Trigg, Rowley, Berry.
Att: 3,000
May 20 v Cork Athletic (a) 5-2
Trigg 2, Higgins, Stewart, Dailey
Merrick; Green, Martin, Boyd, Ferris, Dorman, Stewart, Higgins, Trigg, Dailey, Berry(Rowley).
Att: 2,750

Opening of Floodlights

1956-57
Oct 31 v Borussia Dortmund (h) 3-3
Orritt 2, Govan
Merrick; Farmer, Green, Watts, Newman, Warhurst, Astall, Orritt, Brown, Larkin, Govan.
Att: 45,000

FA Youth Cup

1966-67
Final (1st leg)
May 17 v Sunderland (h) 0-1
D.Latchford; Reynolds, Beckett, Lee, Saunders, Pendrey, Rushworth, Dorsett, R.Latchford, Bowker, Jones.
Att: 10,440
Final (2nd leg)
May 22 v Sunderland (a) 0-1 (aggregate 0-2)
D.Latchford; Reynolds, Beckett, Lee, Saunders, Pendrey, Rushworth, Dorsett, R.Latchford, Bowker, Jones.
Att: 9,273

Anglo-Italian Tournament

1971-72
Jun 1 v Lanerossi Vicenza (a) 0-0
Cooper; Page, Want, Smith, Hynd, Harland, Campbell, Hope, R.Latchford, Hatton, Taylor.
Att: 3,000
Jun 4 v Sampdoria (a) 1-2
Campbell (pen)
Cooper; Page, Want, Smith, Hynd, Harland, Campbell, Hope(Pendrey), R.Latchford, Hatton, Taylor(Summerill).
Att: 15,000
Jun 7 v Lanerossi Vicenza (h) 5-3
Latchford 2, Francis, Hatton, Taylor
Cooper(Kelly); Page, Want, Pendrey, Hynd, Harland, Campbell, Francis, R.Latchford, Hatton, Taylor.
Att: 23,642
Jun 10 v Sampdoria (h) 2-0
Latchford, Hatton
Kelly; Page, Want(Whitehead), Pendrey, Hynd, Harland, Campbell, Francis, R.Latchford, Hatton, Taylor.
Att: 19,510
Birmingham finished fourth in the English group and failed to qualify for the Final.

Centenary Match

1975-76
Nov 25 v Celtic (h) 1-0
Withe
Smith; Martin, Want, Kendall(Emmanuel), Gallagher(Sbragia), Burns, Conway (Hibbitt), Calderwood, Withe, Hatton, Bryant.
Att: 14,670

Anglo-Scottish Tournament

1977-78
Group 'A'
Aug 5 v Plymouth Argyle (a) 1-1
Craven (og)
Montgomery; Rathbone, Pendrey, Towers, Page, Want, Jones, Francis, Bertschin, Hibbitt, Connolly.
Att: 5,176
Aug 9 v Bristol Rovers (a) 1-1
Francis
Montgomery; Page, Pendrey, Towers, Sbragia, Want, Jones(Calderwood), Francis, Bertschin, Hibbitt, Connolly.
Att: 2,317
Aug 12 v Bristol City (h) 1-0
Francis
Montgomery; Rathbone, Pendrey, Page, Sbragia, Want, Jones, Francis, Bertschin, Hibbitt, Connolly.
Att: 9,512

1979-80
Aug 4 v Bristol City (h) 0-4
Wealands; Calderwood(Van den Hauwe), Page, Curbishley, Gallagher, Lees, Lynex, Evans, Bertschin, Towers, Dillon.
Att: 7,631

Aug 6 v Plymouth Argyle (a) 1-1
Bertschin
Freeman; Van den Hauwe, Page, Curbishley, Gallagher, Lees, Lynex, Evans, Bertschin, Calderwood(Dillon), Ainscow.
Att: 3,137
Aug 8 v Fulham (a) 5-0
Bertschin 2, Evans, Ainscow, Dillon
Freeman(Wealands); Calderwood, Page, Curbishley, Gallagher, Van den Hauwe, Ainscow, Evans, Bertschin, Gemmill, Dillon.
Att: 2,899

Texaco Cup

1973-74
Round 1 (1st leg)
Sep 19 v Stoke City (a) 0-0
Cooper(Kelly); Gallagher, Want, Campbell, Hynd, Whitehead, Hope(Emmanuel), Pendrey, Hatton, Phillips, Bryant.
Att: 9,530
Round 1 (2nd leg)
Oct 2 v Stoke City (h) 0-0 (aggregate 0-0; Birmingham won 3-1 on penalties)
D.Latchford(Blackmore); Osborne, Want, Burns, Gallagher, Roberts, Calderwood, Campbell, Francis, Hatton(Emmanuel), Phillips.
Att: 13,433
Round 2 (1st leg)
Oct 22 v Newcastle United (h) 1-1
Latchford
Kelly; Clarke, Want, Pendrey, Gallagher, Roberts, Burns, Francis, R.Latchford(Hope), Hatton, Taylor.
Att: 12,422
Round 2 (2nd leg)
Nov 28 v Newcastle United (a) 1-1 (Match abandoned after 100 minutes because of bad light)
Bowker
D.Latchford; Martin, Gallagher, Want, Whitehead, Roberts, Calderwood, Jenkins, Bowker, Phillips, Taylor.
Att: 5,529
Replay
Dec 5 v Newcastle United (a) 1-3 (aggregate 2-4)
Francis
D.Latchford; Gallagher, Want(Clarke), Jenkins, Hynd, Burns, Campbell, Francis, R.Latchford, Hatton, Hendrie.
Att: 9,762

1974-75
Group 1
Aug 3 v West Bromwich Albion (a) 0-0
D.Latchford; Martin, Pendrey, Kendall, Gallagher, Roberts, Campbell, Morton, Burns, Hatton, Hendrie.
Att: 18,643
Aug 7 v Peterborough United (a) 1-1
Taylor
D.Latchford(Sprake); Page, Pendrey, Kendall, Gallagher, Roberts, Hendrie, Morton(Sbragia), Burns, Hatton, Taylor.
Att: 8,915

Aug 10 v Norwich City (h) 3-1
Campbell, Francis, Hatton
D.Latchford(Sprake); Martin, Pendrey, Kendall, Sbragia, Roberts, Campbell, Francis(Hendrie), Burns, Hatton, Page.
Att: 14,847
Round 2 (1st leg)
Sep 17 v Ayr United (h) 3-0
Burns 2, Calderwood
D.Latchford; Martin(Hope), Styles, Calderwood, Gallagher, Pendrey, Campbell, Francis, Burns, Hatton, Taylor.
Att: 12,327
Round 2 (2nd leg)
Oct 2 v Ayr United (a) 0-0 (aggregate 3-0)
D.Latchford; Calderwood, Bryant, Kendall, Hynd, Pendrey, Hendrie, Phillips(Hope), Allen, Hatton, Taylor.
Att: 4,992
Semi-final (1st leg)
Oct 23 v Newcastle United (a) 1-1
Hatton
D.Latchford; Hynd, Styles, Kendall, Gallagher, Pendrey, Campbell(Emmanuel), Taylor, Burns, Hatton, Calderwood.
Att: 20,556
Semi-final (2nd leg)
Nov 6 v Newcastle United (h) 1-4 (aggregate 2-5)
Burns
D.Latchford; Martin, Pendrey, Kendall, Gallagher, Page, Campbell, Phillips(Taylor), Burns, Hatton, Calderwood.
Att: 17,754

Full Members' Cup

1986-87
Round 1
Oct 1 v Brighton & Hove Albion (a) 3-0
Clarke, Kuhl, O'Regan (og)
Hansbury; Ranson, Dicks(Williams), Hagan, Overson, Rees, Bremner, Clarke, Whitton, Mortimer(Kuhl), Cooke.
Att: 3,794
Round 2
Nov 4 v Charlton Athletic (a) 2-3
Geddis, Shirtliff (og)
Hansbury; Jones(Rees), Dicks, Russell, Overson, Kuhl, Bremner, Clarke, Whitton, Geddis, Lynex(Hagan).
Att: 821

Simod Cup

1987-88
Round 1
Nov 25 v Derby County (a) 1-3
Whitton
Godden; Ranson, Trewick, Williams, Frain, Bird, Bremner, Childs(Rees), Whitton, Kennedy(Ashley), Wigley.
Att: 8,277

1988-89
Round 1
Nov 9 v Aston Villa (a) 0-6
Thomas; Frain, Roberts, Atkins, Bird, Langley, Bremner, Childs, Yates, Sturridge(Morris), Wigley.
Att: 8,324

Leyland DAF Cup

1989-90
Preliminary Round
Nov 28 v Aldershot (a) 0-3
Thomas; Ashley, Frain, Atkins, Clarkson(Tait), Matthewson, Bell, Bailey, Sturridge, Gleghorn, Langley.
Att: 1,148
Preliminary Round
Dec 12 v Hereford United (h) 1-0
Atkins
Thomas; Clarkson(Roberts), Frain, Atkins, Overson, Matthewson, Bell, Bailey, Yates(Deakin), Gleghorn, Langley.
Att: 3,168

1990-91
Preliminary Round
Nov 6 v Walsall (a) 1-0
Skipper (og)
Thomas; Hopkins, Downs, Frain, Overson, Matthewson, Peer, Sturridge(Bailey), Aylott(Clarkson), Gleghorn, Tait.
Att: 5,053
Preliminary Round
Nov 27 v Lincoln City (h) 2-0
Clarke (og), Sturridge
Thomas; Clarkson, Downs, Frain, Overson, Matthewson, Peer, Bailey, Gayle, Gleghorn, Sturridge.
Att: 2,922
Round 1
Feb 18 v Swansea City (h) 0-0
Thomas; Clarkson, Frain, Rodgerson, Overson, Matthewson, Peer, Dolan, Aylott(Harris), Gleghorn, Sturridge.
Att: 3,555
Birmingham won 4-2 on penalties
Southern Area quarter-final
Feb 26 v Mansfield Town (h) 2-0
Matthewson, Gayle
Thomas; Clarkson, Frain, Rodgerson, Overson, Matthewson, Peer, Dolan(Gayle), Aylott, Gleghorn(Bailey), Sturridge.
Att: 5,358
Southern Area semi-final
Mar 5 v Cambridge United (h) 3-1
Peer, Gleghorn, Overson
Thomas; Clarkson, Frain, Rodgerson, Overson, Matthewson, Peer, Gayle, Aylott, Gleghorn, Sturridge.
Att: 9,429
Southern Area Final (1st leg)
Mar 26 v Brentford (h) 2-1
Rodgerson, Gayle
Thomas; Clarkson, Frain, Yates, Overson, Matthewson, Peer, Gayle, Rodgerson (Robinson), Gleghorn, Sturridge.
Att: 16,219
Southern Area Final (2nd leg)
Apr 9 v Brentford (a) 1-0
Sturridge
Thomas; Clarkson, Frain, Peer, Overson, Matthewson, Robinson, Gayle(Aylott), Yates, Sturridge, Gleghorn.
Att: 8,745
Final
May 26 v Tranmere Rovers (at Wembley) 3-2
Sturridge, Gayle 2
Thomas; Clarkson, Frain, Yates, Overson, Matthewson, Peer, Gayle, Robinson, Gleghorn, Sturridge(Bailey).
Att: 58,756

Autoglass Trophy

1991-92
Preliminary Round
Dec 18 v Stoke City (a) 1-3
Tait
Cheesewright; Clarkson, Frain, Peer, Hicks, Mardon, Rodgerson, Tait, Atkins(Okenla), Gleghorn, Cooper.
Att: 5,932
Preliminary Round
Jan 7 v Walsall (h) 0-1
Miller; Clarkson, Frain, Cooper, Hicks, Matthewson, Rodgerson, Peer, Beckford, Gleghorn, Okenla(Hogan).
Att: 5,239

Anglo-Italian Cup

1992-93
Preliminary Round
Sep 15 v Sunderland (a) 1-0
Sale
Gosney; Clarkson, Frain, Hicks, Rogers, Matthewson, Donowa, Tait, Sale, Gleghorn, Rowbotham.
Att: 5,871
Preliminary Round
Sep 29 v Cambridge United (h) 3-3
Gleghorn, Frain, Sale
Thomas; Clarkson, Frain, Matthewson, Hicks, Rogers, Rodgerson, Tait(Sale), Donowa, Gleghorn, Sturridge(Rowbotham).
Att: 3,102
International Stage
Group A
Nov 11 v AS Bari (h) 1-0
Cooper
Sealey; Tait(Donowa), Potter, Rogers, Frain, Matthewson, Rodgerson, Gayle (Peschisolido), Speedie, Cooper, Sturridge.
Att: 4,970
Dec 2 v AC Cesena (a) 2-1
Frain (pen), Sturridge
Thomas; Clarkson, Potter, Tait, Frain, Rogers, Rowbotham(Peer), Gayle, Sturridge, Sale, Rodgerson.
Att: 2,090
Dec 8 v Ascoli Calcio (h) 1-1
Sturridge
Sealey; Clarkson, Potter, Fenwick, Frain, Matthewson, Rodgerson, Tait, Speedie, Sale(Donowa), Sturridge.
Att: 3,963
Dec 16 v Lucchese (a) 0-3
Sealey; Clarkson, Potter, Rennie, Hicks, Matthewson, Rodgerson, Gayle, Rowbotham, Tait, Peschisolido.
Att: 139

1993-94
Preliminary Round
Sep 1 v Stoke City (a) 0-2
Miller; Scott, Rogers, Peer, Clarkson, Mardon, Fenwick, Tait, Moulden (Robinson), Morgan(Black), Potter.
Att: 8,633
Preliminary Round
Sep 14 v Wolverhampton Wanderers (h) 2-2
Wratten 2
Miller; Hicks, Potter, Fenwick, Whyte, Mardon, McMinn, Tait(Wratten), Black, Smith, Donowa.
Att: 2,710

Auto Windscreens Shield

1994-95
Round 1
Sep 27 v Peterborough United (a) 5-3
Bull, Dominguez, Hunt 3
Price; Scott, Frain, Ward, Barnett, Daish,
Hunt, Claridge, Bull(McGavin), Poole,
Dominguez(Wallace).
Att: 2,044
Round 2
Oct 18 v Walsall (h) 3-0
Shearer 2, Donowa
Bennett; Poole, Donowa, Ward, Barnett,
Daish, Hunt, Claridge(McGavin), Bull, De
Souza(Doherty), Shearer.
Att: 10,089
Round 3
Nov 29 v Gillingham (h) 3-0
McGavin, Poole, Tait
Bennett; Poole, Whyte, Ward(Lowe),

Barnett, Daish, Donowa(Cooper), Claridge,
McGavin, Dominguez, Tait.
Att: 17,028
Round 4
Jan 10 v Hereford United 3-1
Claridge, Ward (pen), Otto
Bennett; Poole, Cooper, Ward, Barnett,
Daish,Donowa, Claridge,
Lowe(Dominguez), Otto, Shearer.
Att: 22,351
Southern Area semi-final
**Jan 31 v Swansea City (h) 3-2 aet
'sudden death'**
Claridge, Francis, Tait
Bennett; Scott, Cooper, Ward, Barnett,
Whyte, Donowa(Dominguez), Claridge,
Francis, Otto, Lowe(Tait).
Att: 20,326
Southern Area Final (1st leg)
Feb 28 v Leyton Orient (h) 1-0
Shearer

Bennett; Poole, Cooper, Tait(Whyte),
Barnett, Daish, Donowa, Saville(McGavin),
Francis, Otto, Shearer.
Att: 24,002
Southern Area Final (2nd leg)
**Mar 14 v Leyton Orient (a) 3-2
(aggregate 4-2)**
Claridge 2, Williams
Bennett; Poole, Whyte, Ward, Barnett,
Daish, Esteves(Tait), Claridge, Robinson,
Otto(Doherty), Williams.
Att: 10,830
Final
**Apr 23 v Carlisle United (Wembley) 1-0
aet 'sudden death'**
Tait
Bennett; Poole, Cooper, Ward, Barnett,
Daish, Hunt, Claridge, Francis(Donowa),
Otto, Shearer(Tait).
Att: 76,663

*Steve Claridge breaks through the Carlisle United defence during the 1995 Auto Windscreens Shield Final at Wembley, which was settled
by the first 'sudden death' goal at the stadium.*

International Blues

England

Astall G. v Finland, West Germany 1955-56 (2).
Barton P.H. v Belgium 1920-21; Ireland 1921-22; France 1922-23; Belgium, Wales, Scotland 1923-24; Northern Ireland 1924-25 (7).
Bradford J. v Ireland 1923-24; Belgium 1924-25; Scotland 1927-28; Northern Ireland, Wales, France, Spain 1928-29; Northern Ireland, Scotland, Germany, Austria 1929-30; Wales 1930-31 (12).
Charsley C.C. v Ireland 1892-93 (1).
Corbett W.S. v Austria, Hungary, Bohemia 1907-08 (3).
Francis T.J. v Holland, Luxembourg, Scotland, Brazil 1976-77; Switzerland, Luxembourg, Italy (sub), West Germany (sub), Brazil, Wales, Scotland, Hungary 1977-78 (12).
Grosvenor A.T. v Northern Ireland, Wales, France, 1933-34 (3).
Hall J.J. v Denmark, Wales, Northern Ireland, Spain, Scotland, Brazil, Sweden, Finland, West Germany 1955-56; Northern Ireland, Wales, Yugoslavia, Denmark, Scotland, Republic of Ireland, Denmark, Republic of Ireland 1956-57 (17).

Birmingham and England goalkeeper Harry Hibbs meets the Duke Of Gloucester before a pre-war international.

Hellawell M.S. v France, Northern Ireland 1962-63 (2).
Hibbs H.E. v Wales, Scotland, Germany, Austria 1929-30; Northern Ireland, Wales, Scotland 1930-31; Northern Ireland, Wales, Spain 1931-32; Northern Ireland, Wales, Austria, Scotland, Italy, Switzerland 1932-33; Northern Ireland, Wales, France 1933-34; Wales, Northern Ireland, Scotland, Holland 1934-35; Germany, Wales 1935-36 (25).
Merrick G.H. v Northern Ireland, Scotland, Italy, Austria (twice), Switzerland 1951-52; Northern Ireland, Wales, Belgium, Scotland, Argentina, Chile, Uruguay 1952-53; Wales, Rest of Europe, Northern Ireland, Hungary (twice), Scotland, Yugoslavia, Belgium, Switzerland, Uruguay 1953-54 (23).
Smith T. v Wales, Sweden 1959-60 (2).
Stoker L. v Wales 1932-33; Scotland, Hungary 1933-34 (3).
Tremelling D.R. v Wales 1927-28 (1).

Scotland

Crosbie J.A. v England 1921-22 (1).
Burns K. v West Germany 1973-74; East Germany (sub), Spain (twice) 1974-75; Czechoslovakia (sub), Wales, Sweden, Wales (sub) 1976-77 (8).
Gemmill A. v Austria, Portugal, Northern Ireland, Wales, England, Hungary 1979-80; v Sweden, Portugal, Israel, Northern Ireland 1980-81 (10).
Herriot J. v Northern Ireland, England, Denmark, Cyprus (twice), Wales (sub) 1968-69; v Republic of Ireland (sub), West Germany 1969-70 (8).
McGurk F. v Wales 1933-34 (1).

Wales

Curtis E.R. v Scotland 1931-32, Northern Ireland 1933-34 (2).
Dearson D.J. v Scotland, Northern Ireland, France 1938-39 (3).
Edwards G. v England, Scotland, Northern Ireland 1946-47; England, Scotland, Northern Ireland 1947-48 (6).
Evans S.V.L. v Northern Ireland 1933-34 (1).
Green C.R. v USSR, Italy 1964-65; England, Scotland, USSR, Brazil (twice) 1965-66; England 1966-67; England, Scotland, Northern Ireland, West Germany 1967-68; Scotland, Italy, Northern Ireland (sub) 1968-69 (15).
Hennessey W.T. v Northern Ireland, Brazil (twice) 1961-62; Scotland, England, Hungary (twice) 1962-63; England, Scotland 1963-64; Scotland, England, Denmark, Greece, USSR 1964-65; England, USSR 1965-66 (16).
Hughes W.M. v Scotland, England, Northern Ireland 1937-38; England, Northern Ireland, Scotland, France 1938-39; England, Scotland, Northern Ireland 1946-47 (10).
Jenkyns C.A.L. v England, Scotland, Ireland 1891-92; England 1894-95 (4).
Jones C.W. v Northern Ireland 1934-35; France 1938-39 (2).
Jones F.W. v Scotland 1892-93 (1).
Kinsey N. v Northern Ireland 1953-54; England, Scotland 1955-56 (3).
Leek K. v Brazil (sub), Mexico 1961-62; England 1962-63; Scotland, Greece 1964-65 (5).
Morris S. v England, Scotland 1936-37; England, Scotland 1937-38; France 1938-39 (5).
Page M.E. v Finland 1970-71; Scotland, Northern Ireland 1971-72; England (twice, once as sub), Northern Ireland 1972-73; Scotland, Northern Ireland 1973-74; Hungary,

Luxembourg, Scotland, England, Northern Ireland 1974-75; England (twice), Yugoslavia (twice), Northern Ireland 1975-76; West Germany, Scotland 1976-77; Kuwait (twice, once as sub), West Germany, Iran, England, Scotland 1977-78; Malta, West Germany 1978-79 (28).
Powell A. v Scotland 1950-51 (1).
Rees A.A. v Norway (sub) 1983-84 (1).
Richards D. v Northern Ireland 1936-37; England, Scotland, Northern Ireland 1937-38; England, Scotland 1938-39 (6).
Roberts J.G. v England (twice), Poland, Scotland, Northern Ireland 1972-73; Poland, England, Scotland, Northern Ireland 1973-74; Austria, Hungary, Scotland, England 1974-75; England, Scotland 1975-76 (15).
Sprake G. v Scotland, Northern Ireland 1973-74; Austria, Hungary, Luxembourg 1974-75 (5).
Stevenson W.B. v Spain, Scotland, Northern Ireland, France 1981-82 (4).

Northern Ireland (and Ireland before 1924)
Brennan R.A. v England, Scotland, Wales 1949-50 (3).
Brown J. v Scotland, England, Wales, 1938-39 (3).
Ferris R.O. v Scotland 1949-50; France 1950-51; Scotland 1951-52 (3).

Republic of Ireland
Barber E. v Belgium 1965-66 (1).
Carroll T.R. v Iran, Ecuador, Chile, Portugal 1971-72; v USSR (twice), Poland, France, Norway 1972-73 (9).
Daly G.A. v Mexico (sub), Norway, Spain, Sweden 1984-85; Switzerland 1985-86 (5).
Givens D.J. v Northern Ireland (sub), England, Denmark, Bulgaria, West Germany, Argentina 1978-79; USA (sub) Northern Ireland (sub), Switzerland, Argentina 1979-80; v Holland, Belgium, Cyprus (sub), Wales 1980-81 (14).
Higgins J. v Argentina 1950-51 (1).
Langan D.F. v Holland, Belgium (twice), France, Cyprus, Wales, Czechoslovakia, Poland 1980-81; Holland, France 1981-82 (10).

Canada
P.P.Peschisolido 1992-93 v Bermuda, Costa Rica, Honduras, Mexico (3 goals), El Salvador, Martinique (6).
L.Hooper 1993-94 v Morocco, Brazil, Germany, Spain, Holland (5).

Under-21 Internationals (1976-95)

England
Bertschin K.E. 1976-77 v Scotland; 1977-78 v Yugoslavia (twice) (3).
Curbishley L.C. 1980-81 v Switzerland (1).
Dennis M.E. 1979-80 v Bulgaria; 1980-81 v Norway, Romania (3).
Dillon K.P. 1980-81 v Romania (1).
Gayle H. 1983-84 v Italy, Spain (twice) (3).
Seaman D.A. 1984-85 v Finland, Turkey, Israel, Republic of Ireland, Romania, Finland; 1985-86 v Romania, France, Denmark, Italy (10).

Wales
Rees A.A. 1983-84 v Norway (1).

Under-23 Internationals(1954-76)

England
Francis T.J. 1973-74 v Portugal, Denmark, Wales; 1975-76 v Portugal, Hungary (5).

Greenhoff J. 1968-69 v Wales, Holland (twice, once as sub), Belgium (4).
Latchford R.D. 1973-74 v Denmark, Wales (2).
Neal R.M. 1956-57 v Bulgaria (1).
Smith T. 1954-55 v Italy, Scotland; 1955-56 v Denmark, Scotland; 1956-57 v Denmark, France, Scotland, Bulgaria, Romania, Czechoslovakia; 1957-58 v Bulgaria, Romania, Scotland, Wales; 1958-59 v Italy (15).

Scotland
Burns K. 1973-74 v Wales; 1975-76 v Holland (2).
Calderwood J.R. 1973-74 v England (1).

Wales
Emmanuel J.G. 1974-75 v Scotland (1).
Green C.R. 1962-63 v Northern Ireland; 1963-64 v England, Scotland; 1964-65 v Northern Ireland (4).
Hennessey W.T. 1961-62 v Northern Ireland; 1962-63 v Northern Ireland; 1963-64 v Scotland, Northern Ireland; 1964-65 v England, Scotland (6).
Orritt B. 1957-58 v England; 1958-59 v Scotland; 1959-60 v Scotland (3).
Page M.E. 1965-66 v England, Scotland; 1967-68 v Northern Ireland; 1968-69 v England; 1969-70 v England, Scotland (6).

Great Britain v Rest of Europe

Hughes W.M. 1946-47.

England 'B'

Boyd L. 1951-52 v Holland (1).
Gallagher J.A. 1980-81 v Australia (1).
Green K. 1953-54 v Yugoslavia, Switzerland (2).
Hall J.J. 1954-55 v Germany (1).
Smith T. 1954-55 v Germany; 1956-57 v Scotland (2).

Young England v England

Hall J.J. 1957-58 (1).
Neal R.M. 1956-57 (1).
Smith T. 1953-54; 1954-55; 1956-57; 1958-59 (4).

FA XI

Merrick G.H. 1945-46 v FA XI (1).

APTC XI

Merrick G.H. 1945-46 v FA XI (1).

Football League XI

Francis T.J. 1976-77 v Glasgow XI (Jubilee Fund) (1).

FA Tours
Hall J.J. 1955 (West Indies).
Harris W.A. 1926 (Canada).
Hibbs H.E. 1931 (Canada).

Smith W. 1951 (Australia).
Tewkesbury K.C. 1931 (Canada).
Womack F. 1925 (Australia).

Unofficial Internationals
(Wartime & Victory Internationals, 1919-20, 1939-46)

England
Ball W. 1919-20 v Wales (1).

Scotland
Dougall C. 1945-46 v England (1).

Wales
Dearson D.J. 1939-40 v England (twice); 1940-41 v England (twice); 1941-42 v England (twice); 1942-43 v England (thrice); 1943-44 v England (twice); 1944-45 v England (twice); 1945-46 v England, Scotland. (15).
Edwards G. 1945-46 v England, Scotland (2).
Hughes W.M. 1939-40 v England; 1940-41 v England (twice); 1941-42 v England (twice); 1942-43 v England (thrice); 1943-44 v England; 1944-45 v England (twice); 1945-46 v England, Scotland, Northern Ireland (14).

Other Internationals

England
Hibbs H.E. 1929-30 v South Africa (1).
Leake A. 1901-02 v Germany (1).
Mitchell F.R. 1946-47 v Scotland (Bolton Disaster Find) (1).
Morgan W.A. 1917-18 v Scotland XI (1).
Smith W.H. 1951-52 v Australia (1).
Wharton S.E. 1901-02 v Germany (1).

Scotland
Dougall C. 1946-47 v England (Bolton Disaster Fund) (1).

All-Ireland
Carroll T.R. v Brazil 1973-74 (1).

United Kingdom (Amateur)
Corbett W.S. v Sweden, Holland, Denmark (1908 Olympic Games) (3).

Amateur Internationals

England
Bailey H.P. 1910-13 (4).
Corbett W.S. 1906-11 (18).
Harvey W.H. 1923-25 (3).
Hauser S. 1913-14 (1).
Slater J. 1928-30 (2).
Tewkesbury K.C. 1929-31 (4).

International Trials

The Rest v England
Barton P.H. 1919-20, 1920-21 (2).
Bradford J. 1929-30 (1).
Hibbs H.E. 1928-29 (1).
Stoker L. 1931-32, 1933-4 (2).

England v The Rest
Barton P.H. 1923-24 (1).

Bradford J. 1923-24 (1).
Grosvenor A.T. 1932-33 (1).
Hibbs H.E. 1929-30, 1931-32 (2).
North v South
Barton P.H. 1923-24 (1).
Bradford J. 1923-24 (1).
Jones W.H. 1906-07 (1).
Jones J.W. 1924-25 (1).
Leake A. 1901-02 (1).
Robinson A.C. 1905-06 (1).
Stokes F. 1904-05 (1).
Wilcox F.J. 1904-05 (1).

South v England
Barton P.H. 1919-20, 1920-21 (2).
Womack F. 1913-14 (1).

South v North
Womack F. 1913-14 (1).

Anglo-Scots v Home Scots
Crosbie J.A. 1920-21, 1921-22, 1922-23 (3).

Professionals v Amateurs
Bradford J. 1923-24 (1).
Harris W.A. 1926-27 (1).
Robinson A.C. 1906-07 (1).
Stokes F. 1906-07 (1).
Womack F. 1913-14 (1).

Possibles v Probables
Stoker L. 1935-36 (1).

Amateur Trialist (England)
Pointon T. (North v South) 1914-15.

Football League

Astall G. 1956-57 v League of Ireland (1).
Bradford J. 1923-24 v Irish League, Scottish League; 1927-28 v Scottish League; 1928-29 v Scottish League; 1929-30 v Irish League (5).
Glover J. 1905-06 v Irish League, Scottish League (2).
Green K. 1952-53 v Scottish League; 1953-54 v Irish League (2).
Grosvenor A.T. 1933-34 v Irish League (1).
Harris F. 1948-49 v Scottish League (1).
Hall J.J. 1955-56 v Scottish League; 1956-57 v League of Ireland, Irish League (3).
Hibbs H.E. 1929-30 v Scottish League; 1931-32 v Scottish League; 1932-33 v Scottish League (3).
Hooper H. 1959-60 v Scottish League (1).
Jones J.W. 1924-25 v Scottish League (1).
Jones W.H. 1904-05 v Irish League (1).
McClure A. 1921-22 v Irish League (1).
Merrick G.H. 1947-48 v Irish League; 1948-49 v League of Ireland; 1949-50 v League of Ireland, Irish League; 1951-52 v Scottish League, Irish League; 1952-53 v Irish League, Scottish League; 1953-54 v Irish League, League of Ireland, Scottish League (11).
Morgan W.A. 1918-19 v Scottish League (1).
Robinson A.C. 1906-07 v Irish League, Scottish League (2).
Smith T. 1957-58 v Irish League; 1959-60 v Irish League (2).
Stoker L. 1932-33 v Irish League (1).
Tickle C.H. 1907-08 v Scottish League (1).

Tremelling D.R. 1926-27 v Irish League; 1927-28 v Irish League (2).
Wharton S.E. 1901-02 v Irish League (1).
Wheldon G.F. 1893-94 v Irish League, Scottish League (2).
Wigmore W. 1899-1900 v Scottish League (1).
Womack F. 1918-19 v Scottish League (1).

Other Football League Representative Matches

Francis T.J. v Glasgow XI 1976-7.
Wheldon G.F. v Aston Villa 1894-5.
Womack F. v Nottingham Forest/Notts County XI 1913-14.

England Youth Caps

Beard M. 1959.
Gibson A.S. 1981
Rathbone M.J. 1977

Birmingham's Ian Handyside tries a shot for England against Northern Ireland in a Youth international at Walsall in 1981.

Bird R.P. 1958.
Handysides I.R. 1981.
Roach J. 1955.
Dennis M.E. 1979.
Hawker P.N. 1981.
Smith S.J. 1975.
Dillon K.P. 1978.
Jones D.W.L. 1958.
Summerill P.E. 1966.
Duce N. 1982.
Latchford R.D. 1969.
Thwaites D. 1961, 1963.
Elliott A.M. 1987.
Passey P.T.J. 1970.
Vincent J.V. 1965.
Francis T.J. 1971, 1972.
Phillips S.E. 1973.
Winterburn N. 1982.
Potter G.S. 1992

Staffordshire County & County FA

1870s: W.H.Edmunds - W.Edden - D.Keys - J.H.Sparrow
1927: R.A.Dale - G.R.Briggs

The following players all gained full international honours with other clubs either before or after serving with the Blues:-

England
W.Abbott, W.C.Athersmith, H.P.Bailey, R.J.Barlow, J.J.Berry, B.J.Bridges, F.C.Buckley, J.Conlin, T.J.Francis, W.George, H.Hampton, M.G.Harford, D.Hodgetts, R.D.Latchford, A.Leake, L.V.Lodge, A.W.Morley, S.W..Owen, M.O'Grady, F.B.Pentland, F.Pickering, W.C.Rose, D.A.Seaman, J.Smith, R.A.Thomson, C.Todd, M.A.Towers, G.F.Wheldon, J.E.Windridge, N.Winterburn, P.Withe, F.S.Worthington.

Scotland
R.Auld, J.N.Blyth, D.G.Bremner, D.Bruce, K.Burns, J.Connolly, J.A.Crosbie, A.Gemmill, R.A.Hope, W.M.Johnston, G.Leggett, B.D.Rioch, W.R.Robb, J.Robertson, D.R.Speedie.

Wales
E.R.Curtis, S.C.Davies, G.Edwards, S.L.V.Evans, R.O.Evans, D.Giles, J.Hallam, W.T.Hennessey, T.Hockey, C.A.L.Jenkyns, N.Kinsey, K.Leek, C.Phillips, A.Powell, D.A.Richards, J.G.Roberts, G.Sprake, W.B.Stevenson, M.R.Thomas, P.W.R.Van den Hauwe.

Northern Ireland
R.A.Brennan, J.Brown, O.Madden, J.C.McLaughlin.

Republic of Ireland
E.Barber, J.Brown, T.R.Carroll., G.A.Daly, D.J.Givens, D.F.Langan, J.M.McDonagh, O.Madden.

Netherlands
B.A.Brocken, A.W.M.T.Van Mierlo.

Argentina
A.C.Tarantini.

Canada
P.Fenwick, L.Hooper, P.P.Peschisolido.

Northern Ireland Youth
S.J.Quinn 1992.

Wales Youth
W.T.Hennessey 1958, M.E.Page 1964, C.J.Price, K.J.Oakley, A.J.Hinchey.

Under-21
Portugal
J.M.M.Dominguez 1994-95 v Austria.

Republic of Ireland 'B'
L.S.Daish 1994-95 v England.

Hat-trick Heroes

Football League

1892-93
W.H.Walton (3) v Walsall Town Swifts (h) 17 December
F.Mobley (3) v Walsall Town Swifts (h) 17 December
G.F.Wheldon (3) v Lincoln City (a) 7 January
G.F.Wheldon (3) v Northwich Victoria (h) 14 January
J.Hallam (3) v Bootle (h) 18 February
W.H.Walton (3) v Grimsby Town (h) 25 February

1893-94
C.J.Izon (3) v Walsall Town Swifts (h) 16 September
W.H.Walton (3) v Grimsby Town (h) 7 October
F.Mobley (3) v Lincoln City (a) 11 November
G.F.Wheldon (4) v Northwich Victoria (h) 2 December
F.Mobley (3) v Northwich Victoria (h) 2 December
F.Mobley (3) v Northwich Victoria (1) 6 January
F.Mobley (3) v Ardwick (h) 17 March

1897-98
W.Abbott (3) v Darwen (h) 25 December

1898-99
W.Robertson (3) v Luton Town (h) 12 November
W.Abbott (5) v Darwen (h) 26 November
W.Abbott (3) v Loughborough Town (h) 21 January
W.Abbott (3) v Luton Town (a) 11 March
W.Abbott (3) v Gainsborough Trinity (h) 1 April

1899-1900
R.McRoberts (3) v Middlesbrough (a) 9 September
R.McRoberts (3) v Lincoln City (h) 2 October
R.McRoberts (3) v Gainsborough Trinity (h) 20 January
J.Aston (3) v Loughborough Town (h) 10 February

1900-01
R.McRoberts (5) v Blackpool (h) 2 March

1902-03
B.Leonard (4) v Doncaster Rovers (h) 11 April
F.J.Wilcox (4) v Doncaster Rovers (h) 11 April

1904-05
F.J.Wilcox (3) v Wolverhampton Wanderers (h) 11 February

1905-06
F.J.Wilcox (3) v Nottingham Forest (h) 16 December
B.Green (5) v Middlesbrough (h) 27 December
C.H.Tickle (3) v Sheffield Wednesday (h) 14 April

1908-09
F.J.Chapple (4) v Stockport County (h) 25 December
A.Mounteney (3) v Chesterfield (h) 17 April

1909-10
J.Needham (3) v Gainsborough Trinity (h) 16 October

1911-12
J.H.Hall (4) v Leeds City (h) 30 September
J.H.Hall (3) v Wolverhampton Wanderers (h) 10 February

J.H.Hall (3) v Clapton Orient (h) 23 March

1914-15
A.W.Smith (3) v Leeds City (h) 24 October
A.W.Smith (4) v Glossop (h) 6 January
J.Windridge (5) v Glossop (h) 6 January

1919-20
H.Hampton (4) v Nottingham Forest (h) 10 March
J.Lane (3) v Lincoln City (h) 13 March

1920-21
H.Hampton (3) v Leicester City (h) 2 October

1924-25
J.Bradford (3) v Liverpool (h) 29 November

1925-26
J.Bradford (3) v Tottenham Hotspur (h) 25 December
J.Bradford (3) v Blackburn Rovers (a) 16 January

1927-28
J.Bradford (4) v Blackburn Rovers (a) 24 September
G.Briggs (3) v Sheffield United (h) 10 March
J.Bradford (3) v Burnley (h) 24 March

1928-29
J.Bradford (3) v Sunderland (a) 29 September
J.Bradford (3) v Leeds United (h) 22 December

1929-30
J.Bradford (3) v West Ham United (h) 4 September
J.Bradford (3) v Newcastle United (h) 21 September
J.Bradford (3) v Blackburn Rovers (a) 28 September
J.Bradford (3) v Leicester City (h) 3 May

1930-31
J.Firth (3) v Grimsby Town (h) 22 November
J.Bradford (4) v Blackburn Rovers (h) 7 February

1932-33
R.Gregg (3) v Liverpool (h) 10 December
G.Haywood (3) v Everton (h) 7 January

1933-34
W.Guest (3) v Leicester City (a) 28 April 1934

1934-35
D.Mangnall (3) v Liverpool (a) 13 October
C.W.Jones (3) v Derby County (h) 23 March
F.White (3) v Preston North End (h) 6 April

1935-36
C.W.Jones (3) v Sheffield Wednesday (h) 22 April

1937-38
J.M.Beattie (3) v Middlesbrough (h) 1 September
C.W.Jones (3) v Leicester City (h) 15 September

1938-39
F.White (4) v Brentford (h) 10 December
F.Harris (3) v Charlton Athletic (h) 4 February

Alex Govan's five hat-tricks in 1956-57 were a Birmingham club record from a winger in a single season.

1946-47
C.Trigg (3) v Luton Town (a) 14 December
H.Bodle (3) v Plymouth Argyle (h) 21 December
1948-49
J.Stewart (4) v Manchester City (h) 15 September

1950-51
C.Trigg (3) v Swansea Town (h) 16 December

1951-52
W.Smith (3) v Rotherham United (h) 25 December
R.Murphy (3) v Doncaster Rovers (a) 19 January

1952-53
P.Murphy (3) v Leicester City (a) 29 January

1953-54
P.Murphy (3) v Swansea Town (h) 22 August
P.Murphy (3) v Luton Town (h) 9 September

1954-55
P.Murphy (3) v Port Vale (h) 27 November
E.Brown (3) v Liverpool (h) 11 December

1955-56
E.Brown (3) v Portsmouth (a) 15 October
N.Kinsey (3) v Everton (h) 26 December
E.Brown (3) v Charlton Athletic (h) 4 February

1956-57
A.Govan (3) v Portsmouth (a) 29 August
A.Govan (3) v Newcastle United (h) 5 September
A.Govan (3) v Preston North End (h) 8 September
A.Govan (3) v Leeds United (h) 20 April

1957-58
P.Murphy (3) v Manchester City (h) 5 October

1958-59
E.Brown (4) v Leeds United (h) 10 September
R.Stubbs (3) v Leicester City (a) 18 March

1964-65
M.Beard (3) v Blackburn Rovers (h) 24 April

1965-66
G.Vowden (3) v Rotherham United (a) 11 December

1967-68
B.Bridges (3) v Rotherham United (h) 28 October

1968-69
G.Vowden (3) v Huddersfield Town (h) 7 September
J.Greenhoff (4) v Fulham (h) 5 October
P.Summerill (3) v Hull City (h) 30 October
P.Summerill (3) v Bolton Wanderers (h) 25 March.

When Trevor Francis (above) scored all four goals against Bolton at St Andrew's in February 1971, he was the first 16-year-old to achieve the feat in League football.

1969-70
A.Murray (3) v Queen's Park Rangers (h) 30 August
P.Summerill (3) Carlisle United (a) 17 January

1970-71
T.Francis (4) v Bolton Wanderers (h) 20 February

1971-72
R.Latchford (3) v Charlton Athletic (h) 4 September
R.Latchford (3) v Watford (h) 28 September

1972-73
R.Latchford (3) v Manchester City (h) 9 September

1973-74
R.Latchford (3) v Leicester City (h) 24 November
K.Burns (3) v Leicester City (a) 6 April

1974-75
T.Francis (3) v Luton Town (a) 12 October

1976-77
K.Burns (4) v Derby County (h) 2 October
K.Burns (3) v Leicester City (a) 4 December
T.Francis (3) v Arsenal (h) 19 January
T.Francis (3) v Bristol City (h) 9 April

1979-80
K.Bertschin (3) v Luton Town (a) 24 November
K.Bertschin (3) v Orient (h) 9 February

1981-82
A.Evans (3) v Manchester City (h) 19 September

1984-85
D.Geddis (3) v Portsmouth (a) 13 April

1994-95
J.Hunt (3) v Crewe Alexandra (h) 1 November

FA Cup

1885-86
E.Stanley (4) v Burton Wanderers (h) 31 October

1889-89
E.Devey (4) v Burton Wanderers (h) 8 December
W.Devey (4) v Burton Wanderers (h) 8 December

1889-90
W.Devey (3) v Walsall Town Swifts (h) 7 December

1890-91
G.F.Wheldon (3) v Hednesford Town (h) 4 October

1891-92
F.Wilkes (3) v Brierley Hill Athletic (h) 5 December

1898-99
W.H.Walton (3) v Chirk (h) 29 October
R.McRoberts (3) v Druids (h) 19 November
W.Abbott (3) v Burslem Port Vale (h) 10 December

1899-1900
R.McRoberts (3) v Wrexham (h) 22 November

1919-20
J.Whitehouse (3) v Darlington (h) 31 January

1927-28
J.Bradford (3) v Peterborough United (h) 14 January

1934-35
F.Harris (3) v Coventry City (h) 12 January

1945-46
A.Mulraney (3) v Watford (h) 26 January

1952-53
P.Murphy (3) v Oldham Athletic (a) 10 January

Bob Latchford scored four hat-tricks in his 84 League and Cup goals for Birmingham City.

1955-56
E.Brown (3) v Torquay United (a) 7 January

1956-57
A.Govan (3) v Southend United (a) 26 January

Football League Cup

1973-74
R.Hatton (3) v Blackpool (h) 16 October
R.Latchford (3) v Ipswich Town (a) 21 November

Milk Cup

1983-84
M.Harford (3) v Derby County (h) 25 October

Auto Windscreens Shield

1994-95
J.Hunt (3) v Peterborough United (a) 27 September

Football Alliance

1889-90
W.Devey (6) v Nottingham Forest (h) 8 March
G.Short (3) v Nottingham Forest (h) 8 March

1890-91
C.Short (3) v Stoke (h) 1 November
W.Devey (3) v Crewe Alexandra (h) 7 February
C.Short (3) v Nottingham Forest (h) 28 February
G.F.Wheldon (3) v Bootle (h) 21 March

1891-92
G.F.Wheldon (3) v Lincoln City (h) 26 September

Wartime – 1916-1919

1916-17
J.Whitehouse (3) v Sheffield United (h) 4 November
J.Whitehouse (3) v Nottingham Forest (h) 9 April

1917-18
S.Stevens (3) v Notts County (h) 12 January

1918-19
J.Godfrey (3) v Sheffield United (a) 5 October
D.Brown (3) v Sheffield United (h) 12 October
J.Godfrey (3) v Barnsley (h) 30 November
J.Godfrey (3) v Bradford City (h) 4 January
J.Godfrey (3) v Leicester Fosse (a) 26 April

Wartime – 1939-1946

1940-41
C.Trigg (5) v Stoke City (h) 16 November
C.Trigg (3) v Notts County (a) 30 November
C.Trigg (3) v Walsall (a) 25 December
D.Dearson (3) v Luton Town (a) 1 March

1942-43
D.Dearson (3) v Walsall (h) 7 November
S.Ottewell (3) v West Bromwich Albion (h) 3 April

1943-44
C.Trigg (4) v Walsall (h) 22 April

1944-45
C.Trigg (4) v Port Vale (h) 2 September
C.Trigg (3) v Wolverhampton Wanderers (a) 11 November
C.Trigg (3) v Walsall (h) 30 December
C.Trigg (3) v Coventry City (h) 6 January
D.Massart (3) v West Bromwich Albion (h) 5 May
D.Massart (3) v West Bromwich Albion (a) 12 May

1945-46
C.W.Jones (3) v Plymouth Argyle (a) 1 April